# BUSINESS

## A Changing World

**O.C. Ferrell**
University of New Mexico–Albuquerque

**Geoffrey A. Hirt**
DePaul University

**Linda Ferrell**
University of New Mexico–Albuquerque

**Suzanne Iskander**
Humber ITAL

**Peter Mombourquette**
Mount Saint Vincent University

**BUSINESS: A CHANGING WORLD**
**Seventh Canadian Edition**



ISBN-13: 978-1-26-006586-2
ISBN-10: 1-26-006586-3

1 2 3 4 5 6 7 8 9 M 23 22 21 20

Printed and bound in Canada.



Product Director: *Rhondda McNabb*
Portfolio Manager: *Amy Clarke-Spenceley*
Marketing Manager: *Emily Park*
Content Developer: *Krisha Escobar*
Portfolio Associate: *Christine Albert*
Senior Supervising Editor: *Jessica Barnoski*
Photo/Permissions Editor: *Monika Schurmann*
Copy Editor: *Judy Sturrup*
Plant Production Coordinator: *Joelle McIntyre*
Manufacturing Production Coordinator: *Jason Stubner*
Cover Design: *Katherine Strain*
Cover Image: © *frankies/Shutterstock*
Interior Design: *Michelle Losier*
Page Layout: *MPS Limited*
Printer: *Marquis*

# DEDICATION

To the memory of

Autumn Lea Mombourquette

- P.M., S.I.

# ABOUT THE AUTHORS

## O.C. Ferrell

O.C. Ferrell is professor of management and Creative Enterprise Scholar in the Anderson School of Management, University of New Mexico. He recently served as the Bill Daniels Distinguished Professor of Business Ethics at the University of Wyoming, and the chair of the department of marketing and the Ehrhardt, Keefe, Steiner, and Hottman P. C. Professor of Business Administration at Colorado State University. He also has held faculty positions at the University of Memphis, the University of Tampa, Texas A&M University, Illinois State University, and Southern Illinois University, as well as visiting positions at Queen's University (Ontario, Canada), University of Michigan (Ann Arbor), University of Wisconsin (Madison), and University of Hannover (Germany). He has served as a faculty member for the master's degree program in marketing at Thammasat University (Bangkok, Thailand). Dr. Ferrell received his B.A. and M.B.A. from Florida State University and his Ph.D. from Louisiana State University. His teaching and research interests include business ethics, corporate citizenship, and marketing.

Dr. Ferrell is widely recognized as a leading teacher and scholar in business. His articles have appeared in leading journals and trade publications. In addition to *Business: A Changing World*, he has two other textbooks, *Marketing: Concepts and Strategies* and *Business Ethics: Ethical Decision Making and Cases*, that are market leaders in their respective areas. He also has co-authored other textbooks for marketing, management, business and society, and other business courses, as well as a trade book on business ethics. He chaired the American Marketing Association (AMA) ethics committee that developed its current code of ethics. He was the vice president of marketing education and president of the Academic Council for the AMA. Currently he is vice president of publications for the Academy of Marketing Science.

Dr. Ferrell's major focus is teaching and preparing learning material for students. He has taught the introduction to business course using this textbook. This gives him the opportunity to develop, improve, and test the book and ancillary materials on a first-hand basis. He has travelled extensively to work with students and understands the needs of instructors of introductory business courses. He lives in Albuquerque, New Mexico, and enjoys skiing, golf, and international travel.

## Geoffrey A. Hirt

Geoffrey A. Hirt is currently professor of finance at DePaul University and a Mesirow Financial Fellow. From 1987 to 1997 he was chairman of the finance department at DePaul University. He teaches investments, corporate finance, and strategic planning. He developed and was director of DePaul's M.B.A. program in Hong Kong and has taught in Poland, Germany, Thailand, and Hong Kong. He received his Ph.D. in Finance from the University of Illinois at Champaign–Urbana, his M.B.A. from Miami University of Ohio, and his B.A. from Ohio-Wesleyan University. Dr. Hirt has directed the Chartered Financial Analysts Study program for the Investment Analysts Society of Chicago since 1987.

Dr. Hirt has published several books, including *Foundations of Financial Management* published by McGraw-Hill/Irwin. Now in its thirteenth edition, this book is used at more than 600 colleges and universities worldwide. It has been used in more than 31 countries and has been translated into more than 10 different languages. Additionally, Dr. Hirt is well known for his text, *Fundamentals of Investment Management*, also published by McGraw-Hill/Irwin and now in its ninth edition. He plays tennis and golf, is a music lover, and enjoys travelling with his wife, Linda.

## Linda Ferrell

Dr. Linda Ferrell is associate professor and Creative Enterprise Scholar in the Anderson School of Management at the University of New Mexico. She completed her Ph.D. in business administration, with a concentration in management, at the University of Memphis. She has taught at the University of Tampa, Colorado State University, University of Northern Colorado, University of Memphis, and the University of Wyoming. She also team teaches a class at Thammasat University in Bangkok, Thailand, as well as an online business ethics certificate course through the University of New Mexico.

Her work experience as an account executive for McDonald's and Pizza Hut's advertising agencies supports her teaching of advertising, marketing management, marketing ethics, and marketing principles. She has published in the *Journal of Public Policy and Marketing, Journal of Business Research, Journal of Business Ethics, Journal of Marketing Education, Marketing Education Review, Journal of Teaching Business Ethics,* and *Case Research Journal,* and is co-author of *Business Ethics: Ethical Decision Making and Cases* (Seventh Edition) and *Business and Society* (Third Edition). She is the ethics content expert for the AACSB Ethics Education Resource Center and was co-chair of the 2005 AACSB Teaching Business Ethics Conference in Boulder, Colorado.

Dr. Ferrell is the vice president of programs for the Academy of Marketing Science, vice president of development for the Society for Marketing Advances, and a past president for the Marketing Management Association. She is a member of the college advisory board for Petco Vector. She frequently speaks to organizations on teaching business ethics, including the Direct Selling Education Foundation's training programs and AACSB International Conferences. She has served as an expert witness in cases related to advertising, business ethics, and consumer protection.

## Suzanne Iskander

Suzanne Iskander is a professor, finance and economics, at the Faculty of Business, Humber ITAL. Suzanne taught the undergraduate Introduction to Business course at the University of Guelph–Humber for many years, and using her skills as teacher, trainer, and coach, now teaches finance and economics courses in both degree and diploma programs. At Humber, she currently serves as program coordinator for three business programs and has served as chair, Academic Council; chair, the Sustainability Conference; and as a member of various other committees: Degree Council, Academic Framework, Economics Conference, Program Advisory, and Scholarly Society. She participated in the Moshi–Humber Curriculum Development Workshop in Tanzania and volunteers with various organizations to enhance the business skills and education of students in Canada.

Suzanne holds an MBA from Schulich School of Business and is a holder of the Chartered Financial Analyst (CFA) designation. Her previous experience in business and in the financial services industry include the position of vice-president for an international financial institution.

## Peter Mombourquette

Peter S. Mombourquette is a professor and chair of the Department of Business and Tourism and Hospitality Management at Mount Saint Vincent University, where he teaches introduction to business, strategic management, and entrepreneurship and small business. In addition to teaching and research, Peter founded the Entrepreneurship Skills Program (ESP), a highly intensive, multi-disciplinary entrepreneurship program aimed at encouraging entrepreneurship among university graduates. Peter also founded and chairs the highly successful Social Enterprise for a Day (SE4D) conference, where students and community leaders learn about social enterprise and how to start and run social ventures.

Over Peter's time as chair of the department, he has worked with his colleagues to create an engaging environment for students and provide them with an opportunity to give back to society while learning about career opportunities. Peter has worked collaboratively to create a highly successful Learning Passport program for students, an annual career week, job clubs, a mentorship program with community leaders, an annual Social Enterprise Study Tour, a quarterly newsletter, and an annual sustainable business tour to name a few. Peter was recognized for his efforts by Mount Saint Vincent University when he received the Innovative Teaching Award. Peter has also been nominated on two separate occasions by Mount Saint Vincent University for the Atlantic Canadian Leadership Award in teaching.

Peter completed his D.B.A. at the University of Southern Queensland after graduating with an M.B.A. from Saint Mary's University, a B.Ed. from Saint Francis Xavier University, and a B.A. from Cape Breton University. Peter currently resides in Halifax with his wife, Amanda, and they have had the immense pleasure of having four children—their wonderful son, Jack; a beautiful baby girl, Autumn, who tragically passed away shortly before her first birthday; a young daughter, April Autumn; and a baby boy, Will.

# BRIEF CONTENTS

## PART 1

### Business in a Changing World

## PART 2

### Starting and Growing a Business



## PART 3

### Managing for Quality and Competitiveness

## PART 4

### Creating the Human Resource Advantage

## PART 5

### Marketing: Developing Relationships

## PART 6

### Financing the Enterprise



### Appendixes

# CONTENTS

## PART 1
## Business in a Changing World

### Chapter 1: The Dynamics of Business and Economics 2



### Chapter 2: Business Ethics and Social Responsibility 26

## PART 2
## Starting and Growing a Business

## PART 6
## Financing the Enterprise

# PREFACE

## Welcome

This new edition reflects many dynamic changes in the business environment related to how managers make decisions. It is important for students to understand how the functional areas of business have to be coordinated as the economy, technology, global competition, and the way consumers make decisions continue to evolve. All of these changes are presented in concepts that entry-level students can understand. Our book contains all of the essentials that most students should learn in a semester.

*Business: A Changing World* has, since its inception, been a concise presentation of the essential material needed to teach an introduction to business course. From our experience in teaching the course, we know that the most effective way to engage a student is by making business exciting, relevant, and current. Our teachable, from-the-ground-up approach involves a variety of media, application exercises, and subjects, including up-to-date content supplements, boxed examples, video cases, PowerPoint presentations, and testing materials that work for entry-level business students. We cover major changes in our economy related to sustainability, digital marketing, and social networking, and we have worked hard to make sure that the content of this edition is as current as possible in order to best reflect today's dynamic world of business.

## The Seventh Canadian Edition

The Seventh Canadian Edition represents a complete and comprehensive revision. This is because so many recent events and changes in the business environment affect the foundational concepts. This means that an introduction to business textbook has to provide adequate coverage of these changes as they relate to business decisions. We have listened to your feedback and incorporated needed changes in content, boxes, cases, exercises, support, online resources, and other features.

In this edition we further expand our chapter on digital marketing and social networking in business, a dynamic area that continues to change the face of business. Entrepreneurs and small businesses must be able to increase sales and reduce costs by using social networking to communicate and develop relationships with customers. The sharing, or "gig," economy is transforming entrepreneurial opportunities for employees. The Internet is providing opportunities for peer-to-peer relationships for companies such as Uber as well as health care services. Because this area is a moving target, we have made substantial changes to the seventh edition in Chapter 12, "Dimensions of Marketing Strategy," and Chapter 13, "Digital Marketing and Social Networking." Digital marketing has helped many entrepreneurs launch successful businesses.

Throughout the product, we recognize the importance of sustainability and "green" business. By implementing *reduce, reuse, and recycle* philosophy we believe every business can be more profitable and contribute to a better world through green initiatives. There are Going Green boxes that cover these environmental changes. As well, our Entrepreneurship in Action boxes discuss many innovations and opportunities to use sustainability for business success. Sustainability is not only a goal of many businesses; it is also providing career opportunities for many of our students.

We have been careful to continue our coverage of global business, ethics and social responsibility, and information technology as they relate to the foundations important in an introduction to business course. Our co-author team has a diversity of expertise in these important areas.

The different areas of introduction to business, entrepreneurship, small business management, marketing, accounting, and finance have been revised. Examples have been provided to which students can easily relate. An understanding of core functional areas of business is presented so that students get a holistic view of the world of business. Boxed examples such as Responding to Business Challenges, Entrepreneurship in Action, and Going Green help provide real-world examples in these areas. As a respectful inclusion in our work, we have been mindful of Indigenous contributions, and introduce examples where appropriate.

Our goal is to make sure that the content and teaching package for this book are of the highest quality possible. We wish to seize this opportunity to gain your trust, and we appreciate feedback to help us continually improve these materials. We hope that the real beneficiary of all of our work will be well-informed students who appreciate the role of business in society and take advantage of the opportunity to play a significant role in improving our world. In this new edition, we have additional content to help students understand how our free enterprise system operates and how we fit into the global competitive environment. This course is an opportunity for students to understand how they can create their own success and improve their quality of life.

## Focused, Exciting, Applicable, Happening

***Business: A Changing World,*** Seventh Canadian Edition, offers faculty and students a **focused** resource that is **exciting, applicable,** and **happening**! What sets this learning program apart from the competition? Our text contains all of the essentials that most students should learn in a semester. *Business: A Changing World* has, since its inception, delivered a focused presentation of the essential material needed to teach introduction to business. An unrivalled mixture of exciting content and resources, application-focused material and activities, and fresh topics and examples that show students what is happening in the world of business today set this text apart.

**Focused** It's easy for students taking their first steps into business to become overwhelmed. Longer texts try to solve this problem by chopping out examples or topics to make shorter editions. *Business: A Changing World* carefully builds just the right mix of coverage and applications to give your students a firm grounding in business principles. Instead of sprinting through the semester to get everything in, the text allows you the breathing space to explore topics and incorporate other activities that are important to you and your students. Exceptional resources support you in this effort every step of the way.

**Exciting** It's exciting to see students succeed! It's exciting to see more A's and B's in a course without grade inflation. *Business: A Changing World* makes these results possible for your course with its integrated learning package that is proven effective, tailored to each individual student, and easy to use.

**Applicable** When students see how content applies to them, their life, their career, and the world around them, they are more engaged in the course. *Business: A Changing World* helps students maximize their learning efforts by setting clear objectives, delivering interesting cases and examples, focusing on core issues, and providing engaging activities to apply concepts, build skills, and solve problems.

**Happening** There are no outdated or irrelevant examples or coverage. Everything in the seventh edition reflects the very latest developments in the business world—from the 2008 recession, high unemployment rates, and the financial instability in Europe, to the growth of digital marketing and social networking. In addition, ethics continues to be a key issue, and boxed material is used to instill in students the importance of ethical conduct in business.

## New to This Edition

As always, when revising this material for the current edition, all examples, figures, and statistics have been updated to incorporate any recent developments that affect the world of business. Additionally, content was updated and numerous new examples were included in the text to ensure the most pertinent topical coverage is provided. We have been mindful of the inclusion of Indigenous content and focus on using inclusive language wherever possible.

### Chapter 1

- New Enter the World of Business profile of Prem Watsa with discussion questions
- New boxed features describing real-world business issues
- Updated economic statistics
- New Indigenous content—Consider the Following: Indigenous languages

## Chapter 2

- New Enter the World of Business profile of Greenlid and its founding entrepreneurs Morgan and Jackson Wyatt with discussion questions
- Inclusion of multiple new in-chapter discussion cases on relevant topics to encourage student participation. Features include a look into the business practices of Ticketmaster, food delivery services, the Canada Summer Jobs Program, and the response of pro football to new information about concussions.
- Additional updates have been made to in-chapter boxed features that students will find interesting and relatable. These include The Case of Valeant Pharmaceuticals; The case of ride-sharing and Uber in Canada; Is Facebook acting ethically by making billions off your personal information?; Fracking for Natural Gas: Clean Energy Solution or Environmental Catastrophe?; Are social media sites fair game for employers?; When is organic really organic?; Canada, the counterfeiters' safe haven; and "Are energy drinks safe?"
- Updated boxed features: Going Green, Responding to Business Challenges
- New end of chapter case: Trans Mountain Pipeline

## Chapter 3

- New Enter the World of Business feature on Alibaba with discussion questions
- New boxed features describing describing issues in international business
- New end of chapter case: Electra Bikes

## Chapter 4

- New Enter the World of Business feature on Indigo and Heather Reisman with discussion questions
- Revised boxed features: Going Green, Entrepreneurship in Action, Responding to Business Challenges
- New in-chapter feature on Indigenous entrepreneur Mark Marsolais-Nahwegahbow and his company, Birch Bark Coffee
- Updated in-text material including enhanced coverage of cannabis companies and mergers and acquisitions
- New information on IPOs
- New information on joint ventures
- New end of chapter case on Canada's turbulent cannabis industry

## Chapter 5

- New Enter the World of Business feature on Fiix and its entreprenurial team, Khallil Mangalji, Arif Bhanji, and Zain Manji
- Updated boxed features: Going Green, Entrepreneurship in Action, Responding to Business Challenges
- New in-chapter features on crowdfunding, solar farming, and the use of the term *mompreneur*
- Numerous examples of young entrepreneurs who started digital and/or social enterprises
- Expanded discussion on raising money to start a business, including crowdfunding and peer-to-peer lending in Canada
- Updated Case: Finding a Niche in the Golf Apparel Business

## Chapter 6

- New Enter the World of Business feature on Loblaw with discussion questions
- New boxed features describing current business issues
- Staffing has been removed as a function of management, and the information on staffing has been moved to the Importance of Management
- New definition of brainstorming
- New information on participative decision making
- New end of chapter case: RONA's Turnaround

## Chapter 7

- New Enter the World of Business feature on Keurig Green Mountain with discussion questions
- New boxed features describing current business issues
- A new objective on organizational culture
- New figure describing desired attitudes and behaviours associated with corporate culture
- Information on formal communication has been placed in a table
- New end of chapter case: A Freshii Approach to Food and Business

## Chapter 8

- New Enter the World of Business feature on Costco with discussion questions
- New boxed features describing current operational issues
- A new objective on operations management
- New material on the role of drones in operations
- New information on ISO 19600 related to compliance
- New end of chapter case: Creating Supply Chain Efficiencies at the Cocoa Exchange

## Chapter 9

- New Enter the World of Business feature on Facebook with discussion questions
- New boxed features describing current business issues
- New section on goal-setting theory
- Definition of reinforcement theory

## Chapter 10

- New Enter the World of Business feature on Shopify with discussion questions
- Updated content on recruiting employees, employee training, including the use of virtual reality training, performance management, the importance of diversity
- Updated in-chapter features including information on using social media to recruit (Snapchat), rewarding socially responsible employees, and penalizing employees who smoke.
- New end of chapter case: WestJet Unionizes

## Chapter 11

- New Enter the World of Business Case on Spin Master and founding partners Ronnen Harary and Anton Rabie of Spin Master Toys with new discussion questions
- New and updated boxed features: Going Green, Entrepreneurship in Action, Responding to Business Challenges
- New in-chapter features: Starbucks Refines the Customer Experience; Charmed Playhouse; Online Wedding Shopping
- Increased emphasis on the impact of social media and digital marketing
- New information on the marketing mix, including new trends emerging in pricing and place/location strategies
- New end of chapter case: Will Crowdfunding Replace Traditional Market Research?

## Chapter 12

- New Enter the World of Business feature on Tulip and its CEO, Ali Asaria, with new discussion questions
- New and updated boxed features: Going Green, Entrepreneurship in Action
- In-chapter features highlighting Indigenous entrepreneurs Patrice Mousseau and her company, Satya, and Shar Wilson and her company, Finawear
- New section on Influencers
- New and greatly enhanced information on the promotional mix, including in-depth coverage of digital media and social media, including new examples of Canadian companies using Facebook, LinkedIn, Pinterest, Instagram, Snapchat, Tinder, YouTube, and Ebay
- New material on mobile marketing
- New end of chapter case about Musi and young entrepreneurs Christian Lunny and Aaron Wojnowski

## Chapter 13

- New Enter the World of Business feature on Arlene Dickinson and her focus on investing in entrepreneurs with new discussion questions
- New and updated boxed features: Going Green, Entrepreneurship in Action, Responding to Business Challenges
- Increased emphasis on social media and communications, including Facebook, LinkedIn, Instagram, YouTube
- Updated and detailed discussion of digital marketing
- New information on the legal and social issues of digital marketing with special emphasis on Influencers
- Updated and new in-chapter features including: Famous Folks and Going Viral

## Chapter 14

- New Enter the World of Business feature on Deloitte with discussion questions
- New boxed features describing current accounting issues
- New information on the financial information and ratios of Loblaw
- Financial ratio comparisons of Loblaw and Metro
- New Responding to Business Challenges feature: Auditing First Nations
- New end of chapter case: Goodwill Industries: Accounting in a Non-profit

## Chapter 15

- New Enter the World of Business feature on mobile banking with discussion questions
- New boxed features describing current financial issues
- New material on reward cards
- New Responding to Business Challenges feature—Banking in Indigenous Communities
- New end of chapter case: Crowdfunding: Loans You Can Count On

## Chapter 16

- New Enter the World of Business case on General Electric with discussion questions
- New boxed features describing current financial issues

# Getting a Handle on Business

*Business: A Changing World*'s pedagogy helps students get the most out of their reading, from Learning Objectives at the beginning of each chapter to the Learning Objectives Summary at the end of each chapter.

## Learning Objectives

These appear at the beginning of each chapter to provide goals for students to reach in their reading. The objectives are then used in the **Learning Objectives Summary** at the end of each chapter, and help the students gauge whether they've learned and retained the material.

LEARNING OBJECTIVES

**After reading this chapter, you will be able to:**

LO 1-1 Define basic concepts such as *business*, *product*, and *profit*.

LO 1-2 Identify the main participants in and activities of business and explain why studying business is important.

LO 1-3 Define *economics* and compare the four types of economic systems.

LO 1-4 Describe the role of supply, demand, and competition in a free-enterprise system.

LO 1-5 Specify why and how the health of the economy is measured.

LO 1-6 Trace the evolution of the Canadian economy and discuss the role of the entrepreneur in the economy.

ENTER THE WORLD OF BUSINESS

**Prem Watsa: Canada's Warren Buffet**

When Prem Watsa, chairman of the board of directors and CEO of Fairfax, arrived in Canada from India in 1972, he had $8 in his pocket and $600 to put toward the first year's tuition for the MBA program at the University of Western Ontario. To finance his education, he peddled air conditioners in the summer and furnaces in the winter. After graduating from the Ivey Business School, Watsa worked for Confederation Life, an insurance company. A decade after joining Confederation Life, Watsa and colleagues struck out to form the company that would eventually be called Fairfax. The name means "fair, friendly acquisitions" and, through those acquisitions, he grew the company to assets of over $16 billion dollars by 2018. Most importantly, he believes in his acquisitions and their value, a strategy that has made him one of the wealthiest Canadians.

Watsa conducts detailed research before acquiring any company and develops unique strategies and tactics for growing a company. Today, Watsa's companies are engaged in insurance and reinsurance, as well as investment management in Canada, the United States, Great Britain, Brazil, Poland, Malaysia, Singapore, Barbados, and Hong Kong. Leading such a variety of companies comes with challenges, as well. Companies require leaders who know the business and have specialized expertise—something nearly impossible for one person with so many different business interests. For this reason the insurance and reinsurance companies operate on a decentralized basis, with autonomous management teams applying a focused strategy to each of their markets.

Although Watsa acknowledges that he has benefitted from a good education, he also recognizes that much of his life has been influenced by his father, a teacher, and the advice he passed to his son: "Work as hard as you can, as though everything depended on you. Pray as hard as you can, as though everything depended on God."[1]

DISCUSSION QUESTIONS

1. Describe Watsa's business strategy. Why do you think it was so successful?
2. Why is it important for Fairfax to allow management teams the ability to run the firms as they see fit?
3. What factors led to Watsa's success?

Introduction

We begin our study of business in this chapter by examining the fundamentals of business and economics. First, we introduce the nature of business, including its goals, activities, and participants. Next, we describe the basics of economics and apply them to the Canadian economy. Finally, we establish a framework for studying business using this text.

## Enter the World of Business

Each chapter opens with an introduction to a relevant company or leader in industry, by detailing each company's challenges and opportunities.

## Pedagogical Boxes

An important feature of the book is the **Consider the Following** pedagogical boxes demonstrating real-world examples to drive home the applied lessons to students. These features provide an excellent vehicle for stimulating class discussions.

**Consider the Following: Should views on charter freedoms impact federal government funding?**

The Canadian Summer Jobs Program offers a great example of an ethical dilemma. Each and every summer thousands of corporations and not-for-profit firms, including many charitable groups such as churches, receive funding from the federal government to employ students during the summer months. Students earn valuable experience and much-needed income, and the organizations receive grants to offset the cost of labour. The program is considered a win-win-win for students, employers and government.

In 2017 and 2018, Prime Minister Justin Trudeau's government amended the application process and asked all applicants to confirm they supported all rights protected by the Charter of Rights and Freedoms, including a woman's right to have an abortion and rights associated with the LGBT community. Trudeau argued that church and not-for-profit groups would be eligible as long as they acknowledged support for people's rights as outlined in the Charter. He stated that certain groups, those fighting against Charter freedoms, should not receive government money. Trudeau stated, "...there are certain groups that are specifically dedicated to fighting abortion rights for women and rights for LGBT communities and that is wrong, that is certainly not something the federal government should be funding: to roll back the clock on women's rights."

The federal government's decision was highly criticized by church and anti-abortion groups, and was even discussed on Fox News in the U.S. In 2019, the federal government made an amendment to the application process. Church and charity groups do not have to attest they support all aspects of the Charter but they do have to clarify that the jobs that are being funded will not interfere with people's rights and freedoms.

DISCUSSION QUESTIONS

1. Was the government's requirement that groups state they supported all aspects of the Charter of Rights and Freedoms in order to receive government funding ethical? What are some of the pros and cons of his decision?
2. Do you think the government was right to change the application and approval process to focus on the activities of the jobs and not the beliefs of the organizations applying for funding?

The **Responding to Business Challenges** boxes illustrate how businesses overcome tough challenges, and many also highlight the importance of ethical conduct and how unethical conduct hurts investors, customers, and, indeed, the entire business world.

### RESPONDING TO BUSINESS CHALLENGES

#### Uber Attempts to Make the Right Turn

Uber provides ride-sharing services by connecting drivers and riders through an app. It has expanded its operations to 674 cities in 83 countries worldwide. As it expands, Uber is engaging in strategic partnerships with local companies. These alliances allow Uber to utilize the knowledge of domestic firms familiar with the country's culture. Uber has partnered with Times Internet in India, Baidu in China, and America Movil in Latin America.

Despite its success, Uber has faced problems in expanding internationally. In Spain, a judge ruled that Uber drivers are not legally authorized to transport passengers and that it unfairly competes against licensed taxi drivers. France and Germany instituted similar bans against unlicensed Uber drivers. Uber returned to Spain with UberX, which uses licensed drivers.

India is Uber's second-largest market after the United States. In New Delhi, the taxi industry banned app-based services without radio-taxi permits in the capital for safety reasons. Uber made changes to increase safety. Yet despite these changes, Uber continued to run afoul of Indian authorities. India asked Internet service providers to block Uber's websites because it continued to operate in the city despite being banned.

Uber has taken a global approach to expansion by applying the same practices in other countries as it does in Canada. However, it is realizing that it must take a more customized approach to achieve long-term international market success.*

**DISCUSSION QUESTIONS**

1. What are some of the major advantages Uber is experiencing by creating strategic partnerships with other companies?
2. What are some challenges Uber is facing as it expands globally?
3. What are some of the barriers that Uber is encountering in different countries?

*Rob Davies, "Uber Suffers Legal Setbacks in France and Germany," *The Guardian*, June 9, 2016, https://www.theguardian.com/technology/2016/jun/09/uber-suffersiegal-setbacks-in-france-and-germany (accessed April 15, 2017); "Uberworld," *The Economist*, September 3, 2016, p. 9; Jefferson Graham, "App Greases the Wheels," *USA Today*, May 27, 2015, p. 5B; Karun, "Times Internet and Uber Enter Into a Strategic Partnership, Uber Blog, March 22, 2015, http://blog.uber.com/times-internet (accessed April 15, 2017); R. Jai Krishna and Joanna Sugden, "India Asks Internet Service Providers to Block Uber Website in Delhi," *Wall Street Journal*, May 14, 2015, http://www. wsj.com/articles/india-asks-internet-service-providers-toblock-uber-website-in-delhi-1431606032 (accessed April 15, 2017); Saritha Rai, "Uber Gets Serious about Passenger Safety In India, Introduces Panic Button," *Forbes*, February 12, 2015, http://www.forbes.com/sites/saritharai/2015/02/12/ uber-gets-serious-about-passenger-safety-in-indiaintroduces-panic-button/ (accessed April 15, 2017); Sam Schechner and Tom Fairless, "Europe Steps Up Pressure on Tech Giants," *Wall Street Journal*, April 2, 2015, http://www.wsj.com/articles/europe-steps-up-pressure-ontechnology- giants-1428020273 (accessed April 15, 2017); Aditi Shrivastava, "Uber Resumes Operations in Delhi Post 1.5 Months Ban," *Economic Times*, January 23, 2015, http://articles.economictimes.indiatimes.com/2015-01-23/news/58382689_1_indian-taxi-market-radio-taxischeme-uber-spokesman (accessed April 15, 2017); UNM Daniels Fund Ethics Initiative, "Truth, Transparency, and Trust: Uber Important in the Sharing Economy," PPT presentation, https://danielsethics.mgt.unm.edu/teachingresources/ presentations.asp (accessed April 15, 2017); Maria Vega Paul, "Uber Returns to Spanish Streets in Search of Regulatory U-Turn," Reuters, March 30, 2016, http:// www. reuters.com/article/us-spain-uber-tech-idUSKCN0WW0AO (accessed April 15, 2017).

### ENTREPRENEURSHIP IN ACTION

#### Kenya Counts on Mobile Banking

**M-Pesa**

**Founders:** Nick Hughes and Susie Lonie

**Founded:** 2007, launched in Kenya through Safaricom

**Success:** Originally launched in Kenya, today this mobile-transfer payment system has 30 million users in 10 countries. In 2007, mobile-transfer payment system M-Pesa was launched by British multinational Vodafone's Kenyan mobile operator Safaricom. Little did it know how revolutionary this innovation would be for the economy. M-Pesa uses mobile services to leapfrog existing technological barriers and open up new opportunities for millions of Kenyans.

In Kenya, a less-developed country, banks tended to avoid catering to lower-income populations and the distance to a financial institution could be significant. The mobile-transfer payment service allowed Kenyan residents to quickly and securely transfer funds to merchants and family members through their cell phones. It also allowed for a significant rise in entrepreneurship. It is estimated that M-Pesa extended financial services to 20 million Kenyans, prompting many to start their own small businesses. Unlike in Canada, credit cards are rare in Kenya, and many Kenyans now use M-Pesa to pay for meals and other transactions.

Over the years, M-Pesa has expanded to nine other countries, including Tanzania, Romania, India, the Democratic Republic of the Congo, and Albania. While competition is rising for M-Pesa, the possibilities of worldwide expansion remain high as mobile payments gain traction globally.*

**DISCUSSION QUESTIONS**

1. What conditions in Kenya created the ideal conditions for a mobile banking service?
2. In what ways has M-Pesa paved the way for entrepreneurship in Kenya?
3. How can businesses in different industries profit from opportunities in less-developed countries?

*Daniel Runde, "M-Pesa and the Rise of the Global Mobile Money Market," August 12, 2015, https://www.forbes.com/sites/danielrunde/2015/08/12/m-pesa-and-the-riseof- the-global-mobile-money-market/#64299fd65aec (accessed March 3, 2018); Kieron Monks, "M-Pesa: Kenya's Mobile Money Success Story Turns 10," CNN, February 24, 2017, https://www.cnn.com/2017/02/21/africa/ mpesa-10th-anniversary/index.html (accessed March 3, 2018); BBC, "M-Pesa's Founders on Launching Mobile Wallet," *BBC News*, November 22, 2010, http://www.bbc.com/news/av/business-11793288/m-pesa-founderson-launching-kenya-s-mobile-wallet (accessed March 3, 2018); Janelle Richards, "Kenyan Entrepreneurs Help Youth Thrive In Africa's Emerging 'Silicon Valley,'" *NBC News*, December 4, 2017, https://www.nbcnews.com/news/ nbcblk/kenyan-entrepreneurs-help-youth-thrive-africa-semerging- silicon-valley-n826156 (accessed March 3, 2018); Charles Graeber, "Ten Days in Kenya with No Cash, Only a Phone," Bloomberg Businessweek, June 5, 2014, http:// www.businessweek.com/articles/2014-06-05/safaricoms-mpesa-turns-kenya-into-a-mobile-payment-paradise (accessed March 3, 2018); Vivienne Walt, "Is Africa's Rise for Real This Time?" *Fortune*, September 18, 2014, pp. 166–172.

The **Entrepreneurship in Action** boxes spotlight successful entrepreneurs and the challenges they have faced on the road to success.

The **Going Green** boxes show how issues of sustainability affect all levels of domestic business, and these boxes encourage students to keep their eyes on how "business as usual" now includes an environmentally responsible element.

### GOING GREEN

#### Fracking for Natural Gas: Clean Energy Solution or Environmental Catastrophe?

Hydraulic fracturing, known as fracking, has the potential to reduce Canada's dependence on foreign oil and create significant economic spinoffs. Fracking forces water, sand, and chemicals into underground tunnels of shale rock, bringing natural gas to the surface. Natural gas releases half the carbon dioxide of oil and is praised as a much more environmentally friendly fuel. Some provinces, such as Alberta and British Columbia, have benefited economically from fracking for years as the drilling creates jobs and increases tax revenue.

However, fracking does have a dark side. There have been instances where fracking chemicals have contaminated drinking water and increased levels of methane in water wells. People in the oil and gas industry argue that these cases occurred in the past and had more to do with companies not operating properly than the actual technology. Phil Knoll, former CEO of Corridor Resources, a Nova Scotia–based oil company, notes that fracking has been successfully and safely done for 20-plus years throughout Canada and the U.S.

Yet some provinces, most notably Quebec and recently Nova Scotia, have banned fracking over environmental concerns. While environmental groups have applauded such bans and are lobbying other provincial governments to stop fracking, many people in government and in the oil industry question the economic sense of the ban. Given that both Nova Scotia and Quebec would benefit from the increased tax revenue and investment fracking would bring, Knoll criticized the decision to ban fracking by the Nova Scotia government, stating the government ignored the science that fracking has been done safely for 20 years and turned away investment into the province, which is struggling economically.

Former Cape Breton University President David Wheeler was commissioned by the Nova Scotia government to complete a report on fracking, and he estimated that fracking would likely result in an additional billion dollars a year in revenue through the creation of jobs, investment, and royalties to the government.* Interestingly, both Quebec and Nova Scotia receive money, better known as transfer payments, from other provinces that have stronger economies. In 2017, four provinces (Alberta, Saskatchewan, British Columbia, and Newfoundland) paid into the transfer payment program, which benefited Nova Scotia and Quebec. All of these provinces have a successful oil and gas industry operating within their provincial boundaries and allow for fracking.

©Design Pics/Bilderbuch

The recent decision by the government of Nova Scotia to ban fracking has resulted in criticism from oil and gas companies who claim significant studies have proven that fracking is safe and would result in billions of economic opportunities for the struggling region.

**DISCUSSION QUESTIONS**

1. What is the ethical issue involved with fracking, and why is it so hard to resolve?
2. Examine this issue from the perspective of the gas company as well as from the perspective of concerned stakeholders.
3. Why might a government ban fracking when science appears to indicate it can be safely done?
4. Do you think it is fair for some provinces to ban fracking yet turn around and take money from other provinces who allow for fracking?
5. Use Internet resources and find additional arguments for and against fracking.

*Quentin Casey, "In the Hot Seat," *Progress*, April 2015, http:// www.progressmedia.ca/article/2015/04/hot-seat

# End-of-Chapter Material

The end-of-chapter material provides a great opportunity to reinforce and expand upon the chapter content.

**Key Terms.** Important terms, highlighted in bold face throughout the text with an accompanying definition on the page, are listed in alphabetical order for ease of reference.

### KEY TERMS

budget deficit
budget surplus
business
capitalism, or free enterprise
communism
competition
demand
depression
economic contraction
economic expansion
economic system
economics
entrepreneur
equilibrium price
financial resources
free-market system
gross domestic product (GDP)
human resources (labour)
inflation
mixed economies
monopolistic competition
monopoly
natural resources
non-profit organizations
oligopoly
open economy
products
profit
pure competition
recession
socialism
stakeholders
standard of living
supply
unemployment

### So You Want a Job *in the Business World*

When most people think of a career in business, they see themselves entering the door to large companies and multinationals that they read about in the news and that are discussed in class. Most jobs are not with large corporations but instead are in small companies, non-profit organizations, and government, and even as self-employed individuals. The majority of employees work for small businesses, constituting 71 percent of private sector employment. In addition, with more than 78 percent of the working population employed in service industries, there are jobs available in, for example, health care, finance, education, hospitality, entertainment, and transportation. E-commerce is creating the need for supply chain jobs related to purchasing, transportation, and operations. The world is changing quickly and large corporations replace the equivalent of their entire workforce every four years.

The fast pace of technology today means that you have to be prepared to take advantage of emerging job opportunities and markets. You must also become adaptive and recognize that business is becoming more global, with job opportunities around the world. If you want to obtain such a job, you shouldn't miss a chance to spend some time overseas. To get you started on the path to thinking about job opportunities, consider all of the changes in business today that might affect your possible long-term track and that could bring you lots of success. Companies are looking for employees with skills that can be used to address the changing business environment. For example, the demand for graduates who are good at analyzing data and navigating cloud-based computing is on the rise.

You're on the road to learning the key knowledge, skills, and trends that you can use to be a star in business. Business's impact on our society, especially in the areas of sustainability and improvement of the environment, is a growing challenge and opportunity. Examples of green businesses and green jobs in the business world are provided to give you a glimpse at the possibilities. Along the way, we will introduce you to some specific careers and offer advice on developing your own job opportunities. Research indicates that you won't be that happy with your job unless you enjoy your work and feel that it has a purpose. Because you spend most of your waking hours every day at work, you need to seriously think about what is important to you in a job.[21]

**So You Want a Job.** This end-of-chapter feature offers valuable advice on a wide spectrum of business career choices.

**Build Your Business Plan.** This end-of-chapter feature (along with Appendix A, "Business Plan Development") helps students through the development of their business plan by relating the steps to the content of each chapter. Additional information and resources can be found in the Instructor's Manual.

### BUILD YOUR BUSINESS PLAN

The Dynamics of Business and Economics

Have you ever thought about owning your business? If you have, how did your idea come about? Is it your experience with this particular field? Or might it be an idea that evolved from your desires for a particular product or service not being offered in your community? For example, perhaps you and your friends have yearned for a place to go have coffee, relax, and talk. Now is an opportunity to create the café bar you have been thinking of!

Whether you consider yourself a visionary or a practical thinker, think about your community. What needs are not being met? While it is tempting to suggest a new restaurant (maybe near campus), easier-to-implement business plans can range from a lawn care business or a designated driver business, to a placement service agency for teenagers.

Once you have an idea for a business plan, think about how profitable this idea might be. Is there sufficient demand for this business? How large is the market for this particular business? What about competitors? How many are there?

To learn about your industry you should do a thorough search of your initial ideas of a product/service on the Internet.

## Award-Winning Technology

McGraw Hill connect

McGraw-Hill Connect® is an award-winning digital teaching and learning solution that empowers students to achieve better outcomes and enables instructors to improve efficiency with course management. Within Connect, students have access to SmartBook®, McGraw-Hill's adaptive learning and reading resource. SmartBook prompts students with questions based on the material they are studying. By assessing individual answers, SmartBook learns what each student knows and identifies which topics they need to practice, giving each student a personalized learning experience and path to success.

Connect's key features include analytics and reporting, simple assignment management, smart grading, the opportunity to post your own resources, and the Connect Instructor Library, a repository for additional resources to improve student engagement in and out of the classroom.

Instructor resources for *Business: A Changing World*, Seventh Canadian Edition:

- Instructor's Manual
- Test Bank
- Microsoft® PowerPoint® Presentations
- Manager's HotSeat Videos

## Instructors' Resources

*Business: A Changing World*, Seventh Canadian Edition, offers a complete, integrated supplements package for instructors to address all your needs.

- **Instructor's Manual:** The Instructor's Manual, prepared by the Canadian text authors, Suzanne Iskander and Peter Mombourquette, accurately represents the text's content and supports instructors' needs. Each chapter includes the learning objectives, the glossary of key terms, a chapter synopsis, a complete lecture outline, and solutions to the end-of-chapter discussion questions.
- **Comprehensive Test Bank:** This flexible and easy-to-use electronic testing program allows instructors to create tests from book-specific items. Created by Suzanne Iskander of Humber College, the test bank has undergone a rigorous auditing and revision process for the Seventh Canadian Edition. It contains a broad selection of multiple choice, true/false, and essay questions, and instructors may add their own questions, as well. Each question identifies the relevant page reference and difficulty level. Multiple versions of the test can be created and printed.
- **PowerPoint™ Presentations:** Prepared by Liz McLean of St. Lawrence College, these robust presentations offer high-quality visuals from the text and highlight key concepts from each chapter to bring key business concepts to life.
- **Manager's HotSeat Videos**: This resource allows students to watch real managers apply their years of experience to management and organizational behaviour issues. Students assume the role of the manager as they watch the video and then answer multiple-choice questions following the segment. The Manager's HotSeat Videos are ideal for group or classroom discussions.

## Superior Learning Solutions and Support

The McGraw-Hill Education team is ready to help instructors assess and integrate any of our products, technology, and services into your course for optimal teaching and learning performance. Whether it's helping your students improve their grades, or putting your entire course online, the McGraw-Hill Education team is here to help you do it. Contact your Learning Solutions Consultant today to learn how to maximize all of McGraw-Hill Education's resources.

For more information please visit us online: www.mheducation.ca/he/solutions.

## Acknowledgements

The Seventh Canadian Edition of *Business: A Changing World* would not have been possible without the commitment, dedication, and patience of our excellent task masters and guides at McGraw-Hill: Amy Clarke-Spencley, Portfolio Manager; Krisha Escobar, Content Developer; Jessica Barnoski, Supervising Editor; Joelle McIntyre, Production Coordinator; Monika Schurmann, Photo/Permissions Editor; and Judy Sturrup, Copy Editor. We would also like to thank our digital author, Charissa Lee, from the Southern Alberta Institute of Technology.

Many others have assisted us with their helpful comments, recommendations, and support throughout this and previous editions. We acknowledge and thank David Newhouse, Professor and Director, Chanie Wenjack School for Indigenous Studies, Trent University, for his review and the guidance given in the development of Indigenous content. We would also like to express our thanks to the following reviewers who were among the instructors who reviewed previous editions:

Mohammed Khan—Centennial College
Lara Loze—Durham College
Tony Mallette—Southern Alberta Institute of Technology
Joyce Manu—George Brown College
Kerri Shields—Centennial College
Jeff Short—Humber College
Mike Wade—Seneca College
Dan Wong—Southern Alberta Institute of Technology

*—Suzanne Iskander and Peter Mombourquette*

CHAPTER 1

# The Dynamics of Business and Economics

©The Canadian Press/Nathan Denette

## LEARNING OBJECTIVES

**After reading this chapter, you will be able to:**

- LO 1-1 Define basic concepts such as *business*, *product*, and *profit*.
- LO 1-2 Identify the main participants in and activities of business and explain why studying business is important.
- LO 1-3 Define *economics* and compare the four types of economic systems.
- LO 1-4 Describe the role of supply, demand, and competition in a free-enterprise system.
- LO 1-5 Specify why and how the health of the economy is measured.
- LO 1-6 Trace the evolution of the Canadian economy and discuss the role of the entrepreneur in the economy.

# ENTER THE WORLD OF BUSINESS

**Prem Watsa: Canada's Warren Buffet**

When Prem Watsa, chairman of the board of directors and CEO of Fairfax, arrived in Canada from India in 1972, he had $8 in his pocket and $600 to put toward the first year's tuition for the MBA program at the University of Western Ontario. To finance his education, he peddled air conditioners in the summer and furnaces in the winter. After graduating from the Ivey Business School, Watsa worked for Confederation Life, an insurance company. A decade after joining Confederation Life, Watsa and colleagues struck out to form the company that would eventually be called Fairfax. The name means "fair, friendly acquisitions" and, through those acquisitions, he grew the company to assets of over $16 billion dollars by 2018. Most importantly, he believes in his acquisitions and their value, a strategy that has made him one of the wealthiest Canadians.

Watsa conducts detailed research before acquiring any company and develops unique strategies and tactics for growing a company. Today, Watsa's companies are engaged in insurance and reinsurance, as well as investment management in Canada, the United States, Great Britain, Brazil, Poland, Malaysia, Singapore, Barbados, and Hong Kong. Leading such a variety of companies comes with challenges, as well. Companies require leaders who know the business and have specialized expertise—something nearly impossible for one person with so many different business interests. For this reason the insurance and reinsurance companies operate on a decentralized basis, with autonomous management teams applying a focused strategy to each of their markets.

Although Watsa acknowledges that he has benefitted from a good education, he also recognizes that much of his life has been influenced by his father, a teacher, and the advice he passed to his son: "Work as hard as you can, as though everything depended on you. Pray as hard as you can, as though everything depended on God."[1]

**DISCUSSION QUESTIONS**

1. Describe Watsa's business strategy. Why do you think it was so successful?
2. Why is it important for Fairfax to allow management teams the ability to run the firms as they see fit?
3. What factors led to Watsa's success?

# Introduction

We begin our study of business in this chapter by examining the fundamentals of business and economics. First, we introduce the nature of business, including its goals, activities, and participants. Next, we describe the basics of economics and apply them to the Canadian economy. Finally, we establish a framework for studying business using this text.

## The Nature of Business

**LO 1-1** Define basic concepts such as *business*, *product*, and *profit*.

A **business** tries to earn a profit by offering goods and services that satisfy people's needs. The outcomes of its efforts are **products** that have both tangible and intangible characteristics that provide satisfaction and benefits. When you purchase a product, you are buying the benefits and satisfaction you think the product will provide. A Subway sandwich, for example, may be purchased to satisfy hunger, while a Honda Accord may be purchased to satisfy the need for transportation and the desire to present a certain image.

**business** individuals or organizations trying to earn a profit by providing goods and services that satisfy people's needs

**products** good and services with tangible and intangible characteristics that provide satisfaction and benefits

Most people associate the word *product* with tangible goods—an automobile, smartphone, jeans, or some other tangible item. However, a product can also be a service, which occurs when people or machines provide or process something of value to customers. A vacation, a checkup by a doctor, a movie or sports event—these are examples of services. An Uber ride satisfies the need for transportation and is therefore a service. A product can also be an idea. Accountants and lawyers, for example, generate ideas for solving problems.

©M40S Photos/Alamy Stock Photo

Some services, such as Instagram, a mobile photo management and sharing app, do not charge a fee for use but obtain revenue from ads on their sites.

## The Goal of Business

The primary goal of all businesses is to earn a **profit**, the difference between what it costs to make and sell a product and what a customer pays for it. If a company spends $8 to manufacture, finance, promote, and distribute a product that it sells for $10, the business earns a profit of $2 on each product sold. Businesses have the right to keep and use their profits as they choose—within legal limits—because profit is the reward for the risks they take in providing products. Earning profits contributes to society by creating resources that support our social institutions and government. Businesses that create profits, pay taxes, and create jobs are the foundation of our economy. In addition, profits must be earned in a responsible manner. Not all organizations are businesses, however.

**Non-profit organizations**, such as the United Way, the Canadian Red Cross, and other charities and social causes, do not have the fundamental purpose of earning profits, although they may provide goods or services and engage in fundraising. They also utilize skills related to management, marketing, and finance. Profits earned by businesses support non-profit organizations through donations from employees. Table 1.1 shows Canada's top 10 non-profit organizations in 2019, based on donations.

**profit** the difference between what it costs to make and sell a product and what a customer pays for it

**non-profit organizations** organizations that may provide goods or services but do not have the fundamental purpose of earning profits

To earn a profit, a person or organization needs *management skills* to plan, organize, and control the activities of the business and to find and develop employees so that it can make products consumers will buy. A business also needs *marketing expertise* to learn what products consumers need and want and to develop, manufacture, price, promote, and distribute those products. Additionally, a business needs *financial resources* and *skills* to fund, maintain, and expand its operations.

**Table 1.1** | Canada's Top 10 Non-profit Organizations

1. World Vision Canada
2. Salvation Army
3. Plan Canada
4. Canadian Red Cross
5. Canadian Cancer Society
6. Sick Kids Foundation
7. United Way Toronto & York Region
8. Heart and Stroke Foundation
9. Toronto General and Western Hospital Foundation
10. Princess Margaret Cancer Foundation

Courtesy of Walmart Canada

Sustainability is a growing concern among both consumers and businesses. Walmart Canada operates the sustainable Balzac Fresh Food Distribution Centre in Alberta, a facility that uses solar, thermal, and wind power as well as powering forklifts with hydrogen fuel cells. This cutting-edge facility is an estimated 60 percent more energy efficient than the company's traditional refrigerated distribution centres.[2]

Other challenges for business include abiding by laws and government regulations, and adapting to economic, technological, political, and social changes. Even non-profit organizations engage in management, marketing, and finance activities to help reach their goals.

To achieve and maintain profitability, businesses have found that they must produce quality products, operate efficiently, and be socially responsible and ethical in dealing with customers, employees, investors, government regulators, and the community. Because these groups have a stake in the success and outcomes of a business, they are sometimes called **stakeholders**. Many businesses, for example, are concerned about how the production and distribution of their products affect the environment. New fuel requirements are forcing automakers to invest in smaller, lighter-weight cars to meet increasingly

**stakeholders** people who have a vested interest in the success and outcomes of a business

## GOING GREEN

### Rainforest Alliance Stands Out in a Forest of Non-profits

When you think of the phrase *non-profit organization*, you likely think of a bare-bones operation run by people who are so dedicated that they do not mind working for peanuts. However, the Rainforest Alliance is an international organization that not only has a compelling and motivating mission but also offers excellent benefits and many opportunities for growth to their staff. With thousands of members and supporters, the Rainforest Alliance has been fighting globally to preserve biodiversity and promote sustainability since 1987.

As more consumers and businesses become interested in preserving the world's resources, the Rainforest Alliance has gained widespread support. Interacting with key stakeholders is essential to the Rainforest Alliance's success. For instance, the Rainforest Alliance has many resources for businesses that partner with the organization. The Rainforest Alliance provides auditing and certification services for businesses—such as agricultural, tourism, and forestry organizations—that wish to display the Rainforest Alliance certification seal.

The Rainforest Alliance blog describes how sustainability can positively affect a business, and its seal is one way businesses can inform consumers that they have incorporated sustainability principles into their operations. The Rainforest Alliance even has its own business unit, called RA-Cert, involved with auditing, evaluation, and certification decisions. Additionally, the Rainforest Alliance offers resources to businesses that want to educate their own employees about sustainability.

Stakeholders generally have a positive image of the Rainforest Alliance. One survey noted that coffee drinkers were likely to spend extra on coffee certified by Rainforest Alliance. For individuals looking to aid the environment and support small growers, the Rainforest Alliance is making a positive difference with its strong mission and interaction with stakeholders.*

#### DISCUSSION QUESTIONS

1. Why might investing in sustainability and becoming certified by an organization like the Rainforest Alliance be a good business decision?
2. Who do you feel are Rainforest Alliance's primary customers, consumers or businesses?
3. How does being a non-profit give Rainforest Alliance a competitive advantage over for-profit organizations in the same business?

*Rainforest Alliance, "Annual Report 2012," http://www.rainforest-alliance.org/sites/default/files/about/ annual_reports/AR2012_spreads-optimized.pdf (accessed June 24, 2013); Rainforest Alliance, "About Us," http:// www.rainforest-alliance.org/about (accessed January 1, 2018); Kelly K. Spors, "Top Small Workplaces 2008," *Wall Street Journal*, February 22, 2009, https://www.wsj.com/articles/SB122347733961315417 (accessed January 1, 2018); Richard Donovan, "Rainforest Alliance Launches TREES," Forest Stewardship Council, www.fscus.org/news/ index.php?article=169 (accessed May 29, 2009); Rainforest Alliance, "Marketing Your Commitment to Sustainability," https://www.rainforest-alliance.org/business/marketing (accessed January 1, 2018); Rainforest Alliance, "Raising Awareness . . . Among Employees," https://www.rainforestalliance.org/business/marketing/awareness/employees (accessed January 1, 2018); Rainforest Alliance, "What Does Rainforest Alliance CertifiedTM Mean?" October 25, 2016, https://www.rainforest-alliance.org/faqs/what-doesrainforest- alliance-certified-mean (accessed January 1, 2018).

stringent fuel-economy and greenhouse gas emission standards. Electric vehicles may be a solution, but only about 1 percent of new car sales are plug-in electric.[3] Other businesses are concerned with increasing diversity in their workforce. A Canadian survey showed that a one percent increase in ethnocultural diversity was associated with an average 2.4 percent increase in revenue.[4] Non-profit organizations such as the Canadian Red Cross use business activities to support natural-disaster victims, relief efforts, and a national blood supply.

## The People and Activities of Business

**LO 1-2** Identify the main participants in and activities of business and explain why studying business is important.

Figure 1.1 shows the people and activities involved in business. At the centre of the figure are owners, employees, and customers; the outer circle includes the primary business activities—management, marketing, and finance. Owners have to put up resources—money or credit—to start a business. Employees are responsible for the work that goes on within a business. Owners can manage the business themselves or hire employees to accomplish this task. The president of Loblaw Companies Limited, Sarah Davis, does not own Loblaw, but is an employee who is responsible for managing all the other employees in a way that earns a profit for investors, who are the real owners.

Most importantly, a business's major role is to satisfy the customers who buy its goods or services. Note also that people and forces beyond an organization's control—such as legal and regulatory forces, the economy, competition, technology, and ethical and social concerns—all have an impact on the daily operations of businesses. You will learn more about these participants in business activities throughout this book. Next, we will examine the major activities of business.

**Management.** Notice in Figure 1.1. that management and employees are in the same segment of the circle. This is because management involves coordinating employees' actions to achieve the firm's goals, organizing people to work efficiently and motivating them to reach the business's objectives. Management is also concerned with acquiring, developing, and using resources (including people) effectively and efficiently.

Operations is another element of management. Managers must oversee the firm's operations to ensure that resources are successfully transformed into goods and services. Although most people associate operations with the development of goods, operations management applies just as strongly to services. Managers at the Hilton, for instance, are concerned with transforming resources, such as employee actions and hotel amenities, into a quality customer service experience. In essence, managers plan, organize, staff, and control the tasks required to carry out the work of the company or non-profit organization. We take a closer look at management activities in Parts 3 and 4 of this text.

**Figure 1.1** | Overview of the Business World

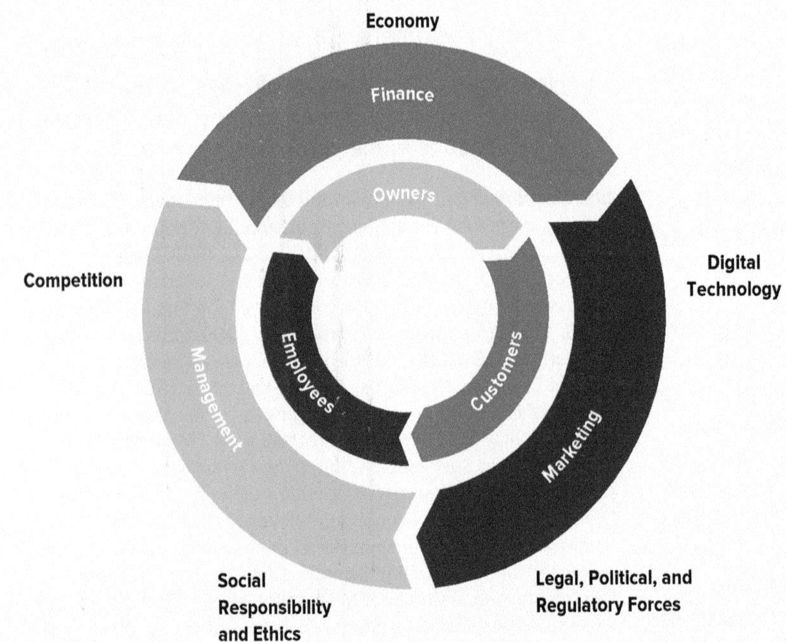


"Managers plan, organize, staff, and control the tasks required to carry out the work of the company or non-profit organization."

**Marketing.** Marketing and consumers are in the same segment of Figure 1.1 because the focus of all marketing activities is satisfying customers. Marketing includes all the activities designed to sell goods and services that satisfy consumers' needs and wants. Marketers gather information and conduct research to determine what customers want. Using information gathered from marketing research, marketers can help plan and develop products as well as make decisions about how much to charge for them and when and where to make them available. They also

**Table 1.2** | The Marketing Mix

| The 4 P's | |
|---|---|
| Product | Product management involves such key management decisions as product adoption or deletion, branding, and product positioning. |
| Price | Selecting the right price for the product is essential to the organization as it relates directly to profitability. |
| Place (or distribution) | Distribution is an important management concern because it involves making sure products are available to consumers in the right place at the right time. Supply chain management involves purchasing and logistics as well as operations to coordinate suppliers, producers, and distributors to create value for customers. |
| Promotion | Marketers use promotion—advertising, personal selling, sales promotion (coupons, games, sweepstakes, movie tie-ins), and publicity—to communicate the benefits and advantages of their products to consumers and increase sales. |

analyze the marketing environment to see if products need to be modified. The retail environment is changing based on competition from online retailing such as Amazon. This has caused some retail stores and malls to close.[5]

©Helen Sessions/Alamy Stock Photo

One of the world's largest customer rewards programs is Tim Hortons' Roll Up the Rim to Win campaign. The marketing initiative was developed by the company's former marketing director, Ron Buist, to gain marketing leverage (strength) from its paper cup and to increase sales.[6]

Marketing focuses on the four P's—also known as the *marketing mix*—shown in Table 1.2. We will examine marketing activities in Part 5 of this text.

**Finance.** Owners and finance are in the same part of Figure 1.1 because, although management and marketing have to deal with financial considerations, it is the primary responsibility of the owners to provide financial resources for the operation of the business. Moreover, the owners have the most to lose if the business fails to make a profit. Finance refers to all activities concerned with obtaining money and using it effectively. People who work as accountants, investment advisors, or bankers are all part of the financial world. Owners sometimes have to borrow money from banks to get started or attract additional investors who become partners or stockholders. Owners of small businesses in particular often rely on bank loans for funding. Part 6 of this text discusses financial management.

## Why Study Business?

Business activities help generate the profits that are essential not only to individual businesses and local economies but also to the health of the global economy. Without profits, businesses find it difficult, if not impossible, to buy more raw materials, hire more employees, attract more

**Consider the Following: Studying business can help you to...**

1. Develop skills and acquire knowledge to prepare for your future career, regardless of whether you plan to work for a multinational firm, start your own business, work for a government agency, or manage or volunteer at a non-profit organization.
2. Explore a variety of interesting and challenging career opportunities throughout the world, such as human resources management, information technology, finance, production and operations, wholesaling and retailing, and many more.
3. Understand the many business activities that are necessary to provide satisfying goods and services.
4. Become a well-informed consumer and member of society.

capital, and create additional products that in turn make more profits and fuel the world economy. Understanding how our free-enterprise economic system allocates resources and provides incentives for industry and the workplace is important to everyone.

## The Economic Foundations of Business

**LO 1-3** Define *economics* and compare the four types of economic systems.

It is useful to explore the economic environment in which business is conducted. In this section, we examine economic systems, the free-enterprise system, the concepts of supply and demand, and the role of competition. These concepts play important roles in determining how businesses operate in a particular society.

**economics** the study of how resources are distributed for the production of goods and services within a social system

**economic system** a description of how a particular society distributes its resources to produce goods and services

**entrepreneurs** individuals who risks their wealth, time, and effort to develop for profit an innovative product or way of doing something

**Economics** is the study of how resources are distributed for the production of goods and services within a social system. Table 1.3 describes those resources or the *factors of production,* consisting of land, labour, capital, and enterprise, used to produce goods and services. The firm can also have intangible resources such as a good reputation for quality products or being socially responsible. The goal is to turn the factors of production and intangible resources into a competitive advantage.

### Economic Systems

An **economic system** describes how a particular society distributes its resources to produce goods and services. A central issue of economics is how to fulfill an unlimited demand for goods and services in a world with a limited supply of resources. Different economic systems attempt to resolve this central issue in numerous ways, as we shall see.

Communism, socialism, and capitalism, the basic economic systems found in the world today (Table 1.4) have fundamental differences in the way they address the distribution of resources. The factors of production in command economies are controlled by government planning. In many cases, the government owns or controls the

**Table 1.3** | The Factors of Production

| Type of Resource | Description |
|---|---|
| **Natural resources** | Land, forests, minerals, water, and other things that are not made by people. |
| **Human resources (labour)** | Physical and mental abilities that people use to produce goods and services. |
| **Financial resources (capital)** | The funds used to acquire the natural and human resources needed to provide products. |
| **Enterprise** | **Entrepreneurs** organize the resources, or factors of production, and take risks. |

©Michael Interisano/Design Pics/Getty Images

Canada's abundant natural resources include vast quantities of oil.

**Consider the Following: Economic systems must address three important issues...**

1. What goods and services, and how much of each, will satisfy consumers' needs?
2. How will goods and services be produced, who will produce them, and with what resources will they be produce.
3. How are the goods and services to be distributed to consumers?

**Table 1.4** | Comparisons of Communism, Socialism, and Capitalism

| | Communism | Socialism | Capitalism |
|---|---|---|---|
| Business ownership | Most businesses are owned and operated by the government. | The government owns and operates major industries; individuals own small businesses. | Individuals own and operate all businesses. |
| Competition | Government controls competition and the economy. | Restricted in major industries; encouraged in small business. | Encouraged by market forces and government regulations. |
| Profits | Excess income goes to the government, which supports social and economic institutions. | Profits earned by small businesses may be reinvested in the business; profits from government-owned industries go to the government. | Individuals and businesses are free to keep profits after paying taxes. |
| Product availability and price | Consumers have a limited choice of goods and services; prices are usually high. | Consumers have some choice of goods and services; prices are determined by supply and demand. | Consumers have a wide choice of goods and services; prices are determined by supply and demand. |
| Employment options | Little choice in choosing a career; most people work for government-owned industries or farms. | More choice of careers; many people work in government jobs. | Unlimited choice of careers. |

production of goods and services. Communism and socialism are, therefore, considered command economies.

**Communism.** Karl Marx (1818–1883) first described **communism** as a society in which the people, without regard to class, own all the nation's resources. In his ideal political–economic system, everyone contributes according to ability and receives benefits according to need. In a communist economy, the people (through the government) own and operate all businesses and factors of production. Central government planning determines what goods and services satisfy citizens' needs, how the goods and services are produced, and how they are distributed. However, no true communist economy exists today that satisfies Marx's ideal.

**communism** first described by Karl Marx as a society in which the people, without regard to class, own all the nation's resources

On paper, communism appears to be efficient and equitable, producing less of a gap between rich and poor. In practice, communist economies have been marked by low standards of living, critical shortages of consumer goods, high prices, and little freedom. Russia, Poland, Hungary, and other Eastern European nations have turned away from communism and toward economic systems governed by supply and demand rather than by central planning. Similarly, China has become the first communist country to make strong economic gains by adopting capitalist approaches to business. As a result of economic challenges, communism is declining and its future as an economic system is uncertain.

**Socialism.** **Socialism** is an economic system in which the government owns and operates basic industries—postal service, telephone system, utilities, transportation, health care, and some manufacturing—but individuals own most businesses. Central planning determines what basic goods and services are produced, how they are produced, and how they are distributed. Individuals and small businesses provide other goods and services based on consumer demand and the availability of resources. Citizens are dependent on the government for many goods and services.

Most socialist nations, such as Norway, India, and Israel, are democratic and recognize basic individual freedoms. Citizens can vote politicians in and out of office, but central government planners usually make decisions about what is best for the nation. People are free to go into the occupation of their choice, but they often work in government-operated organizations. Socialists believe their system permits a higher standard of living than other economic systems, but the difference often applies to the nation as a whole rather than to its individual citizens. Although this may be true, taxes and unemployment are generally higher in socialist countries. However, countries like Denmark have a high standard of living and they rate high in measures of happiness.

**socialism** an economic system in which the government owns and operates basic industries but individuals own most businesses

**capitalism, or free enterprise** an economic system in which individuals own and operate the majority of businesses that provide goods and services

**Capitalism.** **Capitalism, or free enterprise**, is an economic system in which individuals own and operate the majority of businesses that provide goods and services. Competition, supply, and demand determine which goods and services are produced, how they are produced, and how they are distributed. Canada, the United States, Japan, and Australia are examples of economic systems based on capitalism.

There are two forms of capitalism: pure capitalism and modified capitalism. In pure capitalism, also called a **free-market system**, all economic decisions are made without government intervention. This economic system was first described by Adam Smith in *The Wealth of Nations* (1776). Smith, often called the father of capitalism, believed that the "invisible hand of competition" best regulates the economy. He argued that competition should determine what goods and services people need. Smith's system is also called *laissez-faire* ("let it be") *capitalism* because the government does not interfere in business.

**free-market system** pure capitalism, in which all economic decisions are made without government intervention

**mixed economies** economies made up of elements from more than one economic system

Modified capitalism differs from pure capitalism in that the government intervenes and regulates business to some extent. One of the ways in which the Canadian and United States governments regulate business is through laws. Laws such as Canada's Competition Act in Canada, which maintains and enforces antitrust laws, illustrate the importance of the government's role in the economy.

**Mixed Economies.** No country practises a pure form of communism, socialism, or capitalism, although most tend to favour one system over the others. Most nations operate as **mixed economies**, which have elements from more than one economic system. In socialist Sweden, most businesses are owned and operated by private individuals. In capitalist Canada a number of government-owned businesses or Crown corporations exist, such as Canada Post and the Canadian Broadcasting Corporation (CBC). In once-communist Russia, Hungary, Poland, and other Eastern European nations, capitalist ideas have been implemented, including private ownership of businesses.

©Lester Balajadia/Shutterstock

VIA Rail is one of Canada's 49 federal Crown corporations.

Countries such as China and Russia have used state capitalism to advance the economy. State capitalism tries to integrate the powers of the state with the advantages of capitalism. It is led by the government but uses capitalistic tools such as listing state-owned companies on the stock market and embracing globalization.[7] State capitalism includes some of the world's largest companies such as Russia's Gazprom, which is the largest natural gas company. China's ability to make huge investments—to the point of creating entirely new industries—puts many private industries at a disadvantage.[8]

## The Free-Enterprise System

Many economies—including those of Canada, the United States, and Japan—are based on free enterprise, and many communist and socialist countries, such as China and Russia, are applying more principles of free enterprise to their own economic systems. Free enterprise provides an opportunity for a business to succeed or fail on the basis of market demand. In a free-enterprise system, companies that can efficiently manufacture and sell products that consumers desire will probably succeed. Inefficient businesses and those that sell products that do not offer needed benefits will likely fail as consumers take their business to firms that have more competitive products.

A number of basic individual and business rights must exist for free enterprise to work. These rights are the goals of many countries that have recently embraced free enterprise.

Without these rights, businesses cannot function effectively because they are not motivated to succeed. Thus, these rights make possible the open exchange of goods and services. In the countries that favour free enterprise, such as Canada, citizens have the freedom to make many decisions about the employment they choose and to create their own productivity systems. Many entrepreneurs are more productive in free-enterprise societies because personal and financial incentives are available that can aid in entrepreneurial success. For many entrepreneurs, their work becomes a part of their system of goals, values, and lifestyle. Consider the panelists ("dragons") on the CBC program *Dragons' Den*. Panelists on *Dragons' Den* give entrepreneurs a chance to receive funding to realize their dreams by deciding whether to invest in their projects. They include Arlene Dickinson, who built one of Canada's largest independent marketing firms, and Jim Treliving, founder of Boston Pizza.[9]

## Consider the Following: Individual and business rights under free enterprise

1. Individuals must have the right to own property and to pass this property on to their heirs. This right motivates people to work hard and save to buy property.
2. Individuals and businesses must have the right to earn profits and to use the profits as they wish, within the constraints of their society's laws and values.
3. Individuals and businesses must have the right to make decisions that determine the way the business operates. Although there is government regulation, the philosophy in countries like Canada and the United States is to permit maximum freedom within a set of rules of fairness.
4. Individuals must have the right to choose what career to pursue, where to live, what goods and services to purchase, and more. Businesses must have the right to choose where to locate, what goods and services to produce, what resources to use in the production process, and so on.

©AF archive/Alamy Stock Photo

In the U.S., *Shark Tank* allows potential entrepreneurs to receive funding for their businesses, but only if they receive approval from the panel of "sharks," self-made tycoons who choose whether to invest in the projects. Two of the sharks, Robert Herjavec and Kevin O'Leary, are Canadian entrepreneurs.

# The Forces of Supply and Demand

**LO 1-4** Describe the role of supply, demand, and competition in a free-enterprise system.

In Canada and in other free-enterprise systems, the distribution of resources and products is determined by supply and demand. **Demand** is the number of goods and services that consumers are willing to buy at different prices at a specific time. From your own experience, you probably recognize that consumers are usually willing to buy more of an item as its price falls because they want to save money. Consider handmade rugs, for example. Consumers may be willing to buy six rugs at $350 each, four at $500 each, or only two at $650 each. The relationship between the price and the number of rugs consumers are willing to buy can be shown graphically with a *demand curve* (see Figure 1.2).

**Supply** is the number of products that businesses are willing to sell at different prices at a specific time. In general, because the potential for profits is higher, businesses are willing to supply more of a good or service at higher prices. For example, a company that sells rugs may be willing to sell six at $650 each, four at $500 each, or just two at $350 each. The relationship between the price of rugs and the quantity the company is willing to supply can be shown graphically with a *supply curve* (see Figure 1.2).

**demand** the number of goods and services that consumers are willing to buy at different prices at a specific time

**supply** the number of products—goods and services—that businesses are willing to sell at different prices at a specific time

In Figure 1.2, the supply and demand curves intersect at the point where supply and demand are equal. The price

Figure 1.2 | Equilibrium Price of Handmade Rugs

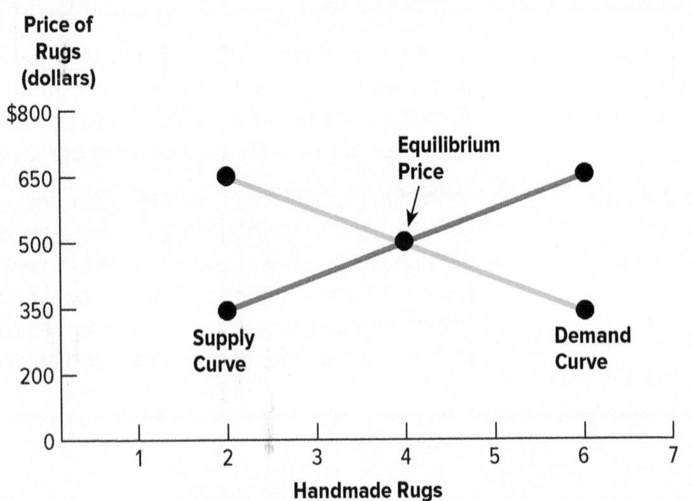


Supply and demand is the force that drives the distribution of resources (goods and services, labour, and money) in a free-enterprise economy.

Critics of supply and demand say the system does not distribute resources equally. The forces of supply and demand prevent participation in the market by sellers who have to sell at higher prices (because their costs are high) and buyers who cannot afford to buy goods at the equilibrium price. According to critics, the wealthy can afford to buy more than they need, but the poor are unable to buy enough of what they need to survive.

at which the number of products that businesses are willing to supply equals the amount of products that consumers are willing to buy at a specific point in time is the **equilibrium price**. In our rug example, the company is willing to supply four rugs at $500 each, and consumers are willing to buy four rugs at $500 each. Therefore, $500 is the equilibrium price for a rug at that point in time, and most rug companies will price their rugs at $500. As you might imagine, a business that charges more than $500 (or whatever the current equilibrium price is) for its rugs will not sell many and might not earn a profit. On the other hand, a business that charges less than $500 accepts a lower profit per rug than could be made at the equilibrium price.

**equilibrium price** the price at which the number of products that businesses are willing to supply equals the amount of products that consumers are willing to buy at a specific point in time

"Demand is the number of goods and services that consumers are willing to buy at different prices at a specific time."

If the cost of making rugs goes up, businesses will not offer as many at the old price. Changing the price alters the supply curve, and a new equilibrium price results. This is an ongoing process, with supply and demand constantly changing in response to changes in economic conditions, availability of resources, and degree of competition. For example, the price of oil can change rapidly and ranged between $45 and $74 a barrel in 2018 alone. Prices for goods and services vary according to these changes in supply and demand.

## The Nature of Competition

**Competition**, the rivalry among businesses for consumers' dollars, is another vital element in free enterprise. According to Adam Smith, competition fosters efficiency and low prices by forcing producers to offer the best products at the most reasonable price; those who fail to do so are not able to stay in business. Thus, competition should improve the quality of the goods and services available or reduce

**competition** the rivalry among businesses for consumers' dollars

©PhotoLink/Getty Images

Atlantic Canadian lobster prices are set by the forces of supply and demand. In recent years, demand has slowed as people are less likely to spend large amounts of money on premium seafood during periods of economic uncertainty. The low prices have forced some fishermen out of business. Other fishermen have taken a more entrepreneurial route and have started to sell directly to the consumer and eliminated the middleman to maximize their earnings. What do you think are the pros and cons of such an approach?

prices. Competition allows for open markets and provides opportunities for both individuals and businesses to successfully compete. Entrepreneurs can discover new technology, ways to lower prices, as well as methods for providing better distribution or services.

Jeff Bezos, founder of Amazon.com, is a prime example. Amazon was able to offer products at competitive prices and continued to succeed even after the dot-com bubble burst. Today, Amazon competes against such retail giants as Walmart in a number of industries, including cloud computing, entertainment, food, and consumer products found in retail stores. Bezos is now the richest person in the world.

Within a free-enterprise system, there are four types of competitive environments, (or market structures) as Table 1.5 shows: pure competition, monopolistic competition, oligopoly, and monopoly.

**Pure competition** exists when there are many small businesses selling one standardized product, such as agricultural commodities. No one business sells enough of the product to influence the product's price. And because there is no difference in the products, prices are determined solely by the forces of supply and demand.

**pure competition** the market structure that exists when there are many small businesses selling one standardized product

**monopolistic competition** the market structure that exists when there are fewer businesses than in a pure-competition environment and the differences among the goods they sell are small

**Monopolistic competition** exists when there are fewer businesses than in a pure competition environment and the differences among the goods they sell are small. The products differ slightly in packaging, warranty, name, and other characteristics, but all satisfy the same consumer need. Businesses have some power over the price they charge in monopolistic competition because they can make consumers aware of product differences through advertising. Consumers value some features more than others and are often willing to pay higher prices for a product with the features they want.

**Table 1.5** | Market Structures

| | Pure Competition | Monopolistic Competition | Monopoly | Oligopoly |
|---|---|---|---|---|
| Number of Firms | Many | Several | One | Few |
| Nature of Product | Standardized | Differentiated | Standardized or Differentiated | Specialized |
| Type of Product | Commodities like oil, wheat, and cotton | Breakfast cereals, soft drinks, and jeans | Utility companies, railways, and airports | Airlines, supermarket chains, and gaming consoles |
| Example | Apples | Cheerios | Microsoft | OPEC |

For example, many consumers are willing to pay a higher price for organic fruits and vegetables rather than receive a bargain on non-organic foods. The same holds true for non–genetically modified foods.

An **oligopoly** exists when there are very few businesses selling a product. In an oligopoly, individual businesses have control over their products' prices because each business supplies a large portion of the products sold in the marketplace. Nonetheless, the prices charged by different firms stay fairly close because a price cut or increase by one company will trigger a similar response from another company.

**oligopoly** the market structure that exists when there are very few businesses selling a product.

**monopoly** the market structure that exists when there is only one business providing a product in a given market

In the airline industry, for example, when one airline cuts fares to boost sales, other airlines quickly follow with rate decreases to remain competitive. On the other hand, airlines often raise prices at the same time. Oligopolies exist when it is expensive for new firms to enter the marketplace. Not just anyone can acquire enough financial capital to build an automobile production facility or purchase enough airplanes and related resources to build an airline.

> "Competition, the rivalry among businesses for consumers' dollars, is another vital element in free enterprise."

A **monopoly** exists when there is one business providing a product in a given market, Utility companies that supply electricity, natural gas, and water are often monopolies. The government permits such monopolies because the cost of creating the good or supplying the service is so great that new producers cannot compete for sales. Government-granted monopolies are subject to government-regulated prices.

Some monopolies exist because of technological developments that are protected by patent laws. Patent laws grant the developer of new technology a period of time (17 or 20 years) during which no other producer can use the same technology without the agreement of the original developer. This monopoly allows the developer to recover research, development, and production expenses and to earn a reasonable profit. A drug can receive a 17-year patent from the time it is discovered or the chemical is identified. For example, Tamiflu lost its patent, and now the generic version can be made by other firms.

## Economic Cycles and Productivity

**LO 1-5** Specify why and how the health of the economy is measured.

**Expansion and Contraction.** Economies are not stagnant; they expand and contract. **Economic expansion** occurs when an economy is growing and people are spending more money. Their purchases stimulate the production of goods and services, which in turn stimulates employment. The standard of living rises because more people are employed and have money to spend. Rapid expansions of the economy, however, may result in **inflation**, a continuing rise in prices. Inflation can be harmful if individuals' incomes do not increase at the same pace as rising prices, reducing their buying power. The worst case of hyperinflation occurred in Hungary in 1946. At one point, prices were doubling every 15.6 hours. More recent cases of hyperinflation have occurred in Zimbabwe and Venezuela. Zimbabwe suffered from hyperinflation so severe that its inflation percentage rate rose into the hundreds of millions. Venezuela's hyperinflation is ongoing note and its inflation percentage rate is expected to reach in the millions.[10]

**economic expansion** the situation that occurs when an economy is growing and people are spending more money; their purchases stimulate the production of goods and services, which in turn stimulates employment

**inflation** a condition characterized by a continuing rise in prices

Figure 1.3 | Unemployment Rate in Canada, 2013–2018

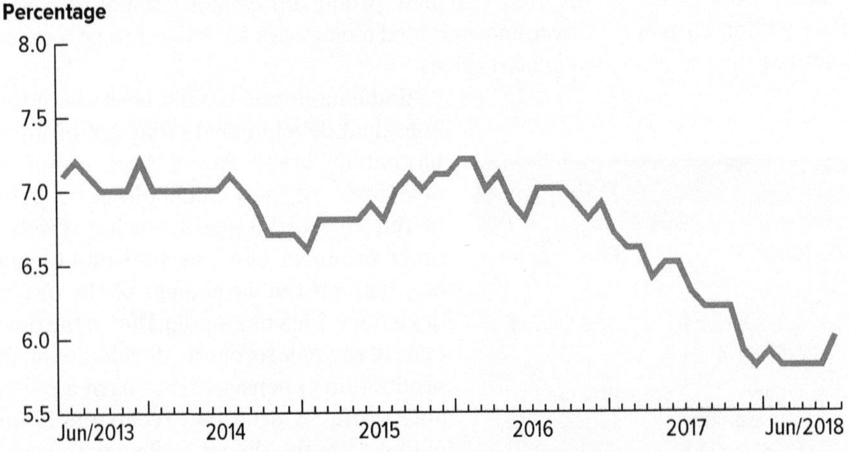


**Economic contraction** occurs when spending declines. Businesses cut back on production and lay off workers, and the economy as a whole slows down. Contractions of the economy lead to **recession**—a decline in production, employment, and income. Recessions are often characterized by rising levels of **unemployment**, which is measured as the percentage of the population that wants to work but is unable to find jobs. Figure 1.3 shows the overall unemployment rate in Canada from 2013 to 2018. Rising unemployment levels tend to stifle demand for goods and services, which can force prices downward, a condition known as *deflation*. Deflation poses a serious economic problem because price decreases could result in consumers delaying purchases. If consumers wait for lower prices, the economy could fall into a recession.

**economic contraction** a slowdown of the economy characterized by a decline in spending and during which businesses cut back on production and lay off workers

**recession** a decline in production, employment, and income

**unemployment** the condition in which a percentage of the population wants to work but is unable to find a job

**depression** a condition of the economy in which unemployment is very high, consumer spending is low, and business output is sharply reduced

Canada has experienced numerous recessions, with the most recent one occurring in 2008–2009. This recession (or economic slowdown) was caused by problems in the housing market in the United States, which led to a crisis in the banking industry and the U.S. government bailing out banks to keep them from failing. This in turn caused a lack of confidence in the overall global financial sector, which had an impact on the economies of Canada and other countries around the world. A severe recession may turn into a **depression**, in which unemployment is very high, consumer spending is low, and business output is sharply reduced, something that occurred worldwide in the early 1930s.

Economies expand and contract in response to changes in consumer, business, and government spending. War also can affect an economy, sometimes stimulating it (as in Canada during World Wars I

**Figure 1.4** | Canada's Gross Domestic Product, 2013–2018

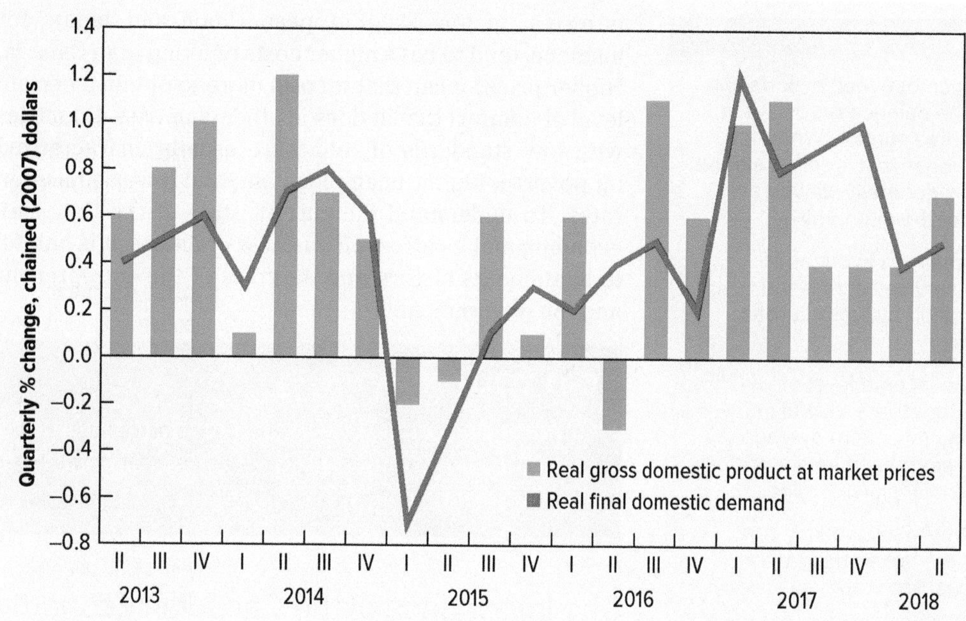


and II) and sometimes stifling it (as in the United States during the Persian Gulf and Iraq wars). Although fluctuations in the economy are inevitable, and to a certain extent predictable, their effects—inflation and unemployment—disrupt lives and thus governments try to minimize them.

**Measuring the Economy.** Countries measure the state of their economies to determine whether they are expanding or contracting and whether corrective action is necessary to minimize the fluctuations. One commonly used measure is **gross domestic product (GDP)**—the sum of all goods and services produced in a country during a year. GDP measures only those goods and services made within a country and, therefore, does not include profits from companies' overseas operations; it does include profits earned by foreign companies within the country being measured. However, it does not take into account the concept of GDP in relation to population (GDP per capita). Figure 1.4 shows Canada's GDP over several years, while Table 1.6 compares a number of economic statistics for a sampling of countries.

**gross domestic product (GDP)** the sum of all goods and services produced in a country during a year

**budget surplus** the condition in which a nation spends less than it takes in from taxes

**budget deficit** the condition in which a nation spends more than it takes in from taxes

Another important indicator of a nation's economic health is the relationship between its spending and income (from taxes). When a nation spends less than it takes in from taxes it has a **budget surplus**, and when it spends more than it takes in from taxes, it has a **budget deficit**.

**Table 1.6** | Economic Indicators of Different Countries

| Country | GDP (in billions of dollars) | GDP per Capita | Unemployment Rate (%) | Inflation Rate (%) |
|---|---|---|---|---|
| Argentina | $586 | $22,400 | 7.6 | 27.6 |
| Brazil | 1,903 | 15,800 | 6.4 | 10.6 |
| Canada | 1,592 | 45,900 | 6.9 | 1.2 |
| China | 11,383 | 14,300 | 4.2 | 1.5 |
| Germany | 3,468 | 47,400 | 4.8 | 0.2 |
| India | 2,289 | 6,300 | 7.1 | 5.6 |
| Japan | 4,413 | 38,200 | 3.3 | 0.7 |
| Mexico | 1,291 | 18,500 | 4.5 | 2.7 |
| Russia | 1,179 | 23,700 | 5.4 | 15.4 |
| United States | 18,558 | 55,300 | 5.2 | 0.2 |

Traditionally, Canada has been fiscally conservative, but in 2016, it moved out of surplus to planned deficits. The federal government's market debt—the debt on which Ottawa pays interest—topped $1 trillion for the first time, in 2018.[11] Deficits are especially worrisome because, to reduce the debt to a manageable level, the government either has to increase its revenues (raise taxes) or reduce spending on social, defense, and legal programs, none of which are politically popular. Table 1.7 describes some of the other ways we evaluate our nation's economy.

**Table 1.7** | How Do We Evaluate Our Nation's Economy?

| Unit of Measure | Description |
|---|---|
| Trade balance | The difference between exports and imports. If the balance is positive, it is called a trade surplus. When the balance is negative it is called a trade deficit and is generally viewed as unhealthy for the economy. |
| Consumer price index | Measures changes in prices of goods and services purchased for consumption by typical urban households. |
| Per capita income | Indicates the income level of "average" Canadians. Useful in determining how much "average" consumers spend and how much money Canadians are earning. |
| Unemployment rate | Indicates how many working age Canadians are not working who otherwise want to work. |
| Inflation | Monitors price increases in consumer goods and services over specified periods of time. Used to determine if costs of goods and services are rising faster than worker compensation over time. |
| Worker productivity | The amount of goods and services produced for each hour worked. |

# The Canadian Economy

**LO 1-6** Trace the evolution of the Canadian economy and discuss the role of the entrepreneur in the economy.

As we said previously, Canada is a mixed economy with a foundation based on capitalism. The answers to the three basic economic issues are determined primarily by competition and the forces of supply and demand, although the federal government does intervene in economic decisions to a certain extent. For instance, the federal government exerts oversight over the airline industry to make sure airlines remain economically viable as well as for safety and security purposes.

**Standard of living** refers to the level of wealth and material comfort that people have available to them. Canada, the United States, Switzerland, Australia, and Norway all have a high standard of living, meaning that most of their citizens are able to afford basic necessities and some degree of comfort. These nations are often characterized by a high GDP per capita. However, a higher GDP per capita does not automatically translate into a higher standard of living. Costs of goods and services is also a factor. The European Union and Japan, for instance, tend to have higher costs of living than Canada. Higher prices mean that it costs more to obtain a certain level of comfort than it does in other countries. Countries with low standards of living are usually characterized by poverty, higher unemployment, and lower education rates. To understand the current state of the Canadian economy and its effect on business practices, it is helpful to examine its history and the roles of the entrepreneur and the government.

**standard of living** refers to the level of wealth and material comfort that people have available to them.

**DID YOU KNOW?**

Canada performs very well in many measures of well-being relative to most other countries in the OECD's Better Life Index.[12]

## The Importance of the Canadian Economy

The Canadian economy is an **open economy** or an economy in which economic activities occur between the country and the international community. Canada is an important player in international trade. Open economies tend to grow faster than economies that do not engage in international trade. This is because international trade is positively related to efficiency and productivity. Companies in Canada have greater access to a wider range of resources and knowledge, including technology. The ability to harness technology is essential for increased innovation. In contrast, research shows a negative relationship between regulatory actions and innovation in firms, suggesting that too much regulation hinders business activities and their contribution to the economy.[13]

**open economy** an economy in which economic activities occur between a country and the international community

## A Brief History of the Canadian Economy

**The Early Economy.** Before the colonization of North America, Aboriginal Peoples lived as hunter/gatherers and farmers, with some trade among tribes. The first European settlers operated primarily as an agricultural economy. Abundant natural resources nourished industries such as farming, fishing, fur trading, and shipping. A few manufactured goods and money for the burgeoning industries came from England and other countries.

Farm families who produced surplus goods sold or traded them for things they could not produce themselves, such as fine furniture and window glass. Some families also spent time turning raw materials into clothes and household goods. Because these goods were produced at home, this system was called the *domestic system.*

## RESPONDING TO BUSINESS CHALLENGES

### The Trix of the Trade: General Mills Brand Strategy

In its 150-year history, General Mills has evolved from a flour mill to a packaged consumer goods company with global revenues of US$16 billion. More recently, General Mills has begun investing heavily in organic and natural foods with its acquisition of organic food brands Cascade Farms and Annie's. Sales of organic products are a $5.4 billion industry in Canada and growing worldwide. Demand for organic food is increasing so rapidly that the supply has been unable to keep up. As a result, General Mills has begun underwriting the costs for farmers to convert their farms to organic crops.

The consumer goods market is characterized by monopolistic competition, meaning that General Mills has many competitors. This requires General Mills to adapt to changing consumer preferences. For example, consumers have been eating less cereal and looking for quick breakfast items like yoghurt and breakfast bars. As a result, General Mills has expanded into more on-the-go products such as yoghurt and granola. Perhaps as a way to meet the competition head-on, General Mills has adopted a new brand strategy: Consumers first.

General Mills wants its customer-centric focus to differentiate it from rival firms. In keeping with this customer emphasis, it has agreed to adopt genetically modified organism (GMO) labelling for some of its products. While General Mills believes GMO products are safe, it wants customers to know that it is listening to their concerns. In fact, General Mills became a first mover in this endeavour by reformulating Cheerios to be GMO-free. However, as competitors also turn toward organic ingredients, it might not be long before other cereal manufacturers begin developing their own non-GMO cereals. General Mills must continue to innovate to maintain its competitive edge.*

#### DISCUSSION QUESTIONS

1. Why does the consumer goods industry operate in an environment of monopolistic competition? What must firms like General Mills do to succeed in this environment?
2. How is General Mills addressing the supply–demand problem that it is facing with organic food?
3. What are some of the ways in which General Mills is differentiating its products from the competition?

*Sarah Elbert, "Food for Thought," Delta Sky, December 2016, pp. 66–70; Annie Gasparro, "General Mills Starts Making Some Cheerios Without GMOs," *Wall Street Journal*, January 2, 2014, http://www.wsj.com/articles/SB10001424052702303370904579297211874270146 (accessed January 6, 2017); Hadley Malcolm, "General Mills to Label GMOs on Products across Country," *USA Today*, March 18, 2016, http://www.usatoday.com/story/money/2016/03/18/general-mills-to-label-gmos-onproducts/ 81981314/ (accessed January 6, 2017); Stephanie Strom, "Paying Farmers to Go Organic, Even Before the Crops Come In," *New York Times*, July 14, 2016, http:// www.nytimes .com/2016/07/15/business/paying-farmers-togo-organic-even-before-the-crops-come-in.html (accessed January 6, 2017); John Kell, "General Mills Reveals How It Plans to 'Renovate' Yogurt Products," *Fortune*, July 14, 2016, http://fortune.com/2016/07/14/general-mills-yogurt/ (accessed January 2, 2018); Nathan Bomey, "Slumping Yogurt, Cereal Sales Spoil General Mills' Performance," *USA Today*, September 20, 2017, https://www.usatoday.com/story/money/2017/09/20/general-mills-first-quarterearnings/ 684218001/ (accessed January 2, 2018); Mary Ellen Shoup, "Chobani Beats Yoplait in Sales and Market Share as Dannon Takes No. 1 Spot in US Yogurt Market," *Dairy Reporter*, March 13, 2017, https://www.dairyreporter.com/Article/2017/03/13/Chobani-surpasses Yoplait-in-sales-and-market-share (accessed January 2, 2018); Sean Rossman, "What Is French Yogurt and Is It the New Greek?" *USA Today*, July 6, 2017, https:// www.usatoday.com/story/money/nation -now/2017/07/06/what-french-yogurt-and-new-greek/439935001/ (accessed January 2, 2018); Bruce Horovitz, "Cheerios Drop Genetically Modified Ingredients," *USA Today*, January 2, 2014, https://www.usatoday.com/story/money/business/2014/01/02/cheerios-gmos-cereals /4295739/ (accessed January 2, 2018); Foodincanada.com. (2018), https://www.foodincanada.com/food-in-canada/canadas-organic-sector -continues-capture-market-share-report-138272/ (retrieved 28 October, 2018).

**The Industrial Revolution.** The nineteenth century and the Industrial Revolution brought the development of new technology and factories. The factory brought together all the resources needed to make a product—materials, machines, and workers. Work in factories became specialized as workers focused on one or two tasks. As work became more efficient, productivity increased, making more goods available at lower prices. In Canada, industrialization mostly occurred in Ontario and Quebec. Due to the size of the country, its relatively small population, and the richness of its resources, most Canadians continued to work in primary industries.[15]

The government of the day established the Canadian Pacific Railway and linked the country coast to coast. Railroads brought major changes, allowing farmers to send their surplus crops and goods all over the nation for barter or for sale. Factories began to spring up along the railways to manufacture farm equipment and a variety of other goods to be shipped by rail.

## Consider the Following: Indigenous languages

The United Nations has declared 2019 the International Year of Indigenous Languages. There is no consensus on the number of Indigenous languages currently in existence in Canada, but UNESCO's list of vulnerable languages includes eighty-seven Indigenous languages in Canada. Thirty-two are designated as critically endangered. Canada's first *Indigenous Languages Act*, implemented in 2019, aims to provide federal support for a multi-faceted approach to Indigenous language revitalization.

But some groups have already found ways to reclaim language. For example, Clarence Louie, Chief of the Osoyoos Band, one of the most prosperous First Nations in Canada, models not only business development but also socio-economic development. Chief Louie stresses the importance of maintaining Okanagan language and culture in all aspects of the Band's activities, including business. The Osoyoos Indian Band's corporate motto is In Business to Preserve Our Past by Strengthening Our Future. In establishing this, Chief Louie has chosen a different path toward capitalism.*

*Shimon Koffler Fogel, "Why Canada's Jewish community supports revitalizing Indigenous languages," *Toronto Star*, February 22, 2019, https://www.thestar.com/opinion/contributors/2019/02/22/why-canadas-jewish-community-supports-revitalizing-indigenous-language.html, (accessed March 10, 2019); Ryan Flannigan, "Jewish advocacy group backs push to revitalize Indigenous languages," CTVNews.ca, January 31, 2019, https://www.ctvnews.ca/canada/jewish-advocacy-group-backs-push-to-revitalize-indigenous-languages-1.4277415, (accessed March 10, 2019); Diane Weber Bederman, "First Nations and the Jews: A Common History," Huffington Post, May 15, 2013, https://www.huffingtonpost.ca/diane-bederman/first-nations-and-jews_b_3237519.html, (accessed March 10, 2019); The National Indigenous Economic Development Board, "Chief Clarence Louie," http://www.naedb-cndea.com/en/the-board/chief-clarence-louie/, (accessed March 10, 2019).

©Wallace Kirkland/The LIFE Picture Collection/Getty Images

The fur trade was important to Canada's early development as it began in the sixteenth century and remained a major industry for almost three hundred years. The first major business competitors in Canada were the North West Trading Company and the Hudson's Bay Company, which remained active in the fur trade until the 1980s.[14]

**The Manufacturing and Marketing Economies.** Industrialization brought increased prosperity, and many Canadians found jobs in the *manufacturing economy*—one devoted to manufacturing goods and providing services rather than producing agricultural products. The assembly line was applied to more industries, increasing the variety of goods available to the consumer. Businesses became more concerned with the needs of the consumer and entered the *marketing economy*. Expensive goods such as cars and appliances could be purchased on a time-payment plan. Companies conducted research to find out what products consumers needed and wanted. Advertising made consumers aware of differences in products and prices.

Because these developments occurred in a free-enterprise system, consumers determined what goods and services were produced. They did this by purchasing the products they liked at prices they were willing to pay. Canada prospered, and Canadian citizens had one of the highest standards of living in the world.

**The Service and New Digital Economy.** After World War II, with the increased standard of living, Canadians had more money and more time. They began to pay others to perform services that made their lives easier. Beginning in the 1960s, more and more women entered the workforce. The profile of the family changed: today there are more single-parent families and individuals living alone; in two-parent families, both parents often work.

One result of this trend is that time-pressed Canadians are increasingly paying others to do tasks they used to do at home, like cooking, laundry, landscaping, and child care. These trends have gradually changed Canada to a *service economy*—one devoted to the production of services that make life easier for busy consumers. Businesses increased their demand for services, especially in the areas of finance and information technology. Service industries such as restaurants, banking, medicines, child care, auto repair, leisure-related industries, and even education are growing rapidly and may account for as much as 70 percent of the Canadian economy.

These trends continue, with advanced technology contributing to new service products based on technology and digital media that provide smartphones, social networking, and virtual worlds. This has led to the growth of e-commerce, or transactions involving goods and services over the Internet. E-commerce has led to firms that would have been unheard of a few decades ago, such as eBay, Shopify, Etsy, and Amazon.ca. Figure 1.5 shows a snapshot of Canadian adults who engage in e-commerce. More about the digital world, business, and new online social media can be found in Chapter 13.

**Figure 1.5** | Online Retailing and E-commerce in Canada

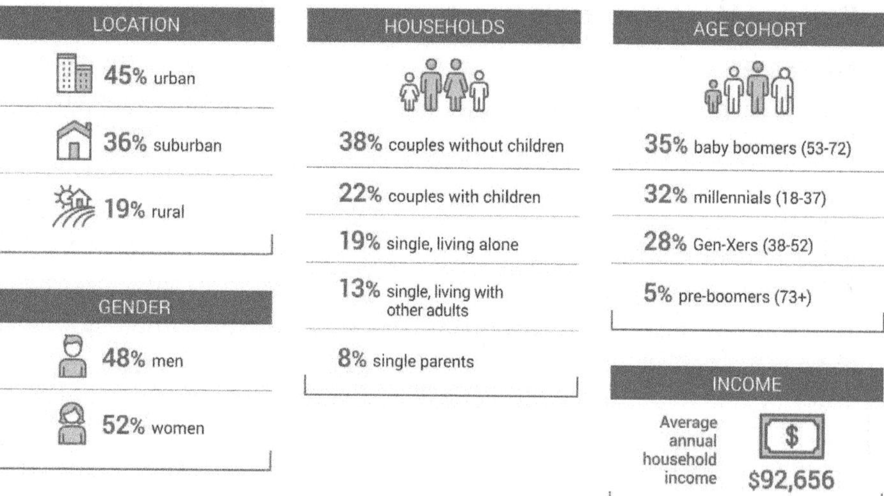

©Canada Post

## The Role of Government in the Canadian Economy

The Canadian economic system is best described as a mixed economy because entrepreneurs and citizens control many of the factors of production and own the majority of businesses, but the government is still active in the economic system through its ownership of Crown corporations and the regulations it maintains to preserve competition and protect consumers and employees. Federal and provincial governments intervene in the economy with laws and regulations designed to promote competition and to protect consumers, employees, and the environment. Many of these laws are discussed in Appendix A.

Additionally, government agencies such as Industry Canada and the Department of Finance measure the health of the economy (GDP, productivity, etc.). Furthermore, the government—through the Bank of Canada, tax policy, and when necessary, spending—takes steps to minimize the disruptive effects of economic fluctuations and reduce unemployment. When the economy is contracting and unemployment is rising, the federal government tries to spur growth so that consumers will spend more money and businesses will hire more employees. To accomplish this, it may, through the Bank of Canada, reduce interest rates or increase its own spending for goods and services. When the economy expands so fast that inflation results, the government may intervene to reduce inflation by slowing down economic growth. This can be accomplished by raising interest rates to discourage spending by businesses and consumers. Techniques used to control the economy are discussed in Chapter 15.

## The Role of the Entrepreneur

An **entrepreneur** is an individual who risks their wealth, time, and effort to develop a product or service that he or she can sell for profit.

The free-enterprise system provides the conditions necessary for entrepreneurs to succeed. In the past, entrepreneurs were often inventors who brought all the factors of production together to produce a new product. Joseph-Armand Bombardier, who invented the snowmobile, and Alexander Graham Bell, who invented the telephone, were early Canadian entrepreneurs. Other entrepreneurs have succeeded by offering consumers both services and products. For example, Garfield Weston Ltd., which was started in the late nineteenth century, now controls a great deal of the retail food business in Canada through its

**entrepreneurs** individuals who risks their wealth, time, and effort to develop for profit an innovative product or way of doing something

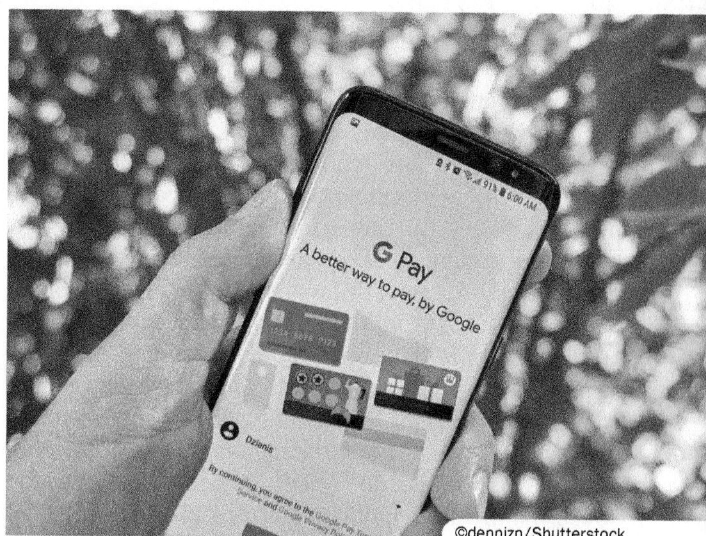

©dennizn/Shutterstock

Google Pay is a mobile payments system that allows users to store their credit card or debit card information. When checking out at stores, users can bring up the app and use the information to pay for their purchases.

## ENTREPRENEURSHIP IN ACTION

### Cashing In on Cannabis

**Aphria Inc.**

**Founders:** Vic Neufeld, John Cervini, and Cole Cacciavillanin

**Founded:** 2014, Ontario

**Success:** Vic Neufeld and his partners have taken their company, Aphria, from zero worth to $2.5 billion after only four years.

The founders have multi-generational expertise in commercial agriculture and began with a sack of seeds. It took more than a year of trial and error to find the best strains. Their goals are to be the best-performing cannabis company globally, and to grow pharmaceutical-grade medical marijuana at a lower cost than other licensed producers. They believe that the regulated system in Canada gives them a competitive head start as foreign markets, where medical marijuana is legal, will play a crucial role in taking up domestic oversupply from Canada.

The international interest in the industry is focused on the potential for Canada to lead the way in the science and production of medicinal cannabis. A report published by consultancy firm Deloitte in 2018 estimates that recreational use of the drug is a $22.6 billion industry in Canada. However, medicinal marijuana is more interesting because the market is global and the size of that market is expected to reach US$146.4 billion by the end of 2025. The owners of Aphria have already put their plans for global domination into action and have a presence in more than 10 countries across 5 continents.*

#### DISCUSSION QUESTIONS

1. What risks did these entrepreneurs take in entering a new industry?
2. Are being a low-cost producer and international expansion enough to be successful?
3. How will the industry change as more competition enters this market?

*Newsinteractivescbc.ca. (2018), https://newsinteractives.cbc.ca/longform/marijuana-moguls (retrieved October 26, 2018); Aphria.ca (2018), Aphria | Medical Marijuana Canada, https://aphria.ca/blog/vic-neufeld-from-a-peach-farm-boy-to-pot-czar/ (retrieved October 26, 2018); Benzingacom (2018), https://www.benzinga.com/fintech/18/07/12018382/cannabis-after-legalization-vic-neufeld-shares-aphrias-plan-for-growth (retrieved October 26, 2018); The Motley Fool (2018), https://www.fool.com/investing/2018/09/12/4-marijuana-stocks-could-control-half-of-canadas-w.aspx (retrieved October 26, 2018); Canadianbusiness.com (2016), https://www.canadianbusiness.com/business-news/from-dime-bag-to-money-bags-businesses-look-forward-to-recreational-marijuana/ (retrieved October 26, 2018); Alison Langley (2018), StCatharinesStandard.ca, https://www.stcatharinesstandard.ca/news-story/8886769-canada-could-be-leader-in-global-cannabis-market-o-leary-says/ (retrieved October 26, 2018).

controlling interest in Loblaw.[16] Although these entrepreneurs were born in another century, their legacy to the Canadian economy lives on in the companies they started, many of which still operate today.

Entrepreneurs are constantly changing business practices with new technology and innovative management techniques. Bill Gates, for example, built Microsoft, a software company whose products include Word and Windows, into a multi-billion dollar enterprise. Steve Jobs co-founded Apple and turned the company into a successful, highly innovative consumer electronics firm with products such as Macintosh computers as well as the iPod, iPhone, and iPad. Entrepreneurs have been associated with such uniquely Canadian concepts as Cirque du Soleil, Boston Pizza, Canada Goose, Lululemon, and Tim Hortons. Tim Horton and Ron Joyce co-founded the Tim Hortons chain in 1967. Today, Tim Hortons is Canada's largest quick service restaurant chain with over 4,000 restaurants in nine countries.[17] We will examine the importance of entrepreneurship further in Chapter 5.

## The Role of Ethics and Social Responsibility in Business

In the past few years, you may have read about a number of ethical issues at several well-known corporations, including Volkswagen, Pfizer, and General Motors. In many cases, misconduct by individuals within these firms had an adverse effect on current and retired employees, investors, and others associated with these firms. In some cases, individuals went to jail for their actions. These scandals undermined public confidence in the free-enterprise system and sparked a new debate about ethics in business. Business ethics generally refer to the standards and principles used by society to define appropriate and inappropriate conduct in the workplace. In many cases, these standards have been codified as laws prohibiting actions deemed unacceptable.

Society is increasingly demanding that business people become more socially responsible toward their stakeholders, including customers, employees, investors, government regulators, communities, and the natural environment. For example, diversity in the workforce

## Consider the Following: Demand eclipses supply of bluefin tuna

Bluefin tuna is immensely popular among sushi lovers, creating a high demand for the fish. Supply, on the other hand, is another matter. The bluefin population is being reduced through global overfishing and pollution. In Canada, the fish are harvested commercially from the Scotian Shelf, St. Margaret's Bay, the southern Gulf of St. Lawrence, the Bay of Fundy, and the Grand Banks.

The Center for Biological Diversity requested endangered species status for the bluefin, fearing current fishing practices might bring about extinction. The U.S. government declined the request. It argued that scientists need time to assess the current status of bluefin. It did, however, place the fish on its watch list. The Government of Canada made the determination not to list Atlantic bluefin tuna under the *Species at Risk Act,* based on a series of western Atlantic bluefin tuna stock assessments that demonstrated continued stock growth.

Most scientists, environmentalists, and lawmakers agree that the bluefin population has significantly declined, but many feel an international agreement on how best to preserve the population is preferable to a moratorium on fishing it. This assumes that fishers will comply with regulations. Many fishers currently fish more than the legal quota, with some fishing 100 percent illegally. Reduced supply and steady demand are driving up the price of bluefin, making it a desirable catch. One fish can bring in $1,000,000. Mitsubishi Corporation (the largest bluefin purchaser globally) has stored a large amount of frozen bluefin in anticipation of extinction. Unless there is an effective way to police fishing and preserve habitats, the bluefin may ultimately need official protection.*

### DISCUSSION QUESTIONS

1. Why is the price of bluefin tuna skyrocketing?
2. What are the ethical issues involved in selling bluefin tuna?
3. Why might the Canadian government be reluctant to place the bluefin tuna on the endangered species list? What are some of the consequences of acting too slowly or too quickly in its assessment?

*Felicity Barringer, "U.S. Declines to Protect the Overfished Bluefin Tuna," *New York Times,* May 27, 2011, www.nytimes.com/2011/05/28/science/earth/28tuna.html (accessed June 15, 2011); David Helvarg, "Oil, Terror, Tuna and You," Huffington Post, May 9, 2011, www.huffingtonpost.com/david-helvarg/oil-terror-tuna-and-you_b_859106.html (accessed June 15, 2011); "Endangered Species Listing for Atlantic Bluefin Tuna Not Warranted," NOAA, May 27, 2011, www.noaanews.noaa.gov/stories2011/20110527_bluefintuna.html (accessed June 18, 2011); David Jolly, "Many Mediterranean Fish Species Threatened With Extinction, Report Says," *New York Times,* April 19, 2011, http://green.blogs.nytimes.com/2011/04/19/mediterranean-fish-species-threatened-with-extinction/ (accessed June 18, 2011); "Giant Bluefin Tuna Sells for Record Breaking Price: Big Pic," Discovery News, January 5, 2011, http://news.discovery.com/animals/bluefin-tuna-record-auction-110105.html (accessed June 18, 2011); "The King of Sushi," CBS—*60 Minutes,* www.youtube.com/watch?v=dsbx6dQuRhQ (accessed June 18, 2011).

is both socially responsible and highly beneficial to the financial performance of companies. According to a McKinsey consulting firm study, organizations that have diverse leadership are more likely to report higher financial returns. (This study defined diversity as women and racial minorities.) Diversity creates increased employee satisfaction and improved decision making.[18]

©asiseeit/Getty Images

Many companies engage in socially responsible behaviour to give back to their communities. Home Depot partners with Habitat for Humanity to build homes for disadvantaged families.

Research has also shown that ethical behaviour can not only enhance a company's reputation but can also drive profits.[19] The ethical and socially responsible conduct of companies such as Whole Foods, Starbucks, and the mining company Teck Resources provides evidence that good ethics is good business. There is growing recognition that the long-term value of conducting business in an ethical and socially responsible manner that considers the interests of all stakeholders creates superior financial performance.[20]

To promote socially responsible and ethical behaviour while achieving organizational goals, businesses can monitor changes and trends in society's values. Businesses should determine what society wants and attempt to predict the long-term effects of their decisions. While it requires an effort to address the interests of all stakeholders, businesses can prioritize and attempt to balance conflicting demands. The goal is to develop a solid reputation of trust and avoid misconduct to develop effective workplace ethics.

# Can You Learn Business in a Classroom?

Obviously, the answer is yes, or there would be no purpose for this textbook! To be successful in business, you need knowledge, skills, experience, and good judgment. The topics covered in this chapter and throughout this book provide some of the knowledge you need to understand the world of business. The opening vignette at the beginning of each chapter, boxes and examples within each chapter, and the case at the end of each chapter describe experiences to help you develop good business judgment.

However, good judgment is based on knowledge and experience plus personal insight and understanding. Therefore, you need more courses in business, along with some practical experience in the business world, to help you develop the special insight necessary to put your personal stamp on knowledge as you apply it. The challenge in business is in the area of judgment, and judgment does not develop from memorizing an introductory business textbook. If you are observant in your daily experiences as an employee, as a student, and as a consumer, you will improve your ability to make good business judgments.

Whether you choose to work in an organization or become an entrepreneur, you will be required to know the basic concepts and principles in this book. It should be exciting to think about your opportunities and the challenges of creating a successful career. Our society needs a strong economic foundation to help people develop their desired standard of living. Our world economy is becoming more digital and competitive, requiring new skills for new kinds of jobs. Individuals like you can become leaders in business, non-profits, and government to create a better life.

"Business ethics generally refers to the standards and principles used by society to define appropriate and inappropriate conduct in the workplace."

Figure 1.6 is an overview of how the chapters in this book are linked together and how the chapters relate to the participants, the activities, and the environmental factors found in the business world. The topics presented will give you the best opportunity to begin the process of understanding the world of business.

**Figure 1.6** | The Organization of This Book

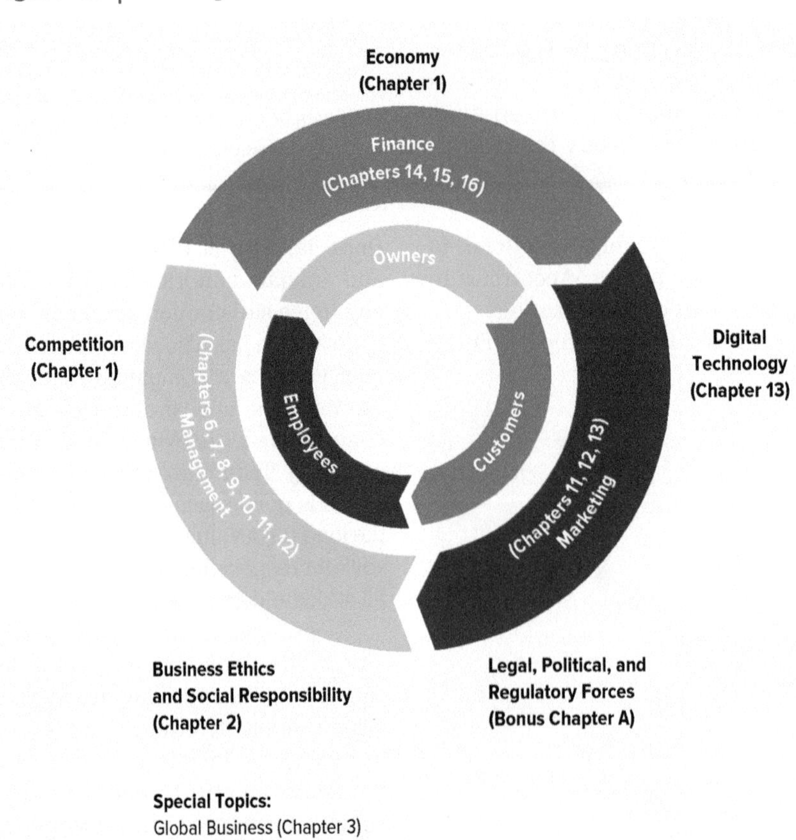

## TEAM EXERCISE

Major economic systems, including capitalism, socialism, and communism, as well as mixed economies, were discussed in this chapter. Assuming that you want an economic system that is best for the majority, not just a few members of society, defend one of the economic systems as the best system. Form groups and try to reach agreement on one economic system. Defend why you support the system you advance.

# LEARNING OBJECTIVES SUMMARY

**LO 1-1** Define basic concepts such as *business*, *product*, and *profit*.

A business is an organization or individual that seeks a profit by providing products that satisfy people's needs. A product is a good or service with tangible and intangible characteristics that provide satisfaction and benefits. Profit is the difference between what it costs to make and sell a product and what a customer pays for it.

**LO 1-2** Identify the main participants in and activities of business, and explain why studying business is important.

The three main participants in business are owners, employees, and customers, but others—government regulators, suppliers, social groups, etc.—are also important. Management involves planning, organizing, and controlling the tasks required to carry out the work of the company. Marketing refers to those activities—research, product development, promotion, pricing, and distribution—designed to provide goods and services that satisfy customers. Finance refers to activities concerned with funding a business and using its funds effectively. Studying business can help you prepare for a career and become a better consumer.

**LO 1-3** Define *economics* and compare the four types of economic systems.

Economics is the study of how resources are distributed for the production of goods and services within a social system; an economic system describes how a particular society distributes its resources. Communism is an economic system in which the people, without regard to class, own all the nation's resources. In a socialist system, the government owns and operates basic industries, but individuals own most businesses. Under capitalism, individuals own and operate the majority of businesses that provide goods and services. Mixed economies have elements from more than one economic system; most countries have mixed economies.

**LO 1-4** Describe the role of supply, demand, and competition in a free-enterprise system.

In a free-enterprise system, individuals own and operate the majority of businesses, and the distribution of resources is determined by competition, supply, and demand. Demand is the number of goods and services that consumers are willing to buy at different prices at a specific time. Supply is the number of goods or services that businesses are willing to sell at different prices at a specific time. The price at which the supply of a product equals demand at a specific point in time is the equilibrium price. Competition is the rivalry among businesses to convince consumers to buy goods or services. Four types of competitive environments are pure competition, monopolistic competition, oligopoly, and monopoly. These economic concepts determine how businesses may operate in a particular society and, often, how much they can charge for their products.

**LO 1-5** Specify why and how the health of the economy is measured.

A country measures the state of its economy to determine whether it is expanding or contracting and whether the country needs to take steps to minimize fluctuations. Commonly used measures include the gross domestic product (GDP), budget deficits/surpluses, the trade balance, the consumer price index, per capita income unemployment rate, inflation, and worker productivity.

**LO 1-6** Trace the evolution of the Canadian economy, and discuss the role of the entrepreneur in the economy.

The Canadian economy is an open economy that engages in significant international trade. Government public policy helps drive the economy through job creation, requiring a tax base to provide for the public interest. Much of the government's revenue comes from individual income taxes, but corporations pay a high corporate tax in Canada. The Canadian economy has evolved through several stages: the early economy, the Industrial Revolution, the manufacturing economy, the marketing economy, and the service and new digital economy of today. Entrepreneurs play an important role because they risk their time, wealth, and efforts to develop new goods, services, and ideas that fuel the growth of the Canadian economy.

# KEY TERMS

budget deficit
budget surplus
business
capitalism, or free enterprise
communism
competition
demand
depression
economic contraction
economic expansion
economic system
economics
entrepreneur
equilibrium price
financial resources
free-market system
gross domestic product (GDP)
human resources (labour)
inflation
mixed economies
monopolistic competition
monopoly
natural resources
non-profit organizations
oligopoly
open economy
products
profit
pure competition
recession
socialism
stakeholders
standard of living
supply
unemployment

# So You Want a Job *in the Business World*

When most people think of a career in business, they see themselves entering the door to large companies and multinationals that they read about in the news and that are discussed in class. Most jobs are not with large corporations but instead are in small companies, non-profit organizations, and government, and even as self-employed individuals. The majority of employees work for small businesses, constituting 71 percent of private sector employment. In addition, with more than 78 percent of the working population employed in service industries, there are jobs available in, for example, health care, finance, education, hospitality, entertainment, and transportation. E-commerce is creating the need for supply chain jobs related to purchasing, transportation, and operations. The world is changing quickly and large corporations replace the equivalent of their entire workforce every four years.

The fast pace of technology today means that you have to be prepared to take advantage of emerging job opportunities and markets. You must also become adaptive and recognize that business is becoming more global, with job opportunities around the world. If you want to obtain such a job, you shouldn't miss a chance to spend some time overseas. To get you started on the path to thinking about job opportunities, consider all of the changes in business today that might affect your possible long-term track and that could bring you lots of success. Companies are looking for employees with skills that can be used to address the changing business environment. For example, the demand for graduates who are good at analyzing data and navigating cloud-based computing is on the rise.

You're on the road to learning the key knowledge, skills, and trends that you can use to be a star in business. Business's impact on our society, especially in the areas of sustainability and improvement of the environment, is a growing challenge and opportunity. Examples of green businesses and green jobs in the business world are provided to give you a glimpse at the possibilities. Along the way, we will introduce you to some specific careers and offer advice on developing your own job opportunities. Research indicates that you won't be that happy with your job unless you enjoy your work and feel that it has a purpose. Because you spend most of your waking hours every day at work, you need to seriously think about what is important to you in a job.[21]

# BUILD YOUR BUSINESS PLAN

## The Dynamics of Business and Economics

Have you ever thought about owning your business? If you have, how did your idea come about? Is it your experience with this particular field? Or might it be an idea that evolved from your desires for a particular product or service not being offered in your community? For example, perhaps you and your friends have yearned for a place to go have coffee, relax, and talk. Now is an opportunity to create the café bar you have been thinking of!

Whether you consider yourself a visionary or a practical thinker, think about your community. What needs are not being met? While it is tempting to suggest a new restaurant (maybe near campus), easier-to-implement business plans can range from a lawn care business or a designated driver business, to a placement service agency for teenagers.

Once you have an idea for a business plan, think about how profitable this idea might be. Is there sufficient demand for this business? How large is the market for this particular business? What about competitors? How many are there?

To learn about your industry you should do a thorough search of your initial ideas of a product/service on the Internet.

# CASE | Apple Stores: The Future of Retail?

Apple is one of the most valuable global brands, along with Google and Amazon. Much of Apple's success can be attributed to its innovative products, such as the iPad. However, Apple has also made a profound mark in the world of retailing. Its stores, which were first opened in 2001, are the fastest growing retail stores in history. An obvious draw is store design—modern and spacious, creating a relaxed, low-pressure atmosphere. The stores are like showrooms that allow customers to test products and take educational classes.

To truly understand Apple's retail success, it is important to look beneath the surface. According to *Forbes* contributor Steve Denning, two keys to Apple's success are delight the customer and avoid selling. Apple focuses extensively on meeting customer needs and wants. This focus significantly alters employee behaviour and complements the avoid-selling mantra. Rather than pushing products on consumers, Apple store employees are asked to listen and assist. Employees have been trained to speak with customers within two minutes of them entering the store. Apple executives are also constantly looking for new innovative ways to enhance customer service. The company recently began installing iPad stations equipped with a customer service app designed to answer customer questions. If the customer requires additional assistance, he or she can press a help button on the app.

Apple has been so successful in the retail arena that other stores are looking to adopt its retail strategies. Microsoft and Sony have opened their own stores, and other industries are using Apple products to enhance their businesses. Apple's blend of exceptional products, appealing stores, and knowledgeable and dedicated employees creates a top-notch customer experience and is having enormous repercussions for the retail industry as a whole.[22]

### DISCUSSION QUESTIONS

1. Why is Apple having such a profound impact on the retail store experience?
2. How is Apple integrating its products into the retail store experience?
3. Describe Apple's approach to customer service.

CHAPTER 2

# Business Ethics and Social Responsibility

©Greenlid Envirosciences

Morgan and Jackson Wyatt, seen here with Adil Qawi, who handles Greenlid's finance and strategy, founded Greenlid shortly after finishing school. The brothers believe that they can make money and help the planet by encouraging people to be socially responsible.

## LEARNING OBJECTIVES

**After reading this chapter, you will be able to:**

- **LO 2-1** Define business ethics and social responsibility, and examine their importance.
- **LO 2-2** Detect some of the ethical issues that may arise in business.
- **LO 2-3** Specify how businesses can promote ethical behaviour by employees.
- **LO 2-4** Explain the four dimensions of social responsibility.
- **LO 2-5** Debate an organization's social responsibilities to owners, employees, consumers, the environment, and the community.

## ENTER THE WORLD OF BUSINESS

### Greenlid: Doing Well by Doing Good

Brothers Morgan and Jackson Wyatt, founders of Greenlid, a socially responsible recycling and mosquito-trap company, state their company's fundamental belief on their website:

*"The world isn't going to change overnight. We believe each small change a person makes is one step closer to a healthier, sustainable earth."*

With this motto in mind the pair created Greenlid, the first fully compostable organic waste container. The container, which is made of newspapers and food grade additives, won't leak and people can fill them with compostable materials and simply place them in a compost bin. The Greenlid product's advantages include the facts that it does not have to be washed out, unlike plastic competitors, and the bins will not leak like other boxes or bags. The Wyatts believe that the easier it is to compost the more likely it is people will engage in the practice, ultimately benefiting the planet. The Wyatts fit the description of social entrepreneurs, a relatively new term that indicates an entrepreneur who not only wants to make money but wants to help make the world a better place.

After inventing the product, the brothers opted to use the crowdfunding site Kickstarter to determine if people would buy the product and received 14,000 pre-orders totalling $26,000. With the pre-orders in hand, the pair successfully went on CBC's *Dragon's Den*, a television show where investors hear pitches from aspiring entrepreneurs and decide whether to invest their money in the company. Arlene Dickinson and David Chilton, two "Dragons," agreed to invest $85,000 in the business for a 20 percent equity share in the firm. With help from Dickinson and Chilton, Greenlid was soon being sold in Home Hardware and Home Depot retail stores. Sales quickly rose from $100,000 in a year to over $1 million, and distribution has increased to Loblaws, Rona, Sobeys, and so forth. Today, Greenlids can be found in almost every major retailer in North America.

Interestingly, others saw a different potential use for the compostable bins. In 2016, the Australian Health Authority contacted the company looking for biodegradable materials or bins that could be used as mosquito traps. Mosquitoes represent a significant health hazard in parts of the world spreading diseases such as Dengue fever and Zika. Most countries that set traps use plastic containers that are expensive, and perhaps more importantly need to be collected and cleaned every six weeks. If the plastic traps are not collected, they become ideal breeding homes for mosquitoes and increase the bug population.

Given that some countries set more than 10,000 traps in an area, relocating and cleaning the traps is a substantial investment. With this information from the Health Authority, the Wyatts created BioTrap, a biodegradable mosquito trap that does not have to be cleaned, is cheaper than the plastic versions, and becomes operational as soon as a small amount of water is added.

Based on the success of their initial crowdfunding campaign, the Wyatts launched BioTrap on the crowdfunding site Indiegogo, where they quickly raised in excess of $50,000 for the new product. Additionally, the company has pledged that for every package of five sold, they will donate one BioTrap to a country in need. Like any new product, BioTrap is still undergoing testing to see how results compare to plastic traps but the company received a big boost when it was used during the Summer Olympics to protect Canadian athletes.

The future appears bright for the socially responsible Greenlid company, a company founded on the belief that helping people make incremental change can lead to a more sustainable planet.

#### DISCUSSION QUESTIONS

1. Greenlid represents a new kind of company, a company that wants to make money, but also wants to be proactive in protecting Earth. Do you think all companies will eventually act proactively toward protecting our planet? Why or why not?

2. What do you think are some of the potential advantages and disadvantages of a proactive socially responsible approach?
3. Greenlid's most successful product is their compost bins. The BioTrap has been slower to develop as it requires substantial investment in testing and many underdeveloped countries with the most pressing mosquito problems lack the funds to make sizeable investments in traps. Based on this information, do you think Greenlid should abandon BioTraps and focus solely on its composting bins? Why or why not?
4. Greenlid relied on some non-traditional funding including both crowdfunding and an investment from angel investors on *Dragons' Den*. Why do you think the founders pursued this type of investment? What are the advantages and disadvantages of non-traditional financing?

## Introduction

As we introduce students to the concept of ethics, it is important that you understand that almost any business decision may be judged as right or wrong or ethical or unethical depending on what stakeholder group you belong to. Think about this in simple terms. If you were a business owner you'd likely want to keep costs low and charge consumers a competitive price for your products. So if you manufacture your products in China, you, your shareholders, and consumers may think you're acting ethically, while other stakeholder groups such as unions, local job-seekers, and perhaps some environmental and human rights groups may think otherwise.

In this chapter, we take a look at the role of ethics and social responsibility in business decision making. First, we define business ethics and examine why it is important to understand the role of ethics in business. Next, we explore a number of business ethics issues to help you learn to recognize such issues when they arise. Finally, we consider steps businesses can take to improve ethical behaviour in their organizations. The second half of the chapter focuses on social responsibility. We survey some important responsibility issues and detail how companies have responded to them.

## Business Ethics and Social Responsibility

**LO 2-1** Define business ethics and social responsibility, and examine their importance.

In this chapter, we define **business ethics** as the principles and standards that determine acceptable conduct in business organizations. The acceptability of behaviour in business is determined by customers, competitors, government regulators, interest groups, and the public, as well as each individual's personal moral principles and values. Readers should realize that determining ethical behaviour is not as easy as one may think and often depends on which stakeholder group an individual belongs.

**business ethics** principles and standards that determine acceptable conduct in business

Consider the Trans Mountain pipeline expansion that is discussed at the end of the chapter. Advocates of the pipelines, including the Canadian government, management of oil sands companies, shareholders, and some people in the public, likely believe their arguments are ethical. People opposing the pipelines, including some aboriginal communities, some government officials, and environmental groups, have stated that approving the pipelines would constitute unethical behaviour.

You may also want to consider the situation with General Motors (GM), Ford, and Chrysler, which all maintain manufacturing facilities in Canada. During the 2008–2010 recession, these companies laid off thousands of workers and essentially tore up contracts that they had negotiated with their employees, claiming that this was the only way to ensure that any manufacturing jobs were left in the local economies.[1] GM went a step further and entered into bankruptcy protection in the United States, enabling the company to avoid paying some creditors, to pass off some expenses to government, and essentially to destroy any shareholder value. Ford opted not to enter into bankruptcy protection but did receive some government support. During the recession, the companies continued to manufacture cars, offered consumers better warranties, and attempted to introduce more environmentally friendly automobiles to the marketplace.

If you worked for these companies, would you consider them ethical? As a consumer, would your opinions differ those of the from employees? One of the reasons Ford avoided bankruptcy was its ability to drastically reduce wages, thus allowing its shareholders to avoid losing everything they had invested. Would shareholders and employees have a different opinion of Ford?

Then, in 2018, GM announced they are closing down their Oshawa plant, laying off 2500 workers. GM notes that the plant was manufacturing unpopular cars. Some labour unions and government officials say that, while this may have been the case, GM failed to invest in the plant, even though the government had clearly supported GM earlier in the decade and the union agreed to significant reductions in wages. Union leaders and some government officials state that without ongoing company investment the plant was always doomed to fail. Canada's largest auto union, Unifor, is now calling for a boycott of all GM vehicles in Canada to stop the Oshawa plant closure. It has been estimated that the federal and provincial governments lost a combined $3.5 billion with their investment in bailing out GM and Chrysler earlier in the decade.

©The Canadian Press/Nathan Denette

Canada's largest labour union, Unifor, called for a boycott of GM vehicles after the car manufacturing company announced the closure of its Oshawa plant, laying off approximately 2500 employees.

Another interesting ethical dilemma is any action that has a perceived negative environmental impact, such as tree cutting by the Irving Group's forestry division. While one may presume that the cutting of trees is unethical behaviour, the Irving Group is the largest private planter of trees in the country. Does knowing this affect your opinion of the company and its business practices?

At other times, determining ethical behaviour is much easier. For example, the Competition Bureau of Canada has alleged that seven Canadian bread companies, including Loblaws under parent company George Weston Ltd., worked together, in an act called collusion, to artificially raise the price of bread in Canada. The bureau states that

## Consider the Following: Should views on charter freedoms impact federal government funding?

The Canadian Summer Jobs Program offers a great example of an ethical dilemma. Each and every summer thousands of corporations and not-for-profit firms, including many charitable groups such as churches, receive funding from the federal government to employ students during the summer months. Students earn valuable experience and much-needed income, and the organizations receive grants to offset the cost of labour. The program is considered a win-win-win for students, employers and government.

In 2017 and 2018, Prime Minister Justin Trudeau's government amended the application process and asked all applicants to confirm they supported all rights protected by the Charter of Rights and Freedoms, including a woman's right to have an abortion and rights associated with the LGBT community. Trudeau argued that church and not-for-profit groups would be eligible as long as they acknowledged support for people's rights as outlined in the Charter. He stated that certain groups, those fighting against Charter freedoms, should not receive government money. Trudeau stated, "...there are certain groups that are specifically dedicated to fighting abortion rights for women and rights for LGBT communities and that is wrong, that is certainly not something the federal government should be funding: to roll back the clock on women's rights."

The federal government's decision was highly criticized by church and anti-abortion groups, and was even discussed on Fox News in the U.S. In 2019, the federal government made an amendment to the application process. Church and charity groups do not have to attest they support all aspects of the Charter but they do have to clarify that the jobs that are being funded will not interfere with people's rights and freedoms.

### DISCUSSION QUESTIONS

1. Was the government's requirement that groups state they supported all aspects of the Charter of Rights and Freedoms in order to receive government funding ethical? What are some of the pros and cons of his decision?
2. Do you think the government was right to change the application and approval process to focus on the activities of the jobs and not the beliefs of the organizations applying for funding?

©lynx/iconotec.com/Glowimages

The Competition Bureau of Canada alleged that Loblaws and six other Canadian companies worked together to overcharge consumers for bread for 16 years.

over a period of 16 years, producers colluded to raise the price of wholesale bread and then strong-armed retailers to also increase their prices.

The end result was that bread increased in price roughly 96 percent over that 16-year time frame compared to food prices generally, which increased 46 percent over a similar period. Employees from Loblaws first brought the matter to the attention of the Competition Bureau. While the matter is still before the courts, Loblaws has offered all Canadian consumers a $25 gift card to ease public criticism of the company. Research indicates that most unethical activities within organizations are supported by an organizational culture that encourages employees to bend the rules.[2]

Many people—including entrepreneurs, employees, consumers, and social advocates—believe that businesses should not only make a profit but also consider the social implications of their activities. We define **social responsibility** as a business's obligation to maximize its positive impact and minimize its negative impact on society. Although many people use the terms *social responsibility* and *ethics* interchangeably, they do not mean the same thing. Business ethics relate to an *individual's* or a *work group's* decisions that society evaluates as right or wrong, whereas social responsibility is a broader concept that concerns the impact of the *entire business's* activities on society. From an ethical perspective, for example, we may be concerned about a drug company overcharging the government for its medications. From a social responsibility perspective, we might be concerned about the impact that this overcharging will have on the ability of the health care system to provide adequate services for all citizens.

**social responsibility** a business's obligation to maximize its positive impact and minimize its negative impact on society

As discussed in the opening profile of this chapter, and in various examples throughout the text, an increased interest in social responsibility has led to a new type of business owner or a entrepreneur—the social entrepreneur. A social entrepreneur or business owner not only wants to make money but also wants to have a positive impact on their environment. There are numerous examples of social entrepreneurs throughout the book, including Morgan and Jackson Wyatt, discussed above, and Dave Luba and Kalen Emsley, founders of tentree, who are planting ten trees for every article of clothing their company sells.

Managing with a social conscience is not limited to small or start-up firms. Numerous large companies, including both TD Bank and RBC, are investing in socially responsible initiatives. Business owners may want to take note of the growing importance of acting in a socially responsible manner. In a recent poll, 77 percent of Canadians said that they would quit their jobs to work at a company that was more environmentally friendly.[3]

"Many people including entrepreneurs, employees, consumers, and social advocates believe that businesses should not only make a profit but also consider the social implications of their activities."

The most basic ethical and social responsibility concerns have been codified as laws and regulations that encourage businesses to conform to society's standards, values, and attitudes. For example, in the early 2000s, corporate scandals involving Nortel, Atlas Cold Storage, Enron, WorldCom, Global Crossing, and Tyco, as well as several major auditing firms, including Arthur Andersen, resulted in hundreds of billions of dollars in corporate and investor losses and shook public confidence in the integrity of the public markets. To help restore confidence in corporations and markets, the U.S. Congress passed the *Sarbanes-Oxley Act*[4] and the Ontario government proclaimed Bill C-198, which criminalized securities fraud and stiffened penalties for corporate fraud.

©Echo/Getty Images

Cell phone companies Rogers and Telus frequently argue about who has the fastest service in Canada.

**Table 2.1** | A Timeline of Ethical and Socially Responsible Concerns

| 1960s | 1970s | 1980s | 1990s | 2000s | 2010s |
|---|---|---|---|---|---|
| • Environmental issues | • Employee militancy | • Bribes and illegal contracting practices | • Sweatshops and unsafe working conditions in third-world countries | • Employee benefits | • Social media |
| • Civil rights issues | • Human rights issues | • Influence peddling | | • Privacy issues | • Financial fraud |
| • Increased employee–employer tension | • Covering up rather than correcting issues | • Deceptive advertising | • Rising corporate liability for personal damages (e.g., cigarette companies) | • Financial mismanagement | • Privacy |
| • Honesty | • Discrimination | • Financial fraud (e.g., savings and loan scandal) | | • Abusive behaviour | • Bullying |
| • Changing work ethic | • Harassment | | | • Cyber crime | |
| • Rising drug use | | • Transparency issues | • Financial mismanagement and fraud | • Intellectual property theft | |

At a minimum, managers are expected to obey all laws and regulations. Yet even obeying laws is open to interpretation. In Canada, Rogers Communications was running advertisements noting that it offered consumers the fastest and most reliable cell phone service. Telus, one of Rogers' competitors, disagreed with the claim and brought the matter before the courts. Telus ultimately succeeded in stopping Rogers from running the ads, but Rogers did not admit to any wrongdoing.[5] Essentially, both businesses felt that they were obeying the laws at the time.

Most legal issues arise as choices that society deems unethical, irresponsible, or otherwise unacceptable. However, all actions deemed unethical by society are not necessarily illegal, and both legal and ethical concerns change over time (see Table 2.1). *Business law* refers to the laws and regulations that govern the conduct of business. Many problems and conflicts in business can be avoided if owners, managers, and employees know more about business law and the legal system. Together, business ethics, social responsibility, and legislation act as a compliance system requiring that businesses and employees act responsibly in society. In this chapter, we explore ethics and social responsibility; Appendix B addresses business law, including securities regulations.

# The Role of Ethics in Business

You only have to pick up the *National Post* or the *Globe and Mail's* "Report on Business" to see examples of the growing concern about legal and ethical issues in business. Volkswagen, for example, installed software in some of its diesel cars to trick emission testers into thinking the cars were more environmentally friendly than they actually were. The result of its unethical, and perhaps illegal, behaviour led to cars on the road emitting up to 40 times the allowable nitrogen oxide limits.[6]

Other examples include the presidential election in the United States, where Google, Twitter, and Facebook admitted in 2017, after previously denying claims, that they did indeed sell online ads to Russian companies who were trying to sway the election in favour of Donald Trump. Additionally, the rent-to-own store Aaron's installed spy software on people's laptops, which enabled Aaron's to record pictures and video of users at home or work without their knowledge. Regardless of what an individual believes about a particular action, if society judges it to be unethical or wrong, whether correctly or not, that judgment directly affects the organization's ability to achieve its business goals.[7]

Well-publicized incidents of unethical and illegal activity—from accounting fraud to using the Internet to steal another person's credit card number, and from deceptive advertising of food and diet products to unfair competitive practices in the computer software industry—strengthen the public's perception that ethical standards and the level of trust in business need to be raised. Author David Callahan has commented, "[People] who wouldn't so much as shoplift a pack of chewing gum are committing felonies at tax time, betraying the trust of their patients, misleading investors, ripping off their insurance companies, lying to their clients, and much more."[8]

Often, misconduct starts as an ethical conflict but evolves into legal disputes when cooperative conflict resolution cannot be accomplished. This is because individuals may have different ethical beliefs and resort to legal activities to resolve issues. Also, there are many ethical gray areas, which occur when a new, undetermined, or ambiguous situation arises. There may be no values, codes, or laws that answer the question about appropriate action. The sharing economy, with peer-to-peer relationships like Uber, Lyft, and Airbnb, provides new business

## Consider the Following: Ticketmaster

If you have attended a live concert or a sporting event chances are you have heard about Ticketmaster. Ticketmaster is the largest seller of event tickets in North America and has established exclusive deals with major sports teams, stadiums, and theatres. This exclusive relationship means Ticketmaster is often the sole provider of event tickets for major events in North America. The result of this exclusivity is that Ticketmaster can often add fees to the ticket prices, which have risen to the point that they have caught the attention of the Canadian Competition Bureau.

The bureau is alleging that Ticketmaster is engaging in the deceptive practice of *drip pricing*, where they advertise a low price for a product, in this case an event ticket—but with the additional fees, consumers actually pay a much higher price. The bureau has found that Ticketmaster fees, including service and order processing fees, usually inflate event ticket prices upward of 20 percent, and in some cases as high as 65 percent.*

While the high fees may upset consumers, information about Ticketmaster working with professional scalpers may be more concerning. Have you ever been unsuccessful in purchasing event tickets even though you logged on to Ticketmaster as soon as sales commenced? Turns out professional scalpers are also logging in but they are doing so with hundreds of accounts, sometimes using automatic bots to ensure they purchase large quantities of tickets.

Ticketmaster has been on the receiving end of negative publicity over their excessive fees and their co-operation with scalpers.

models where existing regulations are inadequate, ambiguous, or in some cases blocking progress. For example, Uber has been accused of price gouging, endangering riders' safety, sexual harassment, stealing secret information on self-driving cars from Google, and violating local regulations on public transportation in some countries, states, and cities. To settle some of its legal fees, it has paid more than $500 million in the last two years.

> "Ethical conduct builds trust among individuals and in business relationships, which validates and promotes confidence in business relationships."

However, it is important to understand that business ethics go beyond legal issues. Ethical conduct builds trust among individuals and in business relationships that validates and promotes confidence in business relationships. Establishing trust and confidence is much more difficult in organizations that have established reputations for acting unethically. If you were to discover, for example, that a manager had misled you about company benefits when you were hired, your trust and confidence in that company would probably diminish. And if you learned that a colleague had lied to you about something, you probably would not trust or rely on that person in the future.

Ethical issues are not limited to for-profit organizations, as evidenced by recent political scandals. In Canada, several prominent politicians have recently resigned due to allegations of improper behaviour toward women. In 2018, both Ontario PC leader Patrick Brown and Nova Scotia PC leader Jamie Baillie resigned due to allegations of inappropriate behaviour.

Several scientists have been accused of making false claims, which could invalidate later research based on their data and jeopardize trust in all scientific research. For example, Andrew Wakefield was the lead author on the research paper that linked common vaccinations to the development of autism. Upon further investigation, the paper was found to suffer from serious problems and was retracted by the journal that originally published it. Wakefield was later stripped of his medical licence by the British

Why would Ticketmaster allow this, you may ask. The answer is rather simple. Ticketmaster then allows the scalpers to resell the tickets through Ticketmaster, where they can generate even more fees. Think about it this way, Ticketmaster originally sells a $100 ticket and collects $25 in fees, then the broker resells the same ticket for $400 and Ticketmaster collects $75 in fees. So Ticketmaster sells the same ticket twice and charges a higher service charge when the broker raises the price of the ticket.

CBC recently sent two reporters to a ticket sales convention in Las Vegas where they learned that Ticketmaster has created a product to allow brokers to upload and resell large quantities of tickets with ease. Furthermore, Ticketmaster has established a rewards program to motivate brokers to sell more tickets through their site rather than using competitor sites such as Stub Hub or Ace Tickets.**

Ticketmaster appears undaunted by all of this negative publicity. While some governments or groups have launched investigations and/or lawsuits, these can take years to complete. In the meantime, Ticketmaster and its partner, Live Nation, continue to make hundreds of millions off the ticket buying public.

### DISCUSSION QUESTIONS

1. Do you think Ticketmaster's business is ethical? Why or why not?
2. Scalpers will often point out that what they are doing amounts to capitalism. They are purchasing a product, which in this case is an event ticket, and reselling the product at a higher price. If a market doesn't exist they will lose money. Do you think ticket scalpers are ethical or unethical? Would you buy a ticket from a scalper?
3. Many artists continue to be happy to work with Ticketmaster as some of Ticketmaster's sales mechanisms allow them to make more money from their shows. For example, Ticketmaster can raise the price of tickets as demand increases, increasing an artist's revenue. Do you think the artists are ethical or unethical for using Ticketmaster?
4. Do you think governments should intervene in the ticket sales market? Why or why not? What solutions would you propose?

*"Competition Bureau sues Ticketmaster over misleading ticket price advertising," January 25, 2018, https://www.newswire.ca/news-releases/competition-bureau-sues-ticketmaster-over-misleading-ticket-price-advertising-671140343.html

**Dave Seglins, Rachel Houlihan, Laura Clemenston, "A public relations nightmare: Ticketmaster recruits pros for secret scalper program," Social Sharing, September 21, 2018, https://www.cbc.ca/news/business/ticketmaster-resellers-las-vegas-1.4828535

General Medical Council. Yet the result of his work has been a decrease in vaccination usage throughout the world, leading to an increase in such diseases as measles and mumps.

Even sports can be subject to ethical lapses. At many universities, for example, coaches and athletic administrators have been put on administrative leave after allegations of improper recruiting practices by team members came to light.[9] In other examples, in 2015 Montreal native Dick Pound completed an investigation on behalf of the World Anti-Doping Agency into the use of illegal drugs by Russian athletes in the Olympic Games. Pound concluded that the Russians were engaged in a massive doping cover-up as the majority of its track team was using performance-enhancing drugs. Pound noted that this was not the case of one or two athletes and stated that the governing body of the sport in Russia had to either have knowledge of the doping or aided in covering it up, saying, "It would be naive in the extreme to think the massive cheating could happen without government backing it."

Asked whether it was state-supported doping, Mr. Pound said: "I don't see how you could call it anything else," adding that it was "not possible" for Russia's top sports bosses to be unaware. While Russia has denied any doping allegations, the Olympic Committee banned Russia from sending athletes to the 2017 Olympic games. The ban was later amended, allowing Russian athletes who had no history of doping violations to compete—but they could not do so as representatives of Russia. The athletes had

©Shutterstock/Monkey Business Images

Who is looking at your social media information? You may be interested to know it's both current and prospective employers.

## RESPONDING TO BUSINESS CHALLENGES

### The Case of Valeant Pharmaceuticals

Bausch Health Companies recently appeared on the public stock exchange. A novice investor, or perhaps someone who doesn't frequently read the news—would see Bausch as a new publicly traded company and perhaps accurately link Bausch to their main product, contact lenses. Seasoned investors and news readers would know otherwise. Bausch is not a new publicly traded company; they were a subsidiary of Valeant Pharmaceuticals, based in Laval, Quebec. Valeant opted to change its name due to the publicity associated with its controversial business practices. Management is clearly hoping that a name change will move the attention of consumers and investors away from the past few years, which were, at the very least, newsworthy.

Valeant was in the news for much of 2015 to 2018 for various reasons. First, the company, which manufactures and distributes roughly 500 drugs globally, became for a brief period of time the largest company in Canada by market cap.* The value of the business almost doubled in 2015 as investors were attracted to strong growth and what shareholders believed was a sound business model. Rather then develop new drugs, Valeant often prefers to purchase companies that have brought drugs from development to the approval process. Once Valeant purchases the companies, it uses its aggressive sales force to improve the sales of the drugs.

The business model on its own appears to be both ethical and practical. Developing drugs can take a significant amount of time and resources, and Valeant doesn't appear able to successfully bring its own drugs to market. Firms that successfully develop drugs normally do so at great cost, and once they are approved, the companies can lack both the resources and marketing abilities to successfully sell the drugs. Valeant purchases the firms and/or their drugs; the company's investors, entrepreneurs, and scientists normally get paid a premium for their time and investment; and Valeant makes money by using its marketing abilities to sell the drugs.

What brought Valeant into the news beyond its financial success was its pricing practices for newly acquired drugs. Valeant has been charged with unethically raising the price of acquired drugs. It is not uncommon for Valeant to raise the price by 100 percent or more, and in rare cases by as much as 500 percent. Valeant has been justifying the price hikes by noting the drugs were originally priced too low for market conditions.**

On average, in 2015 Valeant raised its drug prices by 66 percent, which is five times more than similar-sized companies, and significantly raised the price of

©Ingram Publishing/SuperStock

Canadian pharmaceutical giant Valeant Pharmaceuticals, now Bausch Health Companies, has had its fair share of people question the ethics of the company over its practice of buying other drug businesses and then substantially raising the price of the drugs.

## Consider the Following: Are social media sites fair game for employers?

1. In a 2018 Career Builder survey, 70 percent of employers admitted to visiting social media sites to pre-screen applicants who are applying for a job. Of the employers who pre-screen candidates, a significant majority of them will not allow prospective applicants to explain questionable behaviour they see online. These companies simply remove the person from the pool of candidates they are considering for a job.

While most people know that having pictures of yourself engaging in illegal activity is likely not a good idea for your Instagram or Facebook page, employers are going even further than quickly reviewing photos. Many businesses are reading people's online posts to pre-determine if they have a good attitude and are friendly. Do you think it's ethical for companies to screen potential employees by

two new heart drugs it bought the rights to sell: Nitropress by 212 percent and Isuprel by 525 percent.*** Valeant also charged more for drugs in different parts of the world based on consumers' ability to pay and what insurance would accept. For example, Valeant's Flucytosine drug was 10,000 percent higher in price in the United States than in some European countries.

Former CEO Michael Pearson defended the company's drug-price policies, stating price increases do not drive the company's success; rather, growth in the number of prescriptions being written for Valeant drugs is the major factor fuelling revenue growth, and this is a direct result of its marketing and sales abilities.†

Unfortunately, for Valeant investors, the company's business practices caught the attention of numerous government agencies, which started to investigate the company. In 2016, Michael Pearson stepped down as CEO and was replaced by Joseph Papa. Under Papa's leadership the company has reduced its debt, which had risen to support their purchases of other companies, and settled roughly 70 lawsuits that were pending against the firm. In 2018, as a way to turn the corner on the past, Valeant announced it was changing its name to Bausch. Critics maintain that while Papa is reducing debt, many of the company's old business practices remain.‡

### DISCUSSION QUESTIONS

1. Is Bausch Health, formerly Valeant Pharmaceuticals, an ethical company? Why or why not? Would you invest in the company based on its business model?
2. Do you think governments should regulate the prices that companies can charge for drugs? Why or why not?
3. What are some of the arguments for charging high drug prices?
4. The discussions about Bausch Health and ethics are likely to continue for years to come. Use Internet resources to review the current state of the company and whether any governments have started to regulate their pricing practices. Update the class on what you have found.
5. Do you think changing a company's name will alter the way a firm is perceived by consumers and government? Why or why not? You maybe interested to learn that this is the third time the firm has changed names since 2010. Use Internet resources to discover Valeant's former Canadian name.

*Doug Alexander and Eric Lam, "Valeant passes RBC as Canada's largest company by market value," *Globe and Mail*, July 23, 2015, http://www.theglobeandmail.com/globe-investor/valeant-passes-rbc-as-canadas-largest-company-by-market-value/article25642880/ (accessed November 3, 2015).

**Ranjit Thomas, "Is Valeant An Ethical Company?" Seeking Alpha, November 2, 2015, http://seekingalpha.com/article/3633866-is-valeant-an-ethical-company (accessed November 2, 2015).

***"Valeant's High-Price Drug Strategy," *New York Times*, October 2, 2015, http://www.nytimes.com/2015/10/04/business/valeants-high-price-drug-strategy.html?_r=0 (accessed November 5, 2015).

†Bertrand Morotte, "Valeant revenue not fuelled by drug-price increases, CEO says," *Globe and Mail*, October 15, 2015, www.theglobeandmail.com/report-on-business/valeant-probed-by-us-prosecutors-over-drug-pricing-concerns/article26819873/ (accessed November 9, 2015).

‡Emma Court, "Valeant is back to its old drug-pricing ways," Market Watch, July 1, 2018, https://www.marketwatch.com/story/valeant-is-back-on-to-its-old-drug-pricing-ways-2018-06-29

viewing their entries on social media sites such as Facebook, Twitter, and Instagram? Why or why not?

2. In the same 2018 Career Builder survey, 48 percent of employers stated they visited employees social media sites. Of the 48 percent that do so, 10 percent actually visit their employees sites on a daily basis. Employers found various reasons to be unhappy with their employees' social media actions and 34 percent of employers said they either fired or reprimanded employees for their social media activity. Do you think it's ethical for employers to monitor social media accounts of their employees? Why or why not?

©The Canadian Press/Dave Chidley

Canadian Dick Pound, a member of the World Anti-Doping Association, has found that Russian athletes engaged in the use of performance-enhancing drugs in the last Summer Olympic Games.

to wear non-country-specific Olympic clothing and the Russian anthem would not be played if they won a medal.[10]

> "Many business issues may seem straightforward and easy to resolve, but in reality, a person often needs several years of experience in business to understand what is acceptable or ethical."

Although we will not tell you in this chapter what you ought to do, others—your superiors, co-workers, and family—will make judgments about the ethics of your actions and decisions. Learning how to recognize and resolve ethical issues is an important step in evaluating ethical decisions in business.

## Recognizing Ethical Issues in Business

**LO 2-2** Detect some of the ethical issues that may arise in business.

Learning to recognize ethical issues is the most important step in understanding business ethics. An **ethical issue** is an identifiable problem, situation, or opportunity that requires a person to choose from among several actions that may be evaluated as right or wrong, ethical or unethical. Learning how to choose from alternatives and make a decision requires not only good personal values, but also knowledge competence in the business area of concern. Employees also need to know when to rely on their organizations' policies and codes of ethics or have discussions with co-workers or managers on appropriate conduct.

**ethical issue**
an identifiable problem, situation, or opportunity that requires a person to choose from among several actions that may be evaluated as right or wrong, ethical or unethical

Ethical decision making is not always easy because there are always gray areas that create dilemmas, no matter how decisions are made. For instance, should an employee report on a co-worker engaging in time theft? Or should you report a friend cheating on a test? Should salespeople omit facts about a product's poor safety record in their presentations to customers? Such questions require the decision maker to evaluate the ethics of their choice and decide whether to ask for guidance.

Many business issues may seem straightforward and easy to resolve, but in reality, a person often needs several years of experience in business to understand what is acceptable or ethical. For example, if you are a salesperson, when does offering a gift—such as season basketball tickets—to a customer become a bribe rather than just a sales practice? Clearly, there are no easy answers to such a question. But the size of the transaction and the history of personal relationships within the particular company, as well as many other factors, may determine whether an action will be judged as right or wrong by others.

Ethics is also related to the culture in which a business operates. In Canada, for example, it would be inappropriate for a businessperson to bring an elaborately wrapped gift to a prospective client on their first meeting—the gift could be viewed as a bribe. In Japan, however, it is considered impolite *not* to bring a gift. Experience with the culture in which a business operates is crucial to understanding what is ethical or unethical.

To help you understand ethical issues that perplex businesspeople today, we will take a brief look at some of them in this section. The vast number of news-format investigative programs has increased consumer and employee awareness of organizational misconduct. In addition, the multitude of cable channels and Internet resources has improved the awareness of ethical problems among the general public.

©Verena Matthew/Shutterstock

Canadians currently buy $4.4 billion worth of organic food a year. Once a Canadian farm is labelled organic there is no follow-up testing to see if the farm is maintaining organic standards. Do you think most Canadians know organic products are not routinely tested?

## Consider the Following: When is organic really organic?

The organic food industry boasts that sales have surpassed $4.4 billion, with supermarkets and specialty stores often charging a premium price for products labelled as organic. In Canada, food with the organic label must be certified by the Canadian Food Inspection Agency (CFIA). Once certified, a company's products do not undergo any laboratory testing to confirm they are free of pesticides. The industry operates on what amounts to an honour system. The CFIA states that testing may be done as part of its annual monitoring program, but specific lab tests to confirm products are organic are not used.

In one recent spot test, CFIA documents showed that 24 percent of organic apples contained pesticide residue. The CFIA theorized that many of the tainted apples likely resulted from inadvertent contamination. The CFIA states that while it is not opposed to testing of products, it is not a proponent of excessive tests, arguing that too much testing will increase the price of organic food—something it says consumers do not want to see happen.*

Mischa Popoff, a former organic inspector who worked in both Canada and the U.S., says the lack of testing is laughable and that consumers may be paying for products that are not organic: "It's like a policeman trying to catch speeders without a radar gun. I mean, it's just unthinkable. It's laughable, in fact. Those people [consumers] are doubling their grocery bill, assuming they're getting something organic, whatever that means, and they're not."

### DISCUSSION QUESTIONS

1. Do you think the Canadian Food Inspection Agency is doing enough to ensure foods labelled organic are actually organic?
2. Would you trust producers not to use pesticides in their operations? Why or why not?
3. Do you think consumers would be willing to pay more for organic food if a testing program ensured the food truly was organic? Why or why not?
4. Do you think most Canadians assume that testing is taking place? Should the Canadian Food Inspection Agency do a better job communicating how they approve food to be labelled organic? Why or why not?

*Adrian Humphreys, "Canada's organic food certification system 'little more than an extortion racket' report says," *National Post*, November 24, 2012, http://news.nationalpost.com/2012/11/24/canadas-organic-food-certification-system-little-more-than-an-extortion-racket-report-says/; Mischa Popoff and Patrick Moore, "Canada's Organic Nightmare," Frontier Centre Policy Series, http://mobi.fcpp.org/publication.php/4361; Mischa Popoff, "Opinions and Editorials," Is It Organic? website, http://isitorganic.ca/opinions_and_editorials (accessed June 19, 2013).

The National Business Ethics Survey of more than 5000 U.S. employees found that workers witness many instances of ethical misconduct in their organizations (see Table 2.2). The most common types of observed misconduct were abusive/intimidating behaviour, lying, and placing employee interests over organizational interests.[11]

One of the principal causes of unethical behaviour in organizations is overly aggressive financial or business

**Table 2.2** | Types and Incidences of Observed Misconduct

| Type of Conduct Observed | Employees Observing It |
|---|---|
| Lying to employees, customers, vendors, or the public | 26% |
| Abusive or intimidating behaviour toward employees | 21 |
| Situations placing employee interests over organizational interests | 16 |
| Internet abuse | 16 |
| Health violations | 15 |
| Discrimination on the basis of race, colour, gender, age, or similar categories | 12 |
| Sexual harassment | 12 |
| Stealing | 12 |

©Image 100/Punchstock

Bullying, which was once thought to occur primarily on the playground, is also a problem at work when abusive or intimidating behaviour is directed at employees.

## RESPONDING TO BUSINESS CHALLENGES

### Determining Ethical Behaviour: The Case of Ride-Sharing and Uber in Canada

Uber Technologies Inc., the ride-sharing company that allows regular people to turn their cars into unlicensed taxis has taken the personal transportation industry by storm. Uber, which was founded only 10 years ago, was recently valued at over $72 billion dollars, and the company is currently going public with an estimated $120 billion dollar valuation. Uber ride sharing is available in 600 cities and 65 countries, and had $20 billion in revenue in 2018.*

The concept behind ride-sharing services such as Uber is simple: Consumers download an app and can use it to hail car owners who will take them to their desired location. All transactions are paid for electronically, eliminating the need for cash. Consumers like the concept, as the consensus is that drivers are more professional and their cars are cleaner than traditional taxis, you do not have to stand outside to hail a car, and in many instances, the ride-sharing driver will text you when they arrive. Additionally, consumers can specify car types and can see driver reviews prior to agreeing to be picked up. Ride-share drivers like the service as it enables them to operate as an unlicensed taxi—they can earn money and create their own schedules.

So while riders and drivers clearly like Uber's business model, some government officials and traditional taxi drivers view the service very differently. In most, if not all, Canadian cities, taxi and limousine drivers are heavily regulated and drivers have to have a special licence or permit to operate. In many cities, such as Montreal, there is a limit on the number of legal taxis allowed on the road.** This limit, in theory, is to ensure that drivers earn a livable wage from their work.

The reality is that in most cities drivers treat their licences or permits as assets and sell or rent them to other potential users. For example, in Montreal it is not uncommon to see a driver trying to sell his permit (licence) for upward of $175,000.*** Suni Johal, policy director at the Mowat Centre, a public-policy think tank at the University of Toronto, and Vincent Geloso from the Montreal Economic Institute are in agreement that the traditional taxi industry should be deregulated, and government should think about what's best for citizens rather than maximizing taxi revenue.†

Taxi owners and some city officials do not agree with Johal and Geloso. Both sides point to the fact that traditional Canadian car insurance does not allow people to offer paid-for ride-sharing services, and there is a chance Uber drivers would have their insurance invalidated if they were involved in an accident leaving the driver personally liable for the car and its occupants.‡ The result is that Uber riders might have to personally sue the driver to cover any health and/or legal claims. Taxi owners also point out that anyone can drive for Uber, while the taxi licensing process has checks in place to ensure that drivers are not a threat to passengers.

©ValeStock/Shutterstock

Uber drivers are everywhere in big cities in Canada. While many users prefer some of the Uber advantages, such as knowing who your driver is before they pick you up, taxi drivers often argue Uber should be outlawed in Canada.

Toronto City Council decided in 2016 to allow Uber and other ride-sharing services to operate in the city, but with some hesitation from Mayor John Tory, who admitted that while he doesn't think drivers should continue to operate, shutting down Uber's 16,000 drivers and 400,000 riders is likely an impossible task. "I'm not okay with it, but I guess you have to sort of accept in this job, there's a lot of things that go on in the city every day where people are not in compliance, and we don't have the necessary resources to have every single one of those people overseen and charged. The practicality of having a huge portion of the police service devoted to cracking down on UberX drivers, the practicality of having a huge additional number or even existing bylaw officers cracking down to a point where we could stop the behaviour, I'm not sure is realistic."[§]

Traditional taxi and limousine drivers don't agree with Tory and other government officials who have allowed for ride-sharing services in Canada. Simply put, they want the service shut down. A Toronto taxi owner, Dominik Konjevic, filed a class-action lawsuit against Uber on behalf of Ontario taxi and limousine drivers, seeking $410 million in damages and a court injunction to shut down the service in Ontario. Mr. Konjevic states Uber conspired to break Ontario's *Highway Traffic Act*, which requires a licence to pick up people for money, and caused significant harm to taxi and limo drivers.

"The defendants (Uber) and the UberX drivers knew, or ought to have known, that the natural result of their conspiracy would be injury to the ongoing legitimate business interests of the class members."[‖] Taxi drivers are not just suing Uber, they are also launching lawsuits against cities and provinces that have amended regulations to allow for ride-sharing services. In Quebec, where regulations were amended to allow for Uber, Damas Metellus, who is representing taxi owners and drivers, has launched a $1 billion lawsuit against the province. In Ontario, several lawsuits have been launched against Toronto and Ottawa for allowing Uber to operate. The drivers are all claiming ride-sharing services have reduced their income and the value of their taxi permits/licences.

John Pecman, Canada's Commissioner of Competition, totally disagrees with taxi lawsuits. He notes that the government didn't stop DVD sales to protect people in the VCR industry and are not preventing live streaming services to help with falling DVD sales. He says ride sharing is innovation, which is beneficial to consumers: "...(ride sharing) will allow consumers to benefit from competitive prices on a variety of innovative choices."

Even as lawsuits are launched, ride-sharing companies are reporting continued growth in Canada. More consumers continue to claim they prefer ride-sharing drivers, that there are not enough taxis on the road—especially late at night and in the suburbs—and that they like knowing who their drivers are prior to pick-up. All of which is driving the demand for ride-sharing services.

### DISCUSSION QUESTIONS

1. In your opinion, are ride-sharing services like Uber ethical or unethical? Why?
2. Taxi drivers have advocated for fines for people who use Uber and other similar companies, such as Lyft. Do you think this is a fair and ethical way to prevent ride-sharing services?
3. Do you think all businesses should follow the same rules? Why or why not?
4. Do you think the government should shut down ride-sharing services, allowing traditional taxi drivers to earn a living wage? Why or why not?
5. Do you prefer to have some choice in using a taxi or a ride sharing service? Why?
6. Intact, along with some other insurance companies, is now selling ride-sharing insurance.[#] Given the insurance question, should governments across Canada allow Uber to operate as-is? Why or why not?

*Eugene Kim, "Uber has grown faster in its first five years than Facebook did," *Business Insider*, June 1, 2015, http://www.businessinsider.com/uber-vs-facebook-valuation-in-years-one-through-five-2015-6 (accessed November 4, 2015).

**Giuseppe Valiante, "Uber pushes Canadian cities to re-evaluate taxi industry," CBC News, July 19, 2015, http://www.cbc.ca/news/canada/montreal/uber-pushes-canadian-cities-to-re-evaluate-taxi-industry-1.3159212 (accessed November 2, 2015).

***Ibid.

†Ibid.

‡"Uber drivers and passengers face serious legal and insurance consequences," Kennedy Insurance Brokers Inc., n.d., http://www.kennedyinsurance.ca/uber-drivers-passengers-face-serious-legal-insurance-consequences/ (accessed November 16, 2015).

§Ann Hui, "Uber to continue 'outside the law' in Toronto," *Globe and Mail*, October 1, 2015, http://www.theglobeandmail.com/news/toronto/uber-to-continue-outside-the-law-in-toronto/article26628483/ (accessed November 12, 2015).

‖Ann Hui, "Ontario taxi owner files $410-million class-action suit against Uber Canada," *Globe and Mail*, July 23, 2015, http://www.theglobeandmail.com/news/national/ontario-taxi-files-400-million-class-action-suit-against-uber-canada/article25643753/ (accessed November 13, 2015).

#Sean Silcoff and Jacqueline Nelson, "Insurance Bureau of Canada pushing to get Uber drivers covered," *Globe and Mail*, October 13, 2015, http://www.theglobeandmail.com/report-on-business/insurance-bureau-of-canada-pushing-to-get-uber-drivers-covered/article26792745/ (accessed November 1, 2015).

objectives. Many of these issues relate to decisions and concerns that managers have to deal with daily. It is not possible to discuss every issue, of course. However, a discussion of a few issues can help you begin to recognize the ethical problems with which businesspersons must deal. Many ethical issues in business can be categorized in the context of their relation with abusive and intimidating behaviour, conflicts of interest, fairness and honesty, communications, and business associations.

**Abusive or Intimidating Behaviour.** Abusive or intimidating behaviour is the most common ethical problem for employees. It can mean anything from physical threats, false accusations, annoying behaviour, profanity, insults, yelling, harshness, or ignoring someone, to unreasonableness, and the meaning of these words can differ by person—you probably have some ideas of your own. Abusive behaviour can be placed on a continuum from a minor distraction to a workplace disruption. For example, what one person may define as yelling might be another's definition of normal speech. Civility in our society has become a concern, and the workplace is no exception. The productivity level of many organizations has been damaged by the time spent unraveling abusive relationships.

Abusive behaviour is difficult to assess and manage because of diversities in culture and lifestyle. What does it mean to speak profanely? Is profanity only related to specific words or other such terms that are common in today's business world? If you are using words that are normal in your use of language but others consider profanity, have you just insulted, abused, or disrespected them?

"Bullying is associated with a hostile workplace when someone considered a target (or a group) is threatened, harassed, belittled, or verbally abused or overly criticized."

Within the concept of abusive behaviour, intent should be a consideration. If the employee was trying to convey a compliment but the comment was considered abusive, then it was probably a mistake. The way a word is said (voice inflection) can be important. Add to this the fact that we now live in a multicultural environment—doing business and working with many different cultural groups—and the businessperson soon realizes the depth of the ethical and legal issues that may arise. There are problems of word meanings by age and within cultures. For example, an expression such as "Did you guys hook up last night?" can have various meanings, including some that could be considered offensive in a work environment.

Bullying is associated with a hostile workplace when someone (or a group) considered a target is threatened, harassed, belittled, or verbally abused or overly criticized. While bullying may create what some may call a hostile environment, this term is generally associated with sexual harassment. Although there is legal recourse for those who've experienced sexual harassment, currently there are few options for people who've been bullied.

**Table 2.3 | Actions Associated with Bullies**

1. Spreading rumours to damage others
2. Blocking others' communication in the workplace
3. Flaunting status or authority to take advantage of others
4. Discrediting others' ideas and opinions
5. Use of emails to demean others
6. Failing to communicate or return communication
7. Insulting, yelling, and shouting
8. Using terminology to discriminate by gender, race, or age
9. Using eye contact or body language to hurt others or their reputations
10. Taking credit for others' work or ideas

Bullying can cause psychological damage that can result in health-endangering consequences for the target. As Table 2.3 indicates, bullying can use a mix of verbal, non-verbal, and manipulative threats to damage workplace productivity. You may wonder why workers tolerate such activities. The problem is that 81 percent of workplace bullies are supervisors. A recent study by Jacqueline Power, an assistant professor of management at the University of Windsor's Odette School of Business, found that 40 percent of Canadians experienced one or more acts of workplace bullying at least once a week in a six-month period. Power has determined that bullying leads to the underperformance of organizations, as the injured parties can quit and go elsewhere or are prone to be less productive.[12]

Power's findings are echoed by a 2018 study by Forum Research. The polling company surveyed 1800 Canadians and determined that 55 percent had been bullied or had co-workers who were bullied on the job. Forum Research also found that older employees, those with disabilities, and members of the LGBT community were more likely to be bullied.

**Conflict of Interest.** A conflict of interest exists when a person must choose whether to advance his or her own personal interests or those of others. For example, a manager in a corporation is supposed to ensure that the company is profitable so that its shareholder–owners receive a return on their investment. In other words, the managers have a responsibility to investors. If they, instead, make decisions that give them more power or money but do not help the company, then they have a conflict of interest—they are acting to benefit themselves at the expense of the company and are not fulfilling their responsibilities.

To avoid conflicts of interest, employees must be able to separate their personal financial interests from their business dealings. For example, Global Television suspended Toronto-based news anchor Leslie Roberts after it was revealed that he was a secret partner in public relations firm BuzzPR. BuzzPR was being paid by clients for publicity Roberts was providing them on the news and through his social media accounts. Roberts ultimately resigned over the matter.

As mentioned earlier, it is considered improper to give or accept **bribes**—payments, gifts, or special favours intended to influence the outcome of a decision. A bribe is a conflict of interest because it benefits an individual at the expense of an organization or society. Companies that do business should be aware that bribes are a significant ethical issue and are, in fact, illegal in many countries, including Canada. Yet in other countries bribes or facilitation payments are seen as a normal way of conducting business.

**bribes**
payments, gifts, or special favours intended to influence the outcome of a decision

Even though Canadian law prohibits Canadian firms from engaging in this practice, some still do in order to move projects ahead or to maximize profits. For example, Acres International of Oakville, Ontario, was convicted by the Lesotho High Court in Africa of bribing a local official to secure contracts.[13] Bribery is more prevalent in some countries than in others. For example, bribes are standard practice in Bangladesh, where Niko Resources, a Calgary-based company recently experienced trouble when it was caught purchasing a $190,000 car for a government official.[14] Transparency International has developed a Corruption Perceptions Index (Table 2.4). Note there are seven countries perceived as less corrupt than Canada.

©The Canadian Press/Frank Arcuri

Leslie Roberts, former Global News anchor, resigned when it was discovered he was being secretly paid to generate publicity for businesses and other clients.

**Fairness and Honesty.** Fairness and honesty are at the heart of business ethics and relate to the general values of decision makers. At a minimum, businesspersons are expected to follow all applicable laws and regulations. But beyond obeying the law, they are expected not to harm customers, employees, clients, or competitors knowingly through deception, misrepresentation, coercion, or discrimination.

Table 2.4 | Least Corrupt Countries

| Rank | Country | 2017 CPI Score* |
|---|---|---|
| 1 | New Zealand | 89 |
| 2 | Denmark | 88 |
| 3 | Finland | 85 |
| 3 | Norway | 85 |
| 3 | Switzerland | 85 |
| 6 | Singapore | 84 |
| 6 | Sweden | 84 |
| 8 | Canada | 82 |
| 8 | Luxembourg | 82 |
| 8 | Netherlands | 82 |
| 8 | United Kingdom | 82 |
| 12 | Germany | 81 |
| 16** | United States | 75 |

* CPI score relates to perceptions of the degree of corruption as seen by businesspeople and country analysts, and ranges between 100 (highly clean) and 0 (highly corrupt).

** Included as Canada's main trading partner.

As discussed throughout the chapter, issues of ethics are not always clear, and this can be seen in the case of probiotics, one of the trendiest health products over the past decade. Probiotics are being put into yogurt, sports drinks, and other food products with claims that they improve the digestive system. Advocates of the bacteria cite incidents of people's health improving as a result of ingesting the bacteria.

Yet scientific research does not support these claims. The European Food Safety Authority (EFSA) has studied hundreds of health claims associated with probiotics and rejected them all. The EFSA has gone so far as to ban the use of the word *probiotics* on food labels. Yet some companies that produce these products point to research that they state proves their claim that probiotics are good for you.

Other examples are a bit clearer cut, such as the case of Volkswagen mentioned above, which intentionally installed software on some of its diesel cars to cheat emission tests

## RESPONDING TO BUSINESS CHALLENGES

### What Is Ethical When Bribes Are the Norm?

For years, bribes and corruption in foreign countries were customary and considered acceptable, meaning a Canadian company operating in a part of the world where bribery was the norm would be forgiven for following local customs and could pay bribes. This attitude started to change in 1999, when both the U.S. and Canadian governments started to pass tougher rules governing how North American companies conducted business globally.

©webphotographeer/Getty Images

While bribery is illegal in Canada, facilitation payments or bribes are common in other parts of the world. Would you be willing to pay a facilitation payment if it was common practice in a country where you owned a business?

Like most of what happens in business, though, things are not always straightforward. While large bribes are no longer considered acceptable, it still isn't clear about small bribes, often referred to as "facilitation payments," that get people to perform their jobs. For example, in some European countries it is not unusual for the mailman to knock on your door at Christmas looking for a cash gift. The norm is that you pay the gift or you don't get your mail anymore.

#### DISCUSSION QUESTIONS

1. Do you think it is ethical to pay a bribe in a country where it is a cultural norm? Why or why not?
2. Do you think "facilitation payments" should be considered bribes? If you ran a company in a country where these payments were the norm, would you pay them?
3. Do you think Canada's legal system should be investigating crimes, such as bribes, that occur in other countries? Why or why not?

and then sold the cars as being more environmentally friendly than they were. Other clear cases of dishonesty include Suzy Shier Inc. and The Forzani Group, owners and operators of SportChek and Sports Smart stores, who ended up on the receiving end of a number of consumer complaints as consumer groups noted that the stores frequently overstated the regular selling price on items to make the sales price look more attractive. The result was consumers who felt that they were getting a larger bargain and spent more or bought items that they normally would not have bought.

The Canadian Competition Bureau, an independent law enforcement agency that protects and promotes consumers, brought the matter before the courts; the result was fines of $1 million for Suzy Shier Inc. and total fines and court costs of $1.7 million for The Forzani Group.[15] Vault.com found that 67 percent of employees have taken office supplies from work to use for matters unrelated to their job. Most employees do not view taking office supplies as stealing or dishonest, with 97 percent saying they have never gotten caught and it would not matter if they were found out. In addition, only 3.7 percent say they have taken items like keyboards, software, and memory sticks. Still, an employee should be aware of policies on taking items and recognize how these decisions relate to ethical behaviour.[16]

©Keith Homan/Shutterstock

Consumers are flocking to buy products with added probiotics, hoping to improve their health. Unfortunately, research by the European Food Safety Authority and the U.S. Food and Drug Administration does not support any of these claims. Are companies pushing consumers to purchase probiotic products ethical?

One aspect of fairness relates to competition. For example, the former CEO of Uber was alleged to have conspired with a former Google engineer to steal trade secrets related to driverless cars. Although numerous laws have been passed to foster competition and make monopolistic practices illegal, companies sometimes gain control over markets by using questionable practices that harm competition. For instance, the European Commission started an antitrust investigation into Google's practices to determine whether it was engaging in anti-competitive behaviour. Several companies, including Microsoft, claimed that Google promoted its own search results over those of competitors in spite of their relevance. Because Google holds 90 percent of the search engine market in Europe, the controversy over how it is using its dominant position to remain ahead of competitors is not likely to die down.

Another aspect of fairness and honesty relates to disclosure of potential harm caused by product use. For example, Chipotle had a series of food safety challenges in 2015 and 2016. In the U.S. an outbreak of E. coli was traced to a number of stores. Steve Ells, founder and former co-CEO acted quickly, closing 43 restaurants in two states to rid the stores of contamination and retrain staff on food handling procedures. Maple Leaf Foods announced a series of recalls in 2008 after it discovered that some of its products were tainted with *Listeria monocytogenes*, a bacterium that can cause serious illness and even death if ingested.

While a number of people did become ill and some in fact died, Maple Leaf CEO Michael McCain's handling of the situation was recognized as positive by the business press and many Canadians. McCain claimed full responsibility for the recall and was in constant communication with the public and the press. Right from the start of the outbreak, Maple Leaf reached out to the public using press conferences, web postings, and commercials to keep consumers informed.

## Consider the Following: Restaurant delivery services take a huge bite out of profits.

Food delivery is big business, in excess of $2.6 billion and growing. In Canada almost everyone has heard of Uber Eats, Skip the Dishes, and Foodora, delivery services that allow restaurants to deliver food to customers without employing costly delivery staff. Food delivery operates very much like ride sharing except the rider is the food. Customers use an app to scan through local restaurants, select the food they want to order, and in anywhere from 15 to 60 minutes receive the food at their front door. The food is delivered by contract employees who only work when they want to and often use bicycles instead of cars to make the deliveries.

There is a downside to your receiving food deliveries. Most delivery services are charging restaurants 30 percent of the sales price to deliver the food. So if your order totals $20, Uber for example, is taking $6 from the restaurant in delivery fees. Given that most if not all restaurants make less than 30 percent per order they are losing money on all deliveries. Since most food delivery services also have a rule that restaurants cannot charge more for food being delivered using their app, the restaurant owner is almost guaranteed to lose money. Delivery services tack on a delivery fee, as well, which the customer pays.

Delivery people also have some complaints about the service. They note that they are not treated as employees, meaning they do not receive minimum wage, receive no overtime pay, do not have access to benefits such as Workers Compensation if they are hurt on the job, and so forth. Both Skip the Dishes and Uber Eats are currently involved in lawsuits with contract delivery people who are trying to access traditional employee benefits.

©Jerome Cid/Alamy Stock Photo

Most food delivery services such as Uber Eats treat all delivery people as independent contractors. Do you think they should be classified as contractors or employees? Why?

### DISCUSSION QUESTIONS

1. Do you think food delivery services are running an ethical business, knowing restaurants are likely losing money on every order? Why or why not?
2. Why do you think restaurants are participating in the food delivery service? What are some potential benefits?
3. Do you think people who deliver food are employees and should be treated as such, or do you think they are independent contractors? Why?
4. Some restaurants have been caught charging higher prices for delivered food. Do you think the restaurant owners are acting ethically when they do this? Why or why not?

Testifying before a parliamentary committee on food safety McCain noted, "This tragedy was a defining moment for Maple Leaf Foods and for those that worked there. We are determined to make a terrible wrong, right."[17] Maple Leaf's efforts not only helped consumers realize they may have purchased tainted products but also helped the company's image and bottom line as the decline in the firm's value has not been as significant as industry experts thought it would be as a result of the recall.

Compare the responses of those companies to that of XL Foods, a Canadian beef processing plant where testing for E. coli was not stringent enough. The lack of testing resulted in infected food reaching the marketplace, causing consumers to become ill and requiring the company to institute a large recall of products. Rather than address the problem directly, the company basically went into a media blackout, ignoring requests for additional information. The result was no one trusted the few statements they heard from XL and rumours ran rampant in the press. Consumers seem willing to accept that mistakes, even deadly mistakes, will happen in the manufacturing of consumer goods. What upsets consumers, however, is when companies attempt to avoid the truth to limit financial damage. Both Chipotle and Maple Leaf benefitted from being honest with their customers.

While corrupt business practices in Canada are an issue, the country has recently improved its standing, according to the Corruption Perceptions Index from Transparency International, which annually ranks countries based on perceptions of corruption in business and government circles.[18] As of 2017, Canada is ranked eighth in the world, an improvement from our fourteenth-place ranking a decade ago.

Dishonesty is not only found in business. According to the first major study of academic misconduct in Canada, cheating, deceit, and plagiarism were found to be serious problems. Julia Christensen Hughes of the University of Guelph and Donald McCabe of Rutgers University surveyed 14,913 undergraduate students, 1318 graduate students, 683 teaching assistants, and 1902 faculty from 11 Canadian post-secondary institutions across five provinces.

Students admitted to having engaged in some form of misconduct while completing their academic work. Seventy-three percent admitted to "serious" cheating while in high school and 53 percent of undergrads admitted they are still cheating in university.[19] If today's students are tomorrow's leaders, there is likely to be a correlation between acceptable behaviour today and tomorrow, adding to the argument that the leaders of today must be prepared for the ethical risks associated with this downward trend. According to a poll by Deloitte Touche of teenagers aged 13 to 18, when asked if people who practise good business ethics are more successful than those who don't, 69 percent of teenagers agreed.[20] The same poll found only 12 percent of teens think business leaders today are ethical. On the other hand, another survey indicated that many students do not define copying answers from another student's paper or downloading music or content for classroom work as cheating.[21]

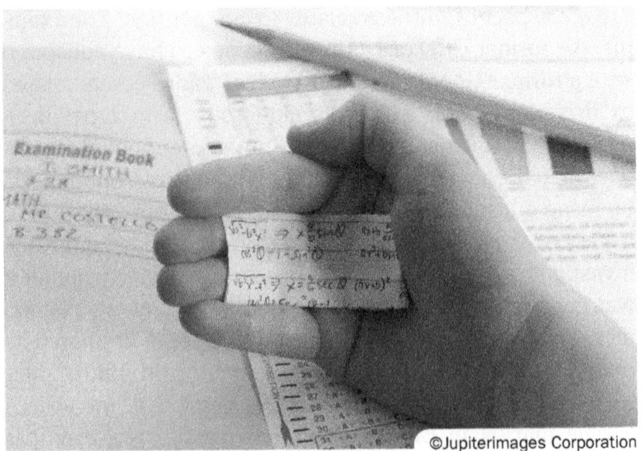


©Jupiterimages Corporation

Seventy-three percent of high school students and 53 percent of university students admitted to serious cheating.

**Communications.** Communications is another area in which ethical concerns may arise. False and misleading advertising, as well as deceptive personal-selling tactics, anger consumers and can lead to the failure of a business. Truthfulness about product safety and quality is also important to consumers.

As discussed above, manufacturers of products with probiotics are starting to come under increased government scrutiny in Europe and the U.S. The bacteria was largely ignored in North America until Danone, producers of Activia yogurt, started spending upward of $130 million annually to promote the health benefits of the product. The issue is that the benefits are not supported by any scientific research.[22] Claims about dietary supplements and weight-loss products can be similarly problematic. For example, Canada, Mexico, and the United States recently announced actions taken to fight weight-loss fraud: they took 734 compliance actions to combat companies promoting bogus and misleading weight-loss schemes.

Canadian investigative news shows *Marketplace* and *W5* have spent considerable effort studying some of the claims of the weight loss industry with surprising results. CBC's *Marketplace* investigated Herbal Magic, one of the biggest weight-loss companies in Canada with more than 300 stores nationwide. The journalists discovered that Herbal Magic clients were being told to purchase two expensive dietary supplements to encourage weight loss. CBC took the supplements to laboratories for independent testing and discovered that there was not enough scientific evidence to justify the claims.

Since the airing of the show, Herbal Magic has announced it will replace the supplements with different formulations.[23] *W5* also uncovered questionable behaviour in its investigation of PhytoPharma, which became known for many weight-loss products including the popular Plant Macerate and Apple Cider Vinegar capsules by Naturalab.

*W5* determined that there was no scientific evidence to support the claim that the products assisted in weight loss.[24]

Unscrupulous activity is not limited to just the diet industry. Governments in Canada, Mexico, and the United States launched 177 compliance and enforcement actions against companies promoting bogus diabetes products and services. Actions include prosecutions, recalls, seizures, import refusals, warnings, and other enforcement programs against false and misleading advertising and labelling, as well as the promotion of industry compliance.[25]

Some companies fail to provide enough information for consumers about differences or similarities between products. For example, driven by high prices for medicines, many consumers are turning to the Internet, Mexico, and overseas sources for drugs to treat a variety of illnesses and conditions. However, research suggests that a significant percentage of these imported pharmaceuticals may not actually contain the labelled drug, and the counterfeit drugs could even be harmful to those who take them. The issue of drug importation is particularly problematic in the United States where millions of people do not have health insurance. Unfortunately, as stated above, people do not always know what they are getting. In a recent FDA seizure, it was discovered that 85 percent of the drugs that were purported to be sold from Canada in fact came from other countries.[26]

Another important aspect of communications that may raise ethical concerns relates to product labelling. In Canada, anti-tobacco legislation requires cigarette manufacturers to include graphic pictures, health warnings, health information messages, and toxic emissions/constituents statements on their packages. The U.S. Surgeon General currently requires cigarette manufacturers to indicate clearly on cigarette packaging that smoking cigarettes is harmful to the smoker's health. In Europe, at least 30 percent of the front side of product packaging and 40 percent of the back needs to be taken up by the warning. The use of descriptors such as "light" or "mild" has been banned.[27]

However, labelling of other products raises ethical questions when it threatens basic rights, such as freedom of speech and expression. This is the heart of the controversy surrounding the movement to require warning labels on movies and video games, rating their content, language, and appropriate audience age. Although people in the entertainment industry believe that such labelling violates their rights, other consumers—particularly parents—believe that such labelling is needed to protect children from harmful influences.

Internet regulation, particularly that designed to protect children and the elderly, is at the forefront of consumer protection legislation. Because of the debate surrounding the acceptability of these business activities, they remain major ethical issues. The Canadian Radio-television and Telecommunications Commission, the body responsible for regulating broadcasting and telecommunications in Canada, does not regulate the Internet. However, certain obligations must be met under consumer protection laws when doing business with consumers on the Internet.

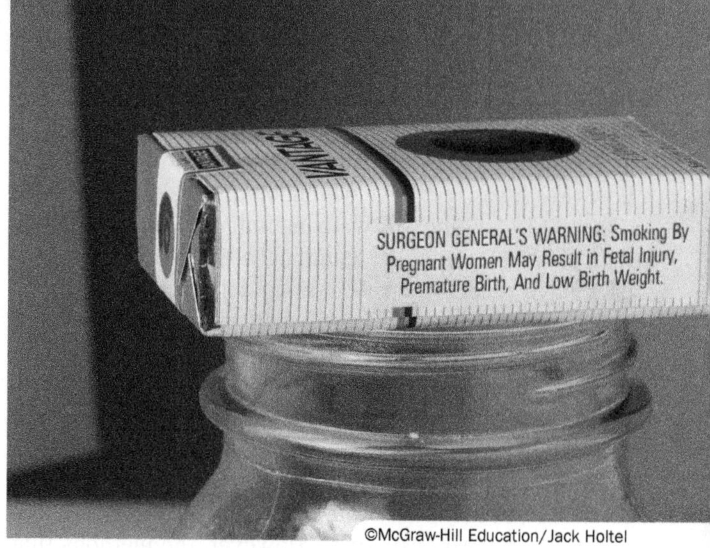


©McGraw-Hill Education/Jack Holtel

Cigarette labels now have to warn about health risks.

Another highly polarized debate concerns the labelling of genetically modified (GM) foods in Canada. Currently, disclosure of GM foods among Canadian food manufacturers and retailers is not required, even though GM foods are said to be present in 60 to 70 percent of all processed foods on the market, according to the Food and Consumer Products Manufacturers of Canada.[28]

Opponents of GM foods argue that they might pose health risks for certain people (for example, foods could become metabolically dangerous or even toxic from the introduction of a fish gene in a plant). Proponents assert that GM foods will promise many health benefits (for example, farmers typically produce GM crops using fewer pesticides, herbicides, and fertilizers). Other arguments against GM crops are that the technology will hurt small farmers and harm the environment, that modification goes against nature, that the industry suffers from poor oversight and regulation, and that biotech companies are profit-driven with little concern for potential risks to people or nature. Proponents maintain that farmers will reap great benefits from biotechnology; that the technology helps the environment, is completely natural, and uses the most thoroughly tested and highly regulated food plants; and that GM crops hold the greatest hope for adequately feeding a rapidly expanding population. Because of the debate surrounding the acceptability of these business activities, they remain major ethical issues.

**Business Relationships.** The behaviour of businesspersons toward customers, suppliers, and others in their workplace may also generate ethical concerns. Ethical behaviour within a business involves keeping company secrets, meeting obligations and responsibilities, and avoiding undue pressure that may force others to act unethically.

Managers, in particular, because of the authority of their position, have the opportunity to influence employees' actions. For example, a manager can influence employees to use pirated computer software to save costs. The use of illegal software puts the employee and the company at legal risk, but employees may feel pressured to do so by their superior's authority. The Canadian Alliance Against Software Theft (CAAST) and the Business Software Alliance (BSA), watchdog groups that represent the world's leading software manufacturers, announced that some 11 Canadian companies from diverse industries have recently agreed to pay a total of $252,093 to settle claims that they were using unlicensed software. According to a study, 33 percent of software installed on computers in Canada was pirated, representing a loss of $943 million. It is estimated that, globally, software piracy resulted in a loss of $46.3 billion.[29]

It is the responsibility of managers to create a work environment that helps the organization achieve its objectives and fulfill its responsibilities. However, the methods that managers use to enforce these responsibilities should not compromise employee rights. Organizational pressures may encourage a person to engage in activities that he or she might otherwise view as unethical, such as invading others' privacy or stealing a competitor's secrets.

In Canada it is estimated that corporate espionage costs companies upward of $20 billion a year. One of the better known examples occurred when Air Canada found that WestJet had gained access to its internal website to acquire commercially sensitive data, and it launched a $220 million lawsuit against the company. In return, WestJet filed a $5 million countersuit claiming that Air Canada had hired private investigators to pilfer the garbage of WestJet's co-founder, Mark Hill. After two years of arguments, WestJet apologized and admitted that its online snooping was unethical. It agreed to pay Air Canada $5.5 million to settle the allegations of corporate espionage, and to donate $10 million to children's charities in the name of both airlines. In return, Air Canada accepted WestJet's apologies and withdrew the legal claims.[30]

Alternatively, a firm may provide only vague or lax supervision on ethical issues, providing the opportunity for misconduct. Managers who offer no ethical direction to employees create many opportunities for manipulation, dishonesty, and conflicts of interest.

> "In Canada, corporate espionage is estimated to cost the economy upward of $20 billion a year as secrets and confidential information is stolen."

**Plagiarism**—taking someone else's work and presenting it as your own without mentioning the source—is another ethical issue. As a student, you may be familiar with plagiarism in school; for example, copying someone else's term paper or quoting from a published work or Internet source without acknowledging it. In business, an ethical issue arises when an employee copies reports or presents the work or ideas of others as his or her own. At *USA Today*, for example, an internal investigation into the work of veteran reporter Jack Kelley identified dozens of stories in which Kelley appeared to have plagiarized material from competing newspapers. The investigation also uncovered evidence Kelley fabricated significant portions of at least eight major stories and conspired to cover up his lapses in judgment. The newspaper later apologized to its readers, and Kelley resigned.[31] A manager attempting to take credit for a subordinate's ideas is engaging in another type of plagiarism.

**plagiarism** the act of taking someone else's work and presenting it as your own without mentioning the source

©Design Pics/Don Hammond

Air Canada and WestJet have both engaged in questionable practices as they fight for market share in Canada.

> "It is the responsibility of managers to create a work environment that helps the organization achieve its objectives and fulfill its responsibilities."

## Making Decisions About Ethical Issues

Although we've presented a variety of ethical issues that may arise in business, it can be difficult to recognize specific ethical issues in practice. Whether a decision maker recognizes an issue as an ethical one often depends on the issue itself. Managers, for example, tend to be more concerned about issues that affect those close to them, as well as issues that have immediate rather than long-term consequences. Thus, the perceived importance of an ethical issue substantially affects choices, and only a few issues receive scrutiny, while most receive no attention at all.[32]

Table 2.5 lists some questions you may want to ask yourself and others when trying to determine whether an action is ethical. Open discussion of ethical issues does not eliminate ethical problems, but it does promote both trust and learning in an organization.[33] When people feel that they cannot discuss what they are doing with their co-workers or superiors, there is a good chance that an

## Consider the Following: Is Facebook acting ethically by making billions off your personal information?

In 2018, Facebook reported $55.8 billion in revenue and saw its total number of active users reach 2.32 billion people. Facebook, which also owns WhatsApp and Instagram, has seen steady growth in revenue and profits since its inception by Mark Zuckerberg 17 years ago. While investors in the company are quite happy with the results, there are a growing number of critics who contend that much of Facebook's advertising revenue is a direct result of Facebook using its users' personal information to sell to advertisers who create targeted ads based on users' browser history, likes, recommendations, and other information. These critics contend that Facebook is combining information from WhatsApp, Instagram, and location proximity apps to create even more detailed user profiles.* The end result is that Facebook is making billions off people's personal information, and often people do not know that this is the case or the extent of personal information Facebook is selling.**

©Stanca Sanda/Alamy Stock Photo

Facebook makes billions from using your personal information and selling it to advertisers. Do you think this is an ethical business model? Why or why not?

### DISCUSSION QUESTIONS

1. Do you think people are aware of the amount of personal information being collected by Facebook? Will awareness hurt the company's business model? Why or why not?
2. Do you think it's ethical for Facebook to collect and sell the personal information of its roughly 2.7 billion users? Why or why not?
3. Facebook originally stated it would not combine the personal information from Facebook and Instagram to create even more detailed user profiles. After a brief period, Facebook has gone back on its word and started to combine user profiles. Is this ethical? Why or why not?

*Stephen Fidler, "Facebook Policies Taken to task in Report for Data-Privacy Issues," *Wall Street Journal*, February 23, 2015, http://www.wsj.com/articles/facebook-policies-taken-to-task-in-report-for-data-privacy-issues-1424725902 (accessed November 9, 2015).

**Olivia Campbell, "Facebook will now track your browsing history on external sites & mobile apps," Abine, June 13, 2014, https://www.abine.com/blog/2014/facebook-tracking-browsing/ (accessed November 6, 2015); Drew Guarini, "Hold your gasps, Facebook is under fire for its privacy policy again," Huffington Post, September 5, 2013, http://www.huffingtonpost.com/2013/09/05/facebook-privacy-ftc_n_3873764.html (accessed November 08, 2015).

ethical issue exists. Once a person has recognized an ethical issue and can openly discuss it with others, he or she has begun the process of resolving the ethical issue.

**Table 2.5** | Questions to Consider in Determining Whether an Action Is Ethical

| |
|---|
| Are there any potential legal restrictions or violations that could result from the action? |
| Does your company have a specific code of ethics or policy on the action? |
| Is this activity customary in your industry? Are there any industry trade groups that provide guidelines or codes of conduct that address this issue? |
| Would this activity be accepted by your co-workers? Will your decision or action withstand open discussion with co-workers and managers and survive untarnished? |
| How does this activity fit with your own beliefs and values? |

## Improving Ethical Behaviour in Business

**LO 2-3** Specify how businesses can promote ethical behaviour.

Understanding how people make ethical choices and what prompts a person to act unethically may reverse the current trend toward unethical behaviour in business. Ethical decisions in an organization are influenced by three key factors: individual moral standards, the influence of managers and co-workers, and the opportunity to engage in misconduct (Figure 2.1). While you have great control over your personal ethics outside the workplace, your co-workers and superiors exert significant control over your choices at work through authority and example. In fact, the activities and examples set by co-workers,

Figure 2.1 | Three Factors That Influence Business Ethics

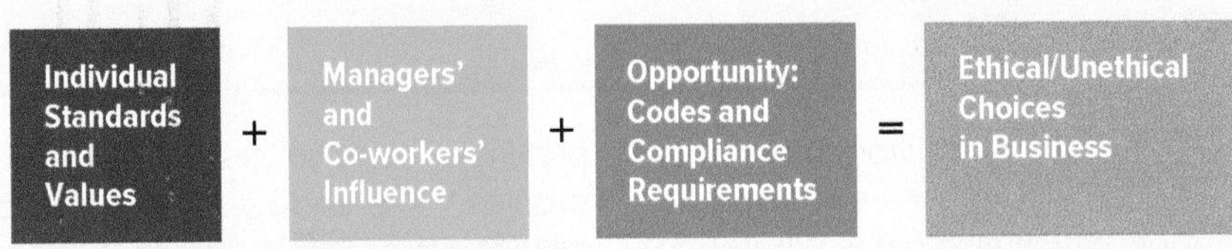


along with rules and policies established by the firm, are crucial in gaining consistent ethical compliance in an organization.

If the company fails to provide good examples and direction for appropriate conduct, confusion and conflict will develop and result in the opportunity for misconduct. If your boss or co-workers leave work early, you may be tempted to do so, as well. If you see co-workers making personal long-distance phone calls at work and charging them to the company, then you may be more likely to do so also. In addition, having sound personal values contributes to an ethical workplace.

Because ethical issues often emerge from conflict, it is useful to examine the causes of ethical conflict. Business managers and employees often experience some tension between their own ethical beliefs and their obligations to the organizations in which they work. Many employees utilize different ethical standards at work than they do at home. This conflict increases when employees feel that their company is encouraging unethical conduct or exerting pressure on them to engage in it.

It is difficult for employees to determine what conduct is acceptable within a company if the firm does not have ethics policies and standards. And without such policies and standards, employees may base decisions on how their peers and superiors behave. Professional **codes of ethics** are formalized rules and standards that describe what the company expects of its employees. Codes of ethics do not have to be so detailed that they take into account every situation, but they should provide guidelines and principles that can help employees achieve organizational objectives and address risks in an acceptable and ethical way. The development of a code of ethics should include not only a firm's executives and board of directors, but also legal staff and employees from all areas of a firm.[34] Table 2.6 lists some key things to consider when developing a code of ethics.

**codes of ethics**
formalized rules and standards that describe what a company expects of its employees

"Many employees utilize different ethical standards at work than they do at home."

Table 2.6 | Key Things to Consider in Developing a Code of Ethics

- Create a team to assist with the process of developing the code (include management and non-management employees from across departments and functions).
- Solicit input from employees from different departments, functions, and regions to compile a list of common questions and answers to include in the code document.
- Make certain that the headings of the code sections can be easily understood by all employees.
- Avoid referencing specific Canadian laws and regulations or those of specific countries, particularly for codes that will be distributed to employees in multiple regions.
- Hold employee group meetings on a complete draft version (including graphics and pictures) of the text using language that everyone can understand.
- Inform employees that they will receive a copy of the code during an introduction session.
- Let all employees know that they will receive future ethics training which will, in part, cover the important information contained in the code document.

Codes of ethics, policies on ethics, and ethics training programs advance ethical behaviour because they proscribe which activities are acceptable and which are not, and they limit the opportunity for misconduct by providing punishments for violations of the rules and standards. According to the National Business Ethics Survey (NBES), employees in organizations that have written standards of conduct, ethics training, ethics offices or hotlines, and systems for anonymous reporting of misconduct are more likely to report misconduct when they observe it. The survey also found that such programs are associated with higher employee perceptions that they will be held accountable for ethical infractions.[35]

The enforcement of such codes and policies through rewards and punishments increases the acceptance of ethical standards by employees. One of the most important components of an ethics program is a means through which employees can report observed misconduct anonymously. The NBES found that although employees are increasingly reporting illegal and unethical activities they observe in the workplace, the majority of surveyed employees indicated they are unwilling to report misconduct because they fear that no corrective action will be taken or that their report will not remain confidential.[36]

The lack of anonymous reporting mechanisms may encourage **whistleblowing**, which occurs when an employee exposes an employer's wrongdoing to outsiders, such as the media or government regulatory agencies. However, more companies are establishing programs to encourage employees to report illegal or unethical practices internally so that they can take steps to remedy problems before they result in legal action or generate negative publicity. The *Federal Accountability Act*, among other measures, provides public-sector workers legal protection against reprisals for reporting government wrongdoing. The legislation is "part of the government's broader commitment to ensure transparency, accountability, financial responsibility and ethical conduct."[37] Currently, whistleblowers in Canada also have special protection with respect to environmental and health and safety matters, and there is a requirement for public companies to have confidential whistleblower hotlines and established procedures for anonymous reporting. Unfortunately, whistleblowers are often treated negatively in organizations.

**whistleblowing**
the act of an employee exposing an employer's wrongdoing to outsiders, such as the media or government regulatory agencies

The current trend is to move away from legally based ethical initiatives in organizations to cultural- or integrity-based initiatives that make ethics a part of core organizational values. Organizations recognize that effective business ethics programs are good for business performance. Firms that develop higher levels of trust function more efficiently and effectively and avoid damaged company reputations and product images. Organizational ethics initiatives have been supportive of many positive and diverse organizational objectives, such as profitability, hiring, employee satisfaction, and customer loyalty.[38] Conversely, lack of organizational ethics initiatives and the absence of workplace values such as honesty, trust, and integrity can have a negative impact on organizational objectives. According to one report on employee loyalty and work practices, 79 percent of employees who questioned their bosses' integrity indicated that they felt uncommitted or were likely to quit soon.[39]

"The Canadian government is hoping to encourage whistleblowers to inform them about tax cheats. Revenue Canada is offering whistleblowers a 15 percent commission on money collected as a result of tips."

## The Nature of Social Responsibility

**LO 2-4** Explain the four dimensions of social responsibility.

There are four dimensions of social responsibility: economic, legal, ethical, and voluntary (including philanthropic) (Figure 2.2).[40] Earning profits is the economic foundation of the pyramid in Figure 2.2, and complying with the law is the next step. However, a business whose *sole* objective is to maximize profits is not likely to consider its social responsibility, although its activities will probably be legal. (We looked at ethical responsibilities in the first half of this chapter.) Finally, voluntary responsibilities are additional activities that may not be required but that promote human welfare or goodwill. Legal and economic

**Figure 2.2** | The Pyramid of Social Responsibility

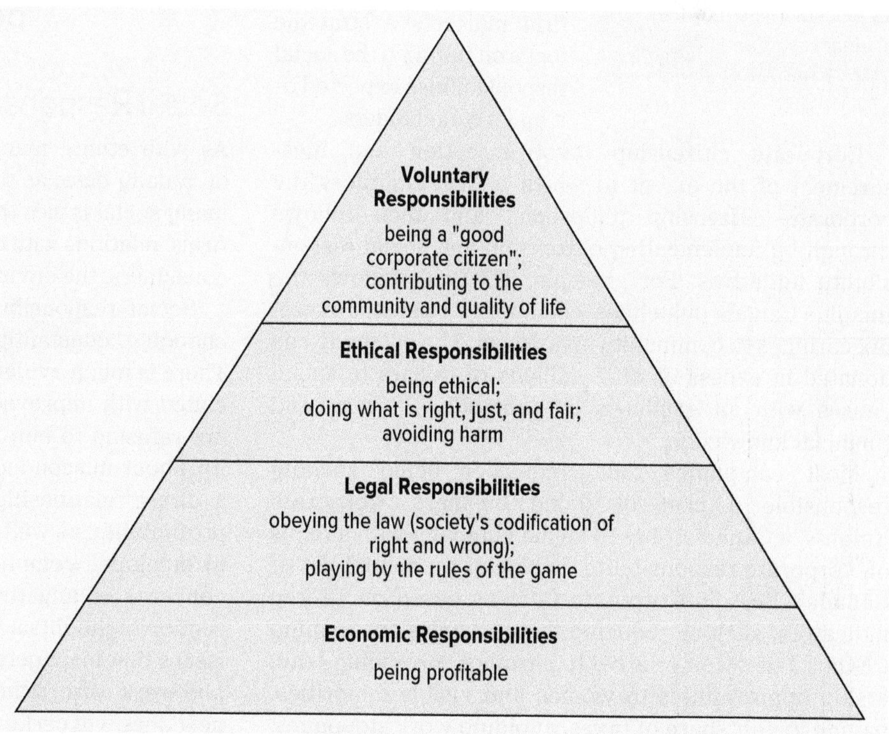

**Table 2.7** | The Arguments For and Against Social Responsibility

**For:**

1. Business helped to create many of the social problems that exist today, so it should play a significant role in solving them, especially in the areas of pollution reduction and cleanup.
2. Businesses should be more responsible because they have the financial and technical resources to help solve social problems.
3. As members of society, businesses should do their fair share to help others.
4. Socially responsible decision making by businesses can prevent increased government regulation.
5. Social responsibility is necessary to ensure economic survival: if businesses want educated and healthy employees, customers with money to spend, and suppliers with quality goods and services in years to come, they must take steps to help solve the social and environmental problems that exist today.

**Against:**

1. It sidetracks managers from the primary goal of business—earning profits. Every dollar donated to social causes or otherwise spent on society's problems is a dollar less for owners and investors.
2. Participation in social programs gives businesses greater power, perhaps at the expense of particular segments of society.
3. Some people question whether business has the expertise needed to assess and make decisions about social problems.
4. Many people believe that social problems are the responsibility of government agencies and officials, who can be held accountable by voters.

concerns have long been acknowledged in business, but voluntary and ethical issues are more recent concerns.

**Corporate citizenship** is the extent to which businesses meet the legal, ethical, economic, and voluntary responsibilities placed on them by their various stakeholders. It involves the activities and organizational processes adopted by businesses to meet their social responsibilities. A commitment to corporate citizenship by a firm indicates a strategic focus on fulfilling the social responsibilities expected of it by its stakeholders.

**corporate citizenship** the extent to which businesses meet the legal, ethical, economic, and voluntary responsibilities placed on them by their stakeholders

Corporate citizenship involves action and measurement of the extent to which a firm embraces the corporate citizenship philosophy and then follows through by implementing citizenship and social responsibility initiatives. For example, TD Bank follows the Imagine Canada guidelines, committing 1 percent of pre-tax earnings to community investment. The company has donated in excess of $107 millions of dollars to social causes with an emphasis on promoting literacy and financial knowledge.

Most companies today consider being socially responsible a cost of doing business. Corporate Knights, a Canadian-based media company with a focus on corporate responsibility, publishes an annual list of Canada's Best 50 Corporate Citizens based on 13 key indicators, such as reducing factory emissions, paying CEOs a fair wage relative to earnings, providing leadership opportunities to women and visible minorities, paying its fair share of taxes, avoiding work stoppages, and making sure workers' pension funds are properly funded.[41]

Although the concept of social responsibility is receiving more and more attention, it is still not universally accepted. Table 2.7 lists some of the arguments for and against social responsibility.

"Organizations recognize that effective business ethics programs are good for business performance."

## Social Responsibility Issues

As with ethics, managers consider social responsibility on a daily basis as they deal with real issues. Among the many social issues that managers must consider are their firms' relations with owners and shareholders, employees, consumers, the environment, and the community.

Social responsibility is a dynamic area with issues changing constantly in response to society's desires. There is much evidence that social responsibility is associated with improved business performance. Consumers are refusing to buy from businesses that receive publicity about misconduct. A number of studies have found a direct relationship between social responsibility and profitability, as well as that social responsibility is linked to employee commitment and customer loyalty—major concerns of any firm trying to increase profits.[42] This section highlights a few of the many social responsibility issues that managers face; as managers become aware of and work toward the solution of current social problems, new ones will certainly emerge.

**LO 2-5** Debate an organization's social responsibilities to owners, employees, consumers, the environment, and the community.

**Relations with Owners and Shareholders.** Businesses must first be responsible to their owners, who are primarily concerned with earning a profit or a return on their investment in a company. In a small business, this responsibility is fairly easy to fulfill because the owner(s) personally manages the business or knows the managers well. In larger businesses, particularly corporations owned by thousands of shareholders, ensuring responsibility to the owners becomes a more difficult task.

A business's responsibilities to its owners and investors, as well as to the financial community at large, include maintaining proper accounting procedures, providing all relevant information to investors about the current and projected performance of the firm, and protecting the owners' rights and investments. In short, the business must maximize the owners' investment in the firm.

**Employee Relations.** Another issue of importance to a business is its responsibilities to employees, for without employees a business cannot carry out its goals. Employees expect businesses to provide a safe workplace, pay them adequately for their work, and tell them what is happening in their company. They want employers to listen to their grievances and treat them fairly.

As noted at the start of the chapter, sometimes it is difficult to determine if businesses are acting ethically and responsibly to their employees as their motives often differ. Businesses usually want to maximize value for their shareholders while employees often want to maximize their own earnings. Thus there is often an ongoing debate about what is considered adequate pay. In Canada's auto sector, assembly workers earned approximately $80 an hour including benefits and received numerous other perks. When General Motors and Ford attempted to cut labour costs, the Canada Auto Workers Union (CAW) fought strongly against the move.[43]

In order to engage employees, many business such as WestJet and Royal Bank offer employees an opportunity to own shares in their company.[44] The result is employees who feel more engaged and interested in the performance of the company. Employee ownership programs are not just limited to large businesses. *Profit* magazine, a Canadian publication that covers small- and mid-size businesses in Canada, has discovered that many small firms are encouraging employees to become shareholders in their company.

The Canadian government has passed several laws regulating safety in the workplace. Labour unions have also made significant contributions to achieving safety in the workplace and improving wages and benefits. Most organizations now recognize that the safety and satisfaction of their employees are critical ingredients in their success, and many strive to go beyond what is expected of them by the law. Healthy, satisfied employees supply more than just labour to their employers, however. Employers are beginning to realize the importance of obtaining input from even the lowest-level employees to help the company reach its objectives.

A major social responsibility for business is providing equal opportunities for all employees regardless of their sex, age, race, religion, or nationality. Women and minorities have been slighted in the past in terms of education, employment, and advancement opportunities; additionally, many of their needs have not been addressed by business. For example, Google is currently being sued by a group of women in a clash action lawsuit noting that the company has underpaid women compared to male employees. Women, who continue to bear most child-rearing responsibilities, often experience conflict between those responsibilities and their duties as employees. Consequently, day care has become a major employment issue for women, and more companies are providing daycare facilities as part of their effort to recruit and advance women in the workforce.

In addition, companies are considering alternative scheduling such as flex-time and job sharing to accommodate employee concerns. Telecommuting has grown significantly over the past five to ten years, as well. Many Canadians today believe business has a social obligation to provide special opportunities for women and minorities to improve their standing in society.

**Consumer Relations.** A crucial issue in business today is business's responsibility to customers, who look to business to provide them with satisfying, safe products and to respect their rights as consumers. The activities that independent individuals, groups, and organizations undertake to protect their rights as consumers are known as **consumerism**. To achieve their objectives, consumers and their advocates write letters to companies, lobby government agencies, make public service announcements, and boycott companies whose activities they deem irresponsible.

**consumerism** the activities that independent individuals, groups, and organizations undertake to protect their rights as consumers

Many of those involved in the consumer movement argue that consumers should have four specific rights. The *right to safety* means that a business must not knowingly sell anything that could result in personal injury or harm to consumers. Defective or dangerous products erode public confidence in the ability of business to serve society. They also result in expensive litigation that ultimately increases the cost of products for all consumers. The right to safety also means businesses must provide a safe place for consumers to shop. In recent years, many large retailers have been under increasing pressure to improve safety in their large warehouse-type stores. At Home Depot, for example, three consumer deaths and numerous serious injuries have been caused by falling

## RESPONDING TO BUSINESS CHALLENGES

### Professional Football and Concussions

Playing professional football is not one of the safest jobs in the world, especially in the National Football League (NFL). Over the past few decades, retired NFL players have raised concerns about how repetitive head injuries/concussions sustained during games have affected them later in life. Many retired NFL players have faced neurological problems, including permanent brain damage, dementia, and higher-than-average incidents of Alzheimer's disease and clinical depression.

Various retired NFL players have brought lawsuits against the NFL, arguing that the NFL knew or should have known the risks and did not do enough to prevent these injuries. The NFL paid nearly $1 billion to retired NFL players who had suffered injuries in this regard and provided $10 million to fund brain injury research and education/safety programs. Researchers later discovered that 177 out of 202 brains from former football players who had played football sometime during their lives showed evidence of brain degenerative disease. These risks have convinced some NFL players to retire early. Parents are faced with an ethical issue about whether they should allow their children to play football in school at the risk of long-term injury. One poll found parents are 44 percent less likely to allow their children to play football.

Some observers note that football players accept the inherent dangers of the game. Seattle Seahawks star cornerback Richard Sherman has pointed out that NFL players have chosen their profession, know the risks, and have decided to play anyway. However, quarterback Brett Favre states that he has experienced memory loss. He believes concussions have had a negative impact on his life and fears he might develop a brain disease experienced by many retired NFL players.

#### DISCUSSION QUESTIONS

1. To what extent should there be something of a *caveat emptor* (buyer beware) when someone chooses to professionally play football in the NFL?
2. Can the NFL ever really make professional football totally safe?
3. Is playing in the NFL different from being a NASCAR driver, a police officer, or an astronaut?
4. Do you think the NFL is an ethical organization? Why or why not?

©ZUMA Press Inc/Alamy Stock Photo

The NFL has recently dealt with a number of concerns about player safety and the long term impact of playing football. Should the government prevent people from playing sports that are dangerous? Why or why not?

merchandise. One lawsuit brought against the company over injuries received in one of its stores resulted in a $1.5 million judgment. To help prevent further deaths, injuries, and litigation, Home Depot now has a corporate safety officer and has hired 130 safety managers to monitor store compliance with new safety measures.[45]

The *right to be informed* gives consumers the freedom to review complete information about a product before they buy it. This means that detailed information about ingredients, risks, and instructions for use are to be printed on labels and packages.

The *right to choose* ensures that consumers have access to a variety of products and services at competitive prices. The assurance of both satisfactory quality and service at a fair price is also a part of the consumer's right to choose. Some consumers are not being given the right to choose. Many are being billed for products and services they never ordered.

The *right to be heard* assures consumers that their interests will receive full and sympathetic consideration when the government formulates policy. It also ensures the fair treatment of consumers who voice complaints about a purchased product.

The role of provincial and federal governments is to protect consumers against unfair, deceptive, or fraudulent

## Consider the Following: Canada, the counterfeiters' safe haven

Up until 2016, Canada's border patrol did not have the right to seize counterfeit products. As a result, Canada became a safe haven for knock-off products. Since 2016, border patrol has only seized 48 shipments of knock-off goods, and of the 48 cases, 36 were later released. This compares to 34,000 seized shipments in the U.S. and 63,000 shipments seized in Europe in 2016.

©The Canadian Press/Aaron Vincent Elkaim

Canada Goose has been investing both money and time trying to prevent knock-offs from coming into North America.

### DISCUSSION QUESTIONS

1. Do you think the border patrol should seize products that they know are counterfeit? Why or why not?
2. Is manufacturing products under another company's label unethical? Should it be considered illegal?
3. Some Canadian companies such as Canada Goose are investing both time and money trying to fight knock-off versions of their products. Should companies bother to do this? Why or why not?
4. Why do you think Canada has seized so few shipments since 2016?

practices. Canada's Office of Consumer Affairs, a part of Industry Canada, works with both the public and private sectors, using information, research, and policy to complement and support consumer protection regulation.[46]

**Environmental Issues.** Environmental responsibility has become a leading issue as both business and the public acknowledge the damage done to the environment in the past. Today's consumers are increasingly demanding that businesses take a greater responsibility for their actions and how they impact the environment.

**Animal Rights.** One area of environmental concern in society today is animal rights. Probably the most controversial business practice in this area is the testing of cosmetics and drugs on animals that may be injured or killed as a result. Animal-rights activists, such as People for the Ethical Treatment of Animals, say such research is morally wrong because it harms living creatures. Consumers who share this sentiment may boycott companies that test products on animals and take their business instead to companies such as The Body Shop and John Paul Mitchell Systems, which

## Consider the Following: Are energy drinks safe?

Since 2003, energy drinks have been suspected in the deaths of upwards of 22 people in North America. Reports indicate that numerous others have visited the hospital after consuming one of the caffeine-filled beverages. One drink, 5-hour Energy, which comes in a small container, has been attracting the most scrutiny of late but others, including Red Bull and Monster, have been plagued by similar incidents. Doctors in Nova Scotia are asking the government to ban the sale of the energy drinks to people under the age of 19, and other provinces are considering putting warning labels on the beverages.

Should energy drink sales be banned for people under the age of 19?

### DISCUSSION QUESTIONS

1. Do you think government should prevent the sale of these drinks to people under the age of 19? Why or why not?
2. Do you think warning labels should be placed on the drinks based on what energy drink makers say is limited evidence? Why or why not?

©McGraw-Hill Companies/Jill Braaten

do not use animal testing. However, researchers in the cosmetics and pharmaceutical industries argue that animal testing is necessary to prevent harm to human beings who will eventually use the products.

Business practices that harm wildlife and their habitats are another environmental issue. The seal hunt is one such controversial issue in Canada and around the world. Many Canadians argue that hunting seals is the same as farming beef cows or pigs, while animal rights groups argue that it is unethical and cruel. The hunt of 25-day-old seals takes place every March in the waters off the coast of Newfoundland. The federal government says the landed value of seals was $26.5 million in 2006 when 350,000 seals were killed, and provides a "significant" source of income for thousands of sealers.[47]

The International Fund for Animal Welfare (IFAW) describes the contribution of sealing to Newfoundland's GDP as "trivial" and says after costs and indirect subsidies are taken into account, Canadians would "likely find that the hunt actually costs the Canadian taxpayer money." It is a pointless activity, in the view of the IFAW, which says, "the only economically valuable part of the seal is its fur, a non-essential luxury product that no one really needs."[48]

Most of the pelts are exported to Russia and China where demand is strong and growing. IFAW and other interest groups, including many consumers, recently struck a blow to the sealing industry when the European Union banned imported seal products. This ban, along with milder weather that prevents sealers from going on the ice, has seriously limited the seal hunt in recent years. The result is that the seal industry has seen a drastic decline in exports from a high of almost $18 million in 2016 to below $2 million in 2019.

"Related to the problem of land pollution is the larger issue of how to dispose of waste in an environmentally responsible manner."

**Pollution.** Another major issue in the area of environmental responsibility is pollution. Water pollution results from dumping toxic chemicals and raw sewage into rivers and oceans, oil spills, and the burial of industrial waste in the ground where it may filter into underground water supplies. Fertilizers and insecticides used in farming and grounds maintenance also run off into water supplies with each rainfall. Water pollution problems are especially notable in heavily industrialized areas. Medical waste—such as used syringes, vials of blood, and AIDS-contaminated materials—has turned up on beaches in Toronto, Halifax, and Vancouver, as well as other places. Society is demanding that water supplies be clean and healthful to reduce the potential danger from these substances.

Air pollution is usually the result of smoke and other pollutants emitted by manufacturing facilities, as well as carbon monoxide and hydrocarbons emitted by motor vehicles. In addition to the health risks posed by air pollution, when some chemical compounds emitted by manufacturing facilities react with air and rain, acid rain results. Acid rain has contributed to the deaths of many valuable forests and lakes in North America as well as in Europe. Air pollution may also contribute to global warming in which carbon dioxide collects in the Earth's atmosphere, trapping the sun's heat and preventing the earth's surface from cooling. Chlorofluorocarbons also harm the Earth's ozone layer, which filters out the sun's harmful ultraviolet light; this too may be a cause of the greenhouse effect.

Land pollution is tied directly to water pollution because many of the chemicals and toxic wastes that are dumped on the land eventually work their way into the water supply. Land pollution results from the dumping of residential and industrial waste, strip mining, forest fires, and poor forest conservation. In Brazil and other South American countries, rain forests are being destroyed—at a rate of one hectare every two minutes—to make way for farms and ranches, at a cost of the extinction of the many animals and plants (some endangered species) that call the rain forest home. Large-scale deforestation also depletes the oxygen supply available to humans and other animals.

**DID YOU KNOW?**

Nearly one-third of Canada's natural gas production is used to generate oil from the oil sands.[49]

Related to the problem of land pollution is the larger issue of how to dispose of waste in an environmentally responsible manner. One specific solid waste problem is being created by rapid innovations in computer hardware that make many computers obsolete after just 18 months. By 2005, 350 million computers had reached obsolescence, and at least 55 million were expected to end up in landfills.[50] Computers contain toxic substances such as lead, mercury, and polyvinyl chloride, which can leach into the soil and contaminate the groundwater when disposed of improperly. In Europe, the Waste of Electrical and Electronic Equipment (WEEE) legislation aims to reduce the waste arising from this equipment. The key elements are that users recycle equipment free of charge, while producers (manufacturers, sellers, and distributors) are responsible for financing the collection, treatment, recovery, and disposal of WEEE from the recycling facilities.[51]

### Response to Environmental Issues

Partly in response to laws and partly due to consumer concerns, businesses are responding to environmental issues. Many small and large companies, including the Irving Group, Suncor, BlackBerry, Walt Disney Company, Chevron, and Scott Paper, have created new positions to help them achieve their business goals in an environmentally responsible manner. A survey indicated that 82 percent of Fortune 500 companies have published

## GOING GREEN

### Fracking for Natural Gas: Clean Energy Solution or Environmental Catastrophe?

Hydraulic fracturing, known as fracking, has the potential to reduce Canada's dependence on foreign oil and create significant economic spinoffs. Fracking forces water, sand, and chemicals into underground tunnels of shale rock, bringing natural gas to the surface. Natural gas releases half the carbon dioxide of oil and is praised as a much more environmentally friendly fuel. Some provinces, such as Alberta and British Columbia, have benefited economically from fracking for years as the drilling creates jobs and increases tax revenue.

However, fracking does have a dark side. There have been instances where fracking chemicals have contaminated drinking water and increased levels of methane in water wells. People in the oil and gas industry argue that these cases occurred in the past and had more to do with companies not operating properly than the actual technology. Phil Knoll, former CEO of Corridor Resources, a Nova Scotia–based oil company, notes that fracking has been successfully and safely done for 20-plus years throughout Canada and the U.S.

Yet some provinces, most notably Quebec and recently Nova Scotia, have banned fracking over environmental concerns. While environmental groups have applauded such bans and are lobbying other provincial governments to stop fracking, many people in government and in the oil industry question the economic sense of the ban. Given that both Nova Scotia and Quebec would benefit from the increased tax revenue and investment fracking would bring, Knoll criticized the decision to ban fracking by the Nova Scotia government, stating the government ignored the science that fracking has been done safely for 20 years and turned away investment into the province, which is struggling economically.

Former Cape Breton University President David Wheeler was commissioned by the Nova Scotia government to complete a report on fracking, and he estimated that fracking would likely result in an additional billion dollars a year in revenue through the creation of jobs, investment, and royalties to the government.* Interestingly, both Quebec and Nova Scotia receive money, better known as transfer payments, from other provinces that have stronger economies. In 2017, four provinces (Alberta, Saskatchewan, British Columbia, and Newfoundland) paid into the transfer payment program, which benefited Nova Scotia and Quebec. All of these provinces have a successful oil and gas industry operating within their provincial boundaries and allow for fracking.

©Design Pics/Bilderbuch

The recent decision by the government of Nova Scotia to ban fracking has resulted in criticism from oil and gas companies who claim significant studies have proven that fracking is safe and would result in billions of economic opportunities for the struggling region.

#### DISCUSSION QUESTIONS

1. What is the ethical issue involved with fracking, and why is it so hard to resolve?
2. Examine this issue from the perspective of the gas company as well as from the perspective of concerned stakeholders.
3. Why might a government ban fracking when science appears to indicate it can be safely done?
4. Do you think it is fair for some provinces to ban fracking yet turn around and take money from other provinces who allow for fracking?
5. Use Internet resources and find additional arguments for and against fracking.

*Quentin Casey, "In the Hot Seat," *Progress*, April 2015, http://www.progressmedia.ca/article/2015/04/hot-seat

corporate sustainability reports, 74.7 percent engage in recycling efforts, and 69.7 percent have made investments in waste-reduction efforts.[52] Many companies, including Alcoa, Dow Chemical, Phillips Petroleum, and Raytheon, now link executive pay to environmental performance.[53] Some companies are finding that environmental consciousness can save them money. DuPont saved more than $3 billion through energy conservation by replacing natural gas with methane in its industrial boilers in many of its plants.[54]

Many firms are trying to eliminate wasteful practices, the emission of pollutants, and/or the use of harmful chemicals. For example, Toronto-based Delta Hotels introduced Delta Greens, a national sustainability program aimed at improving environmental practices. Marriott Hotels of Canada also engaged in similar environmentally friendly practices by using low-energy light bulbs and low-flow shower heads in their guest rooms.[55] Other companies are seeking ways to improve their products to minimize the environmental impact. Lush Fresh Handmade Cosmetics, a Vancouver-based cosmetic retailer, has diverted 6 million plastic bottles from landfills by selling shampoo in bars.[56]

Utility providers, for example, are increasingly supplementing their services with alternative energy sources, including solar, wind, and geothermal power. Many businesses have turned to *recycling,* the reprocessing of materials—aluminum, paper, glass, and some plastic—for reuse. The above-mentioned Lush Fresh Handmade Cosmetics uses recycled material in its packaging 90 percent of the time. Such efforts to make products, packaging, and processes more environmentally friendly have been labelled "green" business or marketing by the public and media. Lumber products at Home Depot may carry a seal from the Forest Stewardship Council to indicate that they were harvested from sustainable forests using environmentally friendly methods.[57] Likewise, most Chiquita bananas are certified through the Better Banana Project as having been grown with more environmentally and labour-friendly practices.[58]

It is important to recognize that, with current technology, environmental responsibility requires trade-offs. Society must weigh the huge costs of limiting or eliminating pollution against the health threat posed by the pollution. Environmental responsibility imposes costs on both business and the public. Although people certainly do not want oil fouling beautiful waterways and killing wildlife, they insist on low-cost, readily available gasoline and heating oil. People do not want to contribute to the growing garbage-disposal problem, but they often refuse to pay more for "green" products packaged in an environmentally friendly manner, to recycle as much of their own waste as possible, or to permit the building of additional waste-disposal facilities (the "not in my backyard," or NIMBY, syndrome). Managers must coordinate environmental goals with other social and economic ones.

**Community Relations.** A final, yet very significant, issue for businesses concerns their responsibilities to the general welfare of the communities and societies in which they operate. Many businesses want to make their communities better places for everyone to live and work. The most common way that businesses exercise their community responsibility is through donations to local and national charitable organizations. Examples of donations include Delta Hotels' support of Habitat for Humanity Canada, CIBC's sponsorship of MADD Canada, and significant contributions by Pfizer Canada and Boardwalk Realty to the Canadian Mental Health Association.[59]

"Many businesses want to make their communities better places for everyone to live and work."

## TEAM EXERCISE

Sam Walton, founder of Walmart, had an early strategy for growing his business related to pricing. The Opening Price Point strategy used by Walton involved offering the introductory product in a product line at the lowest price point in the market. For example, a minimally equipped microwave oven would sell for less than anyone else in town could charge for the same unit. The strategy was that if consumers saw a product, such as the microwave, and saw it as a good value, they would assume that all of the microwaves were good values. Walton also noted that most people don't buy the entry-level product; they want more features and capabilities and often trade up.

Form teams and assign the role of defending this strategy or casting this strategy as an unethical act. Present your thoughts on either side of the issue.

## LEARNING OBJECTIVES SUMMARY

**LO 2-1** Define business ethics and social responsibility and examine their importance.

Business ethics refers to principles and standards that define acceptable business conduct. Acceptable business behaviour is defined by customers, competitors, government regulators, interest groups, the public, and each individual's personal moral principles and values. Social responsibility is the obligation an organization assumes to maximize its positive impact and minimize its negative impact on society. Socially responsible businesses win the trust and respect of their employees, customers, and society, and in the long run, this practice increases profits. Ethics is important in business because it builds trust and confidence in business relationships. Unethical actions may result in negative publicity, declining sales, and even legal action.

**LO 2-2** Detect some of the ethical issues that may arise in business.

An ethical issue is an identifiable problem, situation, or opportunity requiring a person or organization to choose from among several actions that must be evaluated as right or wrong. Ethical issues can be categorized in the context of their relation with conflicts of interest, fairness and honesty, communications, and business associations.

**LO 2-3** Specify how businesses can promote ethical behaviour by employees.

Businesses can promote ethical behaviour by employees by limiting their opportunity to engage in misconduct. Formal codes of ethics, ethical policies, and ethics training programs reduce the incidence of unethical behaviour by informing employees of what is expected of them and providing punishments for those who fail to comply.

**LO 2-4** Explain the four dimensions of social responsibility.

The four dimensions of social responsibility are economic (being profitable), legal (obeying the law), ethical (doing what is right, just, and fair), and voluntary (being a good corporate citizen).

**LO 2-5** Debate an organization's social responsibilities to owners, employees, consumers, the environment, and the community.

Businesses must maintain proper accounting procedures, provide all relevant information about the performance of the firm to investors, and protect the owners' rights and investments. In relations with employees, businesses are expected to provide a safe workplace, pay employees adequately for their work, and treat them fairly. Consumerism refers to the activities undertaken by independent individuals, groups, and organizations to protect their rights as consumers. Increasingly, society expects businesses to take greater responsibility for the environment, especially with regard to animal rights, as well as water, air, land, and noise pollution. Many businesses engage in activities to make the communities in which they operate better places for everyone to live and work.

## KEY TERMS

bribes
business ethics
codes of ethics
consumerism
corporate citizenship
ethical issue
plagiarism
social responsibility
whistleblowing

## So You Want a Job *in Business Ethics and Social Responsibility*

In the words of Kermit the Frog, "It's not easy being green." It may not be easy, but green business opportunities abound. A popular catch phrase, "Green is the new black," indicates how fashionable green business is becoming. Consumers are more in tune with and concerned about green products, policies, and behaviours by companies than ever before. Companies are looking for new hires to help them see their business creatively and bring insights to all aspects of business operations. The American Solar Energy Society estimates that the number of green jobs could rise to 40 million in North America by 2030.

Green business strategies not only give a firm a commercial advantage in the marketplace, but help lead the way toward a greener world. The fight to reduce our carbon footprint in an attempt to reverse climate change has opened up opportunities for renewable energy, recycling, conservation, and increasing overall efficiency in the way resources are used. New businesses that focus on hydro, wind, and solar power are on the rise and will need talented businesspeople to lead them. Carbon emissions trading is gaining popularity as large corporations and individuals alike seek to decrease their footprints. A job in this growing field could be similar to that of a stock trader, or you could lead the search for carbon-efficient companies in which to invest.

In the ethics arena, current trends in business governance strongly support the development of ethics and compliance departments to help guide organizational integrity. This alone is a billion-dollar business, and there are jobs in developing organizational ethics programs, developing company policies, and training employees and management. An entry-level position might be as a communication specialist or trainer for programs in a business ethics department. Eventually there's an opportunity to become an ethics officer with typical responsibilities of meeting with employees, the board of directors, and top management to discuss and advise on ethics issues in the industry; developing and distributing a code of ethics; creating and maintaining an anonymous, confidential service to answer questions about ethical issues; taking actions on possible ethics code violations; and reviewing and modifying the code of ethics of the organization.

There are also opportunities to support initiatives that help companies relate social responsibility to stakeholder interests and needs. These jobs could involve coordinating and implementing philanthropic programs that give back to others important to the organization or developing a community volunteering program for employees. In addition to the human relations function, most companies develop programs to assist employees and their families to improve their quality of life. Companies have found that the healthier and happier employees are, the more productive they will be in the workforce.

Social responsibility, ethics, and sustainable business practices are not a trend; they are good for business and the bottom line. New industries are being created and old ones are adapting to the new market demands, opening up many varied job opportunities that will lead not only to a paycheque, but to the satisfaction of making the world a better place.[60]

## BUILD YOUR BUSINESS PLAN

### Business Ethics and Social Responsibility

Think about which industry you are considering competing in with your product/service. Are there any kind of questionable practices in the way the product has been traditionally sold? Produced? Advertised? Have there been any recent accusations regarding safety within the industry? What about any environmental concerns?

For example, if you are thinking of opening a lawn care business, you need to consider what possible effects the chemicals you are using will have on the client and the environment. You have a responsibility not to threaten your customers' health or safety. You also have the social responsibility to let the community know of any damaging effect you may be directly or indirectly responsible for.

## CASE | Trans Mountain Pipeline

As discussed at the start of the chapter, whether something is ethical or unethical often depends on your personal viewpoint of the world or what stakeholder group you belong to. For example, the Trans Mountain pipeline expansion, which has been discussed a great deal in the media, has many proponents and opponents. The pipeline would not be new but an expansion of the current pipeline that carries refined oil from Alberta to the coast of British Columbia. The expansion would result in an increase of 300,000 barrels of oil a day to 890,000 barrels. Currently, Canadian oil from the oil sands, better known as Western Canada Select, sells at a substantial discount from the North American benchmark, West Texas Intermediate. While Canadian oil is lower in quality, a substantial part of the discount is due to the lack of pipeline capacity, so the oil is priced lower to account for the high transportation costs of shipping the oil using rail. An expansion of the pipeline would allow for more oil to reach tankers on the West Coast.

The Canadians in favour of the project argue that Canada's oil sands industry needs the pipeline to ship oil. They note that Alberta's oil currently sells at a discount because there is a lack of means to transport the oil to refineries, and as a result, tax dollars and jobs are being lost. The Alberta premier at the time, Rachel Notley, stated that the oil price gap was costing the Canadian economy $80 million a day. If the pipeline is approved, Canadian companies will be able to get more money for their oil, resulting in more jobs and additional tax dollars. These tax dollars support health care, scientific research, education, and several positive initiatives. Many politicians, including Prime Minister Justin Trudeau, support the project and in 2018, the federal government bought the current pipeline and the expansion project from Kinder Morgan Energy for $4.5 billion and created the Trans Mountain Corporation.

The government bought the pipeline project with the belief they could complete the project more quickly than Kinder Morgan. Unlike Kinder Morgan, who would only be constructing the pipeline expansion when it was optimal for shareholders, Trudeau planned to build the pipeline as quickly as possible. He argued the federal government could get a return not only in pipeline profits but also from the economic activity construction would create. Trudeau also believed the federal government could successfully manage any provincial objections to the completion of the project voiced by British Columbia.

In addition to government advocates, many labour groups also support the proposed pipeline for the jobs it will create, and shareholders of oil sands companies favour the deal as the pipeline should create further profits for the companies.

Opponents of the Trans Mountain pipeline, including many people in the general public and some politicians, say the oil sands produce more greenhouse gas than traditional oil production and should be discouraged, not encouraged. Furthermore, with any pipeline there is a danger of a spill that can harm the environment.

The government quickly started construction on the pipeline after receiving regulatory approvals in the summer of 2018. However the Federal Court of Appeals blocked the project a few short days later due to lack of consultation and environment concerns. The court essentially ruled that the consultation process was lacking in two-way dialogue. Many advocates in the oil industry were stunned by the decision as they thought the Trans Mountain pipeline had gone through the most extensive consultation and review process to date. Finance Minister Bill Morneau was disappointed with the decision but noted that the pipeline will be built, and the government is committed to the project. He describes the project as one that is good for Canada's national interests, one that will create thousands of good-paying middle-class jobs, and will have positive long-term benefits for Canada.

### DISCUSSION QUESTIONS

1. Based on the information in the case and your own personal views—do you think building or expanding pipelines is ethical or unethical? Why?
2. Do you think the government should have purchased the pipeline from Kinder Morgan? Why or why not? What are some advantages and disadvantages of government ownership?
3. Use Internet resources to check in on the current status of the pipeline. Do you think the pipeline will be built?

CHAPTER 3

# Business in a Borderless World

©Shutterstock

## LEARNING OBJECTIVES

**After reading this chapter, you will be able to:**

- **LO 3-1** Explore some of the factors within the international trade environment that influence business.
- **LO 3-2** Assess some of the economic, legal, political, social, cultural, and technological barriers to international business.
- **LO 3-3** Specify some of the agreements, alliances, and organizations that may encourage trade across international boundaries.
- **LO 3-4** Summarize the different levels of organizational involvement in international trade.
- **LO 3-5** Contrast two basic strategies used in international business.

# ENTER THE WORLD OF BUSINESS

**Alibaba: China's National Treasure**

A former English teacher, Jack Ma founded Alibaba as an e-commerce business in 1999 after taking a trip to the United States as a translator. While there, he saw firsthand how the Internet was transforming the business world. He realized the commercial potential of pioneering an online marketing channel in China so businesses could connect with local and international buyers. The online giant gained attention in Canada in 2014 when it sold 100,000 Nova Scotia lobsters on Singles Day, a Chinese counterpart to Valentine's Day.

Ma named the marketplace he created Alibaba because of the association with opening doors and finding treasure. The initial business-to-business website did so well that Alibaba opened a second online marketplace for selling to consumers called Taobao, followed by an e-commerce mall for multinational retailers targeting Chinese consumers. In 2005, Ma formed a strategic alliance with Yahoo! Inc. co-founder Jerry Yang when he recognized the need for a search engine partner. The deal resulted in Yahoo! purchasing a 40 percent stake in Alibaba for $1 billion.

Ma's launch of a Chinese e-commerce business was not without risk. Obstacles existed in the economic and technological environments. Disposable incomes were still relatively low in China, and Internet connections were slow and expensive. However, as technology improved and disposable incomes increased, more Chinese consumers became interested in e-commerce.

Today, the company's many marketplaces and supporting businesses serve more than 600 million customers in 240 nations. Alibaba has held tightly to its top spot in China. With a 47 percent market share in China's online retail market, Alibaba has made it difficult for Amazon to compete on price, preventing the online retail giant from gaining traction. China, with approximately 890 million online shoppers, is the world's largest e-commerce market.[1]

**DISCUSSION QUESTIONS**

1. What barriers did Alibaba need to overcome in its home country?
2. How do you think Alibaba's strategic alliance with Yahoo! helped it to gain market share?
3. What are some of the barriers that firms such as Amazon face as they try to compete against Alibaba in China?

## Introduction

Consumers around the world can drink Coca-Cola, eat at McDonald's, buy an Apple phone made in China, and watch CNN on Samsung televisions. The products you consume today are just as likely to have been made in China, South Korea, or Mexico as in Canada. Likewise, consumers in other countries buy Western electrical equipment, clothing, and cosmetics, as well as computers, robots, and industrial equipment.

Many Canadian firms are finding that international markets provide tremendous opportunities for growth. Accessing these markets can promote innovation, while intensifying global competition spurs companies to market better and less-expensive products. Today, the more than 7 billion people who inhabit Earth create one tremendous marketplace.

In this chapter, we explore business in this exciting global marketplace. First, we'll look at the nature of international business, including barriers and promoters of trade across international boundaries. Next, we consider the levels of organizational involvement in international business. Finally, we briefly discuss strategies for trading across national borders.

# The Role of International Business

**LO 3-1** Explore some of the factors within the international trade environment that influence business.

**DID YOU KNOW?**

Most of the world's population and two-thirds of its total purchasing power are outside of North America.

**International business** refers to the buying, selling, and trading of goods and services across national boundaries. Falling political barriers and new technology are making it possible for more and more companies to sell their products overseas as well as at home. And, as differences among nations continue to narrow, the trend toward the globalization of business is becoming increasingly important.

When Pizza Hut sells a pizza in Moscow, Sony sells a television in Vancouver, or a Swiss medical supply company sells optical equipment to a hospital in Mexico City, the sale affects the economies of the countries involved. The Canadian market, with 37 million consumers, makes up only a small part of the more than 7.6 billion people in the world to whom global companies must consider marketing. Global marketing requires balancing your global brand with the needs of local consumers.[2] To begin our study of international business, we must first consider some economic issues: why nations trade, exporting and importing, and the balance of trade.

**international business** the buying, selling, and trading of goods and services across national boundaries

**absolute advantage** a monopoly that exists when a country is the only source of an item, the only producer of an item, or the most efficient producer of an item

## Why Nations Trade

Nations and businesses engage in international trade to obtain raw materials and goods that are otherwise unavailable to them or are available elsewhere at a lower price than that at which they themselves can produce them. A nation, or individuals and organizations from a nation, sell surplus materials and goods to acquire funds to buy the goods, services, and ideas its people need. Countries like Belize and Kenya trade with Western nations in order to acquire technology and techniques to advance their economy. Which goods and services a nation sells depends on what resources it has available.

**Absolute advantage** exists when a country is the only source of an item, the only producer of an item, or the most efficient producer of an item. Some nations have a monopoly on the production of a particular resource or product. An example would be an African mining company that possesses the only mine where a specialty diamond can be found. Russia has an absolute advantage in yuksporite, a rare and useful mineral that can be found only in Russia.

**Comparative advantage**, occurs when a country specializes in products that it can supply more efficiently or at a lower cost than it can produce other items. Most international trade is based on comparative advantage. Canada has a comparative advantage in forestry, minerals, and hydroelectric power generation. France has a comparative advantage in making wine because of its agricultural capabilities, reputation, and the experience of its vintners. Other countries, particularly India and Ireland, are also gaining a comparative advantage in the provision of some services, such as call-centre operations, engineering, and software programming.

**comparative advantage** the basis of most international trade, when a country specializes in products that it can supply more efficiently or at a lower cost than it can produce other items

**outsourcing** the transferring of manufacturing or other tasks—such as data processing—to countries where labour and supplies are less expensive

**Outsourcing**, or transferring manufacturing and other tasks to countries where labour and supplies are less expensive, has become a controversial practice because many jobs have moved overseas where those tasks can be accomplished for lower costs. Many Canadian corporations outsource work to other countries to remain efficient, competitive, and keep their costs down. Meanwhile, Canada has also emerged as a significant nearshore outsourcing destination for the United States

©Roberto Westbrook/Blend Images

Many companies choose to outsource manufacturing to factories in Asia due to lower costs of labour.

because of geographic proximity, a well-educated workforce, and similarities in laws, language, and business culture.[3]

> "Outsourcing has become a controversial practice in [many Western nations]."

## Trade Between Countries

To obtain needed goods and services and the funds to pay for them, nations trade by exporting and importing. **Exporting** is the sale of goods and services to foreign markets. Canada exported more than $549 billion in goods and services in 2017.[4] Canadian businesses export many goods and services, particularly energy products, industrial goods and materials (e.g., metals, chemicals, fertilizers), and machinery and equipment products. **Importing** is the purchase of goods and services from foreign sources. Many of the goods you buy in Canada are likely to be imports or have some imported components. Sometimes you may not even realize they are imports. As shown in Table 3.1, Currently, Canada imports almost $600 billion each year.[5]

**exporting** the sale of goods and services to foreign markets

**importing** the purchase of goods and services from foreign sources

**balance of trade** the difference in value between a nation's exports and its imports

**trade deficit** a nation's negative balance of trade, which exists when that country imports more products than it exports

## Balance of Trade

You have probably read or heard about the fact that Canada has a trade deficit, but what is a trade deficit? A nation's **balance of trade** is the difference in value between its exports and imports. Because Canada (and some other nations as well) imports more products than it exports, it has a negative balance of trade, or **trade deficit**. If a nation exports more products than it imports, it has a positive balance of trade, or **trade surplus**. Table 3.1 shows the overall trade deficit for Canada, which is currently around $24 billion.

**Table 3.1** | Canada's Trade Balance, 2012–2017 (in millions of dollars)

| | 2012 | 2013 | 2014 | 2015 | 2016 | 2017 |
|---|---|---|---|---|---|---|
| Exports | 461,511 | 479,225 | 529,334 | 524,972 | 521,470 | 549,618 |
| Imports | 474,800 | 487,370 | 524,661 | 548,707 | 547,341 | 573,573 |
| Trade surplus/ deficit | −13,289 | −8,145 | 4,673 | −23,735 | −25,871 | −23,955 |

**Table 3.2** | Top 5 Countries with which Canada Has Trade Deficits/Surpluses

| Trade Deficit | Trade Surplus |
|---|---|
| 1. China | 1. United States |
| 2. European Union | 2. India |
| 3. Mexico | 3. Indonesia |
| 4. Switzerland | 4. Singapore |
| 5. Brazil | 5. Australia |

Table 3.2 shows Canada's principal trading partners and whether Canada had a trade deficit or a trade surplus with them. In 2017, Canada had a $40 billion trade surplus with the United States and a $17.7 billion trade deficit with China.[6] The trade deficit fluctuates according to such factors as the economic health of Canada and other countries, productivity, perceived quality, and exchange rates. Trade deficits are harmful because they can mean the failure of businesses, the loss of jobs, and a lowered standard of living.

**trade surplus** a nation's positive balance of trade, which exists when that country exports more products than it imports

**balance of payments** the difference between the flow of money into and out of a country

Of course, when a nation exports more goods than it imports, it has a favourable balance of trade, or trade surplus. Until 2008, Canada had a constant trade surplus due to trade in automotive products, machinery and equipment, and an abundance of natural resources, including crude oil and related energy products.[7]

The difference between the flow of money into and out of a country is called its **balance of payments**. A country's balance of trade, foreign investments, foreign aid, loans, military expenditures, and money spent by tourists comprise its balance of payments. As you might expect, a country with a trade surplus generally has a favourable balance of payments because it is receiving more money from trade with foreign countries than it is paying out. When a country has a trade deficit, more money flows out of the country than into it. If more money flows out of the country than into it from tourism and other sources, the country may experience declining production and higher unemployment, because there is less money available for spending.

## International Trade Barriers

**LO 3-2** Assess some of the economic, legal, political, social, cultural, and technological barriers to international business.

Completely free trade seldom exists. When a company decides to do business outside its own country, it will encounter a number of barriers to international trade. Any firm considering international business must research the other country's economic, legal, political, social, cultural, and technological background. Such research will help the company choose an appropriate level of involvement and operating strategies, as we will see later in this chapter.

### Economic Barriers

When looking at doing business in another country, managers must consider basic economic factors, such as economic development and exchange rates.

**Economic Development.** When considering doing business abroad, business people need to recognize that they cannot take for granted that other countries offer the same things as are found in *industrialized nations*. Many countries in Africa, Asia, and Oceania are less economically advanced than those in the Americas and Europe; they are often called *developing nations*. Developing nations represent a potentially profitable market for many businesses because they may be buying technology to improve their infrastructures, and much of the population may desire consumer products. For example, Bhutan's trade with India accounts for about 80 per cent of total exports and 60 per cent of total imports. Bhutan's exports to India are mainly hydroelectricity, while the bulk of imports are essential goods, automobiles, and the services of Indian labourers working in the construction sector.[8]

A country's level of development is determined in part by its **infrastructure**, the physical facilities that support its economic activities, such as railroads, highways, ports, airfields, utilities and power plants, schools, hospitals, communication systems, and commercial distribution systems. When doing business with developing nations a business may need to compensate for rudimentary distribution and communication systems, or even a lack of technology.

**infrastructure** the physical facilities that support a country's economic activities, such as railroads, highways, ports, airfields, utilities and power plants, schools, hospitals, communication systems, and commercial distribution systems

"Devaluation decreases the value of currency in relation to other currencies."

**Exchange Rates.** The ratio at which one nation's currency can be exchanged for another nation's currency is the **exchange rate**. Familiarity with exchange rates is important because they affect the cost of imports and exports. When the value of the Canadian dollar declines relative to other currencies, such as the euro, the price of imports becomes relatively expensive for Canadian consumers. On the other hand, Canadian exports become relatively cheap for international markets—in this example, the European Union.

**exchange rate** the ratio at which one nation's currency can be exchanged for another nation's currency

Occasionally, a government may intentionally alter the value of its currency through fiscal policy. Devaluation decreases the value of currency in relation to other currencies. If the Canadian government were to devalue the dollar, it would lower the cost of Canadian goods abroad and make trips to Canada less expensive for foreign tourists. Thus, devaluation encourages the sale of domestic goods and tourism. On the other hand, when Switzerland's central bank let the value of the Swiss franc rise by 30 percent against the euro in 2015, it resulted in increasing the costs of exports. This made everything exported from Switzerland more expensive, including tourism.[9] Revaluation, as in the Swiss example, increases the value of a currency in relation to other currencies, but occurs rarely.

### Ethical, Legal, and Political Barriers

A company that decides to enter the international marketplace must contend with potentially complex relationships among the different laws of its own nation, international laws, and the laws of the nation with which it will be trading; various trade restrictions imposed on international trade; changing political climates; and different ethical values. Legal and ethical requirements for successful business are increasing globally.

©fine art/Alamy Stock Photo

Damages caused by brand and product piracy to the original producers are substantial. (The real watch, on the left, was created by Rolex SA, a Swiss luxury watch manufacturer based in Geneva, Switzerland.)

## GOING GREEN

### Algae: A Biofuel Breakthrough

If Euglena has its way, algae will become the fuel of the future. The name of this Tokyo-based company comes from the product it sells: the algae Euglena gracilis. Euglena's business is focused on five key areas: food, fibre, feed, fertilizer, and fuel. The firm is also investigating the use of algae for pharmaceuticals. The company has been successful in developing food and cosmetics using algae and is now making its mark in the biofuel industry.

As carbon emissions become an increasing problem—particularly for countries like Canada, the United States, China, and India—governments are looking toward biofuels as an alternative fuel source. Research has shown that the algae in which Euglena specializes has strong potential for biofuel production. Euglena oversees all aspects of the process, including cultivation of the algae and the refining and marketing of the fuel. A strategic alliance with Isuzu Motors has allowed Euglena to successfully mix its algae biofuel with light oil to power city buses. However, Euglena is determined to create its own algae biofuel that will not require oil and further reduce carbon emissions. The company is working with other businesses to develop algae-based jet fuel. These partnerships have allowed Euglena to build the nation's first algae biofuel refinery, which it estimates will produce 125,000 litres of jet fuel yearly.

Euglena has certainly attracted the attention of investors, but any promising breakthrough brings competition. ExxonMobil has partnered with Synthetic Genomics to investigate algae biofuels, and others are trying to create biofuels from garbage. The biofuel industry is growing globally, requiring firms like Euglena to remain innovative as competition heats up.*

#### DISCUSSION QUESTIONS

1. How has partnering with other businesses been crucial to Euglena's success? How would you recommend they approach expansion opportunities into other countries?
2. What are some type of barriers Euglena is likely to face as it grows?
3. What are some of the opportunities Euglena might have expanding into countries like Canada, the United States, China, and India? What are some potential barriers?

*Ted Redmond and Yuko Takeo, "Skimming Profits from Pond Scum," *Bloomberg Businessweek*, July 20–26, 2015, pp. 31–32; Chisaki Watanabe, "Japan's Isuzu, Euglena to Begin Biodiesel Development with Algae," Bloomberg, June 25, 2014, http://www.bloomberg.com/news/articles/2014-06-25/japan-s-isuzu-euglena-to-begin-biodiesel-development-withalgae (accessed March 3, 2018); Durga Madhab Mahapatra, H. N. Chanakya, and T. V. Ramachandra, "Euglena sp. as a Suitable Source of Lipids for Potential Use as Biofuel and Sustainable Wastewater Treatment," *Journal of Applied Psychology* 25, no. 3 (2013), pp. 855–865; Euglena, "Research and Business Strategy," http://www.euglena.jp/en/labo/research.html (accessed March 3, 2018); Sarah Karacs, "Food, Face Cream and Jet Fuel: Japanese Firm Finds Many Uses for Algae," CNN Tech, March 24, 2017, http://money.cnn.com/2017/03/24/technology/japan-algae-euglena/index.html (accessed March 3, 2018); Yoko Shoji, "Euglena Plans Japanese Refinery for Algae-Derived Biofuel," *Nikkei Asian Review*, December 2, 2015, https://asia.nikkei.com/Tech-Science/Tech/Euglena-plans-Japanese-refinery-for-algaederived-jet-fuel (accessed March 3, 2018).

**Laws and Regulations.** Canada has a number of laws and regulations that govern the activities of Canadian firms engaged in international trade and has a variety of trade and investment agreements with other nations. These agreements allow business to be transacted between Canadian companies and citizens of the specified countries.

Once outside Canadian borders, businesspeople are likely to find that the laws of other nations differ from those of Canada. Many of the legal rights that Canadians take for granted do not exist in other countries, and a firm doing business abroad must understand and obey the laws of the host country. Some countries have strict laws limiting the amount of local currency that can be taken out of the country and the amount of foreign currency that can be brought in; others forbid foreigners from owning real property outright.

Some countries have copyright and patent laws that are less strict than those of Canada, and some countries fail to honour Canada's laws. In China and Vietnam, laws protecting copyrights and intellectual property are weak and minimally enforced, and those countries are flooded with counterfeit goods. Companies are angry because the counterfeits harm not only their sales but also their reputations if the knock-offs are of poor quality. Such counterfeiting is not limited to China or Vietnam. It is estimated that nearly half of all software installed on personal computers worldwide is not properly licensed.[10] In countries where these activities occur, laws against them may not be sufficiently enforced, even if counterfeiting is deemed illegal. Thus, businesses engaging in foreign trade may have to take extra steps to protect their products because local laws may be insufficient to do so.

**Tariffs and Trade Restrictions.** Tariffs and other trade restrictions are part of a country's legal structure but may be established or removed for political reasons.

A **tariff** is a tax levied by a nation on imported or exported goods. Most countries allow citizens travelling abroad to bring home a certain amount of merchandise without paying an import tariff. A Canadian citizen may bring up to $200 worth of merchandise into Canada duty free after each absence of 24 hours, and up to $800 worth of goods after each absence of 48 hours. After that, Canadian citizens must pay duty rates according to the goods imported, the country where the goods were made, and the country from which they are imported. Thus, identical items purchased in different countries might have different tariffs.

**tariff** a tax levied by a nation on imported or exported goods

**exchange controls** regulations that restrict the amount of currency that can be bought or sold

©Spaces Images/Blend Images

In 2017, the United States placed a 21 percent tariff on Canadian softwood, claiming the industry was unfairly subsidized. This tariff resulted in driving lumber prices to record highs in the United States because Canadian producers passed the higher tariffs back to U.S. purchasers.[11]

Countries sometimes levy tariffs for political reasons, as when they impose sanctions against other countries to protest their actions. However, import tariffs are more commonly imposed to protect domestic products by raising the price of imported ones. Protective tariffs allow more expensive domestic goods to compete with foreign ones. Such protective tariffs have become controversial, as governments become concerned over their trade deficits, and there are fears that a trade war could develop that damages the world economy.

**Exchange controls** restrict the amount of currency that can be bought or sold. Some countries control their foreign trade by forcing businesspeople to buy and sell foreign products through a central bank. If Bombardier, for example, receives payments for its Learjets in a foreign currency, it may be required to sell the currency to that nation's central bank. When foreign currency is in short supply, as it is in many less-developed and Eastern European countries, the government uses foreign currency to purchase necessities and capital goods and produces other products locally, thus limiting its need for foreign imports.

A **quota** limits the number of units of a particular product that can be imported into a country. A quota may be established by voluntary agreement or by government decree. Quotas are designed to protect the industries and jobs of the country imposing the

**quota** a restriction on the number of units of a particular product that can be imported into a country

(left): ©Ryan McVay/Getty Images RF, (right): ©Stockbyte RF

Dumping can spark trade wars. After the United States imposed tariffs on Chinese-made tires it alleged were being dumped on the U.S. market, China retaliated by slapping tariffs on U.S. chicken products exported to China.

quota. Quotas help domestic suppliers but will lead to higher prices for consumers. In Canada, products subject to quotas include agricultural products, firearms, textiles and clothing, and steel.[12]

An **embargo** prohibits trade in a particular product. Embargoes are generally directed at specific goods or countries and may be established for political, economic, health, or religious reasons. For example, Canada currently prohibits the export, sale, and other provision of arms and related materials to North Korea; the United States maintains a trade embargo with Cuba. Health embargoes prevent the importing of various pharmaceuticals, animals, plants, and agricultural products. Some nations forbid the importation of alcoholic beverages on religious grounds.

**embargo** a prohibition on trade in a particular product

**dumping** the act of a country or business selling products at less than what it costs to produce them

One common reason for setting quotas or tariffs is to prohibit **dumping**, which occurs when a country or business sells products for less than what it costs to produce them. Dumping permits quick entry into a market. Sometimes dumping occurs when the domestic market for a firm's product is too small to support an efficient level of production. In other cases, technologically obsolete products that are no longer saleable in the country of origin are dumped overseas. Dumping is relatively difficult to prove, but even the suspicion of dumping can lead to the imposition of quotas or tariffs. As with other trade restrictions, dumping quotas or tariffs result in higher prices for consumers.

**Political Barriers.** Unlike legal issues, political considerations are seldom written down and often change rapidly. Nations that have been subject to economic sanctions for political reasons in recent years include Cuba, Iran, Syria, and North Korea. While these were dramatic events, political considerations affect international business daily as governments enact tariffs, embargoes, or other types of trade restrictions in response to political events.

Businesses engaged in international trade must consider the relative instability of other countries. Political unrest in countries such as Pakistan, Somalia, and the Democratic Republic of the Congo may create a hostile or even dangerous environment for foreign businesses. Natural disasters can cripple a country's government, making the region even more unstable. Finally, a sudden change in power can result in a regime that is hostile to foreign investment. Some businesses have been forced out of a country altogether, as when a socialist revolution in Venezuela forced out or took over foreign oil companies. Today, Venezuela has a sinking economy with shortages of products and political unrest. Whether they like it or not, companies are often involved directly or indirectly in international politics.

Political concerns may lead a group of nations to form a **cartel**, a group of firms or nations that agree to act as a monopoly and not compete with each other to generate a competitive advantage in world markets. Probably the most famous cartel is OPEC, the Organization of Petroleum Exporting Countries, founded in the 1960s to increase the price of petroleum throughout the world and to maintain high prices. By working to ensure stable oil prices, OPEC hoped to enhance the economies of its member nations.

**cartel** a group of firms or nations that agree to act as a monopoly and not compete with each other in order to generate a competitive advantage in world markets

## Social and Cultural Barriers

Most businesspeople engaged in international trade underestimate the importance of social and cultural differences, but these differences can derail an important transaction. Tiffany & Co. learned that attentive customer service was necessary in order to succeed in Japan, and bold marketing and advertising served as the recipe for success in China.[13] And in Europe, Starbucks took the unprecedented step of allowing its locations to be franchised in order to reach smaller markets that are unfamiliar. This way, Starbucks reduced the cultural and social risks involved in entering such markets.[14] For example, Starbucks opened its first store in Italy in 2018.[15] Starbucks waited to enter Italy because it needed to understand the coffee culture there. Unfortunately, cultural norms are rarely written down, and what is written down may well be inaccurate.

Cultural differences include differences in spoken and written language. Although it is certainly possible to translate words from one language to another, the true meaning is sometimes misinterpreted or lost. Consider some translations that went awry in foreign markets:

- Scandinavian vacuum manufacturer Electrolux used the following in an American campaign: "Nothing sucks like an Electrolux."
- The Coca-Cola name in China was first read as "Ke-kou-ke-la," meaning "bite the wax tadpole."
- In Italy, a campaign for Schweppes Tonic Water translated the name into Schweppes Toilet Water.[16]

Companies cannot just translate slogans, advertising campaigns, and website language literally; they must know the cultural differences that could affect a company's success.

Differences in body language and personal space also affect international trade. Body language is non-verbal, usually unconscious communication through gestures, posture, and facial expression. Personal space is the distance at which one person feels comfortable talking to another. Canadians tend to stand a moderate distance away from the person with whom they are speaking. Arab businessmen tend to stand face-to-face with the object of their conversation. Table 3.3 shows some of the behaviours

Table 3.3 | Cultural Behavioural Differences

| Region | Gestures Viewed as Rude or Unacceptable |
|---|---|
| Japan, Hong Kong, Middle East | Summoning with the index finger |
| Middle and Far East | Pointing with index finger |
| Thailand, Japan, France | Sitting with soles of shoes showing |
| Brazil, Germany | Forming a circle with fingers (e.g., the "O.K." sign in North America) |
| Japan | Winking means "I love you" |
| Buddhist countries | Patting someone on the head |

considered rude or unacceptable in other countries. Such cultural differences may generate uncomfortable feelings or misunderstandings when businesspeople of different countries negotiate with one another.

Family roles also influence marketing activities. Advertising that features people in non-traditional social roles may or may not be successful. Companies should also guard against marketing that could be perceived as reinforcing negative stereotypes. Coca-Cola was forced to pull an online advertisement and issue an apology after releasing a Christmas ad showing fair-skinned people arriving at an indigenous village in Mexico bearing gifts of sodas and a Christmas tree. Mexican activists claimed the advertisement reinforced negative stereotypes of indigenous people and called for the government's anti-discrimination commission to issue sanctions against the company.[17]

The people of other nations quite often have a different perception of time, as well. Canadians value promptness; a business meeting scheduled for a specific time seldom starts more than a few minutes late. Companies engaged in foreign trade must also observe the national and religious holidays and local customs of the host country. In many Islamic countries, for example, workers expect to take a break at certain times of the day to observe religious rites.

The United States, unlike most nations, including Canada, does not use the metric system. This lack of uniformity creates problems for both buyers and sellers in the international marketplace. American sellers, for instance, must produce goods destined for foreign markets in litres or metres, and Canadian sellers must convert to the imperial system if they plan to sell a product in the United States.

The literature dealing with international business is filled with accounts of sometimes humorous but often costly mistakes that occurred because of a lack of understanding of the social and cultural differences between buyers and sellers. Such problems cannot always be avoided, but they can be minimized through research on the cultural and social differences of the host country.

### Technological Barriers

Many countries lack the technological infrastructure found in Canada, and some marketers are viewing such barriers as opportunities. For instance, marketers are targeting many countries such as India and China and some African nations where there are few private phone lines. Citizens of these countries are turning directly to wireless communication through cell phones. Technological advances are creating additional global marketing opportunities. Along with opportunities, changing technologies also create new challenges and competition. For example, out of the top five global PC companies—Lenovo, Hewlett-Packard, Dell, Asus, and Acer Group—three are from Asian countries. On the other hand, Apple Inc.'s iPad and tablets from other computer makers have already begun eroding the market share of traditional personal computers, placing the industry in the maturity stage of the product life cycle.[18]

## Trade Agreements, Alliances, and Organizations

**LO 3-3** Specify some of the agreements, alliances, and organizations that may encourage trade across international boundaries.

Although these economic, political, legal, and sociocultural issues may seem like daunting barriers to international trade, there are also organizations and agreements—such as the General Agreement on Tariffs and Trade, the World Bank, and the International Monetary Fund—that foster international trade and can help companies get involved in and succeed in global markets. Various regional trade agreements, such as the North American Free Trade Agreement and the European Union, also promote trade among member nations by eliminating tariffs and trade restrictions. In this section, we'll look briefly at some of these agreements and organizations.

### General Agreement on Tariffs and Trade (GATT)

During the Great Depression of the 1930s, nations established so many protective tariffs covering so many products that international trade became virtually impossible. By the end of World War II, there was considerable international momentum to liberalize trade and minimize the effects of tariffs. The **General Agreement on Tariffs and Trade (GATT)**, originally signed by 23 nations in 1948, provided a forum for tariff

**General Agreement on Tariffs and Trade (GATT)** a trade agreement, originally signed by 23 nations in 1947, that provided a forum for tariff negotiations and a place where international trade problems could be discussed and resolved

## ENTREPRENEURSHIP IN ACTION

### Kenya Counts on Mobile Banking

**M-Pesa**

**Founders:** Nick Hughes and Susie Lonie

**Founded:** 2007, launched in Kenya through Safaricom

**Success:** Originally launched in Kenya, today this mobile-transfer payment system has 30 million users in 10 countries. In 2007, mobile-transfer payment system M-Pesa was launched by British multinational Vodafone's Kenyan mobile operator Safaricom. Little did it know how revolutionary this innovation would be for the economy. M-Pesa uses mobile services to leapfrog existing technological barriers and open up new opportunities for millions of Kenyans.

In Kenya, a less-developed country, banks tended to avoid catering to lower-income populations and the distance to a financial institution could be significant. The mobile-transfer payment service allowed Kenyan residents to quickly and securely transfer funds to merchants and family members through their cell phones. It also allowed for a significant rise in entrepreneurship. It is estimated that M-Pesa extended financial services to 20 million Kenyans, prompting many to start their own small businesses. Unlike in Canada, credit cards are rare in Kenya, and many Kenyans now use M-Pesa to pay for meals and other transactions.

Over the years, M-Pesa has expanded to nine other countries, including Tanzania, Romania, India, the Democratic Republic of the Congo, and Albania. While competition is rising for M-Pesa, the possibilities of worldwide expansion remain high as mobile payments gain traction globally.*

#### DISCUSSION QUESTIONS

1. What conditions in Kenya created the ideal conditions for a mobile banking service?
2. In what ways has M-Pesa paved the way for entrepreneurship in Kenya?
3. How can businesses in different industries profit from opportunities in less-developed countries?

*Daniel Runde, "M-Pesa and the Rise of the Global Mobile Money Market," August 12, 2015, https://www.forbes.com/sites/danielrunde/2015/08/12/m-pesa-and-the-riseof-the-global-mobile-money-market/#64299fd65aec (accessed March 3, 2018); Kieron Monks, "M-Pesa: Kenya's Mobile Money Success Story Turns 10," CNN, February 24, 2017, https://www.cnn.com/2017/02/21/africa/mpesa-10th-anniversary/index.html (accessed March 3, 2018); BBC, "M-Pesa's Founders on Launching Mobile Wallet," *BBC News*, November 22, 2010, http://www.bbc.com/news/av/business-11793288/m-pesa-founderson - launching-kenya-s-mobile-wallet (accessed March 3, 2018); Janelle Richards, "Kenyan Entrepreneurs Help Youth Thrive in Africa's Emerging 'Silicon Valley,'" *NBC News*, December 4, 2017, https://www.nbcnews.com/news/nbcblk/kenyan-entrepreneurs-help-youth-thrive-africa-semerging- silicon-valley-n826156 (accessed March 3, 2018); Charles Graeber, "Ten Days in Kenya with No Cash, Only a Phone," *Bloomberg Businessweek*, June 5, 2014, http:// www.businessweek.com/articles/2014-06-05/safaricoms-mpesa-turns-kenya-into-a-mobile-payment-paradise (accessed March 3, 2018); Vivienne Walt, "Is Africa's Rise for Real This Time?" *Fortune*, September 18, 2014, pp. 166–172.

©The McGraw-Hill Companies, Inc./Barry Barker

The WTO facilitates trade among nations through the development of trade policies.

negotiations and a place where international trade problems could be discussed and resolved. GATT sponsored rounds of negotiations aimed at reducing trade restrictions.

The **World Trade Organization (WTO)**, an international organization dealing with the rules of trade between nations, was created in 1995 by the Uruguay Round of the GATT. Key to the World Trade Organization are the WTO agreements, which are the legal ground rules for international commerce. The agreements were negotiated and signed by most of the world's trading nations and ratified by their legislative assemblies. The goal is to help producers of goods and services and exporters and importers conduct business.

**World Trade Organization (WTO)** international organization dealing with the rules of trade between nations

In addition to administering the WTO trade agreements, the WTO presents a forum for trade negotiations, monitors national trade policies, provides technical assistance and training for developing countries, and cooperates with other international organizations. Based in Switzerland, the WTO has also adopted a leadership role in negotiating trade disputes among nations.[19] For example, in 2018, Canada lodged a WTO complaint accusing the U.S. of regularly breaching international trade laws through various anti-dumping duties, from Argentine lemon juice to frozen shrimp from India.[20]

## The North American Free Trade Agreement (NAFTA)

The **North American Free Trade Agreement (NAFTA)**, which went into effect on January 1, 1994, effectively merged Canada, the United States, and Mexico into one market of more than 450 million consumers. NAFTA virtually eliminated all tariffs on goods produced and traded among Canada, Mexico, and the United States to create a free trade area. The estimated annual output for this trade alliance is $20.8 trillion. NAFTA makes it easier for Canadian businesses to invest in the U.S. and Mexico; provides protection for intellectual property (of special interest to high-technology and entertainment industries); expands trade by requiring equal treatment of Canadian firms in both countries; and simplifies country-of-origin rules, hindering Japan's use of Mexico as a staging ground for penetration into Canadian and U.S. markets.

**North American Free Trade Agreement (NAFTA)** agreement that eliminated most tariffs and trade restrictions on agricultural and manufactured products to encourage trade among Canada, the United States, and Mexico

"NAFTA makes it easier for Canadian businesses to invest in the U.S. and Mexico."

The United States' 325 million consumers are relatively affluent, with a per capita GDP of $59,000.[21] Trade between the United States and Canada totals approximately $580 billion. About 80 percent of Canada's exports go to the United States, including gold, oil, and uranium.[22] In fact, Canada is the single largest trading partner of the United States.[23]

NAFTA has also increased trade between Canada and Mexico. Mexico is Canada's fifth largest export market and third largest import market.[24] With a per capita GDP of $19,500, Mexico's nearly 125 million consumers are less affluent than American consumers.[25] Many Canadian companies have taken advantage of Mexico's low labour costs and proximity to set up production facilities, sometimes called *maquiladoras*. Mexico attracted major technological industries, including electronics, software, and aerospace. Companies as diverse as Bombardier, Celestica, and Ford have set up facilities in Mexican states.

Despite its benefits, NAFTA has been controversial and disputes continue to arise over the implementation of the trade agreement. While many Canadians feared the agreement would erase jobs in Canada, Mexicans have been disappointed that the agreement failed to create more jobs. Moreover, Mexico's rising standard of living has increased the cost of doing business there; hundreds of *maquiladoras* have closed their doors and transferred work to China and other nations where labour costs are cheaper. Indeed, China has become Canada's second-largest importer.

**The New NAFTA.** More recently, NAFTA has been reviewed and a new agreement has been renegotiated as the United States had concerns about benefits and fairness in NAFTA. The Canada–United States–Mexico Agreement (CUSMA) is a signed, but not ratified, free trade agreement as of November 2018. More recently, the United States announced intentions to withdraw from NAFTA, requiring Congress either to ratify the CUSMA (or USMCA, as it's called in the United States), or else revert to pre-NAFTA trading rules.

## The European Union (EU)

The **European Union (EU)**, also called the *European Community* or *Common Market*, was established in 1958 to promote trade among its members, which initially included Belgium, France, Italy, West Germany, Luxembourg, and the Netherlands. Today, the Euro Zone (countries that have adopted the euro as their currency) consists of 28 member countries with varying political landscapes.[26] Until 1993, each nation functioned as a separate market, but at that time members officially unified into one of the largest single world markets, which today has nearly half a billion consumers with a GDP of more than $17.1 trillion.[27]

**European Union (EU)** community established in 1958 to promote trade within Europe

To facilitate free trade among members, the EU is working toward standardization of business regulations and requirements, import duties, and value-added taxes; the elimination of customs checks; and the creation of a standardized currency for use by all members. Many European nations link their exchange rates together to a common currency, the *euro;* however, several EU members have rejected use of the euro in their countries.

Although the common currency requires many marketers to modify their pricing strategies and will subject them to increased competition, the use of a single currency frees companies that sell goods among European countries from the nuisance of dealing with complex exchange rates.[28] The long-term goals are to eliminate all trade barriers within the EU, improve the economic efficiency of the EU nations, and stimulate economic growth, thus making the union's economy more competitive in global markets, particularly against Japan and other Pacific Rim nations, and North America. However, several disputes and debates still divide the member nations, and many barriers to completely free trade remain. Consequently, it may take many years before the EU is truly one deregulated market.

## Asia–Pacific Economic Cooperation (APEC)

The **Asia–Pacific Economic Cooperation (APEC)**, established in 1989, promotes open trade as well as economic and technical cooperation among member nations, which initially included Australia, Brunei, Darussalam, Canada, Indonesia, Japan, South Korea, Malaysia, New Zealand, the Philippines, Singapore, Thailand, and the United States. Since then the alliance has grown to include Chile, China, Hong Kong, Mexico, Papua New Guinea, Peru, Russia, Chinese Taipei, and Vietnam. The 21-member alliance represents approximately 40 percent of the world's population, 54 percent of world GDP and 44 percent of global trade.[29] APEC differs from other international trade alliances in its commitment to facilitating business and its practice of allowing the business/private sector to participate in a wide range of APEC activities.[30]

**Asia–Pacific Economic Cooperation (APEC)** community established in 1989 to promote international trade and facilitate business; as of 2013, has 21 member countries

Companies of the APEC countries have become increasingly competitive and sophisticated in global business in the last three decades. The Japanese and South Koreans, in particular, have made tremendous inroads on world markets for automobiles, cameras, and audio and video equipment. Products from Samsung, Sony, Canon, Toyota, Daewoo, Mitsubishi, Suzuki, and Lenovo are sold all over the world and have set standards of quality by which other products are often judged.

China, a country of 1.3 billion people, has launched a program of economic reform to stimulate its economy by privatizing many industries, restructuring its banking system, and increasing public spending on infrastructure (including railways and telecommunications).[31] As a result, China has become a manufacturing powerhouse, and its GDP is the world's second-largest, behind the United States.[32] Increased industrialization has also caused China to become the world's largest emitter of greenhouse gases. On the other hand, China has also begun a quest to become a world leader in green initiatives and renewable energy. This is an increasingly important quest as the country becomes more polluted.

Less visible Pacific Rim regions, such as Thailand, Singapore, Taiwan, Vietnam, and Hong Kong, have also become major manufacturing and financial centres. Vietnam, with a socialist-oriented market economy, has bypassed its communist government with private firms moving ahead despite bureaucracy, corruption, and poor infrastructure. In a country of 88 million, Vietnamese firms now compete internationally as a result of trade liberalization, deregulation, and investment in human and physical capital. As China's labour costs continue to grow, more businesses are turning toward Vietnam as a place in which to open factories.[33]

## Association of Southeast Asian Nations (ASEAN)

The **Association of Southeast Asian Nations (ASEAN)**, established in 1967, promotes trade and economic integration among member nations in Southeast Asia, including Malaysia, the Philippines, Singapore, Thailand, Brunei, Vietnam, Laos, Indonesia, Myanmar, and Cambodia.[34] The ten-member alliance represents 600 million people with a GDP of $2.4 trillion.[35] ASEAN's goals include the promotion of free trade, peace, and collaboration between its members.[36]

**Association of Southeast Asian Nations (ASEAN)** trade alliance that promotes trade and economic integration among member nations in Southeast Asia

However, ASEAN is facing challenges in becoming a unified trade bloc. Unlike members of the European Union, the economic systems of ASEAN members are quite different, with political systems including democracies (Philippines and Malaysia), constitutional monarchies (Cambodia), and communism (Vietnam).[37] Major conflicts have also occurred between member nations. For instance, in Thailand the military staged a coup and placed the country under martial law, a change that not only impacted Thailand but also ASEAN as a whole.[38] Unlike the EU, ASEAN will not have a common currency or fully free labour flows between member nations. In this way, ASEAN plans to avoid some of the pitfalls that occurred among nations in the EU during the last worldwide recession.[39]

©Glowimages/Getty Images

Clothing, timber, rice, and fish are among Cambodia's major exports.

## RESPONDING TO BUSINESS CHALLENGES

### Uber Attempts to Make the Right Turn

Uber provides ride-sharing services by connecting drivers and riders through an app. It has expanded its operations to 674 cities in 83 countries worldwide. As it expands, Uber is engaging in strategic partnerships with local companies. These alliances allow Uber to utilize the knowledge of domestic firms familiar with the country's culture. Uber has partnered with Times Internet in India, Baidu in China, and America Movil in Latin America.

Despite its success, Uber has faced problems in expanding internationally. In Spain, a judge ruled that Uber drivers are not legally authorized to transport passengers and that it unfairly competes against licensed taxi drivers. France and Germany instituted similar bans against unlicensed Uber drivers. Uber returned to Spain with UberX, which uses licensed drivers.

India is Uber's second-largest market after the United States. In New Delhi, the taxi industry banned app-based services without radio-taxi permits in the capital for safety reasons. Uber made changes to increase safety. Yet despite these changes, Uber continued to run afoul of Indian authorities. India asked Internet service providers to block Uber's websites because it continued to operate in the city despite being banned.

Uber has taken a global approach to expansion by applying the same practices in other countries as it does in Canada. However, it is realizing that it must take a more customized approach to achieve long-term international market success.*

#### DISCUSSION QUESTIONS

1. What are some of the major advantages Uber is experiencing by creating strategic partnerships with other companies?
2. What are some challenges Uber is facing as it expands globally?
3. What are some of the barriers that Uber is encountering in different countries?

*Rob Davies, "Uber Suffers Legal Setbacks in France and Germany," *The Guardian*, June 9, 2016, https://www.theguardian.com/technology/2016/jun/09/uber-sufferslegal-setbacks-in-france-and-germany (accessed April 15, 2017); "Uberworld," *The Economist*, September 3, 2016, p. 9; Jefferson Graham, "App Greases the Wheels," *USA Today*, May 27, 2015, p. 5B; Karun, "Times Internet and Uber Enter Into a Strategic Partnership, Uber Blog, March 22, 2015, http://blog.uber.com/times-internet (accessed April 15, 2017); R. Jai Krishna and Joanna Sugden, "India Asks Internet Service Providers to Block Uber Website in Delhi," *Wall Street Journal*, May 14, 2015, http://www.wsj.com/articles/india-asks-internet-service-providers-toblock-uber-website-in-delhi-1431606032 (accessed April 15, 2017); Saritha Rai, "Uber Gets Serious about Passenger Safety In India, Introduces Panic Button," *Forbes*, February 12, 2015, http://www.forbes.com/sites/saritharai/2015/02/12/uber-gets-serious-about-passenger-safety-in-indiaintroduces-panic-button/ (accessed April 15, 2017); Sam Schechner and Tom Fairless, "Europe Steps Up Pressure on Tech Giants," *Wall Street Journal*, April 2, 2015, http://www.wsj.com/articles/europe-steps-up-pressure-ontechnology-giants-1428020273 (accessed April 15, 2017); Aditi Shrivastava, "Uber Resumes Operations in Delhi Post 1.5 Months Ban," *Economic Times*, January 23, 2015, http://articles.economictimes.indiatimes.com/2015-01-23/news/58382689_1_indian-taxi-market-radio-taxischeme-uber-spokesman (accessed April 15, 2017); UNM Daniels Fund Ethics Initiative, "Truth, Transparency, and Trust: Uber Important in the Sharing Economy," PPT presentation, https://danielsethics.mgt.unm.edu/teachingresources/ presentations.asp (accessed April 15, 2017); Maria Vega Paul, "Uber Returns to Spanish Streets in Search of Regulatory U-Turn," Reuters, March 30, 2016, http://www. reuters.com/article/us-spain-uber-tech-idUSKCNOWWOAO (accessed April 15, 2017).

## World Bank

The **World Bank**, was established by the industrialized nations in 1946 to loan money to underdeveloped and developing countries. It loans its own funds or borrows funds from member countries to finance projects ranging from road and factory construction to the building of medical and educational facilities. The World Bank and other multilateral development banks (banks with international support that provide loans to developing countries) are the largest source of advice and assistance for developing nations.

**World Bank** an organization established by the industrialized nations in 1946 to loan money to underdeveloped and developing countries; formally known as the International Bank for Reconstruction and Development

## International Monetary Fund

The **International Monetary Fund (IMF)** was established in 1947 to promote trade among member nations by eliminating trade barriers and fostering financial cooperation. It also makes short-term loans to member countries that have balance-of-payment deficits and provides foreign currencies to member nations. The IMF

**International Monetary Fund (IMF)** organization established in 1947 to promote trade among member nations by eliminating trade barriers and fostering financial cooperation

tries to avoid financial crises and panics by alerting the international community about countries that will not be able to repay their debts. The IMF's Internet site provides additional information about the organization, including news releases, frequently asked questions, and members.

The IMF is the closest thing the world has to an international central bank. If countries get into financial trouble, they can borrow from the World Bank. However, the global economic crisis created many challenges for the IMF as it was forced to significantly increase its loans to both emerging economies and more developed nations. The usefulness of the IMF for developed countries is limited because these countries use private markets as a major source of capital.[40] Yet the European debt crisis changed this somewhat. Portugal, Ireland, Greece, and Spain required billions of dollars in bailouts from the IMF to keep their economies afloat.

**Figure 3.1** | Top Exporting Countries (in billions of U.S. dollars)

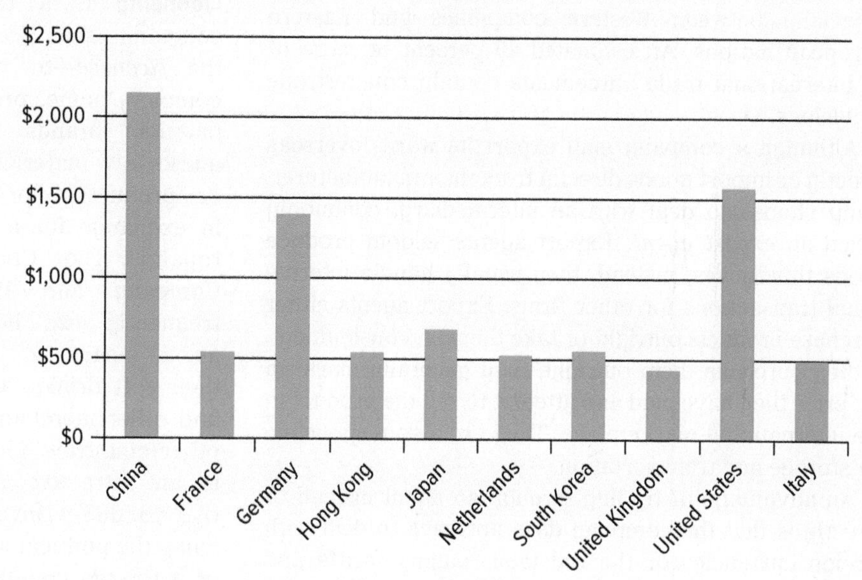


## Getting Involved in International Business

**LO 3-4** Summarize the different levels of organizational involvement in international trade.

Businesses may get involved in international trade at many levels—from a small Kenyan firm that occasionally exports African crafts to a huge multinational corporation such as Shell Oil that sells products around the globe. The degree of commitment of resources and effort required increases according to the level at which a business involves itself in international trade. This section examines exporting and importing, trading companies, licensing and franchising, contract manufacturing, joint ventures, direct investment, and multinational corporations.

### Exporting and Importing

Many companies first get involved in international trade when they import goods from other countries for resale in their own businesses. For example, a grocery store chain may import bananas from Honduras and coffee from Colombia. A business may get involved in exporting when it is called upon to supply a foreign company with a particular product and products often have higher sales growth potential in foreign countries than they have in the parent country. For example, Heinz exports its ketchup to other countries, including Mexico, Africa, and the Middle East, because there exists much greater potential for growth. Mexico in particular has become a crucial part of Heinz's growth strategy because Mexicans consume more ketchup than all but eight other nations.[41] Figure 3.1 shows some of the world's largest exporting countries.

Exporting sometimes takes place through **countertrade agreements**, which involve bartering

**countertrade agreements** foreign trade agreements that involve bartering products for other products instead of for currency

©Glow Images

The ship *Cosco Ran* transports cargo from one side of the globe to the other.

products for other products instead of for currency. Such arrangements are fairly common in international trade, especially between Western companies and Eastern European nations. An estimated 40 percent or more of all international trade agreements contain countertrade provisions.

Although a company may export its wares overseas directly or import goods directly from their manufacturer, many choose to deal with an intermediary, commonly called an *export agent*. Export agents seldom produce goods themselves; instead, they usually handle international transactions for other firms. Export agents either purchase products outright or take them on consignment. If they purchase them outright, they generally mark up the price they have paid and attempt to sell the product in the international marketplace. They are also responsible for storage and transportation.

An advantage of trading through an agent instead of directly is that the company does not have to deal with foreign currencies or the red tape (paying tariffs and handling paperwork) of international business. A major disadvantage is that, because the export agent must make a profit, either the price of the product must be increased or the domestic company must provide a larger discount than it would in a domestic transaction.

## Trading Companies

A **trading company** buys goods in one country and sells them to buyers in another country. Trading companies handle all activities required to move products from one country to another, including consulting, marketing research, advertising, insurance, product research and design, warehousing, and foreign exchange services, to companies interested in selling their products in foreign markets. Trading companies are similar to export agents, but their role in international trade is larger. By linking sellers and buyers of goods in different countries, trading companies promote international trade. Canada has a few trading companies but one of the oldest is the Canadian Commercial Corporation (CCC), a federal Crown corporation in existence since 1946. Its primary goal is to promote and facilitate international trade on behalf of Canadian industry, particularly with government markets.[42] Export Development Canada (EDC) is another Crown corporation and Canada's export credit agency. It helps Canadian exporters and investors expand their international business among other services.[43]

**trading company** a firm that buys goods in one country and sells them to buyers in another country

## Licensing and Franchising

**Licensing** is a trade arrangement in which one company—the *licensor*—allows another company—the *licensee*—to use its company name, products, patents, brands, trademarks, raw materials, and/or production processes in exchange for a fee or royalty. The Coca-Cola Company and PepsiCo frequently use licensing as a means to market their soft drinks, apparel, and other merchandise in other countries. Licensing is an attractive alternative to direct investment when the political stability of a foreign country is in doubt or when resources are unavailable for direct investment. Licensing is especially advantageous for small manufacturers wanting to launch a well-known brand internationally. Yoplait is a French yogurt that is licensed for production in Canada.

**licensing** a trade agreement in which one company–the licensor–allows another company–the licensee–to use its company name, products, patents, brands, trademarks, raw materials, and/or production processes in exchange for a fee or royalty

**franchising** a form of licensing in which a company–the franchisor–agrees to provide a franchisee a name, logo, methods of operation, advertising, products, and other elements associated with a franchiser's business, in return for a financial commitment and the agreement to conduct business in accordance with the franchisor's standard of operations

**Franchising** is a form of licensing in which a company—the *franchisor*—agrees to provide a *franchisee* a name, logo, methods of operation, advertising, products, and other elements associated with the franchisor's business, in return for a financial commitment and the agreement to conduct business in accordance with the franchisor's standard of operations. Subway, McDonald's, and Pizza Hut are well-known franchisers with international visibility. Table 3.4 lists some of the top global franchises.

**Table 3.4** | Top 10 Global Franchises

| Franchise | Industry | Ranking |
|---|---|---|
| McDonald's | Fast food franchises | 1 |
| KFC | Chicken franchises | 2 |
| Burger King | Fast food franchises | 3 |
| Pizza Hut | Pizza franchises | 4 |
| 7-Eleven | Convenience store franchises | 5 |
| Marriott International | Hotel franchises | 6 |
| RE/MAX | Real estate franchises | 7 |
| Dunkin' Donuts | Bakery and doughnut franchises | 8 |
| InterContinental Hotels and Resorts | Hotel franchises | 9 |
| Subway | Sandwich and bagel franchises | 10 |

©WENN Ltd/Alamy Stock Photo

The Canadian frozen yogurt franchise Yogen Früz has operations on four continents.

Licensing and franchising enable a company to enter the international marketplace without spending large sums of money abroad or hiring or transferring personnel to handle overseas affairs. They also minimize problems associated with shipping costs, tariffs, and trade restrictions. And they allow the firm to establish goodwill for its products in a foreign market, which will help the company if it decides to produce or market its products directly in the foreign country at some future date. However, if the licensee (or franchisee) does not maintain high standards of quality, the product's image may be hurt; therefore, it is important for the licensor to monitor its products overseas and to enforce its quality standards.

**contract manufacturing** the hiring of a foreign company to produce a specified volume of the initiating company's product to specification; the final product carries the domestic firm's name

## Contract Manufacturing

**Contract manufacturing** occurs when a company hires a foreign company to produce a specified volume of the firm's product to specification; the final product carries the domestic firm's name. Spalding, for example, relies on contract manufacturing for its sports equipment; Reebok uses Korean contract manufacturers to manufacture many of its athletic shoes.

## Outsourcing

Earlier, we defined *outsourcing* as transferring manufacturing or other tasks (such as information technology operations) to companies in countries where labour and supplies are less expensive. Many firms have outsourced tasks to India, Ireland, Mexico, and the Philippines, where there are many well-educated workers and significantly lower labour costs. Services, such as preparing taxes or customer service, can also be outsourced.

Although outsourcing has become politically controversial in recent years amid concerns over jobs lost to overseas workers, foreign companies sometimes transfer tasks and jobs to Canadian companies—sometimes called *insourcing*. However, some firms are bringing their outsourced jobs back after concerns that foreign workers were not adding enough value. This has to do with increased regulations in foreign countries and concerns over data security. Companies such as General Electric and Caterpillar are returning to the United States due to increasing labour costs in places such as China, the expense of shipping products across the ocean, and fears of fraud or intellectual property theft.

## Offshoring

**offshoring** the relocation of business processes by a company or subsidiary to another country; it differs from outsourcing because the company retains control of the offshored processes

**Offshoring** is the relocation of a business process by a company, or a subsidiary, to another country. Offshoring is different from outsourcing: the company retains control of the process because it is not subcontracting to a different company. Companies may choose to offshore for a number of reasons, ranging from lower wages, skilled labour, or taking advantage of time zone differences in order to offer services around the clock. Some banks have chosen not to outsource because of concerns about data security in other countries. These institutions may instead engage in offshoring, which allows a company more control over international operations because the offshore office is an extension of the company. Shell, for example, opened a delivery centre in India and moved its global IT jobs to that area.[44]

## Joint Ventures and Alliances

Many countries, particularly developing nations, do not permit direct investment by foreign companies or individuals. A company may also lack sufficient resources or expertise to operate elsewhere. In such cases, a company joint venture a partnership established for a specific project or for a limited time involving the sharing of the costs and operation of a business, often between a foreign company and a local partner

strategic alliance a partnership formed to create competitive advantage on a worldwide basis

direct investment the ownership of overseas facilities

multinational corporation (MNC) a corporation that operates on a worldwide scale, without significant ties to any one nation or region

that wants to do business in another region or country may set up a **joint venture** by finding a local partner (occasionally, the host nation itself) to share the costs and operation of the business. Qualcomm formed a joint venture with Chinese chip maker Semiconductor Manufacturing International Corporation to produce semiconductors. Qualcomm hopes this joint venture will help it to gain a foothold in selling chips in the Chinese market.[45]

In some industries, such as automobiles and computers, strategic alliances are becoming the predominant means of competing. A **strategic alliance** is a partnership formed to create competitive advantage on a worldwide basis. In such industries, international competition is so fierce and the costs of competing on a global basis are so high that few firms have the resources to go it alone, so they collaborate with other companies. An example of a strategic alliance is the partnership between LinkedIn and accounting firm Ernst & Young. The companies hope to use their combined expertise to assist other companies in using technology, social networking, and sales effectively.[46]

## Direct Investment

Companies that want more control and are willing to invest considerable resources in international business may consider **direct investment**, the ownership of overseas facilities. Direct investment may involve the development and operation of new facilities—such as when Starbucks opens a new coffee shop in Japan—or the purchase of all or part of an existing operation in a foreign country.

The highest level of international business involvement is the **multinational corporation (MNC)**, a corporation, such as IBM or ExxonMobil, that operates on a worldwide scale, without significant ties to any one nation or region. Table 3.5 lists the ten largest multinational corporations.

MNCs are more than simple corporations. They often have greater assets than some of the countries in which they do business. Nestlé, with headquarters in Switzerland, operates more than 400 factories around the world and receives revenues from Europe; North, Central, and South America; Africa; and Asia.[47] The Royal Dutch/Shell Group, one of the world's major oil producers, is another MNC. Its main offices are located in The Hague and London. Other MNCs include BASF, British Petroleum, Matsushita, Mitsubishi, Siemens, Toyota, and Unilever.

©pcruciatti/Shutterstock

Walmart has chosen to directly invest in China. However, it must still make adjustments to fit with the local culture. For instance, Walmart, which is normally against trade unions, was pressured to allow its Chinese employees to unionize.

Many MNCs have been targeted by anti-globalization activists at global business forums, and some protests have turned violent. The activists contend that MNCs increase the gap between rich and poor nations, misuse and misallocate scarce resources, and exploit the labour markets in developing nations and harm their natural environments.[48]

**Table 3.5** | Large Multinational Companies

| Company | Country | Description |
|---|---|---|
| Royal Dutch Shell | Netherlands | Oil and gas; largest company in the world in terms of revenue |
| Toyota | Japan | Largest automobile manufacturer in the world |
| Walmart | United States | Largest retailer in the world; largest private employer in the world |
| Siemens | Germany | Engineering and electronics; largest engineering company in Europe |
| Nestlé | Switzerland | Nutritional, snack-food, and health-related consumer goods |
| Samsung | South Korea | Subsidiaries specializing in electronics, electronic components, telecommunications equipment, medical equipment, and more |
| Unilever | United Kingdom | Consumer goods including cleaning and personal care, foods, beverages |
| Boeing | United States | Aerospace and defense; largest U.S. exporter |
| Lenovo | China | Computer technology; highest share of PC market |
| Subway | United States | Largest fast-food chain; fastest-growing franchises in 105 countries |

## International Business Strategies

**LO 3-5** Contrast two basic strategies used in international business.

Planning in a global economy requires businesspeople to understand the economic, legal, political, and sociocultural realities of the countries in which they will operate. These factors will affect the strategy a business chooses to use outside its own borders.

### Developing Strategies

Companies doing business internationally have traditionally used a **multinational strategy**, customizing their products, promotion, and distribution according to cultural, technological, regional, and national differences. To succeed in India, for example, McDonald's had to adapt its products to respect religious customs. McDonald's India does not serve beef or pork products and also has vegetarian dishes for its largely vegetarian consumer base. Many soap and detergent manufacturers have adapted their products to local water conditions, washing equipment, and washing habits. For customers in some less-developed countries, Colgate-Palmolive Co. has developed an inexpensive, plastic, hand-powered washing machine for use in households that have no electricity.

**multinational strategy** a plan, used by international companies, that involves customizing products, promotion, and distribution according to cultural, technological, regional, and national differences

Even when products are standardized, advertising often has to be modified to adapt to language and cultural differences. For example, Mars has been in the pet food market in China for more than two decades with brands like Royal Canin, Whiskas, and Pedigree. U.S.-based Mars has competitive advantage because in China people are concerned about the safety of locally produced pet food.

More and more companies are moving from this customization strategy to a **global strategy (globalization)**, which involves standardizing products (and, as much as possible, their promotion and distribution) for the whole world, as if it were a single entity. Examples of globalized products are clothing, movies, music, and cosmetics. Social media sites are important channels that brands are using to connect with their global customers. Pampers, 3M, and Corona had the highest engagement with their global followers on Twitter.[49]

**global strategy (globalization)** a strategy that involves standardizing products (and, as much as possible, their promotion and distribution) for the whole world, as if it were a single entity

Before moving outside their own borders, companies must conduct environmental analyses to evaluate the potential of and problems associated with various markets and to determine what strategy is best for doing business in those markets. Failure to do so may result in losses and even negative publicity. Some companies rely on local managers to gain greater insights and faster response to changes within a country. Astute businesspeople today

### Consider the Following: Airbnb keeps travel local

Globally, people spend around $700 billion a year on travel accommodation, and many travellers are willing to forgo hotel luxuries to get a unique local experience. With an online marketplace that lets people turn spare bedrooms and homes into vacation rentals, Airbnb is now in more than 81,000 cities and 191 countries.

But how have they become global while creating a local accommodation rental market? Airbnb sees it as a "global" challenge. The company has to simultaneously build the global and local markets. Airbnb has made localization smooth. Its app is available in 26 different languages and it creates marketing campaigns by leveraging its network of users who help tailor marketing to their own countries. App redesigns added new elements like neighbourhood reviews and recommendations for Airbnb users.

Airbnb is going to get a lot more local in the coming years. It's all part of owning the entire travel experience, rather than just helping tourists rent a room. As Airbnb demonstrates, a better localized product will also be a more successful product.*

*The University of Texas at Austin, "How Airbnb Became Global," http://sites.utexas.edu/longhornglobalbiznet/airbnb/ (accessed December 13, 2018); Airbnb, "About Us," https://press.airbnb.com/about-us/ (accessed December 13, 2018); *Forbes*, "How Airbnb Expanded To 190 Countries by Thinking 'Glocal,'" https://www.forbes.com/sites/briansolomon/2016/05/03/how-airbnb-expanded-to-190-countries-by-thinking-glocal/#2c6f12527e91 (accessed December 13, 2018); OneSky Blog, "How to Grow a Business in 190 Markets: 4 Lessons from Airbnb," http://www.oneskyapp.com/blog/airbnb-global-growth/, (accessed December, 13 2018); HBR, "Airbnb Is Facing an Existential Expansion Problem," https://hbr.org/2016/07/airbnb-is-facing-an-existential-expansion-problem (accessed December 13, 2018), Inc.com, "Airbnb Is Inc.'s 2014 Company of the Year," https://www.inc.com/magazine/201412/burt-helm/airbnb-company-of-the-year-2014.html (accessed December 13, 2018).

*think globally, act locally.* That is, while constantly being aware of the total picture, they adjust their firms' strategies to conform to local needs and tastes.

## Managing the Challenges of Global Business

As we have pointed out in this chapter, many past political barriers to trade have fallen or been minimized, expanding and opening new market opportunities. Managers who can meet the challenges of creating and implementing effective and sensitive business strategies for the global marketplace can help lead their companies to success. For example, the Canadian Trade Commissioner Service is the global business solutions unit of Foreign Affairs and International Trade Canada that offers Canadian firms wide and deep practical knowledge of international markets and industries, a network of international business professionals, market intelligence, financial support, and expert advice.[50] As mentioned previously, Canadian Commercial Corporation (CCC) promotes and facilitates international trade on behalf of Canadian industry, and Export Development Canada provides Canadian exporters with financing, insurance, and bonding services as well as foreign market expertise. A major element of the assistance that these governmental organizations can provide firms (especially for small- and medium-sized firms) is knowledge of the internationalization process.

Small businesses, too, can succeed in foreign markets when their managers have carefully studied those markets, and prepared and implemented appropriate strategies. Being globally aware is therefore an important quality for today's managers and will become a crucial attribute for managers of the twenty-first century.

### TEAM EXERCISE

Visit Transparency International's Country Corruption Index website: www.transparency.org/. Form groups and select two countries. Research some of the economic, ethical, legal, regulatory, and political barriers that would have an impact on international trade. Be sure to pair a fairly ethical country with a fairly unethical country (e.g., Sweden with Myanmar, Ireland with Haiti). Report your findings.

# LEARNING OBJECTIVES SUMMARY

**LO 3-1** Explore some of the factors within the international trade environment that influence business.

International business is the buying, selling, and trading of goods and services across national boundaries. Importing is the purchase of goods and services from another nation; exporting is the sale of goods and services to foreign markets. A nation's balance of trade is the difference in value between its exports and imports; a positive balance of trade is a trade surplus and a negative balance of trade is a trade deficit. The difference between the flow of money into and out of a country is called the balance of payments. An absolute or comparative advantage in trade may determine what products a company from a particular nation will export.

**LO 3-2** Assess some of the economic, legal, political, social, cultural, and technological barriers to international business.

Companies engaged in international trade must consider the effects of economic, legal, political, social, and cultural differences between nations. Economic barriers are a country's level of development (infrastructure) and exchange rates. Wide-ranging legal and political barriers include differing laws (and enforcement), tariffs, exchange controls, quotas, embargoes, political instability, and war. Ambiguous cultural and social barriers involve differences in spoken and body language, time, holidays and other observances, and customs.

**LO 3-3** Specify some of the agreements, alliances, and organizations that may encourage trade across international boundaries.

Among the most important promoters of international business have been the General Agreement on Tariffs and Trade, the World Trade Organization, the North American Free Trade Agreement, the European Union, the Asia-Pacific Economic Cooperation, the Association of Southeast Asian Nations, the World Bank, and the International Monetary Fund.

**LO 3-4** Summarize the different levels of organizational involvement in international trade.

A company may be involved in international trade at several levels, each requiring a greater commitment of resources and effort, ranging from importing/exporting to multinational corporations. Countertrade agreements occur at the import/export level and involve bartering products for other products instead of currency. At the next level, a trading company links buyers and sellers in different countries to foster trade. In licensing and franchising, one company agrees to allow a foreign company the use of its company name, products, patents, brands, trademarks, raw materials, and production processes, in exchange for a flat fee or royalty.

Contract manufacturing occurs when a company hires a foreign company to produce a specified volume of the firm's product to specification; the final product carries the domestic firm's name. A joint venture is a partnership in which companies from different countries agree to share the costs and operation of the business. The purchase of overseas production and marketing facilities is direct investment. Outsourcing, a form of direct investment, involves transferring manufacturing to countries where labour and supplies are cheap. A multinational corporation is one that operates on a worldwide scale, without significant ties to any one nation or region.

**LO 3-5** Contrast two basic strategies used in international business.

Companies typically use one of two basic strategies in international business. A multinational strategy customizes products, promotion, and distribution according to cultural, technological, regional, and national differences. A global strategy (globalization) standardizes products (and, as much as possible, their promotion and distribution) for the whole world, as if it were a single entity.

# KEY TERMS

absolute advantage
Asia-Pacific Economic Cooperation (APEC)
Association of Southeast Asian Nations (ASEAN)
balance of payments
balance of trade
cartel
comparative advantage
contract manufacturing
countertrade agreements
direct investment
dumping
embargo
European Union (EU)
exchange controls
exchange rate
exporting
franchising
General Agreement on Tariffs and Trade (GATT)
global strategy (globalization)
importing
tariff
infrastructure
international business
International Monetary Fund (IMF)
joint venture
licensing
multinational corporation (MNC)
multinational strategy
North American Free Trade Agreement (NAFTA)
offshoring
outsourcing
quota
strategic alliance
trade deficit
trade surplus
trading company
World Bank
World Trade Organization (WTO)

## So You Want a Job *in Global Business*

Have you always dreamt of travelling the world? Whether backpacking through Central America or sipping espressos at European cafés is your style, the increasing globalization of business might just give you your chance to see what the world has to offer. Most new jobs will have at least some global component, even if located within Canada, so being globally aware and keeping an open mind regarding different cultures is vital in today's business world. Think about the 1.3 billion consumers in China who have already purchased mobile phones. In the future, some of the largest markets will be in Asia.

Many jobs discussed in chapters throughout this book tend to have strong international components. For example, product management and distribution management are discussed as marketing careers in Chapter 12. As more and more companies sell products around the globe, their function, design, packaging, and promotions need to be culturally relevant to many different people in many different places. Products very often cross multiple borders before reaching the final consumer, both in their distribution and through the supply chain to produce the products.

Jobs exist in export and import management, product and pricing management, distribution and transportation, and advertising. Many "born global" companies such as Google operate virtually and consider all countries their market. Many companies sell their products through eBay and other Internet sites and never leave Canada. Today, communication and transportation facilitates selling and buying products worldwide with delivery in a few days. You may have sold or purchased a product on eBay outside of Canada without thinking about how easy and accessible international markets are to business. If you have, welcome to the world of global business.

To be successful you must have an idea not only of differing regulations from country to country, but of different languages, ethics, and communication styles, and varying needs and wants of international markets. From the regulatory side, you may need to be aware of laws related to intellectual property, copyrights, antitrust, advertising, and pricing in every country. Translating is never only about translating the language. Perhaps even more important is ensuring that your message gets through. Whether on a product label or in advertising or promotional materials, the use of images and words varies widely across the globe.

## BUILD YOUR BUSINESS PLAN

### Business in a Borderless World

Think about the product/service you are contemplating for your business plan. If it is an already established product or service, try to find out if the product is currently being sold internationally. If not, can you identify opportunities to do so in the future? What countries do you think would respond most favourably to your product? What problems would you encounter if you attempted to export your product to those countries?

If you are thinking of creating a new product or service for your business plan, think about the possibility of eventually marketing that product in another country. What countries or areas of the world do you think would be most responsive to your product?

Does Canada has trade agreements or alliances with any countries that would make your entry into the market easier? What are the economic, social, cultural, and technological barriers you would have to recognize? Think about the specific cultural differences that would have to be considered before entering the prospective country or countries.

## CASE | Electra Bikes: Better, Cooler, Awesomer!

Twenty-three years ago, Swiss snowboard designer Benno Bänziger and his German business partner Jeano Erforth decided they wanted to make bike riding fun again. At the time, cruiser bikes were out of style and were in danger of disappearing. Bänziger and Erforth converted their T-shirt company in California into a bicycle manufacturer called Electra Bikes. However, they did not want to manufacture just any type of cruiser bike. They wanted their bikes to look hip with a vintage style, based on rockabilly culture and resembling the look of muscle cars. The shop went from selling a few hundred the first year it was in business to becoming a global sensation. Electra eventually caught the attention of Trek Bicycle Corporation, which acquired the firm in 2014.

As Electra began to expand globally, it found that it had a comparative advantage its bigger competitors did not have. First of all, many bike enthusiasts worldwide appreciated the vintage look combined with the most up-to-date technology of Electra bicycles. One particular advantage Electra has is its patented Flat Foot Technology®. This technology enables better leg extension, making the ride more comfortable. Because of its patent, Electra is currently the only company that can use the technology it developed. These advantages combined with its "genuine Americana" message proved to be a hit overseas.

Global expansion offered Electra the unique opportunity to reach new market niches of bicycle enthusiasts. It started slowly, expanding first into markets that were closer, including Canada and Australia. The company currently has distributors in 26 countries that sell its bikes. Electra opened a European office that supports sales for 25 countries. Like many other firms, Electra outsources production to Taiwan and China. Using freight ships, the firm ships its products to markets such as Australia and the European Union. By outsourcing production, the firm is able to save money.

Like most companies that expand globally, Electra is subject to import duties that can vary depending upon where the bicycles are manufactured. It is also subject to regulations that vary from country to country. Sometimes Electra bikes must have additional features due to safety laws. For instance, some bikes shipped to certain countries have front brakes, while others have lighting systems or fenders. While these different features add to costs, they ensure that Electra stays on the right side of the laws within the countries in which they do business.

Regulations can vary by type of product, as well. Kevin Cox, president of Electra Bicycle Company, describes how Electra had to take this into consideration when designing a bicycle with a motor called the Townie Go. According to Cox, "There are certain speed regulations that exist, and those regulations are different in Europe." The company chose to adopt a stricter U.S. standard, although it meant a slower speed, because it would give Electra "one product platform that has global reach."

Electra also faces economic and geographical challenges. "Currency fluctuation in Asia, that's a big one because that in and of itself can skew the cost of our bicycle," Cox says. Additionally, certain areas such as Europe and Canada have highly seasonal weather that limits bike riding to certain times of the year. These weather variations cause fluctuations in demand based upon the season. However, Cox also points out that having a global reach helps to balance out these fluctuations "because while it's winter in North America, I'm enjoying a nice summer in Australia." In other words, there is a constant worldwide demand for bicycles year-round.

As Electra expanded globally, the infrastructure of operating a global network became more complex. This is why, in 2014, Electra made the decision to sell the company to Trek. The decision benefits Electra because it can now utilize Trek's extensive network to reach new markets. At the same time, tapping into Trek's distribution networks frees Electra to focus less on distribution concerns and more on its core competency: developing highquality, durable, vintage-look bicycles.[51]

## DISCUSSION QUESTIONS

1. Describe how Electra maintains a worldwide comparative advantage.
2. What are some global difficulties Electra had to overcome when it expanded into different countries?
3. Why did Electra—which markets itself with a "genuine Americana" message—decide to outsource production to Asia? Do you believe this is appropriate?

CHAPTER 4

# Options for Organizing Business

©Vince Talotta/Toronto Star via Getty Images

## LEARNING OBJECTIVES

**After reading this chapter, you will be able to:**

**LO 4-1** Define and examine the advantages and disadvantages of the sole proprietorship form of organization.

**LO 4-2** Identify three types of partnership, and evaluate the advantages and disadvantages of the partnership form of organization.

**LO 4-3** Describe the corporate form of organization, and cite the advantages and disadvantages of corporations.

**LO 4-4** Define and debate the advantages and disadvantages of mergers, acquisitions, and leveraged buyouts.

## ENTER THE WORLD OF BUSINESS

**Heather Reisman and Indigo**

If you walk into any Chapters or Indigo bookstore in Canada, you are likely to see some books flagged as Heather's Picks. Heather, in case you don't know, is Heather Reisman, founder of Indigo Books and Music and the current CEO of Canada's largest retail chain of bookstores, Indigo, which includes Chapters, Indigo, and Coles branded stores. Reisman maintains she has always had a deep love of books and had originally intended to be a major investor in bringing Borders, an American bookstore, to Canada. Borders' attempts to enter the Canadian market failed to gain approval from the Canadian government, and Reisman opted to start her own book retailer.

During Indigo's early years, the company battled for market share with what at the time was its main rival, Chapters. This competitive rivalry changed dramatically when Indigo, under Reisman's leadership, launched a hostile takeover of Chapters. While Chapters' management tried to prevent the sale of the company to Indigo, Reisman was ultimately successful. The acquisition, or merger, gave Indigo a virtual monopoly on retail bookstores in Canada. Yet the monopoly was fraught with challenges, including the ever-increasing expansion of Amazon in Canada. In fact, numerous business experts wondered if Indigo wasn't going to go the way of other bricks-and-mortar retailers and eventually head toward bankruptcy.

Reisman initially responded to the challenge by improving Indigo and Chapter's online presence and shifting its merchandise mix to include electronics, household items, giftware, stationery, baby gifts, and toys, all with the hopes of increasing its revenue. Building on this strategy, Indigo started to form strategic partnerships, sometimes known as joint ventures, with popular companies including Fitbit and Rifle Paper Co. One of the better known partnerships is with American Girl, which brought the popular dolls to Canada's retail environment. Indigo's exclusive partnership not only increased revenue, but brought new non-traditional shoppers into their retail outlets.

Indigo is now transforming itself once again, into what Reisman is describing as the world's first "cultural department store." The company will not only sell books but offer consumers a variety of lifestyle products and feature store-within-a-store partnerships with American Girl, Fitbit, and others.

Reisman notes they are now featuring products that appeal to taste makers and those who want to create culture. Retailer experts state that part of Indigo's success is attracting customers who want to see what is cool, hot, or chic. In addition to redesigning current stores, Indigo is building brand new stores in major cities in Canada and in 2018 opened its first U.S. store in New Jersey. When many other bricks-and-motor retailers are closing down locations or going out of business, Indigo is doing the opposite and expanding in the hope that their cultural department stores are just what consumers want in the ever-changing world of retail.

**DISCUSSION QUESTIONS**

1. What do you think are some of the advantages and disadvantages of changing Indigo from a traditional bookseller to a "cultural department store?"
2. Why would retailers enter into partnerships allowing store-within-store concepts? What advantages do you see in such partnerships? What are some disadvantages?
3. Do you think Indigo's expansion strategy will be successful? Why or why not?

## Introduction

The legal form of ownership taken by a business is seldom of great concern to you as a customer. When you eat at a restaurant, you probably don't care whether the restaurant is owned by one person (a sole proprietorship), has two or more owners who share the business (a partnership), or is an entity owned by many

Table 4.1 | Various Forms of Business Ownership

| Structure | Ownership | Taxation | Liability | Use |
|---|---|---|---|---|
| Sole proprietorship | One owner | Individual income taxed | Unlimited | Individual starting a business and easiest way to conduct business |
| Partnership | Two or more owners | Individual owners' income taxed | Unlimited (unless it is a limited partnership) | Easy way for two individuals to conduct business |
| Private corporation | Any number of shareholders | Corporate and shareholder income taxed | Varies between limited and unlimited | A legal entity with shareholders or stakeholders |
| Public corporation | Any number of shareholders | Corporate and shareholder income taxed | Limited | A legal entity with shareholders or stakeholders |

shareholders (a corporation); all you want is good food. If you buy a foreign car, you probably don't care whether the company that made it has laws governing its form of organization that are different from those for businesses in Canada. You are buying the car because it is well made, fits your price range, or appeals to your sense of style. Nonetheless, a business's legal form of ownership affects how it operates, how much tax it pays, and how much control its owners have.

This chapter examines three primary forms of business ownership—sole proprietorship, partnership, and corporation—and weighs the advantages and disadvantages of each. These forms are the most often used whether the business is a traditional bricks-and-mortar company, an online-only one, or a combination of both. We also take a look at cooperatives and discuss some trends in business ownership. You may wish to refer to Table 4.1 to compare the various forms of business ownership mentioned in the chapter.

# Sole Proprietorships

**LO 4-1** Define and examine the advantages and disadvantages of the sole proprietorship form of organization.

**Sole proprietorships**, businesses owned and operated by one individual, are the most common form of business organization in Canada. Common examples include service firms, restaurants, hair salons, flower shops, doggie day cares, and independent retail stores. Some entrepreneurs have managed to start quite small businesses and grow their sole proprietorship into a large successful company. For example, Tobias Lütke founded Ottawa-based Shopify, an online business that assists companies in establishing online shopping platforms while working out of his garage. Lütke notes that the company quickly grew to five people working out of a coffee shop and today has 3000 employees, 600,000 customers, revenue in excess of $1.5 billion, and is worth an estimated $17 billion. While most sole proprietors stay small, stories like Lütke's can occur.

**sole proprietorships** businesses owned and operated by one individual; the most common form of business organization in Canada

Sole proprietorships are typically small businesses employing fewer than 50 people. (We'll look at small businesses in greater detail in Chapter 5.) There are approximately 2.3 million businesses in Canada, of which the majority are sole proprietorships.

"Common examples include many restaurants, hair salons, flower shops, doggie day cares, and independent retail stores."

## Advantages of Sole Proprietorships

Sole proprietorships are generally managed by their owners. Because of this simple management structure, the owner/manager can make decisions quickly. This is just one of many advantages of the sole proprietorship form of business.

**Ease and Cost of Formation.** Forming a sole proprietorship is relatively easy and inexpensive. In some instances, all the entrepreneur has to do is to start selling a product or service. For example, when Brian Scudamore started 1-800-GOT-JUNK? he did so by buying a $700 used pickup truck and starting a junk removal business. Scudamore eventually grew the business into the largest junk removal franchise in North America. Other proprietorships, such as barbershops and restaurants, may require provincial and local licences and permits because of the nature of the business. The cost of these permits may run from $25 to $1,000. No lawyer is needed to create such enterprises, and the owner can usually take care of the required paperwork.

©O2E

Brian Scudamore was like many students. He was 18 years old and needed a job. So he bought a $700 truck and started Rubbish Boys, a junk removal business. He grew the business into a multi-million dollar empire, 1-800-GOT-JUNK?

Of course, an entrepreneur starting a new sole proprietorship must find a suitable site from which to operate the business. Some sole proprietors look no farther than their garage or a spare bedroom that they can convert into a workshop or office. Among the more famous businesses that sprang to life in their founders' homes are Shopify, Spin Master, Google, Apple, eBay, and Mattel.[1]

Computers, tablets, and smartphones, all powered by the Internet, have been a boon for small and home-based businesses, permitting entrepreneurs to interact quickly with customers, suppliers, and others. Many independent entrepreneurs can perform their work using a tablet computer or smartphone from their home or as they travel. Email and cell phones have made it possible for many proprietors to develop in the services area. Internet connections also allow small businesses to establish websites to promote their products and even to make low-cost long-distance phone calls with voice over Internet protocol (VOIP) technology such as Skype.

Amazon and eBay also provides small proprietors the opportunity to sell their goods online to millions of potential customers. Both Amazon and eBay take a percentage of the sales and provide entrepreneurs with a variety of online services. This opens up opportunities for small proprietors to compete with much larger competitors. For example, Yossef and Shoshana Vidal started selling cell phones on eBay in 2013. The married couple quickly expanded their business to include branded watches and handbags. To date their cumulative sales are in excess of $10 million.

**Secrecy.** Sole proprietorships allow for the greatest degree of secrecy. The proprietor, unlike the owners of a partnership or corporation, does not have to share his or her operating plans, minimizing the possibility that competitors can obtain trade secrets. Financial reports need not be disclosed, as do the financial reports of publicly owned corporations. For example, when David Reynolds of Halifax, Nova Scotia, founded his sole proprietorship, QuickSnap, selling a unique shoe-fastening device that was later featured on CBC's hit TV series *Dragons' Den*, he did not have to share information on how the product was constructed or his financial results with anyone.

**Distribution and Use of Profits.** All profits from a sole proprietorship belong exclusively to the owner. They do not have to share them with any partners or shareholders. The owner alone decides how the profits are used, which could include to expand the business, to increase salaries, or to find new customers.

**Flexibility and Control of the Business.** The sole proprietor has complete control over the business and can make decisions on the spot without anyone else's approval. This control allows the owner to respond quickly to competitive business conditions or to changes in the economy. Jim Pattison, one of Canada's most successful entrepreneurs and owner of the Pattison Group (www.jimpattison.com), a private corporation that is managed very much like a sole proprietorship, has frequently stated that his company has remained private as it allows him to make quick decisions that focus on the long term without having to answer to a board of directors or shareholders like publicly owned corporate operators.

**Government Regulation.** Sole proprietorships have the most freedom from government regulation. Many government regulations—federal, provincial, and local—apply only to businesses that have a certain number of employees, and securities laws apply only to corporations that issue shares. Nonetheless, sole proprietors must ensure that they follow all laws that do apply to their businesses.

**Taxation.** Profits from the business are considered personal income for the sole proprietor and are taxed at individual tax rates. The owner pays one income tax, but owners of sole proprietorships can deduct losses from their business from their total income. For example, if Bill, a high school teacher, starts a part-time business sealing driveways and loses $10,000 in his first year of operations, he can now deduct $10,000 from the $80,000 he makes as an educator and only pay tax on $70,000. Sole proprietors who work from their homes can also deduct expenses such as their home office from their business income.

> "Sole proprietorships have the most freedom from government regulation."

**Closing the Business.** A sole proprietorship can be dissolved easily. No approval of co-owners or partners is necessary. When Mary Drain of Sudbury, Ontario, closed her home-based craft business, she just told her friends and family she was closing. No other formal notice was required.

## Disadvantages of Sole Proprietorships

What is seen as an advantage by one person may turn out to be a disadvantage to another. The goals and talents of the individual owner are the deciding factors in determining the success of a sole proprietorship. For profitable businesses managed by capable owners, many of the following factors do not cause problems. On the other hand, proprietors starting out with little management experience and little money are likely to encounter many of the disadvantages.

**Unlimited Liability.** The sole proprietor has unlimited liability in meeting the debts of the business. In other words, if the business cannot pay its creditors, the owner may be forced to use personal, non-business holdings such as a car or a home to pay off the debts. Furthermore, the sole proprietor may also be legally responsible for any claims made against the business. For example, if a person walks into a retail store and slips, he or she will be able to personally sue the sole proprietor for the accident. The more wealth an individual has, the greater is the disadvantage of unlimited liability.

**Limited Sources of Funds.** Among the relatively few sources of money available to the sole proprietorship are banks, friends, family, some government programs, and/or his or her own funds. The owner's personal financial condition determines his or her credit standing. Additionally, sole proprietorships may have to pay higher interest rates on funds borrowed from banks than do large corporations because they are considered greater risks. Often, the only way a sole proprietor can borrow for business purposes is to pledge a house, other real estate, or other personal assets to guarantee the loan. If the business fails, the owner may lose the personal assets as well as the business. Publicly owned corporations, in contrast, not only can obtain funds from banks but can sell shares and bonds to the public to raise money. If a public company goes out of business, the owners do not lose personal assets.

**Limited Skills.** The sole proprietor must be able to perform many functions and possess skills in diverse fields such as management, marketing, finance, accounting, bookkeeping, and personnel, although business owners can rely on specialized professionals for advice and services, such as accountants and attorneys. Musicians, for example, can turn to agents for assistance in navigating the complex maze of the recording business. One start-up firm specializing in this type of assistance for online musicians and bands is the Digital Artists Agency, which researches, markets and cultivates online music talent in exchange for a commission on their online sales of music, tickets, and merchandise.[2] In the end, however, it is up to the owner to make the final decision in all areas of the business, and not everyone has the skills to be successful on their own.

> "The sole proprietor has unlimited liability in meeting the debts of the business."

**Lack of Continuity.** The life expectancy of a sole proprietorship is directly related to that of the owner and his or her ability to work. The serious illness of the owner could result in failure if competent help cannot be found.

It is difficult to arrange for the sale of a proprietorship and at the same time assure customers that the business will continue to meet their needs. For instance, how does one sell a veterinary practice? A veterinarian's major asset is patients. If the vet dies suddenly, the equipment can be sold, but the patients will not necessarily remain loyal to the office. On the other hand, a veterinarian who wants to retire could take in a younger partner and sell the practice to the partner over time.

**Taxation.** Although we listed taxation as an advantage for sole proprietorships, it can also be a disadvantage, depending on the proprietor's income. Under current tax rates, sole proprietors pay a higher marginal tax rate than do small corporations. This means sole proprietors may pay more in tax than small corporations.

# Partnerships

**LO 4-2** Identify three types of partnership, and evaluate the advantages and disadvantages of the partnership form of organization.

One way to minimize the disadvantages of a sole proprietorship and maximize its advantages is to have more than one owner. For example, publicly traded Spin Master toys was founded by three partners, Ronnen Harary, Anton Rabie, and Ben Varadi, all with complementary skill sets. The trio has successfully grown the business from a small home-based firm to a $5.3 billion dollar company with such hits as Paw Patrol and Hatchimals.

## Consider the Following: Microlending helps small entrepreneurs start businesses

Sending food and money to disadvantaged communities meets immediate needs, but ending long-term poverty is more difficult. Kiva.org is one business that seeks to tackle this problem head-on. Founded by Stanford University graduates with an interest in business and technology, Kiva was first designed to lend money to impoverished Ugandan entrepreneurs. It soon expanded its reach to include other developing countries. Kiva is a microfinance business, which means it provides small loans—as little as $25 for equipment, for example—to individuals to start their own businesses.

Kiva partners with microfinance institutions worldwide. These field partners approve entrepreneurs and send their profiles to Kiva. The entrepreneurs' profiles are then posted on Kiva's website, and people who want to lend to an entrepreneur send their loans through the site. Kiva's field partners distribute the loans, work with the entrepreneurs, and collect repayments.

Kiva.org does not earn returns on investments for lenders, but most of its partners who distribute the loans do charge interest rates in the range of 23 and 48 percent. These interest rates cover loan costs, transaction costs, defaults, and inflation rates—and are much lower than rates charged by informal lenders or predatory lenders who typically supply loans to those who do not qualify for bank loans. For example, Mukula, a female entrepreneur from India, borrowed $570 from a Kiva partner to purchase yarn to start a sewing business. She has grown the business to the point where she has two employees and hopes one day to save enough money to build a larger house.

Kiva and over 1.6 million lenders have succeeded in providing loans to over 2.6 million entrepreneurs since 2005. The company has loaned entrepreneurs a total of $1 billion since its inception, with an average loan of $412.84 and a repayment rate of roughly 97 percent. The buzz about Kiva is positive, and Kiva.org's future looks bright as microlending continues to receive favourable press.*

©Kiva

Kiva supports entrepreneurs in underdeveloped countries, providing entrepreneurs like Mukula an opportunity to access needed capital to start businesses leading to long term financial stability.

### DISCUSSION QUESTIONS

1. Kiva has been very successful at extending microlending to entrepreneurs in need. What about Kiva has helped make it so successful?
2. Given the strong repayment levels for Kiva borrowers do you think lending partners should be charging such high interest rates? Why or why not? Do you think Kiva lenders would be knowledgeable and supportive of such high interest rates?
3. What is unique about the way Kiva is organized that sets it apart from more traditional businesses?
4. Do you think the Kiva model of extending loans would work for larger loans, or even for other kinds of businesses?

*"Facts & History," Kiva, www.kiva.org/about/facts (accessed March 18, 2011); David M. Ewalt, "Low-Dose Capitalism," *Forbes*, November 2, 2009, p. 40; Leena Rao, "Kiva Brings Microlending Home to U.S. Entrepreneurs in Need," *TechCrunch*, June 10, 2009, www.techcrunch.com/2009/06/10/kiva-brings-microlending-home-tous-entrepreneurs-in-need (accessed December 19, 2009); Peter Greer and Phil Smith, *The Poor Will Be Glad* (Grand Rapids, MI: Zondervan, 2009), pp. 99, 107.

Harary, considered to be the quintessential entrepreneur with an interest in creativity and start-ups, works mainly in the entertainment aspect of the business. Rabie, who is interested in long term growth and financials, works in acquisitions. Varadi deals with product development and innovation. Chris Harrs, executive vice-president and general counsel for Spin Master describes the partnership as the perfect three-headed monster with each head complementing the others. Harrs notes that the business would likely have not reached its level of success without all of the three partners participating in the management of the firm.

Hand-out/TMX Group Limited/Newscom

Spin Master Toys grew from a partnership between Ronnen Harary, Anton Rabie, and Ben Varadi to a private corporation, then to a publicly traded toy giant.

©tentree

Apparel company tentree was founded by Kalen Emsley and David Luba, who shared a passion for giving back to the environment they love.

Other partnerships are formed because people share a passion for the same type of business or hobby. For example, Kalen Emsley and David Luba loved being outdoors and interacting with the environment and were passionate about giving back to nature. While visiting Hawaii, the pair came up with the idea of forming an apparel company that would plant ten trees for every piece of clothing they sold. Based on this simple concept, their company, tentree, was formed.

Today tentree sells men's and women's apparel in specialty shops and online, and has planted over 25 million trees in countries such as Madagascar, Senegal, Nepal, and Haiti. The trees not only help the ecosystem but can provide food and jobs in countries that badly need both. The environmentally friendly company, which uses organic cotton and partners with manufacturers who pay employees a fair wage, hopes to plant one billion trees by 2030.

In Canada, partnerships are formed when two or more people fill out simple forms registering their business with their provincial government. In Ontario, for example, the partnership would then be governed by the *Partnership Act* (see Table 4.2), which outlines the rights and duties of partners toward one another. The rules of the *Partnership Act* apply unless the partners have signed a *partnership agreement*. A **partnership** can be defined as an association of two or more persons who carry on as co-owners of a business for profit. Partnerships are the least-used form of business organization in Canada. They are typically larger than sole proprietorships but smaller than corporations.

**partnership** a form of business organization defined as an association of two or more persons who carry on as co-owners of a business for profit

## Types of Partnerships

There are three basic types of partnership: general partnership, limited partnership, and a limited liability partnership. A **general partnership** involves a complete sharing in the management of a business. In a general partnership, each partner has unlimited liability for the debts of the business. For example, Cirque du Soleil grew from a group of Quebec street performers, who acted as partners, into a half-billion dollar global company.[3] Professionals such as lawyers,

**general partnership** a partnership that involves a complete sharing in both the management and the liabilities of the business

**Table 4.2** | The Ontario *Partnership Act*

The following rules can be found in the Ontario *Partnership Act*, which is similar to those of other provinces:

- All partners are entitled to share equally in the capital and profits of the business and must contribute equally toward the losses, whether of capital or otherwise, sustained by the firm.
- All money or property brought into or acquired by the partnership becomes partnership property.
- No partner should be entitled to remuneration for acting in the partnership of the business.
- No person may be introduced as a partner without the consent of existing partners.

## ENTREPRENEURSHIP IN ACTION

### Business Ownership—An Ever-Changing Structure Story

**Quicksnap**

**Founder:** David Reynolds

**Founded:** 2003

**Success:** After Reynolds' appearance on season three of *Dragons' Den*, sales rose more than twofold, with online orders originating from as far away as Australia and New Zealand.

When David Reynolds of Halifax, Nova Scotia, started university he was, like most students, unsure about what he wanted to do with his life. Reynolds notes, "I had no idea why I was even enrolled in university other than it was what everyone does." Shortly after attending a lecture on entrepreneurship, Reynolds became enthralled with the idea of starting his own company, saying, "I loved the idea of being my own boss, thoughts of getting rich with something I created."

Reynolds searched for an idea and found one when he was getting tired of waiting for his friend to tie his shoes. Reynolds states, "People hate tying their shoes. What if they didn't have to do this? What if there was a way to clip the laces together?" A short time later, QuickSnap, a shoe-fastening device, was born. When the company first started, it was structured as a sole proprietorship; as Reynolds quips, "It was just me and my idea." A short time later, Reynolds realized he needed some help managing his business as well as some extra funding, and recruited two friends to join his company. Thus, the sole proprietor became a partner.

©David Reynolds

Young entrepreneur David Reynolds established QuickSnap while growing tired of watching his friend try to tie his shoes.

Reynolds says that forming a partnership was cheaper and easier than forming a corporation. "We drafted a partnership agreement, we all signed it, and we became partners." Like most start-ups, the business eventually needed more funding, and Reynolds found himself looking for outside investors. Reynolds notes, "At this time I knew that we needed a formal structure and the business went through the process of incorporating. We needed the advantages of a private corporation, we needed to be able to issue shares to investors, ensure that everyone involved in the ownership group had limited liability and so forth."

The product was later sold nationally in various stores. Reynolds was no longer CEO, but still owned shares in the business that he founded as a 19-year-old with an idea he had while watching his friend struggle to tie his shoes.*

*Daryl-Lynn Carlson, "QuickSnap Invention Clicks..." *Financial Post,* December 11, 2008, http://www.financialpost.com/story.html?id=1067682 (accessed September 13, 2010).

accountants, and architects often join together in general partnerships.

A **limited partnership** has at least one general partner, who assumes unlimited liability, and at least one limited partner, whose liability is limited to their investment in the business. Limited partnerships exist for risky investment projects where the chance of loss is great. The general partners accept the risk of loss; the limited partners' losses are limited to their

**limited partnership** a business organization that has at least one general partner, who assumes unlimited liability, and at least one limited partner, whose liability is limited to his or her investment in the business

©Nathan King/Alamy Stock Photo

Cirque du Soleil started with a small partnership between Quebec street performers and has grown into a global company with millions in sales.

initial investment. Limited partners do not participate in the management of the business, but share in the profits in accordance with the terms of a partnership agreement. Usually the general partner receives a larger share of the profits after the limited partners have received their initial investment back. Popular examples are oil-drilling partnerships and real estate partnerships. A **limited liability partnership (LLP)** is a unique partnership agreement where non-negligent partners are not personally responsible for losses created by other partners. This type of partnership is available only in some provinces and is popular among legal and accounting firms.

**limited liability partnership (LLP)** a partnership agreement where partners are not responsible for losses created by other partners

## Partnership Agreement

A **partnership agreement** is a legal document that sets forth the basic agreement between partners. Unless partners sign a partnership agreement, their partnership will be bound by the rules outlined in their provincial partnership act. While not legally required, it makes good sense for partners to sign and follow such an agreement. Partnership agreements usually list the money or assets that each partner has contributed (called *partnership capital*), state each partner's management role or duty, specify how the profits and losses of the partnership will be divided among the partners, and describe how a partner may leave the partnership, as well as any other restrictions that might apply to the agreement. Table 4.3 lists some of the issues and provisions that should be included in articles of partnership.

**partnership agreement** document that sets forth the basic agreement between partners

## Advantages of Partnerships

Law firms, accounting firms, and investment firms with several hundred partners have partnership agreements that are quite complicated in comparison with the partnership agreement among two or three people owning a computer repair shop. The advantages must be compared with those offered by other forms of business organization, and not all apply to every partnership.

**Ease of Organization.** Starting a partnership requires little more than filling out some basic forms with the provincial government including the registration of the business's name. While a partnership agreement is highly recommended, it is not required as each provincial partnership act provides rules for the

**Table 4.3** | Issues and Provisions in Articles of Partnership

1. Name, purpose, location
2. Duration of the agreement
3. Authority and responsibility of each partner
4. Character of partners (i.e., general or limited, active or silent)
5. Amount of contribution from each partner
6. Division of profits or losses
7. Salaries of each partner
8. How much each partner is allowed to withdraw
9. Death of partner
10. Sale of partnership interest
11. Arbitration of disputes
12. Required and prohibited actions
13. Absence and disability
14. Restrictive covenants
15. Buying and selling agreements

business to follow. As evident in the Entrepreneurship in Action box above, forming a partnership is relatively simple.

**Combined Knowledge and Skills.** Successful partners acknowledge each other's talents and avoid confusion and conflict by specializing in a particular area of expertise such as marketing, production, accounting, or service. The diversity of skills in a partnership makes it possible for the business to be run by a management team of specialists instead of by a generalist sole proprietor. For example, Brian Scudamore founder of 1-800-Got-Junk, brought Erik Church in as partner. Scudamore notes he was good at creating a vision but needed someone to help with the execution, "I'm the visionary, the culture guy. He's (Erik) the rigour, the discipline, the execution. And he's able to take ideas and translate them into execution."

Tracey Bochner, co-owner of Paradigm Public Relations, a Toronto-based PR firm, states that a good partnership enables you to achieve more than you could on your own. Boucher says, "In my experience, if you share, the net result can be so much better than what you can achieve alone." She states partners can help you become better problem solvers and prevent you from making stupid mistakes.[4] Service-oriented partnerships in fields such as law, financial planning, and accounting may attract customers because clients think that the service offered by a diverse team is of higher quality than that provided by one person. Larger law firms, for example, often have individual partners who specialize in certain areas of the law—such as family, bankruptcy, corporate, entertainment, and criminal law.

"When a business has several partners, it has the benefit of a combination of talents."

**Availability of Capital and Credit.** When a business has several partners, it has the benefit of a combination of talents and skills and pooled financial resources. The pooling of financial resources is particularly attractive to new firms as they are heavily dependent on the personal investment of the owner for start-up financing. As will be discussed in Chapter 5, personal investment of the owner is responsible for 66 percent of the money raised by new ventures. Partnerships tend to be larger than sole proprietorships and therefore have greater earning power and better credit ratings.

**Decision Making.** Small partnerships can react more quickly to changes in the business environment than can large partnerships and corporations. Such fast reactions are possible because the partners are often involved in day-to-day operations and can make decisions quickly after consultation. Examples of this quick decision making can often be seen by partners on CBC's *Dragons' Den* or ABC's *Shark Tank,* where entrepreneurs are looking to raise money for a fledging business or idea. Often partners are given very little time to make decisions about selling a percentage of their business for much-needed capital.

This was the situation in which the owners of Ellebox, Jessica Bilmer, and Bunny and Taran Ghatrora, found themselves on *Dragons' Den* when Joe Mimran offered them $25,000 for 15 percent of their business. The trio quickly accepted the offer from the Mimran as the capital was needed to help them expand their monthly home delivery of environmentally friendly feminine hygiene products throughout North America. The entrepreneurs have since

©Brett Gundlock

Tracey Bochner, co-owner of Paradigm Public Relations, pictured here with her partner, Michael Abbass, states that a good partner will help you solve problems and keep you from making stupid mistakes.

©Ellebox

Ellebox's partners, Jessica Bilmer, and Bunny and Taran Ghatrora, were able to make a quick decision on CBC's *Dragons' Den* to accept an offer for 15 percent of their business. If they had been in a corporation with multiple shareholders they might have had to consult with various other stakeholders.

renamed the company Blume and are passionate about delivering both products and education to their customers.

**Regulatory Controls.** Like a sole proprietorship, a partnership has fewer regulatory controls affecting its activities than does a corporation. A partnership does, however, have to abide by all laws relevant to the industry or profession in which it operates, as well as provincial and federal laws relating to hiring and firing, food handling, and so on, just as the sole proprietorship does.

## Disadvantages of Partnerships

Partnerships have many advantages compared to sole proprietorships and corporations, but they also have some disadvantages. Limited partners have no voice in the management of the partnership, and they may bear most of the risk of the business while the general partner reaps a larger share of the benefits. There may be a change in the goals and objectives of one partner but not the other, particularly when the partners are multinational organizations. This can cause friction, giving rise to an enterprise that fails to satisfy both parties or even forcing an end to the partnership.

Many partnership disputes wind up in court or require outside mediation. For example, a quarrel among the partners who owned the Montreal Expos baseball team moved to U.S. District Court after new general partner Jeffrey Loria moved the team to Florida and renamed it the Florida Marlins. Twelve of the team's limited partners sued Loria, accusing him of buying the Expos with the intent of moving the team, diluting their share in the team, and effectively destroying "the economic viability of baseball in Montreal."[5] While the Expos are long since gone from Montreal, a new partnership group led by Mitch Garber and fellow billionaire Stephen Bronfman are working together to return Major League Baseball to Montreal.

Major disadvantages of partnerships include the following.

**Disagreements Among Partners.** A partnership is similar to any relationship including a close friendship or a marriage. Partners often work together on a daily basis and disagreements are inevitable. Smaller firms are more likely to suffer from such disagreements as their size often prevents a clear distinction of duties that can be found in larger partnerships. Often disagreements are minor and they can be successfully managed or resolved.

For example, Babak Barkhodaei and his brother Arash started SkyPrep, an online training company. The pair split the duties, with Babak focusing on sales and Arash on product development. While it seemed like the perfect match, Babak admits the partnership was far from perfect as he was so focused on sales he often failed to consider if Arash could actually develop the finished product. Babak says, "We had so many conflicts. I was thinking about growing the business, so any time a person wanted a feature, I would say to Arash, 'do it, do it.' I was focused on getting business and didn't consider the complexity of the solution. At one point, Arash just got really fed up." Rather than end the partnership, the pair brought in another partner, their brother Sepand, who understood their points of view and implemented a conflict resolution system.[6]

Sometimes disputes can go much further and actually spell the end of a partnership, a friendship, and a business. This is what happened to the highly successful partnership of Michel Boucher and Chuck Buchanan. The pair operated Flightexec, a company based in London, Ontario, that went from bankruptcy to $20 million in annual sales in 10 years. But when the two partners differed over the long-term strategy for the company, it ended the partnership, and Buchanan was forced to leave the business.

Partnership disputes can occur in large companies, as well. One of the most talked-about disputes in Canadian business history was the succession battle at the multi-billion dollar McCain Foods frozen food empire. Harrison and Wallace McCain co-managed the business for years with Harrison looking after sales and growth and his brother Wallace dealing with managing the manufacturing facilities. When the pair started to look for a successor, Wallace was insistent that his son Michael receive the job while Harrison objected to the idea. The succession battle ended with Harrison removing Wallace as his co-CEO, the brothers' relationship in tatters, and Wallace buying a large interest in Maple Leaf Foods where his son Michael was eventually named CEO. Table 4.4 lists some suggestions for building a successful partnership.

**Unlimited Liability.** In general partnerships, the general partners have unlimited liability for the debts incurred by the business, just as the sole proprietor has unlimited liability for their business. Such unlimited liability can be a distinct disadvantage to one partner if their personal financial resources are greater than those of the others. A potential partner should make sure that all partners have

**Table 4.4** | Keys to Success in Business Partnerships

1. Keep profit sharing and ownership at 50/50, or you have an employer/employee relationship.
2. Ensure partners have different skill sets to complement one another.
3. Be scrupulously honest with each other.
4. Maintain face-to-face communication in addition to phone and email.
5. Maintain transparency, sharing more information over time.
6. Be aware of funding constraints and do not put yourself in a situation where neither you nor your partner can secure additional financial support.
7. Seek the crucial business experience you need to be successful.
8. While family should be a priority in partnerships involving relatives, be careful to minimize the number of associated problems.
9. Do not become too infatuated with "the idea" as opposed to its implementation.
10. Couple optimism with realism in sales and growth expectations and planning.

©Stavros Rougas

Brothers Babak, Arash, and Sepand Barkhodaei, partners in the online training company SkyPrep, admit their initial partnership suffered from a lot of disagreements before they implemented a conflict management system.

comparable resources to help the business in times of trouble. This disadvantage is eliminated for limited partners, who can lose only their initial investment.

**Business Responsibility.** All partners are responsible for the business actions of all others. Partners may have the ability to commit the partnership to a contract without approval of the other partners, and a bad decision by one partner may put the other partners' personal resources in jeopardy. Personal problems, such as divorce, can eliminate a significant portion of one partner's financial resources and weaken the financial structure of the whole partnership.

**Life of the Partnership.** A partnership is terminated when a partner dies or withdraws. In a two-person partnership, if one partner withdraws, the firm's liabilities would be paid off and the assets divided between the partners. Obviously, the partner who wishes to continue in the business would be at a serious disadvantage. The business could be disrupted, access to financing would be reduced, and the management skills of the departing partner would be lost. The remaining partner would have to find another partner or reorganize the business as a sole proprietorship. In very large partnerships, such as those found in law firms and investment banks, the continuation of the partnership may be provided for in the articles of partnership. The provision may simply state the terms for a new partnership agreement among the remaining partners. In such cases, the disadvantage to the other partners is minimal.

> "All partners are responsible for the business actions of all others."

Selling a partnership interest has the same effect as the death or withdrawal of a partner. It is difficult to place a value on a partner's share of the partnership. No public value is placed on the partnership, as there is on publicly owned corporations. What is a law firm worth? What is the local hardware store worth? Coming up with a fair value to which all partners can agree is not easy. For example, in the McCain partnership dispute discussed above, Wallace maintained 35 percent ownership in the business even after being fired as co-CEO because he could not sell his stake in the company. No buyer wanted to purchase his minority stake, and he and his brother Harrison could never agree on a price for the shares.[7]

Selling a partnership interest is easier if the articles of partnership specify a method of valuation. Even if there is not a procedure for selling one partner's interest, the old partnership must still be dissolved and a new one created. In contrast, in the corporate form of business, the departure of owners has little effect on the financial resources of the business, and the loss of managers does not cause long-term changes in the structure of the organization.

**Distribution of Profits.** Profits earned by the partnership are distributed to the partners in the proportions specified in the articles of partnership. This may be a disadvantage if the division of the profits does not reflect the work each partner puts into the business. You may have encountered this disadvantage while working on a student group project: you may have felt that you did most of the work and that the other students in the group received grades based on your efforts. Even the perception of an unfair profit-sharing agreement may cause tension between the partners, and unhappy partners can have a negative effect on the profitability of the business.

**Limited Sources of Funds.** As with a sole proprietorship, the sources of funds available to a partnership are limited. Because no public value is placed on the business (such as the current trading price of a corporation's shares), potential partners do not know what one partnership share is worth. Moreover, because partnership shares cannot be bought and sold easily in public markets, potential owners may not want to tie up their money in assets that cannot be readily sold on short notice, as is evident in the McCain dispute. Accumulating enough funds to operate a national business, especially a business requiring intensive investments in facilities and equipment, can be difficult. Partnerships also may have to pay higher interest rates on funds borrowed from banks than do large corporations because partnerships may be considered greater risks.

## Taxation of Partnerships

Partnerships do not pay taxes when submitting the partnership tax return to the Canada Revenue Agency. Partners must report their share of profits on their individual tax returns and pay taxes at the income tax rate for individuals. Much like sole proprietors, partners can apply losses from their partnership against other sources of income, but often pay more in taxes compared to corporations due to their tax rate.

## RESPONDING TO BUSINESS CHALLENGES

### Should Partners Have a Shotgun?

"Should partners have a shotgun?" Perhaps the question makes you think of the Old West or organized crime movies, but the term *shotgun* has a very different meaning in partnership agreements.

Essentially the term is used to describe a clause where one business partner can make a cash offer for the other partner's share of the business. The person being offered the money for their share of the business is usually left with only two choices: (1) Accept the offer and take the money, or (2) match the partner's offer and assume the partner's share of the business.

People's opinions of shotgun clauses in partnerships differ. Some argue that they are useful tools, which allow for a quick end to a partnership that is no longer working. Furthermore, the cash offer is usually at a premium as the person making the offer risks getting removed from the business if they make a low offer. Others argue that shotgun clauses are often used too quickly when other dispute resolutions could be used to save partnerships, and that shotguns favour the partner with the most resources.

Joyce Groote, owner of Vancouver-based Holey Soles, did not start the business that she currently runs with her husband. Groote, who was very successful in the pharmaceutical industry, was asked to join the company to offer the founders managerial assistance. Groote eventually invested some cash in the business and ultimately exercised a shotgun clause to oust the founding partners. Groote noted that while her partners were good at starting a company, they were often too slow at making decisions, which negatively impacted growth.

The use of shotgun clauses is not limited to small business, as evident in the case of Tim Hortons and its partner, the Swiss specialist bakery conglomerate Aryzta AG. Tim Hortons and Aryzta AG had formed a partnership whereby the companies jointly owned a baking facility in Brantford, Ontario, that supplied all of the Tim Hortons stores with baked goods. Unexpectedly, the Swiss firm exercised a shotgun clause, forcing Tim Hortons to either pay a substantial amount of money for a key production facility that is essential to its operation or allow Aryzta AG to assume control of an essential part of Tim Hortons' business. Tim Hortons eventually accepted the $475 million offer after Aryzta agreed to continue to supply product to the company until 2016.*

©Tom Wang/Shutterstock

Shotgun clauses allow partners to quickly end their partnership and settle disagreements within a specified time frame.

#### DISCUSSION QUESTIONS

1. If you were ever to join a partnership, would you want to have a shotgun clause?
2. What are some of the advantages and disadvantages of a shotgun clause?
3. What alternatives would you suggest to using a shotgun clause?
4. Would exercising the shotgun clause negatively impact Aryzta AG's ability to form partnerships in the future? Why or why not?

*Dawn Calleja, "How Tim Hortons will take over the world," *Globe and Mail,* September 23, 2010, http://www.theglobeandmail.com/report-on-business/rob-magazine/how-tim-hortons-will-take-over-the-world/article1718843/singlepage/

# Corporations

**LO 4-3** Describe the corporate form of organization, and cite the advantages and disadvantages of corporations.

When you think of a business, you probably think of a huge corporation such as Royal Bank, Amazon, or Shoppers Drug Mart because most of your consumer dollars go to such corporations. A **corporation** is a legal entity, created under law either provincially or federally, whose assets and liabilities are separate from those of its owners. As a legal entity, a corporation has many of the rights, duties, and powers of a person, such as the right

**corporation** a legal entity, whose assets and liabilities are separate from those of its owners

to receive, own, and transfer property. Corporations can enter into contracts with individuals or with other legal entities, and they can sue and be sued in court.

Corporations account for the majority of Canadian sales and employment. Thus, most of the dollars you spend as a consumer probably go to incorporated businesses (see Table 4.5 for the largest corporations in Canada). Not all corporations are mega-companies like Enbridge or Manulife; even small businesses can incorporate and share in many of the advantages of being an incorporated company. In fact, as a business grows, it is normal for its legal ownership structure to change. As discussed above, many business start as a sole proprietorship or a partnership, but as sales climb and the firm and its owner takes on more liability risk, it is considered routine for entrepreneurs and/or managers to incorporate their business. *Globe and Mail* business columnist Chris Griffiths sums up this sentiment when he writes, "For most businesses, the question is not if, but when, to incorporate."[8]

Corporations are typically owned by individuals and organizations who own **shares** of the business sometimes referred to as stocks (thus, corporate owners are often called *shareholders* or *stockholders*). Shareholders can buy, sell, give or receive as gifts, or inherit their shares of stock. As owners, the shareholders are entitled to all profits that are left after all the corporation's other obligations have been paid. These profits may be distributed in the form of cash payments called **dividends**. For example, if a corporation earns $100 million after expenses and taxes and decides to pay the owners $40 million in dividends, the shareholders receive 40 percent of the profits in cash dividends. However, not all after-tax profits are paid to shareholders in dividends. In this example, the corporation retained $60 million of profits to finance expansion.

**shares** units of ownership of a corporation that may be bought or sold

**dividends** profits of a corporation that are distributed in the form of cash payments to shareholders

**Table 4.5** | Market Cap: Top 10 Snapshot

The largest corporations in Canada by market cap from largest to smallest are as follows.[9] Since the information in this table can change quickly, students may want to use Internet resources to see what companies have moved up or down the list.

| |
|---|
| Royal Bank of Canada |
| Toronto-Dominion Bank |
| Canada National Railway |
| Bank of Nova Scotia (Scotiabank) |
| Enbridge |
| Suncor |
| Bank of Montreal |
| Canada Natural Resources Limited |
| CIBC |
| BCE |

©brystock/Alamy Stock Photo

Canadian banks consistently rank as some of the largest and most profitable companies in Canada.

## Creating a Corporation

A corporation is created, or incorporated, under the laws of the provincial or federal government. A business that is incorporated provincially does so under its provincial corporations legislation and can conduct business only in the province in which it is incorporated. Businesses that are incorporated federally do so under the *Canada Business Corporations Act* and can conduct business in all provinces and territories provided that they register their corporation in all the provinces where they carry on business. The main advantages of incorporating federally are the ability to operate anywhere in Canada and to use the same company name. Federal corporations do cost more to start than provincial corporations and have extra paperwork, including filings required by the federal Directors of Corporations Branch and all the filings required by the provinces.

The individuals creating the corporation are known as *incorporators*. Each provincial government and the federal government have specific procedures, sometimes called *chartering the corporation*, for incorporating a business. The first step is often choosing the name of the company, which must have the following:

- Distinctive portion to identify the business
- Descriptive portion that assists in identifying the activities of the company
- Legal element that identifies the business as a corporation, including Limited, Incorporated, or Corporation

After a name is chosen, a search is conducted to determine if the name is original and suitable.

The incorporators must then file legal documents including the *Memorandum*, which lays out the rules for the company's conduct; the *Articles of Incorporation*, which are the rules and regulations that the company's members and directors must follow; and the *Notice of Officers*, which states the location of the required offices for the company—the registered office and the records office. Corporations that are incorporating under federal law must also prepare a *Notice of Directors* with the appropriate provincial or federal government. The following information is necessary when filing for a corporation:

- Name and address of the corporation
- Address for the Registered and Records Office
- Description of the classes of shares and the maximum number of shares that will be issued, as well as a clear description of the rights, privileges, and restrictions for each class of share
- Restrictions on share transfers, which must specify whether shares can be sold or transferred
- Number of directors
- Restrictions on the company's business activities
- Other provisions (While there is no requirement to include this, some incorporators do so to satisfy requirements from other provinces or regulatory agencies.)

Based on the information in the articles of incorporation, the provincial or federal government approves the corporation by issuing a **certificate of incorporation**. After securing approval, the owners hold an organizational meeting at which they establish the corporation's bylaws and elect a board of directors. The bylaws might set up committees of the board of directors and describe the rules and procedures for their operation.

**certificate of incorporation**
a legal document that the provincial or federal government issues to a company based on information the company provides in the articles of incorporation

## Types of Corporations

A corporation may be privately or publicly owned. A **private corporation** is owned by just one or a few people who are closely involved in managing the business. These people, sometimes a family, own the majority if not all of the corporation's shares, and shares are not sold on any of the public stock exchanges. Shares in private corporations can be sold but the details of the transactions usually remain private. Many corporations are quite large, yet remain private, including the Irving Group of New Brunswick. Irving is one of the largest and most diversified companies in Canada with interests in shipbuilding, newspapers, tissue paper, transportation, and oil and gas, yet it remains a large private corporation. Privately owned corporations are not required to disclose financial information publicly, but they must, of course, pay taxes.

**private corporation**
a corporation owned by just one or a few people who are closely involved in managing the business

"A corporation may be privately or publicly owned."

A **public corporation** is one whose shares anyone may buy, sell, or trade on the Toronto Stock Exchange (www.tmx.com) or another public stock exchange. In large public corporations, such as the Royal Bank, the shareholders are often far removed from the management of the company. In other public corporations, the managers are often the founders and the majority shareholders. For example, the late Ted Rogers, founder of Rogers Communications, ran Rogers Communications right up until the time of his death. Other Canadian companies that were or still are controlled by their founders include Magna International (Frank Stronach), Power Corporation of Canada (the late Paul Desmarais), and Onex Corporation (Gerald Schwartz). Publicly owned corporations must disclose financial information to the public under specific laws that regulate the trade of stocks and other securities.

**public corporation**
a corporation whose shares anyone may buy, sell, or trade

©Kobby Dagan/Shutterstock

Facebook CEO Mark Zuckerberg saw the company's share price fall shortly after taking the company public. The share price has recovered and risen sharply as Facebook has managed to increase its revenue by increasing sales of advertising.

"Privately owned corporations are not required to disclose financial information publicly, but they must, of course, pay taxes."

A private corporation sometimes goes public to obtain more financing through the sale of shares, to allow the founders of the company to realize the value of the business, to raise money to pay off debt, to invest the proceeds in the firm, or to enhance the company's ability to raise capital in the future. A company goes public through an **initial public offering (IPO)**, that is, becoming a public corporation by selling its shares so that it can be traded in public markets. For example, Canada Goose went public both in the United States and Canada in 2017 and raised $255 million U.S.

**initial public offering (IPO)** selling a corporation's shares on public markets for the first time

The company intends to use the money to fund further product expansion aimed at diversifying their product line, which is heavily dependent on outerwear. Investors were quick to buy Canada Goose shares as they soared in value on the first day of the IPO climbing 25 percent in one day. Since then the IPO shares in the company have continued to climb from the initial IPO price of US$16 to a high of US$72 in 2018.

Roots, another Canadian company, also went public in 2018, raising $200 million dollars. The clothing company, which operates 120 retail stores in North America and another 136 in Taiwan and China, intends to use the money to open up additional locations. Unfortunately for investors, the share price for Roots plummeted after its IPO, which opened at $12 and closed roughly 20 percent lower on day one. The stock has been in a downward spiral ever since, reaching a low of $3.92 in 2018.

Canada has also seen a surge of IPOs in the cannabis industry since 2015 with numerous companies going public. In anticipation of recreational cannabis becoming legal, over 20 companies have gone public in recent years including ten in a two-month period from May 2018 to August 2018. Tilray, a British Columbia producer of cannabis, made history in 2018 when they become the first cannabis company to raise money through an IPO on an American stock exchange. Tilray, which trades under the stock market symbol TLRY, opened on the Nasdaq at $17 a share and has seen its shares soar since its IPO and trade consistently over $100. Cannabis shares, including IPOs, have been very volatile and it will be interesting to see where the shares are trading in the coming years.

Sometimes, privately owned firms are forced to go public with share offerings when a majority owner dies and the company's family members cannot decide on how best to manage the company or settle a large tax bill due as a result of the owner's death. The Irving Group discussed above has a long history of being a "very private" corporation—meaning very little information about the company has ever been shared with the outside world. The family-owned business is currently controlled by the three sons of founder K.C. Irving, but they are apparently considering

©Rubens Alarcon/Alamy Stock Photo

©Jerome Cid/Alamy Stock Photo

Roots and Canada Goose both filed IPOs in recent years. While investors in Canada Goose were rewarded with sizeable returns, investors in Roots saw their investment value quickly dwindle from an IPO price of $12 to a low of $3.92.

©Stefan Malloch/Shutterstock

Canadian cannabis producer Tilray became the first company to raise money in the United States with its IPO on the Nasdaq.

taking the company public in order to assist in long-term planning for the business and to ensure that all family members are properly compensated. Another example occurred at Adolph Coors Inc. When brewer Adolph Coors died, his business went public and his family sold shares of stock to the public to pay the estate taxes.

When students see the letters IPO, they may recall media stories describing the large amounts of money investors were willing to pay for the initial public offerings of companies such as Google, Facebook, Spin Master Toys, Tilray, or Canada Goose. But these figures are not always the norm. In fact, sometimes the money raised is not as significant as you might imagine, and often the companies are not well known. Listed below are some of the companies that completed IPOs in Canada between 2013 and 2018.[10] How many of these have you heard of? Consider using the Internet to find out how much money their IPOs raised and what they did with the proceeds.

- Canada Goose
- Spin Master Toys
- Shopify
- Tilray
- Roots
- Cronos Group
- Inner Spirit Holding Limited
- 48North Cannabis Corp

On the other hand, public corporations can be "taken private" when one or a few individuals (perhaps the management of the firm) purchase all the firm's shares so that it can no longer be sold publicly. For example, the founder and CEO of Hollywood Video, Mark Wattles, took the video rental chain private in 2004 by buying up all the shares for $14 each.[11]

Taking a corporation private may be desirable when new owners want to exert more control over the firm, or when they want to avoid the necessity of public disclosure of future activities for competitive reasons. For example, Frank Stronach opted to privatize two Canadian auto component manufacturing companies he owns, Intier and Decoma, to avoid the increased scrutiny public companies are now facing in North America. Taking a corporation private is also one technique for avoiding a takeover by another corporation.

Two other types of corporations are Crown corporations and non-profit corporations. **Crown corporations**, such as Canada Post, are owned by the provincial or federal government and focus on providing a service to citizens, such as mail delivery, rather than earning a profit. Examples of federal Crown corporations include the Royal Canadian Mint and Via Rail Canada Inc.

**Crown corporations** corporations owned and operated by government (federal or provincial)

©Blend Images/Ariel Skelley/Getty Images

Habitat for Humanity is a non-profit, non-denominational Christian housing organization that builds simple, decent, and affordable houses in partnership with those who lack adequate shelter. Chosen families work alongside volunteers to build their own home.

Provincial examples often include providers of electricity such as BC Hydro, lottery corporations, and liquor boards, such as the LCBO in Ontario.

Like Crown corporations, **non-profit corporations** focus on providing a service rather than earning a profit, but they are not owned by a government entity. Organizations such as the Children's Wish Foundation, the United Way, the Canadian Cancer Society, museums, and private schools provide services without a profit motive. To fund their operations and services, non-profit organizations sometimes charge for their services (private schools), solicit donations from individuals and companies, and apply for grants from the government and other charitable foundations.

**non-profit corporations** corporations that focus on providing a service rather than earning a profit but are not owned by a government entity

## Elements of a Corporation

**The Board of Directors.** A **board of directors**, elected by the shareholders to oversee the general operation of the corporation, sets the long-range objectives of the corporation. It is the board's responsibility to ensure that the objectives are achieved on schedule. Board members are legally liable for the mismanagement of the firm or for any misuse of funds.

**board of directors** a group of individuals, elected by the shareholders to oversee the general operation of the corporation, who set the corporation's long-range objectives

An important duty of the board of directors is to hire corporate officers, such as the president and the chief executive officer (CEO), who are responsible to the directors for the management and daily operations of the firm. The role and expectations of the board of directors took on greater significance after the accounting scandals of the early 2000s and the passage of much tougher regulations in Canada by the provincial regulatory boards and the *Sarbanes-Oxley Act* in the United States.[12] As a result, the duties and the workload of board members has increased substantially along with their accountability.

Allen Shaw, chairman of the Shaw Group and a director at the Bank of Nova Scotia, says, "Fifteen years ago, it wouldn't have been unusual for very little paper to be sent out before a meeting. Directors could prepare for lots of meetings in an hour. Today it is not unusual to spend a day or more reading documents and studying financial statements while preparing for board meetings."[13]

An example of this increased accountability and scrutiny occurred when former Newfoundland premier Brian Tobin recruited Kevin O'Leary, a well-known TV personality and investor, along with former Ontario premier Mike Harris, Nova Scotia seafood king John Risley, and Toronto governance expert Timothy Rowley, to serve on the board at Environmental Management Solutions Inc. (EMS), today known as EnGlobe Corp. Tobin had agreed to assist then-CEO Frank D'Addario in building a board and quickly assembled what many would consider an all-star team of directors. The public reacted strongly to the move and the company's shares soared.

Unfortunately, the new directors quickly learned about what they characterized as financial misdeeds by D'Addario and were forced to fire him from his post. Some of the new board members considered leaving the company due to the financial mess they inherited, but after hearing from their lawyers that they could be held responsible for the mismanagement of the company, the board stayed on and dealt with the company's problems.

Directors can be employees of the company (*inside directors*) or people unaffiliated with the company (*outside directors*). Inside directors are usually the officers responsible for running the company. For example, when Frank Stronach of Magna sat on its board of directors and acted as CEO, he would have been considered an inside director. Outside directors are often top executives from other companies, lawyers, bankers, or even professors. Directors today are increasingly chosen for their expertise, competence, and ability to bring diverse perspectives to strategic discussions.

Outside directors are also thought to bring more independence to the monitoring function because they are not bound by past allegiances, friendships, a current role in the company, or some other issue that may create a conflict of interest. Many of the corporate scandals uncovered in recent years might have been prevented if each of the companies' boards of directors had been better qualified, more knowledgeable, and more independent.

A survey by *USA Today* found that corporate boards have considerable overlap. More than 1000 corporate board members sit on four or more company boards, and of the nearly 2000 boards of directors, more than 22,000 board members are linked to boards of more than one company.[14] According to Phil Purcell, CEO of Morgan Stanley, "Some director overlap is inevitable when shareholders demand the highest-calibre directors for their board."[15] This overlap creates the opportunity for conflicts of interest in decision making and limits the independence of individual boards of directors. For example, the telecommunications firm Verizon, which shares four board members with prescription-drug producer Wyeth, withdrew from the non-profit organization Business for Affordable Medicine, which had been criticized by Wyeth because of its stance on bringing generic drugs to market sooner.[16]

©Thomas Barwick/Getty Images

After the accounting scandals of the early 2000s and the passage of much tougher regulations, directors on public corporations' boards are expected to be more involved in the running of the company and highly scrutinize management decisions.

**Share Ownership.** Corporations issue two types of shares: preferred and common. Owners of **preferred shares** are a special class of owners because, although they generally do not have any say in running the company, they have a claim to any profits before any other shareholders do. Other shareholders do not receive any dividends unless the preferred shareholders have already been paid. Dividend payments on preferred shares are usually a fixed percentage of the initial issuing price (set by the board of directors). For example, if a preferred share originally cost $100 and the dividend rate was stated at 7.5 percent, the dividend payment will be $7.50 per share per year. Dividends are usually paid quarterly. Most preferred shares carry a cumulative claim to dividends. This means that if the company does not pay preferred-share dividends in one year because of losses, the dividends accumulate to the next year. Such dividends unpaid from previous years must also be paid to preferred shareholders before other shareholders can receive any dividends.

**preferred shares** a special type of share whose owners, though not generally having a say in running the company, have a claim to profits before other shareholders do

**common shares** shares whose owners have voting rights in the corporation, yet do not receive preferential treatment regarding dividends

Although owners of **common shares** do not get such preferential treatment with regard to dividends, they do get some say in the operation of the corporation. Their ownership gives them the right to vote for members of the board of directors and on other important issues. Common share dividends may vary according to the profitability of the business, and some corporations do not issue dividends at all, but instead plough their profits back into the company to fund expansion.

"Corporations issue two types of shares: preferred and common."

Common shareholders are the voting owners of a corporation. They are usually entitled to one vote per share. During an annual shareholders' meeting, common shareholders elect a board of directors. Because they can choose the board of directors, common shareholders have some say in how the company will operate. Common shareholders may vote by *proxy,* which is a written authorization by which shareholders assign their voting privilege to someone else, who then votes for their choice at the shareholders' meeting. It is a normal practice for management to request proxy statements from shareholders who are not planning to attend the annual meeting. Most owners do not attend annual meetings of the very large companies, such as Royal Bank or Suncor, unless they live in the city where the meeting is held.

Common shareholders have another advantage over preferred shareholders. Sometimes when the corporation decides to sell new common shares in the marketplace, common shareholders have the first right, called a *pre-emptive right,* to purchase new shares from the corporation. A pre-emptive right is often included in the articles of incorporation. This right is important because it allows shareholders to purchase new shares to maintain their original positions. For example, if a shareholder owns 10 percent of a corporation that decides to issue new shares, that shareholder has the right to buy enough of the new shares to retain the 10 percent ownership.

"Common shareholders are the voting owners of a corporation."

## Advantages of Corporations

Because a corporation is a separate legal entity, it has some very specific advantages over other forms of ownership. The biggest advantage may be the limited liability of the owners.

**Limited Liability.** Because the corporation's assets (money and resources) and liabilities (debts and other obligations including legal) are separate from its owners', in most cases the shareholders are not held responsible for the firm's debts if it fails. Their liability or potential loss is limited to the amount of their original investment. Although a creditor can sue a corporation for not paying its debts, even forcing the corporation into bankruptcy, it cannot make the shareholders pay the corporation's debts out of their personal assets. This advantage is rarely extended to small private corporations when borrowing money. Most banks and credit unions will insist that the owners of a private corporation pledge personal assets to secure a loan for the corporation unless the business has a long successful history; this would be most unusual for a public corporation. The main advantage of limited liability to small business is against loss to trade creditors/suppliers who granted the business credit and against legal liability.

**Ease of Transfer of Ownership.** Shareholders in public corporations can sell or trade shares to other people without causing the termination of the corporation, and they can do this without the prior approval of other shareholders. The transfer of ownership (unless it is a majority position) does not affect the daily or long-term operations of the corporation. Private corporations also allow shareholders to sell or transfer shares, but the transfer is not always easy, as is evident from the discussion about McCain Foods Ltd. Private corporations often face the same hurdles as partnerships when people are trying to sell shares or a stake in the business.

**Perpetual Life.** A corporation usually is chartered to last forever unless its articles of incorporation stipulate otherwise. The existence of the corporation is unaffected by the death or withdrawal of any of its shareholders. It survives until the owners sell it or liquidate its assets. However, in some cases, bankruptcy ends a corporation's life. Bankruptcies occur when companies are

©Chris Batson/Alamy Stock Photo

RBC is currently Canada's largest public corporation.

unable to compete and earn profits. Eventually, uncompetitive businesses must close or seek protection from creditors in bankruptcy court while the business tries to reorganize.

**External Sources of Funds.** Of all the forms of business organization, the public corporation finds it easiest to raise money. When a corporation needs to raise more money, it can sell more shares or issue bonds (corporate "IOUs," which pledge to repay debt), attracting funds from anywhere in North America and even overseas. The larger a corporation becomes, the more sources of financing are available to it. We take a closer look at some of these in Chapter 16. Research has indicated that a private corporation's ability to raise funds has more to do with the history of the company than its business structure. A private corporation such as the Irving Group or Chapman's Ice Cream (Canada's largest ice cream seller) would have little trouble raising money. A small corporation with an unproven business record would likely face the same hurdles in raising funds that a sole proprietor or partnership would have.

> "Of all the forms of business organization, the public corporation finds it easiest to raise money."

**Expansion Potential.** Because large public corporations can find long-term financing readily, they can easily expand into national and international markets. And as a legal entity, a corporation can enter into contracts without as much difficulty as a partnership.

**Tax Advantages.** Corporations have a number of tax advantages. Public corporations pay a lower tax rate than sole proprietorships and partnerships. Smaller private corporations also pay a lower tax rate, and their owners can often defer tax by leaving money in the corporation, splitting income through payment of dividends to spouses or children, and, if the business is sold, realizing tax-free capital gains of up to $750,000.

## Disadvantages of Corporations

Corporations have some distinct disadvantages resulting from tax laws and government regulation.

**Double Taxation.** As a legal entity, the corporation must pay taxes on its income just like you do. When after-tax corporate profits are paid out as dividends to the shareholders, the dividends are taxed a second time as part of the individual owner's income. This process creates double taxation for the shareholders of dividend-paying corporations. Often, the disadvantage of double taxation is offset by the Dividend Tax Credit program, a tax credit that allows the Canada Revenue Agency to tax dividend income at a lower rate than personal income. For example, if a private corporation earns $200,000, the money is taxed at 16 percent, which creates a $32,000 tax bill. If the owner then pays himself the remaining $168,000 as dividends, which are taxed at 15 percent, his take-home pay will be $142,800. If the owner of the business was a sole proprietor, all of the $200,000 would be taxed at personal rates, which can be as high as 49 percent. Double taxation does not occur with the other forms of business organization.

**Forming a Corporation.** The formation of a corporation can be costly. There are filing fees associated with forming a corporation, and often a lawyer is needed. The total costs of forming a corporation are usually in excess of $1000.

**Disclosure of Information and Regulations.** Corporations must make information available to their owners, usually through an annual report to shareholders. The annual report contains financial information about the firm's profits, sales, facilities and equipment, and debts, as well as descriptions of the company's operations, products, and plans for the future. Public corporations must also file reports with the public stock exchanges and the various provincial exchange commissions.

As discussed above, tougher corporate governance laws and increased scrutiny in Canada and the United States means corporations are faced with increased paperwork and regulations. In fact, some of Canada's most prominent business leaders, including Paul Desmarais, owner of Power Corp., and Dominic D'Allessandro, former CEO of Manulife, have stated that the increased regulations have hindered corporate growth by draining time and money away from the company. Frank Stronach, former CEO of the publicly traded Canadian automobile component manufacturing company Magna, notes, "The time we spend complying with regulations is now enormous."[17]

**Impact on Management Decisions.** Shareholders of publicly traded companies are becoming much more aggressive in demanding share appreciation and short-term results from management teams. As a result, management sometimes feels pressure to make decisions that are beneficial in the short term, but are not good long-term decisions. When Rogers Communications invested hundreds of millions of dollars in technology, shareholders and stock market analysts questioned the decision and some attempted to pressure management to halt the costly investment. As a result of the investment, however, Rogers became the technological leader among cell phone companies in Canada. This leadership position is what allowed the company to be the first cell phone provider to sell the popular iPhone in Canada, giving Rogers a substantial advantage over its competitors, but this shareholder pressure is why some owners prefer to remain private. Jim Pattison of Jim Pattison Group sums up the advantages of remaining private: "We can make better decisions as the owner of a private enterprise where we don't have to worry about daily share prices and analysts' expectations."[18]

**Employee–Owner Separation.** Many employees are not shareholders of the company for which they work. This separation of owners and employees may cause employees to feel that their work benefits only the owners. Employees without an ownership stake do not always see how they fit into the corporate picture and may not understand the importance of profits to the health of the organization. If managers are part owners but other employees are not, management–labour relations take on a different, sometimes difficult, aspect from those in partnerships and sole proprietorships. However, this situation is changing as more corporations establish employee share ownership plans (ESOPs), which give employees shares in the company. Such plans build a partnership between employee and employer and can boost productivity because they motivate employees to work harder so that they can earn dividends from their hard work as well as from their regular wages. In fact, of the 100 fastest-growing businesses in Canada identified by *Profit* magazine, 47 percent run ESOPs.[19]

## ENTREPRENEURSHIP IN ACTION

### Good Coffee Plus Clean Drinking Water

**Birch Bark Coffee**

**Founder:** Mark Marsolais-Nahwegahbow

**Founded:** March 2018

**Success:** Mark Marsolais-Nahwegahbow, Ojibwe and member of the Whitefish River First Nation in Birch Island, Ontario, has owned renovation companies, worked in social services, and is an artist. Recently he has embraced a new title: founder and owner of Birch Bark Coffee, a social enterprise that is dedicated to providing consumers with excellent coffee and First Nations communities with clean drinking water.*

Marsolais-Nahwegahbow says the inspiration for his company came as he became increasingly aware of the poor quality of water in some First Nations communities. He wanted to do something to help, and if he could sell a product and donate some of the revenue to provide clean drinking water, then he would be able create a business for himself, create jobs for others, and most importantly, help First Nations people.

©Birch Bark Coffee

With these goals in mind, Birch Bark coffee was born. Birch Bark purchases coffee beans from Indigenous organic coffee bean farmers, roasts them using a special formula, and then sells the bags to consumers with two dollars from every bag sold donated to purchasing water purification systems for First National families.**

While Birch Bark is a currently a private corporation, sales have been growing at a brisk pace and Marsolais-Nahwegahbow says he cannot keep his product on the shelves. In fact, he is receiving daily calls to expand internationally and announced the product will soon be sold in the United States and Switzerland.***

#### DISCUSSION QUESTIONS

1. Why do you think Birch Bark Coffee has been successful?
2. Birch Bark is a private corporation. Why would Marsolais-Nahwegahbow opt for this form of ownership? What are the advantages and disadvantages?
3. Given Birch Bark's rapid expansion, do you think Marsolais-Nahwegahbow may someday consider an alternate form of business ownership? Why or why not?

*Interview: Mark Marsolais-Nahwegahbow - Birch Bark Coffee, November 9, 2018, ELMNT FM Ottawa, https://www.youtube.com/watch?v=s_d3roFqE40; https://birchbarkcoffeecompany.com/pages/founder (accessed May 18, 2019).
**Meghan McKenna, "5 Indigenous Entrepreneurs Creating Social Change in Their Communities," June 21, 2018, https://fashionmagazine.com/culture/indigenous-entrepreneurs-canada/
***Interview: Mark Marsolais-Nahwegahbow - Birch Bark Coffee, November 9, 2018, ELMNT FM Ottawa, https://www.youtube.com/watch?v=s_d3roFqE40; https://birchbarkcoffeecompany.com/pages/founder, (accessed May 18, 2019).

## Other Types of Ownership

In this section we will take a brief look at joint ventures and cooperatives—businesses formed for special purposes.

### Joint Ventures

A **joint venture** is a partnership established for a specific project, often for a limited time. The partners in a joint venture may be individuals or organizations, as in the case of the international joint ventures discussed in Chapter 3. Control of a joint venture may be shared equally, or one partner may control decision making. Joint ventures are especially popular in situations that call for large investments, such as the development of new products or the emergence of new market which requires investment. Canada saw both such occurrences in 2018, when cannabis became legal. As a result, Constellation Brands, one of the largest alcohol companies in the world, invested billions in Canopy Growth, one of the largest cannabis companies in Canada.

**joint venture** a partnership established for a specific project or for a limited time involving the sharing of the costs and operation of a business, often between a foreign company and a local partner

Constellation views this investment as a partnership whereby they can access cannabis sales in Canada and work with Canopy in producing cannabis-infused drinks and edibles. Canopy benefits from the injection of cash, which it will use to quickly expand its operations in the emerging Canadian marketplace, and access to Constellation's drink and product production knowledge. Joint ventures are also common in the extraction of natural resources in the Western oil patch. Husky Energy and BP plc formed a 50/50 joint venture in the Athabasca Oil Sands in Alberta. BP plc agreed to bring its excess refinery capacity to the agreement and Husky Energy brought its reserves from the oil patch.

Retail joint ventures are also becoming increasingly common as evident in the Indigo and American Girl shop-in-shop example in the opening profile. The host shop, in this case Indigo, allows another retailer, American Girl, access to its Canadian retail and online space. The host shop (Indigo) benefits by increasing revenue often from receiving a percentage of sales and/or rent and increased foot and Web traffic from carrying popular branded products. The expanding company (American Girl), accesses prime retail locations and additional customers for a smaller investment than if they'd entered a market themselves.

The arrangement is mutually beneficial as both companies share increasing revenue with limited risk. Examples of these shop-in-shops can be also be seen at Hudson Bay retail locations both in Canada and Germany where they have partnered with a number of companies including Sephora. Former Hudson's Bay CEO Gerald Storch notes that every time they open a Sephora in one of their stores it generates significant foot traffic. Kiehl's, a retailer of cosmetic products just announced a partnership with Sephora Canada in which their men's products will be carried in Sephora stores and online. While not a shop within a shop concept, Sephora will provide Kiehl's with valuable shelf space and online sales. The result of the partnership should be an increase in revenue for both companies.

While the theory supporting joint ventures such as the pooling of resources and/or the sharing of expertise

©Room 76/Shutterstock

Constellation Brands has invested billions in Canopy Growth, a Canadian cannabis company. Constellation is hoping to generate revenue from the recreational market in Canada and one day infuse cannabis into their drink portfolio.

©Torontonian/Alamy Stock Photo

Indigo has experimented with the shop-in-shop concept with partners such as American Girl.

©Manor Photography/Alamy Stock Photo

When first announced, Tim Hortons' joint venture with Cold Stone Creamery seemed like a perfect match of complementary products. But value-seeking Tim Hortons customers did not like the premium pricing of Cold Stone products, and the venture ultimately failed. The partnership still remains in the U.S., where Tim Hortons is using the Cold Stone name to attract customers to its stores.

is sound in principle, many studies indicate that over 50 percent of joint ventures fail and most will not last five years. For example, Tim Hortons and Cold Stone Creamery formed an ill-fated Canadian joint venture. Tim Hortons agreed to include Cold Stone ice cream in over 150 stores in Canada and Cold Stone would sell Tim Hortons' coffee in some of the more prominent Cold Stone stores in the United States. The venture allowed Cold Stone to quickly gain access to the Canadian market through a proven retailer, and Tim Hortons was able to offer a product with strong summer sales to its customers and franchise owners. Tim Hortons also gained access to some of Cold Stone's U.S. locations as a result of the arrangement. This joint venture didn't last as Tim Hortons ended the partnership citing the premium price attached to Cold Stone products which did not seem to fit in the Tim Hortons restaurants that are known for value food. The partnership still remains in the United States where Tim Hortons is not a well-known brand and they benefit from the co-branded retail locations.

## Cooperatives

Another form of organization in business is the **cooperative (or co-op)**, an organization composed of individuals or small businesses that have banded

**cooperative (or co-op)** an organization composed of individuals or small businesses that have banded together to reap the benefits of belonging to a larger organization

### GOING GREEN

#### CSAs for Everyone

As people become more and more concerned about the state of the environment, *sustainable*, *local*, and *green* are just some of the words being tossed around with increasing frequency. Individuals are looking for ways to reduce their carbon footprint, protect the land, and take better care of their own health. To this end, community-supported agriculture (CSA) is becoming a popular alternative to large-chain grocery stores. The CSA is not a new idea. It originated in Japan around 30 years ago and was adopted in Canada in the 1980s.

A CSA is a way for local farmers to bypass the bureaucracy of traditional corporate grocery stores and to conduct business directly with consumers. Under this model, a farmer first creates a budget for the growing season that includes all costs (such as land payments, seeds, salaries, equipment, and so on). The farmer then divides this budget into the number of shares of crops available for purchase. Usually a CSA share is designed to feed a family of four for a week. People become members of a farm's CSA by purchasing shares. They will then receive a portion of local, often organic, produce each week during the growing season. The CSA creates a sustainable relationship in which members receive quality produce and farmers have a reliable method for distributing their crops.

How does the CSA benefit the environment and contribute to health? The farms offering CSAs are usually small and dedicated to ecologically sound farming practices, such as permaculture and avoiding chemical pesticides. Because the cost of distribution is lower for these farmers, members often receive produce at prices competitive with conventional produce sold in grocery stores. Farmers, knowing that their basic costs are covered, can focus their full attention on growing high-quality produce rather than searching for distributors. In addition, because deliveries are made locally, produce is fresher. The local aspect of delivery also cuts down on pollution because the products do not need to travel great distances.

together to reap the benefits of belonging to a larger organization. In cooperatives, the owners usually are limited to one share per person—although the share structure can be altered to reflect the level of a member's contribution to the co-op.

There are currently over 9000 co-ops in Canada that provide services to 18 million members and employ over 150,000 people.[20] Well-known Canadian co-ops include Farmers Dairy, which is a co-operative of milk producers in Atlantic Canada; the Toronto Renewable Energy Co-operative (TREC), which was Canada's first green power community co-operative; SSQ Groupe Financier in Quebec, which stands out in the financial services industry as its clients are also the company's owners; and Community Health Co-operative Federation in Saskatchewan, which aims to reform health policy and provide community-oriented alternatives to traditional care.

A co-op is set up not to make money as an entity but so that its members can become more profitable or save money. Co-ops are generally expected to operate without profit or to create only enough profit to maintain the co-op organization. For example, Mountain Equipment Co-op is the largest retailer co-operative in Canada, and its goal is to provide accessible and fairly priced outdoor gear to its members. At the end of the year, any surplus money is returned to shareholders.

Many cooperatives exist in small farming communities. The co-op stores can market grain; order large quantities of fertilizer, seed, and other supplies at discounted prices; and reduce costs and increase efficiency with good management. A co-op can purchase supplies in large quantities and pass the savings on to its members. It also can help distribute the products of its members more efficiently than each could on an individual basis. A cooperative can advertise its members' products and thus generate demand. Ace Hardware, a cooperative of independent hardware store owners, allows its members to share in the savings that result from buying supplies in large quantities; it also provides advertising, which individual members might not be able to afford on their own.

In a world where people are looking to take better care of themselves and the environment, as well as to understand where their food came from, the CSA is becoming a popular alternative to traditional stores.*

Farmers and consumers are embracing community-supported agriculture, in which consumers invest in farms and get paid in produce.

While Agriculture Canada has yet to determine the number of CSAs in existence, an Internet search reveals that they exist in every province and news articles indicate that they are growing in popularity with consumers.

### DISCUSSION QUESTIONS

1. What are some of the benefits farmers gain by switching to the CSA model?
2. Why are people opting to use CSAs over traditional grocery stores?
3. Can you think of any drawbacks to the CSA model?

*"What Is Community Supported Agriculture and How Does It Work?" Local Harvest, www.localharvest.org/csa.jsp (accessed February 18, 2008); "Community Supported Agriculture at Indian Line Farm," Indian Line Farm, http://www.indianlinefarm.com/csa.html (accessed February 25, 2008).

## RESPONDING TO BUSINESS CHALLENGES

### Heartland Farm Foods Co-op Helps Preserve Beef—and a Way of Life

Jim Farmer, a lifelong livestock producer in the United States, wants his son and two daughters to be able to carry on the family farm. To help achieve this goal, he formed the Heartland Farm Foods Co-op with about three dozen beef producers to turn 1000 cattle a year into canned beef. The co-op form of organization is not unusual for small businesses that band together to obtain the benefits of a larger organization. The co-op is not set up to make money as an organization, but rather so that all the ranchers involved can become more profitable or, in this case, continue to maintain a lifestyle that they enjoy. In the face of intense competition from large commercial feedlots, Farmer's idea was to offer a different kind of product and to market and support it through the co-op, which has the support of the local Beef Industry Council, and the Department of Agriculture.

The co-op's canned, precooked ground and chunked beef products contain just one ingredient—beef, with no preservatives, not even salt. Any harmful bacteria are removed through a pressure-cooking process. Each animal yields 400 to 500 cans of federally inspected beef from cattle raised without steroids, hormone additives, or routine antibiotics. The precooked beef is targeted at outdoor enthusiasts—from hikers and hunters to anglers and campers. Thanks to a shelf life of two to five years, the cans can be stowed in tackle boxes or backpacks, or even stored in storm shelters in case of a disaster.

The co-op has constructed a 415-square-metre plant on 4 hectares to process the beef. Construction of this facility and first-year operating capital needs were estimated at approximately $750,000. Some of these expenses were partially offset by grants that the co-op received; co-ops that foster economic development in a region often receive grants or other financial support from provincial or federal development initiatives.

Currently, Heartland's canned beef is primarily available in local supermarkets and convenience stores and online at www.heartlandfoods.com. Prices range from $2.69 to $3.99 on the website, although retailers sell the product for $4.99 per can. At this price, consumers surely demand a quality product, but Heartland believes the product's convenience and ingredients support sales. The co-op recently released five new products—Nacho Express, Zesty Beef'n Bean, Beef'n Bean Chili, Chili Con Queso, and Hearty Taco Beef—and is selling steaks to local restaurants and markets. Heartland's initiative offers an example of creativity in bringing back a product—canned meat—that was once a pantry staple before the era of refrigeration. The co-operative form of organization has made it possible for small ranchers to join together to make this product a reality.*

#### DISCUSSION QUESTIONS

1. Why did Heartland Foods employ a cooperative form of organization?
2. What are the advantages for ranchers who belong to the cooperative?
3. Can you think of any other industries where the cooperative form of business ownership would be beneficial?

*"Farmers Offering up Beef in a Can," CNN, March 22, 2004, www.cnn.com/2004/US/Midwest/03/22/canned.beef.asp; Him Suhr, "Farmers Form Canned-Beef Co-op," *Courier-Journal*, March 28, 2004, www.courier-journal.com/business/news2004/03/28/E7-beefcan28-4323.html; Jim Suhr, "Livestock Farmer Hopes Canned Beef Will Catch On," *The Fort Collins Coloradoan*, March 28, 2004, p. E2; Erica Coble, "Trading on Tradition," March 2005, www.rurdev.usda.gov/rbs/pub/mar05/value.htm (accessed March 1, 2006); www.heartlandfarmfoods.com;www.heartlandfarmfoods.com/Company.htm; www.heartlandfarmfoods.com/Catalog_Page%201.htm; www.heartlandfarmfoods.com/Producers.htm (all accessed March 1, 2006).

# Trends in Business Ownership: Mergers and Acquisitions

**LO 4-4** Define and debate the advantages and disadvantages of mergers, acquisitions, and leveraged buyouts.

Companies large and small achieve growth and improve profitability by expanding their operations, often by developing and selling new products or selling current products to new groups of customers in different geographic areas. Such growth, when carefully planned and controlled, is usually beneficial to the firm and ultimately helps it reach its goal of enhanced profitability. But companies also grow by merging with or purchasing other companies.

A **merger** occurs when two companies combine to form a new company. For example, in 2018 two leading Canadian agricultural giants, Potash Corp. of

**merger** the combination of two companies (usually corporations) to form a new company

(©Ivan Marc Sanchez/Alamy Stock Photo

©Collection Christophel/Alamy Stock Photo

With Disney's purchase of Fox, the company added X-Men, Deadpool, and the Fantastic Four to its superhero lineup, which already included the Avengers and Star Wars characters.

Saskatchewan and Agrium Inc. of Alberta, merged to form Nutrien, a brand new publicly traded company. For years, Potash and Agrium where bitter rivals, producing and selling fertilizer and other farm products.

Management of the two companies recognized they would be stronger as one and formed a new company, Nutrien, which would enable them to offer complementary products, cut costs, and expand. Estimated annual cost savings are in the range of $500 million and Nutrien is using some of that money to acquire other firms. An **acquisition** occurs when one company purchases another, generally by buying its shares. The acquired company may become a subsidiary of the buyer, or its operations and assets may be merged with those of the buyer. Nutrien has expanded its operations by purchasing Waypoint Analytical, Inc. in a private sale and has agreed to pay $63 million for Illinois-based Agrible Inc. Waypoint has soil technology that should enable Nutrien to produce more efficient fertilizers, and Agrible produces agricultural software enabling better crop management.

**acquisition** the purchase of one company by another, usually by buying its shares

Other well known acquisitions include Disney purchasing some of Fox's assets for $71.3 billion in 2018. Not only did Disney acquire the streaming service Hulu, various television stations including the National Geographic channel and other properties, Disney also acquired the rights to Fox-owned superheroes including the X-Men, Deadpool, and the Fantastic Four. With Disney's Avenger movie series scheduled to end in 2019 with the release of the sequel to *Infinity War*, this opens up a number of new movie possibilities. Imagine, if you will, Black Panther teaming with Deadpool to defeat Earth's next super villain.

The Fox purchase followed Disney's purchase of Lucasfilm Ltd., including the rights to the Star Wars movies for $4.01 billion.[21] Disney has already released new Star Wars movies, is currently building a Star Wars land at Walt Disney World, including a themed hotel, and plans to expand the Star Wars brand, ensuring children will be playing with light sabres for years to come.[22]

Other well-known examples include Amazon buying Whole Foods for $13.7 billion, Coach purchasing Kate Spade for $2.4 billion, and Burger King's takeover of Tim Hortons for $14.6 billion.[23] The legalization of cannabis has also led to a flurry of merger and acquisition activity in Canada with 48 deals taking place in the first half of 2018 with a dollar value in access of $5 billion. Aurora Cannabis (featured in the end-of-chapter case) was at the forefront of the two largest deals, paying $1.1 billion for CanniMed Therapeutics Inc. and $3.2 billion for MedReleaf.

Acquisitions and mergers are generally driven by (1) *economies of scale*, where a larger company can reduce its costs and offer the same products or level or service at a lower cost; (2) *increased market share*, when the company is acquiring a competitor; (3) *cross-selling*, where the acquired firm can sell different products to the same customer; (4) *integration*, where the acquired firm can act as a supplier or a distributor for the firms' products; and (5) *diversification*, where a firm acquires another firm that operates in a different industry to hedge against an industry downturn. As previously discussed, even when one or more of these advantages are evident in an acquisition/merger, studies indicate that they are only successful 50 percent of the time. Common reasons cited for the lack of success include unanticipated expenses, overestimation of cost savings, and conflicting corporate cultures.

Examples of mergers and acquisitions in Canada or featuring Canadian companies include the following:

- Aurora Cannabis Inc. acquiring MedReleaf for $3.2 billion and CanniMed Therapeutics Inc. for $1.1 billion
- Potash Corp. of Saskatchewan and Agrium Inc. merging to form Nutrien
- Burger King acquiring Tim Hortons for $14.6 billion
- Enbridge Corp. acquiring Specter Energy Corp. for $61 billion
- Suncor purchasing Canada Oil Sands Limited for $4.2 billion
- CIBC's $4.8 billion acquisition of Bancorp Inc.
- Lowe's buying RONA for $3.1 billion

When firms that make similar products and sell them to the same customers merge, it is known as a *horizontal merger*, as when Potash Corp. and Agrium Inc. merged to form Nutrien as discussed above. Horizontal mergers reduce the number of corporations competing within an

©Teri Virbickis/Shutterstock

Merger and acquisition activity in Canada's cannabis industry has soared towards the end of the decade with 48 deals in first half of 2018.

industry and, for this reason, usually are reviewed carefully by federal regulators before the merger is allowed to proceed. Sometimes firms purchase other companies and allow them to continue operating under their brand and to maintain some form of independence. This often happens when the competitor's brand is strong, and it resonates with consumers. For example, when the American retailer Lowe's bought Rona they continued to allow the company to operate under the Rona brand as it is well recognized company in Canada. Another example is the Burger King purchase of Tim Hortons discussed above. Can you imagine the outcry from loyal Tim Hortons consumers if their coffee cup was suddenly labelled with Burger King's BK across the front?

Since most mergers and acquisitions result in larger companies and reduce the level of competition, the government, through various regulatory agencies, often has to approve mergers. As discussed above, various regulatory boards review acquisitions to ensure that a level, competitive playing field exists, that consumers are not negatively impacted as a result of the merger, and (in the case of foreign takeovers of Canadian companies) that the result is of net benefit to Canada. Recently, the Canadian Radio-television and Telecommunications Commission (CRTC) rejected Bell Canada's proposed $3.4 billion takeover of Astral Media, saying it would place too much power in the hands of one company and threaten the competitive media landscape in Canada. Bell then submitted a revised proposal that included the sale of several television and radio stations; the proposal was ultimately approved.[24]

When companies operating at different but related levels of an industry merge, it is known as a *vertical merger*. In many instances, a vertical merger results when one corporation merges with one of its customers or suppliers. For example, if Tim Hortons were to purchase a large coffee bean farm—to ensure a ready supply of beans for its coffee—a vertical merger would result. Vertical mergers allow for quick growth and were a key strategy used by K.C. Irving to grow the Irving Group. Irving noted that he started selling cars, and since cars needed gas, he opened a gas station. Since gas needed refined oil, he started an oil company, and since oil had to be transported, he entered into the transportation and shipping industry.

A *conglomerate merger* results when two firms in unrelated industries merge. For example, the purchase of the Toronto Blue Jays in the 1990s by brewer Labatt and the CIBC represents a conglomerate merger because the two companies are in different industries.

When a company (or an individual), sometimes called a *corporate raider*, wants to acquire or take over another company, it first offers to buy some or all of the other company's shares at a premium over its current price in a *tender offer*. Most such offers are "friendly," with both groups agreeing to the proposed deal, but some are "hostile," as when the second company does not want to be taken over. For example, Aurora Cannabis launched a hostile takeover of CanniMed Therapeutic, which is discussed in the case at the end of the chapter.

Management at CanniMed opposed the bid before agreeing to accept a new, higher offer from Aurora. As discussed in the profile at the start of the chapter, Indigo, a Canadian book retailer, made a hostile bid for Chapters, its largest Canadian competitor. Initially, management at Chapters tried to avert the bid using a number of techniques, including looking for a white knight (see below), which they thought they'd found in Future Shop, but Indigo was persistent in its pursuit of the company and raised the initial offer price. Ultimately, Indigo successfully acquired Chapters.

To head off a hostile takeover attempt, a threatened company's managers may use one or more of several techniques. They may ask shareholders not to sell to the raider; file a lawsuit in an effort to abort the takeover; institute a *poison pill* (in which the firm allows shareholders to buy more shares at prices lower than the current market value) or *shark repellant* (in which management requires a large majority of shareholders to approve the takeover); or seek a *white knight* (a more acceptable firm that is willing to acquire the threatened company).

In some cases, management may take the company private or even take on more debt so that the heavy debt obligation will "scare off" the raider. The result of companies taking actions such as these has been a reduction in the success rate of hostile bids—only 50 percent of hostile takeovers are successful.[25] As a result, the popularity of hostile takeovers has declined sharply since their heyday in the 1990s. From 2006 to 2015 only 5 percent of takeovers would be classified as hostile. In the case of the initial hostile bid by Aurora for CanniMed, CanniMed initially instituted several measures to thwart the takeover attempt, including a poison pill that would prevent Aurora from buying any more CanniMed shares. Only when Aurora significantly raised its offer did CanniMed's board of directors recommend that its shareholders accept the revised offer.

In a **leveraged buyout (LBO)**, a group of investors borrows money from banks and other institutions to acquire a company (or a division of one), using the assets of the purchased company to guarantee repayment of the loan. In some LBOs, as much as 95 percent of the

**leveraged buyout (LBO)** a purchase in which a group of investors borrows money from banks and other institutions to acquire a company (or a division of one), using the assets of the purchased company to guarantee repayment of the loan

buyout price is paid with borrowed money, which eventually must be repaid. The new management then engages in a number of strategies including selling assets, cutting costs including termination of employees, and/or breaking up businesses to restore value to the acquired business. The company uses its improved balance sheet to pay off the debt and the business is often sold at a much higher price than the original purchase price. In Canada, Gerry Schwartz, CEO of Onex Corporation, has made billions by buying distressed businesses, making changes, and then selling the improved companies. Examples of Schwartz's work include Sky Chefs and Loews Cineplex, two companies that he bought at deep discounts using debt and eventually sold for millions in profit.

With the explosion of mergers, acquisitions, and leveraged buyouts in the 1980s and 1990s, some financial journalists coined the term *merger mania*. Many companies joined the merger mania simply to enhance their own operations by consolidating them with the operations of other firms. Mergers and acquisitions enabled these companies to gain a larger market share in their industries, acquire valuable assets, such as new products or plants and equipment, and lower their costs. Mergers also represent a means of making profits quickly, as was the case during the 1980s when many companies' shares were undervalued. Quite simply, such companies represent a bargain to other companies that can afford to buy them. Additionally, deregulation of some industries has permitted consolidation of firms within those industries for the first time, as is the case in the banking and airline industries.

Some people view mergers and acquisitions favourably, pointing out that they boost corporations' share prices and market value, to the benefit of their shareholders. In many instances, mergers enhance a company's ability to meet foreign competition in an increasingly global marketplace. And, companies that are victims of hostile takeovers generally streamline their operations, reduce unnecessary staff, cut costs, and otherwise become more efficient with their operations, which benefits their shareholders whether or not the takeover succeeds.

Critics, however, argue that mergers hurt companies because they force managers to focus their efforts on avoiding takeovers rather than managing effectively and profitably. Some companies have taken on a heavy debt burden to stave off a takeover, later to be forced into bankruptcy when economic downturns left them unable to handle the debt. Mergers and acquisitions also can damage employee morale and productivity, as well as the quality of the companies' products.

Many mergers have been beneficial for all involved; others have had damaging effects for the companies, their employees, and customers. No one can say if mergers will continue to slow, but many experts say the utilities, telecommunications, financial services, natural resources, computer hardware and software, gaming, managed health care, and technology industries are likely targets.

## TEAM EXERCISE

Form groups and find examples of mergers and acquisitions. Mergers can be broken down into traditional mergers, horizontal mergers, and conglomerate mergers. When companies are found, note how long the merger or acquisition took, if there were any requirements by the government before approval of the merger or acquisition, and if any failed mergers or acquisitions were found that did not receive government approval. Report your findings to the class, and explain what the companies hoped to gain from the merger or acquisition.

# LEARNING OBJECTIVES SUMMARY

**LO 4-1** Define and examine the advantages and disadvantages of the sole proprietorship form of organization.

Sole proprietorships—businesses owned and managed by one person—are the most common form of organization. Their major advantages are the following: (1) They are easy and inexpensive to form, (2) they allow a high level of secrecy, (3) all profits belong to the owner, (4) the owner has complete control over the business, (5) government regulation is minimal, (6) taxes are paid only once, and (7) the business can be closed easily. The disadvantages include: (1) The owner may have to use personal assets to borrow money, (2) limited source of external funds, (3) often owners have a limited skill set, (4) lack of continuity, and (5) successful sole proprietors pay a higher tax than they would under the corporate form of business.

**LO 4-2** Identify three types of partnership, and evaluate the advantages and disadvantages of the partnership form of organization.

Partnership is a form of business organization defined as an association of two or more persons who carry on as co-owners of a business for profit. There are three basic types of partnership: general partnership, limited partnership, and limited liability partnership.

Partnerships offer the following advantages: (1) They are easy to organize, (2) partners can complement each other's skills, (3) they may have more access to capital, (4) partnerships can make decisions faster than larger businesses, and (5) government regulations are few. Partnerships also have several disadvantages: (1) All partnerships have to deal with disagreements, (2) general partners have unlimited liability for the debts of the partnership, (3) partners are responsible for each other's decisions, (4) the death or termination of one partner requires a new partnership agreement to be drawn up, (5) it is difficult to sell a partnership interest at a fair price, (6) the distribution of profits may not correctly reflect the amount of work done by each partner, and (7) partnerships may be taxed at a higher rate than corporations.

**LO 4-3** Describe the corporate form of organization, and cite the advantages and disadvantages of corporations.

A corporation is a legal entity created by the province or federal government, whose assets and liabilities are separate from those of its owners. Corporations have a board of directors made up of corporate officers or people from outside the company. Corporations, whether private or public, are owned by shareholders. Common shareholders have the right to elect the board of directors. Preferred shareholders do not have a vote but get preferential dividend treatment over common shareholders.

Advantages of the corporate form of business include: (1) The owners have limited liability, (2) ownership (stock) can be easily transferred, (3) corporations usually last forever, (4) raising money is easier than for other forms of business, and (5) expansion into new businesses is simpler because of the ability of the company to enter into contracts. Corporations also have disadvantages: (1) The company is taxed on its income, and owners pay a second tax on any profits received as dividends although the combined amount of tax paid may still be less than what would be paid by other forms of business, (2) forming a corporation can be expensive, (3) corporations have to disclose a great deal of information to the public (such as future plans) and comply with various government regulations, (4) corporations sometimes make decisions to appease shareholders' goals, and (5) owners and managers are not always the same and can have different goals.

**LO 4-4** Define and debate the advantages and disadvantages of mergers, acquisitions, and leveraged buyouts.

A merger occurs when two companies (usually corporations) combine to form a new company. An acquisition occurs when one company buys most of another company's stock. In a leveraged buyout, a group of investors borrows money to acquire a company, using the assets of the purchased company to guarantee the loan. They can help merging firms to gain a larger market share in their industries, acquire valuable assets such as new products or plants and equipment, and lower their costs. Consequently, they can benefit shareholders by improving the companies' market value and stock prices. However, they also can hurt companies if they force managers to focus on avoiding takeovers at the expense of productivity and profits. They may lead a company to take on too much debt and can harm employee morale and productivity.

## KEY TERMS

acquisition
board of directors
certificate of incorporation
common shares
cooperative (or co-op)
corporation
Crown corporations
dividends
general partnership
initial public offering (IPO)
joint venture
leveraged buyout (LBO)
limited liability partnership (LLP)
limited partnership
merger
non-profit corporations
partnership
partnership agreement
preferred shares
private corporation
public corporation
shares
sole proprietorships

## So You Want *to Start a Business*

If you have a good idea and want to turn it into a business, you are not alone. Small businesses are popping up all over Canada and the concept of entrepreneurship is hot. Entrepreneurs seek opportunities and creative ways to make profits. Business emerges in a number of different organizational forms, each with its own advantages and disadvantages. Sole proprietorships are the most common form of business organization in Canada. They tend to be small businesses and can take pretty much any form—anything from a hair salon to a scuba shop, from an organic produce provider to a financial advisor. Proprietorships are everywhere serving consumers' wants and needs. Proprietorships have a big advantage in that they tend to be simple to manage—decisions get made quickly when the owner and the manager are the same person and they are fairly simple and inexpensive to set up. Rules vary by province, but at most all you will need is a licence from the province.

Many people have been part of a partnership at some point in their life. Group work in school is an example of a partnership. If you ever worked as a DJ on the weekend with your friend and split the profits, then you have experienced a partnership. Partnerships can be either general or limited. General partnerships have unlimited liability and share completely in the management, debts, and profits of the business.

Limited partners, on the other hand, consist of at least one general partner and one or more limited partners who do not participate in the management of the company, but share in the profits. This form of partnership is used more often in risky investments where the limited partner stands only to lose his or her initial investment. Real estate limited partnerships are an example of how investors can minimize their financial exposure. Although it has its advantages, partnership is the least utilized form of business. Part of the reason is that all partners are responsible for the actions and decisions of all other partners, whether or not all of the partners were involved. Usually, partners will have to write up articles of partnership that outline respective responsibilities in the business. Unlike a corporation, proprietorships and partnerships both expire upon the death of one or more of those involved.

Corporations tend to be larger businesses, but do not need to be. A corporation can consist of nothing more than a small group of family members. In order to become a corporation, you have to file in the province in which you wish to incorporate. Each province has its own procedure for incorporation, meaning there are no general guidelines to follow. You can make your corporation private or public, meaning the company issues stocks and shareholders are the owners. While incorporating is a popular form of organization because it gives the company an unlimited lifespan and limited liability (meaning that if your business fails you cannot lose personal funds to make up for losses), there is a downside. You will be taxed as a corporation and as an individual, resulting in double taxation. No matter what form of organization suits your business idea best, there is a world of options out there for you if you want to be or experiment with being an entrepreneur.

## BUILD YOUR BUSINESS PLAN

### Options for Organizing a Business

As discussed above, there are a variety of legal structures for organizing your own business. In addition to reviewing the material in this chapter, students may want to talk to some small-business owners and see what structure they selected and why. Students should ask these entrepreneurs if they are happy with their form of business organization and what they see as its advantages and disadvantages. Students could also describe their business to the entrepreneur and ask them what form of business they would recommend.

# CASE | Cannabis Companies the Result of New Highs

When Canada announced the legalization of cannabis in 2018 there were a lot of jokes with references to Canadians getting "high." While most comedians were referring to people enjoying recreational cannabis, some in the business community were using the term in a different way. Investors were using the term *new high* to describe the rising value attached to Canadian public and private cannabis companies as their values rose sharply in anticipation of firms accessing the estimated $23 billion Canadian recreational cannabis market. Investors pushed cannabis shares up sharply from 2016 to 2018 as the market value for the companies soared. While cannabis companies have been appreciating in value for the past several years, many companies reached new highs in 2017 and 2018. For example, Aurora Cannabis Inc., which was valued at roughly $0.50 a share in 2016 rose to a high of $13.71 in 2018 representing a 2400 percent increase in market capitalization which represents the value of the business.

Business analysts who study Canadian acquisitions and merger activity were are also using the term *high* as an adjective to describe the amount of action among Canadian cannabis firms. In the first half of 2018 there were 48 cannabis deals in Canada worth an estimated $5.2 billion. While the high amount of acquisition and merger activity can be partly attributed to foreign companies investing in Canadian firms and larger players purchasing assets from smaller under-capitalized companies, a portion of the activity can be attributed to the sharp rise in the value of cannabis firms. Companies such as Aurora, which saw a huge jump in share price, now could use their shares as currency to buy other companies or sell additional shares in their company to raise money to make purchases.

Aurora's chief corporate officer, Cam Battley, notes that there is an increased pressure for Canadian cannabis companies to expand as they have higher share prices and almost all of them have raised additional money through equity financing. "They've got the currency, they've got the ammunition, and the market's going to expect people to use it." As a result of its increased value, Aurora purchased Larssen Ltd., a greenhouse company, and H2 Biopharma Inc., a Quebec-based cannabis applicant, in 2017 and early 2018.

Aurora was not finished acquiring firms and made history by announcing the first ever hostile takeover in the Canadian cannabis industry when they made an all-share offer for CanniMed Therapeutics Inc. Aurora's hostile bid of $24 a share offered a 56.9 percent premium on CanniMed's closing share price on the day of the offer. Aurora also announced that they completed agreement with 36 percent of CanniMed's shareholders to support the takeover proposal.

Aurora's offer was quickly denounced by the board of directors at CanniMed, which stated that Aurora's management was simply using their inflated shares to acquire firms and have not demonstrated any ability to execute on long term strategies. In response to the hostile takeover, CanniMed announced a shareholder's rights plan, also known as a poison pill, hoping to stop the proposed takeover. CanniMed's shareholders rights plan would prevent Aurora's management from purchasing any more shares in the company and prevent them from signing deals with other shareholders in support of the acquisition. Aurora responded by stating that CanniMed was a poorly managed company and asking securities regulators to stop the poison pill. In response the Ontario Securities Commission did, in fact, determine that the poison pill was unfair to Aurora and shareholders.

Rather than continue with a hostile bid, Aurora presented management with a combined share and cash offer, valuing CanniMed at $1.1 billion, a 181 percent premium over the closing share price from the original offer. While Aurora did offer a combination of cash and shares the amount of cash was limited to $140 million. CanniMed's management opted to support the takeover rather than continue to fight the bid. As a result of the takeover Aurora aquired CanniMed's 40,000 registered medical customers, increased its production capacity, gained access to CanniMed products, in particular their growing oils business, and can now enhance their expansion efforts in Australia.

Aurora was not done making acquisitions for the year, though, and announced another mega purchase, acquiring MedReleaf in an all-share deal worth $3.2 billion in the summer of 2018. The friendly takeover was supported by MedReleaf and its shareholders, who were happy with the 18.2 percent premium Aurora was willing to pay above current share price. In aquiring MedReleaf, Aurora further increased production capacity, gained access to products such as MedReleaf's cannabis-infused topical cream, and made it possible for the company to piggyback on MedReleaf's expansion efforts in Germany.

Given that roughly 50 percent of acquisitions and mergers are successful, some financial analysts, including Martin Landry, an analyst with GMP Securities L.P., wonder if Aurora is growing too fast and straining its ability to manage the integration of all their acquisitions. Landry would find support in Aurora's 2018 financial reports, which show an increase in costs, specifically operating costs, which can be used as a measure of a firm's success in integrating acquisitions.

Investors in cannabis stocks may also start to wonder about the long term prospects of their investments. Many financial analysts are pointing out that cannabis stocks could be significantly overvalued and in a bubble phase. A bubble is when companies in a sector see their values soar quickly and then drop rapidly. Bubbles are characterized by significant increases in share value, share values that are not supported by earnings, and investors purchasing shares in what they see as hot, hip, cool companies rather than making informed investment decisions.

Interestingly, Aurora and other cannabis companies have seen a huge surge in share value, earnings are considered very low compared to share prices, and many millennials, with limited investment knowledge, appear to be buying cannabis stocks. Alternatively, believers in cannabis companies note that we are in the infancy of a brand-new investment opportunity, the potential for growth justifies the evaluated share values, and large well-established companies, including Constellation Brands and maybe even Coca-Cola, appear to be willing to invest in cannabis firms.

## DISCUSSION QUESTIONS

1. What are some of the advantages and disadvantages of Aurora's strategy of growing quickly and using its shares as currency?
2. Would you invest in cannabis companies based on the information in the case? Why or why not?
3. Investment bubbles are common, including recent investments in Bitcoin and before that the technology bubble in the late 90s. Use the Internet to look up the current value of cannabis companies, including Aurora. Has the company continued to increase in value?

# CHAPTER 5

# Small Business, Entrepreneurship, and Franchising

©Fiix.io

## LEARNING OBJECTIVES

**After reading this chapter, you will be able to:**

- **LO 5-1** Define entrepreneurship and small business.
- **LO 5-2** Investigate the importance of small business in the Canadian economy and why certain fields attract small business.
- **LO 5-3** Specify the advantages of small-business ownership.
- **LO 5-4** Summarize the disadvantages of small-business ownership, and analyze why many small businesses fail.
- **LO 5-5** Describe how you go about starting a small business and what resources are needed.
- **LO 5-6** Evaluate the demographic, technological, and economic trends that are affecting the future of small business.
- **LO 5-7** Explain why many large businesses are trying to "think small."

## ENTER THE WORLD OF BUSINESS

### Changing Tires Leads to a Brand New Business

Have you ever actually watched tires being changed on a car, or brake pads being replaced, and been surprised at the ease of the process? If so, this was the same thought that Khallil Mangalji, Arif Bhanji, and Zain Manji had when they founded the Toronto-based car repair service company, Fiix.io (www.Fiix.io). Bhanji says his eureka moment came about when he was desperately trying to get snow tires replaced on his car and couldn't get into a local repair shop. Growing anxious, he eventually found someone on Kijji who offered to complete the changeover at his home. After watching the mechanic perform the service, Bhanji wondered why all car services couldn't be performed this way, and Fiix was born.

Fiix is an online company that matches mechanics to customers. Fiix's owners describe the company as *Uber for car repair*. Consumers log on to Fiix's website or app, select a car type and the mechanical problem, book a location (often the car owner's home), and select a date and time. Much like with ride-sharing services, mechanics are independent contractors, and potential customers can review their online ratings prior to booking. Fiix mechanics show up with fresh coffee in hand for the customers, complete the service, and the customer pays Fiix. Since Fiix doesn't have the same overhead as a traditional service centre they can actually charge less for fixing a car while earning a 38 percent margin, which is quite good, and offer mechanics the opportunity to make more working for themselves then they would for others. In fact Fiix mechanics can earn roughly double working for Fiix compared to traditional employment.

While the business is only a few years old, reaction from customers and investors has been overwhelmingly positive. Fiix's customers love the lower cost and convenience of the service, their direct access to the mechanics, and that they only pay after a job is complete. Customer satisfaction is evident in both Fiix's online reviews, which are at 4.9/5 for both Yelp and Google, and their revenue, which now exceeds $1 million annually and has been growing by 41 percent a month.

Fiix has also been very popular with the investor community. The company, which has plans eventually to go national, managed to raise $1.5 million from investors in 2017 with a $10 million valuation. Shortly after raising the initial money, Arif Bhanji and Zain Manji appeared on CBC's *Dragons' Den* looking for $100,000 for 1 percent of their company, a $10 million valuation. After the Dragons heard about the sales growth, 38 percent margins, and the growing list of mechanics, a deal was struck with Michelle Romonow, Joe Mimran, and Arlene Dickinson for $700,000 for 7 percent of the company and a 1 percent royalty on sales, which amounts to a roughly $5 million valuation for the company. Other Dragons opted not to invest as some were concerned about potential competition or service centres lowering their prices to compete.

### DISCUSSION QUESTIONS

1. Do you think this is a business that the entrepreneurs will be able to take national? Why or why not?
2. What are some of the barriers to growth for the company?
3. The entrepreneurs visited *Dragons' Den* with a $10 million valuation. Were you surprised they lowered their valuation to $5 million? Even if the entrepreneurs do not close on the deal, what are some of the potential problems with reducing the company value?
4. Use Internet resources and visit the company's website. What is the status of the company today? You may expand your search to online reviews and other sources of information.

## Introduction

Although many business students go to work for large corporations upon graduation, others may choose to start their own businesses or find employment opportunities in small businesses with 500 or fewer employees. There are more than 1.65 million small businesses operating in Canada today.[1] Each small business represents the goal of its entrepreneurial owners to succeed by providing new or better products. Small businesses are the heart of the Canadian economic and social system because they offer opportunities and express the freedom of people to make their own destinies. *Profit* magazine's editor-in-chief, Ian Portsmouth, states, "Canada is in the middle of an entrepreneurial boom . . . and Canada and the world [will be] full of opportunities . . . in coming years."[2] Today, the entrepreneurial spirit is growing around the world, from India and China to Germany, Brazil, and Mexico.

This chapter surveys the world of entrepreneurship and small business. First we define entrepreneurship and small business and examine the role of small business in the Canadian economy. Then we explore the advantages and disadvantages of small-business ownership and analyze why small businesses succeed or fail. Next, we discuss how an entrepreneur goes about starting a small business and the challenges facing small business today. Finally, we look at entrepreneurship in larger businesses.

As you study this chapter, you may be asking yourself why you should study entrepreneurship. Research indicates students who study entrepreneurship are likely to experience the following benefits:

- Be three to four times more likely to start a business
- Earn 20 to 30 percent more than students studying in other fields
- Gain valuable entrepreneurial skills such as business planning, networking, and sales, which are valued by employers
- Improve their ability to think critically and become better problem solvers
- Improve their chance of landing their dream job because entrepreneurial students have many of the characteristics that employers are looking for
- Gain knowledge to supplement their income

Other reasons for studying entrepreneurship include:

- Entrepreneurs have unlimited earning potential.
- Many of society's problems today require entrepreneurial solutions. In fact, charity workers, nurses, and social workers often need to think entrepreneurially in order to solve problems. As discussed in previous chapters, these people are sometimes referred to as social entrepreneurs.
- Because 99.7 percent of businesses in Canada are, in fact, small or medium-sized enterprises (SMEs), even if you don't start an SME, you will probably end up working for one. By studying entrepreneurship, you will understand how to succeed at such a firm.

## The Nature of Entrepreneurship and Small Business

**LO 5-1** Define entrepreneurship and small business.

In Chapter 1, we defined an entrepreneur as a person who risks his or her wealth, time, and effort to develop for profit an innovative product or way of doing something. **Entrepreneurship** is the process of creating and managing a business to achieve desired objectives. Many large businesses you may recognize—Facebook, Tim Hortons, Uber, and Boston Pizza—all began as small businesses based on the entrepreneurial visions of their founders.

**entrepreneurship** the process of creating and managing a business to achieve desired objectives

Some entrepreneurs who start small businesses have the ability to see emerging trends; in response, they create a company to provide a product that serves customer needs. For example, rather than inventing a major new technology, an innovative company may exploit an existing technology to create markets that did not exist before, such as Amazon.com.[3] Or they may offer something familiar but improved or repackaged, such as what Vancouver-based 1-800-GOT-JUNK? did with junk removal.

Prior to Brian Scudamore founding and subsequently franchising 1-800-GOT-JUNK?, most junk and garbage

©Ryan Holmes, CEO of Hootsuite. Photograph courtesy of Hootsuite.

Ryan Holmes is the founder and CEO of Hootsuite. He started the company in 2008 and has helped grow it into the world's most widely used social relationship platform, with 16-million-plus users, including 79 percent of Fortune 500 companies.

removal was done by small independent operators whose customer service practices were often questionable. Scudamore's approach was to first professionalize the service and then franchise the concept, which he has done successfully over 250 times in three different countries. The company that Scudamore started as a university student now generates millions of dollars in annual revenue.[4]

Another way entrepreneurs may innovate is by focusing on a particular market segment and delivering a combination of features that consumers in that segment could not find anywhere else (e.g., REI Outdoor Gear & Clothing for camping, hiking, backpacking, and more).

Of course, smaller businesses do not have to evolve into such highly visible companies to be successful, but those entrepreneurial efforts that result in rapidly growing businesses become more visible with their success. Entrepreneurs who have achieved success—like Gerry Schwartz (Onex Corp.), Jim Pattison (Pattison Group), Ryan Holmes (Hootsuite.com), Tobias Lütke (Shopify.com), Mark Zuckerberg (Facebook)—are the most visible.

The entrepreneurship movement is accelerating with many new, smaller businesses emerging. Technology once available only to the largest firms can now be acquired by a small business. The Internet and cloud computing have reshaped the business landscape and levelled the playing field between large and small businesses by allowing small businesses to offer products globally, present professional marketing campaigns, and conduct customer service at a fraction of what it used to cost.

A recent article in the *National Post* summed this up when the author noted, "The Web has lowered the bar for people with skills and ideas. People don't need a development team or a big budget; they just need a good idea and a laptop."[5] For example, Mike McDerment of Toronto founded FreshBooks, an online accounting company aimed at servicing small businesses throughout North America. While the company is based in Ontario, it now boasts 10 million users—most of them paying $19.95 a month for accounting services—and bills itself as the world's No. 1 cloud-based accounting specialist for small businesses. FreshBooks has grown from four employees to over 200 who service clients from all over the world using the Internet.

Vincent Cheung founded Shape Collage Inc. as a student at the University of Toronto. Cheung's website allows people to take hundreds of photos and, in seconds, automatically arrange them into a collage in any shape. His software has been downloaded over a million times so far. Not only has he managed to pay himself a full salary, but he also captured the 2010 Ontario Entrepreneur of the Year student award.[6]

Much like Cheung, Cameron Laker started Vancouver-based Mindfield Group when he was in his 20s. Within three

©Freshbooks

Mike McDerment founded Freshbooks, an online accounting company for small businesses, after becoming frustrated with the lack of choice in the market. Freshbook currently has millions of users who rave about software's ease of use.

### Consider the Following: What is the difference between an entrepreneur and a small-business person?

This common question can result in much discussion. The authors of the book think an entrepreneur is someone who is always looking to seize opportunities. Whether through expansion of a business or finding better ways to do things, an entrepreneur is consistently looking to create something new. A small business person is someone who works in a small business. They may have even started the company and engaged in one act of entrepreneurship, but if they do not continue to look for additional opportunities to create something new then they stop being an entrepreneur and become a manager. The question for you is: How would you define an entrepreneur and a small business person? Do you think they are different, as we believe?

## Consider the Following: Should you start your own business?

Each day, thousands of individuals ask the difficult question, "Should I start my own business?" When queried, 85 percent of the populace said they would like to be in business for themselves. The driving force behind this desire to start a new venture is the wish to be one's own boss, to be independent. Since there is no definitive measurement developed that allows an individual to determine if they can be a successful entrepreneur, each individual needs to carefully appraise their situation through several different methods and self-assessment models.

One way to determine whether you have what it takes to be an entrepreneur is to fill out the questionnaire below. If you find that you are answering "yes" to most of the questions, you might have all the qualities to be a great entrepreneur. If you answer "no" to many of the questions, it likely means you could still be an entrepreneur and do very well, but you may have to work on some of your weaknesses. There are many exceptions, and there is no such person as a "typical" entrepreneur.

1. Can you start a project and see it through to completion in spite of a myriad of obstacles? ______ Yes ______ No
2. Can you make a decision on a matter and then stick to the decision even when challenged? ______ Yes ______ No
3. Do you like to be in charge and be responsible? ______ Yes ______ No
4. Do other people you deal with respect and trust you? ______ Yes ______ No
5. Are you in good physical health? ______ Yes ______ No
6. Are you willing to work long hours with little immediate compensation? ______ Yes ______ No
7. Do you like meeting and dealing with people? ______ Yes ______ No
8. Can you communicate effectively and persuade people to go along with your dream? ______ Yes ______ No
9. Do others easily understand your concepts and ideas? ______ Yes ______ No
10. Have you had extensive experience in the type of business you wish to start? ______ Yes ______ No
11. Do you know the mechanics and forms of running a business (tax records, payroll records, income statements, balance sheets)? ______ Yes ______ No
12. Is there a need in your geographic area for the product or service you are intending to market? ______ Yes ______ No
13. Do you have skills in marketing and/or finance? ______ Yes ______ No
14. Are other firms in your industrial classification doing well in your geographic area? ______ Yes ______ No
15. Do you have a location in mind for your business? ______ Yes ______ No
16. Do you have enough financial backing for the first year of operation? ______ Yes ______ No
17. Do you have enough money to fund the start-up of your business or have access to it through family or friends? ______ Yes ______ No
18. Do you know the suppliers necessary for your business to succeed? ______ Yes ______ No
19. Do you know individuals who have the talents and expertise you lack? ______ Yes ______ No
20. Do you really want to start this business more than anything else? ______ Yes ______ No

years, the company had grown to be one of the leading retail human resource staffing firms in Canada. Laker notes that the Internet, in particular social media sites, is important to the company's success: "Social media has allowed us to get our name out there very quickly . . . Every one of our deals, except for . . . one, has been attracted to us originally because of our use of social media."[7]

The Internet also allows smaller companies to find great employees no matter where their head office is located. For example, ZipRecuiter (www.ziprecruiter,com), uses the Internet to link employers and employees together. Businesses can post jobs with ZipRecruiter, the jobs are shared to hundreds of job sites and the software identifies the best candidates and notifies them to apply. Other technological advances, such as tablets, smartphones, online meeting software, 3D printers, fax machines, copiers, voicemail, computer bulletin boards, and even overnight delivery services enable small businesses to be more competitive with today's giant corporations. Small businesses can also form alliances with other companies to produce and sell products in domestic and global markets.

### Entrepreneur Characteristics

While entrepreneurs can come from various backgrounds, many of them share certain characteristics including the following:

- Strong desire to act independently
- High need for achievement
- Willingness to take some risks
- Energetic

Do you think you have some of these characteristics? Do you think entrepreneurs need all of them to be successful? Why or why not?

### What Is a Small Business?

This question is difficult to answer because smallness is relative. While recent research has found that the most consistent determinant of business size is the number of employees, there is no consistency in identifying the actual number of employees that make up a small business. Furthermore, researchers and government agencies often consider other variables, such as upper limits on revenue, limits on rank in the industry, and so forth, when determining whether a business is small.

In this book, we will define a **small business** as any independently owned and operated business that is not dominant in its competitive area and does not employ more than 500 people. A local Mexican restaurant may be the most patronized Mexican restaurant in your community, but because it does not dominate the restaurant industry as a whole, the restaurant can be considered a small business. This definition is similar to that of Statistics Canada, which uses 500 employees as the cut-off separating small and large businesses.[8] The Canadian Federation of Independent Businesses (CFIB) also defines small business by the number of employees but uses less than 250 employees as its cut-off. The CFIB website (www.cfib.ca) offers advice on starting a small business and offers a wealth of information to current and potential small-business owners.[9]

**small business** any independently owned and operated business that is not dominant in its competitive area and does not employ more than 500 people

## The Role of Small Business in the Canadian Economy

**LO 5-2** Investigate the importance of small business in the Canadian economy and why certain fields attract small business.

No matter how you define small business, one fact is clear: small businesses are vital to the soundness of the Canadian economy. As you can see in Table 5.1, more than 99 percent of all Canadian firms are classified as small businesses, and they employ 89.6 percent of private workers.[10] Small firms are also important as exporters, representing roughly 41.9 percent of Canadian exporters of goods.[11] In addition, small businesses are largely responsible for fuelling job creation and innovation. Small businesses also provide opportunities for women to succeed in business. There are 950,000 women entrepreneurs in Canada with an ownership interest in approximately 1 million small businesses.[12] For example, Christine Magee, co-founder and president of Sleep Country Canada, started the specialty store in 1994. The firm, which specializes in mattress sales, was purchased in 2008 for $356 million. Today, Magee remains as president of the company, which has become famous for its slogan, "Why buy a mattress anywhere else?"

**Job Creation.** The energy, creativity, and innovative abilities of small-business owners have resulted in jobs for

**Table 5.1** | Facts about Small Businesses (>500 employees)

- 99.8 percent of all employer firms are small businesses.
- They employ 10.7 million people, or 89.6 percent of all private-sector employees.
- Between 2013 and 2017 small businesses created roughly 83.5 percent percent of the jobs created in Canada.
- Approximately 1.5 million Canadians are self-employed.
- Over 99 percent of small businesses are in the service sector.
- Small firms spend approximately $4 billion on R&D annually.

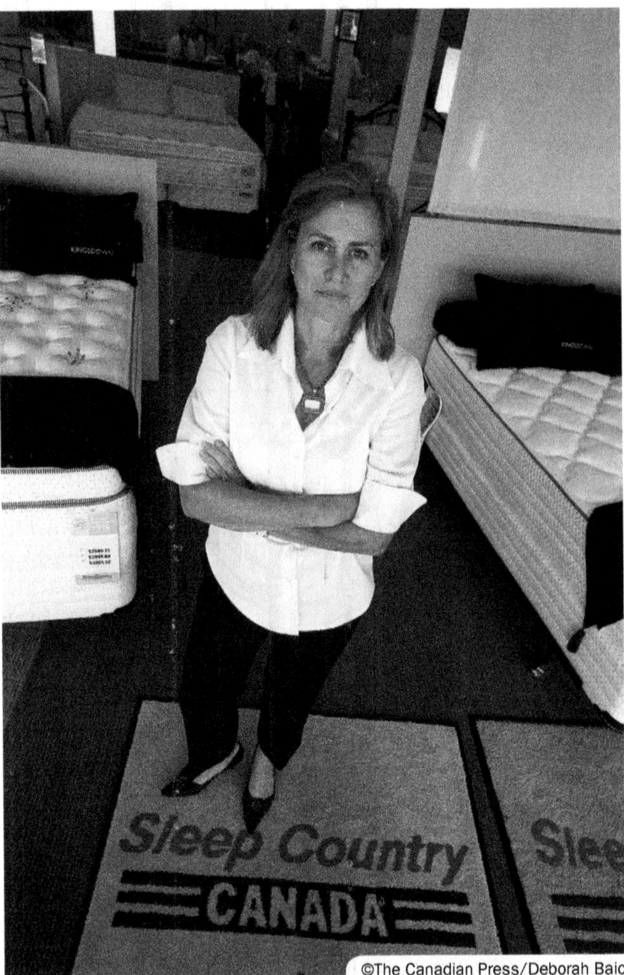

©The Canadian Press/Deborah Baic

Christine Magee is one of the better-known female entrepreneurs in Canada. She co-founded Sleep Country Canada in 1994 and has grown the company from one store to 265 today.

other people. In fact, between 2013 and 2017, 93.5 percent of net new jobs annually were created by small businesses.[13] Table 5.2 indicates that 99.7 percent of all businesses employ fewer than 500 people.

Many small businesses today are being started because of encouragement from larger ones. Many jobs are being created by big-company/small-company alliances. Whether through formal joint ventures, supplier relationships, or product or marketing cooperative projects, the rewards of collaborative relationships are creating many jobs for small-business owners and their employees.

**Innovation.** Perhaps one of the most significant strengths of small businesses is their ability to innovate and bring significant changes and benefits to customers. Small firms produce approximately 58.3 percent of innovations and invest significant resources in the development of new products and services.[14] For example, Toronto-based X-Matik Inc. (https://x-matik.com) has developed an aftermarket add-on to cars that enables them to drive autonomously. Company founder and former Tesla engineer, Nima Ashtar, says people are surprised a company as small as his has been able to develop self-driving technology. X-Matik's system, Lane Cruiser, is an add-on kit that can transform any car into a self-driving automobile. The system, which was originally sold just in Ontario as a test market, sold out in 2018. X-Matik plans on offering national sales of a more advanced but similarly priced product in 2019. Some of the better-known innovations by Canadian small firms are smartphones, insulin, the snowmobile, the pacemaker, the washing machine, the IMAX movie system, and television.

**Table 5.2** | Number of Businesses by Firm Size (Number of Employees), December 2017

| Number of Employees | Cumulative Percent of Employer Businesses | TOTAL |
|---|---|---|
| Employer Business Total | 100.0 | 1,177,634 |
| 1–4 | 53.8 | 634,063 |
| 5–9 | 73.4 | 230,857 |
| 10–19 | 86.4 | 152,801 |
| 20–49 | 95 | 101,353 |
| 50–99 | 97.9 | 33,695 |
| 100–199 | 99.1 | 14,842 |
| 200–499 | 99.8 | 7,084 |
| 500+ | 100.0 | 2,939 |

The innovation of successful firms takes many forms. For example, a group of entrepreneurs and filmmakers noticed how popular multi-screen films were at EXPO '67 in Montreal and decided to build a system using a large screen and a powerful projector. The result of the invention was the IMAX screen and projection system.[15] As mentioned previously, Ryan Holmes, CEO of Vancouver-based HootSuite,

©Alex Segre/Alamy Stock Photo

Nima Ashtar of Toronto founded X-Matik, an aftermarket autonomous driving system that he is selling for roughly $3000.

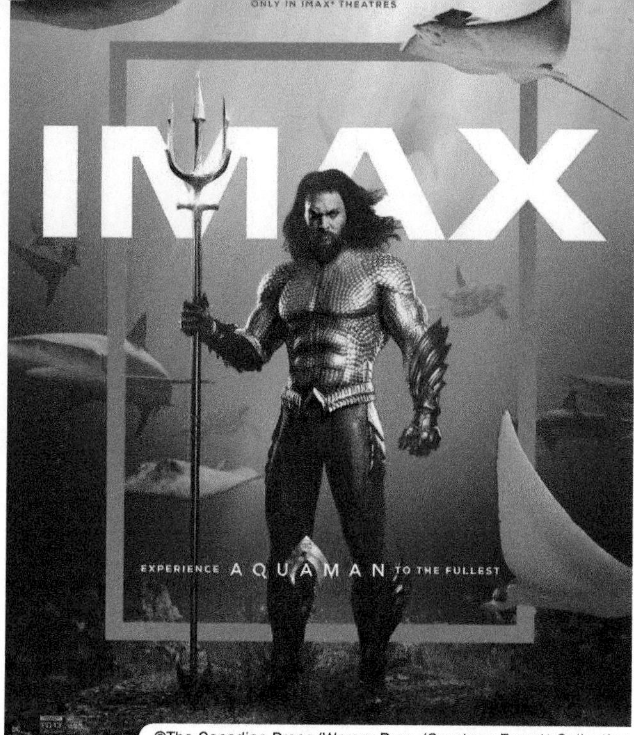

©The Canadian Press/Warner Bros./Courtesy Everett Collection

IMAX screens and projection systems are one of the innovations created by Canadians.

felt that companies should be able to manage their social media messages from one central location. Holmes created a social-media dashboard that is now being used by almost 80 out of the largest 100 companies in America.[16]

Ray Kroc found a new way to sell hamburgers and turned his small business into one of the most successful fast-food franchises in the world—McDonald's. Much like Kroc, Ron Joyce, longtime owner of Tim Hortons, found a way to sell doughnuts and coffee along with other quick-serve items from one store. Joyce's aggressive growth strategy resulted in Canada having more doughnut stores per capita than anywhere else in the world and the company name becoming a cultural icon.[17] Small businesses have become an integral part of our lives. They provide fresh ideas and usually have greater flexibility to change than do large companies.

## Industries that Attract Small Business

Small businesses are found in nearly every industry, but retailing and wholesaling, services, manufacturing, and high technology are especially attractive to entrepreneurs because they are relatively easy to enter and require low initial financing. Small-business owners also find it easier to focus on a specific group of consumers in these fields than in others, and new firms in these industries suffer less from heavy competition, at least in the early stages, than do established firms.

**Retailing and Wholesaling.** Retailers acquire goods from producers or wholesalers and sell them to consumers. Main streets, shopping strips, and shopping malls are lined with independent music stores, sporting-goods shops, dry cleaners, boutiques, drugstores, restaurants, caterers, service stations, and hardware stores that sell directly to consumers. Retailing attracts entrepreneurs because gaining experience and exposure in retailing is relatively easy.

Additionally, an entrepreneur opening a new retail store does not have to spend the large sums of money for the equipment and distribution systems that a manufacturing business requires. All that a new retailer needs is a lease on store space, merchandise, enough money to sustain the business, knowledge about prospective customers' needs and desires, the ability to use promotion to generate awareness, and basic management skills.

Some small retailers are taking their businesses online. For example, Christine Deslauriers, of Sudbury, Ontario, won the 2015 Canadian eBay Entrepreneur of the Year Award. Deslauriers, founder of Boutique Step Up, an online eBay store that started out selling figure-skating equipment, has seen sales grow by 470 percent in two years. As a result of her success, Deslauriers has expanded her product line to gymnastic and dance equipment and opened a bricks-and-mortar store.[18]

©Christine Deslauriers

eBay has enabled Canadians, such as eBay 2015 Entrepreneur of the Year Christine Deslauriers, to start successful retail businesses without establishing a physical location.

Wholesalers supply products to industrial, retail, and institutional users for resale or for use in making other products. Wholesaling activities range from planning and negotiating for supplies, promoting, and distributing (warehousing and transporting) to providing management and merchandising assistance to clients. Wholesalers are extremely important for many products, especially consumer goods, because of the marketing activities they perform. Although it is true that wholesalers themselves can be eliminated, their functions must be passed on to some other organization, such as the producer or another intermediary, often a small business.

For example, FouFou Dog (www.foufoubrands.com) was founded by Cheryl Ng from Richmond Hill, Ontario, to produce trendy, affordable, and high-quality pet clothes. After Ng started manufacturing and designing her own pet clothes, she expanded the business to act as a distributor for other manufacturers of similar products, including Rolf C. Hagen Inc., the world's largest pet products company.[19] FouFou's website notes that the company has a growing portfolio of brands allowing the company to create special moments with their pets.[20] Frequently, small businesses are closer to the final customers and know what it takes to keep them satisfied.

Some smaller businesses start out in manufacturing but find their real niche as a supplier or distributor of larger firms' products. One of the better-known Canadian success stories is Spin Master Toys, the firm founded by Ronnen Harary, Anton Rabie, and Ben Varadi after they graduated from university. They started manufacturing Earth Buddies, small pantyhose heads filled with grass seed, and built the business into the largest toy company in Canada through in-house product development and by acting as a distributor/licensee for the Canadian market for large and small international toy firms.

Today the company sells or distributes a variety of well-known toys including Paw Patrol, Air Hogs, Aqua Doodle, Bella Dancerella, Nano Speed, and the highly acclaimed Bakugan Battle Brawlers. Gerrick Johnson, an expert in the toy industry, notes, "They don't have to develop the toys themselves. If someone brings them the right idea, they'll develop it."[21] In fact, both their break out product, Air Hogs and one of their more successful toy lines, Bakugan Battle Brawlers, were acquired from inventors who had no ties to the company.[22] Anton Rabie states, "We have no ego about where the idea comes from. Lots of ideas come from in-house, but even more come from outside."[23]

**Services.** Services include businesses that work for others but do not actually produce tangible goods. They represent one of the fastest-growing sectors of the Canadian economy, accounting for 66 percent of the economy and employing roughly 75 percent of the workforce.[24] Real estate, insurance, and personnel agencies; barbershops; banks; television and computer repair shops; copy centres; dry cleaners; and accounting firms are all service businesses.

©Niloo/Shutterstock

Gillam Group became Canada's fastest growing company in 2017 by focusing on mid-range buildings, which are an under-serviced market in Toronto.

Services also attract individuals—such as beauticians, morticians, jewellers, doctors, and veterinarians—whose skills are not usually required by large firms. Service businesses are attractive to start as the upfront costs are often quite low and potential profits can be quite high. If entrepreneurs are willing to complete the services themselves, they don't even need employees. Of the 50 fastest-growing companies in Canada as identified in *Profit* magazine, roughly 30 percent are service-based businesses.[25] For example, Toronto-based Gillam Group, a construction service business, was the fastest growing business in Canada in 2017 with revenue growth of 29,000 percent since 2011. Company founder, Marcus Gillam says that the firm stands out by building mid-range projects. He notes there are a lot of firms going after the skyscraper market and many builders on a small scale. But his company's focus on the middle range buildings, an under-serviced market, has allowed Gillam to grow at a rapid pace.[26]

"Services include businesses that work for others but do not actually produce tangible goods."

**Manufacturing.** Manufacturing goods can provide unique opportunities for small businesses. While start-up costs can be higher for manufacturing businesses, entrepreneurs may be able to focus on a specific niche and keep costs down. Such products include unique food items, custom artwork, jewellery, clothing, and furniture. For example, Toronto-based, Love Child Organic was founded by Leah and John Garrad-Cole shortly after the birth of their daughter when they noticed that almost all organic foods on the marketplace contained unnecessary additives and fillers.

Leah, a home cook, started making her own organic baby food and shortly afterward the new company, Love Child, was born. The business has grown to be one of the major players in the children's organic market with distribution throughout North America including Walmart,

©M-image/Getty Images

Love Child Organic was founded by Leah and John Garrad-Cole when they couldn't find any organic food without fillers or additives. The company has grown to be one of the largest businesses in the niche segment.

Whole Foods, and Shoppers Drug Mart.[27] Love Child has become so successful that the company founders created a Spreading the Love campaign where they donate one percent of sales to building playgrounds in war-torn countries. The company recently finished its third playground in Afghanistan at a school that educates 6000 students. Other examples include Canada Goose, which has carved a niche for itself by manufacturing warm, stylish coats in Northern Canada. The company has managed to build a premium brand and sell its products at a premium through marketing and free celebrity endorsements.

**Technology.** *Technology* was once a broad term used to describe businesses that depend heavily on advanced scientific and engineering knowledge. Today, the term also refers to businesses that make use of the Internet and cloud computing to create opportunities for entrepreneurs. As mentioned at the start of the chapter, the Internet has substantially levelled the playing field between large and small business. People previously needed substantial money to engineer new technology products, but this is not the case anymore. People who can innovate or identify new markets in the fields of computers (smartphones and tablets), biotechnology, genetic engineering, robotics, and other markets have the opportunity to become today's high-tech giants.

For example, Kevin Chau, a Toronto student, built and developed the Summary Scanner app in his spare time while earning his degree. The app works by taking pictures of books and summarizing the pages so students and other readers can spend less time reading. The Summary Scanner app, which has over 70,000 downloads, was recently recognized as one of the top scanning apps by Appolicious.[28]

Another example is Hinterland Games, a Vancouver-based gaming company, which created the post-apocalyptic video game The Long Dark. Raphael van Lierop, the company founder, first used Kickstarter to successfully raise $250,000 for the development of the game and then sold alpha versions on Steam's Early Access program to continue to fund the development.[29] As of 2019, The Long Dark had sales in excess of 10 million games and Hinterland had signed a movie deal based on the story in the game.[30]

Other well-known examples include Larry Page and Sergey Brin who started Google in their dorm room, Mark Zuckerberg who launched Facebook from *his* dorm room, and Jeff Bezos who started Amazon in his garage.[31] In general, high-tech businesses require greater capital and have higher initial start-up costs than do other small businesses. The Internet is changing this, however, as the technology is reducing start-up costs and allowing entrepreneurs to reach consumers all over the globe. For example, Lane Merrifield created the world's largest social network for children, Club Penguin, at age 28. Merrifield grew the company to 200 million users before selling it to Disney for $350 million.[32] Merrifield continued to work for Disney on Club Penguin, growing the brand to a billion-dollar valuation that led to such spin-offs as Club Penguin Island, video games for Nintendo, and a television special.

©Kevin Chau

Kevin Chau started Summary Scanner while studying for his degree. His parents didn't even know he'd started the business until he appeared on CBC's *Dragons' Den*.

# Advantages of Small-Business Ownership

**LO 5-3** Specify the advantages of small-business ownership.

There are many advantages to establishing and running a small business. These can be categorized as personal advantages and business advantages.

**DID YOU KNOW?**

Thirty-nine percent of high-tech jobs in the U.S. are in small businesses.[33]

## Independence

According to Statistics Canada, independence is the leading reason that entrepreneurs choose to go into business for themselves. Being a small-business owner means being your own boss. Many people start their own businesses because they believe they will do better for themselves than they could do by remaining with their current employer or by changing jobs. Kenzie MacDonald left his job as vice president at Colliers International, a global commercial real estate firm, to branch off and start his own company in Halifax. MacDonald stated the main reason for leaving his job was a strong desire to be his own boss: "I wanted to be in charge, to do things the way I wanted to do them . . . when you work as an employee for years you always answer to someone . . . it's nice to be able to make all the decisions, to be in control."[34] Sometimes people who venture forth to start their own small business are those who simply cannot work for someone else. Such people may say that they just do not fit the corporate mold.

More often, small-business owners just want the freedom to choose whom they work with, the flexibility to pick where and when to work, and the option of working in a family setting. The availability of the computer, copy machine, business telephone, and fax machine has permitted many people to work at home. Only a few years ago, most of them would have needed the support that an office provides.

The desire for flexible work has given rise to a new type of entrepreneur or small-business owner—the *mompreneur*. Mompreneurs are mothers who are running a business either full-time or part-time and taking care of their children. Mompreneurs often start businesses rather than choose traditional employment as they can establish their own hours and schedule. Kathryn Kolaczek, a mompreneur herself, founded *The Mompreneur*, a Canadian magazine dedicated to this niche group, noting that she wanted to assist other mompreneurs in balancing their family life and business.[35]

## Enjoyment

One of the most commonly cited advantages of owning a business, whether big or small, is how much entrepreneurs enjoy their chosen careers. In fact, over 90 percent of Canadian entrepreneurs would start their businesses again if given the chance. Colin MacDonald, co-founder of Clearwater—a Halifax-based fish wholesale business that he founded out of the back of a pickup truck—notes that one of his biggest motivations in growing his business was how much he enjoyed working. "I really enjoyed the job, the responsibility, the growth," says MacDonald. Today, Clearwater is a publicly traded company and MacDonald says, "I still enjoy running the company . . . there is good and bad but I truly enjoy it."[36]

Young entrepreneur James Cuthbert, founder of the Port Moody, B.C.–based Rocky Point Kayak Ltd., echoes MacDonald's comments. "I love being an entrepreneur because it gives me the ability to earn a living in an area I love. It gives me an opportunity to be flexible with my time and pursue other personal and business interests."[37]

## Financial Rewards

Often people are drawn to entrepreneurship with the hopes of earning a higher salary. Small-business owners know that their earnings are limited only by their skills as an entrepreneur. There is an old saying: "You can't get rich working for someone else." While there are no guarantees you will become wealthy by running your own business—you just may.

## Low Start-Up Costs

As already mentioned, small businesses often require less money to start and maintain than do large ones. Obviously, a service firm with just five people will spend less money on wages and salaries, rent, utilities, and other expenses than does a firm employing tens of thousands of people in several large facilities. And, rather than maintain the expense

©Joaquin Palting/Getty Images

Entrepreneurs like James Cuthbert, founder of Rocky Point Kayak Ltd., enjoy the freedom of being an entrepreneur.

## Consider the Following: Entrepreneurship—with a difference

Entrepreneurs do not just operate in business. The entrepreneurial spirit can also be found in the social sector. A social entrepreneur is someone who is driven to create social change by identifying and implementing solutions to social problems. Emphasis is being placed on the social entrepreneur as a necessary component for future economic growth. One of the most famous social entrepreneurs is Muhammad Yunus, founder of microfinance bank, Grameen. Another example is Canadian Jeff Skoll, founder of the Skoll Foundation, which invests in social entrepreneurs who are helping solve some of the world's most pressing problems. The foundation is the world's largest organization of its type in the world and makes annual grants of $470 million to social entrepreneurs and organizations throughout the world.*

Although social entrepreneurship has long been privately funded, governments are recognizing its importance. For example, the Canadian government and many of its provincial counterparts are in the process of implementing Social Impact Bonds (SIB). The bonds would have private investors lend money to organizations that are trying to make improvements in society, such as increasing literacy rates for prisoners. If the organization succeeds, the government would then pay for the service and the organization could pay back its investors plus interest.

In 2014, Saskatchewan became the first province to approve SIBs as they were approached by Don Meikle, the executive director of EGADZ, a non-profit that provides programs for families. Meikle wanted to build a home for displaced young single mothers, and the province couldn't provide the financing. What they did do was approve an SIB bond, and a short time later, Sweet Dreams shelter was opened thanks to $1 million raised through SIBs.** The investors will only be paid back if Sweet Dreams prevents a minimum of 17 children from entering foster care.

Other examples include the Community Hypertension Prevention Initiative which was founded with a $2.9 million SIB. Ten investors contributed a total of $2.9 million to the Heart and Stroke Foundation who launched a program to reduce hypertension which can lead to heart disease. If the program reaches its participation goals, investors will earn a three-year return of 8.8 percent. If the program is not as successful as planned, the investment payback will be scaled back. SIBs are expanding to other provinces. In 2016 Ontario started a large-scale pilot project to determine the feasibility of SIBs.***

Not everyone is convinced, however, that SIBs are a good idea. In a recent story in the *Globe and Mail*, Darah Hansen cites research by Cameron Graham from York University that the bonds do have a darker side. Hansen writes that the pursuit of bonds can alter an organization's culture and that people in need could be treated as commodities as organizations strive to reach targets.† Hansen's concerns are partially echoed in a study assessing SIBs in Canada, where the researchers noted some concerns about the transparency of some SIBs and potential problems in measuring impacts. The report ultimately concluded that SIBs can save government money and assist charitable organizations.‡

### DISCUSSION QUESTIONS

1. What are the potential benefits of social entrepreneurship in our society?
2. What are some of the advantages and disadvantages of SIBs?
3. Should the government do more to encourage social enterprise? Why or why not?
4. If you were an investor, would you invest money in SIBs? Why or why not?
5. Use the Internet to see what progress SIBs have made in Canada. What other provinces have adopted SIBs? See if you can find what projects are being funded and share them with your class.

*"Skoll Foundation," Wikipedia, http://skoll.org/about/about-skoll/ (accessed March 1, 2019).

** Elisa Birnbaum, "Investing in the Non-Profit Sector: The Social Impact Bond Makes Its Canadian Debut," *Charity Village*, November 5, 2014, https://charityvillage.com/Content.aspx?topic=Investing_in_the_nonprofit_sector_The_Social_Impact_Bond_makes_its_Canadian_debut

***Government of Ontario, "Social Impact Bonds," February 8, 2016, https://www.ontario.ca/page/social-impact-bonds#section-0

†Darah Hansen, "The dark side of social impact bonds." *Globe and Mail*, August 9, 2017, https://www.theglobeandmail.com/report-on-business/careers/business-education/the-dark-side-of-social-impact-bonds/article35793919/

‡ Iryna Khovrenkov and Cindy Kobayashi, "Assessing Social Impact Bonds," January 19, 2018, https://www.schoolofpublicpolicy.sk.ca/research/publications/policy-brief/Assessing-social-impact-bonds-in-Canada.php

## RESPONDING TO BUSINESS CHALLENGES

### Please Don't Call Me a Mompreneur

If you google the term *mompreneur,* the search engine quickly finds millions of websites linked to the word. Readers can find news articles, blogs, online magazines, associations, and even clubs. The term is everywhere. Canada even boasts a number of organizations such as The Mompreneurs, which has established an annual Mompreneur conference and awards (https://themompreneur.com/). It is quite evident that many female entrepreneurs with children embrace the term as they find it to be inspiring. Grace Moores, founder of the Moores Group says she uses the term because it defines who she is, a mom and a business owner, with both being equally important. Moores also notes she finds the support and encouragement from other mompreneurs important to her success and encouraging to other potential female entrepreneurs with families.*

Even with its widespread use, not everyone is sold on the mompreneur term. Many women and men find the term troubling. People who object to the use of *mompreneur* point out that there is no *dadpreneur* term, there are simply men who own businesses.** In a recent article in the *Daily Femme*, titled "Please Stop Calling me a 'Mompreneur,'" the author states the word *mompreneur* is far from empowering. The author says that some people appear to treat mompreneurs as hobbyist entrepreneurs, females who are running a business in between their children's nap times. She states that many female entrepreneurs work 50-plus hours a week on their businesses and the term devalues what they do.*** Objectors to the term also point out that it appears to undervalue female entrepreneurial accomplishments, and the word produces imagery of women selling children's products to other moms as children play.

©Kathryn Kolaczek

Kathryn Kolaczek created *The Mompreneur* magazine to support other mompreneurs who are pursuing their entrepreneurship goals.

#### DISCUSSION QUESTIONS

1. What do you think are some of the advantages and disadvantages with using the term *mompreneur*?
2. Do you think people should continue to use the *mompreneur* term? Why or why not?

*Grace Moore, "What I've Learned About Being a Mompreneur," January 11, 2016, https://themompreneur.com/blog/grace-moores-the-moores-group/

**Grace Moore, "What I've Learned About Being a Mompreneur," January 11, 2016, https://themompreneur.com/blog/grace-moores-the-moores-group/

***Krystal, "Please Stop Calling me a 'Mompreneur," February 7, 2017, https://www.dailyfemme.com/please-stop-calling-mompreneur/

and staff of keeping separate departments for accounting, advertising, and legal counselling, small businesses can hire other firms (often small businesses themselves) to supply these services as they are needed. Additionally, small-business owners trying to produce a difficult project can sometimes rely on the volunteer efforts of friends and family members in order to save money.

## Management

Small businesses usually have only one layer of management—the owners. With small size comes the flexibility to adapt to changing market demands, the ability to build employee relations, and the capacity to create a strong corporate culture. Since decisions can be made and carried out quickly, small firms can change direction faster than larger businesses.

For example, Targray Technology International Inc., a Quebec manufacturer of CD and DVD components, noticed the trend toward green energy and started making inputs for solar panel makers. With the success of their solar panel production Targary expanded its operations into lithium-ion batteries and biofuels. The company has transformed itself into a renewable energy company with annual revenue in excess of $400 million.[38]

A similar situation occurred on a smaller scale for David Ciccarelli, who was acting as an agent and trying to market voice-over work for his wife. Ciccarelli noticed that no firms were offering what he thought was the appropriate level of service to voice-over artists. He quickly changed the focus of his work from drumming up business for his wife to building www.voices.com, a website that markets roughly 200,000 voice-over artists to Fortune

500 companies, advertising agencies, and various types of media.[39] If David had been working for a large marketing agency, this decision might have taken months if not years to come to fruition.

In larger firms, decisions about even routine matters can take weeks because they must pass through two or more levels of management before action is authorized. When McDonald's introduces a new product, for example, it must first research what consumers want, then develop the product and test it carefully before introducing it nationwide, a process that sometimes takes years. An independent snack shop, however, can develop and introduce a new product (perhaps to meet a customer's request) in a much shorter time.

Another advantage of being small is that business owners can build strong relationships with their employees, which can distinguish their businesses from larger competitors. Since managers/owners in smaller firms get to know their employees better than larger counterparts, they can use this knowledge to differentiate themselves from larger competitors. Grant McKeracher of Keen Technology Consulting, a Toronto-based IT staffing agency, states that by being small, they get to know their employees, can monitor them more closely, and provide customers with better service: "It's easy to compete when your company is small. You can easily monitor the quality of work of people you are hiring and the work that's going on, because it's all happening right in front of you."[40]

Small-business owners also get to create their company's corporate culture. In larger, more established firms, the culture of the business can be hard to influence and/or change. In smaller firms, especially new companies, the owner can create the culture desired and often use it to his or her advantage. For example, VersaPay Corp., a credit card and debt payment processing company based in Vancouver, uses its employee ownership program to motivate existing employees and to attract new talent. Michael Gokturk, the CEO, says he wanted employees to be owners of his company right from the start: "I went into this with a very Warren Buffett mindset. If you read his annual report . . . employee ownership is one of the main reasons his subsidiary companies do so well . . . At our company we use our stock as currency to incentivize our current employees."[41]

### Focus

Small firms can focus their efforts on a few key customers or on a precisely defined market niche—that is, a specific group of customers. Many large corporations must compete in the mass market or for large market segments. Smaller firms can develop products for particular groups of customers or to satisfy a need that other companies have not addressed.

For example, Fatheadz (www.fatheadz.com) focuses on producing sunglasses for people with big heads. To be an official "fathead," you need a ball cap size of at least 7⅝ and a head circumference above the ear of at least 23.5 inches. The idea arose when Rico Elmore was walking down the Las Vegas strip with his brother and realized that he had lost his sunglasses. He went to a nearby sunglass shop, and out of 300 pairs of glasses, he could not find one that fit. Customers include the entire starting line of the Indianapolis Colts, Rupert Boneham (of *Survivor* fame), and Tim Sylvia, former Ultimate Fighting Championship heavyweight title holder.[42] By targeting small niches or product needs, small businesses can sometimes avoid fierce competition from larger firms, helping them to grow into stronger companies.

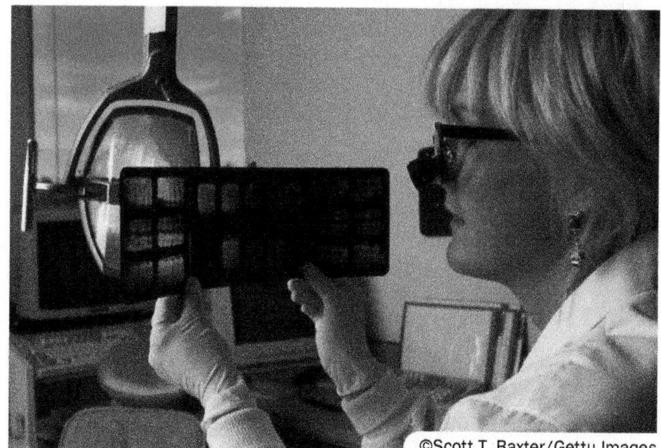

©Scott T. Baxter/Getty Images

Small-business owners, such as dentists, know that maintaining a high-quality reputation is essential to their success.

### Reputation

Small firms, because of their capacity to focus on narrow niches, can develop enviable reputations for quality and service. For example, the above-mentioned VersaPay Corp. knew it was entering a market dominated by the large Canadian banks. The co-founders, Michael Gokturk and Kevin Short, felt that they could capture market share by offering superior customer service at lower fees—especially to smaller firms that frequently complain about how large banks treat them. The company's strategy paid off as they have grown from a small firm with less than $50,000 in sales to a public company with millions in revenue.[43]

## Disadvantages of Small-Business Ownership

**LO 5-4** Summarize the disadvantages of small-business ownership, and analyze why many small businesses fail.

The rewards associated with running a small business are so enticing that it's no wonder many people dream of it. However, as with any undertaking, small-business ownership has its disadvantages.

**Table 5.3** | Top Ten Challenges for Small Businesses

- Underfunding (insufficient startup capital)
- Not understanding your competitive niche
- Lack of effective utilization of websites and social media
- Lack of a marketing and business plan
- If operating a retail store, poor site selection
- Pricing mistakes–too high or too low
- Underestimating the time commitment for success
- Not finding complementary partners to bring in additional experience
- Not hiring the right employees and/or not training them properly
- Not understanding legal and ethical responsibilities

## High Stress Level

A small business is likely to provide a living for its owner, but this often comes with an increase in stress. There are always worries about competition, employee problems, new equipment, expanding inventory, rent increases, or changing market demand. In addition to other stresses, small-business owners tend to be victims of physical and psychological stress. The small-business person is often the owner, manager, human resource specialist, sales force, shipping and receiving clerk, bookkeeper, and custodian. Table 5.3 shows the biggest challenges of small and medium-sized businesses. Many creative persons fail, not because of their business concepts, but rather because of difficulties in managing their business.

## Limited Financial Rewards

While many people start a business with dreams of becoming wealthy, research indicates that this does not always happen. Royal Bank of Canada recently released a study that shows only 34 percent of entrepreneurs were making more money than they made as a paid employee.[44] In a larger study, Statistics Canada determined that the median income of self-employed individuals was only 91.4 percent of the median income of paid employees.[45]

Young entrepreneur Brandon Turner also decided that being a paid employee resulted in more money than being an entrepreneur. Turner, who started his own real estate investing website, RealEstateInYourTwenties.com, left the company to take a job with www.BiggerPockets.com, an online real estate social network. Turner says he could get paid more as an employee and as a result he can invest that money into creating more wealth in the future and enjoying life. "While most of the world would simply buy a larger house, a nicer car, and better wardrobe, I've been sinking this cash into several other more productive avenues, including more real estate investments, paying off debt, and going on some relaxing vacations. Simply put: I'm leveraging this job to create even greater wealth in my future."[46]

## Time Demands

Entrepreneurship usually involves a significant investment in time from the entrepreneur, Statistics Canada, *Profit*, and the U.S. Census all have produced research indicating that entrepreneurs work longer hours than paid employees. For example, Ambareen Musa, founder of Souqalmal.com, a financial website, states, "There's no such thing as a 9-to-5 schedule for the company founder and no holiday when he or she can take a complete break from work . . . and when it comes to maternity leave, forget it. When my second child was born this past summer, I took one week off."[47] Given the time demands of entrepreneurship and the low pay, entrepreneurs must really love what they do. Serial entrepreneur, Chris Neville of Sydney, Nova Scotia, sums up his feelings on entrepreneurship: "I work longer hours and likely get paid less than I would make as an employee. But I love going to work and wouldn't have it any other way."[48]

## High Failure Rate

Despite the importance of small businesses to our economy, there is no guarantee of small-business success. Roughly 90 percent of all new businesses fail within the first five years.[49] Neighbourhood restaurants are a case in point. Look around your own neighbourhood and you can probably spot the locations of several restaurants that are no longer in business.

Small businesses fail for many reasons (see Table 5.4). A poor business concept—such as insecticides for garbage cans (research found that consumers are not concerned with insects in their garbage)—will produce disaster nearly every time. Expanding a hobby into a business may work if a genuine market niche exists, but all too often people start such a business without identifying a real need for the goods or services. Other notable causes of small-business failure include the burdens imposed by

**Table 5.4** | Most Common Mistakes Made by Start-Up Businesses

- Not testing to see if consumers will buy the product or service.
- Setting goals but not establishing a strategy
- Underestimating financial requirements and timing
- Over-projecting sales volume
- Making cost projections that are too low
- Spending too much on offices and facilities
- Being unwilling to take on equity partners
- Inability to manage debt
- Focusing too much on sales volume rather than profit
- Choosing poor partners or partners who do not add value
- Inability to manage growth
- Lacking an exit strategy

©Art Wager/Getty Images

Some external shocks can be so significant they can cause a business to close.

government regulation, insufficient funds to withstand slow sales, and vulnerability to competition from larger companies. However, four major causes of small-business failure deserve a close look: external shocks, undercapitalization, managerial inexperience or incompetence, and inability to cope with growth; roughly 90 percent of small-business failures can be attributed to these faults.[50]

**External Shocks.** Approximately 68 percent of businesses fail in Canada due to what is described as **external shocks**. These are events that occur in a company's external environment that the company could not control. Examples of external shocks can include changes to laws, recessions, or even a new competitor moving into a region.

**external shocks** unanticipated events that occur in a firm's external environment that hurt the company's business

**undercapitalization** the lack of funds to operate a business normally

**Undercapitalization.** The shortest path to failure in business is **undercapitalization**, the lack of funds to operate a business normally. Too many entrepreneurs think that all they need is enough money to get started, that the business can survive on cash generated from sales soon thereafter. But almost all businesses suffer from seasonal variations in sales, making cash tight, and few businesses make money from the start. Without sufficient funds, the best small-business idea in the world will fail.

**Managerial Inexperience or Incompetence.** Poor management is the cause of many business failures. Just because an entrepreneur has a brilliant vision for a small business does not mean he or she has the knowledge or experience to manage a growing business effectively. A person who is good at creating great product ideas and marketing them may lack the skills and experience to make good management decisions in hiring, negotiating, finance, and control. Moreover, entrepreneurs may neglect those areas of management they know little about or find tedious, at the expense of the business's success.

**Inability to Cope with Growth.** Sometimes, the very factors that are advantages turn into serious disadvantages when the time comes for a small business to grow. Growth often requires the owner to give up a certain amount of direct authority, and it is frequently hard for someone who has called all the shots to give up control.[51] For example, Rebecca MacDonald, founder of Toronto-based Energy Saving Income Fund, says that when she first started the business she did everything, but as the company grew she had to let other people do more and more. MacDonald notes that the transition was tough: "It was almost like letting a child leave home. It was hard for me. But I wanted to allow my talented people to do what they were hired to do."[52]

Similarly, growth requires specialized management skills in areas such as credit analysis and promotion—skills that the founder may lack or not have time to apply. David Cynamon, CEO of KIK Corp., a private-label cleaning product producer, openly questions if he has the ability to manage the company as it grows: "It becomes a different game . . . At 700 people (current number of employees), it becomes difficult; 3000 people might be beyond my capability." Cynamon has accepted that fact that his company may outgrow his ability to manage it. "It's not about the job (CEO), it's about the longevity and success of KIK forever. The status of the job means nothing to me."[53]

Poorly managed growth probably affects a company's reputation more than anything else, at least initially. And products that do not arrive on time or goods that are poorly made can quickly reverse a company's success.

## Starting a Small Business

**LO 5-5** Describe how you go about starting a small business and what resources are needed.

We've told you how important small businesses are, and why they succeed and fail, but *how do you go about* starting your own business? To start any business, large or small, you must first have an idea. Sam Walton, founder of Walmart, had an idea for a discount retailing enterprise and spawned the world's largest retailing empire, also changing the way traditional companies look at their business. Next, you need to assess whether the idea is in fact an opportunity that is worth pursuing as a business—the two are not one and the same. You may have an idea to build an amusement park in space, but due to financial and resource limitations, it is unlikely to be considered an opportunity for an entrepreneur. An opportunity is an idea that can be turned into a profitable company. Writing a business plan to guide planning and development in the business comes next. Finally, you must make decisions about form of ownership, the financial resources needed, and whether to buy an existing business, start a new one, or buy a franchise.

## Idea Generation

Ideas can come from anywhere—past jobs and hobbies are two of the most common sources of business ideas, as 80 percent of new businesses in Canada can trace their beginnings to the entrepreneur's previous business experience. For example, Michelle Strum, owner of the Halifax Backpackers Hostel, came up with the idea of a locally owned hostel after travelling extensively overseas and staying and working in different countries.[54] Similarly, Costa Elles, co-owner of Ela, a Greek restaurant that is expanding rapidly in Atlantic Canada, relied heavily on his 10-plus years of work experience in the food and beverage industry to shape the design and management of his restaurants.[55]

Ideas can also come from watching television shows like CBC's *Dragons' Den,* observing consumers as they shop, or paying close attention to emerging trends by following reports by trend watchers such as www.wired.com, www.springwise.com, and www.trendwatching.com. For example, Jay Cho of Coma Food Truck, a gourmet Korean–Mexican–American food truck that operated in Vancouver, states he was inspired to open his business after seeing the popularity of the trucks in Los Angeles. Cho says he always wanted to open his own restaurant but could never come up with the start-up money. The food-truck business would allow him to enter the restaurant business at a much lower cost than opening a bricks-and-mortar establishment.[56] Coma Food Truck opened to rave reviews from customers, but Cho eventually closed the business after a dispute with the city.

The growing number of tutoring companies, especially online tutoring, is a direct result of entrepreneurs watching trends and using the Internet to first reach customers and offer an improved experience. At one time, tutoring was used by struggling students to pass, but more and more parents are including tutoring as part of their children's extracurricular activities with the hope that the extra attention will lead to long-term success. For example, Christopher Ide, co-founder of Pax Learning, is currently offering both in-home and online tutoring in Toronto; his selling point is personalized engagement. "I don't think we need a white paper to tell us that kids' lives are totally immersed in technology these days," he says. "Having a background in the educational-technology sector, I knew that tablets, computers, and smartphones could make learning much more enjoyable for kids."[57]

Other business ideas can come from a deliberate search, where entrepreneurs are engaging in formal methods to generate new ideas. For example, Dr. A.K. Kirumira of BioMedical, a Windsor, Nova Scotia–based diagnostic equipment company, says that when he needs new ideas he starts with a formal review of medical journals, old files, and research to look for opportunities that others may have missed.[58]

©Frances Roberts/Alamy Stock Photo

Michael Duck of Sackville, Nova Scotia, founded Sure Shot Dispensing after observing Tim Hortons was constantly putting different amounts of cream in his morning coffee. His company, which manufactures portion control cream and sweetener dispensers, has annual revenues in the $20 to $25 million range.

## Opportunity Identification and Assessment

All entrepreneurs start with an idea that they hope can be an opportunity. An "opportunity" to an entrepreneur is an idea that can be turned into a profitable business. Prior to spending significant time on the development of an idea, an entrepreneur should first conduct an opportunity assessment. An opportunity assessment is a screening tool that can be used to determine if an entrepreneur should write a full business plan or go back to the drawing board and consider another idea. An opportunity assessment consists of the following:

1. Describing the business and the marketing mix (price, product, place, and promotion).
2. Assessing the entrepreneur's own skills. Does the potential entrepreneur know enough about the industry and have the skills necessary to run this type of business? Additionally, the entrepreneur should want to work in this type of industry.
3. Determining if there is a need for the business. While entrepreneurs do not have to engage in market research at this point, they may want to talk to friends, family, knowledgeable lawyers, accountants, and industry experts.
4. Identifying the competition and assessing their strengths and weaknesses. Start to determine how they would react to a new competitor.
5. Calculating start-up costs, annual expenses, and potential revenue to determine if the idea makes financial sense.
6. Determining if the entrepreneur has the ability to bring together the financial and human resources to start the company.

After completing a thorough opportunity assessment, an entrepreneur should have enough facts to decide if the idea is still worth pursuing. If the idea

## ENTREPRENEURSHIP IN ACTION

### Parsel—Helping People Make Money on YouTube and Instagram

**Parsel, later Brand Lab Partners**

**Founders:** Josh Brandley and Hamid Abbas

**Founded:** 2014

**Success:** The business has recently raised $1.2 million to fuel expansion.*

Josh Brandley and Hamid Abbas recognized that many of the people with significant YouTube and Instagram followings were not making money off their content. In fact, it was Internet giants Google and Facebook that were making the money off people's content, such as their pictures, YouTube channels, and so forth. "We realized it's the distribution platforms that are really making the money out of this—Google owns YouTube and Facebook owns Instagram," Brandley says.**

So Brandley and his partner founded Parsel to help the social media stars make money from their success. Parsel matches up companies who are looking for online personalities with significant followers to endorse their products or services. These companies pay a fee per endorsement or product placement. Additionally, Parsel will help online stars create web pages to sell the products they are endorsing.

Parsel boasts that it pre-screens people before allowing them to use its services, and that its average creator has 100,000 YouTube subscribers, with some at over a million.*** For example, Sylvia Ta, whose YouTube channel has more than 186,000 subscribers, says she has made enough money to pay for a condo in downtown Toronto as a result of working with Parsel.†

In 2016, Parsel pivoted its business and it was renamed Brand Lab Partners. With the new concept its develop brands for influencers who will market and sell the products as partners. The first product was KL Polish, a nail polish brand in partnership with beauty influencer Kathleen Lights.

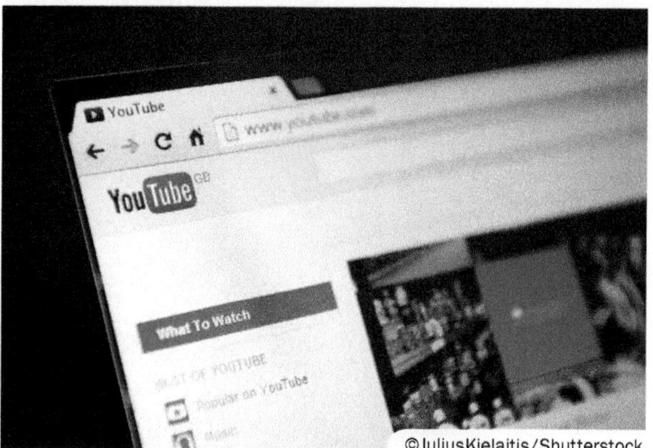

©JuliusKielaitis/Shutterstock

Josh Brandley and Hamid Abbas founded Parsel after they realized online YouTube stars were making very little off their popular videos. Parsel helped online stars monetize their content through the use of endorsements and online stores. Now called Brand Lab Partners, the company shifted its business in 2016 to partnering with influencers to sell products.

*"Parsel.me," *Crunch Base Inc.,* 2016, https://www.crunchbase.com/organization/parsel#/entity

**Jason Tchir, "Toronto startup helps YouTube and Instagram stars make money," *Globe and Mail,* January 21, 2016, http://www.theglobeandmail.com/report-on-business/small-business/startups/toronto-startup-helps-youtube-and-instagram-stars-make-money/article27921680/

***Parsel, "About Me," 2014, http://creators.parsel.me/about

†Jason Tchir, "Toronto startup helps YouTube and Instagram stars make money."

looks promising, the entrepreneur may proceed and write a business plan.

## The Business Plan

A key element of business success is a **business plan**—a precise statement of the rationale for the business and a step-by-step explanation of how it will achieve its goals. The business plan should include an explanation of the business, an analysis of the competition, estimates of income and expenses, and other information. It should establish a strategy for acquiring sufficient funds to keep the business going.

**business plan** a precise statement of the rationale for a business and a step-by-step explanation of how it will achieve its goals

Indeed, many financial institutions decide whether to loan money to a small business based on its business plan. However, the business plan should act as a guide and reference ocument—not a shackle to limit the business's flexibility and decision making. Finally, the business plan should berevised periodically to ensure that the firm's goals and strategies can adapt to changes in the environment.

Julian Brass, founder and CEO of Notablelife.com, an online company that informs people about notable events and people in and around Canada, sums up this sentiment: "Every entrepreneur needs to start with a business plan, and like when you're seeking advice and mentorship, it's an ongoing process. You can say, 'This is a golden plan and we're going to be rich in a year,' but often times when you hit the market things are very different than what you

©Julian Brass, @MrBrass

Julian Brass, founder of Notable, a website for young, professional, and connected people, says entrepreneurs should start their business with a plan. Brass, who recently sold Notable Life, wrote a book, *Own Your Anxiety*, and has embarked on a mission of helping people around the world to redirect their anxiety.

perceived before starting out. It's then that you have to return to the drawing board and tweak some things and go from there."[59]

Numerous websites provide information on how to write a business plan, including www.bdc.ca and www.scotiabank.com. The major points covered in a business plan include the following:

- Executive summary
- Industry analysis
- Description of the venture
- Production plan
- Operational plan
- Marketing plan
- Organizational plan
- Assessment of risk
- Financial plan

## Forms of Business Ownership

After developing a business plan, the entrepreneur has to decide on an appropriate legal form of business ownership—whether it is best to operate as a sole proprietorship, partnership, or corporation—and examine the many factors that affect that decision, which we explored in Chapter 4.

## Financial Resources

The old adage "It takes money to make money" holds true in developing a business enterprise. To make money from a small business, the owner must first provide or obtain money (capital) to start the business and keep it running smoothly. Often, the small-business owner has to put up a significant percentage of the necessary capital. Few new business owners have the entire amount, however, and must look to other sources for additional financing.

Students should recognize that while finding money to start a business is hard, it is never impossible—the world is full of entrepreneurs who came up with creative fund-raising techniques. For example, Susan Squires-Hutchings, owner of a St. John's, Newfoundland, pottery business, was turned down for financing on more than 50 occasions prior to convincing her landlord to lend her the money to get her company off the ground.[60] Jim Treliving and George Melville of Boston Pizza fame did not originally create the restaurant; rather, they purchased the rights to be the franchisor from the original owner. The pair raised the funds needed by convincing two friends to lend them half the money and then persuading the founder to lend them the other half.[61]

**Equity Financing.** The most important source of funds for any new business is the owner. Many owners include among their personal resources ownership of a home or the accumulated value in a life-insurance policy or a savings account. A new business owner may sell or borrow against the value of such assets to obtain funds to operate a business. Gerry Schwartz, one of the richest men in Canada and founder of Onex Corp., says that people should invest in themselves—they shouldn't fear risking their assets if it means attempting to realize their dreams.[62]

Additionally, the owner may bring useful personal assets such as a computer, desks and other furniture, or a car or truck as part of his or her ownership interest in the firm. Such financing is referred to as *equity financing* because the owner uses real personal assets rather than borrowing funds from outside sources to get started in a new business. The owner can also provide working capital by reinvesting profits into the business or simply by not drawing a full salary. These thoughts are evident in the words of Michael Cerny, CEO of Creative Building Maintenance Inc. in Mississauga, Ontario, and Huck Owen, CEO of Toronto-based Owen Media Partners Inc. Cerny states, "The reality is that any grade-A financial institution is going to expect you to put up some kind of your own money up front to show your commitment and belief in your venture."[63] "Be prepared not to get paid,"[64] says Owen, who admits he is the last person in the company to get paid.

## Consider the Following: Check your creativity

The entrepreneurial success stories in this chapter are about people who used their creative abilities to develop innovative products or ways of doing something that became the basis of a new business. Of course, being creative is not just for entrepreneurs or inventors; creativity is an important tool to help you find the optimal solutions to the problems you face on a daily basis. Employees rely heavily on their creativity skills to help them solve daily workplace problems.

According to brain experts, the right brain hemisphere is the source of creative thinking, and the creative part of the brain can "atrophy" from lack of use. Let's see how much "exercise" you're giving your right brain.

**TASK:**

1. Take the following self-test to check your Creativity Quotient.*
2. Write the appropriate number in the box next to each statement according to whether the statement describes your behaviour always (3), sometimes (2), once in a while (1), or never (0).
3. Check your score using the following scale:

   30–36 High creativity. You are giving your right-brain hemisphere a regular workout.

   20–29 Average creativity. You could use your creativity capacity more regularly to guard against "creativity atrophy."

   10–19 Low creativity. You could benefit from reviewing the questions you answered "never" in the assessment and selecting one or two of the behaviours that you could start practising.

   0–9 Undiscovered creativity. You have yet to uncover your creative potential.

| | Always 3 | Sometimes 2 | Once in a While 1 | Never 0 |
|---|---|---|---|---|
| 1. I am a curious person who is interested in other people's opinions. | | | | |
| 2. I look for opportunities to solve problems. | | | | |
| 3. I respond to changes in my life creatively by using them to redefine my goals and revising plans to reach them. | | | | |
| 4. I am willing to develop and experiment with ideas of my own. | | | | |
| 5. I rely on my hunches and insights. | | | | |
| 6. I can reduce complex decisions to a few simple questions by seeing the "big picture." | | | | |
| 7. I am good at promoting and gathering support for my ideas. | | | | |
| 8. I think further ahead than most people I associate with by thinking long term and sharing my vision with others. | | | | |
| 9. I dig out research and information to support my ideas. | | | | |
| 10. I am supportive of the creative ideas from my peers and subordinates and welcome "better ideas" from others. | | | | |
| 11. I read books and magazine articles to stay on the "cutting edge" in my areas of interest. I am fascinated by the future. | | | | |
| 12. I believe I am creative and have faith in my good ideas. | | | | |
| Subtotal for each column | | | | |
| | Grand Total | | | |

*Nitasha Tiku, "Making the Most of a Brush with Fame," *Inc.*, August 2007, p. 19; Recycline, http://www.recycline.com/ (accessed May 4, 2008); "Recycline: Sitting on Mainstream's Doorstep," Sustainable Is Good, http://www.sustainableisgood.com/blog/2007/03/recycline_produ.html (accessed May 4, 2008).

## GOING GREEN

### A New Kind of Farming

Michael Zimmerman, like most Southern Ontario farmers, has a deep appreciation for our environment. Zimmerman has a passion for land, sustainability and making a difference in his community. What separates Zimmerman from other traditional farmers is the crop he has chosen to cultivate. Zimmerman owns one of the first Ontario solar farms. Unlike traditional crops, Zimmerman's farm creates sustainable renewable energy, which is sold back to the Ontario power grid for a profit.

Zimmerman founded Group IV Solar in 2012 and spent roughly three years going through the various bureaucratic hurdles to build one of Ontario's first solar farms. Along the way Zimmerman quit his well-paying job, remortgaged his home several times, and invested over $1 million prior to even breaking ground on the project. While on his entrepreneurial journey he also heard critics point out that no one had managed to build a solar farm in Ontario, that he was wasting his time and money, and he would be an old man by the time the project was complete.

Zimmerman persevered and eventually built, then expanded, his solar farm, which is now producing enough solar energy to power 100,000 homes. Zimmerman is also happy to note that he and his investors netted $5 million over the past several years on a total investment that would have been in the $8 to $10 million range.*

Zimmerman is now on to his next project, which is convincing Ontario home and landowners in the Toronto area to allow him to install solar panels on their properties and to sell the solar electricity back to the power grid.

#### DISCUSSION QUESTIONS

1. Do you think Zimmerman's idea of installing solar panels on private homes will be successful? Why or why not?
2. Based on Zimmerman's story would you advise someone to build a solar farm? Why or why not?
3. Use Internet resources to look into the use of solar farms in your geographical area? Do farms exist? Does the government support the use of solar farms? Report your findings back to the class.

*"These are Canada's Most Successful Dragons' Den Products of All Time," January 23, 2016, https://notablelife.com/these-are-the-most-successful-dragons-den-products-of-all-time/; "Canadian Dragons' Den contestants who went on to make millions," September 20, 2018, https://www.msn.com/en-ca/money/topstories/canadian-dragons-den-contestants-who-went-on-to-make-millions/ss-BBNzjSY

"The most important source of funds for any new business is the owner."

Small businesses can also obtain equity financing by finding investors for their operations. They may sell stock in the business to family members, friends, employees, or other investors. For example, when Eryn Green and Tamar Wagman—founders of Sweetpea Baby Food, an Ontario company that sells frozen organic baby food—needed money, they asked their families and friends to help out. The pair managed to raise $150,000 by selling a 10 percent stake in the company.[65]

©fyletto/123RF.com

Michael Zimmerman created one of Ontario's first solar farms, resulting in millions in profits and electricity for over 100,000 homes.

Other sources of equity financing include the informal risk-capital market or business **angel investors** and venture capitalists. Angels are private, wealthy investors who typically invest anywhere from $10,000 to $500,000 in a business for an equity stake in the company. Angels in Canada are typically older males with entrepreneurship experience and most will want to invest in companies where they can provide some management assistance or mentoring.

**angel investors** private investors who supply equity financing for businesses

While little research has been done in Canada on the total value of dollars invested by angels, research in the U.S. has found that the amount far exceeds the total venture capital pool in the country. Examples of angel investors can be seen on CBC's *Dragons' Den* where entrepreneurs pitch their ideas to wealthy investors with hopes of receiving cash and business mentoring.[66] While the CBC version of angel investing has been spiced up for TV, it does provide some insight into what angel investors are looking for in a company—a motivated owner, strong business plan and presentation skills, an idea where they can add some expertise, and growth potential.

A new trend in angel investing is the formation of angel groups or clubs. These are small organizations of investors who meet on a regular basis to hear pitches from aspiring entrepreneurs. Some of the better-known clubs in Canada include National Angel Capital Organization, Angel One Investor Network, BC Angel Forum, and the First Angel Network. **Venture capitalists** are businesses or organizations that agree to provide some funds for a new business in exchange for an ownership interest or stock. Venture capitalists hope to purchase the stock of a small business at a low price and then sell the stock for a profit after the business has grown successful.

**venture capitalists** persons or organizations that agree to provide some funds for a new business in exchange for an ownership interest or stock

A new form of investment has emerged in Canada in recent years—crowdfunding. Rather than one or two large investors, groups of small investors, or a crowd, pool their money and invest in a business. While crowdfunding was originally started as way for entertainers or social entrepreneurs to raise money in the form of donations, it quickly evolved. For example, the Brooklyn Warehouse, a popular Halifax-based eatery, engaged in a crowdfunding campaign where they asked people for a donation to expand their business. In return, people received free meals and their picture on the wall of the restaurant.[67]

Soon entrepreneurs were using popular crowdfunding sites such as Kickstarter (www.kickstarter.com) and Indiegogo (www.indiegogo.com) to pre-sell product ideas. For example, Navi Cohen and Daniel Blumer of Montreal used Kickstarter to pre-sell Revol, their quick fitting, custom wireless earphones. The business partners, who have been friends for 25-plus years, pre-sold 10,569 pairs raising $3.3 million.[68]

In addition to crowdfunding sites, which pre-sell products a number of sites have emerged which allow investors to sell equity in the business. Investors now can earn a return on their investment in the form of equity in the business, profit sharing debt and so forth.[69] Examples of equity crowdfunding sites include AngelList and EquityNet.

Growth in crowdfunding has been significant with $17.2 billion being raised in crowdfunding in North America by 2017. There appears to be no slow-down in growth with an anticipated $762,400 million expected to be invested in over 140,000 campaigns in 2019.[70] Kickstarter, one of the largest crowdfunding sites, saw contributions top $4 billion in 2018, up from $320 million in 2012.[71] Before 2015, only Ontario allowed entrepreneurs to actually sell equity in their businesses using crowdfunding. This all changed when British Columbia, Saskatchewan, Manitoba, Quebec, New Brunswick, and Nova Scotia all agreed

## RESPONDING TO BUSINESS CHALLENGES

### Crowdfunding Success

Canadian entrepreneurs have been very successful in using crowdfunding to raise funds for a variety of businesses over several years. You can still view their crowdfunding campaigns on the crowdfunding sites inducing updates and customer comments.

Some of the most successful initiatives include:

1. Neptune Pine (https://www.neptune.co/) smart watch raised $802,1224.
2. Bulat (www.bulatkitchen.com), a kitchen knife, raised $942,716.
3. Smart Parka (https://northaware.ca), a winter coat, raised $3.2 million.
4. Smart Halo (www.smarthalo.bike), a GPS for bikes built into the handlebars, raised $538,723.

#### DISCUSSION QUESTIONS

1. Based on the text and Internet resources what do you think are some of the advantages and disadvantages of using crowdfunding sites from a business and consumer perspective?
2. Use Internet resources to review some of the products and companies cited above. What is the current state of the company's business and their products?
3. Use Internet resources to visit some of the more popular crowdfunding sites. Select a product that you would pre-purchase and present it to your peers. Be sure to explain to your peers why you would purchase the product including its strengths compared to competitor products.
4. Use Internet resources to visit some of the more popular equity based crowdfunding sites. Select a firm you would be willing to invest in and present the opportunity to your peers. Be sure to explain why you think the business will be successful.

## Consider the Following: Are these angels from heaven or greedy dragons?

"Stop the madness! You are a crazy chicken and this is a really bad idea," barks Kevin O'Leary at one entrepreneur. Jim Treliving tells another, "This idea is awful." Do these quotes sound like words from angels? Well, it depends on how you see the world. Both O'Leary and Treliving have starred on CBC's show, *Dragons' Den*, where entrepreneurs pitch their ideas to five angel investors in the hopes of receiving much-needed cash and business mentoring. Successful pitches may receive funding and often more than one new partner in their business, while unsuccessful pitches (poor products) are sometimes lambasted by the Dragons. Many viewers of the popular show are left to wonder if pitching ideas to angel investors even remotely resembles this process and if all investors are indeed as greedy as these so-called angels appear to be.

The questions are not easy to answer. Yes, entrepreneurs may pitch their ideas to a group of angel investors in a relatively short time period as seen on the show. Yes, the investors will be mostly interested in the numbers, want a large return, and expect entrepreneurs to know their business inside and out. But the really poor ideas or the unprepared entrepreneurs often seen on the show would almost never get an opportunity to pitch to a group of angel investors.

Almost all angel investors thoroughly pre-screen ideas (by reading a business plan) and would not consider listening to any of the poor, albeit entertaining, concepts that make their way onto the CBC. Furthermore, most angel investors do not want control of a company, whereas these investors almost always do. The question concerning greed is much more difficult to answer. Let's look at two examples, PeerFX and Atomic Tea. Both companies came looking for money and mentorship.

PeerFX, an online peer-to-peer currency exchange, allows customers to exchange money via the Internet at a substantially lower fee than traditional banks charge. At the time of their pitch to the Dragons, 22-year-old business students Robert Dunlop and Florence Leung were presenting an idea to make money, not operate a business. The pair had hoped to receive an investment of $200,000 for 25 percent of their business. What they ended up with was $200,000, but for 50.1 percent of their company, and partners with the knowledge and contacts to bring the project to life. The Dragons, especially Kevin O'Leary, negotiated very strongly with the two students and perhaps bullied them a bit. But both students admitted later that they are soft-spoken and may need a partner like O'Leary to get the business operating successfully. So, were the investors helpful angels or greedy dragons in this case? You decide.

Atomic Tea, an innovative tea company owned by Jessica and Russell Bohrson, presented the Dragons with an operating company and a vision of becoming the next Starbucks, albeit with teas. The brother and sister team hoped to raise $120,000 for 25 percent of their company and use the funds to franchise their business. During the course of their pitch, the Dragons all stated that they loved Atomic Tea's products

to permit the practice. Entrepreneurs are now allowed to raise upward of $500,000 a year for their company using crowdfunding in these provinces.[72]

Although these forms of equity financing have helped many small businesses, they require that the small-business owner share the profits of the business—and sometimes control, as well—with the investors. The trade-off in profits and control may well be worth the risk as research in Canada and the United States has found that businesses that make use of equity investors (angels/venture capitalists) are more financially successful, hire more employees, and bring more products to market than firms that do not use equity financing.

**Debt Financing.** Businesses often borrow the funds necessary to start and run their business. Banks are the main suppliers of external financing to small businesses. Business owners can also borrow money from some government sources such as the Business Development Centre or have some of their bank loans guaranteed by government programs such as the Canadian Small Business Financing Program. Other sources of debt financing can include family and friends, money borrowed from equity investors, and peer-to-peer lending, which is relatively new in Canada. If the business owner manages to borrow money from family or friends, he or she may be able to structure a favourable repayment schedule and sometimes negotiate an interest rate below current bank rates. If the business goes bad, however, the emotional losses for all concerned may greatly exceed the money involved. Anyone lending a friend or family member money for a venture should state the agreement clearly in writing.

The amount a bank or other institution is willing to loan depends on its assessment of the venture's likelihood of success and of the entrepreneur's ability to repay the loan. The bank will often require the entrepreneur to put up *collateral*, a financial interest in the property or fixtures of the business, to guarantee payment of the debt. Additionally, the small-business owner may have to offer some personal property as collateral, such as his or her home, in

and all of them appeared interested in investing in the fledgling company.

Jim Treliving spoke first, offering them $120,000 for 51 percent. Laurence Lewin spoke next and offered to pair with Treliving and suggested that they invest $75,000 each for a total of $150,000 for 50.1 percent of the business. Before the Bohrsons could respond, Dragon Robert Herjavec jumped in and stated that he believed Atomic Tea would need more money to franchise successfully and offered to join Treliving and Lewin to create a syndicate that would invest $225,000 in the business for 50.1 percent equity in the company.

While the three investors were contemplating their offer, fellow Dragon Arlene Dickinson offered the Bohrsons $120,000 for only 40 percent of the business. Meanwhile, the only Dragon not heard from, Kevin O'Leary, told the two Atomic Tea owners to go back behind the curtain and consider their options. The pair left thinking they were going to come back and choose between two offers—one for $225,000 for 50.1 percent of the company, and one for $120,000 for 40 percent of their company.

Back in the Den, the investors were listening to a pitch of a different kind from O'Leary that would see the investors withdraw both offers and counter with a new take-it-or-leave-it, single offer from all the Dragons. When the Atomic Tea owners reappeared in front of the Dragons, they were surprised to hear that both original offers were now gone and they could accept a one-time offer of $120,000 for 50.1 percent of their business. The Bohrsons tried to get the investors to revisit one of the previous offers and were told by O'Leary that they could "take or leave the new offer" as it was the only one that they would get.

After some thought, the Bohrsons accepted the terms and shook on the deal. After the show, Internet chat rooms and blogs were filled with people questioning the ethics of the Dragons and stating the Bohrsons should have walked away from the offer. But the Bohrsons have since said time and time again that they are happy with the terms and the Dragons' vast experience was worth giving up 50.1 percent of their company.

So, were the investors helpful angels or greedy dragons in this case? You decide.*

**DISCUSSION QUESTIONS**

1. If you represented PeerFX or Atomic Tea, would you have agreed to the deals proposed by the Dragons?
2. Did the investors act ethically?
3. Using Internet resources such as YouTube, review some *Dragons' Den* episodes. What were the pitches about? Were they successful? What were the terms of the offer? Communicate your findings to the class.

*Kerry Gold, "Dragons' Den success stories," MSN, December 7, 2009, http://money.ca.msn.com/small-business/gallery/gallery.aspx?cp-documentid=22789615&page=1; Rick Spence, "Dragons' Den: The magic touch," PROFITguide, October 1, 2008, http://www.profitguide.com/article/4487--dragons-146-den-the-magic-touch

which case the loan is called a *mortgage*. If the small business fails to repay the loan, the lending institution may eventually claim and sell the collateral (or the owner's home, in the case of a mortgage) to recover its loss.

Banks and other financial institutions can also grant a small business a *line of credit*—an agreement by which a financial institution promises to lend a business a predetermined sum on demand. A line of credit permits an entrepreneur to take quick advantage of opportunities that require a bank loan. Small businesses may obtain funding from their suppliers in the form of a *trade credit*—that is, suppliers allow the business to take possession of the needed goods and services and pay for them at a later date or in instalments. Occasionally, small businesses engage in *bartering*—trading their own products for the goods and services offered by other businesses. For example, an accountant may offer accounting services to an office supply firm in exchange for printer paper and ink cartridges.

Entrepreneurs know that being persistent is a requirement for raising money. If the idea is sound and an entrepreneur has a strong business plan, then raising debt and/or equity is always possible. For example, when Christopher Frey, Kisha Ferguson, and Matt Robinson began searching for the $300,000 they needed to fund their Toronto-based, Canadian adventure travel magazine *Outpost*, they had to be determined. During a three-month period, the partners telephoned over 200 potential investors. While the trio were initially unsuccessful in raising all the money, they did manage to come up with $50,000—enough to get started. Two years later, the company managed to raise $400,000 from BHVR Communications, a Montreal media and entertainment company.[73] See Table 5.5 for a list of funds requested by Canadian small and medium-sized enterprises (SMEs) in 2015.

## Approaches to Starting a Small Business

**Starting from Scratch versus Buying an Existing Business.** Although entrepreneurs often start new small businesses from scratch, much as we have discussed in this section, they may elect instead to buy an already

©Outpost

In their search for capital, Christopher Frey, Kisha Ferguson, and Matt Robinson, founders of *Outpost,* a travel magazine, contacted over 200 potential investors. Their perseverance eventually paid off and *Outpost* is Canada's top independent travel magazine.

**Table 5.5** | Small Business Funding Requested by SMEs

| | |
|---|---|
| Trade Credit | 29% |
| Bank Debt (Banks, Credit Unions, Government) | 28% |
| Lease Financing | 8% |
| Government Financing (non-debt) | 4% |
| Equity Financing | 1% |

existing business. This has the advantage of providing a network of existing customers, suppliers, and distributors and reducing some of the guesswork inherent in starting a new business. However, an entrepreneur buying an existing business must also deal with whatever problems the business already has, such as human resource issues, declining business, and increasing competition. In addition, it is often difficult to determine a price for a business that satisfies both the buyer and seller.

**Family Business.** Another common method of starting a business is to engage in a family-run business. Entrepreneurs may join an existing family business, start their own family-orientated company, or inherit a firm. In Canada, family businesses account for 80 to 90 percent of all firms, create 50 percent of all new jobs, and represent 40 percent of the largest 100 companies.[74] The advantages of starting or joining a family business include the following:

- Family businesses outperform non-family businesses in terms of profit and longevity.
- Family members' strengths can be combined.
- Family members tend to be more loyal to a firm than people who are not family.
- Owners of family businesses are often more driven to succeed than traditional business owners.
- Family members tend to trust each other more.

Even with these advantages, the long-term survival rate of family businesses is not as high as some people think—in fact, only one-third of family businesses survive to be passed on to the founder's children and fewer than 10 percent of those make it to the third generation. As the founder exits the business, the new owner(s) may not be as competent, the external environment can change, or issues may arise over succession planning that could result in the demise of the business.

The Irving Group represents an example of what can happen to a family business over time. K.C. Irving, the original founder of the company, noted that his succession plan was rather simple. He had three male children and they would inherit the business equally with his oldest son in charge. While the eldest Irving sibling's approach was rather traditional, it did work and the Irving empire continued to grow into a multi-billion dollar firm. Eventually, Irving's sons started to hand the company down to their children, but instead of three successors there were many more heirs. Still, the company remained relatively intact. Now, with the company going through another succession plan, there is loud talk that the firm will break up into separate companies as the family can no longer agree to a succession plan and there are too many shareholders at the table vying for their own interests.

Besides the problems with succession planning, there are other disadvantages associated with family businesses, including disputes among family members, family ties preventing people from being honest with one another, the inability of participants to separate work from home, problems in establishing fair remuneration policies, and difficulty in attracting qualified non-family workers. Still, even with these problems, people gravitate to starting or joining family businesses. For example, when Tyler Gompf of Winnipeg came up with the idea of a customer management company called Tell Us About Us Inc., he enlisted his brother Kirby to help start and eventually manage the business. The brothers have grown TUAU into a full-service customer-feedback research firm. The pair agree that there are advantages and disadvantages of working with family as they communicate easily and trust one another. But they admit that they do argue, which can strain family relations. Their solution was for Tyler to assume the role of CEO and for Kirby to become chief operating officer (COO).[75]

**Franchising.** Many small-business owners find entry into the business world through franchising. A licence to sell another's products or to use another's name in business, or both, is a **franchise**. The company that sells a franchise is the **franchisor**. Tim Hortons, Nurse Next Door, and Boston Pizza are well-known franchisers with national visibility. The purchaser of a franchise is called a **franchisee**.

**franchise** a licence to sell another's products or to use another's name in business, or both

**franchisor** the company that sells a franchise

**franchisee** the purchaser of a franchise

"Many small-business owners find entry into the business world through franchising."

The franchisee acquires the rights to a name, logo, methods of operation, national advertising, products, and other elements associated with the franchiser's business in return for a financial commitment and the agreement to conduct business in accordance with the franchiser's standard of operations. Depending on the franchise, the initial fee to join a system varies. In addition, franchisees buy equipment, pay for training, and obtain a mortgage or lease. The franchisee also pays the franchiser a monthly or annual fee based on a percentage of sales or profits. In return, the franchisee often receives building specifications and designs, site recommendations, management and accounting support, and perhaps most importantly, immediate name recognition. Visit the website of the International Franchise Association or the Canadian Franchise Association to learn more about this topic.

The practice of franchising first began in the United States when Singer used it to sell sewing machines in the nineteenth century. It soon became commonplace in the distribution of goods in the automobile, gasoline, soft drink, and hotel industries. The concept of franchising grew especially rapidly during the 1960s, when it expanded to more diverse industries.

There are both advantages and disadvantages to franchising for the entrepreneur. Franchising allows a franchisee the opportunity to set up a small business relatively quickly, and because of its association with an established brand, a franchise outlet often reaches the break-even point faster than an independent business would. Franchisees often report the following advantages:[76]

- Management training and support
- Brand-name appeal
- Standardized quality of goods and services
- National advertising programs
- Financial assistance
- Proven products and business formats

©yellowdog/Getty Images

Curves is designed for women. It's not a fast-food franchise—it's a fast-exercise franchise.

- Centralized buying power
- Site selection and territorial protection
- Greater chance for success

However, the franchisee must sacrifice some freedom to the franchisor. Furthermore, research has found that franchisees fail at the same rate as traditional small- and medium-sized firms. Some shortcomings experienced by some franchisees include:[77]

- Franchise fees and profit sharing with the franchiser
- Strict adherence to standardized operations
- Restrictions on purchasing
- Limited product line
- Possible market saturation
- Less freedom in business decisions

Strict uniformity is the rule rather than the exception. Entrepreneurs who want to be their own bosses are often frustrated with a franchise. In addition, entrepreneurs should recognize that not all franchises offer the same advantages to their franchisees. While there is value in the brand recognition and training of large franchises such as Tim Hortons, Quiznos, and Subway, an entrepreneur has to question if it is worthwhile to pay the extra costs and ongoing royalties associated with buying into a small, lesser-known company.

Often the entrepreneur could start a business from scratch and create a name and brand for less money than is required to purchase a franchise. For example, a Halifax woman purchased a Western Canada–based tanning franchise. She assumed that buying into a franchise would provide her with training and that she would receive some ongoing assistance for the royalties (fees) she paid to the franchiser. Soon after buying the franchise she received her training, which amounted to a small manual. She then learned that since all of the other franchisees were located in Western provinces, the franchise would not assist her in advertising her company until more franchises were sold in her region.[78]

> "Entrepreneurs can learn critical marketing, management, and finance skills in seminars and university/college courses."

### Help for Small-Business Managers

Because of the crucial role that small business and entrepreneurs play in the Canadian economy, a number of organizations offer programs to improve the small-business owner's ability to compete. These include entrepreneurial training programs and programs sponsored by Industry Canada and the Business Development Centre. Such programs provide small-business owners with invaluable assistance in managing their businesses, often at little or no cost to the owner.

Entrepreneurs can learn critical marketing, management, and finance skills in seminars and university/college courses. In addition, knowledge, experience, and judgment are necessary for success in a new business. While knowledge can be communicated and some experiences can be simulated in the classroom, good judgment must be developed by the entrepreneur. Local chambers of commerce and provincial and federal economic development offices offer information and assistance helpful in operating a small business. National publications and websites such as *Profit*, *Inc.*, and *Entrepreneur* share statistics, advice, tips, and success/failure stories. Additionally, many urban areas—including Halifax, Montreal, Ottawa, Toronto, Calgary, and Vancouver—have weekly or monthly business journals or newspapers that provide stories on local businesses as well as on business techniques that a manager or small business can use.

Additionally, the small-business owner can obtain advice from other small-business owners, suppliers, and even customers. A customer may approach a small business it frequents with a request for a new product, for example, or a supplier may offer suggestions for improving a manufacturing process. Networking—building relationships and sharing information with colleagues—is vital for any businessperson, whether you work for a huge corporation or run your own small business. Communicating with other business owners is a great way to find ideas for dealing with employees and government regulation, improving processes, or solving problems. New technology is making it easier to network. For example, some regions are setting up computer bulletin boards for the use of their businesses to network and share ideas.

## The Future for Small Business[79]

**LO 5-6** Evaluate the demographic, technological, and economic trends that are affecting the future of small business.

Although small businesses are crucial to the economy, they can be more vulnerable to turbulence and change in the marketplace than large businesses. Next, we take a brief look at the demographic, technological, and economic trends that will have the most impact on small business in the future.

### Demographic Trends

Canada's baby boom started in 1946 and ended in 1964. The earliest baby boomers are already past 65, and in the next few years, millions more will pass that mark. The baby boomer generation numbers about 9 million, or roughly 30 percent of Canadian citizens.[80] This segment of the population is probably the wealthiest, and the one that is often pursued by small businesses. For example, Atlantic Tours, a Halifax-based travel company, offers numerous tours aimed at this market. Industries such as travel, financial planning, and health care will continue to grow as baby boomers age.

The baby boom will also influence the labour market in Canada, as many boomers are considering retirement options. The results of this are a shortage of highly trained and skilled labour in various regions, which is a contributing factor to the growth in staffing agencies such as PEOPLEsource Staffing Solutions Inc. and MGA Computer Consulting Ltd., both in Toronto. In fact, when companies were surveyed for a recent *Profit* magazine poll, they noted the lack of skilled workers as the biggest barrier to future growth.[81]

Another market with huge potential for small business is the children of the baby boomers. They are referred to as Millennials. Millennials were born between 1981 and 1996, there are about 10 million people in Canada in this age group. Typically, they are concerned about the environment, spend considerable time using digital media, and tend to spend money on brands they trust. Much like the Baby Boomers, the Millennial generation is large and covers a significant period of time. So early Millennials will behave differently and make different purchases than later Millennials. Younger Millennials are still in school, just starting their careers, and making their first large purchases. Older

©Sneakertub

Kamaj Silva, who founded Sneakertub, gave free products to social media influencers in music and fashion who promoted his sneaker subscription service on their digital channels.

Millennials have children, likely have already purchased a home, and are starting to think about retirement.

Given the difference in ages, you cannot always market to all Millenials in the same way. For example, Sneakertub is an online sneaker subscription company founded by Kamaj Silva, who founded the business with only $700 in his bank account. The company used social media influencers in music and fashion to spread the word about their monthly subscription service of sneakers to younger Millennials. While the marketing channels worked for the company, the product and marketing would be unlikely to appeal to older Millennials who would be more interested in baby products and family vacations.

Post-Millenials are another generation that is becoming an increasingly popular target for businesses. Post-Millenials were born in 1997 or later, and the generation is very technology savvy, global, and open-minded. Many rely on digital devices to check facts and to create relationships.

Yet another trend is the growing number of immigrants living in Canada, as in excess of 300,000 people immigrate to this country each year.[82] This vast number of people provides still another greatly untapped market for small businesses. Retailers who specialize in ethnic products, and service providers who offer bi- or multilingual employees, can find vast potential in this market. Table 5.6 ranks the top cities for doing business in Canada.

## Technological and Economic Trends

Advances in technology have opened up many new markets to small businesses. As previously discussed, the Internet has revolutionized business and allows small firms to compete with larger counterparts. One of the hot areas will be the Internet infrastructure area that enables companies to improve communications with employees, suppliers, and customers.

**Table 5.6** | Top Cities for Doing Business in Canada

1. Grande Prairie, Alberta
2. Edmonton, Alberta
3. Saskatoon, Saskatchewan
4. Lethbridge, Alberta
5. High River Alberta
6. Winnipeg, Manitoba
7. Whitby, Ontario
8. Vaughan, Ontario
9. Moose Jaw, Saskatchewan
10. Burlington, Ontario

Technological advances and an increase in service exports have created new opportunities for small companies to expand their operations abroad. Changes in communications and technology can allow small companies to customize their services quickly for international customers. Also, free trade agreements and trade alliances are helping to create an environment in which small businesses have fewer regulatory and legal barriers.

In recent years, significant economic growth has provided both opportunities and threats for small businesses. With the growth and access to the Internet some smaller firms found new niche markets. Smaller companies can react quickly to change and can stay close to their customers. Many small businesses are learning to maximize the value of the Internet to promote their businesses and sell products online. For example, many arts and crafts dealers and makers of specialty products found they could sell their wares on existing websites, such as eBay and Etsy. Service providers related to tourism, real estate, and construction also found they could reach customers through their own or existing websites.

Interest in alternative fuels and fuel conservation has spawned many small businesses. Earth First Technologies Inc. produces clean-burning fuel from contaminated water or sewage. Southwest Windpower Inc. manufactures and markets small wind turbines for producing electric power

©opturadesign/Alamy Stock Photo

Sirius created value for a product and a market that didn't previously exist.

for homes, sailboats, and telecommunications. Solar Attic Inc. has developed a process to recover heat from home attics to use in heating hot water or swimming pools. As entrepreneurs begin to realize that worldwide energy markets are valued in the hundreds of billions of dollars, the number of innovative companies entering this market will increase. In addition, many small businesses have the desire and employee commitment to purchase such environmentally friendly products.

The future for small business remains promising. The opportunities to apply creativity and entrepreneurship to serve customers are unlimited. While large organizations such as Walmart, which has more than 2.2 million employees,[83] typically must adapt to change slowly, a small business can adapt to customer and community needs and changing trends immediately. This flexibility provides small businesses with a definite advantage over large companies.

## Making Big Businesses Act "Small"

**LO 5-7** Explain why many large businesses are trying to "think small."

The continuing success and competitiveness of small businesses through rapidly changing conditions in the business world have led many large corporations to take a closer look at what makes their smaller rivals tick. More and more firms are emulating small businesses in an effort to improve their own bottom line. Beginning in the 1980s and continuing through the present, the buzzword in business has been to *downsize,* or more recently, to *right-size;* to reduce management layers, corporate staff, and work tasks in order to make the firm more flexible, resourceful, and innovative—like a smaller business.

Many well-known Canadian companies—including Bell Canada and Air Canada—have downsized to improve their competitiveness, as have American, German, British, and Japanese firms. Other firms have sought to make their businesses "smaller" by making their operating units function more like independent small businesses, with each being responsible for its profits, losses, and resources.

Trying to capitalize on small-business success in introducing innovative new products, more and more companies are attempting to instil a spirit of entrepreneurship into even the largest firms. In major corporations, **intrapreneurs**, like entrepreneurs, take responsibility for, or "champion," the development of innovations of any kind *within* the larger organization.[84] Often, they use company resources and time to develop a new product for the company.

**intrapreneurs** individuals in large firms who take responsibility for the development of innovations within the organizations

### TEAM EXERCISE

Explore successful franchises. Go to the companies' websites and find the requirements for applying for three franchises. This chapter provides examples of successful franchises. What do these companies provide, and what is expected to be provided by the franchiser? Compare and contrast each group's findings for the franchises researched. For example, at Subway, the franchisee is responsible for the initial franchise fee, finding locations, leasehold improvements and equipment, hiring employees and operating restaurants, and paying an 8 percent royalty to the company and a fee into the advertising fund. The company provides access to formulas and operational systems, store design and equipment ordering guidance, a training program, an operations manual, a representative on-site during opening, periodic evaluations and ongoing support, and informative publications.

# LEARNING OBJECTIVES SUMMARY

**LO 5-1** Define entrepreneurship and small business.

Entrepreneurship is the process of creating and managing a business to achieve desired objectives. Small business is any independently owned and operated business that is not dominant in its competitive area and does not employ more than 500 people.

**LO 5-2** Investigate the importance of small business in the Canadian economy and why certain fields attract small business.

No matter how you define small business, one fact is clear: Small businesses are vital to the soundness of the Canadian economy as more than 99 percent of all

Canadian firms are classified as small businesses, and they employ 48 percent of private workers. Small firms are also important as exporters, representing roughly 97 percent of Canadian exported goods. In addition, small businesses are largely responsible for fuelling job creation and innovation.

**LO 5-3** Specify the advantages of small-business ownership.

Small-business ownership has many advantages, including (1) independence—the leading reason that entrepreneurs choose to go into business for themselves; (2) enjoyment of chosen career—one of the most commonly cited advantages of owning a business whether big or small; (3) realization that earnings are limited only by their skills as an entrepreneur—they can become wealthy; (4) the requirement for less money to start and maintain a small business compared to a large one; (5) small businesses usually have only one layer of management—the owners—which gives them flexibility to adapt to changing market demands, the ability to build strong employee relations, and the capacity to create a strong corporate culture; (6) the ability to focus efforts on a few key customers or on a precisely defined market niche—that is, a specific group of customers; and (7) the ability, with that narrow focus, to develop enviable reputations for quality and service.

**LO 5-4** Summarize the disadvantages of small-business ownership, and analyze why many small businesses fail.

Small businesses have many disadvantages for their owners, such as expense, physical and psychological stress, and a high failure rate. Small businesses fail for many reasons: undercapitalization, external shocks, management inexperience or incompetence, neglect, disproportionate burdens imposed by government regulation, and vulnerability to competition from larger companies.

**LO 5-5** Describe how you go about starting a small business and what resources are needed.

First you must have an idea for developing a small business. You must decide whether to start a new business from scratch, enter into a family business, buy an existing company, or buy a franchise operation. Next, you need to devise a business plan to guide planning and development of the business. Then you must decide what form of business ownership to use: sole proprietorship, partnership, or corporation. Small-business owners are expected to provide some of the funds required to start their businesses, but funds also can be obtained from friends and family, financial institutions, other businesses in the form of trade credit, investors (angels and or venture capitalists), and government organizations.

**LO 5-6** Evaluate the demographic, technological, and economic trends that are affecting the future of small business.

Changing demographic trends that represent areas of opportunity for small businesses include more elderly people as baby boomers age; a large group known as echo boomers, Millennials, or Generation Y; and an increasing number of immigrants to Canada. Technological advances and an increase in service exports have created new opportunities for small companies to expand their operations abroad, while trade agreements and alliances have created an environment in which small business has fewer regulatory and legal barriers. Economic turbulence presents both opportunities and threats to the survival of small business.

**LO 5-7** Explain why many large businesses are trying to "think small."

More large companies are copying small businesses in an effort to make their firms more flexible, resourceful, and innovative, and generally to improve their bottom line. This effort often involves downsizing (reducing management layers, laying off employees, and reducing work tasks) and intrapreneurship, where an employee takes responsibility for (champions) developing innovations of any kind within the larger organization.

# KEY TERMS

angel investors
business plan
entrepreneurship
external shocks
franchise
franchisee
franchisor
intrapreneurs
small business
undercapitalization
venture capitalists

## So You Want to Be *an Entrepreneur or Small-Business Owner*

In times when jobs are scarce, many people turn to entrepreneurship as a way to find employment. As long as there are unfulfilled needs from consumers, there will be a demand for entrepreneurs and small businesses. Entrepreneurs and small-business owners have been, and will continue to be, a vital part of the Canadian economy, whether in retailing, wholesaling, manufacturing, technology, or services. Creating a business around your idea has a lot of advantages. For many people, independence is the biggest advantage of forming their own small business, especially for those who do not work well in a corporate setting and like to call their own shots. Smaller businesses are also cheaper to start up than large ones in terms of salaries, infrastructure, and equipment. Smallness also provides a lot of flexibility to change with the times. If consumers suddenly start demanding new and different products or services, a small business is more likely to deliver quickly.

Starting your own business is not easy, especially in slow economic times. Even in a good economy, taking a good idea and turning it into a business has a very high failure rate. The possibility of failure can increase even more when money is tight. Reduced revenues and expensive material can hurt a small business more than a large one because small businesses have fewer resources. When people are feeling the pinch from rising food and fuel prices, they tend to cut back on other expenditures—which could potentially harm your small business. However, several techniques can help your company survive.

Set clear payment schedules for all clients. Small businesses tend to be worse about collecting payments than large ones, especially if the clients are acquaintances. However, you need to keep cash flowing into the company in order to keep business going.

Take the time to learn about tax breaks. A lot of people do not realize all of the deductions they can claim on items such as equipment.

Focus on your current customers, and don't spend a lot of time looking for new ones. It is far less expensive for a company to keep its existing customers happy.

Although entrepreneurs and small-business owners are more likely to be friends with their customers, do not let this be a temptation to give things away for free. Make it clear to your customers what the basic price is for what you are selling and charge for extra features, extra services, etc.

Make sure the office has the conveniences employees need—like a good coffee maker and other drinks and snacks. This will not only make your employees happy, but it will also help maintain productivity by keeping employees closer to their desks.

Use your actions to set an example. If money is tight, show your commitment to cost cutting and making the business work by doing simple things like taking the bus to work and bringing your lunch every day.

Don't forget to increase productivity in addition to cutting costs. Try not to focus so much attention on cost cutting that you don't try to increase sales.

In unsure economic times, these measures should help new entrepreneurs and small-business owners sustain their businesses. Learning how to run a business on a shoestring is a great opportunity to cut the fat and establish lean, efficient operations.[85]

## BUILD YOUR BUSINESS PLAN

### Small Business, Entrepreneurship, and Franchising

Now you can get started writing your business plan! Refer to the "Business Plan Development" section following Chapter 1, which provides you with an outline for your business plan. As you are developing your business plan, keep in mind that potential investors might be reviewing it. Or you might have plans to participate in some of the government opportunities aimed at supporting youth in entrepreneurship, such as the Futurpreneurs loans program.

At this point in the process, you should think about collecting information from a variety of (free) resources. For example, if you are developing a business plan for a local business, product, or service, you might want to check out any of the following sources for demographic information: the local Chamber of Commerce, the Economic Development Office, or the Statistics Canada website.

Go on the Internet and see if any recent studies or articles have focused on your specific type of business, especially in your area. Remember, you always want to explore any secondary data before trying to conduct your own research.

# CASE | Finding a Niche in the Golf Apparel Business

Like lots of golf enthusiasts, Linda Hipp loves to golf and played as much as she could. The more she played, though, the less she liked traditional women's golf apparel. Hipp notes that the clothes were mostly baggy shirts and shorts and the colours were bland. Hipp was certain that she could mesh the colours and styles from fashion runways into her own line of golf clothing.

She started to do some research on the idea and discovered that a market was emerging for stylish golf clothing. "After doing research, I found that there was a huge upswing in younger women taking up the game and I thought there would be a demand for more fashionable apparel," says Hipp. Based on this market research, Hipp started manufacturing clothing under the brand name Hyp Golf.

Shortly after starting her firm, Hipp started to realize that she was right; there was in fact a significant market for fashionable women's golf clothing. Retailers were signing up to sell her clothes, and that year Pearl Sinn became the first of many women on the LPGA tour to embrace the brand. "Our customers are women who are fit. They care about what they look like and they care about their health and well-being. They want to look good no matter what they're doing, whether taking kids to school, or out on a golf course, or out to dinner."

Hipp, now armed with positive consumer reaction in Canada, started to look south of the border to the U.S. for expansion opportunities. She says, "We started off in Canada. We made sure that, one, we could sell the product, and second, that we could manufacture and provide the goods completely and on time to customers." Hipp admits that she was hesitant to expand into the U.S., as many people advised her against the idea. "I had a lot of people tell me that we shouldn't [enter the U.S. market], that a Canadian company can never make it into the U.S." But Hipp could see the huge potential for her products, especially in the Southern states where golf is played 12 months a year.

Rather than rush into the market, Hipp opted to spend considerable time conducting research and planning on the right market-entry strategy. "To mitigate the risk, we spent a lot of time researching and finding the right people, and finding the right two or three markets that had the most potential." Hipp also designed a unique marketing program to help her break into new territories using a three-step approach.

The first step is to identify market influencers in the geographical area, such as golf pros, and provide them with free clothes to create awareness for the brand. The second stage involves securing media coverage by targeting newspapers, radio, television, and Internet companies, providing them with free product and encouraging them to write about the company. The final step involves a manager from head office contacting three to five key accounts, establishing a relationship with them, and securing an initial order. Only once a relationship is established with key retailers, along with appropriate demand for the product, does the company find a sales representative to serve the area.

©Linda Hipp

Hyp Golf's entry into the U.S. market has been a huge success, and today the market accounts for more than 75 percent of the company's sales. Hipp has since rebranded her business and product line under the brand LIJA and expanded into yoga, tennis, running, and studio apparel.[86] LIJA has continued to expand globally and has launched its brand into Dubai, the United Arab Emirates, South Africa, and the United Kingdom.

## DISCUSSION QUESTIONS

1. What are some of Linda Hipp's strengths as an entrepreneur? Does she have any apparent weaknesses?
2. Why do you think Hipp was advised to avoid the American market? What did she do to ensure that she would be successful?
3. What are some of the advantages and disadvantages of dropping the Hyp Golf name and rebranding her products under the LIJA name?
4. Given the company's success in the U.S., what are some of the advantages of continuing to expand into other countries? What would some of the challenges be?
5. Hyp's original product, fashionable clothes for young female golfers, could be characterized as a niche product. She has now expanded her product line to include products that compete against much larger competitors such as Nike and Lululemon. Why do you think she diversified her product line? Do you think adding new products is a wise strategy?

CHAPTER 6

# The Nature of Management

©James Hackland/Alamy Stock Photo

## LEARNING OBJECTIVES

**After reading this chapter, you will be able to:**

- **LO 6-1** Explain *management's* role in the achievement of organizational objectives.
- **LO 6-2** Describe the major functions of management.
- **LO 6-3** Distinguish among three levels of management and the concerns of managers at each level.
- **LO 6-4** Specify the skills managers need in order to be successful.
- **LO 6-5** Summarize the systematic approach to decision making used by many business managers.

# ENTER THE WORLD OF BUSINESS

**Loblaw's Restructuring Strategy**

When Galen G. Weston took over his family's Loblaw Companies Ltd. grocery chain at the age of 33, he also took on an obligation to restore value to a good company that had lost its way. Galen crafted a restructuring strategy that scaled back the company's lineup of non-food products. His main objectives have been a greater assortment of foods to attract customers, an improved customer experience, and lower costs. To achieve those goals, the company cut 700 jobs, or approximately 10 percent of its head office and administrative staff, and spent more than $2 billion making its technology and supply chains more efficient.

Under Galen's leadership, his team adopted a business model designed to strengthen its brand and to position itself for growth. To do so, a number of strategic decisions were undertaken, including moving into the higher-margin clothing business, introducing the Joe Fresh clothing line; strengthening the President's Choice (PC) brand; developing organic foods under the PC umbrella; and engineering a takeover of Shoppers Drug Mart. The company also introduced a number of environmentally and socially responsible initiatives, including selling reusable cloth grocery bags and becoming the first grocery chain to have unsold produce converted into energy.

Currently, Canada's largest grocer provides Canada with online grocery services. It has partnered with California-based Instacart to provide delivery services rather than wait to build a distribution centre. Shoppers use the Instacart website or app to order food from participating Loblaws and other chains. Instacart picks up and delivers the orders. It also expanded its click-and-collect program to more than 700 pickup locations. The 99-year-old grocery store is still strong on innovation, which shows that companies don't have to be young to hatch new ideas.[1]

**DISCUSSION QUESTIONS**

1. What are the most important factors contributing to Galen Weston's success?
2. What strategies did Galen Weston use to revitalize the company?
3. How does innovation contribute to the growth of the company?

## Introduction

For any organization—small or large, for-profit or non-profit—to achieve its objectives, it must have equipment and raw materials to turn into products to market, employees to make and sell the products, and financial resources to purchase additional goods and services, pay employees, and generally operate the business. To accomplish this, it must also have one or more managers to plan, organize, staff, direct, and control the work that goes on.

This chapter introduces the field of management. It examines and surveys the various functions, levels, and areas of management in business. The skills that managers need for success and the steps that lead to effective decision making are also discussed.

# The Importance of Management

**LO 6-1** Explain *management's* role in the achievement of organizational objectives.

**Management** is a process designed to achieve an organization's objectives by using its resources effectively and efficiently in a changing environment. *Effectively* means having the intended result; *efficiently* means accomplishing the objectives with a minimum of resources. **Managers** make decisions about the use of the organization's resources and are concerned with planning, organizing, staffing, directing, and controlling the organization's activities so as to reach its objectives. Management is universal. It takes place not only in businesses of all sizes, but also in government, the military, labour unions, hospitals, schools, and religious groups—any organization requiring the coordination of resources.

**management** a process designed to achieve an organization's objectives by using its resources effectively and efficiently in a changing environment

**managers** those individuals in organizations who make decisions about the use of resources and who are concerned with planning, organizing, staffing, directing, and controlling the organization's activities to reach its objectives

Every organization, in the pursuit of its objectives, must acquire resources (people, raw materials and equipment, money, and information) and coordinate their use to turn out a final good or service. Employees are one of the most important resources in helping a business attain its objectives. Hiring people to carry out the work of the organization is known as **staffing**. Beyond recruiting people for positions within the firm, managers must determine what skills are needed for specific jobs, how to motivate and train employees, how much to pay, what benefits to provide, and how to prepare employees for higher-level jobs in the firm at a later date. Sometimes, they must also make the difficult decision to reduce the workforce. This is known as **downsizing**, the elimination of significant numbers of employees from an organization. After a downsizing situation, an effective manager will promote optimism and positive thinking and minimize criticism and fault-finding. These elements of staffing will be explored in detail in Chapter 9 and Chapter 10.

**staffing** the hiring of people to carry out the work of the organization

**downsizing** the elimination of a significant number of employees from an organization

Acquiring suppliers is another important part of managing resources and in ensuring that products are made available to customers. As firms reach global markets, companies such as Walmart, IKEA, and Dell enlist hundreds of diverse suppliers that provide goods and services to support operations. A good supplier maximizes efficiencies and provides creative solutions to help the company reduce expenses and reach its objectives. Finally, the manager needs adequate financial resources to pay for essential activities. Primary funding comes from owners and shareholders, as well as banks and other financial institutions. All these resources and activities must be coordinated and controlled if the company is to earn a profit. Organizations must have adequate resources of all types, and managers must carefully coordinate the use of these resources if they are to achieve the organization's objectives.

©Piotr Swat/Shutterstock

Waze, Google's crowdsourcing map app, taps data from 90 million users to deliver information on traffic patterns and infrastructure problems. Management of Waze sells location-based advertising and traffic data, such as the location of a local McDonald's restaurant. The firm provided organizational structure for the launch, and was involved in directing and controlling implementation of the service.[2]

# Management Functions

**LO 6-2** Describe the major functions of management.

To harmonize the use of resources so that the business can develop, make, and sell products, managers engage in a series of activities: planning, organizing, staffing, directing, and controlling (Figure 6.1). Although we describe each separately, these five functions are interrelated, and managers may perform two or more of them at the same time.

## Planning

**Planning**, the process of determining the organization's objectives and deciding how to accomplish them, is the first function of management. Planning

**planning** the process of determining the organization's objectives and deciding how to accomplish them; the first function of management

Figure 6.1 | The Functions of Management

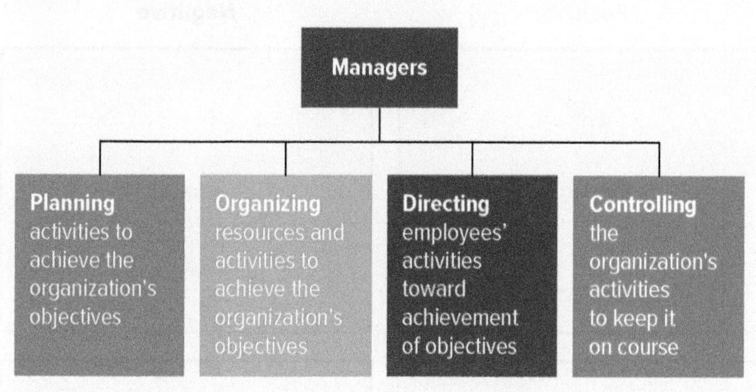


is a crucial activity, for it designs the map that lays the groundwork for the other functions. It involves forecasting events and determining the best course of action from a set of options or choices. The plan itself specifies what should be done, by whom, where, when, and how. For some managers, one major decision that requires extensive planning is selecting the right type of automation for warehouses and distribution facilities. Data gathering is a major phase of the planning process to determine what the facilities need and which automation can maximize order efficiency.

Potential pitfalls in this process that managers should plan for include being swayed by advanced technology that is not needed, under-automating the facility, or over-automating the facility. All businesses—from the smallest restaurant to the largest multinational corporation—need to develop plans for achieving success. But before an organization can plan a course of action, it must first determine what it wants to achieve.

**Mission.** A **mission**, or mission statement, is a declaration of an organization's fundamental purpose and basic philosophy. It seeks to answer the question: What business are we in? Good mission statements are clear and concise statements that explain the organization's reason for existence. A well-developed mission statement, no matter what the industry or size of business, will answer five basic questions:

**mission** the statement of an organization's fundamental purpose and basic philosophy

1. Who are we?
2. Who are our customers?
3. What is our operating philosophy (basic beliefs, values, ethics, etc.)?
4. What are our core competencies and competitive advantages?
5. What are our responsibilities with respect to being a good steward of environmental, financial, and human resources?

A mission statement that delivers a clear answer to these questions provides the foundation for the development of a strong organizational culture, a good marketing plan, and a coherent business strategy. Tesla's mission is "to accelerate the world's transition to sustainable energy."[3]

**Goals.** A goal is the result that a firm wishes to achieve. A goal has three key components:

1. An attribute sought, such as profits, customer satisfaction, or product quality.
2. A target to be achieved, such as the volume of sales or extent of management training to be achieved.
3. A time frame, which is the time period in which the goal is to be achieved.

To be successful at achieving goals, it is necessary to know what is to be achieved, how much, when, and how succeeding at a goal is to be determined. Also, the company goals should be specific. Walmart, for example, set goals to improve its reputation as an environmentally friendly company. Some of its goals involve reducing greenhouse gas emissions, increasing the fuel efficiency of its fleet, and requiring its suppliers to use less packaging. Walmart planned to improve the fuel efficiency of its truck fleet by 25 percent within a specified time frame and implemented systems to measure its progress toward these goals.

**Objectives.** Objectives are the ends or results desired by an organization; they derive from the organization's mission. Objectives provide direction for all managerial decisions; additionally, they establish criteria by which performance can be evaluated and are measurable. A business's objectives may be elaborate or simple. Common objectives relate to profit, competitive advantage, efficiency, and growth (Table 6.1).

One of the most important objectives for businesses is sales. For example, as the consumption of bottled water overtook soda, water marketers took advantage of the trend, and to boost sales, they advertised in Super Bowl LI: Pepsi launched LIFEWTR, and Fiji advertised its water to an audience of more than 111 million.[4]

Table 6.1 | Organizational Objectives

| Objective | Description |
|---|---|
| Profit | To have money and assets left over after paying off business expenses. |
| Competitive Advantage | These are generally stated in terms of percentage of sales increase and market share, with the goal of increasing those figures. |
| Efficiency | Involve making the best use of the organization's resources. |
| Growth | Relate to an organization's ability to adapt and to get new products to the marketplace in a timely fashion. |

"Objectives are the ends or results desired by the organization."

**Plans.** There are three general types of plans for meeting objectives—strategic, tactical, and operational. Planning is a continuous process that defines the organization's objectives, assesses the internal and external environment, implements the strategy, evaluates the progress, and makes the necessary adjustments to stay on track. Basically, planning answers two fundamental questions:

- Where does the organization want to go?
- How does it get there?

Figure 6.2 | SWOT Framework

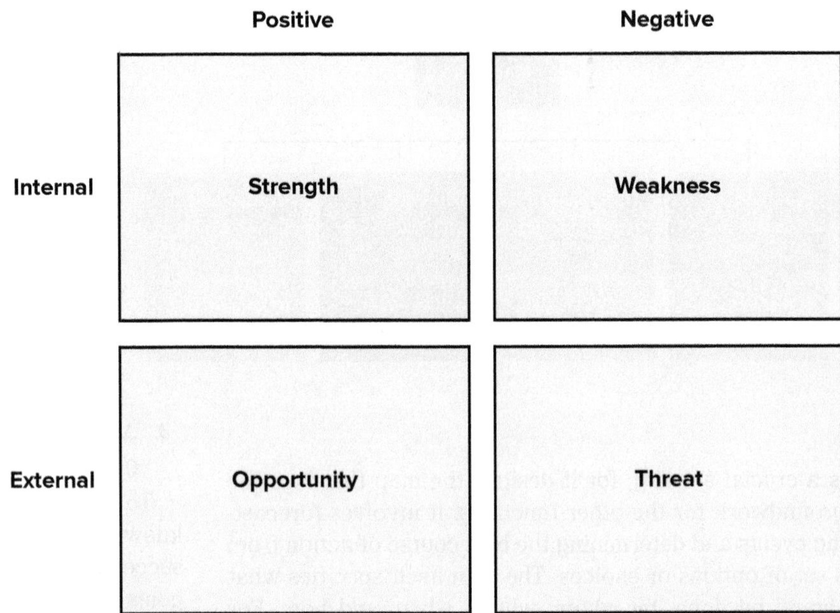


Guided by the business vision, managers then set the financial and strategic objectives. Assessing the environment includes an analysis of the firm, the industry, and the external macro-environment. A framework that helps to identify the organization's strengths, weaknesses, opportunities, and threats is the SWOT analysis (Figure 6.2).

- *Strengths* are things the company does well or characteristics that give it an important capability—for example, access to unique resources.
- *Weaknesses* are things the company does not have or does poorly, or are conditions where it is at a disadvantage—for example, a deteriorating financial position.
- *Opportunities* are found in the external environment and could potentially be an avenue for growth or a source of competitive advantage—for example, online sales.
- *Threats* are also potentially present in the external environment—for example, future demographic changes that would curtail demand for the product the company sells.

For example, strengths for Tim Hortons could include its profits, brand, and reputation as a respected employer. Weaknesses could include the company's reliance on the Canadian market and its main product, coffee. Under opportunities is the potential for global expansion, as well as new products and services or menus. Threats could be changing consumer tastes; price increases of commodities like coffee, sugar, and milk; and the entry of new competition.

An industry analysis can be performed using a framework known as Porter's five forces, shown in Figure 6.3. This framework evaluates entry barriers, suppliers, customers, substitute products, and industry rivalry. For example, industry rivals for Tim Hortons include other coffee retailers, ranging from local operators to national chains such as McDonald's and Starbucks; while the threat of substitutes is pushing Tim Hortons to develop rival strategies in order to keep up with other expanding fast-food restaurants.[5]

- *Threat of new entrants.* How easy is it for new competitors to enter the market? For example, the Internet has made it easy to enter the publishing industry.

Figure 6.3 | Porter's Five Forces Framework

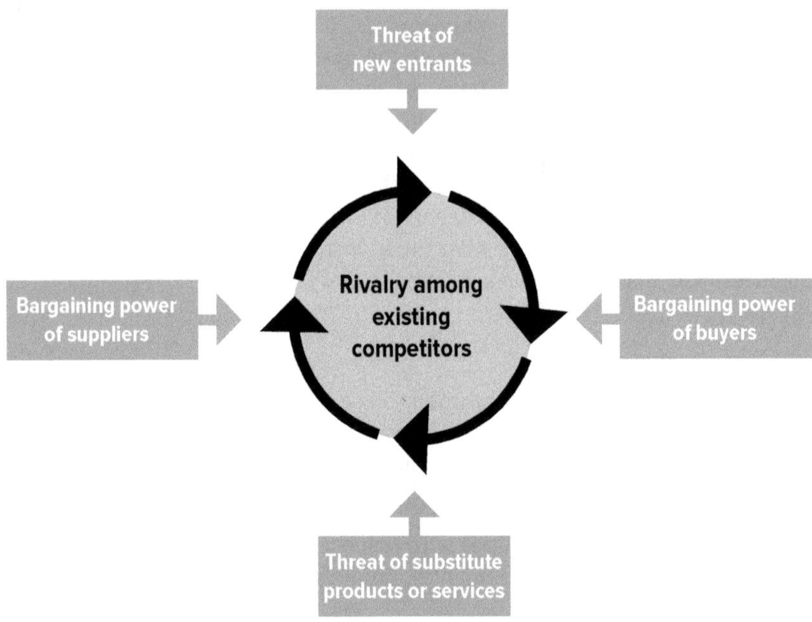

- *Threat of substitutes*. How easy is it for customers to find an alternative to this product or service? For example, there are many substitutes in the soft drinks market.
- *Buyer power*. How strong is the position of buyers? Do they control the market? For example, airlines are very large buyers of jet fuel.
- *Supplier power*. How strong is the position of suppliers? Can they drive up input prices? For example, OPEC can control the supply of oil and oil prices.
- *Rivalry*. Is there strong competition or are there dominant players? For example, the top five suppliers of sugar control 99 percent of market share.[6]

The external macro-environment can be assessed using a PEST analysis. A PEST (political, economic, social, technology) analysis is a macro framework for expanding a SWOT analysis to include political and regulatory issues, economic factors, social norms and attitudes as well as demographics, and technological developments. Some organizations expand the PEST analysis to include environmental and legal concerns (PESTEL).[7]

**Strategic plans**, establish the long-range objectives and overall strategy or course of action by which the firm fulfills its mission and vision statement while attempting to stay true to its values. These plans generally cover periods ranging from two to ten years or even longer. They include plans to add products, purchase companies, sell unprofitable segments of the business, issue stock, and move into international markets. For example, Combekk, a Dutch firm that makes knives and tools, set an objective to increase sales by introducing a heavyweight pot called a Dutch Oven that cost $450. The 100 percent recycled iron collected from bridges and former train rails has an added value to help create an incredible sales success.[8]

**strategic plans** those plans that establish the long-range objectives and overall strategy or course of action by which a firm fulfills its mission

Strategic plans are developed from the information gathered in the environmental assessment to help the organization keep a competitive advantage over its rivals. A competitive advantage exists when a firm can deliver the same benefits as competitors at a lower cost (cost advantage), or deliver benefits that exceed those of competing products (differentiation advantage). This results in profits that exceed the industry average.[9]

Strategic plans must take into account the organization's capabilities and resources, the changing business environment, and organizational objectives. Plans should be market-driven, matching customers' desire for value with operational capabilities, processes, and human resources.[10]

**Tactical plans** are short-range plans designed to implement the activities and objectives specified in the strategic plan. These plans, which usually cover a period of one year or less, help keep the organization on the course established in the strategic plan. General Motors, for instance, developed tactical plans to release redesigned versions of its vehicles that target millennials as part of its strategic plan to grow market share.[11] Because tactical plans permit the organization to react to changes in the environment while continuing to focus on the company's overall strategy, management must periodically review and update them. Declining performance or failure to meet objectives set out in tactical plans may be reasons for revising them.

The differences between strategic and tactical plans result in different activities in the short-term versus the long-term. For instance, a strategic plan might include the use of social media to reach consumers. A tactical plan could involve finding ways to increase traffic to the site or promoting premium content to those who visit the site. A fast-paced and ever-changing market requires companies to develop short-run or tactical plans to deal with the changing environment.

**tactical plans** short-range plans designed to implement the activities and objectives specified in the strategic plan

**operational plans** very short-term plans that specify what actions individuals, work groups, or departments need to accomplish in order to achieve the tactical plan and ultimately the strategic plan

**Operational plans** are very short term and specify what actions specific individuals, work groups, or departments need to accomplish to achieve the tactical plan and ultimately the strategic plan. They may apply to just one month, week, or even day. For example, a work group may be assigned a weekly production quota to ensure there are sufficient products available to elevate market share (tactical goal) and ultimately help the firm be number one in its product category (strategic goal). Returning to our retail store example, operational plans may specify the schedule for opening one new store, hiring new employees, obtaining merchandise, training new employees, and opening for actual business.

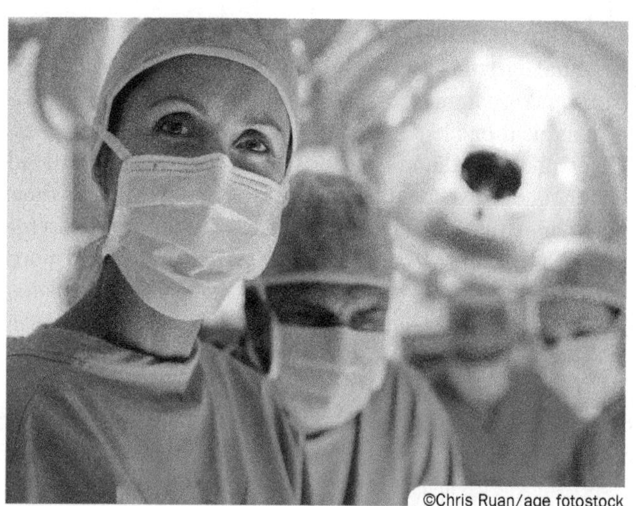

©Chris Ryan/age fotostock

Businesses have to rely on contingency plans when disaster strikes.

## ENTREPRENEURSHIP IN ACTION

### The 7 Virtues: Make Perfume, Not War

**The 7 Virtues Beauty Inc.**

**Founder:** Barbara Stegemann

**Founded:** 2010, in Halifax

**Success:** The business sources oils from farmers in Afghanistan, Haiti, Rwanda, and the Middle East. The fair-trade oils are brought to Canada where they are turned into organic, hypo-allergenic perfumes that are free of phthalates and parabens. The fragrances are available at Hudson's Bay and Sephora stores across Canada.

Barb Stegemann's life was transformed after she met fellow student, Trevor Greene, at King's College in Halifax. Greene, later a military captain, would become the inspiration for her company when he was severely wounded in Afghanistan. To carry on her friend's mission of peace, Stegemann founded The 7 Virtues, a social enterprise selling perfumes made from essential oils sourced in countries rebuilding from war or strife. She wanted to effect change and have an impact on poverty and education and people's ability to help themselves.

Stegemann had read about a man in Afghanistan who was growing orange blossom and rose rather than the illegal poppy crops, which are the source of more than 90 percent of the world's heroin. The same people who attacked her best friend were also destroying this man's distillery. Stegemann travelled to Ottawa to meet with the Canadian International Development Agency. From there, she connected with a non-governmental organization (NGO) that had done a study on how to get farmers off the illegal poppy crop. With the help of the NGO, she connected with the Afghan supplier and began purchasing his oils.

A year later, The 7 Virtues began a relationship with Hudson's Bay, launching its Original collection in 70 stores across Canada. That same year, Stegemann won the chance to make her pitch on the CBC program *Dragons' Den*, and she ended up becoming the first woman from Atlantic Canada to score a deal on the show. "Just like they taught us in school, I did my homework," she says. "That presentation took months to prepare."*

#### DISCUSSION QUESTIONS

1. What management skills did Barbara Stegemann need to found her successful business?
2. How does Barbara Stegemann use the four functions of management to operate her business?
3. What types of decisions did Barbara Stegemann need to make as her business grew?

*The 7 Virtues Peace Perfumes (2018), The 7 Virtues, www.the7virtues.com (retrieved December 23, 2018); *Atlantic Business Magazine*, April 12, 2018, "2018 Top 50 CEO Award Winners," https://www.atlanticbusinessmagazine.net/article/24837/ (retrieved December 23, 2018); Speakers Spotlight, April 12, 2018, Barb Stegemann, https://www.speakers.ca/speakers/barb-stegemann/ (retrieved December 23, 2018; Huffington Post, Barb Stegemann, https://www.huffingtonpost.ca/author/barbara-stegemann/ (retrieved December 23, 2018); BDC (2018), "Perfumes for peace," https://www.bdc.ca/en/articles-tools/business-strategy-planning/manage-business/pages/perfumes_peace_purposeful_entrepreneur_business_cause.aspx?&ccr=ctl00%24ctl35%24ctl00%24h%24BDCMainSearchBoxEntirePortal%24ctl00&k=scss&z=987313520 (retrieved December 23, 2018); University of King's College (2014), Barb Stegemann, http://ukingscommunity.ca/stories/barb-stegemann (retrieved December 23, 2018); Barb Stegemann (2018), "Meet Barb," http://www.barbstegemann.com/meet-barb.html (retrieved December 23, 2018).

**Crisis management or contingency planning**, deals with potential disasters such as product tampering, oil spills, fire, earthquake, computer viruses, or even a reputation crisis due to unethical or illegal conduct by one or more employees. Unfortunately, many businesses do not have updated contingency plans to handle the types of crises that their companies might encounter. Businesses that have correct and well-thought-out contingency plans tend to respond more effectively when problems occur than do businesses who lack such planning.

**crisis management or contingency planning** an element in planning that deals with potential disasters such as product tampering, oil spills, fires, earthquakes, computer viruses, or airplane crashes

Many companies have crisis management teams to deal specifically with problems, permitting other managers to continue to focus on their regular duties. Some companies even hold periodic disaster drills to ensure that their employees know how to respond when a crisis does occur. After a horrific earthquake in Japan, companies in earthquake zones reevaluated their crisis management plans. Crisis management plans generally cover maintaining business operations throughout a crisis and communicating with the public, employees, and officials about the nature of and the company's response to the problem. Communication is especially important to minimize panic and damaging rumours; it also demonstrates that the company is aware of the problem and plans to respond.

Sometimes, disasters occur that no one can anticipate, but companies can still plan for how to react to the disaster. There can be a major crisis when supply that is time sensitive is disrupted. That's what happened to KFC in the U.K. when it pared back its logistics network to cut expenses. The move resulted in two-thirds of its outlets being without chicken

©Ray Tang/REX/Shutterstock

After KFC's chicken shortage in the U.K. went viral on Twitter, the fast-food company acknowledged the issue in a timely manner, addressed guest concerns on social media, and published a series of ads apologizing for the supply chain error.

for several days.[12] Incidents such as this highlight the importance of planning for crises and the need to respond publicly and quickly when a disaster occurs.

## Organizing

Rarely are individuals in an organization able to achieve common goals without some form of structure. **Organizing** is the structuring of resources and activities to accomplish objectives in an efficient and effective manner. Managers organize by reviewing plans and determining what activities are necessary to implement them; then, they divide the work into small units and assign it to specific individuals, groups, or departments. As companies reorganize for greater efficiency, more often than not, they are organizing work into teams to handle core processes such as new product development instead of organizing around traditional departments such as marketing and production. Organizing occurs continuously because change is inevitable and is important for several reasons:

**organizing** the structuring of resources and activities to accomplish objectives in an efficient and effective manner

- Helps create synergy, whereby the effect of a whole system equals more than that of its parts
- Establishes lines of authority
- Improves communication
- Helps avoid duplication of resources
- Improves competitiveness by speeding up decision making

A business model relates to how a firm is organized to operate and provide value to stakeholders. It is the map or blueprint for running a business—a conceptual tool for organizing how a business operates. Examples of business models include a Subway franchise, Avon direct selling, Amazon and online retailing, and Netflix's subscription business model that provides access to entertainment. General business models relate to manufacturing to create a product or a distribution that resells to retailers.

Today many businesses are trying to create new business models that focus on business sectors such as the sharing economy. Uber and Airbnb provide access to but not ownership of products. In the future, many business models will emerge related to the digital economy, driverless vehicles, robotics, drones, and artificial intelligence. Artificial intelligence will allow managers to gain extraordinary control over their workers as well as forecasting demand, developing customer relationships, and managing the supply chain. New business models will develop around artificial intelligence systems.[13] Because organizing is so important, we'll take a closer look at it in Chapter 7.

## Directing

During planning and organizing, staffing occurs and management must direct the employees. **Directing** is motivating and leading employees to achieve organizational objectives. Good directing involves telling employees what to do and when to do it through the implementation of deadlines, and then encouraging them to do their work. For example, as a sales manager, you would need to learn how to motivate salespersons, provide leadership, teach sales teams to be responsive to customer needs, and manage organizational issues as well as evaluate sales results. Finally, directing also involves determining and administering appropriate rewards and recognition.

**directing** motivating and leading employees to achieve organizational objectives

All managers are involved in directing, but it is especially important for lower-level managers who interact daily with the employees operating the organization. For example, an assembly-line supervisor for Frito-Lay in Ancaster, Ontario, must ensure that workers know how to use their equipment properly and have the resources needed to carry out their jobs safely and efficiently, and must motivate her workers to achieve their expected output of packaged snacks.

Managers may motivate employees by providing incentives—such as the promise of a raise or promotion—for them to do a good job. But most workers want more than money from their jobs: they need to know that their employer values their ideas and input. Managers should give younger employees some decision-making authority as soon as possible. Smart managers, therefore, ask workers to contribute ideas for reducing costs, making equipment more efficient, improving customer service, or even developing new products.

For example, Travelocity has made employee engagement a top priority to bring customer service to the highest level. This participation makes workers feel important, and the company benefits. Recognition and appreciation are often the best motivators. Employees who understand more about their effect on the financial success of the company may be induced to work harder for that success, and managers who understand the needs and desires of workers can encourage their employees to work harder and more productively. The motivation of employees is discussed in detail in Chapter 9.

> "Participation makes workers feel important, and the company benefits."

### Controlling

Planning, organizing, staffing, and directing are all important to the success of an organization, whether its objective is earning a profit or something else. But what happens when a firm fails to reach its goals despite a strong planning effort? **Controlling** is the process of evaluating and correcting activities to keep the organization on course. Controlling involves five activities:

**controlling** the process of evaluating and correcting activities to keep the organization on course

1. Measuring performance
2. Comparing present performance with standards or objectives
3. Identifying deviations from the standards
4. Investigating the causes of deviations
5. Taking corrective action when necessary

Controlling and planning are closely linked. Planning establishes goals and standards. By monitoring performance and comparing it with standards, managers can determine whether performance is on target. When performance is substandard, management must determine why and take appropriate actions to get the firm back on course. In short, the control function helps managers assess the success of their plans.

You might relate this to your performance in this class. If you did not perform as well on early projects or exams, you must take corrective action such as increasing studying or using website resources to achieve your overall objective of getting an A or B in the course. When the outcomes of plans do not meet expectations, the control process facilitates revision of the plans. Control can take many forms such as visual inspections, testing, and statistical modelling processes. The basic idea is to ensure that operations meet requirements and are satisfactory to reach objectives.

The control process also helps managers deal with problems arising outside the firm. For example, if a firm is the subject of negative publicity, management should use the control process to determine why and to guide the firm's response.

## Types of Management

**LO 6-3** Distinguish among three levels of management and the concerns of managers at each level.

All managers—whether the sole proprietor of a jewellery store or the hundreds of managers of a large company such as Home Depot—perform the five functions just discussed. In the case of the jewellery store, the owner handles all the functions, but in a large company with more than one manager, responsibilities must be divided and delegated. This division of responsibility is generally achieved by establishing levels of management and areas of specialization—finance, marketing, and so on.

### Levels of Management

As we have hinted, many organizations have multiple levels of management—top management, middle management, and first-line, or supervisory management. These levels form a pyramid, as shown in Figure 6.4. As the pyramid shape implies, there are generally more middle managers than top managers, and still more first-line managers. Very small organizations may have only one manager (typically, the owner), who assumes the responsibilities of all three levels. Large businesses have many managers at each level to coordinate the use of the organization's resources. Managers at all three levels perform all

**Figure 6.4** | Levels of Management

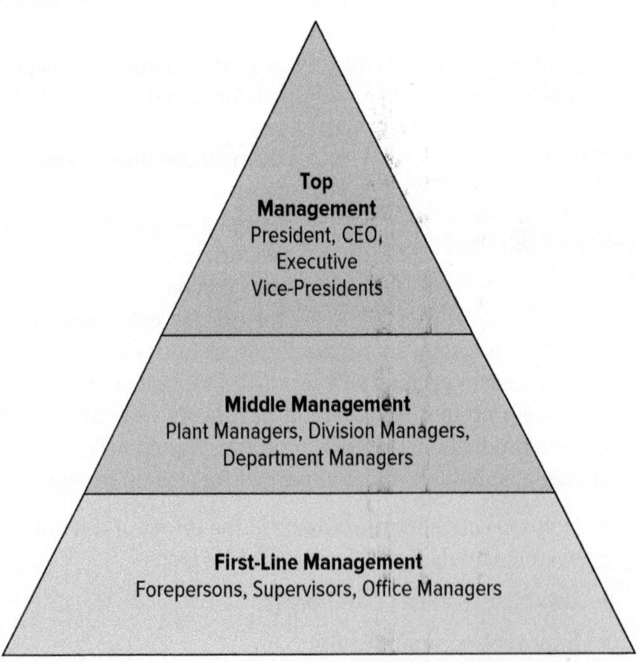

## GOING GREEN

### Feeling the Heat

Canada Goose CEO Dani Reiss is feeling the heat over the company's ethical and sustainable practices, from the sourcing of coyote fur to the treatment of geese on farms. The coat maker, founded more than 35 years ago, knows that being a sustainable and ethical luxury brand can lead to profitability.

Canada Goose and other popular brands like North Face and Patagonia say their businesses operate with animal welfare in mind. On their websites, the companies use terms such as "without unnecessary harm," "traceability," and "ethical sourcing" to demonstrate their concern for animal welfare. However, when a video was released in 2017 showing geese being thrown and crushed at a Manitoba farm that supplies the company with down, it ignited outrage over cruel practices.

There are alternatives available. For example, Canadian company, Wully Outerwear, offers a line of vegan jackets that excel in cold-weather protection. It uses a material called PrimaLoft which was created for the United States Army. The material retains 98 percent of its heating properties even when dampened by sweat or snow. Wully jackets are sold for about the same price as Canada Goose. North Face and Patagonia also offer comparable down-free options.*

#### DISCUSSION QUESTIONS

1. What assurances does Canada Goose give to consumers regarding animal welfare?
2. Describe why consumers tend to be more loyal to sustainable and ethical brands.
3. With comparable down-free options, why do consumers still flock to brands like Canada Goose?

*Jessica Scott-Reid, "Cold comfort: Think of the geese before buying a down winter coat," *Globe and Mail*, November 2017, https://www.theglobeandmail.com/opinion/cold-comfort-think-of-the-geese-before-buying-a-down-winter-coat/article36837532/, (accessed December 23, 2018); Canada Goose (2018), "Fur & Down," https://www.canadagoose.com/ca/en/fur-and-down-policy/fur-and-down-policy.html, (accessed December 23, 2018).

five management functions, but the amount of time they spend on each function varies, as we shall see (Figure 6.5).

**Top Management.** In businesses, **top managers** include the president and other top executives, such as the chief executive officer (CEO), chief financial officer (CFO), and chief operations officer (COO), who have overall responsibility for the organization. For example, the CEO of a company manages the overall strategic direction of the company and plays a key role in representing the company to stakeholders. The COO is responsible for daily operations of the company. The COO reports to the CEO and is often considered to be number two in command.

In public corporations, even the CEO has a boss, which is the firm's board of directors. With technological advances continuing and privacy concerns increasing, some companies are adding a new top management position in the form of a chief privacy officer (CPO). The position of privacy officer has grown in response to

**top managers** the president and other top executives of a business, such as the chief executive officer (CEO), chief financial officer (CFO), chief operations officer (COO), and, more recently, chief privacy officer (CPO), who have overall responsibility for the organization

**Figure 6.5** | Importance of Management Functions to Managers at Each Level

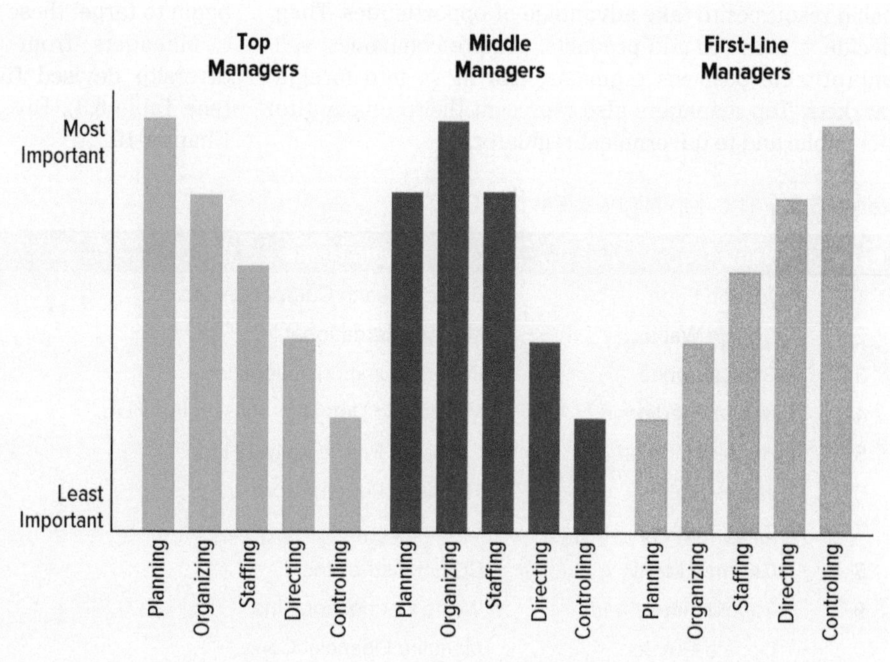

©YURIKO NAKAO/AFP/Getty Images

Interestingly, Mark Zuckerberg is an example of a CEO who does not receive high annual compensation. His annual pay is a token $1 per year.

growing concerns about privacy as well as a requirement in the *Personal Information Protection and Electronic Documents Act* (PIPEDA). In government, *top management* refers to the prime minister, a premier, or a mayor or city manager; in education, a chancellor of a university or a school's superintendent of education.

**DID YOU KNOW?**

Women represent 8 percent of executive positions in Canadian companies and just 3 percent are CEOs.[14]

Top-level managers spend most of their time planning. They make the organization's strategic decisions, decisions that focus on an overall scheme or key idea for using resources to take advantage of opportunities. They decide whether to add products, acquire companies, sell unprofitable business segments, and move into foreign markets. Top managers also represent their company to the public and to government regulators.

Given the importance and range of top management's decisions, top managers generally have many years of varied experience and command top salaries. In addition to salaries, top managers' compensation packages typically include bonuses, long-term incentive awards, stock, and stock options. Table 6.2 lists the ten highest-paid CEOs in Canada, including bonuses, stock options, and other compensation. Top management may also get perks and special treatment that is criticized by stakeholders.

Compensation committees are increasingly working with boards of directors and CEOs to attempt to keep pay in line with performance in order to benefit stockholders and key stakeholders. The majority of major companies cite their concern about attracting capable leadership for the CEO and other top executive positions in their organizations. However, many firms are trying to curb criticism of excessive executive compensation by trying to align CEO compensation with performance. In other words, if the company performs poorly, the CEO will not be paid as well.

Unsuccessful management has negative consequences for leaders, whereas successful management translates into happy stockholders who are willing to compensate their top executives fairly and in line with performance.[15] For example, when Chipotle struggled after attempting to recover from E. coli outbreaks in its restaurants in 2018, the co-CEOs had their pay cut in half, and the stock lost 30 percent of its value in one year.

Workforce diversity is an important issue in today's corporations. Effective managers at enlightened corporations have found that diversity is good for workers and for the bottom line. Putting together different kinds of people to solve problems often results in better solutions. A diverse workforce is better at making decisions regarding issues related to consumer diversity. Reaching fast-growing demographic groups such as new Canadians and others will be beneficial to large companies as they begin to target these markets.

Managers from companies devoted to workforce diversity devised five rules that make diversity work (see Table 6.3). Diversity is explored in greater detail in Chapter 10.

**Table 6.2** | The Ten Highest-Paid CEOs

| Rank | Name | Organization Name | Total Compensation (millions) |
|---|---|---|---|
| 1 | Joseph Papa | Bausch Health Companies Inc. | $83.1 |
| 2 | Donald Walker | Magna International Inc. | $28.6 |
| 3 | Guy Laurence | Rogers Communications Inc. | $24.6 |
| 4 | Daniel Friedmann | Macdonald Dettwiler & Associates Ltd. | $21.4 |
| 5 | Hunter Harrison | Canadian Pacific Railway Ltd. | $18.8 |
| 6 | James Smith | Thomson Reuters Corp. | $17.8 |
| 7 | Doug Suttles | Encana Corp. | $17.6 |
| 8 | Geoffrey Martin | CCL Industries Inc. | $15.9 |
| 9 | Ronald Mittelstaedt | Waste Connections Inc. | $18.6 |
| 10 | Donald Guloien | Manulife Financial Corp. | $15.3 |

Table 6.3 | Five Rules of Successful Diversity Recruiting

| Rule | Action |
|---|---|
| 1. Involve employees | Educate all employees on the tangible benefits of diversity recruiting to garner support and enthusiasm for those initiatives. |
| 2. Communicate diversity | Prospective employees are not likely to become excited about joining your company just because you say that your company is diversity friendly; they need to see it. |
| 3. Support diversity initiatives and activities | By supporting community-based diversity organizations, your company will generate the priceless word-of-mouth publicity that will lead qualified diversity candidates to your company. |
| 4. Delegate resources | If you are serious about diversity recruiting, you will need to spend some money getting your message out to the right places. |
| 5. Promote your diversity initiatives | Employers need to sell their company to prospective diversity employees and present them with a convincing case that their company is a good fit for the diversity candidate. |

**Middle Management.** Rather than making strategic decisions about the whole organization, **middle managers** are responsible for tactical planning that will implement the general guidelines established by top management. Thus, their responsibility is more narrowly focused than that of top managers. Middle managers are involved in the specific operations of the organization and spend more time organizing than other managers. In business, plant managers, division managers, and department managers make up middle management. The product manager for laundry detergent at a consumer products manufacturer, the department chairperson in a university, and the head of a regional public health department are all middle managers. The ranks of middle managers have been shrinking as more and more companies downsize to be more productive.

**middle managers** those members of an organization responsible for the tactical planning that implements the general guidelines established by top management

©NAN104/iStock

This financial manager analyzes data from financial charts. Financial managers are responsible for ensuring the organization has the necessary funding to succeed, both in the short term and in the long term.

**First-Line Management.** Most people get their first managerial experience as **first-line managers**, those who supervise workers and the daily operations of the organization. They are responsible for implementing the plans established by middle management and directing workers' daily performance on the job. They spend most of their time directing and controlling. Common titles for first-line managers are foreperson, supervisor, and office manager.

**first-line managers** those who supervise both workers and the daily operations of an organization

"Most people get their first managerial experience as first-line managers."

## Areas of Management

At each level, there are managers who specialize in the basic functional areas of business: finance, production and operations, human resources (personnel), marketing, IT, and administration.

Each of these management areas is important to a business's success. For instance, a firm cannot survive without someone obtaining needed financial resources (financial managers) or staff (human resources managers). While larger firms will most likely have all of these managers, and even more depending upon that particular firm's needs, in smaller firms, these important tasks may fall onto the owner or a few employees. Yet whether or not companies have managers for specific areas, every company must have someone responsible for obtaining financial resources, transforming resources into finished products for the marketplace, hiring and/or dealing with staff, marketing goods and services, handling the firm's information technology resources, and managing a business segment or the overall business. These different types of managers are discussed in more detail in Table 6.4.

**financial managers** those who focus on obtaining needed funds for the successful operation of an organization and using those funds to further organizational goals

**production and operations managers** those who develop and administer the activities involved in transforming resources into goods, services, and ideas ready for the marketplace

**human resources managers** those who handle the staffing function and deal with employees in a formalized manner

**marketing managers** those who are responsible for planning, pricing, and promoting products and making them available to customers

**information technology (IT) managers** those who are responsible for implementing, maintaining, and controlling technology applications in business, such as computer networks

**administrative managers** those who manage an entire business or a major segment of a business; they are not specialists but coordinate the activities of specialized managers

Table 6.4 | Areas of Management

| Manager | Function |
|---|---|
| **Financial managers** | Focus on obtaining the money needed for the successful operation of the organization and using that money in accordance with organizational goals. |
| **Production and operations managers** | Develop and administer the activities involved in transforming resources into goods, services, and ideas ready for the marketplace. |
| **Human resources managers** | Handle the staffing function and deal with employees in a formalized manner. |
| **Marketing managers** | Have responsibility for planning, pricing, and promoting products and making them available to customers through distribution. |
| **Information technology (IT) managers** | Have responsibility for implementing, maintaining, and controlling technology applications in business, such as computer networks. |
| **Administrative managers** | Manage an entire business or a major segment of a business; do not specialize in a particular function. |

## Skills Needed by Managers

LO 6-4 Specify the skills managers need in order to be successful.

Managers are typically evaluated as to how effective and efficient they are. Managing effectively and efficiently requires certain skills—leadership, technical expertise, conceptual skills, analytical skills, and human relations skills. Table 6.5 describes some of the roles managers may fulfill.

Table 6.5 | Managerial Roles

| Type of Role | Specific Role | Example Activity |
|---|---|---|
| Decisional | Entrepreneur | Changing work process |
| | Disturbance handler | Deciding which unit moves into new facilities |
| | Resource allocator | Deciding who receives new computer equipment |
| | Negotiator | Settling union grievance |
| Informational | Monitor | Contacting government regulatory agencies |
| | Disseminator | Conducting meetings with subordinates to pass along safety policy |
| Interpersonal | Spokesperson | Meeting with consumer group to discuss product safety |
| | Figurehead | Attending award banquet |
| | Leader | Conducting performance appraisal for subordinates |
| | Liaison | Coordinating production schedule with supply manager |

**Technical Expertise.** Managers need **technical expertise**, the specialized knowledge and training needed to perform jobs that are related to their area of management. Accounting managers need to be able to perform accounting jobs, and production managers need to be able to perform production jobs. Although a production manager may not actually perform a job, he or she needs technical expertise to train employees, answer questions, provide

**technical expertise** the specialized knowledge and training needed to perform jobs that are related to particular areas of management

guidance, and solve problems. Technical skills are most needed by first-line managers and least critical to top-level managers.

**Conceptual Skills.** **Conceptual skills**, the ability to think in abstract terms, and to see how parts fit together to form the whole, are needed by all managers, but particularly top-level managers. Top management must be able to evaluate continually where the company will be in the future. Conceptual skills also involve the ability to think creatively. Recent scientific research has revealed that creative thinking, which is behind the development of many innovative products and ideas, can be learned. As a result, top firms hire creative consultants to teach their managers how to think creatively.

**Analytical Skills.** **Analytical skills** refer to the ability to identify relevant issues and recognize their importance, understand the relationships between them, and perceive the underlying causes of a situation. When managers have identified critical factors and causes, they can take appropriate action. All managers need to think logically, but this skill is probably most important to the success of top-level managers. To be analytical, it is necessary to think about a broad range of issues and to weigh different options before taking action.

Because analytical skills are so important, questions that require analytical skills are often a part of job interviews. Queries such as "Tell me how you would resolve a problem at work if you had access to a large amount of data." may be part of the interview process. The answer would require the interviewee to try to explain how to sort data to find relevant facts that could resolve the issue. Analytical thinking is required in complex or difficult situations where the solution is often not clear. Resolving ethical issues often requires analytical skills.

**Human Relations Skills.** People skills, or **human relations skills**, are the ability to deal with people, both inside and outside the organization. Those who can relate to others, communicate well with others, understand the needs of others, and show a true appreciation for others are generally more successful than managers who lack human relations skills. People skills are especially important in hospitals, airline companies, banks, and other organizations that provide services. For example, WestJet's motto is "We succeed because I care." The company believes that highly engaged employees, or in its case, owners, will go above and beyond to provide a truly memorable experience. Its strategy has earned WestJet a spot alongside only five other companies in Canada's Most Admired Corporate Cultures Hall of Fame, J.D. Power has recognized it as a customer service champion, and it is one of the most profitable airlines in North America.[16]

**conceptual skills** the ability to think in abstract terms and to see how parts fit together to form the whole

**analytical skills** the ability to identify relevant issues, recognize their importance, understand the relationships between them, and perceive the underlying causes of a situation

**human relations skills** the ability to deal with people, both inside and outside the organization

©Compassionate Eye Foundation/Getty Images

WestJet Airlines has been able to successfully differentiate itself from its competitors by way of no-frills and low-price fares. But WestJet also is known for its human relations skills. Jovial flight crews often crack jokes over the intercom system to their captive audiences.

## Leadership

**Leadership** is the ability to influence employees to work toward organizational goals. Strong leaders manage and pay attention to the culture of their organizations and the needs of their customers. Table 6.6 offers some tips for successful leadership. The list is compiled annually for *Fortune* magazine by executives and analysts who grade companies according to nine attributes, including quality of management.

**leadership** the ability to influence employees to work toward organizational goals

Managers often can be classified into three types based on their leadership style. *Autocratic leaders* make all the decisions and then tell employees what must be done and how to do it. They generally use their authority and economic rewards to get employees to comply with their directions. Martha Stewart is an example of an autocratic leader. She built up her media empire by paying close attention to every detail.[17]

**Table 6.6** | Requirements for Successful Leadership

- Communicate objectives and expectations.
- Gain the respect and trust of stakeholders.
- Develop shared values.
- Acquire and share knowledge.
- Empower employees to make decisions.
- Be a role model for appropriate behaviour.
- Provide rewards and take corrective action to achieve goals.

*Democratic leaders* involve their employees in decisions. The manager presents a situation and encourages his or her subordinates to express opinions and contribute ideas. The manager then considers the employees' points of view and makes the decision. Clive Beddoe, co-founder of WestJet Airlines, had a democratic leadership style. Under his leadership, employees were encouraged to discuss concerns and provide input.

*Free-rein leaders* let their employees work without much interference. The manager sets performance standards and allows employees to find their own ways to meet them. For this style to be effective, employees must know what the standards are, and they must be motivated to attain them. The free-rein style of leadership can be a powerful motivator because it demonstrates a great deal of trust and confidence in the employee. Larry Page, CEO and co-founder of Google, uses free-rein leadership, and employees are encouraged to pursue any and all ideas.

©Michael Reynolds/Epa/REX/Shutterstock

Twitter CEO Jack Dorsey believes in a democratic leadership style.

"Employees who have been involved in decision making generally require less supervision than those not similarly involved."

The effectiveness of the autocratic, democratic, and free-rein styles depends on several factors. One consideration is the type of employees. An autocratic style of leadership is generally needed to stimulate unskilled, unmotivated employees; highly skilled, trained, and motivated employees may respond better to democratic or free-rein leaders. Employees who have been involved in decision making generally require less supervision than those not similarly involved.

Other considerations are the manager's abilities and the situation itself. When a situation requires quick decisions, an autocratic style of leadership may be best because the manager does not have to consider input from a lot of people. If a special task force must be set up to solve a quality-control problem, a normally democratic manager may give free rein to the task force.

Many managers, however, are unable to use more than one style of leadership. Some are unable to allow their subordinates to participate in decision making, let alone make any decisions. Thus, what leadership style is "best" depends on specific circumstances, and effective managers strive to adapt their leadership style as circumstances warrant. Many organizations offer programs to develop leadership skills. When plans fail, very often leaders are held responsible for what goes wrong. For example, Lululemon chief product officer Sheree Waterson and chief executive officer Christine Day left the company following a product mishap with Lululemon pants.[18]

Another type of leadership style that has been gaining in popularity is *authentic leadership*. Authentic leadership is a bit different from the other three leadership styles because it is not exclusive. Both democratic and free-rein leaders could qualify as authentic leaders depending upon how they conduct themselves among stakeholders. Authentic leaders are passionate about the goals and mission of the company, display corporate values in the workplace, and form long-term relationships with stakeholders.

While leaders might incorporate different leadership styles depending on the business and the situation, all leaders must be able to align employees behind a common vision to be effective.[19] Strong leaders also realize the value that employees can provide by participating in the firm's corporate culture. It is important that companies develop leadership training programs for employees. Because managers cannot oversee everything that goes on in the company, empowering employees to take more responsibility for their decisions can aid in organizational growth and productivity.

©Jen Grantham/iStock

A product mishap with pants led to the resignation of Lululemon's CEO, Christine Day.

## Consider the Following: Home Depot builds effective management system

When Home Depot was founded in 1979, the founders built a strong culture placing customers and employees at the top and executives at the bottom. However, after Robert Nardelli took over as CEO, the style of leadership at Home Depot abruptly changed. Nardelli took a top-down approach to running Home Depot: executives at the top and customers and employees at the bottom.

This new management style was disastrous, and customer satisfaction hit an all-time low. After Nardelli was ousted, new CEO Frank Blake quickly refocused on customers and employees. As an authentic leader, Blake led by example. He quickly admitted to the customer service problems the company faced, apologized for the inconvenience it caused, and encouraged customers to leave feedback so it could make improvements. Each one of the complaints was addressed; some angry stakeholders were appeased by phone calls from managers and personal emails responding to their specific issues. Both customer satisfaction and company morale rose once more.

After Blake stepped down as CEO, he was replaced by Craig Menear. Menear proved that he would continue managing the company in a way that would honour the original culture of Home Depot. This is being put to the test as bricks-and-mortar retailers are experiencing major changes because of online competition. While many companies have struggled because of online retailing, Home Depot has continued to see revenues increase, partly because of the resolve of leadership to invest in a strong e-commerce strategy. The company's online sales have increased since Menear became CEO. Thanks to the transformational leadership of its committed managers, Home Depot is effectively competing in the "Amazon era."*

### DISCUSSION QUESTIONS

1. What type of leader was Robert Nardelli? What type of leaders were CEOs Frank Blake and Craig Menear?
2. What are some ways that Blake used the management functions of leading and controlling to change the culture of Home Depot?
3. As an effective manager, Craig Menear must successfully engage in planning, organizing, leading, and controlling. Why is this especially important for Home Depot's ability to compete against online retailers?

*Brad Tuttle, "Why Home Depot Is Immune to the 'Amazon Effect,'" *Time: Money*, August 16, 2016, http://time.com/money/4453962/home-depot-amazon-effect-sales/ (accessed September 17, 2017); Greenleaf, "How Home Depot Overcame a Difficult Cultural Shift: A Q&A with CFO Carol Tome," Greenleaf Center for Servant Leadership, July 10, 2015, https://www.greenleaf.org/how-home-depotovercame-a-difficult-cultural-shift-a-qa-with-cfo-carol-tome/ (accessed September 27, 2017); Heidi N. Moore, "Chrysler: The End of Bob Nardelli. Again," *Wall Street Journal*, April 21, 2009, https://blogs.wsj.com/deals/2009/04/21/chrysler-the-end-of-bob-nardelli-again/ (accessed September 27, 2017); "CEO Craig Menear Talks Innovation: Follow the Consumer," Home Depot, October 19, 2016, https://corporate.homedepot.com/newsroom/ceo-craig-meneartalks-innovation-aspen-institute (accessed September 27, 2017); "Home Depot Builds Out Its Online Customer Service," Internet Retailer, June 4, 2010, https://www.digitalcommerce360.com/2010/06/04/home-depot-builds-outits-online-customer-service/ (accessed September 27, 2017); Joann Lublin, Matt Murray, and Rick Brooks, "Home Depot Names GE's Nardelli as New CEO in a Surprise Move," *Wall Street Journal*, December 6, 2000, https://www.wsj.com/articles/SB976051062408860254 (accessed September 27, 2017); John Kell, "Home Depot's Former CEO Frank Blake to Retire as Chairman," *Fortune*, January 16, 2015, http://fortune.com/2015/01/16/home-depot-former-ceo-retires-aschairman/ (accessed September 27, 2017); Julie Creswell and Michael Barbaro, "Home Depot Ousts Highly Paid Chief," *New York Times*, January 4, 2007, http://www.nytimes.com/2007/01/04/business/04home.html?mcubz=3 (accessed September 27, 2017); Louis Uchitelle, "Home Depot Girds for Continued Weakness," *The New York Times*, May 18, 2009, http://www.nytimes.com/2009/05/19/business/19depot.html (accessed September 27, 2017); Nathan Owen Rosenberg, "The Key to Home Depot's Success Is Transformational Leadership," Insigniam, http://insigniam.com/blog/the-keyto-home-depots-success-is-transformational-leadership/ (accessed September 27, 2017); Parija B. Kavilanz, "Nardelli Out at Home Depot," CNN Money, January 3, 2007, http://money.cnn.com/2007/01/03/news/companies/home_depot/ (accessed September 27, 2017); "Home Unimprovement: Was Nardelli's Tenure at Home Depot a Blueprint for Failure?" Knowledge, Wharton, http://knowledge.wharton.upenn.edu/article/home-unimprovement-was-nardellis-tenureat-home-depot-a-blueprint-for-failure/ (accessed September 27, 2017); Rachel Tobin, "Frank Blake Is Home Depot's 'Calmer-in-Chief,'" *Seattle Times*, September, 4, 2010, https://www.seattletimes.com/business/frank-blake-is-home-depotscalmer-in-chief/ (accessed September 27, 2017); Rachel Tobin Ramos, "Home Depot Laying Off 1,000 Nationwide," *Atlanta Journal-Constitution*, January 26, 2010, http://www.ajc.com/business/home-depot-laying-off-000-nationwide/ADq8GoBrxpX5h37LIxBxyM/ (accessed September 27, 2017); "Home Depot Builds Out Its Online Customer Service," Internet Retailer, June 4, 2010, https://www.digitalcommerce360.com/2010/06/04/home-depot-builds-outits-online-customer-service/ (accessed September 27, 2017).

## Employee Empowerment

Businesses are increasingly realizing the benefits of participative corporate cultures characterized by employee empowerment. **Employee empowerment** occurs when

**employee empowerment** when employees are provided with the ability to take on responsibilities and make decisions about their jobs

employees are provided with the ability to take on responsibilities and make decisions about their jobs. Employee empowerment does not mean that managers are not needed. Managers are important for guiding employees, setting goals, making major decisions, and other responsibilities emphasized throughout this chapter. However, a participative corporate culture has been found to be beneficial because employees in these companies feel like they are taking an active role in the firm's success.

Leaders who wish to empower employees adopt systems that support an employee's ability to provide input and feedback on company decisions. *Participative decision making*, a type of decision making that involves both manager and employee input, supports employee empowerment within the organization. One of the best ways to encourage participative decision making is through employee and managerial training. As mentioned earlier, employees should be trained in leadership skills, including teamwork, conflict resolution, and decision making. Managers should also be trained in ways to empower employees to make decisions while also guiding employees through challenging situations in which the right decision might not be so clear.[20]

A section on leadership would not be complete without a discussion of leadership in teams. In today's business world, decisions made by teams are becoming the norm. Employees at Precision Nutrition, a sixty-person Toronto firm specializing in tailored life coaching, for instance, often work in teams and are encouraged to make decisions that they believe will reinforce the company's mission and values. Teamwork has often been an effective way for encouraging employee empowerment.

Although decision making in teams is collective, the most effective teams are those in which all employees are encouraged to contribute their ideas and recommendations. Because each employee can bring in their own unique insights, teams often produce innovative ideas or decisions that would not have been reached by only one or two people. Michelle Peluso, IBM's chief marketing officer, tries to pull designers and data scientists, as well as marketers, together in teams. For example, she has teams attend sessions where they review and refine their work using only mobile devices to better understand how consumers use their products.[21]

However, truly empowering employees in team decision making can be difficult. It is quite common for more outspoken employees to dominate the team and others to engage in groupthink, in which team members go with the majority rather than what they think is the right decision. Training employees to listen to one another and then provide relevant feedback can help to prevent these common challenges. Another way is to rotate the team leader so that no one person can assume dominancy.[22]

# Decision Making

**LO 6-5** Summarize the systematic approach to decision making used by many business managers.

Managers make many different kinds of decisions, such as what office hours to set, which employees to hire, what products to introduce, and what price to charge for a product. Decision making is important in all management functions at all levels, whether the decisions are on a strategic, tactical, or operational level. A systematic approach using these six steps usually leads to more effective decision making: (1) recognizing and defining the decision situation, (2) developing options to resolve the situation, (3) analyzing the options, (4) selecting the best option, (5) implementing the decision, and (6) monitoring the consequences of the decision (Figure 6.6).

## Recognizing and Defining the Decision Situation

The first step in decision making is recognizing and defining the situation. The situation may be negative—for example, huge losses on a particular product—or positive—for example, an opportunity to increase sales.

Situations calling for small-scale decisions often occur without warning. Situations requiring large-scale decisions, however, generally occur after some warning signals. Effective managers pay attention to such signals. Declining profits, small-scale losses in previous years, inventory buildup, and retailers' unwillingness to stock a product are signals that may warn of huge losses to come. If managers pay attention to such signals, problems can be contained.

Once a situation has been recognized, management must define it. Huge losses reveal a problem—for example, a failing product. One manager may define the situation as a product quality problem; another may define it as a change in consumer preference. These two definitions may lead to vastly different solutions to the problem. The first manager, for example, may seek new sources of raw materials of better quality. The second manager may believe that the product has reached the end of its lifespan and decide to discontinue it. This example emphasizes the

**Figure 6.6** | Steps in the Decision-Making Process

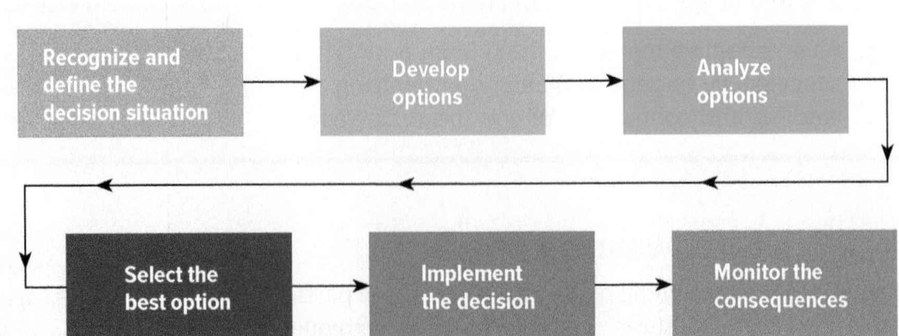

## RESPONDING TO BUSINESS CHALLENGES

### Managers and Employees See Different Corporate Cultures

Many top managers believe that their organizations have values-based cultures in which employees can grow and make ethical decisions. However, employees disagree. In a recent study of the workplace, 43 percent of employee respondents described the workplace as "command-and-control" or "top-down management." This indicates a management style in which the top managers make the rules and employees follow them. However, employers were eight times more likely to respond that their organizations allow employees to make decisions based upon organizational values, thus contributing to a values-based organizational culture.

In a traditional top-down chain of command, managers perform most of the planning, organizing, and directing functions of the firm. However, as views toward management change and employees are expected to take on greater roles, stakeholders are advocating for a self-governance approach. Such an approach calls for employee engagement, a greater emphasis on employee well-being, and the adoption of a culture that inspires through values rather than strictly rules. Additionally, managers must look beyond the bottom line when providing rewards.

The good news is that managers are recognizing the benefits of this system. The bad news is that, according to employees, managers are not successfully implementing this new management style. Better communication is needed to understand employee concerns, disseminate corporate values throughout the company, and create an incentives system that rewards the successful practice of these values in the workplace.*

#### DISCUSSION QUESTIONS

1. How does a values-based culture differ from a top-down chain of command?
2. Why do you think more managers want to adopt a values-based corporate culture?
3. How can managers make sure that they are successfully implementing a values-based managerial approach?

*Dov Seidman, "Upgrade to the Human Operating System," *Bloomberg Businessweek*, November 9, 2010, www.businessweek.com/managing/content/nov2010/ca2010118_005704.htm (accessed October 24, 2011); "The View from the Top, and Bottom," *The Economist*, September 24, 2011, www.economist.com/node/21530171 (accessed October 24, 2011); "The HOW Report SM: Rethinking the Source of Resiliency, Innovation and Sustainable Growth," *LRN*, www.lrn.com/form/43-how-report-form.html (accessed October 24, 2011).

©Kristoffer Tripplaar/Alamy Stock Photo

General Electric's excellent managerial training programs are renowned around the world. The company knows good managers aren't born. They are made.

importance of carefully defining the problem rather than jumping to conclusions.

## Developing Options

Once the decision situation has been recognized and defined, the next step is to develop a list of possible courses of action. The best lists include both standard courses of action and creative ones. **Brainstorming**, a technique in which group members spontaneously suggest ideas to solve a problem, is an effective way to encourage creativity and explore a variety of options.

**brainstorming** a technique in which group members spontaneously suggest ideas to solve a problem.

As a general rule, more time and expertise are devoted to the development stage of decision making when the decision is of major importance. When the decision is of lesser importance, less time and expertise will be spent on this stage. Options may be developed individually, by teams, or through analysis of similar situations in comparable organizations. Creativity is a very important part of selecting the best option. Creativity depends on new and useful ideas, regardless of where the idea originates or the method used to create the ideas. The best option can range from a required solution to an identified problem to a volunteered solution to an observed problem by an outside work group member.[23]

## Analyzing Options

After developing a list of possible courses of action, management should analyze the practicality and appropriateness of each option. An option may be deemed impractical because of a lack of financial resources to implement it, legal restrictions, ethical and social responsibility considerations, authority constraints, technological constraints, economic limitations, or simply a lack of information and expertise to implement the option. For example, a small computer manufacturer may recognize an opportunity to introduce a new type of computer but lack the financial resources to do so. Other options may be more practical for the computer company: It may consider selling its technology to another computer company that has adequate resources or it may allow itself to be purchased by a larger company that can introduce the new technology.

"After developing a list of possible courses of action, management should analyze the practicality and appropriateness of each option."

When assessing appropriateness, the decision maker should consider whether the proposed option adequately addresses the situation. When analyzing the consequences of an option, managers should consider the impact the option will have on the situation and on the organization as a whole. For example, when considering a price cut to boost sales, management must consider the consequences of the action on the organization's cash flow and consumers' reaction to the price change.

### Selecting the Best Option

When all courses of action have been analyzed, management must select the best one. Selection is often a subjective procedure because many situations do not lend themselves to quantitative analysis. For example, how Amazon uses its Alexa virtual assistant involves many alternatives. A decision had to be made whether the voice-activated device could store bank account data and make payments with all the risk associated with this service. Nearly all options create dilemmas that create an assortment of risks and rewards.[24] Of course, it is not always necessary to select only one option and reject all others; it may be possible to select and use a combination of several options.

### Implementing the Decision

To deal with the situation at hand, the selected option or options must be put into action. Implementation can be fairly simple or very complex, depending on the nature of the decision. Effective implementation of a decision to abandon a product, close a plant, purchase a new business, or something similar requires planning. For example, when a product is dropped, managers must decide how to handle distributors and customers and what to do with the idle production facility. Additionally, they should anticipate resistance from people within the organization (people tend to resist change because they fear the unknown). Finally, management should be ready to deal with the unexpected consequences. No matter how well planned implementation is, unforeseen problems will arise. Management must be ready to address these situations when they occur.

### Monitoring the Consequences

After managers have implemented a decision, they must determine whether the decision has accomplished the desired result. Without proper monitoring, the consequences of decisions may not be known quickly enough to make efficient changes. If the desired result is achieved, management can reasonably conclude that it made a good decision. If the desired result is not achieved, further analysis is warranted. Was the decision simply wrong, or did the situation change? Should some other option have been implemented?

If the desired result is not achieved, management may discover that the situation was incorrectly defined from the beginning. That may require starting the decision-making process all over again. Finally, management may determine that the decision was good even though the desired results have not yet shown up or it may determine a flaw in the decision's implementation. In the latter case, management would not change the decision but would change the way in which it was implemented.

## Management in Practice

Management is not exact or easily calculated. There is no mathematical formula for managing an organization and achieving organizational goals, although many managers passionately wish for one! Managers plan, organize, staff, direct, and control, but management expert John P. Kotter says even these functions can be boiled down to two basic activities:

1. Figuring out what to do despite uncertainty, great diversity, and an enormous amount of potentially relevant information, and
2. Getting things done through a large and diverse set of people despite having little direct control over most of them.[25]

Managers spend as much as 75 percent of their time working with others—not only with subordinates but with bosses, people outside their hierarchy at work, and people outside the organization itself. In these interactions they discuss anything and everything remotely connected with their business.

"Managers spend a lot of time establishing and updating an agenda of goals and plans for carrying out their responsibilities."

Managers spend a lot of time establishing and updating an agenda of goals and plans for carrying out their responsibilities. An **agenda** contains both specific and vague items, covering short-term goals and long-term objectives. Like a calendar, an agenda helps the manager figure out what must be done and how to get it done to meet the objectives set by the organization. Technology tools

**agenda** a calendar, containing both specific and vague items, that covers short-term goals and long-term objectives

networking the building of relationships and sharing of information with colleagues who can help managers achieve the items on their agendas

such as smartphones can help managers manage their agendas, contacts, and time.

Managers also spend a lot of time **networking**—building relationships and sharing information with colleagues who can help them achieve the items on their agendas. Managers spend much of their time communicating with a variety of people and participating in activities that on the surface do not seem to have much to do with the goals of their organization. Nevertheless, these activities are crucial to getting the job done.

Networks are not limited to immediate subordinates and bosses; they include other people in the company as well as customers, suppliers, and friends. These contacts provide managers with information and advice on diverse topics. Managers ask, persuade, and even intimidate members of their network in order to get information and to get things done. Networking helps managers carry out their responsibilities. Social media sites have increased the ability of both managers and subordinates to network. Internal social networks allow employees to connect with one another, while social networks such as Facebook or Twitter enable managers to connect with customers.

Sales managers are even using social networks to communicate with their distributors. LinkedIn has been used for job networking and is gaining in popularity as an alternative to traditional job hunting. Some speculate that social networks might eventually replace traditional resumés and job boards.[26]

©JuliusKielaitis/Shutterstock

Websites like LinkedIn help managers and employees network to achieve their professional goals.

Finally, managers spend a great deal of time confronting the complex and difficult challenges of the business world today. Some of these challenges relate to rapidly changing technology (especially in production and information processing), increased scrutiny of individual and corporate ethics and social responsibility, the changing nature of the workforce, new laws and regulations, increased global competition and more challenging foreign markets, declining educational standards (which may limit the skills and knowledge of the future labour and customer pool), and time itself—that is, making the best use of it. But such diverse issues cannot simply be plugged into a computer program that supplies correct, easy-to-apply solutions. It is only through creativity and imagination that managers can make effective decisions that benefit their organizations.

## TEAM EXERCISE

Form groups and research examples of crisis management implementation for companies dealing with natural disasters (explosions, fires, earthquakes, etc.), technology disasters (viruses, plane crashes, compromised customer data, etc.) or ethical or legal disasters. How did these companies communicate with key stakeholders? What measures did the company take to provide support to those involved in the crisis? Report your findings to the class.

# LEARNING OBJECTIVES SUMMARY

**LO 6-1** Explain *management's* role in the achievement of organizational objectives.

Management is a process designed to achieve an organization's objectives by using its resources effectively and efficiently in a changing environment. Managers make decisions about the use of the organization's resources and are concerned with planning, organizing, staffing, directing, and controlling the organization's activities so as to reach its objectives.

**LO 6-2** Describe the major functions of management.

Planning is the process of determining the organization's objectives and deciding how to accomplish them. Organizing is the structuring of resources and activities to accomplish those objectives efficiently and effectively. Staffing obtains people with the necessary skills to carry out the work of the company. Directing is motivating and leading employees to achieve organizational objectives. Controlling is the process of evaluating and correcting activities to keep the organization on course.

**LO 6-3** Distinguish among three levels of management and the concerns of managers at each level.

Top management is responsible for the whole organization and focuses primarily on strategic planning. Middle management develops plans for specific operating areas and carries out the general guidelines set by top management. First-line, or supervisory, management supervises the workers and day-to-day operations. Managers can also be categorized as to their area of responsibility: finance, production and operations, human resources, marketing, IT or administration.

**LO 6-4** Specify the skills managers need in order to be successful.

To be successful, managers need leadership skills (the ability to influence employees to work toward organizational goals), technical expertise (the specialized knowledge and training needed to perform a job), conceptual skills (the ability to think in abstract terms and see how parts fit together to form the whole), analytical skills (the ability to identify relevant issues and recognize their importance, understand the relationships between issues, and perceive the underlying causes of a situation), and human relations (people) skills.

**LO 6-5** Summarize the systematic approach to decision making used by many business managers.

A systematic approach to decision making follows these steps: recognizing and defining the situation, developing options, analyzing options, selecting the best option, implementing the decision, and monitoring the consequences.

## KEY TERMS

administrative managers
agenda
analytical skills
brainstorming
conceptual skills
controlling
crisis management or contingency planning
directing
downsizing
employee empowerment
financial managers
first-line managers
human relations skills
human resources managers
information technology (IT) managers
leadership
management
managers
marketing managers
middle managers
mission
networking
operational plans
organizing
planning
production and operations managers
staffing
strategic plans
tactical plans
technical expertise
top managers

## So You Want to Be *a Manager: What Kind?*

Managers are needed in a wide variety of organizations. Experts suggest that employment will increase by thousands of jobs in upcoming years. But the requirements for the jobs become more demanding with every passing year—with the speed of technology and communication increasing by the day, and the stress of global commerce increasing pressures to perform. However, if you like a challenge and if you have the right kind of personality, management remains a viable field. Even as companies are forced to restructure, management remains a vital role in business.

Management positions in public relations, marketing, and advertising are increasing, and demand for financial, computer and IT managers remains strong. Salaries for managerial positions remain robust overall. Pay can vary significantly depending on your level of experience, the firm where you work, and the province where you live.

In short, if you want to be a manager, there are opportunities in almost every field. There may be fewer middle management positions available in firms, but managers remain a vital part of most industries and will continue to be long into the future—especially as navigating global business becomes ever more complex.

# BUILD YOUR BUSINESS PLAN

## The Nature of Management

The first thing you need to be thinking about is "What is the mission of your business? What is the shared vision your team members have for this business? How do you know if there is demand for this particular business?" Remember, you need to think about the customer's *ability and willingness* to try this particular product.

Think about the various processes or stages of your business in the creation and selling of your product or service. What functions need to be performed for these processes to be completed? These functions might include buying, receiving, selling, customer service, and/or merchandising.

Operationally, if you are opening up a retail establishment, how do you plan to provide your customers with superior customer service? What hours will your customers expect you to be open? At this point in time, how many employees are you thinking you will need to run your business? Do you (or one of your partners) need to be there all the time to supervise?

# CASE | RONA's Turnaround

RONA, the 500-store national chain of hardware, garden, and home-renovation centres, had not seen an improvement in same-store sales in several years. A poorly managed expansion plan had resulted in five consecutive years of declining revenues, even as the larger market grew. In 2013 a new CEO joined the team. Robert Sawyer soon turned things around.

Although Sawyer never attended university, he seemed destined for a career in retail. At 14, he delivered beer and groceries on his bike for a corner store in Montreal, where he grew up. He started working for Steinberg's catalogue distribution business at age 16, and by 19, he was foreman of one of its warehouses. He moved on to Metro in 1979, as director of a fruit and vegetable warehouse, and rose through the ranks of the Montreal-based grocer. Those who have worked with him view him as very direct and demanding. "With him, you always know where you are headed. There are no grey zones: It's either white or it's black," says Christian Bourbonnière, Metro's first vice-president, Quebec division. "He is demanding to the extreme."

In approaching the issues facing RONA, Sawyer took the simple path. Under his leadership, the company cut 375 administrative positions, closed 11 unprofitable stores, sold most of its commercial and professional market division, shaved $110 million from expenses, and developed separate business plans for the four divisions. Sawyer took over just as the job and housing markets were slowing. "If you don't know where to cut, I'm giving you two weeks," he told his new team.

But it wasn't all about cutting costs. Sawyer also searched for opportunities to invest in that would help RONA achieve some wins. He focused on underperforming assets in Quebec, as well as the poorly executed integration of Totem Building Supplies in Calgary. The real focus has been on Réno-Dépôt, one of the company's banners in Quebec, which expanded its seasonal merchandise and put a greater emphasis on big-ticket, high-end products. Even parking spaces were widened to better accommodate trucks driven by contractors—Réno-Dépôt's primary customers.

Two years after taking the helm at RONA, Sawyer was named Top Turnaround CEO of the Year by *Canadian Business* magazine. In 2016, Lowe's Canada took control of RONA in a friendly takeover bid. However, Lowe's soon began consolidating some of those locations with Lowe's stores to streamline operations. Current management is struggling to find ways to catch up with do-it-yourself giant Home Depot, whose stores on average generate almost twice as much in sales as Lowe's locations do.

## DISCUSSION QUESTIONS

1. How was Sawyer a strong leader in helping RONA's recovery?
2. What areas of management do you think Sawyer emphasized in his attempt to re-establish RONA as a leader in home improvement products?
3. What are the challenges for a new CEO when trying to ensure a company such as Lowe's continues to stay successful?

CHAPTER 7

# Organization, Teamwork, and Communication

©Terry Putman/Shutterstock

## LEARNING OBJECTIVES

**After reading this chapter, you will be able to:**

- LO 7-1 Explain the importance of organizational culture.
- LO 7-2 Define *organizational structure*, and describe how organizational structures develop.
- LO 7-3 Describe how specialization and departmentalization help an organization achieve its goals.
- LO 7-4 Determine how organizations assign responsibility for tasks and delegate authority.
- LO 7-5 Compare and contrast some common forms of organizational structure.
- LO 7-6 Distinguish between groups and teams, and identify the types of each that exist in organizations.
- LO 7-7 Describe how communication occurs in organizations.

# ENTER THE WORLD OF BUSINESS

**Keurig Green Mountain Brews Effective Communication**

Keurig Green Mountain is a leader in the specialty coffee industry. The company sells coffee and beverage selections through a coordinated, multi-channel distribution network of wholesale and consumer direct operations. It also sells Keurig single-pack coffee packets and Keurig brewers, which are single-cup brewing systems.

Keurig Green Mountain is decentralized with few layers of management. Although it has functional departments that vary across the company, an openness of communication allows employees access to all levels of the organization. The company uses digital communication channels such as email to inform groups of decisions. Verbal communication is used at meetings, and employees are encouraged to share their views. Written forms of communication, such as agendas, outline the results of meetings and serve to guide efficient decision making. This communication across channels ensures that the collaborative approach to getting things done is spread equally throughout the company.

Corporate social responsibility is a major objective of Keurig Green Mountain. Keurig Green Mountain invests in sustainably grown coffee initiatives, and the company is developing K-cup pods that are increasingly recyclable. This is important, as one major criticism of the company is the large amount of waste its pods create over time. Keurig Green Mountain announced the pods would be 100 percent recyclable by 2020. To ensure employees are on board, Keurig Green Mountain communicates this objective across its various communication channels.

In 2016, JAB Holding Company purchased Keurig Green Mountain for $13.9 billion. The company was also taken private. A privately held company with fewer owners might make it easier for management to strengthen communication channels both internally and externally. The company must continue to display effective communication skills to ensure a collaborative corporate culture focused on developing specialty coffees sustainably and responsibly.[1]

**DISCUSSION QUESTIONS**

1. What types of communication does Keurig Green Mountain use within its organization?
2. Why do you think strong communication is important in a decentralized organization with few layers of management?
3. What are some of the advantages of using functional departmentalization?

# Introduction

An organization's structure determines how well it makes decisions and responds to problems, and influences employees' attitudes toward their work. A suitable structure can minimize a business's costs and maximize its efficiency. Even companies that operate within the same industry may utilize different organizational structures. For example, in the consumer electronics industry, Samsung is organized as a conglomerate with separate business units or divisions. Samsung is largely decentralized. Apple, under CEO Tim Cook, has moved from a hierarchical structure to a more collaborative approach among divisions.[2] On the other hand, Ford Motor Company's board views the CEO, Jim Hackett, as being in charge of the firm's strategy in a more hierarchical structure.[3] A manufacturing firm, like Ford, may require more leadership and control from the top.

Because a business's structure can so profoundly affect its success, this chapter will examine organizational structure in detail. First we discuss how an organization's culture affects its operations. Then we consider the development of structure, including how tasks and responsibilities are organized through specialization and departmentalization. Next we explore some of the forms organizational structure may take. Finally we consider communication within business.

# Organizational Culture

**LO 7-1** Explain the importance of organizational culture.

One of the most important aspects of organizing a business is determining its **organizational culture**, a firm's shared values, beliefs, traditions, philosophies, rules, and role models for behaviour. Also called *corporate culture*, an organizational culture exists in every organization, regardless of size, organizational type, product, or profit objective. Sometimes behaviours, programs, and policies enhance and support the organizational culture. For instance, one of the largest accounting firms in Canada, Grant Thornton, established an unlimited vacation policy to give its employees more freedom.

**organizational culture** a firm's shared values, beliefs, traditions, philosophies, rules, and role models for behaviour

Fewer than 1 percent of firms have this policy, but it seems to be growing in companies like Netflix, where employees have greater autonomy. Some speculate, however, that these policies will only work at firms with employees who are already highly motivated to work hard and are less likely to take vacations in the first place.[4] A firm's culture may be expressed formally through its mission statement, codes of ethics, memos, manuals, and ceremonies, but it is more commonly expressed informally. Examples of informal expressions of culture include dress codes (or the lack thereof), employee engagement, and a creative and enjoyable workplace. In his book, *Work Rules*, Google's former HR Boss, Laszlo Bock, states that keeping things fun discharges employees' creativity juice.

## GOING GREEN

### Connection and Collaboration: How Timberland Works as a Team

From its product development team to its Global Stewards, Timberland is committed to using teamwork to advance its goals of sustainable product offerings. In addition to teamwork among its employees, Timberland has also partnered with suppliers and even competitors to create solutions that will positively affect the environment.

Timberland began by manufacturing footwear and later expanded into clothing and accessories. Timberland is known for its eco-friendly products. One-third of the company's footwear is made at least partially from recycled materials.

Timberland uses teamwork to positively affect the sustainability movement. In 2001, the company started a cross-functional team made up of employees from different areas in the company to determine how it could contribute to sustainability. Timberland formed its Global Stewards Program, teams of passionate employee volunteers who take the time to participate as civic leaders within their communities, empower employees, and lead social responsibility projects.

Timberland has also partnered with other important stakeholders. It partnered with its leather suppliers to decrease energy and water usage at its leather tanneries. Timberland has also teamed with competitors on sustainability initiatives. The company worked with Nike and many other firms to create the Higg Index, a green index for apparel, and with Adidas on a green footwear index. Timberland recognizes that by developing teams among various stakeholders, it can create a major difference within its industry.*

#### DISCUSSION QUESTIONS

1. How does Timberland use teamwork to advance its goals?
2. Why would Timberland partner with the competition?
3. How do you think Timberland's use of teams empowers employees?

*Mindy S. Lubber, "How Timberland, Levi's Use Teamwork to Advance Sustainability," *Green Biz*, May 9, 2011, https://www.greenbiz.com/blog/2011/05/09/howcompanies-court-stakeholders-accelerate-sustainability (accessed December 31, 2017); Engaging Employees: Timberland's Global Stewards Program 2009 Report, Timberland Company, http://responsibility.timberland.com/wp-content/uploads/2011/05/Stewards_Program_2009. pdf (accessed August 6, 2013); Betsy Blaisdell and Nina Kruschwitz, "New Ways to Engage Employees, Suppliers and Competitors in CSR," MIT Sloan, November 14, 2012, https://sloanreview.mit.edu/article/new-ways-toengage-employees-suppliers-and-competitors-in-csr/ (accessed December 31, 2017); Focus—Corporate Social Responsibility Report 2001, Timberland Company, http://responsibility.timberland.com/wp-content/ uploads/2011/05/2001-CSR-Report.pdf (accessed August 6, 2013); Chuck Scofield, "Sharing Strength: Lessons about Getting by Giving," LiNE Zine, http://www.linezine.com/7.2/articles/cssslagbg.htm (accessed December 31, 2017); David Hellqvist, "Timberland: 40 Years of the Yellow Boot," *The Guardian*, April 16, 2013, https://www.theguardian.com/fashion/2013/apr/16/timberland-40-years-yellow-boot (accessed December 31, 2017); About Us, Timberland, https://www.timberland.com/about-us.html (accessed December 31, 2017); "Responsibility," Timberland Company, https://www.timberland.com/responsibility.html (accessed December 31, 2017); "Timberland Employees Around the Globe Take Part in 18th Annual Serv-a-Palooza Service Event," Timberland Company, September 17, 2015, https://www.timberland.com/newsroom/press-releases/timberland-18th-annual-serv-a-palooza-service-event.html (accessed December 31, 2017).

©Uladzik Kryhin/Shutterstock

Google embraces a corporate culture that focuses on employee happiness. The tech company offers perks and benefits like in-office gyms and fitness areas, free meals, and more.

McDonald's has an organizational culture focused on quality, service, cleanliness, and value. Mercedes-Benz stresses a culture of excellent customer service. When such values and philosophies are shared by all members of an organization, they will be expressed in its relationships with customers. However, organizational cultures that fail to understand the values of their customers may experience rejection. The values and integrity of customers must always be considered. When Google focuses on online advertising that is effective and easily measured, the company focuses more on metrics and sales of advertising than customer values.

Organizational culture helps ensure that all members of a company share values and suggests rules for how to behave and deal with problems within the organization. Kevin Johnson took over as CEO of Starbucks, so he has to embrace the corporate culture that founder and former CEO Howard Schultz built. Employees like to work at Starbucks because of the firm's culture. It was troubling to executives when a Starbucks manager in Philadelphia had two minority customers removed from the restaurant. The company's move to support their ethical organizational culture was swift and decisive. They offered a half day of racial sensitivity training in the vast majority of their company-owned restaurants in both the United States and Canada.[5] The key to success in any organization is satisfying stakeholders, especially customers. Establishing a positive organizational culture sets the tone for all other decisions, including building an efficient organizational structure.

## Developing Organizational Structure

**LO 7-2** Define *organizational structure*, and describe how organizational structures develop.

**Structure** is the arrangement or relationship of positions within an organization. Rarely is an organization, or any group of individuals working together, able to achieve common objectives without some form of structure, whether that structure is explicitly defined or only implied. A professional baseball team such as the Toronto Blue Jays is a business organization with an explicit formal structure that guides the team's activities so that it can increase game attendance, win games, and sell souvenirs such as T-shirts. But even an informal group playing softball for fun has an organization that specifies who will pitch, catch, bat, coach, and so on. Governments and non-profit organizations also have formal organizational structures to facilitate the achievement of their objectives. Getting people to work together efficiently and coordinating the skills of diverse individuals requires careful planning. Developing appropriate organizational structures is therefore a major challenge for managers in both large and small organizations.

An organization's structure develops when managers assign work tasks and activities to specific individuals or work groups and coordinate the diverse activities required to reach the firm's objectives. When Best Buy, for example, has a sale, the store manager must work with the advertising department to make the public aware of the sale, with department managers to ensure that extra salespeople are scheduled to handle the increased customer traffic, and with merchandise buyers to ensure that enough sale merchandise is available to meet expected consumer demand. All the people occupying these positions must work together to achieve the store's objectives.

The best way to begin to understand how organizational structure develops is to consider the evolution of a new business such as a clothing store. At first, the business is a sole proprietorship in which the owner does everything—buys, prices, and displays the merchandise; does the accounting and tax records; and assists customers. As the business grows, the owner hires a salesperson and perhaps a merchandise buyer to help run the store. As the business continues to grow, the owner hires more salespeople. The growth and success of the business now require the owner to be away from the store frequently, meeting with suppliers, engaging in public relations, and attending trade shows. Thus, the owner must designate someone to manage the salespeople and maintain the accounting, payroll, and tax functions. If the owner decides to expand by opening more stores, still more managers will be needed. Figure 7.1 shows these stages of growth with three **organizational charts** (visual displays of organizational structure, chain of command, and other relationships).

**structure** the arrangement or relationship of positions within an organization

**organizational charts** visual displays of the organizational structure, lines of authority (chain of command), staff relationships, permanent committee arrangements, and lines of communication

**Figure 7.1** | The Evolution of a Clothing Store, Phases 1, 2, and 3

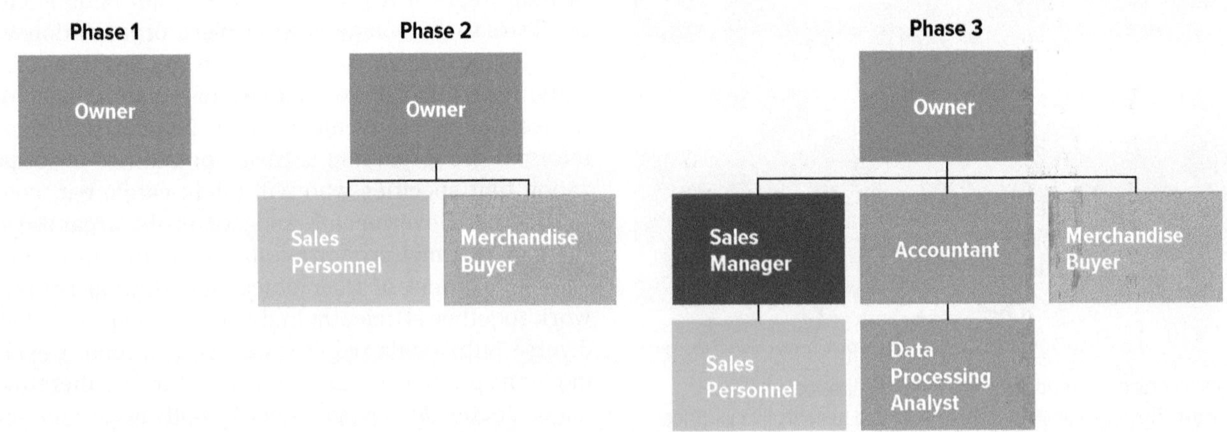


Growth requires organizing—the structuring of human, physical, and financial resources to achieve objectives in an effective and efficient manner. Growth necessitates hiring people who have specialized skills. With more people and greater specialization, the organization needs to develop a formal structure to function

## Consider the Following: Zappos puts the right foot forward

The online shoe and clothing retailer Zappos is famous for its strong customer service and fun corporate culture. Under the leadership of CEO Tony Hsieh, exceptional customer service is a key value of the company. Employees are empowered to engage in Zappos's strong participative culture by identifying problems and working together to come up with solutions.

In 2015, Hsieh changed Zappos from a more traditional top-down structure into what is called a holacracy. Traditional managerial roles were eliminated, and employees became their own leaders with their own roles. Employee teams have tactical meetings to discuss key issues and next actions. Hsieh made this decision because he believes it will help Zappos grow without losing productivity.

One concern is that non-managerial employees may not fully understand the risks and uncertainty that will affect company operations. Some employees are struggling to adapt as Zappos continues to work out the kinks of such a massive structural change. In 2016, Zappos fell off *Fortune* magazine's 100 Best Companies to Work For. Despite these challenges, Hsieh believes that, in the long term, this more fluid organizational structure will allow Zappos to achieve both growth and greater productivity.*

### DISCUSSION QUESTIONS

1. Since Zappos eliminated traditional manager positions, is the new organizational structure still able to achieve the organization's common objectives?
2. What do you think some of the benefits are of this new structure? What might be some disadvantages?
3. Why is it important for Hsieh to take a long-term perspective of the company, even if the decision he makes might hurt the firm in the short run?

*Adapted from "Zappos: Delivering Happiness to Stakeholders," Daniels Fund Ethics Initiative, http://danielsethics.mgt.unm.edu/pdf/Zappos%20Case.pdf (accessed November 25, 2017); Richard Feloni, "Inside Zappos CEO Tony Hsieh's Radical Management Experiment That Prompted 14% of Employees to Quit," *Business Insider*, May 16, 2015, http://www.businessinsider.com/tony-hsiehzappos-holacracy-managementexperiment-2015-5 (accessed May 12, 2017); Rebecca Greenfield, "Zappos CEO Tony Hsieh: Adopt Holacracy or Leave," *Fast Company*, March 30, 2015, https://www.fastcompany.com/3044417/zapposceo-tony-hsieh-adopt-holacracy-or-leave (accessed May 12, 2017); Zack Guzman, "Zappos CEO Tony Hsieh on Getting Rid of Managers: What I Wish I'd Done Differently," CNBC, September 13, 2016, http://www.cnbc.com/2016/09/13/zappos-ceo-tony-hsieh-the-thing-i-regret-aboutgettingrid-of-managers.html (accessed May 12, 2017); "How It Works," HolacracyOne LLC, http://holacracy.org/how-itwork (accessed May 12, 2017); Rachel Emma Silverman, "At Zappos, Some Employees Find Offer to Leave Too Good to Refuse," *Wall Street Journal*, May 7, 2014, http://www.wsj.com/articles/at-zappos-someemployees-findoffer-to-leave-too-good-to-refuse-1431047917 (accessed May 12, 2017); "Holacracy," Zappos Insights, http://www.zapposinsights.com/about/holacrac (accessed May 12, 2017); Zappos.com, Company Statement from Zappos.com, YouTube, April 1, 2016, https://www.youtube.com/watch?v=3zieP6NUWL8 (accessed May 12, 2017).

efficiently. Consider Cirque du Soleil, which started in 1984 with 20 ambitious street artists. Today, with 3,000 employees who encompass 40 nationalities, creativity and business must be balanced through some structure. Cirque returns 10 percent of its profits to employees, and the core team meets 10 times a year to recruit and keep the right people in a team-focused corporate culture.[6] Cirque has a major focus on teamwork, but its structure might not work for a manufacturing firm like Ford that is more hierarchical in its structure. As we shall see, structuring an organization requires that management assign work tasks to specific individuals and departments, and assign responsibility for the achievement of specific organizational objectives.

> "Growth requires organizing—the structuring of human, physical, and financial resources to achieve objectives in an effective and efficient manner."

## Assigning Tasks

**LO 7-3** Describe how specialization and departmentalization help an organization achieve its goals.

For a business to earn profits from the sale of its products, its managers must first determine what activities are required to achieve its objectives. At Celestial Seasonings, for example, employees must purchase herbs from suppliers, dry the herbs and place them in tea bags, package and label the tea, and then ship the packages to grocery stores around the country. Other necessary activities include negotiating with supermarkets and other retailers for display space, developing new products, planning advertising, managing finances, and managing employees. All these activities must be coordinated, assigned to work groups, and controlled. Two important aspects of assigning these work activities are specialization and departmentalization.

### Specialization

After identifying all activities that must be accomplished, managers then break these activities down into specific tasks that can be handled by individual employees. This division of labour into small, specific tasks and the assignment of employees to do a single task is called **specialization**.

**specialization** the division of labour into small, specific tasks and the assignment of employees to do a single task

The rationale for specialization is efficiency. People can perform more efficiently if they master just one task rather than all tasks. In *The Wealth of Nations*, originally published in 1776, eighteenth-century economist Adam Smith discussed specialization, using the manufacture of straight pins as an example. Individually, workers could produce 20 pins a day when each employee produced complete pins. Thus, 10 employees working independently of each other could produce 200 pins a day. However, when one worker drew the wire, another straightened it, a third cut it, and a fourth ground the point, 10 workers could produce 48,000 pins per day. To save money and achieve the benefits of specialization, some companies outsource and hire temporary workers to provide key skills. Many highly skilled workers with diverse experience are available through temp agencies.[7]

Specialization means workers don't waste time shifting from one job to another, and training is easier. However, efficiency is not the only motivation for specialization. Specialization also occurs when the activities that must be performed within an organization are too numerous for one person to handle. Recall the example of the clothing store. When the business was young and small, the owner could do everything, but when the business grew, the owner needed help waiting on customers, keeping the books, and managing other business activities.

**Overspecialization.** Overspecialization can have negative consequences. Employees may become bored and dissatisfied with their jobs, and the result of their unhappiness is likely to be poor-quality work, more injuries, and high employee turnover. In extreme cases, employees in crowded specialized electronic plants are unable to form working relationships with one another. In some factories in Asia, workers are crammed together and overworked.

Fourteen global vehicle manufacturers pledged to increase their oversight of the factories in their supply chain to ensure human rights and healthy working conditions. However, the task is monumental for these global companies because their supply chains encompass many different countries with different labour practices, and it can be difficult to oversee the operations of dozens of supplier and subcontractors.[8] This is

©Adam Hester/Blend Images

Grouping jobs into departments like marketing, customer service, or purchasing can enhance productivity.

why some manufacturing firms allow job rotation so that employees do not become dissatisfied and leave. Although some degree of specialization is necessary for efficiency, because of differences in skills, abilities, and interests, all people are not equally suited for all jobs. We examine some strategies to overcome these issues in Chapter 9.

## Departmentalization

After assigning specialized tasks to individuals, managers next organize workers doing similar jobs into groups to make them easier to manage. **Departmentalization** is the grouping of jobs into working units usually called departments, units, groups, or divisions. As we shall see, departments are commonly organized by function, product, geographic region, or customer (Figure 7.2).

**departmentalization** the grouping of jobs into working units usually called departments, units, groups, or divisions

Most companies use more than one departmentalization plan to enhance productivity. For instance, many consumer goods manufacturers have departments for specific product lines (beverages, frozen dinners, canned goods, and so on) as well as departments dealing with legal, purchasing, finance, human resources, and other business functions. For smaller companies, accounting can be set up online, almost as an automated department. Accounting software can handle electronic transfers so you never have to worry about a late bill.

**functional departmentalization** the grouping of jobs that perform similar functional activities, such as finance, manufacturing, marketing, and human resources

"Specialization means workers do not waste time shifting from one job to another, and training is easier."

**Figure 7.2** | Departmentalization

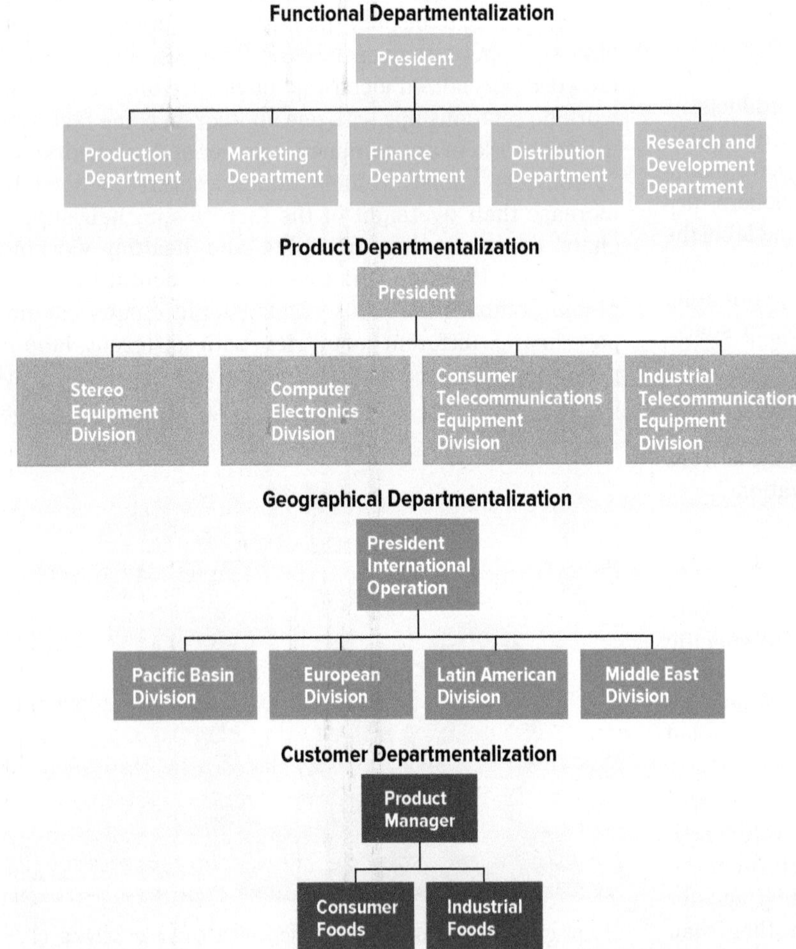


### Functional Departmentalization.

**Functional departmentalization** groups jobs that perform similar functional activities, such as finance, manufacturing, marketing, and human resources. Each of these functions is managed by an expert in the work done by the department—an engineer supervises the production department; a financial executive supervises the finance department. his approach is common in small organizations. Tesla uses functional departmentalization with Finance, Technology, Global Sales and Service, Engineering, and Legal departments in addition to the chairman and CEO. The company also has two divisions: automotive and energy generation and storage.[9]

A weakness of functional departmentalization is that it tends to emphasize departmental units rather than the organization as a whole, so decision making that involves more than one department may be slow, and it requires greater coordination. Thus, as businesses grow, they tend to adopt other approaches to organizing jobs.

### Product Departmentalization.

**Product departmentalization** organizes jobs around the products of the firm. Procter & Gamble has global units, such as laundry and cleaning products, paper products, and health care products. Each division develops and implements its own product

**product departmentalization** the organization of jobs in relation to the products of the firm

©Kristoffer Tripplaar/Alamy Stock Photo

PepsiCo Inc. uses product departmentalization to organize its company. However, the firm also engages in a type of geographical departmentalization for various regions.

plans, monitors the results, and takes corrective action as necessary. Functional activities—production, finance, marketing, and others—are located within each product division. Consequently, organizing by products duplicates functions and resources and emphasizes the product rather than the achievement of the organization's overall objectives. However, it simplifies decision making and helps coordinate all activities related to a product or product group.

PepsiCo Inc. is organized into six business units: (1) North America Beverages; (2) Frito-Lay North America; (3) Quaker Foods North America; (4) Latin America; (5) Europe Sub-Saharan Africa; and (6) Asia, Middle East & North Africa. PepsiCo has actually adopted a combination of two types of departmentalization. While it clearly uses product departmentalization in North America, the company also chooses to divide its segments into geographic regions—a type of geographic departmentalization.[10]

**Geographical Departmentalization.** **Geographical departmentalization** groups jobs according to geographic location, such as state or province, region, country, or continent. Diageo, the premium beverage company known for brands such as Johnnie Walker and Tanqueray, is organized into five geographic regions, allowing the company to get closer to its customers and respond more quickly and efficiently to regional competitors.[11] Multinational corporations often use a geographical approach because of the vast differences between different regions. PepsiCo, General Motors, and McDonalds are organized by region. However, organizing by region requires a large administrative staff and control system to coordinate operations, and tasks are duplicated among the different regions.

**geographical departmentalization** the grouping of jobs according to geographic location, such as state or province, region, country, or continent

**Customer Departmentalization.** **Customer departmentalization** arranges jobs around the needs of various types of customers. Airlines, such as Air Canada and British Airways, provide prices and services customized for either business/frequent travellers or infrequent/vacationing customers. Customer departmentalization, like geographical departmentalization, does not focus on the organization as a whole and therefore requires a large administrative staff to coordinate the operations of the various groups.

**customer departmentalization** the arrangement of jobs around the needs of various types of customers

## Assigning Responsibility

**LO 7-4** Determine how organizations assign responsibility for tasks and delegate authority.

After all workers and work groups have been assigned their tasks, they must be given the responsibility to carry them out. Management must determine to what extent it will delegate responsibility throughout the organization and how many employees will report to each manager.

### Delegation of Authority

**Delegation of authority** means not only giving tasks to employees but also empowering them to make commitments, use resources, and take whatever actions are necessary to carry out those tasks. Let's say a marketing manager at Nestlé has assigned an employee to design a new package that is less wasteful (more environmentally responsible) than the current package for one of the company's frozen dinner lines. To carry out the assignment, the employee needs access to information and the authority to make certain decisions on packaging materials, costs, and so on. Without the authority to carry out the assigned task, the employee would have to get the approval of others for every decision and every request for materials.

**delegation of authority** giving employees not only tasks, but also the power to make commitments, use resources, and take whatever actions are necessary to carry out those tasks

As a business grows, so do the number and complexity of decisions that must be made; no one manager can handle them all. 3M delegates authority to its employees by encouraging them to share ideas and make decisions. The company believes employee ideas can have such an impact on the firm that 3M encourages them to spend 15 percent of their time working on and sharing their own projects. This "15 percent culture" has created the collaboration that drives innovation in the company.[12] Delegation of authority frees a manager to concentrate on larger issues, such as planning or dealing with problems and opportunities.

**responsibility** the obligation, placed on employees through delegation, to perform assigned tasks satisfactorily and be held accountable for the proper execution of work

**accountability** the principle that employees who accept an assignment and the authority to carry it out are answerable to a superior for the outcome

Delegation also gives a **responsibility**, or obligation, to employees to carry out assigned tasks satisfactorily and holds them accountable for the proper execution of their assigned work. The principle of **accountability** means that employees who accept an assignment and the authority to carry it out are answerable to a superior for the outcome. Returning to the Nestlé example, if a packaging design prepared by an employee is unacceptable or late, the employee must accept the blame. If the new design is innovative, attractive, and cost-efficient, as well as environmentally responsible, or is completed ahead of schedule, the employee will accept the credit.

The process of delegating authority establishes a pattern of relationships and accountability between a superior and subordinates. The president of a firm delegates responsibility for all marketing activities to the vice-president of marketing. The vice-president accepts this responsibility and has the authority to obtain all relevant information, make certain decisions, and delegate any or all activities to their subordinates. The vice-president, in turn, delegates all advertising activities to the advertising manager, all sales activities to the sales manager, and so on. These managers then delegate specific tasks to their subordinates. However, the act of delegating authority to a subordinate does not relieve the superior of accountability for the delegated job. Even though the vice-president of marketing delegates work to subordinates, they are still ultimately accountable to the president for all marketing activities.

## Degree of Centralization

The extent to which authority is delegated throughout an organization determines its degree of centralization.

**Centralized Organizations.** In a **centralized organization**, authority is concentrated at the top, and very little decision-making authority is delegated to lower levels. Although decision-making authority in centralized organizations rests with top levels of management, a vast amount of responsibility for carrying out daily and routine procedures is delegated to even the lowest levels of the organization. Many government organizations and Crown corporations, including the Canadian Armed Forces, Canada Post, and the Canada Revenue Agency, are centralized.

**centralized organization** a structure in which authority is concentrated at the top, and very little decision-making authority is delegated to lower levels

Businesses tend to be more centralized when the decisions to be made are risky and when low-level managers are not highly skilled in decision making. In the banking industry, for example, authority to make routine car loans is given to all loan managers, while the authority to make high-risk loans, such as for a large residential development, may be restricted to upper-level loan officers.

Over-centralization can cause serious problems for a company, in part because it may take longer for the organization as a whole to implement decisions and to respond to changes and problems on a regional scale. McDonald's, for example, was one of the last chains to introduce a chicken sandwich because of the amount of research, development, test marketing, and layers of approval the product had to go through. Centralized decision making can also prevent front-line service employees from providing insights and recommendations to improve the customer experience as well as reporting and resolving problems.

**Decentralized Organizations.** A **decentralized organization** is one in which decision-making authority is delegated as far down the chain of command as possible. Decentralization is characteristic of organizations that operate in complex, unpredictable environments. Businesses that face intense competition often decentralize to improve responsiveness and enhance creativity. Lower-level managers who interact with the external environment often develop a good understanding of it and thus are able to react quickly to changes. Johnson & Johnson has a very decentralized, flat organizational structure.

**decentralized organization** an organization in which decision-making authority is delegated as far down the chain of command as possible

Delegating authority to lower levels of managers may increase the organization's productivity. Decentralization requires that lower-level managers have strong decision-making skills. In recent years the trend has been toward more decentralized organizations, and some of the largest and most successful companies, including Google and Nike, have decentralized decision-making authority. Decentralization can be a key to being better, not just bigger. Non-profit organizations benefit from decentralization, as well.

## Span of Management

How many subordinates should a manager manage? There is no simple answer. Experts generally agree, however, that top managers should not directly supervise more than four to eight people, while lower-level managers who supervise routine tasks are capable of managing a much larger number of subordinates. For example, the manager of the finance department may supervise 25 employees, whereas the vice-president of finance may supervise only five managers.

**span of management** the number of subordinates who report to a particular manager (also called *span of control*)

**Span of management** (also called span of control) refers to the number of subordinates who report to a

## ENTREPRENEURSHIP IN ACTION

### An Online Teaching and Learning Platform That's Easy, Flexible, and Smart

**D2L**

**Founder:** John Baker

**Founded:** 1999, in Kitchener, Ontario

**Success:** D2L is already leading a major shift in educational software: it's harnessing data and analytics to become the Netflix of education.

D2L was founded in 1999 by John Baker. When he was a student, his engineering class was challenged to look at the world in new ways by coming up with a question that no one had asked before. The question he wanted to ask was clear: How could we use technology to dramatically transform learning?

John Baker started to imagine designing software that could automatically grade student assignments to provide instant feedback, as well as perform other tasks. In his third year of university, Baker founded D2L to put some of his ideas into practice. Later, Baker signed his first big client, the University of Guelph, which incorporated tools he designed into its new MBA program. These features, which included a way to take notes online, an instant-messaging client, and a discussion board, formed the core of the company's software.

Customer relationships help fuel innovation at D2L, as the company constantly asks clients about how it can meet their needs and tests ideas in the marketplace. Every few months, D2L also holds a weeklong "hackathon," where employees drop what they're doing to work on a new product or bug fix. The events foster the notion that hatching new ideas and solutions is everybody's job, says Baker. Today, D2L is a global cloud software company with offices across Canada, the United States, Europe, Australia, Brazil, and Singapore.*

**DISCUSSION QUESTIONS**

1. How did the founder of D2L use his engineering class to make his company a success?
2. Why is it important for the company to continue to hold "hackathons" to discuss new ideas?
3. Do you think D2L has a centralized or decentralized structure? Why?

* "The 15 Most Innovative Canadian Companies of 2015," *Canadian Business*, March 19, 2015, http://www.canadianbusiness.com/innovation/most-innovative-companies-2015-slideshow/ (accessed January 11, 2016); Sarah Barmak, "How the 'Netflix of education' is using big data in the classroom," *Canadian Business*, March 19, 2015, http://www.canadianbusiness.com/innovation/most-innovative-2015-d2l-brightspace/ (accessed January 11, 2016); "About Us," D2L, n.d., http://www.d2l.com/about (accessed January 11, 2016).

particular manager. A *wide span of management* exists when a manager directly supervises a very large number of employees. A *narrow span of management* exists when a manager directly supervises only a few subordinates (Figure 7.3). At Whole Foods, the best employees are recruited and placed in small teams in one of eight departments. Employees are empowered to discount, give away, and sample products, as well as to assist in creating a respectful workplace where goals are achieved, individual employees succeed, and customers are core in business decisions. This approach allows Whole Foods to offer unique and "local market" experiences in each of its stores. This level of customization is in contrast to more centralized supermarket chains.[13]

Should the span of management be wide or narrow? To answer this question, several factors need to be considered. A narrow span of management is appropriate when superiors and subordinates are not in close proximity, the manager has many responsibilities in addition to the direct supervision, the interaction between superiors and subordinates is frequent, and problems are common. However, when superiors and subordinates are located close to one another, the manager has few responsibilities other than supervision, the level of interaction between superiors and subordinates is low, few problems arise, subordinates are highly competent, and a set of specific operating procedures governs the activities of managers and their subordinates, a wide span of management will be more appropriate. Narrow spans of management are typical in centralized organizations, while wide spans of management are more common in decentralized firms.

"A company with many layers of managers is considered tall."

**Figure 7.3** | Span of Management: Wide Span and Narrow Span

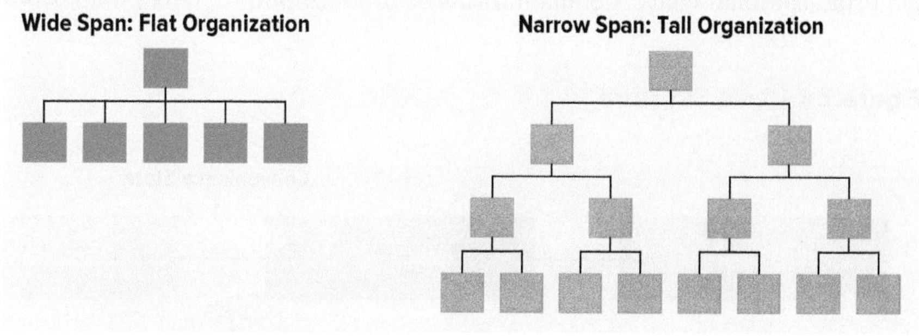

## Organizational Layers

Complementing the concept of span of management are **organizational layers**, the levels of management in an organization.

**organizational layers** the levels of management in an organization

A company with many layers of managers is considered tall; in a tall organization, the span of management is narrow (see Figure 7.3.). Because each manager supervises only a few subordinates, many layers of management are necessary to carry out the operations of the business. McDonald's, for example, has a tall organization with many layers, including store managers, district managers, regional managers, and functional managers (finance, marketing, and so on), as well as a chief executive officer and many vice-presidents. Because there are more managers in tall organizations than in flat organizations, administrative costs are usually higher. Communication is slower because information must pass through many layers.

Organizations with few layers are flat and have wide spans of management. When managers supervise a large number of employees, fewer management layers are needed to conduct the organization's activities. Managers in flat organizations typically perform more administrative duties than managers in tall organizations because there are fewer of them. They also spend more time supervising and working with subordinates. Many of the companies that decentralized also flattened their structures and widened their spans of management, often by eliminating layers of middle management. As mentioned earlier, Johnson & Johnson has both a decentralized and flat organizational structure.

# Forms of Organizational Structure

**LO 7-5** Compare and contrast some common forms of organizational structure.

Along with assigning tasks and the responsibility for carrying them out, managers must consider how to structure their authority relationships—that is, what structure the organization itself will have and how it will appear on the organizational chart. Common forms of organization include line structure, line-and-staff structure, multidivisional structure, and matrix structure.

## Line Structure

The simplest organizational structure, **line structure**, has direct lines of authority that extend from the top manager to employees at the lowest level of the organization. For example, a convenience store employee at 7-Eleven may report to an assistant manager, who reports to the store manager, who reports to a regional manager, while in an independent store they might report directly to the owner (Figure 7.4). This structure has a clear chain of command, which enables managers to make decisions quickly.

**line structure** the simplest organizational structure; direct lines of authority extend from the top manager to the lowest level of the organization

A mid-level manager facing a decision must consult only one person, his or her immediate supervisor. However, this structure requires that managers possess a wide range of knowledge and skills. They are responsible for a variety of activities and must be knowledgeable about them all. Line structures are most common in small businesses.

## Line-and-Staff Structure

The **line-and-staff structure** has a traditional line relationship between superiors and subordinates; specialized managers—called staff managers—are available to assist line managers (Figure 7.5). Line managers can focus on their areas of expertise in the operation of the business, while staff managers provide advice and support to line departments on specialized matters such as finance, engineering, human resources, and the law. Staff managers do not have direct authority over line managers or over the line manager's subordinates, but they do have direct authority over subordinates in their own departments. However, line-and-staff organizations may experience problems with overstaffing and ambiguous lines of communication. Additionally, employees may become frustrated because they lack the authority to carry out certain decisions.

**line-and-staff structure** the a structure having a traditional line relationship between superiors and subordinates and also specialized managers—called staff managers—who are available to assist line managers

**Figure 7.4** | Line Structure

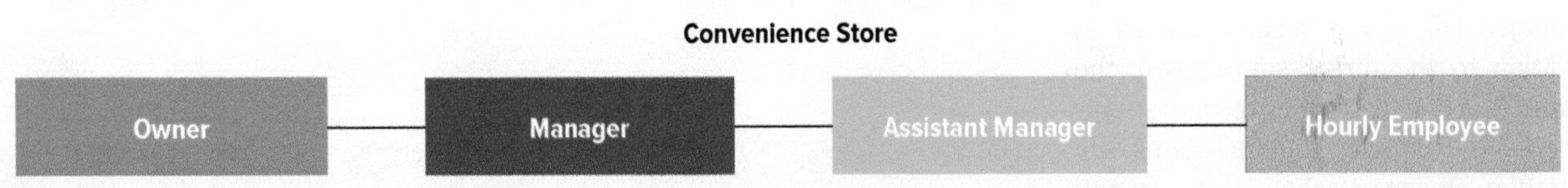

**Figure 7.5** | Line-and-Staff Structure

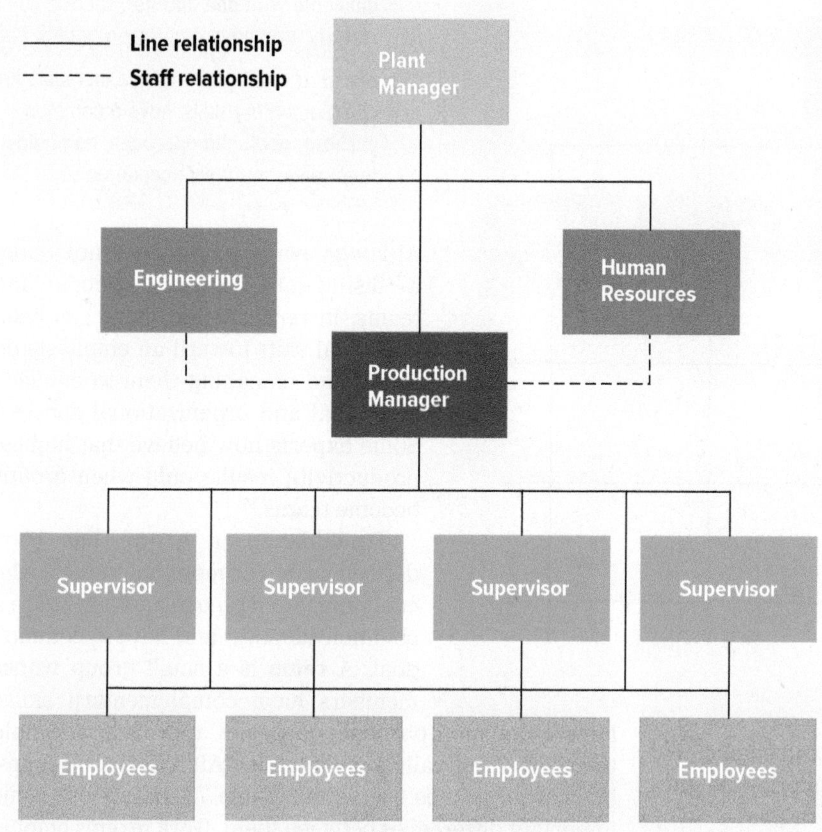


## Multi-divisional Structure

As companies grow and diversify, traditional line structures become difficult to coordinate, making communication difficult and decision making slow. When the weaknesses of the structure—"turf wars," miscommunication, and working at cross-purposes—exceed the benefits, growing firms tend to **restructure**, often into the divisionalized form. A **multi-divisional structure** organizes departments into larger groups called divisions. Just as departments might be formed on the basis of geography, customer, product, or a combination of these, divisions can also be formed based on any of these methods of organizing. Within each of these divisions, departments may be organized by product, geographic region, function, or some combination of all three. Indra Nooyi, CEO of PepsiCo, rearranged the company's organizational structure after taking the helm. Prior to her tenure, PepsiCo was organized geographically. She created new units that span international boundaries and make it easier for employees in different geographic regions to share business practices.[14]

**restructure** to change the basic structure of an organization

**multi-divisional structure** a structure that organizes departments into larger groups called divisions

Multi-divisional structures permit delegation of decision-making authority, allowing divisional and department managers to specialize. They allow those closest to the action to make the decisions that will affect them. Delegation of authority and divisionalized work also mean that better decisions are made faster, and they tend to be more innovative. Most importantly, by focusing each division on a common region, product, or customer, each is more likely to provide products that meet the needs of its particular customers. However, the divisional structure inevitably creates work duplication, which makes it more difficult to realize the economies of scale that result from grouping functions together.

## Matrix Structure

Another structure that attempts to address issues that arise with growth, diversification, productivity, and competitiveness is the matrix. A **matrix structure**, also called a project-management structure, sets up teams that have members from different departments, thereby creating two or more intersecting lines of authority (see Figure 7.6). One of the first organizations to design and implement a matrix structure was the National Aeronautics and Space Administration (NASA) because it needed to coordinate different projects at the same time for the space program.

The matrix structure superimposes project-based departments on the more traditional, function-based departments. Project teams bring together specialists from a variety of areas to work together on a single project, such as developing a new fighter jet. In this arrangement, employees are responsible to two managers—functional managers and project managers. Matrix structures are usually temporary: team members typically go back to their functional or line department after a project is finished. However, more firms are becoming permanent matrix structures, creating and dissolving project teams as needed to meet customer needs. The aerospace industry was one of the first to apply the matrix structure, but today it is used by universities and schools, accounting firms, banks, and organizations in other industries.

**matrix structure** a structure that sets up teams with members from different departments, thereby creating two or more intersecting lines of authority; also called a project-management structure

Matrix structures provide flexibility, enhanced cooperation, and creativity, and they enable the company to respond quickly to changes in the environment by giving special attention to specific projects or problems. However, they

**Figure 7.6** | Matrix Structure

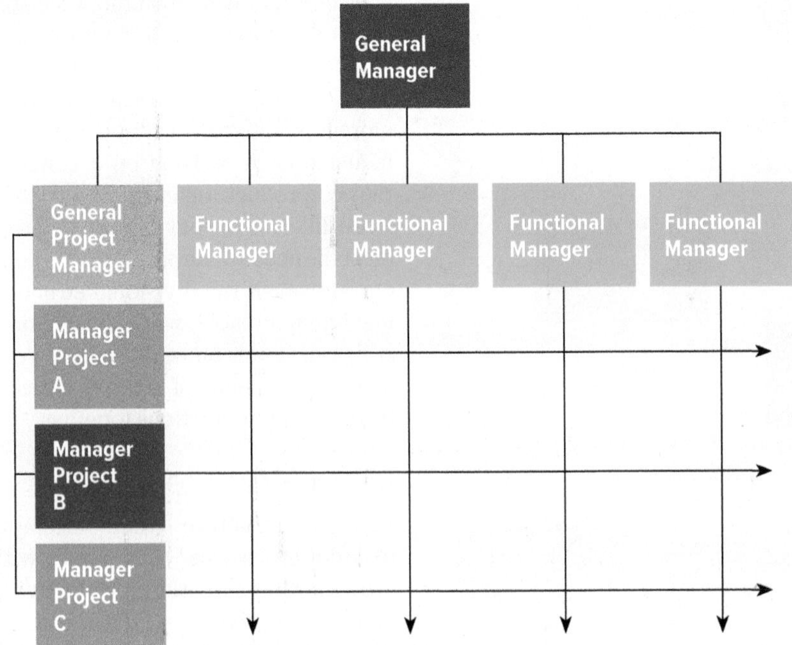


are generally expensive and quite complex, and employees may be confused as to whose authority has priority—the project manager's or the immediate supervisor's.

## The Role of Groups and Teams in Organizations

**LO 7-6** Distinguish between groups and teams, and identify the types of each that exist in organizations.

Regardless of how they are organized, most of the essential work of business occurs in individual work groups and teams, so we'll take a closer look at them now.

**group** two or more individuals who communicate with one another, share a common identity, and have a common goal

**team** a small group whose members have complementary skills; have a common purpose, goal, and approach; and hold themselves mutually accountable

Although some experts do not make a distinction between groups and teams, in recent years there has been a gradual shift toward an emphasis on teams and managing them to enhance individual and organizational success. Some experts now believe that highest productivity results only when groups become teams.[15]

Traditionally, a **group** has been defined as two or more individuals who communicate with one another, share a common identity, and have a common goal. A **team** is a small group whose members have complementary skills; have a common purpose, goal, and approach; and hold themselves mutually accountable.[16] All teams are groups, but not all groups are teams. Table 7.1 points out some important differences between them. Work groups emphasize individual work products, individual accountability, and even individual leadership. Salespeople working independently for the same company could be a work group.

In contrast, work teams share leadership roles, have both individual and mutual accountability, and create collective work products. In other words, a work group's performance depends on what its members do as individuals, while a team's performance is based on creating a knowledge centre and a competency to work together to accomplish a goal. On the other hand, it is also important for team members to retain their individuality and avoid becoming just "another face in the crowd." The purpose

**Table 7.1** | Differences Between Groups and Teams

| Working Group | Team |
|---|---|
| Has strong, clearly focused leader | Has shared leadership roles |
| Has individual accountability | Has individual and group accountability |
| Has the same purpose as the broader organizational mission | Has a specific purpose that the team itself delivers |
| Creates individual work products | Creates collective work products |
| Runs efficient meetings | Encourages open-ended discussion and active problem-solving meetings |
| Measures its effectiveness indirectly by its effects on others (e.g., financial performance of the business) | Measures performance directly by assessing collective work products |
| Discusses, decides, and delegates | Discusses, decides, and does real work together |

Source: Robert Gatewood, Robert Taylor, and O. C. Ferrell, *Management: Comprehension Analysis and Application*, 1995, p. 427. Copyright © 1995 Richard D. Irwin, a Times Mirror Higher Education Group, Inc., company. Reproduced with permission of the McGraw-Hill Companies.

of teams should be collaboration rather than collectivism. Although the team is working toward a common goal, it is important that all team members actively contribute their ideas and work together to achieve this common goal.[17]

The type of groups an organization establishes depends on the tasks it needs to accomplish and the situation it faces. Some specific kinds of groups and teams include committees, task forces, project teams, product-development teams, quality-assurance teams, and self-directed work teams. All of these can be *virtual teams*—employees in different locations who rely on email, audio conferencing, fax, Internet, videoconferencing, or other technological tools to accomplish their goals. Virtual teams are becoming a part of everyday business, with the number of employees working remotely from their employer increasing more than 80 percent in the last several years.[18] Virtual teams have also opened up opportunities for different companies. For instance, inside salespeople use virtual technology such as email and social media to connect with prospects and clients.[19]

## Committees

A **committee** is usually a permanent, formal group that does some specific task. For example, many firms have a compensation or finance committee to examine the effectiveness of these areas of operation as well as the need for possible changes. Ethics committees are formed to develop and revise codes of ethics, suggest methods for implementing ethical standards, and review specific issues and concerns.

**committee** a permanent, formal group that performs a specific task

**DID YOU KNOW?**

A survey of employees revealed that approximately 53 percent consider how senior management communicates with them to be a key factor in their job satisfaction.[20]

## Task Forces

A **task force** is a temporary group of employees responsible for bringing about a particular change. They typically come from across all departments and levels of an organization. Task force membership is usually based on expertise rather than organizational position. Occasionally, a task force may be formed from individuals outside a company. Coca-Cola has often used task forces to address problems and provide recommendations for improving company practices or products. While some task forces might last a few months, others last for years. When Coca-Cola faced lawsuits alleging discrimination practices in hiring and promotion, it developed a five-year task force to examine pay and promotion practices among minority employees. Its experiences helped Coca-Cola realize the advantages of having a cross-functional task force made up of employees from different departments, and it continued to use task forces to tackle major company issues.[21]

**task force** a temporary group of employees responsible for bringing about a particular change

## Teams

Teams are becoming far more common in the Canadian workplace as businesses strive to enhance productivity and global competitiveness. In general, teams have the benefit of being able to pool members' knowledge and skills and make greater use of them than can individuals working alone. Team building is becoming increasingly popular in organizations, with around half of executives indicating their companies had team-building training. Teams require harmony, cooperation, synchronized effort, and flexibility to maximize their contribution.[22]

Teams can also create more solutions to problems than can individuals. Furthermore, team participation enhances employee acceptance of, understanding of, and commitment to team goals. Teams motivate workers by providing internal rewards in the form of an enhanced sense of accomplishment for employees as they achieve more, and external rewards in the form of praise and certain perks. Consequently, they can help get workers more involved. They can help companies be more innovative, and they can boost productivity and cut costs.

According to psychologist Ivan Steiner, team productivity peaks at about five team members. People become less motivated and group coordination becomes more difficult after this size. Jeff Bezos, Amazon.com CEO, says that he has a "two-pizza rule": If a team cannot be fed by two pizzas, it is too large. Keep teams small enough that everyone gets a piece of the action.[23]

**Project Teams.** **Project teams** are similar to task forces, but normally they run their operation and have total control of a specific work project. Like task forces, their membership is likely to cut across the firm's hierarchy and be composed of people from different functional areas. They are almost always temporary, although a large project, such as designing and building a new airplane at Bombardier, may last for years.

**project teams** groups similar to task forces that normally run their operation and have total control of a specific work project

"Teams are becoming far more common in the workplace as businesses strive to enhance productivity and global competitiveness."

**product-development teams** a specific type of project team formed to devise, design, and implement a new product

**quality-assurance teams (or quality circles)** small groups of workers brought together from throughout the organization to solve specific quality, productivity, or service problems

**Product-development teams** are a special type of project team formed to devise, design, and implement a new product. Sometimes product-development teams exist within a functional area—research and development for example—but now they more frequently include people from numerous functional areas and may even include customers to help ensure that the end product meets customers' needs. Intel informs its product development process through indirect input from customers. It has a social scientist on staff who leads a research team on how customers actually use products. This is done mainly by observation and asking questions. Once enough information is gathered, it is relayed to the product-development team and incorporated into Intel's designs.[24]

**Quality-Assurance Teams.** **Quality-assurance teams (or quality circles)** are fairly small groups of workers brought together from throughout the organization to solve specific quality, productivity, or service problems. Although the term *quality circle* is not as popular as it once was, the concern about quality is stronger than ever. Companies such as IBM and Xerox, as well as companies in the automobile industry, have used quality circles to shift the organization to a more participative culture. The use of teams to address quality issues will no doubt continue to increase throughout the business world.

**Self-Directed Work Teams.** A **self-directed work team (SDWT)** is a group of employees responsible for an entire work process or segment that delivers a product to an internal or external customer.[25] SDWTs have the flexibility to change rapidly to meet the competition or respond to customer needs. The defining characteristic of an SDWT is the extent to which it is empowered or given authority to make and implement work decisions. Thus, SDWTs are designed to give employees a feeling of "ownership" of a whole job. Employees at 3M, as well as an increasing number of companies, encourage employees to be active to perform a function or operational task. With shared team responsibility for work outcomes, team members often have broader job assignments and cross-train to master other jobs, thus permitting greater team flexibility.

**self-directed work team (SDWT)** a group of employees responsible for an entire work process or segment that delivers a product to an internal or external customer

# Communicating in Organizations

**LO 7-7** Describe how communication occurs in organizations.

Communication within an organization can flow in a variety of directions and from a number of sources, each using both oral and written forms of communication. The success of communication systems within the organization has a tremendous effect on the overall success of the firm, as mistakes can lower productivity and morale.

Alternatives to face-to-face communications—such as meetings—are growing thanks to technology such as voice mail, email, social media, and online newsletters. Many companies use internal networks called intranets to share information with employees. Intranets increase communication across different departments and levels of management and help with the flow of everyday business activities.

**Cloud Computing.** Rather than using physical products, companies using cloud computing technology can access computing resources and information over a network. Cloud computing allows companies to have more control over computing resources and can be less expensive than hardware or software. Salesforce.com uses cloud computing in its customer relationship management solutions.[26] Companies can even integrate aspects of social media into their intranets, allowing employees to post comments and pictures, participate in polls, and create group calendars.

## Formal and Informal Communication

Formal channels of communication are intentionally defined and designed by the organization. They represent the flow of communication within the formal organizational structure, as shown on organizational charts. Table 7.2 describes the different forms of formal communication. Traditionally, formal communication patterns were classified as vertical and horizontal, but with the

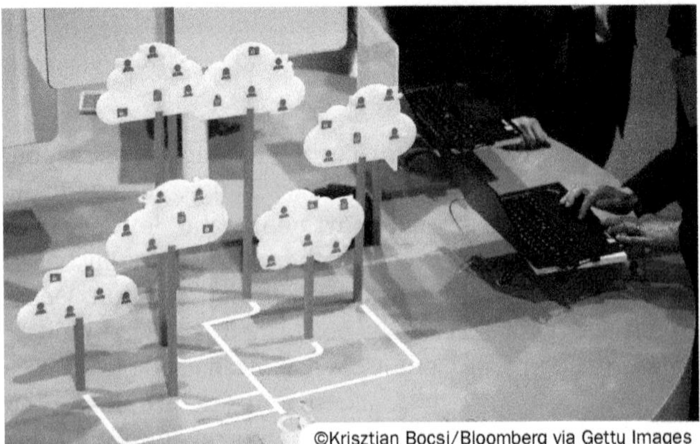



Cloud-based tools like Dropbox, iCloud, Google Drive, Salesforce, and more are transforming internal communication at companies. They allow employees to share documents, collaborate with their teams, and even work from home.

**Table 7.2** | Types of Formal Communication

| Type | Definition | Examples |
|---|---|---|
| Upward | Flows from lower to higher levels of the organization | Progress reports, suggestions for improvement, inquiries, grievances |
| Downward | Traditional flow of communication from upper organizational levels to lower organizational levels | Directions, assignments of tasks and responsibilities, performance feedback, details about strategies and goals, speeches, employee handbooks, job descriptions |
| Horizontal | Exchange of information among colleagues and peers on the same organizational level, such as across or within departments, who inform, support, and early coordinate activities both within the department and between other departments | Task forces, project teams, communication from the finance department to the marketing department concerning budget requirements |
| Diagonal | When individuals from different levels and different departments communicate | A manager from the finance department communicates with a lower-level manager from the marketing department |

## RESPONDING TO BUSINESS CHALLENGES

### Whole Foods Focuses on the Whole Team

Since its founding in 1978, Whole Foods has been committed to great customer service and selling the highest-quality natural and organic products. Employees are essential to achieving these goals as they daily interact with customers. Employees are therefore highly valued at Whole Foods and are labelled *team members* to empower them through their everyday contributions.

At each store, individuals are divided into 8 to 10 self-directed work teams. Initially, when candidates are hired, they are hired on a provisional basis. Before candidates are hired on a provisional basis, they undergo a 60-day process of interviews on the phone, with team members, and with leaders. If two thirds of the team members vote in favour of the candidate, the candidate becomes part of the team. The team approach has been adopted throughout the entire chain of command—even among regional leaders. Through its use of teams, Whole Foods has been able to turn its workers into significant contributors of value to the company.

Despite Whole Foods' success, the company has struggled to get rid of its "whole paycheque" reputation. Due to its financial challenges, Amazon acquired Whole Foods for $13.7 billion. Such a cultural shift might take away some of the team autonomy practiced at individual stores. Amazon and Whole Foods will need to balance these changes with the successful team approach practised at individual stores.*

#### DISCUSSION QUESTIONS

1. What are some of the ways Whole Foods encourages teamwork among employees?
2. Why does the use of teams allow Whole Foods to tap into a variety of talent?
3. How does Whole Foods make use of self-directed work teams?

*"Why We're a Great Place to Work," Whole Foods Market, http://www.wholefoodsmarket.com/careers/why-were-greatplace-work (accessed December 30, 2017); "Whole Foods Market's Core Values," Whole Foods Market, www.wholefoodsmarket.com/values/corevalues.php#supporting (accessed December 30, 2017); "100 Best Companies to Work For: Whole Foods Market," CNN Money, 2011, http://money.cnn.com/magazines/fortune/bestcompanies/2011/snapshots/24.html (accessed December 30, 2017); "100 Best Companies to Work For: Whole Foods Market," CNN Money, 2013, http://money.cnn.com/magazines/fortune/best-companies/2013/snapshots/71.html?iid=bc_fl_list (accessed September 9, 2013); Kerry A. Dolan, "America's Greenest Companies 2011," *Forbes*, April 18, 2011, www.forbes.com/2011/04/18/americas-greenest-companies.html (accessed December 30, 2017); Joseph Brownstein, "Is Whole Foods' Get Healthy Plan Fair?" *ABC News*, January 29, 2010, http://abcnews.go.com/Health/w_DietAndFitnessNews/foods-incentives-make-employeeshealthier/story?id=9680047 (accessed December 30, 2017); Deborah Dunham, "At Whole Foods Thinner Employees Get Fatter Discounts," *That's Fit*, January 27, 2010, www.thatsfit.com/2010/01/27/whole-foods-thin-employeesget-discounts/ (accessed September 9, 2013); David Burkus, "Why Whole Foods Builds Its Entire Business on Teams," *Forbes*, June 8, 2016, https://www.forbes.com/sites/davidburkus/2016/06/08/why-whole-foods-buildtheir- entire-business-on-teams/#47872abc3fa1 (accessed December 30, 2017); Kate Taylor, "Here Are All the Changes Amazon Is Making to Whole Foods," *Business Insider*, November 15, 2017, http://www.businessinsider.com/amazon-changes-whole-foods-2017-9/#whole-foodsimmediately-slashed-prices-and-announced-another-roundof-price-cuts-in-november-1 (accessed December 30, 2017).

increased use of teams and matrix structures, formal communication may occur in a number of patterns (Figure 7.7).

Along with the formal channels of communication shown on an organizational chart, all firms communicate informally, as well. Communication between friends, for instance, cuts across department, division, and even management–subordinate boundaries. Such friendships and other non-work social relationships comprise the *informal organization* of a firm, and their impact can be great.

The most significant informal communication occurs through the **grapevine**, an informal channel of communication, separate from management's formal, official communication channels. Grapevines exist in all organizations. Information passed along the grapevine may relate to the job or organization, or it may be gossip and rumours unrelated to either. The accuracy of grapevine information has been of great concern to managers.

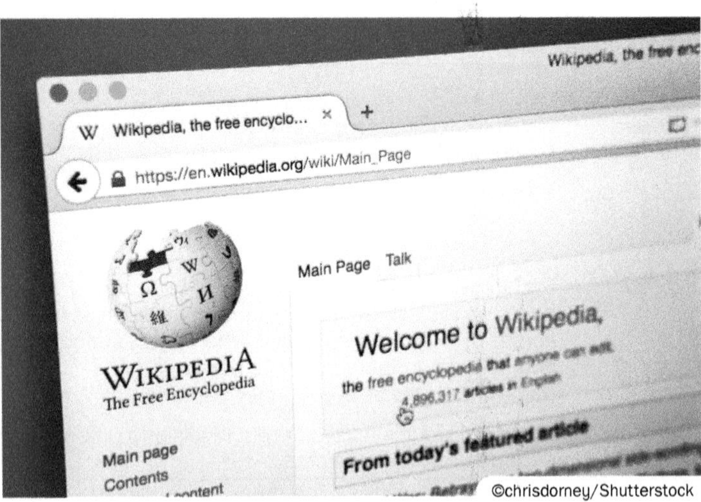

©chrisdorney/Shutterstock

Online sites such as wikis are allowing employee teams to share information and work collaboratively on documents. The most well-known wiki is the online encyclopedia, Wikipedia.

Managers can turn the grapevine to their advantage. Using it as a "sounding device" for possible new policies is one example. Managers can obtain valuable information from the grapevine that could improve decision making. Some organizations use the grapevine to their advantage by floating ideas, soliciting feedback, and reacting accordingly. People love to gossip, and managers need to be aware that grapevines exist in every organization. Managers who understand how the grapevine works also can use it to their advantage by feeding it facts to squelch rumours and incorrect information. For instance, rather than confronting employees about gossip and placing them on the defensive, some employers ask employees—especially those who are the spreaders of gossip—for assistance in squelching the untrue rumours. This tactic turns employees into advocates for sharing truthful information.[27]

**grapevine** an informal channel of communication, separate from management's formal, official communication channels

"Grapevines exist in all organizations. Information passed along the grapevine may relate to the job or organization, or it may be gossip and rumours unrelated to either."

**Figure 7.7** | The Flow of Communication in an Organizational Hierarchy

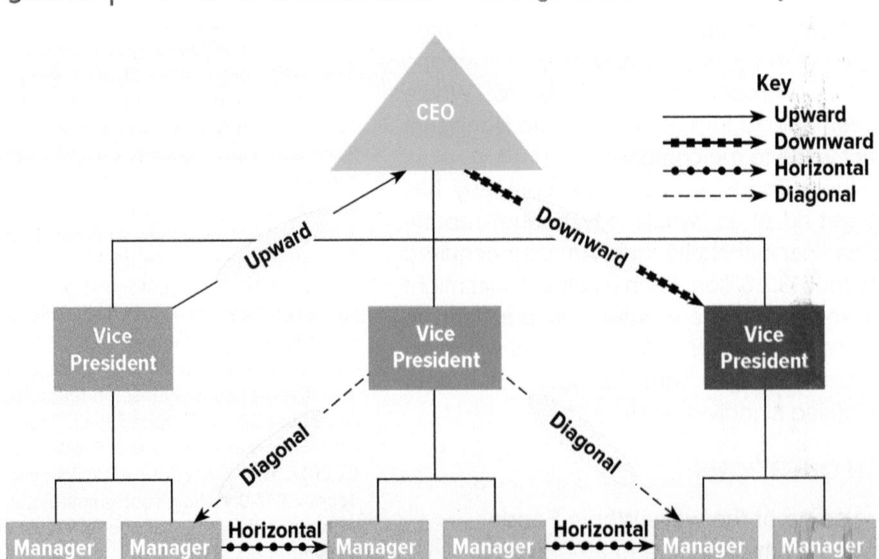

## Monitoring Communications

Technological advances and the increased use of electronic communication in the workplace have made monitoring its use necessary for most companies. Failing to monitor employees' use of email, social media, and the Internet can be costly. Many companies require that employees sign and follow a policy on appropriate Internet use. These agreements often require that employees will use corporate computers only for work-related activities. Additionally, several companies use software programs to monitor employee computer usage.[28] Instituting practices that show respect for employee privacy but do not abdicate employer responsibility are increasingly necessary in today's workplace. Several websites provide model policies and detailed guidelines for conducting electronic monitoring, including the Guide for Businesses and Organizations, "Your Privacy Responsibilities," on the Privacy Commissioner of Canada site.

**Artificial Intelligence (AI).** Artificial intelligence (AI) is having a significant impact on workplace monitoring, benchmarking, and understanding how employees "feel" about their jobs. More than 40 percent of employers globally have implemented AI processes within their organization. One such tool, called Xander, can determine an employee's optimism, confusion, anger, or happiness. With such an understanding of employee attitudes, you can correct or improve the negative experiences in the workplace and enhance the positive ones. Software companies have developed artificial intelligence tools that can make routine human resource decisions such as performance management. There are concerns that AI technology might incorporate biases that can lead to discriminatory decision making.[29]

## Improving Communication Effectiveness

Strong and effective communication channels are a requirement for companies to distribute information to different levels of the company. Without effective communication, the activities and overall productivity of projects, groups, teams, and individuals will be diminished. Apple supplier Foxconn is one example of how essential communication is to a firm. Despite criticisms of unfair labour conditions, the Fair Labor Association determined that Foxconn had formal procedures in place at its factories to prevent many major accidents. However, it concluded that the firm had a communication problem. These procedures were not being communicated to the factory workers, contributing to unsafe practices and two tragic explosions.[30]

**Feedback.** One of the major issues of effective communication is in obtaining feedback. If feedback is not provided, then communication will be ineffective and can drag down overall performance. Managers should always encourage feedback, including concerns and challenges about issues. Listening is a skill that involves hearing, and most employees listen much more than they actively communicate to others. Therefore, managers should encourage employees to provide feedback—even if it is negative. This will allow the organization to identify strengths and weaknesses and make adjustments when needed. At the same time, strong feedback mechanisms help to empower employees as they feel that their voices are being heard.

**Interruptions.** Interruptions can be a serious threat to effective communication. Various activities can interrupt the message. For example, interjecting a remark can create discontinuance in the communication process or disrupt the uniformity of the message. Even small interruptions can be a problem if the messenger cannot adequately understand or interpret the communicator's message. One suggestion is to give the communicator space or time to make another statement rather than quickly responding or making your own comment.

**Email.** It is important for companies to communicate their email policies throughout the organization and for employees to use email correctly. The increasing use of email as a communication tool inundates employees and managers with messages, making it easier to overlook individual communications. For example, it is advised that employees place a specific subject in the subject line, keep emails brief, and avoid using email if a problem would be better solved through telephone contact or face-to-face interaction.[31] It is also quite easy to send the wrong email to the wrong person, and messages sent over email can be misinterpreted. Communicators using email, whether managers or employees, must exert caution before pushing that Send button. Email can also be a distraction or disruptive to productivity. Some guidance on best practices in managing workplace productivity suggests that it's best to check email every 45 minutes. Also, responding too quickly and during evenings and weekends can increase stress and diminish productivity.[32]

Communication is necessary in helping every organizational member understand what is expected of him or her. Many business problems can be avoided if clear communication exists within the company. Even the best business strategies are of little use if those who will oversee them cannot understand what is intended. Communication might not seem to be as important a concern to management as finances, human resources, and marketing, but in reality it can make the difference between successful implementation of business activities or failure.

### TEAM EXERCISE

Assess the organizational structure of a company that one of your team members has worked for. Was the organization centralized or decentralized in terms of decision making? Was the span of control wide or narrow? Were any types of teams, committees, or task forces used in the organization? Report your work to the class.

# LEARNING OBJECTIVES SUMMARY

**LO 7-1** Explain the importance of organizational culture.

Organizational culture is the firm's shared values, beliefs, traditions, philosophies, and role models for behaviour. It helps ensure that all members of a company share values and suggests rules for how to behave and deal with problems within the organization.

**LO 7-2** Define *organizational structure*, and describe how organizational structures develop.

Structure is the arrangement or relationship of positions within an organization; it develops when managers assign work activities to work groups and specific individuals, and coordinate the diverse activities required to attain organizational objectives. Organizational structure evolves to accommodate growth, which requires people with specialized skills.

**LO 7-3** Describe how specialization and departmentalization help an organization achieve its goals.

Structuring an organization requires that management assign work tasks to specific individuals and groups. Under specialization, managers break labour into small, specialized tasks and assign employees to do a single task, fostering efficiency. Departmentalization is the grouping of jobs into working units (departments, units, groups, or divisions). Businesses may departmentalize by function, product, geographic region, or customer, or they may combine two or more of these.

**LO 7-4** Determine how organizations assign responsibility for tasks and delegate authority.

Delegation of authority means assigning tasks to employees and giving them the power to make commitments, use resources, and take whatever actions are necessary to accomplish the tasks. It puts the responsibility on employees to carry out assigned tasks satisfactorily and holds them accountable to a superior for the proper execution of their assigned work. The extent to which authority is delegated throughout an organization determines its degree of centralization. Span of management refers to the number of subordinates who report to particular manager. A wide span of management occurs in flat organizations; a narrow one exists in tall organizations.

**LO 7-5** Compare and contrast some common forms of organizational structure.

Line structures have direct lines of authority that extend from the top manager to employees at the lowest level of the organization. The line-and-staff structure has a traditional line relationship between superiors and subordinates, and specialized staff managers to assist line managers. A multi-divisional structure gathers departments into larger groups called divisions. A matrix, or project-management, structure assembles team members from different departments, thereby creating two or more intersecting lines of authority.

**LO 7-6** Distinguish between groups and teams, and identify the types of each that exist in organizations.

A group is two or more persons who communicate, share a common identity, and have a common goal. A team is a small group whose members have complementary skills, a common purpose, goals, and approach, and who hold themselves mutually accountable. The major distinction is that individual performance is most important in groups, while collective work performance counts most in teams. Special kinds of groups include task forces, committees, project teams, product-development teams, quality-assurance teams, and self-directed work teams.

**LO 7-7** Describe how communication occurs in organizations.

Communication occurs both formally and informally in organizations. Formal communication may be downward, upward, horizontal, and even diagonal. Informal communication takes place through friendships and the grapevine.

# KEY TERMS

accountability
centralized organization
committee
customer departmentalization
decentralized organization
delegation of authority
departmentalization
functional departmentalization
geographical departmentalization
grapevine
group
line-and-staff structure
line structure
matrix structure
multi-divisional structure
organizational charts
organizational culture
organizational layers
product departmentalization
product-development teams
project teams
quality-assurance teams (or quality circles)
responsibility
restructure
self-directed work team (SDWT)
span of management
specialization
structure
task force
team

# So You Want a Job *in Managing Organizational Culture, Teamwork, and Communication*

Jobs dealing with organizational culture and structure are usually at the top of the organization. If you want to be a CEO or high-level manager, you will help shape these areas of business. On the other hand, if you are an entrepreneur or small-business person, you will need to make decisions about assigning tasks, departmentalization, and assigning responsibility. Even managers in small organizations have to make decisions about decentralization, span of management, and forms of organizational structure. While these decisions may be part of your job, there are usually no job titles dealing with these specific areas. Specific jobs that attempt to improve organizational culture could include ethics and compliance positions as well as those who are in charge of communicating memos, manuals, and policies that help establish the culture. These positions will be in communications, human resources, and positions that assist top organizational managers.

Teams are becoming more common in the workplace, and it is possible to become a member of a product-development group or quality-assurance team. There are also human resources positions that encourage teamwork through training activities. The area of corporate communications provides lots of opportunities for specific jobs that facilitate communication systems. Thanks to technology, there are job positions to help disseminate information through online newsletters, intranets, or internal computer networks to increase collaboration.

In addition to the many advances using electronic communications, there are technology concerns that create new job opportunities. Monitoring workplace communications such as the use of email and the Internet have created new industries. There have to be internal controls in the organization to make sure that the organization does not engage in any copyright infringement. If this is an area of interest, there are specific jobs that provide an opportunity to use your technological skills to assist in maintaining appropriate standards in communicating and using technology.

If you go to work for a large company with many divisions, you can expect to find a number of positions dealing with the tasks discussed here. If you go to work for a small company, you will probably engage in most of these tasks as a part of your position. Organizational flexibility requires individual flexibility, and those employees willing to take on new domains and challenges will be the employees who survive and prosper in the future.

# BUILD YOUR BUSINESS PLAN

## Organization, Teamwork, and Communication

Developing a business plan as a team is a deliberate move on the part of your instructor to encourage you to familiarize yourself with the concept of teamwork. You need to realize that you are going to spend a large part of your professional life working with others. At this point, you are working on the business plan for a grade, but after graduation you will be teaming with co-workers, and the success of your endeavours may determine whether you get a raise or a bonus. It is important that you be comfortable as soon as possible with working with others and holding them accountable for their contributions.

Some people are natural leaders, and leaders often feel that if team members are not doing their work, they must take it upon themselves to do it all. This is not leadership, but rather micro-managing.

Leadership means holding members accountable for their responsibilities. Your instructor may provide ideas on how this could be implemented, possibly by utilizing peer reviews. Remember you are not doing team members any favours by doing their work for them.

If you are a follower (someone who takes direction well) rather than a leader, try to get into a team where others are hard workers and you will rise to their level. There is nothing wrong with being a follower; not everyone can be a leader!

# CASE | A Freshii Approach to Food and Business

Freshii is a restaurant franchise that focuses on fast and healthy food options. With more than 395 locations in 18 countries, the company has a variety of customizable food offerings from burritos and salads to frozen yogurt and smoothies. Freshii takes pride in its flat organizational structure, which it believes lets the company cut excess layers of management and allow for easier communication. Its flat organizational structure also empowers employees to have more ownership in their segment of the business.

Matthew Corrin, CEO of Freshii, founded the company in 2005 to offer healthy food that is fast, convenient, and affordable. Surprisingly, the restaurants have no stoves, ovens, fryers, ventilation, or freezers. Since Freshii started, it has become the fastest growing franchise in the world and is leading the industry with 20 consecutive quarters of same-store sales growth. The company took the top spot in FastCasual's Top 100 Movers & Shakers list in recognition of Freshii's efforts to make fundamental changes in the industry.

Freshii aims to have a corporate culture that allows free communication and ideas but isn't bogged down by extra layers of management, and its organizational structure is a big part of this. The company's flat structure allows employees to make critical decisions in a timely manner and empowers employees to be responsible for their own tasks. Freshii considers all employees Partners and rewards each employee with stock in the company so that employees have a real vested interest.

"We really feel that we empower our employees by giving them full ownership of their role for their area. They own their business from project ideation, research, and then all the way through execution and launching it, and then measuring the results out in the field," says Chief People Officer Ashley Dalziel. "And because of this structure, they get to see a project through from ideation, brainstorming, research, all the way through to execution."

Even though employees are given the power to design and execute their own projects, Freshii keeps a strong emphasis on communication. The company has seven key departments that are led by executives who have complete ownership of their area. Freshii's executive team, including its CEO, works in the same room around one large open table. This layout allows the executive team to communicate openly with each other in a space where the entire executive team can stay informed and be involved in the discussion.

Employees at Freshii are given a lot of responsibility to own their segments of the business. Because this can be overwhelming, the company rewards employees and builds chemistry through team activities. Freshii puts on monthly fitness challenges for employees where they are encouraged to run, take spin classes, and exercise with each other. Some of Freshii's core values are to live an energized life and to strive to be better, which the company embraces through these activities. Each Freshii store leader is encouraged to talk to employees and find out what they are passionate about. Then the store leader can assign team members to roles in which they are most likely to succeed. This personal attention from management allows employees to find roles they are best suited for and gives them an opportunity to be in a role they care about.

Franchising has helped Freshii expand internationally and spread its brand. However, Freshii is careful about choosing franchise partners who share its mission. Freshii's mission statement is "To help citizens of the world live better by making healthy food convenient and affordable." It is important that franchise partners embrace this mission in order for the company to maintain its unified culture. Still, Freshii empowers franchise owners to try new things and create new offerings to create innovation.

Freshii's flat organizational structure fits well with its culture of open communication and personal responsibility. Because of its culture, the company finds employees who are competitive and committed to providing healthy, convenient, and affordable food. Freshii strives to continue its rapid expansion while maintaining what made it unique from the start.[33]

## DISCUSSION QUESTIONS

1. How does Freshii's organizational structure shape its culture?
2. In what ways are employees at Freshii empowered to contribute to the company?
3. What effect does Freshii's franchise model have on its company culture?

CHAPTER 8

# Managing Operations and Supply Chains

©Alastair Wallace/Shutterstock

## LEARNING OBJECTIVES

**After reading this chapter, you will be able to:**

- **LO 8-1** Define *operations management*, and differentiate between operations and manufacturing.
- **LO 8-2** Explain how operations management differs in manufacturing and service firms.
- **LO 8-3** Describe the elements involved in planning and designing an operations system.
- **LO 8-4** Specify some techniques managers may use to manage the logistics of transforming inputs into finished products.
- **LO 8-5** Assess the importance of quality in operations management.

# ENTER THE WORLD OF BUSINESS

**Costco's Operational Success**

Founded in 1976, Costco is a multi-billion dollar global retailer with warehouse club operations in eight countries. By carefully choosing products based on quality, price, brand, and features, the company has generated a loyal customer following. Their operating philosophy has been simple: keep costs down and pass the savings on to members. Their large membership base and tremendous buying power, combined with efficiency, is a formula for success. The company has grown worldwide with total sales in recent fiscal years exceeding $64 billion.

The warehouse concept is built around the idea that Costco can achieve unbeatably low prices by offering a small selection of only the quickest-selling products. The combination of lower inventory and higher product turnover creates greater operational efficiencies. The store stocks about 4000 items compared to the 30,000 stocked by a typical grocery store or the 150,000 at a Walmart Supercentre. Inventory control has been a key advantage to reducing costs and focusing on a limited number of quality products. Products that have low demand or high production costs often do not last long.

Another attribute that sets Costco apart is its supply chain. At any given time, management aims to minimize the number of hands that touch a product. Costco will purchase directly from manufacturers, ship straight to distribution centres, and then send products to stores. Costco has crafted its distribution process to create efficiency and reduce costs. This efficiency increases productivity and allows customers to receive premium products consistently.

Additionally, Costco excels at quality and supplier relationships. It employs product developers who travel the world in search of best product/price combinations. Suppliers covet contracts with the store, which charges less in fees and is known for on-time payments. Costco expands only into areas that can support its streamlined distribution system. With its popularity continuing to rise, customers seem impressed by the way Costco has redefined the shopping experience.[1]

**DISCUSSION QUESTIONS**

1. How does Costco use inventory control as a way to control operational efficiencies?
2. Why do you think it is important for Costco to maintain a simple supply chain?
3. How do Costco's strong operational efficiencies allow it to compete against its larger rivals?

# Introduction

All organizations create products—goods, services, or ideas—for customers. Thus, organizations as diverse as Toyota, Subway, UPS, and a hospital share a number of similarities relating to how they transform resources into the products we consume. Most hospitals use similar admission procedures, while online social media companies, like Facebook and Twitter, use their technology and operating systems to create social networking opportunities and sell advertising. Such similarities are to be expected. But even organizations in unrelated industries take similar steps in creating goods or services. The check-in procedures of hotels and commercial airlines are comparable, for example. The way Subway assembles a sandwich and the way Ford assembles a truck are similar (both use assembly lines). These similarities are the result of operations management, the focus of this chapter.

Here, we discuss the role of production or operations management in acquiring and managing the resources necessary to create goods and services. Production and operations management involves planning and designing the processes that will transform those resources into finished products, managing the movement of those resources through the transformation process, and ensuring that the products are of the quality expected by customers.

# The Nature of Operations Management

**LO 8-1** Define *operations management*, and differentiate between operations and manufacturing.

**Operations management (OM)**, the development and administration of the activities involved in transforming resources into goods and services, is of crucial importance. Operations managers oversee the transformation process, and the planning and designing of operations systems, managing logistics, quality, and productivity. Quality and productivity have become fundamental aspects of operations management because a company that cannot make products of the quality desired by consumers, using resources efficiently and effectively, will not be able to remain in business. OM is the core of most organizations because it is responsible for the creation of the organization's goods or services. Some organizations, like Toyota, produce tangible products, but service is an important part of the total product for the customer.

Historically, operations management has been called *production* or *manufacturing* primarily because of the view that it was limited to the manufacture of physical goods. Its focus was on methods and techniques required to operate a factory efficiently. The change from *production* to *operations* recognizes the increasing importance of organizations that provide services and ideas. Additionally, the term *operations* represents an interest in viewing the operations function as a whole rather than simply as an analysis of inputs and outputs.

Today, OM includes a wide range of organizational activities and situations outside of manufacturing, such as health care, food service, banking, entertainment, education, transportation, and charity. Thus, we use the terms **manufacturing** and **production** interchangeably to represent the activities and processes used in making *tangible* products, whereas we use the broader term **operations** to describe those processes used in the making of *both tangible and intangible products.* Manufacturing provides tangible products such as the Apple Watch, and operations provides intangibles such as a stay at the Holiday Inn.

**operations** the activities and processes used in making both tangible and intangible products

**inputs** the resources—such as labour, money, materials, and energy—that are converted into outputs

**outputs** the goods, services, and ideas that result from the conversion of inputs

## The Transformation Process

At the heart of operations management is the transformation process through which **inputs** (resources such as labour, money, materials, and energy) are converted into **outputs** (goods, services, and ideas). The transformation process combines inputs in predetermined ways using different equipment, administrative procedures, and technology to create a product (Figure 8.1). To ensure that this process generates quality products efficiently, operations managers control the process by taking measurements (feedback) at various points in the transformation process and comparing them to previously established standards. If there is any deviation between the actual and desired outputs, the manager may take some sort of corrective action. For example, if an airline has a standard of 90 percent of its flights departing on time but only 80 percent depart on time, a 10 percentage point negative deviation exists. All adjustments made to create a satisfying product are a part of the transformation process.

Transformation may take place through one or more processes. In a business that manufactures oak furniture, for example, inputs pass through several processes before being turned into the final outputs—furniture that has been designed to meet the desires of customers (Figure 8.2).

**Figure 8.1** | The Transformation Process of Operations Management

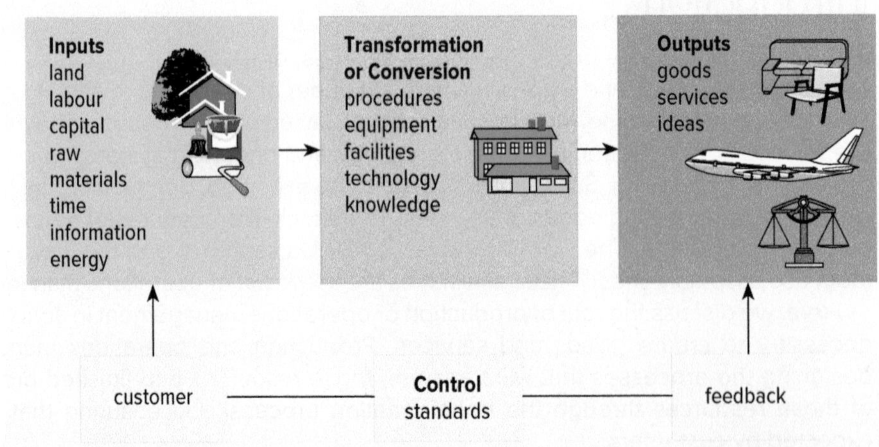


**operations management (OM)** the development and administration of the activities involved in transforming resources into goods and services

**manufacturing** the activities and processes used in making tangible products; also called *production*

**production** the activities and processes used in making tangible products; also called *manufacturing*

**Figure 8.2** | Inputs, Outputs, and Transformation Processes in the Manufacture of Oak Furniture

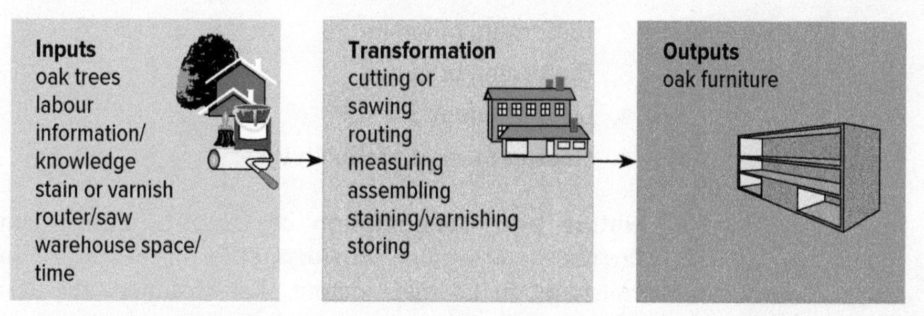


The furniture maker must first strip the oak trees of their bark and saw them into appropriate sizes—one step in the transformation process. Next, the firm dries the strips of oak lumber, a second form of transformation. Third, the dried wood is routed into its appropriate shape and made smooth. Fourth, workers assemble and treat the wood pieces, then stain or varnish the piece of assembled furniture. Finally, the completed piece of furniture is stored until it can be shipped to customers at the appropriate time. Of course, many businesses choose to eliminate some of these stages by purchasing already processed materials—lumber, for example—or outsourcing some tasks to third-party firms with greater expertise.

# Operations Management in Service Businesses

**LO 8-2** Explain how operations management differs in manufacturing and service firms.

Different types of transformation processes take place in organizations that provide services, such as airlines, universities or colleges, and most non-profit organizations. An airline transforms inputs such as employees, time, money, and equipment through processes such as booking flights, flying airplanes, maintaining equipment, and training crews. The output of these processes is flying passengers and/or packages to their destinations.

In a non-profit organization like Habitat for Humanity, inputs such as money, materials, information, and volunteer time and labour are used to transform raw materials into homes for needy families. In this setting, transformation processes include fundraising and promoting the cause in order to gain new volunteers and donations of supplies, as well as pouring concrete, raising walls, and setting roofs. Some companies such as Home Depot feel so strongly about a charitable cause that they donate materials and encourage their employees to volunteer for groups such as Habitat for Humanity. Transformation processes occur in all organizations, regardless of their products or their objectives. For most organizations, the ultimate objective is for the produced outputs to be worth more than the combined costs of the inputs.

Unlike tangible goods, services are effectively actions or performances that must be directed toward the consumers who use them. Thus, there is a significant customer-contact component to most services. Examples of high-contact services include health care, real estate, tax preparation, and food service. The amount of training for service or customer-contact personnel can vary significantly depending on the business, industry, or culture of the company. Low-contact services, such as Amazon, often have a strong high-tech component. Table 8.1 shows common characteristics of services.

Regardless of the level of customer contact, service businesses strive to provide a standardized process, and technology offers an interface that creates an automatic and structured response. The ideal service provider will be high-tech and high-touch. Amazon, for instance, has one of the highest customer service ratings. It provides a site that is easily navigable, and it has fast shipping times to deliver high-quality customer service. Amazon, through the commitment of CEO Jeff Bezos, encourages customers to email him with any concerns. He routes the messages to the appropriate Amazon employee, asking for an explanation of why the problem occurred and how it can be prevented in the future.[2] Thus, service organizations must build their operations around good execution, which comes from hiring and training excellent employees, developing flexible systems, customizing services, and maintaining adjustable capacity to deal with fluctuating demand.[3]

Another challenge related to service operations is that the output is generally intangible and even perishable. Few services can be saved, stored, resold, or returned.[4] A seat on an airline or a table in a restaurant, for example,

**Table 8.1** | Characteristics of Services

| Service Characteristics | Examples |
|---|---|
| Intangibility | Going to a concert or sports event such as baseball, basketball, or football |
| Inseparability of production and consumption | Going to a chiropractor, air travel, veterinary services |
| Perishability | Seats at a speaker's presentation |
| Customization | Haircut, legal services, tax consultation |
| Customer contact | Restaurants, retailers such as The Bay |

©Digital Vision/Alamy

Although service organizations tend to vary depending on the service provider, businesses strive to standardize operations to ensure a high level of quality. The service staff at this hotel wear uniforms and are trained to behave a certain way when interacting with customers.

cannot be sold or used at a later date. Because of the perishability of services, it can be extremely difficult for service providers to accurately estimate the demand to match the right supply of a service. If an airline overestimates demand, for example, it will still have to fly each plane, even with empty seats. The flight costs the same regardless of whether it is 50 percent full or 100 percent full, but the former will result in much higher costs per passenger. If the airline underestimates demand, the result can be long lines of annoyed customers or even the necessity of bumping some customers off an overbooked flight.

Businesses that manufacture tangible goods and those that provide services or ideas are similar yet different. For example, both types of organizations must make design and make operating decisions. But most goods are manufactured prior to purchase, while most services are performed after purchase. Flight attendants at Air Canada, hotel service personnel at the Westin, and even the Montreal Canadiens hockey team engage in performances that are a part of the total product. Though manufacturers and service providers often perform similar activities, they also differ in several respects. We can classify these differences in five basic ways:

1. Nature and consumption of output
2. Uniformity of inputs
3. Uniformity of output
4. Labour required
5. Measurement of productivity

**Nature and Consumption of Output.** First, manufacturers and service providers differ in the nature and consumption of their output. For example, the term *manufacturer* implies a firm that makes tangible products. A service provider, on the other hand, produces more intangible outputs such as Canada Post's delivery of priority mail or a business stay in a Westin hotel. As mentioned earlier, the very nature of the service provider's product requires a higher degree of customer contact. Moreover, the actual performance of the service typically occurs at the point of consumption.

At the Westin, business travellers may be very pleased with the Heavenly Bed and Shower System, both proprietary and luxury amenities. Or customers may like getting points through their reward membership or upgrades based on their status with Starwood Preferred Guests. Automakers, on the other hand, can separate the production of a car from its actual use.

Manufacturing, then, can occur in an isolated environment, away from the customer. On the other hand, service providers, because of their need for customer contact, are often more limited than manufacturers in selecting work methods, assigning jobs, scheduling work, and exercising control over operations. At FedEx, the quality improvement process (QIP) includes sayings such as "Do it right the first time," and "Make the first time you do it the only time anyone has to do it." The quality of the service experience is often controlled by a service contact employee. However, some hospitals are studying the manufacturing processes and quality control mechanisms applied in the automotive industry in an effort to improve their service quality.

By analyzing work processes to find unnecessary steps to eliminate, and by using teams to identify and address problems as soon as they occur, these hospitals are slashing patient waiting times, decreasing inventories of wheelchairs, readying operating rooms sooner, and generally moving patients through their hospital visit more quickly, with fewer errors, and at a lower cost.[5]

"The actual performance of the service typically occurs at the point of consumption."

**Uniformity of Inputs.** A second way to classify differences between manufacturers and service providers has to do with the uniformity of inputs. Manufacturers

## RESPONDING TO BUSINESS CHALLENGES

### Improving the Supply Chain with a Blockchain

Although much of the technological hype revolves around cryptocurrency, perhaps a more important idea resides in the underlying technology: the blockchain. The blockchain could change many industries as we know them today. One of the most evident examples is the improvement throughout supply chains.

A blockchain is a secure database that records all transactions and is spread across multiple computers. Essentially, it is a ledger that, by its public nature, makes it difficult to tamper with. This makes it safer to make transfers (of any variety) without worry of security breaches. Bitcoin and other cryptocurrencies use the blockchain to make online transfers of currency; however, the blockchain is also used in global supply chains. Retailers such as Walmart use blockchain to improve logistics and transparency. Walmart uses blockchain for more than 1.1 million of its items, tracking their journey from suppliers to store shelves.

Companies are also using IBM's blockchain technology to improve their supply chains. For example, Maersk uses the technology to track shipping containers around the world, thus improving cargo tracking throughout its supply chain. IBM's blockchain more accurately displays all transactions in the ledger as it updates in real time and allows participants to see valuable information, including the location of the asset and who has it in their possession. Other companies employing IBM's technology are Kroger, Nestlé, and Tyson Foods.

Blockchain can be altered to fit different processes, participants, and types of networks. Growing rapidly, this technology could impact every future transaction from online voting to goods that we buy and how we buy them.*

#### DISCUSSION QUESTIONS

1. What are some ways that blockchain increases transparency in the supply chain?
2. How can blockchain be used as a tool to manage inventory?
3. What are some ways that you think different industries could use blockchain to improve the quality of their operations and products?

*Christopher Mims, "Why Blockchain Will Survive, Even if Bitcoin Doesn't," *Wall Street Journal*, March 12, 2018, https://www.wsj.com/articles/why-blockchain-willsurvive-even-if-bitcoin-doesnt-1520769600 (accessed April 5, 2018); Steve Banker, "The Growing Maturity of Blockchain for Supply Chain Management," February 22, 2018 https://www.forbes.com/sites/stevebanker/2018/02/22/ the-growing-maturity-of-blockchain-for-supply-chain-management/#3048ec9811da (accessed April 5, 2018); Jon-Amerin Vorabutra, "Why Blockchain Is a Game Changer for Supply Chain Transparency," Supply Chain 24/7, October 3, 2016, http://www.supplychain247.com/article/ why_blockchain_is_a_game_changer_for_the_supply_chain (accessed April 5, 2018); IBM, "Blockchain for Supply Chain," https://www.ibm.com/blockchain/supply-chain/ (accessed April 5, 2018); Deloitte, "Using Blockchain to Drive Supply Chain Transparency," https://www2.deloitte.com/us/en/pages/operations/articles/blockchain-supplychain-innovation.html (accessed April 5, 2018).

typically have more control over the amount of variability of the resources they use than do service providers. For example, each customer calling Service Canada is likely to require different services due to differing needs, whereas many of the tasks required to manufacture a Ford Focus are the same across each unit of output. Consequently, the products of service organizations tend to be more "customized" than those of their manufacturing counterparts. Consider, for example, a haircut versus a bottle of shampoo. The haircut is much more likely to incorporate your specific desires (customization) than is the bottle of shampoo.

**Uniformity of Output.** Manufacturers and service providers also differ in the uniformity of their output, the final product. Because of the human element inherent in providing services, each service tends to be performed differently. Not all grocery cashiers, for example, wait on customers in the same way. If a barber or stylist performs 15 haircuts

©ValeStock/Shutterstock

Subway's inputs are sandwich components such as bread, tomatoes, and lettuce, while its outputs are customized sandwiches.

in a day, it is unlikely that any two of them will be exactly the same. Consequently, human and technological elements associated with a service can result in a different day-to-day or even hour-to-hour performance of that service.

The service experience can even vary at McDonald's or Burger King, despite the fact that the two chains employ very similar procedures and processes. Moreover, no two customers are exactly alike in their perception of the service experience. Health care offers another excellent example of this challenge. Every diagnosis, treatment, and surgery varies because every individual is different. In manufacturing, the high degree of automation available allows manufacturers to generate uniform outputs and, thus, the operations are more effective and efficient. For example, we expect luxury bicycles—such as the Giant TCR Advanced, which sells for $9000, and the Litespeed T1sl Disc Titanium Road Bike, which sells for up to $14,000—to have extremely high standards for quality and performance.

**Labour Required.** A fourth point of difference is the amount of labour required to produce an output. Services are generally more labour-intensive (require more labour) because of the high level of customer contact, perishability of the output (must be consumed immediately), and high degree of variation of inputs and outputs (customization). For example, Adecco provides temporary support personnel. Each temporary worker's performance determines Adecco's product quality. A manufacturer, on the other hand, is likely to be more capital-intensive because of the machinery and technology used in the mass production of highly similar goods. For instance, it would take a considerable investment for Ford to make an electric car that has batteries with a longer life.

**Measurement of Productivity.** The final distinction between service providers and manufacturers involves the measurement of productivity for each output produced. For manufacturers, measuring productivity is fairly straightforward because of the tangibility of the output and its high degree of uniformity. For the service provider, variations in demand (e.g., higher demand for air travel in some seasons than in others), variations in service requirements from job to job, and the intangibility of the product make productivity measurement more difficult. Consider, for example, how much easier it is to measure the productivity of employees involved in the production of Intel computer processors as opposed to serving the needs of CIBC's clients.

It is convenient and simple to think of organizations as being either manufacturers or service providers as in the preceding discussion. In reality, however, most organizations are a combination of the two, with both tangible and intangible qualities embodied in what they produce. For example, Samsung provides customer services such as toll-free hotlines and warranty protection, while banks may sell cheques and other tangible products that complement their primarily intangible product offering. Thus, we consider *products* to include tangible physical goods as well as intangible service offerings. It is the level of tangibility of its principal product that tends to classify a company as either a manufacturer or a service provider. From an OM standpoint, this level of tangibility greatly influences the nature of the company's operational processes and procedures.

## Planning and Designing Operations Systems

**LO 8-3** Describe the elements involved in planning and designing an operations system.

Before a company can produce any product, it must first decide what it will produce and for what group of customers. It must then determine what processes it will use to make these products as well as the facilities it needs to produce them. These decisions comprise operations planning. Although planning was once the sole realm of the production and operations department, today's successful companies involve all departments within an organization, particularly marketing, and research and development, in these decisions.

### Planning the Product

Before making any product, a company first must determine what consumers want and then design a product to satisfy that want. Most companies use marketing research (discussed in Chapter 11) to determine the kinds of goods and services to provide and the features they must possess. Twitter and Facebook provide new opportunities for businesses to discover what consumers want, and then design the product accordingly. Less than 50 percent of companies use social media in the new product development process.[6] Marketing research can also help gauge the demand for a product and how much consumers are willing to pay for it. But, when a market's environment changes, firms have to be flexible. Marketing research is advancing from wearables that measure skin response to geo-located survey delivery. Artificial intelligence can be used to measure people's expressions as they watch events.[7]

Developing a product can be a lengthy, expensive process. For example, Uber and Volvo are partnering to bring a driverless car to consumers. The $300 million alliance brings Volvo's manufacturing and design expertise together with Uber's ride-sharing market and a staff that increasingly consists of former employees of universities' robotics departments.[8] Once a firm has developed an idea for a product that customers will buy, it must then plan how to produce the product.

Within a company, the engineering or research and development department is charged with turning a product idea into a workable design that can be produced economically.

In smaller companies, a single individual (perhaps the owner) may be solely responsible for this crucial activity. Regardless of who is responsible for product design, planning does not stop with a blueprint for a product or a description of a service; it must also work out efficient production of the product to ensure that enough is available to satisfy consumer demand. How does a lawn mower company transform steel, aluminum, and other materials into a mower design that satisfies consumer and environmental requirements? Operations managers must plan for the types and quantities of materials needed to produce the product, the skills and quantity of people needed to make the product, and the actual processes through which the inputs must pass in their transformation to outputs.

## Designing the Operations Processes

Before a firm can begin production, it must first determine the appropriate method of transforming resources into the desired product. Often, consumers' specific needs and desires dictate a process. A province's needs for its highway systems may be very structured and consistent, and engineering and manufacturing would be standardized. On the other hand, a bridge often must be customized so that it is appropriate for the site and expected load; furthermore, the bridge must be constructed on site rather than in a factory. Typically, products are designed to be manufactured by one of three processes: standardization, modular design, or customization.

**Standardization.** Most firms that manufacture products in large quantities for many customers have found that they can make them more quickly and at lower cost by standardizing designs. **Standardization** is making identical, interchangeable components or even complete products. With standardization, a customer may not get exactly what he or she wants, but the product generally costs less than

**standardization** the making of identical interchangeable components or products

## ENTREPRENEURSHIP IN ACTION

### Roads Less Travelled

**Lonely Planet**

**Founders:** Tony and Maureen Wheeler

**Founded:** 1972

**Success:** A sense of adventure led to Lonely Planet with offices in Melbourne, London, and Oakland; 500 staff members; and 300 authors.

Tony and Maureen met on a park bench in London, England, and married a year later. For their honeymoon, they decided to attempt what few people thought possible—crossing Europe and Asia overland, all the way to Australia. It took them several months and all the money they could earn, beg, or borrow, but they made it. The experience was too amazing to keep to themselves. Urged on by their friends, they stayed up nights at their kitchen table writing, typing, and stapling together their very first travel guide, *Across Asia on the Cheap*.

Within a week they had sold 1500 copies and Lonely Planet was born. They wrote their second book, *South-East Asia on a Shoestring,* in a backstreet hotel in Singapore, which led to books on Nepal, Australia, Africa, and India. The Wheelers decided to settle in Australia where Maureen went to La Trobe University in Melbourne and received a bachelor's degree in social work. Faced with a choice between her social work and travelling, she chose to make travel her career.

Travelling with children became a way of life for the Wheelers after the births of their children. This prompted Maureen to write a guidebook about it, *Travel with Children*, which is the result of years of experience on the road with the kids. As Lonely Planet became a globally loved brand, the Wheelers received several offers for the company, finally selling to BBC Worldwide, which in turn sold the company to NC2 Media in 2013.

The Wheelers are still actively involved with Lonely Planet. They are travelling more often than ever, and they are devoting their spare time to charitable projects. And the company is still driven by the philosophy in *Across Asia on the Cheap*: "All you've got to do is decide to go and the hardest part is over. So go!"*

**DISCUSSION QUESTIONS**

1. Is Lonely Planet a service organization or a manufacturing organization?
2. What are the inputs and outputs used in Lonely Planet's production of its guides?
3. Managing quality consistently is important to Lonely Planet's successful operations. What are some of the challenges of managing consistency of service in Lonely Planet's writing business that it may not have with its manufacturing business?

*Lonely Planet, www.lonelyplanet.com/about/ (accessed July 2, 2010); Tony Wheeler, "The Long Journey of Lonely Planet," *Financial Times*, https://www.ft.com/content/67706fe6-5da3-11e8-ad91-e01af256df68, (accessed December 24, 2018).

a custom-designed product. Television sets, ballpoint pens, and tortilla chips are standardized products; most are manufactured on an assembly line. Standardization speeds up production and quality control and reduces production costs. And, as in the example of the highways, standardization provides consistency so that customers who need certain products to function uniformly all the time will get a product that meets their expectations.

Standardization becomes more complex on a global scale because different countries have different standards for quality. To help solve this problem, the International Organization for Standardization (ISO) has developed a list of global standards that companies can adopt to assure stakeholders that they are complying with the highest quality, environmental, and managerial guidelines. ISO standards are discussed later in the chapter.

**Modular Design.** **Modular design** involves building an item in self-contained units, or modules, that can be combined or interchanged to create different products. Dell laptops, for example, are composed of a number of components—LCD screen, AC adapter, keyboard, motherboard, etc.—that can be installed in different configurations to meet customers' needs.[9] Because many modular components are produced as integrated units, the failure of any portion of a modular component usually means replacing the entire component. Modular design allows products to be repaired quickly, thus reducing the cost of labour, but the component itself is expensive, raising the cost of repair materials. Many automobile manufacturers use modular design in the production process. Manufactured homes are built on a modular design and often cost about one-fourth the cost of a conventionally built house.

**modular design** the creation of an item in self-contained units, or modules, that can be combined or interchanged to create different products

**Customization.** **Customization** is making products to meet a particular customer's needs or wants. Products produced in this way are generally unique. Such products include repair services, photocopy services, custom artwork, jewellery, and furniture, as well as large-scale products such as bridges, ships, and computer software. For instance, bicycles are popular products to customize. The company Villy Custom (named after the owner's dog)—supported on *Shark Tank*—has 10 "best seller" models of bicycles that can be customized for consumers. The company also has a customizable line of bikes for corporate use.[10]

**customization** making products to meet a particular customer's needs or wants

Mass customization relates to making products that meet the needs or wants of a large number of individual customers. The customer can select the model, size, colour, style, or design of the product. Dell can customize a computer with the exact configuration that fits a customer's needs. Services such as fitness programs and travel packages can also be custom designed for a large number of individual customers. For both goods and services, customers get to make choices and have options to determine the final product.

**DID YOU KNOW?**

Hershey's has the production capacity to make 390,000 Kit Kats per day.[11]

**Blockchain.** Blockchain information technology could alter processes throughout virtually every industry including supply chain, health care, and even online advertising. The blockchain is a secure, public database (or ledger) that records all transactions and is spread across multiple

©SeongJoon Cho/Bloomberg via Getty Images

Lancôme sells Le Teint Particulier, a custom foundation with 72,000 possibilities. After customers have their skin tone scanned and select their skin type and desired coverage, the foundation is made on the spot. Because of the complexities of offering a customized product, the foundation is only available at select Nordstrom stores in Canada.

©DR MANAGER/Shutterstock

Bitcoin is a decentralized digital currency that works based on the blockchain technology without a central bank or single administrator. Bitcoins are generated at mining farms like this one.

computers. The global blockchain is difficult to tamper with and growing rapidly. In fact, blockchain technology is projected to maintain a compound annual growth rate of over 48 percent between now and 2023.[12]

In the age of tech-savvy consumers and continuous innovation, the adoption of blockchain technology is occurring more quickly than ever. For example, Coda Coffee Co., located in Colorado, is allowing its customers to scan a QR code and get all of the information they could possibly want with regard to their coffee in what they call "the world's first blockchain-traced coffee." They are able to see the date and location of each transaction from collection at the farm through every process until they swipe their credit card at the register. Starbucks Corp. announced that it was launching a two-year pilot program to develop "traceability technology" for farms in Costa Rica, Colombia, and Rwanda. Blockchain technology continues to be tested by companies across all industries and could change the way we do almost everything.[13]

## Planning Capacity

Planning the operational processes for the organization involves two important areas: capacity planning and facilities planning. The term **capacity** basically refers to the maximum load that an organizational unit can carry or operate. The unit of measurement may be a worker or machine, a department, a branch, or even an entire plant. Maximum capacity can be stated in terms of the inputs or outputs provided. For example, an electric plant might state plant capacity in terms of the maximum number of kilowatt-hours that can be produced without causing a power outage, while a restaurant might state capacity in terms of the maximum number of customers who can be effectively—comfortably and courteously—served at any one particular time.

**capacity** the maximum load that an organizational unit can carry or operate

Efficiently planning an organization's capacity needs is an important process for the operations manager. Capacity levels that fall short can result in unmet demand and, consequently, lost customers. On the other hand, when there is more capacity available than needed, operating costs are driven up needlessly due to unused and often expensive resources. To avoid such situations, organizations must accurately forecast demand and then plan capacity based on these forecasts.

Another reason that efficient capacity planning is important has to do with long-term commitment of resources. Often, once a capacity decision—such as factory size—has been implemented, it is very difficult to change the decision without incurring substantial costs. Large companies have come to realize that although change can be expensive, not adjusting to future demand and stakeholder desires will be more expensive in the long run. Responding to consumers' concern for the environment, Toyota and its subsidiaries have acquired ISO 14001 certification for environmental management at many of their locations worldwide.[14] These systems help firms monitor their impact on the environment.

## Planning Facilities

Once a company knows what process it will use to create its products, it then can design and build an appropriate facility in which to make them. Many products are manufactured in factories, but others are produced in stores, at home, or where the product ultimately will be used. Companies must decide where to locate their operations facilities, what layout is best for producing their particular product, and even what technology to apply to the transformation process.

Many firms are developing both a traditional organization for customer contact and a virtual organization. RBC Financial Group maintains traditional branches and has developed complete telephone and Internet services for customers. Through its website, clients can obtain banking services and trade securities without leaving their homes or offices.

**Facility Location.** Where to locate a firm's facilities is a significant question because, once the decision has been made and implemented, the firm must live with it due to the high costs involved. When a company decides to relocate or open a facility at a new location, it must pay careful attention to factors such as proximity to market, availability of raw materials, availability of transportation, availability of power, climatic influences, availability of labour, community characteristics (quality of life), and taxes and inducements.

Inducements and tax reductions have become increasingly important criteria in recent years. Provinces and municipalities are willing to forgo some tax revenue in exchange for job growth as well as good publicity. However, it is still less expensive for many firms to use overseas factories. Apple has followed the lead of other

©China Photos/Getty Images

Apple stores are designed to make the most efficient use of space. The layout of the stores allows customers to test Apple's products before purchasing.

major companies by locating its manufacturing facilities in Asia to take advantage of lower labour and production costs. The facility-location decision is complex because it involves the evaluation of many factors, some of which cannot be measured with precision. Because of the long-term impact of the decision, however, it is one that cannot be taken lightly.

**Facility Layout.** Arranging the physical layout of a facility is a complex, highly technical task. Some industrial architects specialize in the design and layout of certain types of businesses. There are three basic layouts: fixed-position, process, and product.

A company using a **fixed-position layout** brings all resources required to create the product to a central location. The product—perhaps an office building, house, hydroelectric plant, or bridge—does not move. A company using a fixed-position layout may be called a **project organization** because it is typically involved in large, complex projects such as construction or exploration. Project organizations generally make a unique product, rely on highly skilled labour, produce very few units, and have high production costs per unit.

Firms that use a **process layout** organize the transformation process into departments that group related processes. A metal fabrication plant, for example, may have a cutting department, a drilling department, and a polishing department. A hospital may have an X-ray unit, an obstetrics unit, and so on. These types of organizations are sometimes called **intermittent organizations**, which deal with products of a lesser magnitude than do project organizations, and their products are not necessarily unique but possess a significant number of differences. Doctors, makers of custom-made cabinets, commercial printers, and advertising agencies are intermittent organizations because they tend to create products to customers' specifications and produce relatively few units of each product. Because of the low level of output, the cost per unit of product is generally high.

**fixed-position layout** a layout that brings all resources required to create the product to a central location

**project organization** a company using a fixed-position layout because it is typically involved in large, complex projects such as construction or exploration

**process layout** a layout that organizes the transformation process into departments that group related processes

**intermittent organizations** organizations that deal with products of a lesser magnitude than do project organizations; their products are not necessarily unique but possess a significant number of differences

**product layout** a layout requiring that production be broken down into relatively simple tasks assigned to workers, who are usually positioned along an assembly line

The **product layout** requires that production be broken down into relatively simple tasks assigned to workers, who are usually positioned along an assembly line. Workers remain in one location, and the product moves from one worker to another. Each person in turn performs their required tasks or activities. Companies that use assembly lines are usually known as **continuous manufacturing organizations**, so named because once they are set up, they run continuously, creating products with many similar characteristics. Examples of products produced on assembly lines are automobiles, television sets, vacuum cleaners, toothpaste, and meals from a cafeteria. Continuous manufacturing organizations using a product layout are characterized by the standardized product they produce, the large number of units produced, and the relatively low unit cost of production.

**continuous manufacturing organizations** companies that use continuously running assembly lines, creating products with many similar characteristics

**computer-assisted design (CAD)** the design of components, products, and processes on computers instead of on paper

**computer-assisted manufacturing (CAM)** manufacturing that employs specialized computer systems to actually guide and control the transformation processes

Many companies actually use a combination of layout designs. For example, an automobile manufacturer may rely on an assembly line (product layout) but may also use a process layout to manufacture parts.

**Technology.** Every industry has a basic underlying technology that dictates the nature of its transformation process. The steel industry continually tries to improve steelmaking techniques. The health care industry performs research into medical technologies and pharmaceuticals to improve the quality of health care service. Two developments that have strongly influenced the operations of many businesses are computers and robotics.

Computers have been used for decades and on a relatively large scale since IBM introduced its 650 series in the late 1950s. The operations function makes great use of computers in all phases of the transformation process. **Computer-assisted design (CAD)**, for example, enables engineers to design components, products, and processes on a computer instead of on paper. CAD software is used to develop a 3D image. Then the CAD file is sent to a 3D printer. The printer is able to use layers of liquid, powder, paper, or metal to construct a 3D model.[15]

**Computer-assisted manufacturing (CAM)** goes a step further, employing specialized computer systems to actually guide and control the transformation processes. Such systems can monitor the transformation process, gathering information about the equipment used to produce the products and about the product itself as it goes from one stage of the transformation process to the next. The computer provides information to an operator who may, if necessary, take corrective action. In some highly automated systems, the computer itself can take corrective action.

"Every industry has a basic underlying technology that dictates the nature of its transformation process."

Using **flexible manufacturing**, computers can direct machinery to adapt to different versions of similar operations. For example, with instructions from a computer, one machine can be programmed to carry out its function for several different versions of an engine without shutting down the production line for refitting.

**flexible manufacturing** the direction of machinery by computers to adapt to different versions of similar operations

The use of drones in business operations would vastly change the technology landscape. *Drones* are remotely controlled aerial vehicles and have long been used in military operations. Amazon is pursuing methods to use drones for package delivery. Amazon has secured a patent to allow it to drop packages delivered by its fleet of drones by parachute. Currently, however, the use of automated drones without direct supervision is illegal in Canada.[16]

It is surprising that drones have not played a larger role thus far; the adoption of drones in organizations could increase and greatly impact everything from shipping to logistics and delivery in the near future. For example, in one of the current common uses of this technology, drones send automatic signals for reorder when an order has been placed or when inventory for a product is low and thus greatly improves inventory management. Whether it is adapting drones to a specific company to increase efficiency and capability or expanding the available applications as a whole, it is evident that drones could potentially handle many activities associated with operations.[17]

Robots are also becoming increasingly useful in the transformation process. These "steel-collar" workers have become particularly important in industries such as nuclear power, hazardous-waste disposal, ocean research, and space construction and maintenance, in which human lives would otherwise be at risk. Robots are used in numerous applications by companies around the world. Many assembly operations—cars, television sets, telephones, stereo equipment, and numerous other products—depend on industrial robots. The economic impact of robots was quantified by two economists who found that for every robot per 1,000 employees, up to six employees lost their jobs and wages fell by three-fourths of a percent.[18]

Researchers continue to make more sophisticated robots, extending their use beyond manufacturing and space programs to various industries, including laboratory research, education, medicine, and household activities. There are many advantages in using robotics, such as more successful surgeries, re-shoring manufacturing activities, energy conservation, and safer work practices. The strongest market is China, with a 40 percent share of the market for industrial robots projected by the end of the decade.[19]

When all these technologies—CAD/CAM, flexible manufacturing, robotics, computer systems, and more—are integrated, the result is **computer-integrated manufacturing (CIM)**, a complete system that designs products, manages machines and materials, and controls the operations function. Companies adopt CIM to boost productivity and quality and reduce costs. Such technology, and computers in particular, will continue to make strong inroads into operations on two fronts—dealing with the technology involved in manufacturing, and dealing with the administrative functions and processes used by operations managers. The operations manager must be willing to work with computers and other forms of technology and to develop a high degree of computer literacy.

**computer-integrated manufacturing (CIM)** a complete system that designs products, manages machines and materials, and controls the operations function

## Sustainability and Manufacturing

Manufacturing and operations systems are moving quickly to establish environmental sustainability and minimize negative impact on the natural environment. Sustainability deals with conducting activities in such a way as to provide for the long-term well-being of the natural environment, including all biological entities. Sustainability issues are becoming increasingly important to stakeholders and consumers, as they pertain to the future health of the planet.

The Hershey Company is committed to working toward a long-term, sustainable cocoa supply, protecting the natural environment as a part of its Cocoa for Good sustainability initiative.[20] Some sustainability issues include pollution of the land, air, and water; climate change; waste management; deforestation; urban sprawl; protection of biodiversity; and genetically modified foods. Molson Coors Brewing Company was the first major brewer in Canada to convert its brewing by-products, such as spent yeast and waste beer, into fuel-grade ethanol. Molson's aluminum cans are made with a minimum 67 percent recycled content, while kegs are refilled more than 200 times over their 25-year lifespan.[21]

Molson Coors demonstrates that reducing waste, recycling, conserving, and using renewable energy not only protect the environment but also can gain the support of stakeholders. Green operations and manufacturing

©JSMimages/Alamy Stock Photo

The one million square foot Garden Office Tower in Vancouver is certified LEED Platinum. The building uses cutting-edge green technology, such as a geothermal heat exchange that traps heat from a hub of Telus circuits.

can improve a firm's reputation along with customer and employee loyalty, leading to improved profits.

Much of the movement to green manufacturing and operations is the belief that global warming and climate change must decline. The McKinsey Global Institute (MGI) says that just by investing in existing technologies, the world's energy use could be reduced by 50 percent by 2020. Just creating green buildings and more fuel-efficient cars could yield $900 billion in savings per year by 2020.[22] Companies such as Canadian National Railway Company are integrating hybrid and alternative fuel vehicles into their fleets, which are up to 20 percent more fuel efficient and produce 40 percent fewer nitrogen oxides. CN provides customers with web-based carbon emissions and carbon credit calculators to estimate the environmental impact of their rail shipments.[23]

Much of the movement to green manufacturing and operations is driven by the belief that global warming and climate change must decline. In Canada, roughly 12 percent of carbon dioxide emissions are accounted for by buildings; however, Leadership in Energy and Environmental Design (LEED)-certified buildings maintain a 34 percent lower emissions rate and consume 25 percent less energy, 11 percent less water, and produce 80 million tons less waste.[24]

Companies like General Motors and Honda are adapting to stakeholder demands for greater sustainability by producing smaller and more fuel-efficient cars. Tesla has taken sustainability further by making a purely electric vehicle that also ranks at the top in safety. The company also makes sure that its manufacturing facilities operate sustainably by installing solar panels and other renewable sources of energy. Green products produced through green operations and manufacturing are our future. Government initiatives provide space for businesses to innovate their green operations and manufacturing.

# Managing the Supply Chain

**LO 8-4** Specify some techniques managers may use to manage the logistics of transforming inputs into finished products.

A major function of operations is **supply chain management**, which refers to connecting and integrating all parties or members of the distribution system to satisfy customers.[25] *Supply chain* is a part of distribution that will be discussed in more detail in Chapter 12, where we cover marketing channels, which are the groups of organizations that make decisions about moving products from producers to consumers. We discuss supply chains here because it is a major component of operations within a business.

**supply chain management** connecting and integrating all parties or members of the distribution system in order to satisfy customers

It may help to think of the firms involved in a total distribution system as existing along a conceptual line, the combined impact of which results in an effective supply chain. Firms that are "upstream" in the supply chain (for example, suppliers) and "downstream" (for example, wholesalers and retailers) work together to serve customers and generate competitive advantage. Supply chain management requires marketing managers to work with other managers in operations, logistics, and procurement.

Procurement involves the processes to obtain resources to create value through sourcing, purchasing, and recycling materials and information. Procurement for many is synonymous with buying or purchasing, but this is only a small part of what goes into the procurement activities within a supply chain. Decisions about where the supplies (including services) come from are very important. They are not just about price but also relate to where they are sourced and the integrity of the supplier. Also, the impact of recycling on the environment after consumption is an important consideration. An important process is the creation of a digital platform to link everything from production to consumer, and involves sensors, mobile devices, cameras, and other systems that capture information for procurement. We discuss purchasing more in the next section.

Logistical concerns involve physical distribution and the selection of transportation modes. In transportation, digital networks that integrate the movement of products provide insights to import service and reduce cost. Inbound logistics, outbound logistics, and third-party logistics are all important pieces of these transportation nodes.

*Inbound logistics* involves the movement of the raw materials, packaging, information, and other goods and services from the suppliers to the producers. Similarly, *outbound logistics* follows the finished products and

©dpa picture alliance/Alamy Stock Photo

Amazon and drone technology could completely change the way logistics and the supply chain operate in the future.

information from the business customers and then to the final consumer. In order to pull this transportation process together, some companies use *third-party logistics*, which involves employing outside firms to move goods because they can transport them more efficiently.

With predictive analytics and artificial intelligence orders, transportation decisions can be made based on customers' defined requirements, costs, and service options.[26] Manufacturers, distributors, and retailers need to communicate with their supply-chain partners to provide real-time information. This provides the opportunity to advance capabilities and efficiencies in the supply chain. For these same reasons, and with so many variables, logistical disruptions can be massively harmful to the ability to adequately satisfy customer expectations and can even be fatal to the firm.

Logistics management is just as important in managing services, enabling, and communicating with partners. For example, health care providers must rely on manufacturers and distributors to perform many supply-chain activities for various unrelated items; food, medicine, and supplies involve deliveries from vendors with inventories that accommodate the ability to provide health care services.

Drone technology has its challenges but, as noted earlier, is nevertheless growing rapidly, with some estimating that drone services overall are worth more than $127 billion globally, $23 billion coming from transport. For example, Amazon is paving the way for new innovation with its ideas regarding consumer goods delivery. With skepticism and public safety concerns from consumers, Amazon is working more with lower-value, less fragile items to begin with before straying from traditional delivery methods for other goods.[27]

Operations are often the most public and visible aspect of the supply chain. Consumers are increasingly concerned with an important question: How are our products being made? Fair trade, organic food products, working conditions, child labour, concerns with sending jobs overseas, and regulatory mandates create major factors in making decisions about operations. Technology in operations is driving a more digital enterprise system. Robotics, predictive analytics, the Internet of Things (IoT), driverless cars, drones, automation in identification of inventory, and network inventory optimization tools are changing the landscape of operations. By making profitable and responsible use of the materials and products sourced to them, and utilizing the information and capabilities afforded them through logistics, operational personnel can create extensive financial and brand value.

In the next section, we look at elements of supply chain, including purchasing, managing inventory, outsourcing, and scheduling, which are vital tasks in the transformation of raw materials into finished goods. To illustrate logistics, consider a hypothetical small business—we'll call it Rushing Water Canoes Inc.—that manufactures aluminum canoes, which it sells primarily to sporting goods stores and river-rafting expeditions. Our company also makes paddles and helmets, but the focus of the following discussion is the manufacture of the company's quality canoes as they proceed through the logistics process.

## Procurement

**Purchasing**, also known as procurement, is the buying of all the materials needed by the organization. The purchasing department aims to obtain items of the desired quality in the right quantities at the lowest possible cost. Rushing Water Canoes, for example, must procure not only aluminum and other raw materials, and various canoe parts and components, but also machines and equipment, manufacturing supplies (oil, electricity, and so on), and office supplies to make its canoes.

**purchasing** the buying of all the materials needed by the organization; also called procurement

People in the purchasing department locate and evaluate suppliers of these items. They must constantly be on the lookout for new materials or parts that will do a better job or cost less than those currently being used. The purchasing function can be quite complex and is one area made much easier and more efficient by technological advances. Advanced artificial intelligence can uncover the highest value opportunities and empower organizations to unlock savings and increase profit.[28]

Not all companies purchase all the materials needed to create their products. Often, they can make some components more economically and efficiently than can an outside supplier. Coors, for example, manufactures its own cans at a subsidiary plant. On the other hand, firms sometimes find that it is uneconomical to make or purchase an item, and instead arrange to lease it from another organization. Some airlines, for example, lease airplanes rather than buy them. Whether to purchase, make, or lease a needed item generally depends on cost, as well as on product availability and supplier reliability.

"A major function of operations is supply chain management, which refers to connecting and integrating all parties or members of the distribution system in order to satisfy customers."

## Managing Inventory

Once the items needed to create a product have been procured, some provision has to be made for storing them until they are needed. Every raw material, component, completed or partially completed product, and piece of equipment a firm uses—its **inventory**—must be accounted for or controlled.

There are three basic types of inventory. *Finished-goods inventory* includes those products that are ready for sale, such as a fully assembled automobile ready to ship to a dealer. *Work-in-process inventory* consists of those products that are partly completed or are in some stage of the transformation process. At McDonald's, a cooking hamburger represents work-in-process inventory because it must go through several more stages before it can be sold to a customer. *Raw materials inventory* includes all the materials that have been purchased to be used as inputs for making other products. Nuts and bolts are raw materials for an automobile manufacturer, while hamburger patties, vegetables, and buns are raw materials for the fast-food restaurant.

**inventory** all raw materials, components, completed or partially completed products, and pieces of equipment a firm uses

**inventory control** the process of determining how many supplies and goods are needed and keeping track of quantities on hand, where each item is, and who is responsible for it

Our fictional Rushing Water Canoes has an inventory of materials for making canoes, paddles, and helmets, as well as its inventory of finished products for sale to consumers. **Inventory control** is the process of determining how many supplies and goods are needed and keeping track of quantities on hand, where each item is, and who is responsible for it.

Operations management must be closely coordinated with inventory control. The production of televisions, for example, cannot be planned without some knowledge of the availability of all the necessary materials. Also, each item held in inventory—any type of inventory—carries with it a cost. For example, storing fully assembled televisions in a warehouse to sell to a dealer at a future date requires not only the use of space, but also the purchase of insurance to cover any losses that might occur due to fire or other unforeseen events.

Inventory managers spend a great deal of time trying to determine the proper inventory level for each item. The answer to the question of how many units to hold in inventory depends on variables such as the usage rate of the item, the cost of maintaining the item in inventory, the cost of paperwork and other procedures associated with ordering or making the item, and the cost of the item itself.

For example, radio frequency identification (RFID) is a wireless system composed of tags and readers that use radio waves to communicate information (tags communicate to readers) through every phase of handling inventory. RFID has a broad range of applications, particularly throughout the supply chain, and has immensely improved shipment tracking and reduced cycle times. This technology can be used in everything from inventory control to helping to prevent the distribution of counterfeit drugs and medical devices.[29] Several approaches may be used to determine how many units of a given item should be procured at one time and when that procurement should take place.

**The Economic Order Quantity Model.** To control the number of items maintained in inventory, managers need to determine how much of any given item they should order. One popular approach is the **economic order quantity (EOQ) model**, which identifies the optimum number of items to order to minimize the costs of managing (ordering, storing, and using) them.

**economic order quantity (EOQ) model** a model that identifies the optimum number of items to order to minimize the costs of managing (ordering, storing, and using) them

©Katie N. Gardner for the Washington Post via Getty Images

At Walmart, managing inventory involves finding the right balance between excess inventory and not enough inventory. Walmart uses just-in-time inventory management to minimize inventory costs and become more efficient.

**Just-in-Time Inventory Management.** An increasingly popular technique is **just-in-time (JIT) inventory management**, which eliminates waste by using smaller quantities of materials that arrive "just in time" for use in the transformation process and therefore require less storage space and other inventory management expense. JIT minimizes inventory by providing an almost continuous flow of items from suppliers to the production facility. While first used by Toyota, many companies now have adopted JIT to reduce costs and boost efficiency.

**just-in-time (JIT) inventory management** a technique using smaller quantities of materials that arrive "just in time" for use in the transformation process and therefore require less storage space and other inventory management expense

Let's say that Rushing Water Canoes uses 20 units of aluminum from a supplier per day. Traditionally, its inventory manager might order enough for one month at a time: 440 units per order (20 units per day times 22 workdays per month). The expense of such a large inventory could be considerable because of the cost of insurance coverage, record-keeping, rented storage space, and so on. The just-in-time approach would reduce these costs because aluminum would be purchased in smaller quantities, perhaps in lot sizes of 20, which the supplier would deliver once a day. Of course, for such an approach to be effective, the supplier must be extremely reliable and relatively close to the production facility.

On the other hand, there are some downsides to just-in-time inventory management that marketers must take into account. When an earthquake and tsunami hit Japan, resulting in a nuclear reactor crisis, several Japanese companies halted their operations. Some multinationals relied so much upon their Japanese suppliers that their supply chains were also affected. In the case of natural

## GOING GREEN

### Meet Your Meat: This Company Is Disrupting the Global Meat Market

De Vegetarische Slager (The Vegetarian Butcher) is a Dutch vegetarian food producer. At the end of the twentieth century, founder Jaap Korteweg wanted to become a vegetarian. However, he missed meat's taste and texture. After spending years searching and developing meat-like vegetarian products, Jaap founded The Vegetarian Butcher to market his products. His success in managing the firm's operations involved transforming raw materials into plant-based food that taste like meat.

Since its launch, The Vegetarian Butcher has expanded to 3500 stores in 15 countries. To achieve this, The Vegetarian Butcher has focused extensively on product quality. From day one, the development team was committed to producing plant-based products resembling meats without compromising taste or texture. With the right focus on quality, The Vegetarian Butcher convinced not only vegetarian customers to purchase its products, but also many meat eaters.

The meaty quality of its products allows The Vegetarian Butcher to take advantage of a market niche that targets both vegetarians and meat lovers. However, it also places greater pressure on maintaining quality control standards. To ensure the unique taste and texture of each type of "meat," The Vegetarian Butcher has to set up separate production for each product line. Thus, expanding product lines while ensuring the meat-like experience is an operational challenge.

Managing products and the supply chain are necessary for The Vegetarian Butcher to maintain its competitive advantage for meat-like products. The firm has been an innovative leader in establishing standards and managing quality. If The Vegetarian Butcher can overcome operational challenges, global consumers can expect to have tastier vegetarian "meats" in the future.*

#### DISCUSSION QUESTIONS

1. Why do you think it took years for founder Jaap Korteweg to begin marketing his meat-like vegetarian products?
2. Why is quality control so important for The Vegetarian Butcher?
3. What are some of the operational challenges that The Vegetarian Butcher faces?

*Caryn Ginsberg, "The Market for Vegetarian Foods," The Vegetarian Resource Group, http://www.vrg.org/ nutshell/market .htm (accessed December 31, 2017); Jaag Korteweg, Founder of De Vegetarische Slager, November 2017 (J. Wienen, Interviewer); Nielsen, "Green Generation: Millennials Say Sustainability Is a Shopping Priority," November 5, 2015, http://www.nielsen.com/us /en/insights/ news/2015/green-generation-millennials-say -sustainabilityis-a-shopping-priority.html (accessed December 31, 2017); The Vegetarian Butcher, "About Us," 2017, https://www .thevegetarianbutcher.com/about-us/since-1962 (accessed December 31, 2017); Niamh Michail, "Vegetarian Butcher Slams Dutch Food Authority for Double Standards over 'Misleading' Meat Name Ban," Food Navigator, October 5, 2017, https://www .foodnavigator.com/Article/2017/10/05/ Vegetarian-Butcher-slams -Dutch-food-authority-for-doublestandards-over-misleading-meat -name-ban (accessed December 31, 2017); Bryan Walsh, "The Triple Whopper Environmental Impact of Global Meat Production," *Time*, December 16, 2013, http://science.time.com/2013/12/16/ the -triple-whopper-environmental-impact-of-global-meatproduction/ (accessed December 31, 2017).

disasters, having only enough inventory to meet current needs could create delays in production and hurt the company's bottom line. For this reason, many economists suggest that businesses store components that are essential for production and diversify their supply chains. That way, if a natural disaster knocks out a major supplier, the company can continue to operate.[30]

**Material-Requirements Planning.** Another inventory management technique is **material-requirements planning (MRP)**, a planning system that schedules the precise quantity of materials needed to make the product. The basic components of MRP are a master production schedule, a bill of materials, and an inventory status file. At Rushing Water Canoes, for example, the inventory-control manager will look at the production schedule to determine how many canoes the company plans to make. He or she will then prepare a bill of materials—a list of all the materials needed to make that quantity of canoes. Next, the manager will determine the quantity of these items that RWC already holds in inventory (to avoid ordering excess materials) and then develop a schedule for ordering and accepting delivery of the right quantity of materials to satisfy the firm's needs. Because of the large number of parts and materials that go into a typical production process, MRP must be done on a computer. It can be, and often is, used in conjunction with just-in-time inventory management.

**material-requirements planning (MRP)** a planning system that schedules the precise quantity of materials needed to make the product

## Outsourcing

Increasingly, outsourcing has become a component of supply chain management in operations. As we mentioned in Chapter 3, *outsourcing* refers to the contracting of manufacturing or other tasks to independent companies, often overseas. Many companies elect to outsource some aspects of their operations to companies that can provide these products more efficiently, at a lower cost, and with greater customer satisfaction.

Globalization has put pressure on supply chain managers to improve speed and balance resources against competitive pressures. Companies outsourcing to China, in particular, face heavy regulation, high transportation costs, inadequate facilities, and unpredictable supply chain execution. Therefore, suppliers need to provide useful, timely, and accurate information about every aspect of the quality requirements, schedules, and solutions to dealing with problems. Companies that hire suppliers must also make certain that their suppliers are following company standards; failure to do so could lead to criticism of the parent company.

Many high-tech firms have outsourced the production of memory chips, computers, and telecom equipment to Asian companies.[31] The hourly labour costs in countries such as China, India, and Vietnam are far less than in Canada, Europe, or even Mexico. These developing countries have improved their manufacturing capabilities, infrastructure, and technical and business skills, making them more attractive regions for global sourcing. On the other hand, the cost of outsourcing halfway around the world must be considered in decisions.[32] While information technology is often outsourced today, transportation, human resources, services, and even marketing functions can also be outsourced. Our hypothetical Rushing Water Canoes might contract with a local janitorial service to clean its offices and with a local accountant to handle routine bookkeeping and tax-preparation functions.

Outsourcing, once used primarily as a cost-cutting tactic, has increasingly been linked with the development of competitive advantage through improved product quality, reducing the time it takes products to get to the customer, and overall supply-chain efficiencies. Table 8.2 describes five of the top 100 global outsourcing providers that assist mainly in information technology. Outsourcing allows companies to free up time and resources to focus on what they do best and to create better opportunities to focus on customer satisfaction. Many executives view outsourcing as an innovative way to boost productivity and remain competitive against low-wage offshore factories. However, outsourcing may create conflict with labour and negative public opinion when it results in Canadian workers being replaced by lower-cost workers in other countries.

"Many executives view outsourcing as an innovative way to boost productivity and remain competitive against low-wage offshore factories."

**Table 8.2** | The World's Top Five Outsourcing Providers

| Company | Services |
|---|---|
| ISS | Facility services |
| Accenture | Management consulting, technology, and outsourcing |
| Canon Business Process Services | Business process services, document management, and managed workforce services |
| CBRE | Commercial real estate services |
| Kelly Outsourcing and Consulting Group | Talent management solutions |

©AP Photo/Richard Vogel

Many athletic shoe manufacturers such as Nike outsource production to China and Vietnam to take advantage of lower labour costs.

## Routing and Scheduling

After all materials have been procured and their use determined, managers must then consider the **routing**, or sequence of operations through which the product must pass. For example, before employees at Rushing Water Canoes can form aluminum sheets into a canoe, the aluminum must be cut to size. Likewise, the canoe's flotation material must be installed before workers can secure the wooden seats. The sequence depends on the product specifications developed by the engineering department of the company.

**routing** the sequence of operations through which the product must pass

Once management knows the routing, the actual work can be scheduled. **Scheduling** assigns the tasks to be done to departments or even specific machines, workers, or teams. At Rushing Water, cutting aluminum for the company's canoes might be scheduled to be done by the cutting and finishing department on machines designed especially for that purpose.

**scheduling** the assignment of required tasks to departments or even specific machines, workers, or teams

Many approaches to scheduling have been developed, ranging from simple trial and error to highly sophisticated computer programs. One popular method is the *Program Evaluation and Review Technique* (PERT), which identifies all the major activities or events required to complete a project, arranges them in a sequence or path, determines the critical path, and estimates the time required for each event.

Producing a McDonald's Big Mac, for example, involves removing meat, cheese, sauce, and vegetables from the refrigerator; grilling the hamburger patties; assembling the ingredients; placing the completed Big Mac in its package; and serving it to the customer (Figure 8.3). The cheese, pickles, onions, and sauce cannot be put on before the hamburger patty is completely grilled and placed on the bun.

**Figure 8.3** | A Hypothetical PERT Diagram for a McDonald's Big Mac

Start
1 Remove buns, 2 beef patties, cheese, sauce, lettuce, onions, pickle (20)
2 Grill beef patties (120)
3 Apply sauce to bun (10)
4 Place cooked patties on bun (5)
5 Top with cheese and vegetables (15)
6 Place Big Mac in package (5)
7 Place package in heated bin (5)
8 Serve to customer (5)
End

Critical path
Activity
5 Event
(185) Time to complete event (seconds)

The path that requires the longest time from start to finish is called the *critical path* because it determines the minimum amount of time in which the process can be completed. If any of the activities on the critical path for production of the Big Mac fall behind schedule, the sandwich will not be completed on time, causing customers to wait longer than they usually would.

## Managing Quality

**LO 8-5** Assess the importance of quality in operations management.

Quality, like cost and efficiency, is a critical element of operations management, for defective products can quickly ruin a firm. Quality reflects the degree to which a good or service meets the demands and requirements of customers. For example, customers are increasingly dissatisfied with the quality of service provided by many airlines. Flight delays are a common subject of complaints from airline passengers; 20 percent of all flights arrive more than 15 minutes late. However, most consumers select airlines based on price, route, schedule, or membership or status with the airline's frequent-flyer program.[33]

The fuel economy of an automobile or its reliability (defined in terms of frequency of repairs) can be measured with some degree of precision. Although automakers rely on their own measures of vehicle quality, they also look to independent sources such as the J. D. Power & Associates annual initial quality survey for confirmation of their quality assessment as well as consumer perceptions of quality, as indicated in Table 8.3.

It is especially difficult to measure quality characteristics when the product is a service. A company has to decide exactly which quality characteristics it considers important and then define those characteristics in terms that can be measured. The inseparability of production and consumption and the level of customer contact influence the selection of characteristics of the service that are most important. Employees in high-contact services such as hairstyling, education, legal services, and even the barista at Starbucks are an important part of the product.

The Canada Awards for Excellence are given each year to companies that meet rigorous standards of quality. Recipients are role models of excellence in the areas of leadership, governance, strategy, planning, customer experience, employee engagement, innovation, and wellness. The American Malcolm Baldridge National Quality Award is given each year to companies that meet rigorous standards of quality. The Baldridge criteria are leadership, information and analysis, strategic planning, human resource development and management, process management, business results, and customer focus and satisfaction. The criteria have become a worldwide framework for driving business improvement.

**Table 8.3** | Top 10 Initial Automobile Quality Study

| |
|---|
| 1. Genesis |
| 2. Kia |
| 3. Hyundai |
| 4. Ford |
| 5. Lincoln |
| 6. Chevrolet |
| 7. Nissan |
| 8. Dodge |
| 9. Lexus |
| 10. Toyota |

Quality is so important that we need to examine it in the context of operations management. **Quality control** refers to the processes an organization uses to maintain its established quality standards. Quality has become a major concern in many organizations, particularly in light of intense foreign competition and increasingly demanding customers. To regain a competitive edge, a number of firms have adopted a total quality management approach. **Total quality management (TQM)** is a philosophy that uniform commitment to quality in all areas of the organization will promote a culture that meets customers' perceptions of quality. It involves coordinating efforts to improve customer satisfaction, increase employee participation and empowerment, form and strengthen supplier partnerships, and foster an organizational culture of continuous quality improvement. TQM requires continuous quality improvement and employee empowerment.

**quality control** the processes an organization uses to maintain its established quality standards

**total quality management (TQM)** a philosophy that uniform commitment to quality in all areas of an organization will promote a culture that meets customers' perceptions of quality

Continuous improvement of an organization's goods and services is built around the notion that quality is free; by contrast, *not* having high-quality goods and services can be very expensive, especially in terms of dissatisfied customers.[34] A primary tool of the continuous improvement process is *benchmarking,* the measuring and evaluating of the quality of the organization's goods, services, or processes as compared with the quality produced by the best-performing companies in the industry.[35] Benchmarking lets the organization know where it stands competitively in its industry, thus giving it a goal to aim for over time. Now that online digital media are becoming more important in businesses, benchmarking tools are also becoming more popular. These tools allow companies to monitor and compare the success of

## Consider the Following: Stella & Chewy's: The food dogs love

After being told that her dog Chewy was seriously ill, Marie Moody's only chance of saving him was to change his diet. She began purchasing organic meat and vegetables to create her own dog food. Almost immediately, Chewy's health improved. Moody began feeding her other dog, Stella, the same mixture and noticed positive results in her, as well. Stella & Chewy's dog food, consisting of fresh meats and organic produce, was born.

Moody began in her apartment kitchen and later expanded manufacturing. She developed partnerships with organic and antibiotic-free meat producers and hired animal scientists to help create technology to keep the food pathogen-free. Today, Stella & Chewy's uses hydrostatic high pressure to pasteurize without removing nutrients and taste. The company has a third party test each batch of food. Maintaining quality is essential to a raw food diet and for building a product that consumers trust. Stella & Chewy's has flourished, becoming the dog food of choice for many pet lovers.*

### DISCUSSION QUESTIONS

1. How would you describe operations management at Stella & Chewy's?
2. Why is it important to engage suppliers and partnerships to enhance quality?
3. Do you think Stella & Chewy's quality in its production process is a major cost or a benefit that enhances the profits of the company?

*K. Weisul, "The Dog Lover," *Inc.*, October 2010, pp. 68–70; Rebecca Konya, "Marie Moody: Women of Influence 2010," *Business Journal*, 2010, www2.bizjournals.com/milwaukee/events/2010/women_of_influence/marie_moody_women_of_influence_2010.html (accessed October 19, 2010); www.stellaandchewys.com (accessed October 19, 2010).

their websites as they track traffic to their sites versus competitors' sites.

Companies employing total quality management (TQM) programs know that quality control should be incorporated throughout the transformation process, from the initial plans to develop a specific product through the product and production facility design processes to the actual manufacture of the product. In other words, they view quality control as an element of the product itself, rather than as simply a function of the operations process. When a company makes the product correctly from the outset, it eliminates the need to rework defective products, expedites the transformation process itself, and allows employees to make better use of their time and materials. One method through which many companies have tried to improve quality is **statistical process control**, a system in which management collects and analyzes information about the production process to pinpoint quality problems in the production system.

**statistical process control** a system in which management collects and analyzes information about the production process to pinpoint quality problems in the production system

## International Organization for Standardization (ISO)

Regardless of whether a company has a TQM program for quality control, it must first determine what standard of quality it desires and then assess whether its products meet that standard. Product specifications and quality standards must be set so the company can create a product that will compete in the marketplace. Rushing Water Canoes, for example, may specify that each of its canoes has aluminum walls of a specified uniform thickness, that the front and back of each canoe be reinforced with a specified level of steel, and that each canoe contain a specified amount of flotation material for safety. Production facilities must be designed that can build products with the desired specifications.

Quality standards can be incorporated into service businesses as well. A hamburger chain, for example, may establish standards relating to how long it takes to cook an order and serve it to customers, how many fries are in each order, how thick the burgers are, or how many customer complaints might be acceptable. Once the desired quality characteristics, specifications, and standards have been stated in measurable terms, the next step is inspection.

The International Organization for Standardization (ISO) has created a series of quality management standards—**ISO 9000**—designed to ensure the customer's quality standards are met. The standards provide a framework for documenting how a certified business keeps records, trains employees, tests products, and fixes defects. To obtain ISO 9000 certification, an independent auditor must verify that a business's factory, laboratory, or office meets the quality

**ISO 9000** a series of quality assurance standards designed by the International Organization for Standardization (ISO) to ensure consistent product quality under many conditions

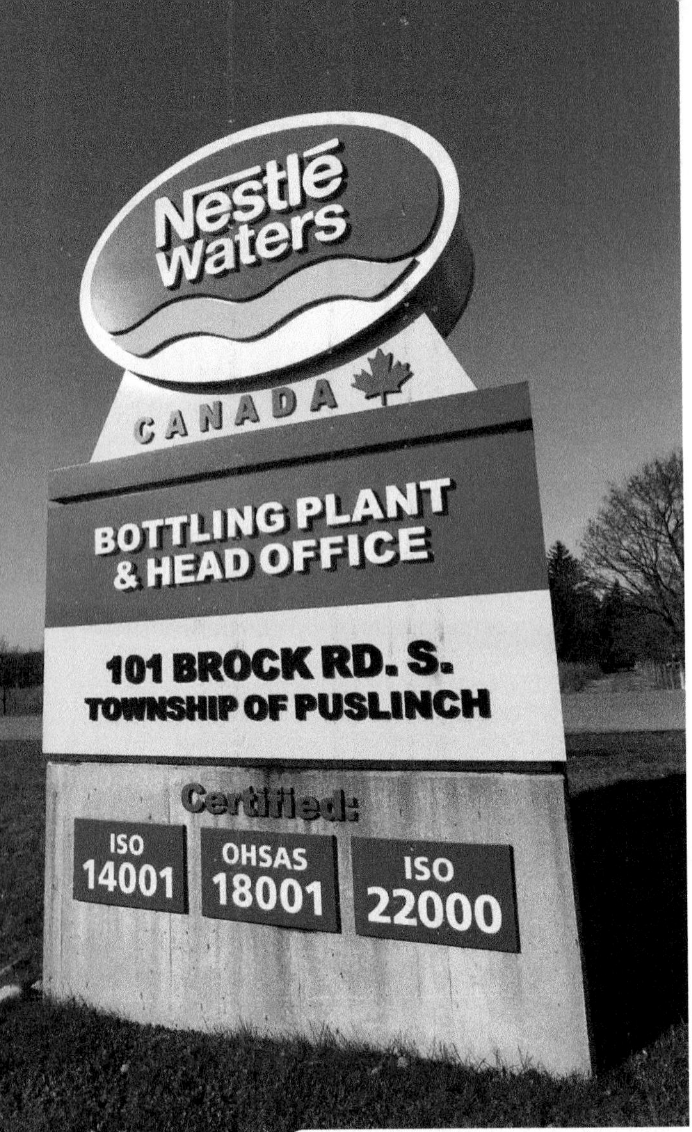

©The Canadian Press/Fred Lum/The Globe and Mail

Nestlé Waters Canada's plants in Hope, British Columbia, and Puslinch, Ontario, have achieved ISO 14001 certification.

standards spelled out by the International Organization for Standardization. The certification process can require significant investment, but for many companies, the process is essential to being able to compete. Thousands of companies have been certified, and many more are working to meet the standards. Certification has become a virtual necessity for doing business in Europe in some high-technology businesses. ISO 9002 certification was established for service providers.

**ISO 14000** is a comprehensive set of environmental standards that encourages a cleaner and safer world. ISO 14000 is a valuable standard because, currently, considerable variation exists between the regulations in different nations, and even regions within a nation. These variations make it difficult for organizations committed to sustainability to find acceptable global solutions to problems. The goal of the ISO14000 standards is to promote a more uniform approach to environmental management and to help companies attain and measure improvements in their environmental performance.

**ISO 14000** a comprehensive set of environmental management standards determined by the ISO that help companies attain and measure improvements in their environmental performance

**ISO 19600** provides guidance for establishing, developing, implementing, evaluating, maintaining, and improving an effective and responsive compliance management system within an organization. The guidelines are applicable to all types of organizations. The extent of the application of these guidelines depends on the size, structure, nature, and complexity of the organization. This guidance is based on the principles of good governance, transparency, and sustainability.[36]

**ISO 19600** a comprehensive set of guidelines for compliance management that address risks, legal requirements, and stakeholder needs.

## Inspection

Inspection reveals whether a product meets quality standards. Some product characteristics may be discerned by fairly simple inspection techniques—weighing the contents of cereal boxes or measuring the time it takes for a customer to receive a hamburger. As part of the ongoing quality assurance program at Hershey Foods, all wrapped Hershey Kisses are checked, and all imperfectly wrapped kisses are rejected. Other inspection techniques are more elaborate. Automobile manufacturers use automated machines to open and close car doors to test the durability of latches and hinges. The food-processing and pharmaceutical industries use various chemical tests to determine the quality of their output. Rushing Water Canoes might use a special device that can precisely measure the thickness of each canoe wall to ensure that it meets the company's specifications.

Organizations normally inspect purchased items, work-in-process, and finished items. The inspection of purchased items and finished items takes place after the fact; the inspection of work-in-process is preventive. In other words, the purpose of inspection of purchased items and finished items is to determine what the quality level is. For items that are being worked on—an automobile moving down the assembly line or a canoe being assembled—the purpose of the inspection is to find defects before the product is completed so that necessary corrections can be made.

## Sampling

An important question relating to inspection is how many items should be inspected. Should all canoes produced by Rushing Water be inspected or just some of them? Whether to inspect 100 percent of the output or only part of it is related to the cost of the inspection process, the destructiveness of the inspection process (some tests last until the product fails), and the potential cost of product flaws in terms of human lives and safety.

Some inspection procedures are quite expensive, use elaborate testing equipment, destroy products, and/or require a significant number of hours to complete. In such cases, it is usually desirable to test only a sample of the output. If the sample passes inspection, the inspector may assume that all the items in the lot from which the sample was drawn would also pass inspection. By using principles of statistical inference, management can employ sampling techniques that assure a relatively high probability of reaching the right conclusion—that is, rejecting a lot that does not meet standards and accepting a lot that does. Nevertheless, there will always be a risk of making an incorrect conclusion—accepting a population that *does not* meet standards (because the sample was satisfactory) or rejecting a population that *does* meet standards (because the sample contained too many defective items).

Sampling is likely to be used when inspection tests are destructive. Determining the life expectancy of lightbulbs by turning them on and recording how long they last would be foolish: there is no market for burned-out lightbulbs. Instead, a generalization based on the quality of a sample would be applied to the entire population of lightbulbs from which the sample was drawn. However, human life and safety often depend on the proper functioning of specific items, such as the navigational systems installed in commercial airliners. For such items, even though the inspection process is costly, the potential cost of flawed systems—in human lives and safety—is too great not to inspect 100 percent of the output.

## Integrating Operations and Supply Chain Management

Managing operations and supply chains can be complex and challenging due to the number of independent organizations that must perform their responsibilities in creating product quality. Managing supply chains requires constant vigilance and the ability to make quick tactical changes. For example, an Australian firm experienced severe supply chain problems when it sent 50 goldfish to media companies as part of a public relations campaign. The fish died in transit, requiring the company to issue an apology and donate money to animal protection organizations.[37]

Even Apple Inc., the most admired company in the world, has had supply chain problems. Reports of forced overtime, underage workers, and dangerous conditions at its Chinese supplier factories have resulted in negative publicity for the company.[38] Therefore, managing the various partners involved in supply chains and operations is important because many stakeholders hold the firm responsible for appropriate conduct related to product quality. This requires that the company exercise oversight over all suppliers involved in producing a product. Encouraging suppliers to report problems, issues, or concerns requires excellent communication systems to obtain feedback. Ideally, suppliers will report potential problems before they reach the next level of the supply chain, which reduces damage.

Despite the challenges of monitoring global operations and supply chains, there are steps businesses can take to manage these risks. All companies who work with global suppliers should adopt a Global Supplier Code of Conduct and ensure that it is effectively communicated. Additionally, companies should encourage compliance and procurement employees to work together to find ethical suppliers at reasonable costs. Those in procurement are concerned with the costs of obtaining materials for the company. As a result, supply chain and procurement managers must work together to make operational decisions to ensure the selection of the best suppliers from an ethical and cost-effective standpoint.

Businesses must also work to make certain that their supply chains are diverse. Having only a few suppliers in one area can disrupt operations should a disaster strike. Finally, companies must perform regular audits on its suppliers and take action against those found to be in violation of company standards.[39] Kellogg's offers a Global Supplier Code of Conduct on its website in 13 different languages, showing the importance of having access to the code throughout its supply chain.[40]

### TEAM EXERCISE

Form groups and assign the responsibility of finding companies that outsource their production to other countries. What are the key advantages of this outsourcing decision? Do you see any drawbacks or weaknesses in this approach? Why would a company not outsource when such a tactic can be undertaken to cut manufacturing costs? Report your findings to the class.

# LEARNING OBJECTIVES SUMMARY

**LO 8-1** Define *operations management* and differentiate between operations and manufacturing.

Operations management (OM) is the development and administration of the activities involved in transforming resources into goods and services. Operations managers oversee the transformation process and the planning and designing of operations systems, managing logistics, quality, and productivity. The terms *manufacturing* and *production* are used interchangeably to describe the activities and processes used in making tangible products, whereas *operations* is a broader term used to describe the process of making both tangible and intangible products.

**LO 8-2** Explain how operations management differs in manufacturing and service firms.

Manufacturers and service firms both transform inputs into outputs, but service providers differ from manufacturers in several ways: they have greater customer contact because the service typically occurs at the point of consumption; their inputs and outputs are more variable than manufacturers', largely because of the human element; service providers are generally more labour intensive; and their productivity measurement is more complex.

**LO 8-3** Describe the elements involved in planning and designing an operations system.

Operations planning relates to decisions about what product(s) to make, for whom, and what processes and facilities are needed to produce them. OM is often joined by marketing and research and development in these decisions. Common facility layouts include fixed-position layouts, process layouts, or product layouts. Where to locate operations facilities is a crucial decision that depends on proximity to the market, availability of raw materials, availability of transportation, availability of power, climatic influences, availability of labour, and community characteristics. Technology is also vital to operations, particularly computer-assisted design, computer-assisted manufacturing, flexible manufacturing, robotics, and computer-integrated manufacturing.

**LO 8-4** Specify some techniques managers may use to manage the logistics of transforming inputs into finished products.

Logistics, or supply chain management, includes all the activities involved in obtaining and managing raw materials and component parts, managing finished products, packaging them, and getting them to customers. The organization must first make or purchase (procure) all the materials it needs. Next, it must control its inventory by determining how many supplies and goods it needs and keeping track of every raw material, component, completed or partially completed product, and piece of equipment, how many of each are on hand, where they are, and who has responsibility for them. Common approaches to inventory control include the economic order quantity (EOQ) model, the just-in-time (JIT) inventory concept, and material-requirements planning (MRP). Logistics also includes routing and scheduling processes and activities to complete products.

**LO 8-5** Assess the importance of quality in operations management.

Quality is a critical element of OM because low-quality products can hurt people and harm the business. Quality control refers to the processes an organization uses to maintain its established quality standards. To control quality, a company must establish what standard of quality it desires and then determine whether its products meet that standard through inspection.

# KEY TERMS

capacity
computer-assisted design (CAD)
computer-assisted manufacturing (CAM)
computer-integrated manufacturing (CIM)
continuous manufacturing organizations
customization
economic order quantity (EOQ) model
fixed-position layout
flexible manufacturing
inputs
intermittent organizations
inventory
inventory control
ISO 9000
ISO 14000
ISO 19600
just-in-time (JIT) inventory management
manufacturing
material-requirements planning (MRP)
modular design
operations
operations management (OM)
outputs
process layout
product layout
production
project organization
purchasing
quality control
routing
scheduling
standardization
statistical process control
supply chain management
total quality management (TQM)

# So You Want a Job *in Operations Management*

While you might not have been familiar with terms such as *supply chain* or *logistics* or *total quality management* before taking this course, careers abound in the operations management field. You will find these careers in a wide variety of organizations—manufacturers, retailers, transportation companies, third-party logistics firms, government agencies, and service firms. Closely managing how a company's inputs and outputs flow from raw materials to the end consumer is vital to a firm's success. Successful companies also need to ensure that quality is measured and actively managed at each step.

Supply chain managers have a tremendous impact on the success of an organization. These managers are engaged in every facet of the business process, including planning, purchasing, production, transportation, storage and distribution, customer service, and more. Their performance helps organizations control expenses, boost sales, and maximize profits.

Warehouse managers are a vital part of manufacturing operations. A typical warehouse manager's duties include overseeing and recording deliveries and pickups, maintaining inventory records and the product tracking system, and adjusting inventory levels to reflect receipts and disbursements. Warehouse managers also have to consider customer service and employee issues.

Operations management is also required in service businesses. With more than 80 percent of the North American economy in services, jobs exist for services operations. Many service contact operations require standardized processes that often use technology to provide an interface that provides an automatic quality performance. Consider jobs in health care, the travel industry, fast food, and entertainment. Think of any job or task that is a part of the final product in these industries. Even an online retailer such as Amazon has a transformation process that includes information technology and human activities that facilitate a transaction. These services have a standardized process and can be evaluated based on their level of achieved service quality.

Total quality management is becoming a key attribute for companies to ensure that quality pervades all aspects of the organization. Quality-assurance managers monitor and advise on how a company's quality management system is performing and publish data and reports regarding company performance in both manufacturing and service industries.

# BUILD YOUR BUSINESS PLAN

## Managing Service and Manufacturing Operations

For your business you need to determine if you are providing raw materials that will be used in further production, or if you are a reseller of goods and services, known as a retailer. If you are the former, you need to determine what processes you go through in making your product.

The text provides ideas for breaking the process into inputs, transformation processes, and outputs. If you are a provider of a service or a link in the supply chain, you need to know exactly what your customer expectations are. Services are intangible so it is all the more important to better understand what exactly the customer is looking for in resolving a problem or filling a need.

# CASE | How Sweet It Is: Creating Supply Chain Efficiencies at the Cocoa Exchange

Looking for a way to create incremental, non-cannibalizing growth, Mars, Incorporated, the world's largest chocolate company, launched The Cocoa Exchange, a stand-alone subsidiary. While Mars focuses on mass producing products like Snickers and M&Ms that are available in all distribution channels, The Cocoa Exchange sells exclusive and premium chocolate products directly to consumers through a commission-based sales force under three product lines: Pod & Bean, Dove Signature, and Pure Dark. The Cocoa Exchange's mission is to create incremental, non-cannibalizing growth for Mars through niche products targeting individual consumers rather than the mass market. The company accomplishes this by creating supply-chain efficiencies, thanks to its parent company, and using the direct selling business model. Direct selling can be a more relationship-driven, customized form of selling and allows for even greater market segmentation.

The Cocoa Exchange is able to source its cocoa beans directly from farmers, just like Mars. Purchasing and sourcing can be challenging in the chocolate industry because cocoa only grows in a few places around the world. Complicating the matter is the fact that cocoa is produced by very small family farmers who often struggle to make ends meet. The majority of the cocoa sourced by The Cocoa Exchange is from developing countries like the Ivory Coast and Ghana in West Africa. The company develops relationships with the farmers to improve their yields and income as well as improve its own supply chain.

This close relationship between Mars, The Cocoa Exchange, and the farmers allows for improvements in sustainability practices. Demand continues to grow for chocolate, however, sourcing cocoa in a sustainable manner is limited, since the crop can only grow in certain areas near the equator. Because of these challenges, The Cocoa Exchange aims to improve conditions for farmers so that they can create a larger supply of cocoa. Mars is working with farmers, as well, to improve their productivity and economic viability through tripling farm yields in three to five years. By partnering with a humanitarian group called CARE, The Cocoa Exchange helps farmers save money and secure loans. By investing in the suppliers from which The Cocoa Exchange sources and purchases its chocolate, the company has greater influence over the sustainability of its supply chain.

Marketing and selling directly to the consumer, through an independent contractor sales force, is called *direct selling*. The Cocoa Exchange embraces the direct selling model and has created a commission-based labour force called "curators" to sell its products through in-house parties. Party attendees can sample a range of products from The Cocoa Exchange and purchase the products they like online. Curators receive a 25 to 40 percent commission on products sold from their individual online store and gain access to exclusive discounts up to 50 percent depending on performance.

Curators also have the opportunity to increase their earning power by building and training a team, receiving 3 to 5 percent commission on team sales. The Cocoa

Exchange subsidizes the starter kits, and curators host parties and provide free shipping on the items ordered. Additionally, as curators sales grow, they earn credits they can use to shop. The company also ships products directly to the consumer, so curators aren't burdened with inventory management and protection. Premium chocolates and other Cocoa Exchange products are carefully handled so that they arrive fresh and in "mint" condition. Direct selling encourages an entrepreneurial spirit in their chocolate sellers, allows The Cocoa Exchange to find new customers, and helps the company maintain a robust and efficient supply chain.

As a subsidiary of Mars, Incorporated, The Cocoa Exchange benefits from an established and extensive supply chain where it can secure all the materials needed to create its chocolate products. The Cocoa Exchange is uniquely poised to sell premium and exclusive products directly to customers because of its premium food products and careful sourcing. Its initiatives to improve the operations of the rural cocoa farmers has benefited the supply chain as well as The Cocoa Exchange's curators, creating a strong, mutually beneficial relationship.[41]

## DISCUSSION QUESTIONS

1. Describe how The Cocoa Exchange benefits from Mars, Incorporated's supply chain.
2. How does The Cocoa Exchange benefit from building relationships with cocoa farmers?
3. Why does the exclusive nature of these products increases engagement in the company's sales force?

CHAPTER 9

# Motivating the Workforce

©Tony Avelar/Bloomberg via Getty Images

## LEARNING OBJECTIVES

**After reading this chapter, you will be able to:**

- **LO 9-1** Define *human relations*, and determine why its study is important.
- **LO 9-2** Summarize early studies that laid the groundwork for understanding employee motivation.
- **LO 9-3** Compare and contrast the human-relations theories of Abraham Maslow and Frederick Herzberg.
- **LO 9-4** Investigate various theories of motivation, including theories X, Y, and Z; equity theory; expectancy theory; and goal-setting theory.
- **LO 9-5** Describe some of the strategies that managers use to motivate employees.

# ENTER THE WORLD OF BUSINESS

**Facebook Knows How to Motivate Employees**

Facebook has been ranked as the second-best company to work for by the job-hunting site Glassdoor. This success largely stems from Facebook's leadership, specifically CEO Mark Zuckerberg. Zuckerberg was awarded a 99.3 percent approval rating by nearly 19,000 Facebook employees.

At Facebook, employees are encouraged to take risks and stay innovative. Zuckerberg has been known to meet with entry-level employees to hear their ideas. Engineers are encouraged to consistently create new software builds and can test this software on 10,000 to 50,000 users. More importantly, engineers are not punished if their testing leads to mistakes. A former intern once crashed Facebook when testing a solution for a bug and was later hired by the company. Not only are engineers and employees given free rein on their work, they are also given the ability to choose the team with which they would like to work. A key success factor of Facebook is that the company focuses on an individual's strengths, rather than fixing his or her weaknesses. This encourages employees to find their "best fit" in the company.

Facebook has great employee benefits, including free lunches, laundry services, shuttle buses, flexible work hours, and the ability to work at home when needed. Research suggests that Facebook pulls employees from Apple 11 times more than Apple does from Facebook, and Facebook holds a 15:1 advantage over Google and 30:1 over Microsoft.

The mission of Facebook is to make the world more open and connected, which is demonstrated by its internal focus on an open and innovative work environment. Creativity and flexibility at Facebook lead to happier employees, allowing Facebook to earn its title as one of the best companies to work for in the United States.[1]

**DISCUSSION QUESTIONS**

1. According to Maslow's hierarchy of needs, what type of needs do you think Facebook is meeting among its employees?
2. What motivational factors used at Facebook contribute to employee satisfaction?
3. How does Facebook align its mission with its employees?

## Introduction

Because employees do the actual work of the business and influence whether the firm achieves its objectives, most top managers agree that employees are an organization's most valuable resource. To achieve organizational objectives, employees must have the motivation, ability (appropriate knowledge and skills), and tools (proper training and equipment) to perform their jobs. Chapter 10 covers topics related to managing human resources, such as those listed earlier. This chapter focuses on how to motivate employees.

We examine employees' needs and motivations, managers' views of workers, and several strategies for motivating employees. Managers who understand the needs of their employees can help them reach higher levels of productivity and thus contribute to the achievement of organizational goals.

# Nature of Human Relations

**LO 9-1** Define *human relations*, and determine why its study is important.

What motivates employees to perform on the job is the focus of **human relations**, the study of the behaviour of individuals and groups in organizational settings. In business, human relations involves motivating employees to achieve organizational objectives efficiently and effectively. The field of human relations has become increasingly important over the years as businesses strive to understand how to boost workplace morale, maximize employees' productivity and creativity, and motivate their ever more diverse employees to be more effective.

**human relations** the study of the behaviour of individuals and groups in organizational settings

**motivation** an inner drive that directs a person's behaviour toward goals

**Motivation** is an inner drive that directs a person's behaviour toward goals. A goal is the satisfaction of some need, and a need is the difference between a desired state and an actual state. Both needs and goals can be motivating. Motivation explains why people behave as they do; similarly, a lack of motivation explains, at times, why people avoid doing what they should do. Motivating employees to do the wrong things or for the wrong reasons can be problematic, however. On the other hand, motivating employees to achieve realistic company objectives can greatly enhance an organization's productivity.

A person who recognizes or feels a need is motivated to take action to satisfy the need and achieve a goal (Figure 9.1). Consider a person who takes a job in sales. If their performance is far below other salespeople's, they will likely recognize a need to increase sales. To satisfy that need and achieve success, the person may try to acquire new insights from successful salespeople or obtain additional training to improve sales skills. In addition, a sales manager might try different means to motivate the salesperson to work harder and improve their skills. Human relations is concerned with the needs of employees, their goals and how they try to achieve them, and the impact of those needs and goals on job performance.

**Figure 9.1** | The Motivation Process

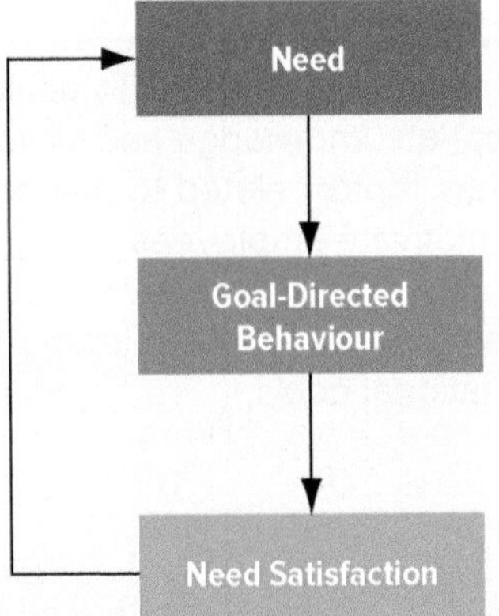


**DID YOU KNOW?**
Absenteeism costs the Canadian economy more than $16 billion a year.[2]

Effectively motivating employees helps keep them engaged in their work. Engagement involves emotional involvement and commitment. Being engaged results in carrying out the expectations and obligations of employment. Many employees are actively engaged in their jobs, while others are not. Some employees do the minimum amount of work required to get by, and some employees are completely disengaged. Motivating employees to stay engaged is a key responsibility of management.

One prominent aspect of human relations is **morale**—an employee's attitude toward their job, employer, and colleagues. High morale contributes to high levels of productivity, high returns to stakeholders, and employee loyalty. Conversely, low morale may cause high rates of absenteeism and turnover (when employees quit or are fired and must be replaced by new employees). Google recognizes the value of happy, committed employees and strives to engage in practices that will minimize turnover. Employees have the opportunity to have a massage every other week, onsite laundry service, free all-you-can-eat gourmet meals and snacks, and the "20 percent a week" rule, which allows engineers to work on whatever project they want for one day each week.[3]

Employees are motivated by their perceptions of extrinsic and intrinsic rewards. An **intrinsic reward** is the personal satisfaction and enjoyment that you feel from attaining a goal. For example, in this class you may feel personal enjoyment in learning how business works and aspire to have a career in business or to operate your own business one day. An **extrinsic reward** is a benefit and/or recognition that you receive from someone else. In this class, your grade is an extrinsic recognition of your efforts and success in the class. In business, praise and recognition, pay increases, and bonuses are extrinsic rewards. If you believe that your job provides an opportunity to contribute to society or the environment, then that aspect would represent an intrinsic reward. Both intrinsic and extrinsic

**morale** an employee's attitude toward their job, employer, and colleagues

**intrinsic reward** the personal satisfaction and enjoyment felt from attaining a goal

**extrinsic reward** a benefit and/or recognition received from someone else

**Table 9.1** | How to Retain Good Employees

1. Offer training and mentoring.
2. Create a positive organizational culture.
3. Build credibility through communication.
4. Blend compensation, benefits, and recognition.
5. Encourage referrals and don't overlook internal recruiting.
6. Give coaching and feedback.
7. Provide growth opportunities.
8. Create work/life balance and minimize stress.
9. Foster trust, respect, and confidence in senior leadership.
10. Make employees feel valued.

rewards contribute to motivation that stimulates employees to do their best in contributing to business goals.

Respect, involvement, appreciation, adequate compensation, promotions, a pleasant work environment, and a positive organizational culture are all morale boosters. Patagonia, for instance, has a positive organizational culture that encourages employees to act ethically and contribute their ideas. Ensuring that employee values are aligned with the company's values is extremely important for Patagonia. The company prides itself on charitable giving and doing what's right, and it hires individuals accordingly. Table 9.1 lists some ways to retain good employees.

Some of the businesses acknowledged as the best companies to work for offer a diverse array of benefits designed to improve the quality of employees' lives and increase their morale and satisfaction. For example, companies, like Suncor in Calgary have onsite daycare facilities for parents, while others, like the Bank of Canada in Ottawa, encourage employees to keep fit with free memberships to onsite fitness facilities.[4]

©IT Stock Free/Alamy Stock Photo

Many companies offer onsite daycare as a benefit for employees who have children. Company benefits such as these tend to increase employee satisfaction and motivation.

## Historical Perspectives on Employee Motivation

**LO 9-2** Summarize early studies that laid the groundwork for understanding employee motivation.

Throughout the twentieth century, researchers have conducted numerous studies to try to identify ways to motivate workers and increase productivity. From these studies have come theories that have been applied to workers with varying degrees of success. A brief discussion of two of these theories—the classical theory of motivation and the Hawthorne studies—provides a background for understanding the present state of human relations.

### Classical Theory of Motivation

The study of human relations can be traced to time and motion studies conducted at the turn of the century by Frederick W. Taylor and Frank and Lillian Gilbreth. Their studies analyzed how workers perform specific work tasks in an effort to improve the employees' productivity. These efforts led to the application of scientific principles to management.

According to the **classical theory of motivation**, money is the sole motivator for workers. Taylor suggested that workers who were paid more would produce more, an idea that would benefit both companies and workers. To improve productivity, Taylor thought that managers should break down each job into its component tasks (specialization), determine the best way to perform each task, and specify the output to be achieved by a worker performing the task. Taylor also believed that incentives would motivate employees to be more productive. Thus, he suggested that managers link workers' pay directly to their output. He developed the piece-rate system, under which employees were paid a certain amount for each unit they produced; those who exceeded their quota were paid a higher rate per unit for all the units they produced.

**classical theory of motivation** theory suggesting that money is the sole motivator for workers

We can still see Taylor's ideas in practice today in the use of mathematical models, statistics, and incentives. Moreover, companies are increasingly striving to relate pay to performance at both the hourly and managerial level. Incentive planners choose an individual incentive to motivate and reward their employees. In contrast, team

©Jason Smith/iStock

Even small symbols of recognition, such as an Employee of the Month parking space, can serve as strong motivators for employees.

incentives are used to generate partnership and collaboration to accomplish organizational goals. Boeing develops sales teams for most of its products, including commercial airplanes. The team dedicated to each product shares in the sales incentive program.

More and more corporations are tying pay to performance in order to motivate—even up to the CEO level. The topic of executive pay has become controversial in recent years, and many corporate boards of directors have taken steps to link executive compensation more closely to corporate performance. Despite these changes, many top executives still receive large compensation packages. Joseph Papa, CEO of Bausch Health Companies Inc., received a total compensation package of $83 million and was Canada's highest paid CEO in 2018.[5]

Like most managers of the early twentieth century, Taylor believed that satisfactory pay and job security would motivate employees to work hard. However, later studies showed that other factors are also important in motivating workers.

## The Hawthorne Studies

Elton Mayo and a team of researchers from Harvard University wanted to determine what physical conditions in the workplace—such as light and noise levels—would stimulate employees to be most productive. From 1924 to 1932 they studied a group of workers at the Hawthorne Works Plant of the Western Electric Company and measured their productivity under various physical conditions.

"Taylor believed that satisfactory pay and job security would motivate employees to work hard. However, later studies showed that other factors are also important in motivating workers."

What the researchers discovered was quite unexpected and very puzzling: productivity increased regardless of the changes in physical conditions. This phenomenon has been labelled the Hawthorne effect. When questioned about their behaviour, the employees expressed satisfaction because their co-workers in the experiments were friendly and, more importantly, because their supervisors had asked for their help and cooperation in the study. In other words, they were responding to the attention they received, not the changing physical work conditions. The researchers concluded that social and psychological factors could significantly affect productivity and morale.

The Hawthorne experiments marked the beginning of a concern for human relations in the workplace. They revealed that human factors do influence workers' behaviour and that managers who understand the needs, beliefs, and expectations of people have the greatest success in motivating their workers.

©Frederic Lewis/Getty Images

Working conditions are important. However, the Hawthorne studies, which were carried out at the electric company shown here beginning in the 1920s, found that the workers became more productive because of the attention they received–regardless of their working conditions.

## GOING GREEN

### Patagonia Attracts and Empowers Passionate Employees

What type of organization lets employees take off during the day to go surfing? The answer is Patagonia, an outdoor clothing and gear company. When founder Yvon Chouinard first developed the company, he was not interested in pursuing profits as the firm's main goal. Instead, he wanted to improve the planet. New employees are hired based in large part on their passion for the firm's goals.

Chouinard decided that the company would produce only products of the highest quality, manufactured in the most responsible way. The company's mission statement is to *build the best product, cause no unnecessary harm, use business to inspire and implement solutions to the environmental crisis.** Patagonia ensures employees understand and support these values, using a mix of in-person training, video training, and online instruction to help employees learn about company expectations.

Patagonia creates excitement for the company's mission with a fun, informal work environment for employees. It instituted a flextime policy that allows employees to go surfing during the day. Solar panels, Tibetan prayer flags, and sheds full of rescued or recuperating owls and hawks are all a part of corporate headquarters. Patagonia also developed an internship program that enables employees to leave the company for two months to volunteer at the environmental organization of their choice. At Patagonia, employees are viewed as important partners toward advancing environmental preservation.**

#### DISCUSSION QUESTIONS

1. How does Patagonia use training and a fun, informal work environment to encourage employees to support Patagonia's mission?
2. Why do you think Yvon Chouinard decided to make his company so focused on employee satisfaction?
3. Do you think that an informal work environment that provides employees freedom to take off during the day will be harmful or helpful in the long run? Why?

*Patagonia, "Our Reason for Being", About Us, https://www.patagoniahalifax.ca/service/about/, (accessed March 11, 2019).

**Patagonia, "Environmental Internship Program," http://www.patagonia.com/us/patagonia.go?assetid=80524 (accessed on December 10, 2017); Giselle Abramovich, "Inside Patagonia's Content Machine," Digiday, January 31, 2013, http://digiday.com/brands/inside-patagonias-contentmachine/ (accessed December 10, 2017); Leigh Buchanan, "How Patagonia's Roving CEO Stays in the Loop," *Inc.*, March 18, 2013, https://www.inc.com/leigh-buchanan/ patagonia-founder-yvon-chouinard-15five.html (accessed December 10, 2017); "Patagonia: A Sustainable Outlook on Business," Daniels Fund Ethics Initiative, http://danielsethics.mgt.unm.edu/pdf/patagonia.pdf (accessed December 10, 2017); "Patagonia: Case Study," Lynda.com, 2013, http://cdn.lynda.com/cms/asset/text/ patagonia-case-study-1931751689.pdf (accessed December 10, 2017); Patagonia, "Patagonia's Mission Statement," http://www.patagonia.com/company-info.html (accessed December 10, 2017).

# Theories of Employee Motivation

**LO 9-3** Compare and contrast the human-relations theories of Abraham Maslow and Frederick Herzberg.

The research of Taylor, Mayo, and many others has led to the development of a number of theories that attempt to describe what motivates employees to perform. In this section, we will discuss some of the most important of these theories. The successful implementation of ideas based on these theories will vary, of course, depending on the company, its management, and its employees. It should be noted, too, that what worked in the past may no longer work today. Good managers must have the ability to adapt their ideas to an ever-changing, diverse group of employees.

## Maslow's Hierarchy of Needs

Psychologist Abraham Maslow theorized that people have five basic needs: physiological, security, social, esteem, and self-actualization. **Maslow's hierarchy** arranges these needs into the order in which people strive to satisfy them (Figure 9.2).

**Physiological needs**, the most basic and first needs to be satisfied, are the essentials for living—water, food, shelter, and clothing. According to Maslow, humans devote all their efforts to satisfying physiological needs until they are met. Only when these needs are met can people focus their attention on satisfying the next level of needs—security.

**Maslow's hierarchy** a theory that arranges the five basic needs of people—physiological, security, social, esteem, and self-actualization—into the order in which people strive to satisfy them

**physiological needs** the most basic human needs to be satisfied— water, food, shelter, and clothing

**Figure 9.2** | Maslow's Hierarchy of Needs

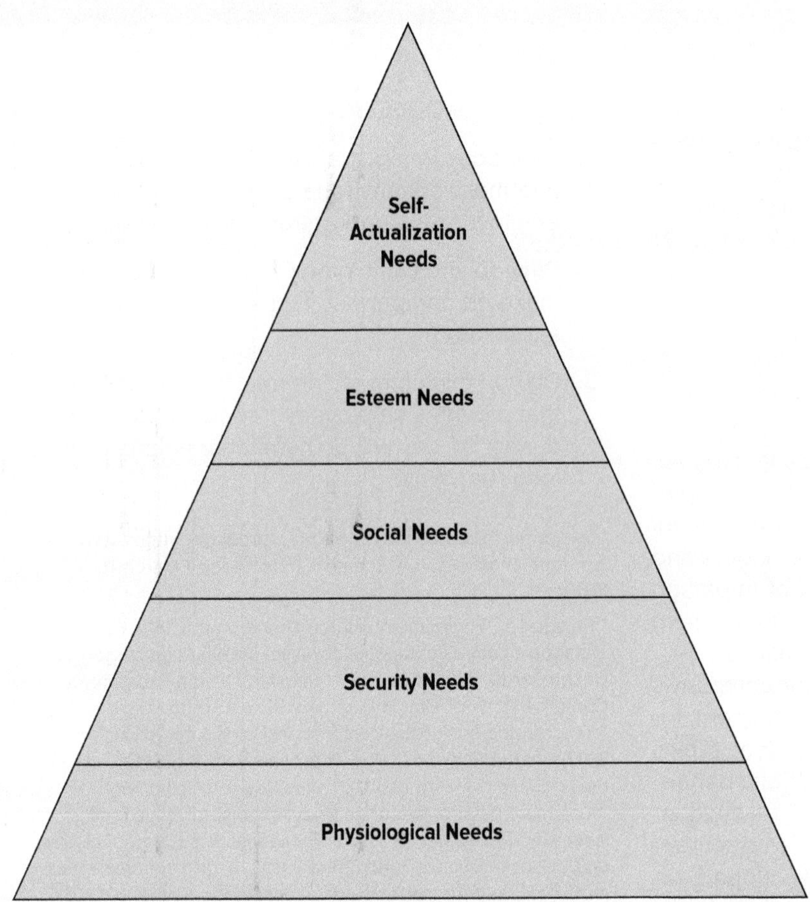


**Security needs** relate to protecting yourself from physical and economic harm. Actions that may be taken to achieve security include reporting a dangerous workplace condition to management, maintaining safety equipment, and purchasing insurance with income protection in the event you become unable to work. Once security needs have been satisfied, people may strive for social goals.

**Social needs** are the need for love, companionship, and friendship—the desire for acceptance by others. To fulfill social needs, a person may try many things: making friends with a co-worker, joining a group, volunteering at a hospital, or throwing a party. Once their social needs have been satisfied, people attempt to satisfy their need for esteem.

**security needs** need to protect oneself from physical and economic harm

**social needs** needs for love, companionship, and friendship—the desire for acceptance by others

**esteem needs** needs for respect—both self-respect and respect from others

**Esteem needs** relate to respect—both self-respect and respect from others. One aspect of esteem needs is competition—the need to feel that you can do something better than anyone else. Competition often motivates people to increase their productivity. Esteem needs are not as easily satisfied as the needs at lower levels in Maslow's hierarchy because they do not always provide tangible evidence of success. However, these needs can be realized through rewards and increased involvement in organizational activities. Until esteem needs are met, people focus their attention on achieving respect. When they feel they have achieved some measure of respect, self-actualization becomes the major goal of life.

**Self-actualization needs**, at the top of Maslow's hierarchy, mean being the best you can be. Self-actualization involves maximizing your potential. A self-actualized person feels that she or he is living life to its fullest in every way. For the Indigenous author Tanya Talaga, self-actualization might mean being praised as the best fiction writer in Canada; for the American actress Regina King, it might mean winning an Oscar.

Maslow's theory maintains that the more basic needs at the bottom of the hierarchy must be satisfied before higher-level goals can be pursued. Thus, people who are hungry and homeless are not concerned with obtaining respect from their colleagues. Only when physiological, security, and social needs have been more or less satisfied do people seek esteem. Maslow's theory also suggests that if a low-level need is suddenly reactivated, the individual will try to satisfy that need rather than higher-level needs. Many laid-off workers probably shift their focus from high-level esteem needs to the need for security.

**self-actualization needs** need to be the best one can be; at the top of Maslow's hierarchy

When unemployment reached 8.3 percent during the last recession and the job market appeared increasingly insecure, many employees, particularly those in manufacturing, banking, and finance, felt they had to shift their focus back to security needs. Managers should learn from Maslow's hierarchy that employees will be motivated to contribute to organizational goals only if they are able to first satisfy their physiological, security, and social needs through their work.

"Maslow's theory maintains that the more basic needs at the bottom of the hierarchy must be satisfied before higher-level goals can be pursued."

©Image Source Plus/Alamy Stock Photo

Some companies let people bring their pets to work as an added incentive to make the workplace feel more friendly.

Table 9.2 | Herzberg's Hygiene and Motivational Factors

| Hygiene Factors | Motivational Factors |
|---|---|
| Company policies | Achievement |
| Supervision | Recognition |
| Working conditions | Work itself |
| Relationships with peers, supervisors, and subordinates | Responsibility |
| Salary | Advancement |
| Security | Personal growth |

## Herzberg's Two-Factor Theory

In the 1950s, psychologist Frederick Herzberg proposed a theory of motivation that focuses on the job and on the environment where work is done. Herzberg studied various factors relating to the job and their relation to employee motivation and concluded that they can be divided into *hygiene* factors and *motivational* factors (Table 9.2).

**hygiene factors** aspects of Herzberg's theory of motivation that focus on the work setting and not the content of the work; these aspects include adequate wages, comfortable and safe working conditions, fair company policies, and job security

**Hygiene factors**, which relate to the work setting and not to the content of

### Consider the Following: Rewarding performers with time off

Companies that reward employees with extra time off include Travelzoo (a global travel deal website), Ontario Public Service (a provincial government entity), and Patagonia (an outdoor gear and clothing company). Travelzoo offers its employees of more than one year an annual $1500 to $3000 stipend to use with three extra vacation days and a travel deal listed on its site. In return, employees are merely required to submit pictures and brief write-ups to the company's subscriber newsletter.

The Ontario Public Service manages a unique volunteer opportunity for high-potential employees to be seconded for a 15-week period to work for United Way (with regular pay).* After one year of employment, Patagonia covers up to 60 days worth of an employee's salary to allow the employee to volunteer with a grassroots organization. Like those at Travelzoo, employees are asked to report back about their experiences.

Several organizations offer paid time off to part-time workers rather than creating full-time positions, which come with their own share of costs.

Studies have suggested that these types of incentives boost bottom-line profits and enhance employee retention. Points of Light Foundation claims that over 80 percent of companies feel that volunteering raises profits. This may be due to the fact that consumers are increasingly doing business with socially responsible companies. Employees also become committed to companies that give back to communities and appreciate their efforts.**

*Diane Jermyn, "Canada's Top 100 Employers make their workplaces exceptional," http://www.theglobeandmail.com/report-on-business/careers/top-employers/canadas-top-100-employers-make-their-workplaces-exceptional/article21427767/

**Charisse Jones, "Great Work. Now Hit the Road—on Us," *USA Today*, May 12, 2010, pp. 1B–2B; V. Dion Haynes," Washington-Baltimore Benefits Survey: Part-Timers Getting More Perks," *Washington Post*, June 8, 2010, www.washingtonpost.com/wp-dyn/content/article/2010/06/07/AR2010060704513.html (accessed June 10, 2010); Kim Covert, "Travel Perks One Way to Keep Employees Engaged," *Vancouver Sun*, April 27, 2010, www.vancouversun.com/life/Travel+perks+keep+employees+engaged/2956071/story.html (accessed June 10, 2010); www.pointsoflight.org (accessed May 2, 2010); "Best Places to Work 2009," Crain's, www.crainsnewyork.com/apps/pbcs.dll/gallery?Site=CN&Date=20091207&Category=GALLERIES&ArtNo=120209998&Ref=PH&Params=Itemnr=31 (accessed May 2, 2010); www.patagonia.com (accessed July 10, 2010).

the work, include adequate wages, comfortable and safe working conditions, fair company policies, and job security. These factors do not necessarily motivate employees to excel, but their absence may be a potential source of dissatisfaction and high turnover. Employee safety and comfort are clearly hygiene factors.

Many people feel that a good salary is one of the most important job factors, even more important than job security and the chance for employees to use their minds and abilities. Salary and security, two of the hygiene factors identified by Herzberg, make it possible for employees to satisfy the physiological and security needs identified by Maslow. However, the presence of hygiene factors is unlikely to motivate employees to work harder.

**Motivational factors**, which relate to the content of the work itself, include achievement, recognition, involvement, responsibility, and advancement. The absence of motivational factors may not result in dissatisfaction, but their presence is likely to motivate employees to excel.

**motivational factors** aspects of Herzberg's theory of motivation that relate to the content of the work itself, include achievement, recognition, involvement, responsibility, and advancement

Many companies are beginning to employ methods to give employees more responsibility and control and to involve them more in their work, which serves to motivate them to higher levels of productivity and quality. Hotels are adopting more employee-centric processes in order to better their offerings. Service businesses, such as hotels and airlines, recognize the benefit of happy employees—they are not only 12 percent more productive, but they work to generate happy customers. Many companies who value employee happiness consider the following benefits, where possible: implementing flexible hours and the ability to work from home (the average commute is over 25 minutes), making the office "pet friendly," maintaining a break room with recreational items (ping-pong, video games, etc.), and celebrating successes and special occasions.[6]

©Daniel Brenner/Bloomberg via Getty Images

Google's employee-friendly offices feature elements like basketball courts, pinball machines, and photo booths to foster creativity and make work more enjoyable.

Herzberg's motivational factors and Maslow's esteem and self-actualization needs are similar. Workers' low-level needs (physiological and security) have largely been satisfied by minimum-wage laws and occupational-safety standards set by various government agencies and are therefore not motivators. Consequently, to improve productivity, management should focus on satisfying workers' higher-level needs (motivational factors) by providing opportunities for achievement, involvement, and advancement, and by recognizing good performance.

## McGregor's Theory X and Theory Y

**LO 9-4** Investigate various theories of motivation, including Theories X, Y, and Z; equity theory; and expectancy theory.

In *The Human Side of Enterprise*, Douglas McGregor related Maslow's ideas about personal needs to management. McGregor contrasted two views of management—the traditional view, which he called Theory X, and a humanistic view, which he called Theory Y.

According to McGregor, managers adopting **Theory X** assume that workers generally dislike work and must be forced to do their jobs. They believe that the following statements are true of workers:

**Theory X** McGregor's traditional view of management in which it is assumed that workers generally dislike work and must be forced to do their jobs

1. The average person naturally dislikes work and will avoid it when possible.
2. Most workers must be coerced, controlled, directed, or threatened with punishment to get them to work toward the achievement of organizational objectives.
3. The average worker prefers to be directed and to avoid responsibility, has relatively little ambition, and wants security.[7]

Managers who subscribe to the Theory X view maintain tight control over workers, provide almost constant supervision, try to motivate through fear, and make decisions in an autocratic fashion, eliciting little or no input from their subordinates. The Theory X style of management focuses on physiological and security needs and virtually ignores the higher needs discussed by Maslow.

The Theory X view of management does not take into account people's needs for companionship, esteem, and personal growth, whereas Theory Y, the contrasting view of management, does. Managers subscribing to the

## ENTREPRENEURSHIP IN ACTION

### Nulogy Embraces Employee Democracy Model of Management

**Nulogy**

**Founders:** Jason Tham, Jason Yuen, and Sean Kirby

**Founded:** 2002, in Toronto, Ontario

**Success:** In 2018, Food Logistics awarded Nulogy the Food Logistics FL100 award and named the company a top technology provider for holding an influential role in the global food and beverage supply chain.

Nulogy, a Toronto-based software supplier, puts new hires through an intensive orientation. They get face time with the CEO, who explains the company's vision. They are taken to customer sites to see first-hand how the company's software is being used. This process not only shows new employees how much they matter but also creates transparency around the company's operations and demonstrates how their work contributes to the whole.

The company also empowers workers to solve problems for themselves. For example, teams vote on disputed issues, like whether a meeting should last five minutes or an hour. By giving employees a clear, formal process to achieve decisions among their peers, they feel a greater sense of ownership and accomplishment in their projects. Plus, a collaborative workforce is a happier workforce.*

#### DISCUSSION QUESTIONS

1. What are some ways that Nulogy motivates employees?
2. Why do you think putting new hires through an intensive orientation encourages employees to ensure Nulogy is successful?
3. How does Nulogy's collaborative culture allow the company to develop innovative new products or processes?

*John Lorinc, "Mass market, custom display: Toronto's Nulogy solves the puzzle," *Globe and Mail*, November 26, 2015, http://www.theglobeandmail.com/report-on-business/rob-magazine/nuology/article27322383/ (accessed January 12, 2016); Mai Nguyen, "Best Employers 2016: How small companies provide big perks," *Canadian Business*, November 5, 2015, http://www.canadianbusiness.com/lists-and-rankings/best-jobs/best-employers-2016-perks/ (accessed January 12, 2016).

**Theory Y** McGregor's humanistic view of management in which it is assumed that workers like to work and that under proper conditions employees will seek out responsibility in an attempt to satisfy their social, esteem, and self-actualization needs

**Theory Y** view assume that workers like to work and that under proper conditions employees will seek out responsibility in an attempt to satisfy their social, esteem, and self-actualization needs. McGregor describes the assumptions behind Theory Y in the following way:

1. The expenditure of physical and mental effort in work is as natural as play or rest.
2. People will exercise self-direction and self-control to achieve objectives to which they are committed.
3. People will commit to objectives when they realize that the achievement of those goals will bring them personal reward.
4. The average person will accept and seek responsibility.
5. Imagination, ingenuity, and creativity can help solve organizational problems, but most organizations do not make adequate use of these characteristics in their employees.
6. Organizations today do not make full use of workers' intellectual potential.[8]

Obviously, managers subscribing to the Theory Y philosophy have a management style very different from managers subscribing to the Theory X philosophy. Theory Y managers maintain less control and supervision, do not use fear as the primary motivator, and are more democratic in decision making, allowing subordinates to participate in the process.

Theory Y managers address the high-level needs in Maslow's hierarchy as well as physiological and security needs. For example, H&R Block is empowering its employees to have "extra help" in interpreting the tax code. Employees can use IBM's Watson to assist them in analyzing returns and maximizing customer refunds. This empowerment gives employees the ability to offer more personalized service and improve customer satisfaction in return.[9] Today, Theory Y enjoys widespread support and may have displaced Theory X.

"Theory Y managers maintain less control and supervision, do not use fear as the primary motivator, and are more democratic in decision making."

Table 9.3 | Comparisons of Theories X, Y, and Z

| | Theory X | Theory Y | Theory Z |
|---|---|---|---|
| **Countries that use this style** | China | United States | Japan |
| **Philosophy** | Tight control over workers | Assume workers will seek out responsibility and satisfy social needs | Employee participation in all aspects of company decision making |
| **Job description** | Considerable specialization | Less control and supervision; address higher levels of Maslow's hierarchy | Trust and intimacy with workers sharing responsibilities |
| **Control** | Tight control | Commitment to objectives with self-direction | Relaxed but required expectations |
| **Worker welfare** | Limited concern | Democratic | Commitment to worker's total lives |
| **Responsibility** | Managerial | Collaborative | Participative |

## Theory Z

**Theory Z** is a management philosophy that stresses employee participation in all aspects of company decision making. It was first described by William Ouchi in his book *Theory Z—How American Business Can Meet the Japanese Challenge.*

Theory Z incorporates many elements associated with the Japanese approach to management, such as trust and intimacy, but Japanese ideas have been adapted for use in North America. In a Theory Z organization, managers and workers share responsibilities, the management style is participative, and employment is long term and often lifelong. Japan has faced a significant period of slowing economic progress and competition from China and other Asian nations. This has led to experts questioning Theory Z, particularly at firms such as Sony and Toyota. Theory Z results in employees feeling organizational ownership. Research has found that such feelings of ownership may produce positive attitudinal and behavioural effects for employees.[10] In a Theory Y organization, managers focus on assumptions about the nature of the worker. The two theories can be seen as complementary. Table 9.3 compares Theory X, Theory Y, and Theory Z.

## Equity Theory

According to **equity theory**, how much people are willing to contribute to an organization depends on their assessment of the fairness, or equity, of the rewards they will receive in exchange. In a fair situation, a person receives rewards proportional to the contribution they make to the organization. However, in practice, equity is a subjective notion. Each worker regularly develops a personal input–output ratio by taking stock of their contributions (inputs) to the organization in time, effort, skills, and experience, and assessing the rewards (outputs) offered by the organization in pay, benefits, recognition, and promotions. The worker compares their ratio to the input–output ratio of some other person—a *comparison other*—who may be a co-worker, a friend working in another organization, or an "average" of several people working in the organization. If the two ratios are close, the individual will feel that they are being treated equitably.

**Theory Z** a management philosophy that stresses employee participation in all aspects of company decision making

**equity theory** an assumption that how much people are willing to contribute to an organization depends on their assessment of the fairness, or equity, of the rewards they will receive in exchange

Let's say you have a high-school education and earn $25,000 a year. When you compare your input–output ratio with that of a co-worker who has a college degree and makes $35,000 a year, you will probably feel that you are being paid fairly. However, if you perceive that your personal input–output ratio is lower than that of your college-educated co-worker, you may feel that you are being treated unfairly and be motivated to seek change. But if you learn that the co-worker who makes $35,000 has only a high-school diploma, you may feel cheated by your employer. To achieve equity, you could try to increase your outputs by asking for a raise or promotion. You could also try to have your co-worker's inputs increased or his or her outputs decreased. Failing to achieve equity, you may be motivated to look for a job at a different company.

Equity theory might explain why many consumers are upset about CEO compensation. Although the job of the CEO can be incredibly stressful, the fact that they take home millions in compensation, bonuses, and stock options has been questioned. The high unemployment rate coupled with the misconduct that occurred at some large corporations prior to the recession contributed largely to the Occupy Wall Street protests. To counter this perception of pay inequality, several corporations have now begun to tie CEO compensation to company performance. If the company performs poorly for the year, then firms will cut bonuses and other compensation.[11] While lower compensation rates might appease the general public, some companies are worried that lower pay might deter talented individuals from wanting to assume the position of CEO at their firms.

Because almost all the issues involved in equity theory are subjective, they can be problematic. Author David Callahan has argued that feelings of inequity may underlie some unethical or illegal behaviour in business. For example, due to employee theft and shoplifting, Walmart experiences billions in inventory losses every year. Some employees may take company resources to restore what they perceive to be equity (inadequate pay, working hours, or other deficient benefits). Theft of company resources is a major ethical issue, based on a survey by the Ethics Resource Center.[12] Callahan believes that employees who do not feel they are being treated equitably may be motivated to equalize the situation by lying, cheating, or otherwise "improving" their pay, perhaps by stealing.[13] Managers should try to avoid equity problems by ensuring that rewards are distributed on the basis of performance and that all employees clearly understand the basis for their pay and benefits.

## Expectancy Theory

Psychologist Victor Vroom described **expectancy theory**, which states that motivation depends not only on how much a person wants something, but also on the person's perception of how likely they are to get it. A person who wants something and has reason to be optimistic will be strongly motivated. For example, say you really want a promotion. And let's say that because you have taken some night classes to improve your skills, and moreover, have just made a large, significant sale, you feel confident that you are qualified and able to handle the new position. Therefore, you are motivated to try to get the promotion. In contrast, if you do not believe you are likely to get what you want, you may not be motivated to try to get it, even though you really want it.

**expectancy theory** the assumption that motivation depends not only on how much a person wants something but also on how likely they are to get it

©Monkey Business Images/Shutterstock

Managers should be transparent with employees about opportunities for advancement. According to expectancy theory, your motivation depends not only on how much you want something, but also on how likely you are to get it.

## Goal-Setting Theory

**Goal-setting theory** refers to the impact that setting goals has on performance. According to this philosophy, goals act as motivators to focus employee efforts on achieving certain performance outcomes. Setting goals can positively affect performance because goals help employees direct their efforts and attention toward the outcome, mobilize their efforts, develop consistent behaviour patterns, and create strategies to obtain desired outcomes.[14] When Cinnabon introduced two new hot chocolates, Ghirardelli and Cinnamon Roll, it had specific goals for sales. To support these sales goals and generate awareness of the new drinks, the company might have employees at the counter suggest these new options or offer other forms of promotional support.

**goal-setting theory** refers to the impact that setting goals has on performance.

In 1954, Peter Drucker introduced the term *management by objectives* (MBO) that has since become important to goal-setting theory. MBO refers to the need to develop goals that both managers and employees can understand and agree upon.[15] This requires managers to work with employees to set personal objectives that will be used to further organizational objectives. When managerial objectives are linked with personal objectives, employees often feel a greater sense of commitment toward achieving organizational goals.

# Strategies for Motivating Employees

**LO 9-5** Describe some of the strategies that managers use to motivate employees.

Based on the various theories that attempt to explain what motivates employees, businesses have developed several strategies for motivating their employees and boosting morale and productivity. Some of these techniques include behaviour modification and job design, as well as the already described employee involvement programs and work teams.

## Behaviour Modification

**Behaviour modification** involves changing behaviour and encouraging appropriate actions by relating the consequences of behaviour to the behaviour itself. Behaviour modification is the most widely discussed application of **reinforcement theory**, the theory that behaviour can be strengthened or weakened through the use

**behaviour modification** changing behaviour and encouraging appropriate actions by relating the consequences of behaviour to the behaviour itself

**reinforcement theory** the theory that behaviour can be strengthened or weakened through the use of rewards and punishments

of rewards and punishments. The concept of behaviour modification was developed by psychologist B. F. Skinner, who showed that there are two types of consequences that can modify behaviour: reward and punishment. Skinner found that behaviour that is rewarded will tend to be repeated, while behaviour that is punished will tend to be eliminated. For example, employees who know that they will receive a bonus, such as an expensive restaurant meal, for making a sale over $2000 may be more motivated to make sales. Workers who know they will be punished for being tardy are likely to make a greater effort to get to work on time.

However, the two strategies may not be equally effective. Punishing unacceptable behaviour may provide quick results but may lead to undesirable long-term side effects, such as employee dissatisfaction and increased turnover. In general, rewarding appropriate behaviour is a more effective way to modify behaviour.

## Job Design

Herzberg identified the job itself as a motivational factor. Managers have several strategies that they can use to design jobs to help improve employee motivation. These include job rotation, job enlargement, job enrichment, and flexible scheduling strategies.

**Job Rotation.** **Job rotation** allows employees to move from one job to another in an effort to relieve the boredom that is often associated with job specialization. Businesses often turn to specialization in hopes of increasing productivity, but there is a negative side effect to this type of job design: employees become bored and dissatisfied, and productivity declines. Job rotation reduces this boredom by allowing workers to undertake a greater variety of tasks and by giving them the opportunity to learn new skills. With job rotation, an employee spends a specified amount of time performing one job and then moves on to another, different job. The worker eventually returns to the initial job and begins the cycle again. World Vision Canada manages an internal secondment policy allowing employees to try a new role within the organization for up to six months while holding their original position.[16] Table 9.4 offers additional benefits of job rotation.

**job rotation** movement of employees from one job to another in an effort to relieve the boredom often associated with job specialization

**Table 9.4** | Benefits of Job Rotation

| |
|---|
| 1. Exposure to a diversity of viewpoints |
| 2. Motivating ongoing lifelong learning |
| 3. Preparing for promotion and leadership roles |
| 4. Building specific skills and abilities |
| 5. Supporting recruitment efforts |
| 6. Boosting overall productivity |
| 7. Retaining employees |

Job rotation is a good idea, but it has one major drawback. Because employees may eventually become bored with all the jobs in the cycle, job rotation does not totally eliminate the problem of boredom. Job rotation is extremely useful, however, in situations where a person is being trained for a position that requires an understanding of various units in an organization. Many executive training programs require trainees to spend time learning a variety of specialized jobs. Job rotation is also used to cross-train today's self-directed work teams.

**Job Enlargement.** **Job enlargement** adds more tasks to a job instead of treating each task as separate. Like job rotation, job enlargement was developed to overcome the boredom associated with specialization. The rationale behind this strategy is that jobs are more satisfying when the number of tasks performed by an individual increases. Employees sometimes enlarge, or craft, their jobs by noticing what needs to be done and then changing tasks and relationship boundaries to adjust. Individual orientation and motivation shape opportunities to craft new jobs and job relationships.[17] Job enlargement strategies have been more successful in increasing job satisfaction than have job rotation strategies.

**job enlargement** the addition of more tasks to a job instead of treating each task as separate

**job enrichment** the incorporation of motivational factors, such as opportunity for achievement, recognition, responsibility, and advancement, into a job

**Job Enrichment.** **Job enrichment** incorporates motivational factors, such as opportunity for achievement, recognition, responsibility, and advancement, into a job. It gives workers not only more tasks within the job but more control and authority over the job. Job enrichment programs enhance a worker's feeling of responsibility and provide opportunities for growth and advancement when the worker is able to take on the more challenging tasks. Statistics Canada allows employees who have been with the firm for four years a chance to request "career broadening," where they request an assignment in another department to build their skill set.[18] The potential benefits of job enrichment are great, but it requires careful planning and execution.

**Flexible Scheduling Strategies.** Many Canadians work a traditional 40-hour workweek consisting of five 8-hour days with fixed starting and ending times. Facing problems of poor morale and high absenteeism, as well as a diverse workforce with changing needs, many managers have turned to flexible scheduling strategies such as flextime, compressed workweeks, job sharing, part-time work, and telecommuting. A survey by CareerBuilder.com showed that 40 percent of working fathers were offered flexible work schedules versus 53 percent of working mothers.[19]

**Figure 9.3** | Flextime, Showing Core and Flexible Hours

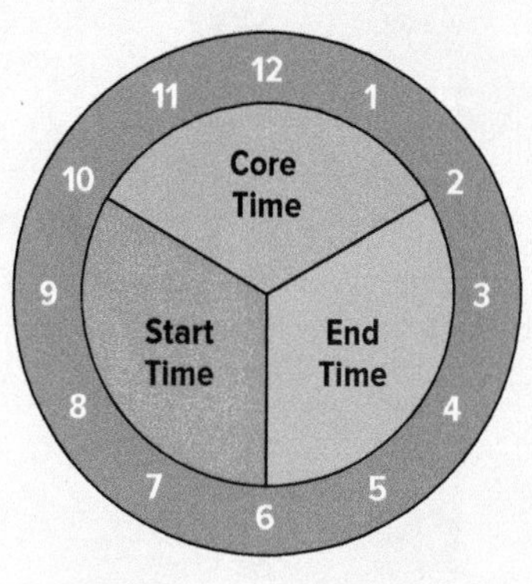


**Flextime** is a program that allows employees to choose their starting and ending times, as long as they are at work during a specified core period (Figure 9.3). It does not reduce the total number of hours that employees work; instead, it gives employees more flexibility in choosing which hours they work. A firm may specify that employees must be present from 10:00 a.m. to 3:00 p.m. One employee may choose to come in at 7:00 a.m. and leave at the end of the core time, perhaps to attend classes at a nearby college after work. Another employee who lives in the suburbs may come in at 9:00 a.m. after dropping off their children at a daycare centre and commuting to work by public transportation.

**flextime** a program that allows employees to choose their starting and ending times, provided that they are at work during a specified core period

**compressed workweek** a four-day (or shorter) period during which an employee works 40 hours

Flextime provides many benefits, including improved ability to recruit and retain workers who wish to balance work and home life. Customers can be better served by allowing more coverage of customers over longer hours, workstations and facilities can be better utilized by staggering employee use, and rush hour traffic may be reduced. In addition, flexible schedules have been associated with an increase in healthy behaviours on the part of employees. More flexible schedules are associated with higher job satisfaction, less burnout, and better work-to-family balance.[20]

> "Flextime provides many benefits, including improved ability to recruit and retain workers who wish to balance work and home life."

Related to flextime are the scheduling strategies of the compressed workweek and job sharing. The **compressed workweek** is a four-day (or shorter) period in which an employee works 40 hours. Under such a plan, employees typically work 10 hours per day for four days and have a three-day weekend. The compressed workweek reduces the company's operating expenses because its actual hours of operation are reduced. It is also sometimes used by parents who want to have more days off to spend with their families. Millennials and Generation Z are groups of employees who value flexibility in their work schedules. Cameco Corp., in Saskatoon, encourages employees' work–life balance with alternative work arrangements including flexible hours, telecommuting, and shortened and compressed workweek options.[21]

**job sharing** performance of one full-time job by two people on part-time hours

**Job sharing** occurs when two people do one job. One person may work from 8:00 a.m. to 12:30 p.m.; the second person comes in at 12:30 p.m. and works until 5:00 p.m. Job sharing gives both people the opportunity to work, as well as time to fulfill other obligations, such as parenting or school. With job sharing, the company has the benefit of the skills of two people for one job, often at a lower total cost for salaries and benefits than one person working eight hours a day would be paid.

Two other flexible scheduling strategies attaining wider use include allowing full-time workers to work part time for a certain period and allowing workers to work at home either full or part time. Employees at some firms may be permitted to work part time for several months in order to care for a new baby or an elderly parent, or just to slow down for a little while to "recharge their batteries."

When the employees return to full-time work, they are usually given a position comparable to their original full-time position. Other firms are allowing employees to telecommute or telework (work at home a few days of the week), staying connected via computers and telephones. Most telecommuters tend to combine going into the office with working from home. At Dell, for instance, an estimated 25 percent of the workforce work from home either full time or a few days a week. Today, 11.2 million Canadians are teleworkers, working most often from home.[22]

©nd3000/Shutterstock

Working remotely is becoming increasingly common. Telecommuting, job sharing, and flextime can be beneficial for employees who cannot work normal work hours.

Although many employees ask for the option of working at home to ease the responsibilities of caring for family members, some have discovered that they are more productive at home without the distractions of the workplace. An assessment of 12 company telecommuting programs found that positive productivity changes occurred. Traveler's Insurance Company reports its telecommuters to be 20 percent more productive than its traditional employees.[23]

Other employees, however, have discovered that they are not suited for working at home. Human resource management executives are split as to whether telecommuting helps or hurts employees' careers. Thirty percent feel telecommuting helps their careers, while 25 percent feel that it hurts; 39 percent feel it does neither.[24] Still, work-at-home programs do help reduce overhead costs for businesses. For example, some companies used to maintain a surplus of office space but have reduced the surplus through employee telecommuting, *hoteling* (being assigned to a desk through a reservation system), and *hot-desking* (several people using the same desk but at different times).

Companies are turning to flexible work schedules to provide more options for employees who are trying to juggle their work duties with other responsibilities and needs. Preliminary results indicated that flexible scheduling plans increase job satisfaction, which, in turn, leads to increases in productivity. Some recent research, however, has indicated there are potential problems with telecommuting. Some managers are reluctant to adopt the practice because the pace of change in today's workplace is faster than ever, and telecommuters may be left behind or actually cause managers more work in helping them stay abreast of changes. Some employers also worry that telecommuting workers create a security risk by creating more opportunities for computer hackers or equipment thieves.

Some employees have found that working outside the office may hurt career advancement opportunities, and some report that instead of helping them balance work and family responsibilities, telecommuting increases the strain by blurring the barriers between the office and home. Co-workers call at all hours, and telecommuters are apt to continue to work when they are not supposed to (after regular business hours or during vacation time).[25]

## Importance of Motivational Strategies

Motivation is more than a tool that managers can use to foster employee loyalty and boost productivity. It is a process that affects all the relationships within an organization and influences many areas such as pay, promotion, job design, training opportunities, and reporting relationships. Employees are motivated by the nature of the relationships they have with their supervisors, by the nature of their jobs, and by characteristics of the organization. Table 9.5 shows companies with excellent motivational strategies.

Single-working-parent families face a tough challenge in balancing work and home life. For single parents, business travel and other routine demands of a corporate career—including overtime and interoffice transfers—can turn life upside down. Sometimes single parents decline promotions or high-profile assignments to preserve time with their children. In some organizations, experts say, it may be assumed single-parent staffers can't handle new duties because of the responsibilities they're shouldering at home.

Even the economic environment can change an employee's motivation. In a slow growth or recession economy, sales can flatten or decrease, and morale can drop because of the need to cut jobs. In the most recent recession, many workers feared losing their jobs and increased the amount they were saving. The firm may have to work harder to keep good employees and to motivate all employees to work to overcome obstacles.

Businesses have come up with different ways to motivate employees, including rewards such as trophies and plaques to show the company's appreciation.

## RESPONDING TO BUSINESS CHALLENGES

### Bad Moods Contribute to Decreased Productivity

There is no getting around it: bad moods produce bad results. Employees who come to work unhappy tend to carry that unhappiness throughout the day. Until recently, just how much bad moods affect the work environment was not clear. However, a study by business professor Steffanie Wilk found that employees who start the day in a bad mood can see their productivity levels reduced by more than 10 percent. Additionally, bad moods tend to be contagious, affecting other employees and customers and reducing the bottom line.

This does not bode well for companies in the current work climate. The Gallup-Healthways Well-Being Index reveals that employees are becoming unhappier with their jobs. Much of this can be attributed to economic uncertainty. With businesses cutting back, employees are often expected to take on greater roles with fewer benefits. As a result, employees experience more dissatisfaction with their jobs and a less positive relationship with their employers. But managers can take steps to improve employees' moods in simple ways. Some companies offer very small incentives that make employees feel appreciated.

For example, 3M gives its employees time to pursue their own projects, an act that not only increases employee morale but has also yielded some of 3M's greatest product ideas. Employers might also encourage short periods of socialization among employees, which can improve moods and build cohesiveness. It seems carrots, not sticks, are the key to creating a more productive work environment.*

#### DISCUSSION QUESTIONS

1. Why might an uncertain economic climate contribute to decreased productivity?
2. Why do employee bad moods have such a negative effect on an organization?
3. What can employers do to improve the moods of their employees?

*Nancy Rothbard, "Put on a Happy Face. Seriously." *Wall Street Journal*, October 24, 2011, p. R2; "How 3M Gave Everyone Days Off and Created an Innovation Dynamo," February 1, 2011, www.fastcodesign.com/1663137/how-3m-gave-everyone-days-off-and-created-aninnovation-dynamo (accessed October 31, 2011); "Americans Increasingly Unhappy at Work," *BusinessNewsDaily*, March 10, 2011, www.businessnewsdaily.com/work-wellness-index-1073/ (accessed October 31, 2011); "Employee Mood Impacts Bottom Line," *BusinessNewsDaily* April 5, 2011, www.businessnewsdaily.com/employee-mood-customer-service-1152/ (accessed October 31, 2011).

In good economic times, employees may be more demanding and be on the lookout for better opportunities. New rewards or incentives may help motivate workers in such economies. Motivation tools, then, must be varied, as well. Managers can further nurture motivation by being honest, supportive, empathetic, accessible, fair, and open. Motivating employees to increase satisfaction and productivity is an important concern for organizations seeking to remain competitive in the global marketplace.

**Table 9.5** | Companies with Excellent Motivational Strategies

| | |
|---|---|
| 3M Canada Company | Gives employees 15–20 percent of their time to pursue own projects |
| Apple | Creates a fast-paced, innovative work environment where employees are encouraged to debate ideas |
| Bell Canada | Offers subsidized membership to a fully equipped onsite fitness facility as well as access to nutritionist, massage therapist, and physiotherapist services |
| Marriott International | Offers discounts at hotels across the world as well as free hotel stays and travel opportunities for employees with exceptional service |
| Mountain Equipment Co-op | Employees work to get Canadians outside, from building new recreation trails to support for urban cycling programs to support for at-risk youth through outdoor recreation and education programs |
| Nike | Offers tuition assistance, product discounts, onsite fitness centres, and the ability for employees to give insights on how to improve the firm |
| Suncor Energy | Offers volunteer awards of up to $1000 per year for employees who are active in their local communities as well as leadership rewards for those who serve as a board member for a community organization |
| Whole Foods | Employees receive 20 percent discounts on company products, the opportunity to gain stock options, and the ability to make major decisions in small teams |

## TEAM EXERCISE

Form groups and outline a compensation package that you would consider ideal in motivating an employee, recognizing performance, and assisting the company in attaining its cost-to-performance objectives. Think about the impact of intrinsic and extrinsic motivation and recognition. How can flexible scheduling strategies be used effectively to motivate employees? Report your compensation package to the class.

# LEARNING OBJECTIVES SUMMARY

**LO 9-1** Define *human relations*, and determine why its study is important.

Human relations is the study of the behaviour of individuals and groups in organizational settings. Its focus is what motivates employees to perform on the job. Human relations is important because businesses need to understand how to motivate their increasingly diverse employees to be more effective, boost workplace morale, and maximize employees' productivity and creativity.

**LO 9-2** Summarize early studies that laid the groundwork for understanding employee motivation.

Time and motion studies by Frederick Taylor and others helped them analyze how employees perform specific work tasks in an effort to improve their productivity. Taylor and the early practitioners of the classical theory of motivation felt that money and job security were the primary motivators of employees. However, the Hawthorne studies revealed that human factors also influence workers' behaviour.

**LO 9-3** Compare and contrast the human-relations theories of Abraham Maslow and Frederick Herzberg.

Abraham Maslow defined five basic needs of all people and arranged them in the order in which they must be satisfied: physiological, security, social, esteem, and self-actualization. Frederick Herzberg divided characteristics of the job into hygiene factors and motivational factors. Hygiene factors relate to the work environment and must be present for employees to remain in a job. Motivational factors—recognition, responsibility, and advancement—relate to the work itself. They encourage employees to be productive. Herzberg's hygiene factors can be compared to Maslow's physiological and security needs; motivational factors may include Maslow's social, esteem, and self-actualization needs.

**LO 9-4** Investigate various theories of motivation, including Theories X, Y, and Z; equity theory; expectancy theory; and goal-setting theory.

Douglas McGregor contrasted two views of management: Theory X (traditional) suggests workers dislike work, while Theory Y (humanistic) suggests that workers not only like work but seek out responsibility to satisfy their higher-order needs. Theory Z stresses employee participation in all aspects of company decision making, often through participative management programs and self-directed work teams. According to equity theory, how much people are willing to contribute to an organization depends on their assessment of the fairness, or equity, of the rewards they will receive in exchange. Expectancy theory states that motivation depends not only on how much a person wants something but also on the person's perception of how likely they are to get it. Goal-setting theory refers to the impact that setting goals has on performance.

**LO 9-5** Describe some of the strategies that managers use to motivate employees.

Strategies for motivating workers include behaviour modification (changing behaviour and encouraging appropriate actions by relating the consequences of behaviour to the behaviour itself) and job design. Among the job design strategies businesses use are job rotation (allowing employees to move from one job to another to try to relieve the boredom associated with job specialization), job enlargement (adding tasks to a job instead of treating each task as a separate job), job enrichment (incorporating motivational factors into a job situation), and flexible scheduling strategies (flextime, compressed workweeks, job sharing, part-time work, and telecommuting).

## KEY TERMS

behaviour modification
classical theory of motivation
compressed workweek
equity theory
esteem needs
expectancy theory
extrinsic reward
flextime
goal-setting theory
human relations
hygiene factors
intrinsic reward
job enlargement
job enrichment
job rotation
job sharing
Maslow's hierarchy
morale
motivation
motivational factors
physiological needs
reinforcement theory
security needs
self-actualization needs
social needs
Theory X
Theory Y
Theory Z

## So You Think *You Might Be Good at Motivating a Workforce*

If you are good at mediation, can smooth over conflict, and have a good understanding of motivation and human relations theories, then you might be a good leader, human resources manager, or training expert. Most organizations, especially as they grow, will need to implement human relations programs. These are necessary to teach employees about sensitivity to other cultures, religions, and beliefs, as well as for teaching the workforce about the organization so that they understand how they fit in the larger picture. Employees need to appreciate the benefits of working together to make the firm run smoothly, and they also need to understand how their contributions help the firm. To stay motivated, most employees need to feel like what they do each day contributes something of value to the firm. Disclosing information and including employees in decision-making processes will also help employees feel valuable and wanted within the firm.

There are many different ways employers can reward and encourage employees. However, employers must be careful when considering what kinds of incentives to use. Different cultures value different kinds of incentives more highly than others. For example, a Japanese worker would probably not like being singled out from the group and given a large cash bonus as a reward for their work. Japanese workers tend to be more group oriented, and therefore anything that singles out individuals would not be an effective way of rewarding and motivating. Canadian workers, on the other hand, are very individualistic, and a raise and public praise might be more effective. However, what might motivate a younger employee (bonuses, raises, and perks) may not be the same as what motivates a more seasoned, experienced, and financially successful employee (recognition, opportunity for greater influence, and increased training). Motivation is not an easy thing to understand, especially as firms become more global and more diverse.

Another important part of motivation is enjoying where you work and your career opportunities. Here's a list of the Best Places to Live in Canada, (Table 9.6). Chances are, workers in these top ten places have encountered fewer frustrations than those in places at the bottom of the list and, therefore, would probably be more content with where they work.

**Table 9.6** | Best Places to Live in Canada

| Rank | City | Population |
|---|---|---|
| 1 | Oakville, Ontario | 209,039 |
| 2 | Ottawa, Ontario | 999,183 |
| 3 | Russell Township, Ontario | 17,155 |
| 4 | Saint-Bruno-de-Montarville, Quebec | 27,171 |
| 5 | Lacombe, Alberta | 13,906 |
| 6 | Milton, Ontario | 120,556 |
| 7 | Canmore, Alberta | 14,930 |
| 8 | Westmount, Quebec | 21,083 |
| 9 | Saint-Lambert, Quebec | 22,432 |
| 10 | Halton Hills, Ontario | 65,782 |

## BUILD YOUR BUSINESS PLAN

### Motivating the Workforce

As you determine the size of your workforce, you are going to face the reality that you cannot provide the level of financial compensation that you would like to your employees, especially when you are starting your business.

Many employees are motivated by other things than money. Knowing that they are appreciated and doing a good job can bring great satisfaction to employees. Known as "stroking," it can provide employees with internal gratification that can be valued even more than financial incentives. Listening to employees' suggestions, involving them in discussions about future growth, and valuing their input can go a long way toward building loyal employees and reducing employee turnover.

Think about what you could do in your business to motivate your employees without spending much money. Maybe you will have lunch brought in once a week or offer tickets to a local sporting event to the employee with the most sales. Whatever you elect to do, you must be consistent and fair with all your employees.

## CASE | Is It Possible Your Dog Could Increase Business Productivity?

In an age in which companies are cutting back health care benefits due to a sluggish economy, many employers are turning to low-cost perks to keep workers happy. In addition to perks such as gym and spa facilities and weight-loss programs, an increasing number of companies are actually allowing employees to bring their pets to work. A survey conducted by Dogster (an online dog forum) and Simply Hired indicates that two-thirds of all dog owners surveyed would work longer hours if allowed to bring their dogs to work. One-third claimed they would accept a 5 percent pay deduction if allowed to bring their dogs to work. Maybe this is because another survey indicated that 69 percent of dog owners view their dog as part of the family.

Having dogs and cats in the workplace can provide many benefits, including a more relaxed and flexible atmosphere, increased staff morale, and even increased employee retention. One company's spokesperson indicated that its pet policy gives employees individual flexibility and shows that the company respects employees enough to let them make choices about their work environment. The American Psychological Association has even honoured companies such as Small Dog Electronics, a computer merchant with 27 employees, as psychologically healthy workplaces in part because of their pet-friendly policies. At this time, many pet-friendly companies have 50 or fewer employees, although a few Fortune 500 companies such as Amazon and Google have pet-friendly policies. At Planet Dog, a company allowing pets in the office daily, the company consists, so to speak, of 16 employees and 14 dogs.

A pet-friendly workplace can be a definite advantage in recruiting and retaining employees. Small Dog Electronics, for example, has boasted an employee turnover rate of 1 percent compared with an industry average of 11 percent. Even non–pet owners often appreciate the informal, flexible environments that characterize workplaces with pets.

To some extent, being pet friendly helps define a corporate culture—as it does at AutoDesk, a software provider. A Pet Products Manufacturers Association survey revealed that 73 percent of surveyed companies believed allowing pets at work increased productivity—compared with a 42 percent productivity increase due to business development or management training. Even when it is not possible for employees to bring pets to work every day, some companies allow them to bring their pets to work occasionally for short periods of time.

Many small businesses, particularly retailers, established pet-friendly policies out of personal necessity. Indeed many small retailers, such as antique dealers and bookstore owners, often have "store cats" or "store dogs" that are appreciated as much by customers as by employees. Although legislation prohibits allowing pets in restaurants in Canada and the United States, many European restaurants allow customers to have their dogs right at their tables where food is served.

While bringing your pet to work can definitely improve morale, there are a few challenges. People with allergies or who are afraid of animals might be distracted from their jobs. Of course, there may be the concern that a dog may bite a person or another dog. However, research by attorneys at Ralston Purina found that lawsuits related to pets in the work environment are quite rare. As long as good judgment is used, allowing animals in the workplace appears to be a great move.[26]

## DISCUSSION QUESTIONS

1. Why can a non-financial benefit such as being able to bring your dog to work motivate employees?
2. What types of businesses are appropriate for a pet-friendly workplace policy?
3. How do you personally feel about having other people's pets in an office where you work or store where you shop?

CHAPTER 10

# Managing Human Resources

©Richard Drew/AP/The Canadian Press

Shopify has grown from a business run in Tobias Lütke's garage to a $30 billion company.

## LEARNING OBJECTIVES

**After reading this chapter, you will be able to:**

- LO 10-1 Define human resources management and explain its significance.
- LO 10-2 Summarize the processes of recruiting and selecting human resources for a company.
- LO 10-3 Discuss how workers are trained and their performance appraised.
- LO 10-4 Identify the types of turnover companies may experience, and explain why turnover is an important issue.
- LO 10-5 Specify the various ways a worker may be compensated.
- LO 10-6 Discuss some of the issues associated with unionized employees, including collective bargaining and dispute resolution.
- LO 10-7 Describe the importance of diversity in the workforce.

# ENTER THE WORLD OF BUSINESS

**Shopify Supports Employees in an Autonomous Environment**

Shopify's growth over the past five years has been substantial. The company which was started by Tobias Lütke in his garage has seen its market cap soar to almost $30 billion with almost 3000 employees. Shopify allows businesses both large and small to build and create websites to sell goods all over the world. To date 600,000 merchants have used Shopify to create websites and they have recorded $63 billion in sales.[1]

With Canada's unemployment rate at its lowest level in almost four decades, many employers are struggling to attract talent. Shopify is not one of the employers, in fact, Shopify routinely attracts many applicants who go through a rather rigorous hiring process in which many prospective candidates are unsuccessful. What attracts prospective employees to Shopify? To some it may be the Silicon Valley–type office perks, including Shopify's work spaces, which resemble an Ikea showroom; they are open, and employees get to enjoy a variety of benefits including an indoor go-kart track, a games room, free food, and generous health and parental benefits.[2]

While all these perks are appealing, what drives many prospective employees to apply is the autonomy Shopify provides employees and the company's concept of trust. Shopify very quickly thrusts new hires into projects where they can play a substantial role and perhaps even lead. Shopify also openly discusses what they refer to as a Trust Battery, which is a measure of how much trust people have in each other.

Lütke says anyone who can make it through their stringent hiring process is assigned a 50 percent rating on their Trust Battery and, based on their interactions and work, this trust can grow or decline. New employees state that starting with such a high trust rating enables them to work independently, to lead projects, to be creative, and the Trust Battery concept provides them with an understanding of how their successes or failures will impact their interactions with their employer and their colleagues.[3, 4]

To ensure Shopify hires appropriate people, they engage in an exhaustive hiring process. The company routinely has candidates complete interviews with numerous people to eliminate bias. Shopify also shuns traditional interview questions such as asking candidates about their strengths and weaknesses. Rather, Shopify tries to make a human connection with people, get to know them, and understand how they respond to changing circumstances. Lütke says that Shopify tends to focus on pivotal moments in people's lives to see how they reacted to understand the type of person they are.

Annie Zhang, a recent hire at Shopify, describes the interview process as being placed in a blender and spun around and coming out alive. She says her selection process took four months and she completed 12 chats/interviews, wrote an article for *Buzzfeed*, completed a case study on a new product, and built a Shopify store. Zhang say the result, a job at Shopify, was worth going through the process but cautions that working for a fast-growing firm and having a great deal of autonomy may not be for everybody. For example, if asked what she does daily Zhang's response is she just figures it out.[5, 6] Overall employee feedback for Shopify is strong, and the company has frequently been recognized as one of the top employers in Canada, dating back to 2014.

### DISCUSSION QUESTIONS

1. What are some of the advantages and disadvantages of Shopify's hiring practices?
2. Based on the information in the case, create a definition for the term Trust Battery. Do you like the concept? Do you think it accurately represents work relationships? Why or why not?
3. Are you surprised Shopify provides employees with such a high level of autonomy? What are the advantages and disadvantages of this type of work environment?

## Introduction

If a business is to achieve success, it must have sufficient numbers of employees who are qualified and motivated to perform the required duties. Thus, managing the quantity (from hiring to firing) and quality (through training, compensating, and so on) of employees is an important business function. Meeting the challenge of managing increasingly diverse human resources effectively can give a company a competitive edge in a global marketplace.

This chapter focuses on the quantity and quality of human resources. First, we look at how human resources managers plan for, recruit, and select qualified employees. Next, we look at training, appraising, and compensating employees, aspects of human resources management designed to retain valued employees. Along the way, we'll also consider the challenges of managing unionized employees and workplace diversity.

# The Nature of Human Resources Management

**LO 10-1** Define human resources management, and explain its significance.

Chapter 1 defined human resources as labour—the physical and mental abilities that people use to produce goods and services. **Human resources management (HRM)** refers to all the activities involved in determining an organization's human resources needs, as well as acquiring, training, and compensating people to fill those needs. Human resources managers are concerned with maximizing the satisfaction of employees and motivating them to meet organizational objectives productively. In some companies, this function is called personnel management.

**human resources management (HRM)** all the activities involved in determining an organization's human resources needs, as well as acquiring, training, and compensating people to fill those needs

©David Lees/Digital Vision/Getty Images

Today's organizations are more diverse, with a greater number of women, minorities, and older workers.

HRM has increased in importance over the last few decades, in part because managers have developed a better understanding of human relations through the work of Maslow, Herzberg, and others. Moreover, the human resources themselves are changing. Employees today are not just concerned about how much a job pays; they are concerned also with job satisfaction, personal performance, leisure, the environment, and the future. Once dominated by white men, today's workforce includes significantly more women, African Canadians, Chinese Canadians, and other minorities, as well as people with disabilities and older workers. Human resources managers must be aware of these changes and make the best use of them to increase the productivity of their employees. Every manager practises some of the functions of human resources management at all times.

# Planning for Human Resources Needs

When planning and developing strategies for reaching the organization's overall objectives, a company must consider whether it will have the human resources necessary to carry out its plans. After determining how many employees and what skills are needed to satisfy the overall plans, the human resources department (which may range from the owner in a small business to hundreds of people in a large corporation) ascertains how many employees the company currently has and how many will be retiring or otherwise leaving the organization during the planning period. With this information, the human resources manager can then forecast how many more employees the company will need to hire and what qualifications they must have.

HRM planning also requires forecasting the availability of people in the workforce who will have the necessary qualifications to meet the organization's future needs. The human resources manager then develops a strategy for satisfying the organization's human resources needs. As organizations strive to increase efficiency through outsourcing, automation, or learning to effectively use temporary workers, hiring needs can change dramatically.

Next, managers analyze the jobs within the organization so that they can match the human resources to the available assignments. **Job analysis** determines, through observation and study, pertinent information about a job—the specific tasks that comprise it; the knowledge, skills, and abilities necessary to perform it; and the environment in which it will be performed. Managers use the information obtained through a job analysis to develop job descriptions and job specifications.

**job analysis** the determination, through observation and study, of pertinent information about a job–including specific tasks and necessary abilities, knowledge, and skills

**job description** a formal, written explanation of a specific job, usually including job title, tasks, relationship with other jobs, physical and mental skills required, duties, responsibilities, and working conditions

**job specification** a description of the qualifications necessary for a specific job, in terms of education, experience, and personal and physical characteristics

A **job description** is a formal, written explanation of a specific job that usually includes job title, tasks to be performed (for instance, waiting on customers), relationship with other jobs, physical and mental skills required (such as lifting heavy boxes or calculating data), duties, responsibilities, and working conditions. Job seekers might turn to online websites or databases to help find job descriptions for specific occupations. For instance, the Labour Market Information (LMI) service helps Canadians find information about occupations and labour market trends and outlooks, including skill or labour shortages and surpluses.[7]

Vancouver based Hootsuite, a global leader in social media management, recently changed their job descriptions to make them more candidate friendly. On top of describing the job, Hootsuite "re-imagined" their job descriptions so they would be easier to read and to highlight to prospective candidates the benefits of working for the company.[8] A **job specification** describes the qualifications necessary for a specific job, in terms of education (some jobs require a post-secondary degree), experience, personal characteristics (recruitment ads frequently request outgoing, hardworking persons), and physical characteristics. Both the job description and job specification are used to develop recruiting materials that can be distributed through the channels that will reach interested candidates.

©chrisdorney/Shutterstock

Hootsuite recently changed its hiring process to make it more candidate friendly. One of their changes included updating job descriptions so they are easier to read, have links, and highlight the benefits of working for the company.

# Recruiting and Selecting New Employees

**LO 10-2** Summarize the processes of recruiting and selecting human resources for a company.

After forecasting the firm's human resources needs and comparing them to existing human resources, the human resources manager should have a general idea of how many new employees the firm needs to hire. With the aid of job analyses, management can then recruit and select employees who are qualified to fill specific job openings.

## Recruiting

**Recruiting** means forming a pool of qualified applicants from which management can select employees. Given that in late 2018 the unemployment rate was 5.6 percent, the lowest it has been in four decades, finding qualified applicants has become increasingly difficult for managers.[9] There are two sources from which to develop this pool of applicants—the internal and external.

**recruiting** forming a pool of qualified applicants from which management can select employees

Internal sources of applicants include the organization's current employees. Many firms have a policy of giving first consideration to their own employees—also known as promoting from within. The cost of filling job openings with current employees is inexpensive when compared with the cost of hiring from external sources, and it is good for employee morale.

Serial entrepreneur Richard Branson, owner of the Virgin Group, which controls more than 400 companies, advocates for promoting from within, stating it is good for employee morale and argues that current employees can become unmotivated if they think they are not being presented with opportunities to advance.[10] Adam Foroughi, co-founder of AppLovin, a firm that specializes in promoting and monetizing online games, agrees with Branson, noting that promoting from within motivates people to work harder, positively impacts retention, and benefits the company because internal hires already understand its culture.[11] Of course, hiring from within does eliminate the new perspective an outsider can bring to a company and creates another job vacancy to be filled.

**DID YOU KNOW?**

Proctor & Gamble only hires people at the entry level and promotes from within. So to work at P&G you'll likely have to start at the bottom.[12]

©Mark Chivers/Alamy Stock Photo

Virgin Group promotes hiring from within because it creates loyal and engaged employees.

External sources consist of advertisements in newspapers and professional journals, employment agencies, colleges, vocational schools, recommendations from current employees, competing firms, unsolicited applications, and online. Internships and/or co-operative work placements are also a good way to solicit potential employees. Many companies hire university students or recent graduates for low-paying internships that give them the opportunity to get hands-on experience on the job. If the intern or co-op student proves to be a good fit, an organization may then hire them as a full-time worker.

There are also hundreds of websites where employers can post job openings and job seekers can post their resumés, including Eluta www.eluta.ca, Glassdoor www.glassdoor.ca, TalentEgg https://talentegg.ca, Workopolis.com, Monster.com, and CareerBuilder.com. Employers seeking employees for specialized jobs can use sites such as computerwork.com.

Increasingly, companies are turning to their own websites for potential candidates. Employers can also use social networking sites such as LinkedIn to post jobs and search for candidates. Many people believe social networking sites are overtaking traditional job-search channels.

Using external sources of applicants is generally more expensive than hiring from within, but it may be necessary if there are no current employees who meet the job specifications or if there are better-qualified people outside of the organization. Recruiting for entry-level managerial and professional positions is often carried out on college and university campuses. For managerial or professional positions above the entry level, companies sometimes depend on employment agencies or executive search firms, sometimes called *headhunters*, which specialize in luring qualified people away from other companies. Employers are also increasingly using professional social networking sites such as LinkedIn and Viadeo as recruitment tools.

## Selection

**Selection** is the process of collecting information about applicants and using that information to decide which ones to hire. It includes the application itself, as well as interviewing, testing, and reference checking. This process can be quite lengthy and expensive. As described in case at the start of the chapter, some companies like Shopify can invest months in employee selection. Other examples include Procter & Gamble Canada, for example, where the steps include application submission, screening and comprehensive interviews, day visits/site visits, and for international applicants, a problem-solving test, all designed to ensure that P&G attracts and

**selection** the process of collecting information about applicants and using that information to make hiring decisions

## RESPONDING TO BUSINESS CHALLENGES

### Recruiters Embrace Non-traditional Recruitment Methods

Traditionally, recruiters have used resumés to gauge an applicant's fitness for a job. However, some organizations are realizing that initially judging applicants' suitability for jobs based on resumés—and immediately discarding those who do not fit the criteria—is a flawed system that can overlook talented candidates.

Part of the problem with using traditional recruiting methods is their inflexibility. Journalist George Anders claims that some of the best candidates are not the ones with great GPAs or job backgrounds, but those who possess analytical and conceptual skills to think outside of the box.

For this reason, some businesses are changing their recruitment methods. Employee referrals remain the top recruitment tool, with 30 percent of all hires recruited this way. Others are taking more unique approaches. Best Buy holds a national hiring day when its locations hold open interviews for store positions. Facebook sends out coding puzzles for programmers to solve; this enables candidates to test their abilities despite their previous work background.

To recruit employees, McDonald's Canada is using a tool called Snapplications. It placed 10-second videos on Snapchat about how great it is to work at McDonald's. Interested candidates will be able to create a 30-second video responding to the job posting and fill in a brief resumé. McDonald's is hoping Snapchat's will enable them to access the next generation of young workers.* Shopify has also used SnapChat to recruit since 2016. The Ottawa-based firm often has potential applicants submit a Snapchat story along with their resumé.**

Although resumés will likely remain an important part of the recruitment process, employers are increasingly finding that resumés only show part of the picture. Using non-traditional recruitment tools gives companies the opportunity to test talents that may not be readily visible in a resumé, such as creativity or problem-solving skills.

#### DISCUSSION QUESTIONS

1. What might be some of the limitations of resumés as the primary recruitment tool?
2. Why do you think referrals are valued so highly as a recruitment tool?
3. Do you believe that resumés are still important, or should they be discarded as a recruitment tool?
4. What are some advantages and disadvantages of using social media to recruit prospective employees?

*Alicja Siekierska, "McDonald's Canada turns to Snapchat to recruit young workers," March 20, 2019, https://ca.finance.yahoo.com/news/mc-donalds-canada-turns-to-snapchat-to-recruit-young-workers-203124248.html

**Rachel Hill, "Snapchat and Recruitment: A match made in heaven or not?" April 28, 2018, https://hirehive.com/snapchat-recruitment/

©ZUMA Press Inc/Alamy Stock Photo

McDonald's is one of the first companies to use SnapChat to recruit in Canada.

retains high-quality employees.[13] Such rigorous scrutiny is necessary to find those applicants who can do the work expected and fit into the firm's structure and culture. If an organization finds the "right" employees through its recruiting and selection process, it will not have to spend as much money later in recruiting, selecting, and training replacement employees.

**The Application.** In the first stage of the selection process, the individual fills out an application form and perhaps has a brief interview. The application form asks for the applicant's name, address, telephone number, education, and previous work experience. The goal of this stage of the selection process is to get acquainted with the applicants and to weed out those who are obviously not qualified for the job. For employees with work experience, most companies ask for the following information before contacting a potential candidate: reason for seeking a new job, years of experience, availability, and level of interest in the position.

In addition to identifying obvious qualifications, the application can provide subtle clues about whether a person is appropriate for a particular job. For instance, an applicant who gives unusually creative answers may be perfect for a position at an advertising agency; a person who turns in a sloppy, hurriedly scrawled application probably would not be appropriate for a technical job requiring precise attention to detail.

Many companies now accept online applications. The online application at Target is designed not only to collect biographical data but to create a picture of the applicant and how the person might contribute within the company. The completion of the survey takes about 45 minutes, depending on the position. To get a better view of the fit between the applicant and the company, the online application contains a questionnaire that asks applicants for more specific information, from how they might react in a certain situation to personality attributes like self-esteem or ability to interact with people.[14]

**The Interview.** The next phase of the selection process involves interviewing applicants. Interviews allow management to obtain detailed information about the applicant's experience and skills, reasons for changing jobs, attitudes toward the job, and an idea of whether the person would fit in with the company. Table 10.1 provides some insights on finding the right work environment. Table 10.2 lists some of the most common questions asked by interviewers while Table 10.3 reveals some common mistakes candidates make in interviewing.

Furthermore, the interviewer can answer the applicant's questions about the requirements for the job, compensation,

**Table 10.1** | Interviewing Tips

1. Evaluate the work environment. Do employees seem to get along and work well in teams?
2. Evaluate the attitude of employees. Are employees happy, tense, or overworked?
3. Are employees enthusiastic and excited about their work?
4. What is the organizational culture, and would you feel comfortable working there?

**Table 10.2** | Top 10 Interview Questions

1. Tell me about yourself.
2. What are your biggest weaknesses?
3. What are your biggest strengths?
4. Where do you see yourself in 5 years?
5. Out of all the other candidates, why should I hire you?
6. How did you learn about the opening?
7. Why do you want the job?
8. What do you consider your biggest professional achievement?
9. Tell me about the last time a co-worker or customer got angry with you. What happened?
10. Describe your dream job.

**Table 10.3** | Mistakes Made by Interviewees

1. Appearing uninterested
2. Using a cell phone
3. Dressing inappropriately
4. Fumbling questions
5. Talking negatively about current or previous employer
6. Talking too much
7. Displaying poor body language
8. Not providing specific examples
9. Falsifying information
10. Failing to follow up

working conditions, company policies, organizational culture, and so on. A potential employee's questions may be just as revealing as his or her answers. Today's students might be surprised to have an interviewer ask them, "What's on your Instagram account?" or have them show the interviewer their social media accounts. Currently, these are legal questions for an interviewer to ask.

Given the high costs of a poor hire, many companies are expanding the interview process over days if not months. As discussed at the start of the chapter, the interview process with Shopify can take months and some candidates are screened by the company founder. Other companies, such as Hilton, are making use of Artificial Intelligence, or AI, to assist them in the hiring process. Hilton uses AllyO, an AI system, to screen applicants and to conduct the first screening interview.[15]

**Testing.** Another step in the selection process is testing. Ability and performance tests are used to determine whether an applicant has the skills necessary for the job.

©Kirby Hamilton/iStockphoto

Personality tests such as Myers-Briggs are used to assess an applicant's potential for a certain kind of job. For instance, extroversion and a love of people would be good qualities for a sales or retail job. Interestingly, there does not seem to be any difference between introversion and extroversion in the qualities that make a good manager.

Aptitude, IQ, or personality tests may be used to assess an applicant's potential for a certain kind of work and their ability to fit into the organization's culture. One of the most commonly used tests is the Myers–Briggs Type Indicator, which is used more than 2.5 million times each year, according to a survey by *Workforce Management.* Employers may use other tests, as well, depending on the position; for example, both Hootsuite and Facebook will often ask people who are applying for information technology positions to spend time solving coding problems, Shopify asks potential candidates to create a case study, and Proctor & Gamble has interviewees complete a presentation.

Applicants may also undergo physical examinations to determine their suitability for some jobs. One difference between Canadian and American human resource practices revolves around the use of drug testing—the practice is no longer legal in Canada (with some exceptions for government positions), but in the United States many companies require applicants to be screened for illegal drug use. In Canada, employers can screen for alcohol but not drugs.[16] If you employ a drug or alcohol abuser, you can expect a 33 percent loss in productivity from this employee.

Because computer knowledge is a requirement for many jobs today, certain companies also require an applicant to take a typing test, or tests to determine their knowledge of Microsoft Word, Excel, PowerPoint, and/or other necessary programs. Like the application form and the interview, testing serves to eliminate those who do not meet the job specifications.

©Jeffrey Coolidge/Digital Vision/Getty Images

Some jobs require potential hires to undergo physical examinations, such as alcohol tests.

**Reference Checking.** Before making a job offer, the company should always check an applicant's references. Reference checking usually involves verifying educational background and previous work experience. Background checking is important because applicants may misrepresent themselves on their applications or resumés. The star of *Dinner: Impossible* on the Food Network fabricated portions of his resumé, including the claim that he'd cooked for Britain's royal family. The Food Network, upon learning of these errors, did not renew Robert Irvine's contract, indicating that viewers place trust in the network and the accuracy of information that it provides and that Irvine "challenged that trust."[17]

Irvine had to work for months to apologize and set the record straight about his chef credentials. The Food Network ultimately did rehire him to host *Dinner: Impossible.* As Table 10.4 illustrates, some of the most common types of resumé lies include the faking of credentials, overstatements of skills or accomplishments, lies concerning education/degrees, omissions of past employment, and the falsification of references.[18]

**DID YOU KNOW?**

According to HireRight's employment survey, 85 percent of employers caught applicants lying on their resumés.[19]

Reference checking is a vital, albeit often overlooked, stage in the selection process. Managers charged with hiring should be aware, however, that many organizations will confirm only that an applicant is a former employee, perhaps with beginning and ending work dates, and will not release details about the quality of the employee's work.

**Table 10.4** | Top 10 Resumé Lies

1. College or university attended
2. Foreign language fluency
3. Academic degree
4. Major (subject)
5. GPA
6. Former employment or work history
7. Awards or accomplishments
8. Minor (subject)
9. Projects or portfolio
10. Job title

"Ability and performance tests are used to determine whether an applicant has the skills necessary for the job."

### Legal Issues in Recruiting and Selecting

Legal constraints and regulations are present in almost every phase of the recruitment and selection process, and a violation of these regulations can result in lawsuits and fines. Therefore, managers should be aware of these restrictions to avoid legal problems. The Charter of Rights and Freedoms guarantees that all people are treated the same way under the law, and the *Canadian Human Rights Act* ensures that all people have equal opportunities for employment.[20]

The Human Rights Act is applicable for all federally regulated organizations, including banks and airlines. Individual provinces and territories have their own laws to protect workers in non-regulated businesses.[21] Another important law that businesses have to be aware of is the *Employment Equity Act*, signed in 1986, which ensures that federally regulated employers with more than 100 employees do not disadvantage women, visible minorities, people with disabilities, or Aboriginal Peoples.

Furthermore, organizations have to make special accommodations to assist people in these categories in gaining meaningful employment. Additionally, if an employer or organization had a disproportionate number of male employees, they were required to develop a plan to balance out the gender of their employees. The same concept applies to skin colour and/or cultural background.[22] Recently, a new category of workers has gone before human rights boards to fight for their rights. Baby boomers, who were being forced to retire due to Canada's mandatory retirement age of 65, successfully challenged the law under the Charter of Rights and Freedoms, and mandatory retirement has effectively been abolished in most of Canada as a result.[23]

## Developing the Workforce

Once the most qualified applicants have been selected and offered positions, and they have accepted their offers, they must be formally introduced to the organization and trained so they can begin to be productive members of the workforce. **Orientation** familiarizes the newly hired employees with fellow workers, company procedures, and the physical properties of the company. It generally includes a tour of the building; introductions to supervisors, co-workers, and subordinates; and the distribution of organizational manuals describing the organization's policy on vacations, absenteeism, lunch breaks, company benefits, and so on. Orientation also involves socializing the new employee into the ethics and culture of the new company. Many larger companies show videos of procedures, facilities, and key personnel in the organization to help speed the adjustment process.

**orientation** familiarizing newly hired employees with fellow workers, company procedures, and the physical properties of the company

### Training and Development

**LO 10-3** Discuss how workers are trained and their performance appraised.

Although recruiting and selection are designed to find employees who have the knowledge, skills, and abilities the company needs, new employees still must undergo **training** to

**training** teaching employees to do specific job tasks through either classroom development or on-the-job experience

©Hero Images/Getty Images

Air Canada, which has been recognized as one of Canada's top diversity employers, has programs in place to support hiring women, Aboriginal Peoples, visible minorities, people with disabilities, and members of the LGBTQ community.

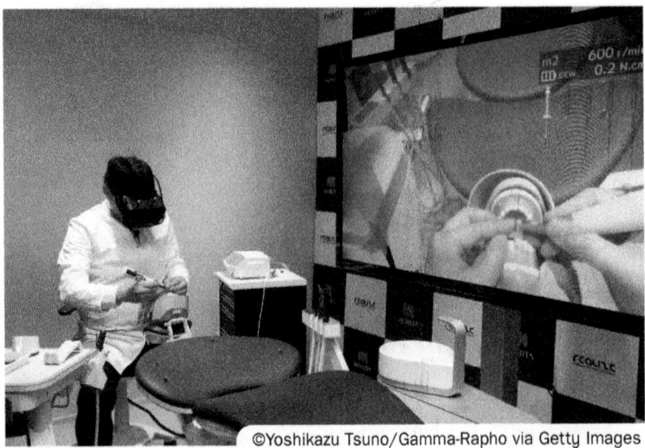

©Yoshikazu Tsuno/Gamma-Rapho via Getty Images

Virtual reality training is growing in popularity as it allows people to mimic real life situations and it appeals to a variety of learning styles.

learn how to do their specific job tasks. *On-the-job training* allows workers to learn by actually performing the tasks of the job, while *classroom training* teaches employees with lectures, conferences, videos, case studies, and web-based training. For instance, McDonald's trains those interested in company operations and leadership development at the Fred L. Turner Training Center, otherwise known as Hamburger University. Hamburger University employs full-time professors to train students in a variety of topics, including crew development, restaurant management, middle management, and executive development. Training includes classroom instruction, hands-on instruction, and computer e-learning.[24]

**Table 10.5 | General Performance Characteristics**

- **Productivity**—rate at which work is regularly produced
- **Quality**—accuracy, professionalism, and deliverability of produced work
- **Job knowledge**—understanding of the objectives, practices, and standards of work
- **Problem solving**—ability to identify and correct problems effectively
- **Communication**—effectiveness in written and verbal exchanges
- **Initiative**—willingness to identify and address opportunities for improvement
- **Adaptability**—ability to become comfortable with change
- **Planning and organization skills**—reflected through the ability to schedule projects, set goals, and maintain organizational systems
- **Teamwork and cooperation**—effectiveness of collaborations with co-workers
- **Judgment**—ability to determine appropriate actions in a timely manner
- **Dependability**—responsiveness, reliability, and conscientiousness demonstrated on the job
- **Creativity**—extent to which resourceful ideas, solutions, and methods for task completion are proposed
- **Sales**—demonstrated through success in selling products, services, yourself, and your company
- **Customer service**—ability to communicate effectively with customers, address problems, and offer solutions that meet or exceed their expectations
- **Leadership**—tendency and ability to serve as a doer, guide, decision maker, and role model
- **Financial management**—appropriateness of cost controls and financial planning within the scope defined by the position

**Development** is training that augments the skills and knowledge of managers and professionals. Training and development are also used to improve the skills of employees in their present positions and to prepare them for increased responsibility and job promotions. Training is therefore a vital function of human resources management. Use of role-plays, simulations, and online training methods are popular in employee training. Virtual reality (VR) training has emerged as a recent trend in training and development. VR training has many advantages, including its ability to mimic real life, simplify complex situations, improve retention and recall of information, and appeal to all learning styles.[25]

**development** training that augments the skills and knowledge of managers and professionals

## Assessing Performance

Assessing an employee's performance—their strengths and weaknesses on the job—is one of the most difficult tasks for managers. However, performance appraisal is crucial because it gives employees feedback on how they are doing and what they need to do to improve their performance. It also provides a basis for determining how to compensate and reward employees, and it generates information about the quality of the firm's selection, training, and development activities. Table 10.5 identifies 16 characteristics that may be assessed in a performance review.

Performance appraisals may be objective or subjective. An objective assessment is quantifiable. For example, a Westinghouse employee might be judged by how many circuit boards they typically produce in one day or by how many of their boards have defects. A Century 21 real estate agent might be judged by the number of houses they have shown or the number of sales they have closed. A company can also use tests as an objective method of assessment. Whatever method they use, managers must take into account the work environment in order to appraise performance objectively.

When jobs do not lend themselves to objective appraisal, the manager must relate the employee's performance to

©bluedog studio/Shutterstock

Performance appraisals are important because they provide employees with feedback on how well they are doing, as well as areas for improvement.

some other standard. One popular tool used in subjective assessment is the ranking system, which lists various performance factors on which the manager ranks employees against each other. Although used by many large companies, ranking systems are unpopular with many employees. Qualitative criteria, such as teamwork and communication skills, used to evaluate employees, are generally hard to gauge.

Such grading systems have triggered employee lawsuits that allege discrimination in grade/ranking assignments. For example, one manager may grade a company's employees one way, while another manager grades a group more harshly, depending on the managers' grading style. If layoffs occur, then employees graded by the second manager may be more likely to lose their jobs. Other criticisms of grading systems include unclear wording or inappropriate words that a manager may unintentionally write in a performance evaluation, like *young* or *good-looking* to describe an employee's appearance. These liabilities can all be fodder for lawsuits should employees allege that they were treated unfairly. It is therefore crucial that managers use clear language in performance evaluations and be consistent with all employees. Several employee grading computer packages have been developed to make performance evaluations easier for managers and clearer for employees.[26]

Another performance appraisal method used by many companies is the 360-degree feedback system, which provides feedback from a panel that typically includes superiors, peers, and subordinates. Because of the tensions it may cause, peer appraisal appears to be difficult for many. However, companies that have success with 360-degree feedback tend to be open to learning and willing to experiment, and are led by executives who are direct about the expected benefits as well as the challenges.[27] Managers and leaders with a high emotional intelligence (sensitivity to their own as well as others' emotions) assess and reflect upon their interactions with colleagues on a daily basis. In addition, they conduct follow-up analysis on their projects, asking the right questions and listening carefully to responses without being defensive about their actions.[28]

Whether the assessment is objective or subjective, it is vital that the manager discuss the results with the employee, so that the employee knows how well he or she is doing the job. The results of a performance appraisal become useful only when they are communicated, tactfully, to the employee and presented as a tool to allow the employee to grow and improve in their position and beyond. Performance appraisals are also used to determine whether an employee should be promoted, transferred, or terminated from the organization.

"The results of a performance appraisal become useful only when they are communicated, tactfully, to the employee and presented as a tool to allow the employee to grow and improve in their position and beyond."

## Consider the Following: Morale among the survivors

Medallion Corporation manufactures quality carpeting and linoleum. A recession and subsequent downturn in home sales sharply cut the company's sales. Medallion found itself in the unenviable position of having to lay off hundreds of employees in the home office (the manufacturing facilities) as well as many salespeople. Employees were called in on Friday afternoon and told about their status in individual meetings with their supervisors. The laid-off employees were given one additional month of work and two weeks' severance pay per year of service, along with the opportunity to sign up for classes to help with the transition, including job search tactics and resumé writing.

Several months after the cutbacks, morale was at an all-time low for the company, although productivity had improved. Medallion brought in consultants, who suggested that the leaner, flatter organizational structure would be suitable for more team activities. Medallion therefore set up task forces and teams to deal with employee concerns, but the diversity of the workforce led to conflict and misunderstandings among team members. Medallion is evaluating how to proceed with this new team approach.*

### DISCUSSION QUESTIONS

1. What did Medallion's HRM department do right in dealing with the employees who were laid off?
2. What are some of the potential problems that must be dealt with after an organization experiences a major trauma such as massive layoffs?
3. What can Medallion do to make the team approach work more smoothly? What role do you think diversity training should play?

*O.C. Ferrell, Geoffrey Hirt, Rick Bates, Elliott Currie, *Business: A Changing World, Second Canadian Edition* (Toronto: McGraw-Hill Ryerson, 2003), p. 258.

©Stephanie De Sakutin/AFP/Getty Images

Amazon holds a job fair in the virtual world Second Life. Companies have started using digital media for posting job applications, holding job fairs, and even training employees.

## Turnover

**LO 10-4** Identify the types of turnover companies may experience, and explain why turnover is an important issue.

**Turnover**, which occurs when employees quit or are fired, promoted, or transferred and must be replaced by new employees, results in lost productivity from the vacancy, fees to recruit replacement employees, management time devoted to interviewing, and training costs for new employees. Some companies are able to manage their employees effectively to minimize turnover. However, some companies have created innovative solutions for reducing turnover.

**turnover** occurs when employees quit or are fired, promoted, or transferred, and must be replaced by new employees

After learning that its employees felt micromanaged, Best Buy implemented a system for some of its employees called Results Only Work Environment (ROWE) to reduce turnover and increase employee morale. Under this program, employees who were able to do their work away from the workplace could choose to do so. The initiative offered flexibility and a better work–life balance for employees. A study that analyzed the impact of ROWE found that employee turnover had decreased by 45 percent.[29, 30] Part of the reason for turnover may be overworked employees as a result of downsizing and a lack of training and advancement opportunities.[31]

Figure 10.1 provides some of the top reasons employees give for leaving the company. Of course, turnover is not always an unhappy occasion when it takes the form of a promotion or transfer.

Many companies in recent years are choosing to downsize by eliminating jobs. Reasons for downsizing might be due to financial constraints or the need to become more productive and competitive.

A **job promotion** is an advancement to a higher-level position with increased authority, responsibility, and pay. In some companies and most labour unions, seniority—the length of time a person has been with the company or at a particular job classification—is the key issue in determining who should be promoted. Most managers base promotions on seniority only when they have candidates with equal qualifications: managers prefer to base promotions on merit.

**job promotion** advancement to a higher-level position with increased authority, responsibility, and pay

**transfer** a move to another job within the company at essentially the same level and wage

**separations** employment changes involving resignation, retirement, termination, or layoff

A **transfer** is a move to another job within the company at essentially the same level and wage. Transfers allow workers to obtain new skills or to find a new position within an organization when their old position has been eliminated because of automation or downsizing.

**Separations** occur when employees resign, retire, are terminated, or are laid off. Employees may be terminated, or fired, for poor performance, violation of work rules, absenteeism, and so on. Businesses have traditionally

**Figure 10.1** | Reasons Employees Do Not Work Out in a Position (aside from poor performance)

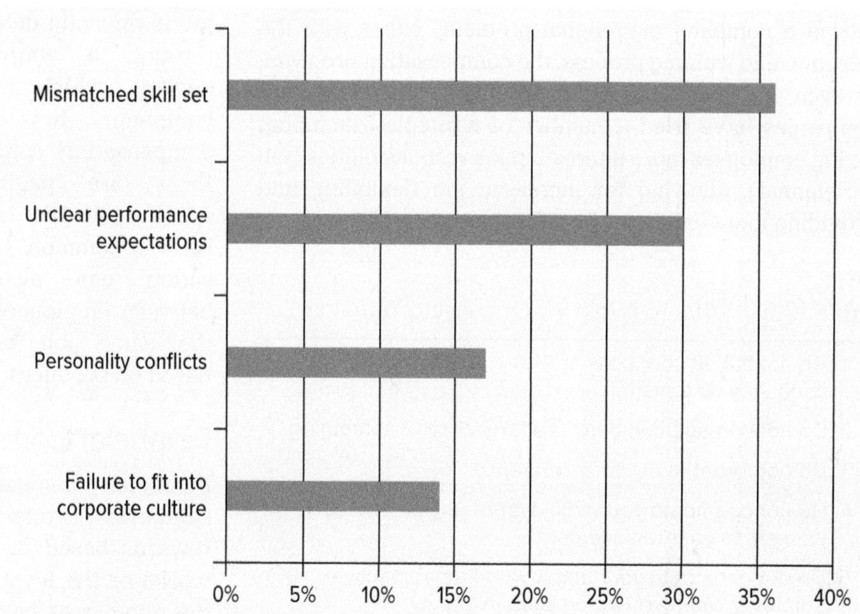

been able to fire employees *at will,* that is, for any reason other than for race, religion, sex, or age, or because an employee is a union organizer. However, legislation and court decisions require that companies fire employees fairly, for just cause only.

Managers must take care, then, to warn employees when their performance is unacceptable and may lead to dismissal. They should also document all problems and warnings in employees' work records. To avoid the possibility of lawsuits from individuals who may feel they have been fired unfairly, employers should provide clear, business-related reasons for any firing, supported by written documentation if possible. Employee disciplinary procedures should be carefully explained to all employees and should be set forth in employee handbooks. Table 10.6 illustrates what *not* to do when you are terminated.

Many companies have downsized in recent years, laying off tens of thousands of employees in their effort to become more productive and competitive. For example, Target had to lay off more than 17,000 workers after it decided to close 133 stores in Canada. Disappointing sales convinced Target to adapt its marketing strategy and suspend its Canadian operations.[32] Layoffs are sometimes temporary; employees may be brought back when business conditions improve. When layoffs are to be permanent, employers often help employees find other jobs and may extend benefits while the employees search for new employment. Such actions help lessen the trauma of the layoffs.

A well-organized human resources department strives to minimize losses due to separations and transfers because recruiting and training new employees is very expensive. For example, Loblaw Companies Ltd. shifted more of its employees to full-time work with plans to convert 10,000 part-time positions to full-time work in the coming years. The company says that the move should reduce staff turnover and improve productivity.[33] Note that a high turnover rate in a company may signal problems either with the selection and training process, the compensation program, or even the type of company. To help reduce turnover, companies have tried a number of strategies, including giving employees more interesting job responsibilities (job enrichment), allowing for increased job flexibility, and providing more employee benefits.

**Table 10.6** | What to Avoid When Leaving Your Job

| |
|---|
| 1. Do not tell off your boss and co-workers, even if you think they deserve it. |
| 2. Do not damage company property or steal something. |
| 3. Do not forget to ask for a reference. |
| 4. Do not badmouth your employer or any of your co-workers to your replacement. |
| 5. Do not badmouth your employer to a prospective employer when you go on a job interview. |

©thodonal88/Shutterstock

Some companies are able to manage their employees more effectively to minimize turnover.

# Compensating the Workforce

**LO 10-5** Specify the various ways a worker may be compensated.

People generally don't work for free, and how much they are paid for their work is a complicated issue. Also, designing a fair compensation plan is an important task because pay and benefits represent a substantial portion of an organization's expenses. Wages that are too high may result in the company's products being priced too high, making them uncompetitive in the market. Wages that are too low may damage employee morale and result in costly turnover. Remember that compensation is one of the hygiene factors identified by Herzberg.

Designing a fair compensation plan is a difficult task because it involves evaluating the relative worth of all jobs within the business while allowing for individual efforts. Compensation for a specific job is typically determined through a **wage/salary survey**, which tells the company how much compensation comparable firms are paying for specific jobs that the firms have in common. Compensation can also vary between employees within the same job category, based on productivity.

**wage/salary survey** a study that tells a company how much compensation comparable firms are paying for specific jobs that the firms have in common

**wages** financial rewards based on the number of hours the employee works or the level of output achieved

## Financial Compensation

Financial compensation falls into two general categories—wages and salaries. **Wages** are financial rewards based on the number of hours the employee works or the level of output achieved. Wages based on the number of hours worked are called time wages. In

Canada, the general minimum wage varies by province or territory, with a high of $13 per hour in Nunavut and a low of $10.50 per hour in Saskatchewan and Newfoundland and Labrador (as of October 2016).[34] Table 10.7 compares the current minimum wage across the country. As previously discussed in this chapter, the impending shortage of labour will result in increased levels of compensation, especially for skilled workers in Canada.

Time wages are appropriate when employees are continually interrupted and when quality is more important than quantity. Assembly-line workers, clerks, and maintenance personnel are commonly paid on a time-wage basis. The advantage of time wages is the ease of computation. The disadvantage is that time wages provide no incentive to increase productivity. In fact, time wages may encourage employees to be less productive.

To overcome these disadvantages, many companies pay on an incentive system, using piece wages or commissions. Piece wages are based on the level of output achieved. A major advantage of piece wages is that they motivate employees to supervise their own activities and to increase output. Skilled craftworkers are often paid on a piece-wage basis.

The other incentive system, **commission**, pays a fixed amount or a percentage of the employee's sales. At GoodLife Fitness trainers are paid minimum wage for the hours they are in clubs prospecting for new clients. For training sessions, they split the hourly rate with GoodLife, from about 40/60 to 50/50, and get paid a 10 percent commission on sales.[35] This method motivates employees to sell as much as they can. Some companies combine payment based on commission with time wages or salaries.

**commission** an incentive system that pays a fixed amount or a percentage of the employee's sales

A **salary** is a financial reward calculated on a weekly, monthly, or annual basis. Salaries are associated with white-collar workers such as office personnel, executives, and professional employees. Although a salary provides a stable stream of income, salaried workers may be required to work beyond the usual hours without additional financial compensation.

**salary** a financial reward calculated on a weekly, monthly, or annual basis

**bonuses** monetary rewards offered by companies for exceptional performance as incentives to further increase productivity

**profit sharing** a form of compensation whereby a percentage of company profits is distributed to the employees whose work helped to generate them

In addition to the basic wages or salaries paid to employees, a company may offer **bonuses** for exceptional performance as an incentive to increase productivity further. Many workers receive a bonus as a thank-you for good work and an incentive to continue working hard. Many owners and managers are recognizing that simple bonuses and perks foster happier employees and reduce turnover. For example, Canadian Western Bank offers employees a number of incentives, including contributions to RSPs and an employee share-purchase plan. Atlantic Canada–based Maritime Travel offers employees free trips and other travel rewards if they meet their sales targets.[36]

Another form of compensation is **profit sharing**, which distributes a percentage of company profits to the employees whose work helped to generate those profits. For example, twice a year WestJet employees share in the company's profits. In addition, performance awards are distributed once a year based on the company reaching targets, including safety and on-time performance.

Some profit-sharing plans involve distributing shares of company stock to employees. Usually referred to as ESOPs—employee stock ownership plans—they have been gaining popularity in recent years. One reason for the popularity of ESOPs is the sense of partnership that they create between the organization and employees. Profit sharing can also motivate employees to work hard, because increased productivity and sales mean that the profits or the stock dividends will increase.

WestJet management attributes much of its success to the fact that approximately 85 percent of its employees own shares in the company. Senior management has noted that employees who own shares in the business have a vested interest in the

**Table 10.7** | Provincial/Territorial Minimum Wage, October 2019

| Jurisdiction | Wage ($C/h) | Effective Date |
|---|---|---|
| Alberta | 15.00 | October 1, 2018 |
| British Columbia | 13.85 | June 1, 2019 |
| Manitoba | 11.65 | October 1, 2019 |
| New Brunswick | 11.50 | April 1, 2019 |
| Newfoundland and Labrador | 11.40 | April 1, 2019 |
| Northwest Territories | 13.46 | April 1, 2019 |
| Nova Scotia | 11.55 | April 1, 2019 |
| Nunavut | 13.00 | April 1, 2016 |
| Ontario | 14.00 | January 1, 2018 |
| Prince Edward Island | 12.25 | April 1, 2019 |
| Quebec | 12.00 | May 1, 2018 |
| Saskatchewan | 11.00 | October 1, 2018 |
| Yukon | 12.71 | April 1, 2019 |

©JGI/Tom Grill/Getty Images

An onsite fitness centre is just one of the benefits that large companies have begun to offer employees. Such onsite benefits as fitness and child care facilities are particularly important for employees who work long hours or who struggle to maintain a healthy work-life balance.

company succeeding, and they will often go the extra mile to ensure that customers are happy.[37]

Many organizations offer employees a stake in the company through stock purchase plans, ESOPs, or stock investments through RRSP plans. Various studies show that 7 to 10 percent of Canadian workers participate in some form of employee ownership. For instance, Flynn Canada, a Toronto-based trade contractor that makes and installs the outer layers of buildings, known as the building envelope, has some 60 owners.[38]

Until recently, employees below senior management levels rarely received stock options. Companies are adopting broad-based stock option plans to build a stronger link between employees' interests and the organization's interests. ESOPs have met with enormous success over the years, and employee-owned stock has even outperformed the stock market during certain periods. Many businesses have found employee stock options a great way to boost productivity and increase morale.

## Benefits

**Benefits** are non-financial forms of compensation provided to employees, such as pension plans for retirement; health, disability, and life insurance; holidays and paid days off for vacation or illness; credit union membership; health programs; child care; elder care; assistance with adoption; and more. According to Statistics Canada, the total cost of employee benefits has risen faster than wages with costs to employers increasing two to three times the rate of inflation. Legally required

**benefits** non-financial forms of compensation provided to employees, such as pension plans, health insurance, paid vacation and holidays, and the like

### GOING GREEN

### Google Rewards Employees for Being Sustainable

Google's environmental mission is clear: the company strives to build sustainability into everything they do. For employees at Google, it pays to be green. Google employees can save money, donate to charities, and receive discounts on eco-friendly technology by taking advantage of the company's green incentives. For instance, employees can save fuel costs by riding to work on Google's biodiesel shuttles. They can also use Google's GFleet car-sharing program, GBikes, or GRide taxi service for travelling across the company campus or attending meetings offsite. If employees choose to bike, walk, or pogo to work, the company provides them with digital stamps, which can be redeemed for company donations to the employee's favourite charity.

Many of Google's green initiatives help both employees and society. Google remains one of the largest supporters of SolarCity with its $280 million fund to support the installation of solar panels on residential homes. While it may be difficult to convince the average consumer to adopt solar technology, Google offers its employees discounts. The company also created the largest corporate electronic-vehicle charging station in the country, not only to support the electric vehicles in its GFleet, but to inspire employees to purchase their own. Google seeks to make a difference in the field of sustainability—starting with its employees.*

#### DISCUSSION QUESTIONS

1. Describe some of Google's green initiatives.
2. How is Google rewarding employees for adopting greener behaviours?
3. Why do you think it might be beneficial for Google to subsidize the cost of installing solar panels on employee houses, even if it costs the company money?

*Alison van Diggelen, "Working@Google: Green Carrots & Pogo Sticks," Fresh Dialogues, www.freshdialogues.com/ (accessed November 9, 2011); "Can We Commute Carbon-Free," Google Green, www.google.com/green/operations/commuting-carbon-free.html (accessed November 9, 2011); Tiffany Hsu, "Google Creates $280-Million Solar Power Fund," *Los Angeles Times*, June 14, 2011, http://articles.latimes.com/2011/jun/14/business/la-fi-google-solar-20110614 (accessed November 9, 2011).

benefits—Canada Pension Plan, workers' compensation, and Employment Insurance—account for some of the increase in costs, but increases in non-mandatory benefits such as health and dental plans account for the majority of the increase.[39] Such benefits increase employee security and, to a certain extent, morale and motivation. Table 10.8 lists some of the benefits that Google offers its employees.

"The most common counselling services offered include drug and alcohol-abuse treatment programs, fitness programs, smoking cessation clinics, stress-management clinics, financial counselling, family counselling, and career counselling."

Surveys have revealed that fewer benefits come with a decrease in employee loyalty. Only 42 percent of employees say they feel a strong sense of loyalty to their employers. However, more than half of respondents indicated that employee benefits were important in decisions to stay with the company. Benefits are particularly important to younger generations of employees.[40] Starbucks recognizes that benefits can significantly impact an employee's health and well-being. As a result, it is the only fast-food company to offer its part-time employees health insurance.

A benefit increasingly offered is the employee assistance program (EAP). Each company's EAP is different, but most offer counselling for and assistance with personal problems that might hurt employees' job performance if not addressed. The most common counselling services offered include drug- and alcohol-abuse treatment programs, fitness programs, smoking cessation clinics, stress-management clinics, financial counselling, family counselling, and career counselling. EAPs help reduce costs associated with poor productivity, absenteeism, and other workplace issues by helping employees deal with personal problems that contribute to these issues. For example, exercise and fitness programs reduce health insurance costs by helping employees stay healthy. Family counselling may help workers trying to cope with a divorce or other personal problems better focus on their jobs.

Companies try to provide the benefits they believe their employees want, but diverse people may want different things. In recent years, some single workers have felt that co-workers with spouses and children seem to get special breaks and extra time off to deal with family issues. Some companies use flexible benefit programs to allow employees to choose the benefits they would like, up to a specified amount.

Fringe benefits include sick leave, vacation pay, pension plans, health plans, and any other extra compensation. Soft benefits include perks that help balance life and work. They include onsite child care, spas, food service, and even laundry services and hair salons. These soft benefits motivate employees and give them more time to focus on their jobs.

Cafeteria-style benefit plans provide a financial amount to employees so that they can select the specific benefits that fit their needs. The key is making benefits flexible, rather than giving employees identical benefits. As firms go global, the need for cafeteria or flexible benefit plans becomes even more important. For some employees, benefits are a greater motivator and differentiator in jobs than wages.

Over the last two decades, the list of fringe benefits has grown dramatically, and new benefits are being added every year.

**Table 10.8** | Google's Employee Benefits

- Health insurance:
  - Dental insurance
  - Vision insurance
- Vacation (15 days per year for one to three years' employment; 20 days off after three years; 25 days for more than five years' employment)
- Unpaid three month leave of absence eligibility
- Twelve paid holidays/year
- Savings plans including matching RRSP contributions in Canada and 50% 401K match up to $8250 in the U.S.
- Disability and life insurance
- Employee assistance program
- Free lunches and snacks
- Massages, gym membership, hair stylist, fitness class, and bike repair
- Weekly activities
- Maternity and parental leave
- Adoption assistance
- Tuition reimbursement
- Employee referral plan
- Onsite doctor
- Backup child care
- Holiday parties, health fair, credit union, roller hockey, outdoor volleyball court, discounts for local attractions
- Dogs are welcome
- Extensive death benefits including for the spouse and children of former Google employees

## Managing Unionized Employees

**LO 10-6** Discuss some of the issues associated with unionized employees, including collective bargaining and dispute resolution.

Employees who are dissatisfied with their working conditions or compensation have to negotiate with management

**labour unions** employee organizations formed to deal with employers for achieving better pay, hours, and working conditions

**collective bargaining** the negotiation process through which management and unions reach an agreement about compensation, working hours, and working conditions for the bargaining unit

**labour contract** the formal, written document that spells out the relationship between the union and management for a specified period of time—usually two or three years

to bring about change. Dealing with management on an individual basis is not always effective, however, so employees may organize themselves into **labour unions** to deal with employers and to achieve better pay, hours, and working conditions. Organized employees are backed by the power of a large group that can hire specialists to represent the entire union in its dealings with management.

Canada has a 28.8 percent unionization rate. However, union growth has slowed in recent years,[41] and prospects for improvement do not look good. One reason is that most blue-collar workers, the traditional members of unions, have already been organized. Factories have become more automated and need fewer blue-collar workers. Canada has shifted from a manufacturing to a service economy, further reducing the demand for blue-collar workers. Moreover, in response to foreign competition, Canadian companies are scrambling to find ways to become more productive and cost efficient. Job enrichment programs and participative management have blurred the line between management and workers. Because workers' say in the way plants are run is increasing, their need for union protection is decreasing.

Nonetheless, labour unions have been successful in organizing blue-collar manufacturing, government, and health care workers, as well as smaller percentages of employees in other industries. Consequently, significant aspects of HRM, particularly compensation, are dictated to a large degree by union contracts at many companies. Therefore, we'll take a brief look at collective bargaining and dispute resolution in this section.

## Collective Bargaining

**Collective bargaining** is the negotiation process through which management and unions reach an agreement about compensation, working hours, and working conditions for the bargaining unit (Figure 10.2). The objective of negotiations is to reach agreement about a **labour contract**, the formal, written document that spells out the relationship between the union and management for a specified period of time, usually two or three years.

In collective bargaining, each side tries to negotiate an agreement that meets its demands; compromise is frequently necessary. Management tries to negotiate a labour contract that permits the company to retain control over things like work schedules; the hiring and firing of workers; production standards; promotions, transfers, and separations; the span of management in each department; and discipline. Unions tend to focus on contract issues such as magnitude of wages; better pay rates for overtime, holidays, and undesirable shifts; scheduling of pay increases; and benefits. These issues will be spelled out in the labour contract, which union members will vote to either accept (and abide by) or reject.

Many labour contracts contain a *cost-of-living allowance* (COLA), or cost-of-living escalator clause, which calls for automatic wage increases during periods of inflation to protect the "real" income of the employees. During tough economic times, unions may be forced to accept *givebacks*—wage and benefit concessions made to

**Figure 10.2** | The Collective Bargaining Process

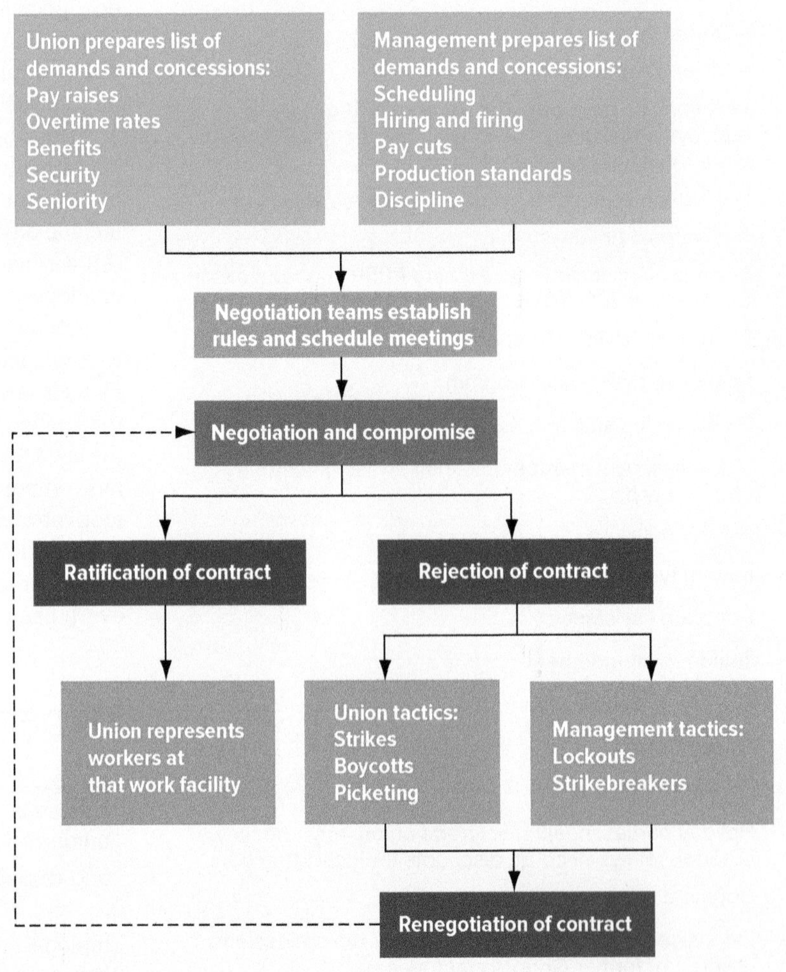

employers to allow them to remain competitive or, in some cases, to survive and continue to provide jobs for union workers.

## Resolving Disputes

Sometimes, management and labour simply cannot agree on a contract. Most labour disputes are handled through collective bargaining or through grievance procedures. When these processes break down, however, either side may resort to more drastic measures to achieve its objectives.

**Labour Tactics.** **Picketing** is a public protest against management practices and involves union members marching (often waving anti-management signs and placards) at the employer's place of business. Picketing workers hope that their signs will arouse sympathy for their demands from the public and from other unions. Picketing may occur as a protest or in conjunction with a strike.

**Strikes** (employee walkouts) are one of the most effective weapons labour has. By striking, a union makes carrying out the normal operations of a business difficult at best and impossible at worst. Strikes receive widespread publicity, but they remain a weapon of last resort. For example, Canada witnessed a significant slowdown in mail delivery when the Canada Postal Union began a series of rotating strikes in 2018. The postal strike started in the fall of 2018 and was timed to negatively impact consumers shopping over the December holidays. The rotating strikes resulted in a significant slow down in mail delivery and it only ended when the federal government adopted legislation forcing the postal workers back to work.[42] The threat of a strike is often enough to get management to back down. In fact, the number of worker-days actually lost to strikes is less than the amount lost to the common cold.

A **boycott** is an attempt to keep people from purchasing the products of a company. In a boycott, union members are asked not to do business with the boycotted organization. Some unions may even impose fines on members who ignore the boycott. To gain further support for their objectives, a union involved in a boycott may also ask the public—through picketing and advertising—not to purchase the products of the picketed firm.

**picketing** a public protest against management practices that involves union members marching and carrying anti-management signs at the employer's plant

**strikes** employee walkouts; one of the most effective weapons labour has

**boycott** an attempt to keep people from purchasing the products of a company

**lockout** management's version of a strike, wherein a worksite is closed so that employees cannot go to work

**Management Tactics.** Management's version of a strike is the **lockout**; management actually closes a worksite so that employees cannot go to work. Lockouts are used, as a general rule, only when a union strike has partially shut down a plant and it seems less expensive for the plant to close completely. Caterpillar locked out workers from its 62-year-old plant in Ontario after failure to reach an agreement with unionized employees over wages. In a controversial move, Caterpillar then announced it would close the plant entirely and relocate to Indiana. The wages of factory workers in Indiana would not be as high as those paid to the company's Canadian workers.[43]

©Cole Burston/Bloomberg via Getty Images

Canadian postal workers engaged in as series of rotating strikes in 2018. The federal government ultimately stepped in and used back-to-work legislation to force the workers to deliver the mail under the terms of their previous contract.

**Strikebreakers**, called "scabs" by striking union members, are people hired by management to replace striking employees. Managers hire strikebreakers to continue operations and reduce the losses associated with strikes—and to show the unions that they will not bow to their demands. Strikebreaking is generally a last-resort measure for management because it does great damage to the relationship between management and labour.

**strikebreakers** people hired by management to replace striking employees; called "scabs" by striking union members

**conciliation** a method of outside resolution of labour and management differences in which a third party is brought in to keep the two sides talking

**Outside Resolution.** Management and union members normally reach mutually agreeable decisions without outside assistance. Sometimes though, even after lengthy negotiations, strikes, lockouts, and other tactics, management and labour still cannot resolve a contract dispute. In such cases, they have three choices: conciliation, mediation, and arbitration.

**Conciliation** is when a neutral third party is brought in to keep labour and management talking. The conciliator has no formal power over union representatives or over management. The conciliator's goal is to get

**mediation** a method of outside resolution of labour and management differences in which the third party's role is to suggest or propose a solution to the problem

**arbitration** settlement of a labour/management dispute by a third party whose solution is legally binding and enforceable

**diversity** the participation of different ages, genders, races, ethnicities, nationalities, and abilities in the workplace

both parties to focus on the issues and to prevent negotiations from breaking down. Like conciliation, **mediation** involves bringing in a neutral third party, but the mediator's role is to suggest or propose a solution to the problem. Mediators have no formal power over either labour or management.

With **arbitration**, a neutral third party is brought in to settle the dispute, but the arbitrator's solution is legally binding and enforceable. Generally, arbitration takes place on a voluntary basis—management and labour must agree to it, and they usually split the cost (the arbitrator's fee and expenses) between them. Occasionally, management and labour submit to *compulsory arbitration,* in which an outside party (usually the federal government) requests arbitration as a means of eliminating a prolonged strike that threatens to disrupt the economy.

# The Importance of Workforce Diversity

**LO 10-7** Describe the importance of diversity in the workforce.

Customers, employees, suppliers—all the participants in the world of business—come in different ages, genders, races, ethnicities, nationalities, and abilities, a truth that business has come to label **diversity**. Understanding this diversity means recognizing and accepting differences as well as valuing the unique perspectives such differences can bring to the workplace.

## The Characteristics of Diversity

When managers speak of diverse workforces, they typically mean differences in gender and race. While gender and race are important characteristics of diversity, others are also important. We can divide these differences into primary and secondary characteristics of diversity. In the lower segment of Figure 10.3, age, gender, race, ethnicity, abilities, and sexual orientation represent *primary characteristics* of diversity which are inborn and cannot be changed. In the upper section of Figure 10.3 are eight *secondary characteristics* of diversity—work background, income, marital status, military experience, religious beliefs, geographic location, parental status, and education—which *can* be changed. We acquire, change, and discard them as we progress through our lives.

Defining characteristics of diversity as either primary or secondary enhances our understanding, but we must remember that each person is defined by the interrelation of all characteristics. In dealing with diversity in the workforce, managers must consider the complete person—not one or a few of a person's differences.

## Why Is Diversity Important?

The Canadian workforce is becoming increasingly diverse. More and more companies are trying to improve HRM programs to recruit, develop, and retain greater diversity among employees to better serve their diverse customers. Some firms are providing special programs, such as sponsored affinity groups, mentoring programs, and special career development opportunities. For example, Manulife has recently included diversity and inclusion accountability into performance goals for its leadership teams and AMEX Canada has introduced a strategy to develop and support women leaders.[44]

**Figure 10.3** | Characteristics of Diversity

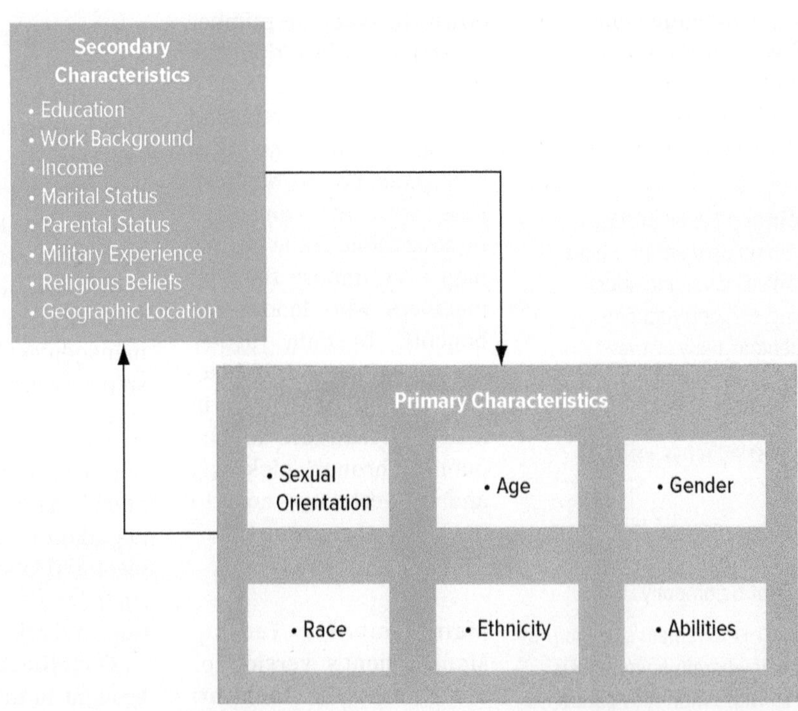


Source: Marilyn Loden and Judy B. Rosener, *Workforce America! Managing Employee Diversity as a Vital Resource*, 1991, p. 20. Used with permission. Copyright © 1991 The McGraw-Hill Companies.

Corporate Canada is also aware of the upcoming labour shortage and is becoming increasingly aware that eliminating barriers to potential employees could eliminate part of this problem. In fact, a recent study completed by RBC found that eliminating age, gender, and cultural barriers could bring an additional 1.6 million Canadians to the workforce.[45] Effectively managing diversity in the workforce involves cultivating and valuing its benefits and minimizing its problems. In order for diversity to thrive, a company's leadership must support the concept and create an organizational culture where diverse workers can succeed.

Business journalist Diane Jermyn states that diversity doesn't just happen on its own, rather, senior leadership must embrace the concept, create a plan, and act in order to create a diverse workplace.[46] For example, Molly Ford, a senior manager at Salesforce, says that at the start of every fiscal year the first thing the company does is outline its values, with equality as a core value. Equality at Salesforce includes equal rights, non-discrimination, and equal access to educational opportunities.[47]

Companies that are championing diversity are also becoming aware of the impact a diverse workforce can have on their financial performance. For example, it has been found that companies with a more diverse leadership teams were 33 percent more likely to see better than average profits. For a list of top Canadian companies that practise diversity in hiring, go to the Canada's Best Diversity Employers website at www.canadastop100.com/diversity.

©FatCamera/Getty Images

Firms that embrace diversity at the leadership level are 33 percent more likely to earn higher profits.

## Consider the Following: Is it ethical for businesses to punish employees for smoking?

For years, companies have offered wellness plans aimed at improving employee health and reducing health care costs. Many of these plans include smoking cessation programs to help employees kick the habit. Statistics reveal that smokers cost businesses 18 percent more than non-smokers.

With health care costs rising, companies are concocting ways to tackle the smoking problem. Many employers are instituting additional insurance charges for employees who smoke. Employees participating in smoking cessation clinics can have their insurance costs deferred. Those who successfully kick the habit—roughly 25 percent—never pay. However, a growing number of employers such as Whirlpool Jet Boat Tours, Union Pacific, Scotts Miracle-Gro, and the Cleveland Clinic simply refuse to hire smokers.*

These choices raise questions concerning employee rights. Critics are accusing these companies of discrimination. They point to the fact that tobacco use is not illegal, and the decision to use it is a private one. However, smoking is not a right protected by law, and legal reactions to this topic are mixed. While a number of courts have backed companies refusing to hire smokers, certain states have passed laws forbidding the practice. Those studying the issue feel the hiring ban is ineffective. They argue that to reduce the number of smokers, one must help them quit. A number of smokers agree, but others are thankful for the incentive to kick a highly addictive habit.**

### DISCUSSION QUESTIONS

1. Why are employers worried about the health care costs of employees who smoke?
2. What are some initiatives employers are adopting to persuade smokers to kick the habit?
3. Do you think it is ethical for employers to create disincentives for smoking?

*Tom Blackwell, "Canadian employer hasn't hire a smoker in 30 years, and 'I am proud of it,' but the policy may be illegal," https://nationalpost.com/health/canadian-employer-hasnt-hired-a-smoker-in-30-years-and-im-proud-of-it-but-the-policy-may-be-illegal, February 28, 2016.

**Pat Wechsler, "And You Thought Cigarettes Were Pricey," *Bloomberg BusinessWeek*, July 4–10, 2011; pp. 24–26; A.G. Sulzberger, "Hospitals Shift Smoking Ban to Smokers Ban," *New York Times*, February 10, 2011, www.nytimes.com/2011/02/11/us/11smoking.html?pagewanted5all (accessed August 12, 2011); Ken Alltucker, "Humana Won't Hire Smokers in Arizona," *USA Today*, July 1, 2011, www.usatoday.com/money/industries/health/2011-06-30-smokers-jobs-humana_n.htm (accessed August 16, 2011).

## The Benefits of Workforce Diversity

There are a number of benefits to fostering and valuing workforce diversity, including the following:

1. More productive use of a company's human resources
2. Reduced conflict among employees of different ethnicities, races, religions, and sexual orientations as they learn to respect each other's differences
3. More productive working relationships among diverse employees as they learn more about and accept each other
4. Increased commitment to and sharing of organizational goals among diverse employees at all organizational levels
5. Increased innovation and creativity as diverse employees bring new, unique perspectives to decision-making and problem-solving tasks
6. Increased ability to serve the needs of an increasingly diverse customer base[48]

Companies that do not value their diverse employees are likely to experience greater conflict, as well as prejudice and discrimination. Among individual employees, for example, racial slurs and gestures, sexist comments, and other behaviours by co-workers harm the individuals at whom such behaviour is directed. The victims of such behaviour may feel hurt, depressed, or even threatened and suffer from lowered self-esteem, all of which harm their productivity and morale. In such cases, women and minority employees may simply leave the firm, wasting the time, money, and other resources spent on hiring and training them. When discrimination comes from a supervisor, employees may also fear for their jobs. A discriminatory atmosphere not only can harm productivity and increase turnover, but may also subject a firm to costly lawsuits and negative publicity.

Astute business leaders recognize that they need to modify their human resources management programs to target the needs of *all* their diverse employees as well as the needs of the firm itself. They realize that the benefits of diversity are long term in nature and come only to those organizations willing to make the commitment. Most importantly, as workforce diversity becomes a valued organizational asset, companies spend less time managing conflict and more time accomplishing tasks and satisfying customers, which is, after all, the purpose of business.

©Inti St Clair/Blend Images LLC

Some of the major benefits of diversity include a wider range of employee perspectives, greater innovation and creativity, and the ability to target a diverse customer base more effectively.

"Companies that do not value their diverse employees are likely to experience greater conflict, as well as prejudice and discrimination."

## Employment Equity

Employee equity emerged in Canada in 1986. The *Employment Equity Act* is designed to ensure that women, Aboriginal Peoples, people with disabilities, and visible minorities receive the same employment opportunities as all Canadians.

# Trends in Management of the Workforce

Because of economic uncertainty, austerity has pervaded the workplace and inflated productivity. While companies are squeezing workers to cut costs, they are also drawing clear lines between workers and managers and are reducing privileges and benefits.

The nature of the workplace is changing as well. The increasing use of smart phones and tablet computers are blurring the lines between leisure and work time, with some employers calling employees after hours.[49] Employees themselves are mixing work and personal time by using social media in the office. In fact, theft of time is the number one ethical issue recorded by the Ethics Resource Center.[50] This is requiring companies to come up with new policies that limit how employees can use social media in the workplace. Clearly, technology is changing the dynamics of the workplace in both positive and negative ways.

It is important for human resources managers to be aware of legal issues regarding worker rights. Interestingly, although it might currently be legal for employers to request an applicant's Facebook password, employees who "rant" about their employers on Facebook can receive some form of legal protection. Threats, on the other hand, are not protected.[51] Hence, human resources managers should understand these issues to ensure that an employee is not wrongfully terminated.

Despite the grim outlook of the past few years, hiring trends appear to be on the rise. Companies are finding that as consumer demands rise, their current employees are hitting the limits of productivity, requiring firms to hire more workers.[52] This will require firms to not only know about relevant employee laws, but also to understand how benefits and employee morale can contribute to overall productivity. Many of the most successful firms have discovered ways to balance costs with the well-being of their employees.

## TEAM EXERCISE

Form groups and go to monster.com. Look up job descriptions for positions in business (account executive in advertising, marketing manager, human resources director, production supervisor, financial analyst, bank teller, etc.). What are the key requirements for the position that you have been assigned (education, work experience, language/computer skills, etc.)? Does the position announcement provide a thorough understanding of the job? Was any key information omitted that you would have expected to see? Report your findings to the class.

# LEARNING OBJECTIVES SUMMARY

**LO 10-1** Define human resources management and explain its significance.

Human resources, or personnel, management refers to all the activities involved in determining an organization's human resources needs and acquiring, training, and compensating people to fill those needs. It is concerned with maximizing the satisfaction of employees and improving their efficiency to meet organizational objectives.

**LO 10-2** Summarize the processes of recruiting and selecting human resources for a company.

The human resources manager must determine the firm's future human resources needs and develop a strategy to meet them. Recruiting is the formation of a pool of qualified applicants from which management will select employees; it takes place both internally and externally. Selection is the process of collecting information about applicants and using that information to decide which ones to hire; it includes the application, interviewing, testing, and reference checking.

**LO 10-3** Discuss how workers are trained and their performance appraised.

Training teaches employees how to do their specific job tasks; development is training that augments the skills and knowledge of managers and professionals, as well as current employees. Appraising performance involves identifying an employee's strengths and weaknesses on the job. Performance appraisals may be subjective or objective.

**LO 10-4** Identify the types of turnover companies may experience, and explain why turnover is an important issue.

A promotion is an advancement to a higher-level job with increased authority, responsibility, and pay. A transfer is a move to another job within the company at essentially the same level and wage. Separations occur when employees resign, retire, are terminated, or are laid off. Turnovers due to separation are expensive because of the time, money, and effort required to select, train, and manage new employees.

**LO 10-5** Specify the various ways a worker may be compensated.

Wages are financial compensation based on the number of hours worked (time wages) or the number of units produced (piece wages). Commissions are a fixed amount or a percentage of a sale paid as compensation. Salaries are compensation calculated on a weekly, monthly, or annual basis, regardless of the number of hours worked or the number of items produced. Bonuses and profit sharing are types of financial incentives. Benefits are non-financial forms of compensation, such as vacation, insurance, and sick leave.

**LO 10-6** Discuss some of the issues associated with unionized employees, including collective bargaining and dispute resolution.

Collective bargaining is the negotiation process through which management and unions reach an agreement on a labour contract—the formal, written document that spells out the relationship between the union and management. If labour and management cannot agree on a contract, labour union members may picket, strike, or boycott the firm, while management may lock out striking employees, hire strikebreakers, or form employers' associations. In a deadlock, labour disputes may be resolved by a third party—a conciliator, mediator, or arbitrator.

**LO 10-7** Describe the importance of diversity in the workforce.

When companies value and effectively manage their diverse workforces, they experience more productive use of human resources, reduced conflict, better work relationships among workers, increased commitment to and sharing of organizational goals, increased innovation and creativity, and enhanced ability to serve diverse customers.

# KEY TERMS

arbitration
benefits
bonuses
boycott
collective bargaining
commission
conciliation
development
diversity
human resources management (HRM)
job analysis
job description
job promotion
job specification
labour contract
labour unions
lockout
mediation
orientation
picketing
profit sharing
recruiting
salary
selection
separations
strikebreakers
strikes
training
transfer
turnover
wage/salary survey
wages

# So You Want to Work *in Human Resources*

Managing human resources is a challenging and creative facet of a business. It is the department that handles the recruiting, hiring, training, and firing of employees. Because of the diligence and detail required in hiring and the sensitivity required in firing, human resources managers have a broad skill set. Human resources, therefore, is vital to the overall functioning of the business because without the right staff a firm will not be able to effectively carry out its plans. Like in basketball, a team is only as strong as its individual players, and those players must be able to work together and to enhance strengths and downplay weaknesses. In addition, a good human resources manager can anticipate upcoming needs and changes in the business, hiring in line with the dynamics of the market and organization.

Once a good workforce is in place, human resources managers must ensure that employees are properly trained and oriented and that they clearly understand some elements of what the organization expects. Hiring new people is expensive, time-consuming, and turbulent; thus, it is imperative that all employees are carefully selected, trained, and motivated so that they will remain committed and loyal to the company. This is not an easy task, but it is one of the responsibilities of the human resources manager. Even with references, a resumé, background checks, and an interview, it can be hard to tell how a person will fit into the organization; the HR manager needs to be able to anticipate how every individual will "fit in." Human resources jobs include compensation, labour relations, benefits, training, ethics, and compliance managers. All of the tasks associated hiring, developing, and maintaining employee motivation come into play in human resources management. Jobs are diverse and salaries will depend on responsibilities, education, and experience.

One of the major considerations for an HR manager is workforce diversity. A multicultural, multi-ethnic workforce consisting of men and women will help bring a variety of viewpoints, and improve the quality and creativity of organizational decision making. Diversity is an asset and can help a company from having blindspots or too much harmony in thought, background, and perspective, which stifles good team decisions.

However, a diverse workforce can present some management challenges. Human resources management is often responsible for managing diversity training and compliance to make sure employees do not violate the ethical culture of the organization or break the law. Different people have different goals, motivations, and ways of thinking that are informed by their cultures, religions, and the people closest to them. No one way of thinking is more right or more wrong than others, and they are all valuable.

A human resources manager's job can become very complicated, however, because of diversity. To be good at human resources, you should be aware of the value of differences, strive to be culturally sensitive, and ideally should have a strong understanding of and appreciation for different cultures and religions. Human resources managers' ability to manage diversity and those differences will affect their overall career success.

# BUILD YOUR BUSINESS PLAN

## Managing Human Resources

Now is the time to start thinking about the employees you will need to hire to implement your business plan. What kinds of background/skills are you going to look for in potential employees? Are you going to require a certain amount of work experience?

When you are starting a business you are often only able to hire part-time staff because you cannot afford to pay the benefits for a full-time employee. Remember at the end of the last chapter we discussed how important it is to think of ways to motivate your employees when you cannot afford to pay them what you would like.

You need to consider how you are going to recruit your employees. When you are first starting your business, it is often a good idea to ask people you respect (and not necessarily members of your family) for any recommendations of potential employees they might have. You probably won't have a large advertising budget, so look for low-cost ways to attract employees. Social networking sites should be considered an excellent way to attract potential candidates with little, if any, investment.

Finally, you need to think about hiring employees from diverse backgrounds—especially if you are considering targeting diverse consumer segments. The more diverse your employees, the greater the chance you will be able to draw in diverse customers.

## CASE | WestJet Unionizes

As WestJet's various employee groups were in the middle of several union drives, then-CEO Greg Saretsky had this to say at an employee pep rally: "There are WestJetters who don't contribute positively to the culture. And if we can't bring them back into the fold, we have to make it uncomfortable for them to stay here. They need to find happiness elsewhere."[53] To union organizers, Saretsky's message was a clear threat; employees who support unions are not welcome, and making them uncomfortable to the point they quit is an acceptable practice. Just in case Saretsky's message wasn't clear, he also vowed to go down fighting against union efforts at WestJet.[54]

When many members of the Canadian public hear Saretsky's message, some may be surprised. After all, this is WestJet, the small(ish) regional Canadian airline that offers direct economy service to various points throughout the country. WestJet employees are funny and approachable, and actual owners in the business, as they are rewarded with generous employee share purchase plans and profit sharing. WestJet employees are treated exceptionally well by management in an employee-focused fun organizational culture. Why would the workers unionize and why would the CEO be using such harsh language toward his employees?

Airline business analysts would point out that Canadians who think this way may be recalling a WestJet from the past. Today, WestJet is much more than a direct regional carrier, the company is embracing a global expansion strategy, including the use of a more traditional hub and spoke system where fliers connect in cities to destinations all over the world, the introduction of premium business class, and the continuation of WestJet-owned low-cost carriers Encore and Swoop.[55]

Many union organizers and WestJet employees would say that their image as happy, well-treated owners in the company is more the result of a successful marketing campaign by management than actual reality. WestJet management often used the term, Owners Care to describe how most of their employees are actual owners in the company and provide customers with superior service as a result. Union organizers and many employees would argue that the motto was part of a carefully orchestrated management strategy to deter union efforts at WestJet and to keep labour costs low.

Union activists state that WestJet has a long history of anti-union activity directly aimed at maintaining low wages and limiting employee rights. For example, all WestJet employees are required to join Proactive Communication Teams (PACTs), in which they pay dues and elect representatives. While PACTs are supposed to represent workers and to facilitate communication between management and employees, they cannot go on strike and are not protected by labour laws. David Camfield, coordinator at the University of Manitoba Labour Studies program, says that WestJet uses PACTs to deter unionization.[56]

WestJet employees also pointed out a number of unfriendly labour practices at the airline. Pilots say that some traditional WestJet routes were being replaced by Swoop and/or Encore flights. Pilots who fly under Swoop or Encore brands are paid less than WestJet pilots even though WestJet owns all the companies. WestJet pilots say sometimes the Encore and Swoop pilots are even flying WestJet branded planes. Pilots also pointed out that there is no seniority in scheduling and new employees have as much access to preferred routes as someone who has been with the company for years.

Flight attendants made similar claims about seniority and scheduling. But flight attendants' dissatisfaction focused on WestJet's compensation practices, which many employees claimed resulted in their earning less than minimum wage. WestJet only pays flight attendants for services when the plane is actually flying. Since flight attendant duties include cleaning planes, assisting passengers on and off the plane, helping with bags, and a host of other pre- and post-flight responsibilities, many noted they were often paid less than minimum wage as they worked many uncompensated hours. For example, flight attendants would normally spend three hours working on a one-hour flight between Edmonton and

Calgary, yet they would only be paid for the one-hour flying time.

As union drives were gaining momentum in 2017, WestJet increased its communication with employees, stating they were better served having direct communication with management and not unionizing. WestJet management also claimed that unions were targeting WestJet, not to improve employee benefits, but to increase union profits by adding more members.[57, 58]

With all of these factors in mind, WestJet pilots voted to unionize in 2017, joining the Air Lines Pilots Association (ALPA). Swoop and Encore pilots joined the same union a short time later. In 2018, ALPA represented the pilots in contract talks that only ended in a new contract after binding conciliation and a threatened pilot strike. The resulting contract saw a significant increase in wages and improvements in seniority and scheduling. WestJet flight attendants officially joined the Canadian Union of Public Employees on August 1, 2018.[59]

## DISCUSSION QUESTIONS

1. What are some of the advantages and disadvantages of unions for management and employees?
2. Do you think the formation of unions at WestJet was inevitable given the company's growth?
3. Do you think WestJet's business practices are ethical? Why or why not?

CHAPTER 11

# Customer-Driven Marketing

©Gary E Perkin/Alamy Stock Photo

## LEARNING OBJECTIVES

**After reading this chapter, you will be able to:**

- **LO 11-1** Define marketing and describe the exchange process.
- **LO 11-2** Specify the functions of marketing.
- **LO 11-3** Explain the marketing concept and its implications for developing marketing strategies.
- **LO 11-4** Examine the development of a marketing strategy, including market segmentation and marketing mix.
- **LO 11-5** Investigate how marketers conduct marketing research and study buying behaviour.
- **LO 11-6** Summarize the environmental forces that influence marketing decisions.

# ENTER THE WORLD OF BUSINESS

## On-Trend Products and Innovative Marketing Drive Spin Master's Success

Ronnen Harary and Anton Rabie are living what, for many, would be a childhood dream. The close friends are co-CEOs of their own toy company—Spin Master Toys. The pair, along with their third partner, Ben Varadi, who is the chief creative officer, started the business with a mere $10,000 as university students[1] and have built an international children's entertainment company that is valued at $4.10 billion.[2]

Spin Master has taken the toy world by storm over the last 18 years with such hot brands as the Paw Patrol television show, toys, and games; Zoomer, including Zoomer Dino and Zoomer Kitty; Star Wars toys, including a talking and interactive Yoda; and Air Hogs, planes that fly on air power. In addition, the company has signed partnership agreements with some of the biggest companies in North America, including Disney and McDonald's, to develop such toys as the SpongeBob SquarePants–inspired Bounce 'Rounds (inflatable, portable play gyms) and a McDonald's McFlurry Maker. As of 2017 the company was on pace to exceed $1 billion in sales.

One of the first and most common questions people ask after hearing the accomplishments of the two entrepreneurs is, "How did they break into a North American toy market that is characterized by large operators with equally large product development and marketing budgets?" The answer is somewhat surprising. They relied on ingenuity and a combination of public relations (PR) and grassroots marketing.

The company's first product was Earth Buddy, a small head constructed of pantyhose and filled with grass seed that would sprout grass when watered. With no money for a major marketing campaign, the entrepreneurs set out to spread their story using non-traditional marketing and PR, selling the product and their story to anyone who would listen. The product was a huge success and they were on their way. They followed with Devil Sticks, a game for children, and they managed to sell 250,000 units in six months without using any traditional promotional campaigns. Instead they hired college and university students to demonstrate the game at playgrounds, local events, and malls, which created a huge demand for the product.

When Devil Sticks became a commercial success, the company received its biggest break when it was approached by two inventors with the idea of an air-powered airplane. The concept was simple enough: children pump the plane full of air and then launch it, watching it soar upward of 15 metres. The result was a flying plane called Air Hogs.

Rather than launch a massive retail and marketing campaign, Spin Master decided to focus on selling the product to specialty educational toy stores and through the Sears catalogue, using what the company did well: PR and unconventional marketing methods. It built a suitcase to serve as a press kit and filled it with the plane plus a plastic airline cup, a bag of peanuts, and a barf bag, sending it out to numerous writers and editors.

The campaign worked wonders; both *Time* and *Popular Science* magazines wrote stories on the airplane, with *Popular Science* calling it one of the best products of the year. Spin Master again hired students to travel from air show to air show demonstrating the product and creating a buzz among airplane enthusiasts. Sales were starting to boom. But the best was yet to come as the PR team at Spin Master managed to get the product on NBC's *Today* and the Rosie O'Donnell talk show, creating major demand. The following year the company was ready to launch Air Hogs in traditional retailers, and the toy became a runaway hit.

One key to Spin Master's ongoing success has been its ability to pay attention to feedback, better known as market research, and emerging trends to develop winning ideas. The toy market is an extremely fickle one, where toys can be popular one year and busts the next. As such, Spin Master had to be extremely shrewd in developing toys and licensing products. For example, one Spin Master toy, aimed at 2015 holiday shoppers, was created to capture the interest of children and fans who had seen the recently released *Star Wars* movie.

The company created an almost life-size interactive Yoda that could speak and teach users to be a Jedi Knight. During product development, Spin Master not only tested the toy with children but also brought in key retailers to provide feedback on important elements of the marketing mix such as price and promotion. By paying attention to customer and retail feedback, Spin Master is more likely to create products that will sell. In fact, the average development time for a Spin Master toy is 18 to 24 months, if not longer, and normally involves the creation of multiple prototypes and the use of play labs and focus groups.[3]

Paying attention to trends has also resulted in the evolution of the company's focus from toys to entertainment. The founders noticed a significant change in how children were playing over the past decade, with a shift from traditional toys to spending time online, playing video and mobile games, and watching television. The co-CEOs concluded that children still want toys, but toys that are connected to their favourite television shows and websites have the most appeal.

Spin Master responded with television shows, websites, a popular YouTube channel, a mobile games division, and of course, toys built with all of this in mind. For example, Spin Master produces the hit television show *Paw Patrol*, sells Paw Patrol toys and mobile games, and has an interactive website aimed at children.[4] By paying attention to consumer trends and market research Spin Master appears to be well poised to be successful for years to come.

**DISCUSSION QUESTIONS**

1. Why is Spin Master Toys successful?
2. What are some of the advantages of non-traditional marketing? What are some of the potential pitfalls?
3. What are the advantages and disadvantages of switching from a toy company to a children's entertainment company?

# Introduction

Marketing involves planning and executing the development, pricing, promotion, and distribution of ideas, goods, and services to create exchanges that satisfy individual and organizational goals. These activities ensure that the products consumers want to buy are available at a price they are willing to pay and that consumers are provided with information about product features and availability. Organizations of all sizes and objectives engage in these activities.

In this chapter, we focus on the basic principles of marketing. First we define and examine the nature of marketing. Then we look at how marketers develop marketing strategies to satisfy the needs and wants of their customers. Next we discuss buying behaviour and how marketers use research to determine what consumers want to buy and why. Finally we explore the impact of the environment on marketing activities.

# Nature of Marketing

**LO 11-1** Define marketing and describe the exchange process.

A vital part of any business undertaking, **marketing** is a group of activities designed to expedite transactions by creating, distributing, pricing, and promoting goods, services, and ideas. These activities create value by allowing individuals and organizations to obtain what they need and want. A business cannot achieve its objectives unless it provides something that customers value. McDonald's, for example, introduced a number of changes over the past few years, all aimed at satisfying consumers. The company began to serve all-day breakfast to satisfy consumers' desires to eat some of their favourite foods all day, stopped using some preservatives in their foods, and starting using fresh beef in some of their hamburgers. The result has been a surge in sales with the hamburger chain reporting their highest growth rates in six years.[5]

**marketing** a group of activities designed to expedite transactions by creating, distributing, pricing, and promoting goods, services, and ideas

EastLink, an Atlantic Canada communications company, recently introduced cell and smartphone service to its Internet, cable, and telephone business to accommodate customers who wanted to purchase all of their communication services from one carrier.[6] Dyson introduced a cordless vacuum as consumers were becoming increasingly tired of getting tangled up in cords. Based

©roger parkes/Alamy Stock Photo

Based on consumer feedback Dyson is halting investment in plug-in vacuums to focus on consumer friendly cordless models.

on positive consumer feedback, Dyson later announced they were halting the development of plug-in vacuums to focus on the cordless models.

But just creating an innovative product that meets many users' needs isn't sufficient in today's volatile global marketplace. Products must be conveniently available, competitively priced, and uniquely promoted.

Of all the business concepts covered in this text, marketing may be the hardest for organizations to master. Businesses try to respond to consumer wants and needs and to anticipate changes in the marketplace. Unfortunately, it is difficult to understand and predict what consumers want. Businesses have found that by using market research (studies of consumers' needs and wants), they can improve their ability to predict consumers' ever-changing desires.

It is important to note what marketing is not: it is not manipulating consumers to get them to buy products they don't want. It is not just selling and advertising. It is a systematic approach to satisfying consumers. Marketing focuses on the many activities—planning, pricing, promoting, and distributing products—that foster exchanges.

## The Exchange Relationship

At the heart of all business is the **exchange**, the act of giving up one thing (money, credit, labour, goods) in return for something else (goods, services, or ideas). Businesses exchange their goods, services, or ideas for money or credit supplied by customers in a voluntary *exchange relationship*, illustrated in Figure 11.1. The buyer must feel good about the purchase, or the exchange will not continue. If your local dry cleaner cleans your nice suit properly, on time, and without damage, you will probably feel good about using its services. But if your suit is damaged or isn't ready on time, you will probably use another dry cleaner next time.

**exchange** the act of giving up one thing (money, credit, labour, goods) in return for something else (goods, services, or ideas)

**Figure 11.1** | The Exchange Process: Giving Up One Thing In Return for Another

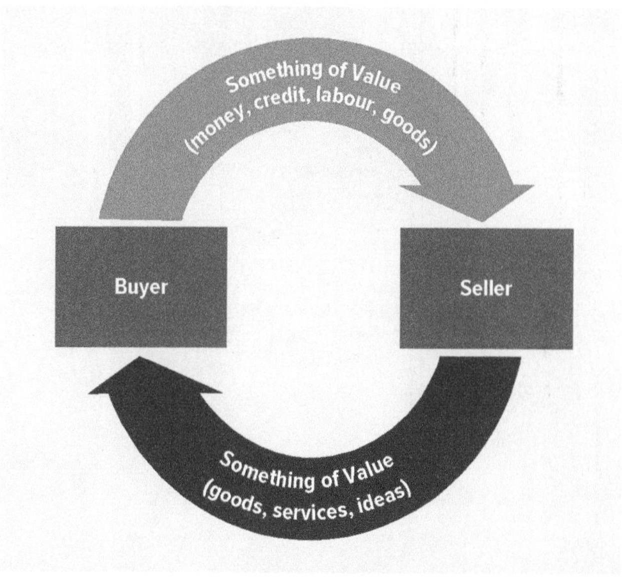


For an exchange to occur, certain conditions are required. As indicated by the arrows in Figure 11.1, buyers and sellers must be able to communicate about the "something of value" available to each. An exchange does not necessarily take place just because buyers and sellers have something of value to exchange. Each participant must be willing to give up their respective something of value to receive something of value held by the other. You are willing to exchange your something of value—your money or credit—for the latest technological gadgets, soft drinks, hockey tickets, or new shoes because you consider those products more valuable or more important than holding on to your cash or credit potential.

> "A business cannot achieve its objectives unless it provides something that customers value."

When you think of marketing products, you may think of tangible things—cars, stereo systems, or tablets, for example. What most consumers want, however, is a way to get a job done, solve a problem, or gain some enjoyment. You may purchase a Booster Juice drink—not because you want a fruit smoothie, but because you are thirsty and want some nourishment. Second Cup provides coffee drinks at a premium price, providing convenience, quality, and an inviting environment. Therefore, the tangible product itself may not be as important as the image or the benefits associated with the product. This intangible "something of value" may be capability gained from using a product or the image evoked by it, such as Gucci jeans, which can sell for over $1000.

©Pietro D'Aprano/Getty Images

People often buy designer products, not for the function they perform, but for the image they portray. For example, Gucci jeans, which can sell for over a $1000 a pair, don't offer any functionality difference compared to much cheaper jeans; what Gucci jeans offers is an image of style and success.

## Functions of Marketing

**LO 11-2** Specify the functions of marketing.

Marketing focuses on a complex set of activities that must be performed to accomplish objectives and generate exchanges. These activities include buying, selling, transporting, storing, grading, financing, marketing research, and risk taking.

**Buying.** Everyone who shops for products (consumers, stores, businesses, governments) decides whether and what to buy. A marketer must understand buyers' needs and desires to determine what products to make available.

**Selling.** The exchange process is expedited through selling. Marketers usually view selling as a persuasive activity that is accomplished through promotion (advertising, personal selling, sales promotion, publicity, and packaging). For example, Natalie Dusome of Penetanguishene,

©Poppy & Peonies. Photo by Jenna Turner.

Natalie Dusome uses influencers to sell her stylish bags at parties and fun social events.

Ontario, started a handbag company, Poppy & Peonies. Her handbags are unique, as one handbag can usually be converted into several functional purses. For example, a large bag can become smaller cross-body bag or a clutch. Dusome also distinguished her company by embracing social selling; her handbags are not in stores but sold by influencers at parties and social events. Dusome's strategy is paying off as her company recently surpassed $1 million in annual revenue.

**Transporting.** Transporting is the process of moving products from the seller to the buyer. Marketers focus on transportation costs and services.

**Storing.** Like transporting, storing is part of the physical distribution of products and includes warehousing goods. Warehouses hold some products for lengthy periods in order to create time utility. Consumers want frozen orange juice year-round, for example, although the production season for oranges is only a few months out of the year. This means that sellers must arrange cold storage for frozen orange juice concentrate all year.

**Grading.** Grading refers to standardizing products and displaying and labelling them so that consumers clearly understand their nature and quality. Many products, such as meat, steel, and fruit, are graded according to a set of standards that often are established by the federal or provincial government.

**Financing.** For many products, especially large items such as automobiles, refrigerators, and new homes, the marketer arranges credit to expedite the purchase.

**Marketing Research.** Through research, marketers ascertain the need for new goods and services. By gathering information regularly, marketers can detect new trends and changes in consumer tastes.

**Risk Taking.** Risk is the chance of loss associated with marketing decisions. Developing a new product creates a chance of loss if consumers do not like it enough to buy it. Spending money to hire a sales force or to conduct marketing research also involves risk. The implication of *risk* is that most marketing decisions result in either success or failure.

## The Marketing Concept

**LO 11-3** Explain the marketing concept and its implications for developing marketing strategies.

A basic philosophy that guides all marketing activities is the **marketing concept**, the idea that an organization should try to satisfy customers' needs through coordinated activities that also allow it to achieve its own goals. According to the marketing concept, a business must find out what consumers need and want and then develop the good, service, or idea that fulfills those needs or wants. The business must then get the product to the customer.

**marketing concept** the idea that an organization should try to satisfy customers' needs through coordinated activities that also allow it to achieve its own goals

In addition, the business must continually alter, adapt, and develop products to keep pace with changing consumer needs and wants. This is sometimes referred to as *relationship marketing* or *customer relationship management*—where the company wants to build a mutually beneficial relationship with a customer that lasts a lifetime. Rather than focus on one sale, a company aims to determine a customer's ever-changing needs and meet those needs over the consumer's lifetime. Art Wilson, a sales consultant, states that firms of all sizes can compete effectively as long as they focus on building relations with customers.

The late retailer, Walter Hachborn, president emeritus and co-founder of Home Hardware, which operates over 1000 stores across Canada, states that "...retailing is all about customer relationships...recognize customers, give customers what they want, and stand behind your products."[7] Simons, the Quebec-based retailer that has recently expanded to Alberta and is eyeing locations in Toronto, is hoping its commitment to customer relations and dedication to knowing its customers' needs and wants will allow the company to successfully expand across Canada.[8] Each business must determine how best to implement the marketing concept, given its own goals and resources.

"According to the marketing concept, a business must find out what consumers need and want, and then develop the good, service, or idea that fulfills those needs or wants."

Although customer satisfaction is the goal of the marketing concept, a business must also achieve its own objectives, such as boosting productivity, reducing costs, or achieving a percentage of a specific market. If it does not, it will not survive. For example, Bell Canada could sell smartphones for five dollars and give customers a lifetime guarantee, which would be great for customers but not so great for Bell. Obviously, the company must strike a balance between achieving organizational objectives and satisfying customer needs and wants.

Doug Kerr, founder and CEO of Vancouver-based Kerr Construction, embraced the marketing concept when he faced a slowing construction market in that city. Rather than give up, Kerr surveyed his customers to better understand their wants and needs and increased his marketing efforts. During this slow period, 75 percent of his business came from previous clients. Kerr increased his focus on customer service to earn even more repeat business, which allowed Kerr Construction to post annual growth rates of 20 to 25 percent while many competitors went out of business.[9]

To implement the marketing concept, a firm must have good information about what consumers want, adopt a consumer orientation, and coordinate its efforts throughout the entire organization; otherwise, it may be awash with goods, services, and ideas that consumers do not want or need. Robb Chase, COO of Toronto-based Blue Ant Media Inc. says, "It's always critical to know what customers' needs are. . .You need to have a monitoring, information-gathering, and communication system to understand what those needs are and if they change you need to be able to adapt your value proposition."[10]

It is getting easier to learn what customers' needs are, according to *Canadian Business* magazine. The publication recently noted that customers now expect to be heard, and companies must let them know that they are listening. Minh Ngo, CEO of Memory Express Computer Products Inc., a Calgary-based retailer, allows customers to post comments on products directly on his website, much like Canadian Tire and Amazon. Ngo, like other marketing managers, knows that companies can gain valuable information from customer comments, including their thoughts on product quality, price, and after-sale service.

Companies are also actively monitoring third-party customer review sites, such as Yelp, TripAdvisor, Angie's List, ConsumerSearch, and Epinions, as well as social media sites, such as Facebook, Twitter, and Pinterest, to determine if customers are satisfied and to identify future consumer wants and needs. In fact, businesses are starting to consider it essential to monitor social media sites to understand their customers and identify opportunities, with 42 percent of companies considering monitoring social media to be one of their top three priorities.[11]

As a result, a number of new businesses have emerged. Meltwater Group has created products such as Meltwater Buzz, a digital private investigator that scans thousands of sites to determine what people are saying about specific issues or companies. Businesses can use the information

## ENTREPRENEURSHIP IN ACTION

### Building a Sustainable Clothing Company Ten Trees at a Time

**tentree**

**Founders:** Dave Luba and Kalen Emsley

**Founded:** 2012

**Success:** Dave Luba and Kalen Emsley have created a branded apparel company that plants 10 trees for every item sold. To date, they have planted over 15 million trees in places such as Madagascar, Nepal, and Ethiopia.*

When Dave Luba went on a student exchange to Hawaii, he never imagined it would lead to the start of an environmentally friendly company. He was studying hard and, in his free time, enjoying the majestic island and, of course, sharing pictures with his friends on Facebook. Luba's friend Kalen was following his friend's photos and was so taken with the beauty of the island that he decided he had to experience Hawaii first-hand.

As the pair explored all the islands had to offer, including hiking, surfing, and swimming, they started to think about companies that give back to society to not only make a profit but also to make the world a better place. One company that stood out was TOMS, a shoe company that donates one pair of shoes for every pair it sells.

Luba and Emsley, inspired by TOMS, came up with the idea of tentree based on a similar model. The pair would develop lifestyle apparel, and for each item of clothing sold, they would plan 10 trees, hence the name tentree. The idea took off, and soon after returning to Canada, they managed to convince 30 retailers to carry tentree branded clothing.

The big break for the company occurred when the entrepreneurs appeared on CBC's television show, *Dragons' Den*. At that time, dragons Arlene Dickinson and Bruce Croxon teamed up to invest $100,000 for a 20 percent stake in the business. Dickinson says, "They are social entrepreneurs to the 10th degree.

©tentree

Dave Luba and Kalen Emsley, two Canadian social entrepreneurs, started tentree, a company dedicated to protecting the environment.

They are the real deal. They are doing something that has serious impact and I think that will resonate with people."** Using the publicity from that appearance, tentree quickly rolled out to other retailers and developed online sales. Now the company, whose motto is Protect the World You Play In, is hoping to further expand globally while protecting the environment at the same time.***

*"Ten Trees Are Planted," *Tentree.com*, http://www.tentree.com/ca/treecode/map/ (accessed May 15, 2019).

**Mary Teresa Bitti, "Dragons See the Seeds of a Good Company in Ten Tree International," Financial Post.com, October 15, 2012, http://business.financialpost.com/entrepreneur/dragons-see-the-seeds-of-a-good-company-in-ten-tree-international (accessed December 10, 2015).

***"Sowing the Seeds of Business Success," *Globe and Mail*, September 30, 2015, http://www.pressreader.com/canada/the-globe-and-mail-metro-ontario-edition/20150930/282054800845019/TextView (accessed December 10, 2015).

from Buzz to see if consumers are satisfied or not, spot developing trends, and address changes in public opinions. Canadian-based HootSuite, much like Buzz, offers companies a vast array of reports and information it gleans from monitoring social media sites.

Successfully implementing the marketing concept requires that a business view customer value as the ultimate measure of work performance and improving value, and the rate at which this is done as the measure of success.[12] Everyone in the organization who interacts with customers—*all* customer-contact employees—must know what customers want. They are selling ideas, benefits, philosophies, and experiences—not just goods and services.

For example, Calgary-based Print Audit, which develops software to track and reduce printing costs, separates itself from the competition by focusing on customer relationships. CEO and founder John MacInnes requires that employees do everything possible to satisfy customers, and if the customer remains unsatisfied they get a refund, no questions asked. MacInnes's firm also surveys clients 15 days after they purchased his products and 15 days later to determine if they are happy. In addition, each employee has access to flower and gift accounts to

©Prathan Chorruangsak/Shutterstock

By determining what customers want and coordinating their efforts, Apple was able to create iPhones that have changed the way people use their phones. To date, Apple has sold over one billion iPhones.

send thank-you gifts to customers or to mark key events in their lives.[13]

Someone once said that if you build a better mousetrap, the world will beat a path to your door. Suppose you do build a better mousetrap. What will happen? Actually, consumers are not likely to beat a path to your door because the market is too competitive. A coordinated effort by everyone involved with the mousetrap is needed to sell the product. Your company must reach out to customers and tell them about your mousetrap, especially how your mousetrap works better than those offered by competitors. If you do not make the benefits of your product widely known, in most cases, it will not be successful.

Consider Apple's retail stores, which market computers and electronics in a way unlike any other computer manufacturer or retail store. The upscale stores, located in high-rent shopping districts, show off Apple's products in sparse, stylish settings to encourage consumers to try new things—like making a movie on a computer. The stores also offer special events like concerts and classes to give customers ideas on how to maximize their use of Apple's products.[14] You must also find—or create—stores willing to sell your mousetrap to consumers. You must implement the marketing concept by making a product with satisfying benefits and making it available and visible.

©Islandstock/Alamy Stock Photo

Apple stores are unique in their wide-open design, large video screens, and tables that display the company's products.

Orville Wright said that an airplane is "a group of separate parts flying in close formation." This is what most companies are trying to accomplish: they are striving for a team effort to deliver the right good or service to customers. A breakdown at any point in the organization—whether it be in production, purchasing, sales, distribution, or advertising—can result in lost sales, lost revenue, dissatisfied customers. Dissatisfied customers lead directly to lost sales as reported by Help Scout, a firm that specializes in helping businesses increase their customer satisfaction. Help Scout found that more than half of consumers stopped a planned purchase due to poor service.[15]

**DID YOU KNOW?**

Millennials are willing to spend an additional 21 percent for good customer service.

## Evolution of the Marketing Concept

The marketing concept may seem like the obvious approach to running a business and building relationships with customers. However, business people are not always focused on customers when they create and operate businesses. Our society and economic system have changed over time, and marketing has become more important as markets have become more competitive. Although this is an oversimplified explanation, the time periods discussed below help readers understand the evolution of marketing.

**The Production Orientation.** During the second half of the nineteenth century, the Industrial Revolution was well under way in Canada. New technologies, such as electricity, railroads, internal combustion engines, and mass-production techniques, made it possible to manufacture goods with ever increasing efficiency. Together with new management ideas and ways of using labour, products poured into the marketplace, where demand for manufactured goods was strong.

**The Sales Orientation.** By the early part of the twentieth century, supply caught up with and then exceeded demand, and businesspeople began to realize they would have to *sell* products to buyers. During the first half of the twentieth century, business people viewed sales as the major means of increasing profits, and this period came to have a sales orientation. They believed that the most important marketing activities were personal selling and advertising. Today some people still inaccurately equate marketing with a sales orientation.

**The Marketing Orientation.** By the 1950s, some business people began to recognize that even efficient production and extensive promotion did not guarantee sales. These

## RESPONDING TO BUSINESS CHALLENGES

### Cool Beans: Starbucks Refines the Customer Experience

Starbucks is brewing up higher sales through new beverages and cafés in global markets. It also continues to refine the retail environment to increase customer value. To speed up purchases, it offers pay-by-cell-phone and order-ahead options. To pay with the Starbucks app, consumers with iPhone, Android, or Windows cell phones download the app and let cashiers scan the Starbucks code on the screen during checkout. The app links to the customer's Starbucks Card, combining the rewards of a loyalty program with the convenience of a prepaid card for making purchases. In the U.S., nearly a third of Starbucks' sales volume now comes through its mobile wallet.

Starbucks aims to open 12,000 additional stores, refocus on its coffee beverages, and expand its focus on technology and its rewards program. With company food sales reaching 21 percent of total sales in the United States, Starbucks aims to elevate its food offerings. The company invested in high-end Italian bakery Princi and opened a bakery inside the company's flagship Reserve Roastery in Seattle. Starbucks' Roasteries are designed to be larger than their traditional café concept and will incorporate Princi bakeries, including stores slated for Shanghai, Milan, New York, Tokyo, and Chicago.

When it comes to innovation, Starbucks proactively monitors the marketing environment to identify new trends. Its many successful initiatives demonstrate that the firm is ready and willing to make changes to maintain its competitive advantage and gain market share.

#### DISCUSSION QUESTIONS

1. How did Starbucks introduce technological changes to speed up purchases?
2. Why must Starbucks remain proactive in monitoring the marketing environment?
3. Do you think a greater investment in food offerings will benefit Starbucks in the long run? Why or why not?

businesses, and many others since, found that they must first determine what customers want and then produce it rather than making the products first and then trying to persuade customers that they need them. Managers at General Electric were among the first to suggest that the marketing concept should be a companywide philosophy of doing business. As more organizations realized the importance of satisfying customers' needs, Canadian and U.S. businesses entered the marketing era, one of marketing orientation.

A **marketing orientation** requires organizations to gather information about customer needs, share that information throughout the entire firm, and use that information to help build long-term relationships with customers. Top executives, marketing managers, non-marketing managers (those in production, finance, human resources, and so on), and customers all become mutually dependent and cooperate in developing and carrying out a marketing orientation. Non-marketing managers must communicate with marketing managers to share information important to understanding the customer.

**marketing orientation** an approach requiring organizations to gather information about customer needs, share that information throughout the firm, and use that information to help build long-term relationships with customers

Consider Tim Hortons. The coffee chain started out by selling coffee and doughnuts. Based on market research and feedback from customers, managers expanded the menu to include cookies, bagels, sandwiches and breakfast. Recently the company started to offer breakfast all day long as the one-time coffee shop has transformed itself into a restaurant that specializes in coffee, breakfast, and lunch.

Trying to assess what customers want is difficult to begin with, and is further complicated by the rate at which trends, fashions, and tastes change. Businesses today want to satisfy customers and build meaningful long-term relationships with them. It is more efficient to retain existing customers and even increase the amount of business each customer provides the organization than to find new customers. As discussed above, Vancouver-based Kerr Construction at one time was securing over 75 percent of its sales from repeat customers. Most companies' success depends on increasing the amount of repeat business, and many companies are turning to technologies associated with customer-relationship management to help build relationships and boost business with existing customers.

"Businesses today want to satisfy customers and build meaningful long-term relationships with them."

Communication remains a major element of any strategy to develop and manage long-term customer relationships. By providing multiple points of interaction with

©Vince Talotta/Toronto Star/Getty Images

Indigo is one of many retailers who use customer information to tailor product offerings to individual customers.

customers—that is, websites, telephone, fax, email, and personal contact—companies can personalize customer relationships.[16] Like many online retailers, Indigo collects, stores, and analyzes purchase data to understand each customer's interests. This information helps the retailer improve its ability to satisfy individual customers and thereby increase sales of books, music, movies, and other products to each customer.

The ability to identify individual customers allows marketers to shift their focus from targeting groups of similar customers to increasing their share of an individual customer's purchases. Regardless of the medium through which communication occurs, customers should ultimately be the drivers of marketing strategy because they understand what they want. Customer relationship management systems should ensure that marketers listen to customers to respond to their needs and concerns and build long-term relationships.

**Social Media Era.** While the marketing orientation era is not over, some would argue that it is slowly being replaced or complemented by the social media era. Social media is redefining marketing, as it allows for the building of online communities, which encourage participation and communication among members. Consumers can communicate in real time with companies, share information with their associates and friends, and search for people's opinions about products online. The results have been significant as Facebook, Instagram, Snapchat, Twitter, LinkedIn, YouTube, Pinterest, blogs, wikis, and podcasts have become both communication and business tools.

Some entrepreneurs, like Ryan Holmes, founder of HootSuite, think that social media is creating a new type of economy, and businesses will have to adapt as social media is vastly changing how business is conducted.[17] Others are less convinced that social media represents a new era in marketing and view social media as a tool, one that complements marketing orientation concepts. After all, social media allows companies to communicate with customers and learn about their wants and needs, and offers another means to establish a long-term relationship with clients—these are some of the major characteristics associated with a marketing orientation.

## Developing a Marketing Strategy

**LO 11-4** Examine the development of a marketing strategy, including market segmentation and marketing mix.

To implement the marketing concept and customer relationship management, a business needs to develop and maintain a **marketing strategy**, a plan of action for developing, pricing, distributing, and promoting products that meet the needs of specific customers. This definition has two major components: selecting a target market and developing an appropriate marketing mix to satisfy that target market.

**marketing strategy** a plan of action for developing, pricing, distributing, and promoting products that meet the needs of specific customers

**market** a group of people who have a need, purchasing power, and the desire and authority to spend money on goods, services, and ideas

**target market** a specific group of consumers on whose needs and wants a company focuses its marketing efforts

### Selecting a Target Market

A **market** is a group of people who have a need, purchasing power, and the desire and authority to spend money on goods, services, and ideas. A **target market** is a more specific group of consumers on whose needs and wants a company focuses its marketing efforts. Nike, for example, introduced a line of golf clubs targeted at recreational golfers.[18]

Marketing managers may define a target market as a relatively small number of people, or they may define it as the total market (Figure 11.2). Rolls-Royce, for example, targets its products at a small, very exclusive, high-income market—people who want the ultimate in prestige in an automobile. General Motors, on the other hand, manufactures vehicles ranging from the Malibu to Cadillac to GMC trucks in an attempt to appeal to varied tastes, needs, and desires. Likewise, Reitmans Canada Ltd., which has grown to include over 950 stores nationwide, operates under seven divisions: Reitmans, Smart Set, Penningtons, Thyme Maternity, Addition Elle, Hyba, and RW & Co., and uses different store concepts to appeal to different target markets.[19]

Effective managers realize that selecting a target market can ultimately determine the success of a company. The Hudson's Bay Company attributed much of its business turnaround to the work of recently retired retail expert, Jeff Sherman. Sherman notes that the key to running a successful retail store is "a maniacal focus on your target customers." Under Sherman's leadership,

Figure 11.2 | Target Market Strategies

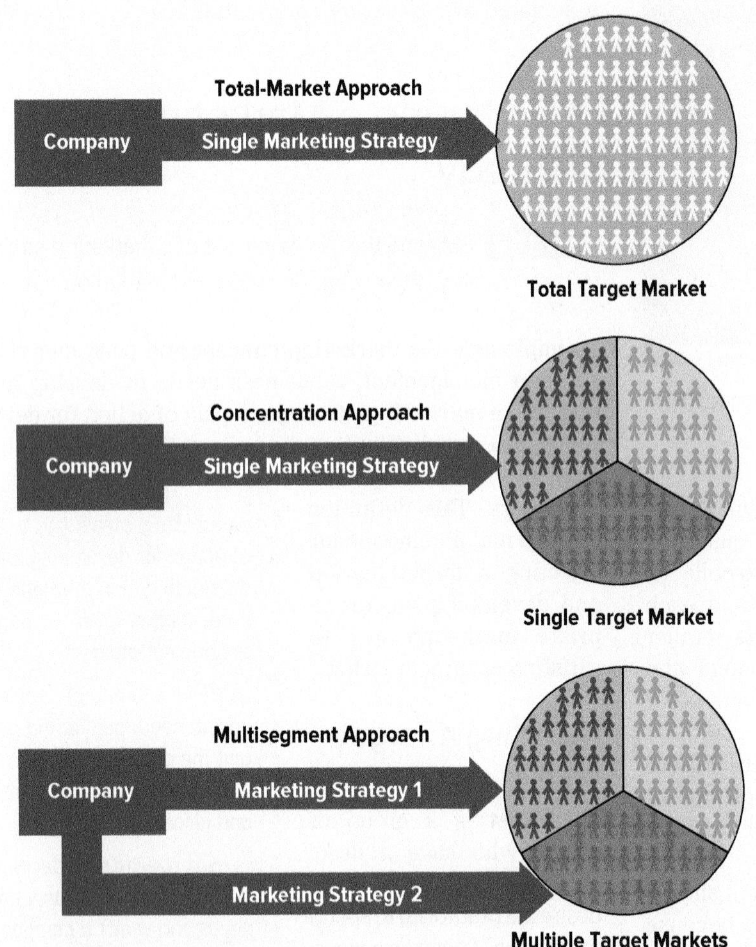


Bonnie Brooks was hired as president and CEO of The Bay and spent several months reviewing data from over 7000 shopper interviews before determining that the retailer would focus on fashion customers who want high-end labels, pragmatists who want good-quality apparel, and value-shoppers who want the best price.

The Bay's target market selection then influenced store design, allocation of advertising dollars, and product selection.[20] The approach at The Bay is no different than the one taken by another Canadian retailer, Shoppers Drug Mart, which had experienced similar business woes over a decade ago. Shoppers spent considerable resources on segmenting and redefining its target markets. The move has paid off and Shoppers is a Canadian retail success story.

As shown in Figure 11.2, some firms use a **total-market approach**, in which they try to appeal to everyone and assume that all buyers have similar needs and wants. Sellers of salt, sugar, and many agricultural products use a total-market approach because everyone is a potential consumer of these products. Most firms, though, use **market segmentation** and divide the total market into groups of people who have relatively similar product needs. A **market segment** is a collection of individuals, groups, or organizations who share one or more characteristics and thus have relatively similar product needs and desires.

**total-market approach** an approach whereby a firm tries to appeal to everyone and assumes that all buyers have similar needs

Prior to selecting its three target markets, The Bay had broken Canada into 12 distinct consumer groups. The Bay then looked internally at its own resources. Women are the largest market segment, with 51 percent of the Canadian population. At the household level, segmentation can unlock each woman's social and cultural characteristics and stage in life to determine preferences and needs.[21]

One market segment that many marketers are focusing on is the growing immigrant population. As immigration rates rise, more and more companies are altering their products or promotion to appeal to this important group. For example, TD Bank has a New to Canada program, which includes a banking package for new immigrants. TD also offers information on its website in a variety of languages and supports a mentoring program to support new immigrants in reaching their full potential in Canada.[22]

Companies use market segmentation to focus their efforts and resources on specific target markets so that they can develop a productive marketing strategy. Two common approaches to segmenting markets are the concentration approach and the multi-segment approach.

"One market segment that many marketers are focusing on is the growing immigrant population."

**Market Segmentation Approaches.** In the **concentration approach**, a company develops one marketing strategy for a single market segment. The concentration approach

**market segmentation** a strategy whereby a firm divides the total market into groups of people who have relatively similar product needs

**market segment** a collection of individuals, groups, or organizations who share one or more characteristics and thus have relatively similar product needs and desires

**concentration approach** a market segmentation approach in which a company develops one marketing strategy for a single market segment allows a firm to specialize, focusing all its efforts on one market segment. Porsche, for example, focuses all its marketing efforts on high-income individuals who want to own high-performance vehicles. A firm can generate a large sales volume by penetrating a single market segment deeply. The concentration approach may be especially effective when a firm can identify and develop products for a particular segment ignored by other companies in the industry.

In the **multi-segment approach**, the marketer aims its marketing efforts at two or more segments, developing a marketing strategy for each. Many firms use a multi-segment approach that includes different advertising messages for different segments. RBC targets many different segments including teens, university students and recent grads, families, baby boomers, and retirees. The bank has products such as mortgages, which appeal to families; RRSPs, which appeal to people saving for their retirement; and student accounts. RBC also targets its promotional efforts to appeal to various customers by communicating through social media, offering services such as Internet banking, and promoting specific products through various commercials.

**multi-segment approach**
a market segmentation approach in which the marketer aims its efforts at two or more segments, developing a marketing strategy for each

*Niche marketing* focuses efforts on one small, well-defined segment that has a unique, specific set of needs. To cater to ice cream "addicts" and people who crave new, exotic flavours, several companies are selling ice cream on the Internet. This niche represents only a fraction of the $20.3 billion per year ice cream business, but online sales at some of the biggest makers increased 30 percent in just one year. Some of the firms focusing on this market are IceCreamSource.com, Nuts About Ice Cream, and Graeter's.[23] Another example, is Nova Scotia-based Blaycation, a travel company that specializes in bucket-list adventures and vacations for high-income individuals who love to travel. Blaycation offers customized trips to allow people to experience such once-in-a-lifetime moments as walking with lions in Africa, having breakfast at a Mt. Everest base camp, or driving a Formula One car in Monaco.[24]

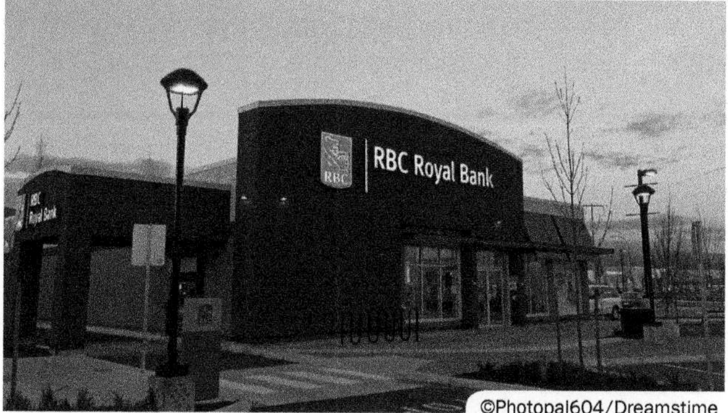

©Photopal604/Dreamstime

RBC targets many different segments with different products and methods of product promotion, as well as different means of communicating with customers.

©Bartosz Hadyniak/Getty Images

Nova Scotia-based Blaycation is a niche tour company. They design individual trips for people who are looking to check things off their bucket lists, such as eating breakfast at a Mt. Everest base camp or walking with lions in Africa.

For a firm to successfully use a concentration or multi-segment approach to market segmentation, several requirements must be met:

1. Consumers' needs for the product must be heterogeneous.
2. The segments must be identifiable and divisible.
3. The total market must be divided in a way that allows estimated sales potential, cost, and profits of the segments to be compared.
4. At least one segment must have enough profit potential to justify developing and maintaining a special marketing strategy.
5. The firm must be able to reach the chosen market segment with a particular market strategy.

**Bases for Segmenting Markets.** Companies segment markets on the basis of several variables:

1. *Demographic*—age, sex, race, ethnicity, income, education, occupation, family size, religion, social class. These characteristics are often closely related to customers' product needs and purchasing behaviour, and they can be readily measured. Some demographers, such as Canada's David Foot, author of *Boom Bust & Echo,* argue that simple demographics can explain upwards of two-thirds of consumer decisions. Foot states that if you know the number of people in each age category, you can make reliable decisions about what products will be popular now and in the future.[25]

   For example, baby boomers, or people born between 1946 and 1966, make up approximately 27 percent of Canada's population and are responsible for the recent rise in spending on cosmetic surgery; they also influence product design. For example, Ford has recently developed the Transit Wagon, a van

## RESPONDING TO BUSINESS CHALLENGES

### Leonard Asper Is Targeting Men in His Return to Media

A decade ago, Leonard Asper was the CEO of CanWest Global Communications, a media giant that controlled such assets as television stations Global Television, Showcase, Slice, and HGTV Canada, as well as other valuable media assets, such as the *National Post*. CanWest was relying on an aggressive acquisition strategy, and when the financial crisis hit, advertising revenue dried up and CanWest's balance sheet, already strapped with a heavy debt load, became unsustainable and the company filed for creditor protection. As a result, Asper stepped down as CEO.

The financial crisis, though, was only part of the story; traditional television viewers have spent the better part of the past decade changing the way they watch programming. No longer are viewers wedded to one show or network; viewers are looking for highly specialized content, and if they cannot find it on television, they can find it online. This point was not lost on Asper, who said, during the final days of CanWest, that the only stations making money were HGTV and the Food Network. Asper says, "You need targeted destinations for communities that are passionate about the subject."*

©Monkey Business Images/Shutterstock

After leaving CanWest, Asper was unsure what direction he would go in professionally, but eventually decided to return to what he knew best—media—and bought a controlling interest in Anthem Media Group Inc., which at the time owned the Fight Network.** Asper was now intent on creating a new media empire, one with a lot more focus on a particular audience. At the time, advertisers were telling Asper, and whoever would listen, that reaching men between the ages of 18 and 65—both on television and online—was increasingly difficult as there were very few stations or shows that targeted this important group.

Asper's approach for Anthem would be to fill this niche, and create and acquire media aimed primarily at male audiences. With this goal in mind, Asper soon added the Pursuit Channel, a hunting and outdoor network; Edge Sports, a channel aimed at extreme sports fans; and the American combat sports channel, My Combat Channel.***

Asper was just getting started building his new media empire when in 2014 he took what might be his biggest risk and started the FNTSY Sports Network. The cable and online outlet is aimed specifically at men who participate in the growing $4 billion fantasy sports industry. The television channel won't actually show any sports but it will provide information and analysis on players, games, and leagues.

Fantasy sports is a growing market, and active fantasy sports players are normally in a number of leagues, enter daily contests, and spend considerable time playing fantasy sports. In fact, some participants in fantasy sports are doing it professionally, taking advantage of the many daily contests and leagues they can enter in order to earn a living. Asper says, "The one thing that convinced me to do this is watching my staff and never being sure if they are working when they have their computers on or if they checking fantasy sites, because they are all doing it."†

Yet some business analysts have expressed concerned about Asper's gamble on fantasy sports.

aimed at Baby Boomers who want to travel with their grandchildren. The largest group of people in Canada is known as the Echo generation, or Millennials, and they are the children of baby boomers. This group, born between 1980 and 2004, was responsible for a renewed interest in child care and kindergarten as they began to have their own families.[26]

2. *Geographic*—climate, terrain, natural resources, population density, subcultural values. These influence consumers' needs and product usage. Climate, for example, influences consumers' purchases of clothing, automobiles, heating and air conditioning equipment, and leisure activity equipment.
3. *Psychographic*—personality characteristics, motives, lifestyles. For example, Canadian smoothie operator Booster Juice presents its products in bright glasses with illustrations of healthy fruit to appeal to customers who want not only to eat healthy but to be seen doing so.
4. *Behaviouristic*—some characteristic of the consumer's behaviour toward the product. These

They maintain that there are not enough dedicated fantasy sports participants to sustain a 24/7 channel, and doubt that Asper will be able to generate enough advertising revenue to make money. Asper counters that channels that focus on a specific target market with focused programming are exactly what consumers and advertisers want. "People thought 'How can there be an entire channel devoted to golf?' but now the Golf Channel is in 82 million homes. It's an obvious trend and we're trying to capture it. . .That's where sports channels are going. The whole world is going to a channel for every sport."[‡]

Asper's ambitious plans of creating specialized programming for men doesn't appear to be slowing down. He recently announced an investment in an eSports data company that specializes in providing statistics on gamers. Asper notes that this is a way for Anthem to learn more about the eSport business, one that expects to reach $1 billion in revenue in the coming years.[§]

**DISCUSSION QUESTIONS:**

1. What are the pros and cons of creating an entire media group aimed specifically at men? Will Asper's company succeed? Why or why not?
2. Asper appears to be creating a media group with a very traditional, if not stereotypical, view of male audiences with a focus on combat sports, hunting, fishing, race cars, and fantasy sports. Do you think enough males are still interested in these pursuits to support independent 24-hour channels? Why or why not?
3. Women are also playing fantasy sports and watching and participating in extreme sports, auto racing, combat sports, and hunting and fishing. Based on this information, should Asper consider changing his message to advertisers that his media company is targeted primarily at men? Why or why not? What would be the advantages and disadvantages of changing his message to advertisers?
4. Assume that you are a corporate marketing expert, and Asper has asked you to change his message to advertisers to make it more inclusive. Develop a new message, which Asper can use, to convince businesses to advertise on his speciality channels.
5. Some critics point out that Asper's focus on males is almost borderline unethical as it treats both men and women in a very stereotypical fashion. Do you think Asper's approach is ethical or unethical? Why?
6. Many media companies, especially those with a television and radio focus, have failed in recent years due the high costs of creating content and the increased time people are spending online. Do you think Asper's company will be successful? Why or why not?

*Joe Castaldo, "The Kid Stays in the Picture," *Canadian Business* online, https://www.canadianbusiness.com/innovation/inside-leonard-aspers-bold-new-venture/ (accessed December 15, 2015).

**Gordon Pitts, "Leonard Asper gets off the mat," *Globe and Mail* online, May 24, 2011, http://www.theglobeandmail.com/report-on-business/leonard-asper-gets-off-the-mat/article585972/?page=2 (accessed December 15, 2015).

***Joe Castaldo, "The Kid Stays in the Picture," *Canadian Business* online, http://site.canadianbusiness.com/longform/asper-fntsy/ (accessed December 15, 2015).

†Steve Ladurantaye, "Leonard Asper places big bet on fantasy sports," *The Globe and Mail* online, January 28, 2013, http://www.theglobeandmail.com/report-on-business/leonard-asper-places-big-bet-on-fantasy-sports/article7900233/ (accessed December 15, 2015).

‡Morgan Campbell, "Fantasy Sports: Can new TV network find an audience among poolies?," thestar.com, http://www.thestar.com/business/2013/03/11/fantasy_sports_can_new_tv_network_find_an_audience_among_poolies.html (accessed December 15, 2015).

§Armina Ligaya, "On my terms: Leonard Asper doubling down on niche sports to build a media empire," March 3, 2017, https://business.financialpost.com/news/on-my-terms-leonard-asper-doubling-down-on-niche-sports-to-build-media-empire

characteristics commonly involve some aspect of product use. The three major issues in this category are the benefits consumers are seeking, consumers' rates of use, and how consumers use and purchase products.

## Developing a Marketing Mix

The second step in developing a marketing strategy is to create and maintain a satisfying marketing mix. The **marketing mix** refers to four marketing activities—product, price, distribution, and promotion—that the firm can control to achieve specific goals within a dynamic marketing environment (Figure 11.3). The buyer or the target market is the central focus of all marketing activities.

**marketing mix** the four marketing activities—product, price, promotion, and distribution—that the firm can control to achieve specific goals within a dynamic marketing environment

## ENTREPRENEURSHIP IN ACTION

### Creating Niche Children's Play Structures

**Charmed Playhouses**

**Founder:** Tyson Leavitt

**Founded:** 2015, in Lethbridge, Alberta

**Success:** Tyson Leavitt was working as a landscaper and noticed that most homes he worked at didn't have any space in the back yard focused solely on children. Recalling days from his youth and his love of playhouses, Leavitt started building tree houses for clients. As his tree houses expanded in popularity, Leavitt realized there might be a market for elaborate, individualized playhouses that could be custom designed around children's interests. Leavitt's dream became a reality when he built a 27-foot-tall Rapunzel castle and displayed it at a local home show. The structure immediately generated interest from potential clients and Leavitt realized there was a market for high-end playhouses.

Soon after the home show, Leavitt quit his landscaping job to focus on building luxury playhouses based on children's interests. To date, Leavitt has built a variety of playhouses including ones with Harry Potter, Disney, superhero, and pirate themes. Leavitt's playhouses are not cheap, ranging in price from $3500 for a base model to $200,000 for his most extravagant structure. Clients tend to be wealthy individuals, celebrities and athletes including basketball star Steph Curry.

Given the uniqueness of Leavitt's story—luxury playhouses being manufactured in a small Alberta town—the TLC network approached Leavitt about being featured in a reality show called *Playhouse Masters*. While initially skeptical, Leavitt and his wife agreed, and the first show aired in 2016.

Leavitt attributes his success to his ability to generate publicity, his focus on quality, and the low Canadian dollar, which allows him to sell his playhouses globally.

©Charmed Playhouses

**Product.** A product—whether a good, a service, an idea, or some combination—is a complex mix of tangible and intangible attributes that provide satisfaction and benefits. A *good* is a physical entity you can touch. A Porsche Cayenne, Lululemon pants, RONA lumber, and a kitten available for adoption at an animal shelter are examples of goods. A *service* is the application of human and mechanical efforts to people or objects to provide intangible benefits to customers. Air travel on WestJet or Air Canada, haircuts at SuperCuts, banking at CIBC, and insurance from Manulife are examples of services.

**Figure 11.3** | The Marketing Mix: Product, Price, Promotion, and Distribution

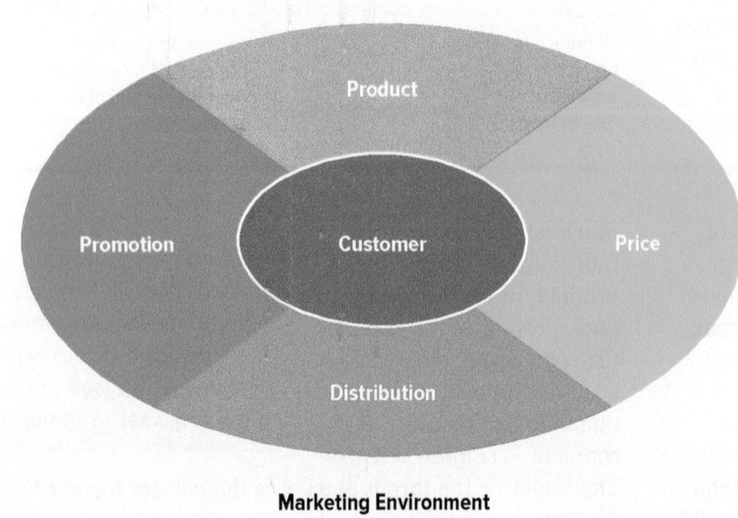


A product has emotional and psychological as well as physical characteristics and encompasses everything that the buyer receives from an exchange. This definition includes supporting services such as installation, guarantees, product information, and promises of repair. Products usually have both favourable and unfavourable attributes; therefore, almost every purchase or exchange involves trade-offs as consumers try to maximize their benefits and satisfaction and minimize unfavourable attributes. For example, a consumer trying to choose between a Xbox One and a PlayStation 4 may have to trade off the superior entertainment features of the Xbox for the

## Consider the Following: RBC's youth marketing strategy

As stated above, marketing strategy consists of selecting a target market and designing your marketing mix—products, price, place, and promotion—to appeal to your targeted market and create value compared to your competitors. RBC, Canada's largest bank, obviously has many different target markets, which results in the bank managing different marketing mixes. One key target market for the bank is university students and recent graduates. This group is particularly important as they are just starting to form relationships with companies and the bank realizes that if it captures a young customer's business now it may be able to retain the customer for a lifetime. To achieve this result, RBC tries to differentiate itself from the other banks by creating a superior student-focused marketing mix.

While all the banks in Canada are offering student banking packages, student lines of credit, credit cards for students, and so forth, RBC is attempting to differentiate itself first and foremost by using promotions that appeal to youth. The bank spent upwards of $120 million to sponsor the 2010 Olympics, including the Own the Podium campaign, which consisted of directing money to athletes who had the best chance to capture an Olympic medal, and the Torch Relay, a 45,000-kilometre trip across the country that stopped in cities and towns and featured youth-focused entertainment. RBC has followed up that promotion with a commitment to the Road to Excellence program, which replaced Own the Podium.

Royal Bank has furthered its commitment to young Canadian athletes with the RBC Training Ground program, which was launched in 2016. The Training Ground program identifies athletes with Olympic potential through regional and then national qualifying competitions. Successful athletes are eligible for funding for their specific sport. In 2018 over 3000 athletes participated in Training Ground competitions in all ten provinces with 100 being selected for the National Finals.*

In addition, RBC is considered the social media leader among the big banks in Canada. RBC has invested heavily in social media including Twitter, Facebook, blogs, avatars, and online competitions and communities to attract young clients. For example, a recent online contest focused on recent university graduates who were asked to provide the best advice they could to new university students.

In 2018, RBC committed an additional $3.2 billion to technology to attract new customers. The company hopes that this investment, which is spread out across areas such as artificial intelligence, digital products, and social media will attract 2.5 million new customers.**

### DISCUSSION QUESTIONS

1. What markets is RBC targeting with social media?
2. Are there other things RBC could be doing with its marketing mix to appeal to the youth market?
3. Do you think RBC's investment in the Olympics and the Torch Relay was a good idea? Will it improve the bank's market share?
4. Will being a leader in social media translate into more young clients for the bank?

*https://www.cbc.ca/olympics/trainingground/#/about, (accessed July 1, 2019).

**Doug Alexander, "RBC to spend $3.2B on technology to attract digital customers," June 13, 2018, https://www.bnnbloomberg.ca/rbc-to-spend-3-2b-on-technology-to-attract-digital-customers-1.1092379

slightly better graphics and wider game library associated with the PS4.[27]

Products are among a firm's most visible contacts with consumers. If they do not meet consumer needs and expectations, sales will be difficult, and product life spans will be brief. The product is an important variable—often the central focus—of the marketing mix; the other variables (price, promotion, and distribution) must be coordinated with product decisions.

**Price.** Almost anything can be assessed by a **price**, a value placed on an object exchanged between a buyer and a seller. Although the seller usually establishes the price, it may be negotiated between buyer and seller. The buyer usually exchanges purchasing power—income, credit, wealth—for the satisfaction or utility associated with a product. Because financial price is the measure of value commonly used in an exchange, it quantifies value and is the basis of most market exchanges.

**price** a value placed on an object exchanged between a buyer and a seller

Marketers view price as much more than a means of assessing value, however. It is a key element of the marketing mix because it relates directly to the generation of revenue and profits. In some industries, prices can also be changed rapidly to stimulate demand or respond to competitors' actions. For example, WestJet will usually drop its prices quickly in response to similar price drops by Air Canada, and Tim Hortons introduced an English

## Consider the Following: Canada—A tale of two segments

Marketers know that if they are going to be successful in Canada, their goods should appeal to one of two market segments—baby boomers or their children (better known as the Millennial generation). Baby boomers, born between 1946 and 1966, represent approximately one-third of Canada's population, and as a group, are quite wealthy. Boomers entered the workforce when there were many jobs. They have often been described as materialistic in nature and consider their time to be very valuable. Businesses that appeal to this group include Nurse Next Door, a Vancouver-based home care company for seniors that boomers hire to help with their aging parents, and Medicard Finance Inc., an Ontario-based company that offers loans and lines of credit to boomers who are interested in cosmetic surgery.*

From a marketer's perspective, the best creation of the baby boomers may be the Millennial generation. This group is the second-largest segment in the population and represents people born from 1980 to 2004. This well-educated generation is interested in the environment and technology, and Millennials expect to be successful, much like their parents. When this generation began to buy their first homes, get married, and have children, many products and services that had fallen out of favour as the baby boomers aged started to become popular again.

### DISCUSSION QUESTIONS

1. What other products or industries should do well as baby boomers continue to age?
2. What do you think are the best ways to promote products or services to baby boomers?
3. What other products or industries should do well now that the Millennial generation is having families?
4. What do you think are the best ways to promote products or services to the Millennial generation?
5. Do some research and determine the size of the baby boomer and Millennial segments.
6. Do you think companies would be wise to consider marketing their products to other groups? Why or why not? What products or industries are aimed at other groups?

*Nurse Next Door, http://www.nursenextdoor.com/index.php (accessed September 1, 2010); Medicard Finance Inc., http://www.medicard.com/ (accessed September 1, 2010).

muffin version of its breakfast sandwich, priced lower than McDonald's Egg McMuffin, to generate sales.

**Place/Distribution.** **Place/distribution** is making products available to customers in the locations and the quantities desired. The Internet and online sales have greatly impacted place/distribution as more and more shoppers make purchases and receive services online. For example, Canadian banks now offer smartphone apps for online banking service. The apps were originally introduced to appeal to the vast number of youth who want to bank using their smartphones.

**place/distribution** making products available to customers in the locations and quantities desired

Almost every product and service can now be purchased on the Internet, including airline tickets from Air Canada and WestJet and sporting goods from SportChek. Matt & Natt, a Montreal-based designer of women's and men's handbags made out of recycled plastic bottles, has used exporting to reach consumers throughout the world as the environmentally friendly nature of the product has resulted in global demand. The company sells handbags in high-end boutique stores in Canada, the United States, the United Kingdom, Japan and Germany.[28]

"Global distribution is becoming increasingly important to Canadian companies. The top 71 exporters identified by *Profit* magazine as the top 100 growth companies sold $17 billion abroad last year."

In addition to making products available in the locations and quantities customers want, *place* also refers to creating a location that consumers find desirable. For example, Dollarama, a Quebec-based chain, became a billion-dollar retailer by offering consumers not just 1000-plus locations to shop at, but by creating a location that customers wanted to visit. Dollarama's stores are organized, clean, and attractive, unlike many mom-and-pop dollar stores, which are often characterized by their unkempt aisles.

Some retailers are now opting to build smaller stores as a way to reduce overhead, focus on items that consumers want, and create a more intimate shopping experience. RONA has recently announced the creation of 11 smaller satellite stores that, according to the company, will have a neighbourhood feel to them.

Other stores are opting to open a store within a store as discussed in Chapter 4. The concept has the a host shop,

## RESPONDING TO BUSINESS CHALLENGES

### Even Wedding Shopping Is Moving Online

For years, when the 4Ps were discussed, *place*, which represents the place where items are sold, rarely changed. Food items were sold in grocery stores, computers in small computer boutiques, music and musical instruments in music stores, clothing in department stores, and so forth. This all changed with the emergence of super-centre department stores, discounters, and ultimately the Internet, as suddenly products had no traditional "place" of sale. Originally, retailers thought items such as books and computers were products deemed perfect for online sales as they were mostly straightforward purchases involving little emotion.

Traditional retailers noted that while non-emotional items could be sold online, specialty goods such as wedding gowns and engagement rings had too much emotional involvement to be sold over the Internet. After all, when people are planning a wedding day, a lot of thought goes into big-ticket items such as the wedding dress and engagement ring. It was thought that consumers would want to see these items in person, try them on, and get feedback from a salesperson before making such a large personal and emotionally charged purchase.

Traditionalists have been proven wrong. Women are flocking to online discount wedding dress stores such as TBDress.com, and NearlyNewlywed.com, OnceWed.com and Tradesy.com have carved out a niche selling used wedding dresses. While the customer experience is not the same as shopping in a store, e-tailers are using videos, pictures, and testimonials to make dresses come to life. Additionally, weddings are becoming more about the overall experience, and not focused solely on the dress. By saving money on a dress, couples can spend money elsewhere.*

Wedding savings don't end there. More couples are using the Internet to cut costs on what is often the most expensive wedding purchase—the engagement ring. BlueNile.com is the world's largest online retailer of diamonds, with global sales in excess of $500 million.** The company boasts that buying a diamond should be a simple process, offers customers deep discounts compared to bricks-and-mortar stores, and provides shoppers with online videos, FAQs, and chat features to assist in the process.

A recent study by the The Diamond Pro, an online consumer-friendly diamond guide, notes that consumers are overpaying by as much as 30 to 40 percent when they purchase rings from a traditional bricks-and-mortar retailer.***

One of the primary reasons BlueNile can sell rings at such a discount is that it does not take possession of the rings until it actually sells them. BlueNile has established relationships with diamond wholesalers throughout the world who will ship the diamonds to BlueNile on demand. While traditionalists may have a problem with not being able to see the diamond in person before buying it, customers do not. In fact, the average engagement ring sold at BlueNile is $5500, which is almost twice the industry average, and BlueNile boasts that it sells $20,000 to $50,000 rings daily. Other online retailers of wedding rings have popped up, including JamesAllen.com, Ice.com, and a variety of companies selling rings on Amazon.

The wedding industry has grown by leaps and bounds, and lower-priced alternatives, especially from online retailers, are starting to reshape what has been a very traditional industry, with consumers benefitting from increased competition and lower prices.

#### DISCUSSION QUESTIONS

1. Are you surprised that people will purchase wedding dresses and engagement rings from online companies? Would you do this? Why or why not?
2. Wedding dresses and engagement rings were thought to be emotional purchases. Is this still true as discount, department, and online stores have become so successful in selling these products?
3. What are some of the reasons that BlueNile has been so successful?
4. Online retailers such as BlueNile are often blamed for putting small local stores out of business. Do you think this could be true? Why or why not?
5. Visit BlueNile's website and try out some of the customization apps. After visiting the site and browsing its merchandise, do you feel you are more or less likely to purchase a ring online?

*Tonya Garcia, "More shoppers are saying 'yes' to their wedding dress by clicking 'buy' online," May 24, 2017, https://www.marketwatch.com/story/more-shoppers-are-saying-yes-to-their-wedding-dress-by-clicking-buyonline-2017-05-23

**Nat Levy, "Two years after $500M acquisition, online jeweler Blue Nile eyes eventual return to public markets," November 21, 2018, https://www.geekwire.com/2018/two-years-500m-acquisition-online-jeweler-blue-nile-eyes-eventual-return-public-markets/

***Michael Fried, "Should I Buy a Diamond Online?" January 5, 2017, https://www.diamonds.pro/education/buy-diamonds-online/

©LWA/Jay Newman/Blend Images LLC

Online retailers such as TBDress.com and Blue Nile are proving that even wedding dresses and engagement rings can be successfully sold online.

for example, Indigo, allowing another retailer access to their floor space. The other retailer sets up a within-store shopping space, for example, American Girl. The host shop gains increased revenue, by charging the other retailer a percentage of sales and/or rent, and because additional shoppers will be drawn to the retail location. The smaller store gets access to prime retail space for a fraction of the cost it would take to establish an independent location. Other examples include fast-food giant McDonald's, which has expanded distribution by opening restaurants in Walmart stores, and Starbucks, which sells its specialty coffee in Target stores throughout the U.S.

Intermediaries, usually wholesalers and retailers, perform many of the activities required to move products efficiently from producers to consumers or industrial buyers. These activities involve transporting, warehousing, materials handling, and inventory control, as well as packaging and communication. For example, Dr. Abdullah Kirumira, founder of Nova Scotia–based BioMedical Diagnostic Inc., which developed the world's first rapid HIV test and "lab in a box" diagnostic tools, notes that marketing and distribution were never his strengths. BioMedical relies on a number of distributors to transport and sell products throughout the world, which allows Kirumira to focus on the development of new drugs and medical applications.[29]

Critics who suggest that eliminating wholesalers and other middlemen would result in lower prices for consumers do not recognize that eliminating intermediaries would not do away with the need for their services. Other institutions would have to perform those services, and consumers would still have to pay for them. For example, Mississauga-based Solutions 2 GO Inc. has achieved approximately $750 million in annual sales by relieving video game manufacturers of the task of getting their games onto the shelves of thousands of stores all on the same day. The company serves as a master distributor for many major game manufacturers. In the absence of wholesalers, all producers would have to deal directly with retailers or customers, keeping voluminous records and hiring people to deal with customers.[30]

**Promotion.** **Promotion** is a persuasive form of communication that attempts to expedite a marketing exchange by influencing individuals, groups, and organizations to accept goods, services, and ideas. Promotion includes advertising, personal selling, social media, publicity, and sales promotion, all of which we will look at more closely in Chapter 12. One aspect of promotion that has been growing rapidly in recent years is the use of non-traditional marketing to achieve corporate goals. Lululemon, for example, once offered customers free clothing if they would wait in line naked at a store's grand opening. The result was national media coverage of the store's opening and extended coverage in the media about the corporation's edgy promotions.[31] Another example is Tim Hortons' successful Roll Up the Rim to Win contest. The contest has been running for over 20 years and still results in increased sales and publicity for the company.

**promotion** a persuasive form of communication that attempts to expedite a marketing exchange by influencing individuals, groups, and organizations to accept goods, services, and ideas

The aim of promotion is to communicate directly or indirectly with individuals, groups, and organizations to facilitate exchanges. When marketers use advertising and other forms of promotion, they must effectively manage their promotional resources and understand product and target-market characteristics to ensure that these promotional activities contribute to the firm's objectives. For example, Tim Hortons is using television advertising to appeal to Canadians across the country who want a fresh cup of coffee in a friendly atmosphere. Tim Hortons' advertisements highlight the fact that every 20 minutes there is a new pot of coffee being brewed. Also, as previously noted, Canadian banks are relying on smartphones and social media to reach the under-30 market segment with their products and services.

"The aim of promotion is to communicate directly or indirectly with individuals, groups, and organizations to facilitate exchanges."

## Marketing Research and Information Systems

**LO 11-5** Investigate how marketers conduct marketing research and study buying behaviour.

Before marketers can develop a marketing mix, they must collect in-depth, up-to-date information about customer needs. **Marketing research** is a systematic,

**marketing research** a systematic, objective process of getting information about potential customers to guide marketing decisions

objective process of getting information about potential customers to guide marketing decisions. For example, when Simple Audiobook, an Oakville, Ontario, company, was contemplating whether to enter the United States market, the company relied on market research to determine if the strategy made sense. CEO Sean Neville says that firms can't guess if there is a market—they need to do research and determine if a market exists, the size of that market, and if customers will purchase the company's product.[32]

Janet and Greta Podleski, authors of two bestselling Canadian cookbooks, *Looneyspoons* and *Crazy Plates*, along with partner David Chilton, discovered the dangers of not doing any market research. They decided to turn some of their favourite recipes into frozen dinners, but were initially quite unsuccessful. Chilton said that almost all of the errors came because they didn't properly research the market. They were making a product for families of four or five priced between $13 and $14—what they found out later was that most people want frozen dinners to feed one or two people and they want to pay much less for them. Since the group had produced a product no one wanted, they were left to repurchase the product from store shelves and re-entered the marketplace only after conducting the necessary market research.

Market research might include data about the age, income, ethnicity, gender, and educational level of people in the target market; their preferences for product features; their attitudes toward competitors' products; and the frequency with which they use the product. For example, Tim Hortons' market research revealed customers wanted larger cups of coffee. As a direct result, the stores started selling extra-large 24-ounce cups.[33]

Toyota's marketing research about Generation Y drivers (born between 1977 and 1994) found that they practically live in their cars, and many even keep a change of clothes handy in their vehicles. As a result of this research, Toyota designed its Scion as a "home on wheels" with a 15-volt outlet for plugging in a computer, reclining front seats for napping, and a powerful audio system, all with a budget-conscious price tag.[34]

Les Mandelbaum, founder of Umbra, a Toronto-based company that is known as one of the world's top designers of products, states that Umbra is very disciplined when it comes to entering the marketplace with new products and spends considerable time analyzing market research including what customers want, what products are already in stores, and what competitors are offering.[35]

Marketing research is vital because the marketing concept cannot be implemented without information about customers. As evident in this chapter's discussion about the revival at The Bay, market research is essential to making decisions for companies. As discussed above, The Bay's senior executives spent several months reviewing data from thousands of interviews prior to making decisions about target markets and store layout. Canadian Tire uses the massive amount of customer information it gathers when customers use their Canadian Tire cards to assist in making decisions on a variety of issues including prices, new product ideas, store layout, and promotional campaigns.

**secondary data** information that is compiled inside or outside an organization for some purpose other than changing the current situation

**primary data** marketing information that is observed, recorded, or collected directly from respondents

The market research process consists of the following steps:

1. *Define the problem or objective.* Objectives could include whether potential customers will buy a product or what price they are willing to pay for a service.
2. *Collect data.* Researchers will normally start their search for information from pre-existing sources known as secondary sources or secondary data. **Secondary data** are compiled inside or outside the organization for some purpose other than changing the current situation. Marketers typically use information compiled by Statistics Canada, business development centres, and other government agencies; databases created by marketing research firms; and sales and other internal reports to gain information about customers.

   To stay on top of consumer demands and emerging trends, Somerset Entertainment Ltd., a Toronto-based music company, hires marketers to read the latest entertainment publications and report back to management. Jason Abbott, founder of Winnipeg-based tour company The Toban Experience, used secondary sources to determine if a market existed for a tour company in his region and if there were any competitors. Abbott relied on secondary data to determine that 6000 visitors travel through Winnipeg in the summer and spring, and no other tour companies were operating in his market.[36]

   If there is not enough secondary information available, marketers will often turn to primary research, or the collection of new data that is specific to the problem at hand. **Primary data** is new data or new information. Primary data is usually collected either by observation, where companies watch what consumers do or how consumers react to certain situations; surveys, where people complete a questionnaire; personal interviews; or focus groups, where groups of consumers come together to discuss a product, service, or business.

   Examples of observation include the use of "mystery shoppers" to visit retail establishments and report on whether the stores are adhering to the company's standards of service. For example, Tell Us About Us Inc. (TUAU) is a Winnipeg-based full-service customer feedback company. TUAU offers companies numerous methods, including social media monitoring, surveys, and secret shoppers, to determine if standards are being met and if consumers are happy and/or would like additional products or services. The province of Nova Scotia used focus groups as part of its effort to develop a formal marketing campaign. Among other things, focus groups suggested the province promote its friendly atmosphere and natural beauty. As noted above, The Bay has used interviews as part of its marketing research efforts, and Shoppers Drug Mart has used surveys.

3. *Analyze the research data.* Data results must then be analyzed and interpreted. Researchers may use a number of software and/or online diagnostic tools to generate different alternatives to a problem.
4. *Choose the best options.* The final step in the research process is determining what alternatives exist and deciding which recommendations to make. For example, when Eryn Green and Tamar Wagman started Sweetpea Baby Food, a Toronto-based fresh-frozen baby food company, they used market research to ensure there was a market for their product. Their first step was to determine if a market did exist for gourmet baby food. The pair collected data from secondary sources, including Statistics Canada, to determine that while birth rates are declining, the number of mothers in their target group (aged 30–35) is rising. The company founders than used primary research and interviewed 50 new moms to see if there was an actual demand for their product. Green and Wagman analyzed the data and concluded a large market did exist for their business.[37]

A marketing information system (MIS) is a framework for accessing information about customers from sources both inside and outside the organization. Inside the organization, there is a continuous flow of information about prices, sales, and expenses. Outside the organization, data are readily available through private or public reports and census statistics, as well as from many other sources. Computer networking technology provides a framework for companies to connect to useful databases and customers with instantaneous information about product acceptance, sales performance, and buying behaviour. This information is important to planning and marketing strategy development.

The marketing of products and collecting of data about buying behaviour—information on what people actually buy and how they buy it—represents the marketing research of the future. New information technologies are changing the way businesses learn about their customers and market their products. Interactive multimedia research, or *virtual testing,* combines sight, sound, and animation to facilitate the testing of concepts as well as packaging and design features for consumer products. Computerization offers a greater degree of flexibility, shortens the staff time involved in data gathering, and cuts marketing research costs. The evolving development of telecommunications and computer technologies is allowing marketing researchers quick and easy access to a growing number of online services and a vast database of potential respondents. Many companies have created private online communities and research panels that bring consumer feedback into the companies 24 hours a day.

Look is an online, real-time service that provides accurate and reliable information, research, and news about trend-setting youths aged 14 to 30. With this age group spending an estimated $140 billion a year, many companies are willing to shell out an annual subscription fee of about $20,000 for access to these valuable data. Look pays more than 35,000 hand-picked, pre-screened young people from all over the world to email the company information about styles, trends, opinions, and ideas.[38]

Other companies are finding that quicker, less-expensive online market research is helping them develop products faster and with greater assurance that the products will be successful. The CEO of Stonyfield Farm (U.S. maker of higher-priced yogurt) is convinced that Web feedback saved his company from a multi-million dollar mistake. The online responses from 105 women caused the company to scrap the name originally planned for its new yogurt from YoFemme (which the respondents did not like) to YoSelf (to which the respondents voted yes).[39]

As discussed above, in addition to online market research, companies are tracking website use, and online feedback via blogs, communities, and social networking sites such as Facebook, Instagram, and Twitter to see how customers are responding to products or messages. This type of activity has resulted in the development of new companies such

©Linqong/Dreamstime

Market research can lead to a whole new market for your product. BMW targets a lower-income consumer than its typical high-end one by selling certified used BMWs at a lower cost, but still with the BMW brand recognition and expectation.

as Cision, a Toronto-based firm that allows companies to listen to social media by tracking and preparing comprehensive reports about what is being said about the company online, measuring what people are saying about their business and competitors, and analyzing the data to assist companies in making marketing decisions.

©The Advertising Archives/Alamy Stock Photo

Polo appeals to people who want to express social roles or identify with a reference group.

## Buying Behaviour

Carrying out the marketing concept is impossible unless marketers know what, where, when, and how consumers buy; marketing research into the factors that influence buying behaviour helps marketers develop effective marketing strategies. **Buying behaviour** refers to the decision processes and actions of people who purchase and use products. It includes the behaviour of both consumers purchasing products for personal or household use and organizations buying products for business use.

Marketers analyze buying behaviour because a firm's marketing strategy should be guided by an understanding of buyers. People view pets as part of their families, and they want their pets to have the best of everything. Iams, which markets the Iams and Eukanuba pet food brands, recognized this trend and shifted its focus. Today, it markets high-quality pet food, fancy pet treats, sauces, and other items that allow pet lovers to spoil their pets.[40]

**buying behaviour** the decision processes and actions of people who purchase and use products

**perception** the process by which a person selects, organizes, and interprets information received from their senses

Both psychological and social variables are important to an understanding of buying behaviour.

### Psychological Variables of Buying Behaviour

Psychological factors include the following:

- **Perception** is the process by which a person selects, organizes, and interprets information received from the senses, as when hearing an advertisement on the radio or touching a product to better understand it.
- *Motivation*, as we said in Chapter 9, is an inner drive that directs a person's behaviour toward goals. A customer's behaviour is influenced by a set of motives rather than by a single motive. A buyer of a home computer, for example, may be motivated by ease of use, ability to communicate with the office, and price.
- **Learning** brings about changes in a person's behaviour based on information and experience. If a person's actions result in a reward, they are likely to behave the same way in similar situations. If a person's actions bring about a negative result, however—such as feeling ill after eating at a certain restaurant—they will probably not repeat that action.
- **Attitude** is knowledge and positive or negative feelings about something. For example, a person who feels strongly about protecting the environment may refuse to buy products that harm Earth and its inhabitants.
- **Personality** refers to the organization of an individual's distinguishing character traits, attitudes, or habits. Although market research on the relationship between personality and buying behaviour has been inconclusive, some marketers believe that the type of car or clothing a person buys reflects his or her personality.

**learning** changes in a person's behaviour based on information and experience

**attitude** knowledge and positive or negative feelings about something

**personality** the organization of an individual's distinguishing character traits, attitudes, or habits

### Social Variables of Buying Behaviour

Social factors include **social roles**, which are a set of expectations for individuals based on some position

## Consider the Following: Using technology to mine customer opinions

Successful company marketers take the time to study and understand what they call *consumer buying behaviour*—in other words, the behaviour of customers buying a company's products for personal or household uses. Marketers pay attention to this behaviour because how customers respond to a company's marketing strategies affects that company's success. They also aim to please customers and undertake research to discover what a company can do to satisfy its customers and keep them coming back.

When marketers have a solid grasp on buying behaviour, they can better predict how customers will react to marketing campaigns. A new strategy being used by large companies such as RBC, TD Canada Trust, Johnson & Johnson, Pfizer, and Procter & Gamble is the use of online software to create large-scale focus groups. Companies that sell this software aim to help marketers listen to what their customers want rather than designing marketing campaigns based on generic strategies.

For years, companies have brought people together for traditional, face-to-face focus groups. In other words, a small group of people was brought together in a room to discuss products while people from the company listened (often from another room) to what they had to say. The advantage of the new, large-scale focus groups is that companies can reach a much larger audience—therefore, getting a much wider range of ideas and opinions.

Perhaps this may create a more accurate picture of what the general public at large is looking for from a company. For example, four years Lego had been producing the same Lego sets based on feedback from traditional focus groups. The company created an online focus group involving 10,000 people—all Lego customers were invited via email to participate in an online contest regarding new products—and the result was essentially brainstorming in cyberspace and customers suggesting departures from Lego's traditional toys.

Here is how this software works: In the case of Lego, customers who had received email invitations were part of an online "popularity contest" regarding new-product suggestions. Customers were shown lists of six proposed products at a time. They were asked to rank the toys they liked and, if they chose, offer their own ideas. The customer ideas were then filtered into the mix and sent to other customers to rank against Lego's proposed toys. The software filtered the selections shown to customers—those receiving the most votes early on most often appear later—and over time, the most popular ideas rose to the forefront.

Although there are many challenges for this new software and its uses (for example, some suggest online research may be skewed toward Internet users), online focus groups are much less expensive than the traditional version. At least for now, this new research method may be a good way to understand more about buying behaviour.*

### DISCUSSION QUESTIONS

1. How can technology be used to determine consumer beliefs and opinions?
2. Compare face-to-face focus groups with online discussions for understanding consumer behaviour.
3. What are the possible biases from using online research to assess consumer beliefs, opinions, and behaviour?

*Allison Fass, "Collective Opinion, Forget the Up-Close Focus Group. Newfangled Software Lets Lego, Procter & Gamble and Others Mine Ideas from Tens of Thousands of Opinionated Customers," *Forbes*, November 28, 2005, pp. 76–79; "About Us," www.informative.com/aboutUs.html; "Solutions and Services," www.informative.com/solutionsServices.html; "Customer Communities," www.communispace.com/customer_c.htm; "The Communispace Difference," www.communispace.com/difference.htm; "Technology and Services," www.communispace.com/technology.htm (all accessed December 10, 2005).

**social roles** a set of expectations for individuals based on some position they occupy

**reference groups** groups with whom buyers identify and whose values or attitudes they adopt

they occupy. A person may have many roles: mother, wife, student, executive. Each of these roles can influence buying behaviour. Consider a woman choosing an automobile. Her father advises her to buy a safe, gasoline-efficient car, such as a Volvo. Her teenaged daughter wants her to buy a cool car, such as a Honda Civic. Her young son wants her to buy a Ford Explorer to take on camping trips. Some of her colleagues at work say she should buy a hybrid Prius to help the environment. Thus, in choosing which car to buy, the woman's buying behaviour may be affected by the opinions and experiences of her family and friends and by her roles as mother, daughter, and employee.

Other social factors include reference groups, social classes, and culture.

- **Reference groups** include families, professional groups, civic organizations, and other groups with whom buyers identify and whose values or attitudes they adopt. A person may use a reference group as a

## Consider the Following: Yelp—where consumers hold the power

If you want recommendations on a business, Yelp may be just what you need. Founded by Jeremy Stoppelman and Russel Simmons, Yelp.com is a website on which consumers can rate and review businesses. Approximately 178 million users visit the site monthly, with roughly 80 percent doing so from a mobile device.* Consumers love this site and other online review sites as they perceive them as objective third-party opinions.

During her stint as marketing director for Yelp Canada, Crystal Henrickson stated that businesses have to be concerned about online review sites as almost 80 percent of regular Internet users consult the Web before making a purchase decision, and the vast majority of all searches on Yelp come from mobile apps. Mobile users are normally in the process of making a purchase decision and not just conducting research, so their impact on a business could be immediate. Henrickson's comments are echoed in a recent Bright Local Consumer Survey which found that 93 percent of shoppers read reviews before making a purchase decision.**

Yet while consumers may love Yelp, the site has a love–hate relationship with many business owners. On the one hand, businesses with loyal customers who post positive reviews on Yelp appreciate the viral nature of the site. A positive review can influence a range of potential customers. For example, Harvard Business School professor Michael Luca recently conducted a study and determined that a one-star increase in Yelp can positively impact revenue.

On the other hand, Yelp makes it easy for consumers to post negative reviews. All a business owner can do is respond either publicly on the site or privately via email to a reviewer. A common complaint from business owners is that responding to complaints can take a significant amount of time. Henrickson's advice is to take the time to respond to consumer comments, as a business would almost always respond to a customer complaining in person. She says a customer complaining online is no different than a complaint in person.

Yelp earns money by selling ad space on the site to represented businesses, but according to co-founder Stoppelman, this does not allow business owners any greater freedom to control review content. What it does give them is the ability to eliminate advertisements of other companies on their pages, the possibility for their ads to appear on other pages, and the opportunity to post photo and video content.

Despite Stoppleman's assurances, businesses have accused Yelp of manipulating reviews either to gain more advertising customers or to punish companies that refuse to advertise through Yelp's paid system. To combat complaints, Yelp has made filtered reviews visible, although they are clearly marked as filtered. Stoppelman continues to support the company's algorithm and claims that Yelp is striving for greater transparency. Whether or not Yelp's actions serve to pacify its detractors, companies are increasingly realizing that the power structure between business and consumer is changing—often in the consumer's favour.***

### DISCUSSION QUESTIONS

1. What is the benefit of Yelp to consumers?
2. What challenges face businesses that are evaluated on Yelp?
3. Do you think businesses should take the time to respond to customer feedback on Yelp? What are the pros and cons of this strategy?
4. How does Yelp contribute to improving competition and the quality of products?

*"An Introduction to Yelp Metrics as of December 31, 2018," https://www.yelp.ca/factsheet, (accessed March 1, 2019).

**Chad Otar, "How Review Sites Can Affect Your Business (And What You Can Do About It)," October 5, 2018, https://www.forbes.com/sites/forbesfinancecouncil/2018/10/05/how-review-sites-can-affect-your-business-and-what-you-can-do-about-it/#2fd8d254266a

***Chris Griffiths, "A Pro's Guide to Managing Your Reputation Online," *Globe and Mail* online, November 6, 2012, http://www.theglobeandmail.com/report-on-business/small-business/sb-digital/biz-categories-technology/a-pros-guide-to-managing-your-reputation-online/article4887679/; and Harvey Schacter, "What's the Real Impact of Online Reviews?", *Globe and Mail* online, October 10, 2011, http://www.theglobeandmail.com/report-on-business/careers/management/whats-the-real-impact-of-online-reviews/article618142/ (both accessed July 9, 2018); Yelp website, www.yelp.com (accessed August 10, 2018); "Yelp Adds a Tiny Bit of Transparency...And Inches Away from Pay for Placement," The Entrepreneur's Corner, TechDirt, ww.techdirt.com/blog/entrepreneurs/articles/20100330/1539268795.shtml (accessed August 20, 2010); Peter Burrows & Joseph Galante, "Yelp: Advertise or Else?," *Bloomberg Businessweek*, March 3, 2010, www.businessweek.com/magazine/content/10_11/b4170027355708.htm (accessed August 10, 2018); Jeremy, YELP CEO, "Additional Thoughts on Last Week's Lawsuit, or How a Conspiracy Theory Is Born," Yelp Web Log, http://officialblog.yelp.com/2010/03/additional-thoughts-on-last-weeks-lawsuit-or-how-a-conspiracy-theory-is-born-.html (accessed August 10, 2010); Kermit Pattison, "Talking to the Chief of Yelp, the Site That Businesses Love to Hate," *New York Times*, March 24, 2010, www.nytimes.com/2010/03/25/business/smallbusiness/25sbiz.html (accessed August 10, 2010); Bill Chappell, "Yelp Goes Unfiltered. Let the Arguments Begin," All Tech Considered, NPR, April 6, 2010, www.npr.org/blogs/alltechconsidered/2010/04/06/125631274/yelp-goes-unfiltered-let-the-arguments-begin (accessed August 10, 2010); Jessica Guynn, "Restaurant Review Site Yelp and Reservation Booking Site OpenTable Team Up," *Los Angeles Times*, June 3, 2010, http://latimesblogs.latimes.com/technology/2010/06/restaurant-review-site-yelp-and-reservationbooking-site-opentable-team-up.html (accessed August 10, 2017).

point of comparison or a source of information. A person new to a community may ask other group members to recommend a family doctor, for example.

- **Social classes** are determined by ranking people into higher or lower positions of respect. Criteria vary from one society to another. People within a particular social class may develop common patterns of behaviour. People in the upper-middle class, for example, might buy a Tesla or a Cadillac as a symbol of their social class.
- **Culture** is the integrated, accepted pattern of human behaviour, including thought, speech, beliefs, actions, and artifacts. Culture determines what people wear and eat and where they live and travel. For example, many Atlantic Canadians restrict travel to that particular region of the country because they are less likely to take longer vacations than other groups of Canadians, people in Quebec are more prone to eat baked beans for breakfast, and people in Alberta are more prone to purchase trucks.

**social classes** a ranking of people into higher or lower positions of respect

**culture** the integrated, accepted pattern of human behaviour, including thought, speech, beliefs, actions, and artifacts

**DID YOU KNOW?**

A recent survey found 85 percent of consumers trusted online reviews as much as reviews from their family and friends.[41]

## Understanding Buying Behaviour

Although marketers try to understand buying behaviour, it is extremely difficult to explain exactly why a buyer purchases a particular product. The tools and techniques for analyzing consumers are not exact. Marketers may not be able to determine accurately what is highly satisfying to buyers, but they know that trying to understand consumer wants and needs is the best way to satisfy them. Marriott International's Innovation Lab, for instance, tests out new hotel designs for its brands to target millennials and other desirable demographics. Wi-Fi, lighting, and more soundproof rooms are among the top desirable traits travellers desire. Another trend is that travellers are not unpacking their suitcases as much. As a result, Marriott has begun reducing the size of closets and the number of hangers to save room.[42]

## GOING GREEN

### Monsanto Faces Threats from New Superweeds

Superweeds are bad news for Monsanto, one of the world's leading agricultural products companies. Monsanto's Roundup is the best-selling herbicide in the nation. However, because of the wide-scale use of Roundup, superweeds—weeds that are resistant to herbicides and are therefore harder to control—are becoming a major challenge for farmers. When first introduced, Roundup was heralded for its remarkable ability to ward off weeds. Even when Roundup resistance first became a problem less than a decade ago, Monsanto officials claimed that resistance was rare and "manageable." Today, despite continued reassurance from Monsanto, this is no longer the case. Superweeds are increasing, with 11 species now resistant to the herbicide.

Competitors such as Dow Chemical and Syngenta are jumping at the chance to grab market share from Monsanto. They have begun promoting older herbicides and herbicide mixtures to combat superweeds. However, scientists caution that even mixing herbicides can eventually lead to resistance.

The problem is not the herbicides themselves, but the way they are used. For many years, farmers and scientists have known that crop rotation prevents pests from developing resistance to certain chemicals. However, because Roundup was so effective, many farmers would rotate one Roundup Ready (seeds that are genetically engineered to resist the herbicide) crop with another. In order to prevent future resistance, many farmers and companies will have to change their tactics. To help in this endeavour, Monsanto has the responsibility to promote and design its products in a way that will better consider their long-term impact on the environment.*

#### DISCUSSION QUESTIONS

1. Why are superweeds becoming a problem for Monsanto?
2. How are competitors capitalizing on Roundup-resistant superweeds?
3. What are some of the reasons weeds have become resistant to Roundup herbicide?

*Jack Kaskey, "The Superweed Strikes Back," *Bloomberg Businessweek*, September 12–18, 2011, pp. 21–22; Andrew Pollack, "Widely Used Crop Herbicide Is Losing Weed Resistance," *New York Times*, January 14, 2003, www.nytimes.com/2003/01/14/business/widely-used-crop-herbicide-islosing-weed-resistance.html (accessed September 26, 2011).

©Egna Laura Ojeda hernandez/Alamy Stock Photo

Marriott has created Innovative Lab to test out new hotel designs.

## The Marketing Environment

**LO 11-6** Summarize the environmental forces that influence marketing decisions.

A number of external forces directly or indirectly influence the development of marketing strategies; the following political, legal, regulatory, social, competitive, economic, and technological forces comprise the marketing environment:

- *Political, legal, and regulatory forces*—laws and regulators' interpretation of laws; law enforcement and regulatory activities; regulatory bodies, legislators and legislation, and political actions of interest groups. Specific laws, for example, require that advertisements be truthful and that all health claims be documented. Changing laws can greatly impact a business. For example, some provinces are substantially increasing minimum wage.

  The result has been an increase in the cost of doing business for many companies. Of course, the legalization of cannabis is perhaps the most substantial law to impact business in Canada in recent years. Not only has the legalization allowed companies to compete for the estimated $8 billion dollar recreational market, it has led to the development of number of new businesses servicing recreational cannabis users. For example, student entrepreneur Ron Paul of Toronto has started selling kits enabling cannabis users to grow their own products at home.
- *Social forces*—the public's opinions and attitudes toward issues such as living standards, ethics, the environment, lifestyles, and quality of life. For example, Ontario-based Crystal Head Vodka attempted to sell its vodka in a clear, skull-shaped bottle. The response from the Liquor Control Board of Ontario was to ban the booze as it deemed that the message was not appropriate, reflecting society's changing opinion about

©Hafiez Razali/Shutterstock

As more and more evidence emerges about the negative implications of children eating too much sugar, companies such as Kellogg are working to make their products healthier.

liquor consumption. Other examples include social concerns that have led marketers to design and market safer toys for children.

- *Competitive and economic forces*—competitive relationships, unemployment, purchasing power, and general economic conditions (prosperity, recession, depression, recovery, product shortages, and inflation).
- *Technological forces*—computers and other technological advances that improve distribution, promotion, and new-product development.

**DID YOU KNOW?**

The legalization of edible cannabis products has resulted in a new $4 billion market in Canada. Businesses large and small are trying to grab as much market share as possible with a variety of products including drinks and candy.

Marketing environment forces can change quickly and radically, which is one reason that marketing requires creativity and a customer focus. For example, *Rolling Stone* magazine did a business analysis before entering the Chinese market. Unfortunately, after a successful debut, the Chinese government had concerns about its licence to publish in China. The success of *Rolling Stone* concerned other lifestyle and music magazines, and they informed the authorities that the licence was not appropriate.[43]

Because such environmental forces are interconnected, changes in one may cause changes in others. Consider that, because of evidence linking children's consumption of soft drinks and fast foods to health issues such as obesity, diabetes, and osteoporosis, marketers of such products have experienced negative publicity and calls for legislation regulating the sale of soft drinks in public schools.

When Morgan Spurlock saw an evening news story about two teenagers who unsuccessfully sued McDonald's for their poor health, he decided to make the movie *Super Size Me.* As director, he went on a supersized diet of fast food and gained 25 pounds, suffered from depression, and experienced heart pain.[44] Some companies have responded to these concerns by reformulating products to make them healthier. Kellogg Company has reformulated many of its popular child-targeted products to make them more healthy. The goal is to cut sugar and fat to help fight childhood obesity. In addition, the company has launched new healthier plant-based cereals.[45]

The fast-food industry's frantic race to cook up the first "better-for-you" french fry appears to have been won by Wendy's. The number-three fast-food chain announced that it will change its cooking oil to a blend of non-hydrogenated corn and soy oils containing nearly no artery-clogging trans fats.[46]

Although the forces in the marketing environment are sometimes called *uncontrollables*, they are not totally so. A marketing manager can influence some environmental variables. For example, businesses can lobby legislators to dissuade them from passing unfavourable legislation. Figure 11.4 shows the variables in the marketing environment that affect the marketing mix and the buyer.

**Figure 11.4** | The Marketing Mix and the Marketing Environment

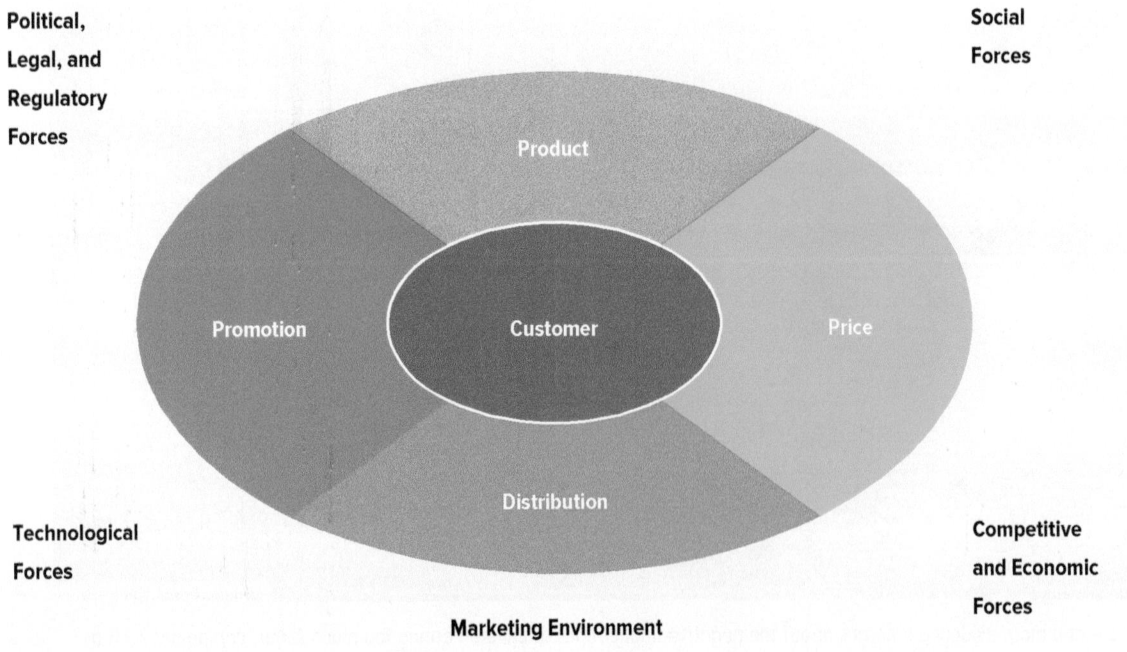

## TEAM EXERCISE

Form groups and divide the responsibility for finding examples of companies that excel in one dimension of the marketing mix (price, product, promotion, and distribution). Provide several company and product examples, and defend why each is an exemplary case. Present your research to the class.

# LEARNING OBJECTIVES SUMMARY

**LO 11-1** Define marketing and describe the exchange process.

Marketing is a group of activities designed to expedite transactions by creating, distributing, pricing, and promoting goods, services, and ideas. Marketing facilitates the exchange, the act of giving up one thing in return for something else. The central focus of marketing is to satisfy needs.

**LO 11-2** Specify the functions of marketing.

Marketing includes many varied and interrelated activities: buying, selling, transporting, storing, grading, financing, marketing research, and risk taking.

**LO 11-3** Explain the marketing concept and its implications for developing marketing strategies.

The marketing concept is the idea that an organization should try to satisfy customers' needs through coordinated activities that also allow it to achieve its goals. If a company does not implement the marketing concept, by providing products that consumers need and want while achieving its own objectives, it will not survive.

**LO 11-4** Examine the development of a marketing strategy, including market segmentation and marketing mix.

A marketing strategy is a plan of action for creating a marketing mix (product, price, promotion, distribution) for a specific target market (a specific group of consumers on whose needs and wants a company focuses its marketing efforts). Some firms use a total-market approach, designating everyone as the target market. Most firms divide the total market into segments of people who have relatively similar product needs. A company using a concentration approach develops one marketing strategy for a single market segment, whereas a multi-segment approach aims marketing efforts at two or more segments, developing a different marketing strategy for each.

**LO 11-5** Investigate how marketers conduct marketing research and study buying behaviour.

Carrying out the marketing concept is impossible unless marketers know what, where, when, and how consumers buy. Marketing research into the factors that influence buying behaviour helps marketers develop effective marketing strategies. Marketing research is a systematic, objective process of getting information about potential customers to guide marketing decisions. Buying behaviour is the decision processes and actions of people who purchase and use products.

**LO 11-6** Summarize the environmental forces that influence marketing decisions.

There are several forces that influence marketing activities: political, legal, regulatory, social, competitive, economic, and technological.

# KEY TERMS

| | | |
|---|---|---|
| attitude | learning | marketing concept |
| buying behaviour | market | marketing mix |
| concentration approach | market segment | marketing orientation |
| culture | market segmentation | marketing research |
| exchange | marketing | marketing strategy |

multi-segment approach
perception
personality
place/distribution
price
primary data
promotion
reference groups
secondary data
social classes
social roles
target market
total-market approach

## So You Want a Job *in Marketing*

You probably did not think as a child how great it would be to grow up and become a marketer. That's because often marketing is associated with sales jobs, but opportunities in marketing, public relations, product management, advertising, e-marketing, customer relationship management, and beyond represent almost one-third of all jobs in today's business world. To enter any job in the marketing field, you must balance an awareness of customer needs with business knowledge while mixing in creativity and the ability to obtain useful information to make smart business decisions.

Marketing starts with understanding the customer. Marketing research is a vital aspect in marketing decision making and presents many job opportunities. Market researchers survey customers to determine their habits, preferences, and aspirations. Activities include concept testing, product testing, package testing, test-market research, and new-product research. Salaries vary, depending on the nature and level of the position as well as the type, size, and location of the firm. An entry-level market analyst may make between $24,000 and $50,000, while a market research director may earn from $75,000 to $200,000 or more.

One of the most dynamic areas in marketing is direct marketing, where a seller solicits a response from a consumer using direct communication methods such as telephone, online communications, direct mail, or catalogues. Jobs in direct marketing include buyers, catalogue managers, research/mail-list managers, or order fulfillment managers. Most positions in direct marketing involve planning and market analysis. Some require the use of databases to sort and analyze customer information and sales history.

Use of the Internet for retail sales is growing, and the Internet continues to be very useful for business-to-business sales. E-marketing offers many career opportunities including customer relationship management (CRM). CRM helps companies market to customers through relationships, maintaining customer loyalty. Information technology plays a huge role in such marketing jobs, as you need to combine technical skills and marketing knowledge to effectively communicate with customers. Job titles include e-marketing manager, customer relationship manager, and e-services manager. A CRM customer service manager may receive a salary in the $40,000 to $45,000 range, and experienced individuals in charge of online product offerings may earn up to $100,000.

A job in any of these marketing fields will require a strong sense of the current trends in business and marketing. Customer service is vital to many aspects of marketing so the ability to work with customers and to communicate their needs and wants is important. Marketing is everywhere from the corner grocery or local non-profit organization to the largest multinational corporation, making it a shrewd choice for an ambitious and creative person. We will talk about additional job opportunities in marketing in Chapter 12.

## BUILD YOUR BUSINESS PLAN

### Customer-Driven Marketing

The first step is to develop a marketing strategy for your product or service. Who will be the target market you will specifically try to reach? What group or groups of people have the need, ability, and willingness to purchase this product? How will you segment customers within your target market? Segmenting by demographic and geographic variables are often the easiest segmentation strategies to attempt. Remember that you would like the customers in your segment to be as homogeneous and accessible as possible. You might target several segments if you feel your product or service has broad appeal.

The second step in your marketing strategy is to develop the marketing mix for your product or service. Whether you are dealing with an established product or you are creating your own product or service, you need to think about what differential advantage your product offers. What makes it unique? How should it be priced? Should the product be priced below, above, or at the market? How will you distribute the product? And last but certainly not least, you need to think about the promotional strategy for your product.

What about the uncontrollable variables you need to be aware of? Is your product something that can constantly be technologically advanced? Is your product a luxury that will not be considered by consumers when the economy is in a downturn?

## CASE | Will Crowdfunding Replace Market Research?

When Olivia Lattimore and Dave Bethune from Kingston appeared on CBC's *Dragons' Den*, the duo believed they had a winning product. As you may recall from Chapter 5, *Dragons' Den* is a show where entrepreneurs pitch ideas looking for an investment from highly successful business people.

Lattimore and Bethune's company, Limestone Technologies Plant Choir, uses polygraph technology to allow plants to play computer-based musical instruments. Limestone's technology works by taking a plant's natural rhythmic vibrations and converting it into sound using computer-generated musical instruments. Plants respond to different stimuli, including wind or interacting with humans, and produce different vibrations as a result. Several plants together, playing different instruments, provide users with relaxing sounds and a unique way to interact with nature. Limestone is hoping that users will purchase multiple instruments, which will sell for $89.99 each, allowing plants to play a symphony of sounds.

When the entrepreneurs were asked if a market existed for their product, they responded that they were in the initial stages of conducting market research. In limited research, the pair had determined that yoga studios and some individuals would be interested in their musical plant technology. To many in the business world, this would be an acceptable way to determine market potential for a new product. The entrepreneurs built the product and were using surveys to determine if people would purchase the technology which enabled their house plants to play musical instruments.

But with the advent of the Internet, social media, and crowdfunding, this may no longer be the case. Dragon investor Manjit Minhas asked them why they would waste their time conducting market research. In her opinion, market research wouldn't confirm if a market existed, as it isn't real. She advised the entrepreneurs to try to sell the product on a crowdfunding site such as Kickstarter. If there were sales, then a market exists, and that was all the market research they would need.[47]

While a few years ago Minhas's comments would have been seen as shocking, the sentiment is far from unique. In fact, fellow Dragon investor Michelle Romanow takes the thought a step further and says aspiring entrepreneurs shouldn't waste their time and money finalizing a product or conducting market research. Romanow argues entrepreneurs and businesses should build a prototype, create a video, and pre-sell the product on a crowdfunding site to see if a market exists. If sales come in, the entrepreneur should go ahead and try to build the product and business. If not, they can move on to their next idea.[48]

Fortunately for Lattimore and Bethune, one of the Dragon investors didn't have a problem that the pair hadn't yet used crowdfunding. Lane Merrifield, the creator of Club Penguin, the world's largest social network for children, which he later sold to Disney, is also an investor in a yoga studio and he thought the musical plant idea had potential. He agreed to invest $50,000 in Limestone Technologies Plant Choir for 30 percent of the business. Merrifield thinks yoga and meditation studios, and people who want to get in touch with nature, are potential customers for the product.

### DISCUSSION QUESTIONS

1. How can traditional market research offer entrepreneurs an advantage over just opting to use crowdfunding to find out if a market exists for their product?
2. Do you think companies should skip traditional market research and use crowdfunding to determine if a market exists for a product? Why or why not?
3. What are some of the potential advantages and disadvantages of pre-selling a product that is not fully developed on a crowd funding site?
4. Do you think people will purchase individual musical instruments for their plants to play at $89.99 each? Why or why not?
5. Develop a marketing strategy for Limestone, including a brief description of the product, price, place, and promotion.
6. Would you invest money in the Limestone Technologies Plant Choir? Why or why not?

# CHAPTER 12

# Dimensions of Marketing Strategy

©Tulip

## LEARNING OBJECTIVES

**After reading this chapter, you will be able to:**

- **LO 12-1** Describe the role of product in the marketing mix, including how products are developed, classified, and identified.
- **LO 12-2** Define price and discuss its importance in the marketing mix, including various pricing strategies a firm might employ.
- **LO 12-3** Identify factors affecting distribution decisions, such as marketing channels and intensity of market coverage.
- **LO 12-4** Specify the activities involved in promotion, as well as promotional strategies and promotional positioning.

# ENTER THE WORLD OF BUSINESS

**Ali Asaria Believes Traditional Retailers Can Still Thrive**

If you go out shopping, one cannot help but notice that some of the most popular stores of the past decades don't exist anymore. For example, Aeropostale, H&M Canada, Payless Shoes, Sears Canada, BCBG, Home Outfitters, Gymboree, and Crabtree have all permanently shut down their retail operations, and many on the list have declared bankruptcy and ceased any operations.

In addition to the stores that have disappeared, numerous other retailers are announcing significant store closings, including Victoria's Secret, Gap, RONA, J. Crew, and Le Chateau.[1] The trend is clear: more and more consumers are shopping online, and bricks-and-mortar retail, while not dead, is in a steep decline. While many people think traditional retail is an unattractive market, Toronto entrepreneur Ali Asaria sees opportunity. Asaria, founder and former CEO of Well.ca, an online pharmacy company, believes traditional retail is not dead, retail just needs to refocus on one of its strengths, something online websites cannot offer—human assistance. With this thought in mind, Asaria left Well.ca to start Tulip, a cloud-based app business focused on helping retailers succeed in the face of online competition.[2]

Tulip's business model is based on enhancing the retail experience by enabling sales associates to provide vastly superior customer service to in-store customers. Tulip allows sales associates to use their smartphones to quickly learn about customers' past purchases, offer recommendations that can be presented to the client, page other associates to bring products to customers while they continue assisting them, and even collect payments from anywhere in the store.

For example, if a customer visits Toys "R" Us, which is a Tulip user, looking for a crib, the sales associate can quickly learn about all the cribs on-site and online, they can show the consumer videos, social media posts, and customer reviews. Sales associates can also view competitor pricing and offer to match online prices keeping the sale in the store. Additionally, if this is a repeat customer, they know what price range of products they have traditionally bought, the brand, and even the colour. The result is an enhanced customer experience. Sales associates can also offer consumers additional product recommendations leading to increased in-store revenue.[3]

Since Asaria started the business, Tulip has enhanced the app to provide retailers with even more data and analytical tools. Tulip has launched Tulip Prism, which allows retailers to create specific customer lists based on buying behaviour and reach out to customers. For example, if Michael Kors, a Tulip adopter, brings in new spring handbags selling at $600, Tulip Prism can identify customers who buy new $600 bags every spring, and the retailer can start conversations with individual customers either face-to-face or through social media. In addition, Tulip offers Tulip Advisor, which makes suggestions to sales associates on client interactions; Tulip Analytic, to understand sales associate impact on customer sales; and Tulip Runner, which enables customers to ask for help from anywhere in the store.[4]

Tulip's customer list is growing. The company boasts that it has many of the top retailers in North America using its service, including Tory Burch, Saks, Coach, Michael Kors, Hudson's Bay Company, and Indigo. Asaria says, "I recently visited many of our customers and it was clear they all want associates to deliver great customer experiences and that great mobile tools have become the key to doing that. The intimacy and personal experience that defined retail decades ago is being brought back by brands that are investing in tech for associates that enhances the engagement with customers."[5]

As Tulip presses to move the service from early adopters to mainstream clients, they can boast some significant performance analytics. To date, retailers who adopt Tulip have seen an increase in store sales from a minimum of 2 percent to as high as 10 percent, customer's repeat purchases and order size have increased from 5 to 20 percent, and customer satisfaction has improved ranging from 10 to 30 percent.[6] Investors clearly believe in Tulip's business model, as Asaria has raised $52 million to fuel growth and technology development.[7]

## DISCUSSION QUESTIONS

1. What are some of the advantages retailers gain by using Tulip? Students may use Internet resources to see latest upgrades to the Tulip app.
2. Do you think Tulip will be successful? Why or why not?
3. Tulip's business model is based on retailers having motivated and engaged sales associates. What are some challenges with this concept? What are some potential solutions?
4. Do you think Tulip will be able to expand their business to mass merchants such as Walmart and Canadian Tire? Why or why not?

# Introduction

Creating an effective marketing strategy is important. Getting just the right mix of product, price, promotion, and distribution is essential if a business is to satisfy its target customers and achieve its own objectives (implement the marketing concept).

In Chapter 11, we introduced the concept of marketing and the various activities important in developing a marketing strategy. In this chapter, we'll take a closer look at the four dimensions of the marketing mix—product, price, distribution, and promotion—used to develop the marketing strategy. The focus of these marketing mix elements is a marketing strategy that builds customer relationships and satisfaction.

# The Marketing Mix

The key to developing a marketing strategy is maintaining the right marketing mix that satisfies the target market and creates long-term relationships with customers. To develop meaningful customer relationships, marketers have to develop and manage the dimensions of the marketing mix to give their firm an advantage over competitors. Successful companies offer at least one dimension of value that surpasses all competitors in the marketplace in meeting customer expectations. However, this does not mean that a company can ignore the other dimensions of the marketing mix; it must maintain acceptable and—if possible—distinguishable differences in the other dimensions, as well.

Tim Hortons, for example, is known for always having fresh coffee. Rogers Communications and Bell Canada are well known for their product bundles that allow consumers to save money by purchasing their smartphone, home phone, Internet, and TV programming as one package. Domino's Pizza is recognized for its superiority in distribution after developing the largest home-delivery pizza company in the world and its innovative product introductions.

> "The key to developing a marketing strategy is maintaining the right marketing mix that satisfies the target market and creates long-term relationships with customers."

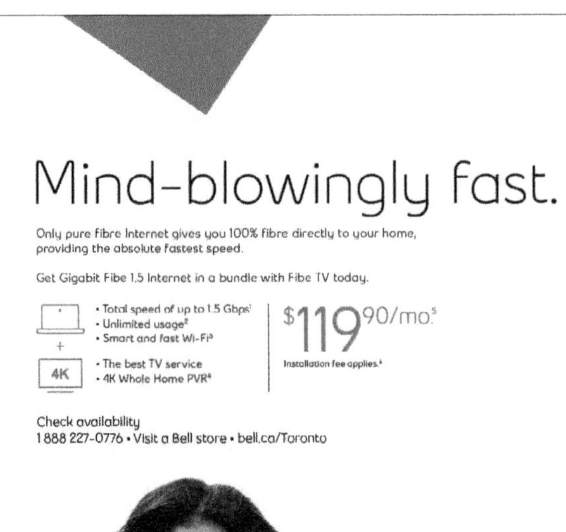

©Bell Canada

Bell Canada ad used in specific Toronto markets in 2019.

# Product Strategy

**LO 12-1** Describe the role of product in the marketing mix, including how products are developed, classified, and identified.

As mentioned previously, the term *product* refers to goods, services, and ideas. Because the product is often the most visible of the marketing mix dimensions, managing product decisions is crucial. In this section, we'll consider product development, classification, mix, life cycle, and identification.

## Developing New Products

Each year thousands of products are introduced, but few of them succeed. For example, Samsung was the world's largest smartphone manufacturer in 2016 when it launched the Note 7 phone. A few weeks later Samsung was forced to recall the phone due to batteries catching on fire. Amazon lost $170 million trying to create its own smartphone, called the Fire.[8] While their phones didn't catch on fire, they were so poorly received Amazon could not sell them even when they reduced the price to 99 cents.[9]

Umbra, a Toronto-based leader in original designs for the home, sells its products through 25,000 retailers in more than 75 countries. Umbra's co-founder and chairman, Les Mandelbaum, notes that while developing products is a key to the company's success, there are many failures that occur on the way to developing a successful product. The company operated for ten years prior to developing its first breakthrough product, which was a swing-top plastic trash can. Mandelbaum says he came up with the idea after purchasing a similar toy-sized trash can in a children's shop in Paris. He states that when he brought the product back to Canada, his staff doubted it would ever result in a profitable product for the company, but he pushed forward anyway.[10]

Even though new product development can be risky, companies can build a competitive advantage by developing new products. For example, Apple has built a very profitable company by developing the iPod, iPhone, and iPad. Readers should recognize that developing new products does not result in success every time. BlackBerry had built a dominant position in the market by developing what amounted to the world's first smartphone. Unfortunately for the company they failed to deliver products customers want, such as smartphones with advanced browsers and game capabilities, and as a result, the company's share of the handset market has fallen to less than one percent.[11] Even Apple has developed products that have not succeeded commercially, such as Apple TV, and sales results from the Apple Watch have been less than stellar.[12]

Some companies opt to acquire and create new products to establish a competitive advantage. For example, Coca-Cola has created or acquired thousands of new products, including Costa, a leading international coffee brand. Adding to its line of sparkling soft drinks, water, enhanced waters, and sports drinks, the company plans to add a range of new products such as Coke Coffee and Coke Energy drinks.

Firms can take considerable time to get a product ready for the market: it took more than 20 years for the first photocopier, for example. General Motors has trimmed the time required to develop and introduce a new vehicle model from 4 years to 18 months. *Canadian Business* columnist Rick Spence notes that senior management must employ and support innovators if a company hopes to develop new products and processes. Before introducing a new product, a business must follow a multi-step process: idea development, the screening of new ideas, business analysis, product development, test marketing, and commercialization.

©PG Pictures/Alamy

Apple, the global technology company that has made billions by developing iPhones and iPads, is not always successful with its product development. The Apple Watch has yet to catch on with consumers. Do you think the Apple Watch will ultimately succeed?

**DID YOU KNOW?**

Apple spent $15 billion on research and development in 2018.[13]

**Idea Development.** New ideas can come from marketing research, engineers, and outside sources such as advertising agencies and management consultants. Microsoft has a separate division—Microsoft Research—where scientists devise the technology of the future. The division has more than 700 full-time employees who work in a university-like research atmosphere. Research teams then present their ideas to Microsoft engineers who are developing specific products.[14]

As stated in Chapter 11, ideas sometimes come from customers too. For example, in preparation for the Winter Olympic Games, Speed Skating Canada relied heavily on feedback from skaters (customers) to develop new skating suits designed to reduce wind traction and improve race times.[15] Ideas can also come from observing trends in the marketplace and paying attention to what competitors are doing. For example, Instagram introduced Stories in 2016, a feature that allows users to share photos and videos that automatically delete in 24 hours. Instagram, which added 250 million Stories users, likely took the concept from Snapchat, which had introduced the idea a few years earlier.[16]

Oded Shenkar, a business expert, notes that many successful entrepreneurs and companies copy ideas from others, including such giants as Walmart and Procter & Gamble. Shenkar states that while many business and aspiring entrepreneurs think they have to come up with a truly original idea in order to be successful, this is not the case. In fact, copying effectively can also be a good strategy.[17] Other sources for new products are brainstorming and intracompany incentives or rewards for good ideas. New ideas can even create a company. For example, Alexander Peters and Rohan Mahimker were completing their fourth year at Waterloo University when they created Prodigy Education. The partners thought if they could combine math and gaming they would have a product that both parents and children would want to buy. The result was a successful game with over 50 million users and a brand new company.[18]

©Prodigy Education

While enrolled at the University of Waterloo, Alexander Peters and Rohan Mahimker created a new game-based educational software for students to practise math. In addition to creating a new game, the partners created a new company.

**New Idea Screening.** The next step in developing a new product is idea screening. In this phase, a marketing manager should look at the organization's resources and objectives, and assess the firm's ability to produce and market the product. Important aspects to be considered at this stage are consumer desires, the competition, technological changes, social trends, and political, economic, and environmental considerations.

Basically, there are two reasons new products succeed: they are able to meet a need or solve a problem better than products already available, or they add variety to the product selection currently on the market. For example, Goodyear has developed a tire that will self-inflate as soon as the air pressure in the tire starts to drop. The tire passed through the screening stage as Goodyear obviously has experience manufacturing and marketing innovative tires, and management felt there would be a demand for such a product.[19]

*Dragons' Den*, a show in which entrepreneurs pitch businesses as well as inventions, usually showcases a number of products that shouldn't have gotten past the screening stage. For example, in a recent telecast, an entrepreneur introduced the Fenis, a device that allows women to use the washroom while standing upright.[20] If the entrepreneurs had screened their idea, they may have realized that the invention was not desired by consumers and did not solve a problem or improve on a current product.

Bringing together a team of knowledgeable people, including design, engineering, marketing, and customers, is a great way to screen ideas. Using the Internet to encourage collaboration is the next sea of innovation for marketers to screen ideas.[21] After many ideas were screened, Heinz introduced kid-targeted Silly Squirts ketchup with three cool drawing nozzles to keep kids amused and entertained at dinner. In addition, Easy Squeeze upside-down bottles added to convenience.[22] Most new-product ideas are rejected during screening because they seem inappropriate or impractical for the organization, but many, which go on to fail, still make it to market. Indeed, GfK Custom Research has established a collection, nicknamed the Museum of Product Failures, just outside Ann Arbor, Michigan. While not open to the public, companies considering a product idea can visit—for a $5000 entrance fee—this massive physical database of products as a stark reminder of the consequences of poor market research.[23]

**Business Analysis.** Business analysis is a basic assessment of a product's compatibility in the marketplace and its potential profitability. Both the size of the market and competing products are often studied at this point. The most important question relates to market demand: How will the product affect the firm's sales, costs, and profits?

**Product Development.** If a product survives the first three steps, it is developed into a prototype that should reveal the intangible attributes it possesses as perceived by the consumer. Product development is often expensive, and few product ideas make it to this stage. New product research and development costs vary. Adding a new colour to an existing item may cost $100,000 to $200,000, but launching a completely new product can cost millions of dollars. For example, Andrew Scott of Vancouver spent over $1 million developing a replacement for traditional parking meters. Scott's parking meters enable remote monitoring by parking enforcement, six locking points to detect theft, full-colour graphic screens, and a wide variety of payment options including coins, bank cards, and credit cards.[24]

The Coca-Cola Company reduced the time and cost of product development research by 50 percent when it created an online panel of 100 teenagers and asked them how to remake its Powerade sports drink.[25] During product development, various elements of the marketing mix must be tested. Copyrights, tentative advertising copy, packaging, labelling, and descriptions of a target market are integrated to develop an overall marketing strategy.

**Test Marketing.** **Test marketing** is a trial mini-launch of a product in limited areas that represent the potential market. It allows a complete test of the marketing strategy in a natural environment, giving the organization an opportunity to discover weaknesses and eliminate them before the product is fully launched. For example, Burger King has recently announced that they are rolling out the Impossible Whopper, a vegetarian hamburger that Burger King claims tastes the same as a traditional Whopper, across North America. Prior to the North American launch Burger King tested the products out in 59 St. Louis restaurants to gauge consumer reaction, which the company described as overwhelmingly positive.[26]

**test marketing** a trial mini-launch of a product in limited areas that represent the potential market

©Grzegorz Czapski/Shutterstock

Burger King has recently announced a rollout of the Impossible Whopper, a vegetarian Whopper, after first testing the product at 59 St. Louis restaurants.

Test marketing is not limited to new products; companies will also test new packaging, labels, and so forth before rolling them out in larger geographical areas. For example, Tim Hortons is testing a new coffee cup lid in 100 locations across Canada. Prior to testing the lid at 100 stores, Tim Hortons introduced the lids in just six Ontario stores to gauge consumer feedback.[27] Product testing is certainly not new to Tim Hortons. When the company was considering introducing steeped tea, it first tried the product in Atlantic Canada to determine what the public reaction would be. And when Tim Hortons was considering increasing the size of its coffee cups, it tested the concept in two Ontario markets, Sudbury and Kingston, to gauge customer reaction.[28]

**commercialization** the full introduction of a complete marketing strategy and the launch of the product for commercial success

**Commercialization.** **Commercialization** is the full introduction of a complete marketing strategy and the launch of the product for commercial success. During commercialization, the firm gears up for full-scale production, distribution, and promotion. When Research In Motion introduced the BlackBerry Storm, it spent millions on production, distribution, advertising, and publicity for the product. The original product did not catch on with consumers and was replaced by the Storm2 a short time later.

A more successful example of a product launch may be Procter & Gamble's introduction of the Fusion razor, when it used its large distribution and retail network and spent more than $6 million for just two Super Bowl ads for the five-blade product. It blanketed stores with 180,000 displays in the first week, coverage that had taken a year to achieve with the Mach3 razor in 1998. The Fusion razor commands 30 percent higher prices than Mach3 products, which—at a time when Procter & Gamble cannot increase the prices on Tide or Crest—will boost earnings by $120 million and increase market share to 15 percent.[29]

It's often not until commercialization that companies will know if a product is going to be successful. New products released in 2019 include a connected door lock, a television which rolls out, and a precision skincare system which uses a tiny camera to detect skim blemishes and automatically applies make-up or serum. Only time will tell if these products will be successful, even though the companies have spent countless hours and millions of dollars ensuring that consumers will want to buy them.

©Satya Organic Skincare

Patrice Mousseau, 2017 Aboriginal Entrepreneur of the Year, says her entrepreneurship journey started when she wanted to find an organic treatment for her young daughter's eczema. Today her product, Satya, is being sold nationally in 700 stores and expanding globally.

## ENTREPRENEURSHIP IN ACTION

### Indigenous Entrepreneur Patrice Mousseau Solves a Common Skin Problem

**Company:** Satya

**Founder:** Patrice Mousseau

**Founded:** 2013

**Success:** Satya cream is now available in 700 stores across Canada.

Patrice Mousseau, an Ojibway from the Fort William First Nation community in Ontario, says her entrepreneurship journey started with a need to solve a problem. Shortly after the birth of her daughter, her new baby developed red welts on her body and was subsequently diagnosed with eczema. The most common treatment for eczema is steroid cream and Mousseau was concerned about the long-term impact of using steroids on her young child.

Given her past work experience as a journalist, Mousseau notes that she was used to doing research and started investigating alternate treatments. Mousseau says she essentially took everything she could learn from academic journals and medical research, combined this with her knowledge about Indigenous medicine in her crock-pot, and cooked up a treatment. Mousseau says she tested the chemical- and fragrance-free cream and all her daughter's eczema cleared up in two days.

Mousseau's product development journey might have ended there, but she was inspired at a entrepreneurship conference and says that, as an Indigenous woman, she wanted to create a business that would inspire others. With this in mind, Satya cream was born. Mousseau says *satya* is a Sanskrit word that means *truth and virtue,* and this is what her product represents.

Mousseau started to sell her product at farmers markets, and her first day revenues were $110. She soon expanded to craft fairs and made contacts at local shops, leading to roughly 70 stores carrying her cream. Her big break came when distributor Purity Life Health Products learned about Satya and started to distribute the products nationally. Satya is now available in 700 stores across Canada and employs six working mothers in Vancouver. Mousseau notes that to support working mothers she allows them to work when they can, given their busy lives, and she pays them what is living wage in Vancouver, $22 an hour.

Mousseau's future plans include international expansion and one day building her own manufacturing centre on Aboriginal land near Vancouver. Mousseau says her short-term plans are to continue to introduce new products and to serve as a role model for other Indigenous women. Mousseau notes that business practices are changing such that people are concerned about hearing everyone's ideas and valuing their opinions. She says this trait comes naturally to Indigenous women and they are well positioned for entrepreneurial success as a result.*

#### DISCUSSION QUESTIONS

1. Explain what new product development steps Mousseau went through as she developed her company and cream, Satya.
2. Given Mousseau's business and her actions, do you think she qualifies as a social entrepreneur? Why or why not? Students may wish to use Internet resources to revisit the term.
3. How would you classify Mousseau's cream using the categories directly discussed below. Why?

*Karen Kwan, "From Home Remedy to Worldwide Organic Skincare Success." February 19, 2019, https://satya.ca/blogs/satya-organics/start-up-here-toronto-article; Satya website, "From Crockpots to Whole Foods: The Launch of Satya Organic Skincare," October 18, 2018, https://satya.ca/blogs/satya-organics/from-crockpots-to-whole-foods-the-launch-of-satya-organic-skin-care; Rick Spence, "Fire Up the crock pot – the baby has eczema and mom has the answer," January 12, 2018, https://satya.ca/blogs/satya-organics

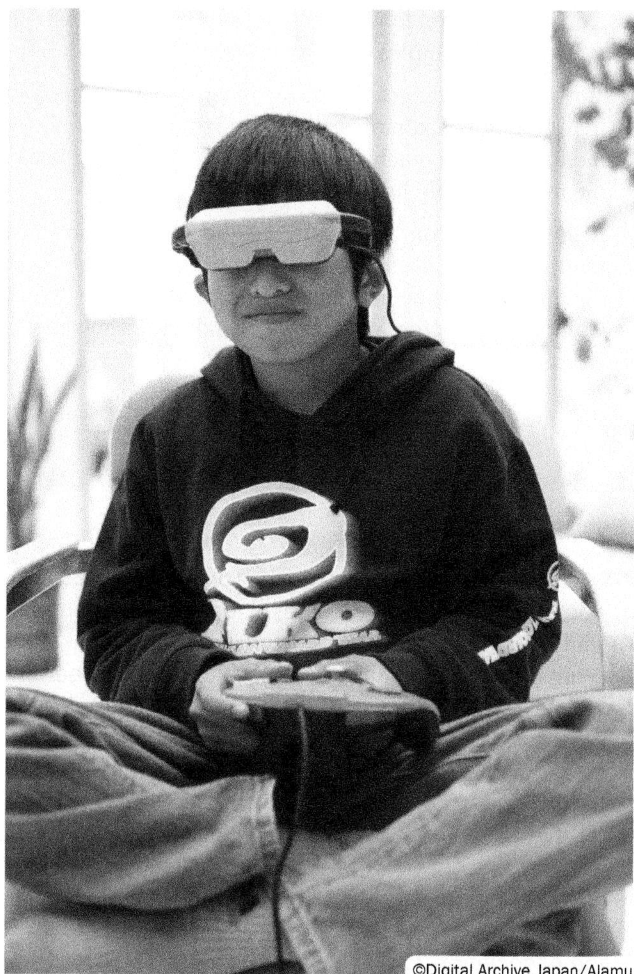

©Digital Archive Japan/Alamy

Virtual reality headsets are predicted to be the next big thing in technology and gaming. Yet only time will tell if people will be willing to buy and wear the devices.

## Classifying Products

Products are usually classified as either consumer products or business products. **Consumer products** are for household or family use; they are not intended for any purpose other than daily living. They can be further classified as convenience products, shopping products, and specialty products on the basis of consumers' buying behaviour and intentions.

**consumer products** products intended for household or family use

- *Convenience products*, such as eggs, milk, bread, and newspapers, are bought frequently, without a lengthy search, and often for immediate consumption. Consumers spend virtually no time planning where to purchase these products and usually accept whatever brand is available.
- *Shopping products*, such as furniture, audio equipment, clothing, and sporting goods, are purchased after the consumer has compared competitive products and

©hurricanehank/Shutterstock

Hoverboards started being sold in late 2015 and into 2016. Would you purchase one of these?

"shopped around." Price, product features, quality, style, service, and image all influence the decision to buy.

- *Specialty products*, such as ethnic foods, designer clothing and shoes, art, and antiques require even greater research and shopping effort. Consumers know what they want and go out of their way to find it; they are not willing to accept a substitute.

©Waxart/Dreamstime

Milk is a convenience product. It is bought frequently by consumers for relatively quick consumption without their conducting a lengthy search.

**Business products** are used directly or indirectly in the operation or manufacturing processes of businesses. They are usually purchased for the operation of an organization or the production of other products; thus, their purchase is tied to specific goals and objectives. They, too, can be further subdivided:

**business products** products that are used directly or indirectly in the operation or manufacturing processes of businesses

- *Raw materials* are natural products taken from the earth or from the oceans, and recycled solid waste. Iron ore, bauxite, lumber, cotton, and fruits and vegetables are examples.
- *Major equipment* covers large, expensive items used in production. Examples include earth-moving equipment, stamping machines, and robotic equipment used on auto assembly lines.
- *Accessory equipment* includes items used for production, office, or management purposes, which usually do not become part of the final product. Computers, copiers, calculators, and hand tools are examples.

## GOING GREEN

### Levi's Blue Jeans Go Green

Levi Strauss & Co. has long been known for its 501s and affordable prices. Recently, the company delved into the premium denim market, dominated by brands such as Earl Jeans, 7 for All Mankind, Citizens for Humanity, and True Religion, by launching its Premium collection. Now, in an attempt to break into yet another hot market, Levi's is going green.

According to the research group Mintel, about 35 million people in the United States regularly purchase "green" products. Consumers are increasingly willing to pay more for earth-friendly products and services. As a result, companies are going to great lengths to prove that they are part of the green movement. Many are switching to Earth-friendly packaging or new production methods that conserve energy. Levi's is producing 100 percent organic cotton jeans.

These new jeans, priced at $250 a pair, are made with 100 percent organic cotton, natural dyes, tags composed of recycled paper and soy ink, and recycled rivets. The company is also releasing less expensive lines composed partly of organic and recycled materials.

Although many of us might be willing to switch to green jeans, we may wonder at the price and find it prohibitive. Why is going green sometimes so expensive? In the case of Levi's jeans, it's the organic cotton. The demand for organic cotton is currently much greater than the supply, making it expensive. For cotton to be certified organic, it cannot be genetically modified and must be pesticide and fungicide free. In 2005, more than 50 percent of cotton in the United States was genetically modified. Many companies are turning to farmers overseas, but certification for these farmers can be a challenge. As of 2007, certified organic cotton composed less than 1 percent of the world's cotton supply. For now, Levi's can only produce a limited number of green jeans, hence the high price.

However, the very issue that drives up prices can be used as a marketing strategy to gain customers. Many people are willing to pay more to support farmers committed to harvesting through organic methods. In fact, at the recent Cannes Lions International Advertising Festival, *eco-marketing* was an extremely popular topic. Consumers are excited about green products and services, and companies are spending big bucks to promote their stances on going green. According to TNS Media Intelligence, marketers spent $18 million on green-focused television advertising in a three-month time span.

While going green may seem to some like a current fad, indicators point to a prolonged increase in demand for such products. According to the Organic Trade Association, Canadian organic retail sales have grown every year since 1990. It seems that companies can only benefit from a continued investment in eco-friendly items, and Levi's appears committed to incorporating organic cotton and other eco-friendly materials into its product lines.*

#### DISCUSSION QUESTIONS

1. Why can companies charge a premium price for green products?
2. What else might Levi's do to increase its offering of moderately priced green products?
3. How much more would you be willing to pay for environmentally friendly clothing such as Levi's new green jeans?

*Reena Jana, "Green Threads for the Eco Chic," *BusinessWeek*, September 27, 2006, www.businessweek.com/print/innovate/content/sep2006/id20060927_111136.htm (accessed June 20, 2007); Laura Petrecca and Theresa Howard, "Eco-marketing a Hot Topic for Advertisers at Cannes," *USA Today*, June 22, 2007, www.usatoday.com/money/advertising/2007-06-22-cannes-green-usat_N.htm?csp=34 (accessed June 23, 2007); Laura McClure, "Green Jeans," *Reader's Digest*, June 2007, p. 213; "Levi's Brand Launches 100% Organic Cotton Jeans," www.levistrauss.com, July 5, 2006, https://www.businesswire.com/news/home/20060705005220/en/Levis-Brand-Launches-100-Organic-Cotton-Jeans (accessed June 20, 2007).

- *Component parts* are finished items, ready to be assembled into the company's final products. Tires, window glass, batteries, and spark plugs are component parts of automobiles.
- *Processed materials* are things used directly in production or management operations but not readily identifiable as component parts. Varnish, for example, is a processed material for a furniture manufacturer.
- *Supplies* include materials that make production, management, and other operations possible, such as paper, pencils, paint, cleaning supplies, and so on.
- *Industrial services* include financial, legal, marketing research, security, janitorial, and exterminating services. Purchasers decide whether to provide these services internally or to acquire them from an outside supplier.

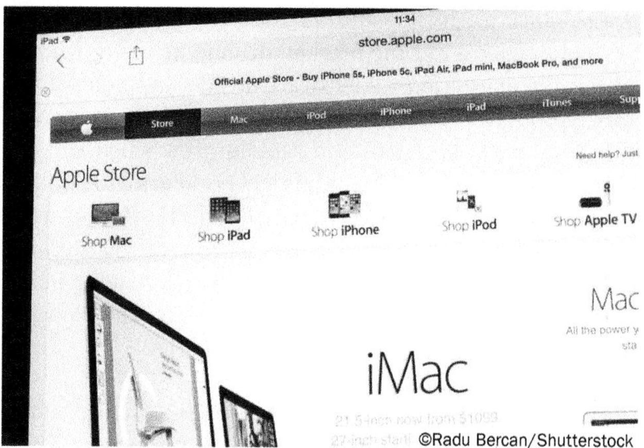

©Radu Bercan/Shutterstock

Apple's product mix and its many product lines are visible on the company's website.

## Product Line and Product Mix

Product relationships within an organization are of key importance. A **product line** is a group of closely related products that are treated as a unit because of similar marketing strategy. At Colgate-Palmolive, for example, the oral-care product line includes Colgate toothpaste, toothbrushes, and dental floss. A **product mix** is all the products offered by an organization. For example, a product line at Lululemon could be all of the company's yoga gear while its product mix would be its full range of products—clothing, equipment, and accessories. Figure 12.1 displays a sampling of the product mix and product lines of the Colgate-Palmolive Company.

**product line** a group of closely related products that are treated as a unit because of similar marketing strategy, production, or end-use considerations

**product mix** all the products offered by an organization

## Product Life Cycle

Like people, products are born, grow, mature, and eventually die. Some products have very long lives. Ivory Soap was introduced in 1879 and is still popular. In contrast, a new computer chip is usually outdated within a year because of technological breakthroughs and rapid changes in the computer industry. There are four stages in the life cycle of a product: introduction, growth, maturity, and decline (Figure 12.2). The stage a product is in helps determine marketing strategy.

**Figure 12.2** | Product Life Cycle

| Introduction | Growth | Maturity | Decline |
|---|---|---|---|
| 3D television | DVRs | Flat-screen televisions | AM/FM radios |
| YouTube movies | Blu-ray players | Laptop computers | VCRs |
| Electric cars | Tablet computers | Chevrolet Corvette | Desktop computers |

In the *introductory stage*, consumer awareness and acceptance of the product are limited, sales are zero, and profits are negative. Profits are negative because the firm has spent money on research, development, and marketing to launch the product. During the introductory stage, marketers focus on making consumers aware of the product and its benefits. When Procter & Gamble introduced the Tide Stainbrush to reach the 70 percent of consumers who pre-treat stains when doing laundry, it employed press releases as well as television and magazine advertising to make consumers aware of the new product.[30] Sales accelerate as the product enters the growth stage of the life cycle.

In the *growth stage*, sales increase rapidly and profits peak, then start to decline. One reason

**Figure 12.1** | Colgate-Palmolive's Product Mix and Product Lines

Product Mix (columns) / Product Lines (rows)

| *Oral Care* | *Personal Care* | *Household Care* | *Pet Nutrition* |
|---|---|---|---|
| Toothpaste | Men's antiperspirant/deodorant | Dishwashing | Science diet |
| Toothbrushes | Women's antiperspirant/deodorant | Fabric conditioner | Prescription diet |
| Kids' products | Bar soap | Household cleaners | |
| Whitening products | Body wash | Institutional products | |
| Over the counter | Liquid hand wash | | |
| From the dentist | Toiletries for men | | |

profits start to decline during the growth stage is that new companies enter the market, driving prices down and increasing marketing expenses. Consider Apple's iTunes store. Apple developed iTunes to sell music and compete with Sony and Microsoft, and rapidly grew sales and the brand. In recent years, iTunes has lost popularity to Spotify, which has emerged as a strong competitor, offering what consumers perceive to be a superior product.[31] During the growth stage, the firm tries to strengthen its position in the market by emphasizing the product's benefits and identifying market segments that want these benefits.

> "During the *decline stage*, sales continue to fall rapidly. Profits also decline and may even become losses as prices are cut and necessary marketing expenditures are made."

Sales continue to increase at the beginning of the *maturity stage*, but then the sales curve peaks and starts to decline while profits also decline. This stage is characterized by severe competition and heavy expenditures. Automobiles are an example of a mature product; intense competition in the auto industry requires Toyota, GM, and other automakers to spend huge sums to make their products stand out in a crowded marketplace.

During the *decline stage*, sales continue to fall rapidly. Profits also decline and may even become losses as prices are cut and necessary marketing expenditures are made. As profits drop, firms may eliminate certain models or items. To reduce expenses and squeeze out any remaining profits, marketing expenditures may be cut back, even though such cutbacks accelerate the sales decline.

Finally, plans must be made for phasing out the product and introducing new ones to take its place. Unfortunately for Mattel, the Barbie doll has seen her status and sales slide as she has been replaced on retail shelves with more edgy products such as Bratz. Barbie became vulnerable to competition from Bratz and other toys, and to the growth of toy sales in stores such as Walmart when they chose to allocate shelf space to products they considered more profitable.[32] CanJet airlines, founded in Halifax, Nova Scotia, was pulled from the market after two years after its owner decided the marketplace would not sustain the airline. The company later re-emerged, specializing in charter flights and southern destinations.

## Identifying Products

Branding, packaging, and labelling can be used to identify or distinguish one product from others. As a result, they

### Consider the Following: Disney English—a new market niche for Disney

Although Disney had high hopes for developing a theme park in Hong Kong, it was soon disappointed. Attendance at Hong Kong Disneyland was below expectations, costing Disney millions of dollars. Although attendance has risen in recent years, Hong Kong Disneyland still faced 2011 losses of more than $30 million. The company plans to open a bigger $4.4 billion resort on the Chinese mainland in Shanghai. Although this new venture might be successful, it could also further cannibalize Hong Kong Disneyland sales. Disney theme parks face many challenges as the company tries to adapt to different cultures.

Ironically, there is one business niche in China where Disney appears to be thriving: English education. In 2008, the Walt Disney Company launched Disney English in China. Teaching English to children in China is big business, and the growing private education sector is a $3.7 billion market. Chinese parents are determined that their children learn English early as a component of future academic and job success. Disney English caters to children aged 2 through 6 and to grade-school children. Its locations tripled to 22 in a one-year period. Lessons, books, songs, exercises, and more are based on Disney stories and characters, fully immersing children in all things Disney. The program is expensive for the average Chinese citizen, but many parents are willing to pay.

Disney claims its schools in China were created solely to teach English, saying that it saw an opportunity to use its characters to motivate learning. However, it also offers the unique marketing opportunity to make both parents and children aware of Disney offerings. Many parents and children appear happy with the program, which could cause them to view Disney favourably in the future. One has to wonder whether these favourable relationships with Disney English participants will help to increase demand for its Hong Kong and Shanghai theme parks.*

#### DISCUSSION QUESTIONS

1. Why do you think Disney decided to open up a larger park in Shanghai?
2. Why has Disney English been such a successful program?
3. How might the Disney English program indirectly market the theme parks?

*Allison Enright, "The Urge to Merge," *Marketing News*, March 15, 2006, pp. 9–10.

are key marketing activities that help position a product appropriately for its target market.

**Branding.** **Branding** is the process of naming and identifying products. A *brand* is a name, term, symbol, design, or combination of these that identifies a product and distinguishes it from other products. Consider that Tim Hortons, Google, and iPhone are brand names that are used to identify entire product categories, much like Xerox has become synonymous with photocopying and Kleenex with tissues. Protecting a brand name is important in maintaining a brand identity.[33]

**branding** the process of naming and identifying products

Recently a Cape Breton, Nova Scotia–based company, Glenora Distilleries, makers of Glen Breton Whisky, emerged from a nine-year fight over the right to use the word *Glen* in its brand and on its labels. The Scotch Whisky Association claimed that the use of the name was leading consumers to believe the product was manufactured in Scotland. Throughout the legal proceedings, the Association stated it was protecting the Scottish brand and reputation as the premier manufacturer of whisky and scotch in the world. Lauchie MacLean, owner of Glenora, argued that the company name is derived from the company's home community—Glenville, Cape Breton. After a lengthy dispute, the Supreme Court of Canada found that MacLean could continue to use the name Glen, which prompted the company to release a new product aptly called The Battle of the Glen.[34]

A new trend has emerged in marketing, where the CEO or founder of the firm actually becomes the brand or unique feature that distinguishes the company from its competitors. Christine Magee, co-founder of Sleep Country Canada, Heather Reisman from Indigo/Chapters, and Galen Weston Jr. from President's Choice and Loblaws are three Canadian examples. While this strategy appears to be becoming more popular, challenges exist if the CEO leaves the company or fails to live up to the brand image, as was the case with Martha Stewart in the U.S., who actually spent time in prison.

Students should realize that successful brands can on their own become very valuable and sometimes be worth more than the products that they represent. For example, Polaroid, a brand that was once synonymous with instant cameras, is making a comeback and at one point even hired Lady Gaga as the firm's creative director. The company, which was bought by private investors including Toronto-based Hilco Consumer Capital, is returning to the photo business with a slew of new products, including some of its classic instant cameras.[35]

*Brand equity* refers to the awareness, loyalty, perceived quality, image, and emotions that people feel toward certain brands. Brands that are well established enjoy brand equity, which is the degree to which customers are committed to future purchases of the brand. The world's ten most valuable brands are shown in Table 12.1 and the ten most valuable brands in Canada are displayed in Table 12.2.

©BAKOUNINE/Shutterstock

Polaroid is making a comeback, and the firm even employed Lady Gaga as the firm's creative director for a time. The company, which was bought by private investors including Toronto-based Hilco Consumer Capital, is returning to the photo business and even selling some of its classic instant cameras.

**Table 12.1** | The Ten Most Valuable Brands in the World–2018[36]

| Rank | Brand | Brand Value (US$billion) |
|---|---|---|
| 1 | Apple | $182.8 |
| 2 | Google | 132.1 |
| 3 | Microsoft | 104.9 |
| 4 | Facebook | 94.8 |
| 5 | Amazon | 70.9 |
| 6 | Coca-Cola | 57.3 |
| 7 | Samsung | 47.6 |
| 8 | Disney | 47.5 |
| 9 | Toyota | 44.7 |
| 10 | AT&T | 41.9 |

**Table 12.2** | The Ten Most Valuable Brands in Canada–2018[37]

| Rank | Brand | Brand Value (C$billion) |
|---|---|---|
| 1. | Royal Bank of Canada | $17.3 |
| 2. | TD | 15.6 |
| 3. | Bell | 13.5 |
| 4. | Scotiabank | 12.7 |
| 5. | BMO | 10.2 |
| 6. | Rogers | 9.8 |
| 7. | Telus | 9.6 |
| 8. | CIBC | 8.9 |
| 9. | Brookfield Asset Management | 8.4 |
| 10. | Thomson Reuters | 6.6 |

©Bayne Stanley/Alamy Stock Photo

Generic products like these appeal to consumers who are less concerned about quality and consistency, but want lower prices.

The brand name is the part of the brand that can be said aloud and consists of letters, words, and numbers—such as *WD-40 lubricant*. A *brand mark* is the part of the brand that is a distinctive design, such as the silver star on the hood of a Mercedes or the McDonald's golden arches logo. A **trademark** is a brand that is registered with the Canadian Intellectual Property Office and is thus legally protected from use by any other firm. Examples of well-known trademarks include the National Hockey League's logo and the Stanley Cup and the Nike swoosh.

**trademark** a brand that is registered with the Canadian Intellectual Property Office and is thus legally protected from use by any other firm

**manufacturer brands** brands initiated and owned by the manufacturer to identify products from the point of production to the point of purchase

**private distributor brands** brands, which may cost less than manufacturer brands, that are owned and controlled by a wholesaler or retailer

Two major categories of brands are manufacturer brands and private distributor brands. **Manufacturer brands** are brands initiated and owned by the manufacturer to identify products from the point of production to the point of purchase. Bell, Bombardier, Canadian Tire, and Petro-Canada are examples. **Private distributor brands**, which may be less expensive than manufacturer brands, are owned and controlled by a wholesaler or retailer, such as Kenmore appliances (Sears) and President's Choice grocery products (Loblaws).

While private-label brands were once considered cheaper and of poorer quality, such as Walmart's Ol' Roy dog food, many private-label brands are increasing in quality and image, and competing with national brands. For example, many President's Choice products are considered to be on par with or superior to branded products. The brand was launched by former Loblaws president Dave Nichol, and his first major success was The Decadent, a chocolate chip cookie made with butter and President's Choice–brand Decadent chocolate chips, which became Canada's best-selling cookie. Sobeys, in response to President's Choice, re-launched its own private brand, which was originally called Sobeys, changing the name to Our Best then to Our Compliments brand, and finally today to Compliments or Sensations by Compliments for premium products.[38]

Another type of brand that has developed is **generic products**. They often come in plain, simple packages that carry only the generic name of the product—peanut butter, tomato juice, aspirin, dog food, and so on. They appeal to consumers who may be willing to sacrifice quality or product consistency to get a lower price.

**generic products** products that often come in simple packages and carry only their generic name

**packaging** the external container that holds and describes the product

Companies use two basic approaches to branding multiple products. In one, a company gives each product within its complete product mix its own brand name. Warner-Lambert, for example, sells many well-known consumer products—Dentyne, Chiclets, Listerine, Halls, Rolaids, and Trident—each individually branded. This branding policy ensures that the name of one product does not affect the names of others, and different brands can be targeted at different segments of the same market, increasing the company's market share (its percentage of the sales for the total market for a product). Another approach to branding is to develop a family of brands with each of the firm's products carrying the same name or at least part of the name. Gillette, Sara Lee, and Dell use this approach.

**Packaging.** The **packaging**, or external container that holds and describes the product, influences consumers' attitudes and their buying decisions. A survey of over 1200 consumers found that 40 percent are willing to try a

©The Canadian Press/Jonathan Hayward

Coca-Cola's bottle was changed for the 2010 Winter Olympic Games into a canvas for Aboriginal art.

new product based on its packaging.[39] It is estimated that consumers' eyes linger only 2.5 seconds on each product on an average shopping trip; therefore, product packaging should be designed to attract and hold consumers' attention.

A package can perform several functions, including protection, economy, convenience, and promotion. Beverage manufacturers have been redesigning their bottles to make them more convenient for consumers and to promote them to certain markets. Scientists videotaped people drinking from different types of bottles and made plaster casts of their hands. They found that the average gulp is 190.45 mL (6.44 ounces) and that half the population would rather suck liquid through a pop-up top than drink it.

Packaging also helps create an overall brand image. Coca-Cola is partnering with Disney to bring custom bottles of Coke to the new Star Wars land, Galaxy's Edge. The bottles will resemble droids and have a unique texture and feel.[40] Coke similarly transformed its bottle for the 2010 Winter Olympic Games in Vancouver into a canvas for Aboriginal art. In this way, the corporation was able to connect with Canadians, and the bottles have become collector's items.[41]

**Labelling.** **Labelling**, the presentation of important information on the package, is closely associated with packaging. The content of labelling, often required by law, may include ingredients or content, nutrition facts (calories, fat, etc.), care instructions, suggestions for use (such as recipes), the manufacturer's address, toll-free number, and website, and other useful information. In Canada, all labels must be bilingual. McDonald's introduced packaging that lets consumers know the nutritional value of Big Macs as well as other products. It was the first fast-food chain to adopt the initiative.[42] This information can have a strong impact on sales. The labels of many products, particularly food and drugs, must carry warnings, instructions, certifications, or manufacturers' identifications.

**labelling** the presentation of important information on a package

**Product Quality.** **Quality** reflects the degree to which a good, service, or idea meets the demands and requirements of customers. Quality products are often referred to as reliable, durable, easily maintained, easily used, a good value, or a trusted brand name. The level of quality is the amount of quality that a product possesses, and the consistency of quality depends on the product maintaining the same level of quality over time.

**quality** the degree to which a good, service, or idea meets the demands and requirements of customers

Quality of service is difficult to gauge because it depends on customers' perceptions of how well the service meets or exceeds their expectations. In other words, service quality is judged by consumers, not the service providers. A bank may define service quality as employing friendly and knowledgeable employees, but the bank's customers may be more concerned with waiting time, ATM access, security, and statement accuracy. Similarly, an airline traveller considers on-time arrival, on-board food service, and satisfaction with the ticketing and boarding process. J.D. Power, a global market information service firm, ranks customer satisfaction in many Canadian and worldwide industries.

The quality of services provided by businesses on the Internet can be gauged by consumers on such sites as ConsumerReports.org and BBBOnline. The subscription service offered by ConsumerReports.org provides consumers with a view of e-commerce sites' business, security, and privacy policies. BBBOnline is dedicated to promoting responsibility online. The Web Credibility Project focuses on how health, travel, advocacy, news, and shopping sites disclose business relationships with the companies and products they cover or sell, especially when such relationships pose a potential conflict of interest.[43]

## Pricing Strategy

**LO 12-2** Define price and discuss its importance in the marketing mix, including various pricing strategies a firm might employ.

In Chapter 11, we defined *price* as the value placed on an object exchanged between a buyer and a seller. Buyers' interest in price stems from their expectations about the usefulness of a product or the satisfaction they may derive from it. Because buyers have limited resources, they must allocate those resources to obtain the products they most desire. They must decide whether the benefits gained in an exchange are worth the buying power sacrificed.

Almost anything of value can be assessed by a price. Many factors may influence the evaluation of value, including time constraints, price levels, perceived quality, and motivations to use available information about prices.[44] Indeed, consumers vary in their response to price: some focus solely on the lowest price, while others consider quality or the prestige associated with a product and its price. Two of Canada's retail success stories have used opposing strategies when setting prices for their items. Dollarama has risen to become the largest dollar store in Canada based on its low-price policy, while Harry Rosen, a high-end clothing store for men that has been in business in Canada since 1954, is known to charge premium prices for many of its prestigious items.

Price is a key element in the marketing mix because it relates directly to the generation of revenue and profits. Sobeys, for example, has generated more revenue from its premium private-label brand Sensations by Compliments by charging more for those items than for its regular private-label goods—Compliments. McDonald's has increased profits with upscale items such as its higher-priced Cobb salad.[45]

In large part, the ability to set a price depends on the supply of and demand for a product. For most products, the quantity demanded goes up as the price goes down, and as the price goes up, the quantity demanded goes down. This has been evident in the price of oil and gas in Canada in recent years. When the price per litre has fallen below one dollar, consumers have been much more willing to purchase gas than when the price exceeds one dollar per litre. The change in gas prices has also impacted the sale of other items, such as the sales decline of larger, less fuel-efficient sport utility vehicles, especially when the price of gas rose in recent years and topped $1.20 per litre. Of course, price also depends on the cost to manufacture a good or provide a service or idea.

Changes in buyers' needs, variations in the effectiveness of other marketing mix variables, the presence of substitutes, and dynamic environmental factors can influence demand. A firm may temporarily sell products below cost to match competition, to generate cash flow, or even to increase market share, but in the long run it cannot survive by selling its products below cost. For example, many small independent stores in Halifax sold milk well below cost during the early part of 2017 to increase sales of other more profitable items. Sobeys executives have stated that they are not worried about this trend as the practice is not sustainable in the long term.[46]

Price is probably the most flexible variable in the marketing mix. Although it may take years to develop a product, establish channels of distribution, and design and implement promotion, a product's price may be set and changed in a few minutes. Under certain circumstances, of course, the price may not be so flexible, especially if government regulations prevent dealers from controlling prices.

## Pricing Objectives

Pricing objectives specify the role of price in an organization's marketing mix and strategy. They usually are influenced not only by marketing mix decisions but also by finance, accounting, and production factors. Maximizing profits and sales, boosting market share, maintaining the status quo, and survival are four common pricing objectives.

## Specific Pricing Strategies

Pricing strategies provide guidelines for achieving the company's pricing objectives and overall marketing strategy. They specify how price will be used as a variable in the marketing mix. Significant pricing strategies relate to price lining, pricing new products, psychological pricing, and price discounting.

**Price Lining.** Price lining occurs when a company sells multiple products in the same product category. For example, Peoples Jewellers sells three different one-carat diamond rings and has labelled them as good, better, and best. Research indicates people are willing to move up one product/price category if the price difference is not perceived as significant. So if a ring labelled as "good" is priced at $2000 and cost Peoples $1200, the company would make $800. But a ring labelled as "better" could sell for $2500 and cost People's $1500, resulting in a $1000 profit. Peoples knows that by creating these labels, consumers will be inclined to jump to the better product description, and as a result Peoples will make more money by selling the ring that is priced slightly higher. As discussed below, Tim Hortons uses a type of product line pricing in its coffee sales to generate additional sales volume and more revenue per cup of coffee sold.

**Pricing New Products.** Setting the price for a new product is crucial: The right price leads to profitability; the wrong price may kill the product. In general, there are two basic strategies to setting the base price for a new product. **Price skimming** is charging the highest possible price that buyers who want the product will pay and gradually lowering it over time. For example, when the new gaming console Xbox One was introduced into the marketplace, it was priced at $699. Over time, Microsoft gradually lowered the price to appeal to more consumers and to maintain sales. This strategy allows companies to generate much-needed revenue to help offset the costs of research and development.

Conversely, a **penetration price** is a low price designed to help a product enter the market and gain market share rapidly. For example, many discount real estate brokers have started to emerge in Canada in recent years. Many of these, such as PropertyGuys.com, have been charging much lower fees than traditional real estate agents as a way to break into the market. The discount brokers have been dealing with strong resistance from traditional real estate agents who charge thousands more than discount real estate companies. Penetration pricing is less flexible than price skimming; it is more difficult to raise a penetration price than to lower a skimming price. Penetration pricing is used most often

**price skimming** charging the highest possible price that buyers who want the product will pay

**penetration price** a low price designed to help a product enter the market and gain market share rapidly when marketers suspect that competitors will enter the market shortly after the product has been introduced.

**Psychological Pricing.** **Psychological pricing** encourages purchases based on emotional rather than rational responses to the price. For example, the assumption behind *even/odd pricing* is that people will buy more of a product for $9.99 than $10 because it seems to be a bargain at the odd price. The assumption behind *symbolic/prestige pricing* is that high prices connote high quality. Thus the prices of certain fragrances are set artificially high to give the impression of superior quality. Some over-the-counter drugs are priced high because consumers associate a drug's price with potency.

**psychological pricing** encouraging purchases based on emotional rather than rational responses to the price

**Price Discounting.** Temporary price reductions, or **discounts**, are often employed to boost sales. Although there are many types, quantity, seasonal, and promotional discounts are among the most widely used. Quantity discounts reflect the economies of purchasing in large volume. Seasonal discounts appeal to buyers who purchase goods or services out of season and help even out production capacity. Promotional discounts attempt to improve sales by advertising price reductions on selected products to increase customer interest.

Often promotional pricing is geared to increased profits. However, many companies such as Walmart, Home Depot, and Toys "R" Us have shunned promotional price discounts and, with everyday low pricing, are focusing more on relationships with

**discounts** temporary price reductions, often employed to boost sales

## Consider the Following: Tim Hortons' pricing strategy—tricking you into buying more coffee, or giving you what you want?

A recent article in *Canadian Business* explains that Canadian icon Tim Hortons is tricking consumers into buying more coffee. The trick, if you want to call it that, is a well-established pricing strategy similar to price lining. You offer consumers a little more of a product, in this case coffee, while you more than offset the extra product by charging more. In this specific case, Tim Hortons increased the size of its extra-large coffee to 24 liquid ounces up from 20 ounces, which results in an extra 0.19 cents in profit per cup sold.

While 0.19 cents may not seem like a lot, think about the thousands of cups of coffee sold daily in every Tim Hortons' store. Tim Hortons states that the change in cup size had more to do with customer demand than raising profit, as marketing research indicated that their old extra-large cup was not large enough. The result of the change was an increase in all cup sizes, as the old extra-large became large, large became medium, and medium became small. The original "small" cup size was abandoned.

Koert Van Ittersum, a marketing expert in behavioural bias that leads to overconsumption, says, "Most consumers will continue to order the same size of coffee out of habit and not pay attention to the size difference. The result is consumers will pay more and consume more." Tim Hortons, of course, is not the only restaurant chain to embrace upsizing as a way to increase consumption and profit. Starbucks, with its 31-ounce Trenta, and 7-Eleven's 32-ounce Big Gulp are still much larger than Tim Hortons' extra-large offering. Still, health experts are wondering how much bigger drinks and food servings can get, and if consumers won't ultimately say no to bigger and bigger portions.*

### DISCUSSION QUESTIONS

1. Are companies acting ethically when they increase the size of their portions as a way to get consumers to consume more and ultimately pay more for a product?
2. What are some of the potential advantages and disadvantages of increasing the size of your products?
3. Do you notice when your favourite restaurant or coffee shop changes the size of its portions? If so, does it impact your purchasing behaviour? Why or why not?
4. Using the Internet, do some market research to determine what companies are selling the largest soft drinks and cups of coffee. Has there been any backlash to these extra-large sizes from health experts and consumer advocates? Can you find any incidences where companies reduced the size of their products as a result?

*"Tim Hortons Changing Cup Sizes Across the Country," CTV, January 16, 2012, http://www.ctvnews.ca/tim-hortons-changing-cup-sizes-across-the-country-1.75466; Wency Leung, "Tim Hortons' Extra-Large Coffee to Get Even Larger," *Globe and Mail*, January 16, 2012, http://www.theglobeandmail.com/life/food-and-wine/food-trends/tim-hortons-extra-large-coffee-to-get-even-larger/article1358604; Emily Jackson, "Tim Hortons Supersizes Its Coffee Cups," *Toronto Star*, January 16, 2012, http://www.thestar.com/business/2012/01/16/tim_hortons_supersizes_its_coffee_cups.html; James Cowan, "Tim Hortons' New Coffee Cup: Why the Supersize?" *Canadian Business*, February 14, 2012, http://www.canadianbusiness.com/business-strategy/tim-hortons-new-coffee-cup-why-the-supersize/ (all accessed July 11, 2013).

©Keith Homan/Shutterstock

Microsoft often uses a price skimming strategy when they first introduce new products such as the Xbox One. The company sets the price high when the unit is first introduced, then lowers the price significantly to maintain sales.

customers. Polo killed its Polo jeans brand because the price of this product hurt its luxury image.[47] In the airline industry, lower-cost airlines like WestJet's Encore and Air Canada Rouge are competing head-to-head with the major airlines by offering sharply discounted fares. Additionally, websites like iTravel.com, Expedia.ca, Priceline.com, Orbitz.com, and Travelocity.com help flyers find the lowest fares quickly, forcing airlines to become even more price competitive.

# Distribution Strategy

**LO 12-3** Identify factors affecting distribution decisions, such as marketing channels and intensity of market coverage.

The best products in the world will not be successful unless companies make them available where and when customers want to buy them. In this section, we will explore dimensions of distribution strategy, including the channels through which products are distributed, the intensity of market coverage, and the physical handling of products during distribution.

## Marketing Channels

A **marketing channel**, or channel of distribution, is a group of organizations that moves products from their producer to customers. Marketing channels make products available to buyers when and where they desire to purchase them. Organizations that bridge the gap between a product's manufacturer and the ultimate consumer are called *middlemen* or intermediaries. They create time, place, and ownership utility. Two intermediary organizations are retailers and wholesalers.

**Retailers** buy products from manufacturers (or other intermediaries) and sell them to consumers for home and household use rather than for resale or for use in producing other products. Hudson's Bay, for example, buys products from Spin Master and resells them to consumers. Retailing usually occurs in a store, but the Internet, vending machines, mail-order catalogues, and entertainment, such as going to a Montreal Canadiens hockey game, also provide opportunities for retailing.

**marketing channel** a group of organizations that moves products from their producer to customers; also called a channel of distribution

**retailers** intermediaries who buy products from manufacturers (or other intermediaries) and sell them to consumers for home and household use rather than for resale or for use in producing other products

With more than 20 million Canadians accessing the Internet, consumers spent an estimated at $40 billion in 2018, and with more and more people engaging in online and mobile shopping, the amount is expected to grow to almost $55 billion by 2023.[48] By bringing together an assortment of products from competing producers, retailers create utility. Traditional retailers arrange for products to be moved from producers to a convenient retail establishment (place utility). They maintain hours of operation for their retail stores to make merchandise available when consumers want it (time utility). They also assume the risk of ownership of inventories (ownership utility).

New online retailers have altered the landscape as they do not have all the costs associated with operating a retail location and can offer consumers access to products 24 hours a day. However, Internet retailing has given rise to a new term, *showrooming*. This is where consumers visit a traditional merchant location to see and touch a product and then purchase it for less money online. Many traditional retailers, such as Canadian Tire and Sport-Chek, have created online shopping sites to retain customers and compete with online-only retailers. One of the best-known online-only, or cyber, merchants is Amazon. Amazon offers millions of products from which to choose, all from the privacy and convenience of the purchaser's home. In some cases, Web merchants offer wide selections, ultra-convenience, superior service, knowledge, and the best products. More detail on the Internet's effect on marketing is presented in Chapter 13.

Table 12.3 describes various types of general merchandise retailers.

Today, competition between retailers in Canada has never been more intense due to the growth in online retailers, Even with the challenging times, an additional 30 new retailers entered the Canadian market in 2018 including Nordstrom Rack, a high-end discount store; Decathlon, the world's largest sports store; and clothing store Kenneth Cole to name a few.[49] Furthermore, competition between different types of stores is changing the nature of retailing. Supermarkets compete with specialty food stores, wholesale clubs,

**Table 12.3** | General Merchandise Retailers

| Type of Retailer | Description | Examples |
|---|---|---|
| Department store | Large organization offering wide product mix and organized into separate departments | Hudson's Bay Sears |
| Discount store | Self-service, general merchandise store offering brand name and private brand products at low prices | Dollarama |
| Supermarket | Self-service store offering complete line of food products and some non-food products | Sobeys Loblaws |
| Superstore | Giant outlet offering all food and non-food products found in supermarkets, as well as most routinely purchased products | Walmart Real Canadian Superstores |
| Warehouse club | Large-scale, members-only establishments combining cash-and-carry wholesaling with discount retailing | Costco |
| Warehouse showroom | Facility in a large, low-cost building with large on-premises inventories and minimum service | Ikea |
| Catalogue showroom | Type of warehouse showroom where consumers shop from a catalogue and products are stored out of buyers' reach and provided in manufacturer's carton | Sears Catalogue |

Source: William M. Pride and O. C. Ferrell, *Marketing: Concepts and Strategies, 2008*, p. 428. Copyright 2008 by Houghton Mifflin Company. Reprinted with permission.

and discount stores. Department stores compete with nearly every other type of store including specialty stores, off-price chains, category killers, discount stores, and online retailers.

"Internet retailing has given rise to a new term, *showrooming*. This is where consumers visit a traditional merchant location to see and touch a product and then purchase it for less money online."

**Wholesalers** are intermediaries who buy from producers or from other wholesalers and sell to retailers. They usually do not sell in significant quantities to end users. Wholesalers perform the functions listed in Table 12.4.

Wholesalers are extremely important because of the marketing activities they perform, particularly for consumer products. Although it is true that wholesalers can be eliminated, their functions must be passed on to some other entity, such as the producer, another intermediary, or even the customer. Wholesalers help consumers and retailers by buying in large quantities, then selling to retailers in smaller quantities. By stocking an assortment of products, wholesalers match products to demand.

**wholesalers** intermediaries who buy from producers or from other wholesalers and sell to retailers

"Although it is true that wholesalers can be eliminated, their functions must be passed on to some other entity, such as the producer, another intermediary, or even the customer."

**Table 12.4** | Major Wholesaling Functions

| Supply Chain Management | Creating Long-Term Partnerships Among Channel Members |
|---|---|
| Promotion | Providing a sales force, advertising, sales promotion, and publicity |
| Warehousing, shipping, and product handling | Receiving, storing, and stock-keeping |
| | Packaging |
| | Shipping outgoing orders |
| | Materials handling |
| | Arranging and making local and long-distance shipments |
| Inventory control and data processing | Processing orders |
| | Controlling physical inventory |
| | Recording transactions |
| | Tracking sales data for financial analysis |
| Risk taking | Assuming responsibility for theft, product obsolescence, and excess inventories |
| Financing and budgeting | Extending credit |
| | Making capital investments |
| | Forecasting cash flow |
| Marketing research and information systems | Providing information about market |
| | Conducting research studies |
| | Managing computer networks to facilitate exchanges and relationships |

Source: William M. Pride and O. C. Ferrell, *Marketing: Concepts and Strategies, 2008*, p. 389. Copyright 2008 by Houghton Mifflin Company. Reprinted with permission.

**Supply Chain Management.** In an effort to improve distribution channel relationships among manufacturers and other channel intermediaries, supply chain management creates alliances between channel members. In Chapter 8, we defined *supply chain management* as connecting and integrating all parties or members of the distribution system to satisfy customers. It involves long-term partnerships among marketing channel members working together to reduce costs, waste, and unnecessary movement in the entire marketing channel in order to satisfy customers.[50] It goes beyond traditional channel members (producers, wholesalers, retailers, customers) to include *all* organizations involved in moving products from the producer to the ultimate customer. In a survey of business managers, a disruption in the supply chain was viewed as the number-one crisis that could decrease revenue.[51]

The focus shifts from one of selling to the next level in the channel to one of selling products *through* the channel to a satisfied ultimate customer. Information, once provided on a guarded, "as needed" basis, is now open, honest, and ongoing. Perhaps most importantly, the points of contact in the relationship expand from one-on-one at the salesperson–buyer level to multiple interfaces at all levels and in all functional areas of the various organizations.

**Channels for Consumer Products.** Typical marketing channels for consumer products are shown in Figure 12.3. In Channel A, the product moves from the producer directly to the consumer. Farmers who sell their fruit and vegetables to consumers at roadside stands use a direct-from-producer-to-consumer marketing channel.

In Channel B, the product goes from producer to retailer to consumer. This type of channel is used for products such as textbooks, automobiles, and appliances. In Channel C, the product is handled by a wholesaler and a retailer before it reaches the consumer. Producer-to-wholesaler-to-retailer-to-consumer marketing channels distribute a wide range of products including refrigerators, televisions, soft drinks, cigarettes, clocks, watches, and office products. In Channel D, the product goes to an agent, a wholesaler, and a retailer before going to the consumer. This long channel of distribution is especially useful for convenience products. Candy and some kinds of produce are often sold by agents who bring buyers and sellers together.

Services are usually distributed through direct marketing channels because they are generally produced *and* consumed simultaneously. For example, you cannot take a haircut home for later use. Many services require the customer's presence and participation: the sick patient must visit the physician to receive treatment, the child must be at the daycare centre to receive care, the tourist must be present to sightsee and consume tourism services.

**Channels for Business Products.** In contrast to consumer goods, more than half of all business products, especially expensive equipment or technically complex products, are sold through direct marketing channels. Business customers like to communicate directly with producers of such products to gain the technical assistance and personal assurances that only the producer can offer. For this reason, business buyers prefer to purchase expensive and highly complex mainframe computers directly from Dell, HP, and other mainframe producers. Other business products may be distributed through channels employing wholesaling intermediaries such as industrial distributors and/or manufacturer's agents.

**Figure 12.3** | Marketing Channels for Consumer Products

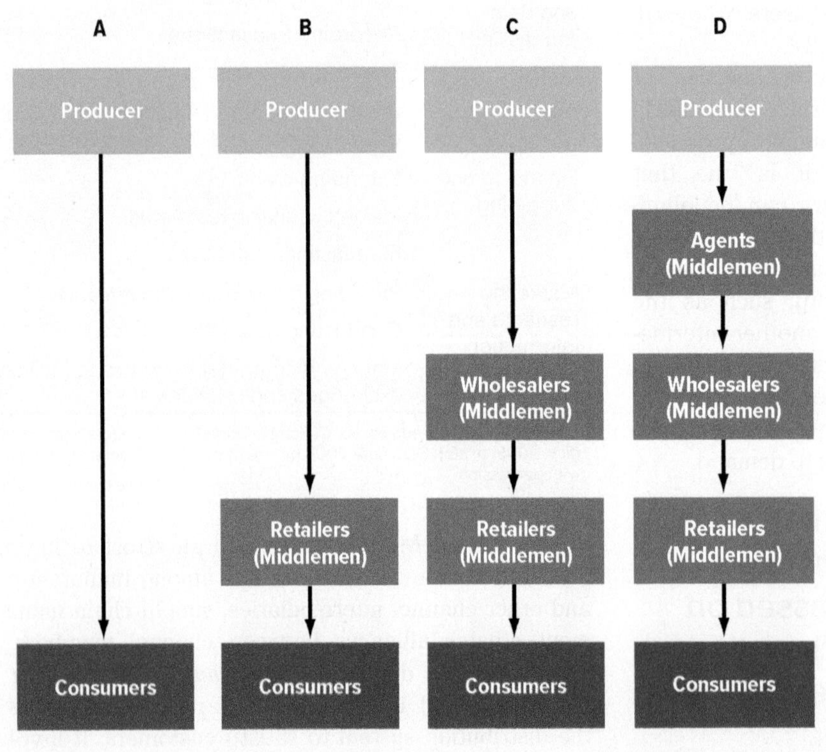


## Intensity of Market Coverage

A major distribution decision is how widely to distribute a product—that is, how many and what type of outlets should carry it. The intensity of market coverage depends on buyer behaviour, as well as the nature of the target market and the competition. Wholesalers and retailers provide various intensities of market coverage and must be selected carefully to ensure success. Market coverage may be intensive, selective, or exclusive.

**Intensive distribution** makes a product available in as many outlets as possible. Because

**intensive distribution** a form of market coverage whereby a product is made available in as many outlets as possible

availability is important to purchasers of convenience products such as bread, milk, gasoline, soft drinks, and chewing gum, a nearby location with a minimum of time spent searching and waiting in line is most important to the consumer. To saturate markets intensively, wholesalers and many varied retailers try to make the product available at every location where a consumer might desire to purchase it. For example, at one time, to market its single-use Max cameras, Eastman Kodak rolled out 10,000 climate-controlled, Internet-connected vending machines. The machines allowed credit card transactions and were refrigerated to protect the film. The vending machine's Internet connection allowed Kodak to know who bought each camera, where customers lived, the specific location of the machine, and the machine's inventory level. The machines were found at zoos, stadiums, parks, hotels, and resorts—all places where consumers typically desired a single-use camera.[52]

**Selective distribution** uses only a small number of all available outlets to expose products. It is used most often for products that consumers buy only after shopping and comparing price, quality, and style. Many products sold on a selective basis require salesperson assistance, technical advice, warranties, or repair service to maintain consumer satisfaction. Typical products include automobiles, major appliances, clothes, and furniture.

**selective distribution** a form of market coverage whereby only a small number of all available outlets are used to expose products

**Exclusive distribution** exists when a manufacturer gives an intermediary the sole right to sell a product in a defined geographic territory. Such exclusivity provides an incentive for a dealer to handle a product that has a limited market. Exclusive distribution is the opposite of intensive distribution in that products are purchased and consumed over a long period of time, and service or information is required to develop a satisfactory sales relationship. Products distributed on an exclusive basis include high-quality musical instruments, yachts, airplanes, and high-fashion leather goods.

**exclusive distribution** a manufacturer awards to an intermediary the sole right to sell a product in a defined geographic territory

## Physical Distribution

**Physical distribution** includes all the activities necessary to move products from producers to customers—inventory control, transportation, warehousing, and materials handling. Physical distribution creates time and place utility by making products available when they are wanted, with adequate service and at minimum cost. Retail legend, the late Walter Hachborn, former president of Home Hardware, said that the firm's distribution system is one characteristic that allows it to compete against much larger firms such as Home Depot and RONA. "We have four warehouses across Canada. We likely have one of the most efficient hardware packing and shipping operations in the world."[53] Both goods and services require physical distribution. Many physical distribution activities are part of supply chain management, which we discussed in Chapter 8; we'll take a brief look at a few more now.

**physical distribution** all the activities necessary to move products from producers to customers—inventory control, transportation, warehousing, and materials handling

**Transportation.** **Transportation**, the shipment of products to buyers, creates time and place utility for products, and thus is a key element in the flow of goods and services from producer to consumer. The five major modes of transportation used to move products between cities in Canada are railways, motor vehicles, inland waterways, pipelines, and airways.

**transportation** the shipment of products to buyers

Railroads offer the least expensive transportation for many products. Heavy commodities, foodstuffs, raw materials, and coal are examples of products carried by railroads. Trucks have greater flexibility than railroads because they

Left to right: ©Jeff Greenberg/Alamy Stock Photo, ©Lars Niki

Most consumer packaged goods companies, such as Pepsi, strive for intensive distribution—they want to be everywhere. But many cosmetics firms use an exclusive distribution strategy by limiting their distribution to a few select, higher-end retailers in each region.

## ENTREPRENEURSHIP IN ACTION

### Finawear—Authentic Indigenous Art

**Founder:** Shar Wilson

**Business:** Finawear

**Founded:** 2014

**Success:** Shar Wilson, who is Tsimshian of Gitxsan and Nisga'a ancestry, noticed a trend in Indigenous art. A lot of the art was being produced by non-Indigenous people—and not in Canada.

Wilson wanted to change this and thought combining clothing and art would provide her with the opportunity to do so. She set out to create wearable Indigenous art featuring different designs to represent different Indigenous cultures. Wilson, who was an accountant by trade, had to teach herself how to draw and create the art that is now featured in her clothing line.

Wilson's product mix consists of tops and leggings which are being sold online and with some retailers and manufactured in Canada. Wilson sees herself as successful as she is teaching people the difference between cultural appropriation and cultural appreciation.*

*Shalu Mehta, "Entrepreneur's wearable Indigenous art appears on *Dragons' Den* tonight," November 22, 2018, https://www.haidagwaiiobserver.com/business/entrepreneurs-wearable-indigenous-art-appears-on-dragons-den-tonight/

can reach more locations. Trucks handle freight quickly and economically, offer door-to-door service, and are more flexible in their packaging requirements than are ships or airplanes. Air transport offers speed and a high degree of dependability but is the most expensive means of transportation; shipping by boat is the least expensive and slowest form. Pipelines are used to transport petroleum, natural gas, semi-liquid coal, wood chips (in a slurry), and certain chemicals. Many products can be moved most efficiently by using more than one mode of transportation.

Factors affecting the selection of a mode of transportation include cost, capability to handle the product, reliability, and availability, and as suggested, selecting transportation modes requires trade-offs. Unique characteristics of the product and consumer desires often determine the mode selected.

**Warehousing.** **Warehousing** is the design and operation of facilities to receive, store, and ship products. A warehouse facility receives, identifies, sorts, and dispatches goods to storage; stores them; recalls, selects, or picks goods; assembles the shipment; and finally, dispatches the shipment.

**warehousing** the design and operation of facilities to receive, store, and ship products

Companies often own and operate their own private warehouses that store, handle, and move their own products. They can also rent storage and related physical distribution services from public warehouses. Regardless of whether a private or a public warehouse is used, warehousing is important because it makes products available for shipment to match demand at different geographic locations.

**Materials Handling.** **Materials handling** is the physical handling and movement of products in warehousing and transportation. Handling processes may vary significantly due to product characteristics. Efficient materials-handling procedures increase a warehouse's useful capacity and improve customer service. Well-coordinated loading and movement systems increase efficiency and reduce costs.

**materials handling** the physical handling and movement of products in warehousing and transportation

### Importance of Distribution in a Marketing Strategy

Distribution decisions are among the least flexible marketing mix decisions. Products can be changed over time, prices can be changed quickly, and promotion is usually changed regularly. But distribution decisions often commit resources and establish contractual relationships that are difficult if not impossible to change. As a company attempts to expand into new markets, it may require a complete change in distribution. Moreover, if a firm does not manage its marketing channel in the most efficient manner and provide the best service, then a new competitor will evolve to create a more effective distribution system.

## Promotion Strategy

**LO 12-4** Specify the activities involved in promotion, as well as promotional strategies and promotional positioning.

The role of promotion is to communicate with individuals, groups, and organizations to facilitate an exchange directly or indirectly. It encourages marketing exchanges by attempting to persuade individuals, groups, and organizations to accept goods, services, and ideas. Promotion is used not only to sell products but also to influence opinions and attitudes toward an organization, person, or cause.

The province of Prince Edward Island, for example, has successfully used promotion to educate potential tourists about beautiful beaches and golf courses on the island. The provincial tourism board and the Atlantic Canada Opportunities Agency spent $1 million to bring popular daytime television personalities Regis Philbin and Kelly Ripa to host their show, *Live!*, from the island for three days. On day one of the show Prince Edward Island skyrocketed to the number two spot on Google search in the United States.[54] Most people probably equate promotion with advertising, but it also includes personal selling, publicity, and sales promotion. The role that these elements play in a marketing strategy is extremely important.

©Foto by M/Shutterstock

To convince consumers that the S60 model is both safe and sporty, Volvo used an integrated marketing communication program that included print and broadcast advertising as well as new communication technologies such as social media.

## The Promotion Mix

Advertising, personal selling, publicity, and sales promotion are collectively known as the promotion mix because a strong promotion program results from the careful selection and blending of these elements. The process of coordinating the promotion mix elements and synchronizing promotion as a unified effort is called **integrated marketing communications**. When planning promotional activities, an integrated marketing communications approach results in the desired message for customers. Different elements of the promotion mix are coordinated to play their appropriate roles in delivery of the message on a consistent basis. For example, RBC uses TV commercials, social media, Internet marketing, and publicity to reach its target market. The main components of a promotional campaign are to:

**integrated marketing communications** coordinating the promotion mix elements and synchronizing promotion as a unified effort

1. *Determine objectives.* What are you hoping to accomplish? Objectives must be quantifiable so that they are measurable. Examples include "Increase sales by 2 percent," "Generate 20 leads," "Increase website traffic," and so on.
2. *Define customers.* Whom are you targeting? Are you targeting new customers, current customers, frequent shoppers, holiday shoppers, or some other group?
3. *Determine benchmarks.* Establish measures/controls to measure the effectiveness of a promotion, such as the number of website hits, sales figures, information requests, and so on.
4. *Get the message out.* Determine the method including what you will say to your audience and medium to use: the Internet, TV, radio, direct mail, or some other.
5. *Implement the plan.*
6. *Evaluate the plan.* Look at the controls that you have established and determine if the plan has been successful.

**Advertising.** Perhaps the best-known form of promotion, **advertising** is a paid form of non-personal communication transmitted through a mass medium, such as television commercials, magazine advertisements, or online ads. Commercials featuring celebrities, customers, or unique creations (baby animals for Telus or the Tim Hortons commercials with Sidney Crosby and Nathan MacKinnon) serve to grab viewers' attention and pique their interest in a product.

**advertising** a paid form of non-personal communication transmitted through a mass medium, such as television commercials or magazine advertisements

Advertisers are doing more and more to make their advertising stand out. Examples include Red Bull with the tag line Red Bull Gives You Wings, and Molson beer and Coca-Cola, which rely on making emotional appeals to Canadians by using advertisements that highlight national pride and hockey. During the NHL lockout, both Bauer with its Own the Moment advertisements

©Reefertilizer

Advertisers often use celebrities and humour in their ads to generate public interest.

and Nike's Hockey is Ours marketing campaign, which went viral, used emotional pitches to connect to viewers. Other advertisers are relying on humour to create a buzz for their product. For example, Reefertilizer, a fertilizer designed for growing cannabis has become a viral sensation with their #growgoodweed ad thanking Prime Minister Justin Trudeau for legalizing cannabis.[55]

An **advertising campaign** involves designing a series of advertisements and placing them in various media to reach a particular target audience. The basic content and form of an advertising campaign are a function of several factors. A product's features, uses, and benefits affect the content of the campaign message and individual ads. Characteristics of the people in the target audience—gender, age, education, race, income, occupation, lifestyle, and other attributes—influence both content and form. When Procter & Gamble promotes Crest toothpaste to children, the company emphasizes daily brushing and cavity control, whereas it promotes tartar control and whiter teeth when marketing to adults. To communicate effectively, advertisers use words, symbols, and illustrations that are meaningful, familiar, and attractive to people in the target audience.

**advertising campaign** designing a series of advertisements and placing them in various media to reach a particular target market

An advertising campaign's objectives and platform also affect the content and form of its messages. If a firm's advertising objectives involve large sales increases, the message may include hard-hitting, high-impact language and symbols. When campaign objectives aim at increasing brand awareness, the message may use much repetition of the brand name and words and illustrations associated with it. Thus, the advertising platform is the foundation on which campaign messages are built.

Advertising media are the vehicles or forms of communication used to reach a desired audience. Print media include newspapers, magazines, direct mail, and billboards, and electronic media include television, radio, and cyber ads. Newspapers, television, and direct mail are the most widely used advertising media. According to a recent article in the *Globe and Mail*, advertising spending is on the rise in Canada, reaching $114 billion in 2015.[56]

Choice of media influences the content and form of the message. Effective outdoor displays and short broadcast spot announcements require concise, simple messages. Magazine and newspaper advertisements can include considerable detail and long explanations. Because several kinds of media offer geographic selectivity, a precise message can be tailored to a particular geographic section of the target audience. For example, a company advertising in *Maclean's* might decide to use one message in Ontario and another in the rest of the nation. A company may also choose to advertise in only one region. Such geographic selectivity lets a firm use the same message in different regions at different times.

"Choice of media influences the content and form of the message."

**Online Marketing and Social Media.** The use of online advertising is increasing as companies are attracted to its wide reach and ability to interact with customers. Businesses are also aware that Canadians are spending more time online than citizens in other countries in the world. For example, recent research revealed that Canadians are spending 158 minutes a day online, with 74 percent of Canadians spending three to four hours online each day, and over the course of a month Canadians will visit on average 80 websites.[57] Interestingly much of their time is spent on social media where Canadians spent on average the equivalent of 10,000 minutes on Facebook alone.[58] In addition to spending more time online, Canadians are following, if not leading, the global trend of accessing the Internet, especially social media sites, using mobile devices such as smartphones and tablets.[59] Table 12.5 illustrates the most popular social media/network sites in Canada.

"New technology, such as *behavioural tracking*, is allowing companies to track user information including demographics, location, and search terms to tailor online advertisements and target their online messages to be more effective and appealing."

**Table 12.5** | Most Popular Social Media Sites in Canada

| | Percent of Canadians Using the Site |
|---|---|
| Facebook | 80% |
| LinkedIn | 45% |
| Google+ | 40% |
| Instagram | 39% |
| Pinterest | 36% |
| Twitter | 35% |
| YouTube Channel Subscriptions | 27% |
| Snapchat | 24% |
| Own YouTube Channel | 13% |
| Online discussion (excluding Reddit) | 10% |

Because Chapter 13 discusses the use of social media and digital marketing in greater detail, the coverage here will be condensed. Prior to reading Chapter 13, readers should recognize that the Internet and social media have become a vital part of most companies' integrated marketing communication plan. Online marketing is growing at a phenomenal rate in Canada, especially since consumers not only are accessing the Internet through computers but also are using smartphones and tablets to stay online when on the move. For example, 86 percent of Canadians own smartphones, they spend on average almost three hours a day on their phones, and they look at the device once every ten minutes.[60] Additionally, new technology, such as *behavioural tracking*, is allowing companies to track user information including demographics, location, and search terms to tailor online advertisements and target their online messages to be more effective and appealing.

Following are some ways in which companies increase their online marketing presence:

- *Company websites:* Websites allow companies to provide stakeholders with a significant amount of information, including their entire marketing mix, provide an opportunity for people to make direct purchases, and present significant company information. The sites also allow businesses the chance to interact and communicate with customers using a variety of channels, including emails, reviews, and so forth.

  A good example of website development and operation is the Chapters/Indigo online bookstore (ChaptersIndigo.ca). The site was developed to keep current customers returning and to provide easy navigation for new visitors. The site stores customer account information to allow for easy processing of payment, provides customer reviews, and allows for the tracking of shipping information. In addition, the site contains a search function that allows new users to easily find what they are looking for, provides graphics so that consumers can ensure they are ordering the right material, and allows for immediate feedback so that consumers know whether their order or question has been received. The site is coordinated in both content and graphics with the other marketing divisions of the company, with the front page of the site updated on a weekly basis to draw people in and give them another reason to come back.
- *Search engine optimization:* Companies want to be sure that their site will not only appear on the results page when consumers use popular search engines such as Google or Yahoo, but also that they appear in the first few results. This is referred to as *search engine optimization* (SEO), where companies design websites using title tags (also referred to as *metatags*) that explain the intent of the website, have content pages that use words that relate to the purpose of the site, clearly link all documents, use appropriate external links, update content frequently, and have lots of pages.
- *Pay-per-click (PPC) advertising:* Businesses are now making significant use of PPC advertising. This advertising method allows firms to bid on key words or phrases relevant to their target market. Then, when a consumer enters the phrase or word in the search engine, the company will appear under the results section and their ads will appear on the side of the viewer's screen. The largest PPC advertisers are Google Ads, Yahoo! Search Marketing, and Microsoft adCenter.
- *Social media websites:* Social media sites such as Facebook, LinkedIn, Instagram (see Chapter 13) and Pinterest are online communities where people can create and share information. As noted above, Canadians are spending a significant amount of time on these sites, and they are becoming increasingly important to businesses. Facebook is the third most visited site in Canada, and worldwide boasts over 2.23 billion monthly users, of which more than 66 percent visit the site daily.[61, 62]

  Facebook allows companies to create profiles, join online communities, send out flyers, share videos, post pictures, and write blogs, as well as encouraging people to comment on their walls (bulletin boards), join or create discussion groups, and promote themselves with banner and interactive advertisements.[63] For example, TD Bank's Facebook page alerts customers about company news and also answers customer questions posted to its wall. After the earthquake disaster in Haiti, the bank posted and emailed all its Facebook friends, describing what the bank was doing to help.

  Facebook's targeted ads are becoming increasingly popular with businesses both large and small as they allow firms to target groups of people who are likely to be interested in their products or services. Facebook compiles data on its users, including interests, likes, and web-browsing history, and then allows companies to target groups of people who share similar interests.

  For example, if you have liked baby products, searched out baby information, and viewed baby-centric pages, chances are Facebook would place you in a group of people who are interested in baby products. So companies that sell baby products, such as Pampers, would buy advertising space from Facebook but the ads would appear only to people who have been classified as interested in babies and baby products.

  Terre Bleu Lavender Farm, a Milton, Ontario–based tourist destination, doubled its number of visitors and tripled sales year over year using Facebook targeted ads. Ian Baird, CEO of Terre Bleu Lavender Farm, says Facebook gave him confidence to start the business, and its use helped the company stay in touch with the customers from opening day on: "Ours has

©Ingram Publishing

Terre Bleu Lavender Farm used Facebook to double its visitors and triple its annual sales.

been an ongoing campaign with Facebook. We used Facebook to build momentum for our farm business even before we opened, thereby creating a pre-demand for when we actually opened the farm to the public. It gave us far more confidence to invest in the business as we built the farm and helped us launch with keen customers searching us out right from day one."[64]

Facebook is also engaged in significant efforts to attract more users to its site and increase its attractiveness to businesses. Facebook is investing a substantial amount of money into Facebook Search, which allows users to search for information on the social media site. Facebook's search, unlike Google, is built to give you results directly for your search term and also results based on the context. Facebook has also created Instant Articles, an online platform that allows businesses to create professional articles and videos to distribute through various social media channels.

**DID YOU KNOW?**

Facebook remains the top choice for reaching the broadest audience yet only 50 percent of North American teens are using the site. Teens are visiting YouTube, Instagram, and Snapchat in much greater numbers than Facebook.

LinkedIn is often described as a professional Facebook site where professionals can post their resumé, network, and gather information. LinkedIn is often used by professional companies to make and maintain initial contacts with clients and to source opportunities.

Pinterest is the fifth-largest social media website in North America. Pinterest allows users to save and manage images and video content called *pins* to an online bulletin board known as a *pinboard*. Pinboards can be themed to allow users to easily manage pins, to share their content, and to search for similar content or pins posted by other users. Users can also pin content they find on the Internet and easily upload it to their pinboard. Businesses are particularly interested in Pinterest as it allows users to create their own business page, run contests, and engage with consumers. Victoria's Secret and AMC Theatres are using Pinterest to promote their businesses and actively engage with consumers.

- *Snapchat:* A new form of social networking that relies on messaging over mobile devices. Snapchat allows users to share pictures, create content, comment on posts and so forth. Snapchat is especially popular with users under the age of 34. Numerous companies are making use of Snapchat as marketing tool to reach young Canadians on their smartphones. For example, Jägermeister invests a considerable amount of money in Snapchat advertising as they believe it's the best way to reach young consumers when they are out in a social environment.[65]
- *Tinder/Dating Apps:* Tinder and other dating apps represent a relatively new form of social media/networking. Tinder relies on location-based interaction that allows users to acknowledge if they are interested in someone socially and Tinder supports chat functions. While advertisers are just starting to use Tinder, expectations are its use will grow, as it will enable companies to market to consumers in specific regions using targeted advertisements. One of the most successful Tinder campaigns was created by the marketing team behind the movie *Ex Machina*. The company used a picture of an attractive woman

©Pressureua/Dreamstime

Social media sites have become increasingly important to companies in connecting with consumers.

to create matches and then chatted with potential customers eventually showing people a trailer for the movie. Domino's Pizza is another company that has invested in Tinder advertising.[66]

- *Twitter/Blogs:* These are websites where people can voice their opinion on any issue that they see fit to post about. Twitter is a special blogger website that limits people to messages, or tweets, of 140 characters in length and is frequently in the top ten monthly visited websites by Canadians.[67] Twitter and other similar blogging sites allow companies to communicate with key stakeholders. Jim Estill, CEO of Symex Canada, notes that he produces a blog to stay in touch with key stakeholders.[68]

  Michael Jagger, president of Vancouver-based Provident Security and Event Management Corp., dedicates four hours a week to his blog and states that it is part of the company's overall marketing strategy.[69] Jagger feels that his blog allows him to build closer bonds with current customers and generate new sales.

  David Mandelstam, president and CEO of Markham, Ontario–based Sangoma Technologies Inc., a manufacturer of telephone hardware, takes a different approach to using blogs. His firm identified the most popular blogs on technology and sends the bloggers press releases a few days before they are released to the public. Mandelstam notes that the practice costs very little and the payoff is significant. For example, on days when his firm is mentioned by a blogger it is not uncommon for the company to be contacted by four or five prospective customers and/or potential investors.[70] The advantages of blogging include low costs, ability to reach wide audiences, and ability to reach customers on a personal level.

- *YouTube:* YouTube is the second-most visited site in Canada, and it enables people and companies to share videos with millions of daily visitors. The sites allow participants to load video clips onto their websites and display them for the public to see. The videos can act as commercials, infomercials for a product or service, educational content, or can be used to attract prospective employees or as a means to generate PR. For example, Home Depot uses YouTube to offer potential customers information on home improvement projects. To date the company has posted over 2000 videos to its YouTube channel and has 190,000 subscribers.[71]

- *Direct email to customers:* Email marketing has an almost unlimited number of uses and can be used to welcome customers, encourage people to visit your website, and encourage people to buy a product or service. In addition, emails can convert leads, provide additional information, and/or be used as a mechanism to send videos, blogs, newsletters, and podcasts. Emails can also be used to supplement other forms of marketing, and research indicates that including email as part of a direct mail campaign increases response rates by 40 percent; when used in conjunction with telemarketing the response rate jumps by 76 percent.[72] It should be noted that email marketing is not spamming, a practice where companies send out emails to random lists of people. Rather, it is permission-based marketing.

- *Advertainments:* Advertainments are 6- to 11-minute made-for-the-Web ads. Prominent companies making use of advertainments include BMW, Ford, Diet Coke, and Absolut vodka, all of which are making movies featuring a product as the star. BMW, a leader in advertainment has recently announced a new set of ads that will feature James Brown, who sold his soul to the devil and is trying to escape payment.[73] Other popular BMW movies feature a man who drives difficult passengers (in one film, Madonna stars as a difficult, foul-mouthed celebrity) around in flashy BMWs and gives them the ride of their lives. The Ford advertainments feature a Ford vehicle in different scenarios—the promise of a Ford Focus to a teenager if he can make the team; another advertainment features a young man who drives around in a Ford trying to save his goldfish.[74]

- *Banner advertisements:* Banner ads are interactive display advertising for the Internet. Just use the Internet and you will see examples of banner advertising by numerous Canadian companies such as Porter Airlines, EastLink, and many of Canada's banks. Banner ad placement has become more effective as companies are using information on consumers' Web usage to create personalized interactive ads that people will find more appealing. For example, Paramount Pictures has used targeted interactive banner ads to promote Mission Impossible movies. Based on web usage, the ads appear to prospective movie goers; when users click on the ad they're shown the viewpoints Tom Cruise would experience as he flies a helicopter.[75]

- *Online classified advertising sites:* Sites such as eBay, Kijiji, Craigslist, and Facebook Marketplace are frequently used by businesses to promote and sell their products and services. eBay is one of the most commonly visited sites in the world, and many small businesses use the site for its global reach. eBay allows businesses to sell individual products as well as maintain a virtual storefront. Canadian eBay Micro-Multinational Entrepreneur of the Year winners in 2017, Kalina Koleva and Maria Petrova, successfully sell modestly priced shoes and accessories on their eBay store, RunwayCatalog, and the pair have earned millions in revenue with 95 percent of their sales coming from people who live outside of Canada.[76]

Kijiji has become the 13th most visited site in Canada and businesses are using the site to advertise products and services through individual postings or banner advertisements.[77] Car companies, real estate agents, and landscaping companies are frequent users of Kijiji as they find it to be highly effective in reaching consumers. For example, Chris Neville owns a landscaping business in Nova Scotia and states, "Kijiji is actually my most effective form of advertising. I use Facebook and other forms of social media but most calls for our services come as a direct result from Kijiji."[78]

Craigslist works similarly to Kijiji and many companies are promoting their products and services using multiple sites. Facebook Marketplace is a new addition to online classified advertising. Facebook users including businesses can post both products and service for sale in specific geographic regions. Facebook Marketplace has over 800,000 users so expectations are it will quickly grow into a new marketing channel for businesses both large and small.[79, 80]

- *Online games:* Many companies are delivering promotional messages during game play or sponsoring games as a way to communicate with consumers. For example, Jägermeister recently combined Snapchat with online games to promote its product during Halloween. Snapchat users played a small game revealing messages on tarot cards supporting the Jägermeister brand.[81]
- *Podcasts:* These online broadcasts use audio and/or video clips that can be downloaded on mobile devices. Podcasts are increasing in popularity and offer businesses many of the same benefits as posting clips on YouTube or Facebook.
- Other methods of using the Internet for marketing include deal-of-the-day websites such as Groupon; affiliate programs where companies post information or links on other companies' sites and do the same in turn; webinars, which are Web-based seminars where you can engage in a full sales pitch with a customer regardless of their location; online newsletters; contributing to online bulletin boards/message boards; and posting to live online chat rooms.

**Mobile Marketing.** **Mobile marketing** is the use of a mobile device to communicate marketing messages. Given the growth in mobile device usage, especially globally, mobile marketing is expected to grow significantly in coming years. While mobile devices, in particular their Web browsers, can be used for many of the activities discussed above, such as searching the Internet and using social media, this section of the chapter is going to discuss mobile marketing methods that can be used primarily on mobile devices. The most common mobile marketing methods are as follows:

**mobile marketing** using a mobile device to communicate marketing messages

©Hero Images Inc./Alamy Stock Photo

Jägermeister is using Snapchat and gaming to target young consumers in bars.

- *Apps* or *applications:* Companies are now creating apps to be used on smartphones and mobile devices. Given that Canadians are spending more time using apps than watching television, we can expect the importance of apps to grow steadily in the next few years.[82] For example, *The Score* has been a first mover in apps marketing. Their app allows viewers to receive stats, blogs, sports headlines, and real-time updates. CIBC, the first Canadian bank to develop an app, allows customers to complete most of their daily banking on their smartphone and ties into the smartphone's GPS capabilities to assist customers in finding the nearest bank.

  The use of apps is certainly not limited to large businesses, however. Checkout 51 is a Canadian coupon app that was created by young entrepreneurs Noah Godfrey, Pema Hegan, and Andrew McGrath. The app provides consumers with online coupons that are updated on a regular basis. Rather than redeem the coupons in stores, consumers take a picture of the receipt showing they bought the item and submit the image through their mobile device. When consumers accumulate at least $20 in savings, they can request a cheque.[83]
- *Text/SMS/MMS messages:* Many companies use smartphones to send quick messages to potential customers. For example, at a recent Youth World Beach Volleyball Championship in Halifax, one of the alcoholic beverage sponsors used text messages to alert people about drink specials and

opportunities to win prizes. As text messages are normally read within four minutes of receipt, customers are likely to receive them and respond. MMS messaging is also used to send pictures and videos to further engage consumers.

- *QR codes:* These are block bar codes that link print and other forms of media advertising to websites using a mobile device that scans and reads the code. QR codes have become increasingly popular as companies can add them to virtually any form of advertising, and consumers can use them to link to additional information. One recent study found that 6.2 percent (or 14 million) of mobile users in the U.S. clicked on a QR code in one month alone. The advertisements with the highest click rates are most often printed in magazines and newspapers.[84] Store owners are also using them at the entrance of their stores to entice people in by offering coupons, links to food items, and additional information that consumers will find attractive.

©Vincenzo Lombardo/Getty Images

Businesses are using QR codes like this one to allow consumers to link to additional corporate or product information.

- *Proximity/location-based marketing*: Software embedded or downloaded in a mobile device can allow companies to send out real-time advertising and communication to potential customers when they are in close proximity to a business. For example, restaurants located on Spring Garden Road in Halifax, Nova Scotia, would be able to send ads, menus, and/or coupons to potential customers—pedestrians walking in the area—via their mobile devices. Skincare retailer Kiehls, with locations throughout North America, recently engaged in a proximity-based mobile marketing campaign. Kiehls first ran in-store and online promotions motivating consumers to opt into receiving text messages from the company. The company then sent both SMS and MMS text messages to customers based on their proximity to stores. The result was that 73 percent of customers who received messages made a purchase as a direct result of the campaign.[85]

**Influencer Marketing. Influence marketing** is the use of influencers to sell a product or service or to build a brand. Influencers are trusted people within a community who have loyal online followers and can use their influence to influence others. Influencers create online content, often to express opinions, and companies can use them to promote their products or services.[86] Given the importance followers place on an influencers' opinions, they can be highly effective marketers for a company.

Original influencers were celebrities, and some continue to make significant money by promoting brands and products on social media. For example, Kylie Jenner charges $1 million for every sponsored Instagram post.[87] But other influencers appeal to a more narrow niche and their support for a product or service can be highly effective. For example, Intrepid Travel worked with several vegan influencers to promote its newly introduced vegan tours. There are currently more than 500,000 active influencers and by 2020 it is estimated that companies will spend upwards of $10 billion globally on influencer marketing.

Some of the top Canadian influencers include fashion blogger Krystin Lee, who has 187,000 Instagram followers and has partnered with top designer brands such as Lancôme and Louis Vuitton; Filipa Jackson, a Toronto stylist with 43,000 Instagram followers who works with L'Oreal and Starbucks; and Jeremy Rupke of How to Hockey, with 143,000 Instagram followers.[88]

**influence marketing** the use of influencers to sell a product or service or to build a brand

©Stefanie Keenan/Getty Images for UOMA Beauty

Patrick Starr is a very influential influencer in North America.

**DID YOU KNOW?**

Ninety-four percent of marketers say influence marketing is an effective way to reach audiences and two-thirds of retailers use some form of influencer marketing.[89]

**Personal Selling.** **Personal selling** is direct, two-way communication with buyers and potential buyers. For many products—especially large, expensive ones with specialized uses, such as cars, appliances, and houses—interaction between a salesperson and the customer is probably the most important promotional tool. Robert Herjavec, founder of The Herjavec Group and former panelist on *Dragons' Den*, states that the key to building successful firms is to develop a culture that focuses on sales. Herjavec's IT company has amassed millions in sales by having all employees, whether they be front-line workers or salespeople, focus on sales.[90]

**personal selling** direct, two-way communication with buyers and potential buyers

Personal selling is the most flexible of the promotional methods because it gives marketers the greatest opportunity to communicate specific information that might trigger a purchase. Only personal selling can zero in on a prospect and attempt to persuade that person to make a purchase. Although personal selling has a lot of advantages, it is one of the most costly forms of promotion. A sales call on an industrial customer can cost as much as $200 or $300. One Canadian firm that has mastered personal selling is Energy Saving Plus Income Fund. The company allows people to lock in the price of natural gas for five years at a time using door-to-door salespeople who specialize in cold calls. Former CEO Rebecca MacDonald notes that training salespeople is a key to long-term success.[91]

There are three distinct categories of salespersons: order takers (for example, retail sales clerks and route salespeople), creative salespersons (for example, automobile, furniture, and insurance salespeople), and support salespersons (for example, customer educators and goodwill builders who usually do not take orders). For most of these salespeople, personal selling is a six-step process:

1. *Prospecting:* Identifying potential buyers of the product.
2. *Approaching:* Using a referral or calling on a customer without prior notice to determine interest in the product.
3. *Presenting:* Getting the prospect's attention with a product demonstration.
4. *Handling objections:* Countering reasons for not buying the product.
5. *Closing:* Asking the prospect to buy the product.
6. *Following up:* Checking customer satisfaction with the purchased product.

**Content Marketing.** One of the emerging trends in marketing is the creation of valuable content by companies to attract consumers to their products and further build a company's brand. Rather than focus on selling a product, the company creates either valuable or entertaining content which brings consumers back to their website on a regular basis. Content marketing campaigns have been used to (1) improve brand awareness, (2) increase traffic to a website, (3) increase the number of registered users for a website, and (4) create sales.

Mint.com, an online provider of financial information for young people, effectively used content marketing to build its business. When the site was first created, it sold no products, instead publishing articles such as "How to Pay Off Your Student Loans" that site visitors found interesting. Later on, when Mint started to introduce products, it already had loyal visitors to the site who trusted the brand. Mint was ultimately so successful that Intuit eventually bought the company for $170 million.[92]

Red Bull is another example of a company that embraces content marketing. Rather than creating educational information, Red Bull creates engaging and entertaining information that keeps users coming back time and time again.

**Guerrilla Marketing.** Guerrilla marketing is pursuing traditional marketing through unconventional means. Essentially, guerrilla marketing consists of attracting consumer attention to a company using unique and/or creative methods. For example, Montreal-based Lezza Distribution Inc., a high-end manufacturer of countertops and

©mobil11/Shutterstock

Red Bull has successfully used entertaining content marketing to create traffic to its website.

## Consider the Following: Examining Red Bull's marketing prowess

Red Bull is not meant to taste good, but to provide energy and enhance endurance. At least, this was the intention of Austrian founder Dietrich Mateschitz. Indeed, while Red Bull has frequently been compared to cough syrup in tests of the product, the drink is beloved for its intense caffeine boost. Red Bull markets its $4 drink to those wanting to think and perform at top capacity. With the slogan Red Bull Gives You Wings, the drink has enough caffeine to equal one cup of strong coffee and contains an amino acid called taurine. Taurine occurs naturally in meat, eggs, and human breast milk but is a questionable additive. To date, evidence of its short- and long-term impacts remain inconclusive.

Despite being dubbed "speed in a can" and "liquid cocaine," Red Bull pulled in more than $7 billion in a recent year. Its red and blue can and distinctive logo infiltrate our lives, but when and where we see them is what sets Red Bull apart. Because Red Bull is marketed as a performance enhancer, the company focuses on extreme sports and its athletes. The company's stable of roughly 500 sponsored athletes promotes the brand far more effectively than commercials and other traditional methods. For example, Red Bull offers thousands of YouTube videos of extreme sports, some of which have received millions of views. While the videos do not distinctly urge consumers to buy the product, the brand is always present. The product is rarely talked about, but the plug is always there visually.

The company's online content includes shows, films, and games; it also runs a magazine called the *Red Bulletin* (published by the Red Bull Media House). Rebecca Lieb, a marketing analyst, praised Red Bull's content marketing strategy as one of the best in the industry. "Look, Red Bull has introduced its content marketing around and about the product, but it is never directly correlated to the drink itself," Lieb says. "Nobody is going to go to a website and spend 45 minutes looking at video about a drink. But Red Bull has aligned its brand consistently and unequivocally with extreme sports and action. They are number one at creating content so engaging that consumers will spend hours with it, or at least significant minutes."*

### DISCUSSION QUESTIONS

1. You have likely seen either intentionally or unintentionally some of Red Bull's content marketing. Were you aware that their sponsorships, online presence, and advertising were part of a content marketing strategy? What is your opinion of the company's marketing efforts?
2. What do you think are the pros and cons of content marketing?
3. Red Bull's marketing, both traditional and content-based, has become popular with people in their teens and even children. Given some of the controversy surrounding energy drinks, is it ethical for Red Bull to create videos and ads that young teens and children find appealing? Why or why not?
4. Think about your school or place of business. How could it create a content marketing campaign that would build its brand. What content could it promote and how would it distribute it to consumers?

*James Obrien, "How Red Bull Takes Content Marketing to the Extreme", December 19, 2012, http://mashable.com/2012/12/19/red-bull-content-marketing/#.X5vmjOF75qu (accessed February 14, 2016).

flooring surfaces, is known for its risky marketing efforts. At a recent trade show, the company had barely clothed male models serving drinks, and it has recently started hosting an annual Seven Sins party where there are half-naked models and strip poker. Company president Mark Hanna says, "Parties give us a chance to showcase our core values of passion, risk, and creativity and they give us a cool factor that distinguishes us from our competitors."[93]

Other examples include Atlantic Lotto's introduction of the Lotto Max game. The company placed large balls on smashed cars with the words Lotto Max printed on the balls. Other methods include contests or raffles like Roll Up the Rim to Win; sample giveaways—a strategy successfully used by Swiss Medica Inc., a Mississauga-based company that develops over-the-counter health food products, to compete with much larger drug companies; public demonstrations such as the ones used by Sweetpea, which used new moms as product ambassadors in Vancouver, Calgary, and Montreal to demonstrate organic frozen baby food products at local events; speaking at public events; and so forth. The difference between guerrilla marketing and publicity, which is discussed below, is that guerrilla marketing focuses on creating sales and creating awareness.

**Publicity.** **Publicity** is non-personal communication transmitted through the mass media. Publicity can be free or sometimes paid for directly by the firm. As

**publicity** non-personal communication transmitted through the mass media but not paid for directly by the firm

already discussed, Prince Edward Island paid *Live! With Regis and Kelly* to come to the island and tape three episodes. The investment resulted in strong interest from potential tourists. Sometimes, firms don't pay the media cost for publicity, nor will they be identified as the originator of the message; instead, the message is presented in news story form. Obviously, a company can benefit from publicity by releasing to news sources newsworthy messages about the firm and its involvement with the public. Many companies have public relations departments to try to gain favourable publicity and minimize negative publicity for the firm.

Although advertising and publicity are both carried by the mass media, they differ in several major ways. Advertising messages tend to be informative, persuasive, or both; publicity is mainly informative. Advertising is often designed to have an immediate impact or to provide specific information to persuade a person to act; publicity describes what a firm is doing, what products it is launching, or other newsworthy information, but seldom calls for action although action is sometimes implied or is seen by businesses and consumers as the next logical step.

For example, Spin Master, Canada's largest children's entertainment company, originally did no advertising at all and relied on PR to increase brand awareness and sell products. When advertising is used, the organization must pay for media time and select the media that will best reach target audiences—this is not always the case with publicity. The mass media often willingly carry publicity because they believe it has general public interest. Advertising can be repeated a number of times; most publicity appears in the mass media once and is not repeated. One of the keys to success in generating positive PR is to create value for all participants.

Advertising, personal selling, and sales promotion are especially useful for influencing an exchange directly. Publicity is extremely important when communication focuses on a company's activities and products and is directed at interest groups, current and potential investors, regulatory agencies, and society in general. Yet, as noted above, companies do expect advertising to result in an increase in sales. Brian Scudamore, CEO of Vancouver-based 1-800-GOT-JUNK? spent a considerable amount of time and effort getting the company onto the *Oprah* show. While this would be considered publicity, Scudamore knew that the spot would generate sales to customers and increase interest among entrepreneurs who might want to purchase a franchise. In fact, in the days after the spot on *Oprah* aired, the firm received 3000 calls from customers—up 300 percent from usual—and 500 franchise inquiries.[94]

Examples of good public relations include the following:

- Develop a press kit
- Write articles for a newspaper, newsletter, or community guide
- Write letters to the editor
- Participate in discussions either online or through traditional mediums
- Host events
- Offer services as a guest speaker

One of the keys to success in generating positive PR is to create value for all participants. Just going to a newspaper and announcing the grand opening of a store or an expansion may not be enough. Furthermore, you do not have to spend a great deal of money to generate positive PR. Publishers are interested in business events and/or ideas that are interesting to their readers.

**Sales Promotion.** **Sales promotion** involves direct inducements offering added value or some other incentive for buyers to enter into an exchange. The major tools of sales promotion are store displays, premiums, samples and demonstrations, coupons, contests and sweepstakes, refunds, and trade shows. Recently, online companies such as Save.ca, Retailmenot.ca, and Groupon have been promoting online coupons some with significant savings to consumers. One of the challenges of Groupon coupons is the deep discounts companies are expected to offer consumers in order to participate. The normal discount on Groupon is 50 percent off the purchase price, so a $100 lawn care service would be sold for $50. Groupon normally charges 50 percent of the deal's sale price, meaning in this example they would charge the business $25, leaving the business to perform $100 worth of service for $25.

**sales promotion** direct inducements offering added value or some other incentive for buyers to enter into an exchange

**push strategy** an attempt to motivate intermediaries to push the product down to their customers

Sales promotion stimulates customer purchasing and increases dealer effectiveness in selling products. It is used to enhance and supplement other forms of promotion. Test drives allow salespersons to demonstrate vehicles, which can help purchase decisions. Sampling a product may also encourage consumers to buy. PepsiCo, for example, used sampling to promote its Sierra Mist soft drink to reach more than 5 million potential consumers at well-travelled sites such as Times Square and Penn Station.[95] In a given year, almost three-fourths of consumer product companies may use sampling.

Sales promotions are generally easier to measure and less expensive than advertising. Although less than 2 percent of the 3.2 billion coupons distributed annually are redeemed, offering them in weekend paper inserts is cheaper than producing a television commercial.

## Promotion Strategies: To Push or to Pull

In developing a promotion mix, organizations must decide whether to fashion a mix that pushes or pulls the product (Figure 12.4). A **push strategy** attempts to motivate

## Consider the Following: Lululemon's unconventional marketing

Dennis Wilson founded Vancouver-based Lululemon in 1998 as yoga began to increase in popularity across North America. Wilson opened his first store with the goal of producing products that encourage people to be active and stress free. The first store opened in Vancouver and sales immediately exceeded expectations, fuelled by the popularity of the products and growth in yoga. Today the company revenue exceeds $15 billion, they operate over 440 stores and sells not only yoga attire but also sports apparel.*

A hallmark of the company's success is its unique promotional campaigns, which range from providing local yoga instructors with free clothing to having customers receive discounts for engaging in wacky activities such as shopping with barely anything on. The company also relies heavily on the Internet and buzz from social media to promote its products. Lululemon has amassed over two million social media followers with a heavy emphasis on Instagram and Pinterest.**

Former CEO Christine Day describes the company's marketing as selling in the moment without the aid of large promotions this way: "Our number one goal is to sell to customers where they are at. . .We don't do gift-giving and we don't do, like, special promotions, discounts, whatever. That's not our MO, and we don't do big." The company also doesn't engage in market research. Rather, it relies on employees to gather information on customers and Lululemon pays close attention to customer feedback on chalkboards in stores.

Unconventional marketing appears to be working, as Interbrand recently concluded that Lululemon was the ninth most valuable brand in Canada with a $2.92 billion value.***

Much like anything in life, if you do things unconventionally you are going to get some negative feedback, and Lululemon is no exception.† For example, during the 2010 Vancouver Olympic games, Lululemon received some negative reaction to its Cool Sporting Event That Takes Place in British Columbia Between 2009 & 2011 Edition promotional campaign for its Cheer Gear, which included mitts, toques, and jackets.

The company did not sponsor the games and was technically not allowed to use the word *Olympic* in its promotional efforts. Officials at the 2010 Vancouver games felt that while Lulelemon did not break the law, the company did not follow its spirit, noting the games would not be possible without official sponsors, many of which paid over $100 million to be associated with the 2010 games.‡ Lululemon eventually saw value in official Olympic sponsorship and started sponsoring athletes in 2016.

©Eric Broder Van Dyke/Shutterstock

Lululemon has built a brand by engaging in non-conventional sales techniques.

### DISCUSSION QUESTIONS

1. What are the pros and cons of using unconventional marketing campaigns?
2. Do you think customers know that their feedback to employees and on in-store chalkboards is impacting company decisions? Would they appreciate this or feel that to some extent their privacy is being violated?
3. Do you think Lulelemon should have produced and sold Cheer Gear? Why or why not?
4. What are the long-term consequences to the Olympics if companies produce and sell merchandise without paying any sponsorship dollars?

*Lululemon Athletica Inc. Company Profile, May 8, 2019, https://money.cnn.com/quote/profile/profile.html?symb=LULU

**Dejan Gajsek, "Lululemon Athletica - How One Company Succeeded In One of the Most Ruthless Industries," July 8, 2018, https://medium.com/@dgajsek/lululemon-athletica-how-one-company-succeeded-in-one-of-the-most-ruthless-industries-bd3f2bf685aa

***Interbrand, Best Canadian Brands, https://www.interbrand.com/wp-content/uploads/2015/08/Interbrand-Best-Canadian-Brands-2014.pdf, (accessed July 1, 2019).

†Disruptive Dave, "Meeting Customers Where They Are At," My Disruption Blog, October 2, 2012, http://mydisruption.wordpress.com/2012/10/02/meeting-customers-where-they-are-at (accessed July 14, 2013).

‡"VANOC accuses Lululemon of bad sportsmanship," *Marketing*, December 16, 2009, http://www.marketingmag.ca/english/news/marketer/article.jsp?content=20091216_150310_9752 (accessed June 17, 2010); "Lululemon Athletica," http://en.wikipedia.org/wiki/Lululemon_Athletica, (accessed June 17, 2010).

**Figure 12.4** | Push and Pull Strategies

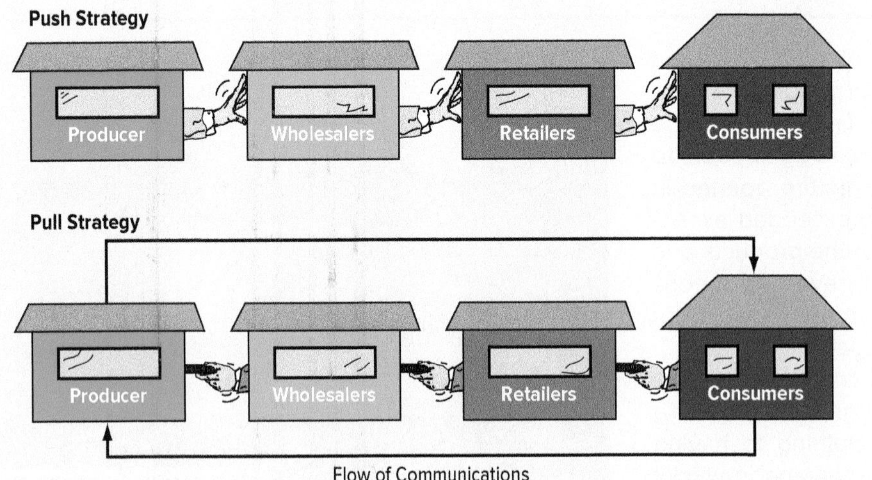


intermediaries to push the product down to their customers. When a push strategy is used, the company attempts to motivate wholesalers and retailers to make the product available to their customers. Sales personnel may be used to persuade intermediaries to offer the product, distribute promotional materials, and offer special promotional incentives for those who agree to carry the product.

A great example of using successful push strategies comes from Jewel Pop, a Dartmouth, Nova Scotia–based jewellery company that recently reached $3 million in sales. Company founder and president Robert Smith developed a Kameleon jewellery line where beads and silver rings are interchangeable, allowing customers to intermingle and colour-coordinate their outfits and jewellery. After taking samples of the product to an Atlanta gift show, Smith found a number of retailers that were willing to sell the product.

Smith, who has years of experience in the jewellery industry, knows that retailers may offer to sell a product but not push it to the customers. So Smith devised an incentive plan providing retailers with exclusive territories, free shipping, and other bonuses to push the unique jewellery. The strategy is working, as Smith notes that some independent retailers are selling in excess of $100,000 a year in jewellery and he hopes to reach $100 million in sales in the next five to six years.[96] Chrysler manufacturing plants operate on a push system. They assemble cars according to forecasts of sales demand. Dealers then sell to buyers with the help of incentives and other promotions.[97]

**pull strategy** the use of promotion to create consumer demand for a product so that consumers exert pressure on marketing channel members to make it available

A **pull strategy** uses promotion to create consumer demand for a product so that consumers exert pressure on marketing channel members to make it available. For example, when the Coca-Cola Company launched its new product Orange Vanilla Coke, the company gave away samples throughout the United States via sampling teams. Coke distributed ice-cold Orange Vanilla Coke at targeted retail outlets, sporting events, and other locations.[98] Such sampling prior to a product roll-out encourages consumers to request the product from their favourite retailer.

A company can use either strategy, or it can use a variation or combination of the two. The exclusive use of advertising indicates a pull strategy. Personal selling to marketing channel members indicates a push strategy. The allocation of promotional resources to various marketing mix elements probably determines which strategy a marketer uses.

## Objectives of Promotion

The marketing mix a company uses depends on its objectives. It is important to recognize that promotion is only one element of the marketing strategy and must be tied carefully to the goals of the firm, its overall marketing objectives, and the other elements of the marketing strategy. Firms use promotion for many reasons, but typical objectives are to stimulate demand, to stabilize sales, and to inform, remind, and reinforce customers. For example, Tim Hortons will advertise in Canada to stimulate demand at certain times of the year, but it will also advertise to remind consumers and Canadians that Tim Hortons is a national brand in the country.

Increasing demand for a product is probably the most typical promotional objective. Stimulating demand, often through advertising and sales promotion, is particularly important when a firm is using a pull strategy.

Another goal of promotion is to stabilize sales by maintaining the status quo—that is, the current sales level of the product. During periods of slack or decreasing sales, contests, prizes, vacations, and other sales promotions are sometimes offered to customers to maintain sales goals. Advertising is often used to stabilize sales by making customers aware of slack use periods. For example, both Air Canada and WestJet use Internet advertising to promote air travel and vacation specials during slow times of the year. During the 2018 Olympics, Air Canada announced a new special the day after any Canadian won a gold medal—most of which were aimed at increasing sales during traditionally slow periods.

An important role of any promotional program is to inform potential buyers about the organization and its products. A major portion of advertising in Canada, particularly in daily newspapers, is informational. Providing information about the availability, price, technology, and features of a product is very important in encouraging a buyer to move toward a purchase decision. Nearly all forms of promotion involve an attempt to help consumers learn more about a product and a company.

Promotion is also used to remind consumers that an established organization is still around and sells certain products that have uses and benefits. Often advertising reminds customers that they may need to use a product more frequently or in certain situations. Canadian Tire, for example, has used a variety of promotions reminding car owners that they need to change their oil every 5000 kilometres to ensure proper performance of their cars.

Reinforcement promotion attempts to assure current users of the product that they have made the right choice and tells them how to get the most satisfaction from the product. Also, a company could release publicity statements through the news media about a new use for a product. Additionally, firms can have salespeople communicate with current and potential customers about the proper use and maintenance of a product—all in the hope of developing a repeat customer.

## Promotional Positioning

**Promotional positioning** uses promotion to create and maintain an image of a product in buyers' minds. It is a natural result of market segmentation. In both promotional positioning and market segmentation, the firm targets a given product or brand at a portion of the total market. A promotional strategy helps differentiate the product and make it appeal to a particular market segment. For example, VIA Rail advertises ease of boarding and comfort to appeal to consumers who want the freedom to move about as they travel and others who do not want the long security check-ins that are common at airports. Volvo heavily promotes the safety and crashworthiness of Volvo automobiles in its advertising. Volkswagen has done the same thing with its edgy ads showing car crashes. Promotion can be used to change or reinforce an image. Effective promotion influences customers and persuades them to buy.

**promotional positioning** the use of promotion to create and maintain an image of a product in buyers' minds

### TEAM EXERCISE

Form groups and search for examples of convenience products, shopping products, specialty products, and business products. How are these products marketed? Provide examples of any ads that you can find to show examples of the promotional strategies for these products. Report your findings to the class.

# LEARNING OBJECTIVES SUMMARY

**LO 12-1** Describe the role of product in the marketing mix, including how products are developed, classified, and identified.

Products (goods, services, ideas) are among a firm's most visible contacts with consumers and must meet consumers' needs and expectations to ensure success. New product development is a multi-step process: idea development, the screening of new ideas, business analysis, product development, test marketing, and commercialization. Products are usually classified as either consumer or industrial products. Consumer products can be further classified as convenience, shopping, or specialty products. The industrial product classifications are raw materials, major equipment, accessory equipment, component parts, processed materials, supplies and industrial services. Products also can be classified by the stage of the product life cycle (introduction, growth, maturity and decline). Identifying products includes branding (the process of naming and identifying products); packaging (the product's container); and labelling (information, such as content and warnings, on the package).

**LO 12-2** Define price and discuss its importance in the marketing mix, including various pricing strategies a firm might employ.

Price is the value placed on an object exchanged between a buyer and a seller, and is probably the most flexible variable of the marketing mix. Pricing objectives include survival, maximization of profits and sales volume, and maintaining the status quo. When a firm introduces a new product, it may use price skimming or penetration pricing. Psychological pricing and price discounting are other strategies.

**LO 12-3** Identify factors affecting distribution decisions, such as marketing channels and intensity of market coverage.

Making products available to customers is facilitated by intermediaries who bridge the gap between the producer of the product and its ultimate user. A marketing channel is a group of marketing organizations that direct the flow of products from producers to consumers. Market coverage relates to the number and variety of outlets that make products available to the customers; it may be intensive, selective, or exclusive. Physical distribution is all the activities necessary to move products from producers to consumers, including inventory planning and control, transportation, warehousing, and materials handling.

**LO 12-4** Specify the activities involved in promotion, as well as promotional strategies and promotional positioning.

Promotion encourages marketing exchanges by persuading individuals, groups and organizations to accept advertising (a paid form of non-personal communication transmitted through a mass medium); personal selling (direct, two-way communication with buyers and potential buyers); publicity (non-personal communication transmitted through mass media but not paid for directly by the firm); and sales promotion (direct inducements offering added value or some other incentive for buyers to enter into an exchange). A push strategy attempts to motivate intermediaries to push the product down to their customers, whereas a pull strategy tries to create consumer demand for a product so that consumers exert pressure on marketing channel members to make the product available. Typical promotion objectives are to stimulate demand, stabilize sales, and inform, remind, and reinforce customers. Promotional positioning is the use of promotion to create and maintain in the buyer's mind an image of the product.

# KEY TERMS

advertising
advertising campaign
branding
business products
commercialization
consumer products
discounts
exclusive distribution
generic products
influence marketing
integrated marketing communications
intensive distribution
labelling
manufacturer brands
marketing channel
materials handling
mobile marketing
packaging
penetration price
personal selling
physical distribution
price skimming
private distributor brands
product line
product mix
promotional positioning
psychological pricing
publicity
pull strategy
push strategy
quality
retailers
sales promotion
selective distribution
test marketing
trademark
transportation
warehousing
wholesalers

# So You Want to Be *a Marketing Manager*

Many jobs in marketing are closely tied to the marketing mix functions: distribution, product, promotion, and price. Often the job titles could be sales manager, distribution or supply chain manager, advertising account executive, or store manager.

A distribution manager arranges for transportation of goods within firms and through marketing channels. Transportation can be costly, and time is always an important factor, so minimizing their effects is vital to the success of a firm. Distribution managers must choose one or a combination of transportation modes from a vast array of options, taking into account local, federal, and international regulations for different freight classifications; the weight, size, and fragility of products to be shipped; time schedules; and loss and damage ratios. Manufacturing firms are the largest employers of distribution managers.

A product manager is responsible for the success or failure of a product line. This requires a general knowledge of advertising, transportation modes, inventory control, selling and sales management, promotion, marketing research, packaging, and pricing. Frequently, several years of selling and sales management experience are prerequisites for such a position as well as college training in business administration. Being a product manager can be rewarding both financially and psychologically.

Some of the most creative roles in the business world are in the area of advertising. Advertising pervades our daily lives, as businesses and other organizations try to grab our attention and tell us about what they have to offer. Copywriters, artists, and account executives in advertising must have creativity, imagination, artistic talent, and expertise in expression and persuasion. Advertising is an area of business in which a wide variety of educational backgrounds may be useful, from degrees in advertising itself, to journalism or liberal arts degrees. Common entry-level positions in an advertising agency are found in the traffic department, account service (account coordinator), or the media department (media assistant). Advertising jobs are also available in many manufacturing or retail firms, nonprofit organizations, banks, professional associations, utility companies, and other arenas outside of an advertising agency.

Although a career in retailing may begin in sales, there is much more to retailing than simply selling. Many retail personnel occupy management positions, focusing on selecting and ordering merchandise, promotional activities, inventory control, customer credit operations, accounting, personnel, and store security. Many specific examples of retailing jobs can be found in large department stores. A section manager coordinates inventory and promotions and interacts with buyers, salespeople, and consumers. The buyer's job is fast-paced, often involving much travel and pressure. Buyers must be open-minded and forward-looking in their hunt for new, potentially successful items. Regional managers coordinate the activities of several retail stores within a specific geographic area, usually monitoring and supporting sales, promotions, and general procedures. Retail management can be exciting and challenging. Growth in retailing is expected to accompany the growth in population and is likely to create substantial opportunities in the coming years.

While a career in marketing can be very rewarding, marketers today agree that the job is getting tougher. Many advertising and marketing executives say the job has gotten much more demanding in the past ten years, viewing their number-one challenge as balancing work and personal obligations. Other challenges include staying current on industry trends or technologies, keeping motivated/inspired on the job, and measuring success. If you are up to the challenge, you may find that a career in marketing is just right for you to utilize your business knowledge while exercising your creative side as well.

# BUILD YOUR BUSINESS PLAN

## Dimensions of Marketing Strategy

If you think your product/business is truly new to or unique to the market, you need to substantiate your claim. After a thorough exploration on the Web, you want to make sure there has not been a similar business/service recently launched in your community. Check with your chamber of commerce or economic development office, which might be able to provide you with a history of recent business failures. If you are not confident about the ability or willingness of customers to try your new product or service, collecting your own primary data to ascertain demand is highly advisable.

The decision of where to initially set your prices is a critical one. If there are currently similar products in the market, you need to be aware of competitors' prices before you determine yours. If your product/service is new to the market, you can price it high (market skimming strategy) as long as you realize that the high price will probably attract competitors to the market more quickly (they will think they can make the same product for less), which will force you to drop your prices sooner than you would like. Another strategy to consider is market penetration pricing, a strategy that sets prices lower and discourages competition from entering the market as quickly. Whatever strategy you decide to use, don't forget to examine your product/service's elasticity.

At this time, you need to start thinking about how to promote your product. Why do you feel your product/service is different or new to the market? How do you want to position your product/service so customers view it favourably? Remember that this is all occurring *within the consumer's mind.*

# CASE | Musi: A Long-Term Sustainable Business?

Christian Lunny and Aaron Wojnowski were attending high school in Winnipeg, Manitoba and both had heard about one another. Unlike many high school exploits that focus on partying or sports, Lunny and Wojnowski were known to one another as the *other teen* who was also doing cool things with computers. Wojnowski had taught himself to code in grade nine, and Lunny was always interested in digital media. They both recall thinking they should meet and perhaps one day start a business together.[99]

A short time after meeting, they had their business inspiration. Lunny and Wojnowski were hanging out with friends and accessing free music on YouTube. The pair note that while YouTube is great for streaming music videos, especially given the large volume of free content, it's not great for playing music on your phone. They found YouTube music was hard to organize, songs would play randomly, users couldn't create a playlist to use when exercising or working, and so forth. With these problems in mind, the app Musi was born. Musi is an IOS/Apple app that allows users to easily stream music from free content providers such as YouTube and SoundCloud on their phones. Musi can organize songs into multiple playlists and it allows users to share their favourite songs and artists.[100]

After launching the app on the App Store, Lunny and Wojnowski started to share their free app with their friends and the pair got a big break when their company was featured on the local news. Soon free daily downloads were numbering in the thousands and the app was receiving strong reviews from users. Wojnowski also discovered an interesting way to generate favourable five-star reviews. He created a pop-up ad that would only appear to current users not new adopters. The pop-up would ask users if they were happy with the app and if they were the app would play one of their favourite songs. The happy user would then be asked to rate the app. If the user wasn't happy, the pop-up wouldn't ask the user to rate the app. Rather the app would ask why the user was unhappy and Wojnowski would respond to their concerns via email. Once the user was satisfied, Wojnowski would then ask them to rate the app through a personal email.[101]

As downloads continued to grow the business partners started to work on App Store optimization. App Store optimization is the process of using key words to describe your app. When users search in the App Store they use certain terms, if entrepreneurs use the correct descriptors in their key words, an app will appear near the top of the search results. If entrepreneurs don't use words to describe their app that users would use, then the app will not appear high in search results. Originally, Musi used key words such as *YouTube organizer*, which no one was searching for or even understood. When they changed their key words to *free* and *music downloads* the daily downloads of their app took off. Soon the app was being downloaded 20 then 30 thousand times a day. Today the app has reached over 12 million downloads in 150 countries with 50,000 downloads a day.[102]

Lunny and Wojnowski then wondered if they could monetize the app, the process of making money from advertisers or perhaps selling content. Originally Wojnowski had concerns that placing ads on the app would destroy the user experience. But after experimenting with ads and earning enough money a day to cover a lot of their expenses, including Wojnowski's tuition, the pair were hooked. Wojnowski says the key was not to overload the app with advertisements while Lunny notes they always remained focused on their vision to create the best streaming app for free YouTube content. The business partners then started working with ad companies that specialize in monetizing apps for entrepreneurs such as MoPub and their revenues tripled overnight. Given that their monthly expenses to run the Musi are estimated to be $25, Lunny and Wojnowski are clearly quite successful with their business which they now do on the side as they pursue other entrepreneurial ventures.[103]

While Lunny and Wojnowski believe they have created a sustainable business some business advisers have expressed concerns. For example, some potential investors have noted that Musi could eventually be sued by YouTube and SoundCloud as Musi uses some of their interface. Other concerns include questions about what would happen if YouTube started to charge for some content or limited third party use.[104]

## DISCUSSION QUESTIONS

1. What are some of the strengths, weaknesses, opportunities and threats (SWOT analysis) for Musi? List all the factors you can think of. Try to develop solutions for the weaknesses and methods or strategies to mitigate the threats.
2. Do you think the Musi founders were acting ethically when they created a pop-up ad that encouraged favourable ratings and deterred unsatisfied users from rating the app? Why or why not?
3. Musicians have attempted to stop websites that enable users to download their songs for free. They have claimed such sites are illegal and unethical. Do you think the same musicians will eventually try to stop users from accessing free content on Musi? Why or why not? Do you think Musi is an ethical business?
4. Do you think Musi is a sustainable business, meaning a business that will last for years? Why or why not?

# CHAPTER 13

# Digital Marketing and Social Networking

©The Canadian Press/Frank Arcuri

## LEARNING OBJECTIVES

**After reading this chapter, you will be able to:**

- **LO 13-1** Define digital media and digital marketing, and recognize their increasing value in strategic planning.
- **LO 13-2** Understand the characteristics of digital media and how these methods are different from traditional marketing activities.
- **LO 13-3** Demonstrate the role of digital marketing and social networking in today's business environment.
- **LO 13-4** Show how digital media affect the marketing mix.
- **LO 13-5** Define social networking and illustrate how businesses can use different types of social networking media.
- **LO 13-6** Identify legal and ethical considerations in digital media.

# ENTER THE WORLD OF BUSINESS

### Arlene Dickinson: Investing in Entrepreneurs

Arlene Dickinson, CEO of Venture, a fully integrated marketing firm, and YouInc.com, a website dedicated to encouraging entrepreneurship, is living proof that the Canadian dream is possible.

Dickinson, star of CBC's *Dragons' Den*, is the owner of Venture, one of the largest marketing and communications companies in the country. She also has an ownership stake in over 50 businesses and has won numerous business awards, including being included in Canada's Most Powerful Women: Top 100 Hall of Fame, and *PROFIT* and *Chatelaine* magazines' Top 100 Business Owners. Today, Dickinson's net worth is estimated to be in excess of $125 million.

Dickinson immigrated to Canada with her parents who, by the time they arrived here from South Africa, only had $50 left to support the family of five. Dickinson's family struggled so much during their early years in Canada that her mother had to sell her engagement ring as their car broke down moving from Edmonton to Calgary and the family had no money to fix the car or buy a replacement.

Things improved in Calgary, and Dickinson graduated from high school at the age of 16, but didn't have an interest in pursuing anything that resembled a career. Her main goal was to have a family, which started when she married at the age of 19. Dickinson soon became a working mother, paying her husband's way through teacher's college. The marriage was very rocky, and Dickinson divorced her husband when she was 27, leaving her with four children and no job.

At this point, Dickinson had her first break when she was offered a job selling advertising for a TV station. While she had no experience in sales, she excelled at the position and spent 18 months working on what she assumed was a new career. Unfortunately, the station went through a cost-cutting program and Dickinson lost her job. One of Dickinson's co-workers had recently started a company called Venture Communications and he asked if Dickinson would like to become a partner. According to Dickinson, becoming a partner meant working for no pay and hoping that the company became successful. Dickinson says, "I joined the company with no income and we barely scraped by the first few years living off credit cards and whatever money I could scrape together."

The firm continued to grow, and in 1998 Dickinson took over as owner of the company. By 2014, Venture Communications had established itself as one of the largest marketing and communications firms in Canada, with estimated annual gross sales in excess of $45 million.

While on *Dragons' Den*, Dickinson founded Arlene Dickinson Enterprises, which is a venture capital firm committed to supporting entrepreneurship. Shortly afterward, Dickinson founded YouInc.com, a website committed to promoting entrepreneurship as a lifestyle. Visitors to YouInc.com can read articles on social media promotions, share their entrepreneurship successes, and even pose questions to informal focus groups to get feedback from other entrepreneurs.

During this time, Dickinson took Venture through a re-visioning process, as she thought the firm needed to emphasis its entrepreneurial roots. The company dropped *Communications* from its name and started to position itself as the entrepreneur's marketing company. Venture positions itself as the best company to work with entrepreneurs as it is run by one of the premiere entrepreneurs in Canada: Dickinson. Venture also features YouInc.com prominently on its website and states that Venture's involvement in the site and its mission of encouraging entrepreneurship is fundamental to who they are as a firm. The company says they are looking to service three distinct groups of clients: businesses that are run by entrepreneurs, companies that wish to sell to entrepreneurs, and companies that want to be more entrepreneurial.

Given the new entrepreneurial positioning of the firm, some potential clients maybe wondering if Venture is focusing on start-ups. But this is not the case, Dickinson says the firm is concentrating on existing small and medium businesses that need marketing to get them to the next level. She believes that there has been too much emphasis on going after large clients and not enough on helping entrepreneurs tell their stories.

Venture's new positioning also comes with message that they are more than just a marketing company. The firm is promoting itself as one that is forging partnerships with entrepreneurs to not only provide marketing assistance but also consulting and strategic management direction.[1]

**DISCUSSION QUESTIONS**

1. Do you think positioning Venture as an entrepreneurial firm, one that knows entrepreneurs, will make the company more or less attractive to large corporate clients? Why?
2. Venture is clearly using Arlene Dickinson as their main promotional spokesperson. What are some short- and long-term advantages and disadvantages of such a strategy?
3. On their website, Venture communicates to start-ups that they may lack the resources to hire the firm. Will this messaging result in start-ups being more or less willing to use the firm in the future? Why?

# Introduction

The Internet and information technology have dramatically changed the environment for business. Marketers' new ability to convert all types of communications into digital media has created efficient, inexpensive ways of connecting businesses and consumers and has improved the flow and the usefulness of information. Businesses have the information they need to make more informed decisions, and consumers have access to a greater variety of products and more information about choices and quality.

The defining characteristic of information technology in the twenty-first century is accelerating change. New systems and applications advance so rapidly that it is almost impossible to keep up with the latest developments. Start-up companies emerge that quickly overtake existing approaches to digital media. When Google first arrived on the scene, a number of search engines were fighting for dominance, including Excite, Infoseek, Lycos, and WebCrawler. With its fast, easy-to-use search engine, Google became number one and is now challenging the status quo in many industries, including advertising, newspapers, mobile phones, and book publishing.

Despite its victory, Google is constantly being challenged itself by competitors like Yahoo! and Baidu. The Chinese search engine Baidu represents a particular threat as it is the fifth-largest "pure-play" Internet company (after Google, Amazon, Tencent, and eBay) and has the majority of the Chinese Internet market.

Google is also being challenged by social networks, which most observers believe will dominate digital communication in the future.[2] Today, people spend more time on social networking sites, such as Facebook, than they spend on email. Facebook, in an attempt to compete directly against Google in search, has actually launched Facebook Search (http://search.fb.com), which allows users to find information on the social network. Facebook's search engine not only searches for keywords but will also give you results based on the context of your search items, which is something Google does not do. In 2019 Facebook started to test search engine advertising that could eventually bring them into direct competition with Google for search-based advertising.[3]

In this chapter we first provide some key definitions related to digital marketing and social networking. Next we discuss using digital media in business and marketing. We look at marketing mix considerations when using digital media and pay special attention to social networking. Then we focus on digital marketing strategies—particularly new communication channels like social networks—and consider how consumers are changing their information searches and consumption behaviour to fit emerging technologies and trends. Finally, we examine the legal and social issues associated with information technology, digital media, and e-business.

# What Is Digital Marketing?

**LO 13-1** Define digital media and digital marketing, and recognize their increasing value in strategic planning.

Let's start with a clear understanding of our focus in this chapter. First, we can distinguish **e-business** from traditional business by noting that conducting e-business means carrying out the goals of business through the use of the Internet. **Digital media** are electronic media that function using digital codes—when we refer to digital media, we mean media available via computers and other digital devices, including mobile and wireless ones like cell phones and smartphones.

**e-business** carrying out the goals of business using the Internet

**digital media** electronic media that function using digital codes via computers, cellular phones, smartphones, and other digital devices

**digital marketing** uses all digital media, including the Internet and mobile and interactive channels, to develop communication and exchanges with customers

**Digital marketing** uses all digital media, including the Internet and mobile and interactive channels, to develop communication and exchanges with customers. *Digital marketing* is a term we will use often because we are interested in all types of digital communications, regardless of the electronic channel that transmits the data.

©Rawpixel.com/Shutterstock

Digital media, including the Internet and mobile and interactive channels, has changed the way businesses can reach customers. Consumers often expect multiple touch points and two-way communication to help facilitate the purchase decision.

# Growth and Benefits of Digital Communication

**LO 13-2** Understand the characteristics of digital media and how these methods are different from traditional marketing activities.

The Internet has created tremendous opportunities for businesses to forge relationships with consumers and business customers, target markets more precisely, and even reach previously inaccessible markets at home and around the world. The Internet also facilitates business transactions, allowing companies to network with manufacturers, wholesalers, retailers, suppliers, and outsource firms to serve customers more quickly and more efficiently. The telecommunication opportunities created by the Internet have set the stage for digital marketing's development and growth.

Digital communication offers a completely new dimension in connecting with others. Some of the characteristics that distinguish digital from traditional communication are addressability, interactivity, accessibility, connectivity, and control. Let's look at what these mean and how they enhance marketing.

The ability of a business to identify customers before they make a purchase is **addressability**. Digital media make it possible for visitors on a website like Amazon.ca and Chapters.Indigo.ca to provide information about their needs and wants before they buy. A social network such as Facebook lets users create a profile to keep in touch or to build a network of identified contacts, including friends, colleagues, and businesses. Companies such as Porter Airlines, Canada's third-largest airline, use social networks such as Facebook to announce new promotions, share company news, collect customer feedback, and answer questions. Porter uses Twitter primarily to answer questions from customers and YouTube to share videos about the company.

**addressability** the ability of a business to identify customers before they make purchases

©Robseguin/Dreamstime.com

Porter Airlines uses social media, especially Twitter, to interact with customers.

**DID YOU KNOW?**

The average Canadian sits in front of a computer for 45.3 hours a month, taking in content from some 98 websites.[4]

**Interactivity** allows customers to express their needs and wants directly to the firm in response to its communications. In traditional one-way forms of communication, such as television advertising, the customer must contact the company by phone or other means. Interactivity relies on digital media that can make a conversation between the firm and the customer happen without any delay; thus, real relationships become possible.

**interactivity** allows customers to express their needs and wants directly to the firm in response to its communications

**accessibility** allows consumers to find information about competing products, prices, and reviews, and become more informed about a firm and the relative value of its products

Digital media, such as blogs and social networks, allow marketers to engage with customers, shape their expectations and perceptions, and benefit from broader market reach at lower cost. As mentioned above, Porter Airlines uses social media sites to communicate with customers in real time. Customers can ask questions about promotions, flight times, and so forth, and Porter will respond. Other customers who may not be directly involved in the interaction can also read and benefit from the information.

Ken Tencer, a branding and innovation expert, says that conversations with customers are better than a strong communication strategy. Tencer uses the example of Fluevog, a Vancouver-based specialty shoe and accessory store with fourteen North American locations. According to Tencer, Fluevog's website and digital strategy have been successful because the company engages customers and asks them to participate in a conversation about products and the brand.[5]

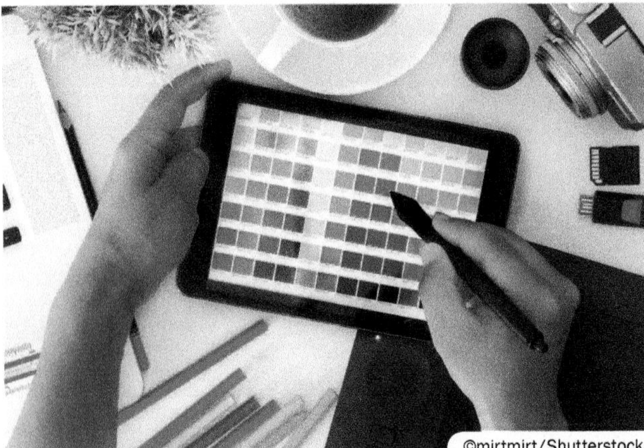

©mirtmirt/Shutterstock

Benjamin Moore's iPhone app allows customers to match paint colour samples and photographs, with shades of Benjamin Moore paint

**Accessibility** allows consumers and to find information about competing products, prices, and reviews, and become more informed about a firm and the relative value of its products. Mobile devices—including smartphones and mobile computing devices like the iPad—allow customers to leave their desktops and access digital networks from anywhere. Thanks to the popularity of the iPhone, businesses and their customers can stay in constant touch. Benjamin Moore & Co. has an iPhone app that allows customers to match anything, such as their own home-decorating colour samples and photographs, with shades of Benjamin Moore paint. Many companies are adopting a digital media philosophy of open communication with customers; for example, a firm can go to a site such as https://en.eyeka.com/ or https://tongal.com/, marketing firms that provide customized services linking businesses with creators and in some cases customers, to request ideas for new products, advertising, or the solicitation of other feedback.

**Connectivity** keeps customers, employees, and businesses connected with each other. It involves the use of digital networks to provide linkages between information providers and users. Social networking is a key form of connectivity made easier on a global scale by Facebook, LinkedIn, Twitter, Tumblr, Pinterest, and other networking sites. Facebook has a larger audience than any television network that has ever existed. Firms can also target precise markets through local social networking sites such as Orkut, a Google-owned service operating in India and Brazil.

**connectivity** the use of digital networks to provide linkages between information providers and users

**control** consumers' ability to regulate the information they receive via the Internet, and the rate and sequence of their exposure to that information

**Control** refers to consumers' ability to regulate the information they receive via the Internet, and the rate and sequence of their exposure to that information. Consumers choose the websites they view, the blogs they follow, and the social networking sites to which they belong. This trend toward a consumer-controlled market requires marketers to approach their jobs in a different way than they did in traditional marketing.

## Using Digital Media in Business

**LO 13-3** Demonstrate the role of digital marketing and social networking in today's business environment.

The phenomenal growth of digital media has provided new ways of conducting business. Given almost instant communication with precisely defined consumer groups, firms can use real-time exchanges to stimulate interactive communication, forge closer relationships, and learn more accurately about consumer and supplier needs. Consider that Amazon, one of the most successful e-businesses, ranked eighth on the Fortune 500 list of America's largest corporations.[6] Amazon is a true global e-business, with a presence in 58 countries, reaching over 1.2 billion people, and international sales account for more than 50 percent of its $241 billion in revenue.[7,8] Many of you may not remember a world before Amazon because it has completely transformed how many people shop. Previously, consumers had to travel store to store in order to find goods and compare prices.

Because it is fast and inexpensive, digital communication is making it easier for businesses to conduct marketing research, provide and obtain price and product information, and advertise, as well as to fulfill their business goals by selling goods and services online. For example, Lululemon uses social media—and has amassed a loyal following on a variety of sites. For example, Lululemon boasts 2.9 million Instagram followers, 2.1 million Facebook fans, 1.05 million Twitter followers, and almost 251,000 LinkedIn followers—the company uses social media to create links with customers, get immediate feedback on products, and promote its brand. By getting feedback online, the company can save significant time and money in determining what products are likely to appeal to different segments of the marketplace. Even the government engages in digital marketing activities—marketing everything from bonds and other financial instruments to oil-drilling leases and surplus equipment.

New businesses and even industries are evolving that would not exist without digital media. As discussed in Chapter 12, YouTube lets consumers watch a broad collection of videos, anytime and from anywhere.

The reality, however, is that Internet markets are more similar to traditional markets than they are different. Thus, successful e-business strategies, like traditional business strategies, focus on creating products that customers need or want, not merely developing a brand name or reducing the costs associated with online transactions. Instead of changing all industries, e-business has had much more impact in certain industries where the cost of business and customer transactions has been very high. For example, investment trading is less expensive online because customers can buy and sell investments, such as stocks and mutual funds, on their own. Firms such as TD Waterhouse, the biggest online brokerage firm, have been innovators in promoting online trading. As a result, traditional brokers such as Nesbitt Burns have had to follow with online trading for their customers.

Because the Internet lowers the cost of communication, it can contribute significantly to any industry or activity that depends on the flow of digital information, such as entertainment, health care, government services, education, and computer services like software development. The publishing industry is transitioning away from print newspapers, magazines, and books as more consumers purchase e-readers, like the Kobo or Kindle, or read the news online. For example, *Fifty Shades of Grey* has been downloaded millions of times over the past few years. Even your textbook is available electronically. Because publishers save money on paper, ink, and shipping, sometimes electronic versions of books are cheaper than their paper counterparts.

Digital media can also improve communication within and between businesses. In the future, most significant gains will come from productivity improvements within businesses. Communication is a key business function, and improving the speed and clarity of communication can help businesses save time and improve employee problem-solving abilities. Digital media can be a communications backbone that helps to store knowledge, information, and records in management information systems so co-workers can access it when faced with a problem to solve. A well-designed management information system that makes use of digital technology can, therefore, help reduce confusion, improve organization and efficiency,

©Wavebreakmedia Ltd/Getty Images

Athletic apparel retailer Lululemon has amassed millions of social media followers. The company uses Instagram, Facebook, Twitter, and other sites to promote yoga clothes and a fit lifestyle.

©Hero Images/Getty Images

Digital media are changing the way people read. Electronic readers and tablets are taking the place of traditional books and newspapers.

and facilitate clear communication. Given the crucial role of communication and information in business, the long-term impact of digital media on economic growth is substantial, and it will inevitably grow over time.

The dynamic nature of digital marketing can quickly change opportunities and create challenges. For example, smartphones and tablets now function as personal information managers and are being used to assist professionals in medicine, engineering, and other business areas. And they, along with social networking, drones, and driverless cars are shaping a new marketing environment. While digital marketing has many benefits, however, challenges exist, especially in giving up privacy.

## Digital Media and the Marketing Mix

**LO 13-4** Show how digital media affect the marketing mix.

While digital marketing shares some similarities with conventional marketing techniques, a few valuable differences stand out. Digital media make customer communications faster and interactive. Digital media also help companies reach new target markets more easily, affordably, and quickly than ever before. And digital media provide marketers with access to new resources in seeking out and communicating with customers.

One of the most important benefits of digital marketing is the ability of marketers and customers to easily share information. Through websites, social networks, and other digital media, consumers can learn about everything they consume and use in their lives, ask questions, voice complaints, indicate preferences, and otherwise communicate about their needs and desires. Many marketers use email, mobile phones, social networking, wikis, video sharing, podcasts, blogs, videoconferencing, and other technologies to coordinate activities and communicate with employees, customers, and suppliers.

Twitter, considered both a social network and a micro blog, illustrates how these digital technologies can combine to create new robust communication opportunities. For example, the Bell Let's Talk campaign, which is aimed at reducing the stigma and silence surrounding mental illness, used social media such as Twitter to encourage people to participate on Bell Let's Talk Day and donated five cents to mental health programs for every eligible interaction.[9]

Nielsen Marketing Research revealed that consumers now spend more time on social networking sites than they do on email, and social network use is still growing. In Canada, it is estimated that 74 percent of Canadians spend three to four hours a day online and the third most popular activity is using social media (67 percent). In

©Bell Canada

Every time people use the #BellLetsTalk hashtag on Bell Let's Talk Day, Bell donates money to Canadian mental health programs. The hashtag was the most used on Twitter in Canada in 2018.

Canada roughly 23.8 million people, or approximately 67 percent of the population, use Facebook.[10] Other popular social media sites include LinkedIn (with 45 percent of social media users active on the site); Instagram (39 percent of social media users); Pinterest (36 percent); and Twitter (35 percent).[11]

With digital media, even small businesses can reach new markets through these inexpensive communication channels. For example, FreshBooks, a Toronto-based accounting service for small companies, has expanded to reach 24 million users in 160 countries. FreshBooks uses social media to communicate with customers and promote its products and services.[12] Bricks-and-mortar companies like Canadian Tire and Best Buy use online catalogues and company websites and blogs to supplement their retail stores. Internet companies like Amazon and BlueNile, which lack physical stores, let customers post reviews of their purchases, creating company-sponsored communities.

One aspect of marketing that has not changed with digital media is the importance of achieving the right marketing mix. Product, distribution, promotion, and pricing are as important as ever for successful online marketing strategies. More than 56.8 percent of the world's population now uses the Internet.[13] That means it is essential for businesses large and small to use digital media effectively, not only to grab or maintain market share but also to streamline their organizations and offer customers entirely new benefits and convenience. Let's look at how businesses are using digital media to create effective marketing strategies on the Web.

**Product Considerations.** Like traditional marketers, digital marketers must anticipate consumer needs and preferences, tailor their products and services to meet these needs, and continually upgrade them to remain competitive. The connectivity created by digital

©Alberto Pomares/Getty Images

Amazingly, 74 percent of Canadians spend three to four hours a day online with 67 percent of users visiting social media/networking sites.

media provides the opportunity for adding services and can enhance product benefits. For example, L'Oreal, the world's largest cosmetic company, has created the L'Oreal Makeup Genius App. The app allows customers to virtually try on products, and to mix and match colour combinations, allowing them to experiment with different products and looks.[14]

Other examples include streaming services such as Netflix, which have virtually eliminated traditional movie rental stores as the company can offer a much wider array of movies and games, a monthly subscription service, and of course, no late fees. Netflix also prides itself on its recommendation engine, which suggests movies to users based on their previous viewing history and how they rate movies they have seen. As Netflix demonstrates, the Internet can make it much easier to anticipate consumer needs. However, fierce competition makes quality product and service offerings more important than ever.[15]

**Distribution Considerations.** The Internet is a new distribution channel for making products available at the right time, at the right place, and in the right quantities. Marketers' ability to process orders electronically and increase the speed of communication via the Internet reduces inefficiencies, costs, and redundancies while increasing speed throughout the marketing channel. Shipping times and costs have become an important consideration in attracting customers, prompting many

## ENTREPRENEURSHIP IN ACTION

### Etsy: The Site for the Creative Entrepreneur

**Etsy**

**Founders:** Robert Kalin, Chris Maguire, and Haim Schoppik

**Founded:** 2005

**Success:** Etsy has 54 million members and 39.4 million shoppers who spent $3.93 billion in 2019 shopping on Etsy.*

Humpty Dumpty mugs, T-shirts featuring texting zombies, and pet beds made from suitcases—all have been listed for sale on Etsy, the digital marketing website for handmade, vintage, and do-it-yourself products. The company is popular with artists and small businesses and reached profitability in just four years.

Etsy allows entrepreneurs a central site to distribute handmade creations at a fraction of the cost of setting up a traditional website or selling the goods in retail locations. Etsy also allows business owners access to thousands of daily visitors who come to a central site to see what is new, unique, and/or unusual.

Co-founder Rob Kalin expresses Etsy's goal as "restoring community and culture to our commerce." Etsy therefore refuses manufactured goods on its website—all products must be handmade. Etsy charges US$0.20 to list a seller's product on its website for four months along with 5 percent on each sale. Sellers can also advertise their products on the website for a fee.

Despite its initial success, Etsy faces many challenges. Some analysts believe Etsy's insistence on only handmade goods might limit its growth.

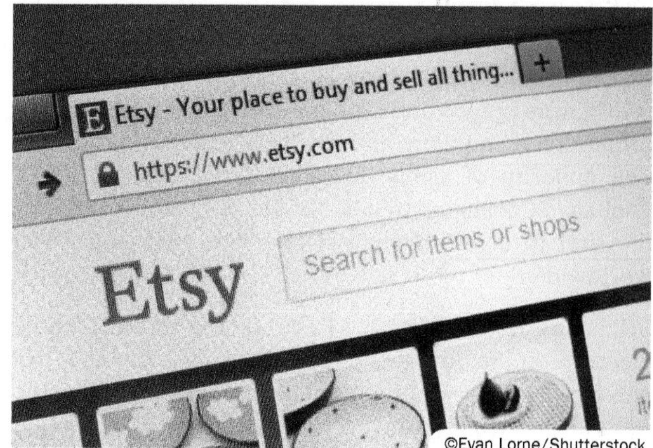


©Evan Lorne/Shutterstock

Etsy allows home-based business owners a central website with millions of users to sell their homemade products.

*"70 Amazing Etsy Stats and Facts (2019)/By the Numbers," https://expandedramblings.com/index.php/etsy-statistics/, (accessed August 18, 2019).

companies to offer consumers low shipping costs or next-day delivery.

For example, Coastal Contacts, which operates as Clearly Contacts in Canada, is successfully taking customers away from traditional optometrists and eyeglass retailers. The company, founded in 2000, was expected to have revenue in excess of $250 million in recent years.[16] Coastal Contacts is thriving as it sells contacts and glasses at a cheaper price than traditional retailers and is often considered more convenient by consumers. Rather than visit a retailer, consumers can order contacts or glasses online and have them arrive at their home within 48 hours. Coastal has also established an automatic refill program where contact lenses are shipped automatically at a predetermined time.

**Promotion Considerations.** Perhaps one of the best ways businesses can utilize digital media is for promotion purposes—whether they are increasing brand awareness, connecting with consumers, or taking advantage of social networks or virtual worlds (discussed later) to form relationships and generate positive publicity or "buzz" about their products. Thanks to online promotion, consumers can be more informed than ever, including reading customer-generated content before making purchasing decisions. Consumer consumption patterns are radically changing, and marketers must adapt their promotional efforts to meet them. For example, more and more travellers are using the Internet to purchase flights and to compare prices when planning a trip. WestJet has gone to great lengths to make it easy for consumers to buy airline tickets online using its website, and it relies on digital marketing to promote sales and special events, and to stay connected with customers.

These effects are not limited to the Western world. In a revolutionary shift in China, where online shopping had not been widely adopted by consumers, businesses are now realizing the benefits of marketing online. One of the first adopters of Internet selling was the Chinese company Taobao, a consumer auction site that also features sections for Chinese brands and retailers. Taobao provides online promotion of retailers and products featured on its site. The majority of online sales in China take place on Taobao.[17] Consumer trends like these demonstrate that the shift to digital media promotion is well under way worldwide.

**Pricing Considerations.** Price is the most flexible element of the marketing mix. Digital marketing can enhance the value of products by providing extra benefits such as service, information, and convenience. Through digital media, discounts and other promotions can be quickly communicated. As consumers have become better informed about their options, the demand for low-priced products has grown, leading to the creation of deal sites where consumers can directly compare prices. Expedia, for instance, provides consumers with a wealth of travel information about everything from flights to hotels, which lets them compare benefits and prices. Many marketers offer buying incentives like online coupons or free samples to generate consumer demand for their products.

**Social Media Marketing.** Social media marketing involves communicating with consumers through social media sites. Social media marketing enables firms to promote a message and create online conversations through multiple platforms. Large markets can be targeted and reached through paid media, owned media, and earned media.[18] Traditional paid media includes print and broadcast, but it is now joined by paid advertising on social networks such as Facebook and Twitter as discussed in Chapter 12. Marketers can place ads on Google just like they place an ad on television. On Facebook, which has more than 6 million advertisers, brands can pay to boost posts, create compelling photo carousel ads, promote their pages, and more.[19]

In addition to placing ads, marketers can own their own media outlets and create messages on social networks. Most firms have their own websites, but can also develop websites such as Facebook and LinkedIn. Finally, markets can have earned media when consumers are communicating on social media sites. These digital word-of-mouth posts or interactions can promote a product or firm. Although it is not controllable like advertising, if the communication is positive, it can result in an increase in sales.[20]

User-generated content relates to consumers who create, converse, rate, collect, join, or simply read online materials. Marketers can't always access the creative efforts of consumers who post or publish on publicly accessible websites, such as blogs like A Beautiful Mess and Modern Martha, or on social networking sites such as LinkedIn. These user-generated sites often involve self-disclosure, where consumers share their knowledge, interests, and desire to join or associate with others. Participating in discussions to connect and network with others is a major motivating factor to influence others or to promote an interest or cause.

There are many critics involved in user-generated content. These consumers post evaluations on blogs or post ratings and reviews. If you have ever posted a product review or rated a movie, you have engaged in this activity. Evaluating what critics post should be an important part of a company's digital marketing strategy. Of course, consumers read ratings to aid their shopping purchases. As discussed in Chapter 11, Yelp is one of the most comprehensive review sites on products and businesses. With more than 171 million reviews, Yelp continues to expand its platform, adding Questions and Answers for users to ask venue-specific questions for other users to answer.[21] Therefore these rating sites can be helpful to collect information used in marketing research and to monitor firm reputation.

Marketers need to analyze their target markets and determine the social media approach that will best

## ENTREPRENEURSHIP IN ACTION

### Building Brands on Digital Media

**Famous Folks**

**Founders:** Jay Dingwall and Ryan Joseph

**Founded:** 2006

**Success:** Re-developed brand strategy for Pizzatown

Jay Dingwall was pursuing his corporate dream. He earned a business degree from St. Mary's University and completed a Masters in Business Administration at Florida Atlantic University. His plans were simple: return home to Canada and start to work in a marketing or public relations agency to gain some meaningful work experience. Specifically, Dingwall opted to bypass his home province of Nova Scotia, and move to Toronto where he thought he could quickly land a job at an agency and work with some of Canada's largest companies. Unfortunately, as Dingwall described it, no matter how hard he tried, he couldn't actually get a job. He wasn't sure why. At times he appeared to be overqualified, and at other times underqualified.

Given his lack of success in the job market, Dingwall decided if no one would hire him he would start his own firm. At that point very few people had heard about influencers and Jay thought he saw an opportunity to help famous people build their online brands though digital media. Hence the name of the company, Famous Folks. Dingwall says he was a bit too early for the influencer trend but was correct about building brands through digital media.

Dingwall was soon joined by new business partner Ryan Joseph, a designer, and the pair started to look for opportunities to take current brands and redevelop them using both print and digital media. They noticed that Pizzatown, a Nova Scotia restaurant landmark, was in serious need of a re-brand and they approached the company's founder, Rob Toulany. Dingwall and Joseph recall they had no guarantee of any work but presented their ideas and concepts to Toulany. A short time later they signed their first major contract.

©Jazz Aviation/Famous Folks

Famous Folks CEO Jay Dingwall says that by staying small the digital branding firm has managed to create long term relationships with such great clients as Jazz Aviation.

While Famous Folks has kept its original name, the company's focus is on digital branding. Dingwall says their desire to remain a boutique entrepreneurial firm has enabled them to invest significant time in client relationships and the result is that their customers love the results. While staying small, Famous Folks has worked for some of the largest firms in the nation including Jazz Aviation and Cadillac Fairview along with numerous small and midsize firms.*

*Interview with Jay Dingwall, May 25, 2019.

support marketing objectives. Social media should be included in both the corporate and marketing strategy. It should be a part of the firm's marketing plan and implementation efforts. Social media can be used to monitor market competitors and understand the social and economic environment as a whole. Social media has the potential to build campaigns that produce advocates for and enthusiasts of a firm's products. For example, Dodge uses social media to release product teasers and news to its engaged fans. The brand rewarded its most engaged social media fans by inviting a limited number to the unveiling of the 2018 Dodge Challenger SRT Demon.[22] Marketing should be focused on relationship building, and social media can influence consumer behaviour and deliver value to the firm.

# Types of Consumer-Generated Marketing and Digital Media

**LO 13-5** Define social networking and illustrate how businesses can use different types of social networking media.

While digital marketing has generated exciting opportunities for companies to interact with their customers, digital media are also more consumer-driven than traditional media. Internet users are creating and reading consumer-generated content as never before and are having a profound effect on marketing in the process.

Two factors have sparked the rise of consumer-generated information:

1. The increased tendency of consumers to post their own thoughts, opinions, reviews, and product discussions through blogs or digital media.
2. Consumers' tendencies to trust other consumers over corporations.

Consumers often rely on the recommendations of friends, family, and fellow consumers when making purchasing decisions. Marketers who know where online users are likely to express their thoughts and opinions can use these forums to interact with them, address problems, and promote their companies. Types of digital media in which Internet users are likely to participate include social networks, blogs, wikis, video-sharing sites, podcasts, virtual reality sites, and mobile applications. Let's look a little more closely at each.

©Nik Taylor/Getty Images

Chris Webb, co-owner of Pavia Café, a well-known Halifax company, says they use both Facebook and Instagram as they appeal to completely different demographics. Webb says young people are on Instagram and older consumers are on Facebook.

## Social Networks

A **social network** is "a Web-based meeting place for friends, family, co-workers, and peers that lets users create a profile and connect with other users for purposes that range from getting acquainted, to keeping in touch, to building a work-related network."[23] Social networks are a valued part of marketing because they are changing the way consumers communicate with each other and with firms. As discussed in Chapter 12, sites such as Facebook, Instagram, Twitter, LinkedIn, Pinterest, and Snapchat have emerged as opportunities for marketers to build communities, provide product information, and learn about consumer needs.

**social network** a Web-based meeting place for friends, family, co-workers, and peers that lets users create a profile and connect with other users for a wide range of purposes

Social media use has become an integral part of daily Canadian life. Sherpa Marketing, a Canadian digital firm, estimates that 75 percent of Canadians use Facebook, 75 percent use YouTube, 37 percent Twitter, 34 percent Instagram, 31 percent Pinterest, 28 percent LinkedIn, and 20 percent Snapchat.[24] Most Canadians visit their social media environment of choice numerous times a day and spend a significant amount of their online time on social networks.[25] As social networks evolve, both marketers and the owners of social networking sites are realizing the opportunities such networks offer—an influx of advertising dollars for site owners and a large reach for the advertiser. As a result, marketers have begun investigating and experimenting with promotion on social networks. Some of the most prominent sites are highlighted below.

**Facebook.** As discussed in Chapter 12, Facebook is the third most visited site in Canada and boasts 2.23 billion active users, with the majority (66 percent) logging on daily.[26] Users of Facebook are very diverse. For example there are slightly more 45 to 54 year old people (15.5 percent) using Facebook than 18 to 24 year old people (15.1 percent). The largest users of Facebook (25 percent) are between the ages of 25 and 34, and the site is hardly used by younger people under the age of 17 (1.7 percent). Chris Webb, owner of Pavia Café, who was discussed earlier, says his company uses both Facebook and Instagram as they appeal to different demographics. He uses Instagram for younger consumers and Facebook for older ones to ensure he reaches the largest possible audience.[27]

As discussed in Chapter 12, many marketers are using Facebook to market products, interact with consumers, and gain publicity. It is possible for a consumer to become a "fan" of a major company like Starbucks by clicking on the Like icon on the coffee retailer's Facebook page. Companies are also using Facebook to generate awareness about themselves and encourage repeat visits. Many companies, such as RBC and CBC, have online contests to keep people coming back to their social media sites.

Facebook, like other social networking sites, is also allowing companies to sell goods directly to users; this is known as F-commerce when talking purely about Facebook, and as *social commerce* when discussing this new emerging trend. As noted in Chapter 12, Facebook is also well known for its targeted advertisements. Facebook compiles information about users, including what they like or search for on Facebook, along with their other Web browsing history, to identify groups of consumers with similar interests. Facebook then allows companies to post advertising specific to this group.

For example, the Stratford Festival, an Ontario-based theatre group, successfully used targeted Facebook ads to post a one-day coupon aimed at increasing ticket sales among new and lapsed patrons. As a result, Stratford sold three times the normal number of tickets. Stratford's social media coordinator, Aaron George, says, "Using

Facebook as a media tool has definitely been beneficial for us. It's given us the reach of television with the targeting capabilities of a direct mail campaign. It allows us to target lapsed patrons or reach those who came to a performance a few years ago, and gave us a great return on ad spend. Facebook ads have helped us strengthen our digital brand presence, increase ticket sales, and cultivate new audiences."[28]

Social networking sites are also useful for small businesses. Ela restaurant in Halifax, Nova Scotia, uses interactive marketing on a social networking outlet to drum up more business. The company provides users with coupons, special seating, and updates on new menu items on Facebook and other social media sites.[29] Some small businesses are actually abandoning traditional websites and just maintain a Facebook page.

**DID YOU KNOW?**

In a recent global survey on the effectiveness of social marketing, researchers determined that:

- 95 percent of consumers ages 18–34 are likely to follow a brand through social media.
- 71 percent of consumers who have a good social media experience will recommend the brand to others.
- 63 percent of consumers think companies should offer customer service through social network.
- Global mobile social media users total 3.3 billion.[30]

Other companies that have used relationship marketing to help consumers feel more connected to their products are Pepsi and the Walt Disney Co. The Pepsi Refresh Project (PRP) invites consumers to suggest local charities that are making a positive impact. Consumers vote for their favourites, and Pepsi donates money to the winning causes. Facebook, Twitter, and blogging helped the company to spread the word about PRP.[31]

The Walt Disney Co. has created many different Facebook pages, which have succeeded in generating over 100 million Facebook fans. Some of its success is attributed to the Disney Pages promotion tab on its main Disney Facebook page. The tab allows users to access promotional content without having to navigate away from Facebook. In many ways, Facebook is becoming an e-commerce platform whereby companies can sell products. DigiSynd, Disney's social media agency, was able to use a platform on Facebook called Disney Tickets Together that allowed fans to purchase tickets for movies like *Toy Story 3.* These new opportunities for businesses demonstrate the evolution of Facebook into a marketing destination.[32]

**LinkedIn.** LinkedIn is a social networking site geared toward professionals from all over the world. With 630 million professional members, including executives from all the Fortune 500 companies, it is one of the most popular social networking sites.[33] Roughly 28 percent of Canadians are on LinkedIn, with the slight majority being aged 25 to 34.[34] A LinkedIn profile resembles a resumé. It contains information about past and current job experiences, qualifications, goals, and educational background.

Like all social networking sites, it lets users locate and connect with other members and join groups, which are often professional organizations. LinkedIn facilitates job searches and allows companies to search the network for potential employees with the necessary skills. Scotiabank, Delta Hotels, Microsoft, eBay, and Netflix have all used the LinkedIn network to recruit new employees.[35]

Employees are also using LinkedIn to search for potential employers. Although a professional networking site like LinkedIn seems more like a recruiting site than a marketing tool, companies do use it to familiarize users with their businesses. In addition to listing job openings, most company LinkedIn profiles also offer a link to the company website, some background on the business, links to news updates on company activities and products, and stock information. Smart marketers can use LinkedIn to reach professionals not only for recruiting purposes but to spread information about and generate interest in the company. For example, Oakville, Ontario, firm ClubRunner, which creates sports management software, used LinkedIn as part of a marketing campaign. The company shared information about software to targeted firms and eventually asked readers to review the company's information and products. The result of their efforts was a 40 percent increase in inbound leads.[36]

**Twitter.** Twitter is a hybrid of a social networking site and a micro-blogging site that asks users one simple question: "What are you doing?" Members can post answers of up to 140 characters, which are then available for their registered "followers" to read. It sounds simple enough, but Twitter's effect on digital media has been immense. The site quickly progressed from a novelty to a social networking staple, attracting millions of viewers each month.[37]

Globally, Twitter has in excess of 1.2 billion registered users, with 326 million monthly users who send on average 500 million tweets a day .[38, 39] In Canada, 37 percent of the population uses Twitter, and Canadian users visit the site five times a week.[40] The thrill of Twitter is that users get to tell the world about their daily lives in short messages, known as tweets. These tweets can be mundane, such as "I'm eating a sandwich," to interesting. Prime Minister Justin Trudeau is an active Twitter user, using the forum to make various announcements and often respond to questions. Current American President Donald Trump is likely the most famous Twitter user.

©Everything You Need/Shutterstock

Starbucks made heavy use of Twitter to promote its Blonde Roast coffee in Canada.

Twitter has quickly transformed from novelty to serious marketing tool, with the company announcing plans to generate revenue through sponsored tweets and working to make the service more user-friendly.[41] Although 140 characters may not seem like enough for companies to send an effective message, some have become experts at using Twitter in their marketing strategies. Starbucks Canada has used Twitter in marketing campaigns to promote new store openings, offer coupons, and respond to questions. Twitter and social networks were heavily used by Starbucks when it released its Blonde Roast coffee, which was aimed primarily at Canadians.[42] On a small scale, many local restaurants have turned to Twitter to share nightly specials, interact with customers, and book reservations. Restaurants such as Ryan Duffy's in Halifax use the social media site to promote specials and solicit consumer response.

Like other social networking tools, Twitter is also being used to build customer relationships. Media experts almost universally agree that the most effective use of Twitter involves creating conversation, not just pushing information onto followers. As discussed earlier, Porter Airlines is a service business that effectively uses Twitter to communicate with followers.

Finally, companies are using Twitter to gain a competitive advantage. Microsoft's search engine, Bing, developed a partnership with Twitter in which Bing sorts the millions of tweets by relevance and the popularity of the person tweeting. By doing a Bing–Twitter search, Twitter fans can get the most important tweets in real time.[43] Firms also have a chance to utilize promoted tweets, promoted accounts, and promoted trends offered on the site. Marketers can pay Twitter to highlight advertisements or company brands to a wider array of users while they search for specific terms or top notes.[44] The race is on among companies that want to use Twitter to gain a competitive edge.

**Snapchat.** Snapchat has 188 million global users and is the seventh most popular social networking site in Canada. The majority of users are under the age of 34, and 90 percent of those users are between the ages of

## RESPONDING TO BUSINESS CHALLENGES

### Social Media Monitoring

By this point in your reading, it should be clear that social media monitoring has become quite important for businesses. Not only do companies want to share information on social media sites, but they want to learn what you are saying about their organizations. Social media dashboards (discussed below) are becoming increasingly common tools to monitor what people are saying about a company on the Internet.

Still, other tools exist. For example, Google Alerts notifies a business if its name comes up anywhere online. As discussed above, Facebook tracks not only its users' activity on its site but other Web-browsing activity. Businesses such as Vancouver's Hootsuite identify trends in online communities and assist businesses in dealing with complaints. Other software tools, such as KISSmetrics, have been developed to help businesses identify the behaviour of Web users. Users of KISSmetrics can identify not only who is visiting their site but their actions as well. This information can be used to tailor offerings and improve sales. Since the company's inception, it has tracked the Web use of 4.5 billion people and their 36 billion interactions.*

#### DISCUSSION QUESTIONS

1. Do you think organizations should be able to track who visits their websites and their online behaviour?
2. Do you think it is a worthwhile investment for businesses to monitor and respond to social media discussions about their companies? Why or why not?

*"Neil Patel (entrepreneur)," Wikipedia, http://en.wikipedia.org/wiki/Neil_Patel_%28entrepreneur%29 (accessed July 17, 2013).

©Crystal Eye Studio/Shutterstock

Facebook, Google, and KISSmetrics are all tracking social media and Web-browsing activity. They then sell this information to corporations. Do you think this is ethical?

13 and 24. Businesses using Snapchat can share photos, storyboards, and content, and communicate with consumers, including sharing information on promotions.[45]

## Media Sharing

Businesses can also share their corporate messages in more visual ways through media sharing sites. Media sharing sites allow marketers to share photos, videos, and podcasts. Media sharing sites are more limited in scope in how companies interact with consumers. They tend to be more promotional than reactive. This means that while firms can promote their products through videos or photos, they usually do not interact with consumers through personal messages or responses. At the same time, the popularity of these sites provides the potential to reach a global audience of consumers.

Video sharing sites allow virtually anybody to upload videos, from professional marketers at Fortune 500 corporations to the average Internet user. Businesses are using video sharing sites to post advertisements prior to videos playing, to create and share entertaining and/or educational content, and to interact with consumers. Some of the most popular video sharing sites include YouTube, Video, Yahoo!, Metacafe, and Hulu. Video sharing sites give companies the opportunity to upload ads and informational videos about their products. YouTube use in Canada and globally is significant, and YouTube has recently released the following statistics about traffic to its site:[46]

- YouTube is the second most visited site in Canada.
- One billion unique users visit the site monthly in 91 countries and 80 languages.
- YouTube and YouTube mobile reach more people aged 18 to 49 than cable TV.
- YouTube is localized in 56 countries and across 61 languages.
- Over 1 billion hours of video are watched daily.[47]

Video sharing sites are increasingly being used as a low-cost promotional method to educate and entertain potential consumers. Almost all major North American companies make use of YouTube. For example, Epic Games, makers of the popular online game Fortnight, uses YouTube to promote its online game using ads and content. Other examples include Budweiser, which ran the most popular YouTube advertisement in the winter of 2018 featuring an anthem to hockey legend Wayne Gretzky.[48] Many small organizations are using the video sharing site as well. For example, many schools—such as Mount Saint Vincent University with 4500 students—are using YouTube to create promotional videos about student experiences and to showcase campus events on the Internet.

Ontario-based Roger Neilson's Hockey Camp is using YouTube to advertise annual hockey camps and highlight some of the instruction that occurs in its programs. Global pop sensation Justin Bieber actually owes a lot of his fame and fortune to YouTube and other social media sites. After finishing second in a local singing contest, Bieber started posting videos on both YouTube and Myspace. This eventually led to his being offered his first music contract.

A few videos become viral at any given time, and although many of these gain popularity because they are unusual in some way, others reach viral status because people find them entertaining. **Viral marketing** occurs when a message gets sent from person to person to person. It can be an extremely effective tool for marketers—particularly on the Internet, where one click can send a message to dozens or hundreds of people simultaneously.

> **viral marketing** a marketing tool that uses the Internet, particularly social networking and video sharing sites, to spread a message and create brand awareness

However, viral marketing often requires marketers to develop an offbeat sense of humour and creativity in order to catch the viewers' attention—something with which some marketers may not be comfortable. For instance, April Fool's Day has become a day when Canadian

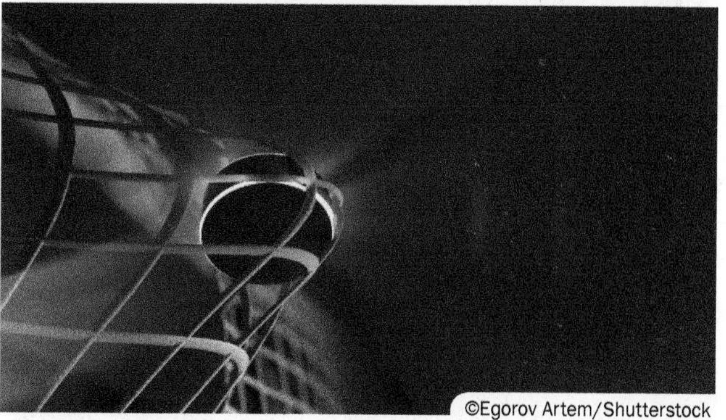

©Egorov Artem/Shutterstock

YouTube videos have been successfully used to promote small businesses including regional hockey camps as well as global brands such as Budweiser, whose 2018 video with hockey legend Wayne Gretzky, was the most viewed YouTube commercial in Canada.

companies try to generate some added attention for their company and products by offering some offbeat ads and often fake products. Recently, WestJet, McDonalds, and Phillips Brewing all offered gag products on April Fool's Day in Canada. WestJet used April Fool's Day to promote a new in-flight music festival; McDonalds introduced the mock product, the McPickle, a pickle-only burger; and Phillips Brewing introduced its own ride-sharing service, the Phüber, which consisted of one 2006 Pontiac Wave.

Such campaigns can be successful; WestJet's gag promotion video had roughly one million hits on YouTube and boosted the company's rank in search engines.[49] Companies such as IBM have created an entire video series to generate publicity for the company. IBM's six videos, called "The Art of the Sale," present three attributes of the company's mainframe computer in a humorous format reminiscent of episodes of *The Office.* Though some wrote off the videos as a forced attempt at humorous marketing, they received hundreds of thousands of hits on YouTube.[50]

Businesses have also begun to use consumer-generated video content, saving money they would have spent on hiring advertising firms to develop professional ad campaigns. For example, many universities and colleges throughout Canada are creating their own content with students and staff, and running video contests to promote their school or a particular field of academic study. The Ontario government has recently started using a similar strategy, asking people to create their own videos stressing job safety in the It's Your Job video contest.[51]

Perhaps the most successful campaign was Frito Lay's Crash the Super Bowl contest, which ended in 2017. Frito Lay would invite customers to create ads that might be selected for broadcast during the football game. One of the most recent winners created an ad featuring dogs trying to get into a supermarket to buy bags of Doritos. The advertisement was widely considered to be the best commercial played during the 2016 Super Bowl and attracted significant attention from social and mainstream media.[52] Marketers believe consumer videos appear more authentic and create enthusiasm for the product among consumer participants.

©Debby Wong/Shutterstock

Justin Bieber's singing career actually started on YouTube with videos he created himself. Bieber's videos were eventually discovered and he has gone on to sing numerous number one hits and star in his own movie.

## Photo Sharing

Photo sharing sites allow users to upload and share their photos and short videos with the world. The most popular site is Instagram with over 1.1 billion monthly users of which 500 million log on every day. Instagram users tend to be young and are willing to follow brands and purchase products they see online.[53] Chris Webb co-owner of PAVIA, a Halifax café, says Instagram works exceptionally well for his company, especially among young customers. Webb says a well placed Instagram post can actually drive sales for new items or remind consumers of past favourites. He says Instagram allows PAVIA to professionally highlight their all-natural, healthy products. Other well-known photo sharing sites include Pinterest, Imgur, Shutterfly, and Photobucket. Pinterest is the fifth most visited social media site in Canada. The site allows users to share photos and videos as pins to individual bulletin boards.[54]

Photo sharing represents an opportunity for companies to market themselves visually by displaying snapshots of company products, events, and/or company staff. Companies can direct viewers to their photostreams (their sets of photographs) by marking their pictures with the appropriate keywords, or tags, and also communicate with consumers to find out what they like and don't like about products, brands and services.[55] Companies are also using photo sharing sites to urge consumers to purchase products and to offer consumers promotions. As one Web marketer puts it, companies that use photo sharing "add a personal touch to their businesses."[56]

## Blogs and Wikis

Today's marketers must recognize that the impact of consumer-generated material like blogs and wikis, and their significance to online consumers have increased a

©Earl Gibson III/Getty Images

## Consider the Following: Going viral

As social media increases in importance, more and more companies are relying on the public to create a buzz for their products and/or their online promotions. Companies are often hoping that their online advertisements will "go viral," meaning that the public will become so interested in an ad campaign or product that they will share it within their own online social networks, thus spreading the company's brand, products, or advertisement to thousands if not millions of computers. For example Canadian Tire's recent advertisement showing boys making makeshift wheelchairs to include a boy who thought he might not be welcome to play due to his own wheelchair, went viral wth almost 60 million views. The ad, part of Canadian Tire's, We All Play for Canada campaign, promotes inclusiveness and relates it back to who are are as Canadians and what Canadian Tire stands for as a company.*

Other viral marketing videos include Bauer's Own the Moment and Nike's Hockey is Ours campaigns, which went viral, as the ads connected with Canadians during an NHL lockout. Old Spice had a viral hit on its hands with the Old Spice Guy advertisements. The ads, which were originally intended only for TV use, resonated with viewers and became a YouTube sensation. Old Spice supported the campaign by releasing hundreds of videos on YouTube in which the actor in the commercials answered questions using the popular video sharing network and Twitter. The campaign spread like wildfire on the Internet as consumers used Facebook, Twitter, and other social media sites to share the advertisements on their networks.

### DISCUSSION QUESTIONS

1. Do you think companies' sales benefit from viral ads such as the ones discussed above and throughout this chapter? Why or why not?
2. Do you think advertising with a strong emotional appeal is effective?
3. Given that firms are intentionally trying to generate viral campaigns, such as creating mock ads on April Fool's Day, do you think consumers will eventually grow tired of such campaigns?

*"Canadian Tire ad promoting inclusivity goes viral; shines light on Canadian values," February 28, 2017, https://www.newswire.ca/news-releases/canadian-tire-ad-promoting-inclusivity-goes-viral-shines-light-on-canadian-values-615004023.html; "This beautiful advertisment from Canada is going viral for all the right reasons," February 21, 2017, https://timesofindia.indiatimes.com/blogs/everything-social/this-beautiful-advertisement-from-canada-is-going-viral-for-all-the-right-reasons/

**blog** a Web-based journal in which a writer can editorialize and interact with other Internet users

great deal. A **blog** (short for Web log) is a Web-based journal in which writers can editorialize and interact with other Internet users. Two-thirds of Internet users read blogs, and more than half of bloggers say they blog about topics and brands about which they feel strongly.[57] The blogging phenomenon is not limited to North America. In South Korea, for example, more than two-thirds of the online population creates blogs or similar material.[58] Blogs have also grown significantly from their origin as shorter, less interactive sources of information. For example, popular Canadian travel blog www.departful.com features full length articles on travelling, videos, and beautiful pictures.

**DID YOU KNOW?**

Searching is the most popular online activity.[59]

Blogs give consumers power, sometimes more than companies would like. Bloggers can post whatever they like about a company or its products, whether their opinions are positive or negative, true or false. When a Korean Dunkin' Donuts worker created a blog alleging that a company factory had unsanitary conditions, the company forced him to delete the blog. However, readers had already created copies of it and spread it across the Internet after the original's removal.[60] In other cases, a positive review of a product or service posted on a popular blog can result in large increases in sales. Thus, blogs can represent a potent threat or opportunity to marketers.

Rather than trying to eliminate blogs that cast their companies in a negative light, some firms are using their own blogs, or employee blogs, to answer consumer concerns or defend their corporate reputations. For example, when Electronic Arts' SimCity game failed to work properly, the company used blogs to respond to consumer complaints and questions. Electronic Arts also used blogs to highlight some of the company's news and promotions.[61] As blogging changes the face of media, smart companies are using blogs to build enthusiasm for their products and create relationships with consumers. As noted in Chapter 12, many CEOs, such as Ryan Holmes of Hootsuite are using blogs to reach out and connect with consumers and provide information that customers find relevant and interesting.

**DID YOU KNOW?**

Longer blogs result in nine times more leads for companies compared to shorter blogs.[62]

A **wiki** is a website where users can add to or edit the content of posted articles. One of the best known is Wikipedia, an online encyclopedia with over 40 million entries in over 301 languages on nearly every subject imaginable (*Encyclopedia Britannica* only has 120,000 entries).[63, 64] Wikipedia is one of the ten most popular sites on the Web, and because much of its content can be edited by anyone, it is easy for online consumers to add detail and supporting evidence and to correct inaccuracies in content. Wikipedia used to be completely open to editing, but in order to stop vandalism, the site had to make some topics off-limits, now editable only by a small group of experts.

Like all digital media, wikis have advantages and disadvantages for companies. Wikis about controversial companies like Walmart and Nike often contain negative publicity, such as posts about workers' rights violations. However, monitoring relevant wikis can provide companies with a better idea of how consumers feel about the company or brand. Some companies have also begun to use wikis as internal tools for teams working on projects that require a great deal of documentation.[65] There is too much at stake financially for marketers to ignore wikis and blogs. Despite this fact, only 36 percent of Fortune 500 companies have blogs.[66] Marketers who want to form better customer relationships and promote their company's products must not underestimate the power of these two media outlets.

**wiki** software that creates an interface that enables users to add or edit the content of some types of websites

**podcast** an audio or video file that can be downloaded from the Internet with a subscription and automatically deliver new content to listening devices or personal computers

## Podcasting

A **podcast** is made up of audio or video files that can be downloaded from the Internet via a subscription and automatically deliver new content to listening devices or personal computers. Podcasting offers the benefit of convenience, giving users the ability to listen to or view content when and where they choose.

Podcasting is rapidly gaining in popularity and there are 700,000 active podcasts with 29 million podcast episodes. It is estimated that roughly half of North Americans have listed to a podcast.[67] Dozens of online programs, such as Apple's iPodderX and Podcast Studio, or Android's dPod, offer podcasting services. Business can use podcasts to improve traffic to their Web or social media sites, create better relationship with customers and boost sales. Recent research indicates that 63 percent of podcast listeners will buy products featured in the podcast.[68]

"Podcasting offers the benefit of convenience, giving users the ability to listen to or view content when and where they choose."

## Social Media Dashboards

Given the popularity of social networking/media sites, businesses—especially larger businesses—often attempt to maintain an active presence on all the sites. Posting and then managing responses to numerous social networking sites can be time consuming, and businesses often simultaneously monitor numerous websites. A recent emerging solution has been social media dashboards, which enable companies to submit information to a central location, and software posts the information to various social media sites.

For example, RBC could enter information about a new promotion into a social media dashboard, and the dashboard would then distribute the information to RBC's various social networks such as Facebook, Twitter, Tumblr, and YouTube. The dashboard could then monitor the consumer feedback about the posting and summarize the information for RBC. As previously mentioned in the text, the most common social media dashboard is HootSuite, which is based in British Columbia. HootSuite is popular as it allows companies to post and manage information on multiple sites—Twitter, Facebook, LinkedIn, and Instagram to name a few.[69]

## Mobile Marketing

Digital marketing is becoming increasingly sophisticated as consumers are beginning to use mobile devices such as smartphones as highly functional communication methods. The iPhone and Android phones have changed the way consumers communicate, and a growing number of travellers are using their smartphones to find online maps, travel guides, and taxis. In industries such as hotels, airlines, and car rental agencies, mobile phones have become a primary method for booking reservations and

Social media dashboards such as Hootsuite allow companies to message dozens of social media sites using a single point of entry.

## Consider the Following: Pinterest successfully combines social networking and photo sharing to overtake Flickr

As discussed in Chapter 12, Pinterest is the fifth-largest, social media website in North America. In a very short time, the company has overtaken Flickr and become the second largest photo sharing site by combining photo sharing with elements of social media.

Pinterest allows users to manage pictures and videos, called *pins*, to an online bulletin board, known as a pinboard. Themed pinboards allow users to easily manage pins, to share their content, and to search pins posted by other users. Users can also pin content they find on the Internet and easily upload it to their pinboard. Pinboard users take great pride in creating attractive pinboards to share.

According to experts, Pinterest's success can be attributed to many subtle differences when it is compared to traditional photo sharing sites. Pinterest is, first and foremost, free, and its focus is on social networking. The site refers to users as friends and lets you know when friends are logged on to Twitter and Facebook. Additionally, the company allows you to follow others, comment on their pinboards, and quickly load embedded photos to an attractive website.

These subtle differences stand out when compared to Flickr, the previous leader in the online photo sharing industry. Flickr, while allowing for some free sharing of photos, charges for a premium account, does not alert you when contacts are online, and, while having a social network element, has stayed fairly rigid in its business model. Charlotte Henry, an online journalist, says Pinterest has clearly surpassed Flickr. "In terms of advertising and building an online presence, the choice is simple. The ability to categorize images, the deep social interaction, not to mention the attractive interface, make Pinterest the clear winner. You can really build a brand image on Pinterest, and display your products. Flickr remains important to photographers, but has been overtaken by Pinterest by almost every other kind of user."*

### DISCUSSION QUESTIONS

1. Why do you think Pinterest has surpassed Flickr?
2. Do you think Flickr charging for a premium account has hindered its ability to grow?
3. Flickr has recently added some additional social networking elements to its website. Do you think it will be able to re-establish itself as the leader in photo sharing?
4. Given what you have learned about Pinterest, Flickr, and Instagram, which photo-sharing site would you recommend for a company to use if it were trying to appeal to young women between the ages of 25 and 40 with a new product? Why?

*Charlotte Henry, "Pinterest vs. Flickr: the Battle for Photo Dominance," *The Wall* website, March 6, 2013, http://wallblog.co.uk/2013/03/06/pinterest-vs-flickr-the-battle-for-photo-dominance/ (accessed July 17, 2013).

communicating about services. They can act as airline boarding passes, GPS devices, and even hotel room keys.

Travel companies are collecting personal information so they can send consumers relevant updates about travel opportunities. Farelogix, a travel software company, is working with a number of airlines to introduce features that allow airlines to sell services such as priority boarding. While airlines already make these services available on their websites, they also want to communicate with travellers who experience unexpected changes on their trips. Other marketing uses of mobile phones include sending shoppers timely messages related to discounts and shopping opportunities.[70]

"New businesses and even industries are evolving that would not exist without digital media."

Marketing over mobile devices has been made possible largely by apps—programs that can be loaded onto certain mobile devices to allow users to perform a variety of functions, from playing games to comparing product prices from different stores. The latter is becoming particularly useful for consumers. The smartphone's ability to find retailers and entertainment and to organize an itinerary is changing the nature of consumer and business relationships. Large hotel chains, such as Delta Hotels, are increasingly using iPhone apps that allow guests to check in early, order room service so food is waiting for them when they arrive, and even specify bed and pillow types.

The most important feature of apps is the convenience and cost savings they offer the consumer. To remain competitive, companies are beginning to use mobile marketing to offer additional customer incentives, with some success. Jiffy Lube offered coupons for one of its franchises over mobile devices. The company estimated that 50 percent of the new customers who came to the franchise did so as a result of its mobile marketing.[71]

Another application that marketers are finding useful is the QR scanning app. The black-and-white squares on magazines, posters, storefront displays, and so forth contain messages not visible to the naked eye. To read these messages, smartphone users must download a QR

©Chimeandsense/Dreamstime

The use of mobile marketing is growing as people perform more and more daily tasks using a mobile device.

scanning application. When they come across a QR code, they simply scan the black-and-white square. The QR scanning app will recognize the code and open up the link, video, or image on the phone's screen. Marketers are using QR codes to market their companies and offer consumer discounts. As more people and companies use these codes they are likely to add a whole new layer to digital marketing.[72] In fact, Juniper Research predicts by 2022, 5.3 billion QR coupons will be redeemed and over 1 billion phones will have an active QR code scanner.[73]

Mobile payments are also gaining traction, and companies like Google are working to capitalize on this opportunity.[74] Google Wallet is a mobile app that stores credit card information on the smartphone. When the shopper is ready to check out, they tap the phone at the point of sale for the transaction to be registered.[75] The success of mobile payments in revolutionizing the shopping experience will largely depend upon retailers to adopt this payment system, but companies such as Starbucks have already jumped at the opportunity. An estimated 262.2 million North Americans will use smartphones in 2019, so businesses cannot afford to miss out on the chance to profit from these new trends.[76]

Widgets are small bits of software on a website, desktop, or mobile device that enables users "to interface with the application and operating system." Marketers might use widgets to display news headlines, clocks, or games on their Web pages.[77] Widgets have been used by companies such as A&E television network as a form of viral marketing—users can download the widget and send it to their friends with a click of a button.[78] Widgets downloaded to a user's desktop can update the user on the latest company or product information, enhancing relationship marketing between companies and their fans. For instance, Krispy Kreme Doughnuts developed a widget that alerts users when their Original Glazed doughnuts are hot out of the oven at their favourite Krispy Kreme shop.[79] Widgets are an innovative digital marketing tool to personalize Web pages, alert users to the latest company information, and spread awareness of the company's products.

As previously discussed in Chapter 12, the major uses of mobile marketing by firms both large and small include:

- *SMS messages:* SMS messages are text messages of 160 words or less. SMS messages have been an effective way to send coupons to prospective customers.[80]
- *Multimedia messages:* Multimedia messaging takes SMS messaging a step further by allowing companies to send video, audio, photos, and other types of media over mobile devices. Motorola's House of Blues multimedia campaign allowed users to receive access to discounts, tickets, music, and other digital content on their mobile phones.[81]
- *Mobile advertisements:* Mobile advertisements are visual advertisements that appear on mobile devices. Companies might choose to advertise through search engines, websites, or even games accessed on mobile devices. Orville Redenbacher has used mobile advertisements to promote its healthy snack notes.[82]
- *Mobile websites:* Mobile websites are websites designed for mobile devices. Mobile devices constitute 52.2 percent of Web traffic.[83]
- *Mobile applications:* Apps are software programs that run on mobile devices and give users access to certain content.[84] Businesses release apps to help consumers access more information about their company or to provide incentives. Apps are discussed in further detail in the next section.

## Online Monitoring and Analytics

Without digital media monitoring and evaluation, it will not be possible to maximize resources and minimize costs in social media marketing. The strength of measurement relates to the ability to have online analytics and metrics. Social media monitoring involves activities to track, measure, and evaluate a firm's digital marketing initiatives.[85] An advantage of digital marketing evaluations is that there are methods to capture the metrics that indicate the outcomes of strategies. Therefore, an expected level of performance can be compared with actual performance.

Metrics develop from listening and tracking. For example, a firm could set up a hashtag and promote it. Metrics can be quantitative or qualitative. For example, click-through rate (CTR) determines the percentage of consumers who clicked on a link on a site as a quantitative measure. In addition, a qualitative metric could relate how consumers feel about a product.

Key performance indicators (KPIs) should be embedded at the onset of a social media strategy that can allow almost real-time measurement and evaluation. This provides a foundation for making iterative changes to implementation and tactical execution. Marketing analytics uses tools and methods to measure and interpret the effectiveness of marketing activities. Applying analytics to social media performance can help develop better targeted social media campaigns. Selecting valid metrics requires specific objectives that the social media strategy is to obtain. Objectives that are quantitative could include the number of likes on an Instagram post or the CTR of a Facebook post.

A comprehensive performance evaluation requires gathering all valid metrics and understanding the way the strategy meets performance standards or underperforms based on expectations. One way to approach this is to use Google Analytics, the largest analytics platform monitoring more than 30 million websites.[86] The Google Analytics dashboard is broken down into five sections: real time, audience, acquisition, behaviour, and conversions:

- *Real Time*: Data updates are live so you can see page views, top social traffic, top referrals, top keywords, top active pages, and top locations in real time.
- *Audience*: Audience reports provide insight into demographics, interests, geography, behaviour, mobile use, and more.
- *Acquisition*: In-bound traffic is monitored through acquisition reports, allowing you to compare traffic from search, referrals, email, and social media.
- *Behaviour*: Use RSS feeds. Add tags to web pages or photos. Vote for websites online.
- *Joiners*: Evaluate your site's content by seeing how visitors interact with your content. Monitor landing pages, exit pages, site speed, bounce rate, and more.
- *Conversions*: Google Analytics allows users to set goals and objectives to monitor web conversions, like signing up for an email newsletter or completing a purchase.

Using this tool allows you to identify your website's strengths and weaknesses and uncover opportunities for growth. For example, you may find that organic search traffic is very high, but that your social media traffic is quite low, or you may see a spike in weekday traffic while weekends are slow. KPIs for your social media strategy can include likes, shares, reach, engagement rate, CTR, and conversions. In the conversions dashboard, marketers can set up custom conversion goals to see the impact social media has on their business. By analyzing rich site traffic data, marketers can better understand their customers and measure the effectiveness of their marketing efforts.

For example, PBS uses Google Analytics to monitor the web performance for multiple properties and track key events like user registrations and video views. After analyzing search engine trends, PBS experienced 30 percent more site traffic in the first year after implementation.[87] Google Analytics is arguably the most robust web analytics tool available, and it is free to anyone with a Google account. A premium version, Google Analytics 360 Suite, designed to help companies target potential customers, is available for even more in-depth analytics. The tool identifies someone's habits, from Web and television time to mobile usage, competing with companies like Salesforce and Oracle.[88]

## Using Digital Media to Reach Consumers

We've seen that customer-generated communications and digital media connect consumers. These connections let consumers share information and experiences without company interference so they get more of the "real story" on a product or company feature. In many ways, these media take some of the professional marketer's power to control and dispense information and place it in the hands of the consumer.

However, this shift does not have to spell doom for marketers, who can choose to harness the power of the consumer and Internet technology to their advantage. While consumers use digital media to access more product information, marketers can use the same sites to get better and more targeted information about the consumer—often more than they could gather through traditional marketing methods. Marketers increasingly use consumer-generated content to aid their own marketing efforts, even going so far as to incorporate Internet bloggers in their publicity campaigns. Finally, marketers are using the Internet to track the success of their online marketing campaigns, creating an entirely new way of gathering marketing research.

The challenge for digital media marketers is to constantly adapt to new technologies and changing consumer patterns. Unfortunately, the attrition rate for digital media channels is very high, with some dying off each year as new ones emerge. Social networks are no exception: the earliest ones, like Six Degrees, disappeared when they failed to catch on with the general public, and Friendster, though still active, has been far surpassed by newer networks. As time passes, digital media are becoming more sophisticated so as to reach consumers in more effective ways. Those that are not able to adapt and change eventually fail.

Mastering digital media presents a daunting task for businesses, particularly those used to more traditional means of marketing. For this reason, it is essential that marketers focus on the changing social behaviours of consumers, the ways in which they gather and use

## GOING GREEN

### Mobile Apps Help Consumers to Become Greener

Although support for the green movement is growing, most consumers want to know how going green can save them money. Until recently, acquiring this information was difficult for the average consumer. Now the explosive growth of mobile apps is creating a solution to this problem. These "green" apps enable users to save money and/or locate green products by making small changes in their everyday lives. For instance, zerogate's MeterRead iPhone app allows users to monitor their energy meters and then suggests ways that users could further reduce their energy usage. Founder Mark Barton claims that by adopting these suggestions, he was able to decrease his monthly energy bill by $50.

In addition to helping consumers save money, apps can help to combat greenwashing. Greenwashing occurs when marketers claim that a product is greener than it really is. Because there are very few guidelines on what constitutes a green product, consumers must often research products before they enter the store. One of the most popular green apps, known as GoodGuide, is eliminating this problem. Consumers with the app can use their phones to photograph product barcodes. The app will then provide information on the sustainability of the product while the consumer is still in the store.

Green apps have the potential to revolutionize the green movement, particularly as it meets consumer desires for cost savings and convenience. Perhaps best of all, many of the apps are relatively inexpensive, ranging from free to a few dollars.*

#### DISCUSSION QUESTIONS

1. What are some of the barriers preventing consumers from buying green products?
2. How can apps help consumers to be more "green"?
3. What are some ways that apps are combating greenwashing?

*Jefferson Graham, "Mobile Apps Make It Easier to Go Green," *USA Today*, May 12, 2011, www.usatoday.com/tech/products/2011-05-12-green-tech_n.htm (accessed October 6, 2011); "Green Apps That Can Save You Money," Reuters, February 18, 2011, http://blogs.reuters.com/environment/2011/02/18/green-apps-that-can-save-you-money/ (accessed October 6, 2011); Jefferson Graham, "GoodGuide App Helps Navigate Green Products," *USA Today*, May 13, 2011, www.usatoday.com/tech/products/2011-05-12-GoodGuideapp_n.htm (accessed October 6, 2011).

information, and the way the Internet is enabling them to get involved in the marketing process.

Charlene Li and Josh Bernoff of Forrester Research, a technology and market research company, emphasize the need for marketers to understand these changing relationships in the online media world. By grouping consumers into different segments based on how they make use of digital media, marketers can gain a better understanding of the online market and how best to proceed.[89] Table 13.1 shows six ways to group consumers based on their Internet activity (or lack thereof). The categories are not mutually exclusive; online consumers can participate in more than one at a time.

*Creators* are consumers who create their own media outlets, such as blogs, podcasts, consumer-generated videos, and wikis.[90] Consumer-generated media are increasingly important to online marketers as a conduit for addressing consumers directly. The second category, *critics*, consists of people who comment on blogs or post ratings and reviews. Because many online shoppers read ratings and reviews to aid their purchasing decisions, critics should be a primary component in a company's digital marketing strategy. *Collectors* are the most recently recognized category. They collect information and organize content generated by critics and creators.[91] Because collectors are active members of the online community, a company story or site that catches the eye of a collector is likely to be posted, discussed on collector sites, and made available to other online users looking for information.

*Joiners* include all who become users of Twitter, Facebook, LinkedIn, Pinterest, Tumblr, or other social

**Table 13.1** | Social Technographics

| | |
|---|---|
| **Creators** | • Publish a blog<br>• Publish your own Web pages<br>• Upload video you created<br>• Upload audio/music you created<br>• Write articles or stories and post them |
| **Critics** | • Post ratings/reviews of products or services<br>• Comment on someone else's blog<br>• Contribute to online forums<br>• Contribute to/edit articles in a wiki |
| **Collectors** | • Use RSS feeds<br>• Add tags to Web pages or photos<br>• Vote for websites online |
| **Joiners** | • Maintain profile on a social networking site<br>• Visit social networking sites |
| **Spectators** | • Read blogs<br>• Watch video from other users<br>• Listen to podcasts<br>• Read online forums<br>• Read customer ratings/reviews |
| **Inactives** | • None of the activities |

networking sites. It is not unusual for consumers to be members of several social networking sites at once. Joiners use these sites to connect and network with other users, but as we've seen, marketers too can take significant advantage of these sites to connect with consumers and form customer relationships.[92] The last two segments are spectators and inactives. *Spectators,* who read online information but do not join groups or post anywhere, are the largest group in most countries. *Inactives* are online users who do not participate in any digital online media, but their numbers are dwindling.

Marketers who want to capitalize on social and digital media marketing need to consider what proportion of online consumers is creating, rating, collecting, joining, or simply reading online materials. As in traditional marketing efforts, they need to know their target market. For instance, where spectators make up the majority of the online population, companies should post their own corporate messages through blogs and websites promoting their organizations.

## Using Digital Media to Learn About Consumers

Marketing research and information systems can use digital media and social networking sites to gather useful information about consumers and their preferences. Sites such as Twitter, Facebook, Instagram, LinkedIn, Pinterest, and Snapchat can be good substitutes for focus groups. Online surveys can serve as an alternative to mail, telephone, or personal interviews.

*Crowdsourcing* describes how marketers use digital media to find out the opinions or needs of the crowd (or potential markets). Communities of interested consumers join sites like threadless.com, which designs T-shirts, or crowdspring.com, which creates logos, and print and Web designs. These companies give interested consumers opportunities to contribute and give feedback on product ideas. Crowdsourcing lets companies gather and utilize consumers' ideas in an interactive way, if the company uses the ideas it is often referred to as user-generated content (UGC).

Examples of sites that help clients to facilitate user-generated content include https://www.shortstack.com/, https://www.yotpo.com/, and https://www.tintup.com/. Some companies such as Barilla, the Italian pasta brand, get consumers involved in designing new pasta for little expense—far less than the cost of banner ads on websites. The Ottawa-based company Ideavibes has built a crowdsourcing app that will allow companies to engage with consumers in crowdsourcing campaigns. Ideavibes states, "Crowdsourcing can lead to the creation of cool products, which are customer focused and easy to use."[93] Chaordix is another Canadian company that is enabling businesses to use crowdsourcing. The company has built a platform using feedback from a 50,000-member crowd. The platform allows companies to engage crowds online in a user-friendly environment.

There is no end to the opportunities to gain information, insights, and new-product ideas from consumers. For instance, Rupert Barksfield developed the Multi-Pet Feeder to end pet feeding-time frenzy when one greedy pet eats the other pet's food. Barksfield paid $99 to post a concept and some drawings at quirky.com, and 30,000 people passed judgment on his idea.[94] Consumer feedback is an important part of the digital media equation. Some of the oldest forms of digital media are online forums, where participants post and respond to messages and discuss specific topics. About one-fifth of U.S. and Japanese Internet users participate in discussion forums, whose topics can range from consumer products to movies. Ratings and reviews have become exceptionally popular; 25 percent of the U.S. online population reads this type of consumer-generated feedback.[95] Retailers such as Amazon, Netflix, and Priceline allow consumers to post comments on their sites about the books, movies, and travel arrangements they sell. Today, most online shoppers search the Internet for ratings and reviews before making major purchase decisions.

**DID YOU KNOW?**

About three-quarters of people shopping on the Web read online ratings and reviews before making a purchasing decision.[96]

While consumer-generated content about a firm can be either positive or negative, digital media forums do allow businesses to closely monitor what their customers are saying. In the case of negative feedback, businesses can communicate with consumers to address problems or complaints much more easily than through traditional communication channels. Hotels and resorts, for example, have begun monitoring social media sites to see what their guests are saying about them. In some cases, guests who

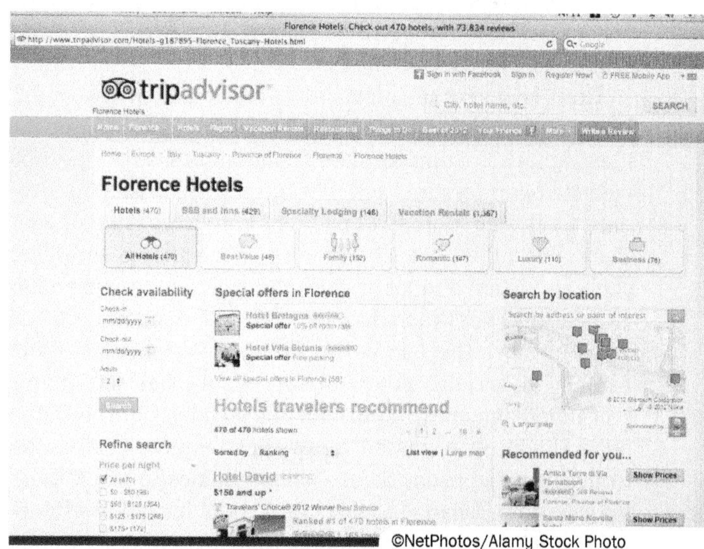


©NetPhotos/Alamy Stock Photo

Hotels have been some of the quickest firms to engage with and respond to online reviews. In cases of poor reviews, some hotels have offered free upgrades or other incentives to get guests to return.

have complained about their rooms using digital media have found themselves upgraded to better rooms that very night.[97] Yet despite the ease and obvious importance of online feedback, many companies do not yet take full advantage of the digital tools at their disposal.

## Legal and Social Issues in Internet Marketing

**LO 13-6** Identify legal and ethical considerations in digital media.

The extraordinary growth of information technology, the Internet, and e-business has generated many legal and social issues for consumers and businesses. The major issues related to digital media are privacy, identify theft, online fraud, and intellectual property, which are discussed below.

### Privacy

Businesses have long tracked consumers' shopping habits with little controversy. However, observing the contents of a consumer's shopping cart or the process a consumer goes through when choosing a box of cereal generally does not result in the collection of specific, personally identifying data. Although using credit cards, shopping cards, and coupons forces consumers to give up a certain degree of anonymity in the traditional shopping process, they can still choose to remain anonymous by paying cash. Shopping on the Internet, however, allows businesses to track them on a far more personal level, from what they buy online to the websites they favour. Current technology has made it possible for marketers to amass vast quantities of personal information, often without consumers' knowledge, and to share and sell this information to interested third parties.

How is personal information collected on the Web? Many sites follow users online by storing a *cookie*, or an identifying bit of data, on users' computers. Cookies permit website operators to track how often a user visits the site, plus what they look at while there and in what sequence. They also allow website visitors to customize services, such as virtual shopping carts, as well as the particular content they see when they log on to a Web page.

Users have the option of turning off cookies on their machines, but the potential for misuse has left many consumers uncomfortable with this technology. The European Union even passed a law that requires companies to get users' consent before using cookies to track their information. Because of this law, Yahoo! Inc. allows Internet users in the United Kingdom to choose whether to opt out of having their Internet habits tracked.[98]

Some companies have become even more creative when tracking users. Aaron's, a rent-to-own store, got into hot water for installing software in laptops that enabled the company to use the computer's webcam to see what its customers were doing. The software, called PC Rental Agent, has been the subject of a number of consumer complaints as it has been used to capture pictures and video of people in very intimate moments, including playing with their children and in some cases having sex. Governments subsequently disallowed the use of such software in Canada and the United States.

Influencer marketing, which we discussed earlier as a form of promotion, is relatively new compared with other forms of advertising, so it should be no surprise there have been road bumps for early adopters. In Canada influencer advertising is administered by the Competition Bureau, which has issued several papers reminding firms and influencers of the importance of honesty in advertising.[99] In America, the Federal Trade Commission (FTC) requires influencers to clearly disclose any connection they have with brands they promote. Neglecting to make a disclosure is viewed as deceptive advertising. Cases have been filed against Warner Bros. Home Entertainment, which paid PewDiePie, YouTube's number one most subscribed channel, for an endorsement of its video game Middle-Earth: Shadow of Mordor, and Lord & Taylor, which paid various influencers to promote their dresses, all without disclosures. According to the FTC, any level of compensation much be disclosed, whether a partner is paid or an influencer simply receives free product.[100]

### Identity Theft

**Identity theft** occurs when criminals obtain personal information that allows them to impersonate someone else in order to use the person's credit to access financial accounts and make purchases. Many of these breaches occur at banks, universities, and other businesses that hold sensitive consumer information.[101] This requires organizations

©Simon Jarratt/Corbis

Businesses may be taking online monitoring to a whole new level. PC Rental Agent was software installed on people's laptops that enabled the rental agent to capture pictures and video of users.

identity theft when criminals obtain personal information that allows them to impersonate someone else in order to use their credit to access financial accounts and make purchases

online fraud any attempt to conduct fraudulent activities online

to implement increased security measures to prevent database theft, and while these usually work, problems do still occur. For example, in 2013, the Canadian government announced it lost a portable hard drive containing the personal information of over 500,000 people who took out student loans. The lost drive included vast amounts of information including names, social insurance numbers, dates of birth, addresses, and other personal information. The most common complaints about identity theft relate to credit card fraud, followed by utility fraud, bank fraud, employment-related fraud, government document fraud, and loan fraud.[102]

The Internet's relative anonymity and speed make possible both legal and illegal access to databases storing social insurance numbers, driver's licence numbers, dates of birth, mothers' maiden names, and other information that can be used to establish a credit card or bank account in another person's name in order to make fraudulent transactions. One growing scam used to initiate identity theft fraud is the practice of *phishing,* in which con artists counterfeit a well-known website and send out emails directing victims to it. There visitors find instructions to reveal sensitive information such as their credit card numbers. Phishing scams have faked websites and/or emails for PayPal, Western Canada Summer Games, and Canada Post.

Some identity theft problems are resolved quickly, while other cases take weeks and hundreds of dollars before a victim's bank balances and credit standings are restored.

## Online Fraud

**Online fraud** includes any attempt to conduct fraudulent activities online, such as by deceiving consumers into releasing personal information. It is becoming a major source of frustration among users of social networking sites, because cybercriminals are finding new ways to use sites like Facebook and Twitter to commit fraudulent activities. For instance, they will create profiles under a company's name to either damage the company's reputation (particularly larger, more controversial companies) or lure that company's customers into releasing personal information the perpetrators can use for monetary gain.

Another tactic is to copy a blog entry from a reputable company and repost it with a link that connects the user to the criminal's own fraudulent site, where he or she attempts to sell the user goods (under the reputable company's name) or collect personal information. For instance, a fraudster may repost a blog written by a professional sports organization with a fraudulent link that connects users to a site that sells unlicensed sporting goods.[103] Criminals may also use social networking sites to pose as

©Perry Mastrovito/Creatas/Picture Quest

Even the government is prone to mistakes in managing people's information, as was evident in the 2013 announcement that Canada lost a file containing personal information about 500,000 Canadians.

charitable institutions. After the 2018 Humboldt Broncos bus crash, fraudsters set up fake accounts to scam social media users into donating money for the fraudsters' own financial gain.[104] Despite any number of safeguards, the best protection for consumers is to be careful when they divulge information online. The surest way to stay out of trouble is never to give out personal information, like a social insurance number or credit card number, unless it is a site you trust and that you know is legitimate.

## Intellectual Property

In addition to protecting personal privacy, Internet users and others want to protect their rights to property they may create, including songs, movies, books, and software. Such intellectual property consists of the ideas and creative materials developed to solve problems, carry out applications, and educate and entertain others.

Although intellectual property is generally protected by patents and copyrights, each year losses from the illegal copying of computer programs, music, movies, compact discs, and books reaches billions of dollars in North America. This has become a particular problem with digital media sites. For example, YouTube has faced lawsuits over its users' possible infringement of other companies' copyrights. In one case, Viacom Inc. sued YouTube's owner, Google, claiming Google had violated its copyrights by allowing users to post protected film clips on YouTube.[105] Although YouTube is responsible for the video content shown on its sites, it can be difficult for Google to monitor and remove all the videos that may contain copyrighted content, given the many millions of clips that are loaded onto YouTube daily.

Illegal sharing of content is another major intellectual property problem. Some consumers rationalize the pirating of software, video games, movies, and music for a number of reasons. First, many feel they just don't have the money to pay for what they want. Second, because their friends engage in piracy and swap digital content, some users feel influenced to engage in this activity. Others enjoy the thrill of getting away with something with a low risk of consequences. And finally, some people feel being tech-savvy allows them to take advantage of the opportunity to pirate content.[106]

There are also a number of consumers who simply do not feel they are doing anything wrong when they share or download software. For example, Gary Fung, founder of Vancouver-based isoHunt, does not think there is anything wrong with sharing TV shows, films, and so forth and has made millions selling advertising on his website. The U.S. courts do not agree with Mr. Fung and have levied a $150 million fine against his company. Fung's argument is that his site, much like Google, is a search engine that organizes data. What users do with that data is not for him to control and when asked to remove a movie or TV show due to copyright he complies.

"Developing a strategic understanding of how digital marketing can make business more efficient and productive is increasingly necessary."

The software industry loses over $52 billion globally each year due to theft and illegal use of software products.[107] About 90 percent of illegal software copying is actually done by businesses. For example, a firm may obtain a licence to install a specific application on 100 of its computers but actually installs it on 300. In some cases, software is illegally made available through the Internet by companies that have taken the software from the producer and set up their own distribution system. Both the Canadian and U.S. governments are pursuing tougher laws against online piracy.

## Digital Media's Impact on Marketing

To be successful in business, you need to know much more than how to use a social networking site to communicate with friends. Developing a strategic understanding of how digital marketing can make business more efficient and productive is increasingly necessary. If you are thinking of becoming an entrepreneur, then the digital world can open doors to new resources and customers. Smart phones, mobile broadband, and webcams are among the tools that can make the most of the online business world, creating greater efficiency at less cost. For example, rather than using traditional phone lines, Skype helps people make and receive calls via the Internet and provides free video calling and text messaging for a fraction of the cost of a land line.[108] It is up to businesses and entrepreneurs to develop strategies that achieve business success using existing and future technology, software, and networking opportunities.

Traditional businesses accustomed to using print media can find the transition to digital challenging. New media may require employees with new skills or additional training for current employees. There is often a gap between technical knowledge of how to develop sites and how to develop effective digital marketing strategies to enhance business success. Determining the correct blend of traditional and new media requires careful consideration; the mix will vary depending on the business, its size, and its target market. Future career opportunities will require skills in both traditional and digital media areas so that marketers properly understand and implement marketing strategies that help businesses achieve a competitive advantage.

### TEAM EXERCISE

Develop a digital marketing promotion for a local sports team. Use Twitter, Facebook, and other social networking media to promote ticket sales for next season's schedule. In your plan, provide specific details and ideas for the content you would use on the sites. Also, describe how you would encourage fans and potential fans to go to your site. How would you use digital media to motivate sports fans to purchase tickets and merchandise and attend games?

# LEARNING OBJECTIVES SUMMARY

**LO 13-1** Define digital media and digital marketing, and recognize their increasing value in strategic planning.

Digital media are electronic media that function using digital codes via computers, cellular phones, smartphones, and other digital devices. Digital marketing uses all digital media, including the Internet and mobile and interactive channels, to develop communication and exchanges with customers.

Because both have impacted strategic planning by allowing for instant communication with precisely defined consumer groups, firms can use real-time exchanges to stimulate interactive communication, forge closer relationships, and learn more accurately about consumer and supplier needs. Thus, firms who use digital media and digital marketing should have a better understanding of consumers, be able to communicate with them more efficiently, and be able to manage their marketing mix to appeal to a broad range of people.

**LO 13-2** Understand the characteristics of digital media and how these methods are different from traditional marketing activities.

While digital marketing shares some similarities with conventional marketing techniques, a few valuable differences stand out. First, digital media make customer communications faster and interactive. Second, digital media help companies reach new target markets more easily, affordably, and quickly than ever before. Finally, digital media help marketers utilize new resources in seeking out and communicating with customers.

**LO 13-3** Demonstrate the role of digital marketing and social networking in today's business environment.

One of the most important benefits of digital marketing is the ability of marketers and customers to easily share information. Through websites, social networks, and other digital media, consumers can learn about everything they consume and use in their lives, ask questions, voice complaints, indicate preferences, and otherwise communicate about their needs and desires. Many marketers use email, mobile phones, social networking, wikis, video sharing, podcasts, blogs, videoconferencing, and other technologies to coordinate activities and communicate with employees, customers, and suppliers. Twitter, considered both a social network and a micro blog, illustrates how these digital technologies can combine to create new communication opportunities.

**LO 13-4** Show how digital media affect the marketing mix.

**Product Considerations.** Like traditional marketers, digital marketers must anticipate consumer needs and preferences, tailor their products and services to meet these needs, and continually upgrade them to remain competitive. The connectivity created by digital media provide the opportunity for adding services and enhancing product benefits.

**Distribution/Place.** The Internet is a new distribution channel for making products available at the right time, at the right place, and in the right quantities. The ability of marketers to process orders electronically and increase the speed of communication via the Internet reduces inefficiencies, costs, and redundancies while increasing speed throughout the marketing channel. Shipping times and costs have become an important consideration in attracting customers, prompting many companies to offer consumers low shipping costs or next-day delivery.

**Promotion Considerations.** Perhaps one of the best ways businesses can utilize digital media is for promotion purposes—whether they are increasing brand awareness, connecting with consumers, or taking advantage of social networks or virtual worlds to form relationships and generate positive publicity or "buzz" about their products. Thanks to online promotion, consumers can be more informed than ever, including reading customer-generated content before making purchasing decisions. Consumer consumption patterns are radically changing, and marketers must adapt their promotional efforts to meet them.

**Pricing Considerations.** Price is the most flexible element of the marketing mix. Digital marketing can enhance the value of products by providing extra benefits such as service, information, and convenience. Through digital media, discounts and other promotions can be quickly communicated.

**LO 13-5** Define social networking and illustrate how businesses can use different types of social networking media.

A social network is "a Web-based meeting place for friends, family, co-workers, and peers that lets users create a profile and connect with other users for purposes that range from getting acquainted, to keeping in touch, to building a work-related network." Social networks are a valued part of marketing because they are changing the way consumers communicate with each other and with firms. Sites such as Facebook, Instagram, Twitter, and LinkedIn have emerged as opportunities for marketers to build communities, provide product information, and learn about consumer needs. By the time you read this, it is possible there will be new social network sites that continue to advance digital communication and opportunities for marketers. The uses of social networking are widespread. Companies can use blogs to answer questions, YouTube to post videos, and social network sites such as Facebook to communicate with customers.

**LO 13-6** Identify legal and ethical considerations in digital media.

The major issues related to legal and ethical concerns are privacy, identity theft, online fraud, and intellectual property.

# KEY TERMS

accessibility
addressability
blog
connectivity
control
digital marketing
digital media
e-business
identity theft
interactivity
online fraud
podcast
social network
viral marketing
wiki

# So You Want to Be *a Digital Marketer*

The business world has grown increasingly dependent on digital marketing to maintain communication with stakeholders. Reaching customers is often a major concern, but digital marketing can also be used to communicate with suppliers, concerned community members, and special interest groups about issues related to sustainability, safety practices, and philanthropic activities. Many types of jobs exist: account directors of social media and directors of marketing for digital products, as well as digital advertisers, online marketers, global digital marketers, and brand managers are prominently listed on career opportunity websites.

Entrepreneurs are taking advantage of the low cost of digital marketing, building social networking sites to help market their products. In fact, some small businesses such as specialty publishing, personal health and beauty, and other specialty products can use digital marketing as the primary channel for reaching consumers. Many small businesses are posting signs outside their stores with statements such as "Follow us on Twitter" or "Check out our Facebook page."

To create effective digital marketing, especially in the area of social networking, requires more than information technology skills related to constructing websites, graphics, videos, podcasts, and so on. Most importantly, marketers must be able to determine how digital media can be used in implementing a marketing strategy. All marketing starts with identifying a target market and developing a marketing mix. Digital marketing is just another way to reach customers, provide information, and develop relationships. Therefore, your opportunity for a career in this field is greatly based on understanding the messages, desired level of interactivity, and connectivity that helps achieve marketing objectives.

As social media use skyrockets, digital marketing professionals will be in demand. The experience of many businesses and research indicate digital marketing is a powerful way to increase brand exposure and generate traffic. In fact, a study conducted on Social Media Examiner found that 85 percent of marketers surveyed believe generating exposure for their business is their number-one advantage in Internet marketing. As consumers use social networking for their personal communication, they will be more open to obtaining information about products through this channel. Digital marketing could be the fastest-growing opportunity in business.

To prepare yourself for a digital marketing career, learn not only the technical aspects, but also how social media can be used to maximize marketing performance. A glance at careerbuilder.com indicates that management positions such as account manager, digital marketing manager, and digital product manager can pay from $60,000 to $170,000 or more per year.

# BUILD YOUR BUSINESS PLAN

## Digital Marketing and Social Networking

As you are building your business plan, one thing that is virtually certain is that you will need a digital marketing strategy. Digital marketing including social networking sites allows businesses to engage with more consumers, establish a two-way communication relationship with customers, and ultimately should enable a business to be more successful.

The question many new businesses face is not whether they should use online marketing tools, but what tools are most appropriate for their business. As discussed throughout the chapter, there are a number of different online techniques a business can use, and each involves an investment of time and sometimes money. Given that new businesses often have a shortage of both, it is crucial that as an entrepreneur you develop a clear strategy for digital marketing.

A successful way to do this is to evaluate each marketing tool in a table or spreadsheet as they relate to your business. Create a table where you assess and highlight the user demographics of the various sites—Facebook, Twitter, and so forth—and how you may use the site in your business. You can start to think about which tools you will use, and which tools would likely not work best for your business. You could then extend the table further and state specifically how you could incorporate these digital marketing sites into your company's overall marketing plan. After completing this analysis you should have a sense of what digital marketing tools would work best with your prospective business.

## CASE | Should Employees Use Social Media Sites At Work?

As social media sites have gained popularity and expanded, managing their use at work has become an increasingly hot topic. Studies on the use of social media in the workplace don't agree about how much it inhibits productivity. Should employees be allowed to access social media at work? Many offices have banned access to the sites.

A study conducted by Nucleus Research (an IT research company) revealed a 1.5 percent loss of productivity for businesses allowing social media access. It found that 77 percent of Facebook users used the site during work for as much as two hours a day; 87 percent of those surveyed admitted they were using social media sites to waste time. The National Business and Economics Society found that active social networkers were more likely to find certain questionable behaviours to be acceptable—such as criticizing the company or its managers—on social networking sites. Procter & Gamble realized that many of its employees were using social networking sites for non-work purposes. Its investigations revealed that employees across the company were watching an average of 50,000 five-minute YouTube videos and listening to 4000 hours of music on Pandora daily.

However, an outright ban could cause problems. Some younger employees have said that they do not want to work for companies without social media access; they view restricting or eliminating access like removing a benefit. Employees at companies with an outright ban often resent the lack of trust associated with such a move and feel that management is censoring their activities. Additionally, Procter & Gamble uses YouTube and Facebook extensively for marketing purposes. Banning these sites would disrupt the firm's marketing efforts.

An Australian study indicates that employees taking time out to pursue Facebook and other social media were actually 9 percent more productive than those who did not. Brent Coker, the study's author and University of Melbourne faculty member, says people are more productive when they take time to "zone out" throughout the work day. Doing so can improve concentration. Coker's study focused on those using less than 20 percent of the workday on such breaks, which is less than the amount of time "active" social networkers spend on these sites. In the sales industry, a study of 100,000 employees revealed that social media users had a higher rate of sales conversions.

Some companies actually encourage employees to use social networking as part of the company's integrated marketing strategy. For example, Patrick Hoover Law Offices charges employees with the responsibility to use social media in ways that the employees believe can benefit the company. Although this does potentially allow employees to use social media for personal purposes rather than for work, this tactic has been effective in getting new clients and publicizing the organization. By trusting its employees and giving them leeway to use social media in ways they see fit, Patrick Hoover Law Offices has taken a potential problem and reworked it to its own advantage.

Despite the benefits that companies like Patrick Hoover Law Offices have received from allowing their employees to use social media, many companies have gone ahead with social media bans. For example, Procter & Gamble has restricted the use of Netflix and Pandora, but not Facebook or YouTube. Companies all need to ask, "Can management use social media to benefit the company?" If so, it may be more advantageous to take the risks of employees using social media for personal use if they can also be encouraged to use social networks to publicize their organizations, connect with customers, and view consumer comments or complaints. By restricting social media use, companies may be forfeiting an effective marketing tool.

### DISCUSSION QUESTIONS

1. Why do you think results are so mixed on the use of social networking in the workplace?
2. What are some possible upsides to using social media as part of an integrated marketing strategy, especially in digital marketing?
3. What are the downsides to restricting employee access to social networking sites?

CHAPTER 14

# Accounting and Financial Statements

©Amer Ghazzal/Shutterstock

## LEARNING OBJECTIVES

**After reading this chapter, you will be able to:**

LO 14-1 Define *accounting* and describe the different uses of accounting information.

LO 14-2 Demonstrate the accounting process.

LO 14-3 Examine the various components of an income statement in order to evaluate a firm's bottom line.

LO 14-4 Interpret a company's balance sheet to determine its current financial position.

LO 14-5 Analyze financial statements, using ratio analysis, to evaluate a company's performance.

# ENTER THE WORLD OF BUSINESS

**By the Numbers: Deloitte Excels in the Big Four**

When it comes to accounting, the Big Four dominate. What are the Big Four? *The Big Four* refers to the four largest accounting firms in the world: Ernst & Young, PricewaterhouseCoopers, KPMG, and Deloitte. These accounting firms provide a range of services to their clients, including external audit, taxation services, management and business consultancy, and risk assessment and control. The Big Four audit more than 80 percent of all U.S. public companies.

Deloitte was ranked number one in revenue, earning $36.8 billion globally with approximately 244,400 employees in more than 150 countries. Deloitte believes the best measure of success is the effect it has on the world. It does not want to be known for the size or services that it offers; instead, it wants to make an impact. Deloitte strives to have intelligent people work across more than 20 industry sectors, and its purpose is "to deliver measurable, lasting results . . . and help lead the way toward a stronger economy and a healthy society."

As part of the Big Four, it is important for Deloitte to continue its long-standing commitment to communities. The Deloitte Foundation runs a number of projects including fundraising activities and supports charitable organizations with grants. To focus on education, Deloitte's strategy has been to improve higher education readiness. It commits time, talent, and resources to help students persist through high school, college or university, and transition into a great career.

Deloitte is not only highly profitable, but also has a reputation for innovative processes, technologies, governance, and policy. This places it at a competitive advantage with the other Big Four.[1]

**DISCUSSION QUESTIONS**

1. What is unique about Deloitte that would be important to clients?
2. What is the difference between a CPA at Deloitte and a bookkeeper?
3. Why is it important to have a high-integrity accounting firm provide services to clients?

## Introduction

Although you may cover some of this material in your accounting course, reading this chapter will only strengthen your understanding of accounting. What professors find is that a little duplication and repetition goes a long way in helping the brain retain material.

Accounting is the financial "language" that organizations use to record, measure, and interpret all of their financial transactions and records and is very important in business. All businesses—from a small family farm to a giant corporation—use the language of accounting to make sure they use their money wisely and to plan for the future. Non-business organizations such as charities and governments also use accounting to demonstrate to donors and taxpayers how well they are using their funds and meeting their stated objectives.

This chapter explores the role of accounting in business and its importance in making business decisions. First, we discuss the uses of accounting information and the accounting process. Then, we briefly look at some simple financial statements and accounting tools that are useful in analyzing organizations worldwide.

# The Nature of Accounting

**LO 14-1** Define *accounting* and describe the different uses of accounting information.

Simply stated, **accounting** is the recording, measurement, and interpretation of financial information. Large numbers of people and institutions, both within and outside businesses, use accounting tools to evaluate organizational operations. The Accounting Standards Board (AcSB) is the body with the authority to establish accounting standards for use by all Canadian companies outside the public sector.[2] These rules are called *generally accepted accounting principles*, or GAAP. GAAP is a framework that includes a common set of rules and a standard format for public companies to use when they prepare their reports. Public companies must follow the principles and rules set out in the International Financial Reporting Standards (IFRS). This is a single set of high-quality, understandable, and enforceable global standards.[3] Private companies follow *accounting standards for private enterprises* (ASPE), and not-for-profit organizations follow *accounting standards for not-for-profit organizations* (ASNPO). To better understand the importance of accounting, we must first understand who prepares accounting information and how it is used.

©Lars A. Niki

Ernst & Young is part of the Big Four, the four largest international accounting firms. The other three are KPMG, PricewaterhouseCoopers, and Deloitte.

## Accountants

Many of the functions of accounting are carried out by public or private accountants. Large corporations, government agencies, and other organizations may employ their own **accountants** to prepare and analyze their financial statements. With titles such as controller, treasurer, or tax auditor, accountants are deeply involved in many of the most important financial decisions of the organizations for which they work. Accountants can be chartered professional accountants (CPAs) by completing the CPA certification program.

**accounting** the recording, measurement, and interpretation of financial information

**accountants** professionals employed by large corporations, government agencies, and other organizations to prepare and analyze their financial statements

Other accountants are either self-employed or members of large public accounting firms such as Ernst & Young, KPMG, Deloitte, and PricewaterhouseCoopers, together referred to as the *Big Four*. In addition, many CPAs work for one of the second-tier accounting firms that are much smaller than the Big Four firms, as illustrated in Table 14.1.

Although there will always be companies and individual money managers who can successfully hide illegal or misleading accounting practices for a while, eventually they are exposed. After the accounting scandals of Enron and Worldcom in the early 2000s, the U.S. Congress passed the *Sarbanes-Oxley Act*, which required firms to be more rigorous in their accounting and reporting practices. Canadian regulators favoured a more gradual approach, such as Bill 198 in Ontario. This allowed Canadian participants to better reflect the fundamental differences between the Canadian and U.S. capital markets.[4]

Only five years after the passage of the *Sarbanes-Oxley Act*, the world experienced a financial crisis starting in 2008—part of which was due to excessive risk taking and inappropriate accounting practices. Many U.S. banks had developed questionable lending practices and investments based on subprime mortgages made to individuals who

**Table 14.1** | Leading Accounting Firms

| Company | 2017 Revenues (millions) | Number of Offices |
|---|---|---|
| Deloitte LLP | $2,300 | 56 |
| KPMG LLP | $1,446 | 40 |
| PricewaterhouseCoopers Canada | $1,428 | 25 |
| Ernst & Young LLP | $1,397 | 16 |
| Grant Thornton Canada | $597 | 135 |
| MNP LLP | $660 | 58 |
| BDO Canada LLP | $609.5 | 111 |
| Collins Barrow | $213.5 | 41 |

had poor credit. When housing prices declined and people suddenly found that they owed more on their mortgages than their homes were worth, they began to default. The global financial crisis that resulted led to a series of significant regulatory changes to international banking rules, which are designed to reduce the risk of another financial crisis occurring. While these rules were set internationally, Canadian regulators have also implemented them.[5]

A growing area for public accountants is *forensic accounting*, which involves analyzing financial documents in search of fraudulent entries or financial misconduct. Functioning as much like detectives as accountants, forensic accountants have been used since the 1930s. In the wake of the accounting scandals of the early 2000s, many auditing firms are rapidly adding or expanding forensic or fraud-detection services. Additionally, many forensic accountants root out evidence of "cooked books" for federal agencies like the RCMP. The Association of Certified Fraud Examiners, which certifies accounting professionals as *certified fraud examiners* (CFEs), has grown to more than 75,000 members, with chapters in Canada and around the world.[6]

**DID YOU KNOW?**

Corporate fraud costs are estimated at $4 trillion annually.[7]

## Accounting or Bookkeeping?

The terms *accounting* and *bookkeeping* are often mistakenly used interchangeably. Much narrower and far more mechanical than accounting, bookkeeping is typically limited to the routine, day-to-day recording of business transactions. Bookkeepers are responsible for obtaining and recording the information that accountants require to analyze a firm's financial position. They generally require less training than accountants. Accountants, on the other hand, usually complete course work beyond their basic four- or five-year accounting degrees. This additional training allows accountants not only to record financial information but also to understand, interpret, and even develop the sophisticated accounting systems necessary to classify and analyze complex financial information.

## The Uses of Accounting Information

Accountants summarize the information from a firm's business transactions in various financial statements (which we'll look at in a later section of this chapter) for a variety of stakeholders, including managers, investors, creditors, and government agencies. Many business failures may be directly linked to ignorance of the information "hidden" inside these financial statements. Likewise, most business successes can be traced to informed managers who understand the consequences of their decisions. While maintaining and even increasing short-run profits is desirable, the failure to plan sufficiently for the future can easily lead an otherwise successful company to insolvency and bankruptcy court.

Basically, managers and owners use financial statements (1) to aid in internal planning and control, and (2) for external purposes such as reporting to the Canada Revenue Agency, shareholders, creditors, customers, employees, and other interested parties. Figure 14.1 shows some of the users of the accounting information generated by a typical corporation.

**RESPONDING TO BUSINESS CHALLENGES**

### Auditing First Nations

The *First Nations Financial Transparency Act* requires that First Nations bands make their audited consolidated financial statements, and a Schedule of Remuneration and Expenses of chief and council, available to their members. Since then, the Government of Canada and First Nations have been working together to develop an accountability framework that is mutually acceptable.

Researchers from Queen's University in Ontario found that auditors face significant challenges when completing the required audits for a First Nations, Métis, or Inuit group. Challenges include the logistics of working in remote areas, auditors being on site for brief periods, and lack of on-the-ground expertise to prepare proper financial reports.

Auditors must adapt to those challenges by reshaping their mindset and focusing on the needs of the communities, helping with some of the accounting tasks, and re-evaluating the importance of requests for additional information. For example, auditors may work collaboratively with First Nations employees preparing financial reports, spend more time training their clients, or acknowledge that the process might result in some unanswered questions that cannot be resolved by pedantry.*

*Alan Morantz, "How Auditors Find Their Footing in the Indigenous World," May 6, 2018, https://smith.queensu.ca/insight/articles/how_auditors_find_their_footing_in_the_indigenous_world (accessed March 10, 2019); Government of Canada, "A New Approach: Co-development of a New Fiscal Relationship," December 6, 2017, https://www.aadnc-aandc.gc.ca/DAM/DAM-INTER-HQ-ACH/STAGING/texte-text/reconciliation_new_fiscal_rel_approach_1512565483826_eng.pdf, (accessed March 10, 2019).

Figure 14.1 | The Users of Accounting Information

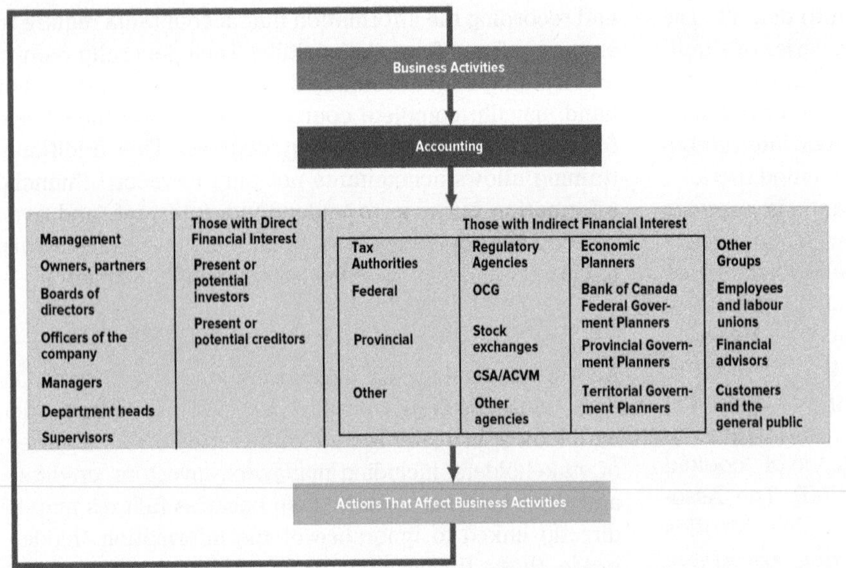


**Internal Uses.** **Managerial accounting** refers to the internal use of accounting statements by managers in planning and directing the organization's activities. Perhaps management's greatest single concern is **cash flow**, the movement of money through an organization over a daily, weekly, monthly, or yearly basis. Obviously, for any business to succeed, it needs to generate enough cash to pay its bills as they fall due. However, it is not at all unusual for highly successful and rapidly growing companies to struggle to make payments to employees, suppliers, and lenders because of an inadequate cash flow. One common reason for a so-called cash crunch, or shortfall, is poor managerial planning

Managerial accountants also help prepare an organization's **budget**, an internal financial plan that forecasts expenses and income over a set period of time. It is not unusual for an organization to prepare separate daily, weekly, monthly, and yearly budgets. Think of a budget as a financial map, showing how the company expects to move from Point A to Point B over a specific period of time. While most companies prepare *master budgets* for the entire firm, many also prepare budgets for smaller segments of the organization such as divisions, departments, product lines, or projects. "Top-down" master budgets begin at the top and filter down to the individual department level, while "bottom-up" budgets start at the department or project level and are combined at the chief executive's office. Generally, the larger and more rapidly growing an organization, the greater will be the likelihood that it will build its master budget from the ground up.

**managerial accounting** the internal use of accounting statements by managers in planning and directing the organization's activities

**cash flow** the movement of money through an organization over a daily, weekly, monthly, or yearly basis

**budget** an internal financial plan that forecasts expenses and income over a set period of time

Regardless of focus, the major value of a budget lies in its breakdown of cash inflows and outflows. Expected operating expenses (cash outflows such as wages, materials costs, and taxes) and operating revenues (cash inflows in the form of payments from customers) over a set period of time are carefully forecasted and subsequently compared with actual results. Deviations between the two serve as a "trip wire" or "feedback loop" to launch more detailed financial analyses in an effort to pinpoint trouble spots and opportunities.

**External Uses.** Managers also use accounting statements to report the business's financial performance to outsiders. Such statements are used for filing income taxes, obtaining credit from lenders, and reporting results to the firm's shareholders. They become the basis for the information provided in the official corporate **annual report**, a summary of the firm's financial information, products, and growth plans for owners and potential investors. While frequently presented between slick, glossy covers prepared by major advertising firms, the single most important component of an annual report is the signature of a certified public accountant attesting that the required financial statements are an accurate reflection of the underlying financial condition of the firm. Financial statements meeting these conditions are termed *audited*. The primary external users of audited accounting information are government agencies, shareholders and potential investors, and lenders, suppliers, and employees.

**annual report** summary of a firm's financial information, products, and growth plans for owners and potential investors

Financial statements evaluate the return on shareholders' investment and the overall quality of the firm's management team. As a result, poor financial statements often result in changes in top management. Potential investors study the financial statements in a firm's annual report to determine whether the company meets their investment requirements and whether the returns from a given firm are likely to compare favourably with other similar companies.

## GOING GREEN

### Stranded Assets Pose a Financial and Environmental Risk

The term *stranded assets* is becoming more popular in financial reporting, especially for the oil and gas industry. Stranded assets are assets that are not recoverable. These assets come with a high environmental price and have the potential to be left unused if tougher environmental regulations are passed. For the oil and gas industry, this may mean more untapped oil and gas reserves. Stranded assets create significant risk for companies and their shareholders. According to the CDP—a group that gathers environmental data for shareholders—deforestation alone could result in $1 trillion of stranded assets for public companies, particularly those in the oil, lumber, and cattle industries.

As a result, more companies have begun to report environmental risks in their financial reports. One survey found that 27 percent of the risks identified in company sustainability reports were being reported in financial reports, as well. Attracting (or appeasing) investors is one of the largest drivers of this trend. Additionally, if climate risk could potentially impact a firm's bottom line or the value of its assets, failing to report this information could be seen as misleading. For instance, ExxonMobil was investigated to see if it had valued some of its assets correctly to account for increasing environmental regulations. This shift toward greener accountability has implications for the possible development of generally accepted accounting principles for sustainability concerns.*

#### DISCUSSION QUESTIONS

1. Should companies include environmental costs, or "stranded assets," in their accounting statements?
2. How might climate change and other environmental risks negatively impact a firm's assets or bottom line?
3. What might be some advantages to reporting and monitoring environmental costs?

*Terry Slavin, "Green Finance: Deforestation Brings Risk of $1trn in Stranded Assets, Warns CDP," Ethical Corporation, November 23, 2017, http://www.ethicalcorp.com/green-finance-deforestation-brings-risk-1trn-strandedassets-warns-cdp (accessed April 12, 2018); Kevin McCoy, "New York Attorney General Probing ExxonMobil's Accounting Amid Oil Slide," *USA Today*, September 16, 2016, https://www.usatoday.com/story/money/2016/09/16/exxonmobil-accounting-disclosuresexamined/90476826/(accessed April 12, 2018); Bradley Olson and Aruna Viswanatha, "SEC Probes Exxon over Accounting for Climate Change," *Wall Street Journal*, September 20, 2016, https://www.wsj.com/articles/sec-investigating-exxon-on-valuing-of-assets-accountingpractices-1474393593 (accessed April 12, 2018); "How to Deal with Worries about Stranded Assets," *The Economist*, November 24, 2016, https://www.economist.com/news/special-report/21710632-oil-companies-needheed-investors-concerns-how-deal-worries-about-stranded (accessed April 12, 2018); Felicia Jackson, "Disclosure Is about Risks and Opportunities, Not Politics," *Forbes*, April 12, 2018, https://www.forbes.com/sites/feliciajackson/2018/04/12/disclosure-is-about-risks-andopportunities-not-politics/#50a8b1cf63be (accessed April 12, 2018).

©pandpstock001/iStockphoto/Getty Images

The annual report is a summary of the firm's financial information, products, and growth plans for owners and potential investors. Many investors look at a firm's annual report to determine how well the company is doing financially.

"A corporation's shareholders use financial statements to evaluate the return on their investment and the overall quality of the firm's management team."

Banks and other lenders look at financial statements to determine a company's ability to meet current and future debt obligations if a loan or credit is granted. To determine this ability, a short-term lender examines a firm's cash flow to assess its ability to repay a loan quickly with cash generated from sales. A long-term lender is more interested in the company's profitability and indebtedness to other lenders.

Labour unions and employees use financial statements to establish reasonable expectations for salary and other benefit requests. Just as firms experiencing record profits are likely to face added pressure to increase employee wages, so too are employees unlikely to grant employers wage and benefit concessions without considerable evidence of financial distress.

## The Accounting Process

**LO 14-2** Demonstrate the accounting process.

Many view accounting as a primary business language. It is of little use, however, unless you know how to "speak" it. Fortunately, the fundamentals—the accounting equation and the double-entry bookkeeping system—are not difficult to learn. These two concepts serve as the starting point for all currently accepted accounting principles.

"Many view accounting as a primary business language."

### The Accounting Equation

Accountants are concerned with reporting an organization's assets, liabilities, and owners' equity. To help illustrate these concepts, consider a hypothetical flower shop called Anna's Flowers, owned by Anna Rodriguez. A firm's economic resources, or items of value that it owns, represent its **assets**—cash, inventory, land, equipment, buildings, and other tangible and intangible things. The assets of Anna's Flowers include counters, refrigerated display cases, flowers, decorations, vases, cards, and other gifts, as well as something known as *goodwill*, which in this case is Anna's reputation for preparing and delivering beautiful floral arrangements on a timely basis.

**Liabilities**, on the other hand, are debts the firm owes to others. Among the liabilities of Anna's Flowers are a loan from the Business Development Bank of Canada and money owed to flower suppliers and other creditors for items purchased. The **owners' equity** category contains all of the money that has ever been contributed to the company that never has to be paid back. The funds can come from investors who have given money or assets to the company, or it can come from past profitable operations. In the case of Anna's Flowers, if Anna were to sell off, or liquidate, her business, any money left over after selling all the shop's assets and paying off its liabilities would comprise her owner's equity. The relationship between assets, liabilities, and owners' equity is a fundamental concept in accounting and is known as the **accounting equation**:

**assets** a firm's economic resources, or items of value that it owns, such as cash, inventory, land, equipment, buildings, and other tangible and intangible things

**liabilities** debts that a firm owes to others

**owners' equity** equals assets minus liabilities and reflects historical values

©Jose Luis Pelaez Inc/Blend Images LLC

The owners' equity portion of this florist's balance sheet includes the money invested in the firm.

Assets = Liabilities + Owners' equity

### Double-Entry Bookkeeping

**Double-entry bookkeeping** is a system of recording and classifying business transactions in separate accounts in order to maintain the balance of the accounting equation. Returning to Anna's Flowers, suppose Anna buys \$325 worth of roses on credit from the Antique Rose Emporium to fill a wedding order. When she records this transaction, she will list the \$325 as a liability or a debt to a supplier. At the same time, however, she will also record \$325 worth of roses as an asset in an account known as *inventory*. Because the assets and liabilities are on different sides of the accounting equation, Anna's accounts increase in total size (by \$325) but remain in balance:

**accounting equation** assets equal liabilities plus owners' equity

**double-entry bookkeeping** a system of recording and classifying business transactions that maintains the balance of the accounting equation

Assets = Liabilities + Owners' equity
\$325 = \$325

Thus, to keep the accounting equation in balance, each business transaction must be recorded in two separate accounts.

In the final analysis, all business transactions are classified as either assets, liabilities, or owners' equity. However, most organizations further break down these three accounts to provide more specific information about a transaction. For example, assets may be broken down into specific categories such as cash, inventory, and equipment, while liabilities may include bank loans, supplier credit, and other debts.

Figure 14.2 shows how Anna used the double-entry bookkeeping system to account for all of the transactions that took place in her first month of business. These transactions

**Figure 14.2** | The Accounting Equation and Double-Entry Bookkeeping for Anna's Flowers

| | Assets | | | = Liabilities | | + Owners' Equity |
|---|---|---|---|---|---|---|
| | *Cash* | *Equipment* | *Inventory* | *Debts to suppliers* | *Loans* | *Equity* |
| *Cash invested by Anna* | $2,500.00 | | | | | $2,500.00 |
| *Loan from SBA* | $5,000.00 | | | | $5,000.00 | |
| *Purchase of furnishings* | –$3,000.00 | $3,000.00 | | | | |
| *Purchase of inventory* | –$2,000.00 | | $2,000.00 | | | |
| *Purchase of roses* | | | $325.00 | $325.00 | | |
| *First month sales* | $2,000.00 | | –$1,500.00 | | | $500.00 |
| *Totals* | $4,500.00 | $3,000.00 | $825.00 | $325.00 | $5,000.00 | $3,000.00 |

$8,325 = $5,325 + $3,000

$8,325 Assets = $8,325 Liabilities + Owners' Equity

include her initial investment of $2500, the loan from the the Business Development Bank of Canada (BDC), purchases of equipment and inventory, and the purchase of roses on credit. In her first month of business, Anna generated revenues of $2000 by selling $1500 worth of inventory. Thus, she deducts, or (in accounting notation that is appropriate for assets) *credits*, $1500 from inventory and adds, or *debits*, $2000 to the cash account. The difference between Anna's $2000 cash inflow and her $1500 outflow is represented by a credit to owners' equity, because it is money that belongs to her as the owner of the flower shop.

## The Accounting Cycle

In any accounting system, financial data typically pass through a four-step procedure sometimes called the **accounting cycle**. The steps include examining source documents, recording transactions in an accounting journal, posting recorded transactions, and preparing financial statements. Figure 14.3 shows how Anna works through them. Traditionally, all of these steps were performed using paper, pencils, and erasers (lots of erasers!), but today the process is often fully computerized.

**accounting cycle** the four-step procedure of an accounting system: examining source documents, recording transactions in an accounting journal, posting recorded transactions, and preparing financial statements

**Step One: Examine Source Documents.** Like all good managers, Anna Rodriguez begins the accounting cycle by gathering and examining source documents—cheques, credit card receipts, sales slips, and other related evidence concerning specific transactions.

**Step Two: Record Transactions.** Next, Anna records each financial transaction in a **journal**, which is basically just a time-ordered list of account transactions. While most businesses keep a general journal in which all transactions are recorded, some classify transactions into specialized journals for specific types of transaction accounts.

**Step Three: Post Transactions.** Anna next transfers the information from her journal into a **ledger**, a book or computer program with separate files for each account. This process is known as *posting*. At the end of the accounting period (usually yearly, but occasionally quarterly or monthly), Anna prepares a *trial balance*, a summary of the balances of all the accounts in the general ledger. If, upon totalling, the trial balance doesn't balance (that is, the accounting equation is not in balance), Anna or her accountant must look for mistakes (typically an error in one or more of the ledger entries) and correct them. If the trial balance is correct, the accountant can then begin to prepare the financial statements.

**journal** a time-ordered list of account transactions

**ledger** a book or computer file with separate sections for each account

**Step Four: Prepare Financial Statements.** The information from the trial balance is also used to prepare the company's financial statements. In the case of public

**Figure 14.3** | The Accounting Process for Anna's Flowers

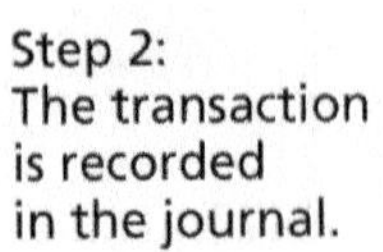

Step 1:
Source documents show that a transaction took place.

**Receipt**
**Anna's Flowers**

| | |
|---|---|
| July 7 Wedding floral arrangements | $500.00 |
| Consultation services | 250.00 |

Step 2:
The transaction is recorded in the journal.

| Assets | |
|---|---|
| | Cash |
| July 7 Brown wedding | $750.00 |

Step 3:
The transaction is posted to the general ledger under the appropriate account (asset, liability, or some further breakdown of these main accounts).

| Date | | Explanation | PR | Debit | Credit | Balance Debit | Balance Credit |
|---|---|---|---|---|---|---|---|
| 2017 | | | | | | | |
| July | 1 | | 1 | 2,000 | | 2,000 | |
| | 3 | | 1 | | 1,250 | | 1,250 |
| | 4 | | 1 | | | | |
| | 7 | Brown wedding | 1 | | 750 | | 750 |
| | 14 | | 1 | | | | |

Step 4: At the end of the accounting period, the ledger is used to prepare the firm's financial statements.

Anna's Flowers
Income Statement
December 31, 2017

| | | |
|---|---|---|
| Revenues: | | |
| Net sales | | $123,850 |
| Consulting | | 73,850 |
| Total revenues | | $197,700 |
| Expenses: | | |
| Cost of goods sold | $72,600 | |
| Selling expenses | 37,700 | |
| General and admin. | 18,400 | |
| Other expenses | 5,600 | |
| Total expenses | | 134,300 |
| Net income | | $ 63,400 |

Anna's Flowers
Balance Sheet
December 31, 2017

| | | |
|---|---|---|
| Assets | | |
| Current assets: | | |
| **Cash** | **$17,850** | |
| Accounts receivable | 10,200 | |
| Merch. Inventory | 8,750 | |
| Tot. assets | | $36,800 |
| Property and Equipment | | |
| Equipment | 11,050 | |
| Office building | 73,850 | |
| Tot. prop. & equip. | | 84,900 |
| Total assets | | $121,700 |
| Liabilities and Owners' Equity | | |
| Current liabilities | | |
| Accounts payable | $12,600 | |
| Tot. cur. liabilities | | 12,600 |
| Long-term liabilities | | |
| Mortgage payable | | 23,600 |
| Total liabilities | | 36,200 |
| Owners' equity: | | |
| **Anna Rodriguez, capital** | | **$ 85,500** |
| Tot. liabilities and owners' equity | | $ 121,700 |

Anna's Flowers
Annual Budget
for 2017

| | Sales | Consulting | Total |
|---|---|---|---|
| January | 10,500 | 4,500 | 15,000 |
| February | 10,000 | 5,500 | 15,500 |
| March | 10,800 | 5,700 | 16,500 |
| April | 10,100 | 6,050 | 16,150 |
| May | 12,000 | 6,000 | 18,000 |
| June | 12,100 | 6,250 | 18,350 |
| July | 13,000 | 6,600 | 19,600 |
| August | 9,950 | 6,000 | 15,950 |
| September | 9,700 | 6,200 | 15,900 |
| October | 9,900 | 7,000 | 16,900 |
| November | 8,500 | 7,150 | 15,650 |
| December | 7,300 | 6,900 | 14,200 |
| Annual | $123,850 | $73,850 | $197,700 |

corporations and certain other organizations, a CPA must *attest*, or certify, that the organization followed generally accepted accounting principles in preparing the financial statements. When these statements have been completed, the organization's books are "closed," and the accounting cycle begins anew for the next accounting period.

# Financial Statements

**LO 14-3** Examine the various components of an income statement to evaluate a firm's bottom line.

The end result of the accounting process are a series of financial statements. The income statement, the balance sheet, and the statement of cash flows are the best-known examples of financial statements. These statements are provided to shareholders and potential investors in a firm's annual report as well as to other relevant outsiders such as creditors, government agencies, and the Canada Revenue Agency.

It is important to recognize that not all financial statements follow precisely the same format. The fact that different organizations generate income in different ways suggests that when it comes to financial statements, one size definitely does not fit all. Manufacturing firms, service providers, and non-profit organizations each use a different set of accounting principles or rules upon which the public accounting profession has agreed. As we have already mentioned, these are sometimes referred to as generally accepted accounting principles (or GAAP).

Each country has a different set of rules that the businesses within that country are required to use for their accounting process and financial statements; however, many countries (including Canada) have adopted International Financial Reporting Standards (IFRS) for listed or large companies so that statutory reporting is comparable across international jurisdictions. Still, as is the case in many other disciplines, certain concepts have more than one name. For example, *sales* and *revenues* are often interchanged, as are *profits*, *income*, and *earnings*. Table 14.2 lists a few common equivalent terms that should help you decipher their meaning in accounting statements.

**Table 14.2** | Equivalent Terms in Accounting

| Term | Equivalent Term |
|---|---|
| Revenues | Sales |
| | Goods or services sold |
| Gross profit | Gross income |
| | Gross earnings |
| Operating income | Operating profit |
| | Earnings before interest and taxes (EBIT) |
| | Income before interest and taxes (IBIT) |
| Income before taxes (IBT) | Earnings before taxes (EBT) |
| | Profit before taxes (PBT) |
| Net income (NI) | Earnings after taxes (EAT) |
| | Profit after taxes (PAT) |
| Income available to common shareholders | Earnings available to common shareholders |

## The Income Statement

The question, "What's the bottom line?" derives from the income statement, where the bottom line shows the overall profit or loss of the company after taxes. Thus, the **income statement** is a financial report that shows an organization's profitability over a period of time, be that a month, quarter, or year. By its very design, the income statement offers one of the clearest possible pictures of the company's overall revenues and the costs incurred in generating those revenues. Other names for the income statement include profit and loss (P&L) statement or operating statement. A sample income statement with line-by-line explanations is presented in Table 14.3, while Table 14.4 presents the income statement of Loblaw. The income statement indicates the firm's profitability or income (the bottom line), which is derived by subtracting the firm's expenses from its revenues.

**income statement** a financial report that shows an organization's profitability over a period of time—month, quarter, or year

**Revenue. Revenue** is the total amount of money received (or promised) from the sale of goods or services, as well as from other business activities such as the rental of property and investments. Non-business entities typically obtain revenues through donations from individuals and/or grants from governments and private foundations. One of the controversies in accounting has been when a business should recognize revenue. For instance, should an organization book revenue during a project or after the project is completed? Differences in revenue recognition have caused similar organizations to book different accounting results. A proposed rule states that firms should book revenue when "it satisfies a performance obligation by transferring a promised good or service to a customer."[8]

**revenue** the total amount of money received from the sale of goods or services, as well as from related business activities

**cost of goods sold** the amount of money a firm spent to buy or produce the products it sold during the period to which the income statement applies

For most manufacturing and retail concerns, the next major item included in the income statement is the **cost of goods sold**, the amount of money the firm spent (or promised to spend) to buy and/or produce the products

**Table 14.3 | Sample Income Statement**

| Company Name for the Year Ended December 31 | |
|---|---|
| The following presents an income statement in word form with all the terms defined and explained. | |
| Revenues (sales) | Total dollar amount of products sold (includes income from other business services such as rental-lease income and interest income). |
| Less: Cost of goods sold | The cost of producing the goods and services, including the cost of labour and raw materials as well as other expenses associated with production. |
| Gross profit | The income available after paying all expenses of production. |
| Less: Selling and administrative expense | The cost of promoting, advertising, and selling products as well as the overhead costs of managing the company. This includes the cost of management and corporate staff. One non-cash expense included in this category is *depreciation*, which approximates the decline in the value of plant and equipment assets due to use over time. In most accounting statements, depreciation is not separated from selling and administrative expenses. However, financial analysts usually create statements that include this expense. |
| Income before interest and taxes (operating income or EBIT) | This line represents all income left over after operating expenses have been deducted. This is sometimes referred to as *operating income* since it represents all income after the expenses of operations have been accounted for. Occasionally, this is referred to as EBIT, or earnings before interest and taxes. |
| Less: Interest expense | Interest expense arises as a cost of borrowing money. This is a financial expense rather than an operating expense and is listed separately. As the amount of debt and the cost of debt increase, so will the interest expense. This covers the cost of both short-term and long-term borrowing. |
| Income before taxes (earnings before taxes—EBT) | The firm will pay a tax on this amount. This is what is left of revenues after subtracting all operating costs, depreciation costs, and interest costs. |
| Less: Taxes | The tax rate is specified in the federal tax code. |
| Net income | This is the amount of income left after taxes. The firm may decide to retain all or a portion of the income for reinvestment in new assets. Whatever it decides not to keep, it will usually pay out in dividends to its shareholders. |
| Less: Preferred dividends | If the company has preferred shareholders, they are first in line for dividends. That is one reason why their stock is called "preferred." |
| Income to common shareholders | This is the income left for the common shareholders. If the company has a good year, there may be a lot of income available for dividends. If the company has a bad year, income could be negative. The common shareholders are the ultimate owners and risk takers. They have the potential for very good or very poor returns since they get whatever is left after all other expenses. |
| Earnings per share | Earnings per share is found by taking the income available to the common shareholders and dividing by the number of shares of common stock outstanding. This is income generated by the company for each share of common stock. |

it sold during the accounting period. This figure may be calculated as follows:

$$\text{Cost of goods sold} = \text{Beginning inventory} + \text{Interim purchases} - \text{Ending inventory}$$

Let's say that Anna's Flowers began an accounting period with an inventory of goods for which it paid $5000. During the period, Anna bought another $4000 worth of goods, giving the shop a total inventory available for sale of $9000. If, at the end of the accounting period, Anna's inventory was worth $5500, the cost of goods sold during the period would have been $3500 ($5000 + $4000 – $5500 = $3500). If Anna had total revenues of $10,000 over the same period of time, subtracting the cost of goods sold ($3500) from the total revenues of $10,000 yields the store's **gross income (or profit)** (revenues minus the cost of goods sold required to generate the revenues): $6500.

**Expenses.** **Expenses** are the costs incurred in the day-to-day operations of an organization. Three common expense accounts shown on income statements are (1) selling, general, and administrative expenses; (2) research, development, and engineering expenses; and (3) interest expenses (remember that the costs directly attributable to selling goods or services are included in the cost of goods sold). Selling expenses include

**gross income (or profit)** revenues minus the cost of goods sold required to generate the revenues

**expenses** the costs incurred in the day-to-day operations of an organization

Table 14.4 | Loblaw's Consolidated Statements of Earnings (millions of Canadian dollars except where otherwise indicated)

| Fiscal Year Ended | Dec 2017 | Dec 2016 |
|---|---|---|
| **Revenue** | **$46,702** | **$46,385** |
| Cost of merchandise inventories sold | (32,913) | (33,213) |
| Selling, general and administrative expenses | (11,295) | (11,080) |
| **Operating income** | **2,494** | **2,092** |
| Net interest expense and other financing charges | (525) | (653) |
| **Earnings before income taxes** | **1,969** | **1,439** |
| Income taxes | (443) | (449) |
| **Net earnings** | **1,526** | **990** |
| Net earnings per share—basic | $ 3.78 | $ 2.40 |
| Net earnings per share—diluted | $ 3.75 | $ 2.37 |
| **Weighted average shares outstanding (millions)** | | |
| Basic | 393.8 | 405.1 |
| Diluted | 397.3 | 409.1 |

advertising and sales salaries. General and administrative expenses include salaries of executives and their staff and the costs of owning and maintaining the general office. Research and development costs include scientific, engineering, and marketing personnel and the equipment and information used to design and build prototypes and samples. Interest expenses include the direct costs of borrowing money.

The number and type of expense accounts vary from organization to organization. Included in the general and administrative category is a special type of expense known as **depreciation**, the process of spreading the costs of long-lived assets such as buildings and equipment over the total number of accounting periods in which they are expected to be used.

**depreciation** the process of spreading the costs of long-lived assets such as buildings and equipment over the total number of accounting periods in which they are expected to be used

Consider a manufacturer that purchases a $100,000 machine expected to last about ten years. Rather than showing an expense of $100,000 in the first year and no expense for that equipment over the next nine years, the manufacturer is allowed to report depreciation expenses of $10,000 per year in each of the next ten years because that better matches the cost of the machine to the years the machine is used. Each time this depreciation is written off as an expense, the book value of the machine is also reduced by $10,000. The fact that the equipment has a zero value on the firm's balance sheet when it is fully depreciated (in this case, after ten years) does not necessarily mean that it can no longer be used or is economically worthless. Indeed, in some industries, machines used every day have been reported as having no book value whatsoever for over 30 years.

**Net Income.** **Net income** (or net earnings) is the total profit (or loss) after all expenses including taxes have been deducted from revenue. Generally, accountants divide profits into individual sections such as operating income and earnings before interest and taxes. Most companies present not only the current year's results but also the previous two years' income statements to permit comparison of performance from one period to another.

**net income** (or net earnings) the total profit (or loss) after all expenses including taxes have been deducted from revenue

©Scott Sroka/National Geographic/Getty Images

The bees in Miels D'Anicet's 1200 beehives help pollinate crops and make organic honey. Two-thirds of edible crops require pollination by the Western honey bee (*apis mellifera*).

## ENTREPRENEURSHIP IN ACTION

### A Buzzing Success

**Miels d'Anicet**

**Founder: Anne-Virginie Schmidt**

**Founded:** 2000

**Success:** Between 2000 and 2015, Miels D'Anicet's sales grew by nearly 50 percent every year, with annual sales now at more than $2 million.

Anne-Virginie Schmidt, a professional accountant, was an auditor at KPMG's downtown Montreal office and dreaming of becoming an entrepreneur. Lacking a particular business idea, she had decided to develop general skills in finance and accounting that would serve her when the right opportunity arose. That dream became a reality when she joined Anicet Desrochers, a beekeeper, as both a business and life partner.

Together, the couple devised an organic honey brand that would appeal to foodies, and grew that brand by getting their honey into the kitchens of fashionable restaurants. Schmidt differentiated Miels d'Anicet by packaging, marketing, and selling all its honey independently and used her skill set to establish margins and calculate the true costs of products.

She also brought risk-management expertise to her new profession by diversifying their revenue. Apart from producing honey and breeding queen bees, she added an organic skincare line, expanded into food products, and opened a restaurant, the Pollens & Nectars Canteen. The strategies are working and Schmidt says her training as an accountant is part of what makes it all possible.*

#### DISCUSSION QUESTIONS

1. Why does Anne-Virginie Schmidt need to possess good accounting skills in her management of Miels d'Anicet?
2. How did Anne-Virginie Schmidt use her skills developed as a CPA?
3. As companies grow, do you think it is a good idea for the founders to continue assuming their firms' accounting responsibilities? Why or why not?

*Miels d'Anicet, About Us, https://mielsdanicet.com/en-ca/about-us/, (accessed February 24, 2019); Mark Mann, *Pivot Magazine*, "The CPA who's making a buzz in the beekeeping biz," https://www.cpacanada.ca/en/news/pivot-magazine/2019-01-02-cpa-beekeeper, (accessed February 1, 2019).

**Temporary Nature of the Income Statement Accounts.** Companies record their operational activities in the revenue and expense accounts during an accounting period. Gross profit, earnings before interest and taxes, and net income are the results of calculations made from the revenue and expense accounts; they are not actual accounts. At the end of each accounting period, the dollar amounts in all the revenue and expense accounts are moved into an account called Retained Earnings, one of the owners' equity accounts. Revenues increase owners' equity, while expenses decrease it. The resulting change in the owners' equity account is exactly equal to the net income.

This shifting of dollar values from the revenue and expense accounts allows the firm to begin the next accounting period with zero balances in those accounts. Zeroing out the balances enables a company to count how much it has sold and how many expenses have been incurred during a period of time. The basic accounting equation (assets = liabilities + owners' equity) will not balance until the revenue and expense account balances have been moved or *closed out* to the owners' equity account.

One final note about income statements. You may remember from Chapter 4 that corporations may choose to make cash payments called dividends to shareholders out of their net earnings. When a corporation elects to pay dividends, it decreases the cash account (in the assets category) as well as a capital account (in the owners' equity category). During any period of time, the owners' equity account may change because of the sale of stock (or contributions/withdrawals by owners), the net income or loss, or from the dividends paid.

©Quality HD/Shutterstock

Walmart is the world's largest company, according to Fortune Global 500, with more than $500 billion in revenue.

# The Balance Sheet

**LO 14-4** Interpret a company's balance sheet to determine its current financial position.

The second basic financial statement is the **balance sheet**, which presents a "snapshot" of an organization's financial position at a given moment. As such, the balance sheet indicates what the organization owns or controls and the various sources of the funds used to pay for these assets, such as bank debt or owners' equity.

**balance sheet** a "snapshot" of an organization's financial position at a given moment

The balance sheet takes its name from its reliance on the accounting equation: assets *must* equal liabilities plus owners' equity. Table 14.5 provides a sample balance sheet with line-by-line explanations. Unlike the income statement, the balance sheet does not represent the result of transactions completed over a specified accounting period. Instead, the balance sheet is, by definition, an accumulation of all financial transactions conducted by an organization since its founding. Following long-established traditions, items on the balance sheet are listed on the basis of their original cost less accumulated depreciation, rather than their present values.

**Table 14.5** | Sample Balance Sheet

| Typical Company December 31 | |
|---|---|
| The following presents a balance sheet in word form with each item defined or explained. | |
| Assets | This is the major category for all physical, monetary, or intangible goods that have some dollar value. |
| Current assets | Assets that are either cash or are expected to be turned into cash within the next 12 months. |
| Cash | Cash or chequing accounts |
| Marketable securities | Short-term investments in securities that can be converted to cash quickly (liquid assets). |
| Accounts receivable | Cash due from customers in payment for goods received. These arise from sales made on credit. |
| Inventory | Finished goods ready for sale, goods in the process of being finished, or raw materials used in the production of goods. |
| Prepaid expense | A future expense item that has already been paid, such as insurance premiums or rent. |
| Total current assets | The sum of the above accounts. |
| Fixed assets | Assets that are long term in nature and have a minimum life expectancy that exceeds one year. |
| Investments | Assets held as investments rather than assets owned for the production process. Most often, the assets include small ownership interests in other companies. |
| Gross property, plant, and equipment | Land, buildings, and other fixed assets listed at original cost. |
| Less: Accumulated depreciation | The accumulated expense deductions applied to all plant and equipment over their life. Land may not be depreciated. The total amount represents in general the decline in value as equipment gets older and wears out. The maximum amount that can be deducted is set by the Canada Revenue Agency (CRA) and varies by type of asset. |
| Net property, plant, and equipment | Gross property, plant, and equipment minus the accumulated depreciation. This amount reflects the book value of the fixed assets and not their value if sold. |
| Other assets | Any other asset that is long term and does not fit into the above categories. It could be patents or trademarks. |
| Total assets | The sum of all the asset values. |
| Liabilities and shareholders' equity | This is the major category. Liabilities refer to all indebtedness and loans of both a long-term and short-term nature. Shareholders' equity refers to all money that has been contributed to the company over the life of the firm by the owners. |
| Current liabilities | Short-term debt expected to be paid off within the next 12 months. |
| Accounts payable | Money owed to suppliers for goods ordered. Firms usually have between 30 and 90 days to pay this account, depending on industry norms. |
| Wages payable | Money owed to employees for hours worked or salary. If workers receive cheques every two weeks, the amount owed should be no more than two weeks' pay. |
| Taxes payable | Firms are required to pay corporate taxes quarterly. This refers to taxes owed based on earnings estimates for the quarter. |
| Notes payable | Short-term loans from banks or other lenders. |
| Other current liabilities | The other short-term debts that do not fit into the above categories. |
| Total current liabilities | The sum of the above accounts. |

Table 14.5 | (Continued)

| Typical Company December 31 | |
|---|---|
| Long-term liabilities | All long-term debt that will not be paid off in the next 12 months. |
| Long-term debt | Loans of more than one year from banks, pension funds, insurance companies, or other lenders. These loans often take the form of bonds, which are securities that may be bought and sold in bond markets. |
| Deferred income taxes | This is a liability owed to the government but not due within one year. |
| Other liabilities | Any other long-term debt that does not fit the above two categories. |
| Shareholders' equity | The following categories are the owners' investment in the company. |
| Common stock | The tangible evidence of ownership is a security called common stock. The par value is stated value and does not indicate the company's worth. |
| Capital in excess of par (a.k.a. contributed capital) | When shares of stock were sold to the owners, they were recorded at the price at the time of the original sale. If the price paid was $10 per share, the extra $9 per share would show up in this account at 100,000 shares times $9 per share, or $900,000. |
| Retained earnings | The total amount of earnings the company has made during its life and not paid out to its shareholders as dividends. This account represents the owners' reinvestment of earnings into company assets rather than payments of cash dividends. This account does not represent cash. |
| Total shareholders' equity | This is the sum of the above equity accounts representing the owners' total investment in the company. |
| Total liabilities and shareholders' equity | The total short-term and long-term debt of the company plus the owners' total investment. This combined amount *must* equal total assets. |

"The balance sheet takes its name from its reliance on the accounting equation: assets must equal liabilities plus owners' equity."

Balance sheets are often presented in two different formats. The traditional balance sheet format placed the organization's assets on the left side and its liabilities and owners' equity on the right. More recently, a vertical format, with assets on top followed by liabilities and owners' equity, has gained wide acceptance. Loblaw's balance sheet is presented in Table 14.6. In the sections

Table 14.6 | Loblaw's Consolidated Balance Sheets (millions of Canadian dollars)

| ASSETS | Dec. 30, 2017 | Dec. 31, 2016 |
|---|---|---|
| **Current assets** | | |
| Cash and cash equivalents | $1,798 | $1,314 |
| Short-term investments | 546 | 241 |
| Accounts receivable | 1,188 | 1,122 |
| Credit card receivables | 3,100 | 2,926 |
| Inventories | 4,438 | 4,371 |
| Prepaid expenses and other assets | 224 | 190 |
| Assets held for sale | 33 | 40 |
| **Total current assets** | **11,327** | **10,204** |
| Fixed assets | 10,669 | 10,559 |
| Investment properties | 235 | 218 |
| Intangible assets | 8,251 | 8,745 |
| Goodwill | 3,922 | 3,895 |
| Deferred income tax assets | 134 | 130 |
| Franchise loans receivable | 166 | 233 |
| Other assets | 402 | 452 |
| **Total Assets** | **$35,106** | **$34,436** |

Table 14.6 | (Continued)

| LIABILITIES AND EQUITY | | |
|---|---|---|
| **Current liabilities** | | |
| Bank indebtedness | 110 | 115 |
| Trade payables and other liabilities | 5,646 | 5,091 |
| Provisions | 283 | 99 |
| Income taxes payable | 117 | 329 |
| Short term debt | 640 | 665 |
| Long term debt due within one year | 1,635 | 400 |
| Associate interest | 263 | 243 |
| **Total current liabilities** | **8,694** | **6,942** |
| Provisions | 169 | 120 |
| Long-term debt | 9,542 | 10,470 |
| Trust unit liability | 972 | 959 |
| Deferred income tax liabilities | 1,977 | 2,190 |
| Other liabilities | 700 | 727 |
| **Total liabilities** | **22,054** | **21,408** |
| **Equity** | | |
| Share Capital | 7,666 | 7.913 |
| Retained earnings | 5,198 | 4,944 |
| Contributed Surplus | 110 | 112 |
| Accumulated other comprehensive income | 38 | 33 |
| Total equity attributable to shareholders of the company | 13,012 | 13,002 |
| Non-controlling interests | 40 | 26 |
| **Total equity** | **13,052** | **13,028** |
| **TOTAL LIABILITIES AND EQUITY** | **$35,106** | **$34,436** |

that follow, we'll briefly describe the basic items found on the balance sheet; we'll take a closer look at a number of these in Chapter 16.

**Assets.** All asset accounts are listed in descending order of *liquidity*—that is, how quickly each could be turned into cash. **Current assets**, also called short-term assets, are those that are used or converted into cash within the course of a calendar year. Thus, cash is followed by temporary investments, accounts receivable, and inventory, in that order. **Accounts receivable** refers to money owed the company by its clients or customers who have promised to pay for the products at a later date. Accounts receivable usually includes an allowance for bad debts that management does not expect to collect. The bad-debts adjustment is normally based on historical collections experience and is deducted from the accounts receivable balance to present a more realistic view of the payments likely to be received in the future, called net receivables. Inventory may be held in the form of raw materials, work-in-progress, or finished goods ready for delivery.

Long-term or fixed assets represent a commitment of organizational funds of at least one year. Items classified as fixed include long-term investments, plant and equipment, and intangible assets, such as corporate goodwill, or reputation, as well as patents and trademarks.

**current assets** assets that are used or converted into cash within the course of a calendar year

**accounts receivable** money owed a company by its clients or customers who have promised to pay for the products at a later date

**Liabilities.** As seen in the accounting equation, total assets must be financed either through borrowing (liabilities) or through owner investments (owners' equity). **Current liabilities** include a firm's financial obligations to short-term creditors, which must be repaid within one year, while long-term liabilities have longer repayment terms. **Accounts payable** represents amounts owed to suppliers for goods and services purchased with credit. For example, if you buy gas with a Shell credit card, the purchase represents an account payable for you (and an account receivable for Shell). Other liabilities include wages earned by employees but not yet paid and taxes owed to the government. Occasionally, these accounts are consolidated into an **accrued expenses** account, representing all unpaid financial obligations incurred by the organization.

**current liabilities** a firm's financial obligations to short-term creditors, which must be repaid within one year

**accounts payable** the amount a company owes to suppliers for goods and services purchased with credit

**accrued expenses** an account representing all unpaid financial obligations incurred by the organization

**Owners' Equity.** Owners' equity includes the owners' contributions to the organization along with income earned by the organization and retained to finance continued growth and development. If the organization were to sell off all of its assets and pay off all of its liabilities, any remaining funds would belong to the owners. Not surprisingly, the accounts listed as owners' equity on a balance sheet may differ dramatically from company to company.

Corporations sell stock to investors, who become the owners of the firm. Many corporations issue two, three, or even more different classes of common and preferred stock, each with different dividend payments and/or voting rights. Google has three classes of stock, with the class B stock having more voting rights than class A shares. These are sometimes called founder's shares and allow the founders to maintain control over the company even though they do not own the majority of the shares. Because each type of stock issued represents a different claim on the organization, each must be represented by a separate owners' equity account, called contributed capital.

## The Statement of Cash Flow

Another primary financial statement is called the **statement of cash flows**, which explains how the company's cash changed from the beginning of the accounting period to the end. Users of financial statements want information about the cash flowing into and out of the firm than is provided on the balance sheet to better understand the company's financial health. The statement of cash flow takes the cash balance from one year's balance sheet and compares it to the next while providing detail about how the firm used the cash. The change in cash is explained through details in three categories: cash from (used for) operating activities, cash from (used for) investing activities, and cash from (used for) financing activities.

**statement of cash flows** explains how the company's cash changed from the beginning of the accounting period to the end

*Cash from operating activities* is calculated by combining the changes in the revenue accounts, expense accounts, current asset accounts, and current liability accounts. If this amount is positive, then the business is making extra cash that it can use to invest in increased long-term capacity or to pay off debts such as loans or bonds. A negative number may indicate a business that is still in a growing stage or one that is in a declining position with regards to operations.

*Cash from investing activities* is calculated from changes in the long-term or fixed asset accounts. If this amount is negative the company is purchasing long-term assets for future growth. A positive figure indicates a business that is selling off existing long-term assets and reducing its capacity for the future.

*Cash from financing activities* is calculated from changes in the long-term liability accounts and the contributed capital accounts in owners' equity. If this amount is positive, the company is either borrowing more money or raising money from investors by selling more shares of stock. If

©Andrey Rudakov/Bloomberg via Getty Images

This type of machinery would be considered a long-term asset on the balance sheet.

this amount is negative, the company is likely paying off long-term debt or returning contributed capital to investors.

## Ratio Analysis: Analyzing Financial Statements

LO 14-5 Analyze financial statements, using ratio analysis, to evaluate a company's performance.

The income statement shows a company's profit or loss, while the balance sheet itemizes the value of its assets, liabilities, and owners' equity. Together, the two statements provide the means to answer two critical questions: (1) How much did the firm make or lose? and (2) How much is the firm currently worth based on historical values found on the balance sheet? **Ratio analysis**, calculations that measure an organization's financial health, brings the complex information from the income statement and balance sheet into sharper focus so that managers, lenders, owners, and other interested parties can measure and compare the organization's productivity, profitability, and financing mix with other similar entities.

As you know, a ratio is simply one number divided by another, with the result showing the relationship between the two numbers. Financial ratios are used to weigh and evaluate a firm's performance. Interestingly, an absolute value, such as earnings of $70,000 or accounts receivable of $200,000, almost never provides as much useful information as a well-constructed ratio. Whether those numbers are good or bad depends on their relation to other numbers. If a company earned $70,000 on $700,000 in sales (a 10 percent return), such an earnings level might be quite satisfactory. The president of a company earning this same $70,000 on sales of $7 million (a 1 percent return), however, should probably start looking for another job!

**ratio analysis** calculations that measure an organization's financial health

**profitability ratios** ratios that measure the amount of operating income or net income an organization is able to generate relative to its assets, owners' equity, and sales

Ratios by themselves are not very useful. It is the relationship of the calculated ratios to both prior organizational performance and the performance of the organization's "peers," as well as its stated goals, that really matters. Remember, while the profitability, asset utilization, liquidity, debt ratios, and per share data we'll look at here can be very useful, you will never see the forest by looking only at the trees.

### Profitability Ratios

**Profitability ratios** measure how much operating income or net income an organization is able to generate relative to its assets, owners' equity, and sales. The numerator (top number) used in these examples is always the net income after taxes. Common profitability ratios include profit margin, return on assets, and return on equity. The following examples are based on the 2016 income statement and balance sheet for Loblaw, as shown in Tables 14.4 and 14.6. Except where specified, all data are expressed in millions of dollars.

The **profit margin**, computed by dividing net income by sales, shows the overall percentage profits earned by the company. It is based solely upon data obtained from the income statement. The higher the profit margin, the better the cost controls within the company and the higher the return on every dollar of revenue. Loblaw's profit margin is calculated as follows:

$$\text{Profit margin} = \frac{\text{Net income}}{\text{Sales}} = \frac{\$1{,}526}{\$46{,}702} = 3.27\%$$

Thus, for every $1 in sales, Loblaw generated profits after taxes of 3.27 cents.

**Return on assets**, net income divided by assets, shows how much income the firm produces for every dollar invested in assets. A company with a low return on assets is probably not using its assets very productively—a key managerial failing. By its construction, the return on assets calculation requires data from both the income statement and the balance sheet.

$$\text{Return on assets} = \frac{\text{Net income}}{\text{Assets}} = \frac{\$1{,}526}{\$35{,}106} = 4.35\%$$

In the case of Loblaw, every $1 of assets generated a return of 4.53 percent, or profits of 4.35 cents per dollar.

Shareholders are always concerned with how much money they will make on their investment, and they frequently use the return on equity ratio as one of their key performance measures. **Return on equity** (also called return on investment [ROI]), calculated by dividing net income by owners' equity, shows how much income is generated by each $1 the owners have invested in the firm. Obviously, a low return on equity means low shareholder returns and may indicate a need for immediate managerial attention. Because some assets may have been financed with debt not contributed by the owners, the value of the owners' equity is usually considerably lower than the total value of the firm's assets. Starbucks' return on equity is calculated as follows:

**profit margin** net income divided by sales

**return on assets** net income divided by assets

**return on equity** net income divided by owners' equity; also called *return on investment* (ROI)

$$\text{Return on equity} = \frac{\text{Net income}}{\text{Equity}} = \frac{\$1{,}526}{\$13{,}052} = 11.69\%$$

For every dollar invested by Loblaw stockholders, the company earned a 11.69 percent return, or 11.69 cents per dollar invested.

"Profitability ratios measure how much operating income or net income an organization is able to generate relative to its assets, owners' equity, and sales."

## Asset Utilization Ratios

**Asset utilization ratios** measure how well a firm uses its assets to generate each $1 of sales. Obviously, companies using their assets more productively will have higher returns on assets than their less efficient competitors. Similarly, managers can use asset utilization ratios to pinpoint areas of inefficiency in their operations. These ratios (receivables turnover, inventory turnover, and total asset turnover) relate balance sheet assets to sales, which are found on the income statement.

The **receivables turnover**, sales divided by accounts receivable, indicates how many times a firm collects its accounts receivable in one year. It also demonstrates how quickly a firm is able to collect payments on its credit sales. Obviously, no payments mean no profits. Loblaw collected its receivables a little less than 11 times per year. Loblaw's sales are for cash and credit.

$$\text{Receivables turnover} = \frac{\text{Sales}}{\text{Receivables}} = \frac{\$46{,}702}{\$1{,}188 + \$3{,}100} = 10.89\ \textit{times}$$

**Inventory turnover**, sales divided by total inventory, indicates how many times a firm sells and replaces its inventory over the course of a year. A high inventory turnover ratio may indicate great efficiency but may also suggest the possibility of lost sales due to insufficient stock levels. Loblaw's inventory turnover indicates that it replaced its inventory times 10.52 times the previous year, or slightly less than once a month.

**asset utilization ratios** ratios that measure how well a firm uses its assets to generate each $1 of sales

**receivables turnover** sales divided by accounts receivable

**inventory turnover** sales divided by total inventory

**total asset turnover** sales divided by total assets

$$\text{Inventory turnover} = \frac{\text{Sales}}{\text{Inventory}} = \frac{\$46{,}702}{\$4{,}438} = 10.52\ \textit{times}$$

**Total asset turnover**, sales divided by total assets, measures how well an organization uses all of its assets in creating sales. It indicates whether a company is using its assets productively. Loblaw generated $1.33 in sales for every $1 in total corporate assets.

$$\text{Total asset turnover} = \frac{\text{Sales}}{\text{Total assets}} = \frac{\$46{,}702}{\$35{,}106} = 1.33\ \textit{times}$$

## Liquidity Ratios

**Liquidity ratios** compare current (short-term) assets to current liabilities to indicate the speed with which a company can turn its assets into cash to meet debts as they fall due. High liquidity ratios may satisfy a creditor's need for safety, but ratios that are too high may indicate that the organization is not using its current assets efficiently. Liquidity ratios are generally best examined in conjunction with asset utilization ratios because high turnover ratios imply that cash is flowing through an organization very quickly—a situation that dramatically reduces the need for the type of reserves measured by liquidity ratios.

**liquidity ratios** ratios that measure the speed with which a company can turn its assets into cash to meet short-term debt

**current ratio** current assets divided by current liabilities

**quick ratio (acid test)** a stringent measure of liquidity that eliminates inventory

**debt utilization ratios** ratios that measure how much debt an organization is using relative to other sources of capital, such as owners' equity

The **current ratio** is calculated by dividing current assets by current liabilities. Loblaw's current ratio indicates that for every $1 of current liabilities, the firm had $1.30 of current assets on hand.

$$\text{Current ratio} = \frac{\text{Current assets}}{\text{Current liabilities}} = \frac{\$11{,}327}{\$8{,}694} = 1.30\ \textit{times}$$

The **quick ratio (acid test)** is a far more stringent measure of liquidity because it eliminates inventory, the least liquid current asset. It measures how well an organization can meet its current obligations without resorting to the sale of its inventory. In 2017, Loblaw had $0.79 invested in current assets (after subtracting inventory) for every $1 of current liabilities, a decrease over previous years.

$$\text{Quick ratio} = \frac{(\text{Current assets} - \text{Inventories})}{\text{Current liabilities}}$$

$$= \frac{(\$11{,}327 - \$4{,}438)}{\$8{,}694} = 0.79\ \textit{times}$$

## Debt Utilization Ratios

**Debt utilization ratios** provide information about how much debt an organization is using relative to other sources of capital, such as owners' equity. Because the use of debt carries an interest charge that must be paid regularly regardless of profitability, debt financing is much riskier than equity. Unforeseen negative events such as recessions affect heavily indebted firms to a far greater extent than those financed exclusively with owners' equity. Because of this and other factors, the managers of most firms tend to keep debt-to-asset levels below 50 percent. However, firms in very stable and/or regulated industries, such as electric utilities, often are able to carry debt ratios well in excess of 50 percent with no ill effects.

The **debt to total assets ratio** indicates how much of the firm is financed by debt and how much by owners' equity. To find the value of Loblaw's total debt, you must add current liabilities to long-term debt and other liabilities.

$$\text{Debt to total assets} = \frac{\text{Debt (Assets} - \text{Equity)}}{\text{Total assets}} = \frac{\$22{,}054}{\$35{,}106} = 62.82\%$$

Thus, for every $1 of Loblaw's total assets, approximately 63 percent is financed with debt. The remaining 37 percent is provided by owners' equity.

The **times interest earned ratio**, operating income divided by interest expense, is a measure of the safety margin a company has with respect to the interest payments it must make to its creditors. A low times interest earned ratio indicates that even a small decrease in earnings may lead the company into financial straits. Loblaw had little interest expense and a lender would not have to worry about receiving interest payments.

$$\text{Times interest earned ratio} = \frac{\text{EBIT}}{\text{Interest}} = \frac{\$2{,}494}{\$525} = 4.75\ \textit{times}$$

## Per Share Data

Investors may use **per share data** to compare the performance of one company with another on an equal, or per share, basis. Generally, the more shares of stock a company issues, the less income is available for each share.

**debt to total assets ratio** a ratio indicating how much of the firm is financed by debt and how much by owners' equity

**times interest earned ratio** operating income divided by interest expense

**per share data** data used by investors to compare the performance of one company with another on an equal, per share basis

**earnings per share** net income or profit divided by the number of stock shares outstanding

**Earnings per share** is calculated by dividing net income or profit by the number of shares outstanding. This ratio is important because yearly changes in earnings per share, in combination with other economy wide factors, determine a company's overall stock price. When earnings go up, so does a company's stock price—and so does the wealth of its shareholders.

$$\text{Earnings per share} = \frac{\text{Net income}}{\text{Number of shares outstanding}}$$

$$= \frac{\$1{,}526}{393.3} = \$3.88$$

Our calculations differ slightly as Loblaw made further adjustments to net earnings for earnings attributable to non-controlling interests. Notice also that Loblaw lists diluted earnings of $3.75 per share in 2017. You can see from the income statement that diluted earnings per share include more shares than the basic calculation; this is because diluted shares include potential shares that could be issued due to the exercise of stock options or the conversion of certain types of debt into common stock. Investors generally pay more attention to diluted earnings per share than basic earnings per share.

**Dividends per share** are paid by the corporation to the shareholders for each share owned. The payment is made from earnings after taxes by the corporation but is taxable income to the shareholder. Thus, dividends result in double taxation: The corporation pays tax once on its earnings, and the shareholder pays tax a second time on the dividend income. The annual dividend for 2017 was $1.13 per share.

**dividends per share** the actual cash received for each share owned

## Industry Analysis

We will use Metro Inc. and industry ratios as comparisons with Loblaw Companies Ltd. While Loblaw's is almost three times larger than Metro in terms of market capitalization, they both have a national presence and, to some extent, compete for the consumer's dollars. Metro is also the nation's third-largest grocery store chain after Sobeys. Table 14.7 indicates that Metro is extremely efficient, well-run, and matches Loblaw in several categories.

In 2017 Loblaw sold its gas station business to Brookfield Business Partners and increased earnings per share from $2.40 to $3.78 or by 57.50 percent. The grocer expected to incur extra costs in 2018 from the minimum wage hike and is looking to cut costs where it can to offset those increases. Loblaw also announced that it would close unprofitable stores and has partnered with Instacart to launch home delivery services. Metro, which has stores in Quebec and Ontario, now offers home delivery service in Quebec, and is looking to expand its online grocery services to Ontario.[9]

Both companies have little accounts receivables relative to the size of their sales, however, Metro has a very high ratio, indicating a lot of cash sales. Both have similar higher inventory turnover ratios and current ratios

**Table 14.7** | Industry Analysis, Year Ending 2017

| | Loblaw | Metro |
|---|---|---|
| Profit margin | 3.27 | 4.08 |
| Return on assets | 4.35 | 6.37 |
| Return on equity | 11.69 | 12.48 |
| Receivables turnover | 10.89 | 30.69 |
| Inventory turnover | 10.52 | 11.46 |
| Total asset turnover | 1.33 | 1.56 |
| Current ratio | 1.30 | 1.41 |
| Quick ratio | 0.79 | 0.52 |
| Debt to total assets | 62.82 | 51.90 |
| Earnings per share | 3.88 | 2.59 |
| Dividends per share | 1.13 | 0.63 |

©Niloo/Shutterstock

When comparing Loblaw and Sobeys, investors generally think Loblaw has better growth prospects and a stronger balance sheet.

that are reasonably solid given their level of profitability. Both companies are in good financial health, and Metro is regaining profitability, after losses due to costs associated with the purchase offer for the Jean Coutu Group. One thing is for sure: the grocery business is more competitive due to large players like Costco, Walmart, and Amazon.

## Importance of Integrity in Accounting

The financial crisis and the recession that followed provided another example of a failure in accounting reporting. Many firms attempted to exploit loopholes and manipulate accounting processes and statements. Banks and other financial institutions often held assets off their

### RESPONDING TO BUSINESS CHALLENGES

#### How Data Analytics Is Changing the World of Accounting

Data analytics is the next frontier in accounting. While data analytics can be simple, today the term is most often used to describe the analysis of large volumes of data and/or high-velocity data, which presents unique computational and data-handling challenges.

Accountants are constantly using data analytics in daily tasks. There are four types of data analytics: descriptive analytics (What's happening?), diagnostic analytics (Why did it happen?), predictive analytics (What's going to happen?), and prescriptive analytics (What should happen?).

Descriptive analytics includes the categorization and classification of information. Accurate reporting with large quantities of data is a hallmark of solid accounting practices. Diagnostic analytics monitors changes in data. Accountants regularly analyze variances and calculate historical performance as an indicator of future performance. Predictive analytics assesses the likelihood of future outcomes. Accountants are instrumental in building forecasts and identifying patterns that shape those forecasts. Prescriptive analytics is used to create tangible actions and crucial business decisions. Accountants use these forecasts to make recommendations for future growth opportunities.

Data analytics offers challenges and opportunities for the accounting field. The challenges include obtaining the skills needed to initiate and support data analytics activities, as well as altering the present audit model to include appropriate audit analytics techniques. Opportunities include a technology-rich audit model and the ability to provide data analytics expertise to clients. With the mastery of data analytics, businesses can generate a higher profit margin and gain meaningful competitive advantages.*

**DISCUSSION QUESTIONS**

1. What types of opportunities are data analytics providing for accountants?
2. Describe the different types of analytics and how they can be utilized in the accounting field.
3. What do you think will happen to accountants who do not master data analytics techniques?

©Vasyl Dolmatov/Getty Images

Data analytics extracts meaning from large volumes of raw data to identify patterns, draw conclusions, and support decision making.

*Norbert Tschakert, Julia Kokina, Stephen Kozlowski, and Miklos Vasarhelyi, "The Next Frontier in Data Analytics," *Journal of Accountancy*, August 1, 2016, https://www.journalofaccountancy.com/issues/2016/aug/data-analyticsskills.html (accessed April 14, 2018); "What Is Data Analytics?" Informatica, (accessed April 14, 2018).

books by manipulating their accounts. If the accountants, the securities regulators, and the bank regulators had been more careful, these types of transactions would have been discovered and corrected.

Strong compliance with accounting principles creates trust among stakeholders. Integrity in accounting is crucial to creating that trust, understanding the financial position of an organization or entity, and making financial decisions that will benefit the organization.

It is most important to remember that integrity in accounting processes requires ethical principles and compliance with both the spirit of the law and professional standards in the accounting profession. Accountants are required to take professional exams and to take accounting ethics courses. Transparency and accuracy in reporting revenue, income, and assets develops trust from investors and other stakeholders.

©JHVEPhoto/Shutterstock

Deloitte must maintain high standards of accounting ethics to secure its reputation for integrity.

## Consider the Following: Can you trust an auditor?

Even large accounting firms like Deloitte can occasionally find themselves in trouble. In 2018, the Public Company Accounting Oversight Board (PCAOB) fined Deloitte Canada $350,000 for failing to maintain its independence during three consecutive audits of Canada-based Banro Corporation, a gold mining company. Under Rule 204, CPAs are required to maintain auditor independence during engagements they undertake or participate in.

The case began in November 2012 when Deloitte South Africa acquired Venmyn Rand, a mining services consultancy business based in South Africa, and changed its name to Venmyn Deloitte. In early 2012, prior to its acquisition, the managing director of Venmyn Rand prepared a technical report on a gold mining operation operated by Banro. When Deloitte South Africa bought Venmyn Rand, the individual became managing director of Venmyn Deloitte.

The 2012 report issued by Venmyn Rand's managing director had valued the Namoya mine at US$366 million. By 2017, after the collapse of global gold prices, the company filed for creditor protection. Because the company was registered for trading on the TSX and the NYSE markets, Deloitte Canada issued audit reports on Banro's financial statements for the 2012–14 fiscal years and filed them with the U.S. Securities and Exchange Commission.

The PCAOB found that Venmyn Deloitte had been an associated entity of Deloitte Canada and is considered part of Deloitte Canada for purposes of the Commissions auditor independence rules. The PCAOB also found that Deloitte Canada's audit independence was impaired because its engagement team used the 2012 Namoya Report as audit evidence to support key management representations and conclusions in its audit reports. In effect, the engagement team audited its own work because the report now belonged to an associated entity of the firm.*

*PCAOB, "PCAOB Fines Deloitte Canada $350,000 for Failing to Maintain Independence Over Three Consecutive Audits," October 16, 2018, https://pcaobus.org/News/Releases/Pages/PCAOB-Fines-Deloitte-Canada-$350,000.aspx, (accessed February 22, 2019); Joe Pickard, "PCAOB fines Deloitte Canada for Lack of Independence," *International Accounting Bulletin*, October 17, 2018, (accessed February 22, 2019); Colin Ellis, "PCAOB fines Deloitte Canada for impaired audit independence," *Canadian Accountant*, October 19, 2018, (accessed February 22, 2019).

## TEAM EXERCISE

You can look at websites such as Yahoo! Finance (http://finance.yahoo.com/), under the company's Key Statistics link, to find many of its financial ratios, such as return on assets and return on equity. Have each member of your team look up a different company, and explain why you think there are differences in the ratio analysis for these two ratios among the selected companies.

# LEARNING OBJECTIVES SUMMARY

**LO 14-1** Define *accounting* and describe the different uses of accounting information.

Accounting is the language businesses and other organizations use to record, measure, and interpret financial transactions. Financial statements are used internally to judge and control an organization's performance and to plan and direct its future activities and measure goal attainment. External organizations such as lenders, governments, customers, suppliers, and the CRA are major consumers of the information generated by the accounting process.

**LO 14-2** Demonstrate the accounting process.

Assets are an organization's economic resources; liabilities are debts the organization owes to others; owners' equity is the difference between the value of an organization's assets and its liabilities. This principle can be expressed as the accounting equation: Assets = Liabilities + Owners' equity. The double-entry bookkeeping system is a system of recording and classifying business transactions in accounts that maintains the balance of the accounting equation. The accounting cycle involves examining source documents, recording transactions in a journal, posting transactions, and preparing financial statements on a continuous basis throughout the life of the organization.

**LO 14-3** Examine the various components of an income statement to evaluate a firm's bottom line.

The income statement indicates a company's profitability over a specific period of time. It shows the bottom line, the total profit (or loss) after all expenses (the costs incurred in the day-to-day operations of the organization) have been deducted from revenue (the total amount of money received from the sale of goods or services and other business activities). The statement of cash flow shows how much cash is moving through the firm and thus adds insight to a firm's bottom line.

**LO 14-4** Interpret a company's balance sheet to determine its current financial position.

The balance sheet, which summarizes the firm's assets, liabilities, and owners' equity since its inception, portrays its financial position as of a particular point in time. Major classifications included in the balance sheet are current assets (assets that can be converted to cash within one calendar year), fixed assets (assets of greater than one year's duration), current liabilities (bills owed by the organization within one calendar year), long-term liabilities (bills due in more than one year), and owners' equity (the net value of the owners' investment).

**LO 14-5** Analyze financial statements, using ratio analysis, to evaluate a company's performance.

Ratio analysis is a series of calculations that brings the complex information from the income statement and balance sheet into sharper focus so that managers, lenders, owners, and other interested parties can measure and compare the organization's productivity, profitability, and financing mix with other similar entities. Ratios may be classified in terms of profitability (dollars of return for each dollar of employed assets), asset utilization (how well the organization uses its assets to generate $1 in sales), liquidity (assessing organizational risk by comparing current assets to current liabilities), debt utilization (how much debt the organization is using relative to other sources of capital), and per share data (comparing the performance of one company with another on an equal basis).

## KEY TERMS

accountants
accounting
accounting cycle
accounting equation
accounts payable
accounts receivable
accrued expenses
annual report
asset utilization ratios
assets
balance sheet
budget
cash flow
cost of goods sold
current assets
current liabilities
current ratio
debt to total assets ratio
debt utilization ratios
depreciation
dividends per share
double-entry bookkeeping
earnings per share
expenses
gross income (or profit)
income statement
inventory turnover
journal
ledger
liabilities
liquidity ratios
managerial accounting
net income
owners' equity
per share data
profit margin
profitability ratios
quick ratio (acid test)
ratio analysis
receivables turnover
return on assets
return on equity
revenue
statement of cash flows
times interest earned ratio
total asset turnover

## So You Want to Be *an Accountant*

Do you like numbers and finance? Are you detail oriented, a perfectionist, and highly accountable for your decisions? If so, accounting may be a good field for you. If you are interested in accounting, there are always job opportunities available no matter the state of the economy. Accounting is one of the most secure job options in business. Of course, becoming an accountant is not easy. You will need at least a bachelor's degree in accounting to get a job, and many positions require additional training. If you are really serious about getting into the accounting field, you will probably want to consider getting your master's in accounting and obtaining your accounting designation. The field of accounting can be complicated, and the extra training provided through a master's program will prove invaluable when you go out looking for a good job. Accounting is a volatile discipline affected by changes in legislative initiatives.

With corporate accounting policies changing constantly and becoming more complex, accountants are needed to help keep a business running smoothly and within the bounds of the law. In fact, the number of jobs in the accounting and auditing field is expected to increase 10 percent between 2016 and 2026. If you go on to get your master's degree in accounting, expect to see a high starting wage. Of course, your earnings could be higher or lower than the average, depending on where you work, your level of experience, the firm, and your particular position

Accountants are needed in the public and the private sectors, in large and small firms, in for-profit and not-for-profit organizations. Accountants in firms are generally in charge of preparing and filing tax forms and financial reports. Public-sector accountants are responsible for checking the veracity of corporate and personal records in order to prepare tax filings. Basically, any organization that has to deal with money and/or taxes in some way or another will be in need of an accountant, either for in-house service or occasional contract work. Requirements for audits are creating more jobs and increased responsibility to maintain internal controls and accounting ethics The fact that accounting rules and tax filings tend to be complex virtually ensures that the demand for accountants will never decrease.

# BUILD YOUR BUSINESS PLAN

## Accounting and Financial Statements

After you determine your initial *reasonable selling price,* you need to estimate your sales forecasts (in terms of units and dollars of sales) for the first year of operation. Remember to be conservative and set forecasts that are modest.

While customers may initially try your business at any time, many businesses have seasonal patterns. A good budgeting/planning system allows managers to anticipate problems, coordinate activities of the business (so that subunits within the organization are all working toward the common goal of the organization), and control operations (know whether spending is "in line").

The first financial statement you need to prepare is the income statement. Beginning with your estimated sales revenue, determine what expenses will be necessary to generate that level of sales revenue. Refer to Table 14.3 to assist you with this process.

The second financial statement you need to create is your balance sheet. Your balance sheet is a snapshot of your financial position in a moment in time. Refer to Table 14.5 to help you list assets, liabilities, and owners' equity.

The last financial statement, the statement of cash flow, is the most important one to a bank. It is a measure of the ability to get and repay the loan from the bank. Be as realistic as possible as you are completing it. Allow yourself enough cash on hand to survive until the point at which the business starts to support itself.

# CASE | Goodwill Industries: Accounting in a Non-profit

Goodwill Industries International Inc. consists of a network of 164 independent, community based organizations located throughout Canada and the United States. The mission of this non-profit is to enhance the lives of individuals, families, and communities "through learning and the power of work." Local Goodwill stores sell donated goods and then donate the proceeds to fund job training programs, placement services, education, and more. Despite their non-profit status, the way Goodwill establishments are run is very similar to for-profit businesses. One of these similarities involves the accounting function.

Like for-profit firms, non-profit organizations like Goodwill must provide detailed information about how they are using the donations that are provided to them. Indeed, fraud can occur just as easily at a non-profit organization as at a for-profit company, making it necessary for non-profits to reassure stakeholders that they are using their funds legitimately. Additionally, donors want to know how much of their donation is going toward activities such as job creation and how much is going toward operational and administrative expenses. It sometimes surprises people that non-profits use part of the funds they receive for operational costs. Yet such a perspective fails to see that non-profits must also pay for electricity, rent, wages, and other services.

"We have revenue and support for the revenue pieces, and then we have direct and indirect expenses for our program services, and then we have G and A, general services. And we have what's called the bottom line, or other people call net profit. We have what's called net change in assets. The concept is pretty much the same as far as accounting," says Jeff McCaw, CFO of Goodwill.

Goodwill creates the equivalent of a balance sheet and income statement. Yet because Goodwill is a non-profit entity, its financials are known as the *statement of financial position* and the *statement of activities*. These financials have some differences compared to financial statements of for-profit companies. For instance, Goodwill's statement of financial position does not include shareholder's equity but, instead, has net assets. The organization's financials are audited, and stakeholders can find the firm's information in the T3010 Registered Charity Information Return through Goodwill's public website (T3010 is the CRA form for non-profits).

Because Goodwill sells goods at its stores, the company must also figure in costs of goods sold. In fact, most of the organization's revenue comes from its store activities. In one year, for Goodwill International, the retail division's sale of donated and contributed goods generated \$3.94 billion. The contracts division, which provides custodial, janitorial, and lawn maintenance service contracts to government agencies, generated \$666 million. Grants from foundations, corporations, individuals, and government accounted for \$185 million. The fact that Goodwill is able to generate much of its own funding through store activities and contracts is important. Many non-profits that rely solely on donated funds find it hard to be sustainable in the long run, particularly during economic downturns.

Remember that even though non-profits are different from for-profit companies, they must still make certain that their financial information is accurate. This requires non-profit accountants to be meticulous and thorough in gathering and analyzing information. Like all accountants, accountants at Goodwill record transactions in journals and then carefully review the information before it is recorded in the general ledger. The organization uses trial balances to ensure that everything balances out, as well as advanced software to record transactions, reconcile any discrepancies, and provide an idea of how much cash the organization has on hand.

Finally, Goodwill uses ratio analysis to determine the financial health of the company. For instance, the common ratio allows Goodwill to determine how much revenue it brings in for every dollar it spends on costs. The organization also uses ratio analysis to compare its results to similar organizations. It is important for Goodwill to identify the best performers in its field so that it can generate ideas and even form partnerships with other organizations. By using accounting to identify how best to use its resources, Goodwill is advancing its mission of helping others.[10]

## DISCUSSION QUESTIONS

1. What are some similarities between the type of accounting performed at Goodwill compared to accounting at for-profit companies?
2. What are some differences between the type of accounting performed at Goodwill compared to accounting at for-profit companies?
3. How can Goodwill use ratio analysis to improve its operations?

CHAPTER 15

# Money and the Financial System

©panuwat phimpha/Shutterstock

## LEARNING OBJECTIVES

**After reading this chapter, you will be able to:**

LO 15-1 Define *money*, its functions, and its characteristics.

LO 15-2 Describe various types of money.

LO 15-3 Specify how the Bank of Canada manages the money supply and regulates the Canadian banking system.

LO 15-4 Compare and contrast chartered banks, trust companies, and credit unions/*caisses populaires*.

LO 15-5 Distinguish among non-banking institutions such as insurance companies, pension funds, mutual funds, and finance companies.

LO 15-6 Investigate the challenges ahead for the banking industry.

## ENTER THE WORLD OF BUSINESS

### How Mobile Banking Is Breaking the Bank

Mobile banking has created a world of convenience and ease of use for consumers. Basic tasks like depositing checks and monitoring accounts can easily be done whenever and wherever the customer pleases. However, this increase in convenience can come at a price.

Transferring tasks to mobile devices escalates risks of cyberattacks and identity fraud. Most experts agree that mobile banking is generally secure and that many security issues do not stem from the technology itself, but because consumers do not understand how to properly use it.

Over the past decade, banks in Canada have spent $84.5 billion on technology, which includes technology dedicated to security measures. While banks have extensive security systems in place to protect customers from fraud, consumers have a role to play in protecting themselves, as well. Consumers fail to consider that their phones work similarly to their computers. Antivirus software should be installed and regular security updates exercised. Incorrect perceptions around the safety of banking apps and Wi-Fi usage increase consumer vulnerability. According to a survey of senior IT executives, around 47 percent say their organizations are adopting mobile applications without assessing associated risks.

While there will always be some risk with regard to cyberspace, there are ways to minimize the potential for information theft. Consumers should educate themselves in how this technology works and its vulnerabilities. Just like a laptop, mobile phones offer security software that can monitor for attacks. Making sure all mobile banking and other apps are up-to-date is crucial. Older and outdated apps are more vulnerable. Consumers should closely monitor all activity and report anything suspicious. Doing so will allow them to reap the rewards of online banking without making themselves vulnerable to cyberattacks.[1]

#### DISCUSSION QUESTIONS

1. What are some of the benefits of mobile banking? The risks?
2. Why do you think consumers fail to understand the risk factors of using online banking apps without taking appropriate security precautions?
3. What are some ways consumers can significantly reduce the risk of cyberattacks when engaging in mobile banking activities?

## Introduction

From Bay Street to Wall Street, both overseas and at home, money is the one tool used to measure personal and business income and wealth. **Finance** is the study of how money is managed by individuals, companies, and governments. This chapter introduces you to the role of money and the financial system in the economy. Of course, if you have a chequing account, automobile insurance, a student loan, or a credit card, you already have personal experience with some key players in the financial world.

**finance** the study of how money is managed by individuals, companies, and governments

We begin our discussion with a definition of money and then explore some of the many forms money may take. Next, we examine the roles of the Bank of Canada and other major institutions in the financial system. Finally, we explore the future of the finance industry and some of the changes likely to occur over the course of the next several years.

# Money in the Financial System

**LO 15-1** Define *money*, its functions, and its characteristics.

Strictly defined, **money**, or *currency*, is anything generally accepted in exchange for goods and services. Materials as diverse as salt, cattle, fish, rocks, shells, and cloth, as well as precious metals such as gold, silver, and copper, have long been used by various cultures as money. Most of these materials were limited-supply commodities that had their own value to society (for example, salt can be used as a preservative or as jewellery). The supply of these commodities therefore determined the supply of "money" in that society.

**money** anything generally accepted in exchange for goods and services

The next step was the development of "IOUs," or slips of paper that could be exchanged for a specified supply of the underlying commodity. "Gold" notes, for instance, could be exchanged for gold, and the money supply was tied to the amount of gold available. While paper money was first issued in Canada in 1817 (and even earlier in Europe), the concept of *fiat money*—a paper money not readily convertible to a precious metal such as gold—did not gain full acceptance until the Great Depression in the 1930s. Canada abandoned its gold-backed currency standard largely in response to the Great Depression and converted to a fiduciary, or fiat, monetary system. In Canada, paper money is really a government "note" or promise, worth the value specified on the note.

## Functions of Money

No matter what a particular society uses for money, its primary purpose is to enable a person or organization to transform a desire into an action. These desires may be for entertainment actions, such as party expenses; operating actions, such as paying for rent, utilities, or employees; investing actions, such as buying property or equipment; or financing actions, such as starting or growing a business. Money serves three important functions: as a medium of exchange, a measure of value, and a store of value.

**Medium of Exchange.** Before fiat money, the trade of goods and services was accomplished through *bartering*—trading one good or service for another of similar value. As any school-age child knows, bartering can become quite inefficient—particularly in the case of complex, three-party transactions involving peanut butter sandwiches, baseball cards, and hair barrettes. There had to be a simpler way, and that was to decide on a single item—money—that could be freely converted to any other good upon agreement between parties.

©DanLinPhotography/Getty Images

For centuries, people on the Micronesian island of Yap have used giant round stones, like the ones shown here, for currency. The stones aren't moved, but their ownership can change.

"No matter what a particular society uses for money, its primary purpose is to enable a person or organization to transform a desire into an action."

**Measure of Value.** As a measure of value, money serves as a common standard for the value of goods and services. For example, $2 will buy a dozen large eggs and $25,000 will buy a nice car in Canada. In Japan, where the currency is known as the yen, these same transactions would cost about 210 yen and 2.75 million yen, respectively. Money, then, is a common denominator that allows people to compare the different goods and services that can be consumed on a particular income level. While a star athlete and a minimum-wage earner are paid vastly different wages, each uses money as a measure of the value of yearly earnings and purchases.

**Store of Value.** As a store of value, money serves as a way to accumulate wealth (buying power) until it is needed. For example, a person making $500 per week who wants to buy a $500 computer could save $50 per week for each of the next ten weeks. Unfortunately, the value of stored money is directly dependent on the health of the economy. If, due to rapid inflation, all prices double in one year, then the purchasing power value of the money "stuffed in the mattress" would fall by half. On the other hand, deflation occurs when prices of goods fall.

Deflation might seem like a good thing for consumers, but in many ways it can be just as problematic as inflation. Periods of major deflation often lead to decreases in wages and increases in debt burdens.[2] Deflation also tends to be an indicator of problems in the economy. Over the past 25 years, we have seen deflation in Japan, and Europe has continued to struggle with deflation off and on since the financial crisis. Given a choice, central banks like the Bank of Canada would rather have a small amount of inflation than deflation.

## Characteristics of Money

To be used as a medium of exchange, money must be acceptable, divisible, portable, stable in value, durable, and difficult to counterfeit.

**Acceptable.** To be effective, money must be readily acceptable for the purchase of goods and services and for the settlement of debts. Acceptability is probably the most important characteristic of money: If people do not trust the value of money, businesses will not accept it as a payment for goods and services, and consumers will have to find some other means of paying for their purchases.

**Divisible.** Given the widespread use of quarters, dimes, and nickels in Canada, it is no surprise that the principle of divisibility is an important one. With barter, the lack of divisibility often makes otherwise preferable trades impossible, as would be an attempt to trade a steer for a loaf of bread. For money to serve effectively as a measure of value, all items must be valued in terms of comparable units—dimes for a piece of bubble gum, loonies for laundry machines, and dollars (or dollars and coins) for everything else.

**Portable.** Clearly, for money to function as a medium of exchange, it must be easily moved from one location to the next. Large coloured rocks could be used as money, but you couldn't carry them around in your wallet. Paper currency and metal coins, on the other hand, are capable of transferring vast purchasing power into small, easily carried (and hidden!) bundles.

**Stable.** Money must be stable and maintain its declared face value. A $10 bill should purchase the same amount of goods or services from one day to the next. The principle of stability allows people who wish to postpone purchases and save their money to do so without fear that it will decline in value. As mentioned earlier, money declines in value during periods of inflation, when economic conditions cause prices to rise. Thus, the same amount of money buys fewer and fewer goods and services. In some countries, particularly in South America, people spend their money as fast as they can in order to keep it from losing any more of its value. Instability destroys confidence in a nation's money and its ability to store value and serve as an effective medium of exchange. Ultimately, people faced with spiralling price increases avoid the increasingly worthless paper money at all costs, storing all of their savings in the form of real assets such as gold and land.

**Durable.** Money must be durable. The crisp new dollar bills you trade for products at the mall will make their way all around town for about 20 months before being replaced (see Table 15.1). Were the value of an old, faded bill to fall in line with the deterioration of its appearance, the principles of stability and universal acceptability would fail (but, no doubt, fewer bills would pass through the washer!). Although metal coins, due to their much longer useful life, would appear to be an ideal form of money, paper currency is far more portable than metal because of its light weight. Today, coins are used primarily to provide divisibility.

**Table 15.1** | The Life Expectancy of Paper Currency

| Denomination of Bill | Life Expectancy (Years) |
|---|---|
| $ 5 | 1–2 |
| $ 10 | 1–2 |
| $ 20 | 2–4 |
| $100 | 7–9 |

**Difficult to Counterfeit.** Finally, to remain stable and enjoy universal acceptance, it almost goes without saying that money must be very difficult to counterfeit—that is, to duplicate illegally. Every country takes steps to make counterfeiting difficult. Most use multicoloured money, and many use specially watermarked papers that are virtually impossible to duplicate. In spite of this, it is becoming increasingly easy for counterfeiters to print money.[3] This illegal printing of money is fuelled by hundreds of people who often circulate only small amounts of counterfeit bills. To thwart the problem of counterfeiting, the Bank of Canada issued the Polymer series, which uses innovative security features that can be seen in transparent areas on both sides of the notes.[4] Many countries are discontinuing large-denominated bills that are used in illegal trade such as drugs or terrorism.

**DID YOU KNOW?**

There were approximately 8000 counterfeit notes detected in each of the first three quarters of 2018, with $100 and $20 denominations being the most common.[5]

©Vstock LLC/Getty Images

The Bank of Canada redesigns currency in order to stay ahead of counterfeiters and protect the public.

## Consider the Following: Will the yuan become the next global currency?

As the world's second-largest economy, China is increasing efforts to make the yuan a global currency. China hopes that the yuan will achieve the status of the dollar, euro, and yen as an international currency for trade and investment. In order to encourage the yuan's internationalization, China allows other countries, including the United States, to trade in the yuan (previously such trade was restricted to the Chinese mainland). An increase in yuan trading and investment should help to buffer China against the dollar's decrease in value. Currently, 62 percent of the world's foreign reserves consist of the U.S. dollar and are used to help stabilize the global economy during economic unrest. A massive decrease in the dollar's value could, therefore, disrupt the world economy.

Making the yuan a global currency could be beneficial for businesses, as well. For example, Caterpillar and McDonald's finance China-based projects using the yuan. According to Caterpillar, this is more efficient and less expensive than having to convert U.S. dollars to the yuan first. Despite these possibilities, China has many obstacles to overcome before the yuan can achieve status as a global currency. Demand among foreign businesses for trading and investing in the yuan is not high, and the yuan must be convertible to be used as a major currency in the foreign reserves.

*Convertibility* means that currency must be easily converted into other currencies, which requires the currency to be valued at the current market rate. China is reluctant to do this, and prefers to keep its currency rates lower than market value in order to maintain its competitive advantage in international trade. China has a preference for "managed convertibility" and imposes discretionary capital controls on inflows and outflows of currency. Currently, the yuan's internationalization is waiting for its liberalization.*

*"Yuan Will Be Fully Convertible by 2015, Chinese Officials Tell EU Chamber," *Bloomberg Businessweek*, September 8, 2011, www.bloomberg.com/news/2011-09-08/yuan-to-be-fully-convertible-by-2015-eu-chamber.html (accessed November 1, 2011); Kersi Jilla, "Global Common Currency—Part 1—Understanding Convertible Currency," Forex Metrics Blog, www.forexmetrics.com/blog/?p=1114 (accessed November 1, 2011); "Foreign Reserve," *Business Dictionary*, www.businessdictionary.com/definition/foreign-reserve.html (accessed November 1, 2011); IMF, COFER data, http://data.imf.org/?sk=E6A5F467-C14B-4AA8-9F6D-5A09EC4E62A4, (accessed September 6, 2019); David Lubin, "Waiting and Waiting for the Global Renminbi," Asia Global Online, February 4, 2019, (accessed September 6, 2019).

# Types of Money

**LO 15-2** Describe various types of money.

While paper money and coins are the most visible types of money, the combined value of all of the printed bills and all of the minted coins is actually rather insignificant when compared with the value of money kept in chequing accounts, savings accounts, and other monetary forms.

You probably have a **chequing account** (also called a *demand deposit*), money stored in an account at a bank or other financial institution that can be withdrawn without advance notice. One way to withdraw funds from your account is by writing a *cheque*, a written order to a bank to pay the indicated individual or business the amount specified on the cheque from money already on deposit. As legal instruments, cheques serve as a substitute for currency and coins, and are preferred for some transactions due to their lower risk of loss.

**chequing account** money stored in an account at a bank or other financial institution that can be withdrawn without advance notice; also called a *demand deposit*

**savings accounts** accounts with funds that usually cannot be withdrawn without advance notice; also known as *time deposits*

**Savings accounts** (also known as *time deposits*) are accounts with funds that usually cannot be withdrawn without advance notice and/or have limits on the number of withdrawals per period. While seldom enforced, the "fine print" governing most savings accounts prohibits withdrawals without two or three days' notice. Savings accounts are not generally used for transactions, but their funds can be moved to a chequing account or turned into cash. There are several types of savings accounts, with different features available for different monthly fee levels or specific minimum account balances. Most savings accounts earn interest. The interest rate paid on such accounts varies with the interest rates available in the economy but is typically quite low.

**Money market funds** are similar to interest-bearing chequing accounts, but with more restrictions. Generally, in exchange for slightly higher interest rates, the owner of a money market account can write only a limited number of cheques each month, and there may be a restriction on the minimum amount of each cheque.

**Certificates of deposit (CDs)** are savings accounts that guarantee a depositor a set interest rate over a specified interval of time as long as the funds are not withdrawn

**money market funds** accounts that offer higher interest rates than standard bank rates but with greater restrictions

**certificates of deposit (CDs)** savings accounts that guarantee a depositor a set interest rate over a specified interval as long as the funds are not withdrawn before the end of the period—six months or one year, for example

before the end of the interval—six months, one year, or five years, for example. Money may be withdrawn from these accounts prematurely only after paying a substantial penalty. In general, the longer the term of the CD, the higher the interest rate it earns. As with all interest rates, the rate offered and fixed at the time the account is opened fluctuates according to economic conditions. Financial institutions issue CDs under a variety of names, for example, Guaranteed Investment Certificates (GICs).

**Credit cards** allow you to promise to pay at a later date by using pre-approved lines of credit granted by a bank or finance company. They are popular substitutes for cash payments because of their convenience, easy access to credit, and acceptance by merchants around the world. The institution that issues the credit card guarantees payment of a credit charge to merchants and assumes responsibility for collecting the money from the cardholders. Card issuers charge a transaction fee to the merchants for performing the credit check, guaranteeing the payment, and collecting the payment. Cardholders are required to make instalment payments and the card has a maximum balance. There is a minimum monthly payment with interest charged on the remaining balance. Some people pay off their credit cards monthly, while others make monthly payments. Charges for unpaid balances can run 18 percent or higher at an annual rate, making credit card debt one of the most expensive ways to borrow money.

Besides the major credit card companies, many stores—Hudson's Bay, Canadian Tire, and others—have their own branded or co-branded credit cards. They use credit rating agencies to check the credit of the cardholders and they generally make money on the finance charges. Unlike the major credit cards discussed, these "private label" cards are generally accepted only at stores associated with the issuing company. **Reward cards** are credit cards that carry a benefit to the user. For example, gas stations such as Esso and Petro-Canada have branded credit cards so that when you use the card you can get gas rewards. Others—such as Air Canada and WestJet—reward you with miles that you can use for flights. And there are cash-back credit cards that give you one percent or more cash back on everything you spend.

**credit cards** means of access to preapproved lines of credit granted by a bank or finance company

**reward cards** credit cards made available by stores that carry a benefit to the user

Consumers with credit cards from banks are protected by *Bank Act* regulations and a Code of Conduct which has been adopted by all payment card networks. These regulations are important to all companies and cardholders. The regulations enhance consumers' access to clear information about key details, such as interest rates, fees, and penalty charges. They also strengthen consumers' rights by limiting certain business practices of financial institutions.[6] This Code of Conduct is important to all companies and cardholders.

©Piotr Adamowicz/123RF

Credit cards have many advantages, including allowing people to buy expensive items and pay them off a little at a time. However, this can easily lead an individual to incur spiralling credit card debt that is hard to pay off.

Research indicates that credit card debt makes up five per cent of total household debt in Canada and credit card debt has remained stable over the past years.[7]

A **debit card** looks like a credit card but works like a cheque. The use of a debit card results in a direct, immediate, electronic payment from the cardholder's account to a merchant or other party. While they are convenient to carry and profitable for banks, they lack credit features, offer no purchase grace period, and provide no hard paper trail. Consumers like debit cards because of the ease of getting cash from an increasing number of ABMs. Financial institutions also want consumers to use debit cards because they reduce the number of teller transactions and cheque processing costs.

**debit card** a card that looks like a credit card but works like a cheque; using it results in a direct, immediate, electronic payment from the cardholder's bank account to a merchant or third party

"Two major credit cards—MasterCard and Visa—represent the vast majority of credit cards held in Canada."

A new type of money called cryptocurrency has become popular over the last several years with technology-oriented people. Bitcoin is the most well known, but it has a fluctuating price, which makes it less desirable than fiat money like dollars, yen, and euros that are backed by governments.

**Credit Card Fraud.** Computer hackers have managed to steal credit card information and either use the information for Internet purchases or actually make a card exactly the same as the stolen card. Losses on credit card theft run into the billions worldwide, but Canadian consumers are usually not liable for the credit or debit card losses, provided they took reasonable care to keep their account and PIN safe.

# The Canadian Financial System

**LO 15-3** Specify how the Bank of Canada manages the money supply and regulates the Canadian banking system.

The Canadian financial system fuels our economy by storing money, fostering investment opportunities, and making loans for new businesses and business expansion as well as for homes, cars, and post-secondary educations. This amazingly complex system includes banking institutions, non-banking financial institutions such as finance companies, and systems that provide for the electronic transfer of funds throughout the world. Over the past 20 years, the rate at which money turns over, or changes hands, has increased exponentially. The combination of this increased turnover rate and increasing interactions with people and organizations from other countries has created a complex money system. First, we need to meet the guardian of this complex system.

> "The Bank of Canada establishes and enforces banking rules that affect monetary policy and the overall level of the competition between different banks."

## The Bank of Canada

The nation's central bank is the **Bank of Canada** (the Bank), a crown corporation of the federal government founded in 1934 "to promote the economic and financial welfare of Canada." The Bank tries to create a positive economic environment capable of sustaining low inflation, high levels of employment, and long-term economic growth. To this end, the Bank has four major responsibilities: (1) to conduct monetary policy; (2) to issue Canada's bank notes and be responsible for their design and security, distribution, and replacement; (3) to promote safe, sound, and efficient financial systems; and (4) to provide high-quality, effective, and efficient funds-management services for the federal government, the Bank, and other clients.

**Bank of Canada** an independent agency of the federal government established in 1934 to regulate the nation's banking and financial industry

**monetary policy** means by which the Bank of Canada controls the amount of money available in the economy

**Monetary Policy.** The Bank controls the amount of money available in the economy through **monetary policy**. Without this intervention, the supply of and demand for money might not balance. This could result in either rapid price increases (inflation), because of rapid growth in money supply, or economic recession and falling prices (deflation), because of too little growth in the money supply. In very rare cases (such as the depression of the 1930s), Canada has suffered from deflation, where the actual purchasing power of the dollar increased as prices declined.

To effectively control the supply of money in the economy, the Bank must have a good idea of how much money is in circulation at any given time. Using several different measures of the money supply, the Bank establishes specific growth targets that, presumably, ensure a close balance between money supply and money demand. The Bank carries out monetary policy by influencing short-term interest rates. It does this by raising and lowering the target for the overnight rate. (The *overnight rate* is the interest rate at which major financial institutions, banks, credit unions, and similar credit-granting organizations borrow and lend one-day funds among themselves. This is different from the *bank rate*, which is the midpoint of the range for the overnight rate.) There is generally a lag of 6 to 18 months before the effect of these changes shows up in economic activity. As with other central banks, notably the European Central Bank and the Federal Reserve, the Bank of Canada has other tools at its disposal to fine-tune money growth, including open market operations, desired reserves, the bank (discount) rate, and credit controls (see Table 15.2).

**Open market operations** refer to decisions to buy or sell Treasury bills (short-term debt issued by a government, also called T-bills) and other investments in the open market.

**open market operations** decisions to buy or sell Treasury bills (short-term debt issued by the government) and other investments in the open market

**Table 15.2** | Tools for Regulating the Money Supply

| Activity | Effect on the Money Supply and the Economy |
|---|---|
| Buy government securities | The money supply increases; economic activity increases. |
| Sell government securities | The money supply decreases; economic activity slows down. |
| Raise bank rate | Interest rates increase; the money supply decreases; economic activity slows down. |
| Lower bank rate | Interest rates decrease; the money supply increases; economic activity increases. |
| Increase reserves | Banks make fewer loans; the money supply declines; economic activity slows down. |
| Decrease reserves | Banks make more loans; the money supply increases; economic activity increases. |
| Relax credit controls | More people are encouraged to make major purchases, increasing economic activity. |
| Restrict credit controls | People are discouraged from making major purchases, decreasing economic activity. |

The actual purchase or sale of the investments is performed by the Bank. This monetary tool, the most commonly employed of all operations, is performed almost daily in an effort to control the money supply.

When the Bank buys securities, it writes a cheque on its own account to the seller of the investments. When the seller of the investments (usually a large bank) deposits the cheque, the Bank transfers the balance from its account into the seller's account, thus increasing the supply of money in the economy and, hopefully, fuelling economic growth. The opposite occurs when the Bank sells investments. The buyer writes a cheque to the Bank, and when the funds are transferred out of the purchaser's account, the amount of money in circulation falls, slowing economic growth to a desired level.

The second major monetary policy tool is the requirement of **desired reserves**, the percentage of deposits that banking institutions must hold in reserve ("in the vault," as it were). Funds so held are not available for lending to businesses and consumers. For example, a bank holding $10 million in deposits with a 10 percent desired reserves requirement must have reserves of $1 million. If the Bank were to withdraw liquidity to, say, 5 percent, the financial institution would need to keep only $500,000 in reserves. It could then lend to customers the $500,000 difference between the old reserve level and the new lower reserve level, thus increasing the supply of money. Because reserves have such a powerful effect on the money supply, the Bank uses market operations to implement monetary policy by changing reserves in the banking system.

The third monetary policy tool, the **bank rate**, is the rate of interest the Bank charges to loan money to any banking institution to meet reserve requirements. The Bank is the lender of last resort for these banks. When a bank borrows from the Bank of Canada, the interest rates charged there are often higher than those charged on loans of comparable risk elsewhere in the economy. This added interest expense, when it exists, serves to discourage banking institutions from borrowing unnecessarily from the Bank. When the Bank wants to expand the money supply, it lowers the bank rate to encourage borrowing. Conversely, when the Bank wants to decrease the money supply, it raises the bank rate. Not surprisingly, economists watch changes in this sensitive interest rate as an indicator of the Bank's monetary policy.

**desired reserves** the percentage of deposits that banking institutions hold in reserve

**bank rate** the rate of interest the Bank of Canada charges to loan money to any banking institution to meet reserve requirements

**credit controls** the authority to establish and enforce credit rules for financial institutions and some private investors

The final tool in the Bank's arsenal of weapons is **credit controls**—the authority to establish and enforce credit rules for financial institutions and some private investors. For example, the Bank can determine how large a down payment individuals and businesses must make on credit purchases of expensive items such as automobiles, and how much time they have to finish paying for the purchases. By raising and lowering minimum down payment amounts and payment periods, the Bank can stimulate or discourage credit purchases of "big ticket" items. The Bank also has the authority to set the minimum down payment investors must use for the credit purchases of stock. Buying stock with credit—buying on margin—is a popular investment strategy among individual speculators. By altering the margin requirement (commonly set at 50 percent of the price of the purchased stocks), the Bank can effectively control the total amount of credit borrowing in the stock market.

©Sml/Dreamstime.com

One of the roles of the Bank of Canada is to use its policies to keep money flowing. Money is the lifeblood of the economy. If banks become too protective of their funds and stop lending money, the economy can grind to a halt.

**Currency.** Another responsibility of the Bank is for Canada's bank notes. The Bank is the country's sole bank note–issuing authority and is responsible for designing, producing, and distributing Canada's bank notes. The Bank must supply financial institutions with enough bank notes to satisfy public demand. Financial institutions get bank notes through the country's Bank Note Distribution System, and return notes that are considered unfit for further circulation to the Bank. These notes are verified on high-speed, note-processing equipment and then shredded.[8]

**The Financial System.** The Bank of Canada works to promote safe, sound, and efficient financial systems. A stable financial system is essential to the health of Canada's economy. The Bank works with other agencies and market participants to promote the safe and efficient operation of the system's key elements. The Bank provides liquidity to the system, gives policy advice to the federal government on the design and development of the financial system, oversees major clearing and settlement systems, provides banking services to these systems and their participants, and collaborates with other domestic and international bodies involved in financial-stability issues.[9]

**Funds Management.** The Bank acts as the fiscal agent for the Government of Canada. As a government banker and treasury manager, the Bank manages the accounts of the Receiver General, through which almost all money collected and spent by the government flows. The Bank ensures that these accounts have enough cash to meet daily requirements and invests any surpluses in term deposits. The Bank also manages the government's foreign exchange reserves. These reserves promote stability in the Canadian-dollar foreign exchange market. The Bank also provides policy advice to the government on the efficient management of the government debt and sells securities at auction to financial market distributors and dealers. The main goal of the Bank's debt-management activities is to help provide stable and low-cost funding to the government.[10]

©Torontonian/Alamy Stock Photo

The Royal Bank of Canada is a Canadian multinational financial services company and the largest bank in Canada by market capitalization.

"Banks are quite diversified and offer a number of services."

# Banking Institutions

**LO 15-4** Compare and contrast chartered banks, trust companies, and credit unions/*caisses populaires*.

Banking institutions accept money deposits from and make loans to individual consumers and businesses. Some of the most important banking institutions include chartered banks, trust companies, and credit unions/*caisses populaires*. Historically, these have all been separate institutions. However, new hybrid forms of banking institutions that perform two or more of these functions have emerged over the last two decades. The following banking institutions all have one thing in common: they are businesses whose objective is to earn money by managing, safeguarding, and lending money to others. Their sales revenues come from the fees and interest that they charge for providing these financial services.

## RESPONDING TO BUSINESS CHALLENGES

### Banking in Indigenous Communities

From complex energy-sector investments to infrastructure projects and businesses, the increased capital flowing into Canada's Indigenous communities represents an emerging market for the country's big banks. Despite this, the majority of First Nations communities do not have a bank within their boundaries, and the lack of on-reserve branches impacts the ability of Indigenous entrepreneurs to seize opportunities. As of 2018, 54 banks and credit union branches were located on reserves. In addition to the major banks there are Indigenous-owned banking institutions, including the Peace Hills Trust and the First Nations Bank of Canada, that offer business banking services.

Banks have taken different approaches to better engage Indigenous communities by creating unique programs tailored to the needs and preferences of Indigenous individuals. For example, in 1978, Scotiabank established the Department of Indian and Inuit Financial Services. By 2005, the bank had four on-reserve branches and a network of twenty-two Aboriginal Banking Centres. More recently, in addition to targeted services for entrepreneurs, the Royal Bank of Canada developed a program called the Royal Eagles with the goal of acting as a resource for Aboriginal communities. The Bank of Montreal and the Canadian Imperial Bank of Commerce, have established dedicated banking services to make development capital more accessible.*

*The Conference Board of Canada–Northern and Aboriginal Policy," Opportunities to improve the financial ecosystem for Aboriginal entrepreneurs and SMEs in Canada," February 14, 2017, https://nacca.ca/wp-content/uploads/2017/04/ProjectSummary_NACCA-BDC_Feb14_2017.pdf, (accessed March 10, 2019); Armina Ligaya, "Indigenous Banking A Bright Spot For Canada's Big Banks," Huffington Post, February 14, 2018, https://www.huffingtonpost.ca/2019/02/14/indigenous-banking-canada_a_23669779/, (accessed March 10, 2019); Barbara Shecter, "An 'emerging market' at home: Canada's banks making a big push into aboriginal communities," *Financial Post*, January 10, 2015, https://business.financialpost.com/news/fp-street/an-emerging-market-at-home-how-canadian-banks-are-making-a-big-push-into-aboriginal-banking, (accessed March 10, 2019); Scotiabank, "Diversity and Inclusion Journey", https://www.scotiabank.com/ca/common/pdf/about_scotia/Diversity_and_inclusion_timeline_accessible_final_v1.pdf, (accessed September 26, 2019).

**Chartered Banks.** The largest and oldest of all financial institutions are **chartered banks**, which perform a variety of financial services. They rely mainly on chequing and savings accounts as their major source of funds and use a portion of these deposits to make loans to businesses and individuals. Because it is unlikely that all the depositors of any one bank will want to withdraw all of their funds at the same time, a bank can safely loan out a large percentage of its deposits.

**chartered banks** the largest and oldest of all financial institutions, relying mainly on chequing and savings accounts as sources of funds for loans to businesses and individuals

Today, banks are quite diversified and offer a number of services. Chartered banks make loans for virtually any conceivable legal purpose, from vacations to cars, from homes to post-secondary educations. Banks offer *home equity loans*, by which home owners can borrow against the appraised value of their already purchased homes. Banks also issue Visa and MasterCard credit cards and offer CDs and trusts (legal entities set up to hold and manage assets for a beneficiary). Many banks rent safe-deposit boxes in bank vaults to customers who want to store jewellery, legal documents, artwork, and other valuables. The banking industry in Canada includes domestic banks, foreign bank subsidiaries, and foreign bank branches. The Office of the Superintendent of Financial Institutions (OSFI), along with the Bank of Canada and the Canada Deposit Insurance Corporation (CDIC), regulate and supervise federally registered financial institutions.[11] Table 15.3 gives an overview of the Canadian financial system.

**Trust Companies.** **Trust companies** act as fiduciaries or corporate trustees and operate under either provincial or federal legislation and conduct the same activities as a bank. Like a bank, they operate through a network of branches. However, because of its fiduciary role, a trust company can administer estates, trusts, pension plans, and agency contracts, which banks cannot do.[12] The *Bank Act* has allowed regulated federal financial institutions to own trust companies. As a result, and with the

**trust companies** corporations that act as a trustee and usually also provide banking services

## GOING GREEN

### Is the World Bank Serious About Sustainability?

The World Bank raises money through donations, bond sales, and shareholder support. This money is then used to provide loans and other financial assistance to developing countries. The loans fund a variety of projects, including education, infrastructure, and public administration. Realizing that funding certain projects could negatively affect the environment, the World Bank adopted policies to assess the sustainability of proposed projects.

Despite these policies, environmental groups have accused the World Bank of funding projects that harm the environment. One project, the Sardar Sarovar Dam on India's River Narmada, was criticized for causing environmental degradation. Yet advocates for the dam argue that it provides irrigation and drinking water. The World Bank must juggle both the human and environmental impacts when determining which projects to fund.

As the importance of sustainability grows, the World Bank has taken steps to curb climate change and support renewable energy initiatives. While projects with "clean" and "resilient" components, such as climate change mitigation and climate change adaptation, have risen, support has declined in some areas, such as biodiversity conservation and water resource management.

In August 2016, the World Bank adopted a new set of environment and social policies called the Environmental and Social Framework (ESF). As of October 1, 2018, the ESF applies to all new World Bank investment project financing. Whether these actions will lead to significant change or whether they are merely window-dressing to reduce criticism remains to be seen.*

#### DISCUSSION QUESTIONS

1. Describe what the World Bank does. Why is it important?
2. Why is sustainability becoming a major issue for the World Bank?
3. Do you feel that the World Bank should make sustainability a priority?

*"C40 and World Bank Form Groundbreaking Climate Change Action Partnership," The World Bank, June 1, 2011, http://web.worldbank.org/WBSITE/EXTERNAL/TOPICS/EXTSDNET/0,,pagePK:64885161~contentMDK:22928707~piPK:5929285~theSitePK:5929282,00.html (accessed November 9, 2011); World Bank Confronts Sustainability Criticism," *Business Ethics*, March 19, 2011, http://business-ethics.com/2011/03/19/1900-world-bank-confronts-sustainability-criticism/ (accessed November 9, 2011); "Benefits," Support Narmadadam.org, www.supportnarmadadam.org/sardar-sarovar-benefits.htm (accessed November 9, 2011); "About Us," The World Bank, http://web.worldbank.org/WBSITE/EXTERNAL/EXTABOUTUS/0,,pagePK:50004410~piPK:36602~theSitePK:29708,00.html (accessed November 9, 2011); "Renewables Almost a Quarter of World Bank's Energy Lending," The World Bank, http://climatechange.worldbank.org/content/world-bank-renewable-energy-lending-rises (accessed November 9, 2011).

**Table 15.3** | Overview of the Canadian Financial Services Sector

| Sector | Number of Active Firms |
|---|---|
| Banks | 88 |
| Trust companies | 44 |
| Loan companies | 18 |
| Credit unions/*caisses populaires* (outside Quebec) | 252 |
| Life and health insurance companies | 68 |
| Property and casualty insurance companies | 152 |
| Mutual fund companies | 106 |
| Investment dealers | 120 |
| Finance and leasing companies | 200 |

acquisition of Canada Trust by the Toronto Dominion Bank, trust companies are a small market segment.

**Credit Unions and *Caisses Populaires*.** A **credit union/*caisse populaire*** is a co-operative financial institution that is owned and controlled by its depositors, who often have a common employer, profession, trade group, or religion. Because the credit union is tied to a common organization, the credit unions are operated democratically and owned by their depositors as members. Members are allowed to vote for directors and share in the credit union's profits in the form of higher interest rates on accounts and/or lower loan rates.

**credit union/*caisse populaire*** a financial institution owned and controlled by its depositors, who usually have a common employer, profession, trade group, or religion

While credit unions were originally created to provide depositors with a short-term source of funds for low-interest consumer loans for items such as cars, home appliances, vacations, and post-secondary education, today they offer a wide range of financial services. They are subject to provincial regulation and are usually small and locally oriented. This sector is almost exclusively regulated at the provincial level in Canada. However, the Credit Union Central of Canada is chartered and regulated by the federal government.[13]

**Insurance for Banking Institutions.** The **Canada Deposit Insurance Corporation (CDIC)**, a federal Crown corporation that insures individual bank accounts, was established in 1967 and insures deposits in banks and trust and loan companies against loss in the event of member failure. It insures eligible deposits up to $100,000 per depositor in each member institution, which must pay premiums to cover CDIC's insurance obligations.

**Canada Deposit Insurance Corporation (CDIC)** a federal Crown corporation that insures bank accounts

Should a member bank fail, its depositors can recover all of their funds, up to $100,000. Deposits of credit unions and *caisses populaires* are protected under provincial stabilization funds and/or deposit insurance and guarantee corporations. Deposit insurance coverage ranges from $60,000 to unlimited coverage, with the amount varying by province.[14]

When they were originally established, the federal government hoped that these insurance funds would make people feel secure about their savings so that they would not panic and withdraw their money when news of a bank failure was announced. During the Great Depression, many banks failed and their depositors lost everything. The fact that a number of financial institutions in the United States failed in the 1980s and 1990s—without a single major banking panic—underscores the effectiveness of the current insurance system. While the future may yet bring unfortunate surprises, most depositors go to sleep every night without worrying about the safety of their savings.

## Non-banking Institutions

**LO 15-5** Distinguish among non-banking institutions such as insurance companies, pension funds, mutual funds, and finance companies.

Non-banking financial institutions offer some financial services, such as short-term loans or investment products, but do not accept deposits. These include insurance companies, pension funds, mutual funds, brokerage firms, non-financial firms, and finance companies.

**Diversified Firms.** Recently, a growing number of traditionally non-financial firms have moved into the financial field. These firms include manufacturing organizations, such as General Motors and General Electric, that traditionally confined their financial activities to financing their customers' purchases. GE was once so successful in the financial arena that its credit subsidiary accounted for more than 40 percent of the company's revenues and earnings. Unfortunately, GE Capital became a liability to GE during the financial crisis and is in the process of recovery as GE cuts the size of its finance unit and writes off billions of dollars in bad loans.

"A growing number of traditionally non-financial firms have moved into the financial field."

**Insurance Companies.** **Insurance companies** are businesses that protect their clients against financial losses from certain specified risks (death, injury,

**insurance companies** businesses that protect their clients against financial losses from certain specified risks (death, accident, and theft, for example)

disability, accident, fire, theft, and natural disasters, for example) in exchange for a fee, called a premium. Because insurance premiums flow into the companies regularly, but major insurance losses cannot be timed with great accuracy (although expected risks can be assessed with considerable precision), insurance companies generally have large amounts of excess funds. They typically invest these or make long-term loans, particularly to businesses in the form of commercial real estate loans.

**Pension Funds.** **Pension funds** are managed investment pools set aside by individuals, corporations, unions, and some non-profit organizations to provide retirement income for members. One type of pension fund is the *registered retirement savings plan* (RRSP), which is established by individuals to provide for their personal retirement needs. RRSP funds can be invested in a variety of financial assets, including shares, bonds, mutual funds, and low-risk financial "staples" such as Treasury securities. The choice is up to each person and is dictated solely by individual objectives and tolerance for risk. The interest earned by all of these investments may be deferred tax-free until retirement.

**pension funds** managed investment pools set aside by individuals, corporations, unions, and some non-profit organizations to provide retirement income for members

In *tax-free savings accounts* (TFSAs), investors may contribute up to a set amount per year ($6000 in 2019); the contribution is considered an after-tax contribution. When the money is withdrawn at retirement, or at any other time, no tax is paid on the distribution. The TSFA is beneficial to young people who can allow a long time for their money to compound.

Most major corporations provide some kind of pension plan for their employees. Many of these are established with bank trust departments or life insurance companies. Money is deposited in a separate account in the name of each individual employee, and when the employee retires, the total amount in the account can be either withdrawn in one lump sum or taken as monthly cash payments over some defined time period (usually for the remaining life of the retiree).

All employed Canadians contribute to either the Canada Pension Plan (CPP) or the Quebec Pension Plan (QPP) through payroll deductions. The funds are managed separately from

©chrisdorney/Shutterstock

Manulife Financial is the largest insurance company in Canada, the second largest in North America, and the world's fifth largest, based on market capitalization.

## ENTREPRENEURSHIP IN ACTION

### Making E-commerce Easy

**Shopify**

**Founder:** Tobias Lütke

**Founded:** 2006

**Success:** Shopify is a Canadian e-commerce company headquartered in Ottawa. The company has more than 800,000 businesses in approximately 175 countries using its platform, and sales exceeded $41 billion for 2018.

Merchants use Shopify to design, set up, and manage their stores across multiple sales channels, including mobile, Web, social media, marketplaces, brick-and-mortar locations, and pop-up shops. The platform also provides merchants with a powerful back-office and a single view of their business, from payments to shipping.

Lütke created Shopify after recognizing that existing e-commerce software was mediocre. The company markets its role as a partner rather than a competitor to differentiate itself from Amazon. Many online merchants want their products on Amazon because it's the busiest shopping platform, but they're also wary of being too dependent on the Seattle-based company, which also makes its own products.

Shopify plans to continue adding capabilities that make it easier for more entrepreneurs to start selling, further simplify merchant operations, and catalyze their growth.*

*Shopify, https://news.shopify.com/ (accessed February 21, 2019); Natalie Wong and Spencer Soper, "Shopify CEO Says Amazon Is Encroaching on Its Turf," Bloomberg, September 25, 2018, https://www.bloomberg.com/news/articles/2018-09-25/shopify-ceo-lutke-says-amazon-is-encroaching-on-its-turf (accessed February 21, 2019); Trevor Cole, "Our Canadian CEO of the year you've probably never heard of," *Globe and Mail*, https://www.theglobeandmail.com/report-on-business/rob-magazine/meet-our-ceo-of-the-year/article21734931/, (accessed February 21, 2019).

general tax dollars and all the monies generated are used to pay benefits to eligible plan members. The plans offer similar benefits including pensions after age 60, survivor benefits for spouses and dependants, and disability payments.

**Mutual Funds.** A **mutual fund** pools individual investor dollars and invests them in large numbers of well-diversified securities. Individual investors buy shares in a mutual fund in the hope of earning a high rate of return and in much the same way as people buy shares of stock. Because of the large numbers of people investing in any one mutual fund, the funds can afford to invest in hundreds (if not thousands) of securities at any one time, minimizing the risks of any single security that does not do well. Mutual funds provide professional financial management for people who lack the time and/or expertise to invest in particular securities, such as government bonds. While there are no hard-and-fast rules, investments in one or more mutual funds are one way for people to plan for financial independence at the time of retirement.

**mutual fund** an investment company that pools individual investor dollars and invests them in large numbers of well-diversified securities

**brokerage firms** firms that buy and sell stocks, bonds, and other securities for their customers and provide other financial services

**investment banker** underwrites new issues of securities for corporate and government clients

A special type of mutual fund called a *money market fund* invests specifically in short-term debt securities issued by governments and large corporations. Money market funds usually offer slightly higher rates of interest than bank money market accounts.

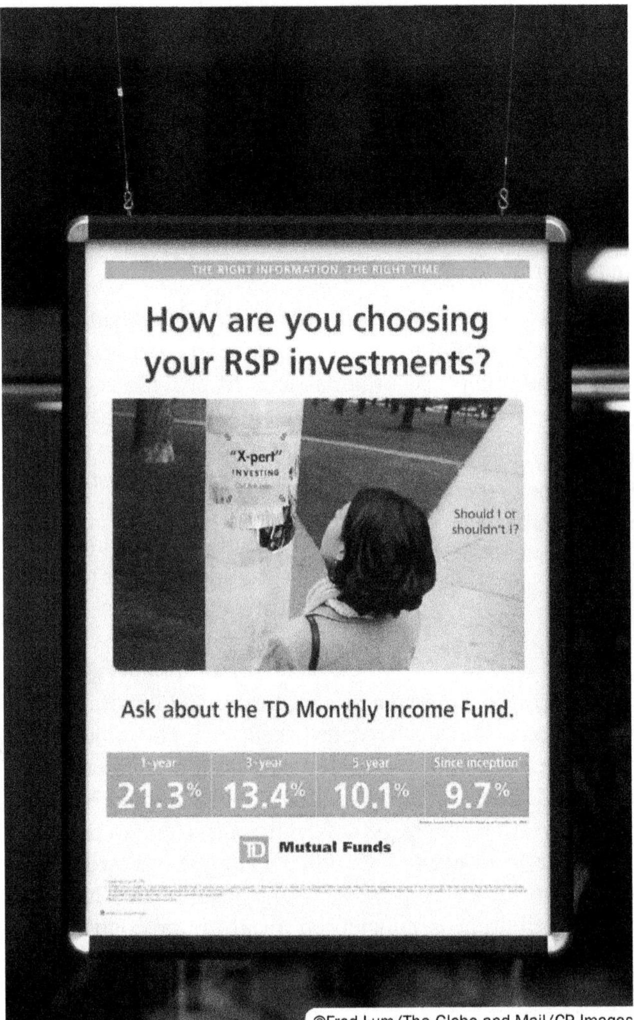

©Fred Lum/The Globe and Mail/CP Images

Mutual funds are considered an excellent method of investing for retirement.

**Brokerage Firms and Investment Banks.** **Brokerage firms** buy and sell stocks, bonds, and other securities for their customers and provide other financial services. The rise of online brokerage firms has helped investors who want to do it themselves at low costs. Firms like Scotia iTRADE and Questrade offer investors the ability to buy and sell securities for less than $10 per trade; the same trade at a full-service broker might cost $100. Some discount brokers offer banking services, debit cards, wire transfers, and many of the same services that the traditional brokerage firms offer.

Most brokerage firms, like RBC Dominion Securities and TD Securities, are really part of financial conglomerates that provide many different kinds of services besides buying and selling securities for clients, such as investment banking. The investment banker underwrites new issues of securities for corporations, states, and municipalities that need to raise money in the capital markets. The new issue market is called a *primary market* because the sale of the securities is for the first time. After the first sale, the securities are traded in the *secondary markets* by brokers. The **investment banker** advises on the price of the new securities and generally guarantees the sale while overseeing the distribution of the securities through the selling brokerage houses. Investment bankers also act as dealers who make markets in securities. They do this by offering to sell the securities at an asked price (which is a higher rate) and buy the securities at a bid price (which is a lower rate)—the difference in the two prices represents the profit for the dealer.

**Finance Companies.** **Finance companies** are businesses that offer short-term loans at substantially higher rates of interest than banks. Commercial finance companies make loans to businesses, requiring their borrowers to pledge assets such as equipment, inventories, or unpaid accounts as collateral for the loans. Consumer finance companies make loans to individuals. Like commercial finance companies, these firms require some sort of personal collateral as security against the borrower's possible inability to repay the loans. Because of the high interest rates they charge and other factors, finance companies typically are the lender of last resort for individuals and businesses whose credit limits have been exhausted and/or those with poor credit ratings.

**finance companies** businesses that offer short-term loans at substantially higher rates of interest than banks

## Electronic Banking

Since the advent of the computer age, a wide range of technological innovations have made it possible to move money all across the world electronically. Such paperless transactions have allowed financial institutions to reduce costs in what has been (and what appears to continue to be) a virtual competitive battlefield. **Electronic funds transfer (EFT)** is any movement of funds by means of an electronic terminal, telephone, computer, or magnetic tape. Such transactions order a particular financial institution to subtract money from one account and add it to another. The most commonly used forms of EFT are automated banking machines and home banking systems.

**Automated Banking Machines.** Probably the most familiar form of electronic banking is the **automated banking machine (ABM)**, which dispenses cash, accepts deposits, and allows balance inquiries and cash transfers from one account to another. ABMs provide 24-hour banking services—both at home (through a local bank) and far away (via worldwide ABM networks such as Cirrus and Plus). Rapid growth, driven by both strong consumer acceptance and lower transaction costs for banks (about half the cost of teller transactions), has led to the installation of hundreds of thousands of ABMs worldwide. Table 15.4 presents some interesting statistics about banks and technology.

**electronic funds transfer (EFT)** any movement of funds by means of an electronic terminal, telephone, computer, or magnetic tape

**automated banking machine (ABM)** the most familiar form of electronic banking, which dispenses cash, accepts deposits, and allows balance inquiries and cash transfers from one account to another

**Table 15.4 | Bank Fact Sheet**

| | |
|---|---|
| Number of bank-owned ABMs in Canada | 18,640 |
| Number of online banking transactions completed | 574 million |
| Number of transactions logged at bank-owned ABMs in Canada | 643 million |
| Amount six largest Canadian banks spent on technology in the last decade | $84.5 billion |
| Amount six largest Canadian banks have spent on technology in 2017 | $13.3 billion |

### RESPONDING TO BUSINESS CHALLENGES

#### Cost of Borrowing Poses a Threat to Brazilian Consumers

Debt is not necessarily a bad thing. Many companies borrow in order to finance projects that can lead to greater profits. Consumers borrow to obtain objects that they value. The problem arises when businesses or individuals incur so much debt that they cannot pay it off. This is becoming a serious concern for consumers in Brazil.

The economic boom between 2004–2013 created a growing middle class in Brazil, and with their newfound wealth, consumers spent and used credit like never before. Unfortunately, many Brazilian consumers had little experience with credit, which contributed to widespread consumer borrowing and a rising number of loan defaults. As the economy cooled, consumers found themselves trapped in credit card debt.

Consumer spending has become such a problem that the central bank of Brazil has increased interest rates. However, some banks charge even higher rates than the central bank. Credit cards have an annual interest rate of 290 percent on average, whereas the cost of borrowing for personal loans is 130 percent for retailers and 47 percent for banks.

The ethics of charging such high interest rates are questionable. On the one hand, higher interest rates tend to deter spending. Additionally, inflation in Brazil has risen significantly, which in turn increases the cost of borrowing. On the other hand, the lack of knowledge that many Brazilian consumers have of credit puts them at a major disadvantage in understanding the financial dangers of too much debt.*

**DISCUSSION QUESTIONS**

1. Why are Brazilians having difficulty with borrowing and paying back debt?
2. Do you feel that it is ethical for banks to charge such high rates for borrowing?
3. What would you suggest as a way to reduce the debt problems that Brazilian consumers are facing?

*Harry Maurer and Alexander Ragir, "Brazil's New Middle Class Goes on a Spree," *Bloomberg Businessweek*, May 12, 2011, www.businessweek.com/magazine/content/11_21/b4229010792956.htm (accessed October 12, 2011); Kenneth Rapoza, "No Major Slowdownas Brazil Consumers Still Happily Spending," Forbes, August 12, 2011, www.forbes.com/sites/kenrapoza/2011/08/12/no-major-slowdown-as-brazil-consumers-still-happily-spending/ (accessed October 12, 2011); "FACTBOX-Bright and Troubled Spots in Brazil's Economy," Reuters, August 18, 2011, www.reuters.com/article/2011/08/18/brazil-economy-idUSN1E77E1EZ20110818 (accessed October 12, 2011); Rodrigo Zeidan, "Four Reasons for Brazil's Credit Dysfunction–and How to Fix It," *America's Quarterly*, January 10, 2018, https://www.americasquarterly.org/content/four-reasons-brazils-credit-dysfunction-and-how-fix-it-0, (accessed February 21, 2019).

©Kite_rin/Shutterstock

Computers and handheld devices have made online banking extremely convenient. However, hackers have stolen millions from banking customers by tricking them into visiting websites and downloading malicious software that gives the hackers access to customers' passwords.

**Online Banking.** Many banking activities may now be carried out on a computer at home or at work, or through wireless devices such as cell phones and tablets anywhere there is a wireless "hot point." Consumers and small businesses can now make a bewildering array of financial transactions at home or on the go, 24 hours a day. Functioning much like a vast network of personal ABMs, banks allow their customers to make sophisticated banking transactions, buy and sell stocks and bonds, and purchase products and airline tickets without ever leaving home or speaking to another human being. Banks also allow customers to log directly into their accounts to check balances, transfer money between accounts, view their account statements, and pay bills via home computer or other Internet-enabled devices. Computers and advanced telecommunications technologies have revolutionized world commerce.

# Future of Banking

**LO 15-6** Investigate the challenges ahead for the banking industry.

Rapid advances and innovations in technology are challenging the banking industry and requiring it to change. As we said earlier, most, if not all banks, both large and small, are offering electronic access to their financial services. ABM technology is rapidly changing, with machines now performing more functions than simply dispensing cash. Online financial services, ABM technology, and bill presentation are just a few of the areas where rapidly changing technology is causing the banking industry to change, as well.

Whether or not banks will get bigger over the next ten years is uncertain. During 2007–2008, the financial markets collapsed under the weight of declining housing prices, subprime mortgages (mortgages with low-quality borrowers), and risky securities backed by these subprime mortgages. Because the value of bank assets declined dramatically, most large U.S. banks had a shrinking capital base; that is, the amount of debt in relation to their equity was so high that they were below the minimum required capital requirements. This was a financial environment where banks did not trust the counter-parties to their loans and asset-backed securities. In this environment, the markets ceased to function in an orderly fashion. To keep the banking system from total collapse, central banks around the world created different programs, including providing increased liquidity and lowering interest rates, to stimulate the economy.

There have been very few bank failures in Canada, which is widely acknowledged as having one of the safest and soundest financial sectors in the world.[15] In response to technological innovation and globalization, the financial services sector has undergone rapid change. The sector is increasingly competitive as changes to federal laws and regulations have resulted in the entry of new domestic and foreign competitors in the Canadian market. The hunt will continue for other merger partners that will globally expand institutions' customer reach and the services they are able to offer.

Indeed, the recent trend toward ever bigger banks and other financial institutions is not happening by chance. Financial services may be an example of a *natural oligopoly*, meaning that the industry may be best served by a few very large firms rather than a host of smaller ones. As the largest banks merge into even larger international entities, they will erase the relative competitive advantages now enjoyed by the largest banks. It is by no means implausible that the financial services industry in the future will be dominated by ten or so internationally oriented "megabanks."

In addition to consolidation, there are the peer-to-peer lenders and other sources of funding by Internet websites such as GoFundMe, which helps people enhance their life skills, raise money for health care issues, and more. There is also the budding use of virtual money and other futuristic ideas, so only time will tell how the world of banking changes over time and how bank regulators will deal with these non-bank institutions.

## TEAM EXERCISE

Mutual funds pool individual investor dollars and invest them in a number of different securities. Go to http://finance.yahoo.com/ and select some top-performing funds using criteria such as sector, style, or strategy. Assume that your group has $100,000 to invest in mutual funds. Select five funds in which to invest, representing a balanced (varied industries, risk, etc.) portfolio, and defend your selections.

# LEARNING OBJECTIVES SUMMARY

**LO 15-1** Define *money*, its functions, and its characteristics.

Money is anything generally accepted as a means of payment for goods and services. Money serves as a medium of exchange, a measure of value, and a store of wealth. To serve effectively in these functions, money must be acceptable, divisible, portable, durable, stable in value, and difficult to counterfeit.

**LO 15-2** Describe various types of money.

Money may take the form of currency, chequing accounts, or other accounts. Chequing accounts are funds left in an account in a financial institution that can be withdrawn (usually by writing a cheque) without advance notice. Other types of accounts include savings accounts (funds left in an interest-earning account that usually cannot be withdrawn without advance notice), money market accounts (an interest-bearing chequing account that is invested in short-term debt instruments), certificates of deposit (deposits left in an institution for a specified period of time at a specified interest rate), credit cards (access to a pre-approved line of credit granted by a bank or company), and debit cards (means of instant cash transfers between customer and merchant accounts).

**LO 15-3** Specify how the Bank of Canada manages the money supply and regulates the Canadian banking system.

The Bank of Canada regulates the Canadian financial system. The Bank manages the money supply indirectly through its influence on the target overnight rate. Increases in interest rates reduce the demand for loans and lead to debtors paying down existing debt. This results in slower growth or even a reduction in money supply. The Bank's other activities include the issuance of Canadian bank notes, provision of banking services for the federal government, and promotion of a safe financial system. Other central bank tools for the conduct of monetary policy are buying and selling government securities, raising or lowering the bank rate (the rate of interest at which banks may borrow cash reserves from the central bank).

**LO 15-4** Compare and contrast chartered banks, trust companies, and credit unions/*caisses populaires*.

Chartered banks are federally regulated under the *Bank Act*. They take and hold deposits in accounts and make loans to individuals and businesses. Trust companies may be incorporated federally or provincially. Trust companies accept and hold deposits in accounts and make loans to individuals but are restricted in commercial lending. Only trust companies can offer trustee services. Credit unions/*caisses populaires* are provincially regulated co-operatives. Both offer deposit accounts and loan services to their members.

**LO 15-5** Distinguish among non-banking institutions such as insurance companies, pension funds, mutual funds, and finance companies.

Insurance companies are businesses that protect their clients against financial losses due to certain circumstances, in exchange for a fee. Pension funds are investments set aside by organizations or individuals to meet retirement needs. Mutual funds pool investors' money and invest in large numbers of different types of securities. Brokerage firms buy and sell stocks and bonds for investors. Finance companies make short-term loans at higher interest rates than do banks.

**LO 15-6** Investigate the challenges ahead for the banking industry.

Future changes in financial regulations are likely to result in fewer but larger banks and other financial institutions.

## KEY TERMS

automated banking machine (ABM)
Bank of Canada
bank rate
brokerage firms
Canada Deposit Insurance Corporation (CDIC)
certificates of deposit (CDs)
chartered banks
chequing account
credit cards
credit controls
credit union/*caisse populaire*
debit card
desired reserves
electronic funds transfer (EFT)
finance
finance companies
insurance companies
investment banker
monetary policy
money
money market funds
mutual fund
open market operations
pension funds
reward cards
savings accounts
trust companies

## So You're Interested *in Financial Systems or Banking*

You think you might be interested in going into finance or banking, but it is so hard to tell when you are a full-time student. Classes that seem interesting when you take them might not translate into an interesting work experience after you graduate. A great way to see if you would excel at a career in finance is to get some experience in the industry. Internships, whether paid or unpaid, not only help you figure out what you might really want to do after you graduate but they are also a great way to build up your resumé, put your learning to use, and start generating connections within the field.

Internship opportunities are available, although you may need to do some research to find them. To start, talk to your program advisor and your professors about opportunities. Also, you can check company websites where you think you might like to work to see if they have any opportunities available. Municipal, provincial, or federal government offices often provide student internships as well. No matter where you end up interning, the real-life skills you pick up, as well as the résumé boost you get, will be helpful in finding a job after you graduate. When you graduate, chartered banks and other financial institutions offer major employment opportunities.

## BUILD YOUR BUSINESS PLAN

### Money and the Financial System

This chapter provides you with the opportunity to think about money and the financial system and just how many new businesses fail every year. In some industries, the failure rate is as high as 80 percent. One reason for such a high failure rate is the inability to manage the finances of the organization. From the start of the business, financial planning plays a key role. Try getting a loan without an accompanying budget/forecast of earnings and cash flow.

While obtaining a loan from a family member may be the easiest way to fund your business, it may cause more problems for you later on if you are unable to pay the money back as scheduled. Before heading to a lending officer at a bank, contact your local Small Business Enterprise Centre (SBEC) to see what assistance they might provide.

## CASE | Crowdfunding: Loans You Can Count On

Kiva is a non-profit organization that accepts donations to crowdfund loans around the world. It was founded in 2005 when Premal Shah recognized that small business owners in developing countries didn't have access to funding. Kiva takes donations on its site from people around the world who can donate a minimum of $25 for specific projects. Money is then given to recipients who are expected to pay back the loan over a set period of time. As the loan is paid back, the original lenders can then either withdraw the money they donated or use it to fund another loan. Kiva now backs thousands of loans each week at a variety of price points and has surpassed $1 billion in loans. Most Kiva loans go to help recipients build inventory or buy assets that will improve their productivity.

Technology is constantly changing the world around us. This is true in the financial world, too. Traditional banks and other financial entities are competing with new structures, like Kiva, that can provide similar services in an innovative way. By using crowdfunding on the Internet to award loans to broader audiences, Kiva has found a way to innovate in the financial loan industry. This is a form of shadow banking where a company performs banking functions, like awarding loans, when the company is not a traditional banking institution and is not encumbered by traditional banking regulations. Lenders like Kiva, known as peer-to-peer lenders, create a human connection.

Even though Kiva does not have to follow many traditional banking regulations, the company must comply with regulations imposed by countries around the world that they are operating in. Developing countries often have poor regulations that increase costs for Kiva and complicate the loan process. For example, money invested in India must stay in India for at least three years, which can create major cash flow problems. Another challenge for Kiva is dealing with infrastructure. These countries have very poor financial infrastructure systems, which is another challenge that Kiva has to overcome when trying to fund those in need.

One of the most fascinating aspects of the Kiva system is Kiva's choice to crowdfund loans instead of using donations. While donations are very helpful for aiding crisis efforts and natural disaster relief, Kiva believes that lending is a more effective way to combat poverty. The company believes that by lending, recipients will have a stable and ongoing source of capital for their business. Loan recipients can also use their Kiva loans as a credit history in order to try and secure loans with traditional financial institutions. Because of the payback structure of Kiva's loans, Kiva is able to reinvest money that is paid back to fund other projects.

"Access to capital isn't enough to end global poverty, but it is clearly necessary," says Elliot Collins, a research and evaluations manager for Kiva. "Kiva's network is reducing the cost of lending to entrepreneurs around the world, and our goal is to ensure that everybody can benefit from financial markets and help build their local economy."

Thanks to its innovative take on crowdfunding loans, Kiva is able to reach those in need all around the world. Donors can give money and then reinvest paid-back loans into other projects. Because of Kiva's non-traditional structure, it is able to avoid many banking regulations. However, Kiva continues faces many challenges due to different government regulations and infrastructures. To stay competitive across the world, Kiva must closely monitor regulations in in the countries in which it operates and how governments will treat shadow banking entities in the future.[16]

### DISCUSSION QUESTIONS

1. Explain the benefit of awarding loans instead of donations.
2. What are the differences between Kiva and more traditional financial institutions?
3. What challenges does Kiva currently face, and what future challenges could it face?

CHAPTER 16

# Financial Management and Securities Markets

©Carsten Reisinger/Shutterstock

## LEARNING OBJECTIVES

**After reading this chapter, you will be able to:**

- LO 16-1 Describe some common methods of managing current assets.
- LO 16-2 Identify some sources of short-term financing (current liabilities).
- LO 16-3 Summarize the importance of long-term assets and capital budgeting.
- LO 16-4 Specify how companies finance their operations and manage fixed assets with long-term liabilities, particularly bonds.
- LO 16-5 Discuss how corporations can use equity financing by issuing stock through an investment banker.
- LO 16-6 Describe the various securities markets in Canada.

# ENTER THE WORLD OF BUSINESS

**No Shock: General Electric Struggles After Poor Financial Management**

General Electric (GE) started out as a light bulb company founded by Thomas Edison. In 2017 it listed the following divisions: Power, Renewable Energy, Oil & Gas, Aviation, Healthcare, Transportation, Lighting, and GE Capital.

Perhaps the biggest mistake was expanding GE Capital into consumer loans. Originally, GE Capital helped customers finance their purchases of its locomotives and airplane engines. However, GE expanded into consumer products such as credit cards, insurance, and mortgage lending through GE Capital. When the financial crisis hit, GE was forced to be regulated by the U.S. Federal Reserve as a bank. The decision was made to shrink GE Capital back to its original focus of lending to industrial customers. It sold off Synchrony Financial, its consumer finance area, and liquidated most of its consumer-oriented subsidiaries. GE Capital got out from under government regulation but lost almost $7 billion in the process.

The shareholder outrage at declining earnings peaked in 2017 when GE cut its dividend in half because of cash flow problems. After becoming the worst-performing stock in the Dow Jones Industrial Average, GE was booted from the Dow in 2018, causing the stock to plunge. The common stock continued to decline to under $10 per share as the company once again cut the dividend to $0.01 per quarter in October of 2018.

The problem GE faced was a mix of bad decisions and market conditions. It sold at a loss divisions it had bought earlier, bought companies that did not perform, and was in the wrong industries at the wrong time. To recover, GE plans to sell several divisions to create a simpler company. Time will tell whether GE can regain its reputation.[1]

**DISCUSSION QUESTIONS**

1. Describe the financial mistakes GE made with GE Capital.
2. Do you think GE Capital's decision to expand into consumer financial products was a decision of bad timing (right before the financial crisis), or was it just a bad business move? Support your argument with reasoning.
3. Is a breakup of GE the best option for the company? Why or why not?

## Introduction

While it's certainly true that money makes the world go 'round, financial management is the discipline that makes the world turn more smoothly. Indeed, without effective management of assets, liabilities, and owners' equity, all business organizations are doomed to fail—regardless of the quality and innovation of their products. Financial management is the field that addresses the issues of obtaining and managing the funds and resources necessary to run a business successfully. It is not limited to business organizations; all organizations, from the corner store to the local non-profit art museum, from giant corporations to county governments, must manage their resources effectively and efficiently if they are to achieve their objectives.

In this chapter, we look at both short- and long-term financial management. First, we discuss the management of short-term assets, which companies use to generate sales and conduct ordinary day-to-day business operations. Next, we turn our attention to the management of short-term liabilities, the sources of short-term funds used to finance the business. Then, we discuss the management of long-term assets such as plant and equipment, and the long-term liabilities such as stocks and bonds used to finance these important corporate assets. Finally, we look at the securities markets, where stocks and bonds are traded.

# Managing Current Assets and Liabilities

**LO 16-1** Describe some common methods of managing current assets.

Managing short-term assets and liabilities involves managing the current assets and liabilities on the balance sheet (discussed in Chapter 14). Current assets are short-term resources such as cash, investments, accounts receivable, and inventory. Current liabilities are short-term debts such as accounts payable, accrued salaries, accrued taxes, and short-term bank loans. We use the terms *current* and *short-term* interchangeably because short-term assets and liabilities are usually replaced by new assets and liabilities within three or four months, and always within a year. Managing short-term assets and liabilities is sometimes called **working capital management** because short-term assets and liabilities continually flow through an organization and are thus said to be "working."

## Managing Current Assets

The chief goal of financial managers who focus on current assets and liabilities is to maximize the return to the business on cash, temporary investments of idle cash, accounts receivable, and inventory.

**Managing Cash.** A crucial element facing any financial manager is effectively managing the firm's cash flow. Remember that cash flow is the movement of money through an organization on a daily, weekly, monthly, or yearly basis. Ensuring that sufficient (but not excessive) funds are on hand to meet the company's obligations is one of the single most important facets of financial management.

Idle cash does not make money, and corporate chequing accounts typically do not earn interest. As a result, astute money managers try to keep just enough cash on hand, called **transaction balances**, to pay bills—such as employee wages, supplies, and utilities—as they fall due. To manage the firm's cash and ensure that enough cash flows through the organization quickly and efficiently, companies try to speed up cash collections from customers.

More companies are now using electronic funds transfer systems to pay and collect bills online. It is interesting that companies want to collect cash quickly but pay out cash slowly. When companies use electronic funds transfers between buyers and suppliers, the speed of collections and disbursements becomes one day. Only with the use of cheques can companies delay the payment of cash quickly and have a three- or four-day waiting period until the cheque is presented to their bank and the cash leaves their account.

**working capital management** the managing of short-term assets and liabilities

**transaction balances** cash kept on hand by a firm to pay normal daily expenses, such as employee wages and bills for supplies and utilities

**Investing Idle Cash.** As companies sell products, they generate cash on a daily basis, and sometimes cash comes in faster than it is needed to pay bills. Organizations often invest this "extra" cash, for periods as short as one day (overnight) or for as long as one year, until it is needed. Such temporary investments of cash are known as **marketable securities**. Examples include Treasury bills, Banker's Acceptances, commercial paper (corporate paper), and eurodollar loans. Table 16.1 summarizes a number of different marketable securities used by businesses and some sample interest rates on these investments. The safety rankings are relative. While all of the listed securities are very low risk, the Bank of Canada securities are the safest.

Many large companies invest idle cash in Government of Canada **Treasury bills (T-bills)**, which are short-term debt obligations the federal government sells to raise money. Auctioned biweekly by the Bank of Canada, T-bills carry maturities of one week to one year. T-bills are generally considered to be the safest of all investments and are called risk-free because the federal government will not default on its debt.

**Commercial certificates of deposit (CDs)** are issued by commercial banks and brokerage companies. They are available in minimum amounts of $100,000 but are typically in units of $1 million for large corporations investing excess cash. Unlike consumer CDs (discussed in Chapter 15), which must be held until maturity, commercial CDs may be traded prior to maturity. Should a cash shortage occur, the organization can simply sell the CD on the open market and obtain needed funds.

One of the most popular short-term investments for the largest business organizations is **commercial paper**—a written promise from one company to another to pay a specific amount of money. Because commercial paper is backed only by the name and reputation of the issuing company, sales of commercial paper are restricted to only the largest and most financially stable companies. As commercial paper is frequently bought and sold for durations of as

**marketable securities** temporary investment of "extra" cash by organizations for up to one year in Treasury bills, certificates of deposit, commercial paper, or eurodollar loans

**Treasury bills (T-bills)** short-term debt obligations the Canadian government sells to raise money

**commercial certificates of deposit (CDs)** certificates of deposit issued by commercial banks and brokerage companies, available in minimum amounts of $100,000, which may be traded prior to maturity

**commercial paper** a written promise from one company to another to pay a specific amount of money

## GOING GREEN

### How Making Sustainability a Top Priority Helps the Bottom Line

Can sustainability improve a firm's bottom line? Chemical company DowDuPont proves the answer is yes. At DowDuPont, sustainability is seen as a market-driven process that enhances the bottom line and creates social value. Sustainability assists in the effective management of assets, liabilities, and owners' equity.

DowDuPont's quest for sustainability began two decades ago when the firm began analyzing how its plants were affecting the environment. It next turned its attention to energy and found that adopting more energy-efficient processes decreased energy costs. Since then, sustainability has morphed into a strategic tool. The company has reduced global greenhouse gas emissions by over 30 percent and water usage by over 19 percent since 2004. Its 2020 Sustainability Goals include reducing greenhouse gas emissions intensity by 7 percent (2015 baseline) and energy intensity by 10 percent (2010 baseline), developing business-specific waste goals, and establishing water risk mitigation plans for select sites.

Finally, DowDuPont believes it can share what it has learned from best practices in sustainability with other companies. Its DowDuPont Sustainable Solutions business helps organizations adopt a triple-bottom-line (people-planet-profits) approach. This approach goes beyond the bottom line to incorporate human and environmental concerns. The company shares many of these practices with its suppliers to increase the sustainability of the supply chain. DowDuPont is an example of a successful company that has turned sustainability into a competitive advantage.*

#### DISCUSSION QUESTIONS

1. How is DowDuPont using sustainability as a competitive advantage?
2. Why is it important for DowDuPont to develop market driven sustainability goals?
3. How can DowDuPont's sustainability initiatives improve financial management?

*DuPont 2017 Global Reporting Initiative Report, 2017, http://www.dupont.com/content/dam/dupont/corporate/our-approach/sustainability/2017-Documents/2017%20DuPont%20Sustainability%20Report.pdf (accessed April 19, 2018); DuPont, CDP 2017 Climate Change 2017 Information Request, 2017, http://www.dupont.com/content/dam/dupont/corporate/ourapproach/sustainability/documents/2016-sustainabilitydocuments/Programme ResponseClimate%20Change%202017.pdf (accessed April 19, 2018); DuPont, "Performance and Reporting," 2018, http://www.dupont.com/corporate-functions/sustainability/sustainabilitycommitments/performance-reporting.html (accessed April 19, 2018).

**Table 16.1** | Short-Term Investment Possibilities for Idle Cash

| Type of Security | Maturity | Issuer of Security | Interest Rate (on Feb. 20, 2019) | Safety Level |
|---|---|---|---|---|
| Treasury Bills | 1 month | Bank of Canada | 1.63 | Excellent |
| Treasury Bills | 6 months | Bank of Canada | 1.74 | Excellent |
| Commercial Paper | 3 months | Corporations | 1.98 | Very Good |
| Certificates of Deposit | 12 months | Chartered Banks | 2.50 | Very Good |
| Eurodollars | 3 months | European Commercial Banks | 2.81 | Very Good |

short as one business day, many players in the market find themselves buying commercial paper with excess cash on one day and selling it to gain extra money the following day.

Some companies invest idle cash in international markets such as the **eurodollar market**, a market for trading U.S. dollars in foreign countries. Because the eurodollar market was originally developed by London banks, any dollar-denominated deposit in a non-U.S. bank is called a eurodollar deposit, regardless of whether the issuing bank is actually located in Europe, South America, or anyplace else. For example, if you travel overseas and deposit $1000 in a German bank, you will have "created" a eurodollar deposit in the amount of $1000. Since the U.S. dollar is accepted by most countries for international trade, these dollar deposits can be used by international companies to settle their accounts. The market created for trading such investments offers firms with extra dollars a chance to earn a slightly higher rate of return with just a little more risk than they would face by investing in Treasury bills.

**eurodollar market** a market for trading U.S. dollars in foreign countries

**Managing Accounts Receivable.** After cash and marketable securities, the balance sheet lists

The Canadian Bankers Association developed the YourMoney seminars as part of its commitment to improving financial literacy among Canadians.

accounts receivable and inventory. Remember that accounts receivable are money owed to a business by credit customers. Many businesses make the vast majority of their sales on credit, so managing accounts receivable is an important task.

Each credit sale represents an account receivable for the company, the terms of which typically require customers to pay the full amount due within 30, 60, or even 90 days from the date of the sale. To encourage quick payment, some businesses offer some of their customers discounts of 1 to 2 percent if they pay off their balance within a specified period of time (usually between 10 and 30 days). On the other hand, late payment charges of between 1 and 1.5 percent serve to discourage slow payers from sitting on their bills forever. The larger the early payment discount offered, the faster customers will tend to pay their accounts.

Unfortunately, while discounts increase cash flow, they also reduce profitability. Finding the right balance between the added advantages of early cash receipt and the disadvantages of reduced profits is no simple matter. Similarly, determining the optimal balance between the higher sales likely to result from extending credit to customers with less than sterling credit ratings and the higher bad-debt losses likely to result from a more lenient credit policy is also challenging. Information on company credit ratings is provided by local credit bureaus, national credit-rating agencies such as Dun and Bradstreet, and industry trade groups.

**Optimizing Inventory.** While the inventory that a firm holds is controlled by both production needs and marketing considerations, the financial manager has to coordinate inventory purchases to manage cash flows. The object is to minimize the firm's investment in inventory without experiencing production cutbacks as a result of critical materials shortfalls or lost sales due to insufficient finished goods inventories. Every dollar invested in inventory is a dollar unavailable for investment in some other area of the organization. Optimal inventory levels are determined, in large part, by the method of production. If a firm attempts to produce its goods just in time to meet sales demand, the level of inventory will be relatively low. If, on the other hand, the firm produces materials in a constant, level pattern, inventory increases when sales decrease and decreases when sales increase.

One way that companies are attempting to optimize inventory is through the use of radio frequency identification (RFID) technology. For example, Walmart manages its inventories by using RFID tags. An RFID tag, which contains a silicon chip and an antenna, allows a company to use radio waves to track and identify the products to which the tags are attached. These tags are primarily used to track inventory shipments from the manufacturer to the buyer's warehouses and then to the individual stores and also cut down on trucking theft because the delivery truck and its contents can be tracked in real time.

Although less publicized, inventory shortages can be as much of a drag on potential profits as too much inventory. Not having an item on hand may send the customer to a competitor—forever. Complex computer inventory models are frequently employed to determine the optimum level of inventory a firm should hold to support a given level of sales. Such models can indicate how and when parts inventories should be ordered so that they are available exactly when required—and not a day before. Developing and maintaining such an intricate production and inventory system is difficult, but it can often prove to be the difference between experiencing average profits and achieving spectacular ones.

## Managing Current Liabilities

**LO 16-2** Identify some sources of short-term financing (current liabilities).

While having extra cash on hand is a delightful surprise, the opposite situation—a temporary cash shortfall—can be a crisis. The good news is that there are several potential sources of short-term funds. Suppliers often serve as an important source through credit sales practices. Also, banks, finance companies, and other organizations offer short-term funds through loans and other business operations.

**Accounts Payable.** Remember from Chapter 14 that accounts payable consist of money an organization owes to suppliers for goods and services. Just as accounts receivable must be actively managed to ensure proper cash collections, so too must accounts payable be managed.

The most widely used source of short-term financing, and therefore the most important account payable,

©Steven Puetzer/Photographer's Choice/Getty Images

From materials management, race timing, or attendee tracking, RFID technology has many practical applications.

is **trade credit**—credit extended by suppliers for the purchase of their goods and services. While varying in formality, depending on both the organizations involved and the value of the items purchased, most trade credit agreements offer discounts to organizations that pay their bills early. A supplier, for example, may offer trade terms of "1/10 net 30," meaning that the purchasing organization may take a 1 percent discount from the invoice amount if it makes payment by the 10th day after receiving the bill. Otherwise, the entire amount is due within 30 days.

**trade credit** credit extended by suppliers for the purchase of their goods and services

For example, pretend that you are the financial manager in charge of payables. You owe Ajax Company $10,000, and it offers trade terms of 2/10 net 30. By paying the amount due within 10 days, you can save 2 percent of $10,000, or $200. Assume you place orders with Ajax

## Consider the Following: Y Combinator gives boost to start-up companies

Although thousands of companies failed during the most recent recession, Y Combinator and the companies it assists were among those thriving. Founder Paul Graham (famous in tech circles for creating Viaweb—sold to Yahoo! for $49 million) launched Y Combinator in 2005. His method is somewhat like a school for start-ups, and his funding somewhat like financial aid. Graham gathers entrepreneurs for three-month periods, during which time he provides them with small loans (typically under $20,000) to meet basic needs, allowing them to focus on developing their fledgling companies. In exchange, Y Combinator receives a 2 to 10 percent company stake.

Graham offers something more valuable than a simple loan—an experienced eye, solid advice, and a positive and creative environment. Y Combinator focuses on tech start-ups, with an emphasis on Web-based applications. Graham's experience allows him to help direct, or redirect, founders toward workable concepts attractive to larger investors. His business motto is "Make something people want." Graham also addresses running businesses, handling investors, and dealing with acquisitions. Y Combinator was rated number 11 in *Businessweek*'s list of top angel investors.

Small businesses like those funded by Y Combinator are making some Fortune 500 companies nervous. For example, eBay, for all of its success, does not often update its auction system. This leaves room for a small start-up to gain market share if it can provide a superior service. These small companies are often less expensive and more flexible, making them better equipped to do well in a recession. Although Graham takes a risk with each start-up, graduates such as Scribd (which partnered with literary giants and received over $12 million in venture capital funding) and Omnisio (purchased by Google for more than $15 million) make it worthwhile. Some of the companies flourish—and when they do, Graham makes a substantial profit.*

### DISCUSSION QUESTIONS

1. Why has Y Combinator succeeded while many other firms in the financial industry have failed?
2. What are the risks involved in creating a business like Y Combinator?
3. What are the rewards for Graham in taking a risk in small tech start-ups?

*http://ycombinator.com (accessed September 15, 2010); Ira Sager, Kimberly Weisul, and Spencer Ante, "Tech Investing: How Smart Is the Smart Money?" *Bloomberg Businessweek*, February 2010, http://images.businessweek.com/ss/10/02/0225_angel_investors/12.htm (accessed October 7, 2010); Om Malik, "Notes From a Conversation With Y Combinator's Paul Graham," Gigaom, February 1, 2010, http://gigaom.com/2010/02/01/ycombinator-paul-graham/ (accessed September 20, 2010); Paul Graham, "A New Venture Animal," March 2008, www.paulgraham.com/ycombinator.html (accessed June 20, 2009); Sean Ellis, "Y Combinator Hatches Brilliant Entrepreneurs," Start Up Marketing Blog by Sean Ellis, December 2, 2008, http://startup-marketing.com/y-combinator-hatches-brilliant-entrepreneurs/ (accessed June 20, 2009); Andy Louis-Charles, "Ignore Y Combinator at Your Own Risk," The Motley Fool, April 28, 2009, www.fool.com/investing/general/2009/04/28/ignore-y-combinator-at-your-own-risk.aspx (accessed June 20, 2009); Josh Quittner, "The New Internet Start-Up Boom: Get Rich Slow," *Time*, April 9, 2009, www.time.com/time/magazine/article/0,9171,1890387-1,00.html (accessed June 20, 2009).

once per month and have 12 bills of $10,000 each per year. By taking the discount every time, you will save 12 times $200, or $2400, per year. Now assume you are the financial manager of Gigantic Corp., and it has monthly payables of $100 million per month. Two percent of $100 million is $2 million per month. Failure to take advantage of such trade discounts can, in many cases, add up to large opportunity losses over the span of a year.

**Bank Loans.** Virtually all organizations—large and small—obtain short-term funds for operations from banks. In most instances, the credit services granted these firms take the form of a line of credit or fixed dollar loan. A **line of credit** is an arrangement by which a bank agrees to lend a specified amount of money to the organization upon request—provided that the bank has the required funds to make the loan. In general, a business line of credit is very similar to a consumer credit card, with the exception that the preset credit limit can amount to millions of dollars.

In addition to credit lines, banks also make **secured loans**—loans backed by collateral that the bank can claim if the borrowers do not repay the loans—and **unsecured loans**—loans backed only by the borrowers' good reputation and previous credit rating. Both individuals and businesses build their credit rating from their history of borrowing and repaying borrowed funds on time and in full.

**line of credit** an arrangement by which a bank agrees to lend a specified amount of money to an organization upon request

**secured loans** loans backed by collateral that the bank can claim if the borrowers do not repay them

**unsecured loans** loans backed only by the borrowers' good reputation and previous credit rating

**prime rate** the interest rate that commercial banks charge their best customers (usually large corporations) for short-term loans

A lack of credit history or a poor credit history can make it difficult to get loans from financial institutions. The *principal* is the amount of money borrowed; *interest* is a percentage of the principal that the bank charges for use of its money. As we mentioned in Chapter 15, banks also pay depositors interest on savings accounts and some chequing accounts. Thus, banks charge borrowers interest for loans and pay interest to depositors for the use of their money. In addition, these loans may include origination fees.

The **prime rate** is the interest rate commercial banks charge their best customers (usually large corporations) for short-term loans. For many years, loans at the prime rate represented funds at the lowest possible cost. For some companies, other alternatives may be cheaper, such as borrowing at the London Interbank Offer Rate (LIBOR) or using commercial paper.

The interest rates on commercial loans may be either fixed or variable. A variable, or floating-rate loan offers an advantage when interest rates are falling but represents a distinct disadvantage when interest rates are rising. Between 1999 and 2004, interest rates plummeted, and borrowers refinanced their loans with low-cost fixed-rate loans. Nowhere was this more visible than in the mortgage markets, where homeowners lined up to refinance their high-percentage home mortgages with lower-cost loans. Individuals and corporations have the same motivation: to minimize their borrowing costs. During what was then a period of historically low interest rates, companies ramped up their borrowing, bought back stock, and locked in large amounts of debt at low rates.

©Comstock/Getty Images

Because both businesses and individuals want to keep their financing costs to a minimum, when interest rates drop, their investment in assets tends to increase.

**Non-bank Liabilities.** Banks are not the only source of short-term funds for businesses. Indeed, virtually all financial institutions, from insurance companies to pension funds, from money market funds to finance companies, make short-term loans to many organizations. The largest companies also actively engage in borrowing money from the eurodollar and commercial paper markets. As noted earlier, both of these funds' sources are typically slightly less expensive than bank loans.

In some instances, businesses actually sell their accounts receivable to a finance company known as a **factor**, which gives the selling organizations cash and assumes responsibility for collecting the accounts. For example, a factor might pay $60,000 for receivables with a total face value of $100,000 (60 percent of the total). The factor profits if it can collect more than it paid for the accounts. Because the selling organization's customers send their payments to a lockbox, they may have no idea that a factor has bought their receivables.

**factor** a finance company to which businesses sell their accounts receivable—usually for a percentage of the total face value

Additional non-bank liabilities that must be efficiently managed to ensure maximum profitability are taxes owed to the government and wages owed to employees. Clearly, businesses are responsible for many different types of taxes and similar payments, including federal, provincial, and municipal income taxes; property taxes; mineral rights taxes; unemployment insurance; CPP contributions; workers' compensation taxes; excise taxes; and even more! While the public tends to think that the only relevant taxes are on income and sales, many industries must pay other taxes that far exceed those levied against income. Taxes and employees' wages represent debt obligations of the firm, which the financial manager must plan to meet as they fall due.

## Managing Fixed Assets

**LO 16-3** Summarize the importance of long-term assets and capital budgeting.

Up to this point, we have focused on the short-term aspects of financial management. While most business failures are the result of poor short-term planning, successful ventures must also consider the long-term financial consequences of their actions. Managing the long-term assets and liabilities and the owners' equity portion of the balance sheet is important for the long-term health of the business.

**Long-term (fixed) assets** are expected to last for many years—production facilities (plants), offices, equipment, heavy machinery, furniture, automobiles, and so on. In today's fast-paced world, companies need the most technologically advanced, modern facilities and equipment they can afford. Automobile, oil refining, and transportation companies are dependent on fixed assets.

**long-term (fixed) assets** production facilities (plants), offices, and equipment—all of which are expected to last for many years

Modern and high-tech equipment carries high price tags, and the financial arrangements required to support these investments are by no means trivial. Leasing is just one approach to financing. Obtaining major long-term financing can be challenging for even the most profitable organizations. For less successful firms, such challenges can prove nearly impossible. One approach is leasing assets such as equipment, machines, and buildings. In the case of leasing, or not taking ownership but paying a fee for usage, potential long-term assets can be taken off the balance sheet as a debt. Still, the company has the asset and an obligation to pay money that is a contractual obligation. We'll take a closer look at long-term financing in a moment, but first let's address some issues associated with fixed assets, including capital budgeting, risk assessment, and the costs of financing fixed assets.

### Capital Budgeting and Project Selection

One of the most important jobs performed by the financial manager is to decide what fixed assets, projects, and investments will earn profits for the firm beyond the costs necessary to fund them. The process of analyzing the needs of the business and selecting the assets that will maximize its value is called **capital budgeting**, and the capital budget is the amount of money budgeted for investment in such long-term assets. But capital budgeting does not end with the selection and purchase of a particular piece of land, equipment, or major investment. All assets and projects must be continually re-evaluated to ensure their compatibility with the organization's needs. If a particular asset does not live up to expectations, then management must determine why and take necessary corrective action. Budgeting is not an exact process, and managers must be flexible when new information is available.

**capital budgeting** the process of analyzing the needs of the business and selecting the assets that will maximize its value

"All assets and projects must be continually re-evaluated to ensure their compatibility with the organization's needs."

### Assessing Risk

Every investment carries some risk. Figure 16.1 ranks potential investment projects according to estimated risk. When considering investments overseas, risk assessments must include the political climate and economic stability of a region. The decision to introduce a product or build a manufacturing facility in England would be much less risky than a decision to build one in the Middle East, for example.

The longer a project or asset is expected to last, the greater its potential risk because it is hard to predict whether a piece of equipment will wear out or become obsolete in five or ten years. Predicting cash flows one year down the road is difficult, but projecting them over the span of a ten-year project is a gamble.

©RosalreneBetancourt 5/Alamy Stock Photo

Although pharmaceutical manufacturers may want to undertake many projects, the costs involved require them to use capital budgeting to determine which projects will lead to the greatest profits.

**Figure 16.1** | Qualitative Assessment of Capital Budgeting Risk

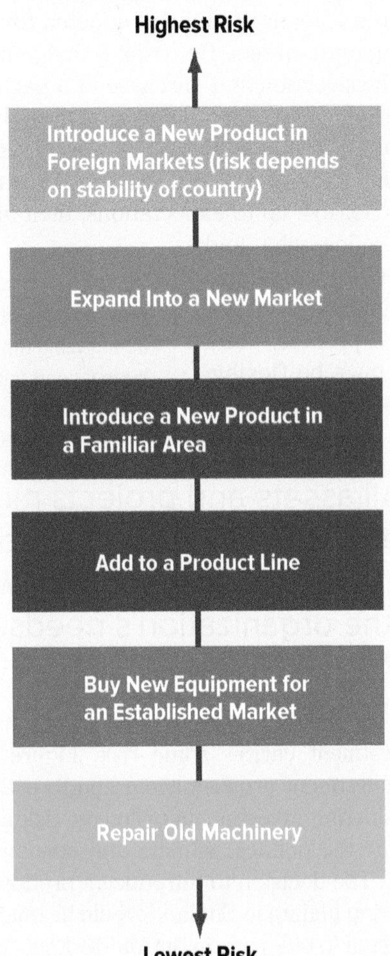


The level of a project's risk is also affected by the stability and competitive nature of the marketplace and the world economy as a whole. IBM's latest high-technology computer product is far more likely to become obsolete overnight than is a similar $10 million investment in a manufacturing plant. Dramatic changes in the marketplace are not uncommon. Indeed, uncertainty created by the rapid devaluation of Asian currencies in the late 1990s wrecked a host of assumptions in literally hundreds of projects worldwide. Financial managers must constantly consider such issues when making long-term decisions about the purchase of fixed assets.

## Pricing Long-Term Money

The ultimate profitability of any project depends not only on accurate assumptions of how much cash it will generate but also on its financing costs. Because a business must pay interest on money it borrows, the returns from any project must cover not only the costs of operating the project but also the interest expenses for the debt used to finance its construction. Unless an organization can effectively cover all of its costs—both financial and operating—it will eventually fail.

Clearly, only a limited supply of funds is available for investment in any given enterprise. The most efficient and profitable companies can attract the lowest-cost funds because they typically offer reasonable financial returns at very low relative risks. Newer and less prosperous firms must pay higher costs to attract capital because these companies tend to be quite risky. One of the strongest motivations for companies to manage their financial resources wisely is that they will, over time, be able to reduce the costs of their funds and in so doing increase their overall profitability.

In our free-enterprise economy, new firms tend to enter industries that offer the greatest potential rewards for success. However, as more and more companies enter an industry, competition intensifies, eventually driving profits down to average levels. The digital music player market of the early 2000s provides an excellent example of the changes in profitability that typically accompany increasing competition. The sign of a successful capital budgeting program is that the new products create higher than normal profits and drive sales and the stock price up. This has certainly been true for Apple since it made the decision to enter the electronics industry.

In 2001, Apple introduced the first iPod, and as the iPod became more popular, it made the iTunes Store possible. The iPhone, introduced in 2007, has now gone through many updates, and over time, iPhones took the place of iPods as music players and have become sophisticated cameras and mini televisions. The iPad was introduced in 2010 and is now the third most popular product after second-place Mac computers. In 2015, Apple introduced the Apple Watch, which is now in its fourth upgrade. Financial analysts always talk about Apple's ecosystem, which allows all Apple products to be synchronized and be updated on whatever products the user owns.

Even with a well-planned capital budgeting program, it may be difficult for Apple to stay ahead of the competition, and many people think Apple has lost its innovation lead to Samsung and Amazon. However, Apple is now the most valuable company in the world, valued at over $1 trillion on October 3, 2018. On June 9, 2014, Apple split its stock seven for one, meaning that for every share you owned, you would get six more, for a total of seven shares. There is no real gain involved because the stock price is divided by 7, so stockholders still have the same value, just more shares at a lower price. An investor who bought $1,000 of Apple stock in 2003 for $0.91 (price adjusted for stock splits) would have had Apple stock worth $229,109 on November 8, 2018. The problem is having the patience to continue to hold such a winner without taking some profits along the way.[2]

Maintaining market dominance is also difficult in the personal computer industry, particularly because tablet computers are taking away market share. With increasing competition, prices have fallen dramatically. Weaker

©The McGraw-Hill Companies, Inc./Jill Braaten

Apple stock trades at approximately 100 times what it did nearly ten years ago.

companies have failed, leaving the most efficient producers/marketers scrambling for market share. The expanded market for personal computers dramatically reduced the financial returns generated by each dollar invested in productive assets. The "glory days" of the personal computer industry—the time in which fortunes could be won and lost in the space of an average-sized garage—have long since passed into history. Personal computers have essentially become commodity items, and profit margins for companies in this industry have shrunk as the market matured and sales declined.

# Financing with Long-Term Liabilities

**LO 16-4** Specify how companies finance their operations and manage fixed assets with long-term liabilities, particularly bonds.

As we said earlier, long-term assets do not come cheap, and few companies have the cash on hand to open a new store across town, build a new manufacturing facility, research and develop a new life-saving drug, or launch a new product worldwide. To develop such fixed assets, companies need to raise low-cost, long-term funds to finance them. Two common choices for raising these funds are attracting new owners *(equity financing)*, which we'll look at in a moment, and taking on long-term liabilities *(debt financing)*, which we'll look at now.

**Long-term liabilities** are debts that will be repaid over a number of years, such as long-term bank loans and bond issues. These take many different forms, but in the end, the key word is *debt*. Companies may raise money by borrowing it from commercial banks or other financial institutions in the form of lines of credit, short-term loans, or long-term loans. Many corporations acquire debt by borrowing money from pension funds, mutual funds, or life-insurance funds.

Companies that rely too heavily on debt can get into serious trouble should the economy falter; during these times, they may not earn enough operating income to make the required interest payments (remember the times interest earned ratio in Chapter 14). In severe cases, when the problem persists too long, creditors will not restructure loans but will instead sue for the interest and principal owed and force the company into bankruptcy.

**long-term liabilities** debts that will be repaid over a number of years, such as long-term loans and bond issues

**bonds** debt instruments that larger companies sell to raise long-term funds

## Bonds: Corporate IOUs

Aside from loans, much long-term debt takes the form of **bonds**, which are debt instruments that larger companies sell to raise long-term funds. In essence, the buyers of bonds (bondholders) loan the issuer of the bonds cash in exchange for regular interest payments until the loan is repaid on or before the specified maturity date. The bond itself is a certificate, much like an IOU, that represents the company's debt to the bondholder. Bonds are issued by a wide variety of entities, including corporations; federal, provincial, and local governments; public utilities; and non-profit corporations. Most bondholders need not hold their bonds until maturity; rather, the existence of active secondary markets of brokers and dealers allows for the quick and efficient transfer of bonds from owner to owner.

The bond contract, or *indenture*, specifies all of the terms of the agreement between the bondholders and the issuing organization. The indenture, which can run more than a hundred pages, specifies the basic terms of the bond, such as its face value, maturity date, and annual interest rate. Table 16.2 briefly explains how to determine these and more things about a bond from a bond quote, as it might appear in the *National Post*.

**Table 16.2** | A Basic Bond Quote

| Issuer (1) | Coupon (2) | Maturity Date (3) | Bid $ (4) | Yield % (5) |
|---|---|---|---|---|
| Loblaw | 5.22 | June 18/2020 | 103.32 | 2.78 |

(1) Issuer—the name or abbreviation of the name of the company issuing the bond, in this case, Loblaw.

(2) Coupon—the annual percentage rate specified on the bond certificate: Loblaw's is 5.22 percent so a $1000 bond will earn $52.20 per year in interest.

(3) Maturity Date—the bond's maturity date; the year in which the issuer will repay bondholders the face value of each bond; 2020.

(4) Bid $—the closing price; 103.32 percent of $1000 per value or $1033.20 per bond.

(5) Yield %—yield to maturity; the percentage return based on the closing price; if you buy a bond with a $1000 par value at today's closing price of 103.32 ($1033.20) and receive $52.20 per year to maturity, your return will be 2.78 percent.

The face value of the bond, its initial sales price, is typically $1000. After this, however, the price of the bond on the open market will fluctuate along with changes in the economy (particularly, changes in interest rates) and in the creditworthiness of the issuer. Bondholders receive the face value of the bond along with the final interest payment on the maturity date. The annual interest rate (often called the *coupon rate*) is the guaranteed percentage of face value that the company will pay to the bond owner every year. For example, a $1,000 bond with a coupon rate of 7 percent would pay $70 per year in interest. In most cases, bond indentures specify that interest payments be made every six months. In the preceding example, the $70 annual payment would be divided into two semiannual payments of $35.

In addition to the terms of interest payments and maturity date, the bond indenture typically covers other important areas, such as repayment methods, interest payment dates, procedures to be followed in case the organization fails to make the interest payments, conditions for the early repayment of the bonds, and any conditions requiring the pledging of assets as collateral.

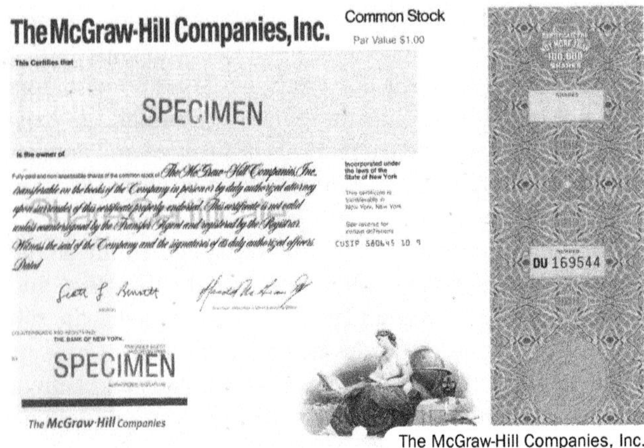

The McGraw-Hill Companies, Inc.

A McGraw-Hill stock certificate.

## Types of Bonds

Not surprisingly, there are a great many different types of bonds. Most are **unsecured bonds**, meaning that they are not backed by specific collateral; such bonds are termed *debentures.* **Secured bonds**, on the other hand, are backed by specific collateral that must be forfeited in the event that the issuing firm defaults. Whether secured or unsecured, bonds may be repaid in one lump sum or with many payments spread out over a period of time. **Serial bonds**, which are different from secured bonds, are actually a sequence of small bond issues of progressively longer maturity. The firm pays off each of the serial bonds as they mature. **Floating-rate bonds** do not have fixed interest payments; instead, the interest rate changes with current interest rates otherwise available in the economy.

High-yield bonds, or **junk bonds** as they are popularly known, offer relatively high rates of interest because they have higher inherent risks. Historically, junk bonds have been associated with companies in poor financial health and/or start-up firms with limited track records. In the mid-1980s, however, junk bonds became a very attractive method of financing corporate mergers; they remain popular today with many investors as a result of their very high relative interest rates. But higher risks are associated with those higher returns (upward of 12 percent per year in some cases) and the average investor would be well advised to heed those famous words: Look before you leap! The best strategy is to buy a mutual fund specializing in high yield bonds. This provides diversification across lots of risky bonds.

**unsecured bonds** debentures, or bonds that are not backed by specific collateral

**secured bonds** bonds that are backed by specific collateral that must be forfeited in the event that the issuing firm defaults

**serial bonds** a sequence of small bond issues of progressively longer maturity

**floating-rate bonds** bonds with interest rates that change with current interest rates otherwise available in the economy

**junk bonds** a special type of high interest-rate bond that carries higher inherent risks

## ENTREPRENEURSHIP IN ACTION

### Sounds Like Spotify's Non-IPO Was a Hit

**Spotify**

**Founders:** Daniel Ek and Martin Lorentzon

**Founded:** 2008 (launch date) in Stockholm, Sweden

**Success:** Spotify ended its first week as a public company with a market capitalization (total market value) of $27 billion. Just like any entrepreneurial journey, Spotify started with an idea. Entrepreneurs Daniel Ek and Martin Lorentzon were looking up music on Ek's home-theatre computer and thought the process could be improved. They began working on the Spotify application in 2005 and officially launched the application in 2008.

Spotify offers a free service where users can create, edit, and share playlists and tracks on social media, as well as make playlists with other users. Spotify provides access to more than 30 million songs and has more than 140 million monthly active users. Spotify pays royalties based on the number of artists' streams as a proportion of total songs streamed, instead of the traditional way of paying a fixed price per song or album sold.

On April 3, 2018, Spotify made its debut on the New York Stock Exchange with an opening price of $165.90 per share. The founders decided to do a direct listing, foregoing investment-banking underwriters and opting not to raise any money for itself. This saved the company tens of millions of dollars. About $940 million worth of Spotify's shares exchanged hands on the first day, making it the fourth largest opening trade in a company going public since 2010.*

**DISCUSSION QUESTIONS**

1. Why do you think Spotify was so popular among investors when it went public?
2. What were the benefits of doing a direct listing when going public? What does this indicate about how Spotify sees itself from a financial perspective?
3. How does Spotify's business royalty model differ from more traditional models, and why do you think this is important?

*Maureen Farrell and Alexander Osipovich, "Spotify's Splashy Debut Pressures Banks," *Wall Street Journal*, April 3, 2018, https://www.wsj.com/articles/spotify-sharesjump-in-market-debut-1522773951 (accessed April 14, 2018); Ben Sisario, "As Spotify Goes Public, Sony Cashes In," *New York Times*, April 4, 2018, https://www.nytimes.com/2018/04/04/business/media/as-spotify-goespublic-sony-cashes-in.html (accessed April 14, 2018); Adam Holownia, "How Spotify Started," *Medium*, February 1, 2017, https://medium.com/@obtaineudaimonia/how-spotifystarted-257e713fcd8f (accessed April 14, 2018).

# Financing with Owners' Equity

**LO 16-5** Discuss how corporations can use equity financing by issuing stock through an investment banker.

A second means of long-term financing is through equity. Remember from Chapter 14 that owners' equity refers to the owners' investment in an organization. Sole proprietors and partners own all or a part of their businesses outright, and their equity includes the money and assets they have brought into their ventures. Corporate owners, on the other hand, own stock or shares of their companies, which they hope will provide them with a return on their investment. Shareholders' equity includes common stock, preferred stock, and retained earnings.

"A second means of long-term financing is through equity."

Common stock (introduced in Chapter 4) is the single most important source of capital for most new companies. On the balance sheet, the common stock account is separated into two basic parts—common stock at par and capital in excess of par. The *par value* of a stock is simply the dollar amount printed on the stock certificate and has no relation to actual *market value*—the price at which the common stock is currently trading. The difference between a stock's par value and its offering price is called *capital in excess of par.* Except in the case of some very low-priced stocks, the capital in excess of par account is significantly larger than the par value account. Table 16.3 briefly explains how to gather important information from a stock quote, as it might appear in financial newspapers.

Preferred stock was defined in Chapter 14 as corporate ownership that gives the shareholder preference in the distribution of the company's profits but not the voting and control rights accorded to common shareholders. Thus, the primary advantage of owning preferred stock is that it is a safer investment than common stock.

All businesses exist to earn profits for their owners. Without the possibility of profit, there can be no incentive to risk investors' capital and succeed. When a corporation has profits left over after paying all of its expenses

**Table 16.3** | A Basic Stock Quote

| Stock (1) | Ticker (2) | Close (3) | Net Change (4) | Volume (5) | Day High/Low (6) | % Yield (7) | 52-Week High/Low (8) |
|---|---|---|---|---|---|---|---|
| **Loblaw Companies Ltd.** | L | 65.50 | −$1.04 | 644,470 | 65.90/63.01 | 1.46 | 69.94/51.90 |

(1) Stock—the name of the issuing company.

(2) Ticker—the ticker tape symbol for the stock; for **Loblaw Companies Ltd.**, L.

(3) Close—the last sale of the day; for **Loblaw**, $65.50.

(4) Net Change—the difference between the previous day's close and the close on the day being reported; **Loblaw** was down $1.04.

(5) Volume—the number of shares traded on this day; for **Loblaw**, 644,470.

(6) Day High/Low—the highest and lowest prices, respectively, paid for the stock during the day; for **Loblaw**, the highest was $65.90 and the lowest price, $63.01.

(7) Percent Yield—the dividend return on one share of common stock; 1.46%.

(8) 52-Week High/Low—the highest and lowest prices, respectively, paid for the stock in the last year; for **Loblaw's** stock, the highest was $69.94 and the lowest price, $51.90.

and taxes, it has the choice of retaining all or a portion of its earnings and/or paying them out to its shareholders in the form of dividends. **Retained earnings** are reinvested in the assets of the firm and belong to the owners in the form of equity. Retained earnings are an important source of funds and are, in fact, the only long-term funds that the company can generate internally.

When the board of directors distributes some of a corporation's profits to the owners, it issues them as cash dividend payments. But not all firms pay dividends. Many fast-growing firms retain all of their earnings because they can earn high rates of return on the earnings they reinvest. Companies with fewer growth opportunities typically pay out large proportions of their earnings in the form of dividends, thereby allowing their shareholders to reinvest their dividend payments in higher-growth companies.

Table 16.4 presents two companies and the dividend each paid on a single share of stock. As shown in the table, when the dividend is divided by the price, the result is the **dividend yield**. The dividend yield is the cash return as a percentage of the price but does not reflect the total return an investor earns on the individual stock. If the dividend yield is 1.3 percent on a company and the stock price increases by 10 percent, then the total return would be 11.3 percent. It is not clear that stocks with high dividend yields will be preferred by investors to those with little or no dividends. Most large companies pay their shareholders dividends on a quarterly basis.

**retained earnings** earnings after expenses and taxes that are reinvested in the assets of the firm and belong to the owners in the form of equity

**dividend yield** the dividend per share divided by the stock price

**DID YOU KNOW?**

A single share of Coca-Cola stock purchased during its original 1919 IPO would be worth more than $5 million today.[3]

The last column in Table 16.4 is the price-to-earnings (P/E) ratio, which measures the current share price relative to the per-share earnings (EPS).

## Investment Banking

A company that needs more money to expand or take advantage of opportunities may be able to obtain financing by issuing stock. The first-time sale of stocks and bonds directly to the public is called a new issue or an initial public offering (IPO) and creates a stock that can be traded in the secondary market. Companies that already have stocks or bonds outstanding may offer more stock or a new issue of bonds to raise additional funds for specific projects.

**Table 16.4** | Estimated Common Stock Price–Earnings Ratios and Dividends for Two Companies

| Ticker Symbol | Company Name | Price Per Share | Annualized Dividend Per Share | Dividend Yield | Earnings Per Share | P/E Ratio |
|---|---|---|---|---|---|---|
| L | Loblaw | 65.50 | 1.13 | 1.46 | 4.38 | 14.97 |
| MRU | Metro | 48.98 | 0.72 | 1.52 | 2.51 | 19.38 |

New issues of stocks and bonds are sold directly to the public and to institutions in what is known as the **primary market**—the market where firms raise financial capital. The primary market differs from **secondary markets**, which are stock exchanges and over-the-counter markets where investors can trade their securities with other investors rather than the company that issued the stock or bonds. Primary market transactions actually raise cash for the issuing corporations, while secondary market transactions do not. For example, when Facebook went public on May 18, 2012, its IPO raised $16 billion for the company and stockholders, who were cashing in on their success. Once the investment bankers distributed the stock to retail brokers, the brokers sold it to clients in the secondary market for $38 per share. The stock got off to a rocky start and hit a low of $17.73 in September 2012. However, by March 2014, it was at $71.97, and it was $168.10 on April 19, 2018.

**primary market** the market where firms raise financial capital

**secondary markets** stock exchanges and over-the-counter markets where investors can trade their securities with others

**investment banking** the sale of stocks and bonds for corporations

**Investment banking**, the sale of stocks and bonds for corporations, helps such companies raise funds by matching people and institutions who have money to invest with corporations in need of resources to exploit new opportunities. Corporations usually employ an investment banking firm to help sell their securities in the primary market. An investment banker helps firms establish appropriate offering prices for their securities. In addition, the investment banker takes care of the myriad details and securities regulations involved in any sale of securities to the public.

Gerald Schwartz runs Onex, one of Canada's largest private equity firms.

Just as large corporations such as BCE and Bombardier have a client relationship with a law firm and an accounting firm, they also have a client relationship with an investment banking firm. An investment banking firm

## Consider the Following: Building shareholder value

**Gerald Schwartz** is founder, chairman, and CEO of Onex, Canada's largest private equity firm. The only son of a Winnipeg auto parts dealer and a lawyer, Schwartz spent his childhood in an apartment upstairs from his grandparents and worked at his father's auto parts store on Friday nights and Saturdays. His high school ambition, he says, was to be an executive and to have a big job that would pay at least $10,000 a year. He studied law at the University of Manitoba and later moved to Boston to earn a Harvard MBA. From there, he went to New York City, where he became part of a team of investment bankers that pioneered leveraged-buyout techniques on Wall Street. He also did deals with Michael Milken, the junk-bond king.

In the late 1970s, Schwartz and a partner, Izzy Asper, founded a media company, later known as CanWest Global Communications. He left CanWest in 1983 and went on to establish Onex. Onex began as a private company financed by a variety of Canadian pension funds, banks, and trust companies. Its mission: to seek out and acquire under-managed companies, preferably ones with brand-name recognition or divisions of large companies. His preference for friendly acquisitions has helped Onex amass a group of companies with 110,000 employees and $17 billion in revenue. Notable components of the $20 billion portfolio are the Cineplex movie chain and Celestica, the huge electronics manufacturer. He is known as a long-term, patient investor who knows how to create shareholder value.*

*Graham F. Scott, "Canada's Top 100 highest paid CEOs," *Canadian Business,* January 20, 2015, http://www.canadianbusiness.com/lists-and-rankings/richest-people/top-100-highest-paid-ceos-2015; Kimberley Noble, "Gerry Schwartz (Profile)," retrieved from *The Canadian Encyclopedia,* last edited December 16, 2013, http://www.thecanadianencyclopedia.ca/en/article/gerry-schwartz-profile/; "The World's Billionaires: Gerald Schwartz," Forbes, n.d.,http://www.forbes.com/profile/gerald-schwartz/; "Gerald Schwartz," Onex.com, n.d., http://www.onex.com/gerald_w_schwartz.aspx; "The Power 25," *Globe and Mail,* October 27, 2005, http://www.theglobeandmail.com/report-on-business/the-power-25/article20429456/?page=all; "The success secrets of Gerry Schwartz," *Profit,* May 16, 2011, http://www.profitguide.com/manage-grow/success-stories/the-success-secrets-of-gerry-schwartz-29394 (all accessed January 11, 2016).

©Lester Balajadia/Shutterstock

CIBC World Markets has almost 1300 employees who work with corporate, government, and institutional clients to tailor solutions to help them access capital, expand their operations, and actively invest.[4]

©EdStock/iStockphoto.com

The New York Stock Exchange is the world's largest stock exchange by market capitalization.

such as CIBC World Markets can provide advice about financing plans, dividend policy, or stock repurchases, as well as advice on mergers and acquisitions. Many now offer additional banking services, making them "one-stop shopping" banking centres.

When companies merge, they often use investment bankers to help them value the transaction. Each firm will want an outside opinion about what it is worth to the other. Sometimes mergers fall apart because the companies cannot agree on the price each company is worth or the structure of management after the merger. The advising investment banker, working with management, often irons out these details. Of course, investment bankers do not provide these services for free. They usually charge a fee of between 1 and 1.5 percent of the transaction. A $20 billion merger can generate between $200 and $300 million in investment banking fees. The merger mania of the late 1990s allowed top investment bankers to earn huge sums. Unfortunately, this type of fee income is dependent on healthy stock markets, which seem to stimulate the merger fever among corporate executives.

# The Securities Markets

**LO 16-6** Describe the various securities markets in Canada.

**Securities markets** provide a mechanism for buying and selling securities. They make it possible for owners to sell their stocks and bonds to other investors. Thus, in the broadest sense, stocks and bonds markets may be thought of as providers of liquidity—the ability to turn security holdings into cash quickly and at minimal expense and effort. Without liquid securities markets, many potential investors would sit on the sidelines rather than invest their hard-earned savings in securities. Indeed, the ability to sell securities at well-established market prices is one of the very pillars of the capitalistic society that has developed over the years in Canada.

**securities markets** the mechanism for buying and selling securities

Unlike the primary market, in which corporations sell stocks directly to the public, secondary markets permit the trading of previously issued securities. There are many different secondary markets for both stocks and bonds. If you want to purchase 100 shares of Google common stock, for example, you must purchase this stock from another investor or institution. It is the active buying and selling by many thousands of investors that establishes the prices of all financial securities. Secondary market trades may take place on organized exchanges or in what is known as the over-the-counter market. Many brokerage houses exist to help investors with financial decisions, and many offer their services through the Internet. One such broker is TD Waterhouse. Its site offers a wealth of information and provides educational material to individual investors.

## Stock Markets

Stock markets exist around the world in New York, Toronto, Tokyo, London, Frankfurt, Paris, and other world locations. The TMX Group operates cash and derivatives markets for multiple asset classes—such as equities, fixed income, and energy—as well as Canada's two national stock exchanges: the Toronto Stock Exchange serving the senior equity market and the TSX Venture Exchange serving the public venture equity market. Now owned by the TMX Group, the Montreal Exchange was Canada's oldest exchange and has leadership in the financial derivatives market. The two biggest stock markets in the United States are the New York Stock Exchange (NYSE) and the NASDAQ.

Exchanges used to be divided into organized exchanges and over-the-counter markets, but during the last several years, dramatic changes have occurred. The TSX, NYSE, and NASDAQ became publicly traded companies. They were previously not-for-profit organizations but are now for-profit companies. In an attempt to expand their markets, NASDAQ acquired the OMX, a Nordic stock exchange headquartered in Sweden, and the New York Stock Exchange merged with Euronext, a large European electronic exchange that trades options and futures contracts as well as common stock.

Traditionally, the NASDAQ market has been an electronics market, and many of the large technology companies such as Microsoft and Apple trade on it. The NASDAQ operates through dealers who buy and sell common stock (inventory) for their own accounts.

The NYSE used to be primarily a floor-traded market, where brokers meet at trading posts on the floor of the New York Stock Exchange to buy and sell common stock, but now more than 80 percent of NYSE trading is electronic. The brokers act as agents for their clients and do not own their own inventory. This traditional division between the two markets is becoming less significant as the exchanges become electronic.

**Electronic Markets.** Electronic markets have grown quickly because of the speed, low cost, and efficiency of trading that they offer over floor trading. One of the fastest-growing electronic markets has been the Intercontinental Exchange (referred to as ICE). ICE, based in Atlanta, Georgia, primarily trades financial and commodity futures products. It started out as an energy futures exchange and has broadened its futures contracts into an array of commodities and derivative products.

©Photographer's Choice/Getty Images

The Toronto Exchange is the world's ninth-biggest stock exchange in terms of market capitalization.

In December 2012, ICE made an offer to buy the New York Stock Exchange. When the NYSE became a public company and had common stock trading in the secondary market, rather than being the hunter, it became the prey. On November 13, 2013, ICE completed its takeover of the NYSE. One condition of the takeover was for ICE to divest itself of Euronext because international regulators thought the company would have a monopoly on European derivative markets. Also acquired as part of the NYSE family of exchanges was LIFFE, the London International Financial Futures Exchange. Many analysts thought that LIFFE was the major reason ICE bought the NYSE—not for its equity markets trading common stocks. What we are seeing is the globalization of securities markets and the increasing reliance on electronic trading.

The rise of electronic markets has led to the rise of robotic trading, sometimes referred to as "bots" or "algos," use algorithmic trading formulas to buy and sell based on market trends. Robotic trading looks for patterns in the market that will trigger a trade to buy or sell. These trading systems rely on programmed instructions that have the advantage of eliminating psychological trading errors. These systems also react to market trends faster than human traders. Using artificial intelligence to enhance trading systems is continuing to transform financial trading, making it more data-driven and efficient.

## The Over-the-Counter Market

Unlike the organized exchanges, the **over-the-counter (OTC) market** is a network of electronically linked dealers. It has no central location. Today, the OTC market for stocks consists of small stocks, illiquid bank stocks, penny stocks, and companies whose stocks trade on the "pink sheets." However, as most corporate bonds and all government debt securities are also traded over the counter, the OTC market regularly accounts for the largest total dollar value of all of the secondary markets.

**over-the-counter (OTC) market** a network of electronically linked dealers

## Measuring Market Performance

Investors, especially professional money managers, want to know how well their investments are performing relative to the market as a whole. Financial managers also need to know how their companies' securities are performing when compared with their competitors'. Thus, performance measures—averages and indexes—are very

## RESPONDING TO BUSINESS CHALLENGES

### Improving Gender Diversity in Finance

While more than half of accounting majors in university undergraduate programs are women, only a few companies on the TSX 60 index have a woman as CFO. This discrepancy is a concern to companies that are trying to emphasize diversity in management. Although discrimination is still a problem, studies suggest that other factors contribute to this low percentage.

One theory is that women do not have as many connections with higher-level finance executives as men. According to a former portfolio consultant, because female employees do not often connect as well with male supervisors, they may be passed up for future management opportunities. The support of senior executives is often essential for career advancement because these executives can successfully advocate on behalf of the employee.

A solution that some companies have implemented is formal mentorship programs for women, but even these efforts have not seemed very successful. Instead, certain businesses have created programs to encourage female executives to form long-lasting relationships with female finance employees. In one such program, female finance executives agree to spend a year mentoring employees recommended by their managers. It is believed that this longer time period will enable the executive and the employee to form a closer relationship; this in turn could result in more female employees being sponsored for financial leadership positions.*

#### DISCUSSION QUESTIONS

1. Why do you think there are so few female CFOs?
2. Describe some ways that companies are trying to promote management positions to female finance employees.
3. Do you feel that a mentorship program will help close the gap?

*Marielle Segarra, "Taking the Next Step," *CFO*, July 15, 2011, www.cfo.com/article.cfm/14586563?f5singlepage (accessed November 3, 2011); Dan Fitzpatrick and Lisa Rappaport, "Financial Firms' Ceiling," *Wall Street Journal*, September 8, 2011, http://online.wsj.com/article/SB10001424053111904103404576557100384026220.html?KEYWORDS5Financial1Firms%275Ceiling (accessed November 3, 2011); Kyle Stock, "Ranks of Women on Wall Street Thin," *Wall Street Journal*, September 20, 2010, http://online.wsj.com/article/SB10001424052748704858304575498071732136704.html (accessed November 3, 2011); Ligaya and Deschamps, " Women still a significant minority at the top rungs of Canada's corporate ladder," *Globe and Mail*, July 31, 2018, https://www.theglobeandmail.com/business/article-women-still-a-significant-minority-at-the-top-rungs-of-canadas/, (accessed February 21, 2019).

important to many different people. They not only indicate the performance of a particular securities market but also provide a measure of the overall health of the economy.

Indexes and averages are used to measure stock prices. An *index* compares current stock prices with those in a specified base period, such as 1944, 1967, or 1977. An *average* is the average of certain stock prices. The averages used are usually not simple calculations, however. Some stock market averages (such as the S&P/TSX Composite Index) are weighted averages, where the weights employed are the total market values of each stock in the index (in this case 500). The Dow Jones Industrial Average is a price-weighted average. Regardless of how constructed, all market averages of stocks move closely together over time.

Many investors follow the activity of stock indexes like the S&P/TSX or the Dow Jones Industrial Average very closely to see whether the stock market has gone up or down. Table 16.5 lists the top ten constituents that currently make up the S&P/TSX 60.

The numbers listed in an index or average that tracks the performance of a stock market are expressed not as dollars but as a number on a fixed scale. A period of large increases in stock prices is known as a *bull market*, with the bull symbolizing an aggressive, charging market and rising stock prices. A declining stock market is known

**Table 16.5** | Top Ten Constituents by Index Weight on the S&P/TSX 60 (as of December 31, 2018)

| Constituent | Symbol | GICS® Sector |
|---|---|---|
| Royal Bank of Canada | RY | Financials |
| Toronto-Dominion Bank | TD | Financials |
| Enbridge Inc. | ENB | Energy |
| Bank of Nova Scotia | BNS | Financials |
| Canadian National Railways | CNR | Industrials |
| Suncor Energy Inc. | SU | Energy |
| Bank of Montreal | BMO | Financials |
| BCE Inc. | BCE | Telecommunications |
| TransCanada Corp | TRP | Energy |
| Brookfield Asset Management Inc. | BAM.A | Financials |

as a *bear market*, with the bear symbolizing sluggish, retreating activity. When stock prices decline very rapidly, the market is said to *crash*.

For investors to make sound financial decisions, it is important that they stay in touch with business news, markets, and indexes. Of course, business and investment publications, such as the *Financial Post*, the *Report on Business*, and *Money*, offer this type of information. Many Internet sites—including CNN Business, Globe Investor, TMX Money, Yahoo! Finance, and others—offer this information as well. Many sites offer searchable databases of information by topic, company, or keyword. However investors choose to receive and review business news, doing so is a necessity in today's market.

"Many investors follow the activity of the S&P/TSX to see whether the stock market has gone up or down."

**TEAM EXERCISE**

Compare and contrast financing with long-term liabilities such as bonds versus financing with owners' equity—typically retained earnings, common stock, and preferred stock. Form groups and suggest a good mix of long-term liabilities and owners' equity for a new firm that makes wind turbines for generating alternative energy and aims to grow quickly.

# LEARNING OBJECTIVES SUMMARY

**LO 16-1** Describe some common methods of managing current assets.

Current assets are short-term resources such as cash, investments, accounts receivable, and inventory, which can be converted to cash within a year. Financial managers focus on minimizing the amount of cash kept on hand and increasing the speed of collections through lockboxes and electronic funds transfer and investing in marketable securities. Marketable securities include Treasury bills, certificates of deposit, commercial paper, and money market funds. Managing accounts receivable requires judging customer creditworthiness and creating credit terms that encourage prompt payment. Inventory management focuses on determining optimum inventory levels that minimize the cost of storing and ordering inventory without sacrificing too many lost sales due to inventory shortages.

**LO 16-2** Identify some sources of short-term financing (current liabilities).

Current liabilities are short-term debt obligations that must be repaid within one year, such as accounts payable, taxes payable, and notes (loans) payable. Trade credit is extended by suppliers for the purchase of their goods and services. A line of credit is an arrangement by which a bank agrees to lend a specified amount of money to a business whenever the business needs it. Secured loans are backed by collateral; unsecured loans are backed only by the borrower's good reputation.

**LO 16-3** Summarize the importance of long-term assets and capital budgeting.

Long-term, or fixed, assets are expected to last for many years, such as production facilities (plants), offices, and equipment. Businesses need modern, up-to-date equipment to succeed in today's competitive environment. Capital budgeting is the process of analyzing company needs and selecting the assets that will maximize its value; a capital budget is the amount of money budgeted for the purchase of fixed assets. Every investment in fixed assets carries some risk.

**LO 16-4** Specify how companies finance their operations and manage fixed assets with long-term liabilities, particularly bonds.

Two common choices for financing are equity financing (attracting new owners) and debt financing (taking on long-term liabilities). Long-term liabilities are debts that will be repaid over a number of years, such as long-term bank loans and bond issues. A bond is a long-term debt security that an organization sells to raise money. The bond indenture specifies the provisions of the bond contract—maturity date, coupon rate, repayment methods, and others.

**LO 16-5** Discuss how corporations can use equity financing by issuing stock through an investment banker.

Owners' equity represents what owners have contributed to the company and includes common stock, preferred stock, and retained earnings (profits that have been reinvested in the assets of the firm). To finance operations, companies can issue new common and preferred stock through an investment banker that sells stocks and bonds for corporations.

**LO 16-6** Describe the various securities markets in Canada.

Securities markets provide the mechanism for buying and selling stocks and bonds. Primary markets allow companies to raise capital by selling new stock directly to investors through investment bankers. Secondary markets allow the buyers of previously issued shares of stock to sell them to other owners. The major secondary market is the S&P/TSX Composite Index in Canada. Investors measure stock market performance by watching stock market averages and indexes such as the S&P/TSX Composite Index and the Dow Jones Industrial Average.

# KEY TERMS

bonds
capital budgeting
commercial certificates of deposit (CDs)
commercial paper
dividend yield
eurodollar market
factor
floating-rate bonds
investment banking
junk bonds
line of credit
long-term (fixed) assets
long-term liabilities
marketable securities
over-the-counter (OTC) market
primary market
prime rate
retained earnings
secondary markets
secured bonds
secured loans
securities markets
serial bonds
trade credit
transaction balances
Treasury bills (T-bills)
unsecured bonds
unsecured loans
working capital management

# So You Want to Work *in Financial Management or Securities*

Taking classes in financial and securities management can provide many career options, from managing a small firm's accounts receivable to handling charitable giving for a multinational to investment banking to stock brokerage. Practically every organization—whether in manufacturing, communications, finance, education, health care, or government—has one or more financial managers and/or financial analysts. Working under titles such as treasurer, controller, cash manager, or financial analyst, these financial managers and analysts prepare and interpret the financial reports required by organizations seeking to ensure that the resources under their control are optimally employed.

Financial management differs from accounting chiefly by its differential focus. By nature, accounting is based almost exclusively on summaries of past organizational transactions and prior account history. In contrast, financial management, despite its frequent reliance on many accounting statements, primarily looks forward. Forward-looking questions, such as how to invest excess cash, determine whether a project should be implemented, when to issue stocks or bonds, or when to initiate loans, are addressed by financial managers and analysts.

Many different industries require people with finance skills. So do not despair if you have a difficult time finding a job in exactly the right firm. Most students switch companies a number of times over the course of their careers. Many organizations require individuals trained in forecasting, statistics, economics, and finance. Even unlikely places like museums, aquariums, and zoos need people who are good at numbers. It may require some creativity, but if you are committed to a career in finance, look to less obvious sources—not just the large financial firms.[5]

# BUILD YOUR BUSINESS PLAN

## Financial Management and Securities Markets

This chapter helps you realize that once you are making money, you need to be careful in determining how to invest it. Meanwhile, your team should consider the pros and cons of establishing a line of credit at the bank.

Remember that the key to building your business plan is to be realistic!

# CASE | Hershey Foods: Melts in Your Mouth and May Melt Your Heart

Hershey Foods is the leading North American producer of quality chocolate and candy products, including much-loved brands such as Hershey's milk chocolate bar, Hershey's syrup, Hershey's cocoa, Almond Joy, Mr. Goodbar, Hershey's Kisses, Kit Kat, and Reese's peanut butter cups.

A century after its founding, the company continues to operate by the values of its founder. Milton Hershey was born in 1857 and was of Pennsylvania Dutch descent. He became an apprentice to a candy maker in 1872, at age 15. By age 30, he had founded the Lancaster Caramel Company. After visiting the Chicago Exhibition in 1893, he became interested in a new chocolate-making machine. He sold his caramel factory and built a large chocolate factory in Derry Church, Pennsylvania, in 1905; the city was renamed Hershey in 1906.

Hershey pioneered modern confectionery mass-production techniques by developing much of the machinery for making and packaging his milk chocolate products. The Hershey Foods Corporation as it exists today was organized under the laws of the state of Delaware on October 24, 1927, as a successor to the original business founded in 1894 by Milton Hershey. The company's stock was first publicly traded on December 1, 1927, and investors can still purchase shares today.

Milton Hershey was not only interested in innovative candy making, he wanted to help the members of his community. An example of his concern for the community was the founding of a home and school for orphan children, the Hershey Industrial School (now called the Milton Hershey School) in 1909. Many of the children who attended the school became Hershey employees, including former Hershey chairman William Dearden (1976–1984).

Today, the 10,000-acre campus houses and provides education for nearly 1300 financially and socially disadvantaged children. Although Hershey remains a public corporation, the Milton Hershey School Trust, which financially supports the school, owns about 30 percent of Hershey Foods' total equity. The Milton Hershey School Trust also owns 100 percent of the Hershey Entertainment and Resort Company, which operates a number of Hershey's non-chocolate properties, including the Hersheypark theme park, the Dutch Wonderland theme park for younger children, the Hershey Hotel, the Hershey Lodge and Convention Center, the Hershey Bears minor league hockey team, Hershey's zoo, a four-course golf club, an outdoor sports stadium, and an indoor sports arena.

Because of Milton Hershey's original funding and the wise investment management by the trust managers, the assets of the Milton Hershey School Trust have grown to a value of more than $7 billion. Milton Hershey was a visionary in terms of using a public corporation to support his philanthropic dreams.[6]

### DISCUSSION QUESTIONS

1. Do you think that Milton Hershey made the right decision in leaving his foundation the controlling voting interest in the Hershey Foods Corporation?
2. Is Hershey Foods' example of founders willing stock for philanthropic purposes something that you believe that companies could do today? Why or why not?
3. Knowing that a large share of Hershey's profits support philanthropic causes, would you be more likely to purchase the company's stock?

# ENDNOTES

## Chapter 1


1. Fairfax (2018), **https://www.fairfax.ca/Corporate/company-profile/default.aspx** (retrieved October 22, 2018); **Gurufocus.com** (2016), **http://www.gurufocus.com/StockBuy.php?GuruName=Prem Watsa** (retrieved January 17, 2016); **Wikipedia.org** (2018), **https://en.wikipedia.org/wiki/Fairfax_Financial** (retrieved October 22, 2018); **http://business.financialpost.com/news/fp-street/fairfax-financial-holdings-ltd-chief-executive-prem-watsa-tells-his-horatio-alger-story**; John Boyko, "Prem Watsa," *The Canadian Encyclopedia*, January 26, 2018; Historica Canada, **https://www.thecanadianencyclopedia.ca/en/article/prem-watsa** (accessed October 22, 2018); Forbes (2018), **https://www.forbes.com/companies/fairfax-financial/#4482d412750e**, (accessed October 22, 2018).
2. Walmartcanada.ca. (2018), **http://www.walmartcanada.ca/newsroom/press-releases/2010/11/10/walmart-canada-opens-its-first-sustainable-distribution-centre** (retrieved November 22, 2018).
3. Jay Young and Janet Loehrke, "Ward's Automotive Reports," US Bureau of Economic Analysis, reported in *USA Today*, March 14, 2017, p. 1B. **Corporateknights.com** (2018). Peter Gorrie, "The 2018 Canadian Clean Cars Guide," **https://www.corporateknights.com/channels/transportation/2018-canadian-clean-cars-guide-15282612/** (retrieved October 28, 2018).
4. Bessma Momani and Jillian Stirk, "Diversity Dividend: Canada's Global Advantage," **https://www.cigionline.org/sites/default/files/documents/DiversitySpecialReportWEB_0.pdf** (retrieved October 28, 2018).
5. Esther Fung, "Mall Owners Head for Exits as Retail Tenants Move Out," *Wall Street Journal*, January 25, 2017, p. A1.
6. Ron Joyce, *The Untold Story of Tim Hortons by the Man Who Created a Canadian Empire*, (Toronto: Harper Collins Publisher's Ltd., 2006), p. 180; Adam Lauzon, "Can I Get a Large Double-Double, Please?" **http://adamlauzon.wordpress.com/**, (accessed July 17, 2010); Newswireca. (2018). **Newswire.ca**, **https://www.newswire.ca/news-releases/tim-hortons-roll-up-the-rim-to-win-celebrates-25-years-with-better-odds—one-in-six-chances—and-more-prizes-than-ever-507719601.html** (retrieved October 25, 2018).
7. Adrian Wooldridge, *The Economist* online, "Special Report: The Visible Hand," **https://www.economist.com/special-report/2012/01/21/the-visible-hand**
8. "Special Report: The World in Their Hands," *The Economist*, January 21, 2012, p. 15–17.
9. "The Dragons," CBC website, n.d., **http://www.cbc.ca/dragonsden/dragons/** (accessed October 25, 2018).
10. Paul Toscano, "The Worst Hyperinflation Situations of All Time," CNBC, February 14, 2011, **http://www.cnbc.com/id/41532451** (accessed May 1, 2017); P. Laya and A. Rosati, "Venezuela's 2018 Inflation to Hit 1.37 Million Percent, IMF Says," *Bloomberg Markets*, **https://www.bloomberg.com/news/articles/2018-10-09/venezuela-s-2018-inflation-to-hit-1-37-million-percent-imf-says**, (accessed October 9, 2018).
11. CBC, "Federal government's total 'market debt' now tops $1 trillion, documents show," **https://www.cbc.ca/news/politics/federal-market-debt-1.4590441** (accessed October 10, 2018).
12. OECD Economic Surveys: Canada 2016, **http://www.oecdbetterlifeindex.org/countries/canada/** (retrieved October 10, 2018).
13. "The Criminalisation of American Business," *The Economist*, August 30–September 5, 2014, pp. 21–24; Tracy Gonzalez-Padron, G. Tomas M. Hult, and O.C. Ferrell, "Stakeholder Marketing Relationships to Social Responsibility and Firm Performance," Working paper, 2015.
14. Arthur Ray, "Hudson's Bay Company," *Canadian Encyclopedia* online, **https://www.thecanadianencyclopedia.ca/en/article/hudsons-bay-company**, (accessed October 10, 2018).
15. Terry Long, "The History of New France: The First European Settlers in Canada," Suite101.com, May 31, 2009, **http://www.suite101.com/content/the-history-of-new-france-a121662**.
16. Peter J. Nicholson, "The Growth Story: Canada's Long-run Economic Performance and Prospects," *International Productivity Monitor*, 2003, **www.csls.ca/ipm/7/nicholson-e.pdf**, pp. 3–23.
17. Royal Bank of Canada (2018), **http://www.rbi.com/About-Us** (retrieved October 28, 2018).
18. Joann S. Lublin, "New Report Finds a Diversity Dividend at Work," *Wall Street Journal*, January 20, 2015, **http://blogs.wsj.com/atwork/2015/01/20/new-report-finds-a-diversity-dividend-at-work/** (accessed February 22, 2016).
19. "The 2011 World's Most Ethical Companies," *Ethisphere*, 2011, Q1, pp. 37–43.
20. Isabelle Maignon, Tracy L. Gonzalez-Padron, G. Tomas M. Hult, and O.C. Ferrell, "Stakeholder Orientation: Development and Testing of a Framework for Socially Responsible Marketing," *Journal of Strategic Marketing* 19, no. 4 (July 2011), pp. 313–338. Corporateknightscom (2018), Corporate Knights, **https://www.corporateknights.com/magazines//2018-best-50-results-15283499/** (retrieved October 26, 2018).
21. Small Business Administration Office of Advocacy, *Frequently Asked Questions*, 2012, **www.sba.gov/sites/default/files/FAQ_Sept_2012.pdf** (accessed February 23, 2016); Joel Holland, "Save the World, Make a Million," *Entrepreneur*, April 2010, **http://www.entrepreneur.com/article/205556** (accessed February 23, 2016); iContact, **www.icontact.com** (accessed May 1, 2017); Leigh Buchanan, "The U.S. Now Has 27 Million Entrepreneurs," Inc., **http://www.inc.com/leigh-buchanan/us-entrepreneurshipreaches-recordhighs.html** (accessed May 1, 2017); "Key Small Business Statistics - August 2013," Industry Canada, June 2016, **http://www.ic.gc.ca/eic/site/061.nsf/eng/h_02800.html** (accessed October 10, 2018).
22. Scott Martin, "How Apple Rewrote the Rules of Retailing," *USA Today*, May 19, 2011, p. 1B; Steve Denning, "Apple's Retail Success Is More Than Magic," *Forbes*, June 17, 2011, **www.forbes.com/sites/stevedenning/2011/06/17/apples-retail-stores-more-than-magic/3/** (accessed August 22, 2011); Jefferson Graham, "At Apple Stores, iPads at Your Service," *USA Today*, May 23, 2011, p. 1B; "Apple Becomes World's Most Valuable Brand, Ending Google's Four-Year Term at the Top, says WPP's BrandZ,"

Millward Brown, May 8, 2011, **www.millwardbrown.com/Global/News/PressReleases/PressReleaseDetails/11-05-08/Apple_Becomes_World_s_Most_Valuable_Brand_Ending_Google_s_Four_Year_Term_at_the_Top_says_WPP_S_BrandZ.aspx** (accessed September 20, 2011).

## Chapter 2

1. "A timeline of auto sector layoffs," CBC News, February 9, 2009, **http://www.cbc.ca/canada/story/2008/10/21/f-autolayoffs.html**
2. Greg Farrell, "Lay, Skilling Found Guilty," *USA Today*, May 26, 2006, pp. A1, B1; *New York Times* coverage of the Enron trial, **www.nytimes.com/business/businessspecial3/index.html?adxnnl=1&adxnnlx=1147986237-z56Vd16RUkp6eHnHTTXBHw** (accessed May 18, 2006); "RCMP charge former Nortel CEO, 2 other execs," CBC News online, June 19, 2008, **http://www.cbc.ca/money/story/2008/06/19/nortel-rcmp.html#ixzz11ROltiTM**; Marguerite Reardon, "Former Nortel execs face criminal charges," cnet News, June 19, 2008, **http://news.cnet.com/8301-10784_3-9973257-7.html#ixzz11RQKFGJr**; "Enron," Wikipedia, **http://en.wikipedia.org/wiki/Enron** (accessed July 17, 2010).
3. Kristen Smalley, "How Important is Corporate Social Responsibility to Canadian Workers?" October 30, 2018, **https://www.randstad.ca/workforce360-trends/archives/do-canadians-care-about-corporate-social-responsibility_1810/**
4. "Sarbanes-Oxley Act," Wikipedia, accessed July 17, 2010, **http://en.wikipedia.org/wiki/Sarbanes%E2%80%93Oxley_Act**
5. Simon Houpt, "Telus sues Rogers over ad claims," *Globe and Mail*, November 18, 2009, **http://www.theglobeandmail.com/news/technology/telus-sues-rogers-over-ad-claims/article1368486/**; "Rogers stands behind its Internet advertising as fastest and most reliable," *Cape Breton Post*, February 17, 2010, **http://www.capebretonpost.com/Living/Technologies/2010-02-17/article-837486/Rogers-stands-behind-its-Internet-advertising-as-fastest-and-most-reliable/1**
6. Russell Hotten, "Volkswagen: The scandal explained," BBC News, December 10, 2015, **http://www.bbc.com/news/business-34324772** (accessed November 7, 2015).
7. O. C. Ferrell, John Fraedrich, Linda Ferrell, *Business Ethics: Ethical Decision Making and Cases*, 6th ed. (Boston: Houghton Mifflin, 2005), p. 7.
8. David Callahan, as quoted in Archie Carroll, "Carroll: Do We Live in a Cheating Culture?", *Athens Banner-Herald*, February 21, 2004, **www.onlineathens.com/stores/022204/bus_20040222028.shtml**
9. "Colorado Places Barnett on Administrative Leave," SI.com, February 19, 2004, **http://sportsillustrated.cnn.com/**
10. David Ebner, "Anti-doping agency calls for ban on Russian track-and-field athletes" *Globe and Mail*, November 10, 2015, **http://www.theglobeandmail.com/sports/anti-doping-agency-accuses-russia-of-coverup-calls-for-ban-on-athletes/article27172282/** (accessed November 10, 2015).
11. "National Business Ethics Survey 2005," "Survey Documents State of Ethics in the Workplace," and "Misconduct" (n.d.), Ethics Resource Center, accessed April 11, 2006, **www.ethics.org/nbes/2005/release.html.**
12. "40% of Canadians bullied at work, experts say," CBC News, December 6, 2011, **http://www.cbc.ca/news/canada/windsor/40-of-canadians-bullied-at-work-expert-says-1.987450** (accessed November 9, 2015).
13. Karen MacGregor, "Acres International convicted in African bribery case," Probe International, September 18, 2002, **http://www.probeinternational.org/odious-debts/acres-intl-convicted-african-bribery-case**
14. Greg McArthur, "NIKO Resources: Ottawa's corruption test case," *Report on Business*, August 25, 2011, **http://www.theglobeandmail.com/report-on-business/rob-magazine/niko-resources-ottawas-corruption-test-case/article542842/** (accessed June 18, 2013).
15. Canadian Competition Bureau, June 13, 2003, **http://www.competitionbureau.gc.ca/eic/site/cb-bc.nsf/eng/01863.html**; and July 6, 2004, **http://www.competitionbureau.gc.ca/eic/site/cb-bc.nsf/eng/01863.html**
16. "Pens and Post-Its Among Most Pilfered Office Supplies, Says New Vault Survey," Vault, November 16, 2005, **www.vault.com/nr/newsmain.jsp?nr_page=3&ch_id=420&article_id=25720773** (accessed June 2, 2006).
17. "Maple Leaf Foods plant linked to Listeria outbreak," CTV News, August 23, 2008, **http://www.ctv.ca/CTVNews/EdmontonHome/20080823/recall_listeria_080823/**; Sarah Schmidt and Mike De Souza, "Maple Leaf CEO says food industry must improve safety regime," *National Post*, April 20, 2009, **http://www.nationalpost.com/news/canada/story.html?id=1516299**; Our Journey to Safe Leadership (Maple Leaf blog), accessed July 17, 2010, **http://blog.mapleleaf.com/**
18. Transparency International, **http://www.transparency.org/** (accessed July 17, 2019).
19. Alex Gillis, "Cheating themselves," University Affairs online, March 12, 2007, **http://www.universityaffairs.ca/cheating-themselves.aspx**
20. "Teens Respect Good Business Ethics," *USA Today*, Snapshots, December 12, 2005, p. 13–1.
21. Marianne Jennings, "An Ethical Breach by Any Other Name," College of Business Master Teacher Initiative, Colorado State University, January/February 2006, **http://www.biz.colostate.edu/MTI/TeachingTips/Academic_Integrity/EthicalBreach.aspx**
22. Matthew McClearn, "Probiotics: Yogurt's secret ingredient," *Canadian Business*, November 1, 2012, **http://www.canadianbusiness.com/lifestyle/probiotics-yogurts-secret-ingredient/** (accessed June 19, 2013).
23. Erica Johnson, "Questioning the Magic at Herbal Magic," CBC.ca *Marketplace* blog, February 5, 2010, **http://www.cbc.ca/marketplace/blog/2010/02/questioning-the-magic-at-herbal-magic.html**
24. "Tracking a diet scam," CTV News, February 22, 2002, **http://www.ctv.ca/CTVNews/SpecialEvent1/20020222/ctvnews836330/**
25. "Mexico, United States, Canada Combat Weight Loss Fraud," U.S. Food and Drug Administration, October 24, 2005, **http://www.fda.gov/NewsEvents/Newsroom/PressAnnouncements/2005/ucm108504.htm**
26. "Campaign Warns about Drugs from Canada," CNN, February 5, 2004, **www.cnn.com**; Gardiner Harris and Monica Davey,

"FDA Begins Push to End Drug Imports," *New York Times*, January 23, 2004, p. C1.

27. "Briefing: Tobacco Packaging and Labelling," Information Resource Center, accessed July 31, 2006, **http://infolink.cancerresearchuk.org/publicpolicy/briefings/prevention/tobacco**
28. Food and Consumer Products of Canada, Consumer Products Safety, **http://www.fcpc.ca/issues/safety/index.html** (accessed July 18, 2010).
29. Nestor E. Arellano. "Toronto firm fined for unlicensed software use," *IT World Canada*, October 4, 2006, **http://www.itworldcanada.com/news/toronto-firm-fined-for-unlicensed-software-use/100124** (accessed July 17, 2010).
30. "WestJet to sue Air Canada for corporate spying," CTV News, June 30, 2004, **http://www.ctv.ca/CTVNews/Canada/20040630/westjet_suesaircanada_20040629/**; "WestJet apologizes to Air Canada for snooping," *National Post*, May 30, 2006, **http://www.canada.com/topics/technology/story.html?p=1&k=30762&id=6138fbd4-c3db-44ca-83a7-bfb6bcc0cbdb**; "Air Canada, WestJet settle spying lawsuit," CBC News, May 30, 2006, **http://www.cbc.ca/money/story/2006/05/29/westjet-aircansettle.html**
31. Blake Morrison, "Ex-USA Today Reporter Faked Major Stories," *USA Today*, March 19, 2004, **www.usatoday.com/**
32. Thomas M. Jones, "Ethical Decision Making by Individuals in Organizations: An Issue-Contingent Model," *Academy of Management Review* 2 (April 1991), pp. 371–73.
33. Sir Adrian Cadbury, "Ethical Managers Make Their Own Rules," *Harvard Business Review* 65 (September–October 1987), p. 72.
34. Ferrell, Fraedrich, and Ferrell, *Business Ethics*, pp. 174–75.
35. Ethics Resource Center, "Misconduct" (n.d.), accessed April 11, 2006, **www.ethics.org/nbes/2005/release.html**
36. Ethics Resource Center, "2005 National Business Ethics Survey: Executive Summary" (n.d.), accessed July 17, 2010, **www.ethic.org/nbes2005/2005nbes_summary.html**, p. 29.
37. "Whistleblower legislation: Bill C-25, Disclosure Protection," CBC News, April 28, 2004, **http://www.cbc.ca/news/background/whistleblower/** (accessed July 27, 2010).
38. Ferrell, Fraedrich, and Ferrell, *Business Ethics*, p. 13.
39. John Galvin, "The New Business Ethics," **SmartBusinessMag.com**, June 2000, p. 99.
40. Archie B. Carroll, "The Pyramid of Corporate Social Responsibility: Toward the Moral Management of Organizational Stakeholders," *Business Horizons* 34 (July/August 1991), p. 42.
41. Corporate Knights, **http://www.corporateknights.ca/** (accessed July 17, 2010).
42. Ferrell, Fraedrich, and Ferrell, *Business Ethics*, pp. 13–19.
43. "Canadian Auto Workers," Wikipedia, **http://en.wikipedia.org/wiki/Canadian_Auto_Workers** (accessed July 17, 2010); "Deadline passes with no deal between CAW, GM," CBC News, May 16, 2009, **http://www.cbc.ca/canada/story/2009/05/15/gm-canada-caw-talks497.html**
44. "WestJet Airlines Ltd.—Company Profile, Information, Business Description, History, Background Information on WestJet Airlines Ltd.," **http://www.referenceforbusiness.com/history2/70/WestJet-Airlines-Ltd.html** (accessed July 17, 2010); Richard Yerema and R. Caballero, "Employer Review: Royal Bank of Canada," Mediacorp Canada Inc., November 2, 2009, **http://www.eluta.ca/top-employer-rbc**
45. Chad Terhune, "Jury Says Home Depot Must Pay Customer Hurt by Falling Merchandise $1.5 Million," *Wall Street Journal*, July 16, 2001, p. A14.
46. "About Us," Office of Consumer Affairs, **http://www.ic.gc.ca/eic/site/oca-bc.nsf/eng/ca00038.html** (accessed June 28, 2010).
47. Loren Drummond, "EU representative condemns seal hunt after Canada visit," The Humane Society of the United States, March 28, 2007, **http://www.hsus.org/marine_mammals/marine_mammals_news/eu_representative_condemns_hunt.html**; "Seal hunting," Wikipedia, **http://en.wikipedia.org/wiki/Seal_hunting** (accessed July 17, 2010); "Bring on the seal war, fisheries minister tells activists," CBC News, September 7, 2006, **http://www.cbc.ca/canada/newfoundland-labrador/story/2006/09/07/seal-war.html**; "FAQs: The Atlantic seal hunt," CBC News, July 27, 2009, **http://www.cbc.ca/canada/story/2009/05/05/f-seal-hunt.html**
48. "FAQs: The Atlantic seal hunt," CBC News, July 27, 2009, **http://www.cbc.ca/canada/story/2009/05/05/f-seal-hunt.html** (accessed July 27, 2010).
49. "Oils sands production using nearly one-third of Canada's natural gas," April 19, 2017, **https://www.bnnbloomberg.ca/oil-sands-production-using-nearly-one-third-of-canada-s-natural-gas-1.728578**
50. Cahal Milmo, "The biggest environmental crime in history," *The Independent*, **http://www.independent.co.uk/environment/the-biggest-environmental-crime-in-history-764102.html** (accessed July 18, 2010).
51. Laura Judy, "Green from the Ground Up," *Atlanta Home Improvement*, January 2006, **www.homeimprovementmag.com/Articles/2006/06Jan_ground_up.html** (accessed June 15, 2007); Earthcraft House, **www.earthcrafthouse.com** (accessed October 5, 2007); "Earthcraft House Program," "Green Fast Facts: Did You Know…" **www.atlantahomebuilders.com/education/earthcraft.cfm** (accessed October 5, 2007); Melanie Lindner, "Living Green" EarthCraft House," Atlanta Intown Newspaper, January 2007, **www.atlantaintownpaper.com/features/EarthCraftHouseJAN07.php** (accessed October 5, 2007).
52. Alan K. Reichert, Marion S. Webb, and Edward G. Thomas, "Corporate Support for Ethical and Environmental Policies: A Financial Management Perspective," *Journal of Business Ethics* 25 (2000), pp. 53–64.
53. "Trend Watch," *Business Ethics*, March/April 2001, p. 8.
54. David J. Lynch, "Corporate America Warms to Fight Against Global Warming," *USA Today*, June 1, 2006, p. B1.
55. Laurie Goldstein, "Marriott Meetings Go Green," *Marriott News*, July 22, 2008, **http://www.marriott.com/news/detail.mi?marrArticle=347592** (accessed July 16, 2010).
56. Lush Fresh Handmade Cosmetics, accessed July 27, 2010, **http://www.lush.ca/shop/about-lush/articles/our-green-initiatives/packaging.html**
57. "Certification" (n.d.), Home Depot, accessed April 6, 2004, **www.homedepot.com/HDUS/EN_US/corporate/corp_respon/certification.shtml**
58. "Yes, We Have No Bananas: Rainforest Alliance Certifies Chiquita Bananas" (n.d.), *Ag Journal*, **www.agjournal.com/story.cfm?story_id_1047** (accessed April 6, 2004).
59. "Delta Hotels and Resorts Wraps Up Cross-Canada Tour to Build Stronger Communities," Habitat for Humanity Canada, accessed Nov. 3, 2010, **http://habitat.ca/deltap4088.php**;

MADD Canada, accessed Nov 3. 2010, **http://www.madd.ca/english/donating/sponsors_complete.html**; "CMHA Corporate Donors," Canadian Mental Health Association, accessed November 3, 2010, **http://www.cmha.ca/bins/content_page.asp?cid=7-19**

60. "Who Really Pays for CSR Initiatives," *Environmental Leader*, February 15, 2008, **www.environmentalleader.com/2008/02/15/who-really-paysfor-csr-initiatives/** (accessed February 25, 2010); "Global Fund," **www.joinred.com/globalfund** (accessed February 25, 2010); Reena Jana, "The Business of Going Green," *BusinessWeek*, June 22, 2007, **www.businessweek.com/innovate/content/jun2007/id20070622_491833.htm?chan=search** (accessed June 19, 2008).

## Chapter 3

1. Lulu Yilun Chen, "Online Giant Alibaba Aims beyond China and E-Commerce: QuickTake," *Washington Post*, November 13, 2017, **https://www.washingtonpost.com/business/online-giant-alibaba-aims-beyond-china-and-ecommerce-quicktake/2017/11/13/9147da86-c846-11e7-b506-8a10ed11ecf5_story.html** (accessed November 19, 2017); Katherine Rushton, "Alibaba Is Now the Biggest Retailer in the World," *Telegraph* (U.K.), October 28, 2014, **http://www.telegraph.co.uk/finance/newsbysector/retailandconsumer/11193340/Alibaba-is-now-the-biggestretailer-in-the-world.html** (accessed November 25, 2017); Laura Lorenzetti, "Alibaba Heads to Hollywood with Its New Cash Stockpile," *Fortune*, October 28, 2014, **http://fortune.com/2014/10/28/alibaba-heads-to-hollywood-withits-new-cash-stockpile/** (accessed November 25, 2017); Bill George, "Jack Ma on Alibaba, Entrepreneurs, and the Role of Handstands," *New York Times*, September 22, 2014, **http://dealbook.nytimes.com/2014/09/22/jack-ma-on-alibabaentrepreneurs-and-the-role-of-handstands/?_r=0** (accessed November 25, 2017); Frank Langfitt, "From a Chinese Apartment to Wall Street Darling: The Rise of Alibaba," National Public Radio, September 8, 2014, **http://www.npr.org/blogs/parallels/2014/09/08/326930271/from-a-chineseapartment-to-wall-street-darling-the-rise-of-alibaba** (accessed November 25, 2017); Aaron Pressman and Adam Lashinsky, "Data Sheet–Alibaba's Vast and Growing Reach," *Fortune*, November 13, 2017, **http://fortune.com/2017/11/13/datasheet-alibaba-payments-shopping/** (accessed November 19, 2017); Daniel Keyes, "Amazon Is Struggling to Find its Place in China," *Business Insider*, August 30, 2017, **http://www.businessinsider.com/amazon-is-struggling-to-find-its-placechina-2017-8** (accessed November 19, 2017); Kathy Chu, "Alibaba to Act Faster Against Counterfeits," *Wall Street Journal*, May 15, 2014, p. B1; "E-commerce with Chinese characteristics," *The Economist*, November 15, 2007, **http://www.economist.com/node/10125658** (accessed November 25, 2017); Eric Markowitz, "From Start-up to Billion-Dollar Company," Inc., April 6, 2012, **https://www.inc.com/eric-markowitz/alibaba-film-dawn-of-the-chinese-internetrevolution.html** (accessed November 25, 2017); "#21 Jack Ma," Forbes.com (2018), **https://www.forbes.com/profile/jack-ma/** (retrieved December 13, 2018).
2. Elisabeth Sullivan, "Choose Your Words Wisely," *Marketing News*, February 15, 2008, p. 22.
3. Findlaw.com (2018), Findlaw. Retrieved November 26, 2018, from https://corporate.findlaw.com/business-operations/u-s-canada-outsourcing-a-canadian-perspective.html; **www.cbc.ca.** (2018), CBC, **https://www.cbc.ca/news/business/cibc-outsourcing-jobs-india-1.4045759** (retrieved 26 November, 2018).
4. Statistics Canada, Table 12-10-0011-01, International Merchandise Trade for All Countries and by Principal Trading Partners (x 1,000,000), **http://www.statcan.gc.ca/tables-tableaux/sum-som/l01/cst01/gblec02a-eng.htm** (accessed November 26, 2018).
5. Statistics Canada, Table 12-10-0011-01, International Merchandise Trade for All Countries and by Principal Trading Partners (x 1,000,000), **http://www.statcan.gc.ca/tables-tableaux/sum-som/l01/cst01/gblec02a-eng.htm** (accessed November 26, 2018).
6. Adapted from Statistics Canada, Table 12-10-0011-01, International merchandise trade for all countries and by Principal Trading Partners (x 1,000,000), (accessed November 26, 2018).
7. Adapted from Statistics Canada, "Canadian international merchandise trade," *The Daily*, February 11, 2009, **http://www.statcan.gc.ca/daily-quotidien/090211/dq090211a-eng.htm** (accessed August 17, 2009).
8. Unctad.org (2018), **https://unctad.org/en/PublicationsLibrary/aldc2015d5_en.pdf** (retrieved November 27, 2018).
9. "Shaken, Not Stirred," *The Economist*, January 24, 2015, p. 48.
10. BSA, "Security Threats Rank as Top Reason Not to Use Unlicensed Software," **http://globalstudy.bsa.org/2013/** (accessed May 3, 2017).
11. Jen Skerritt, "Timber Tariffs Are Hammering U.S. Builders," *Bloomberg Businessweek*, March 12, 2018, p. 35.
12. Foreign Affairs and International Trade Canada website, **www.international.gc.ca/controls-controles/about-a_propos/impor/importing-importation.aspx** (accessed August 17, 2009).
13. Laurie Burkitt, "Tiffany Finds Sparkle in Overseas Markets," *Wall Street Journal*, December 26, 2013, p. B4.
14. Julie Jargon, "Starbucks Shifts in Europe," *Wall Street Journal*, November 30–December 1, 2013, p. B3.
15. Kyle Stock, "Movers," *Bloomberg Businessweek*, March 6–12, 2017, p. 19.
16. "Slogans Gone Bad," **www.joe-ks.com/archives_apr2004/slogans_gone_bad.htm** (accessed June 6, 2006).
17. Nina Lakhani, "Coca-Cola Apologizes for Indigenous People Ad Intended as 'Message of Unity,'" *The Guardian*, December 5, 2015, **http://www.theguardian.com/world/2015/dec/05/coca-cola-mexico-ad-indigenous-people** (accessed May 3, 2017).
18. Gartner, "Gartner Says Worldwide PC Shipments Declined 9.5 Percent in Second Quarter of 2015," July 9, 2015, **http://www. gartner.com/newsroom/id/3090817** (accessed May 3, 2017).
19. "What Is the WTO?" World Trade Organization (n.d.), **www.wto.org** (accessed February 25, 2004).
20. "Canada has just detonated a bomb," *Financial Post*, January 10, 2018, **https://business.financialpost.com/news/economy/u-s-lashes-out-over-ottawas-wto-trade-claim-just-after-higher-tariffs-announced-for-canadian-newsprint-producrs** (accessed December 15, 2018).
21. *CIA—The World Factbook*, https://**www.cia.gov/library/publications/the-world-factbook/geos/us.html**
22. U.S. Census Bureau, "Trade in Goods with Canada," **https://www.census.gov/foreign-trade/balance/c1220.html** (accessed April 1, 2018).

23. "America's Biggest Partners," CNBC.com, **www.cnbc.com/id/31064179?slide=11** (accessed February 24, 2010).

24. Statistics Canada, "Table 1 Merchandise Trade: Canada's Top 10 Principal Trading Partners—Seasonally Adjusted, Current Dollars," December 5, 2014, **http://www.statcan.gc.ca/daily-quotidien/141205/t141205b001-eng.htm** (accessed May 3, 2017).

25. "North America: Mexico," *CIA World Factbook*, **https://www.cia.gov/library/publications/the-world-factbook/geos/mx.html** (February 24, 2010); International Monetary Fund, **www.imf.org/external/pubs/ft/weo/2010/02/weodata/weorept.aspx?sy=2008&ey=2015&scsm=1&ssd=1&sort=country&ds=.&br=1&c=273&s=PPPGDP%2CPPPPC&grp=0&a=&pr.x=67&pr.y=136** (accessed January 10, 2011).

26. "Crisis Revisited," *The Economist*, December 13, 2014, p. 17; "Euro Area," European Commission, **https://ec.europa.eu/info/business-economy-euro/euro-area_en** (accessed January 28, 2017).

27. "IMF World Economic Outlook Database," International Monetary Fund, October 2017, **www.imf.org/external/pubs/ft/weo/2017/02/weodata/weorept.aspx?pr.x=89&pr.y=6&sy=2017&ey=2017&scsm=1&ssd=1&sort=country&ds=.&br=1&c=998&s=NGDPD%2CPPPGDP%2CPPPPC&grp=1&a=1** (accessed February 11, 2018).

28. Stanley Reed with Ariane Sains, David Fairlamb, and Carol Matlack, "The Euro: How Damaging a Hit?" *BusinessWeek*, September 29, 2003, p. 63; "The Single Currency," CNN (n.d.), **www.cnn.com/SPECIALS/2000/eurounion/story/currency/** (accessed July 3, 2001).

29. Asia-Pacific Economic Cooperation, "About APEC," **www.apec.org/About-Us/About-APEC.aspx** (accessed November 21, 2014); "U.S.-APEC Trade Facts," Office of the Unites States Trade Representative, **https://ustr.gov/trade-agreements/other-initiatives/asia-pacific-economic-cooperation-apec/us-apec-trade-facts** (accessed January 31, 2017).

30. "About APEC," Asia-Pacific Economic Cooperation, **www.apec.org/apec/about_apec.html** (accessed December 15, 2018).

31. Geri Smith and Cristina Lindblad, "Mexico: Was NAFTA Worth It?" *Bloomberg Businessweek*, **https://www.bloomberg.com/news/articles/2003-12-21/mexico-was-nafta-worth-it**

32. Charles Riley and Feng Ke, "China to Overtake U.S. as World's Top Trader," CNN, January 10, 2014, **http://money.cnn.com/2014/01/10/news/economy/china-us-trade/** (accessed May 3, 2017).

33. Kathy Chu, "China Loses Edge on Labor Costs," *Wall Street Journal*, December 3, 2015, p. B1, B4; World Economic Forum, September 11, 2018, **https://www.weforum.org/agenda/2018/09/how-vietnam-became-an-economic-miracle/**, (accessed July 30, 2019).

34. Association of Southeast Asian Nations, "Overview," **www.aseansec.org/64.htm** (accessed April 10, 2014).

35. "ASEAN Economic Community: 12 Things to Know," Asian Development Bank, December 29, 2015, **http://www.adb.org/features/asean-economic-community-12-things-know** (accessed January 6, 2016).

36. Simon Long, "Safety in Numbers," *The Economist*, The World in 2015 Edition, p. 68.

37. R.C., "No Brussels Sprouts in Bali," *The Economist*, November 18, 2011, **www.economist.com/banyan/2011/11/18/no-brussels-sprouts-in-bali** (accessed May 3, 2017).

38. "Thaksin Times," *The Economist*, January 31, 2015, p. 31.

39. Eric Bellman, "Asia Seeks Integration Despite EU's Woes," *Wall Street Journal*, July 22, 2011, A9

40. David J. Lynch, "The IMF Is . . . Tired Fund Struggles to Reinvent Itself," *USA Today*, April 19, 2006. p. B1.

41. Ilan Brat and Paul Kiernan, "Heinz Seeks to Tap Mexico's Taste for Ketchup," *Wall Street Journal*, November 24, 2009, pp. B1–B2.

42. Canadian Commercial Corporation (n.d), **www.ccc.ca/eng/home.cfm**

43. Export Development Canada (n.d.), **www.edc.ca/english/corporate.htm**

44. Sobia Khan, "Shell to Open Largest Offshore Delivery Centre Globally in Bengaluru," *Economic Times*, June 5, 2015, **http://economictimes.indiatimes.com/jobs/shell-toopen-largest-offshore-delivery-centre-globally-in-bengaluru/articleshow/47548572.cms** (accessed May 3, 2017).

45. Paul Mozer, "Qualcomm in Venture with Chinese Chip Maker," *New York Times*, June 23, 2015, **http://www.nytimes.com/2015/06/24/business/international/qualcomm-in-venturewith-chinese-chip-maker.html?_r=0** (accessed May 3, 2017).

46. Calum Fuller, "EY and LinkedIn Announce Strategic Alliance," *Accountancy Age*, October 30, 2015, **http://www.accountancyage.com/aa/news/2432737/ey-and-linkedinannounce-strategic-alliance** (accessed May 3, 2017).

47. Guo Changdong and Ren Ruqin, "Nestle CEO visits Tianjin," *China Daily*, August 12, 2010, **www.chinadaily.com.cn/m/tianjin/e/2010-08/12/content_11146560.htm** (accessed May 3, 2017); Nestlé, "How Many Factories Do You Have," **http://www.nestle.com/ask-nestle/our-company/answers/how-manyfactories-do-you-have** (accessed May 3, 2017).

48. O. C. Ferrell, John Fraedrich, and Linda Ferrell, *Business Ethics*, 6th ed. (Boston: Houghton Mifflin, 2005), pp. 227–230.

49. Kimberlee Morrison, "Who Are the Most (and Least) Engaged Brands on Twitter?" *Ad Week*, March 16, 2015, **http://www.adweek.com/socialtimes/the-most-and-leastengaged-brands-on-twitter/617045** (accessed May 3, 2017).

50. Canadian Trade Commissioner (n.d.), **http://www.tradecommissioner.gc.ca/eng/services.jsp**

51. McGraw-Hill video, **http://www.viddler.com/embed/50051953/?f=1&autoplay=0&player=full&disablebranding=0** (accessed April 11, 2016); Brain Staff, "Trek Announces Acquisition of Electra," *Bicycle Retailer*, January 6, 2014, **http://www.bicycleretailer.com/north-america/2014/01/06/trek-announces-acquisition-electra#.Vwu7TjArLIV** (accessed April 11, 2016); Ron Callahan, "Electra Bicycle Company Opens Global Headquarters with Slowest Bicycle Race," *Bike World News*, November 10, 2012, **http://www.bikeworldnews.com/2012/11/10/electra-bicycle-companyopens-global-headquarters-slowest-bicycle-race/** (accessed April 11, 2016); Electra Bicycle Company website, **http://www.electrabike.com/** (accessed April 11, 2016).

## Chapter 4

1. Maggie Overfelt, "Start-Me-Up: The California Garage," *Fortune Small Business*, July/Aug. 2003, **www.fortune.com/fortune/smallbusiness/articles/0,15114,475872,00.html**

2. "1: Digital Artists Agency," *Business 2.0*, April 2004, p. 90.

3. Linda Tischles, "Join the Circus," *Fast Company*, July 2005, pp. 53–58.

4. Tracey Bochner, "The Case for Having a Partner," *PROFIT Guide*, September 18, 2014, **http://www.profitguide.com/manage-grow/strategy-operations/the-case-for-having-a-partner-69106**

5. Alexis Muellner, "Marlins Partners in Dispute, Still Want Rings," *South Florida Business Journal*, February 27, 2004, **www.bizjournals.com/southflorida/stories/2004/03/01/story5.html**

6. Sissi Wang, "Why You Should Treat Your Business Partnership like a Marriage," *PROFIT Guide*, June 30, 2015, **http://www.profitguide.com/manage-grow/leadership/why-you-should-treat-your-business-partnership-like-a-marriage-84545**

7. Sabrina Tavernise, "Harrison McCain, 76, King Of the Frozen French Fry," *New York Times*, March 21, 2004, **http://www.nytimes.com/2004/03/21/world/harrison-mccain-76-king-of-the-frozen-french-fry.html**

8. Chris Griffiths, "When it's time to incorporate your business," *Globe and Mail*, June 12, 2012, **http://www.theglobeandmail.com/report-on-business/small-business/sb-money/when-its-time-to-incorporate-your-business/article4242051/**

9. The Upside, "Stocks by Market Capitalization – Toronto Stock Exchange", March 6, 2015, **http://www.theupside.ca/list-tsx-stocks-market-capitalization/.**

10. Jeff Lagerquist, "Getting in on the Ground Floor: Canada's IPO Winners and Losers," *Business News Network*, June 3, 2015, **http://www.bnn.ca/News/2015/6/3/Getting-in-on-the-ground-floor-Canadas-IPO-winners-and-losers.aspx**

11. Merissa Marr, "Video Chain CEO to Take Company Private in Buyout," *Wall Street Journal*, March 30, 2004, **http://online.wsj.com**

12. O. C. Ferrell, John Fraedrich, and Linda Ferrell, *Business Ethics: Ethical Decision Making and Cases*, 6th ed. (Boston: Houghton Mifflin, 2005), p. 84.

13. "Report to the Congress: Increased Penalties under the *Sarbanes-Oxley Act* of 2002," **http://www.ussc.gov/r_congress/s-oreport.pdf**

14. Matt Krantz, "Web of Board Members Ties Together Corporate America," *USA Today*, November 23, 2002, pp. 1B, 3B.

15. Emily Thornton and Aaron Pressman, "Phil Purcell's Credibility Crisis," *BusinessWeek*, March 21, 2005.

16. Jesus Diaz, "The web of board members that link American corporations, mapped," July 30, 2018, **https://www.fastcompany.com/90209537/the-web-of-board-members-that-link-american-corporations-mapped**

17. Thomas Watson, "His way or the highway: Frank Stronach is God's gift to shareholders. Don't believe it? Just ask him." *Canadian Business*, May 23, 2005, **http://www.canadianbusiness.com/managing/strategy/article.jsp?content=20060109_103241_4508**

18. Sarah Efron, "RBC, Canada's biggest company, has revenue equal to the GDP of Latvia," *FP Magazine Daily*, June 2, 2009, **http://network.nationalpost.com/np/blogs/fpmagazinedaily/archive/2009/06/02/rbc-canada-s-biggest-company-has-revenue-equal-to-the-gdp-of-latvia.aspx**

19. Eleanor Beaton, "The lure of ESOPs," *PROFITguide*, May 31, 2007, **http://www.profitguide.com/manage-grow/strategy-operations/the-lure-of-esops-29171** (accessed June 20, 2013).

20. Cooperatives in Canada, February 9, 2016 **http://www.cooperativedifference.coop/co-operatives-in-canada/**

21. Devin Leonard, "How Disney Bought Lucasfilm—and Its Plans for 'Star Wars,'" Bloomberg Businessweek, March 7, 2013, **http://www.businessweek.com/articles/2013-03-07/how-disney-bought-lucasfilm-and-its-plans-for-star-wars** (accessed July 15, 2013).

22. Dirk Libby, "How Often Disney Is Planning to Release Star Wars Movies," *CinemaBLEND*, December 12, 2015, **http://www.cinemablend.com/new/How-Often-Disney-Planning-Release-Star-Wars-Movies-94987.html**

23. Jamie Sturgeon, "It's Official, Tim Hortons, Burger King Become One," *Global News*, December 12, 2014, **http://globalnews.ca/news/1724238/its-official-tim-hortons-burger-king-become-one/**

24. "CRTC Rejects Bell-Astral Merger," *Canadian Business Journal* online, October 18, 2012, **http://www.cbj.ca/business_news/canadian_business_news/crtc_rejects_bell-astral_merger.html** (accessed July 15, 2013).

25. James Chen, "Hostile Takeover," May 5, 2019, **https://www.investopedia.com/terms/h/hostiletakeover.asp**

## Chapter 5

1. Statistics Canada, **https://www.ic.gc.ca/eic/site/061.nsf/eng/h_03018.html#point1-1** (accessed January 1, 2019).

2. Ian Portsmouth (Ed.), *Profit*, March 2013, **http://www.pdfmagazines.org/magazines/business/44338-profit-march-2013.html**

3. "The Power of Innovation," *Inc. State of Small Business*, 23, no. 7 (2001), p. 103.

4. Scott Allen, "Entrepreneur Success Story: Brian Scudamore of 1-800-GOT-JUNK?", About.com: Entrepreneurs, **http://entrepreneurs.about.com/od/casestudies/a/1800gotjunk.htm** (accessed July 17, 2010).

5. Robert D. Hisrich, Michael P. Peters, Dean A. Shepherd, and Peter Mombourquette, *Entrepreneurship* (2nd Canadian edition), (Toronto: McGraw-Hill Ryerson Ltd., 2009), p. 75.

6. "U of T student named 2010 Student Entrepreneur Ontario Champion," ACE, February 17, 2010, **http://www.acecanada.ca/news/newsItem.cfm?cms_news_id=372**

7. Tony Martin, "Profit Hot 50: Simple ways to sell more," *PROFITguide*, September 1, 2009, **http://www.profitguide.com/article/4360--profit-hot-50-simple-ways-to-sell-more**

8. "Survey on Financing of Small and Medium Enterprises," Statistics Canada, March 11, 2009, **http://www.statcan.gc.ca/cgi-bin/imdb/p2SV.pl?Function=getSurvey&SDDS=2941&lang=en&id=imdb&adm=8&dis=2**

9. Canadian Federation of Independent Business, **www.cfib.ca/** (accessed July 17, 2010).

10. "Key Small Business Statistics," Industry Canada: Small Business and Tourism Branch, January 2019, **http://www.ic.gc.ca/eic/site/061.nsf/eng/h_03090.html#point1-1**

11. "Key Small Business Statistics," Industry Canada: Small Business and Tourism Branch, January 2019, **http://www.ic.gc.ca/eic/site/061.nsf/eng/h_03090.html#point1-1**

12. Susan Ward, "Statistics on Canadian Women in Business," February 22, 2018, **https://www.thebalancesmb.com/statistics-on-canadian-women-in-business-2948029**

13. Key Small Business Statics, **https://www.ic.gc.ca/eic/site/061.nsf/eng/h_03018.html#point2-3** (accessed January 1, 2018).
14. "Summary of the Survey on Financing an Growth of Small and Medium Enterprise," 2014, **https://www.ic.gc.ca/eic/site/061.nsf/eng/02998.html**
15. Diane Disse, "The Birth of IMAX," **http://www.ieee.ca/millennium/imax/imax_birth.html** (accessed July 17, 2010).
16. Trevor Melanson, "Is HootSuite Canada's Next Billion-Dollar Tech Titan?", *Canadian Business*, Winter 2012/13, **http://www.canadianbusiness.com/technology-news/is-hootsuite-canadas-next-tech-titan/**
17. Ron Joyce, *Always Fresh: The Untold Story of Tim Hortons by the Man Who Created a Canadian Empire* (Toronto: Harper Collins Publishers Ltd., 2006).
18. Export insights from eBay Canada's Entrepreneur of the Year, May 30, 2017, **https://www.edc.ca/en/article/export-insights-from-boutique-step-up.html**
19. Jerry Langton, "Canine couture," *Toronto Star*, November 17, 2008, **http://www.thestar.com/Business/SmallBusiness/article/538014.**
20. **www.foufoubrands.com** (accessed March 1, 2019).
21. Douglas Quenqua, "To Create Its Hits, a Company Takes Its Toys on Tour," *New York Times*, June 9, 2008, **http://www.nytimes.com/2008/06/09/business/media/09spin.html**
22. Kristine Orwram, "How Spin Master has defied the odds to transform into a $5.3-billion toy powerhouse," *Financial Post*, April 30, 2018, **https://business.financialpost.com/news/retail-marketing/spin-master-defies-tears-in-toy-land-with-175-rally-since-ipo**
23. Ibid.
24. Peter Svensson, "U.S. Economy Grows at a Slower Pace," *Washington Post*, June 5, 2006, **www.washingtonpost.com/wp-dyn/content/article/2006/06/05/AR2006060500376.html** (accessed June 5, 2006).
25. "STARTUP 50: The Complete Ranking of Canada's Top New Growth Companies," *Profit* and *Canadian Business*, September 14, 2017, **https://www.canadianbusiness.com/profit500/2017-ranking-startup-50/**
26. John Lorinc, "How construction firm Gillam Group became Canada's Fastest Growing Company," *Canadian Business*, September 14, 2017, **https://www.canadianbusiness.com/lists-and-rankings/profit-500/2017-gillam-group/**
27. "Canadian Dragons' Den contestants who went on to make millions," MSN Money, September 20, 2018, **https://www.msn.com/en-ca/money/topstories/canadian-dragons-den-contestants-who-went-on-to-make-millions/ss-BBNzjSY**
28. "Top Scanning Apps for iPhone and Android," October 25, 2017, **https://appolicious.com/top-scanning-apps-for-iphone-and-android/**
29. Chad Sapieha, "B.C.'s Hinterland reflects on The Long Dark's lengthy development and success," *Financial Post*, September 7, 2017.
30. Kirk McKeand, "The Long Dark passes one million sales and lands a movie deal," Accessed March 1, 2019, **https://www.pcgamesn.com/the-long-dark/the-long-dark-sales-numbers-movie**
31. Rachel Knuttel, "The 12 Coolest Dorm Room Startups," **http://thelala.com/12-coolest-dorm-room-startups/** (accessed March 1, 2019).
32. Meet the Dragons: Lane Merrifield, **https://www.cbc.ca/dragonsden/blog/new-dragon-lane-merrifield** (accessed March 1, 2019).
33. "Small Business Statistics" (n.d.), Small Business Administration, **www.sba.gov/aboutsba/sbastats.html** (accessed March 16, 2004).
34. Author interview with Kenzie MacDonald, 2017.
35. Andrea Gordon, "Mompreneurs boom," *Toronto Star*, April 4, 2008, **http://www.thestar.com/article/409934**
36. Colin MacDonald, guest speaker, Mount Saint Vincent University's 35th Annual Business and Tourism Conference, October 2009, Halifax, NS.
37. "Entrepreneur Success Story," Canadian Youth Business Foundation, September 2009, **http://www.cybf.ca/story-gallery/success-stories/bc/Rocky%20Point%20Kayak.pdf**
38. Andy Holloway, "Problem Solvers: To boldly grow…carefully, that is," *Profit*, **http://list.canadianbusiness.com/rankings/profit100/2009/growth/article.aspx?id=20090601_30010_30010** (accessed July 18, 2010); and **https://www.targray.com/company** (accessed March 1, 2019.)
39. Kym Wolfe, "The Sound of Success," *Alumni Gazette* (University of Western Ontario), September 7, 2010, **http://communications.uwo.ca/com/alumni_gazette/alumni_gazetteprofiles/the_sound_of_success_20100907446732/**
40. Laura Pratt, "PROFIT HOT 50: Safer Passage," *Profit*, October 2009, p. 36.
41. Ibid.
42. Dana Knight, "Big Headed Guy Gets a Big Idea for Sunglasses Business," *USA Today*, March 21, 2006, p. 4B; Fatheadz Eyewear, **www.fatheadz.com** (accessed June 5, 2006).
43. "CEO Michael Gokturk interviewed on BNN," VersaPay, January 27, 2010, **http://www.versapay.com/video/ceo-mike-gokturk-interviewed-on-bnn/**; Jennifer Myers, "The Little Shop with a Big Friend," *Profit*, October 2009, pp. 28–30.
44. RBC Study, as reported in *Business Research Newsletter*, February 2005, p. 5.
45. *Small Business Quarterly*, Statistics Canada, August 2010.
46. Brandon Turner, "Why I quit my own business to work with someone else," *Globe and Mail*, February 27, 2015, **http://www.theglobeandmail.com/report-on-business/small-business/sb-tools/sb-how-to/why-i-quit-my-own-busines-to-work-for-someone-else/article23210898/** (accessed March 17, 2015).
47. Ambareen Musa, "Six things they don't tell you when you start your own business," *Globe and Mail*, January 30, 2015, **http://www.theglobeandmail.com/report-on-business/small-business/sb-tools/sb-how-to/six-things-they-dont-tell-you-when-you-leave-the-corporate-world-to-start-your-own-business/article22829151/** (accessed April 2, 2015).
48. Interview with entrepreneur Chris Neville, December 24, 2015.
49. "You're Not the Boss of Me Now," *Weekend Today*, October 21, 2005, **www.msnbc.msn.com/id/9762771/** (accessed June 5, 2006).
50. "Small Business Resource," **www.2-small-business.com** (accessed June 5, 2006).
51. Robert Hisrich, Michael Peters, Dean Shepherd, Peter Mombourquette, *Entrepreneurship*, 2nd ed. (Toronto: McGraw-Hill Ryerson, 2009), p. 542.

52. Robert Hisrich, Michael Peters, Dean Shepherd, Peter Mombourquette, *Entrepreneurship*, 2nd ed. (Toronto: McGraw-Hill Ryerson, 2009), p. 543; Jennifer Myers, "To Boldly Grow," PROFITguide, October/November 2003, **www.profitguide.com/w100/2003/article.asp?ID=1276&p.=1**
53. Jennifer Myers, "The man with the Midas touch," *Profit*, April 2005, **http://www.canadianbusiness.com/entrepreneur/managing/article.jsp?content=20050407_004729_4968&page=3** (accessed July 18, 2010).
54. Rodney Tanake, "Clothier a Favorite of Vegans, PETA Honors Pasadena 'Animal-Friendly' Firm," *Pasadena Star-News*, **www.pasadenastarnews.com/** (accessed January 14, 2006); "About Us," Alternative Outfitters, **www.alternativeoutfitters.com/index.asp?PageAction=COMPANY**; "Alternative Outfitters News," **www.alternativeoutfitters.com/index.asp?PageAction=Custom&ID=10**; "Pasadena-based Alternative Outfitters Wins Second Straight National PETA Award," **www.alternativeoutfitters.com/index.asp?PageAction=Custom&ID=45**; "The 2005 Veggie Awards," **www.vegnews.com/veggieawards_2005.html** (all accessed January 12, 2006).
55. Centre for Entrepreneurship, Education & Development, **http://www.ceed.ca/default.asp?id=190&pagesize=1&sfield=content.id&search=919&mn=1.212.256.305** (accessed March 1, 2019).
56. Wency Leung, "Kimchi on Wheels: Food Truck Trend Gears Up in Canada," *Globe and Mail*, June 14, 2011, **http://www.theglobeandmail.com/life/food-and-wine/food-trends/kimchi-on-wheels-food-truck-trend-gears-up-in-canada/article4261217/** (accessed June 24, 2013).
57. Kim Hart Macneill, "An Apple for the Tutor," PROFITguide, February 11, 2013, **http://www.profitguide.com/opportunity/an-apple-for-the-tutor-48089** (accessed June 24, 2013).
58. Nova Scotia Business Inc., **http://www.nsbi.ca/next/kiru.shtml** (accessed July 18, 2010).
59. Adapted from Carol Kinsey Gorman, *Creativity in Business: A Practical Guide for Creative Thinking*, Crisp Publications Inc., 1989, pp. 5–6. © Crisp Publications Inc., 1200 Hamilton Court, Menlo Park, CA 94025.
60. Patrick Maloney, "Make your banker say yes," PROFITguide, November 7, 2001, **www.profitguide.com/maximize/article.jsp?content=694**
61. **http://www.bostonpizza.com/en/about/PressKit.aspx** (accessed July 18, 2010).
62. Robert Hisrich, Michael Peters, Dean Shepherd, Peter Mombourquette, *Entrepreneurship*, 2nd ed. (Toronto: McGraw-Hill Ryerson, 2009), p. 381; "Ask the Legends," *Profit*, March 2008, p. 72.
63. Rebecca Gardiner, "PROFIT 100 Fundraising Secrets," *Canadian Business*, May 12, 2005, **http://www.canadianbusiness.com/entrepreneur/financing/article.jsp?content=20050511_120413_4152**
64. Ibid.
65. Rick Spence, "Sweetpea Baby Food: Stuck in the middle," *Profit*, October 2007, **http://www.canadianbusiness.com/entrepreneur/sales_marketing/article.jsp?content=20071002_12233_122337**
66. Robert Hisrich, Michael Peters, Dean Shepherd, Peter Mombourquette, *Entrepreneurship*, 2nd ed. (Toronto: McGraw-Hill Ryerson, 2009), pp. 397–398.
67. "The Success of Crowdfunding," The Brooklyn Warehouse website, February 26, 2013, **http://brooklynwarehouse.ca/theblog/2013/2/26/the-success-of-crowdfunding** (accessed July 15, 2013).
68. "Top Ten Most Crowdfunded Kickstarter Canadian Campaigns Ever, January 19, 2017, **http://www.planetweb.ca/news/top-10-funded-canadian-campaigns-ever/**
69. Howard Marks, "What is Equity Crowdfunding?," *Forbes*, December 19, 2018, **https://www.forbes.com/sites/howardmarks/2018/12/19/what-is-equity-crowdfunding/**
70. Crowdfunding North America Highlights, **https://www.statista.com/outlook/335/104/crowdfunding/north-america** (accessed March 1, 2019).
71. "Stats," Kickstarter, March 1, 2019, **https://www.kickstarter.com/help/stats**
72. "Crowdfunding," **https://canadabusiness.ca/grants-and-financing/crowdfunding/** (accessed March 2, 2019).
73. Robert Hisrich, Michael Peters, Dean Shepherd, Peter Mombourquette, *Entrepreneurship*, 2nd ed. (Toronto: McGraw-Hill Ryerson, 2009), pp. 397–398; *Outpost*, **www.outpostmagazine.com**; W.S. Good, *Building a Dream* (6th ed.) (Toronto: McGraw-Hill Ryerson, 2005), p. 277.
74. Robert Hisrich, Michael Peters, Dean Shepherd, Peter Mombourquette, *Entrepreneurship*, 2nd ed. (Toronto: McGraw-Hill Ryerson, 2009), p. 372.
75. Robert Hisrich, Michael Peters, Dean Shepherd, Peter Mombourquette, *Entrepreneurship*, 2nd ed. (Toronto: McGraw-Hill Ryerson, 2009), pp. 589, 592; Susanne Ruder, "A Tale of Two Brothers," *Profit*, March 2007.
76. Thomas W. Zimmerer and Norman M. Scarborough, *Essentials of Entrepreneurship and Small Business Management* (4th ed.) (Upper Saddle River, NJ: Pearson Prentice Hall, 2005), pp. 118–24.
77. Ibid.
78. Peter Mombourquette, March 2010, in-class interview.
79. Adapted from "Tomorrow's Entrepreneur," *Inc. State of Small Business*, 23, no. 7 (2001), pp. 80–104.
80. Population Estimates on July 1, 2018, **https://www150.statcan.gc.ca/t1/tbl1/en/tv.action?pid=1710000501** (accessed March 2, 2019).
81. Andrew Hepburn, "How to hire and retain talent like Canada's fastest-growing companies," *Canadian Business*, November 23, 2017, **https://www.canadianbusiness.com/lists-and-rankings/profit-500/how-to-hire-and-retain-talent-like-canadas-fastest-growing-companies/**
82. "How Many Immigrants Come to Canada Each Year?" August 1, 2018, **https://www.immigration.ca/how-many-immigrants-come-to-canada-each-year**
83. "50 Amazing Walmart Statistics and Facts (2019) by the Numbers," January 26, 2019, **https://expandedramblings.com/index.php/walmart-statistics/**
84. Gifford Pinchott III, *Intrapreneuring* (New York: Harper & Row, 1985), p. 34.
85. Paul Brown, "How to Cope With Hard Times," *New York Times*, June 10, 2008.
86. "Companies to Watch", October 26, 2017. Accessed March 1, 2019; Robert Hisrich, Michael Peters, Dean Shepherd, Peter

Mombourquette, *Entrepreneurship*, 2nd ed. (Toronto: McGraw-Hill Ryerson, 2009), pp. 130, 217, 522; "Lija puts a new spin on golfwear," PROFITguide, July 28, 2005, **http://www.profitguide.com/article/4406--lija-puts-a-new-spin-on-golfwear**; "Lija by Linda Hipp Named One of British Columbia's 50 Fastest Growing Companies," press release (2004), **www.lijastyle.com/press.html**; Karen VanKampen, "Golfers looking hip, stylish and colourful, too," CanWest News Services, June 21, 2005; Kim Shiffman, "Canada's Fastest Growing Companies," *Profit*, June 2005, p. 38; A. Holloway, "The Right Way to Tee Off," *Profit* (December /January 2007), p. 69; Hal Quinn, "Lady of Lija," *Canadian Business*, April 25, 2005, **http://www.canadianbusiness.com/managing/article.jsp?content=20050425_66971_66971**

## Chapter 6

1. W. Nickels et al., *Understanding Canadian Business,* 8th ed. (Toronto: McGraw-Hill Ryerson, 2013); Mark Brown, "How Loblaws stays on the cutting edge after 96 years," *Canadian Business*, March 23, 2015, **http://www.canadianbusiness.com/innovation/most-innovative-companies-2015-loblaw/** (accessed January 11, 2016); Tara Perkins, "Galen G. Weston's plan to grow his family's legacy," *Globe and Mail*, July 15, 2013, **http://www.theglobeandmail.com/report-on-business/galen-gs-big-gamble/article13237442/** (accessed January 11, 2016); The Canadian Press, "Loblaw expanding online grocery business across Canada and hiking quarterly dividend," CBC, May 2, 2018, **https://www.cbc.ca/news/business/loblaws-financial-results-1.4644650**, (accessed December 23, 2018).
2. "Waze: For Clearing the Roads," *Fast Company*, March/April 2018, p. 67.
3. "About Tesla," Tesla, **https://www.tesla.com/about** (accessed April 7, 2017).
4. Kristina Monllos, "As Soda Sales Suffer, Beverage Marketers Are Shifting to a New Stream of Income: Water," *Adweek*, March 20, 2017, **http://www.adweek.com/brandmarketing/as-soda-sales-suffer-beverage-marketers-areshifting-to-a-new-stream-of-income-water/** (accessed April 7, 2017).
5. "Tim Hortons vows faster service to fend off rivals," UBC Blogs, October 7, 2013, **https://blogs.ubc.ca/melodylin/2013/10/07/tim-hortons-vows-faster-service-to-fend-off-rivals/** (accessed January 10, 2016).
6. Adapted from "Outside in business unit strategy: Summary of the Five Forces Model by Porter," ValueBasedManagement.net, January 6, 2016, **http://www.valuebasedmanagement.net/methods_porter_five_forces.html** (accessed January 10, 2016).
7. "Strategic Planning Tools," Chartered Global Management Accountant website, n.d., **http://www.cgma.org/Resources/Tools/essential-tools/Pages/strategic-planning-tools.aspx** (accessed January 10, 2016).
8. "The Dutch Oven, Disrupted," *Bloomberg Businessweek*, March 19, 2018, p. 75.
9. **http://www.quickmba.com/strategy/strategic-planning/**
10. "Strategic Management," Wikipedia, **http://en.wikipedia.org/wiki/Strategic_management** (accessed June 25, 2013).
11. "Chevrolet Remains the Industry's Fastest-Growing Full-Line Brand, with 11 Consecutive Months of Growth," General Motors, March 1, 2016, **https://www.gm.com/investors/sales/us-sales-production.html** (accessed May 4, 2017).
12. James E. Ellis, "At KFC, A Bucketful of Trouble," *Bloomberg Businessweek*, March 5, 2018, pp. 20–21.
13. "AI-Spy," *The Economist*, March 31–April 6, 2018, p. 13.
14. "Fewer Women Leading Canada's Corporations Today Than 5 Years Ago," Huffington Post, July 31, 2018, **https://www.huffingtonpost.ca/2018/07/31/women-workplace-canada_a_23493002/** (accessed December 21, 2018).
15. Melissa Behrend, "More Companies Are Reducing CEO Compensation Due to Poor Quarterly Results," *Chief Executive*, March 21, 2016, **http://chiefexecutive.net/morecompanies-are-reducing-ceo-compensation-due-to-poorquarterly-results/** (accessed April 7, 2017).
16. Mark Colgate, "How to crack the code of great customer service, *Globe and Mail*, September 25, 2014, **http://www.theglobeandmail.com/report-on-business/careers/leadership-lab/how-to-crack-the-code-of-great-customer-service/article20786869/** (accessed January 10, 2016).
17. Del Jones, "Autocratic Leadership Works—Until It Fails," *USA Today*, June 5, 2003, **www.usatoday.com/news/nation/2003-06-05-raines-usat_x.htm** (accessed March 6, 2012).
18. Hayley Peterson, "Lululemon hit with its first major recall since the sheer-pants disaster," *Business Insider*, June 25, 2015, **http://www.businessinsider.com/lululemon-hit-with-another-clothing-recall-2015-6** (accessed January 10, 2016).
19. John P. Kotter, "What Leaders Really Do," *Harvard Business Review*, December 2001, **http://fs.ncaa.org/Docs/DIII/What%20Leaders%20Really%20Do.pdf** (accessed May 4, 2017).
20. C. L. Pearce and C. C. Manz, "The New Silver Bullets of Leadership: The Importance of Self-and Shared Leadership in Knowledge Work," *Organizational Dynamics* 34, no. 2 (2005), pp. 130–140.
21. Michelle Peluseo, "Watson's New Champion," *Fast Company*, April 2017, p. 24.
22. Deborah Harrington-Mackin, *The Team Building Tool Kit* (New York: New Directions Management, 1994); Joseph P. Folger, Marshall Scott Poole, and Randall K. Stutman, *Working through Conflict: Strategies for Relationships, Groups, and Organizations*, 6th ed. (Upper Saddle River, NJ: Pearson Education, 2009).
23. Kerrie Unsworth, "Unpacking Creativity," *Academy of Management Review*, 26 (April 2001), pp. 289–97.
24. Anna Maria Andriotos and Lara Stevens, "Amazon Voices Payment Strategy," *Wall Street Journal*, April 7–8, 2018, pp. B1, B2.
25. *Harvard Business Review* 60 (November–December 1982), p. 160.
26. Dan Schwabel, "5 Reasons Why Your Online Presence Will Replace Your Resume in 10 Years," *Forbes*, February 21, 2012, **www.forbes.com/sites/danschawbel/2011/02/21/5-reasons-why-your-online-presence-will-replace-your-resume-in-10-years/** (accessed March 6, 2012).

## Chapter 7

1. Jena McGregor, "Online Extra: Learning on the Front Lines," *Bloomberg Businessweek*, July 10, 2006, **http://www.businessweek.com/stories/2006-07-09/online-extra-learning-on-the-front-lines** (accessed January 1, 2018); Keurig Green Mountain website, **http://www.keuriggreenmountain.com/** (accessed January 1, 2018); Dun & Bradstreet Inc., "Keurig

Green Mountain," Hoovers Online, **http://www.hoovers.com/companyinformation/cs/company-profile.keurig_green_mountain_inc.09ca839579577b55.html** (accessed January 1, 2018); "Green Mountain Coffee Roasters Brews Formula for Success," in O.C. Ferrell, Geoffrey Hirt, and Linda Ferrell, *Business: A Changing World*, 6th ed. (New York: McGraw-Hill Irwin, 2008), pp. 233–234; Leslie Patton and Nikolaj Gammeltoft, "Green Mountain Drops as David Einhorn Says Market 'Limited,'" *Bloomberg Businessweek*, October 17, 2011, **www.businessweek.com/news/2011-10-17/green-mountain-drops-as-david-einhorn-says-marketlimited.html** (accessed November 6, 2013); Christopher Faille, "Green Mountain Coffee's Trouble with Bean Counting," *Forbes*, June 23, 2011, **https://www.forbes.com/sites/greatspeculations/2011/06/23/green-mountaincoffees-trouble-with-bean-counting/#2578180296dc** (accessed January 1, 2018); GMCR Fiscal 2012 Annual Report, **http://files.shareholder.com/downloads/GMCR/2774887737x0x630863/FDBC5F63-78E8-493C-9BB9-8F33000C0465/GMCR_2012_ANNUAL_REPORT.pdf** (accessed November 6, 2013); "Green Mountain Coffee: Starbucks Bursts Its Bubble," *Seeking Alpha*, March 9, 2012, **http://seekingalpha.com/article/422241-green-mountaincoffee-starbucks-bursts-its-bubble** (accessed January 1, 2018); "2016 By the Numbers," Keurig Green Mountain, January 3, 2017, https://**www.keuriggreenmountain.com/en/OurStories/Business/2016ByTheNumbers.aspx**(accessed January 1, 2018); "Sustainability," Keurig Green Mountain, **http://www.keuriggreenmountain.com/en/Sustainability/Overview.aspx** (accessed January 1, 2018); Steven Bruce, "HRWorks Sits Down with Keurig Green Mountain Coffee," *HR Daily Advisor*, October 9, 2017, **http://hrdailyadvisor.blr.com/2017/10/09/hrworks-sits-keurig-green-mountain-coffee/** (accessed January 1, 2018); "World's Most Innovative Companies: #43 Keurig Green Mountain," *Forbes*, May 2015, **https://www.forbes.com/companies/keurig-greenmountain/** (accessed January 1, 2018).

2. Horace Dediu, "Understanding Apple's Organizational Structure," *Asymco*, July 3, 2013, **www.asymco.com/2013/07/03/understanding-apples-organizationalstructure/** (accessed May 4, 2107); Sam Grobart, "How Samsung Became the World's No. 1 Smartphone Maker," *Bloomberg Businessweek*, March 28, 2013, **www.businessweek.com/articles/2013-03-28/how-samsungbecame-the-worlds-no-dot-1-smartphone-maker#p1** (accessed May 4, 2017); Jay Yarow, "Apple's New Organizational Structure Could Help It Move Faster," *Business Insider*, May 1, 2013, **www.businessinsider.com/apples-new-organizational-structure-could-help-it-movefaster-2013-5** (accessed May 4, 2017).
3. John D. Still, "Ford Aims to Pivot in Raising CEO's Pay," *Wall Street Journal*, April 1, 2017, p. B1.
4. Megan McArdle, "'Unlimited Vacation' Is Code for 'No Vacation,'" September 30, 2015, Bloomberg, September 30, 2015, **http://www.bloombergview.com/articles/2015-09-30/-unlimited-vacation-is-code-for-no-vacation-** (accessed May 4, 2017).
5. Starbucks Stories and News, "Starbucks to Close All Stores Nationwide for Racial-Bias Education on May 29," April 17, 2018, **https://stories.starbucks.com/press/2018/starbucks-to-close-stores-nationwide-for-racial-bias-education-may-29/** (accessed August 19, 2019).
6. Telis Demos, "Cirque du Balancing Act," *Fortune*, June 12, 2006, p. 114.
7. Jyoti Thottam, "When Execs Go Temp," *Time*, April 26, 2004, pp. 40–41.
8. Ben Dipietro, "Automakers Face 'Herculean' Task in Implementing Supply Chain Guidelines," *Wall Street Journal*, May 28, 2014, **http://blogs.wsj.com/riskandcompliance/2014/05/28/automakers-face-herculeantask-in-implementing-supply-chain-guidelines/** (accessed May 4, 2017).
9. "Tesla's Organizational Structure & Its Characteristics (Analysis)," Panmore, January 28, 2018, **http://panmore.com/tesla-motors-inc-organizational-structure-characteristics-analysis** (accessed April 18, 2018).
10. Global Divisions, PepsiCo Inc., **http://www.pepsico.com/About/global-divisions** (accessed April 18, 2018).
11. "Regions," Diageo, **www.diageo.com/en-row/ourbusiness/ourregions/Pages/default.aspx** (accessed March 10, 2016).
12. Matt Scholz, "The Three-Step Process That's Kept 3M Innovative for Decades," *Fast Company*, July 10, 2017, **https://www.fastcompany.com/40437745/the-three-stepprocess-thats-kept-3m-innovative-for-decades** (accessed April 19, 2018).
13. "Why Work Here?" **www.wholefoodsmarket.com/careers/workhere.php** (accessed March 3, 2010).
14. "PepsiCo Unveils New Organizational Structure, Names CEOs of Three Principal Operating Units," PepsiCo Media, November 5, 2007, **www.pepsico.com/PressRelease/PepsiCo-Unveils-New-Organizational-Structure-Names.html** (accessed March 22, 2011); "The PepsiCo Family," PepsiCo, **www.pepsico.com/Company/The-Pepsico-Family/PepsiCo-Americas-Beverages.html** (accessed January 12, 2011).
15. Jon R. Katzenbach and Douglas K. Smith, "The Discipline of Teams," *Harvard Business Review* 71 (March–April 1993), pp. 111–20.
16. Ibid.
17. "The Secret to Team Collaboration: Individuality," *Inc.*, January 18, 2012, **www.inc.com/john-baldoni/the-secret-to-team-collaboration-is-individuality.html** (accessed February 17, 2012).
18. Gregory Ciotti, "Why Remote Teams Are the Future (and How to Make Them Work)," Help Scout, October 23, 2013, **www.helpscout.net/blog/virtual-teams/** (accessed March 11, 2016).
19. Anneke Seley, "Outside In: The Rise of the Inside Sales Team," **Salesforce.com** Blog, February 3, 2015, **http://blogs.salesforce.com/company/2015/02/outside-in-rise-insidesales-team-gp.html** (accessed May 4, 2017).
20. "2017 Employee Job Satisfaction and Engagement: The Doors of Opportunity Are Open," Society for Human Resource Management, April 24, 2017, **https://www.shrm.org/hr-today/trends-and-forecasting/research-and-surveys/pages/2017-job-satisfaction-and-engagement-doors-ofopportunity-are-open.aspx** (accessed April 21, 2018).
21. Patrick Kiger, "Task Force Training Develops New Leaders, Solves Real Business Issues and Helps Cut Costs," *Workforce*, September 7, 2011, **www.workforce.com/article/20070521/NEWS02/305219996/task-force-training-develops-new-leaders-solves-realbusiness-issues-and-helps-cut-costs** (accessed March 10, 2016); Duane D. Stanford, "Coca-Cola Woman Board Nominee Bucks Slowing Diversity Trend," Bloomberg, February 22, 2013, **www.bloomberg.com/news/2013-02-22/coca-cola-s-woman-director-nominee-bucks-slowingdiversity-trend.html** (accessed May 4, 2017).

22. Jia Lynnyang, "The Power of Number 4.6," *Fortune*, June 12, 2006, p. 122.

23. Richard S. Wellins, William C. Byham, and Jeanne M. Wilson, *Empowered Teams: Creating Self-Directed Work Groups That Improve Quality, Productivity, and Participation* (San Francisco: Jossey-Bass Publishers, 1991), p. 5.

24. Natasha Singer, "Intel's Sharp-Eyed Social Scientist," *New York Times*, February 15, 2014, **www.nytimes.com/2014/02/16/technology/intels-sharp-eyed-socialscientist.html?_r=0** (accessed May 4, 2017).

25. Matt Krumrie, "Are Meetings a Waste of Time? Survey Says Yes," *Minneapolis Workplace Examiner*, May 12, 2009, **www.examiner.com/workplace-in-minneapolis/are-meetings-a-waste-of-time-survey-says-yes** (accessed March 21, 2011).

26. Peter Mell and Timothy Grance, "The NIST Definition of Cloud Computing," National Institute of Standards and Technology, Special Publication 800-145, September 2011, **http://csrc.nist.gov/publications/nistpubs/800-145/SP800-145.pdf** (accessed April 9, 2012).

27. Sue Shellenbarger, "They're Gossiping About You," *Wall Street Journal*, October 8, 2014, pp. D1–D2.

28. Kim Komando, "Why You Need a Company Policy on Internet Use," **www.microsoft.com/business/en-us/resources/management/employee-relations/why-you-need-a-company-policy-on-internet-use.aspx?fbid=abWQUsC20hw#WhyyouneedacompanypolicyonInternetuse** (accessed March 22, 2011).

29. Imani Moise, "New Tools Tell Bosses How You're Feeling," *Wall Street Journal*, March 29, 2018, p. B6.

30. *PBS News Hour*, "Apple Supplier Foxconn Pledges Better Working Conditions, but Will It Deliver?" **www.youtube.com/watch?v5ZduorbCkSBQ** (accessed April 9, 2012).

31. Verne Harnish, "Five Ways to Liberate Your Team from Email Overload," *Fortune*, June 16, 2014, p. 52.

32. Gloria Mark, Shamsi T. Iqbal, Mary Czerwinski, Paul Johns, Akane Sano, and Yuliya Lutchyn, "Email Duration, Batching and Self-interruption: Patterns of Email Use on Productivity and Stress," Proceedings of the 2016 CHI Conference on Human Factors in Computing Systems (CHI '16), ACM, New York, NY, USA, pp. 1717–1728; Andrew Blackman, "The Smartest Way to Use Email at Work," *Wall Street Journal*, March 12, 2018, p. R1.

33. "How Did Freshii Become One of the Fastest Growing Restaurant Chains in the World?" QSR, June 2018, p. 1; William G. Nickels, James M. McHugh, and Susan M. McHugh, *Understanding Business* (New York: McGraw-Hill, 2019), p. 214; "Freshii Named FastCasual's Top Brand of the Year," FastCasual, May 22, 2018, **https://www.fastcasual.com/articles/freshii-named-top-brandof-the-year/** (accessed June 3, 2018); S. A. Whitehead, "Freshii Founder Tells How Missteps Can Be Key Teacher on Path to Success," QSR Web, April 16, 2018, **https://www.qsrweb.com/articles/freshii-founder-tellshow-missteps-can-be-key-teachers-on-path-to-success/** (accessed June 3, 2018).

## Chapter 8

1. Costco's website, **www.costco.com** (accessed December 24, 2018); Hollie Shaw, "How Costco Canada breaks retail rules to win," *Financial Post*, February 23, 2017, **https://business.financialpost.com/news/retail-marketing/how-costco-canada-breaks-retail-rules-to-win** (accessed December 24, 2018); Demitrios Kalogeropoulos, "Why Does Costco Have Less Merchandise On Its Shelves Than Other Retailers?," The Motley Fool, April 26, 2015, **https://www.fool.com/investing/general/2015/04/26/why-does-costco-have-less-merchandise-on-its-shelv.aspx** (accessed December 24, 2018); Marc Wulfraat, "The secret to Costco's success lies in supply chain efficiency," *Canadian Grocer*, May 13, 2014, **http://www.canadiangrocer.com/blog/the-secret-to-costcos-success-lies-in-supply-chain-efficiency-40691** (accessed December 24, 2018).

2. "Personified: 11 Things You Didn't Know about Amazon's CEO Jeff Bezos," Gadgets Now, January 12, 2017, **http://www.gadgetsnow.com/checklist/personified-11-things-you-didnt-know-about-amazons-ceo-jeff-bezos/checklistshow/56500597.cms** (accessed April 11, 2017).

3. Leonard L. Berry, *Discovering the Soul of Service* (New York: The Free Press, 1999), pp. 86–96.

4. Zeithaml and Bitner, *Services Marketing*, pp. 3, 22.

5. Bernard Wysocki Jr., "To Fix Health Care, Hospitals Take Tips from the Factory Floor," *Wall Street Journal*, April 9, 2004, via **www.chcanys.org/clientuploads/downloads/Clinical_resources/Leadership%20Articles/LeanThinking_ACF28EB.pdf** (accessed May 4, 2017).

6. Deborah L. Roberts and Frank T. Piller, "Finding the Right Role for Social Media in Innovation," *MIT Sloan Management Review*, March 15, 2016, **http://sloanreview.mit.edu/article/finding-the-right-role-for-social-media-ininnovation/** (accessed April 11, 2017).

7. Debbie Qaqish, "So You Want to Do Experiential Marketing? Consider These 4 Things First," *Marketing News*, April 2018, pp. 4–6.

8. Danielle Muoio, "These 19 Companies Are Racing to Put Driverless Cars on the Road by 2020," *Business Insider*, August 18, 2016, **http://www.businessinsider.com/companies-making-driverless-cars-by-2020-2016-8/** (accessed April 11, 2017).

9. "Dell Laptop Parts," Partspeople, **www.parts-people.com/** (accessed March 23, 2012).

10. "Best Sellers," Villy Customs, 2017, **https://villycustoms.com/collections/the-10** (accessed April 12, 2017).

11. Micheline Maynard, "Kit Kat Lovers, Listen Up: Hershey Is Betting Big That You'll Break Off More," *Forbes*, March 11, 2018, **https://www.forbes.com/sites/michelinemaynard/2018/03/11/kit-kat-loverslisten-up-hershey-is-betting-big-that-youll-break-offmore/#7c61790d7975** (accessed April 22, 2018).

12. Jonathan Dyble, "Global Blockchain in Supply Chain Market to Reach $424 Million by 2023," Supply Chain Digital, **www.supplychaindigital.com/technology/global-blockchain-supplychain- market-reach-424mn-2023** (accessed April 13, 2018).

13. Jonathan Dyble, "Global Blockchain in Supply Chain Market to Reach $424 Million by 2023," Supply Chain Digital, **www.supplychaindigital.com/technology/global-blockchain-supplychain- market-reach-424mn-2023** (accessed April 13, 2018); Erica E. Phillips, "Bringing Blockchain to the Coffee Cup," *Wall Street Journal*, **https://www.wsj.com/articles/bringing-blockchain-to-the-coffee-cup-1523797205**, (accessed December 24, 2018).

14. "Improvements to the Engineering Planning and Development Process," Toyota, 2017, **http://www.toyota-global.com/company/history_of_toyota/75years/data/automotive_ business/products_technology/research/engineering_planning/details_window.html** (accessed April 12, 2017).

15. Ross Toro, "How 3D Printers Work (Infographic)," Live Science, June 18, 2013, **www.livescience.com/37513-how- 3d-printers-work-infographic.html** (accessed May 4, 2017).

16. Matt McFarland, "Amazon's Delivery Drones May Drop Packages via Parachute," CNN Tech, February 14, 2017, **http://money.cnn.com/2017/02/14/technology/amazondrone-patent/** (accessed April 12, 2017).

17. Stuart Hodge, "SAP—Why Drones Have a Key Role to Play in the Future of Procurement," **http://www.supplychaindigital.com/procurement/sap-why-drones-havekey-role-play-future-procurement** (accessed April 16, 2018).

18. Alanna Petroff, "U.S. Workers Face Higher Risk of Being Replaced by Robots. Here's Why," CNN Tech, March 24, 2017, **http://money.cnn.com/2017/03/24/technology/robotsjobs- us-workers-uk/** (accessed April 12, 2017).

19. "Are There Enough Robots?" Robotics Tomorrow, February 14, 2017, **http://www.roboticstomorrow.com/article/2017/02/are-there-enough-robots/9507** (accessed April 12, 2017).

20. James Henderson, "Hershey Pledges $500mn to Improve Supply Chain Sustainability," Supply Chain Digital, **http://www.supplychaindigital.com/technology/hershey-pledges-500mn-improve-supply-chain-sustainability** (accessed April 5, 2018).

21. "Best in Class: Top 50 Socially Responsible Companies 2013," *Maclean's*, **http://www.macleans.ca/canada-top-50-socially-responsible-corporations-2013/** (accessed January 11, 2016).

22. Bryan Walsh, "Why Green Is the New Red, White and Blue," *Time*, April 28, 2008, p. 53.

23. "Best in Class," *Maclean's*, **http://www.macleans.ca/canada-top-50-socially-responsible-corporations-2013/** (accessed January 11, 2016).

24. "Benefits of Green Building," USGBE, April 1, 2016, **http://www.usgbc.org/articles/green-building-facts** (accessed April 12, 2017).

25. O. C. Ferrell and Michael D. Hartline, *Marketing Strategy* (Mason, OH: South-Western, 2005), p. 215.

26. "E-Commerce: Cultivating a New Logistics Landscape," Inbound Logistics, March 22, 2018, p. 13.

27. Mike Danby, "Innovation Beyond Drones—Transforming the Supply Chain," Supply Chain Digital, **http://www .supplychaindigital.com/technology/comment-innovationbeyond-drones-transforming-supply-chain** (accessed April 14, 2018).

28. James Henderson, "AI-Driven Procurement Platform, Suplari, Attracts $10.3 Million in Funding," Supply Chain Digital, **http://www.supplychaindigital.com/technology/ai-driven-procurement-platform-suplari-attracts-103mnfunding** (accessed April 6, 2018).

29. William Pride and O.C. Ferrell, *Marketing,* (Boston: Cengage Learning, 2018), p. 443.

30. "Broken Links," *The Economist*, March 31, 2011, **www.economist.com/node/18486015** (accessed May 4, 2017).

31. Bruce Nussbaum, "Where Are the Jobs?" *BusinessWeek*, March 22, 2004, pp. 36–37.

32. Lisa H. Harington, "Balancing on the Rim," *Inbound Logistics*, January 2006, pp. 168–170.

33. Scott McCartney, "The Best and Worst Airlines of 2016," *Wall Street Journal*, January 11, 2017, **https://www.wsj.com/articles/the-best-and-worst-airlines-of-2016-1484149294** (accessed April 11, 2017).

34. Philip B. Crosby, *Quality Is Free: The Art of Making Quality Certain* (New York: McGraw-Hill, 1979), pp. 9–10.

35. Nigel F. Piercy, *Market-Led Strategic Change* (Newton, MA: Butterworth-Heinemann, 1992), pp. 374–385.

36. "Compliance Management Systems—Guidelines," International Organization for Standardization, 2017, **https://www.iso.org/standard/62342.html** (accessed April 12, 2017).

37. "Mouthing Off by the Numbers," *Ethisphere*, 2011, Q3, p. 9.

38. Charles Duhigg and David Barboza, "Apple's iPad and the Human Costs for Workers in China," *New York Times*, January 25, 2012, **www.nytimes.com/2012/01/26/business/ieconomy-apples-ipad-and-the-human-costs-for-workers-in-china.html?pagewanted5all** (accessed February 8, 2012).

39. "Employment Opportunities," Careers in Supply Chain Management, **www.careersinsupplychain.org/career-outlook/empopp.asp** (accessed March 5, 2010).

40. "Global Supplier Code of Conduct," Kellogg's, 2017, **http://www.kelloggcompany.com/en_US/supplier-relations/transparency-in-supply-chain.html** (accessed April 12, 2017).

41. International Cocoa Organization, "How Exactly is Cocoa Harvested?" May 26, 1998, **https://www.icco.org/faq/58-cocoa-harvesting/130-how-exactly-is-cocoa-harvested.html** (accessed June 19, 2018); The Cocoa Exchange, "Sustainable and Responsibly-Sourced Cocoa," **http://www.mytcesite.com/pws/homeoffice/tabs/sustainable-cocoa.aspx** (accessed June 19, 2018); Ashley Beyer, "The Cocoa Exchange Visits Fresh Living," KUTV, May 31, 2018, **http://kutv.com/features/fresh-living/the-cocoa-exchange-visits-fresh-living** (accessed June 19, 2018); Oliver Nieburg, "'The Cocoa Exchange': Mars Sets Up E-Commerce Party Program for Chocolate," *Confectionary News*, May 16, 2017, **https://www.confectionerynews.com/Article/2017/05/15/Cocoa-Exchange-Mars-sets-up-e-commerce-party-program-for-chocolate** (accessed June 19, 2018); Keith Loria, "Candy Maker Mars Gets into the Party Business," Food Dive, May 10, 2017, **https://www.fooddive.com/news/candy-maker-mars-getsinto-the-party-business/442160/** (accessed June 19, 2018); Bernie Pacyniak, "One-on-One: Berta de Pablos-Barbier, President of Mars Wrigley Confectionary U.S.," *Candy Industry*, November 1, 2017, **https://www.candyindustry.com/articles/87940-one-on-one-berta-de-pablos-barbier-presidentof-mars-wrigley-confectionery-us** (accessed June 19, 2018); "Cocoa-Caring for the Future of Cocoa," **https://www.mars.com/global/sustainable-in-a-generation/our-approach-tosustainability/raw-materials/cocoa** (accessed July 10, 2018).

## Chapter 9

1. Tanner Christensen, "How Facebook Keeps Employees Happy in the World's Largest Open Office," *Inc.*, March 9, 2016, **https://www.inc.com/tanner-christensen/howfacebook-keeps-employees-happy-in-the-worlds-largest-open-office.html** (accessed December 5, 2017); Catherine Clifford, "How Mark

Zuckerberg keeps Facebook's 18,000+ Employees Innovating: 'Is This Going to Destroy the Company? If Not, Let Them Test It,'" CNBC, June 5, 2017. **https://www.cnbc.com/2017/06/05/how-markzuckerberg-keeps-facebook-employees-innovating.html** (accessed December 5, 2017); Mike Hoefflinger, "How Facebook Keeps Its Employees the Happiest, According to a Former Insider," *Business Insider*, April 11, 2017, **http://www.businessinsider.com/how-facebook-keepsemployees-happy-2017-4** (accessed December 5, 2017); Steve Kux, "10 Reasons Why 99% of Facebook Employees Love Mark Zuckerberg," Lifehack, **http://www.lifehack.org/articles/work/10-reasons-why-99-facebook-employeeslove-mark-zuckerberg.html** (accessed December 5, 2017); Marguerite Ward, "The 25 Best Companies to Work For in America," CNBC, December 7, 2016. **https://www.cnbc.com/2016/12/07/the-25-best-companies-to-work-for-inamerica.html** (accessed December 5, 2017).

2. Nicole Stewart, *Missing in Action: Absentee Trends in Canadian Organizations* (Ottawa: The Conference Board of Canada, 2013), retrieved January 12, 2016, from **http://www.sunlife.ca/static/canada/Sponsor/About%20Group%20Benefits/Focus%20Update/2013/Special%20Edition%20-%20Sept.%2023%20-%20%20Sun%20Life%20co-sponsors%20major%20new%20Conference%20Board%20of/MissinginAction_SUN%20LIFE_EN.pdf**
3. "100 Best Companies to Work For 2010," *Fortune*, **http://money.cnn.com/magazines/fortune/bestcompanies/2010/snapshots/4.html** (accessed February 18, 2010); "Benefits," Google Jobs, **www.google.com/support/jobs/bin/static.py?page=benefits.html** (accessed February 18, 2010).
4. Diane Jermyn, "Canada's Top 100 Employers make their workplaces exceptional," *Globe and Mail*, November 4, 2014, **http://www.theglobeandmail.com/report-on-business/careers/top-employers/canadas-top-100-employers-make-their-workplaces-exceptional/article21427767/** (accessed January 12, 2016).
5. "These are Canada's top 100 highest-paid CEOs for 2018," *Maclean's*, January 2, 2018, **https://www.macleans.ca/economy/money-economy/these-are-canadas-top-100-highest-paid-ceos-for-2018/** (accessed December 24, 2018).
6. Shelia Eugenio, "4 Innovative Ways to Motivate Your Team," *Entrepreneur*, March 6, 2017, **https://www.entrepreneur.com/article/289560** (accessed April 22, 2018).
7. Douglas McGregor, *The Human Side of Enterprise* (New York: McGraw-Hill, 1960), pp. 33–34.
8. Ibid.
9. Scott Koegler, "The Empowered Employee: How 6 Companies Are Arming Their Teams with Data," IBM Watson, March 24, 2017, **https://www.ibm.com/blogs/watson/2017/03/empowered-employee-6-companiesarming-teams-data/** (access April 22, 2018).
10. Jon L. Pierce, Tatiana Kostova, and Kurt T. Kirks, "Toward a Theory of Psychological Ownership in Organizations," *Academy of Management Review* 26, no. 2 (2001), p. 298.
11. Liz Rappaport, "Goldman Cuts Blankfein's Bonus," *Wall Street Journal*, February 4, 2012, **http://online.wsj.com/article/SB10001424052970204662204577201483347787346.html** (accessed April 17, 2012).
12. Ethics Resource Center, *2011 National Business Ethics Survey®: Ethics in Transition* (Arlington, VA: Ethics Resource Center, 2012), p. 16.
13. Archie Carroll, "Carroll: Do We Live in a Cheating Culture?" *Athens Banner-Herald*, February 21, 2004, **www.onlineathens.com/stories/022204/bus_20040222028.shtml** (accessed March 12, 2010).
14. Edwin A. Locke, K. M. Shaw, and Gary P. Latham, "Goal Setting and Task Performance: 1969–1980," *Psychological Bulletin* 90 (1981), pp. 125–152.
15. Peter Drucker, *The Practice of Management*, (New York: Harper & Row, 1954).
16. Diane Jermyn, "Canada's Top 100 Employers make their workplaces exceptional," **http://www.theglobeandmail.com/report-on-business/careers/top-employers/canadas-top-100-employers-make-their-workplaces-exceptional/article21427767/**
17. Amy Wrzesniewski and Jen E. Dutton, "Crafting a Job: Revisioning Employees as Active Crafters of Their Work," *Academy of Management Review* 26, no. 2 (2001), p. 179.
18. **http://www.careerbuilder.com/Jobs/Company/C8D7BN6GV5F6ZYT9WDZ/Hyatt-Hotels/**; **http://www.generalmills.com/en/Responsibility/Community_Engagement/Grants/Minneapolis_area/Communities_of_color/grant_recipients_2006.aspx**; "Seminar on Human Resources and Training Session I," Conference of European Statisticians, United Nations Economic and Social Council, June 2006, **http://www.unescap.org/stat/apex/2/APEX2_S.1_Human_Resources&Training_Canada.pdf**
19. My Guides, USA.com, "Which Jobs Offer Flexible Work Schedules?" **http://jobs.myguidesusa.com/answers-to-myquestions/which-jobs-offer-flexiblework-schedules?/** (accessed March 12, 2010).
20. Robert Preidt, "Workplace Flexibility Can Boost Healthy Behaviors," Wake Forest University Baptist Medical Center, news release, December 10, 2007, via **http://yourtotalhealth.ivillage.com/workplaceflexibility-can-boost-healthy-behaviors.html** (accessed March 12, 2010).
21. DIane Jermyn, "Canada's Top 100 Employers make their workplaces exceptional," **http://www.theglobeandmail.com/report-on-business/careers/top-employers/canadas-top-100-employers-make-their-workplaces-exceptional/article21427767/**
22. Statistics Canada, "Working at home: An update," December 7, 2010, **http://www.statcan.gc.ca/pub/11-008-x/2011001/article/11366-eng.htm#a13** (accessed January 16, 2013).
23. "Telecommuting Benefits," **http://www.telecommutect.com/employees/benefits.php**, Telecommute Connecticut! (accessed June 21, 2006); Nicole Demerath, "Telecommuting in the 21st century: Benefits, issues, and leadership model which will work," AllBusiness.com, April 1, 2002, **http://www.allbusiness.com/buying_exiting_businesses/3503510-1.html**; Fran Irwin, "Gaining the Air Quality and Climate Benefit from Telework," January 2004, **http://pdf.wri.org/teleworkguide.pdf**; "The State of California Telecommuting Pilot Project: Final Report Executive Summary," JALA Associates Inc., June 1990, **http://www.jala.com/caexecsumm.pdf**
24. "HR Executives Split on Telecommuting," *USA Today*, March 1, 2006, p. B1.
25. Stephanie Armour, "Telecommuting Gets Stuck in the Slow Lane," *USA Today*, June 25, 2001, pp. 1A, 2A.
26. "Employers Reap Awards and Rewards for Psychologically Healthy Workplaces," *Employee Benefit News*, April 15, 2004,

www.benefitnews.com/pfv.cfm?id=5832; Susan McCullough, "Pets Go to the Office," *HR Magazine* 43 (June 1998), pp. 162–68; "Pets Provide Relief to Workplace Stress," *BenefitNews Connect*, July 1, 2003, **www.benefitnews.com/detail.cfm?id=4736**; "Taking Your Best Friend to Work," *Toronto Star*, December 13, 2004, p. C11; "Working Like a Dog—Survey of Owners Reveals They Would Work More Hours or for Less Pay if They Could Bring Their Pooch to Work," CNNMoney.com, January 24, 2006, **http://money.cnn.com/2006/01/24/news/funny/dog_work/index.htm?cnn=yes** (accessed January 27, 2006); "Every Day Is 'Take Your Dog to Work Day' at Planet Dog," Press Releases, **www.planetdog.com/Press.asp?id=6** (accessed January 27, 2006); Best Friends Survey taken March 27, and 30, 2006, of 1,000 registered voters, "All in the Family," *USA Today Snapshots*, June 21, 2006.

## Chapter 10

1. Craig Smith, "48 Interesting Statistics and Facts(2019) By the Numbers," March 1, 2019, **https://expandedramblings.com/index.php/shopify-statistics/**
2. Richard Yerema and Kristian Leung, "Shopify, Recognized as One of Canada's Top 100 Employers (2019) and National Capital Region's Top Employer (2019), November 8, 2018, **https://content.eluta.ca/top-employer-shopify**
3. Adam Bryant, "Tobi Lütke of Shopify: Powering a Team With a 'Trust Battery,'" April 22, 2016, **https://www.nytimes.com/2016/04/24/business/tobi-lutke-of-shopify-powering-a-team-with-a-trust-battery.html**
4. Annie Zhang, "Shopify? You Mean Spotify? (1/2), July 21, 2016, **https://medium.com/inside-shopify/shopify-you-mean-spotify-1-2-b7469e9d7e4d**
5. Annie Zhang, "Shopify? You Mean Spotify? (1/2), July 21, 2016, **https://medium.com/inside-shopify/shopify-you-mean-spotify-1-2-b7469e9d7e4d**
6. Annie Zhang, "Shopify? You Mean Spotify? (2/2), August 10, 2016, **https://medium.com/inside-shopify/shopify-you-mean-spotify-2-2-974cb9da34a1**
7. "Labour Market Information," Service Canada website, n.d., **http://www.servicecanada.gc.ca/eng/sc/lminfo//index.shtml** (accessed January 12, 2016).
8. Ambrosia Vertesi, "Rethinking Candidates Experience with #HootHROS," September 1, 2015, **https://blog.hootsuite.com/rethinking-candidate-experience-with-hoothros/**
9. Vicky Valet, "Canada's Best Employers 2019," January 29, 2019, **https://www.forbes.com/sites/vickyvalet/2019/01/29/canadas-best-employers-2019/#1430d3f1c558**
10. Jackelyn Ho, "Should You Promote From Within or Bring on an Outsider? According to Richard Branson, the Answer is Obvious," March 28, 2018, **https://www.inc.com/jackelyn-ho/richard-branson-says-promoting-from-within-is-best-thing-you-can-do-for-your-company.html**
11. Adam Foroughi, "3 Reasons Promoting From Within Is Better for Growing Your Business," May 25, 2016, **https://www.entrepreneur.com/article/274346**
12. Neha Aggarwal, "Decoding the P&G Interview," October 20, 2016, **https://medium.com/kraftshala/decoding-the-p-g-interview-4ed2bd47aeb4**
13. Procter & Gamble, "U.S. Recruiting process," **www.pg.com/jobs/jobs_us/recruitblue/recprocess.jhtml** (accessed July 5, 2006); "The Recruitment Process," Procter & Gamble, **http://www.pg.com/en_CA/careers/view_jobs/index.shtml** (accessed June 4, 2010).
14. "Job Opportunities," *Borders*, **https://wss6a.unicru.com/hirepro/C406/applicant.jsp?Eurl564%2Fhirepro%2FC406%2Fapplicant.jsp%3FSite%3D-3%26C%3D406%26k%3Dno%26content%3Dsearch%26Lang%3Den&Site5100585&C5406&k5no&content5start&Lang5en** (accessed March 9, 2010).
15. Amy Elisa Jackson,"Popular Companies Using AI to Interview & Hire You," January 1, 2019, **https://www.glassdoor.com/blog/popular-companies-using-ai-to-interview-hire-you/**
16. "Canadian Human Rights Commission Policy on Alcohol and Drug Testing," Canadian Human Rights Commission, **http://www.chrc-ccdp.ca/pdf/poldrgalceng.pdf** (accessed May 17, 2010).
17. Associated Press, "Food Network Chef Fired After Resume Fraud," *USA Today*, March 3, 2008, **www.usatoday.com/news/nation/2008-03-03-chef-fired_N.htm** (accessed April 14, 2011).
18. Christopher T. Marquet and Lisa J.B. Peterson, "Résumé Fraud: The Top Ten Lies," Marquet International, Ltd., **www.marquetinternational.com/pdf/Resume%20Fraud-Top%20Ten%20Lies.pdf** (accessed April 14, 2011).
19. J.T. O'Donnell, "85 Percent of Job Applications Lie on Resumes. Here's How to Spot a Dishonest Candidate," April 15, 2017, **https://www.inc.com/jt-odonnell/staggering-85-of-job-applicants-lying-on-resumes-.html**
20. The Canadian Charter of Rights and Freedoms, Canadian Heritage, **http://dsp-psd.pwgsc.gc.ca/Collection/CH37-4-3-2002E.pdf** (accessed July 17, 2010).
21. *Canadian Human Rights Act*, **http://www.efc.ca/pages/law/canada/canada.H-6.head.html** (accessed July 17, 2010).
22. "Overview," Canadian Human Rights Commission (n.d.), **http://www.chrc-ccdp.ca/about/icm_page2_gci-eng.aspx** (accessed July 17, 2010).
23. George Waggott and Lang Michener, "Mandatory Retirement: 65 or Not?" Supreme Court Law, **http://www.supremecourtlaw.ca/default_e.asp?id=68** (accessed July 17, 2010).
24. "Our Curriculum," Hamburger University, **www.aboutmcdonalds.com/mcd/careers/hamburger_university/our_curriculum.html** (accessed April 14, 2011).
25. Michael Goeden, "How 4 Industries Are Using Virtual Reality to Train Employees," November 8, 2017, **https://elearningindustry.com/using-virtual-reality-to-train-employees-4-industries**
26. Doug Stewart, "Employee-Appraisal Software," *Inc.*, **www.inc.com/magazine/19940615/3288_pagen_2.html** (accessed April 14, 2011).
27. Maury A. Peiperl, "Getting 360-Degree Feedback Right," *Harvard Business Review*, January 2001, pp. 142–48.
28. Chris Musselwhite, "Self Awareness and the Effective Leader," Inc.com, October 1, 2007, **www.inc.com/resources/leadership/articles/20071001/musselwhite.html** (accessed April 14, 2011).
29. Rick Nauert, "Flexible Work Place Improves Family Life, Reduces Turnover," PsychCentral, April 7, 2011, **http://psychcentral.com/news/2011/04/07/flexible-workplace-improves-family-life-reduces-turnover/25094.html** (accessed April 5, 2012).

30. Elliot Maras, "Best Buy CEO talks melding digital with physical for a winning retail strategy," March 29, 2019, **https://www.retailcustomerexperience.com/articles/best-buy-ceo-describes-its-turnaround/**
31. Marcia Zidle, "Employee Turnover: Seven Reasons Why People Quit Their Jobs," **http://ezinearticles.com/?Employee-Turnover:-Seven-Reasons-Why-People-Quit-Their-Jobs&id=42531** (accessed April 14, 2011).
32. Angela Mulholland, "Target leaving Canada: 'Losing money every day,'" CTV News, January 15, 2015, **http://www.ctvnews.ca/business/target-leaving-canada-losing-money-every-day-1.2189973** (accessed January 12, 2016).
33. Tavia Grant, "Canada's job market in deep freeze," *Globe and Mail* online, November 6, 2009, **https://www.theglobeandmail.com/report-on-business/economy/canadas-job-market-in-deep-freeze/article1205298/** (accessed July 30, 2019).
34. "Current and Forthcoming Minimum Hourly Wage Rates for Experienced Adult Workers in Canada," Government of Canada, **http://srv116.services.gc.ca/dimt-wid/sm-mw/rpt1.aspx** (accessed October 20, 2016).
35. John Daly, "Bulking up: How GoodLife became Canada's dominant gym," *Globe and Mail*, March 27, 2014, **http://www.theglobeandmail.com/report-on-business/rob-magazine/the-secret-of-goodlifes-success/article17673987/?page=4** (accessed January 13, 2016).
36. Robert Lachowiez, presenter, Business & Tourism Conference 2017, Mount Saint Vincent University, Halifax, Nova Scotia.
37. "WestJet Airlines' winning strategy for engagement," Internal Comms Hub, 1(8), December/January 2008, pp. 10–11: **http://www.bridgesconsultancy.com/newsroom/articles/youve_got_the%20strategy.pdf**
38. Marjo Johne, "Why you should give your employees a piece of the company," *Globe and Mail*, March 22, 2012, **http://www.theglobeandmail.com/report-on-business/careers/business-education/why-you-should-give-your-employees-a-piece-of-the-company/article535271/** (accessed January 13, 2016).
39. Katherine Marshall, "Benefits of the Job," Perspectives on Labour and Income, The Online Edition, May 2003, Vol. 4, No. 5, **http://www.statcan.gc.ca/pub/75-001-x/00503/6515-eng.html** (accessed July 17, 2010).
40. Stephan Miller, "Employee Loyalty Hits 7-Year Low; Benefits Promote Retention," Society for Human Resource Management, March 22, 2012, **www.shrm.org/hrdisciplines/benefits/Articles/Pages/LoyaltyLow.aspx** (accessed April 5, 2012).
41. "Unionization rates falling," **https://www150.statcan.gc.ca/n1/pub/11-630-x/11-630-x2015005-eng.htm** (accessed January 13, 2019).
42. "Canada Post Strike to End As Senate Passes Back-To-Work Legislation," November 27, 2018, **https://www.huffingtonpost.ca/2018/11/26/canada-post-strike-end-back-to-work_a_23601685/**
43. James R. Hagerty, "Caterpillar Closes Plant in Canada after Lockout," *Wall Street Journal*, February 3, 2012, **http://online.wsj.com/article/SB10001424052970203889904577200953014575964.html** (accessed April 5, 2012).
44. Diane Jermyn, "Canada's best diversity employers build respectful, inclusive workplaces," March 6, 2019, **https://www.theglobeandmail.com/business/careers/top-employers/article-canadas-best-diversity-employers-build-respectful-inclusive/**
45. **http://www.rbc.com/diversity/research.html** (accessed November 3, 2010).
46. Diane Jermyn, "Canada's best diversity employers build respectful, inclusive workplaces," March 6, 2019, **https://www.theglobeandmail.com/business/careers/top-employers/article-canadas-best-diversity-employers-build-respectful-inclusive/**
47. Shruti Shekar, "Big tech companies talk best practices for more diverse and inclusive workplace at #MoveTheDial," November 9, 2018, **https://www.itworldcanada.com/article/big-tech-companies-talk-best-practices-for-more-diverse-and-inclusive-workplace-at-movethedial/411637**
48. Taylor H. Cox, Jr., "The Multicultural Organization," Academy of Management Executives 5 (May 1991), pp. 34–47; Marilyn Loden and Judy B. Rosener, *Workforce America! Managing Employee Diversity as a Vital Resource* (Homewood, IL: Business One Irwin, 1991).
49. Paul Davidson, "Overworked and Underpaid?" *USA Today*, April 16, 2012, pp. 1A–2A.
50. Ethics Resource Center, 2011 *National Business Ethics Survey®: Ethics in Transition* (Arlington, VA: Ethics Resource Center, 2012), pp. 39–40.
51. Melanie Trottman, "For Angry Employees, Legal Cover for Rants," *Wall Street Journal*, December 2, 2011, **http://online.wsj.com/article/SB10001424052970203710704577049822809710332.html** (accessed April 23, 2012).
52. Martin Crutsinger, "Hiring Grows as Companies Hit Limits with Workers," *NPR News*, March 7, 2012, **http://minnesota.publicradio.org/display/web/2012/03/07/hiring-grows-as-companies-hit-limit/** (accessed April 23, 2012).
53. Tracy Johnson, "WestJet at 20: Grown-up airline, grown-up problems," April 22, 2016, **https://www.cbc.ca/news/business/westjet-20-grown-up-problems-1.3515255**
54. Amanda Stephenson, "WestJet CEO Saretsky will 'go down fighting' to prevent unionization," **https://calgaryherald.com/business/local-business/westjet-ceo-saretsky-will-go-down-fighting-to-prevent-unionization**, (accessed December 22, 2016).
55. Justin Dallaire, "WestJet rebrands to reflect global ambitions," October 11, 2018, **http://strategyonline.ca/2018/10/11/westjet-rebrands-to-reflect-global-ambitions/**
56. P. David Ball, "Could Unions Ground WestJet's 'Owners Care' Motto?" April 8, 2016, **https://thetyee.ca/News/2016/04/08/WestJet-Union-Model/**
57. Canadian Press, "WestJet pilots' union files complaint over recruitment for new low-cost airline," February 9, 2018.
58. Meagan Gillmore, "Multiple union drives reflect turbulence at WestJet," August 2, 2017, **http://rabble.ca/news/2017/08/multiple-union-drives-reflect-turbulence-westjet**
59. Darryl Dyck, "WestJet loses another unionization battle as CUPE to represent flight attendants," August 1, 2018, **https://business.financialpost.com/pmn/business-pmn/westjet-flight-attendants-to-be-represented-by-cupe**


## Chapter 11


1. Dawn Calleja, "How Spin Master got its mojo back," *Globe and Mail*, January 28, 2015, **http://www.theglobeandmail.com/report-on-business/rob-magazine/how-spin-master-got-its-mojo-back/article22639332/** (accessed December 7, 2015).

2. "Spin Master Corp. Company Information," Bloomberg, March 28, 2019, **https://www.bloomberg.com/quote/TOY:CN**

3. Dawn Calleja, "How Spin Master got its mojo back," **http://www.theglobeandmail.com/report-on-business/rob-magazine/how-spin-master-got-its-mojo-back/article22639332/**

4. Billy Langsworthy, "Paw Patrol and Hatchimals success drive Spin Master to record-breaking Q3," November 13, 2017, **https://mojo-nation.com/paw-patrol-hatchimals-success-drive-spin-master-record-breaking-q3/**

5. Dana Hatic, "Five Reasons McDonald's Is Back on Top," January 30, 2018, **https://www.eater.com/2018/1/30/16937672/mcdonalds-comeback-stock-price-all-day-breakfast-delivery**

6. "Wireless," EastLink website, **http://www.eastlink.ca/Wireless.aspx** (accessed July 9, 2013).

7. Tony Martin, "Ask the Legends: Walter Hachborn," *CBOnline*, March 2009, **http://www.canadianbusiness.com/article.jsp?content=20090201_30016_30017** (accessed July 7, 2010).

8. Jennifer Kwan, "Quebec's Simons Eyes Toronto Sears Locations," Yahoo! Finance online, June 17, 2013, **http://ca.finance.yahoo.com/blogs/insight/quebec-simons-eyes-toronto-sears-locations-180217911.html** (accessed July 9, 2013).

9. Jamie Beliveau, "Does Size Matter When You Want to Hire a Construction Company?", Kerr Construction, **http://www.kerrconstruction.ca/articles.html** (accessed July 7, 2010).

10. "Success of Herbal Magic Franchise," The Franchise Mall, June 18, 2008, **http://www.thefranchisemall.com/news/articles/21579-0.htm** (accessed July 7, 2010).

11. Avi Dan, "When It Comes to Social Media Consumers Tell Brands to Speak Only When Spoken To," *Forbes* online, March 31, 2013, **http://www.forbes.com/sites/avidan/2013/03/31/when-it-comes-to-social-media-consumers-tell-brands-to-speak-only-when-spoken-to/** (accessed July 9, 2013).

12. Michael Treacy and Fred Wiersema, *The Discipline of Market Leaders* (Reading, MA: Addison Wesley, 1995), p. 176.

13. "Print Audit," ASTech Awards, **http://www.printaudit.com/downloads/pdf/ASTech_Profile.pdf** (accessed July 6, 2010).

14. MacRumors Staff, "Apple Stores," February 6, 2019, **https://www.macrumors.com/roundup/apple-retail-stores/**

15. Help Scout, "75 Customer Service Facts, Quotes & Statistics," **https://www.helpscout.com/75-customer-service-facts-quotes-statistics/**, (accessed May 15, 2019).

16. Venky Shankar, "Multiple Touch Point Marketing," American Marketing Association Faculty Consortium on Electronic Commerce, Texas A&M University, July 14–17, 2001.

17. Ryan Holmes, "Why Businesses Can't Survive Without Social Media," November 15, 2018, **http://fortune.com/2015/11/18/businesses-cant-survive-social-media/**

18. Stephanie Kang, "The Swoosh Finds Its Swing, Targeting Weekend Golfers," *Wall Street Journal*, April 8, 2004, p. B1.

19. "About the Company," Reitmans, **http://www.reitmans.com/en/company/** (accessed September 1, 2010).

20. Hollie Shaw, "Hudson's Bay CEO Lost in Space," *Financial Post*, **http://www.nationalpost.com/life/health/Hudson+lost+space/857928/story.html** or **https://www.pressreader.com/** (accessed July 7, 2019).

21. Allison Marr, "Household-Level Research Gives Clearer Picture," *Marketing News*, April 15, 2006, p. 18.

22. New to Canada Website, **https://www.tdcanadatrust.com/m/planning/life-events/new-to-canada/**, (accessed May 15, 2019).

23. Charles Passy, "Your Scoop Is in the Mail," *Wall Street Journal*, May 25, 2001, pp. W1, W6.

24. **http://blaycation.com/about-us/**, (accessed June 1, 2019).

25. Sara Carson, "Five lessons from economist and author David K. Foot," June 26, 2017, **https://www.simcoe.com/news-story/7390859-five-lessons-from-economist-and-author-david-k-foot/**

26. Denise R., "Understanding Millennials is Key to Capturing More of the Child Care Market," September 28, 2018, **https://childwatch.com/blog/2018/09/28/understanding-millennials-is-key-to-capturing-more-of-the-child-care-market/**

27. Michael Andronico, "PS4 vs. Xbox One: Which Console Is Right for You?" April 1, 2019, **https://www.tomsguide.com/us/xbox-one-vs-ps4,review-2543.html**

28. Matt & Nat Website, **https://mattandnat.com/our-story/**, (accessed August 9, 2019).

29. Dr. Abdullah Kirumira, BioMedical Diagnostic Inc., in a personal interview with Peter Mombourquette, 2010. Information reconfirmed 2013.

30. **https://www.solutions2go.ca/about.html**, (accessed May 1, 2019).

31. "Lululemon: Building the Brand From the Ground—Yoga Mat—Up," Strategyonline.ca, January 13, 2003, **http://strategyonline.ca/2003/01/13/lululemon-20030113/** (accessed August 5, 2013).

32. Ellen Roseman, "Blockbuster of Books," thestar.com, **http://www.thestar.com/article/269013** (accessed July 7, 2010).

33. Wency Leung, "Tim Hortons' Extra-Large Coffee to Get Even Larger," *Globe and Mail* online, January 16, 2012, **http://www.theglobeandmail.com/life/food-and-wine/food-trends/tim-hortons-extra-large-coffee-to-get-even-larger/article1358604/** (accessed August 5, 2013).

34. Michael J. Weiss, "To Be About to Be," *American Demographics* 25 (September 2003), pp. 29–36.

35. "Ask the Legends: Les Mandelbaum," CBOnline, December 2009, **http://www.canadianbusiness.com/entrepreneur/managing/article.jsp?content=20091130_145811_9872**

36. Rasha Mourtada, "Tour business," *Globe and Mail* online, August 29, 2007, **http://www.theglobeandmail.com/report-on-business/tourbusiness/article778331/singlepage/#articlecontent**

37. Rick Spence, "Sweetpea Baby Food: Stuck in the Middle," CBOnline, October 2007, **http://www.canadianbusiness.com/entrepreneur/sales_marketing/article.jsp?content=20071002_12233_12233&page=1**

38. Look, lookaheadstayahead.com (accessed June 16, 2019).

39. Faith Keenan, "Friendly Spies on the Net," BW Online, July 9, 2001, **http://www.businessweek.com/magazine/content/01_28/b3740624.htm**

40. Diane Brady, "Pets Are People, Too, You Know," *BusinessWeek*, November 28, 2005, p. 114.

41. "Local Consumer Review Survey 2018," **https://www.brightlocal.com/research/local-consumer-review-survey/**, (accessed March 1, 2019).

42. "Marriott's First-Ever, Pop-Up Innovation Lab Further Evolves Its Cutting Edge Aloft and Element Hotel Brands," January 23, 2017,

**https://news.marriott.com/2017/01/marriotts-first-ever-pop-innovation-lab-evolves-cutting-edge-aloft-element-hotel-brands/**

43. Normandy Madden, "'Rolling Stone' Smacks into Great Wall of China," *Advertising Age,* April 3, 2006, p. 8.

44. Karen Valby, "The Man Who Ate Too Much," *Entertainment Weekly,* May 21, 2004, p. 45.

45. Sharon Vega, "Kellogg's UK Launches Healthier Plant-Based Cereal With Fruits and Veggies," January 31, 2019, **https://www.onegreenplanet.org/vegan-food/kellogg-uk-launches-healthier-plant-based-cereal-with-fruits-and-veggies/**

46. Bruce Horovitz, "Wendy's Will Be 1st Foodie with Healthier Oil," *USA Today,* June 8, 2006, p. 1A.

47. "Limestone Technologies," *Dragons' Den,* February 2019, **https://www.cbc.ca/dragonsden/pitches/limestone-technologies-plant-choir**

48. Canada Post, "Michele Romanow's tips on how to launch your e-commerce business," **https://www.canadapost.ca/blogs/business/ecommerce/michele-romanows-tips-on-how-to-launch-your-e-commerce-business/**, (accessed May 1, 2019).

## Chapter 12

1. **https://www.huffingtonpost.ca/news/retail-canada/**, (accessed May 18, 2019).

2. **https://www.forbes.com/sites/forbestreptalks/2017/11/14/tulip-retail-thinks-it-can-save-brick-and-mortar-and-become-a-100-billion-business-really/#18fc3c8463ac**

3. **https://tulip.com/**, (accessed June 1, 2019).

4. **https://tulip.com/**, (accessed June 1, 2019); **https://www.forbes.com/sites/forbestreptalks/2017/11/14/tulip-retail-thinks-it-can-save-brick-and-mortar-and-become-a-100-billion-business-really/#18fc3c8463ac**

5. PR Newswire, **https://tulip.com/articles/top-retailers-choose-tulip-to-drive-more-intimate-shopping-experiences/**, January 1, 2019.

6. **https://tulip.com/**, (accessed June 1, 2019).

7. Peter Carbonara, "Tulip Retail Thinks It Can Save Brick-And-Mortar and Become a $100 Billion Business. Really." November 14, 2017, **https://www.forbes.com/sites/forbestreptalks/2017/11/14/tulip-retail-thinks-it-can-save-brick-and-mortar-and-become-a-100-billion-business-really/#18fc3c8463ac**

8. Mary Hanbury, "Amazon hints that it may return to the smartphone market after its $170 million Fire phone Fiasco," **https://www.businessinsider.com/amazon-may-experiment-with-new-smartphone-after-fire-phone-disaster-2019-5**, May 13, 2019.

9. Adam Clarke Estes, "The Worst Fire Gadget Amazon Ever Made Is Even Worse Than I Remember," **https://gizmodo.com/the-worst-fire-gadget-amazon-ever-made-is-even-worse-th-1836274935**, July 11, 2019.

10. Umbra, **http://www.umbra.com/**; "Ask the Legends: Les Mandelbaum," *Canadian Business,* December 2009, **https://www.canadianbusiness.com/innovation/les-mandelbaum/** (accessed September 1, 2010).

11. Aaron Mamiit, "BlackBerry Mobile 'Here To Stay,' Aims For 3 Percent Market Share Over Next Few Years," **https://www.techtimes.com/articles/221844/20180226/blackberry-mobile-here-to-stay-aims-for-3-percent-market-share-over-next-few-years.htm**, February 26, 2018.

12. Galen Gruman, "Rotten Apple: Apple's 12 Biggest Failures," *CIO,* **http://www.cio.com/article/507483/Rotten_Apple_Apple_s_12_Biggest_Failures?page=13#slideshow** (accessed July 11, 2013).

13. Troy Wolverton, "Apple is now one of the biggest investors in research and development, and critics are wondering what it's getting for its money," March 9, 2019, **https://www.businessinsider.com/apple-research-and-development-self-driving-cars-augmented-reality-2019-3**

14. "About Microsoft Research," Microsoft Research, **http://research.microsoft.com/en-us/about/default.aspx** (accessed September 1, 2010).

15. "Karen Crouse, "A Fashion Statement Designed to Grab Gold," NYTimes.com, February 11, 2010, **http://www.nytimes.com/2010/02/12/sports/olympics/12speedsuits.html**

16. Andrew Zaleski, "7 businesses that cloned others and made millions," October 4, 2017, **https://www.cnbc.com/2017/10/03/7-businesses-that-cloned-others-and-made-millions.html**

17. Joe Castaldo, "The Case for Stealing Your Success," ProfitGuide, June 12, 2014, **http://www.profitguide.com/manage-grow/innovation/steal-your-success-66165** (accessed January 12, 2016).

18. Rose Behar, "Meet the company that teaches 24 million students math through RPG," January 18, 2018, **https://mobilesyrup.com/2018/01/18/burlington-educational-game-prodigy-24-million-players/**

19. "Best Inventions of the Year 2012: Self-Inflating Tires," *Time,* October 31, 2012, **http://techland.time.com/2012/11/01/best-inventions-of-the-year-2012/slide/self-inflating-tires/** (accessed July 11, 2013).

20. The Five Funniest Dragon's Den Pitches of All Time, **https://www.cbc.ca/dragonsden/blog/the-5-funniest-dragons-den-pitches**, (accessed June 1, 2019).

21. Brett Shevack, "Open Up to a New Way to Develop Better Ideas," *Point,* June 2006, p. 8.

22. Judann Pollack, "The Endurance Test, Heinz Ketchup," *Advertising Age,* November 14, 2005, p. 39.

23. Oliver Burkman, "Happiness is a Glass Half-Empty," *The Guardian* online, June 15, 2012, **http://www.guardian.co.uk/lifeandstyle/2012/jun/15/happiness-is-being-a-loser-burkeman**; Dan Gould, "The Museum of Product Failures," *PSFK* online, August 12, 2008, **http://techland.time.com/2012/11/01/best-inventions-of-the-year-2012/slide/self-inflating-tires/** (both accessed July 11, 2013).

24. "Digital Payment Technologies Named to Deloitte's 2010 Technology Fast 500™" in North America," Digital Payment Technologies, October 25, 2010, **http://www.digitalpaytech.com/news/press_releases/2010/101025_Fast_500.pdf** (accessed November 17, 2010).

25. Faith Keenan, "Friendly Spies on the Net," *Business Week,* July 9, 2001.

26. Danielle Wiener-Bronner, "Burger King plans to roll out the Impossible Whopper across the United States," April 29, 2019, **https://www.cnn.com/2019/04/29/business/burger-king-impossible-rollout/index.html**

27. Sophia Harris, "New Tim Hortons coffee lids leak too much, some customers say," December 5, 2018, **https://www.cbc.ca/news/business/tim-hortons-new-lids-leaks-1.4933959**

28. James Cowan, "Tim Hortons' New Coffee Cup: Why the Supersize?" *Canadian Business*, February 14, 2012, **http://www.canadianbusiness.com/business-strategy/tim-hortons-new-coffee-cup-why-the-supersize/** (accessed July 11, 2013); "Tim Horton's tempest in a tea cup," CBC News, November 26, 2001, **http://www.cbc.ca/news/story/2001/11/23/TimmysTea_011123.html** (accessed June 15, 2006).

29. William C. Symonds, "Gillette's New Edge: P&G Is Helping Pump Up the Fusion Razor," *BusinessWeek*, February 6, 2006, p. 44.

30. "Tide Unveils Milestone in Fabric Care with New Tide Stainbrush," Procter & Gamble, press release, February 13, 2004, **www.pg.com/news/**

31. Daniel Eran Dilger, "Editorial: After disrupting iTunes, Spotify demands a free ride from Apple's App Store," March 14, 2019, **https://appleinsider.com/articles/19/03/14/editorial-after-disrupting-itunes-spotify-demands-a-free-ride-from-apples-app-store**

32. T. L. Stanley, "Barbie Hits the Skids," *Advertising Age*, October 31, 2005, pp. 1, 33.

33. Eric Wellweg, "Test Time for TiVo," *Business2.0*, May 24, 2004, **www.business2.com/**

34. "Glenora Distillers," Wikipedia, **http://en.wikipedia.org/wiki/Glenora_Distillers**; The Glenora Inn & Distillery website, **http://www.glenoradistillery.com/glen.html** (accessed July 11, 2013).

35. David Goldman and Julianne Pepitone, "Lady Gaga is the new face of Polaroid," CNN Money, January 8, 2010, **http://money.cnn.com/2010/01/06/news/companies/lady_gaga_polaroid/** (accessed June 17, 2010); Jason Kirby, "Polaroid goes Gaga," CBOnline, February 15, 2010, **http://www.canadianbusiness.com/managing/strategy/article.jsp?content=20100113_10010_10010** (accessed June 17, 2010).

36. "The World's Most Valuable Brands," **https://www.forbes.com/powerful-brands/list/#tab:rank**, (accessed March 1, 2019).

37. Hollie Shaw, "In ranking of Canada's most valuable brands, this widely criticized company is still growing," May 24, 2018, **https://business.financialpost.com/news/retail-marketing/in-ranking-of-canadas-most-valuable-brands-this-widely-criticized-company-is-still-growing**

38. "Loblaw Companies," **http://en.wikipedia.org/wiki/Loblaw_Companies** (accessed June 17, 2010); "Sobeys," **http://en.wikipedia.org/wiki/Sobeys** (accessed June 17, 2010).

39. Alessandra Galloni, "Advertising," *Wall Street Journal*, June 1, 2001, p. B6.

40. Frank Pallotta, "Coca-Cola and Disney partner for new 'Star Wars: Galaxy's Edge' land," April 13, 2019, **https://www.cnn.com/2019/04/13/media/star-wars-galaxys-edge-coke-disney/index.html**

41. Madhuri Katti, "Coke Displays Aboriginal Art on Bottles at Vancouver Winter Olympics 2010," Trends Updates, February 18, 2010, **http://trendsupdates.com/coke-displays-aboriginal-art-on-bottles-at-vancouver-winter-olympics-2010/** (accessed June 17, 2010).

42. Pallavi Gogoi, "McDonald's New Wrap," *BusinessWeek*, February 17, 2006, **www.businessweek.com/print/bwdaily/dnflash/feb2006/nf20060217_8329_db016.htm?chan=db** (accessed February 2006).

43. Stephanie Miles, "Consumer Groups Want to Rate the Web," *Wall Street Journal*, June 21, 2001, p. B13.

44. Rajneesh Suri and Kent B. Monroe, "The Effects of Time Constraints on Consumers' Judgments of Prices and Products," *Journal of Consumer Research* 30 (June 2003), pp. 92+.

45. Steven Gray, "McDonald's Menu Upgrade Boosts Meal Prices and Results," *Wall Street Journal*, February 18, 2006, p. A1.

46. Craig Sutherland, in a personal interview with Peter Mombourquette, August 4, 2010. Information reconfirmed 2018.

47. Stephanie Thompson, "Polo Jeans Thrown in the Hamper," *Advertising Age*, June 5, 2006, p. 3.

48. "Retail e-commerce revenue in Canada from 2017 to 2023," **https://www.statista.com/statistics/289741/canada-retail-e-commerce-sales/**, (accessed June 1, 2019).

49. "List of International Retailers that Entered Canada in 2018," February 27, 2019, **https://www.retail-insider.com/retail-insider/2019/2/list-of-international-retailers-that-entered-canada-in-2018-feature**

50. O. C. Ferrell and Michael D. Hartline, *Marketing Strategy* (Mason, OH: South-Western, 2005), p. 215.

51. "Top Threats to Revenue," *USA Today*, February 1, 2006, p. A1.

52. Todd Wasserman, "Kodak Rages in Favor of the Machines," *BrandWeek*, February 26, 2001, p. 6.

53. Tony Martin, "Ask the Legends: Walter Hachborn," *Canadian Business*, March 2009, **http://www.canadianbusiness.com/article.jsp?content=20090201_30016_30017** (accessed June 17, 2010).

54. Amber MacArthur, "PEI's (million dollar) Google juice," *Globe and Mail*, July 14, 2010, **http://www.theglobeandmail.com/news/technology/trending-tech/peis-million-dollar-google-juice/article1639896/** (accessed August 3, 2010).

55. Nicole Hui, "This Hilarious Marijuana Ad Is Going Viral In Canada and You Need to Watch It Right Now," November 13, 2018, **https://www.narcity.com/news/this-hilarious-marijuana-ad-is-going-viral-in-canada-and-you-need-to-watch-it-right-now-video**

56. "Where advertisers are spending their money in Canada," *Globe and Mail*, September 30, 2015, **http://www.theglobeandmail.com/report-on-business/industry-news/marketing/where-advertisers-are-spending-their-money-in-canada/article26597480/** (accessed November 14, 2016).

57. "Daily time spent using the Internet in Canada from 2010 to 2018 (In minutes), **https://www.statista.com/statistics/237502/daily-time-spent-using-the-internet-among-adults-in-canada/**, (accessed June 1, 2019).

58. "Canadians Lead in Time Spent Online," CBC News website, March 2, 2012, **http://www.cbc.ca/news/canada/story/2012/03/02/canadians-more-time-online.html** (accessed July 14, 2013).

59. Julia Alexander, "Canadians spend the most time online: Study," *Toronto Sun*, March 27, 2015, **http://www.torontosun.com/2015/03/27/canadians-spend-the-most-time-online-study** (accessed January 14, 2016).

60. eMarketer Editors, "In Two Years Users in Canada Will Spend More Time with Mobile than TV," September 14, 2018, **https://www.emarketer.com/content/in-two-years-users-in-canada-will-spend-more-time-with-mobile-than-tv**

61. "41 Facebook Stats That Matter to Marketers in 2019, November 13, 2018, https://blog.hootsuite.com/facebook-statistics/"

62. Craig Smith, "By The Numbers: 200+ Amazing Facebook Statistics" DMR Digital Stats/Gadgets, January 2016, **http://expandedramblings.com/index.php/by-the-numbers-17-amazing-facebook-stats/** (accessed January 16, 2016).

63. Derek Thompson, "The Profit Network: Facebook and Its 835-Million Man Workforce," *The Atlantic* online, February 2, 2012, **http://www.theatlantic.com/business/archive/2012/02/the-profit-network-facebook-and-its-835-million-man-workforce/252473/** (accessed July 30, 2013).

64. "Terre Bleu Lavender Farm," Facebook.com, Success Stories, **https://www.facebook.com/business/success/terre-bleu-lavender-farm** (accessed January 16, 2016).

65. Ilyse Liffreing, "Jagermeister turns to Snapchat for Halloween Push," October 22, 2018, **https://digiday.com/marketing/jagermeister-turns-snapchat-halloween-push/**

66. Vikas Agrawal, "Swipe Right: How Brands Are Using Tinder for Marketing," July 2017, **https://www.relevance.com/swipe-right-how-brands-are-using-tinder-for-marketing/**

67. "Top Sites in Canada," Alexa website, **http://www.alexa.com/topsites/countries/CA** (accessed July 30, 2013).

68. Tony Martin, "They blog, therefore they are ... better CEOs," March 15, 2008, GlobeAdvisor.com, **http://www.globeadvisor.com/servlet/ArticleNews/story/gam/20080315/RWORKOUT15** (accessed June 17, 2010); Grant Robertson, "CEO blogs: The new company 'water cooler,'" *Globe and Mail* online, February 6, 2006, **http://www.theglobeandmail.com/news/technology/ceo-blogs-the-new-company-water-cooler/article810687/singlepage/** (accessed June 17, 2010).

69. Kara Aaserud, "Bonding by Blogging," Provident Security Press, October 1, 2006, **http://www.providentsecurity.ca/press/31** (accessed June 17, 2010).

70. Eleanor Beaton, "How to sell more, more, more," **https://www.s2h.ca/blog/how-sell-more-more-more/**

71. In Katelyn, "7 YouTube Social Media Strategies for Success," September 20, 2018, **https://www.juicer.io/blog/7-youtube-social-media-strategies-for-success**

72. "Direct Mail," Answers.com, **http://www.answers.com/topic/direct-marketing** (accessed June 17, 2010).

73. "That's advertainment!" *NBC News*, October 9, 2018.

74. Jefferson Graham, "Web Pitches, That's 'Advertainment'," *USA Today,* June 26, 2011, p. 3D.

75. "The 6 Best Banner Ads in 2018," **https://www.omnivirt.com/blog/best-banner-ads-2018/**, (accessed July 1, 2019).

76. 2018 eBay Entrepreneur of the Year Awards, **https://pages.ebay.ca/eoy/** (accessed July 1, 2019).

77. "Top Sites in Canada," Alexa website (accessed July 1, 2019).

78. Chris Neville, in a personal interview with Peter Mombourquette, April 1 2019.

79. Corinne Watson, "How to Sell on Facebook Marketplace: A New 2019 Growth Channel," **https://www.bigcommerce.com/blog/selling-on-facebook-marketplace/#what-is-facebook-marketplace** (accessed March 1, 2019).

80. Katie Sehl, "Facebook Marketplace: A Comprehenisive Guide for Marketers," January 8, 2019, **https://blog.hootsuite.com/facebook-marketplace/**

81. Ilyse Liffreing, "Jagermeister turns to Snapchat for Halloween Push," October 22, 2018, **https://digiday.com/marketing/jagermeister-turns-snapchat-halloween-push/**

82. Ritesh Bhavnani, "Top Ten Mobile Marketing Trends for 2016," LuxuryDaily.com, January 5, 2016, **http://www.luxurydaily.com/top-10-mobile-marketing-trends-for-2016/** (accessed January 15, 2016).

83. Christine Dobby, "Checkout 51 App Lets You Shop Anywhere, Snap Pics of Receipt for Savings, *Financial Post,* December 14, 2012, **http://business.financialpost.com/entrepreneur/fp-startups/checkout-51-app-lets-you-shop-anywhere-snap-pics-of-receipt-for-savings?__lsa=6930-d566** (accessed January 15, 2016).

84. Paul Skeldon, "14 Million Americans Scanned QR and Barcodes with Their Mobiles in June 2011," *Internet Retailing* online, August 16, 2011, **http://www.internetretailing.net/2011/08/14m-americans-scanned-qr-and-bar-codes-with-their-mobiles-in-june-2011** (accessed July14, 2013).

85. Derek Johnson, "10 Amazing Retail Mobile Marketing Examples" Tatango, February 18, 2014, **http://www.tatango.com/blog/10-amazing-retail-mobile-marketing-examples/**

86. Joel Mathew, "Understanding Influencer Marketing And Why It Is So Effective," July 30, 2018, **https://www.forbes.com/sites/theyec/2018/07/30/understanding-influencer-marketing-and-why-it-is-so-effective/#2b30d55f71a9**

87. Zameena Mejia, "Kylie Jenner reportedly makes $1 million per paid Instagram post - here's how much other top influencers get," July 31, 2018, **https://www.cnbc.com/2018/07/31/kylie-jenner-makes-1-million-per-paid-instagram-post-hopper-hq-says.html**

88. Izea, "Top 25 Canadian Social Media Influencers," April 6, 2017, **https://izea.com/2017/04/06/canadian-social-media-influencers/?utm_medium=ppc&utm_source=adwords&utm_term=&utm_campaign=Dynamic+Search+Ads&hsa_kw=&hsa_tgt=dsa-395157765570&hsa_ver=3&hsa_mt=b&hsa_ad=283762836197&hsa_net=adwords&hsa_acc=1792975533&hsa_src=g&hsa_grp=62909196848&hsa_cam=1482430957&gclid=EAIaIQobChMI_Kn257aR4gIVhoizCh3jqAIWEAAYAyAAEgJZA_D_BwE**

89. Christina Newberry, "Influencer Marketing in 2019: How to Work With Social Media Influencers," May 2, 2019, **https://blog.hootsuite.com/influencer-marketing/**

90. Chris Atchison, "Entrepreneurial success: Masters of one," *Canadian Business*, May 2009, **http://www.canadianbusiness.com/entrepreneur/sales_marketing/article.jsp?content=20090501_30008_30008**

91. Jim McElgunn and Kim Shiffman, "Canada's Entrepreneurs of the Decade," CBOnline, December 2009, **http://www.canadianbusiness.com/entrepreneur/managing/article.jsp?content=20091201_30044_30044**; Just Energy Income Fund, **http://www.je-un.ca/SiteResources/ViewContent.asp?DocID=3&v1ID=&RevID=730&lang=1** (accessed July 17, 2010).

92. Zach Bulygo, "How Mint Grew to 1.5M Users, and Sold for over $170M in just 2 Years," Kissmetrics, January 22, 2016, **https://blog.kissmetrics.com/how-mint-grew/**

93. Eleanor Beaton, "How to sell more, more, more," May 27, 2010, **https://www.s2h.ca/blog/how-sell-more-more-more/**

94. Susanne Baillie and Kim Shiffman, "How to get on Oprah," *Canadian Business* online, February 2004, **http://www.canadianbusiness.com/entrepreneur/sales_marketing/article.jsp?content=20040213_155625_4316** (accessed June 17, 2010).

95. Kate MacArthur, "Sierra Mist: Cie Nicholson," *Advertising Age*, November 17, 2003, p. S-2.

96. "A tale of two customers," Canada Export Achievement Awards, **http://www.exportawards.ca/exportawards/atlantic.html** (accessed June 17, 2010).

97. Micheline Maynard, "Amid the Turmoil, A Rare Success at DaimlerChrysler," *Fortune*, January 22, 2001, p. 112.

98. Chris Morris, "Coke Is Getting Its First New Flavor in More Than a Decade," February 8, 2019, **http://fortune.com/2019/02/08/new-coke-flavor-orange-vanilla/**

99. "MoPub Publisher Spotlight: Aaron Wojnowski & Christian Lunny, Musi," March 26, 2018, **https://www.youtube.com/watch?v=xxTGJpzHC_A**

100. "MoPub Publisher Spotlight: Aaron Wojnowski & Christian Lunny, Musi," March 26, 2018, **https://www.youtube.com/watch?v=xxTGJpzHC_A**; **Musi**, CBC *Dragons' Den*, **https://www.cbc.ca/dragonsden/pitches/musi**, (accessed February 1, 2019).

101. Aaron Wojnowski, "How I hacked App Store ratings for a consistently perfect five stars," January 2, 2015, **https://medium.com/@awojnowski/how-i-hacked-app-store-ratings-for-a-consistently-perfect-5-stars-3de17d40ca1f**

102. Musi, CBC *Dragons' Den*, **https://www.cbc.ca/dragonsden/pitches/musi**, (accessed February 1, 2019); "Musi – Simple Music Streaming," **https://thinkgaming.com/app-sales-data/110741/musi-unlimited-free-musiyoutube/c-for-**, (accessed May 8, 2019); "MoPub Publisher Spotlight: Aaron Wojnowski & Christian Lunny, Musi," March 26, 2018, **https://www.youtube.com/watch?v=xxTGJpzHC_A**

103. Musi, CBC *Dragons' Den*, **https://www.cbc.ca/dragonsden/pitches/musi**, (accessed February 1, 2019); "Musi – Simple Music Streaming," **https://thinkgaming.com/app-sales-data/110741/musi-unlimited-free-musiyoutube/c-for-** (accessed May 8, 2019); "MoPub Publisher Spotlight: Aaron Wojnowski & Christian Lunny, Musi," March 26, 2018, **https://www.youtube.com/watch?v=xxTGJpzHC_A**

104. Mary Theresa Bitti, "*Dragons' Den*: Why popular music streaming app Musi ended up being too risky a play," March 3, 2016, **https://business.financialpost.com/entrepreneur/small-business/dragons-den-why-popular-music-streaming-app-musi-ended-up-being-too-risky-a-play**

## Chapter 13

1. Bio, Arlene Dickinson website, **http://arlenedickinson.com/bio/**; Angus Gillespie, "Power of Persuasion-The Inspirational Life Story of Arlene Dickinson," *Canadian Business Journal* online, **http://www.cbj.ca/features/may_12_features/power_of_persuasion_the_inspirational_life_story_of_arlene_dicki.html** (both accessed July 16, 2018); and Venture Communications website, **https://venturecommunications.ca/**, (accessed July 2, 2019).

2. Brad Stone and Bruce Einhorn, "Baidu China," *Bloomberg Businessweek*, November 15–21, 2010, pp. 60–67; Loretta Chao, "China's Baidu Brings App Craze to Web," *Wall Street Journal*, September 3, 2010, p. B8.

3. Jake Hundley, "Facebook is a local search engine. Are you treating it like one?" February 11, 2019, **https://searchenginewatch.com/2019/02/11/facebook-local-search-engine/**

4. Steve Ladurantaye, "Canada Tops Globe in Internet Usage," *Globe and Mail*, March 1, 2012, **http://www.theglobeandmail.com/technology/tech-news/canada-tops-globe-in-internet-usage/article551593/** (accessed July 16, 2013).

5. Ken Tencer, "What's Better than a Great Communication Strategy? Conversation," *Globe and Mail*, March 13, 2013, **http://www.theglobeandmail.com/report-on-business/small-business/sb-digital/innovation/whats-better-than-a-great-communication-strategy-conversation/article9600803/** (accessed July 16, 2013).

6. Zameena Meja, "Jeff Bezos finally got Amazon into the top tier of the Fortune 500," May 23, 2018, **https://www.cnbc.com/2018/05/23/jeff-bezos-finally-got-amazon-into-the-top-tier-of-the-fortune-500.html**

7. Dan Alaimo, "Amazon dominates international marketplace reach," September 10, 2018, **https://www.retaildive.com/news/amazon-dominates-international-marketplace-reach/531926/**

8. Amazon Revenue 2006–2019, **https://www.macrotrends.net/stocks/charts/AMZN/amazon/revenue**, (accessed July 1, 2019).

9. Jamie Michaels, "Canada's most memorable Twitter brand campaigns & brand voices for 2018," December 12, 2018, **https://blog.twitter.com/en_ca/topics/insights/2018/Canadian_Twitter_brand_campaigns_2018.html**

10. Number of Facebook Users in Canada from 2017 to 2023, **https://www.statista.com/statistics/282364/number-of-facebook-users-in-canada/**, (accessed July 1, 2019).

11. Melody McKinnon, "2018 Social Media Use in Canada," July 17, 2018, **https://canadiansinternet.com/2018-social-media-use-canada/**

12. "The Freshbooks Story," **https://www.freshbooks.com/about/ourstory**, (accessed July 1, 2019).

13. "Internet Usage Statistics, The Internet Big Picture, World Internet Users and 2019 Population Stats," **https://www.internetworldstats.com/stats.htm**, (accessed June 6, 2019).

14. "How L'Oreal is Using Augmented Reality & VR to Build In-Store Experiences," **https://futurestores.wbresearch.com/loreal-augmented-reality-virtual-reality-in-store-experience-strategy-ty-u** (accessed June 9, 2019).

15. Michael V. Copeland, "Tapping Tech's Beautiful Mind," *Fortune*, October 12, 2009, pp. 35–36.

16. Jacqueline Nelson, "Business without Borders: Coastal Contacts," *Canadian Business* online, March 13, 2012, **http://www.canadianbusiness.com/business-news/industries/consumer-goods/business-without-borders-coastal-contacts/** (accessed July 30, 2013).

17. Aaron Back, "China's Big Brands Tackle Web Sales," *Wall Street Journal*, December 1, 2009, p. B2.

18. Melissa S. Barker, Donald I. Barker, Nicholas F. Bormann, Mary Lou Roberts, and Debra Zahay, *Social Media Marketing*, 2nd ed. (Mason, OH: Cengage Learning, 2016).

19. "Facebook Business, Facebook IQ," **https://www.facebook.com/iq/insights-to-go/6m-there-are-more-than-6-million-active-advertisers-on-facebook**, (accessed June 7, 2019).

20. Melissa S. Barker, Donald I. Barker, Nicholas F. Bormann, Mary Lou Roberts, and Debra Zahay, *Social Media Marketing*, 2nd ed. (Mason, OH: Cengage Learning, 2016).

21. Migs Bassig, "Yelp Factsheet: Stats Your Business Needs to Know," December 4, 2018, **https://www.reviewtrackers.com/yelp-factsheet/**

22. "Dodge Brand Connecting with Its Fans by Inviting a Limited Number to the Hotly Anticipated Reveal of the All-New 2018 Dodge Challenger SRT Demon in NYC," Yahoo! Finance, February 22, 2017, **http://finance.yahoo.com/news/dodge-brand-connecting-fansinviting-130000410.html**

23. "2009 Digital Handbook," *Marketing News,* April 30, 2009, p. 13.

24. "Canadian Social Media Stats (Updated 2018)," **https://www.sherpamarketing.ca/canadian-social-media-stats-updated-2018-471**, (accessed May 23, 2019).

25. Melody McKinnon, "2015 Canadian Social Media Usage Statistics," CanadiansInternet.com, January 12, 2015, **http://canadiansinternet.com/2015-canadian-social-media-usage-statistics/**

26. Facebook Stats That Matter to Marketers in 2019, November 13, 2018, **https://blog.hootsuite.com/facebook-statistics/**

27. Interview with Chris Webb, May 25 2019.

28. "Measure for Measure Facebook Ads Deliver," Facebook, **https://www.facebook.com/business/success/stratford-festival** (accessed February 11, 2016).

29. "Canada Facebook Statistics," Socialbakers website, **http://www.socialbakers.com/facebook-statistics/canada** (accessed July 17, 2013).

30. Liis Hainla, "21 Social Media Marketing Statistics You Need to Know in 2019," July 5, 2018, **https://www.dreamgrow.com/21-social-media-marketing-statistics/**

31. "Pepsi Refresh Project," www.refresheverything.com/index (accessed April 13, 2011); Stuart Elliot, "Pepsi Invites the Public to Do Good," *New York Times,* January 31, 2010, **www.nytimes.com/2010/02/01/business/media/01adco.html** (accessed April 13, 2011).

32. "Facebook Needs to Be a Marketing Destination, Not Just a Conduit," *Marketing News,* March 15, 2011, p. 12.

33. "Linkedin by the Numbers: Stats, Demographics & Fun Facts," May 29, 2019, **https://www.omnicoreagency.com/linkedin-statistics/**

34. "LinkedIn user reach among internet users in Canada as of July 2017, by age group," **https://www.statista.com/statistics/437459/linkedin-user-penetration-canada-age/**, (accessed May 31, 2019).

35. Alison Doyle, "LinkedIn and Your Job Search," About.com, **http://jobsearch.about.com/od/networking/a/linkedin.htm** (accessed April 13, 2011).

36. Jennifer Goldberg, "How to turn social media engagement into real sale," September 14, 2017, **https://www.canadianbusiness.com/lists-and-rankings/profit-500/2017-social-media-marketing/**

37. Jefferson Graham, "Cake Decorator Finds Twitter a Tweet Recipe for Success," *USA Today,* April 1, 2009, p. 5B.

38. Paige Cooper, "28 Twitter Statistics All Marketers Need to Know in 2019," January 16, 2019, **https://blog.hootsuite.com/twitter-statistics/**

39. Craig Smith, "By the Numbers: 170+ Amazing Twitter Statistics," *DMR Digital Stats/Gadgets,* February 26, 2016, **http://expandedramblings.com/index.php/march-2013-by-the-numbers-a-few-amazing-twitter-stats/**

40. Melody McKinnon, "2015 Canadian Social Media Usage Statistics," CanadiansInternet.com, January 12, 2015, **http://canadiansinternet.com/2015-canadian-social-media-usage-statistics/**

41. Claire Cain Miller, "Twitter Loses Its Scrappy Start-Up Status," *New York Times,* April 15, 2010, **www.nytimes.com/2010/04/16/technology/16twitter.html** (accessed April 13, 2011).

42. **https://twitter.com/@StarbucksCanada** and **https://twitter.com/Starbucks/status/304274571845054465** (accessed July 17, 2013).

43. Josh Tyrangiel, "Bing vs. Google: The Conquest of Twitter," *Time,* October 22, 2009, **www.time.com/time/business/article/0,8599,1931532,00.html** (accessed April 13, 2011).

44. "As Twitter Grows and Evolves, More Manpower Is Needed," *Marketing News,* March 15, 2011, p. 13.

45. Eddie Shleyner, "Snapchat for Business: The Ultimate Marketing Guide," February 13, 2019, **https://blog.hootsuite.com/snapchat-for-business-guide/**

46. Jeff Bullas, "30 Mind-Numbing YouTube Facts, Figures, and Statistics," jeffbullas.com, **http://www.jeffbullas.com/2012/05/23/35-mind-numbing-youtube-facts-figures-and-statistics-infographic/** (accessed July 30, 2013).

47. "YouTube by the Numbers," https://www.youtube.com/yt/about/press/, (accessed July 9, 2019).

48. "YouTube Canada 2018 Ads Leaderboard: Spotlighting the ads Canadians chose to watch in Q1," **https://www.thinkwithgoogle.com/intl/en-ca/advertising-channels/video/youtube-canada-2018-ads-leaderboard-spotlighting-ads-canadians-chose-watch-q1/**, (accessed May 5, 2019).

49. Estefania Duran, "April Fool's Day 2019 Winners," April 1, 2019, **https://edmonton.citynews.ca/2019/04/01/april-fools-day-stunts/**

50. David Meerman Scott, *The New Rules of Marketing & PR* (Hoboken, NJ: John Wiley & Sons, Inc., 2009), p. 224; "Mainframe: The Art of the Sale, Lesson One," YouTube, **www.youtube.com/watch?v=MSqXKp-00Hm**; Ryan Rhodes, "The Mainframe: It's Like a Barn," IBM Systems, March–April 2007, **www.ibmsystemsmag.com/mainframe/marchapril07/stoprun/11984p1.aspx** (both accessed April 13, 2011).

51. "It's Your Job Video Contest," Ontario Ministry of Labour, **http://www.labour.gov.on.ca/english/contest/index.php** (accessed July 30, 2013).

52. "Crash the Superbowl Winners and Finalists," Frito Lay Facebook page, **https://apps.facebook.com/crashthesuperbowl/**; "Crash the Superbowl,"*Wikipedia,* **http://en.wikipedia.org/wiki/Crash_the_Super_Bowl** (both accessed July 30, 2013).

53. Todd Clarke, "22+ Instagram Stats That Marketers Can't Ignore," March 5, 2019, **https://blog.hootsuite.com/instagram-statistics/**

54. Paige Cooper, "23 Pinterest Statistics That Matter to Marketers in 2019," February 27, 2019, **https://blog.hootsuite.com/pinterest-statistics-for-business/**

55. Bianca Male, "How to Promote Your Business on Flickr," *Business Insider,* December 1, 2009, **www.businessinsider.com/how-to-promote-your-business-on-flickr-2009-12?**

**utm_source=feedburner&utm_medium=feed&utm_campaign=Feed%3A+businessinsider+(The+Business+Insider)** (accessed April 13, 2011).

56. Sage Lewis, "Using Flickr for Marketing," YouTube, uploaded February 13, 2007, **www.youtube.com/watch?v=u2Xyzkfzlug** (accessed January 11, 2010).
57. "2009 Digital Handbook," *Marketing News,* April 30, 2009, p. 11.
58. Charlene Li and Josh Bernoff, *Groundswell* (Boston: Harvard Business Press, 2008), p. 43.
59. A.C. Nielsen, "Global Faces and Networked Places: A Nielsen Report on Social Networking's New Global Footprint," March 2009, **http://blog.nielsen.com/nielsenwire/wp-content/uploads/2009/03/nielsen_globalfaces_mar09.pdf** (accessed April 19, 2011).
60. "Couldn't Stop the Spread of the Conversation in Reactions from Other Bloggers," from Hyejin Kim's May 4, 2007, blog post "Korea: Bloggers and Donuts" on the blog Global Voices at **http://groundswell.forrester.com/site1-16** (accessed April 19, 2011).
61. Mia Pearson, "Why corporate blogging is on the rebound," *Globe and Mail,* March 21, 2013, **http://www.theglobeandmail.com/report-on-business/small-business/sb-digital/biz-categories-technology/why-corporate-blogging-is-on-the-rebound/article10003057/** (accessed July 17, 2013).
62. Jeremy Moser "101 Blogging Statistics for 2019," **https://getcodeless.com/blogging-statistics/**, (accessed May 28, 2019).
63. Drake Bennett, "Assessing Wikipedia, Wiki-Style, on Its 10th Anniversary," *Bloomberg Businessweek,* January 10–16, 2011, pp. 57–61.
64. Wikipedia: Statistics, **https://en.wikipedia.org/wiki/Wikipedia:Statistics**, (accessed July 3, 2019).
65. Li and Bernoff, *Groundswell,* pp. 25–26.
66. "Percent of Fortune 500 and Inc. 500 companies with public blogs from 2010 to 2017," **https://www.statista.com/statistics/262466/share-of-fortune-500-inc-500-companies-with-public-blogs/**, (accessed June 9, 2019).
67. "The Meteoric Rise of Podcasting, Podcasting Statistics 2019," **https://musicoomph.com/podcast-statistics/**, (accessed June 4, 2019).
68. Steven Scheck, "6 Reasons Why Your Business Should Use Podcasting," June 8, 2018, **https://smallbiztrends.com/2017/01/benefits-of-podcasting.html**
69. Margot da Cunha, "The 7 Best Free Social Media Management Tools in 2019," January 22, 2019, **https://www.wordstream.com/blog/ws/2018/01/17/best-free-social-media-management-tools**
70. Roger Yu, "Smartphones Help Make Bon Voyages," *USA Today,* March 5, 2010, p. B1.
71. Mickey Alam Khan, "Jiffy Lube Mobile Coupons Bring 50 Percent New Households," *Mobile Marketer,* January 30, 2009, **www.mobilemarketer.com/cms/news/commerce/2551.html** (accessed April 13, 2011).
72. Umika Pidaparthy, "Marketers Embracing QR Codes, for Better or Worse," *CNN Tech,* March 28, 2011, **http://articles.cnn.com/2011-03-28/tech/qr.codes.marketing_1_qr-smartphone-users-symbian?_s=PM:TECH** (accessed April 11, 2011).
73. "Juniper Research: Mobile QR Code Coupon Redemptions to Surge, Surpassing 5.3 Billion by 2022," **https://www.businesswire.com/news/home/20180103005014/en/Juniper-Research-Mobile-QR-Code-Coupon-Redemptions**, (accessed August 21, 2019).
74. Brad Stone and Olga Kharif, "Pay As You Go," *Bloomberg Businessweek,* July 18–24, 2011, pp. 66–71.
75. "Google Wallet," **www.google.com/wallet/what-is-google-wallet.html** (accessed May 29, 2014).
76. "Number of smartphone users in North America from 2014 to 2019 (in millions," **https://www.statista.com/statistics/494561/smartphone-users-in-north-america/**, (accessed August 21, 2019).
77. "All About Widgets," Webopedia™, September 14, 2007, **www.webopedia.com/DidYouKnow/Hardware_Software/widgets.asp** (accessed May 29, 2014).
78. Rachael King, "Building a Brand with Widgets," *Bloomberg Businessweek,* March 3, 2008, **www.businessweek.com/technology/content/feb2008/tc20080303_000743.htm** (accessed May 29, 2014).
79. "Barkley Develops Krispy Kreme ® 'Hot Light' App and Widget," *Wall Street Journal,* December 23, 2011, **http://online.wsj.com/article/PR-CO-20111223-904499.html** (accessed February 28, 2012).
80. Mark Milian, "Why Text Messages Are Limited to 160 Characters," *Los Angeles Times,* May 3, 2009, **http://latimesblogs.latimes.com/technology/2009/05/invented-text-messaging.html** (accessed May 29, 2014); "Eight Reasons Why Your Business Should Use SMS Marketing," Mobile Marketing Ratings, **www.mobilemarketingratings.com/eight-reasons-sms-marketing.html** (accessed May 29, 2014).
81. Lauren Folino and Michelle V. Rafter, "How to Use Multimedia for Business Marketing," *Inc.*, January 25, 2010, **www.inc.com/guides/multimedia-for-business-marketing.html** (accessed February 28, 2012); "Motorola Powers House of Blues(R)," PR Newswire, **www.prnewswire.com/news-releases/motorola-powers-house-of-bluesr-54990822.html** (accessed February 28, 2012).
82. Lauren Johnson, "Orville Redenbacher Promotes Healthy Snacks with Mobile Banner Ads," *Mobile Marketer,* October 26, 2011, **www.mobilemarketer.com/cms/news/advertising/11321.html** (accessed February 28, 2012).
83. "Percentage of all global web pages served to mobile phones from 2009 to 2018" July 22, 2019, (accessed September 3, 2019), **https://www.statista.com/statistics/241462/global-mobile-phone-website-traffic-share/**
84. Anita Campbell, "What the Heck Is an App?" Small Business Trends, March 7, 2011, **http://smallbiztrends.com/2011/03/what-is-an-app.html** (accessed March 29, 2014).
85. Melissa S. Barker, Donald I. Barker, Nicholas F. Bormann, Mary Lou Roberts, and Debra Zahay, *Social Media Marketing,* 2nd ed. (Mason, OH: Cengage Learning, 2016).
86. Matt McGee, "As Google Analytics Turns 10, We Ask: How Many Websites Use It?" Marketing Land, November 12, 2015, **http://marketingland.com/as-google-analyticsturns-10-we-ask-how-many-websites-use-it-151892**
87. "By Tailoring the Features of Google Analytics, LunaMetrics Helps PBS Increase Both Conversions and Visits by 30%," Google Analytics, **https://static.googleusercontent.com/media/www.google.com/en//intl/pt_ALL/analytics/customers/pdfs/pbs.pdf** (accessed March 24, 2019).

88. Quentin Hardy, "Google Introduces Products That Will Sharpen Its Ad Focus," The New York Times, March 15, 2016, **https://www.nytimes.com/2016/03/16/technology/google-introduces-products-that-will-sharpen-its-ad-focus.html**

89. Charlene Li and Josh Bernoff, "Groundswell," *Harvard Business Review*, Revised ed., May 24, 2011, p. 41.

90. Ibid., pp. 41–42.

91. Ibid., p. 44.

92. Ibid., pp. 44–45.

93. Rebecca MacLary, "New Canadian User Friendly Crowdfunding and Crowdsourcing Apps," Daily Crowdsource website, **http://dailycrowdsource.com/crowdsourcing/company-reviews/341-new-canadian-user-friendly-crowdfunding-and-crowdsourcing-apps** (accessed July 17, 2013).

94. Mya Frazier, "CrowdSourcing," *Delta Sky Mag,* February 2010, p. 70.

95. Li and Bernoff, *Groundswell,* pp. 26–27.

96. "Why Social Media Marketing?" Digital Visitor website, **http://www.digitalvisitor.com/why-social-media-marketing/** (accessed July 30, 2013).

97. Sarah Nassauer, "'I Hate My Room,' The Traveler Tweeted. Ka-Boom! An Upgrade!" *Wall Street Journal,* June 24, 2010, p. D1.

98. John W. Miller, "Yahoo Cookie Plan in Place," *Wall Street Journal,* March 19, 2011, **http://online.wsj.com/article/SB10001424052748703512404576208700813815570.html** (accessed April 11, 2011).

99. Rene Bissonnette, "Influence and Responsibility: New Canadian Influencer Marketing Guidelines," July 24, 2018.

100. "FTC Cracking Down on Social Influencers' Labeling of Paid Promotions," AdAge, August 5, 2016, **http://adage.com/article/digital/ftc-cracking-social-influencers-labeling promotions/305345/**

101. Larry Barrett, "Data Breach Costs Surge in 2009: Study," *eSecurityPlanet,* January 26, 2010, **www.esecurityplanet.com/features/article.php/3860811/Data-Breach-Costs-Surgein-2009-Study.htm** (accessed April 13, 2011).

102. Steve Rennie, "Government Faces Class-Action Lawsuits Over Student Loan Borrowers' Lost Data," *Globe and Mail,* January 17, 2013, **http://www.theglobeandmail.com/news/politics/government-faces-class-action-lawsuits-over-student-loan-borrowers-lost-data/article7492261/** (accessed July 30, 2013).

103. Sarah E. Needleman, "Social-Media Con Game," *Wall Street Journal,* October 12, 2009, p. R4.

104. Karen Bartko, "Family of Humboldt Bronco player Ryan Straschnitzki angry over fake Facebook account," May 3, 2018, **https://globalnews.ca/news/4184365/ryan-straschnitzki-humboldt-broncos-fake-facebook/**

105. Abigail Field, "Viacom v. YouTube/Google: A Piracy Case in Their Own Words," Daily Finance, March 21, 2010, **https://www.aol.com/2010/03/21/viacom-v-youtube-google-a-piracy-case-in-their-own-words/** (accessed April 13, 2011).

106. Kevin Shanahan and Mike Hyman "Motivators and Enablers of SCOURing," *Journal of Business Research* 63 (September–October 2010), pp. 1095–1102.

107. "Software Piracy Stat Watch, 2018 Software Piracy Statistics," **https://www.revulytics.com/resources/stat-watch**, (accessed March 11, 2019).

108. Max Chafkin, "The Case, and the Plan, for the Virtual Company," *Inc.,* April 2010, p. 68.

## Chapter 14

1. Big 4 Accounting Firms," AccountingVerse, **http://www.accountingverse.com/articles/big-4-accounting-firms.html** (accessed April 7, 2018); "The Big 4 Accounting Firms," **http://big4accountingfirms.org/** (accessed April 7, 2018); "About Deloitte," Deloitte, **https://www2.deloitte.com/us/en/pages/about-deloitte/articles/about-deloitte.html** (accessed April 7, 2018); "Our Approach to Innovation—in Business and Beyond," Deloitte, **https://www2.deloitte.com/us/en/pages/about-deloitte/articles/business-innovation-approach.html** (accessed April 7, 2018); "Corporate Citizenship," Deloitte, **https://www2.deloitte.com/us/en/pages/about-deloitte/articles/deloittecorporate-citizenship.html?icid=top_deloitte-corporatecitizenship** (accessed April 7, 2018); The Deloitte Foundation, **https://www2.deloitte.com/ro/en/pages/about-deloitte/articles/deloitte-foundation.html** (accessed September 6, 2019).

2. "About the AcSB," Financial Reporting & Assurance Standards Canada, n.d., **http://www.frascanada.ca/accounting-standards-board/what-we-do/about-the-acsb/index.aspx** (accessed January 14, 2016).

3. Adapted from Financial Reporting & Assurance Standards Canada, **http://www.frascanada.ca/index.aspx** (accessed January 22, 2013).

4. See, for example, Tara Gray, "Canadian Response to the U.S. Sarbanes-Oxley Act of 2002: New Directions for Corporate Governance," Library of Parliament Economics Division, October 4, 2005, **http://www.parl.gc.ca/content/lop/researchpublications/prb0537-e.htm** (accessed January 14, 2016).

5. "Issue Brief: Global Banking Regulations and Banks in Canada," Canadian Bankers Association, last updated May 2016, **http://www.cba.ca/global-banking-regulations-and-banks-in-canada**

6. "About the ACFE," ACFE website, www.acfe.com/about-the-acfe.aspx (accessed September 28, 2016).

7. "Report to the Nations: 2018 Global Study On Occupational Fraud and Abuse," Association of Certified Fraud Examiners, 2018, **https://s3-us-west-2.amazonaws.com/acfepublic/2018-report-to-the-nations.pdf** (accessed April 24, 2018).

8. Sarah Johnson, "Averting Revenue-Recognition Angst," *CFO,* April 2012, p. 21.

9. Stephanie Bedard-Chateauneuf, "Metro, Inc. vs. Loblaw Companies Ltd.: Which Grocer Is Doing Better?," Decemebr 11, 2017 *The Motley Fool,* **https://www.fool.ca/**, (accessed February 22, 2018).

10. Goodwill website, **www.goodwill.org/** (accessed April 21, 2016); "About Us— Revenue Sources," Goodwill Industries International Inc., **www.goodwill.org/about-us/** (accessed April 21, 2016).

## Chapter 15

1. Dan Weil, "How Secure Is Mobile Banking?" *Wall Street Journal*, March 18, 2018, **https://www.wsj.com/articles/how-secure-is-mobile-banking-1521424920** (accessed April 7, 2018); Haider Pasha, "5 Ways to Improve Your Digital Banking Security," Gulf News—Personal Finance, March 20, 2018, **http://gulfnews.com/gn-focus/personal-finance/banking/5-ways-to-improveyour-digital-banking-security-1.2191358** (accessed April 7, 2018); Dan DiPietro, "Survey Roundup: Cost, Frequency of Cyberattacks Rise for Banks," *Wall Street Journal*, February 14, 2018, **https://blogs.wsj.com/riskandcompliance/2018/02/14/survey-roundup-costfrequency-of-cyberattacks-rises-for-banks/**; **https://cba.ca/banks-and-cyber-security** (accessed February 21, 2019).
2. Paul Krugman, "Why Is Deflation Bad?" *New York Times*, August 2, 2010, **http://krugman.blogs.nytimes.com/2010/08/02/why-is-deflation-bad/** (accessed May 29, 2012).
3. "Weird and Wonderful Money Facts and Trivia," Happy Worker, **www.happyworker.com/magazine/facts/weird-andwonderful-money-facts** (accessed April 25, 2016).
4. Bank of Canada, "Polymer Series (2011)," **www.bankofcanada.ca/banknotes/bank-note-series/polymer/** (accessed January 21, 2012).
5. CTVNews.ca, "Careful, Canada! This counterfeit cash could fool you," (2019), **https://www.ctvnews.ca/canada/careful-canada-this-counterfeit-cash-could-fool-you-1.4256236** (accessed February 21, 2019).
6. Financial Consumer Agency of Canada, "New Credit Card Rules," **www.fcac-acfc.gc.ca/eng/partners/campaign/rulescc/index-eng.asp** (accessed January 21, 2012); Canadian Bankers Association, "Credit Cards: Statistics and Facts," **https://cba.ca/credit-cards**, (accessed February 21, 2019).
7. Jessica Dickler, "Americans Still Relying on Credit Cards to Get By," CNN Money, May 23, 2012, **http://money.cnn.com/2012/05/22/pf/credit-card/index.htm** (accessed May 5, 2017); Martin Merzer, "Survey: Students Fail the Credit Card Test," Fox Business, April 16, 2012, **www.creditcards.com/credit-card-news/survey-students-fail-credit-cardtest-1279.php** (accessed May 5, 2017); Canadian Bankers Association, "Household Borrowing in Canada," **https://cba.ca/household-borrowing-in-canada**, (accessed February 21, 2019).
8. **www.bankofcanada.ca/en/about/currency.html** (accessed August 20, 2009).
9. **www.bankofcanada.ca/en/financial/financial_system.html** (accessed August 20, 2009).
10. **www.bankofcanada.ca/en/about/funds.html** (accessed August 20, 2009).
11. **www.cba.ca/en/section.asp?fl=2&sl=204&tl=&docid** (accessed August 20, 2009).
12. **http://www.fin.gc.ca/toc/2005/fact-cfss-eng.asp** (accessed August 9, 2010).
13. **http://www.fin.gc.ca/toc/2005/fact-cfss-eng.asp** (accessed August 9, 2010).
14. **www.cdic.ca/1/2/1/8/index1.shtml** (accessed August 20, 2009).
15. **www.fin.gc.ca/toce/1999/banke.html** (accessed August 20, 2009).
16. "Leadership," Kiva, **https://www.kiva.org/about/leadership** (accessed May 22, 2018); Devishobha Chandramouli, "Study Details Why Women Entrepreneurs Have Greater Crowdfunding Success," *Entrepreneur*, May 17, 2018, **https://www.entrepreneur.com/article/312964** (accessed June 3, 2018); Elizabeth MacBride, "Kiva Hits $1B in Loans, $25 at a Time. Here's One of the Hidden Keys to its Success," *Forbes*, July 31, 2017, **https://www.forbes.com/sites/elizabethmacbride/2017/07/31/can-online-lenders-assess-your-character-to-a-certain-extent-yes/#6c984c5c1b2f** (accessed June 3, 2018); Connie Loizos, "This Young Lending Startup Just Secured $70 Million to Lend $2 at a Time," TechCrunch, March 28, 2018, **https://techcrunch.com/2018/03/28/this-young-lending-startup-just-secured-70-million-to-lend-2-at-a-time/** (accessed June 3, 2018).

## Chapter 16

1. Matt Egan, "General Electric Gets Booted from the Dow," CNN, June 19, 2018, **https://money.cnn.com/2018/06/19/investing/ge-dow-jones-walgreens/index.html** (accessed September 6, 2018); Drake Bennett, "What the Hell Is Wrong with General Electric," *Bloomberg Businessweek*, February 5, 2018, pp. 42–49; Jeff Desjardins, "Chart: The Largest Companies by Market Cap over 15 Years," Visual Capitalist, August 12, 2016, **http://www.visualcapitalist.com/chart-largest-companies-market-cap-15-years/** (accessed April 26, 2018); Tomas Gryta, Dana Mattiolo, and David Benoit, "GE Explores Further Deals," *Wall Street Journal*, April 13, 2018, p. A1; Matt Egan, "What's Wrong with GE? An American Icon Is in 'Crisis' Mode," CNN Money, October 11, 2017, **http://money.cnn.com/2017/10/11/investing/general-electric-stock-crisis-mode/index.html** (accessed April 26, 2018).
2. Calculated by Geoff Hirt from Apple's annual reports and website on November 8, 2018.
3. Joshua Kennon, "Should You Invest in an IPO?" About.com, **http://beginnersinvest.about.com/od/investmentbanking/a/aa073106a.htm** (accessed May 4, 2016).
4. CIBC, About Us, **http://www.cibccm.com/cibc-eportal-web/portal/wm?pageId=about-cibc&language=en_CA**, (accessed May 12, 2019).
5. Vincent Ryan, "From Wall Street to Main Street," *CFO Magazine*, June 2008, pp. 85–86.
6. Hershey Trust, "About Hershey Trust Company" (n.d.), **www.hersheytrust.com/cornerstones/about.shtml** (accessed March 26, 2006); O. C. Ferrell, "Hershey Foods' Ethics and Social Responsibility," case developed for classroom use, Colorado State University, revised edition, 2004; Hershey Foods, "Frequently Asked Questions," (n.d.), **www.hersheyinvestorrelations.com/ireye/ir_site.zhtml?ticker5HSY&script51801** (accessed June 10, 2004), "Company History," **www.hersheys.com/discover/history/company.asp** (accessed March 27, 2006); William C. Smith, "Seeing to the Business of Fun: Franklin A. Miles Jr., Hershey Entertainment & Resorts Co.," *National Law Journal*, December 22, 2003, p. 8; "Funding the School Trust," **www.hersheys.com/discover/milton/fund_school_trust.asp** (accessed March 27, 2006).

# GLOSSARY

**absolute advantage** a monopoly that exists when a country is the only source of an item, the only producer of an item, or the most efficient producer of an item

**accessibility** allows consumers to find information about competing products, prices, and reviews, and become more informed about a firm and the relative value of its products

**accountability** the principle that employees who accept an assignment and the authority to carry it out are answerable to a superior for the outcome

**accountants** professionals employed by large corporations, government agencies, and other organizations to prepare and analyze their financial statements

**accounting** the recording, measurement, and interpretation of financial information

**accounting cycle** the four-step procedure of an accounting system: examining source documents, recording transactions in an accounting journal, posting recorded transactions, and preparing financial statements

**accounting equation** assets equal liabilities plus owners' equity

**accounts payable** the amount a company owes to suppliers for goods and services purchased with credit

**accounts receivable** money owed a company by its clients or customers who have promised to pay for the products at a later date

**accrued expenses** an account representing all unpaid financial obligations incurred by the organization

**acquisition** the purchase of one company by another, usually by buying its shares

**addressability** the ability of a business to identify customers before they make purchases

**administrative managers** those who manage an entire business or a major segment of a business; they are not specialists but coordinate the activities of specialized managers

**advertising** a paid form of non-personal communication transmitted through a mass medium, such as television commercials or magazine advertisements

**advertising campaign** designing a series of advertisements and placing them in various media to reach a particular target market

**agency** a common business relationship created when one person acts on behalf of another and under that person's control

**agenda** a calendar, containing both specific and vague items, that covers short-term goals and long-term objectives

**agent** in an agency relationship, the one who acts on behalf of the principal to accomplish the task

**analytical skills** the ability to identify relevant issues, recognize their importance, understand the relationships between them, and perceive the underlying causes of a situation

**angel investors** private investors who supply equity financing for businesses

**annual report** summary of a firm's financial information, products, and growth plans for owners and potential investors

**arbitration** settlement of a labour/management dispute by a third party whose solution is legally binding and enforceable

**Asia–Pacific Economic Cooperation (APEC)** community established in 1989 to promote international trade and facilitate business; as of 2013, has 21 member countries

**asset utilization ratios** ratios that measure how well a firm uses its assets to generate each $1 of sales

**assets** a firm's economic resources, or items of value that it owns, such as cash, inventory, land, equipment, buildings, and other tangible and intangible things

**Association of Southeast Asian Nations (ASEAN)** trade alliance that promotes trade and economic integration among member nations in Southeast Asia

**attitude** knowledge and positive or negative feelings about something

**automated banking machine (ABM)** the most familiar form of electronic banking, which dispenses cash, accepts deposits, and allows balance inquiries and cash transfers from one account to another

**balance of payments** the difference between the flow of money into and out of a country

**balance of trade** the difference in value between a nation's exports and its imports

**balance sheet** a "snapshot" of an organization's financial position at a given moment

**Bank of Canada** an independent agency of the federal government established in 1934 to regulate the nation's banking and financial industry

**bank rate** the rate of interest the Bank of Canada charges to loan money to any banking institution to meet reserve requirements

**behaviour modification** changing behaviour and encouraging appropriate actions by relating the consequences of behaviour to the behaviour itself

**benefits** non-financial forms of compensation provided to employees, such as pension plans, health insurance, paid vacation and holidays, and the like

**blog** a Web-based journal in which a writer can editorialize and interact with other Internet users

**board of directors** a group of individuals, elected by the shareholders to oversee the general operation of the corporation, who set the corporation's long-range objectives

**bonds** debt instruments that larger companies sell to raise long-term funds

**bonuses** monetary rewards offered by companies for exceptional performance as incentives to further increase productivity

**boycott** an attempt to keep people from purchasing the products of a company

**brainstorming** a technique in which group members spontaneously suggest ideas to solve a problem.

**branding** the process of naming and identifying products

**breach of contract** the failure or refusal of a party to a contract to live up to his or her promises

**bribes** payments, gifts, or special favours intended to influence the outcome of a decision

**brokerage firms** firms that buy and sell stocks, bonds, and other securities for their customers and provide other financial services

**budget** an internal financial plan that forecasts expenses and income over a set period of time

**budget deficit** the condition in which a nation spends more than it takes in from taxes

**budget surplus** the condition in which a nation spends less than it takes in from taxes

**business** individuals or organizations trying to earn a profit by providing goods and services that satisfy people's needs

**business ethics** principles and standards that determine acceptable conduct in business

**business plan** a precise statement of the rationale for a business and a step-by-step explanation of how it will achieve its goals

**business products** products that are used directly or indirectly in the operation or manufacturing processes of businesses

**buying behaviour** the decision processes and actions of people who purchase and use products

**Canada Deposit Insurance Corporation (CDIC)** a federal Crown corporation that insures bank accounts

**capacity** the maximum load that an organizational unit can carry or operate

**capital budgeting** the process of analyzing the needs of the business and selecting the assets that will maximize its value

**capitalism, or free enterprise** an economic system in which individuals own and operate the majority of businesses that provide goods and services

**cartel** a group of firms or nations that agree to act as a monopoly and not compete with each other in order to generate a competitive advantage in world markets

**cash flow** the movement of money through an organization over a daily, weekly, monthly, or yearly basis

**centralized organization** a structure in which authority is concentrated at the top, and very little decision-making authority is delegated to lower levels

**certificate of incorporation** a legal document that the provincial or federal government issues to a company based on information the company provides in the articles of incorporation

**certificates of deposit (CDs)** savings accounts that guarantee a depositor a set interest rate over a specified interval as long as the funds are not withdrawn before the end of the period—six months or one year, for example

**chartered banks** the largest and oldest of all financial institutions, relying mainly on chequing and savings accounts as sources of funds for loans to businesses and individuals

**chequing account** money stored in an account at a bank or other financial institution that can be withdrawn without advance notice; also called a *demand deposit*

**classical theory of motivation** theory suggesting that money is the sole motivator for workers

**codes of ethics** formalized rules and standards that describe what a company expects of its employees

**collective bargaining** the negotiation process through which management and unions reach an agreement about compensation, working hours, and working conditions for the bargaining unit

**commercial certificates of deposit (CDs)** certificates of deposit issued by commercial banks and brokerage companies, available in minimum amounts of $100,000, which may be traded prior to maturity

**commercialization** the full introduction of a complete marketing strategy and the launch of the product for commercial success

**commercial paper** a written promise from one company to another to pay a specific amount of money

**commission** an incentive system that pays a fixed amount or a percentage of the employee's sales

**committee** a permanent, formal group that performs a specific task

**common shares** shares whose owners have voting rights in the corporation, yet do not receive preferential treatment regarding dividends

**communism** first described by Karl Marx as a society in which the people, without regard to class, own all the nation's resources

**comparative advantage** the basis of most international trade, when a country specializes in products that it can supply more efficiently or at a lower cost than it can produce other items

**competition** the rivalry among businesses for consumers' dollars

**compressed workweek** a four-day (or shorter) period during which an employee works 40 hours

**computer-assisted design (CAD)** the design of components, products, and processes on computers instead of on paper

**computer-assisted manufacturing (CAM)** manufacturing that employs specialized computer systems to actually guide and control the transformation processes

**computer-integrated manufacturing (CIM)** a complete system that designs products, manages machines and materials, and controls the operations function

**concentration approach** a market segmentation approach in which a company develops one marketing strategy for a single market segment

**conceptual skills** the ability to think in abstract terms and to see how parts fit together to form the whole

**conciliation** a method of outside resolution of labour and management differences in which a third party is brought in to keep the two sides talking

**connectivity** the use of digital networks to provide linkages between information providers and users

**consumerism** the activities that independent individuals, groups, and organizations undertake to protect their rights as consumers

**consumer products** products intended for household or family use

**continuous manufacturing organizations** companies that use continuously running assembly lines, creating products with many similar characteristics

**contract** a mutual agreement between two or more parties that can be enforced by law

**contract manufacturing** the hiring of a foreign company to produce a specified volume of the initiating company's product to specification; the final product carries the domestic firm's name

**control** consumers' ability to regulate the information they receive via the Internet, and the rate and sequence of their exposure to that information

**controlling** the process of evaluating and correcting activities to keep the organization on course

**cooperative (or co-op)** an organization composed of individuals or small businesses that have banded together to reap the benefits of belonging to a larger organization

**corporate citizenship** the extent to which businesses meet the legal, ethical, economic, and voluntary responsibilities placed on them by their stakeholders

**corporation** a legal entity, whose assets and liabilities are separate from those of its owners

**cost of goods sold** the amount of money a firm spent to buy or produce the products it sold during the period to which the income statement applies

**countertrade agreements** foreign trade agreements that involve bartering products for other products instead of for currency

**credit cards** means of access to preapproved lines of credit granted by a bank or finance company

**credit controls** the authority to establish and enforce credit rules for financial institutions and some private investors

**credit union/*caisse populaire*** a financial institution owned and controlled by its depositors, who usually have a common employer, profession, trade group, or religion

**crisis management or contingency planning** an element in planning that deals with potential disasters such as product tampering, oil spills, fires, earthquakes, computer viruses, or airplane crashes

**Crown corporations** corporations owned and operated by government (federal or provincial)

**culture** the integrated, accepted pattern of human behaviour, including thought, speech, beliefs, actions, and artifacts

**current assets** assets that are used or converted into cash within the course of a calendar year

**current liabilities** a firm's financial obligations to short-term creditors, which must be repaid within one year

**current ratio** current assets divided by current liabilities

**customer departmentalization** the arrangement of jobs around the needs of various types of customers

**customization** making products to meet a particular customer's needs or wants

**debit card** a card that looks like a credit card but works like a cheque; using it results in a direct, immediate, electronic payment from the cardholder's bank account to a merchant or third party

**debt to total assets ratio** a ratio indicating how much of the firm is financed by debt and how much by owners' equity

**debt utilization ratios** ratios that measure how much debt an organization is using relative to other sources of capital, such as owners' equity

**decentralized organization** an organization in which decision-making authority is delegated as far down the chain of command as possible

**delegation of authority** giving employees not only tasks, but also the power to make commitments, use resources, and take whatever actions are necessary to carry out those tasks

**demand** the number of goods and services that consumers are willing to buy at different prices at a specific time

**departmentalization** the grouping of jobs into working units usually called departments, units, groups, or divisions

**depreciation** the process of spreading the costs of long-lived assets such as buildings and equipment over the total number of accounting periods in which they are expected to be used

**depression** a condition of the economy in which unemployment is very high, consumer spending is low, and business output is sharply reduced

**desired reserves** the percentage of deposits that banking institutions hold in reserve

**development** training that augments the skills and knowledge of managers and professionals

**digital marketing** uses all digital media, including the Internet and mobile and interactive channels, to develop communication and exchanges with customers

**digital media** electronic media that function using digital codes via computers, cellular phones, smartphones, and other digital devices

**directing** motivating and leading employees to achieve organizational objectives

**direct investment** the ownership of overseas facilities

**discounts** temporary price reductions, often employed to boost sales

**diversity** the participation of different ages, genders, races, ethnicities, nationalities, and abilities in the workplace

**dividends** profits of a corporation that are distributed in the form of cash payments to shareholders

**dividends per share** the actual cash received for each share owned

**dividend yield** the dividend per share divided by the stock price

**double-entry bookkeeping** a system of recording and classifying business transactions that maintains the balance of the accounting equation

**downsizing** the elimination of a significant number of employees from an organization

**dumping** the act of a country or business selling products at less than what it costs to produce them

**earnings per share** net income or profit divided by the number of stock shares outstanding

**e-business** carrying out the goals of business using the Internet

**economic contraction** a slowdown of the economy characterized by a decline in spending and during which businesses cut back on production and lay off workers

**economic expansion** the situation that occurs when an economy is growing and people are spending more money; their purchases stimulate the production of goods and services, which in turn stimulates employment

**economic order quantity (EOQ) model** a model that identifies the optimum number of items to order to minimize the costs of managing (ordering, storing, and using) them

**economics** the study of how resources are distributed for the production of goods and services within a social system

**economic system** a description of how a particular society distributes its resources to produce goods and services

**electronic funds transfer (EFT)** any movement of funds by means of an electronic terminal, telephone, computer, or magnetic tape

**embargo** a prohibition on trade in a particular product

**employee empowerment** when employees are provided with the ability to take on responsibilities and make decisions about their jobs.

**entrepreneur** an individual who risks their wealth, time, and effort to develop for profit an innovative product or way of doing something

**entrepreneurship** the process of creating and managing a business to achieve desired objectives

**equilibrium price** the price at which the number of products that businesses are willing to supply equals the amount of products that consumers are willing to buy at a specific point in time

**equity theory** an assumption that how much people are willing to contribute to an organization depends on their assessment of the fairness, or equity, of the rewards they will receive in exchange

**esteem needs** needs for respect—both self-respect and respect from others

**ethical issue** an identifiable problem, situation, or opportunity that requires a person to choose from among several actions that may be evaluated as right or wrong, ethical or unethical

**eurodollar market** a market for trading U.S. dollars in foreign countries

**European Union (EU)** community established in 1958 to promote trade within Europe

**exchange** the act of giving up one thing (money, credit, labour, goods) in return for something else (goods, services, or ideas)

**exchange controls** regulations that restrict the amount of currency that can be bought or sold

**exchange rate** the ratio at which one nation's currency can be exchanged for another nation's currency

**exclusive distribution** a manufacturer awards to an intermediary the sole right to sell a product in a defined geographic territory

**expectancy theory** the assumption that motivation depends not only on how much a person wants something but also on how likely they are to get it

**expenses** the costs incurred in the day-to-day operations of an organization

**exporting** the sale of goods and services to foreign markets

**express warranty** warranty that stipulates the specific terms a seller will honour

**external shocks** unanticipated events that occur in a firm's external environment that hurt the company's business

**extrinsic reward** a benefit and/or recognition received from someone else

**factor** a finance company to which businesses sell their accounts receivable—usually for a percentage of the total face value

**finance** the study of how money is managed by individuals, companies, and governments

**finance companies** businesses that offer short-term loans at substantially higher rates of interest than banks

**financial managers** those who focus on obtaining needed funds for the successful operation of an organization and using those funds to further organizational goals

**financial resources (capital)** the funds used to acquire the natural and human resources needed to provide products; also called capital

**first-line managers** those who supervise both workers and the daily operations of an organization

**fixed-position layout** a layout that brings all resources required to create the product to a central location

**flexible manufacturing** the direction of machinery by computers to adapt to different versions of similar operations

**flextime** a program that allows employees to choose their starting and ending times, provided that they are at work during a specified core period

**floating-rate bonds** bonds with interest rates that change with current interest rates otherwise available in the economy

**franchise** a licence to sell another's products or to use another's name in business, or both

**franchisee** the purchaser of a franchise

**franchising** a form of licensing in which a company—the franchisor—agrees to provide a franchisee a name, logo, methods of operation, advertising, products, and other elements associated with a franchiser's business, in return for a financial commitment and the agreement to conduct business in accordance with the franchisor's standard of operations

**franchisor** the company that sells a franchise

**fraud** a purposeful unlawful act to deceive or manipulate in order to damage others

**free-market system** pure capitalism, in which all economic decisions are made without government intervention

**functional departmentalization** the grouping of jobs that perform similar functional activities, such as finance, manufacturing, marketing, and human resources

**General Agreement on Tariffs and Trade (GATT)** a trade agreement, originally signed by 23 nations in 1947, that provided a forum for tariff negotiations and a place where international trade problems could be discussed and resolved

**general partnership** a partnership that involves a complete sharing in both the management and the liabilities of the business

**generic products** products that often come in simple packages and carry only their generic name

**geographical departmentalization** the grouping of jobs according to geographic location, such as state or province, region, country, or continent

**global strategy (globalization)** a strategy that involves standardizing products (and, as much as possible, their promotion and distribution) for the whole world, as if it were a single entity

**goal-setting theory** refers to the impact that setting goals has on performance.

**grapevine** an informal channel of communication, separate from management's formal, official communication channels

**gross domestic product (GDP)** the sum of all goods and services produced in a country during a year

**gross income (or profit)** revenues minus the cost of goods sold required to generate the revenues

**group** two or more individuals who communicate with one another, share a common identity, and have a common goal

**human relations** the study of the behaviour of individuals and groups in organizational settings

**human relations skills** the ability to deal with people, both inside and outside the organization

**human resources (labour)** the physical and mental abilities that people use to produce goods and services; also called labour

**human resources management (HRM)** all the activities involved in determining an organization's human resources needs, as well as acquiring, training, and compensating people to fill those needs

**human resources managers** those who handle the staffing function and deal with employees in a formalized manner

**hygiene factors** aspects of Herzberg's theory of motivation that focus on the work setting and not the content of the work; these aspects include adequate wages, comfortable and safe working conditions, fair company policies, and job security

**identity theft** when criminals obtain personal information that allows them to impersonate someone else in order to use their credit to access financial accounts and make purchases

**implied warranty** warranty that is imposed on the producer or seller by law

**importing** the purchase of goods and services from foreign sources

**income statement** a financial report that shows an organization's profitability over a period of time—month, quarter, or year

**inflation** a condition characterized by a continuing rise in prices

**influence marketing** the use of influencers to sell a product or service or to build a brand

**information technology (IT) managers** those who are responsible for implementing, maintaining, and controlling technology applications in business, such as computer networks

**infrastructure** the physical facilities that support a country's economic activities, such as railroads, highways, ports, airfields, utilities and power plants, schools, hospitals, communication systems, and commercial distribution systems

**initial public offering (IPO)** selling a corporation's shares on public markets for the first time

**inputs** the resources—such as labour, money, materials, and energy—that are converted into outputs

**insurance companies** businesses that protect their clients against financial losses from certain specified risks (death, accident, and theft, for example)

**integrated marketing communications** coordinating the promotion mix elements and synchronizing promotion as a unified effort

**intellectual property** property, such as musical works, artwork, books, and computer software, that is generated by a person's creative activities

**intensive distribution** a form of market coverage whereby a product is made available in as many outlets as possible

**interactivity** allows customers to express their needs and wants directly to the firm in response to its communications

**intermittent organizations** organizations that deal with products of a lesser magnitude than do project organizations; their products are not necessarily unique but possess a significant number of differences

**international business** the buying, selling, and trading of goods and services across national boundaries

**International Monetary Fund (IMF)** organization established in 1947 to promote trade among member nations by eliminating trade barriers and fostering financial cooperation

**intrapreneurs** individuals in large firms who take responsibility for the development of innovations within the organizations

**intrinsic reward** the personal satisfaction and enjoyment felt from attaining a goal

**inventory** all raw materials, components, completed or partially completed products, and pieces of equipment a firm uses

**inventory control** the process of determining how many supplies and goods are needed and keeping track of quantities on hand, where each item is, and who is responsible for it

**inventory turnover** sales divided by total inventory

**investment banker** underwrites new issues of securities for corporate and government clients

**investment banking** the sale of stocks and bonds for corporations

**ISO 9000** a series of quality assurance standards designed by the International Organization for Standardization (ISO) to ensure consistent product quality under many conditions

**ISO 14000** a comprehensive set of environmental management standards determined by the ISO that help companies attain and measure improvements in their environmental performance

**ISO 19600** a comprehensive set of guidelines for compliance management that address risks, legal requirements, and stakeholder needs.

**job analysis** the determination, through observation and study, of pertinent information about a job—including specific tasks and necessary abilities, knowledge, and skills

**job description** a formal, written explanation of a specific job, usually including job title, tasks, relationship with other jobs, physical and mental skills required, duties, responsibilities, and working conditions

**job enlargement** the addition of more tasks to a job instead of treating each task as separate

**job enrichment** the incorporation of motivational factors, such as opportunity for achievement, recognition, responsibility, and advancement, into a job

**job promotion** advancement to a higher-level position with increased authority, responsibility, and pay

**job rotation** movement of employees from one job to another in an effort to relieve the boredom often associated with job specialization

**job sharing** performance of one full-time job by two people on part-time hours

**job specification** a description of the qualifications necessary for a specific job, in terms of education, experience, and personal and physical characteristics

**joint venture** a partnership established for a specific project or for a limited time involving the sharing of the costs and operation of a business, often between a foreign company and a local partner

**journal** a time-ordered list of account transactions

**junk bonds** a special type of high interest-rate bond that carries higher inherent risks

**just-in-time (JIT) inventory management** a technique using smaller quantities of materials that arrive "just in time" for use in the transformation process and therefore require less storage space and other inventory management expense

**labelling** the presentation of important information on a package

**labour contract** the formal, written document that spells out the relationship between the union and management for a specified period of time—usually two or three years

**labour unions** employee organizations formed to deal with employers for achieving better pay, hours, and working conditions

**leadership** the ability to influence employees to work toward organizational goals

**learning** changes in a person's behaviour based on information and experience

**ledger** a book or computer file with separate sections for each account

**leveraged buyout (LBO)** a purchase in which a group of investors borrows money from banks and other institutions to acquire a company (or a division of one), using the assets of the purchased company to guarantee repayment of the loan

**liabilities** debts that a firm owes to others

**licensing** a trade agreement in which one company—the licensor—allows another company—the licensee—to use its company name, products, patents, brands, trademarks, raw materials, and/or production processes in exchange for a fee or royalty

**limited liability partnership (LLP)** a partnership agreement where partners are not responsible for losses created by other partners

**limited partnership** a business organization that has at least one general partner, who assumes unlimited liability, and at least one limited partner, whose liability is limited to his or her investment in the business

**line-and-staff structure** a structure having a traditional line relationship between superiors and subordinates and also specialized managers—called staff managers—who are available to assist line managers

**line of credit** an arrangement by which a bank agrees to lend a specified amount of money to an organization upon request

**line structure** the simplest organizational structure; direct lines of authority extend from the top manager to the lowest level of the organization

**liquidity ratios** ratios that measure the speed with which a company can turn its assets into cash to meet short-term debt

**lockout** management's version of a strike, wherein a worksite is closed so that employees cannot go to work

**long-term (fixed) assets** production facilities (plants), offices, and equipment—all of which are expected to last for many years

**long-term liabilities** debts that will be repaid over a number of years, such as long-term loans and bond issues

**management** a process designed to achieve an organization's objectives by using its resources effectively and efficiently in a changing environment

**managerial accounting** the internal use of accounting statements by managers in planning and directing the organization's activities

**managers** those individuals in organizations who make decisions about the use of resources and who are concerned with planning, organizing, staffing, directing, and controlling the organization's activities to reach its objectives

**manufacturer brands** brands initiated and owned by the manufacturer to identify products from the point of production to the point of purchase

**manufacturing** the activities and processes used in making tangible products; also called *production*

**market** a group of people who have a need, purchasing power, and the desire and authority to spend money on goods, services, and ideas

**marketable securities** temporary investment of "extra" cash by organizations for up to one year in Treasury bills, certificates of deposit, commercial paper, or eurodollar loans

**marketing** a group of activities designed to expedite transactions by creating, distributing, pricing, and promoting goods, services, and ideas

**marketing channel** a group of organizations that moves products from their producer to customers; also called a channel of distribution

**marketing concept** the idea that an organization should try to satisfy customers' needs through coordinated activities that also allow it to achieve its own goals

**marketing managers** those who are responsible for planning, pricing, and promoting products and making them available to customers

**marketing mix** the four marketing activities—product, price, promotion, and distribution—that the firm can control to achieve specific goals within a dynamic marketing environment

**marketing orientation** an approach requiring organizations to gather information about customer needs, share that information throughout the firm, and use that information to help build long-term relationships with customers

**marketing research** a systematic, objective process of getting information about potential customers to guide marketing decisions

**marketing strategy** a plan of action for developing, pricing, distributing, and promoting products that meet the needs of specific customers

**market segment** a collection of individuals, groups, or organizations who share one or more characteristics and thus have relatively similar product needs and desires

**market segmentation** a strategy whereby a firm divides the total market into groups of people who have relatively similar product needs

**Maslow's hierarchy** a theory that arranges the five basic needs of people—physiological, security, social, esteem, and self-actualization—into the order in which people strive to satisfy them

**material-requirements planning (MRP)** a planning system that schedules the precise quantity of materials needed to make the product

**materials handling** the physical handling and movement of products in warehousing and transportation

**matrix structure** a structure that sets up teams with members from different departments, thereby creating two or more intersecting lines of authority; also called a project-management structure

**mediation** a method of outside resolution of labour and management differences in which the third party's role is to suggest or propose a solution to the problem

**merger** the combination of two companies (usually corporations) to form a new company

**middle managers** those members of an organization responsible for the tactical planning that implements the general guidelines established by top management

**mission** the statement of an organization's fundamental purpose and basic philosophy

**mixed economies** economies made up of elements from more than one economic system

**mobile marketing** using a mobile device to communicate marketing messages

**modular design** the creation of an item in self-contained units, or modules, that can be combined or interchanged to create different products

**monetary policy** means by which the Bank of Canada controls the amount of money available in the economy

**money** anything generally accepted in exchange for goods and services

**money market funds** accounts that offer higher interest rates than standard bank rates but with greater restrictions

**monopolistic competition** the market structure that exists when there are fewer businesses than in a pure-competition environment and the differences among the goods they sell are small

**monopoly** the market structure that exists when there is only one business providing a product in a given market

**morale** an employee's attitude toward their job, employer, and colleagues

**motivation** an inner drive that directs a person's behaviour toward goals

**motivational factors** aspects of Herzberg's theory of motivation that relate to the content of the work itself, include achievement, recognition, involvement, responsibility, and advancement

**multi-divisional structure** a structure that organizes departments into larger groups called divisions

**multinational corporation (MNC)** a corporation that operates on a worldwide scale, without significant ties to any one nation or region

**multinational strategy** a plan, used by international companies, that involves customizing products, promotion, and distribution according to cultural, technological, regional, and national differences

**multi-segment approach** a market segmentation approach in which the marketer aims its efforts at two or more segments, developing a marketing strategy for each

**mutual fund** an investment company that pools individual investor dollars and invests them in large numbers of well-diversified securities

**natural resources** land, forests, minerals, water, and other things that are not made by people

**net income** (or net earnings) the total profit (or loss) after all expenses including taxes have been deducted from revenue

**networking** the building of relationships and sharing of information with colleagues who can help managers achieve the items on their agendas

**non-profit corporations** corporations that focus on providing a service rather than earning a profit but are not owned by a government entity

**non-profit organizations** organizations that may provide goods or services but do not have the fundamental purpose of earning profits

**North American Free Trade Agreement (NAFTA)** agreement that eliminated most tariffs and trade restrictions on agricultural and manufactured products to encourage trade among Canada, the United States, and Mexico

**offshoring** the relocation of business processes by a company or subsidiary to another country; it differs from outsourcing because the company retains control of the offshored processes

**oligopoly** the market structure that exists when there are very few businesses selling a product.

**online fraud** any attempt to conduct fraudulent activities online

**open economy** an economy in which economic activities occur between a country and the international community

**open market operations** decisions to buy or sell Treasury bills (short-term debt issued by the government) and other investments in the open market

**operational plans** very short-term plans that specify what actions individuals, work groups, or departments need to accomplish in order to achieve the tactical plan and ultimately the strategic plan

**operations** the activities and processes used in making both tangible and intangible products

**operations management (OM)** the development and administration of the activities involved in transforming resources into goods and services

**organizational charts** visual displays of the organizational structure, lines of authority (chain of command), staff relationships, permanent committee arrangements, and lines of communication

**organizational culture** a firm's shared values, beliefs, traditions, philosophies, rules, and role models for behaviour

**organizational layers** the levels of management in an organization

**organizing** the structuring of resources and activities to accomplish objectives in an efficient and effective manner

**orientation** familiarizing newly hired employees with fellow workers, company procedures, and the physical properties of the company

**outputs** the goods, services, and ideas that result from the conversion of inputs

**outsourcing** the transferring of manufacturing or other tasks—such as data processing—to countries where labour and supplies are less expensive

**over-the-counter (OTC) market** a network of electronically linked dealers

**owners' equity** equals assets minus liabilities and reflects historical values

**packaging** the external container that holds and describes the product

**partnership** a form of business organization defined as an association of two or more persons who carry on as co-owners of a business for profit

**partnership agreement** document that sets forth the basic agreement between partners

**penetration price** a low price designed to help a product enter the market and gain market share rapidly

**pension funds** managed investment pools set aside by individuals, corporations, unions, and some non-profit organizations to provide retirement income for members

**perception** the process by which a person selects, organizes, and interprets information received from their senses

**per share data** data used by investors to compare the performance of one company with another on an equal, per share basis

**personality** the organization of an individual's distinguishing character traits, attitudes, or habits

**personal property** property that consists of basically everything else; can be subdivided into tangible and intangible property

**personal selling** direct, two-way communication with buyers and potential buyers

**physical distribution** all the activities necessary to move products from producers to customers—inventory control, transportation, warehousing, and materials handling

**physiological needs** the most basic human needs to be satisfied—water, food, shelter, and clothing

**picketing** a public protest against management practices that involves union members marching and carrying anti-management signs at the employer's plant

**place/distribution** making products available to customers in the locations and quantities desired

**plagiarism** the act of taking someone else's work and presenting it as your own without mentioning the source

**planning** the process of determining the organization's objectives and deciding how to accomplish them; the first function of management

**podcast** an audio or video file that can be downloaded from the Internet with a subscription and automatically deliver new content to listening devices or personal computers

**preferred shares** a special type of share whose owners, though not generally having a say in running the company, have a claim to profits before other shareholders do

**price** a value placed on an object exchanged between a buyer and a seller

**price skimming** charging the highest possible price that buyers who want the product will pay

**primary data** marketing information that is observed, recorded, or collected directly from respondents

**primary market** the market where firms raise financial capital

**prime rate** the interest rate that commercial banks charge their best customers (usually large corporations) for short-term loans

**principal** in an agency relationship, the one who wishes to have a specific task accomplished

**private corporation** a corporation owned by just one or a few people who are closely involved in managing the business

**private distributor brands** brands, which may cost less than manufacturer brands, that are owned and controlled by a wholesaler or retailer

**process layout** a layout that organizes the transformation process into departments that group related processes

**product departmentalization** the organization of jobs in relation to the products of the firm

**product-development teams** a specific type of project team formed to devise, design, and implement a new product

**production** the activities and processes used in making tangible products; also called *manufacturing*

**production and operations managers** those who develop and administer the activities involved in transforming resources into goods, services, and ideas ready for the marketplace

**product layout** a layout requiring that production be broken down into relatively simple tasks assigned to workers, who are usually positioned along an assembly line

**product liability** a business's legal responsibility for any negligence in the design, production, sale, and consumption of products

**product line** a group of closely related products that are treated as a unit because of similar marketing strategy, production, or end-use considerations

**product mix** all the products offered by an organization

**products** good and services with tangible and intangible characteristics that provide satisfaction and benefits

**profit** the difference between what it costs to make and sell a product and what a customer pays for it

**profitability ratios** ratios that measure the amount of operating income or net income an organization is able to generate relative to its assets, owners' equity, and sales

**profit margin** net income divided by sales

**profit sharing** a form of compensation whereby a percentage of company profits is distributed to the employees whose work helped to generate them

**project organization** a company using a fixed-position layout because it is typically involved in large, complex projects such as construction or exploration

**project teams** groups similar to task forces that normally run their operation and have total control of a specific work project

**promotion** a persuasive form of communication that attempts to expedite a marketing exchange by influencing individuals, groups, and organizations to accept goods, services, and ideas

**promotional positioning** the use of promotion to create and maintain an image of a product in buyers' minds

**psychological pricing** encouraging purchases based on emotional rather than rational responses to the price

**public corporation** a corporation whose shares anyone may buy, sell, or trade

**publicity** non-personal communication transmitted through the mass media but not paid for directly by the firm

**pull strategy** the use of promotion to create consumer demand for a product so that consumers exert pressure on marketing channel members to make it available

**purchasing** the buying of all the materials needed by the organization; also called procurement

**pure competition** the market structure that exists when there are many small businesses selling one standardized product

**push strategy** an attempt to motivate intermediaries to push the product down to their customers

**quality** the degree to which a good, service, or idea meets the demands and requirements of customers

**quality-assurance teams (or quality circles)** small groups of workers brought together from throughout the organization to solve specific quality, productivity, or service problems

**quality control** the processes an organization uses to maintain its established quality standards

**quick ratio (acid test)** a stringent measure of liquidity that eliminates inventory

**quota** a restriction on the number of units of a particular product that can be imported into a country

**ratio analysis** calculations that measure an organization's financial health

**real property** property consisting of real estate and everything permanently attached to it

**receivables turnover** sales divided by accounts receivable

**recession** a decline in production, employment, and income

**recruiting** forming a pool of qualified applicants from which management can select employees

**reference groups** groups with whom buyers identify and whose values or attitudes they adopt

**reinforcement theory** the theory that behavior can be strengthened or weakened through the use of rewards and punishments

**responsibility** the obligation, placed on employees through delegation, to perform assigned tasks satisfactorily and be held accountable for the proper execution of work

**restructure** to change the basic structure of an organization

**retailers** intermediaries who buy products from manufacturers (or other intermediaries) and sell them to consumers for home and household use rather than for resale or for use in producing other products

**retained earnings** earnings after expenses and taxes that are reinvested in the assets of the firm and belong to the owners in the form of equity

**return on assets** net income divided by assets

**return on equity** net income divided by owners' equity; also called *return on investment* (ROI)

**revenue** the total amount of money received from the sale of goods or services, as well as from related business activities

**reward cards** credit cards made available by stores that carry a benefit to the user

**routing** the sequence of operations through which the product must pass

**salary** a financial reward calculated on a weekly, monthly, or annual basis

**sales promotion** direct inducements offering added value or some other incentive for buyers to enter into an exchange

**savings accounts** accounts with funds that usually cannot be withdrawn without advance notice; also known as *time deposits*

**scheduling** the assignment of required tasks to departments or even specific machines, workers, or teams

**secondary data** information that is compiled inside or outside an organization for some purpose other than changing the current situation

**secondary markets** stock exchanges and over-the-counter markets where investors can trade their securities with others

**secured bonds** bonds that are backed by specific collateral that must be forfeited in the event that the issuing firm defaults

**secured loans** loans backed by collateral that the bank can claim if the borrowers do not repay them

**securities markets** the mechanism for buying and selling securities

**security needs** need to protect oneself from physical and economic harm

**selection** the process of collecting information about applicants and using that information to make hiring decisions

**selective distribution** a form of market coverage whereby only a small number of all available outlets are used to expose products

**self-actualization needs** need to be the best one can be; at the top of Maslow's hierarchy

**self-directed work team (SDWT)** a group of employees responsible for an entire work process or segment that delivers a product to an internal or external customer

**separations** employment changes involving resignation, retirement, termination, or layoff

**serial bonds** a sequence of small bond issues of progressively longer maturity

**shares** units of ownership of a corporation that may be bought or sold

**small business** any independently owned and operated business that is not dominant in its competitive area and does not employ more than 500 people

**social classes** a ranking of people into higher or lower positions of respect

**social needs** needs for love, companionship, and friendship—the desire for acceptance by others

**social network** a Web-based meeting place for friends, family, co-workers, and peers that lets users create a profile and connect with other users for a wide range of purposes

**social responsibility** a business's obligation to maximize its positive impact and minimize its negative impact on society

**social roles** a set of expectations for individuals based on some position they occupy

**socialism** an economic system in which the government owns and operates basic industries but individuals own most businesses

**sole proprietorships** businesses owned and operated by one individual; the most common form of business organization in Canada

**span of management** the number of subordinates who report to a particular manager (also called *span of control*)

**specialization** the division of labour into small, specific tasks and the assignment of employees to do a single task

**staffing** the hiring of people to carry out the work of the organization

**stakeholders** people who have a vested interest in the success and outcomes of a business

**standard of living** refers to the level of wealth and material comfort that people have available to them.

**standardization** the making of identical interchangeable components or products

**statement of cash flows** explains how the company's cash changed from the beginning of the accounting period to the end

**statistical process control** a system in which management collects and analyzes information about the production process to pinpoint quality problems in the production system

**strategic alliance** a partnership formed to create competitive advantage on a worldwide basis

**strategic plans** those plans that establish the long-range objectives and overall strategy or course of action by which a firm fulfills its mission

**strikebreakers** people hired by management to replace striking employees; called "scabs" by striking union members

**strikes** employee walkouts; one of the most effective weapons labour has

**structure** the arrangement or relationship of positions within an organization

**supply** the number of products—goods and services—that businesses are willing to sell at different prices at a specific time

**supply chain management** connecting and integrating all parties or members of the distribution system in order to satisfy customers

**tactical plans** short-range plans designed to implement the activities and objectives specified in the strategic plan

**target market** a specific group of consumers on whose needs and wants a company focuses its marketing efforts

**tariff** a tax levied by a nation on imported or exported goods

**task force** a temporary group of employees responsible for bringing about a particular change

**team** a small group whose members have complementary skills; have a common purpose, goal, and approach; and hold themselves mutually accountable

**technical expertise** the specialized knowledge and training needed to perform jobs that are related to particular areas of management

**test marketing** a trial mini-launch of a product in limited areas that represent the potential market

**Theory X** McGregor's traditional view of management in which it is assumed that workers generally dislike work and must be forced to do their jobs

**Theory Y** McGregor's humanistic view of management in which it is assumed that workers like to work and that under proper conditions employees will seek out responsibility in an attempt to satisfy their social, esteem, and self-actualization needs

**Theory Z** a management philosophy that stresses employee participation in all aspects of company decision making

**times interest earned ratio** operating income divided by interest expense

**top managers** the president and other top executives of a business, such as the chief executive officer (CEO), chief financial officer (CFO), chief operations officer (COO), and, more recently, chief privacy officer (CPO), who have overall responsibility for the organization

**tort** a non-criminal act other than breach of contract

**total asset turnover** sales divided by total assets

**total quality management (TQM)** a philosophy that uniform commitment to quality in all areas of an organization will promote a culture that meets customers' perceptions of quality

**total-market approach** an approach whereby a firm tries to appeal to everyone and assumes that all buyers have similar needs

**trade credit** credit extended by suppliers for the purchase of their goods and services

**trade deficit** a nation's negative balance of trade, which exists when that country imports more products than it exports

**trademark** a brand that is registered with the Canadian Intellectual Property Office and is thus legally protected from use by any other firm

**trade surplus** a nation's positive balance of trade, which exists when that country exports more products than it imports

**trading company** a firm that buys goods in one country and sells them to buyers in another country

**training** teaching employees to do specific job tasks through either classroom development or on-the-job experience

**transaction balances** cash kept on hand by a firm to pay normal daily expenses, such as employee wages and bills for supplies and utilities

**transfer** a move to another job within the company at essentially the same level and wage

**transportation** the shipment of products to buyers

**Treasury bills (T-bills)** short-term debt obligations the Canadian government sells to raise money

**trust companies** corporations that act as a trustee and usually also provide banking services

**turnover** occurs when employees quit or are fired, promoted, or transferred, and must be replaced by new employees

**undercapitalization** the lack of funds to operate a business normally

**unemployment** the condition in which a percentage of the population wants to work but is unable to find a job

**unsecured bonds** debentures, or bonds that are not backed by specific collateral

**unsecured loans** loans backed only by the borrowers' good reputation and previous credit rating

**venture capitalists** persons or organizations that agree to provide some funds for a new business in exchange for an ownership interest or stock

**viral marketing** a marketing tool that uses the Internet, particularly social networking and video sharing sites, to spread a message and create brand awareness

**wage/salary survey** a study that tells a company how much compensation comparable firms are paying for specific jobs that the firms have in common

**wages** financial rewards based on the number of hours the employee works or the level of output achieved

**warehousing** the design and operation of facilities to receive, store, and ship products

**whistleblowing** the act of an employee exposing an employer's wrongdoing to outsiders, such as the media or government regulatory agencies

**wholesalers** intermediaries who buy from producers or from other wholesalers and sell to retailers

**wiki** software that creates an interface that enables users to add or edit the content of some types of websites

**working capital management** the managing of short-term assets and liabilities

**World Bank** an organization established by the industrialized nations in 1946 to loan money to underdeveloped and developing countries; formally known as the International Bank for Reconstruction and Development

**World Trade Organization (WTO)** international organization dealing with the rules of trade between nations

# SOURCES

## Chapter 1

**Table 1.1:** "Canada's top 100 non-profit organizations (registered charities)," *Globe and Mail*, https://www.theglobeandmail.com/report-on-business/top-100-non-profit-organizations-registered-charities/article34067186/, (accessed October 9, 2018).
**Figure 1.3:** Statistics Canada. 2018. "Unemployment Rate," June 2018 (chart). Statistics Canada Table 14-10-0287-01. Released: 2018-07-06. https://www150.statcan.gc.ca/n1/daily-quotidien/180706/cg-a002-png-eng.htm (accessed October 9, 2018).
**Figure 1.4:** Statistics Canada. 2018. "Gross domestic product and final domestic demand," August 2018 (chart). Statistics Canada Table 36-10-0104-01. Released: 2018-08-30. https://www150.statcan.gc.ca/n1/daily-quotidien/180830/cg-a001-png-eng.htm (accessed October 25, 2018).
**Table 1.6:** *CIA, The World Fact Book,* https://www.cia.gov/library/publications/the-world-factbook/rankorder/rankorderguide.html (accessed February 22, 2016; International Monetary Fund, http://www.imf.org/external/index.htm (accessed July 1, 2016).

## Chapter 2

**Table 2.1:** Adapted from "Business Ethics Timeline," Copyright © 2003, *Ethics Resource Center* (n.d.), www.ethics.org, updated 2006.
**Table 2.2:** "National Business Ethics Survey 2018," "Survey Documents State of Ethics in the Workplace," and "Misconduct," Ethics Resource Center (n.d.), https://www.ethics.org/wp-content/uploads/2019/01/Global_Business_Ethics_Survey_2018_Q4_Final.pdf and http://www.boeingsuppliers.com/GBES2018-Final.pdf (accessed January 01, 2019).
**Table 2.3:** © O. C. Ferrell, 2011.
**Table 2.4:** This information is extracted from the CPI; the CPI is measuring perceived public sector corruption. © Transparency International 2017. All Rights Reserved. For more information, visit http://www.transparency.org.
**Table 2.6:** Based on William Miller, "Implementing an Organizational Code of Ethics," *International Business Ethics Review* 7 (Winter 2004), pp. 1, 6–10.
**Figure 2.2:** Based on A. B. Carroll, "The Pyramid of Corporate Social Responsibility: Toward the Moral Management of Organizational Stakeholders," *Business Horizons*, July/August 1991. Copyright © 1991 by the Board of Trustees at Indiana University, Kelley School of Business.

## Chapter 3

**Table 3.1:** Adapted from Statistics Canada. Table 12-10-0011-01. International merchandise trade for all countries and by Principal Trading Partners (x 1,000,000). http://www.statcan.gc.ca/tables-tableaux/sum-som/l01/cst01/gblec02a-eng.htm (accessed November 26, 2018).
**Table 3.2:** Adapted from Statistics Canada. Table 12-10-0011-01. International merchandise trade for all countries and by Principal Trading Partners (x 1,000,000), (accessed November 26, 2018).
**Table 3.3:** Adapted from Judie Haynes, "Communicating with Gestures," *Everything ESL* (n.d.), www.everythingesl.net/inservice/body_language.php (accessed March 2, 2004).
**Figure 3.1:** Central Intelligence Agency, "Country Comparison: Exports," https://www.cia.gov/library/publications/the-world-factbook/rankorder/2078rank.html (accessed April 2, 2017).
**Table 3.4:** "Top 100 Global Franchises—Rankings (2018)," Franchise Direct, https://www.franchisedirect.com/top100globalfranchises/rankings/ (accessed December 15, 2018).
**Table 3.5:** "Top 100 Global Franchises—Ranking," Franchise Direct, www.franchisedirect.com/top100globalfranchises/rankings/ (accessed July 29, 2016).

## Chapter 4

**Table 4.3:** Adapted from "Partnership Agreement Sample," State of New Jersey, http://www.state.nj.us/njbusiness/start/biztype/partner/agreement_sample.shtml (accessed June 13, 2007).
**Table 4.4:** Abstracted from J. Watananbe, "14 Reasons Why 80 Percent of New Business Partnerships Would Fail Within Their First 5 Years of Existence," http://ezinearticles.com/?14-Reasons-Why-80-Percent-Of-New-Business-Partnerships-Would-Fail-Within-Their-First-5-Years-Of-Exis&id=472498 (accessed June 20, 2013).

## Chapter 5

**Consider the Following:** Hisrich et al., *Entrepreneurship*, 2nd Canadian edition. McGraw-Hill Ryerson.
**Table 5.1:** http://www.ic.gc.ca/eic/site/061.nsf/eng/h_03090.html#point1-1 and http://www.ic.gc.ca/eic/site/061.nsf/eng/h_03018.html#point6-1.
**Table 5.2:** http://www.ic.gc.ca/eic/site/061.nsf/eng/h_03090.html#point1-1
**Table 5.4:** John Osher, in Mark Henricks, "What Not to Do," *Entrepreneur*, February 2004, www.entrepreneur.com/article/0,4621,312661,00.html.
**Table 5.5:** Based on data from "Survey on Financing and Growth of Small and Medium Enterprises, 2017," Innovation, Science and Economic Development Canada.
**Table 5.6:** Based on data from: https://www.canadianbusiness.com/innovation/canadas-best-places-for-business-2016-top-25/, accessed March 1, 2019.

## Chapter 6

**Table 6.2** Based on Graham F. Scott, "Canada's Top 100 highest-paid CEOs," *Canadian Business*, January 4, 2016, http://www.canadianbusiness.com/lists-and-rankings/richest-people/canadas-top-100-highest-paid-ceos-2018 (accessed December 10, 2018).
**Table 6.3:** Adapted from Juan Rodriguez, "The Five Rules of Successful Diversity Recruiting," Diversityjobs.com, www.diversityjobs.com/Rules-of-Successful-Diversity-Recruiting (accessed February 25, 2010).
**Table 6.4:** Mintzberg on Management by Henry Mintzberg, Free Press, 1989.

## Chapter 8

**Table 8.1:** Adapted from Valerie A. Zeithaml, A. Parasuraman, and Leonard L. Berry, *Delivering Quality Service: Balancing Customer Perceptions and Expectations* (New York: Free Press, 1990); K. Douglas Hoffman and John E.G. Bateson, *Essentials of Services Marketing* (Mason, OH; Cengage Learning, 2001); Ian P. McCarthy, Leyland Pitt, and Pierre R. Berthon, "Service Customization Through Dramaturgy," *Mass Customization*, 2011, pp. 45–65.
**Table 8.2:** International Association of Outsourcing, The Global Outsourcing 100, 2016, https://www.iaop.org/FORTUNE (accessed April 12, 2017).
**Table 8.3:** J.D. Power & Associates, "New-Vehicle Initial Quality is Best Ever, J.D. Power Finds," June 21, 2017, http://www.jdpower.com/press-releases/2017-us-initial-quality-study-iqs (accessed April 21, 2018).

## Chapter 9

**Table 9.1:** Sarah K. Yazinski, "Strategies for Retaining Employees and Minimizing Turnover," HR.BLR.com, August 3, 2009, https://hr.blr.com/whitepapers/Staffing-Training/Employee-Turnover/Strategies-for-Retaining-Employees-and-Minimizing-Turnover (accessed April 25, 2018).

**Figure 9.2:** Adapted from Abraham H. Maslow, "A Theory of Human Motivation," *Psychology Review* 50 (1943), pp. 370–396. American Psychology Association.

**Table 9.4:** Tim Hird, "The Lasting Benefits of Job Rotation," Treasury & Risk, January 24, 2017, https://www.treasuryandrisk.com/sites/treasuryandrisk/2017/01/24/the-lasting-benefits-of-job-rotation/ (accessed April 30, 2018).

**Table 9.6:** https://www.macleans.ca/news/canadas-top-25-best-places-to-live-in-2018.

## Chapter 10

**Table 10.1:** Adapted from "What to Look for During Office Visits," http://careercenter.tamu.edu/guides/interviews/lookforinoffice.cfm?sn=parents (accessed April 23, 2012).

**Table 10.2:** Jeff Haden, "27 Most Common Job Interview Questions and Answers," *Inc.*, 2017, https://www.inc.com/jeff-haden/27-most-common-job-interview-questions-and-answers.html (accessed April 27, 2018).

**Table 10.3:** "Top 10 Job Interview Mistakes," May 26, 2017, https://theundercoverrecruiter.com/avoid-top-10-job-interview-mistakes-infographic/.

**Table 10.4:** Mike Timmermann, "The #1 Resume Lie That Could Cost You a New Job," Clark, http://clark.com/employment-military/worst-resume-lies/ (accessed April 26, 2018).

**Table 10.5:** "Performance Characteristics," Performance Review from www.salary.com/Careerresources/docs/related_performance_review_part2_popup.html (accessed June 12, 2001).

**Figure 10.1:** Based on Robert Half Finance & Accounting survey of 1,400 chief financial officers. Reprinted in *USA Today*, October 26, 2011.

**Figure 10.3:** Based on Robert Half Finance & Accounting survey of 1,400 chief financial officers. Reprinted in *USA Today*, October 26, 2011.

**Table 10.6:** Dawn Rosenberg McKay, "Five Things Not to Do When You Leave Your Job," http://careerplanning.about.com/od/jobseparation/a/leave_mistakes.htm (accessed April 13, 2011).

**Table 10.8:** Caine, Aine, "8 unbelievable perks that come with working for Google," November 17, 2017, https://www.businessinsider.com/google-employee-best-perks-benefits-2017-11, and D'Onfro, Jillian, England, Lucy, "An Inside Look at Google's Best Employer Perks," September 21, 2015, https://www.inc.com/business-insider/best-google-benefits.html.

## Chapter 12

**Figure 12.1:** Based on Colgate Products, http://www.colgate.com/app/Colgate/US/Corp/Consumers/HomePage.cvsp (accessed June 17, 2007).

**Table 12.5:** Mckinnon, Melody, "2018 Social Media Use in Canada," July 17, 2018, https://canadiansinternet.com/2018-social-media-use-canada/.

## Chapter 13

**Table 13.2:** Charlene Li and Josh Bernoff, *Groundswell* (Boston: Harvard Business Press, 2008), p. 43.

## Chapter 14

**Table 14.1:** Adapted from "Canada's Accounting Top 30," *The Bottom Line*, April 2014, http://www.thebottomlinenews.ca/documents/canadas_accounting_top_30.pdf (accessed September 28, 2016) and WallStreetMojo, Accounting Firms in Canada, http://www.wallstreetmojo.com/accounting-firms-in-canada/ (accessed December 28, 2018).

**Table 14.4:** Source: Data from Loblaw Annual Report, 2017.

**Table 14.6:** Source: Data from Loblaw Annual Report, 2017.

**Table 14.7:** Source: Data calculated from 2017 annual reports and Morningstar (2018), retrieved February 22, 2019.

## Chapter 15

**Table 15.1:** Based on Doug Hanchard, "Polymer to replace cotton in Canadian currency notes," *ZDNet*, March 9, 2010, http://www.zdnet.com/article/polymer-to-replace-cotton-in-canadian-currency-notes/ (accessed February 21, 2019).

**Table 15.3:** Sources: Office of the Superintendent of Financial Institutions, http://www.osfi-bsif.gc.ca/Eng/wt-ow/Pages/wwr-er.aspx; Credit Union Central of Canada, https://www.ccua.com/about/facts_and_figures; Investment Funds Institute of Canada, https://www.ific.ca/en/stats/; Investment Dealers Association of Canada, http://www.iiroc.ca/industry/Pages/Dealers-We-Regulate.aspx; Investment Industry Association of Canada, https://iiac.ca/who-we-are/; Canadian Finance & Leasing Association, https://www.cfla-acfl.ca/information/about-cfla (all accessed February 21, 2019).

**Table 15.4:** Source: Based on "Fast Facts About the Canadian Banking System," Canadian Bankers Association, https://cba.ca/fast-facts-the-canadian-banking-system (accessed February 21, 2019).

## Chapter 16

**Table 16.1:** Sources: Adapted from "Interest Rates," Bank of Canada, http://www.bankofcanada.ca/rates/interest-rates; IIROC, http://www.iiroc.ca/Pages/default.aspxand; FP, Guaranteed Investment Certificates - Annual: www.financialpost.com/personal-finance/rates/gic-annual.html; "Selected Interest Rates," Federal Reserve Statistical Release, http://www.federalreserve.gov/releases/h15/update (both accessed February 21, 2019).

**Table 16.2:** Source: Data from *Business Insider*, "Markets Insider," February 21, 2019, https://markets.businessinsider.com/bonds/5_220-loblaw-companies-bond-2020-ca53947zbt36.

**Table 16.3:** Source: Data from *Financial Post*, February 21, 2019, https://business.financialpost.com/markets/stock/symbol/l/exchange/tor.

**Table 16.4:** Source: Data from *National Post*, January 19, 2016, http://www.financialpost.com/markets/company/index.html?symbol=L&id=33668.

**Table 16.5:** Source: Based on data from S&P Dow Jones Indices, http://www.spindices.com/indices/equity/sp-tsx-60-index (accessed February 21, 2019).

# INDEX

## A

## B

## C

## F

## G

## H



## I

## J

## K



## L

## N



## O

## P

## Q



## R

## S

## T

## U



## V



## W

## X



## Y



## Z